The Persecution and Murder of the Jews, 1933–1945

The Persecution and Murder of the
European Jews by Nazi Germany,
1933–1945

Series edited on behalf of the German Federal Archives,
the Institute of Contemporary History Munich-Berlin,
and the Chair for Modern History
at the Albert Ludwig University of Freiburg

In cooperation with Yad Vashem

Volume 1

edited by
Götz Aly, Wolf Gruner, Susanne Heim, Ulrich Herbert,
Hans-Dieter Kreikamp, Horst Möller,
Dieter Pohl, and Hartmut Weber

English edition also edited by
Michael Hollmann, Sybille Steinbacher,
Simone Walther-von Jena, and Andreas Wirsching

International Advisory Board for the English edition
Nomi Halpern, Elizabeth Harvey, Dan Michman,
and Alan E. Steinweis

The Persecution and Murder of the
European Jews by Nazi Germany,
1933–1945

Volume 1
German Reich
1933–1937

Executive Editor
Wolf Gruner

Coordinator of the English-language edition
Caroline Pearce,
with the assistance of Dorothy Mas

The original German edition was published under the title:
Die Verfolgung und Ermordung der europäischen Juden
durch das nationalsozialistische Deutschland 1933–1945,
hrsg. im Auftrag des Bundesarchivs, des Instituts für Zeitgeschichte und des Lehrstuhls
für Neuere und Neueste Geschichte an der Albert-Ludwigs-Universität Freiburg
von Götz Aly, Wolf Gruner, Susanne Heim, Ulrich Herbert, Hans-Dieter Kreikamp,
Horst Möller, Dieter Pohl und Hartmut Weber,
Bd. 1, Deutsches Reich 1933–1937, bearbeitet von Wolf Gruner,
© München: Oldenbourg Wissenschaftsverlag GmbH, 2008

Coordinator of the English-language edition between 2014–2016
Alex J. Kay,
with assistance of Carla MacDougall

ISBN 978-3-11-035359-4
e-ISBN (PDF) 978-3-11-043519-1
e-ISBN (EPUB) 978-3-11-043321-0

Library of Congress Control Number: 2018019475

Bibliographic information published by the Deutsche Nationalbibliothek
The Deutsche Nationalbibliothek lists this publication in the Deutsche Nationalbibliografie;
detailed bibliographic data are available on the Internet at http://dnb.dnb.de.

© 2019 Walter de Gruyter GmbH, Berlin/Boston
Typesetting: Meta Systems Publishing & Printservices GmbH, Wustermark
Cover and dust jacket: Frank Ortmann and Martin Z. Schröder
Printing and binding: Beltz Grafische Betriebe GmbH, Bad Langensalza

www.degruyter.com

Contents

Foreword to the English Edition	7
Editorial Preface	11
Introduction	15
List of Documents	61
Documents	79
Glossary	801
Approximate Rank and Hierarchy Equivalents	817
List of Abbreviations	821
List of Archives, Sources, and Literature Cited	827
Index	843

Foreword to the English Edition

The Persecution and Murder of the European Jews by Nazi Germany, 1933–1945 presents a broad range of primary sources in a scholarly edition. A total of sixteen English-language volumes will be published in this series, organized according to chronology and geography. The series documents the horrific historical events embodied by the terms Holocaust and Shoah. This English-language edition reproduces all the materials in the German edition but has been adapted for an English-speaking readership. Apart from those originally written in English, all documents have been translated from the language of the original source.

This first volume contains documents on the persecution of Germany's Jews between 1933 and 1937. The second volume covers the period from January 1938 to the beginning of the Second World War in September 1939, thereby encompassing the antisemitic policies pursued in Austria and the Sudetenland following their annexation to the Third Reich. The subsequent volumes focus on the persecution and murder of the Jews in the large swathes of Europe that were occupied by the Wehrmacht, came under German control after the start of the Second World War, or were allies of Nazi Germany. Particular attention is paid to those regions in which the most Jews lived, especially Poland, the occupied Soviet Union, and Hungary. The murder of the Jews of Central and Eastern Europe is described using a wealth of new documents. The Jews in North Africa were also affected by Nazi policies, either directly (in Tunisia and Libya) or indirectly via the Vichy government (Algeria and Morocco). Their fate is documented in a number of the sources included in volumes 5 and 12 on Western Europe, though it does not form a focal point of this series.

The sources used for this edition are written documents and, occasionally, transcribed audio materials, dating from the period of National Socialist rule between 1933 and 1945. The decision was taken not to include memoirs, reports, and judicial documents produced in the period after 1945. However, the footnotes make extensive reference to such retrospective testimonies and historical accounts.

The documents within each volume are arranged chronologically. The editors have chosen not to group documents thematically in an attempt to avoid oversimplified or teleological interpretations of events. At the same time, the aim is to record the responses, whether restrained or more vocal, to Germany's anti-Jewish policies. Hence, the documents indicate how some of the non-Jewish population displayed empathy and a desire to help the persecuted, while others gloated or blatantly encouraged murder. The varied responses from the victims themselves include trust, confusion, fear, determination, or desperation. Functionaries of all kinds are given a voice, as are ordinary citizens, intellectuals, and domestic and foreign observers. The documents shed light on the actions and reactions of people with differing backgrounds and convictions and in different places, and indicate their intentions as well as the frequently limited options available to them. The editors place particular significance on private letters, diary entries, and appeals by the persecuted Jews. As the historian Saul Friedländer has noted, 'theirs were the only voices that conveyed both the clarity of insight and the total blindness of human beings confronted with an entirely new and utterly horrifying reality'.[1] It is also important that this primary source collection contains a representative selection of documents left behind by the perpetrators, especially as it is being compiled in Germany, where the central planning of the persecution and murder occurred.

This first volume illustrates the blend of coldly calculating actions and violence that brought about the disenfranchisement of the Jews, and the variety of reactions to these policies up to the end of 1937. The documents present a wide variety of perspectives: from Königsberg to Stuttgart, from the Jewish family bulletin to the antisemitic smear-sheet, from the law courts to the spa, from the sports club to the school, from the Post Office official fired for racial reasons to the speeches of Hitler. This multi-perspective approach will also be adopted in subsequent volumes, although the focus of the sources selected will be adapted in each case in accordance with the regional circumstances and the course and impact of the German-instigated 'final solution to the Jewish question'. The continuously shifting focus and the chronological presentation of the sources result in a juxtaposition of documents that may appear confusing or contradictory. However, this necessarily fragmentary but also differentiated version of events opens up the possibility of varying approaches and interpretations.

It goes without saying that a primary source collection such as this bears witness to the time and place of its compilation, as well as to the editors involved. Moreover, it reflects the contemporary state of knowledge of events, which inevitably has gaps. And yet the editors consider such a collection to be of enduring relevance, for a number of reasons. First, it adds to the scholarly literature underpinning what is now a broad consensus on how and why the murder of nearly 6 million Jews came about. Second, it reflects the increased range of archival sources that have become available since the end of the Cold War, not only in the former Eastern Bloc but also in Western Europe. Third, the growing temporal distance from the National Socialist period and the dwindling number of those who experienced it directly emphasize the importance of undertaking such a project, which places the historical events and context in the foreground. Fourth, it seems important to produce such a source collection in Germany in view of the country's direct involvement in the events described and its continued academic and public discourse on responsibility for them. Fifth, the series is an invaluable supplement to the wealth of publications now available on the subject, and also to the documents that have already been reproduced. Primary source collections with a thematic focus are shaped almost exclusively by their educational objectives. Such collections focus on specific political aspects or themes depending on the editors' aims and the country of publication. From a historiographical perspective, objections can be raised against almost all such publications. The sources are generally printed in abridged form due to a lack of space, and they are often reproductions of documents already in print. Moreover, and more crucially, the contents are often presented out of context. In other words, the editors of such source collections tacitly assume that the documents 'speak for themselves' on account of the monstrous events concerned. This results in compilations of abridged documents that are arranged in a way that dramatizes events for effect.

---

1 Saul Friedländer, *Nazi Germany and the Jews*, vol. 1: *The Years of Persecution*, 1933–1939 (New York: HarperCollins, 1997), p. 2.

As well as providing a scholarly reference work, this series of volumes seeks to contribute to the commemoration of the murdered Jews of Europe. It is designed for teachers, researchers, or members of the general public who wish to learn about and reflect upon the persecution and murder of the European Jews under the German National Socialist regime and would like to draw on authentic testimonies.

The production of the series has been generously funded by the German Research Foundation (DFG) as a long-term humanities project. The S. Fischer Foundation kindly provided a grant to fund the one-year pilot project for the original German edition. The English edition, which is also DFG funded, is a joint project with the Yad Vashem International Institute for Holocaust Research. In addition to the sponsors, the editors are most grateful to the large number of archivists, public officials, historians, and private individuals who have lent assistance to the project. They have provided the editors with advice and comments on sources and with information for the annotations, including the biographical details of the persons featured in the documents. John Bendix, A. G. Blunden, Todd Brown, Alex J. Kay, Charlotte Kreutzmüller, Sophie Leighton, Kathleen Luft, Jennifer E. Neuheiser, Charlton Payne, and Nicola Varns translated the German-language documents for this first English-language volume in the series. Alicia Brudney translated the Yiddish-language document. Alicia Brudney, Joseph Dunlop, Ashley Kirspel, Benedict Oldfield, Barbara Uchdorf, Ana Lena Werner, and Max Zeterberg contributed to this volume as student assistants. Technical assistance was provided by Johannes Gamm. The following people contributed to the original German volume as student assistants: Romina Becker, Giles Bennett, Natascha Butzke, Florian Danecke, Ulrike Heikaus, Ivonne Meybohm, Titus Milosovic, Remigius Stachowiak, and Elisabeth Weber. Gudrun Schroeter contributed in her capacity as research fellow. Despite all the care taken, occasional inaccuracies cannot be entirely avoided in such a source collection. We would be grateful for any notifications to this effect. They will be taken into account for future publications. The address of the editorial board is: Institut für Zeitgeschichte München–Berlin, Edition 'Judenverfolgung', Finckensteinallee 85/87, 12205 Berlin, Germany.

Berlin/Munich/Freiburg/Klagenfurt, December 2018

Editorial Preface

This primary source collection on the persecution and murder of the European Jews should be cited using the abbreviation PMJ. This citation style is also used in the work itself where there are cross references between the individual volumes. The documents are consecutively numbered, beginning anew with each volume. Accordingly, 'PMJ 1/ 200' refers to document number 200 in the first volume of this edition. The individual documents are presented as follows: title (in bold type), header, document, footnotes.

The titles have been formulated by the editor(s) of the respective volume and provide information on the date of origin of the document, its core message, author, and recipient(s). The header, placed underneath the title, is part of the document itself. It specifies the type of source (letter, draft law, minutes, and so on), the name of the author, the place of origin, the file reference (where applicable), remarks indicating confidential or classified status, and other special features of the document. The location of the ministries or other central agencies in Berlin at the time, for instance the Reich Security Main Office or the Chancellery of the Führer, is not cited. The header also contains details about the addressee and, where applicable, the date of the receipt stamp, and it concludes with the date of origin and reference to the stage of processing of the source, for instance 'draft', 'carbon copy', or 'copy'.

The header is followed by the document text. Salutations and valedictions are printed, though signatures are only included once, in the header. Instances of emphasis by the author in the original document are retained. Irrespective of the type of emphasis used in the original source (for example, underlined, spaced, bold, capitalized, or italicized), they always appear in italics in the printed version. Where necessary, additional particulars on the document are to be found in the footnotes. In order to enhance readability, letters and words are added in square brackets where they are missing in the original due to obvious mistakes, or where the meaning would otherwise be unclear in the translation.

A list of abbreviations can be found at the back of the volume. Uncommon abbreviations, primarily from private correspondence, are expanded in a footnote at the first mention in a given document.

Handwritten additions in typewritten originals have been adopted by the editors without further indication insofar as they are formal corrections and most probably inserted by the author. If the additions significantly alter the content – either by mitigating or radicalizing it – this is mentioned in the footnotes, and, if known, the author of the addition(s) is given.

As a rule, the documents are reproduced here in full. Only in exceptional cases, where individual documents are very long, for instance in the case of antisemitic diatribes, is the document abridged. The same applies to minutes of meetings that do not address in their entirety National Socialist anti-Jewish policy or the associated responses. Such editing is indicated by an ellipsis in square brackets; the contents of the omitted text are outlined in a footnote. Undated monthly or annual reports are dated to the end of the month or year that they appear. Only in a few exceptional cases is a deviation made from the chronological organization of the documents: in this volume in the case of the life stories of Jewish émigrés written in 1939/1940 for a competition organized by Harvard University. These descriptive texts, which were written soon after the period covered but nonetheless retrospectively, are classified in some cases according to the date of the events portrayed rather than the date of origin.

The first footnote for each document, which is linked to the title, contains the location of the source and, insofar as it denotes an archive, the reference number, as well as the folio number(s) if available. Reference to copies of archival documents in research institutions and in the German Federal Archives in Berlin are always made if the original held at the location first mentioned was not consulted there. In the case of printed sources, for instance newspaper articles or legislative texts, this footnote contains standard bibliographical information. If the source has already been published in English in a document collection on National Socialism or on the persecution of the Jews, reference is made to its first publication, alongside the original location of the source. The next footnote explains the origins of the document and, where appropriate, mentions related discussions, the specific role of authors and recipients, and activities accompanying or immediately following its genesis. Subsequent footnotes provide additional information related to the theme of the document and the persons relevant to the content. They refer to other – published or unpublished – sources that contribute to historical contextualization.

The footnotes also point out individual features of the documents, for instance handwritten notes in the margin, underlining, or deletions, whether by the author or the recipient(s). Annotations and instructions for submission are referred to in the footnotes where the editors consider them to contain significant information. Where possible, the locations of the treaties, laws, and decrees cited in the source text are provided in the footnotes, while other documents are given with their archival reference number. If these details could not be ascertained, this is also noted.

Where biographical information is available on the senders and recipients of the documents, this is provided in the footnotes. The same applies to persons mentioned in the text if they play an active role in the events described. As a general rule, this information is given in the footnote inserted after the first mention of the name in question in the volume.

The short biographies are based on data found in reference works, scholarly literature, or the Central Database of Shoah Victims' Names established and run by Yad Vashem. In many cases, the information was retrieved by consulting personnel files and indexes, municipal and company archives, registry offices, restitution and denazification files, or specialists in the field. Indexes and files on persons from the Nazi era held in archives were also used, primarily those of the former Berlin Document Center, the Federal Commissioner for the Records of the State Security Service of the former German Democratic Republic (Bundesbeauftragte für die Unterlagen des Staatssicherheitsdienstes der ehemaligen Deutschen Demokratischen Republik), and the Central Office of the Judicial Authorities of the Federal States for the Investigation of National Socialist Crimes (Zentrale Stelle der Landesjustizverwaltungen zur Aufklärung nationalsozialistischer Verbrechen) in Ludwigsburg, the last of these now stored in the German Federal Archives.

Despite every effort, it has not always been possible to obtain complete biographical information. In such cases, the footnote in question contains only verified facts such as the year of birth. Where a person could not be identified, there is no footnote reference.

Biographical footnotes are not added in the case of extremely well-known individuals such as Adolf Hitler, Thomas Mann, or Albert Einstein.

As a rule, in the titles and footnotes inverted commas are not placed around terms that were commonplace in National Socialist Germany, such as Führer, Jewish Council, or Aryanization. In line with the circumstances of the time, the terms Jew and Jewish are used for people who did not regard themselves as Jewish but were defined as such on the basis of racial legislation and thus subjected to persecution. References in the documents to the 'Gestapo', an acronym of the German GEheime STAatsPOlizei, and to the 'State Police' denote one and the same institution: the Secret State Police.

The Glossary contains concise descriptions of key terms and concepts that are repeated on multiple occasions or are related to the events and developments described in the volume.

All primary and secondary sources consulted are listed in the footnotes and bibliography. Where English-language versions of these sources are available, these are included. If a document has already been published in English translation but has been retranslated for this volume, this is indicated in a footnote.

The index includes all names referred to in the volume and all places significant to the content of the respective documents. It also contains organizations and institutions, as well as terms and concepts relevant to the volume.

Note on the translation

British English is used in all translations into English. Where a document was originally written in British or American English, the spelling, grammar, and punctuation of the original have been retained, with silent correction of minor typographical or grammatical errors and insertions in square brackets to clarify the meaning if necessary.

The spelling and style of the translated documents broadly conform to the guidelines in *New Hart's Rules: The Oxford Style Guide* (2014). Accordingly, the ending -ize rather than -ise is preferred throughout.

SS, Wehrmacht, and certain other ranks are given in the original German, as are titles where there is no standard equivalent in English or where there may be confusion with contemporary usage. A table of these terms and an indication of their position in the National Socialist hierarchy is included after the Glossary. In addition, terms commonly used in German in scholarly literature on the period are presented in German in this volume and explained in the Glossary.

All laws and institutions are translated into English in the documents. In the introduction and footnotes, foreign-language terms and expressions are added in brackets after the translation where this is considered important for understanding or context.

If a word or phrase appears in German in a non-German document, the German is retained in the translated text and its meaning explained in a footnote or, if necessary, the Glossary. The original spelling of foreign organizations is retained in the footnotes. The titles of published works not in the English language are not translated unless the work in question is of contextual or substantial relevance.

In order to avoid confusion between British and American English, dates are spelt out in the order day, month, and year. Foreign proper names are not italicized. Thus, names of institutions, organizations, and places are written in roman type in the footnotes, but legislation and conceptual terms are in italics.

In the titles, footnotes, and translated documents, place names are written according to the contemporary (English) name or the name commonly used in scholarly literature on the period. This also applies to places that have since been renamed, so, for example, 'Danzig' not 'Gdańsk'. Diacritical marks in languages such as Czech and Polish are retained, with the exception of the names of the extermination camps in Eastern Europe, where they have been removed in order to emphasize that these camps were established by the German National Socialist regime. Hebrew and Yiddish terms are described in the footnotes along with any other words requiring explanation.

Introduction*

For well over half a century, scholars have been exploring the origins of Nazi Germany's extensive and uncompromising campaign of terror and persecution against the Jews. The antisemitic state policy that was introduced in 1933 and culminated in the Holocaust, or Shoah, has also been thoroughly scrutinized. Many other aspects of the period, such as Jewish daily life, the interaction between a variety of institutions, organizations, and individuals in the process of victimization, and the role of ideology, have additionally been described and analysed. Nonetheless, the passing of the generations that witnessed the persecution and genocide of Europe's Jews by Nazi Germany highlights the need to present a comprehensive collection of contemporary documents from the viewpoints of victims, perpetrators, and those not directly involved in the crimes. That is the purpose of this series.

There is broad consensus that the decision taken by the Nazi leadership to murder the European Jews was not based on a preconceived plan. Although in only a matter of months Germany's anti-Jewish policy had exceeded the forms of discrimination against minorities that were common in many countries at the time, it was not yet clear to most contemporaries that it would culminate in Europe-wide mass murder. In the words of the renowned Holocaust scholar Raul Hilberg: 'No bureaucrat in 1933 could have predicted what kind of measures would be taken in 1938, nor was it possible in 1938 to foretell the configuration of the undertaking in 1942.'[1] After Germany unleashed the Second World War in September 1939, the Wehrmacht subjugated much of Europe, thereby bringing millions of Jews under German control, including many who had managed to flee Germany beforehand. The process leading to genocide developed in a large number of complex and distinct stages. It culminated in summer 1941 in the unprecedented plan to exterminate a people consisting of close to 10 million individuals in Europe who, though extremely diverse and scattered across nations, had been defined

---

* Götz Aly was the lead author for the introduction, which has undergone minor revisions and updating for the English-language edition.

1 Raul Hilberg, *The Destruction of the European Jews*, 3rd edn, vol. 1 (New Haven, CT/London: Yale University Press, 2003 [1961]), p. 50. Hans Mommsen describes this process using the term 'cumulative radicalisation': Hans Mommsen, 'Cumulative Radicalisation and Progressive Self-Destruction as Structural Determinants of the Nazi Dictatorship', in Ian Kershaw and Moshe Lewin (eds.), *Stalinism and Nazism: Dictatorships in Comparison* (Cambridge: Cambridge University Press, 1997), pp. 75–87. See also Karl Schleunes, *The Twisted Road to Auschwitz: Nazi Policy towards German Jews, 1933–39* (London: Andre Deutsch, 1972); Uwe Dietrich Adam, *Judenpolitik im Dritten Reich* (Düsseldorf: Droste, 1972); Leni Yahil, *The Holocaust: The Fate of European Jewry, 1932–1945*, trans. Ina Friedman and Haya Galai (New York: Oxford University Press, 1990 [Hebrew edn, 1987]); Saul Friedländer, *Nazi Germany and the Jews*, vol. 1: *The Years of Persecution, 1933–1939* (New York: HarperCollins, 1997) and vol. 2: *The Years of Extermination, 1939–1945* (New York: HarperCollins, 2007); Peter Longerich, *Holocaust: The Nazi Persecution and Murder of the Jews*, new edn, trans. Shaun Whiteside (Oxford: Oxford University Press, 2010 [German edn, 1998]); Christian Gerlach, *The Extermination of the European Jews* (Cambridge: Cambridge University Press, 2016).

as a 'race'. The extermination would essentially take place without distinction of age or gender, and be carried out within the shortest possible time. German officials called this the 'final solution to the Jewish question'. By 8 May 1945, close to 6 million people had been murdered because they were Jews or defined as such.

Between 1933 and 1941 the decisions to progressively deprive the German Jews of their rights, jobs, and property were instigated, influenced, and agreed upon by the representatives of various institutions and organizations, as well as by individuals, most notably Adolf Hitler. They were driven by ideologically inspired mass hatred, as well as by material, political, and, ultimately, military considerations. Moreover, the hatred of Jews and the desire to wipe out Jewish existence were directed not only against Jews as a physical presence, but also against preconceived notions of the Jewish spirit, and the idea of human equality underlying modern political, social, and economic systems. In this way, Nazi Germany's foreign, social, economic, cultural, and linguistic policies became intertwined with the 'Jewish question'. Once the Nazi regime had decided upon mass murder, it was primarily, though not exclusively, carried out by Germans. It was Germans who developed and implemented the methods of persecution, mass shooting, and ultimately the construction of the extermination camps, even though they enlisted the support of governments, bureaucracies, police units, and many individuals in different ways and to different degrees to carry out the 'final solution' in the occupied European countries. The evidence of collaboration does not lessen either the guilt or the responsibility of the Germans. In reconstructing the events, however, we must also ask how the persecution of the Jews was facilitated by non-Germans in the countries occupied by and allied with Germany.

The electoral successes of the racist and antisemitic National Socialist German Workers' Party (hereafter Nazi Party, NSDAP) from 1928 onwards and Hitler's entry to power in 1933 resulted from the political and economic climate in Germany, which had its origins in Germany's defeat in the First World War, the humiliation of Versailles, and the subsequent period of inflation. Many Germans were haunted by the fear of losing their livelihoods, and their outlook was dominated by despair, poverty, and resentment. From 1929 on, the Great Depression fostered a climate of political radicalization.

Unquestionably the National Socialist state mobilized both Christian anti-Judaism, which had evolved over centuries, and the nationalist resentment that had developed during the nineteenth century. After 1938 such sentiments were similarly mobilized in the annexed and occupied countries of Europe. Nonetheless, it would be wrong to assume that a unique, unusually malignant form of antisemitism had taken root in Germany in the decades before 1933, an antisemitism that would inevitably lead to Auschwitz. Such teleological explanations, questionable from a methodological and theoretical perspective, constitute an attempt to provide a 'causal explanation whereby the monstrousness of the annihilation of the Jews was the outcome of a monstrous history', and thus to exorcise the horror of the crimes.[2] The reflections that follow on Germany's national history and the situation of the Jews in the centuries prior to the National Socialist regime should be read with these reservations in mind.

2 Reinhart Koselleck, 'Deutschland – eine verspätete Nation?', in Reinhart Koselleck, *Zeitschichten: Studien zur Historik* (Frankfurt am Main: Suhrkamp, 2000), pp. 359–380, here p. 377. On Koselleck's critique in this essay of the so-called *Sonderweg* thesis, see Niklas Olsen, *History in the Plural: An Introduction to the Work of Reinhart Koselleck* (New York: Berghahn, 2012), pp. 246–249.

Emancipation of the Jews and German Nationhood in the Eighteenth and Nineteenth Centuries

In the German principalities that existed within the politically decentralized Holy Roman Empire, the enlightened statism of the late eighteenth century gave rise to calls to abolish special taxes and tolls, residential restrictions, and prohibitions for Jews that had been passed down from the Middle Ages. At the forefront of this development were the playwright Gotthold Ephraim Lessing, with his drama *Die Juden* (The Jews, 1749), and the poet Friedrich Gottlieb Klopstock, acclaimed during his lifetime, who lamented in his 'Ode an den Kaiser' ('Ode to the Kaiser', 1782): 'how our mob dehumanizes the people of Canaan!' In 1781 Christian Wilhelm Dohm's exposé *Über die bürgerliche Verbesserung der Juden* (Concerning the Amelioration of the Civil Status of the Jews) was published in Berlin. A product of the Protestant north, it was one of the standard texts on Jewish emancipation in Europe, and it put forward an argument that was rarely accepted by Christians in those times: 'The Jew is even more man than Jew.'[3]

The epochal caesura wrought by the French Revolution (1787–1799) and the Napoleonic Wars (1803–1815) increased the pressure for change in the German principalities, which had up to then remained largely feudal in nature. In Prussia, a government commission had begun work in 1787 on a law concerning the legal status of the Jews. In 1812 King Friedrich Wilhelm III signed the edict 'concerning the civil status of the Jews' as part of the Stein-Hardenberg reforms, which were instigated in an attempt to rationalize Prussia's administration after it had lost half its territory in the Second Treaty of Tilsit (1807) signed after Napoleon's victory over Prussia and Russia. The edict guaranteed citizenship to the Jews in the Old Prussian territories, but restricted their access to public and elective office. During the politically reactionary period after the founding of the German Confederation in 1815, the restrictions were tightened somewhat, but distinctly eased again during the period of the 1848 revolutions. The emancipation of the Jews was finalized in constitutional law in the German states of the Confederation around 1860 and extended to the whole of the Reich upon the establishment of Imperial Germany in 1871.

There had not been a straightforward or uniform approach to Jewish emancipation in either the principalities of the Holy Roman Empire or the individual sovereign states in the loose-knit German Confederation. By contrast, although France did not emancipate the Jews in the course of the 1789 Revolution, it did so overnight with a law passed two years later in November 1791. This was followed by the imposition of certain restrictions during the Napoleonic era. Both concepts, the liberal-revolutionary in France and the reformist-autocratic in Germany, aimed at assimilation, that is, 'that the Jew should be de-Jewified', as a Württemberg commission report put it in 1828.[4] If one considers

---

3 Christian Wilhelm von Dohm, *Concerning the Amelioration of the Civil Status of the Jews*, trans. Helen Lederer (Cincinnati, OH: Hebrew Union College, 1957 [German edn, 1781]), cited in Paul R. Mendes Flohr and Jehuda Reinhard, *The Jew in the Modern World: A Documentary History* (Oxford: Oxford University Press, 1995), pp. 28–36, here p. 30.
4 Cited in Reinhard Rürup, *Emanzipation und Antisemitismus: Studien zur 'Judenfrage' der bürgerlichen Gesellschaft* (Göttingen: Vandenhoeck & Ruprecht, 1975), p. 24.

the actual situation of the Jews in French Alsace and that of the Jews in neighbouring Baden, there were few substantive differences.

In the nineteenth century, Russia still encompassed large parts of Poland and was home to most of the world's Jews. If one compares the emancipation of the Jews in Germany not with France but instead with the Russian Empire, which directly bordered Germany at the time, the process in Germany was swift and efficient. The Jews in tsarist Russia were regulated in their freedom of movement and repeatedly subject to outbursts of violence from their Christian neighbours. After 1812 the Prussian west just across the border offered them the reverse image of the anti-Jewish despotism that would not be overcome until the Kerensky government that came to power during the February Revolution of 1917: an almost utopian degree of legal security, economic freedom, and opportunities.[5]

Within Germany, Jewish emancipation, positively construed as a necessary aspect of civil progress and the law of reason, found committed advocates for more than a century. But these advocates were held in check for a long time and caught up in public discussions that stalled their efforts. Once the Jews had finally become citizens with equal rights, many of those in the majority society continued to believe that the long-disputed people of another faith could not be 'real' Germans. The enduring strife had further stigmatized them and reinforced the sense of 'infamous birth', even among Jews who were well integrated.

'How loathsome it is always having to establish one's identity first! That alone is enough to make it so repulsive to be a Jew.' With these words, Rahel Varnhagen described her attitude towards life in Berlin in the early nineteenth century.[6] Decades later the compulsion to justify oneself continued after the founding of Imperial Germany in 1871. In the context of the 'Berlin Antisemitism Dispute' in 1879, Hermann Cohen, a professor of philosophy at the University of Marburg, noted how 'the old trepidation [was] reawakened'.[7] Although Theodor Mommsen, a liberal proponent of integration, stood up for the Jews, unlike his historian colleague Heinrich von Treitschke, he still asked these same Jews to 'dispense with [their] special ways as much as possible'.[8] Nonetheless, it would be incorrect to assert that a general attitude of antisemitism prevailed among the middle classes and petty bourgeoisie at this time.

Prior to 1871, policy in the German states was characterized by overcautious reforms, and not only with respect to the Jews. In a parallel development, the aspiring middle

---

5 For a comparison of the various paths toward Jewish emancipation across Europe, see Pierre Birnbaum and Ira Katznelson (eds.), *Paths of Emancipation: Jews, States, and Citizenship* (Princeton, NJ: Princeton University Press, 1995).
6 Cited in Hannah Arendt, *Rahel Varnhagen: The Life of a Jewess*, new edn, ed. Liliane Weissberg (Baltimore, MD: Johns Hopkins University Press, 1997 [1957]), p. 252.
7 Cited in Karsten Krieger (ed.), *Der 'Berliner Antisemitismusstreit' 1879–1881: Eine Kontroverse um die Zugehörigkeit der deutschen Juden zur Nation. Eine kommentierte Quellenedition*, 2 vols. (Munich: Saur, 2003), p. 338. Also see Walter Boehlich (ed.), *Der Berliner Antisemitismusstreit* (Frankfurt am Main: Insel, 1965); Marcel Stoetzler, *The State, the Nation, and the Jews: Liberalism and the Antisemitism Dispute in Bismarck's Germany* (Lincoln, NE: University of Nebraska Press, 2009).
8 Cited in Shulamit Volkov, *Die Juden in Deutschland 1780–1918* (Munich: Oldenbourg, 2000), p. 49.

classes, craftsmen, and farmers, who would be legally held in check for a long time to come, and later the industrial workers, championed a limited conception of the fundamental values of liberty and equality. Significantly, at the Congress of Vienna in 1814/1815, which established the political boundaries in Europe following the Napoleonic Wars, the delegates from Frankfurt am Main, Hamburg, Bremen, and Lübeck turned against the aristocratic advocates of Jewish emancipation, as did those representing the interests of the southern German bourgeois cities. 'There was indeed a struggle for equal rights and human dignity,' historian Franz Schnabel wrote of the feebly principled representatives of the third estate: 'there was a desire to bring down the barriers that were an obstacle to the freedom to earn a living, but there was also opposition to peddling, people were interested in suppressing the Jews, and flogging was regarded as essential in criminal matters.'[9]

A prime example of this narrow interpretation of civil liberty was Friedrich List. Born in Reutlingen and later professor at the University of Tübingen, List was an advocate of the Customs Union (Zollverein) and the extension of the railway system. He commented in 1817: 'In addition, no community should be burdened with certain classes of people whose religion or general character is incompatible with civil society, e.g. Jews, separatists, etc.' In 1818 he emphatically championed equal rights for Catholics in the predominantly Lutheran Kingdom of Württemberg, 'but one must not go to the opposite extreme and, for example, now force on the communities citizens and proprietors from the tribe of Israel'.[10]

In 1806, after the dissolution of the Holy Roman Empire, there was – in the language of the day – a *deutsche Völkerschaft*, a 'German people'. The notion of the German *Volk* expressed hopes that were long left unfulfilled and were still evident at the start of the National Socialist regime. Hence, Albert Einstein was expatriated in 1934 as a Prussian, not a German. It was not until 5 February 1934 that the designation 'German' was added to passports, following an edict from Hitler's interior minister, Wilhelm Frick. Because the German nationalist revolutionaries of the *Vormärz* period (1830–1848) had not inherited a consolidated feudal state, they had to formulate their vision in two ways: first, as a republican overthrow of a political system that was no longer practicable, and, second, according to a concept of a transnational, and as such treasonous, union. They referred – 'as far as the German tongue can be heard', 'from the Meuse to the Memel, from the Adige to the Little Belt', lyrics to what would become the German national anthem in 1922 – to the supposed commonality of language and history, of German character and blood. The socio-political process of inclusion encouraged a corresponding exclusion, a shutting out of 'strangers'. The statutes of the nationalist revolutionary German Societies (Deutsche Gesellschaften) founded by Ernst Moritz Arndt, one of the leading proponents of German nationalism and unification, declared that only Christians could become members, while 'the French, Jews, and philistines' were not allowed

---

9 Franz Schnabel, *Deutsche Geschichte im neunzehnten Jahrhundert*, vol. 2: *Monarchie und Volkssouveränität* (Freiburg im Breisgau: Herder, 1933), p. 225; see also Volkov, *Die Juden*, p. 20.
10 Friedrich List, *Schriften, Reden, Briefe*, vol. 1: *Der Kampf um die politische und ökonomische Reform 1815–25* (Aalen: Scientia, 1971), part 1, p. 158, and part 2, p. 853; Franz Schnabel, *Deutsche Geschichte im neunzehnten Jahrhundert*, vol. 3: *Erfahrungswissenschaft und Technik* (Freiburg im Breisgau: Herder, 1934), p. 351.

to join. Shortly after 1815 the original student fraternity in Jena, which adopted black, red, and gold as its colours, included in its by-laws a passage that had previously been rejected by a narrow margin, stating that only someone who was 'a German and a Christian' could become a member. The anti-Jewish provisions were deleted from the by-laws of the fraternities in 1831, but were reintroduced after 1880.[11]

During the following decades, German linguistic and cultural nationalism, which had been canonized by the brothers Jacob and Wilhelm Grimm and extolled by the poets of German romanticism, served as inspiration for the intellectual and spiritual leaders of the many European nation states which did not take shape until later: from Athens to Helsinki, from Turin to Bucharest, from Belgrade via Budapest and Prague to Warsaw and Riga, finally to the Zionist Congress in Basel in 1897. They adapted the Germans' romantic idea of the nation state and used it as a conceptual basis for new nationalist movements. By 1918, if not before, national revolutionaries had become state leaders. They combined the German idea of linguistic nationalism with the French model of the unitary state, to the double misfortune of the respective national minorities.

What the pioneers in the nineteenth century had interpreted as the arrival of the 'Springtime of the Peoples', what Prince Klemens von Metternich, Chancellor of the Habsburg Empire, sought to suppress as 'the Teutonism of universities and gymnasts',[12] degenerated during and after the First World War into a hyper-nationalism that was as intolerant as it was widespread. It ultimately justified itself by reference to the peoples' right to self-determination, which US President Woodrow Wilson had brought into play in January 1918 as the future blueprint for lasting peace in Europe. Scarcely had that transpired when Wilson's secretary of state, Robert Lansing, noted in alarm: 'The phrase [self-determination] is simply loaded with dynamite. [...] What a calamity that the phrase was ever uttered! What misery it will cause!'[13] Among the European minorities, there was one minority par excellence that was unable to rely on a state and, if necessary, on that state's army for its protection: the Jews, especially those in Eastern Europe. At the Paris Peace Conference of 1919/1920, the chief negotiators of the Western states, who drew thousands of kilometres of new nation-state borders through Europe as part of the terms for peace, were quite aware of the dangers looming for minorities. For this reason they made provision in the agreement, if only half-heartedly, for the protection of national, religious, ethnic, and cultural minorities. But they 'did not foresee the possibility of wholesale population transfers or the problem of people who had become "undeport-

---

11 Georg Simmel, *Sociology: Inquiries into the Construction of Social Forms*, trans. and ed. Anthony J. Blasi, Anton K. Jacobs, and Mathew Kanjirathinkal (Leiden/Boston, MA: Brill, 2009 [German edn, 1908]), pp. 601–620 ('Excursus on the Stranger'); Schnabel, *Deutsche Geschichte*, vol. 2, pp. 248–249; Norbert Kampe, *Studenten und 'Judenfrage' im deutschen Kaiserreich: Die Entstehung einer akademischen Trägerschicht des Antisemitismus* (Göttingen: Vandenhoeck & Ruprecht, 1988); Lisa Fetheringill Zwicker, *Dueling Students: Conflict, Masculinity, and Politics in German Universities* (Ann Arbor, MI: University of Michigan Press, 2011), pp. 103–117.
12 Klemens Wenzel Lothar von Metternich, 'Die Deutsche Frage: Genesis, Verlauf und gegenwärtiger Stand derselben. Denkschrift an Erzherzog Johann, Reichsverweser, London, August 1848', in Richard von Metternich-Winneburg (ed.), *Aus Metternichs nachgelassenen Papieren*, vol. 8 (Vienna: Braumüller, 1884), pp. 443–453.
13 Robert Lansing, *The Peace Negotiations: A Personal Narrative* (New York/Boston, MA: Houghton Mifflin, 1921), pp. 97–98.

able".¹⁴ Furthermore, in those countries of Central, Western, and Southern Europe which had adapted liberal democratic systems from the first half of the nineteenth century, and where Jews had been emancipated for decades, most Jews did not regard themselves as an ethnic minority akin to their co-religionists in Eastern Europe.

From Imperial Germany to the First World War

Industrialization began appreciably later in Germany than in Britain but then took place far more swiftly. Both countries mined almost equal amounts of coal in 1913, but German mining had increased more than sixfold since 1891, while British mining had increased by only 150 per cent. In 1875 British blast furnaces had produced three times the amount of pig iron yielded by German ones; in 1913 Imperial Germany produced 30 per cent more than Britain. The disparity in steel production was even greater. These indicators of an industrial boom concealed enormous social and cultural upheavals such as social dislocation on a huge scale, fear of a loss of livelihood and destitution, and the decline of entire occupational groups, trades, towns, and regions.

Britain had more than sixty years to grapple with the consequences of industrialization. It was able to mitigate problems with the help of its colonial resources, and it benefited from tried and tested political institutions that had matured over a period of many decades. Owing to its federal tradition and constitutional structure, the German Reich, which had only been created in 1871, did not even have a proper finance ministry or independent tax revenue until 1919. The politicians and ministry officials had to get to grips with rapid progress and social dislocation, but in order to do so they first had to create the necessary institutional tools. These efforts were only partially successful. Measured against the rapid pace of development, however, the accomplishments of Imperial Germany in the areas of legislation, education, science, transport, social policy, and hygiene were substantial.

Many Jews took on the challenges of the new era successfully. They were forced to seize the new opportunities and did so unreservedly, while substantial sections of the Christian majority population experienced the end of the established order as both a loss and a threat. The long-established middle classes made up of craftsmen, shopkeepers, those running medium-sized farms, officials, and persons of authority declined and a new middle class appeared on the scene, consisting of lawyers, doctors, procurators, merchants, brewers, stock exchange traders, theatre managers, and founders of department stores.¹⁵ The Jews had a thirst for education and proved to be high achievers, and soon they accounted for a percentage of the middle class disproportionate to their overall share of the population.

---

14 Hannah Arendt, *The Origins of Totalitarianism*, new edn (New York: Harcourt, 1973 [1951]), p. 276. For a general overview, see Carole Fink, *Defending the Rights of Others: The Great Powers, the Jews, and International Minority Protection, 1878–1938* (Cambridge: Cambridge University Press, 2004).

15 Hans Paul Barth, 'Gesellschaftliche Voraussetzungen des Antisemitismus', in Werner E. Mosse (ed.), *Entscheidungsjahr 1932: Zur Judenfrage in der Endphase der Weimarer Republik* (Tübingen: Mohr, 1966), pp. 135–155.

In 1867 Jews comprised 14.8 per cent of Berlin's grammar school (Gymnasium) pupils, although only 4 per cent of the city's residents were Jewish. At the humanistic Mommsen Grammar School in Charlottenburg, the vast majority of first-year pupils in 1910 were Jews. 'Intellectual arrogance was not altogether absent, but there was nevertheless a good sense of comradeship', Rudolf Schottlaender noted in his memoirs. 'The teachers too, almost all of them non-Jews, avoided anti-Jewish remarks.' The proportion of Jewish students at Prussian universities was 9.6 per cent in 1886/1887, while the proportion of Jews in the overall population was less than 1 per cent.[16]

From 1870 to 1884 Leopold Guggenheim served as the mayor of Gailingen in southern Baden. The example of this town provides an insight into the situation of the Jewish population at the time. In 1875 the town had around 1,700 inhabitants, of whom 700 were Jews. A passage in the inspection report of the Grand Ducal District Office, dated 12 September 1878, commented on relations between Christians and Jews: 'As recently as forty to fifty years ago, the vast majority of the Jews [had] belonged to the less well-off segment of the population', but now they had overtaken the Christian citizens 'to a significant extent in terms of assets'. 'Almost all of them live from trading (specifically, cattle trading), while the Christian inhabitants, with few exceptions, are dependent upon agriculture and daily wages. Almost all the sizeable houses are in the possession of Jews. [...] This inequality of wealth, which came about gradually, might also explain why a certain tension is evident between the two denominational groups.'[17]

According to 1895 statistics, one in two working Jews was self-employed, but only one in four Christians. While 11 per cent of the Jews were salaried employees, the comparable figure among the Christians was 3 per cent. As the historian Shulamit Volkov demonstrates by using the example of tax liability, this situation led to distinct economic discrepancies:

> In the early twentieth century, the Jews in Frankfurt am Main, for instance, paid on average four times the amount of taxes paid by a typical Protestant town citizen and eight times the amount paid by a Catholic. In Berlin, the payments amounted to 30 per cent of the city's tax revenue, while the Jews made up only 15 per cent of the taxpayers and just over 4 per cent of the city's population.[18]

The German Jews had nothing to lose in the old system, which had worked to their disadvantage and had been more or less static for centuries. Their opportunity lay in the new dynamics, in entrepreneurship, in science, in the corridors of business, law, and the media. Those who rose to affluence were frequently involved in local councils. They initiated foundations for welfare, education, and research. In Frankfurt am Main they were among the founders of the university. The Jewish hospital in Gailingen naturally

---

16 Rudolf Schottlaender, *Trotz allem ein Deutscher: Mein Lebensweg seit Jahrhundertbeginn* (Freiburg im Breisgau: Herder, 1986), p. 8.
17 Eckhardt Friedrich and Dagmar Schmieder-Friedrich (eds.), *Die Gailinger Juden: Materialien zur Geschichte der jüdischen Gemeinde Gailingen aus ihrer Blütezeit und den Jahren der gewaltsamen Auflösung* (Konstanz: Arbeitskreis für Regionalgeschichte e. V., 1981), pp. 23 and 48.
18 Volkov, *Die Juden*, pp. 53–54.

admitted Christians too, although the government of Baden was critical that: 'Jewish charity also attracts many "scroungers".'[19]

German Jews considered themselves part of national and local culture. Concurrently, separate Jewish associations and lodges developed. Once merely tolerated as subordinates, they had become active citizens. This transformation was symbolized by the New Synagogue on Oranienburger Straße in Berlin, built between 1859 and 1866, shortly before formal legal equality was granted to Jews. Rising up alongside the domes of the Protestant cathedral and the City Palace of the Hohenzollern dynasty, its magnificent gilded dome made a self-assured impression and stood out from those of other European cities.

In this context, new kinds of enemies of the Jews emerged after 1871. They twisted the discourse on the 'Jewish question' so that it became negatively charged. The change is reflected, for example, in the publisher's advertisement for an anti-Jewish pamphlet dating from 1879:

> At one time there was a 'Jewish question' that went like this: Are we entitled to suppress and persecute the Jews? This question is settled; we have granted them rights equal to our own, everywhere (this is under way even in Romania). And what is the result? There is now a new Jewish question, and it goes like this: Shall the Jews suck us dry and eventually dominate us?[20]

The shift took place against the backdrop of developing political democratization, with its multiparty system and mass politics. This provided fertile ground for inflammatory rhetoric, simplified arguments, and the scapegoating of allegedly dangerous elements. Antisemitism, thus reformulated, absorbed the fears of the long-established members of society, the disorientated, those who had lost out as a result of modernization, and those who were threatened by it. Tied in with this development was the famous essay 'Unsere Aussichten' (Our Prospects), also written in 1879, with which Heinrich von Treitschke sparked the aforementioned 'Berlin Antisemitism Dispute'. He took aim at the desire for upward mobility among the Jewish immigrants from Eastern Europe: the 'multitudes of assiduous trouser-selling youths', whose 'children and grandchildren are to be the future rulers of Germany's stock exchanges and Germany's press'. As the dispute continued, Treitschke castigated the Jews' 'continuous mocking invective' and their 'offensive self-overestimation', which, he said, were detrimental to German Christians' moral rectitude and their 'ancient good natured willingness to work'.[21]

In 1930 the historian Arthur Rosenberg analysed the strong response evoked by Treitschke's scholarly antisemitism which he viewed as an 'ideological buttress' for Christian university students and graduates who lacked the status conferred in Wilhelmine

---

19 Reinhard Rürup, 'Emanzipation und Krise: Zur Geschichte der "Judenfrage" in Deutschland vor 1890', in Werner E. Mosse and Arnold Paucker (eds.), *Juden im Wilhelminischen Deutschland* (Tübingen: Mohr, 1976), pp. 1–56, here p. 47.
20 'Annonce für das Buch "Kulturgeschichte des Judentums" von Dr. Otto Henne-am Rhyn', in Wilhelm Marr, *Der Sieg des Judenthums über das Germanenenthum* (Bern: Costenoble, 1879).
21 Heinrich von Treitschke, 'Our Prospects', in Stoetzler, *The State, the Nation, and the Jews*, pp. 309–316, here pp. 312 and 313.

society[22] by aristocratic birth, and who, in their subservient quandary, had no idea how to make use of the opportunities presented by civil liberties. They envied their Jewish fellow students for their thirst for education, confidence, and desire to get ahead, their obvious joy in the present and their optimistic curiosity about the future. 'In defence of their social position', Rosenberg believed, many Christian students regressed to a Germanophile racial ideology because they could in this way elevate themselves to the nobility vis-à-vis their Jewish fellow students.[23]

After 1880 numerous associations emerged that excluded Jews – from the Reich German Association of the Middle Class (Reichsdeutscher Mittelstandsverein) to the German Agrarian League (Bund der Landwirte), the German National Association of Commercial Employees (Deutschnationaler Handlungsgehilfenverband), the Union of Christian Farmers' Associations (Vereinigung Christlicher Bauernvereine), and the student fraternities. In addition, there were old and new antisemitic groups such as the German League (Deutschbund), the Wagner Society, the Gobineau Society, and the Reich Hammer League. In response, the Central Association of German Citizens of the Jewish Faith (Centralverein deutscher Staatsbürger jüdischen Glaubens, CV) was founded in 1893 with the aim of combating antisemitism and defending the rights of German Jews. In paragraph 1 of its charter, the CV's most important task was defined as the 'strengthening' of Germans of the Jewish faith 'in the energetic preservation of their civic and social equality and in the unswerving cultivation of German convictions'.[24]

The Jews repeatedly found prominent defenders among their Christian compatriots. One such advocate was Gerhart Hauptmann, who addressed the new antisemitism in his tragicomedy *Der rote Hahn* (The Conflagration), first performed in 1901. One of the protagonists is the sympathetically portrayed, upstanding Dr Boxer – 'a vigorous man of thirty-six. Physician. Of Jewish birth', as he is described in the list of characters. In this play, malice, treachery, speculation, and arson originate exclusively from Christian protagonists. Hauptmann exposes the openly antisemitic foreman Schmarowski as a conniving, 'poisonous little devil', but also shows the subtle nature of the anti-Jewish misgivings. In reaction to Boxer's intention to practise medicine in his native community after years spent working as a ship's doctor, the chief official, Baron von Wehrhahn, offers the following objection: 'I wonder whether this is an appropriate territory for [you]?' Von Wehrhahn turns out to be irritated at the social mobility of the returning resident ('Your mother still has the little [corner] shop here'), and Boxer must explicitly call his attention to the soldierly merits of his late father ('a tradesman'): he 'was in the reserve forces and was decorated with the Iron Cross in 1870'. Instead of replying, von Wehrhahn mumbles faint approval: 'Ah, yes. Of course. I recall.' The fact that Boxer's mother's windows had just been smashed suggests to him: 'Mischievous boys, no doubt.' Exactly who the culprits were remains a mystery.[25]

---

22 'Wilhelmine' denotes the period between 1890 and 1918 when Germany was under the rule of Kaiser Wilhelm II.
23 See Arthur Rosenberg, 'Treitschke und die Juden: Zur Soziologie der deutschen akademischen Reaktion', *Die Gesellschaft: Internationale Revue für Sozialismus und Politik*, vol. 7/2 (1930), pp. 78–83, here p. 82.
24 *Jüdisches Lexikon*, vol. 1 (Berlin: Jüdischer Verlag, 1927); Avraham Barkai, *'Wehr Dich!' Der Centralverein deutscher Staatsbürger Jüdischen Glaubens (C. V.) 1893–1938* (Munich: Beck, 2002), pp. 219–220.

The staunchly antisemitic organizations in Wilhelmine Germany were not especially strong in terms of their membership numbers, but their propaganda was not without influence.[26] The intellectual centre of these movements was ultimately the Pan-German League (Alldeutscher Verband), which was founded in the late 1800s. In 1912 its chairman, Heinrich Claß, under the pseudonym Daniel Frymann, published a diagnosis of the times. His book *Wenn ich der Kaiser wär* (If I were the Kaiser) exemplified the lines of reasoning behind post-1871 modern antisemitism.

Claß integrated clichés from Charles Darwin's theory of the evolution of species in the struggle for existence, from the nascent science of genetics, and from the racially orientated science of anthropology that had blossomed in the age of colonialism. Placing his considerations against the culturally pessimistic backdrop of 'decay', he described the population agglomerations in the industrial centres, the decline of the established middle class, and the sapping of German national vitality. He railed against debauchery and pomposity in the upper class, against social democracy, and against the tendency towards decadence and Americanization in contemporary art. Claß perceived German Jews as the fundamental root of these evils. In this variant of antisemitism, later refined by the NSDAP, the Jews were described as rootless, eternally wandering elements, constantly assimilating anew, and signifying a source of 'infection' for the main threats that millions of people associated with the modern world: the uprooting of what was time-honoured and traditional, the destruction of familiar ways of life, a compulsion to move into the new metropolitan areas, continuing uncertainty, and constant pressure to adapt. According to Claß, the 'heyday' of the Jews had coincided with the advent of industrialization. Their 'instinct', he said, had no other object than 'acquisition'. 'With their unscrupulousness, their avarice, their indifference to right and wrong, honour and dishonour', he asserted, they would decisively influence German economic life and, moreover, would dominate posts in journalism, the theatre, the legal profession, and medicine, which had the potential to shape public opinion.

To fight off these efforts, Claß demanded that all Jews be deprived of their civil rights. He wanted the Law of Aliens to be applied to them, and called for their taxes to be doubled and further immigration to be banned. In addition, he demanded that their right to hold public and military office and to work as lawyers, teachers, or theatre directors be revoked, as well as their right to vote and to stand for election. At the same time, he believed that a person who embraced the Jewish faith was not the only one who should be regarded as a Jew. Instead, ancestry should be the determining factor, he thought, as it was a matter of immutable inherited characteristics. Claß also ascribed distinctive hereditary traits, albeit noble ones, to the German Christian majority population. He explicitly rejected the idea of a universal humanism, reduced it to the 'solidarity of the Germanic peoples', and enquired polemically:

---

25 Gerhart Hauptmann, 'The Conflagration' [Der rote Hahn], in Ludwig Lewisohn (ed.), *The Dramatic Works of Gerhart Hauptmann*, 7 vols. (New York: B. W. Huebsch, 1912–1917), vol. 1: *Social Dramas*, pp. 511–649, here pp. 512, 570, and 586.

26 Fritz Stern, *The Politics of Cultural Despair: A Study in the Rise of the Germanic Ideology* (Berkeley: University of California Press, 1961); Peter G. J. Pulzer, *The Rise of Political Anti-Semitism in Germany and Austria* (New York: J. Wiley, 1964).

> Where does it start and where does it end, this [group] we are expected to love as a part of mankind? Is the depraved or half-brutish Russian peasant of the commune, the black in East Africa, the half-blood of German South-West Africa or [are] the insufferable Jews of Galicia or Romania part of mankind?[27]

In 1913 the Czech sociologist Thomas Masaryk, speaking about the pan-Slavic variant, coined concepts such as 'zoological patriotism'.[28] In political terms, racial antisemitism, with its peremptory, imperial tone, was directed against the two most significant currents of the day – liberalism and socialism – that were both allegedly under Jewish influence.

Jews in the First World War

With the outbreak of the First World War, antisemitic spite faded into the background. The Kaiser, political parties, and social groups sought to establish a domestic truce. Most Jewish Germans wanted to prove themselves as patriots and soldiers. The patriotically minded Jew Ernst Lissauer composed the battle hymn 'Hassgesang auf England' (Song of Hate against England) – 'We all have only one enemy, England!' With Walther Rathenau, Albert Ballin, Max Warburg, and Carl Melchior, distinguished Jewish industrialists and bankers joined the leading ranks of the German wartime economy. There was a brief period of national solidarity, but the tide turned with the military crisis.

In the summer of 1916 Matthias Erzberger, a Reichstag delegate from the Catholic Centre Party – supported by members of the National Liberal Party and even a few Social Democrats – submitted a formal question in parliament:

> How many individuals of Jewish stock are at the front lines? How many in the rear supply area? How many in garrison administrations, departments for the supply of food and equipment, etc.? How many Jews have been subjects of complaint or declared to be unavailable for military service?[29]

Owing to the loss of files during the Second World War, the details of the background to this cannot be ascertained. In any event, the Minister of War set a deadline of 1 November 1916 for a 'Jew census' (*Judenzählung*) in the army. In fact, on a percentage basis, the proportions of Jewish and Christian soldiers serving at the front in the First World War were equal, as were the proportions of those killed in action. Yet, what Walther Rathenau had predicted as early as the summer of 1916 finally came to pass: 'The more Jews who are killed in this war, the more strongly their opponents will give evidence that they all sat back behind the front lines to engage in war profiteering.'[30]

---

27 Daniel Frymann [Heinrich Claß], *Wenn ich der Kaiser wär': Politische Wahrheiten und Notwendigkeiten* (Leipzig: Dieterich, 1912), p. 186.
28 Thomas G. Masaryk, *Zur russischen Geschichte und Religionsphilosophie: Soziologische Skizzen* (Jena: Diederichs, 1913), p. 257.
29 Cited in Götz Aly, *Why the Germans? Why the Jews? Envy, Race Hatred, and the Prehistory of the Holocaust*, trans. Jefferson Chase (New York: Metropolitan, 2014 [German edn, 2011]), p. 101.

Nonetheless, it would be erroneous to consider policy in Imperial Germany solely from the perspective of antisemitism. Indeed, as early as 1878, at the Congress of Berlin, which reorganized the territories of the states in south-eastern Europe, the German Chancellor Otto von Bismarck had contributed decisively to forcing a decision to include Articles 43 and 44 in the constitution of henceforth sovereign Romania. Owing to the frequent pogroms, the European Great Powers agreed to afford protection to the Jews of the country, and the two articles provided that the difference of religion and denomination could not be cited as grounds to exclude anyone from civil rights, occupations, honorary posts, and business. However, in the decades that followed, the governments of the new Romanian nation state circumvented the provisions with every means imaginable.

In the First World War, Romania fought on the side of the Entente against the Central Powers. In early 1918, however, Germany and Austria-Hungary succeeded in concluding separate peace agreements with both Russia and Romania. Despite the extremely tense military and domestic political situation, Germany forced through Articles 27 and 28 in the Treaty of Bucharest, which was ratified at the end of March 1918. Mindful of the unpleasant experiences of the previous forty years, the authors of the treaty once again placed the country under an obligation to respect the legal equality of all religious faiths and to 'naturalize the stateless population of Romania, including the Jews, regarded there as aliens until now'. Max Warburg, the financial adviser to the German delegation, warmly congratulated the chief German negotiator, State Secretary Richard von Kühlmann, although the German right-wing press reproached him for having bowed to 'pan-Jewish interests' and for embittering 'the Romanians against Germany unnecessarily'.[31]

In 1914 approximately 50,000 immigrants from Eastern Europe, characterized as *Ostjuden*, were living in Germany without having acquired citizenship. The different Jewish experiences of the emancipation and democratization processes in the eighteenth and nineteenth centuries had created a distinction between Eastern European Jews on the one hand and Western and Central European Jews on the other. Emancipation and secularization had brought about the decline of the traditional Jewish community structure in Western and Central Europe and the estrangement of many Jews from Judaism and Jewish communal life. Due to the enormous waves of Jewish emigration, predominantly from Eastern Europe from the 1880s onwards, a number of Jewish religious and political groups had moved to other countries, and as a result Jewish life was both fragmentary

---

30 Letter from Rathenau to Wilhelm Schwaner, 4 August 1916, cited in Werner Jochmann, *Gesellschaftskrise und Judenfeindschaft in Deutschland* (Hamburg: Christians, 1988), p. 111; Egmont Zechlin, *Die deutsche Politik und die Juden im Ersten Weltkrieg* (Göttingen: Vandenhoeck & Ruprecht, 1969); Werner T. Angress, 'Das deutsche Militär und die Juden 1914–1918', *Militärgeschichtliche Mitteilungen*, vol. 19 (1976), pp. 77–146; Jacob Rosenthal, *'Die Ehre des jüdischen Soldaten': Die Judenzählung im Ersten Weltkrieg und ihre Folgen* (Frankfurt am Main: Campus, 2007); Tim Grady, *The German-Jewish Soldiers of the First World War in History and Memory* (Liverpool: Liverpool University Press, 2011); David J. Fine, *Jewish Integration in the German Army in the First World War* (Berlin: De Gruyter, 2012); Peter G. Appelbaum, *Loyal Sons: Jews in the German Army in the Great War* (Edgware/Portland, OR: Vallentine Mitchell, 2014); Tim Grady, *A Deadly Legacy: German Jews and the Great War* (New Haven, CT: Yale University Press, 2017).

31 Benjamin Segel, *Rumänien und seine Juden: Zeitgemäße Studien* (Berlin: Nibelungen, 1918); Hans Schuster, *Die Judenfrage in Rumänien* (Leipzig: Meiner, 1939), pp. 108 ff., Elke Bornemann, *Der Frieden von Bukarest 1918* (Frankfurt am Main: Peter Lang, 1978).

and diverse. Consequently, in no country were all Jews organized in a monolithic, united body, and they certainly did not speak with one voice.[32]

During the First World War the number of *Ostjuden* in Germany rose by an additional 30,000 after the German wartime economic authorities began in 1915 to recruit workers from the occupied Russian part of Poland, including Jews with an explicitly 'Orthodox orientation'. By that summer, Jewish workers were, for the most part, forcibly recruited and soon became targets of antisemitic agitation. In response to this pressure the military authorities closed the borders to *Ostjuden*, claiming that they had proved to be 'reluctant to work, unclean, morally unsound'. Moreover, it was asserted that they had frequently failed to fulfil their contractual obligations and had drifted away to the large cities, where they represented a potential source of unrest that was difficult to control.[33]

Some of the East European Jewish labourers remained in Germany after the war's end. As a result of the Russian Revolution and the civil wars in Europe that were waged under the slogan of the 'right to self-determination', hundreds of pogroms took place in Romania, Hungary, and the regions reclaimed either by Soviet Russia or by Poland and the Baltic states.[34] Such acts of violence and the deliberate economic pressure placed upon the Jewish minorities in the fledgling nation states forced hundreds of thousands of Jews to flee to Western Europe and the United States. In 1923 the number of *Ostjuden* in Germany was estimated at 130,000.[35]

Jewish Life and Antisemitism during the Weimar Republic (1918–1933)

Jews constituted less than 1 per cent of the population of Germany during the Weimar Republic. Though they had lived almost exclusively in villages and small towns at the beginning of the nineteenth century, by 1900 the majority of German Jews lived in big cities. In 1910, 60 per cent of German Jews lived in urban areas of more than 100,000 inhabitants, and this figure had risen to more than 70 per cent by 1933. By that time, only 10 per cent of German Jews lived in the countryside, while 20 per cent lived in small towns and villages. According to the 1925 census, 564,973 registered Jews lived in the Weimar Republic, 71.5 per cent of whom resided in Germany's largest federated state, Prussia.

---

32 Trude Maurer, *Ostjuden in Deutschland: 1918–1933* (Hamburg: Christians, 1986); Frank M. Schuster, *Zwischen allen Fronten: Osteuropäische Juden während des Ersten Weltkrieges (1914–1919)* (Cologne: Böhlau, 2004).
33 Ulrich Herbert, *Geschichte der Ausländerpolitik in Deutschland: Saisonarbeiter, Zwangsarbeiter, Gastarbeiter, Flüchtlinge* (Munich: Beck, 2001), pp. 99–103.
34 Robert Gerwarth and John Horne (eds.), *War in Peace: Paramilitary Violence in Europe after the Great War* (Oxford/New York: Oxford University Press, 2012).
35 Steven E. Aschheim, *Brothers and Strangers: The East European Jew in German and German Jewish Consciousness, 1800–1923* (Madison, WI: University of Wisconsin Press, 1982); Ezra Mendelsohn, *The Jews of East-Central Europe between the World Wars* (Bloomington: Indiana University Press, 1983), pp. 40 ff.; Jack Wertheimer, *Unwelcome Strangers: East European Jews in Imperial Germany* (New York: Oxford University Press, 1987); Israel Bartal, *The Jews of Eastern Europe, 1772–1881*, trans. Chaya Naor (Philadelphia, PA: University of Pennsylvania Press, 2002 [Hebrew edn, 2002]); Heiko Haumann, *A History of East European Jews*, trans. James Patterson (New York: Central European University Press, 2002 [German edn, 1998]).

An organization unique to Central Europe, the 'community' (*Gemeinde*), served as a focal point of German Jewish life. Created to centralize local Jewish activities, the Jewish Community embraced all Jews, including non-citizens. Jewish communities that became public corporations during the Weimar Republic were empowered by the government to organize local Jewish communal and ritual affairs. They recruited rabbis and religious functionaries, maintained and built synagogues, and ran a variety of institutions, among them newspapers, social associations, libraries, hospitals, and charity funds. Tax revenues, collected either by the government on behalf of the Jews or by the community itself, supported communal activities. Nonetheless, despite several attempts to create an umbrella organization for all German Jews, such an organization did not come into being until after Hitler's ascendance to power.

Attempts to promote a sense of Jewish identity in Germany were in sharp contrast to Jewish associational life in Eastern Europe. German Jews established no trade unions and very few professional associations. Although many individual Jews enjoyed acclaim in the arts, cultural activities such as music and theatre were only rarely organized under Jewish auspices. The occupational profile of German Jews differed markedly from that of the general population. Though the Jews had been historically barred from many professional endeavours, Judaism's emphasis on learning and knowledge allowed them to take advantage of the benefits offered by modern society, first and foremost education, in order to climb the social and professional ladder. It was for this reason that in some professions, such as journalism, law, medicine, and retail, Jews were overrepresented in relation to their overall share of the population. Concentrated in a small number of professions (more often than not in urban areas), Jews were particularly conspicuous to the Weimar Republic's often vehement critics. While most German Jews were middle class, a significant proportion of the Jews living in Weimar Germany, many of them Yiddish-speaking refugees from Eastern Europe, eked out a humble existence as industrial workers, artisans, or pedlars. The hyperinflation of the early 1920s and the Great Depression greatly complicated the lives of virtually all German Jews.[36]

The immediate post-war period saw a resurgence of hostility towards Jews across Europe. This radicalization had several causes, above all the devastating social, political, and moral consequences of the First World War. The Jews were blamed not only for military setbacks on the battlefield but also for social conflicts on the home front. This 'new antisemitism', which naturally stemmed from older cultural and economic prejudices, now spread widely to social circles that had not previously been hostile to Jews. Antisemitism was also radicalized as a result of the revolutionary movements that developed from 1917 onwards, in which some Jews played a leading role. This in turn gave antisemites a pretext for blaming Jews for the political upheavals and for combating socialism and Bolshevism as allegedly Jewish inventions. In Central European countries, counter-revolutions by *völkisch* groups and authoritarian, anti-democratic combat leagues accentuated antisemitic sentiments. Groups whose social and economic status had

---

36 Michael Brenner, *The Renaissance of Jewish Culture in Weimar Germany* (New Haven, CT/London: Yale University Press, 1996); Wolfgang Benz, Arnold Paucker, and Peter Pulzer (eds.), *Jüdisches Leben in der Weimarer Republik / Jews in the Weimar Republic* (Tübingen: Mohr Siebeck, 1998); Donald L. Niewyk, *The Jews in Weimar Germany*, new edn (New Brunswick, NJ/London: Transaction, 2001 [1980]); Aly, *Why the Germans? Why the Jews?*, pp. 18–32.

been ruined by the First World War were among the main pillars of these radical right-wing movements. These included former soldiers who were unable to reintegrate into civilian society, dismissed civil servants, debt-ridden farmers, or students, who were particularly susceptible to antisemitic racial theories. The frequently problematic process of establishing successor states out of the debris of Austria-Hungary or the Russian Empire led in many instances to violent national conflicts, which affected the often large Jewish minorities.[37]

In the early years of the Weimar Republic, antisemites in Germany also regrouped in unprecedented numbers. At first they gathered mainly in the German-*Völkisch* Protection and Defiance League (Deutschvölkischer Schutz- und Trutzbund), which had around 600 local associations in 1922, with 200,000 members.[38] It was only in this post-war climate with its susceptibility to theories of conspiracy, betrayal, and doom that *The Protocols of the Elders of Zion*, published in a German edition in 1920, began to have a greater impact. The book, a crude hoax written by the secret police in tsarist Russia, purported to document a plot to take control of the world hatched by leading Jewish representatives on the fringes of the 1897 Zionist Congress in Basel. In addition, the novel *Die Sünde wider das Blut* (The Sin against Blood) became a success, selling 250,000 copies between 1917 and 1934. It was written by a chemist, Artur Dinter, who espoused the theory of 'blood protection' based on racial biology. Given the large number of Germans who had died in the war, and a lost war at that, the concept of 'blood protection' attracted the interest of a public that felt extremely vulnerable and weakened.

The Kaiser Wilhelm Society, which fostered scientific research, founded the Kaiser Wilhelm Institute of Anthropology, Human Heredity, and Eugenics in the Berlin district of Dahlem in 1927, and appointed the anthropologist Eugen Fischer as its director. Together with the botanist Erwin Baur, the director of the Kaiser Wilhelm Institute for Breeding Research, and his pupil Fritz Lenz, Fischer had published the two-volume work *Menschliche Erblichkeitslehre und Rassenhygiene* (Human Heredity Theory and Racial Hygiene) in 1920/1921. The so-called 'Baur-Fischer-Lenz' was published in several editions until 1944, and it purported to be serious science. Yet the scholarly work also allowed the ideas of racial hygiene and eugenics to become socially acceptable in circles that were repelled by gutter antisemitism. Baur, Fischer, and Lenz converted coarse prejudice into seemingly well-founded, biologically substantiated knowledge and turned the 'Jewish beak' into a genetically dominant 'convex nose'.

In the section written by Fischer, one could read that 'the special position of the Jews' was attributable to the fact that they 'are wholly out of the ordinary in the domain of the Europeans'. From this it followed that in the 'hybrid population', meaning the joint descendants of Jews and Fischer's 'normal' Europeans, the dominant characteristics of the Jews broke through: 'the black hair, the convex nose, and perhaps some of the facial features'. In his section, Lenz outlined the threats that allegedly originated from Jews from the standpoint of genetics. Accompanying his arguments with statistics, he asserted that Jews had a far higher incidence of genetically caused blindness, deafness, and mute-

---

37 William I. Brustein, *Roots of Hate: Anti-Semitism in Europe before the Holocaust* (Cambridge: Cambridge University Press, 2003), pp. 47, 270–273, 282–285, 288, 339.
38 Uwe Lohalm, *Völkischer Radikalismus: Die Geschichte des Deutschvölkischen Schutz- und Trutzbundes 1919-1923* (Hamburg: Leibniz, 1970).

ness, developed diabetes more frequently, and were particularly susceptible to 'manic and melancholic disorders'. By contrast, he said, 'the Nordic man' surpassed all other races in terms of 'steadfast will and solicitous forethought'; he marched ahead 'in the vanguard of mankind with respect to intellectual gifts'. Lenz concluded that the Near Eastern race, of which he deemed Jews a branch, had genes that were orientated 'less towards the domination and exploitation of nature than towards the domination and exploitation of human beings'. He ascribed to the Jews an 'astonishing ability' to 'get into the minds of other people and guide them according to their will'.[39]

From 1920 onwards a *völkisch* group that campaigned against the Jews in an especially radical and uncompromising way became a subject of debate: the NSDAP. In the *Jüdisches Lexikon* published in Berlin in 1927, the Bavarian lawyer Wilhelm Levinger wrote in the section 'Antisemitism, History (Germany)':

> In early 1920 the 'National Socialist German Workers' Party' was founded in Munich; its leader soon was Adolf Hitler, who, as a young architectural draughtsman in Vienna, had absorbed the thinking of the [antisemitic] Christian Social Party and cried out for revenge for the treachery of the 'November Criminals',[40] because Germany, he said, could free itself from its external enemies only after destroying the Marxists and Jews, whom he viewed as the 'internal enemy'.

The 'large numbers of determined supporters', initially acquired only in Bavaria, came, according to Levinger, 'mainly from academic circles but also from among workers, who, disappointed, [had turned away] from communism'. Although the election successes had quickly diminished, Levinger warned in 1927

> that the *völkisch* idea, and thus antisemitism as well, scarcely separable from it, still dominates broad segments of the German people, who regard the Jews as an element of a foreign nation, an element one may approach only with mistrust in matters concerning the Fatherland.[41]

After the lost war, the NSDAP and other radical right-wing splinter groups placed unity and concord at the heart of their agenda. They built on the popular belief that the nation had too frequently been at odds with itself and had failed to take advantage of its historical opportunities precisely because, as at the end of the war and then during the peace negotiations, it had been betrayed from within its own ranks. This notion was associated with a phantasmagoria of malevolent forces alien to the German *Volk*, forces that, it was

---

39 Erwin Baur, Eugen Fischer, and Fritz Lenz, *Menschliche Erblichkeitslehre und Rassenhygiene*, vol. 1, 3rd edn (Munich: Lehmann, 1927 [1921]), pp. 119, 138, 148–149, 215, 290, 368, 538, 547, and 557–559; Peter Weingart, Jürgen Kroll, and Kurt Bayertz, *Rasse, Blut und Gene: Geschichte der Eugenik und Rassenhygiene in Deutschland* (Frankfurt am Main: Suhrkamp, 1988); Alan E. Steinweis, *Studying the Jew: Scholarly Antisemitism in Nazi Germany* (Cambridge, MA/London: Harvard University Press, 2006).
40 The reference is to the German leaders who signed the armistice agreement on 11 November 1918.
41 'Antisemitismus, Geschichte (Deutschland)', in *Jüdisches Lexikon*, vol. 1, pp. 342–348, here pp. 345–346.

claimed, had repeatedly undermined the more or less natural drive for unity. At the centre of this obsession the NSDAP placed several variants of 'the Jew', tailored to appeal to different audiences: for example, the Jew was described sometimes as the barely discernible and therefore especially wily 'Jewish assimilant', at other times as an *Ostjude* who allegedly rejected integration and was part of a shadowy parallel society. To both these artificially created figures the shapers of public opinion on antisemitism imputed characteristics hostile to the nation, such as 'defeatist', 'part of an international conspiracy', and 'self-serving'.

The *völkisch* propagandists presented the figure thus sketched either as a 'plutocratic Jew' or as a 'Jewish Bolshevik'. While the former was allegedly destroying the middle class and driving both the rural and the proletarian underclasses into 'big money' bondage, the latter was blamed for the communist revolution, that is, the perceived end to decency, morals, and religion, and of law and honestly acquired property. The threatening scenario that was thus described to an obsessive degree had no lack of apparent support in factual events: the internal collapse during the war; the October Revolution in Russia; the 'war guilt' clause in the Treaty of Versailles, which almost every German considered shameful; the ethnic struggles on the eastern fringes of the Reich; the bloody left-wing and right-wing coup attempts within its borders; and, finally, inflation. In addition, young right-wing intellectuals preached a dry, purportedly 'factual' form of antisemitism: 'We hate [...] the Jew not because he is a Jew; rather, we reject him as a *Volksgenosse*, because his inner values are alien to ours.'[42] Nonetheless, that did not cause the modern antisemites to abandon the traditional stereotypes of Christian animosity towards the Jews. In 1920, when Adolf Hitler gave an address in Munich's Circus Krone building entitled 'Politics and Race – Why Are We Antisemites?', he concluded with the exclamation: 'We want to prevent our Germany from also suffering, as Another did, death on the cross!'[43]

Antisemites justified their agitation as a defensive measure. The final chapter of Hitler's *Mein Kampf* is titled 'The Right of Self-Defence'. The same message is contained in the title of the Law for the Restoration of the Professional Civil Service (*Gesetz zur Wiederherstellung des Berufsbeamtentums*), issued in April 1933. The draft for the partial expropriation of the Jews, which officials from the Reich Ministry of Finance devised in the summer of 1937, was headed 'Law on the Settlement of Damages Inflicted on the German Reich by Jews' (Doc. 285). Underlying these articles was the assertion that the Jews had enriched themselves at the expense of the German people.

The NSDAP's manifesto was based on two forms of the principle of equality that had been developed during the nineteenth century. Both could readily be combined with antisemitism. As *National* Socialists, on the one hand, the party preached the political idea of the ethnic homogeneity of the nation. As national *socialists*, on the other hand, they promised a greater degree of social equality. Of course, they did not conceive their egalitarian demand in universal terms, as the socialists had done in theory. Instead, they reduced the scope of their ideal of equality, limiting it to a large, ethnically defined col-

---

42 Cited in Ulrich Herbert, '"Generation der Sachlichkeit": Die völkische Studentenbewegung der frühen zwanziger Jahre', in Ulrich Herbert, *Arbeit, Volkstum, Weltanschauung: Über Fremde und Deutsche im 20. Jahrhundert* (Frankfurt am Main: Fischer, 1995), pp. 31–58, here p. 49.

43 Alan Bullock, *Hitler: A Study in Tyranny* (London: Hamlyn, 1973), p. 96; Eberhard Jäckel and Axel Kuhn (eds.), *Hitler: Sämtliche Aufzeichnungen* (Stuttgart: Deutsche Verlags-Anstalt, 1980), pp. 906–909.

lective: 'the German *Volk*'. To those who were members of this group, they promised social equilibrium and improved chances of advancement.

Point 4 of the NSDAP programme of 25 February 1920 read: 'None but members of the nation may be citizens of the State. None but those of German blood, whatever their creed, may be members of the nation. No Jew, therefore, may be a member of the nation.' Point 23 dealt with the forces 'of a kind likely to disintegrate our life as a nation'. The economic policy section of the programme was directed against department store magnates, war profiteers, and land speculators, against usurers and black marketeers, whom it was deemed important to dispossess. This meant Jews.[44]

In addition to the NSDAP, the right-wing German National People's Party (DNVP) offered a political home to notorious antisemites. The Stahlhelm (literally 'steel helmet'), a nationalist conservative paramilitary association, introduced a so-called 'Aryan Paragraph' in 1924 for its nearly 400,000 members. This clause reserved membership solely for people belonging to the 'Aryan race' and excluded 'non-Aryans', particularly Jews and those of Jewish descent. The same step was taken by the Young German Order (Jungdeutscher Orden), with 200,000 members; the Reich Agricultural League (Reichslandbund), with 1 million members; the German Student Fraternities; and the German League of Gymnasts.[45] The charter of the German National Association of Commercial Employees, with its 400,000 members, had featured an 'Aryan clause' since the founding of the association in 1893.

Antisemitism found violent expression in the paramilitary Freikorps and in the secret societies. In the post-war years they carried out assassinations of alleged traitors to the national cause, such as the leader of the Catholic Centre Party, Matthias Erzberger, along with prominent politicians of Jewish origin in particular. The left-wing revolutionaries Rosa Luxemburg and Kurt Eisner and the German Foreign Minister, Walther Rathenau, were the best-known victims of such political murders, which were intended as punishment by example and propaganda by deed.

After the failed attempt by Hitler and his nationalist allies to seize power in the so-called Munich Beer Hall Putsch of 8/9 November 1923, and the successful currency reform in the autumn of the same year, the Weimar Republic stabilized and the number of antisemitically motivated acts of violence declined. Until 1932 there were, as a national average, fewer than twenty instances per year of synagogues being defaced with graffiti or Jewish cemeteries being desecrated. Such incidents indicated a suppressed potential for anti-Jewish aggression that erupted only in the form of clandestine activity. Usually, youths were found to be the offenders, and their actions did not always have political motives.[46]

---

44 Gottfried Feder, *The Programme of the N.S.D.A.P. and Its General Conceptions*, trans. E. T. S. Dugdale (Munich: Eher, 1932 [German edn, 1927]), pp. 18–20.
45 Jochmann, *Gesellschaftskrise*, pp. 99–194.
46 Martin Sabrow, *Der Rathenaumord: Rekonstruktion einer Verschwörung gegen die Republik von Weimar* (Munich: Oldenbourg, 1994); Dirk Walter, *Antisemitische Kriminalität und Gewalt: Judenfeindschaft in der Weimarer Republik* (Bonn: Dietz, 1999). According to the records of the CV, between 1923 and June 1932 there were 125 cemetery desecrations and 48 instances of graffitied slogans and vandalism at synagogues in the German Reich: Harry Pross (ed.), *Die Zerstörung der deutschen Politik: Dokumente 1871–1933* (Frankfurt am Main: Fischer, 1959), pp. 260–262.

The situation was different in the student milieu. The German University Circle (Deutscher Hochschulring), in which a majority of the traditional student fraternities had banded together, swiftly assumed an antisemitic orientation and began to set the tone as early as 1921. During this period the University Circle won an average of two thirds of the seats in the student parliaments and was thus able to assume leadership of the Deutsche Studentenschaft (German Students' Union, DSt). When the Prussian Minister of Culture forbade the DSt leadership to exclude students of Jewish ancestry, the result was a strike ballot at Prussian universities in December 1926. Turnout was high, and 77.6 per cent of the voters were in favour of continuing to deny membership to Jewish fellow students.[47]

The outcome of the vote is significant because it indicates how deeply many students, even in the calm phase of the Weimar Republic, harboured *völkisch* ideas. Quite soon, many of the students became involved in the emerging anti-bourgeois and anti-academic National Socialist German Association of Students (NSDStB).[48] There the tone was casual and sarcastic. For example, in the spring of 1929 a Rostock student joked that word should be given in advance as to when the Jews would be sailing for Madagascar from the emigrants' quay in Hamburg: 'The Hamburg SA Band is ready and willing to play the farewell song.' In the elections to the General Students' Committee (AStA) in 1930, the NSDStB won 32.4 per cent of the valid votes cast at German universities. In 1931 it garnered 44.8 per cent of the vote, and by 1932 the share had risen to 49.1 per cent.[49] Given the political climate at German universities, it is not surprising that tens of thousands of young students shortly afterwards became supporters and beneficiaries of the National Socialist state. They immediately put their energies into fleshing out the vague and variable Nazi ideology from within so that it corresponded to a 'rational' concept of rule. Scarcely had the NSDAP come to power before it engineered a change of leadership and a generational shift more far-reaching than Germany had ever known – 'the National Socialist revolution was in large measure a revolution of the younger generation'.[50]

Varieties of latent antisemitism were felt in daily life and could be detected in a multitude of settings. This fact was well recorded in letters written by Jewish holidaymakers attesting to their encounters with everyday forms of antisemitism and sent to the CV.[51] Until 1933, however, the Jews' enemies in Germany also encountered stiff opposition. During the Weimar years, there were multiple waves of protest against antisemitism, which involved all the newspapers from the moderate right all the way to the left. This

---

47 Ulrich Herbert, *Best: Biographische Studien über Radikalismus, Weltanschauung und Vernunft 1903–1989* (Bonn: Dietz, 1996).
48 Geoffrey J. Giles, *Students and National Socialism in Germany* (Princeton, NJ: Princeton University Press, 1985).
49 Michael Grüttner, *Studenten im Dritten Reich* (Paderborn: Schöningh, 1995), pp. 26 ff. and table 25, p. 496; on Rostock: *Akademischer Beobachter: Kampfblatt des Nationalsozialistischen Deutschen Studentenbundes*, vol. 1 (1929), p. 96.
50 Horst Möller, *Die Weimarer Republik: Eine unvollendete Demokratie*, new edn (Munich: DTV, 2006 [1985]), pp. 283–284.
51 Jacob Borut, 'Antisemitism in Tourist Facilities in Weimar Germany', *Yad Vashem Studies*, vol. 28 (2000), pp. 7–50; Frank Bajohr, *'Unser Hotel ist judenfrei': Bäder-Antisemitismus im 19. und 20. Jahrhundert* (Frankfurt am Main: Fischer, 2003).

was the case after the serious antisemitic violence and looting in Berlin's Scheunenviertel neighbourhood (1923), the murder of Rathenau (1922), and the increasingly frequent desecrations of cemeteries in 1924/1925.

The left-liberal German Democratic Party (DDP) declared to its constituents in 1927: 'Antisemitism, in German "hatred against Jews", is an immoral movement, because it appeals to the basest instinct.' In 1930 the Berlin newspaper *Der Abend* launched an attack on the Nazis' antisemitism: 'It is the distinguishing mark of all ethical inadequacy to consider oneself more valuable or innately superior,' the newspaper stated, and shortly afterwards: 'It is proof of the German people's political shortcomings that we must go through a second period of rowdy antisemitism. But we obviously are not yet past the political teething problems in this country.' German bishops routinely opposed the myths alleging that Jews carried out ritual murder, and the republican association of combat veterans known as Reich Banner Black-Red-Gold also staunchly opposed antisemitism. On 25 March 1928 the Holy See issued a decree stating that it condemned 'especially the hatred against the people once chosen by God, namely the hatred that commonly goes by the name of "antisemitism". This declaration was in keeping with older Vatican doctrines regarding the 'duties of love' towards 'Jewish fellow citizens' that had been issued during the controversy with the antisemitically orientated Christian Social Party in Austria. After the anti-Jewish riots on Berlin's Kurfürstendamm in 1931, which were instigated by the city's branch of the NSDAP under the leadership of police chief Count Helldorf, the *Welt am Montag* newspaper used the word 'pogrom', the *Berliner Volkszeitung* wrote of a 'cowardly assault', the *Berliner Tageblatt* referred to 'terrorists', and *Vorwärts* discerned the 'mob' at work.[52]

The mayor of the aforementioned town of Gailingen in southern Baden, who was a member of the Catholic Centre Party, mounted energetic resistance to the NSDAP's antisemitic machinations there, which began in 1928. He prohibited public bell-ringing to announce Nazi meetings, stating that it was a breach of the peace. He ordered the confiscation of antisemitic swastika stickers which read 'Selling cloth and silk is something every Jew can do, but what he won't do is sit at the loom!' He further requested that the town of Konstanz send mounted police to keep forty activists in check. In addition, all the democratic parties organized a protest demonstration in Gailingen in 1930, 'to put an end to the dreadful swastika nuisance'. The Baden regional government provided legal and political support for the demonstration.[53]

These examples say little about the specific attitude of individual Catholics, Protestants, Social Democrats, or middle-class liberals, but it is clear that there were some determined efforts made during the Weimar years to confront antisemitism. In addition, as a constitutional state, the Weimar Republic afforded protection to all citizens, including Jewish ones. In isolated instances, of course, there were court decisions in which sympathy with the antisemites was evident – but these decisions provoked scandals. In the case of attacks, insults, or defamatory propaganda, going to court remained the most effective measure against antisemites throughout the existence of the republic. The CV employed this method with success. When the synagogue at Kottbusser Tor in Berlin was defaced on the night of 16–17 February 1930 with twenty swastikas and the slogan

---

52 Walter, *Antisemitische Kriminalität*, pp. 151–154 and 211–221.
53 Friedrich and Schmieder-Friedrich (eds.), *Die Gailinger Juden*, pp. 55–64.

'Perish Judah, death to Judas, vengeance draws near', a Berlin court of lay judges sentenced each of the five perpetrators to five months in prison. The public prosecutor's office had requested nine months.[54]

German Jews at the Beginning of the Nazi Era

According to the findings of the June 1933 census, the German Reich had more than 65 million inhabitants, 502,799 of whom professed the Jewish faith. Of these Jews, 160,564 lived in Berlin. Only there and in Frankfurt am Main did they reach a proportion of around 4 per cent of the population. In other big cities, Jews constituted approximately 1 per cent of the inhabitants. Moreover, 15.5 per cent of the Jewish population lived in localities numbering fewer than 10,000 inhabitants and 13.6 per cent in towns ranging from 10,000 to 100,000 inhabitants (Doc. 52). One fifth of the Jewish population did not hold German citizenship. Most members of this group had arrived as immigrants in Germany from the countries of Central and Eastern Europe in the decades prior to 1933: 56,000 were Polish citizens, more than 4,000 were citizens of Austria, more than 4,000 others were Czechoslovaks, and just under 20,000 were considered stateless.[55]

Most of the German Jews belonged to the urban middle class. In 1933, 61 per cent of those who were employed worked in trade and commerce, 23 per cent worked in industry and the skilled crafts, 12.5 per cent described themselves as members of the civil service, and 1.7 per cent worked in the agricultural sector. While only one in six Christians in the workforce was self-employed, among Jews it was one in two. Because the self-employment statistics also included farmers, the actual proportions in the cities differed even more significantly than the statistical picture indicates (Doc. 53). In Prussia in 1933, of 11,674 lawyers admitted to practice, 3,370 were Jewish. Among the approximately 52,000 physicians in the territory of the German Reich as a whole, there were 8,500 Jews.[56]

---

54 Pross (ed.), *Die Zerstörung*, p. 262.
55 *Statistik des Deutschen Reichs*, vol. 451: *Volks-, Berufs- und Betriebszählung vom 16. Juni 1933: Volkszählung. Die Bevölkerung des Deutschen Reichs nach den Ergebnissen der Volkszählung 1933*, no. 5: *Die Glaubensjuden im Deutschen Reich*, compiled by the Statistisches Reichsamt (Berlin: Verlag für Sozialpolitik, Wirtschaft und Statistik, 1936), pp. 13–14.
56 Esra Bennathan, 'Demographische und wirtschaftliche Struktur der Juden', in Mosse (ed.), *Entscheidungsjahr 1932*, pp. 87–131; Werner F. Kümmel, 'Die Ausschaltung rassisch und politisch missliebiger Ärzte', in Fridolf Kudlien (ed.), *Ärzte im Nationalsozialismus* (Cologne: Kiepenheuer und Witsch, 1985), pp. 56–81, here p. 76; Tillmann Krach, *Jüdische Rechtsanwälte in Preußen: Über die Bedeutung der freien Advokatur und ihre Zerstörung durch den Nationalsozialismus* (Munich: Beck, 1991), pp. 39 and 416; Konrad H. Jarausch, 'Jewish Lawyers in Germany, 1848–1938: The Disintegration of a Profession', *Leo Baeck Institute Year Book*, vol. 36 (1991), pp. 171–190, here p. 181; Thomas Beddies (ed.), *Jüdische Ärztinnen und Ärzte im Nationalsozialismus: Entrechtung, Vertreibung, Ermordung* (Berlin: De Gruyter, 2014); Douglas G. Morris, 'Discrimination, Degradation, Defiance: Jewish Lawyers under Nazism', in Alan E. Steinweis and Robert D. Rachlin (eds.) *The Law in Nazi Germany: Ideology, Opportunism, and the Perversion of Justice* (New York: Berghahn, 2015).

Rapid urbanization and a fall in the birth rate, which began relatively early in Jewish families, led to the number of German Jews decreasing by 56,000 between the 1925 census and the June 1933 census (20,000 at most may have fled Germany for political reasons during the first half of 1933). In the 1920s, representatives of German Jewry feared the imminent decline of German Jewish communities. The *Jüdisches Lexikon*, published in 1927, reported that 'despite a 29 per cent increase in marriages in the previous fifty years', the number of births had fallen by more than 43 per cent during this period. In Berlin, it said, maintaining the Jewish population at the same level would require 'a relentless influx of Jewish persons from outside'.[57] Moreover, the Jewish population, classified on the basis of religious affiliation, was decreasing as a result of the strong assimilationist trend. After the First World War, more and more Jews converted to Christianity or chose to marry partners of different faiths. In 1927 one third of all German Jews entered into marriage with non-Jews. Their children were generally raised as Christians or received a secular upbringing.

Most Jews considered themselves socially, culturally, and politically as part of German society. At the same time many maintained a significantly loosened yet genuine sense of connection to their origins and faith. Among the schools of religious thought, the Reform Liberal current was dominant. By contrast, the Orthodox communities had few members. Up to the end of the Weimar Republic, the Zionist movement did not play a major role within German Jewry. Even though the German Jews were mostly inclined towards the liberal political parties, among them were also numerous supporters of communist and socialist, conservative and German nationalist opinions.[58] It could not have been further from their minds to regard themselves as a national minority and to found a special party. Unlike, for instance, the Jews of Poland or Romania, they did not take part in the 'Congress of Organized National Groups in the European States', a non-governmental advocacy group created in Geneva in 1925. They regarded themselves as Germans of the Jewish faith, who were, and intended to remain, loyal citizens.

Antisemitism as a State Objective

On 30 January 1933 the NSDAP attained power in Germany. The author of the editorial published in the *Jüdische Rundschau* the next day described the Party as a 'movement hostile to the Jews'. Nonetheless, he placed hope in those forces in German society that would oppose 'barbaric anti-Jewish politics' (Doc. 1). German President Paul von Hindenburg had only reluctantly appointed Adolf Hitler as Reich Chancellor and he instructed him to form a coalition cabinet. Overcoming the economic and constitutional crisis, reversing the ignominy of Versailles, putting an immediate halt to reparations payments,

---

57 'Antisemitismus, Geschichte (Deutschland)', in *Jüdisches Lexikon*, vol. 1, pp. 345–346.
58 Martin Liepach, *Das Wahlverhalten der jüdischen Bevölkerung: Zur politischen Orientierung der Juden in der Weimarer Republik* (Tübingen: Mohr, 1996).

and rearming Germany – in short, 'strong-arm' politics, as common goals, united the National Socialists and the nationalist conservative forces in the new government.⁵⁹

Decisive for the success of the NSDAP was the fact that it appeared outwardly as a unified force. As the first modern *Volkspartei*, a broad-based party with mass appeal, it presented itself as neither regional, nor religious, nor tied to any specific social class.⁶⁰ Many Germans hoped that such a policy could overcome the old national trauma of internal fragmentation: the separation into clans and denominations, which was viewed as historically calamitous; the self-destruction in the Thirty Years War; the particularism, and the social antagonisms, which had intensified dramatically during the Great Depression. 'For a long time, the most varied enemies of our people have thrived on the conflicts and the issues of a thirty-year-long war of religion', as Carl Schmitt expressed it in 1934. He continued: 'We almost pulverized ourselves by being for generations on end, inwardly as well, a war zone for all intellectual and spiritual conflicts.'⁶¹ According to this reading of German history, the welfare of the state and the people had all too long been neglected in favour of particular interests. This situation, many Germans believed, had brought about the collapse of the home front at the end of the First World War, had persisted in the squabbling among the political parties in the Weimar Republic, and had ultimately led to the brink of civil war.

Once the NSDAP was in power, it made antisemitism a fundamental component of its government programme, one that strove for the national 'self-liberation' of Germany. The programme combined anti-Jewish prejudices with small shopkeepers' fear of department stores, craftsmen's dread of industrialization, and farmers' worries about cheap imports, falling prices, and insolvency. There followed specific measures providing debt relief for farmers, stabilizing the producer prices for foodstuffs, halting property seizure and eviction notices that were already legally binding, and prohibiting discounts in order to protect retailers from being undercut by department stores. For workers, protection against wrongful dismissal was markedly increased.

University graduates, the number of whom had risen as a result of the Weimar Republic's educational policies, feared for their employment prospects. They considered the demand for a quota for Jews at universities and grammar schools – corresponding to their proportion of the overall population in Germany – to be a fair means of ensuring equalization. In the summer of 1932 almost 4,000 Jewish students were enrolled in German universities, but by the summer of 1934 their number had dropped to 656. Research assistants and unsalaried lecturers eagerly applied for the positions newly vacated by

---

59 Karl Dietrich Bracher, *The German Dictatorship: Origins, Structure, and Consequences of National Socialism*, trans. Jean Steinberg (New York: Praeger, 1970 [German edn, 1969]); Martin Broszat, *The Hitler State: The Foundation and Development of the Internal Structure of the Third Reich*, trans. John W. Hiden (London: Longman, 1981 [German edn, 1969]); Ludolf Herbst, *Das nationalsozialistische Deutschland 1933–1945* (Frankfurt am Main: Suhrkamp, 1996); Klaus Hildebrand, *The Third Reich*, trans. P. S. Falla (London: Allen & Unwin, 1984 [German edn, 1979]); Norbert Frei, *National Socialist Rule in Germany: The Führer State, 1933–1945*, trans. Simon B. Steyne (Oxford: Blackwell, 1993 [German edn, 1987]); Richard J. Evans, *The Third Reich in Power, 1933–1939* (London: Allen Lane, 2005).
60 Jürgen W. Falter, *Hitlers Wähler* (Munich: Beck, 1991).
61 Radio address by Carl Schmitt (directional transmission to America on 15/16 April 1934), published in *Die Deutsche Studentenschaft: Nachrichtendienst*, vol. 7, issue B, no. 6, 17 April 1934: BArch, NS 38/I90p194/IV.

Jews, who were summarily dismissed. Between 1933 and 1936, around 940 professors, assistant professors, and university employees were forced to leave the German universities, mostly because they were Jews. The same thing occurred in other sectors of the civil service and, at a later stage, in the private sector. The mass dismissal of Jewish teachers in 1933 made it possible, despite all the compulsory economic measures and spending freezes, to immediately hire 60 per cent of the 1,320 'Aryan' applicants.

Self-employed retailers and entrepreneurs suddenly lauded their firms as 'purely German', and profited from the politically desired downfall of their Jewish competitors: they took over their public contracts, wooed their customers, expanded, and finally bought at a ridiculously low price the stock of merchandise belonging to their competitors, who had been driven into bankruptcy. The pressure on Jewish-owned firms made it easier to consolidate and restructure medium-sized companies, and shifted the costs of this process on to a population group suffering discrimination. Managers of firms, banks, and insurance companies participated in their own way in the process of economic modernization that was funded by racial discrimination. The number of private banks in Germany thus fell from 1,350 to 520 between 1932 and 1939. At the end of 1935, 915 private banks were still in existence, 345 of which were considered 'non-Aryan'. By 1939 they had all, without exception, been absorbed by 'Aryan' entities.[62] During the years of the Great Depression, millions were looking for work, and only a few had any objection to the immigration of *Ostjuden* being halted.

Academics immediately devised new projects that met the requirements for public funding. Many managed the transition with seeming ease. Thanks to the government's guidelines and as a result of the emigration of entire academic faculties,[63] scholars who had long thought along *völkisch* lines, and junior researchers who were willing to adapt, gained control over terms and definitions, topics, research methods, grant awards, and appointments to tenured professorships. The members of every academic discipline worked more or less intensively on formulating their fields of study according to antisemitic principles. Even physics was not spared, although it was easier for the humanities scholars, biologists, and medical professionals to give their subjects a racial and *völkisch*-social scientific slant. The following examples illustrate this.

In 1936 the Munich historian Karl Alexander von Müller, who was influenced by nationalist conservative thought, became a co-founder of the 'Research Department for the Jewish Question at the Reich Institute for History of the New Germany'. In his opening address he rhapsodized about the fact that historical and comparative race research

---

62 Michael Grüttner and Sven Kinas, 'Die Vertreibung von Wissenschaftlern aus den deutschen Universitäten', *Vierteljahrshefte für Zeitgeschichte*, vol. 55, no. 1 (2007), pp. 123–188, here p. 126; Marion A. Kaplan, *Between Dignity and Despair: Jewish Life in Nazi Germany* (New York: Oxford University Press, 1998), p. 25; Bennathan, 'Demographische und wirtschaftliche Struktur', p. 131; Günther Keiser, 'Der jüngste Konzentrationsprozeß', *Die Wirtschaftskurve*, vol. 18 (1939), p. 148, cited in Franz Neumann, *Behemoth: The Structure and Practice of National Socialism, 1933–1944* (Chicago: Ivan R. Dee, 2009 [1942/1944]), p. 117; Albert Fischer, 'Jüdische Privatbanken im "Dritten Reich"', *Scripta Mercaturae*, vol. 28, nos. 1–2 (1994), pp. 1–54, here p. 19.

63 Institut für Zeitgeschichte, Munich, and Research Foundation for Jewish Immigration, New York, *International Biographical Dictionary of Central European Emigrés, 1933–1945*, 3 vols. (Munich: Saur, 1999 [1980–1983]); Horst Möller, *Exodus der Kultur: Schriftsteller, Wissenschaftler und Künstler in der Emigration nach 1933* (Munich: Beck, 1984).

was no longer 'taboo'. He celebrated the newly created focus of research and third-party funding as an 'arsenal for the battle of the minds'. The same year, Carl Schmitt opened a conference of the Reich Group of University Teachers on the topic 'Jewry in the German Legal Profession' with statements such as the following:

> What the Führer has said about Jewish dialectics is something we must repeatedly instil in our own minds and in those of our students, in order to avoid the great danger of ever-new attempts to dissemble and to talk an issue to death. Emotional antisemitism alone does not accomplish the task; what is required is conviction founded on knowledge.[64]

Emanuel Hirsch, who held the chair of systematic theology at the University of Göttingen, described Marxism in 1934 'as the product of a German–Jewish mixed marriage and as evidence for the impossibility of Jewish emancipation on the soil of Christian nationhood'. He interpreted Bolshevism as 'perhaps even an unbelieving aberration of the Jewish religion'. The biologist Ernst Lehmann, a professor of botany in Tübingen, was working on a 'German biology' that was up to the task of recording, in 'endless work carried out by one individual', the 'hereditary factors and characteristics of various human races': 'Where necessary and possible, the ensuing consequences will have a legal underpinning (laws pertaining to Jews).'[65]

A similar willingness to adapt was found among musicians, visual artists, journalists, film directors, and theatre people. The theatre critic Herbert Ihering took over from his rival Alfred Kerr at the *Berliner Tageblatt* after Kerr, who had a Jewish background, fled into exile with his family. Later, Werner Höfer began his career as a writer for the culture section of the same newspaper by cautioning the public against Heinrich Heine's lyric poetry, which he described as 'mouldy' fruits of 'political conditioning' and as 'posturing'. The renowned theatrical director Max Reinhardt was forced to leave Germany. His disciple Veit Harlan rose to become Joseph Goebbels's film director of choice. Among his films was the propaganda feature *Jud Süß* (Jew Süss), which premiered at the Venice Film Festival in 1940 and was screened to considerable acclaim in many European cinemas. The name of the musician and composer Felix Mendelssohn-Bartholdy, who had rediscovered the works of Johann Sebastian Bach, vanished immediately from the concert playbills in 1933. Conversely, Bach was turned into the embodiment of 'German ethnic stock' – by means of an appeal in the spring of 1933, in which leading choirmasters and organists sought to prevent 'non-native, cosmopolitan church music from being

---

64 Cited in *Das Judentum in der Rechtswissenschaft: Ansprachen, Vorträge und Ergebnisse der Tagung der Reichsgruppe Hochschullehrer des NSRB am 3. und 4. Oktober 1936*, vol. 1 (Berlin: Deutscher Rechtsverlag, 1936), p. 14.
65 Address by Professor Karl Alexander von Müller, in Walter Frank (ed.), *Deutsche Wissenschaft und Judenfrage: Schriften des Reichsinstituts für Geschichte des neuen Deutschlands* (Hamburg: Hanseatische Verlagsanstalt, 1937), pp. 5–14; Hirsch cited in Robert P. Ericksen, *Theologians under Hitler: Gerhard Kittel, Paul Althaus and Emanuel Hirsch* (New Haven, CT/London: Yale University Press, 1985), p. 154; Lehmann cited in Ute Deichmann, *Biologen unter Hitler: Vertreibung, Karrieren, Forschung* (Frankfurt am Main: Campus, 1992), pp. 289–303. On Müller, see Matthias Berg, *Karl Alexander von Müller: Historiker für den Nationalsozialismus* (Göttingen: Vandenhoeck & Ruprecht, 2014).

presented to our people'. Among the appeal's initiators was Günther Ramin, the musical director of the St Thomas Choir of Leipzig from 1940 until his death in 1956. In 1936 he had played at the wedding of Hermann Göring, and in March 1941 he produced the first German recording of the entire St Matthew Passion.[66]

After the Second World War, the historian Joseph Wulf documented the opportunism of the artists and journalists and the alacrity with which they had jumped on to the totalitarian bandwagon. Wulf, who was born in Chemnitz in 1912 and educated as a rabbi in Cracow,[67] concluded: 'In our century, one might almost say that the concentration camp inmate has understood the nature and purpose of the concepts of freedom and public opinion far more concretely than the intellectual.'[68] Wulf was speaking from personal knowledge: as a member of the Jewish resistance movement in Poland, he had been arrested in 1941 and went on to survive Auschwitz.

In February 1933, in a number of localities, SA and SS forces organized the first, frequently violent boycotts targeting Jewish business people and university lecturers (Doc. 3). After the Reichstag election on 5 March 1933, which produced a narrow majority for the nationalist coalition, though not for the NSDAP alone, Hitler instructed his Minister of the Interior, Wilhelm Frick, to draft anti-Jewish laws. As previously discussed by conservative politicians in 1923 and 1932, Frick wanted to begin by expelling all Jews of Polish or Russian origin, the so-called *Ostjuden*, from the country and by putting a stop to any further immigration (Doc. 8). On the surface the behaviour of the Nazi leadership was contradictory. While Hitler, on 10 March 1933, publicly expressed opposition to spontaneous acts of antisemitism, Hermann Göring refused the following day to extend police protection to Jewish businesses. On 19 March 1933 the National Socialist leaders encouraged the propensity of their grass-roots supporters for engaging in violent disruption by publishing a demand in the *Völkischer Beobachter* newspaper calling for Jews to be ousted from Berlin's local courts.

From the outset a part of the foreign press reported critically on the discrimination against Jews in Germany. Jewish and non-Jewish organizations, particularly in the USA and Britain, discussed the provision of aid to German Jews and organized public protests (Docs. 14 and 20). Some called on consumers to refuse to buy German goods, in order to put economic pressure on the National Socialist government. In reaction Hitler decided to stage an anti-Jewish boycott. On 1 April 1933, a Saturday, SA guards and activists from the German nationalist Stahlhelm organization blocked access to Jewish-owned businesses, law firms, and medical practices throughout the German Reich. They daubed anti-Jewish slogans on shop windows, doors, and pavements. In his radio address the

---

66 On Harlan, see Erwin Leiser, *'Deutschland Erwache!' Propaganda und Film des Dritten Reiches*, new edn (Reinbek bei Hamburg: Rowohlt, 1978 [1968]), pp. 141–146, and Franck Noach, *Veit Harlan: The Life and Work of a Nazi Filmmaker* (Lexington, KY: University Press of Kentucky, 2016). On Höfer: 'Zeitalter des Namenlosen?', 12 Uhr Blatt, 1 Nov. 1943, cited in Friedrich Lambart (ed.), *Tod eines Pianisten: Karlrobert Kreiten und der Fall Werner Höfer* (Berlin: Hentrich, 1988), pp. 179–180. On Ramin: Fred K. Prieberg, *Musik im NS-Staat* (Frankfurt am Main: Fischer, 1982), p. 346.

67 On Wulf, see Klaus Kempter, *Joseph Wulf: Ein Historikerschicksal in Deutschland* (Göttingen: Vandenhoeck & Ruprecht, 2013).

68 Joseph Wulf, *Presse und Funk im Dritten Reich* (Gütersloh: S. Mohn, 1964), p. 5; Joseph Wulf, *Musik im Dritten Reich; Die bildenden Künste im Dritten Reich; Literatur und Dichtung im Dritten Reich; Theater und Film im Dritten Reich*, 4 vols. (Gütersloh: S. Mohn, 1963).

same day, Joseph Goebbels encouraged 'the German people' to seek 'recompense' from the Jews. In many places, shops were looted and customers who resisted the boycott were photographed or filmed, and sometimes mistreated. Murders were committed in Chemnitz, Plauen, and Kiel (Doc. 22).[69]

The evening before, university professor Victor Klemperer had written in Dresden: 'Ever more hopeless. The boycott begins tomorrow. Yellow placards, men on guard. Pressure to pay Christian employees two months' salary, to dismiss Jewish ones.' The next day, he observed: 'People poured down Prager Straße and looked at it all. [...] There will be an explosion – but we may pay for it with our lives, we Jews.' A directive from the Baden Ministry of State shows how quickly the state's antisemitic policy had lodged itself in children's minds. On 3 April 1933 the ministry pointed out in the Baden newspapers 'that insults directed at Jewish school pupils by their fellow pupils cannot be tolerated'.[70]

Behaviour of the 'Aryan' Majority

It is difficult to estimate the extent and nature of popular antisemitism at the beginning of National Socialist rule. There are some indications that most Germans did not embrace state-propagated hatred in the early years of Nazi rule. The 1 April boycott, for example, lasted only one day due to a lack of resonance with German shoppers. Nonetheless, the vast majority reacted with indifference to the state's anti-Jewish policies. As early as 1932 Otto von Harling, a clergyman who was involved in a Christian mission to the Jews, complained: 'The crudeness with which not only everything Jewish is dragged through the mire but also the Jew is personally insulted, [...] all that is barely considered to be disgraceful and unjust by large parts of the population; [...] while in America the representatives of various churches have issued statements opposing the excesses of antisemitism.'[71] Looking back at the final years of the Weimar Republic, Franz Böhm, who later became a Bundestag delegate for the Christian Democratic Union (CDU) and after 1952 led the restitution talks with Israel on behalf of West German Chancellor Konrad Adenauer, said: 'If and when anti-Hitler slogans were to be heard at all in those days, they placed emphasis on other things, but they did not focus on revulsion for

---

69 Armin Nolzen, 'The Nazi Party and Its Violence against the Jews, 1933–1938/39: Violence as a Historiographical Concept', *Yad Vashem Studies*, vol. 31 (2003), pp. 245–285; Robert Gellately, *Backing Hitler: Consent and Coercion in Nazi Germany* (Oxford/New York: Oxford University Press, 2001), p. 27; Michael Wildt, *Hitler's Volksgemeinschaft and the Dynamics of Racial Exclusion: Violence against Jews in Provincial Germany, 1919–1939*, trans. Bernard Heise (New York: Berghahn, 2012 [German edn, 2007]), pp. 77–84; Hannah Ahlheim, *'Deutsche, kauft nicht bei Juden!' Antisemitismus und politischer Boykott in Deutschland 1924 bis 1935* (Göttingen: Wallstein, 2011), pp. 241–262.

70 Victor Klemperer, *I Shall Bear Witness: The Diaries of Victor Klemperer, 1933–1941*, trans. Martin Chalmers (London: Weidenfeld & Nicolson, 1998 [German edn, 1995]), pp. 12–13 (entries for 31 March and 3 April 1933); newspaper excerpt cited in Friedrich and Schmieder-Friedrich (eds.), *Die Gailinger Juden*, p. 80.

71 Quotations from Mosse (ed.), *Entscheidungsjahr 1932*: Hans-Joachim Kraus, 'Die evangelische Kirche', pp. 249–270, here p. 259; Karl Thieme, 'Deutsche Katholiken', pp. 271–288, here pp. 272–273; P. B. Wiener, 'Die Parteien der Mitte', pp. 288–321, here pp. 290–291; Hans-Helmuth Knütter, 'Die Linksparteien', pp. 323–345, here p. 332.

antisemitism.'[72] In addition, historian Saul Friedländer wrote with respect to the year 1935: 'The populace appears to have been mainly passive in the face of such ongoing party agitation: Although there was no resistance to it, outright anti-Jewish violence often encountered disapproval.'[73]

From this perspective, lack of concern for the fate of persons not deemed part of the *Volksgemeinschaft* was perhaps the most significant behavioural tendency of German society that facilitated the killing of the European Jews. Documentary evidence was provided in April 1933 in the reply of Cardinal Michael von Faulhaber, spiritual leader of the Archdiocese of Munich and Freising, to a letter from a Catholic who was deeply troubled by the Jew-baiting. Faulhaber's reaction presaged the slippery slope down which the civil forces of German society began to slide. 'These actions against the Jews', he wrote:

> are so very unchristian that every Christian, not merely every cleric, ought to speak out against them. For the higher Church authorities, [however,] there are far more important questions of our time; because schooling, the continued existence of the Catholic associations, and sterilization are even more important issues for Christianity in our homeland, especially as we may assume, and to some extent have already seen, that the Jews can help themselves and we therefore have no cause to give the government a reason to turn the Jew-baiting into Jesuit-baiting. (Doc. 30)

In addition to the reactions of the many whose own interests mattered more to them than their persecuted neighbours, there was also a widespread attitude that can be characterized as passive antisemitism. A sizeable number of 'Aryan' Germans regarded the Jewish Germans as alien elements that had seemingly prospered disproportionately in the past. For the most part this attitude resulted in the rejection of direct violence, but not to any disapproval of the state-ordered deprivation of rights.

Since Jews were quickly excluded from associations and from public life in general, colleagues from the world of business and the civil service vanished, and social contacts were almost automatically lost. Anyone who was not particularly courageous could simply let these contacts wane. This was by no means the universal approach, as the example of Ernst Loewenberg demonstrates. He had taught German at the Lichtwark School in Hamburg, a reform-friendly, coeducational institution, and, as a holder of the Iron Cross, he did not lose his position until March 1934. The pupils, even those who joined the Hitler Youth, maintained contact with their greatly respected teacher. In the allotment garden, Loewenberg spoke with their parents: 'Where they are unobserved, they too behave as before.' At the end of 1934, at the wish of his former pupils, a study group headed by Loewenberg was created, in which poems by Rainer Maria Rilke were read and discussed. Only after the headmaster summoned a few pupils and accused them of

---

[72] Cited in Jochmann, *Gesellschaftskrise*, p. 193.
[73] Friedländer, *Nazi Germany*, vol. 1, p. 125; David Bankier (ed.), *Probing the Depths of German Anti-Semitism: German Society and the Persecution of the Jews, 1933–1941* (New York: Berghahn, 1999); Susanna Schrafstetter and Alan Steinweis (eds.), *The Germans and the Holocaust: Popular Responses to the Persecution and Murder of the Jews* (New York: Berghahn, 2015).

having 'proved their moral immaturity in such a blatant manner by working with a Jew' did Loewenberg put an end to the meetings, against the wishes of the pupils. He wondered: 'Has a Nazi living in our building reported us to the authorities? It's more likely that word got round at school.'[74]

This story is probably atypical. However, it shows how even if Jews and non-Jews sought to maintain friendly relationships these could be brought to an abrupt end. Fairly rapidly, invisible barriers arose, such as those described by Rabbi Joachim Prinz in 1935: 'The Jew's lot is to be neighbourless.' He added: 'We would not find it all so painful if we did not have the feeling that we once *did have* neighbours' (Doc. 161). For the officials of the SS Security Service (hereafter SD), including Adolf Eichmann, who were responsible for monitoring the Jews, this was not enough. In their opinion, at the end of 1937 the 'unanimous repudiation of the Jews by all parts of the population' was still largely absent.[75]

Reactions of the Persecuted

The representatives of the Jewish associations in Germany reacted to the unexpectedly strong threat by going on the offensive. In April 1933, putting all their differences aside, they founded the Central Committee of German Jews for Relief and Reconstruction (Zentralausschuss der deutschen Juden für Hilfe und Aufbau), which was financed by Jewish communities and foreign relief organizations. All the large Jewish organizations joined forces in the committee: the CV, the Zionist Federation for Germany, the Relief Association of German Jews, the League of Jewish Women, the Prussian Regional Association of Jewish Communities, the Jewish Community of Berlin, and the Orthodox association Agudat Yisrael. The Central Committee undertook social welfare work and economic aid, arranged for the expansion of Jewish schools, a step that quickly became necessary, and offered help and advice to those who wanted to emigrate. In terms of its practical activities it was to become the most important component of the Reich Representation of German Jews (Reichsvertretung der deutschen Juden), which was founded on 17 September 1933 as an umbrella association of the major political Jewish organizations.[76] The Reich Representation was largely composed of the groups that had already made up the Central Committee, but with the addition of the Reich League of Jewish Combat Veterans, which was as influential as it was patriotically German in attitude. The representatives of the Jewish associations chose Leo Baeck as president of the Reich Representation. Born near Posen in 1873, Baeck was a religious scholar, rabbi, and philosopher who had served as a military rabbi in the imperial field army in the First

---

74 Account by Ernst Loewenberg, written in 1940 in Boston, in Monika Richarz (ed.), *Bürger auf Widerruf: Lebenszeugnisse deutscher Juden 1780–1945* (Munich: Beck, 1989), pp. 449–458.
75 Cited in Michael Wildt (ed.), *Die Judenpolitik des SD 1935 bis 1938: Eine Dokumentation* (Munich: Oldenbourg, 1995), p. 165.
76 Otto Dov Kulka (ed.), *Deutsches Judentum unter dem Nationalsozialismus*, vol. 1: *Dokumente zur Geschichte der Reichsvertretung der deutschen Juden 1933–1939* (Tübingen: Mohr Siebeck, 1997); Avraham Barkai, 'Jewish Self-Help in Nazi Germany, 1933–1939: The Dilemmas of Cooperation', in Francis R. Nicosia and David Scrase (eds.), *Jewish Life in Nazi Germany: Dilemmas and Responses* (New York: Berghahn, 2012), pp. 71–88.

World War. He was widely considered the recognized representative of Liberal German Judaism, the main sub-current of Reform Judaism to develop in Germany in the first half of the nineteenth century as a secession from Orthodoxy.[77] Guided by his sense of duty, Baeck assumed the appointment. The first public statement of the Reich Representation bears his imprint:

> At a time that is as hard and difficult and trying as any in Jewish history, but also significant as few times have been, we have been entrusted with the leadership and representation of the German Jews by a joint decision [...]. We must understand [the new regime in Germany] and not deceive ourselves.[78]

While the German Zionists redoubled their efforts to awaken a sense of Jewish national identity in 1933, expedited emigration to Palestine, and, as a movement that opposed assimilation, were supported in all this by the National Socialist state, the Association of National German Jews (Verband Nationaldeutscher Juden) continued to battle for the rights of the Jews in Germany until the organization was banned in 1935. Beyond such differences of opinion, the Reich Representation considered itself the overall spokesperson for Jews with regard to the National Socialist government and repeatedly protested against despotism. For example, in January 1934 the Reich Representation sent the position paper 'On the Present Situation of the Jews' to the Reich government. The almost eighty-page text documented the various forms of discrimination against the Jewish population in Germany, particularly in the economy (Doc. 99). Organizations such as the Reich League of Jewish Combat Veterans, the Central Association of German Citizens of the Jewish Faith, and several synagogue congregations also addressed petitions and complaints to Reich ministries, regional authorities, and municipal administrations (Docs. 47, 110, and 141).

The persecuted fought back. But they did so with civility, as if their adversaries were bound by the same notion of justice and would act in good faith. The Nazi persecutors, however, behaved improperly, constantly changed the rules, and were themselves uncertain what their next steps would be. They had no well-thought-out plan, but rather for the most part made ad hoc decisions – impelled and intoxicated by the self-generated pull of continual radicalization. They acted in the conviction that there was 'only the constant move forward on the road toward ever-new fields'.[79]

---

77 See Michael A. Meyer, *Response to Modernity: A History of the Reform Movement in Judaism* (Detroit, MI: Wayne State University Press, 1988).
78 Statement by the Reich Representation in *C.V.-Zeitung*, 21 Sept. 1933, cited in Yahil, *Holocaust*, pp. 77–78, Barkai, *'Wehr Dich!'*; Georg Heuberger and Fritz Backhaus (eds.), *Leo Baeck 1873–1956: Aus dem Stamme von Rabbinern* (Frankfurt am Main: Jüdischer Verlag, 2001).
79 Cited in Arendt, *Origins*, p. 394, with reference to Theodor Maunz, *Gestalt und Recht der Polizei* (Hamburg: Hanseatische Verlagsanstalt, 1943). Also see Martin Broszat, 'Zur Erklärung des nationalsozialistischen Judenmords', in Hermann Graml and Klaus-Dietmar Henke (eds.), *Nach Hitler: Der schwierige Umgang mit unserer Geschichte. Beiträge von Martin Broszat* (Munich: Oldenbourg, 1988 [1986]), p. 247; Hans Mommsen, 'The Realization of the Unthinkable: The "Final Solution of the Jewish Question in the Third Reich", in Gerhard Hirschfeld (ed.), *The Policies of Genocide: Jews and Soviet Prisoners of War in Nazi Germany* (London: Allen & Unwin, 1986), pp. 97–144.

The trust that German Jews continued to place in state institutions was demonstrated, for example, when the Jews of Treuchtlingen still turned to the local police in 1936 after teenagers intruded on a funeral ceremony and threw stones at the mourners. In 1937 Martha Beerwald, the mother of the philosopher Hannah Arendt, devised 'dinner party menus in the event of Hitler's overthrow', dreamed of her daughter's return to Germany, and, in light of the relative calm after the issuing of the Nuremberg Laws, had 'completely reconciled with Germany again, generally speaking'.[80] What is notable about this story is not so much the credulity of the mother as that of the astute, extremely well-informed daughter, who had emigrated to Paris back in 1933. The two women met up in Geneva, but Hannah Arendt apparently did not try to prevent her mother from returning home to Königsberg.

Violence and Special Legislation

At the beginning of National Socialist rule, there were no clear terms of reference for anti-Jewish policy. Discrimination and persecution were initially not the result of 'Führer orders' and Party resolutions. Following the principle of trial and error, the new state-sponsored antisemitism took shape gradually in an open process lasting many years and escalating on repeated occasions. Politicians and administrators in the nerve centres of the Reich took part in the process, as did local councils, active supporters of the NSDAP, work colleagues, apolitical clubmates, or the initiators of spontaneous popular campaigns.

Factors and interests of many kinds had an influence on antisemitic practices, sometimes slowing them down, sometimes speeding them up. The National Socialist leadership would regularly instigate brief waves of violent antisemitism only to then rein them in again by means of legislation – legislation that imposed restrictions on the Jews but also appeared to guarantee them residual freedoms and exceptions. In this way, out of numerous individual measures and practical suggestions, which were often not embraced immediately, there emerged an unclear but consistent manner of governing. The antisemitism of the street gave way to less conspicuous administrative routine, but it could be reactivated at the 'right' moment. The treacherous interplay between arbitrary violence and temporary moderation was characteristic of German policy towards the Jews prior to the November pogroms of 1938, in accordance with the pattern described by Ian Kershaw: 'pressure from below; green light from above; further violence from below; brakes from above assuaging the radicals through discriminatory legislation. The process had ratcheted up the persecution several notches.'[81]

Regardless of the methods, the aim from the very outset was to intimidate and terrify German Jews and to compel them to flee the country. The fact that in so doing the National Socialist leadership did not initially follow a clear strategy, but rather acted

---

80 Michael Wildt, 'Gewalt gegen Juden in Deutschland 1933–1939', *WerkstattGeschichte*, vol. 6, no. 18 (1997), pp. 5–80, here p. 65; Hannah Arendt and Heinrich Blücher, *Briefe 1936–1968*, ed. Lotte Köhler (Munich: Piper, 1996), letter from Arendt to Blücher, 13 Sept. 1937, p. 80.

81 Ian Kershaw, *Hitler, 1889–1936: Hubris* (London: Allen Lane, 1998), p. 571. Also see Wolf Gruner, 'Die NS-Judenverfolgung und die Kommunen: Zur wechselseitigen Dynamisierung von zentraler und lokaler Politik 1933–1941', *Vierteljahrshefte für Zeitgeschichte*, vol. 48, no. 1 (2000), pp. 75–126.

spontaneously and in accordance with the particular situation, is demonstrated by the 'Law on the Status of the Jews', which was drafted right after the boycott in early April 1933. An interdepartmental group, which was probably headed by Hitler's deputy, Rudolf Heß, had prepared it in order that 'legal' means could be used in the future to avoid direct violence and prevent foreign protests. The draft provided for occupational bans and the expulsion of foreign Jews, and prohibited sexual contact between Jews and non-Jews. Jews were to be labelled with a 'J' after their name and forced to join a state-supervised 'Association of Jews in Germany'. The preamble to the draft emphasized that the fundamental aim of the law was 'to take full advantage of the historically unique moment in order to cleanse the German people and to free it from an alien power, which has openly and secretly ruled it in its own house in ways that constituted an existential threat' (Doc. 27).

Hitler did not approve the bill. He preferred a slower approach. The first antisemitic laws were thus directed against Jewish members of specific occupational groups, e.g. lawyers, civil servants, salaried employees, and labourers in the public sector. For this purpose, in the context of the Civil Service Law (*Berufsbeamtengesetz*) of 7 April 1933, a regulation was required defining who was to be considered a Jew or 'intermarried with a Jew' (*jüdisch versippt*). By implication, the so-called 'Aryan Paragraph' also established who was to be considered an 'Aryan *Volksgenosse*' (Doc. 32). The ensuing legal provisions applied only to officials working for the state, regional, and municipal authorities. But in the following months it was used by the boards of most German associations and non-governmental entities to exclude all Jews or deprive them of their salaried or voluntary offices. By 31 December 1933 even the League of Blind War Veterans had expelled seventeen members on account of their 'non-Aryan' ancestry.[82] Jews who had converted to Protestantism suddenly became 'Jew Christians' (*Judenchristen*). In September 1933 the General Synod of the Protestant Church of the Old Prussian Union passed a resolution adopting the 'Aryan Paragraph' for its clergymen and officials (Doc. 75). Other Protestant regional churches and organizations followed suit.

The Law on the Revocation of Naturalization and the Deprivation of German Nationality, which was promulgated in mid July 1933, created the legal basis to revoke the German citizenship of people who were considered 'undesirable' from a *völkisch* standpoint, especially Jews of Polish or Russian origin naturalized after 1918.[83] In his seminal work on fascism published in 1963, the historian Ernst Nolte wrote: 'A state which deprives a section of its citizens of citizenship, through no fault of their own, in fact abrogates all other contracts and commitments from the past'.[84] Concurrently, ministry officials were discussing a law that was intended to deprive the German Jews as a whole of their civil rights and to distinguish between 'Aryan' citizens of the Reich and 'non-Aryan' subjects of the Reich. It was not issued until the end of 1935, as one of the two

---

82 Gabriel Richter, 'Blindheit und Eugenik: Zwischen Widerstand und Integration', in *Blinde unterm Hakenkreuz: Erkennen, Trauern, Begegnen* (Marburg an der Lahn: Deutscher Verein der Blinden und Sehbehinderten in Studium und Beruf, 1991), pp. 16–34, here p. 21.
83 *Gesetz über den Widerruf von Einbürgerungen und die Aberkennung der deutschen Staatsangehörigkeit*, 14 July 1933, *Reichsgesetzblatt*, 1933, I, p. 480.
84 Ernst Nolte, *Three Faces of Fascism: Action Française, Italian Fascism, National Socialism*, trans. Leila Vennewitz (New York: Holt, Rinehart & Winston, 1966 [German edn. 1963]), p. 378.

Nuremberg Laws.[85] In July 1933 Göring put a halt to prosecution of the antisemitically motivated murders and acts of violence committed up to that time, as they had taken place, he said, during the course of the National Socialist revolution. Those already sentenced were granted amnesty (Doc. 69).

Following the April boycott, various foreign governments had intervened in opposition to the persecution of the Jews. The Polish ambassador in particular made repeated visits to the Reich Foreign Office. Inside Germany, the Jewish organizations and communities protested, but non-Jewish Germans did so as well. To the extent that the press had not been subjected to *Gleichschaltung*, the reporting of some individual newspapers continued to be critical. For example, on 11 April 1933 the *Deutsche Allgemeine Zeitung* published Wilhelm Furtwängler's letter protesting against the exclusion of Jewish musicians from the German stage. 'Ultimately, there is only one dividing line I recognize,' the chief conductor of the Berlin Philharmonic had written to Goebbels, 'that between good and bad art.'

In September 1933 Martin Bormann from the staff of the Deputy of the Führer ordered the lifting of the bans enacted in some places that prohibited Jews from going to public baths, markets, or certain villages (Doc. 76). This directive, however, in no way altered the fundamentally ambivalent policy. For example, on 17 January 1934 Minister of the Interior Frick criticized the blanket application of the 'Aryan Paragraph', but conveyed to the Reich and regional authorities that his intention was by no means to prevent the 'special treatment of non-Aryans'.[86]

From late 1933 until the end of 1934, the initiative with regard to the persecution of the Jews shifted to local authorities. While some cities lifted their anti-Jewish regulations again in the second half of 1933, municipal officials in other areas made arbitrary decisions against Jewish citizens and organizations. In many places, NSDAP groups such as the SA or the National Socialist Organization of Crafts, Trade, and Commerce (NS-Hago) boycotted Jewish firms without having received any central directives (Docs. 12, 15, 141, 143, and 147). A sizeable number of innkeepers, hoteliers, and business people denied Jews access to their premises. In the public display cases of the Nazi smear-sheet *Der Stürmer*, Germans who continued to make purchases in Jewish shops were named and shamed, occasionally even with accompanying photos.

On several occasions Hjalmar Schacht, the Reich minister of economics and president of the Reichsbank, intervened in instances of discrimination not regulated by law. He was not motivated primarily by humanitarian considerations and matters of legal principle. Rather, he mainly feared that arbitrary action at local level would be detrimental to the country's economic interests, particularly abroad (Doc. 189). In addition, in the first years of the National Socialist regime, by no means all German judges were

---

85 Kurt Pätzold, *Faschismus, Rassenwahn, Judenverfolgung: Eine Studie zur politischen Strategie und Taktik des faschistischen Imperialismus 1933–1935* (Berlin: Deutscher Verlag der Wissenschaften, 1975), p. 140.
86 Herbert Michaelis and Ernst Schraepler (eds.), *Ursachen und Folgen: Vom deutschen Zusammenbruch 1918 und 1945 bis zur staatlichen Neuordnung Deutschlands in der Gegenwart. Eine Urkunden- und Dokumentensammlung zur Zeitgeschichte*, vol. 9: *Das Dritte Reich: Die Zertrümmerung des Parteienstaates und die Grundlegung der Diktatur* (Berlin: H. Wendler, 1964), doc. 216, p. 397; Kurt Pätzold (ed.), *Verfolgung, Vertreibung, Vernichtung: Dokumente des faschistischen Antisemitismus 1933–1942* (Leipzig: Reclam, 1983), doc. 25, pp. 70–71.

willing to issue verdicts that were desirable from the standpoint of racial policy. Until 1937, several rulings were issued in favour of Jewish pedlars whom municipal offices for public order had denied permission to set up market stalls. In 1935 the Prussian Higher Administrative Court reversed a lower-court opinion, which had stated: 'Owing to the observations made over the course of centuries' and the 'approach that is characteristic of the German people', Jewish pedlars as a whole ought to be 'regarded as unreliable and therefore excluded'. The high court's decision became legally binding and *Jugend und Recht*, a journal for trainee lawyers, seethed: 'The German people do not stand behind this verdict rendered in their name.'[87]

Withdrawal, Self-Help, and Emigration

While the economic situation of most Germans stabilized after 1933 and soon improved, Jewish families experienced a drastic social decline and often had acute financial difficulties. In the very first year of National Socialist rule, tens of thousands of Jews were laid off or forced to accept substantial losses of income. Of the approximately 100,000 Jewish-owned firms and shops in 1933, 25,000 vanished in the two years that followed. Most small and medium-sized firms suffered serious losses of revenue due to ongoing local boycotts. They were forced to dismiss personnel or went bankrupt. Jewish physicians had already lost their accreditation with health insurance companies by the summer of 1933, and thus a substantial proportion of their patients, and half of their practices closed by 1937. The experience of Jewish lawyers was similar: to protect their interests, a non-Jewish client was de facto dependent on an 'Aryan' lawyer.[88] Increasing numbers of Jewish women entered the workforce in order to contribute to the family's income. Many retailers who lost their businesses as a result of persecution sought to make ends meet as door-to-door or travelling salesmen.

The feeling of growing isolation affected the assimilated families in particular, especially the men. They had been more strongly integrated than their wives into the world of work and the activities of non-Jewish clubs and associations. Out of necessity, they soon changed their behaviour. They sought to avoid drawing attention to themselves or causing any conflict, and now did something that never would have crossed their minds before: they gave preference to restaurants with Jewish proprietors, who advertised in the Jewish newspapers to which they had recently begun to subscribe. The Jewish community and family newspapers urged their readers not to behave in a way that might attract attention. They published job advertisements in which Jews sought Jewish employers, and notices in which shops run by Jews tried to woo new Jewish customers.

---

[87] Memorandum from the German Council of Municipalities, Department IV [1937], LAB, Rep. 142/7, 4-10-2/Nr. 13; Ernst Fraenkel, *Der Doppelstaat: Recht und Justiz im 'Dritten Reich'*, new edn. (Frankfurt am Main: Fischer, 1984 [English edn, 1941]), p. 121 (this example is not in the English-language original, *The Dual State: A Contribution to the Theory of Dictatorship*, (New York: Oxford University Press, 1941).

[88] Kümmel, 'Die Ausschaltung', p. 76; Jacob Boas, 'The Shrinking World of German Jewry, 1933–1938', *Leo Baeck Institute Year Book*, vol. 31 (1986), pp. 241–266, here pp. 254–255; Avraham Barkai and Paul Mendes-Flohr, *Deutsch-Jüdische Geschichte in der Neuzeit*, vol. 4: *Aufbruch und Zerstörung 1918–1945* (Munich: Beck, 1997), p. 232.

Within a matter of months, German Jews and Germans who scarcely remembered their Jewish roots became Jews again. This change was seen in the rapid upswing in the activities of Jewish clubs and associations, a boom fuelled by isolation and fear. The Reich League of Jewish Combat Veterans and its youth and sports clubs gained almost 50,000 new members in only a few years. Despite the substantial increase in emigration to Palestine, which began without delay in 1933, the Zionist Federation for Germany saw its membership swell from 7,000 in 1932 to 22,000 in 1935. Young people in particular turned to the Zionists, and thus the Zionist youth organization Hehalutz (The Pioneer) swelled from 500 members in 1933 to 16,000 at the end of 1935.

In the schools the situation was similar. In 1933, 75 per cent of all Jewish schoolchildren attended state schools, but by the end of 1937 the figure was only 40 per cent. In Berlin, over the same time period, the number of Jewish pupils at state schools declined from 12,746 to 2,704. Simultaneously, enrolment at Jewish schools rose from 2,000 to 8,845. For most pupils, as W. Michael Blumenthal reports, school was 'comforting and protective, and the teachers were dedicated and sympathetic and did their best to shield us from outside pressures'. Most of the children were from assimilated family households and received here their 'first exposure to Jewish religion and […] traditions'. Their parents reacted with a 'mixture of embarrassment and bemusement' when their children suddenly began to chant Hebrew prayers.[89]

The enforced retreat from what had now become 'Aryan' German public life was reflected in the upsurge in newly formed Jewish cultural leagues (Kulturbünde). The first such organization came into being in Berlin in the summer of 1933, with an initial membership of 12,500.[90] It was headed by the physician and musicologist Kurt Singer. Leo Baeck served as honorary chairman along with the painter Max Liebermann and the novelist Jakob Wassermann. Soon the culture leagues numbered more than 70,000 members in around 100 German cities. The Berlin Culture League was able to open its first theatre season in October 1933 with Gotthold Ephraim Lessing's *Nathan der Weise* (Nathan the Wise). It did not take long for the authorities to forbid Jewish actors and musicians to perform the works of 'German composers' and 'German dramatists'.

After a while, the nature of the Jewish communities changed. Once primarily religious centres, they now became providers of legal advice and welfare. They granted microloans to shopkeepers who had been harmed by the boycott, helped those who had been laid off to search for new employment, and placed young people in apprenticeships. The possibilities for providing such help dwindled as the number of those in need of advice and aid increased and – conversely – the receipts of donations and contributions decreased. State interventions additionally hampered the work. In individual provinces of the German Reich, Jewish communities lost the tax privileges they had previously enjoyed as public

---

89 Barkai and Mendes-Flohr, *Deutsch-Jüdische Geschichte*, pp. 237–240; Wolf Gruner, 'Die Reichshauptstadt und die Verfolgung der Berliner Juden 1933–1945', in Reinhard Rürup (ed.), *Jüdische Geschichte in Berlin: Essays und Studien* (Berlin: Hentrich, 1995), pp. 229–266, here table 2, p. 257; quotation from W. Michael Blumenthal, *The Invisible Wall: Germans and Jews. A Personal Exploration* (Washington, DC: Counterpoint, 1998), p. 342.

90 Eike Geisel and Henryk M. Broder, *Premiere und Pogrom: Der jüdische Kulturbund 1933–1941. Texte und Bilder* (Berlin: Siedler, 1992); Rebecca Rovit, *The Jewish Kulturbund Theatre Company in Nazi Berlin* (Iowa City, IA: University of Iowa Press, 2012); Gabriele Fritsch-Vivié, *Gegen alle Widerstände: Der Jüdische Kulturbund 1933–1941* (Berlin: Hentrich & Hentrich, 2013).

corporations. Associations and foundations were shut down by the Gestapo and dispossessed by the tax offices. Jewish employment agencies were banned. In late 1936 the Reich Fiscal Court revoked, with retroactive effect, the exemption of Jewish foundations and communities from the payment of the wealth tax, an exception enjoyed until then by charitable organizations in general.

When the municipal social security offices began to reduce benefits for the Jewish poor in 1935, Jewish welfare offices stepped in to assist. In October of the same year, impoverished Jews were excluded from the aid provided by the Winter Relief Agency of the German People. As a result, the Jewish communities were forced to set up, within a matter of weeks, their own winter relief organization funded by donations. While the number of 'Aryan' unemployed dropped by two thirds between 1933 and the summer of 1936, the number of Jews out of work rose steadily. In mid 1936, more unemployed Jews were counted than at the start of the National Socialist dictatorship, in total 37,204[91] – despite the fact that more than 80,000 Jews had already emigrated, the vast majority of them of prime working age. In order to relieve German Jews of their growing financial burden, Jewish organizations outside Germany contributed substantial funds, especially to the Reich Representation of Jews in Germany and the Central Committee of the German Jews for Relief and Reconstruction. The main sources of financial aid were the American Jewish Joint Distribution Committee (JDC), the Central British Fund for German Jewry, and the Jewish Colonization Association.[92]

In 1933 alone, 37,000 German Jews left their homeland.[93] At first the neighbouring European countries of France, the Netherlands, Switzerland, and Czechoslovakia were the main destinations of the refugees, in addition to Britain and Palestine. International Jewish aid organizations supported the immigrants, many of whom had fled in haste during the first few months, carrying only a single suitcase. In 1934 and 1935 the number of Jewish emigrants decreased to 23,000 and 21,000, respectively. By the end of 1937 more than 125,000 had left Germany. Of a total of 116,000 children and young people between the ages of six and twenty, 67,000 had emigrated. As a result of the rapid decline in membership, many smaller Jewish communities disbanded as early as 1933 and 1934 (Doc. 101).

Tens of thousands of Jewish Germans took an alternative path. They fled from the smaller communities to the big cities. In general, people there were more liberal-minded, though many were simply more indifferent. The Jews there experienced far less social pressure to adapt than people in the smaller municipalities, villages, and market towns.

---

91 Clemens Vollnhals, 'Jüdische Selbsthilfe bis 1938', in Wolfgang Benz (ed.), *Die Juden in Deutschland 1933–1945: Leben unter nationalsozialistischer Herrschaft* (Munich: Beck, 1988), pp. 314–411, here p. 374. Also see Salomon Adler-Rudel, *Jüdische Selbsthilfe unter dem Naziregime 1933–1939: Im Spiegel der Berichte der Reichsvertretung der Juden in Deutschland* (Tübingen: Mohr, 1974); Wolf Gruner, *Öffentliche Wohlfahrt und Judenverfolgung: Wechselwirkung lokaler und zentraler Politik im NS-Staat (1933–1942)* (Munich: Oldenbourg, 2002).
92 Yehuda Bauer, *My Brother's Keeper: A History of the American Jewish Joint Distribution Committee, 1929–1939* (Philadelphia, PA: Jewish Publication Society of America, 1974), pp. 105–137.
93 On emigration, see Werner Rosenstock, 'Exodus, 1933–1939: A Survey of Jewish Emigration from Germany', *Leo Baeck Institute Year Book*, vol. 1 (1956), pp. 373–390; Herbert A. Strauss, 'Jewish Emigration from Germany: Nazi Policies and Jewish Responses', *Leo Baeck Institute Year Book*, vol. 25 (1980), pp. 313–361, here p. 26, and vol. 26 (1981), pp. 343–409.

A good indicator of this trend is the disappearance of Jewish retail businesses. All told, their number was halved in Germany between 1933 and 1937.[94] In the villages and small towns, almost all the Jewish-owned retail shops soon had to be abandoned. Because social control was so much tighter in such places, customers stayed away. While around 20 per cent of such businesses in Hamburg and 30 per cent of those in Berlin had to close, the figures were 47 per cent in Heidelberg, 57 per cent in Göttingen, and 69 per cent in Marburg.[95]

When looking back at the history of the Holocaust, it becomes clear that the more antisemitic the behaviour of 'Aryan' neighbours, customers, and work colleagues at the beginning of the National Socialist regime, the more quickly the embattled Jews chose to flee, thereby saving their lives. However, if long-standing Christian friends and acquaintances were helpful and supportive, the persecuted Jews were more likely to opt to stay. That choice dramatically reduced their chances of survival.[96]

After 1935, emigrants no longer focused on Europe and Palestine but looked instead towards South Africa, the USA, and Latin America. In those regions, however, the number of immigrants remained small at first. Between 1933 and June 1937, approximately 17,000 Jews made it to the USA, distinctly fewer than allowed by the annual quota of 26,000 German immigrants. In the first few years the German state supported and facilitated emigration to Palestine and, to this end, concluded the 'Haavara' (Transfer) Agreement, which simultaneously increased the export of German goods by means of an indirect transfer of the emigrants' capital. Between 1933 and 1937, 40,000 German Jews arrived as immigrants in Palestine.[97]

Aid organizations in Germany and in the neighbouring European states arranged and paid for visas, railway tickets, and passage on ships for emigrants who did not possess the requisite wealth. Jewish newspapers, particularly community papers, reported in detail on the conditions of travel and admission to various countries, and on the possibilities for learning trades and languages or sitting additional examinations that could be helpful for immigrants. Lawyers such as Robert M. W. Kempner, later assistant US chief counsel at the post-war trial of the major Nazi war criminals before the International Military Tribunal in Nuremberg, offered their services 'for the proper and speedy completion of your emigration'. Both young women and young men published personal ads in search of a spouse: 'I'm looking for a man who is prepared to establish a life in Palestine with me. I am twenty-three years old, pretty, and well-to-do.'[98]

---

[94] Avraham Barkai, *From Boycott to Annihilation: The Economic Struggle of German Jews, 1933–1943*, trans. William Templer (Hanover, NH: University Press of New England, 1989 [German edn, 1987]), pp. 110–113.

[95] Frank Bajohr and Dieter Pohl, *Der Holocaust als offenes Geheimnis: Die Deutschen, die NS-Führung und die Alliierten* (Munich: Beck, 2006), p. 29. On Berlin, see Christoph Kreutzmüller, *Ausverkauf: Die Vernichtung der jüdischen Gewerbetätigkeit in Berlin 1930–1945* (Berlin: Metropol, 2012).

[96] Konrad Kwiet, 'Gehen oder bleiben? Die deutschen Juden am Wendepunkt', in Walter Pehle (ed.), *Der Judenpogrom 1938: Von der 'Reichskristallnacht' zum Völkermord* (Frankfurt am Main: Fischer, 1988), pp. 132–145.

[97] Rosenstock, 'Exodus', p. 376; Werner Feilchenfeld, Dolf Michaelis, and Ludwig Pinner, *Haavara-Transfer nach Palästina und Einwanderung deutscher Juden 1933–1939* (Tübingen: Mohr, 1972); Francis R. Nicosia, *The Third Reich and the Palestine Question*, new edn (New Brunswick, NJ/London: Transaction, 2000 [1985]).

Because Palestine and Latin America both gave priority to immigrants who were farmers and craftsmen, Zionist organizations in particular intensified a strategy they had already developed in the 1920s: offering occupational training on farms and courses in skilled crafts and trades. In 1936 there were approximately thirty such training sites in Germany and one non-Zionist training camp in Groß-Breesen in Silesia (Doc. 266). Similar facilities were open to German Jews in many European countries. The young people thus trained were given priority when immigration certificates for Palestine were issued.

At the training centres the young people learned about raising livestock, tilling the soil, and horticulture in order to prepare themselves for the hardships of a new life in Palestine or elsewhere. Ideologically they drew upon an existing set of ideas: socialism, belief in the constructive role of the vanguard and in the German youth movement, the adventurous spirit of the pioneer, national self-discovery, and the romanticizing of ordinary life, in opposition to an increasingly arduous present. In particular, however, the young people could feel relatively free there. Joel König reported on the retraining camp at Steckelsdorf, west of Berlin. Even after the war had begun, he said, it was 'a peaceful enclave – and there we were allowed to live'.[99]

Nonetheless, in the mid 1930s a considerable number of German Jews, deeply attached to their homeland, still hoped that the National Socialist regime would fail and collapse within a short time. Consequently, they tried to persevere in the country, even if they understood clearly that the basic situation in German society had changed.[100] Outside Germany, there were Jewish organizations that feared that a collapse and emigration of German Jewry would boost anti-emancipation policies in other countries, such as Poland. James Marshall of the JDC was quoted in April 1935 as stating that emigration was a concession to the Hitler theory that the Jews must get out. There were other groups in Germany 'that have seriously suffered', he said, and he 'felt that in trying to emigrate, German Jews tended to set themselves off from other groups who in the long run would be helpful to them'.[101]

1935: *The Year of the Nuremberg Laws*

In December 1934 the top-ranking officials of the National Socialist state placed on the agenda the 'complete elimination of the Jew from the German community'. They discussed the comprehensive 'legislative settlement of the Jewish question', a matter that

---

98 Advertisements in the *Jüdische Rundschau* in 1935, published in Susanne Heim, "Deutschland muß ihnen ein Land ohne Zukunft sein': Die Zwangsmigration der Juden 1933 bis 1938', in Eberhard Jungfer et al. (eds.), *Arbeitsmigration und Flucht: Vertreibung und Arbeitskräfteregulierung in Zwischeneuropa* (Berlin: Schwarze Risse; Göttingen: Rote Strasse, 1993), pp. 48–81, here p. 50.
99 Werner T. Angress, *Between Fear and Hope: Jewish Youth and the Third Reich*, trans. Christine Granger (New York: Columbia University Press, 1988 [German edn, 1985]); citation from Joel König [Ezra Ben-Gershom], *David: Aufzeichnungen eines Überlebenden* (Frankfurt am Main: Fischer, 1979), p. 115.
100 For an analysis of the changing strategies of German Jews for coping with conditions in their homeland, see Guy Miron, *The Waning of Emancipation: Jewish History, Memory, and the Rise of Fascism in Germany, France, and Hungary*, Part 1: 'Germany, 1929–1938' (Detroit, MI: Wayne State University Press, 2011), pp. 30–53.
101 Bauer, *My Brother's Keeper*, p. 116.

had already been pondered repeatedly. It included the prohibition of marriages between Jews and non-Jews, and its objective was the complete social isolation of Jewish Germans (Doc. 146). In January 1935 a centrally steered propaganda campaign began once again, followed by acts of violence in which the Hitler Youth participated to an increasing degree, along with the SA and SS (Doc. 169). Concurrently, the state-controlled press vilified Jews, calling them 'race defilers' and 'criminals'.

On 20 August 1935 an inter-ministerial meeting was held in the Reich Ministry of Economics to discuss the economic consequences of certain Party activities (Doc. 189). Hjalmar Schacht reported on the head of the Reichsbank branch in Arnswalde, who had been named and shamed in one of *Der Stürmer*'s public display cases because he had made a purchase in a Jew's shop. Schacht spoke 'of the utmost perfidy and infamy' of this tactic and demanded that an end be put to the practice of denunciation. While a representative of the Ministry of Propaganda saw 'nothing reprehensible' in it, Minister of the Interior Frick spoke out in opposition to such abuse and announced that his ministry would soon submit a number of orders intended to 'solve the Jewish question in a completely legal manner'. That same day he proclaimed in a decree that Hitler had categorically prohibited any independent action.[102] In the case of such directives, local Party offices frequently held the view that 'certain orders, particularly in the area of the Jewish question, would have to be formulated with foreign countries in mind'. But it was known to every 'authentic National Socialist', they believed, how 'the true will of the Führer [is] to be carried out'.[103]

At the Nuremberg rally a few weeks later, Hitler, Goebbels, Frick, and Heß discussed what became known as the Nuremberg Laws.[104] Even before this Party congress had ended, the laws were passed by acclamation in a special session of the German Reichstag. They consisted of two parts: the Reich Citizenship Law (*Reichsbürgergesetz*) and the Law for the Protection of German Blood and German Honour, or Blood Protection Law (*Gesetz zum Schutz des deutschen Blutes und der deutschen Ehre*, or *Blutschutzgesetz*). The former revoked the political rights of the German Jews and declared them mere subjects of the state (*Staatsangehörige*). Henceforth, only 'Aryan' Germans could be citizens of the Reich (*Reichsbürger*). The Blood Protection Law forbade marriages and extramarital sexual relations between Jews and non-Jews. In addition, 'for the protection of German honour', Jews were forbidden to display the Reich flag and the swastika flag (Docs. 198–199). From this point on, German criminal law recognized the crime of race defilement (*Rassenschande*). In the years that followed, Jewish men in every part of Germany were denounced, by neighbours and others motivated by resentment and sexual envy, for actual sexual relationships with 'Aryan' women or a merely suspected *occasio*

---

102 Hilberg, *Destruction*, pp. 35–36.
103 Report by the Regierungspräsident in Wiesbaden, 31 August 1935, documented in Otto Dov Kulka and Eberhard Jäckel (eds.), *The Jews in the Secret Nazi Reports on Popular Opinion in Germany, 1933–1945*, trans. William Templer (New Haven, CT/London: Yale University Press, 2010 [German edn, 2004]), enclosed CD, no. 1141 (in German).
104 Neumann, *Behemoth*, p. 151; Hans Mommsen, *Das NS-Regime und die Auslöschung des Judentums in Europa* (Göttingen: Wallstein, 2014), pp. 49–66; Cornelia Essner, *Die 'Nürnberger Gesetze' oder die Verwaltung des Rassenwahns 1933–1945* (Paderborn: Schöningh, 2002), pp. 113–154; Magnus Brechtken et al. (eds.), *Die Nürnberger Gesetze – 80 Jahre danach: Vorgeschichte, Entstehung, Auswirkungen* (Göttingen: Wallstein, 2017); John J. Michalczyk (ed.), *Nazi Law: From Nuremberg to Nuremberg* (London: Bloomsbury Academic, 2017).

proxima, the 'proximate occasion of sin'. They were persecuted by the Gestapo and sentenced by the courts to imprisonment or penal servitude. The German women involved were not prosecuted, but quite often they were publicly humiliated for 'race betrayal'[105] (Doc. 186).

The Reich Supreme Court in Leipzig availed itself of the new laws in a noteworthy way and declared that the German Jews had undergone 'civil death'. On 27 June 1936 it rejected the claim for damages filed by a Jewish film director whose contract had been cancelled in February 1933 by his non-Jewish producer, who had acted out of racially based political opportunism. On the basis of the clause stating that no remuneration would be forthcoming if the director could not fulfil the contract because of illness or death, the highest German court ruled that 'civil death', a concept stemming from the older law of aliens and now introduced by the new race laws for Jews, was equivalent to 'physical death'. The exact words of the judges' ruling were that the 'change in the legal validity of personhood arising from legally recognized, race-related political viewpoints' was to be 'treated as equivalent' to the event of physical death as provided for in the director's contract.[106]

After the passage of the two laws in Nuremberg, the definition of the term 'Jew' became the subject of heated debate. On one side were the racial science experts, who wanted to use all manner of complicated methods to trace every conceivable 'drop of Jewish blood', if possible. On the other side were the officials of the Reich Ministry of the Interior, who sought a bureaucratic procedure that would be as efficient as possible, one that would function 'automatically'. Hitler aligned himself with the administrative pragmatists. The First Regulation to the Reich Citizenship Law was thus issued on 14 November 1935 (Doc. 210). It provided that anyone with at least three grandparents of the Jewish faith must in the future be regarded as a 'Jew by race' (*Rassejude*). Under this regulation, someone who had two such grandparents was defined as a *Mischling* (half-caste) of the first degree, while someone with only one grandparent of the Jewish faith was henceforth considered a *Mischling* of the second degree.

In 1933 the *Mischling* category included approximately 150,000 persons. Discrimination often came as a greater surprise to them than to so-called full Jews (*Volljuden*), especially as the National Socialist definition of a Jew diverged from that under Jewish religious law. Almost without exception they thought of themselves as Germans and had difficulty understanding why, often as early as 1933, they were denied access to clubs and associations, the Hitler Youth, or careers as military officers. For that reason, in June 1933, the Reich Association of Christian German Citizens of Non-Aryan or Not Pure Aryan Descent was founded to represent the interests of those termed *Mischlinge*.[107]

---

105 Alexandra Przyrembel, '*Rassenschande*': *Reinheitsmythos und Vernichtungslegitimation im Nationalsozialismus* (Göttingen: Vandenhoeck & Ruprecht, 2003); Patricia Szobar, 'Telling Sexual Stories in the Nazi Courts of Law: Race Defilement in Germany, 1933 to 1945', in Dagmar Herzog (ed.), *Sexuality and German Fascism* (New York: Berghahn, 2005), pp. 131–163.

106 Fraenkel, *Der Doppelstaat*, p. 127 (this passage is not in the English-language original, *The Dual State*).

107 Aleksandar-Saša Vuletić, *Christen jüdischer Herkunft im Dritten Reich: Verfolgung und organisierte Selbsthilfe 1933–1939* (Mainz: P. von Zabern, 1999). After the compulsory exclusion of all 'full Jews', the Reich Association was renamed in 1936 as the St Paul's Covenant (Paulus-Bund), Association of Non-Aryan Christians.

In addition to the *Mischlinge*, a further 50,000 Jews lived in so-called mixed marriages (*Mischehen*). Their partners were classified as 'intermarried with a Jew', and stigmatized for that reason.[108] Thousands of married couples divorced in order to secure the professional future of the 'Aryan' spouse (Doc. 109). If the couple decided nonetheless to remain married, in the great majority of cases that protected the Jewish spouse from deportation later on. For the Christian spouse, the mixed marriage entailed enormous disadvantages (Doc. 191). Victor Klemperer dedicated his book *LTI: Notizbuch eines Philologen* (*The Language of the Third Reich*), published in 1947, to his non-Jewish wife, Eva, who had endured with him the humiliation, the Dresden 'Jew houses' (*Judenhäuser*), the fear, and the hunger: 'For without you this book would not exist today and neither would its author.'[109]

From the very outset – and in increasing measure after 1935 – many officials were dismissed because they were married to Jewish women or because they had Jewish grandparents as well as Christian ones (Doc. 303). The scope was never precisely delineated in the case of the *Mischlinge* and mixed marriages, for pragmatic reasons and in order to keep the 'Aryan' relatives quiet. As a result, the informally defined sphere of contact between non-Jewish and Jewish Germans was transformed into a murky zone of separation characterized by fearful and considerate silence, beyond which the 'full Jews', above all, were isolated.

Because the Nuremberg Laws aimed to segregate the German Jews from the Christian majority population, the Gestapo Central Office (Gestapa) shut down the Association of National German Jews on 14 November 1935 on the grounds that it was hostile to the state, and confiscated its assets.[110] The Central Association of German Citizens of the Jewish Faith was forced to change its name to the Central Association of Jews in Germany (Centralverein der Juden in Deutschland). The Reich Representation of German Jews now had to be called the Reich Representation of Jews in Germany (Reichsvertretung der Juden in Deutschland).

The Centralization of Policy towards Jews

An organization that later acquired central importance in the persecution of the German and the European Jews played only a minor role in the first few years: the SD. It had been established in 1931 as the NSDAP's own intelligence organization by Reinhard Heydrich, at the time a 27-year-old former naval officer. From April 1933 to 1934 Heydrich, together with his mentor Heinrich Himmler, ran the Bavarian Political Police. Just one

---

108 H[ans] G[ünther] Adler, *Der verwaltete Mensch: Studien zur Deportation der Juden aus Deutschland* (Tübingen: Mohr, 1974), pp. 278–322; Beate Meyer, *'Jüdische Mischlinge': Rassenpolitik und Verfolgungserfahrung 1933–1945* (Hamburg: Dölling und Galitz, 1999).
109 'To my wife Eva Klemperer', dedication, Dresden, Christmas 1946, in Victor Klemperer, *The Language of the Third Reich: LTI, Lingua Tertii Imperii: A Philologist's Notebook*, trans. Martin Brady (London: Athlone, 2000 [German edn, 1947]).
110 Decree issued by the Gestapo Central Office (Gestapa) (II 1 B 2–64 640/J. 577/35), 18 Nov. 1935, cited in Joseph Walk (ed.), *Das Sonderrecht für die Juden im NS-Staat: Eine Sammlung der gesetzlichen Maßnahmen und Richtlinien. Inhalt und Bedeutung* (Heidelberg: Müller Juristischer, 1981), p. 141.

year later the two men succeeded in taking over the Gestapo Central Office in Prussia and, step by step, in unifying the political police forces of the various provinces under the Gestapo and placing them, along with the Criminal Police (Kripo), under central state control.[111]

From mid 1935 the Gestapo attempted to catalogue individual Jews on the basis of the membership rolls of Jewish organizations. The local Gestapo offices monitored the Jewish organizations in their jurisdiction. They persecuted individual Jews for violation of anti-Jewish regulations, for currency offences, and, later, for so-called race defilement. Such action was ordinarily taken on the basis of denunciations. Primarily, however, the Gestapo dealt at first with the political opponents of the regime: between 1933 and 1937 the Gestapo in Krefeld thus took action against a total of 180 persons, 19 of whom were Jews, between 1933 and 1937.[112]

In October 1935 Hitler adopted the proposal of Reichsführer SS Heinrich Himmler to give the entire police force an ideological mission. This meant assigning it complex tasks that went beyond the usual functions of ensuring public order, conducting surveillance, and, if necessary, employing terror. The police now became, as Heydrich's deputy Werner Best expressed it, the 'guardian of the political health of the German people's body [*Volkskörper*]'. On 17 June 1936 Hitler appointed Himmler Chief of the German Police in the Reich Ministry of the Interior. Himmler restructured the police and created two main offices: the Order Police and the Security Police. The latter was an amalgamation of the Criminal Police and the Gestapo under the control of Heydrich. In addition, Heydrich continued to head the SD, which slowly turned from a Party agency into a state institution. In both organizations, sections for Jewish affairs were established, though they only slowly gained influence. From now on, the police and the SS were firmly linked. Himmler referred to himself as Reichsführer SS and Chief of the German Police. Heydrich held dual functions as head of the SD and head of the Security Police. Formally, however, he did not receive the title Chief of the Security Police and the SD until 27 September 1939.[113]

In 1936, with the Olympic Winter and Summer Games approaching, the Reich government paid increased attention to international reactions. The Winter Olympics were held from 6 to 16 February in Garmisch-Partenkirchen. When the Jewish student David Frankfurter shot the leader of the NSDAP Regional Group for Switzerland, Wilhelm Gustloff, in Davos on 4 February, the National Socialist leadership made sure that no acts of

---

111 Hans Buchheim, 'The SS: Instrument of Domination', in Hans Buchheim, Martin Broszat, Hans-Adolf Jacobsen, and Helmut Krausnick, *Anatomy of the SS State*, trans. Richard Barry, Marian Jackson, and Dorothy Long (London: Collins, 1968 [German edn, 1965]), pp. 127–301, here pp. 145–156; Robert Gellately, *The Gestapo and German Society: Enforcing Racial Policy, 1933–1945* (Oxford: Clarendon, 1990); Carsten Dams and Michael Stolle, *The Gestapo: Power and Terror in the Third Reich* (Oxford: Oxford University Press, 2014). On Heydrich, see Robert Gerwarth, *Hitler's Hangman: The Life of Heydrich* (New Haven, CT: Yale University Press, 2011). On Himmler, see Peter Longerich, *Heinrich Himmler: A Life*, trans. Jeremy Noakes and Lesley Sharpe (Oxford: Oxford University Press, 2012 [German edn, 2008]).
112 Eric A. Johnson, *Nazi Terror: The Gestapo, Jews, and Ordinary Germans* (New York: Basic Books, 2000), pp. 143–158.
113 Buchheim, 'The SS', pp. 166–172; George C. Browder, *Foundations of the Nazi State: The Formation of Sipo and SD* (Lexington, KY: University Press of Kentucky, 1990), pp. 208–249; Herbert, *Best*, pp. 168–180 and 186–191; Best quotation: p. 169.

anti-Jewish violence took place (Doc. 225). On 7 March the Wehrmacht entered the Rhineland, which had been designated a demilitarized zone under the terms of the Treaty of Versailles (1919) and the Treaty of Locarno (1926). Neither Britain nor France intervened. As a result, this risky undertaking helped to strengthen Hitler's domestic standing and substantially increased his freedom of action: 'Without wavering and hesitating, literally regardless of the consequences, the regime relied from now on upon momentum, military build-up, and war. Inaction was something it rejected as a threat to its existence.'[114]

Hitler had scarcely opened the Summer Olympics in Berlin on 1 August 1936 when he wrote the secret position paper on the Four-Year Plan. The memorandum outlined the goal of arming Germany within four years for a war of aggression. In this secret text Hitler spoke in thinly veiled terms of the planned dispossession of the Jews. They were to be held liable collectively for all damage 'inflicted on the German economy and thus on the German people by individual members of this criminal group'.[115] To fund the military build-up, such large loans were taken out that they could be paid off only with the spoils of a predatory war. To the various objections to the unprofitable arms build-up and the manifestly dubious methods of financing it, Göring, as Plenipotentiary for the Four-Year Plan, responded with this comment on 17 December 1938: 'No end to the military build-up is foreseen. The only thing that matters here is victory or defeat. If we are victorious, the economy will be sufficiently compensated.'[116]

The SD, with only about 200 employees in the entire Reich in 1934, had neither the human resources nor the requisite authority to influence anti-Jewish policy in a significant way. Only after the passage of the Nuremberg Laws did the systematic 'fight against Jewry' begin in the SD. In January 1936 Department II 112 was established especially for this purpose. Adolf Eichmann and Dieter Wisliceny, who were later two of the main organizers of the deportation of the European Jews, worked there from the beginning. In 1937 they were joined by Herbert Hagen and Theodor Dannecker. In April 1937 Wisliceny considered it the mission of the department to provide 'absolutely solid information to the state and Party', on the basis of which 'legislative and police measures' against the Jews could follow.[117] To make the use of terror as unerring as possible, the SD's section for Jewish affairs attempted in 1937 to create a registry of all 'Jews and persons of Jewish descent'. After a certain amount of back and forth, it was decided at the suggestion of the Reich Ministry of the Interior to compile the registry with the help of the census scheduled for the early summer of 1938, as such a method was apparently a great deal cheaper and, above all, more reliable (Doc. 288). Due to the *Anschluss* of Austria, the census was postponed by one year, to 1939. Then, however, the personal data of all German Jews and Jewish *Mischlinge* was gathered and put on record in the registries of residents.[118]

---

114 Klaus Hildebrand, *Das vergangene Reich: Deutsche Außenpolitik von Bismarck bis Hitler 1871–1945* (Stuttgart: Deutsche Verlags-Anstalt, 1995), p. 611.
115 Wilhelm Treue, 'Hitlers Denkschrift zum Vierjahresplan 1936', *Vierteljahrshefte für Zeitgeschichte*, vol. 3, no. 2 (1955), pp. 184–210, here p. 210.
116 Cited in Hildebrand, *Das vergangene Reich*, p. 623.
117 Michael Wildt, *An Uncompromising Generation: The Nazi Leadership of the Reich Security Main Office*, trans. Tom Lampert (Madison, WI: University of Wisconsin Press, 2010 [German edn, 2002]); Wildt (ed.), *Die Judenpolitik*, pp. 108–110 (note by Wisliceny, 7 April 1937); Herbert, *Best*, pp. 203–211.

On 1 November 1937 sixty-six SD department heads, section heads, and support staff assembled for a meeting. They all had responsibility for the Jewish question, either in the Berlin central office or in the SD district branches. They listened to twelve short papers and took three hours to discuss the agenda item 'General Debate'. In his paper Dannecker explained the 'methodology' with which the SD men were supposed to make life unbearable for the Jews:

> Don't let up for an instant, use admonitions to keep the leading Jews in suspense at all times, react immediately to every aspiration or sentiment, even the slightest, that goes against our principles – in short: complete penetration into Jewish private life and particularly Jewish political life. In this way the thought of emigration will inevitably be fostered and the idea of possibly continuing to stay in Germany after all will be increasingly undermined.[119]

Even before Göring had been officially appointed Plenipotentiary for the Four-Year Plan, he had held a forerunner position as head of the Raw Materials and Foreign Currency Staff, created in the spring of 1936. In this capacity, on 7 June 1936, he had tasked SD chief Heydrich with setting up a Foreign Exchange Investigation Office (Devisenfahndungsamt). This body was under the 'personal and direct' authority of Göring, and it subsequently ensured that the relevant customs and foreign exchange inspection centres applied the exchange regulations to German Jews with exceptional harshness. Göring needed foreign currency. It was the only way to pay for the imports necessary for the arms build-up, and the only way to buy the 5 million tons of grain in foreign markets that were stockpiled as a national grain reserve in the event of war. In the twelve months that followed, the newly created office collected foreign currency with an equivalent value of 473 million Reichsmarks.[120]

To carry out the process of dispossession, which was extraordinarily successful by the standards of the times, two laws targeting affluent Jews were passed. First, the Law against Economic Sabotage, which punished the illegal transfer of assets into a foreign country with lengthy prison sentences or even death; second, the Law for the Amendment of the Law on Foreign Exchange Control. This allowed the tax offices to confiscate a substantial part of the assets of persons 'suspected of pursuing emigration' as security for the Reich Flight Tax (*Reichsfluchtsteuer*), which was to be paid later. Officially, Jews could transfer their assets to other countries through the Deutsche Golddiskontbank. To do so, they had to accept a deduction amounting to 20 per cent in January 1934. In June 1935 this was raised to 68 per cent and in October 1936 to 81 per cent.[121] Emigration continued to be encouraged, but it was not intended to result in 'any disadvantages to

---

118 Wildt (ed.), *Die Judenpolitik*, pp. 35–37 and 153–154; Götz Aly and Karl Heinz Roth, *Die restlose Erfassung: Volkszählen, Identifizieren, Aussondern im Nationalsozialismus*, new edn (Frankfurt am Main: Fischer Taschenbuch; 2000 [1984]), pp. 92–95.
119 Agenda item cited in Wildt (ed.), *Die Judenpolitik*, pp. 127–156, here p. 150.
120 Adam Tooze, *The Wages of Destruction: The Making and Breaking of the Nazi Economy* (London: Allen Lane, 2006), p. 214.
121 Peter Longerich, *Politik der Vernichtung: Eine Gesamtdarstellung der nationalsozialistischen Judenverfolgung* (Munich: Piper, 1998), pp. 118–121 and 125–126; laws dated 1 Dec. 1936: *Reichsgesetzblatt*, 1936, I, pp. 999–1001.

the German state'. The 'encouragement' consisted primarily of elevating the use of terror against 'the Jewish minority to such an extent that its emigration became cheaper – in other words, as much foreign currency as possible could be conserved, as much property as possible confiscated'.[122]

The dispossession of the Jews to the advantage of the German public coffers thus began in the summer of 1936. Not only that: from this point onwards, the fate of the persecuted was linked to a plan for war that, as proclaimed, allowed only 'victory or downfall'. By May 1937 the SD was considering how the Jews should be dealt with in the event of war (Doc. 283). In this context it becomes clear why in 1938 Göring pushed through the laws with which the Jews were compelled to report their assets and with which they were ultimately deprived of the freedom to dispose of these assets.

In April 1933 the German state had denied Jews the right to work in the public sector and to perform official duties as civil servants. In so doing, the National Socialist government dislodged from the constitutional edifice the capstone of the emancipation of the German Jews, which for all practical purposes had not been set in place until 1919. Next, in May 1935, Jews were denied the right to carry arms in the defence of the nation, an entitlement not gained until the First World War.[123] With the passage of the Nuremberg Laws, the ancient European ban on marriage between Jews and Christians was restored. Between 1933 and 1937 the Jews were subjected to various restrictions on their economic activities in the different regions, communities, and branches of the economy. Not until 1938, however, were they 'excluded from the German economy', both legally and in practice. The first right that had been granted to the Jews in Germany at the beginning of their emancipation was thus the last to be lost.

---

[122] Heim, 'Deutschland', p. 50.
[123] Military Service Law, 21 May 1935, *Reichsgesetzblatt*, 1935, I, p. 609.

List of Documents

1 Jüdische Rundschau, 31 January 1933: editorial on the appointment of Adolf Hitler as Reich Chancellor
2 Nationalsozialistische Monatshefte, January 1933: editorial on the struggle against international Jewry
3 C.V.-Zeitung, 9 February 1933: report on anti-Jewish riots in Gersfeld, Hesse
4 C.V.-Zeitung, 23 February 1933: article criticizing anti-Jewish propaganda on the streets of Berlin and in the Nazi press
5 Völkischer Beobachter, 5/6 March 1933: appeal by the NSDAP to 'German artists' to vote at the parliamentary elections
6 Walter Gyssling describes riots and abuses in Munich on 9/10 March 1933
7 On 14 March 1933 Hermann Badt offers the Deputy Minister President his resignation as Prussian representative to the Constitutional Court
8 On 15 March 1933 the Reich Minister of the Interior recommends that the immigration and naturalization of Ostjuden be prevented
9 Max Moses Polke reports on the persecution of Jewish judges and lawyers in Breslau between 11 and 17 March 1933
10 On 18 March 1933 the Combat League for German Culture calls on the Prussian Minister of Culture to exclude Jews from the cultural institutions of the Ruhr
11 On 20 March 1933 the German ambassador in the USA sends a telegraph to the Reich Foreign Office regarding press reports about the persecution of Jews in Germany
12 On 24 March 1933 the mayor of Munich orders that municipal contracts no longer be awarded to Jews and foreigners
13 On 25 March 1933 the metal trader Fritz Schünemann encourages the mayor of Munich not to sell scrap metal to Jewish firms
14 New York Times, 27 March 1933: article regarding preparations for mass protests in the USA against Hitler's anti-Jewish policies
15 On 28 March 1933 the Frankfurt city administration orders the dismissal of its Jewish civil servants
16 On 30 March 1933 the state commissioner for Berlin prohibits the municipal administration from placing announcements in the 'Jewish press'
17 Völkischer Beobachter, 30 March 1933: the NSDAP calls for an anti-Jewish boycott across Germany
18 On 30 March 1933 the private tutor Johann Ackermann proposes a boycott of Jewish tutors in Munich
19 On 30 March 1933 the Association of German Engineering Institutions calls on its member firms to combat 'international atrocity and boycott propaganda'

20 Discussion between representatives of Jewish organizations on 31 March 1933 in Paris regarding the persecution of Jewish Germans

21 Henriette Necheles-Magnus describes expressions of solidarity during the anti-Jewish boycott on 1 April 1933 in Wandsbek

22 The Times, 3 April 1933: article regarding the murder of the Jewish lawyer Schumm and other acts of violence on the day of the boycott

23 On 3 April 1933 Director Eugen Feuchtmann reports to the chairman of the board of directors of Johannes Jeserich AG on the forced resignation of two Jewish directors

24 On 3 April 1933 patent lawyer Richard Wirth declares his solidarity with his Jewish colleagues

25 On 4 April 1933 the Jüdische Rundschau calls for the development of a new Jewish self-assertiveness in response to the boycott

26 On 5 April 1933 the student Heinrich Marx deliberates whether to remain in Berlin following the boycott or to leave

27 The unimplemented draft of a law 'for the regulation of the status of the Jews', 6 April 1933

28 On 7 April 1933 the Reich Foreign Office opposes the granting of minority rights to Jews in Upper Silesia

29 Law for the dismissal of Jewish and politically undesirable civil servants, 7 April 1933

30 On 8 April 1933 Cardinal Faulhaber writes to Alois Wurm about the latter's protest against the persecution of Jews

31 On 10 April 1933 the Regional Contract Office for the State of Saxony proposes that Jewish firms no longer be permitted to supply the army, navy, or police

32 The Aryan Paragraph introduces the first legal definition of the term 'non-Aryan', 11 April 1933

33 The business representative Walter Hoffmann writes to Göring on 12 April 1933 to intervene following press reports in the USA concerning acts of violence on the day of the boycott

34 On 15 April 1933 Karl Jarres writes to Theodor Lewald following the latter's resignation as president of the German Reich Committee for Physical Exercise

35 On 16 April 1933 Hertha Nathorff records her impressions of a meeting of the League of German Female Physicians in Berlin

36 Jüdische Rundschau, 25 April 1933: article on the suicide of a Jew with German nationalist convictions

37 On 26 April 1933 Charlotte Gumpert informs Minni Steinhardt in Palestine about the political situation in Germany and conditions for emigrants

38 Otto Marx reports on his arrest in Weiden and his imprisonment in Dachau concentration camp in March/April 1933

39 On 3 May 1933 a resident of Bonn protests to Minister President Hermann Göring against the persecution of German Jews

40 On 6 May 1933 the National Socialist German Reich Estate Agents' League criticizes the approach taken by the Reich Association of German Estate Agents during the process of Gleichschaltung

41 On 9 May 1933 Heinrich Marx reflects on his personal situation in Berlin and on conditions in higher education institutions

42 On 13 May 1933 the Israelite Religious Community in Munich complains to the Reich Foreign Office about measures against Jewish associations in Munich

43 Report by company representative Oskar Vangerow on the Jews and the mood in Poland, 16 May 1933

44 On 18 May 1933 Karl Landau asks retired Vienna senior municipal councillor Engelbert Siegl about employment opportunities

45 On 22 May 1933 the Polish Legation protests against attacks on Polish nationals in Germany

46 Directive issued to the German delegation in Geneva on 24 May 1933 to prevent a discussion in the Council of the League of Nations on the persecution of Jews in German Upper Silesia

47 On 29 May 1933 the Jewish Community of Berlin complains to the state commissioner for Berlin about the city administration's anti-Jewish measures

48 Nationalsozialistische Monatshefte, May 1933: article about the 'solution to the Jewish question'

49 On 11 June 1933 a representative of the American Jewish Joint Distribution Committee reports on a discussion with Leo Baeck in Berlin regarding the organization of the emigration of German Jews

50 New York Times, 12 June 1933: report regarding a campaign to support German Jews

51 On 12 June 1933 the Juvenile Court with Lay Judges in Frankfurt sentences Jewish youths for distributing political leaflets

52 The Reich Statistical Office reports on the regional distribution of Jews by faith according to the results of the census of 16 June 1933

53 The Reich Statistical Office reports on the occupational distribution of Jews by faith according to the results of the census of 16 June 1933

54 On 17 June 1933 the street vendor Luise Rupprecht asks the Breslau Chief of Police to expel a competing Jewish street vendor from the square

55 Deutsche Allgemeine Zeitung, 19 June 1933: report concerning a speech by Berlin's mayor to American local politicians

56 On 19 June 1933 Max Osborn writes to Minni Steinhardt about his plans to emigrate to Palestine

57 On 22 June 1933 the director of the Institute of Physics intervenes with the Breslau University administration on behalf of the lecturer Hedwig Kohn

58 On 22 June 1933 Professor James Goldschmidt protests to the Prussian Ministry of Science, Art, and Education against the withdrawal of his authorization to teach

59 The board of the Talmud Torah School in Hamburg discusses the situation of Jewish schools at a meeting on 28 June 1933

60 A regional organization of the Central German Association of German Citizens of the Jewish Faith reports on the situation of Jews in Saxony and Saxony-Anhalt in June 1933

61 On 1 July 1933 Hans Kantorowitz refuses to leave the Berlin Gymnastics Association

62 On 13 July 1933 Isaac Meyer writes to the Senckenberg Natural History Society in Frankfurt to justify his resignation

63 On 18 July 1933 scientists at the Potsdam Observatory denounce their colleague Professor Erwin Finlay Freundlich as an 'anti-nationalist descendant of Jews'

64 On 26 July 1933 the German Council of Municipalities permits the city of Preußisch Friedland to partially exclude Jews from public baths

65 The executive board of the Hamburg Medical Association resigns in July 1933 because of an anti-Jewish amendment to the statutes

66 In late July 1933 a member of Deutsche Bank's management board, Franz Urbig, reports on the dismissal of board members Theodor Frank and Oscar Wassermann

67 On 4 August 1933 the Association of Synagogue Congregations of the province of Upper Silesia lodges a complaint with the Reich Foreign Office regarding discrimination against Jews

68 On 11 August 1933 the Reich Representation of Jewish Regional Associations in Germany complains to the Reich Minister of Labour about occupational restrictions placed on physicians

69 The Prussian Ministry of Justice quashes criminal proceedings on 11 August 1933 in the case of the murder of a Jewish dentist

70 On 14 August 1933 the Reich Ministry of the Interior sends the Reich Foreign Office and the Prussian Minister of the Interior a preliminary list of persons to be deprived of citizenship

71 Advertisement from mid August 1933 for the programme of the newly established Culture League of German Jews

72 On 23 August 1933 Johannes Schräpel informs the Reich Minister of the Interior about the Gleichschaltung of the Association of Budgerigar Enthusiasts

73 Special session of the board of directors of the Jewish Community of Berlin on 24 August 1933 to ensure kosher food in spite of the ban on shechitah

74 On 25 August 1933 the Hamburg Mayor Vincent Krogmann notes a request by Jewish organizations for negotiations with the NSDAP

75 On 6 September 1933 the Protestant Church of the Old Prussian Union introduces the Aryan Paragraph

76 On 12 September 1933 Martin Bormann calls on the Gauleiter to stop local anti-Jewish measures

77 Juristische Wochenschrift, 16 September 1933: article on legal possibilities for the annulment of mixed marriages

78 From the debate of the Congress of European Nationalities on 18 September 1933 on the persecution of Jews in Germany

79 Junge Kirche: report, dated 20 September 1933, by the Faculty of Theology at the University of Marburg opposing a limitation of the rights of non-Aryan Christians

80 The chairman of the German Gymnastics Association writes to Rupert Naumann on 23 September 1933 in response to his concerns about banning all Jews from the Berlin Gymnastics Association

81 On 25 September 1933 the Reich Ministry of Economics criticizes the banning of Jewish dealers from trade fairs and markets

82 On 5 October 1933 the billboard-advertising company Städte-Reklame GmbH asks the Trustee of Labour in Hesse for an opinion on putting up advertising for Jewish firms

83 On 9 October 1933 the dismissed civil servant Johanna Rosenthal asks the Berlin Main Post Office Headquarters to grant her a pension on compassionate grounds

84 On 10 October 1933 conductor Erich Erck applies to the Bavarian State Minister for Education and Culture for the authorization of a Jewish Culture League

85 On 19 October 1933 the Reich Association of Christian German Citizens of Non-Aryan or Not Pure Aryan Descent writes to the government to offer its support

86 On 24 October 1933 the Reich leader of the German Medical Association urges the Association of Statutory Health Insurance Physicians to use lists of non-Aryan doctors discreetly

87 Deutsches Philologen-Blatt, 1 November 1933: article on the introduction of racial studies in schools

88 Völkischer Beobachter, 15 November 1933: article on the demand of the 'German Christians' that 'Jewish Christians' are excluded from the Protestant Church

89 On 15 November 1933 the trader Louis Skalawski complains to the Reich Minister of Economics about being barred from a Berlin market

90 On 4 December 1933 the municipal school inspector of Berlin forbids teachers to marry Jewish partners

91 New York Times, 24 December 1933: article on the work of the High Commissioner of the League of Nations and aid for Jewish refugees

92 On 29 December 1933 Fritz Wolfes asks the mayor of Hanover to lease a sports hall to the Jewish Gymnastics Association

93 Ernst Hofmann reports on mistreatment at the hands of SS and SA men, 1933

94 Pariser Tageblatt, 4 January 1934: commentary on the cancellation of the boxing match between Max Schmeling and King Levinsky

95 On 4 January 1934 businessman Julius Fromm protests against the planned retraction of his German citizenship

96 Der National-Sozialistische Erzieher, 13 January 1934: article on 'racial separation'

97 Juristische Wochenschrift, 13 January 1934: article on two Reich Labour Court rulings concerning the dismissal of Jewish employees

98 Letter dated 26 January 1934 from a German to the Foreign Policy Office of the NSDAP, describing her impressions from a trip to Poland

99 Memorandum dated January 1934 on the situation of the Jewish population, sent by the Reich Representation of German Jews to the Reich government

100 The Gestapo Central Office informs the Prussian Minister of the Interior about a meeting of the Central Association of German Citizens of the Jewish Faith held in Deutsch-Krone on 4 February 1934

101 On 5 February 1934 Rabbi Wahrmann reports on the mounting social and pastoral problems in his Silesian district

102 On 7 February 1934 the Dresden Chamber of Industry and Commerce calls on the Saxon Ministry of Economics to exclude Jews from serving as sworn experts

103 On 9 February 1934 the Central Germany Branch of the Central Association of German Citizens of the Jewish Faith (CV) reports on the representation of the interests of Jewish salaried employees

104 On 13 February 1934 the hotelier Hanns Kilian complains to the municipality of Garmisch about the denunciation of an Austrian performer as a Jew

105 On 18 February 1934 a Jewish pupil and her parents write to a teacher who emigrated to Palestine

106 Report on the performance of the school puppet show Till Ülespegel in late February 1934 in Cologne-Ehrenfeld

107 On 27 February 1934 State Secretary Herbert Backe voices misgivings to the Gestapo Central Office over the retraining of Jews for agricultural occupations

108 On 4 March 1934 Gertrud Baumgart writes to Paula Tobias about the women's movement and about the Jewish question as a vital issue for Europe

109 Deutsche Justiz, 23 March 1934: article disagrees with a court decision precluding 'racial differences' as grounds for applying to annul a marriage

110 On 23 March 1934 the Reich League of Jewish Combat Veterans protests to Reich President Hindenburg over the exclusion of Jewish soldiers from the German armed forces

111 Frankfurter Zeitung, 28 March 1934: article about the ongoing elimination of Jews from the economy

112 Printed form of the NSDAP Kreisleitung in Ansbach, dated March 1934 for submitting a declaration of honour to sever all contact with Jews

113 Die Neue Welt, 5 April 1934: news reports about anti-Jewish riots in Gunzenhausen and the increasing Nationalist Socialist propaganda against 'race defilement'

114 On 10 April 1934 the Groß-Karben gendarmerie reports on the public humiliation of a woman on the grounds of race defilement

115 A clipping from the Pariser Tageblatt along with a letter from the Reich Minister of Labour to the Deputy of the Führer, dated 25 April 1934, about the exclusion of non-Aryan business managers from the 1 May celebrations

116 Report, dated April 1934, by the Gestapo Central Office in Berlin on the surveillance of Jewish organizations and their activities in Germany

117 Völkischer Beobachter, 11 May 1934: excerpt from a speech by Josef Goebbels criticizing detractors, the Jews, the churches, and the foreign press

118 On 26 May 1934 the Regierungspräsident of Frankfurt an der Oder issues a statement to the Prussian Minister of Finance justifying the confiscation of Hugo Simon's estate

119 Excerpt from the Sopade report for May/June 1934 about reactions to the persecution of Jews in Germany

120 On 2 June 1934 Legation Counsellor Hermann von Stutterheim reports on a discussion with Leo Löwenstein, the chairman of the Reich League of Jewish Combat Veterans

121 Report by Vice President Fritz Grau during a session of the Criminal Law Commission on 5 June 1934 about 'race protection' and the social segregation of the Jews

122 On 13 June 1934 State Secretary Hans Pfundtner writes to the Reich Minister of Agriculture proposing the creation of closed camps for the agricultural retraining of Jews

123 On 14 June 1934 the Gestapo Central Office orders the seizure of the assets of the League of Jewish Employees in Prussia

124 On 14 June 1934 Julius Plaut asks Hamburg's Reichsstatthalter, Karl Kaufmann, to retract his dismissal

125 Haynt, 15 June 1934: article on the establishment of an 'antisemitic international' in Nuremberg

126 On 23 June 1934 Kurt Rathenau informs his brother Fritz about the catastrophic situation of his company Ernst Rosenberg & Co. in Berlin

127 Petition to the Regional Tax Office in Silesia dated 4 July 1934 requesting exemption from the Reich Flight Tax for Erich Frank, appointed professor at the University of Istanbul

128 Margot Littauer describes her everyday school life in Breslau in mid 1934

129 Internationales Ärztliches Bulletin, July/August 1934: article about the murder of Erich Mühsam in Oranienburg concentration camp

130 On 2 August 1934 the Gestapo prohibits members of Jewish youth organizations from wearing uniforms and participating in military sports training

131 Verordnungsblatt der Obersten SA-Führung: on 16 August 1934 the Deputy of the Führer, Rudolf Heß, prohibits NSDAP members from consorting with Jews

132 On 29 August 1934 the Tenants' Protection Association in Frankfurt proposes that the mayor rename certain streets and squares

133 On 29 August 1934 the Reich Office for Emigration Affairs provides information concerning the state and problems of Jewish emigration from Germany in the second quarter of the year

134 On 31 August 1934 Reichsstatthalter Fritz Sauckel urges Hitler and Heß to expropriate the Simson Arms Factory in Suhl

135 On 16 September 1934 the historian Willy Cohn describes a visit to a Zionist Hachsharah camp

136 On 21 September 1934 the state commissioner for Berlin makes arrangements on the occasion of the Jewish Feast of Tabernacles

137 Der National-Sozialistische Erzieher, 13 October 1934: draft syllabus regarding the treatment of the Jewish question on so-called State Youth Days

138 On 13 October 1934 the Regional Farmers' Leader for Saxony-Anhalt writes to the Reich Farmers' Leader to justify the removal of Jews from the local economy

139 On 16 October 1934 the Regierungspräsident in Liegnitz reports to the Prussian Minister of the Interior about an incident in Görlitz in connection with a 'Jewish department store' hoisting a swastika flag

140 On 29 October 1934 SA member Werner Siemroth denounces his Hamburg employer for employing Jews

141 On 12 November 1934 the Central Association of German Citizens of the Jewish Faith informs the Reich Ministry of Economics about the hindrance to Jewish traders in town markets

142 On 22 November 1934 Heinrich Himmler asks Hitler to oblige the Federation of Bavarian Regimental Officers' Associations to expel its Jewish members

143 On 26 November 1934 an NSDAP member sends an anonymous letter to the ministries in Berlin in protest against the ongoing boycott of Jewish shops in Braunschweig

144 New York Times, 4 December 1934: report on Germany's pledge to take heed of the rights of Jews for one year in the event of a reincorporation of the Saar territory

145 Juristische Wochenschrift, 7 December 1934: the Hanau Labour Court overturns the dismissal of a Jewish employee

146 Discussion at the Staff of the Deputy of the Führer in Munich on 20 December 1934 regarding 'special legislation on Jews'

147 On 22 December 1934 the management of the Hermann Tietz department store informs the Reich Ministry of Economics about an antisemitic pamphlet

148 On 27 December 1934 the Gestapo Central Office dissolves the Association of German Motor Car Owners for having Jewish members

149 Pariser Tageblatt, 30 December 1934: article regarding a conference of East Prussian communities on the decline and destitution of the Jewish population

150 The Aid Committee of Hamburg's United Jewish Organizations reports on financial aid, emigration assistance, and professional training provided in 1933 and 1934

151 Martin Andermann describes the political and social changes that took place in the city of Königsberg in 1934

152 On 4 January 1935 Hamburg's health and relief authority writes to SA-Oberführer Heusser to insist on the necessity of buying from Jewish traders

153 On 19 January 1935 the SS-Standortführer in Berlin prohibits SS men and their families from having private contact with Jews

154 Report by the Gestapo Central Office in Berlin on the situation of Germany's Jews in December 1934 and January 1935

155 On 17 March 1935 the NSDAP member Walter Tanke denounces participants in a 'Jew-friendly' church gathering to the Stettin Gestapo

156 On 22 March 1935 the Catholic Church establishes the Aid Committee for Catholic Non-Aryans

157 On 22 March 1935 the Central Association of German Citizens of the Jewish Faith reports on anti-Jewish incidents in Mecklenburg communities

158 On 23 March 1935 the gendarmerie informs the regional council in Hünfeld about an attack on visitors to the Rhina Synagogue

159 On 3 April 1935 the Reich Ministry of the Interior informs the Office of the Wehrmacht Adjutant to the Führer and Reich Chancellor about the estimated number of Jews in the German Reich

160 On 8 April 1935 the Central Association of German Citizens of the Jewish Faith protests to Mayor Goerdeler against the boycott of Jewish doctors in Leipzig

161 Jüdische Rundschau, April 1935: speech by Rabbi Joachim Prinz concerning the social and cultural isolation of the Jewish population

162 Berliner Tageblatt, 20 April 1935: article on the call of the German Council of Municipalities to abolish municipal financial subsidies for Jewish schools

163 On 2 May 1935 Victor Klemperer describes his dismissal as professor of Romance languages at the Dresden Institute of Technology

164 On 8 May 1935 Naftali Unger briefs the Palestine Shipping Company on the difficulties in obtaining training positions for Jewish youth on ships

165 Discussion between the German Army Ordnance Department and the Flick Corporation on 22 May 1935 concerning the Aryanization of the Simson Arms Factory in Suhl

166 Werdauer Zeitung, 23 May 1935: report concerning an antisemitic speech at a meeting of the Women's Office of the German Labour Front

167 On 24 May 1935 Paula Tobias protests to the Reich Ministry of the Army about the discrimination against her sons caused by the new Military Law

168 On 26 May 1935 the lawyer Leopold Weinmann urges the Reich Ministry of the Interior to take action against the instigators of anti-Jewish violence in Munich

169 A mother's complaint about her 15-year-old son's participation in nocturnal activities of the Hitler Youth against Jews in Munich (around 26 May 1935)

170 On 28 May 1935 the Gestapo Central Office demands that the Reich Minister of Justice prevent marriages between Jews and non-Jews

171 In a letter of 29 May 1935 Professor Johann Plesch responds to the Kaiser Wilhelm Society's demand for additional contributions

172 Der Stürmer, May 1935: the mayor of Meißen is insulted as a 'slave to Jews' in a purported letter to the editor

173 Antisemitic polemic by Adolf Stein on Jews in Berlin, dated 4 July 1935

174 Meeraner Zeitung, 12 July 1935: article on cases of so-called race defilement

175 On 13 July 1935 the Regierungspräsident in Düsseldorf asks the Reich Minister of the Interior for instructions regarding the handling of Polish Jews by the Police for Foreign Nationals

176 Neue Zürcher Zeitung: article dated 16 July 1935 about anti-Jewish violence on Kurfürstendamm associated with the screening of an antisemitic film from Sweden

177 On 17 July 1935 the head of the Regional Welfare Office in Berlin reduces welfare benefits for newly arriving Jews in need

178 On 19 July 1935 Reich Minister of the Interior Frick informs Hitler about the practice of changing Jewish names

179 On 20 July 1935 Mr and Mrs Lau complain to the newspaper Das Schwarze Korps about Jews in a Berlin allotment garden area

180 On 24 July 1935 the Central Association of German Citizens of the Jewish Faith informs the Reich Minister of the Interior about acts of violence in East Prussia, Mecklenburg, Hesse, Westphalia, and Berlin

181 In anticipation of a future law, Reich Minister of the Interior Frick bans marriages between Jews and non-Jews on 27 July 1935

182 Anti-Jewish prejudices within the Confessing Church: a letter from schoolmistress Elisabeth Schmitz to Walter Künneth, 28 July 1935

183 On 31 July 1935 the Gestapo Central Office reports to Reinhard Heydrich on new plans for discriminating against the Jewish population in Berlin

184 On 31 July 1935 the German Labour Front writes to the SD Main Office to propose name changes for Jews

185 Das Schwarze Korps, 7 August 1935: article calling on the population to arrest Jews

186 On 8 August 1935 the Gestapo informs the Reich Foreign Office about the public humiliation of a woman in Beuthen

187 On 15 August 1935 the head of the NSDAP Gau organization in East Prussia demands that the Landrat in Marienwerder be excluded from the Party

188 On 17 August 1935 the Gestapo Central Office orders the State Police offices to provide material for a central 'Jewish registry'

189 Ministers' conference on 20 August 1935 concerning the next steps in anti-Jewish policy

190 On 22 August 1935 Walter Kühne's section in the Reich Ministry of Finance airs proposals for tax discrimination against Jews

191 On 25 August 1935 the historian Willy Cohn reports on the situation of an acquaintance living in a mixed marriage

192 In late August/early September 1935 a citizen of Leipzig writes to Mayor Haake with suggestions for the further marginalization of the city's Jews

193 On 7 September 1935 the Reich Railways ask its agencies to take action against the posting of anti-Jewish signs on Reich Railways premises

194 On 7 September 1935 a colleague assembles material for Reichsbank President Hjalmar Schacht concerning future burdens on the economy due to Jewish emigration

195 On 9 September 1935 the Gestapo Central Office outlines to Reich Minister Walther Darré its own proposals for the 'solution of the Jewish question'

196 On 10 September 1935 the German News Agency comments on the decree of Reich Minister Bernhard Rust ordering the creation of separate schools for Jewish children

197 On 11 September 1935 the State Political Police departments are requested to report Jews to the Regional Tax Authorities prior to their emigration

198 The Reich Citizenship Law, proclaimed in Nuremberg on 15 September 1935, turns German Jews into second-class citizens

199 The 'Blood Protection Law', promulgated in Nuremberg on 15 September 1935, prohibits marriage and extramarital sexual relations between Jews and non-Jews

200 On 22 September 1935 State Secretary Wilhelm Stuckart explains drafts of the First and Second Regulations to the Reich Citizenship Law to Reich Physicians' Leader Gerhard Wagner

201 Jüdische Rundschau, 24 September 1935: statement by the Reich Representation of Jews in Germany regarding the Nuremberg Laws

202 Comments from 25 September 1935 concerning a presentation by the head of the NSDAP's Racial Policy Office, Walter Groß, about Hitler's new approach to the Jewish question

203 On 25 September 1935 the head of the Department of National Health in the Reich Ministry of the Interior uses Mendel's principles of heredity to justify the prohibition of marriage between Jews and non-Jews

204 On 27 September 1935 the Swiss ambassador in Berlin reports on the increased number of applications for immigration permits by German Jews

205 On 9 October 1935 State Secretary Wilhelm Stuckart informs Reich Minister of the Interior Wilhelm Frick about the planned law for restricting the economic activity of Jews

206 Frankfurter Zeitung, 11 October 1935: report on a statement made by the Racial Policy Office of the NSDAP about mystical tendencies in 'racial theory'

207 On 16 October 1935 Reich Minister of the Interior Wilhelm Frick protests to Robert Ley against the marking of non-Jewish shops by the German Labour Front in Saxony

208 On 27 October 1935 NSDAP member Peters urges Mayor Krogmann to dismiss Jewish collectors from the Hamburg State Lottery

209 On 1 November 1935 the Branch Group for Private Health Insurance asks the relevant Economic Group for permission to exclude Jewish policyholders

210 The First Regulation to the Reich Citizenship Law of 14 November 1935 defines the term 'Jew'

211 On 16 November 1935 Albert Herzfeld reports on the compulsory dismissal of his non-Jewish household help

212 Pariser Tageblatt, 25 November 1935: editorial regarding the absurdity of the definition of race according to the Nuremberg Laws

213 Travel report dated 29 November 1935 about the dramatic situation of the Jewish population after the enactment of the Nuremberg Laws

214 On 12 December 1935 Reich Minister of Justice Franz Gürtner discusses with Hitler the removal of Jews from the liberal professions

215 A leading official in the Reich Ministry of Education reports on the top-level conference on 12 December 1935 regarding the continuation of anti-Jewish policies

216 On 14 December 1935 the city of Radeberg reports to the Saxon State Minister for Economics and Labour on the boycott of Jewish businesses

217 On 17 December 1935 ministry representatives discuss the economic and financial advantages and disadvantages of Jewish emigration

218 On 19 December 1935 the Gestapo Central Office in Berlin announces how the concept of 'prohibited individual actions' against Jews is to be interpreted

219 Die neue Weltbühne, December 1935: Heinrich Mann protests against the persecution of Jews in Germany

220 In early January 1936 the Jewish Telegraphic Agency provides information on plans to finance the mass emigration of Jews from Germany

221 Danziger Echo, 7 January 1936: article on the resignation of the High Commissioner of the League of Nations over the persecution of Jews in Germany

222 Der Stürmer: letter from a National Socialist Christian warning the churches against baptizing Jews en masse, January 1936

223 From the Sopade reports of January 1936 regarding reactions in Germany to the Nuremberg Laws

224 On 4 February 1936 the Regierungspräsident in Potsdam informs Gauleiter Wilhelm Kube of his planned circular directive concerning the Jewish question

225 On 5 February 1936 the Reich Minister of the Interior orders that anti-Jewish excesses occasioned by the assassination of Wilhelm Gustloff in Davos must be prevented

226 On 13 February 1936 the sales representative Bernhard Eidmann complains to the retailer Ludwig Bertram about the selling of goods from Jewish firms in Aryan shops

227 On 3 March 1936 the Karlsruhe Regional Tax Office reports to the Reich Minister of Finance on cooperation with the Gestapo in monitoring Jews

228 On 3 March 1936 the German Council of Municipalities lets the mayor of Stuttgart introduce restrictions on Jews in municipal public baths

229 The Beck publishing house pitches its annotated edition of the Nuremberg Laws to the National Socialist Association of Teachers on 5 March 1936

230 On 12 March 1936 the emigration advisor for the Jewish Community in Leipzig reports on those seeking advice and their financial situations

231 The Potsdam government circumvents a directive issued by Reich Minister of Justice Franz Gürtner on the purchase of plots of land by Jews (around 26 April 1936)

232 Slaughterhouse director Karl Boerner terminates business relations with Gustav Schroeder in Waren (Müritz) on 30 May 1936

233 On 17 June 1936 the Regierungspräsident in Königsberg writes to the Reich Minister of the Interior to outline an amendment to the charter of the Driesen Foundation discriminating against Jews

234 Historische Zeitschrift: the establishment of the column 'History of the Jewish Question', spring 1936

235 Pariser Tageszeitung, 23 June 1936: article about conditions for the German Jews shortly before the Olympic Games in Berlin

236 On 1 July 1936 Albert Herzfeld reports on his expulsion from the Reich Association of German Artists and on being banned from practising his profession as an artist

237 On 9 July 1936 the government of Silesia plans to make it compulsory for Landräte and mayors to compile a civil registry of the Jews

238 On 16 July 1936 the Reich Circle for Propaganda and Public Enlightenment issues recommendations for the conduct of the SA towards foreigners and Jews during the Olympic Games

239 On 21 July 1936 the historian Willy Cohn criticizes the behaviour of Eastern European Jews during a convalescent stay

240 Jüdische Rundschau, 24 July 1936: article on the number and destinations of Jewish emigrants

241 On 30 July 1936 Medical Officer Wilhelm Dopheide from Hagenow justifies his boycott of Dr Hans Sommerfeld to the Mecklenburg Ministry of State

242 On 31 July 1936 Martin Gumpert writes to his sister in Palestine about the problem of transferring money and assets when emigrating to the USA

243 On 14 August 1936 the Jewish Social Service and Youth Welfare Office in Berlin asks the Foreign Currency Department of the Regional Tax Office to authorize support for a Jewish refugee family

244 On 30 August 1936 State Secretary Hans Pfundtner complains to the Bavarian Minister President about Jewish spa guests in Bad Kissingen

245 On 2 September 1936 Mally Dienemann reports on antisemitism in Offenbach am Main

246 On 16 September 1936 the Reich Ministry of Economics informs the Reich Minister of Food about the complaints of Jewish grain-trading companies

247 On 28 September 1936 Alex Löwenstein gives Rosalie Gehrike in Berlin an account of his new life in Argentina

248 Meeting of state secretaries in the Reich Ministry of the Interior on 29 September 1936 about the further course of anti-Jewish policy

249 On 6 October 1936 the German embassy in Warsaw reports to the Reich Foreign Office on Polish initiatives concerning Jewish emigration

250 Amtsblatt der Preußischen Regierung zu Königsberg: regulation issued by the Oberpräsident on 7 October 1936 regarding name changes for towns

251 Pariser Tageszeitung, 11 October 1936: article about the expulsion of German Jews from economic life

252 On 12 October 1936 the Chief of the Security Police asks the Chief of the Order Police in Berlin to alter the registration system so as to improve the collection of data on baptized Jews

253 Invitation from the People's Association for the German Reich Church to a Reformation church service to be held in Grabow on 2 November 1936

254 On 14 November 1936 the Gestapo Central Office informs local Gestapo offices about the regulations for the Jewish Winter Relief in 1936/1937

255 On 19 November 1936 the retailer Julius Block asks the Berlin police to make an exception and grant him a passport valid for five years

256 Deutsches Recht, 15 December 1936: article on a court judgement against a bequeathal to Jews instead of the legal heirs

257 On 18 December 1936 State Secretary Wilhelm Stuckart communicates the draft for an anti-Jewish special tax law to the Reich Ministry of Finance

258 On 21 December 1936 the Gestapo Central Office issues a ban on the public gathering of Jews

259 Zeitschrift des Vereins für Geschichte Schlesiens: review of the antisemitic book The Jews in Germany (1936)

260 Reports on antisemitic measures and incidents in Germany (1936)

261 Walter Gottheil talks about his life in a small German town in 1936

262 Ernst Marcus reports on the fears of the Jewish middle class in Breslau in 1936/1937

263 Pariser Tageszeitung, 28 January 1937: article on the practice of pursuing and punishing cases of race defilement in Germany

264 On 1 February 1937 Reinhard Heydrich informs the Deputy of the Führer about the granting of public house licences to Jews

265 On 8 February 1937 the Israelite Association for Old Age Benefits and Nursing Care applies to the Regierungspräsident in Hanover for a permit to collect donations

266 On 18 February 1937, 16-year-old Werner Angress describes his reaction to the suicide of his group leader in the Groß-Breesen retraining camp

267 Advertisement for the antisemitic play The Dancing Jew, enclosed in a letter from the Franz Wulf publishing house dated 20 February 1937

268 On 2 March 1937 the head of the personnel section of the City of Munich criticizes a staff official in the welfare section for granting too extensive welfare to a Jew

269 Die Kameradschaft, 10 March 1937: proposal for an antisemitic social evening topic for the Hitler Youth

270 Jüdische Rundschau, 16 March 1937: article about two court decisions on making purchases in Jewish shops

271 On 9 April 1937 Karl Scherk invites the Jewish landowners and householders in Stettin to found an interest group

272 On 16 April 1937 Rabbi Wahrmann reports on the grave problems confronting Jewish communities in Silesia

273 On 17 April 1937 the Düsseldorf leather goods salesman Paul Malsch writes to his son from the Netherlands to describe the political situation in Germany

274 Joseph B. Levy describes the B'nai B'rith Lodge in Frankfurt and how it was closed down by the Gestapo on 19 April 1937

275 Hermann Lesser writes to the Reich Association of German Small-Animal Breeders on 27 April 1937 to propose the establishment of a Jewish dog breeders' organization

276 On 29 April 1937 Adolf Hitler outlines his anti-Jewish strategy to NSDAP Kreisleiter at the Vogelsang National Socialist Castle elite training school

277 On 3 May 1937 the Office of the Plenipotentiary for the Four-Year Plan summarizes the effects of the Aryanization of the Jewish art trade

278 On 7 May 1937 the Office of the Plenipotentiary for the Four-Year Plan discusses the classification of Wertheim as an Aryan company

279 On 14 May 1937 Bertha Meyer, who had emigrated to Prague, asks the Foreign Currency Office of the Greater Berlin Tax Office to waive the fees for storage of her household effects

280 Frankfurter Zeitung, 16 May 1937: article on the increased revenue from the Reich Flight Tax as a result of the mass emigration of Jews

281 On 19 May 1937 the chief official of the Civil Registry Offices in Frankfurt reports to the mayor about his plan to marry Jewish couples on designated days

282 On 21 May 1937 the German Council of Municipalities summarizes the results of a survey on the treatment of Jewish patients in municipal hospitals

283 On 28 May 1937 the SS Security Service discusses preliminary measures against Jews in the event of war

284 Lecture by Theodor Oberländer on the strengthening of German influence in Eastern Europe, spring 1937

285 On 16 June 1937 the Reich Ministry of Finance asks the Deputy of the Führer for a response on the planned introduction of special taxes for Jews

286 On 22 June 1937 the Reich Foreign Office informs the embassies of the German position towards the establishment of a Jewish state in Palestine

287 Zwischen Weichsel und Nogat, June 1937: article demanding that a Jewish farmer leave the village of Gnojau

288 On 12 July 1937 the SS Security Service holds talks with the Gestapo to discuss the next census and the racial registration of the Jews

289 Der Fremdenverkehr: reproduction of the decree issued by State Secretary Hans Pfundtner on 24 July 1937 concerning the separation of Jewish from non-Jewish guests in baths and spa resorts

290 Pariser Tageszeitung, 24 July 1937: article about the introduction of a defence tax targeting Jews in the National Socialist state

291 In summer 1937 Max Warburg submits to State Secretary Wilhelm Stuckart proposals to encourage Jewish emigration

292 Report by the Jewish Central Information Office dated 11 August 1937 regarding anti-Jewish riots in Upper Silesia following the expiry of the treaty on minorities

293 On 11 August 1937 the émigré Günter Bodlaender in Prague asks a relief organization to support his emigration to the Philippines

294 On 13 September 1937 the historian Willy Cohn comments on the failure of his attempts to emigrate to Palestine

295 Völkischer Beobachter: Adolf Hitler's closing address on Jewry and Bolshevism at the ninth NSDAP rally in Nuremberg, 13 September 1937

296 On 15 September 1937 the chief public prosecutor in Frankfurt requests permission from the Reich Minister of Justice to initiate criminal proceedings on account of defamation of the SS newspaper Das Schwarze Korps

297 On 30 September 1937 a Berlin local branch of the NSDAP demands the termination of leases to Jewish tenants of the municipal housing associations

298 On 3 October 1937 Gary Samuelis writes to Kurt Polley in Berlin about his difficult start in the USA

299 Position paper dated 16 October 1937 on the establishment in Munich of Europe's largest library for the study of the Jewish question

300 Haynt, 17 October 1937: article on the situation in Germany and resistance on the part of Jews in Poland

301 Conference at the Reich Ministry of the Interior on 18 October 1937 on the mass emigration of Jews

302 On 18 October 1937 Julius Salinger writes to Kaspar Arendt in Berlin to tell him about conditions for immigrants in South Africa

303 On 18 October 1937 Police Detective Ernst Patzer appeals to Adolf Hitler for a new post after being dismissed due to his 'mixed marriage'

304 On 26 October 1937 the Reich Office for Foreign Exchange Control disseminates information about changes in the financing of mass Jewish emigration

305 Jüdisches Gemeindeblatt für Rheinland und Westfalen, 29 October 1937: article on conditions for the Jews in the communities of Cologne and Breslau

306 On 9 November 1937 the chairman of the Berlin City Council writes to the Reich Minister of Education to justify his decision to limit the number of pupils at a Jewish private school

307 Paul Malsch from Düsseldorf writes about the opening of the propaganda exhibition 'The Eternal Jew' (around 10 November 1937)

308 On 12 November 1937 the Relief Association of Jews in Germany issues a report on the progress and organization of emigration

309 On 18 November 1937 the physician Hertha Nathorff bemoans the surveillance by the Gestapo of her lecture at the League of Jewish Women

310 On 20 November 1937 the 17-year-old Werner Angress describes his flight from Germany

311 On 23 November 1937 the Reich Foreign Office urges the head of the Reich Chancellery to ensure that Jewish shops are marked as such

312 On 26 November 1937 Minister of Propaganda Joseph Goebbels advocates the exclusion of Jews from German cultural life

313 The Jewish Community of Merzig writes to the Reich commissioner for the Saarland on 29 November 1937 regarding the repair of the damaged synagogue

314 On 7 December 1937 the German Labour Front plans to push through the legal exclusion of Jews as factory leaders

315 On 15 December 1937 Hermann Göring, as acting Reich Minister of Economics, limits the foreign currency and raw material allocations for Jewish companies

316 On 18 December 1937 State Secretary Hans Pfundtner sends the head of the Reich Chancellery the draft of a regulation directed against Jewish physicians

317 On 28 December 1937 the SS Security Service demands information from the SD Main Districts on the practice of approving itinerant trade licences for Jews

318 In the 1937 Reich Medicinal Almanac, Jewish physicians are indicated with a colon

319 The executive of the Jewish Community of Berlin reports on vocational training and retraining measures in 1937

320 The Reich Representation of Jews in Germany reports on the development and the problems of Jewish welfare support in 1937

DOCUMENTS

DOC. 1
Jüdische Rundschau, 31 January 1933: editorial on the appointment of Adolf Hitler as Reich Chancellor[1]

Hitler's government

The appointment of Hitler as Reich Chancellor and the formation of a government in which the National Socialists hold the most important positions of power puts an end to the condition of ambiguity and constantly repeated confusion that has characterized the preceding epoch of Germany's domestic history. As Jews we are confronted by the fact that a power inimical to us has taken over the government in Germany. Whoever had a sense of reality and was not misled by the reassurances of the liberal press, which again and again believed it had witnessed the demise of the National Socialist movement, could make no mistake about the fact that the political restructuring and changes in the mentality of the German people that have come to light in the major electoral successes of the National Socialists would sooner or later have to find their counterpart in the composition of the government as well.

National Socialism is a *movement hostile to the Jews*. Its antisemitism is programmatic to a degree that no other party has been. It owes a large part of its propagandistic success to the unscrupulous smear campaign against the Jews. This could never prevent us, however, from recognizing the fact that National Socialism has become a decisive force within the German nation, which it would be a mistake to disregard. For that reason, when Hitler was rejected by the Reich President[2] on 13 August and 25 November, we did not in any way appear as relieved and satisfied as did a part of the Jewish community that refuses to see the big picture and clings to isolated political phenomena of the day. Hitler was met with opposition and resistance, but if his path to power was obstructed in the last half-year, it was certainly not because of his antisemitic programme. If anything, one can say that, even without Hitler's seizure of power, the exclusion of the Jews was already being conducted under pressure from Hitler's party.[3]

When Hitler was rejected for the first time, the *Jüdische Rundschau* made striking parallels with the creator of the Christian Social Party in Vienna, Dr *Lueger*.[4] Lueger, who in his time was as much the symbolic figure of antisemitism for the world as Hitler is today, was twice rejected by Emperor Franz Josef after his election as mayor of Vienna. He had to be confirmed on the third occasion and in this way triumphed over the old

---

1 'Regierung Hitler', *Jüdische Rundschau*, 31 Jan. 1933, p. 1. This document has been translated from German. The *Jüdische Rundschau* emerged in 1902 as the organ of the Zionist Federation for Germany from the *Berliner Vereinsbote*, which had been founded in 1895 (from 1901 the *Israelitische Rundschau*). As one of the largest Jewish weeklies in the German-speaking countries, it propagated the goals of the Zionist movement. In 1933 it appeared twice weekly in Berlin, edited by Heinrich Loewe. In 1934 it had a circulation of 37,000. Banned in Germany after the pogroms of Nov. 1938, it was published from March 1939 to 1940 in Jerusalem as the *Jüdische Weltrundschau*.
2 Paul von Hindenburg (1847–1934) was Reich President from 1925 to 1934.
3 Thus, Leo Kestenberg, for instance, was dismissed by the Reich government from the post of head of music in the Prussian Ministry of Culture in 1932: for his biography, see Doc. 5, 5/6 March 1933, fn. 2.
4 Dr Karl Lueger (1844–1910), lawyer; practised law in Vienna, 1874–1896; founder of the antisemitic Christian Social Party in Austria, 1891; mayor of Vienna, 1897–1910.

emperor. Our speculation that Hitler would follow the same path has been confirmed. Less than twenty-four hours ago, the solution to the cabinet crisis was still thoroughly unclear. An agreement between the individual groups on the right, who only a short time ago had bitterly fought among themselves, still seemed impossible. Even the role of individual personalities in this endgame is difficult to comprehend, but it is not our concern to assess them. The right-wing *DAZ*[5] claimed in its Sunday edition that until now Hindenburg had resolutely refused to accept Hitler as leader of a presidential cabinet, and since Hitler's chances for a parliamentary majority are slim, the *DAZ* raised the question: 'Does the Reich President hope that Hitler's movement will relent, or has he himself decided to relent?' By this the newspaper meant that the one option excludes the other.[6]

As these lines go to press, the foundations on which the new cabinet is to be built are as yet unknown. It is unclear above all whether the Centre [Party][7] can supply a viable parliamentary form for the cabinet. The regime appears to depend on the support of groups that are bound by their principles and the imperative of political acumen to safeguard the fundamental rights of citizens as guaranteed by the constitution. The Reich President, who has appointed Hitler, is bound by his constitutional oath, his moral authority, and his international reputation. The civic equality of German Jews is, however, *anchored in the constitution of the Reich*. We can only repeat what we wrote in these pages on 12 August:[8] 'If Hitler becomes Reich Chancellor, the programme of the National Socialist Party, with its well-known anti-Jewish statutes, must not become the programme of the German Reich. As party leader, Hitler could draw upon the support of the masses he has fanaticized, but as Reich Chancellor he has to recognize that Germany consists of different elements that have a right to respect for their distinctiveness.' The German Jews, constantly threatened and offended, demeaned and maligned by the Reich Chancellor's party, demand from *every* government, whichever it may be, respect for their existence, their honour and kind. The entire world is now looking at Germany, especially the Jewish people. Despite the numerical insignificance of German Jewry, the fate of the German Jews is the focus of attention for all Jews in the world. We are convinced that even among the *German people* forces are still alive that will turn against barbaric anti-Jewish politics. Furthermore, Germany's status among all the cultural nations depends upon its behaviour with regard to the Jewish question. Even a National Socialist-ruled Germany cannot ignore the entanglement of international relations.

The *German Jews*, for whom the new turn of events cannot have been unexpected, have to maintain their inner calm and dignity. It goes without saying that German Jewry *will fight with all means and energy* against every attempt at formal and factual disenfranchisement and dispossession. This battle can only be led by a Jewry that is filled with unfaltering pride for its heritage. Attempts at assimilation and self-denial have come to

---

5 *Deutsche Allgemeine Zeitung*. The newspaper appeared from 1861 to 1918 as the *Norddeutsche Allgemeine Zeitung* and thereafter until 1945 as the *Deutsche Allgemeine Zeitung*.
6 Report in the section 'Unsere Meinung' (Our View), *Deutsche Allgemeine Zeitung* (Reich edition), 29 Jan. 1933, p. 1.
7 The author means the Catholic Centre Party (Zentrumspartei), which was represented Catholic Germany. It was founded in 1870 and active until 1933.
8 'Hitler Reichskanzler?', editorial, *Jüdische Rundschau*, 12 August 1932, p. 1.

an end. Those German Jews who trusted the false slogans of their past leaders and devoted themselves to faith in progressive improvement through 'enlightenment' have lost the ground beneath their feet. In the face of the conditions created, German Jewry must more than ever unite to help itself. To keep the spirit of Judaism alive and active – that is the task at hand. Never was it so important as it is now to keep the faith in Judaism and its future strong and unwavering. The Jewish people are the bearer of imperishable values, the inheritor of an incomparable history. In times of danger and in times of hardship, we must make every effort to raise awareness of this fact.

DOC. 2

Nationalsozialistische Monatshefte, January 1933: editorial on the struggle against international Jewry[1]

Arno Schickedanz,[2] *Berlin:*
A concluding word on the Jewish question[3]
Introduction

Recognizing that after the spiritual and material collapse a völkisch renewal of Germany can only take place on an idealistic basis that corresponds to the ancestral character of the German people and its inherent disposition, and leads it again to dominance, National Socialism felt compelled from the outset to take a stand against all alien influences. If it wanted to achieve a rebirth of Germany, then it had to harken back to the eternally renewing forces of its race and soul, restore them to victory, and repel and eliminate as far as possible any influence of a foreign race on the psyche that prevented the unfolding of our own, or adulterated it. It was thus compelled to nationalize the nation in order to save it, and in the process encountered the opposition of those forces that internationalized the nation, in order, whether consciously or unconsciously, to corrupt it for their own benefit. National or international, those are the two solutions from which all others recede; the destiny of the German people will be decided between them. For this reason, however, the confrontation between the nation reawakened in National Socialism and Jewry is unavoidable. All internationalizing tendencies were embodied in Jewry, the – strange as it may sound – national people par excellence, which ceaselessly influenced the other nations and the German people in particular, both spiritually and materially. This influence was already prevalent in the French Revolution, which distorted a

---

1 'Ein abschließendes Wort zur Judenfrage', *Nationalsozialistische Monatshefte*, vol. 4, no. 34 (1933), pp. 1–3. This document has been translated from German. The so-called Academic Journal of the NSDAP was edited by Adolf Hitler until the end of 1933; Alfred Rosenberg was its editorial director. The journal appeared from 1930 to 1944.
2 Arno Schickedanz (1892–1945), journalist; joined the NSDAP in 1923 and took part in the Beer Hall Putsch the same year; director of the Berlin office of the *Völkischer Beobachter*, 1930–1933; chief of staff of the Foreign Policy Office of the NSDAP, 1934–1945; head of the main office in the task force known as Einsatzstab Reichsleiter Rosenberg, 1940–1945; author of *Die Juden: Eine Gegenrasse* (1927).
3 A detailed summary of the article appeared in the *Völkischer Beobachter* under the title 'Die Judenfrage': *Völkischer Beobachter* (northern German edition), 5/6 Feb. 1933, 2nd supplement.

misunderstood and unfortunate ideal of humanity into the [notion of the] equality of everything human and contrasted its outward pacifistic expressions of liberation with an inward reign of blood, only to then acquire a greater scale and significance in the recent past with growing affluence and the utilization of all technological progress. On the one hand, international financial obligations among states sprouted up under Jewish leadership as creeping plants that threatened to strangle national economies. This process was supported by unhealthy parallel phenomena developing simultaneously within the individual national economies, within which industrial and merchant giants grew. These were controlled or managed by Jews who, disregarding or even in direct opposition to national needs, formed their cartels or waged wars of competition. On the other hand, an inner front was established under Jewish leadership that ran through all Volksgemeinschaften and broke up the Volksgemeinschaften under the pretext of wanting to combat those parasitical phenomena. If the call to arms during the French Revolution was 'liberty, equality, and fraternity', which in practice then materialized on the scaffold, it is now, in the next stage, based on the false doctrine of the Jew Marx-Mordechai:[4] 'class rule' and the annihilation of all that is rooted in the soil, organically conditioned and natural, in favour of a shadowy, construed notion of an international community of interest formed by all those supposedly exploited by a 'capitalism per se'. In this way, the German people are threatened like all others by this intellectualized falsification of real life, and in fact from two sides, both of which are under an international slogan as well as Jewish leadership: through Jewish speculation in financial capital and through Marxism.

The ultimate victory of either side would mean the demise of the German Volk. In the first instance, this would be through a slowly worsening ailment that would definitively sap all remaining healthy life forces and dynamism of the nation, which could be furthered by artificial measures such as exporting slave labourers, emigration, and so on and so forth, while other, stronger peoples occupy the space vacated. In the second instance, it would be through having an internal bloodstream like no other, which would mean the extermination of the most valuable racial elements, the most creative and headstrong, the most German in character and essence, which could never ever bow to such a reign of deluded notions alien to its nature. In both cases, the fate of Germany would be sealed. It would be eliminated from the history of peoples, and Judaism would then have experienced not its first, but certainly its greatest, triumph.

In this respect, the fight against the Jews has entailed the attack on the hostile centre of power. Naturally, it can only be won after the defeat of its Jewish support, in particular of its bodyguard, Marxism. However, to have taken it up and declared it an item on its agenda, without deviating from it despite an unprecedented reaction from an opponent at the height of his powers, is already in and of itself to the enormous historical credit of National Socialism, which only later generations will fully appreciate. The awareness that has already arisen among the broadest swathes of the German people to the effect that there will be no recovery of the German people, no liberation from the reign of inferiors, no salvation from empty talk as a cloak for anti-national efforts without the elimination of Jewry and the overcoming of its deluded notions is itself a result of this

---

4 The author means Karl Marx. Mordecai or Mordechai is a central figure in the Old Testament Book of Esther.

struggle for German rebirth. It is thus stated in the NSDAP manifesto: 'Only those of German blood, whatever their creed, may be citizens of the state. No Jew, therefore, may be a Volksgenosse.' This provides the basis for the next demand: 'Whoever is not a citizen of the state, shall only be able to live in Germany as a guest and must be subject to legislation pertaining to foreign nationals.'[5]

DOC. 3

C.V.-Zeitung, 9 February 1933: report on anti-Jewish riots in Gersfeld, Hesse[1]

Terror in Gersfeld

Over the course of the last week the windows of various Jewish families in Gersfeld were smashed. Moreover, a Jewish businessman who gave chase when the windows were shattered was stabbed with a knife and seriously injured. The perpetrators fled but left behind a cap and gloves, so that one can expect them to be identified.

Larger riots broke out on the evening of Saturday 4 February. The leader of the NSDAP, the carpenter Heun,[2] called on his followers at the marketplace to fetch the Jewish inhabitants from their houses. The fanaticized multitude hereupon marched to the house of the respected businessman Bachrach[3] from the Liebstädter company. Three National Socialists forced entry into the house and injured the unsuspecting businessman Bachrach, who was sitting in the company of his family, with punches and kicks that were so severe that he collapsed and required medical attention. The barbarous attack is all the more incomprehensible since businessman Bachrach has never been active politically and enjoyed widespread popularity both personally and in business.

---

5 Cited here are points 4 (misquoted) and 5 of the NSDAP manifesto from 24 Feb. 1920: Walther Hofer (ed.), *Der Nationalsozialismus: Dokumente 1933–1945*, new edn (Frankfurt am Main: Fischer Taschenbuch, 1988 [1957]), p. 28.

1 'Terror in Gersfeld', *C.V.-Zeitung*, 9 Feb. 1933, p. 41. This document has been translated from German. A weekly newspaper with the subtitle '*Blätter für Deutschtum und Judentum*' (Newspaper for Germandom and Jewry), from May 1922 the *C.V.-Zeitung* was the organ of the Central Association of German Citizens of the Jewish Faith (CV) and successor to the CV organ *Im Deutschen Reich*, published from 1895–1922. The *C.V.-Zeitung* reported on Jewish life in German society and addressed the topic of antisemitism. It had a circulation of 40,000 in 1935.

2 Wilhelm Heun (b. 1894), carpenter; joined the NSDAP in 1930.

3 Correctly: Sally Bacharach (b. 1881), businessman; lived from 1909 in Gersfeld and moved to Fulda in March 1934 with his wife, Ida.

DOC. 4
C.V.-Zeitung, 23 February 1933: article criticizing anti-Jewish propaganda on the streets of Berlin and in the Nazi press[1]

Who benefits from it?
New antisemitic agitation. Falsehood about ritual murder. The 'Protocols'. The 'Jewish Hoarder Slogan' and other accusations. What do our friends say?

I

L. H.[2] On Kurfürstendamm and on Tauentzienstraße in Berlin the sale of a brochure has been announced over the last few days: *The Demand of the Hour: Jews Out!*[3] The decree of 4 February protecting the German people (section 2, § 9, no. 6) threatens printed periodicals with prohibition 'if a religious community recognized under public law, its institutions, customs, and objects of religious worship are insulted or maliciously degraded in them.' The meaning of these paragraphs unambiguously aims to remove religious communities and their institutions, which are already protected as such under the penal code (§ 166), from the daily political struggle. Respect for religion should also be held sacred by dissenters. It cannot be the aim of the legislator to restrict this *meaning* of the emergency decree, of which we also approve, merely to *periodical* print matter. It must for this reason be utterly disconcerting that Dr von Leers,[4] a well-known member of the National Socialist Party, whose takeover of government was immediately followed by that emergency decree, has composed a flyer containing severe insults not only towards Jewry as an alleged political power but also towards the *Jewish religion*. We are the last ones who would call for censorship of printed matter. But we regard it as our duty to point out that writings such as this *Demand of the Hour* are liable to provoke an *atmosphere of civil war and pogrom*, and that their dissemination in these times constitutes an immediate threat, not only to the Jews but also to the German people in their entirety. Even if Dr von Leers writes in his afterword: 'National Socialism fights against Judah, not to do violence to the poor Jews, but to remove the opportunity for influence from a domineering foreign people, not to organize pogroms, but to expel the Ostjuden who are detrimental to the country, to make the remaining Jews politically and economically innocuous as foreigners', he does not thereby diminish the effect.

---

1 'Wem nützt das?', *C.V.-Zeitung*, 23 Feb. 1933, pp. 58–59. This document has been translated from German.
2 Dr Ludwig Holländer (1877–1936), lawyer; counsel, 1908; later director of the Central Association of Jews in Germany (CV); editor-in-chief of the *C.V.-Zeitung*, 1932; author of works including *Deutsch-Jüdische Probleme der Gegenwart* (1929).
3 The brochure *Die Forderung der Stunde: Juden raus!* was distributed by National Socialists in uniform in front of buildings such as the department store Kaufhaus des Westens (KaDeWe) with the slogan: 'Jews out! From the secret files of the Public Prosecutor's Office, from Minister Göring': quoted from a petition by Jean Sklarz dated 23 Feb. 1933. Sklarz had complained to Göring that his name was referred to in the brochure as 'Jewish and Galician': GStA PK, I HA, Rep. 90b/133, fol. 1.
4 Dr Johann von Leers (1902–1965), lawyer and journalist; attaché in the foreign service, 1926–1928; joined the NSDAP in 1929 and the SS in 1936; from 1929 editor-in-chief of the Nazi journal *Wille und Weg*; professor in Jena, 1938; in Italy (after 1945), in Argentina (1950), and in Egypt (1955); author of works including *Juden sehen dich an* (1933) and *Die Verbrechernatur der Juden* (1944).

Dr von Leers would probably dismiss as slander the reproach that he harms Jewry as a religious community. However, we can prove it to him from his own writing. He dedicates a large chapter of his text to alleged Talmud citations and the ritual murder commandment. 'For hours on end', he thus concludes his chapter, 'one could list cases of Jewish ritual murder, where poor, innocent little children have been butchered and tortured to death by Jewish devils.' He adds in bold type: 'Mothers, make sure that the Jewish menace to your poor children is removed from the country.'

The Reich Supreme Court has repeatedly recognized in Talmud trials that the claims of Jewish ritual murders are absurd. Yet even if Dr Leers is not familiar with the jurisprudence of the Reich Supreme Court, as someone who has delved into the question of ritual murder he must have also read contrary studies and the numerous statements of leading Christian academics who have clearly stated there is no such Jewish ritual murder. He would have to know that even noted opponents of the Jews have rejected this allegation and that the very same blood libels were made by the Romans against the Christians, by the Chinese against the European missionaries, by the French Catholics against the French Protestants; in short, wherever religious minorities sought to hold their own in the midst of prevailing views. He should have read the work *Blood in the Faith and Superstition of Men*[5] by the prominent Protestant theologian *Strack* and the collections of papal bulls, which defend themselves against such accusations of murder. Dr von Leers, who roots around in cases dating back centuries, should have rather cited the bull of *Pope Paul III* of 14 May 1450, which states:

> We have heard with displeasure that for several years now certain men, as firebrands and, as is said, mortal enemies of those Jews, blinded by hate and envy or, what seems more likely, by avarice, so that they might be in a position to appropriate the possessions and property of those same Hebrews with a certain appearance of legitimacy, falsely accuse them of killing small children, drinking their blood, and committing all manner of monstrous crimes which specifically target our said faith – and in such a way strive to stir up the resentment of ordinary Christians against them, whereby it so happens that the Jews are frequently unjustly robbed not only of their possessions and property, but even of their life.

Or he could have cited that bull of *Pope Innocent IV* of 25 September 1253 which threatens to punish the dissemination of *accusations of ritual murder with excommunication*. He should have read the official document dating from July 1236 in which the *Hohenstaufen Emperor Friedrich II* prohibits the accusing of Jews of ritual murder 'once and for all'. Finally, in the course of his studies he must have also found the resolution of the *Congress of Orientalists* to Rome dating from October 1899 which, at the request of the consistory Professor *Kautzsch*,[6] unanimously pronounced: 'The accusation that

---

5 Correctly: *Blood in the Faith and Superstition of Mankind*; Hermann L. Strack, *Das Blut im Glauben und Aberglauben der Menschheit: Mit besonderer Berücksichtigung der Volksmedizin und des jüdischen 'Blutritus'* (Munich: Beck, 1900); originally published under the title *Blutaberglaube bei Juden und Christen* in 1891. Strack (1848–1922) was professor of Protestant theology and a committed critic of antisemitism.
6 Dr Emil Kautzsch (1841–1910), Protestant theologian; professor of the Old Testament.

some commandment pertaining to followers of the Jewish religion might have ever prescribed or even alluded to the use of Christian blood for ritual purposes is downright absurd and does not befit the century that is now coming to an end.'

Dr von Leers draws a second important element for the demand in his title 'Jews Out!' from *The Protocols of the Elders of Zion*. He asserts that the authenticity of these 'Protocols' has been wrongly doubted and that they are in fact a compilation of decrees from a secret Jewish conference held in the year 1897.[7] It is unnecessary to discuss in greater detail this book, which has long been branded as a forgery and even recognized as such by the anti-Jewish side. Enough of this; we have to point out these things that are humiliating for the entire German nation because we consider it our duty. But unfortunately we also see just how little the fanatical Jew haters whom we meet *are concerned with rectifying factual errors.*

II

On 18 February this year the *Angriff*[8] wrote: in Lübeck, *the Jew* and SPD leader *Leber*[9] was released from custody. The Jew Leber had allegedly called for the murder of [SA] Marinesturmmann and Party Comrade Brüggemann.[10] In the last edition of the *C.V.-Zeitung* we already pointed out that Leber has nothing whatsoever to do with Jewry.[11] Why does the *Angriff* repeat this assertion? Only in order to incite the people against the Jews? Using the same method, it designates as Jewish the notorious scandals of recent years which also have nothing whatsoever to do with Jewishness and Jewry. Karl Marx, who is referred to as Mordechai,[12] allegedly wrote his work *Capital* at the behest of the international Jewish masonic lodges. Utter nonsense, which does not become any more true by its constantly being repeated.[13] So it is with everything else.

III

German Jews shake their heads as they observe the monstrous figments of a foolhardy imagination that have to date found their way into the National Socialist newspapers! What has happened in the economy over the last fourteen years has supposedly been

---

7 The 'Protocols' comprise a fraudulent compilation of different texts (parts of which date from the 1860s), which were first published in their current version in Russia in 1903; see the critical edition: Jeffrey L. Sammons (ed.), *Die Protokolle der Weisen von Zion: Die Grundlage des modernen Antisemitismus – eine Fälschung. Text und Kommentar* (Göttingen: Wallstein, 1998), pp. 8–16. For an English translation, see *The Jewish Peril: Protocols of the Learned Elders of Zion*, trans. George Shanks (London: Eyre & Spottiswoode, 1920 [Russian edn, 1905]). See also Doc. 25, 4 April 1933, fn. 4.
8 *Der Angriff* (The Attack): the newspaper of the Berlin NSDAP.
9 Julius Leber (1891–1945), economist; Reichstag delegate for the Social Democratic Party of Germany (SPD), 1924–1933; held in a concentration camp and in prison, 1933–1937; member of the Kreisau Circle; arrested after the assassination attempt of 20 July 1944 and executed in 1945.
10 The article appeared in the section 'Kurzmeldungen' (News in Brief): *Der Angriff*, 18 Feb. 1933, p. 2. The *Völkischer Beobachter* also referred to Leber as a Jew: *Völkischer Beobachter* (northern German edition), 19/20 Feb. 1933, p. 2.
11 The *C.V.-Zeitung* criticized a corresponding report in the *Westdeutscher Beobachter* from 2 Feb. 1933: *C.V.-Zeitung*, 16 Feb. 1933, p. 50.
12 Central figure in the Old Testament Book of Esther.
13 See also similar claims in an article published in the *NS-Monatshefte*, Jan. 1933, Doc. 2.

born of a prevalent Jewish influence. Jewish people have supposedly, as vampires of the German people, facilitated and capitalized on war, inflation, and deflation, and have ultimately become rich from the economic crisis that is destroying Germany. The *Angriff* even traces the rise of the price of lard to the *slogan about Jews being hoarders*, rather than tariff increases. The *Völkischer Beobachter* calls us 'bed bugs' and demands our extermination.[14] Many friends reckon that it is not worth stooping down to this level; every word of argument is superfluous, for whoever writes something like this knows that he won't be taken seriously, doesn't even want to be taken seriously. One should not, they say, waste thoughts and energy on these concoctions. Such are the words of the confident type of critical, worldly German Jew. Over there, deep in the ranks of the National Socialist electorate, the same verdict. The sorrow and complaints of the German Jews are indeed understandable, but as politically experienced people, German Volksgenossen of the Jewish faith ought not to let themselves get worked up. Nothing, they say, is as bad as it seems, and one must distinguish between exaggerated chants of the masses and the actual goals of German National Socialist politics. The propaganda that refers to us as bed bugs, will, they continue, also abate, and therefore wise restraint is advisable, rather than protest.

We can no longer follow this advice without a second thought. We still believe that editors and agitators are not prompted by exuberance and indiscretion, but that we have to seek the intention and system behind the tone and direction of all fomentation. The fact that anti-Jewish propaganda was circulating *before* the accomplishment of the political goal, in order to bind the masses together and to symbolize the opponent for them, was known to us. The fact that even *after* taking power the tone of the outpourings of official organs such as the *Angriff* and *Völkischer Beobachter* is increasingly and vehemently anti-Jewish should worry us. What good is the propaganda that compares us to bed bugs when one needs to know which issues are really at stake? The German people want work and bread, and they desire the resolution of *actual* problems, which in reality have nothing to do with the so-called Jewish question. We cannot be content with the repudiation of these monstrous and base attacks. We cannot casually dismiss the outpourings of National Socialist organs, as the former NSDAP Reichsleiter for organizational affairs, Gregor Strasser,[15] has recently done in a statement in the *Fränkischer Kurier*, because the standard of the *Stürmer* and its editor define the character of the attacks themselves. In the case of statements by organs of a political, fundamental, indeed now official nature, such as the *Völkischer Beobachter* and the *Angriff*, we must raise the

---

14 An article signed 'KL.' states that 'foreign Jews' can be observed in the Berlin cityscape. The author equates them with lice that nest in crevices and rapidly reproduce. According to the article, they must be subjected to radical treatment. Only the 'fiercest fumigation of the infected space' can drive them out: 'Berliner Spaziergang: Die Wanzen' (Berlin stroll: The bed bugs), *Völkischer Beobachter* (Berlin edition), 12/13 Feb. 1933, *Berliner Beobachter*, daily supplement to the *Völkischer Beobachter*, p. 2.

15 Correctly: Gregor Straßer (1892–1934), pharmacist; joined the NSDAP and the SA in 1921; participated in the Beer Hall Putsch in 1923; imprisoned in Landsberg am Lech; NSDAP Gauleiter for Lower Bavaria, 1925–1929; NSDAP Reichsleiter for propaganda, 1926–1928; NSDAP Reichsleiter for organizational affairs, 1928–1932; resigned from all Party posts in Dec. 1932; managing director of the firm Schering-Kahlbaum, 1933–1934; murdered during the Night of the Long Knives on 30 June 1934.

question 'Who benefits?' and reveal the dangers that arise from the unopposed accordance with such uninhibited methods of combat. Today it is no longer possible to shrug off such a campaign as the nonchalant utterances of some journalists or agitators. If a spark is ignited and results in misfortune, then it will be impossible to absolve of responsibility those who are aware of this spiteful and deceitful activity and nevertheless do nothing about it. It is important to clearly establish responsibility.

DOC. 5
Völkischer Beobachter, 5/6 March 1933: appeal by the NSDAP to 'German artists' to vote at the parliamentary elections[1]

It is time to draw the line!
German men! German women!

At this point in the course of the recent election campaign, which was one of the fiercest and most earnest in our history, we have submitted *the cultural sins of the former system* to a *general reckoning* in a way that pillories once and for all the fairy tale of the Reich of 'beauty and dignity' in all its base dishonesty. It was not pleasant work, but it had to be done, so that it will never be forgotten just how close to the precipice the people of thinkers and poets were brought by the depths and blind fanaticism of elements of a foreign nation and race. It is an incontrovertible, atrocious fact *that it is precisely in the realm of cultural life* that *the most severe internal damages* have been inflicted on the German people as a whole. No branch of cultural life was spared from the erosive and corrosive influences of the systematic agitators. *For that, they will never be forgotten!*
German poet! German writer!
Never forget that the so-called 'heads of the system', all those Jews and their associates whom we have pilloried, and who today hysterically call for '*freedom*', have for decades been *systematically undermining* all freedom of self-discipline, will to defence, reconstruction, and national honour. *Never forget* that for decades they have been allowed to turn the German book market into a stamping ground for their obscene, pacifist, treasonous, and atheistic literary works, while you had to stand aside in determined rage, condemned to inaction!

German playwright! German actor!
Never forget that during the post-war years, to this very day, *hundreds of Jews and foreigners* were allowed to rule German theatres with the loving acceptance of irresponsible theatre managers, that artists of a foreign race and nation were paid huge salaries while there was no place for you in your own homeland, while you had to look on starving as others were fattened up! *Never forget the time* when nigger and mutineer plays,

---

1 'Jetzt wird der Schlußstrich gezogen!', *Völkischer Beobachter* (northern German edition), 5/6 March 1933, 2nd supplement. This document has been translated from German. The *Völkischer Beobachter* was the daily newspaper of the NSDAP and was published from 1927, initially as a nationwide edition. Between 1933 and 1945 a Berlin and a northern German edition also appeared, and from 1938 a Vienna edition.

dramas with a communist tendency, underworld and sensationalist thrillers filled the repertoires and dragged into the dirt everything that was noble and sacred to a German!

German architect! German sculptor!

Never forget that in the 'German artistic empire of the Jewish nation' of the post-war years everything that the German propensity for creation had built over centuries was allowed to be vilified and torn down in unscrupulous, presumptuous, criminal hubris. Constructivists, psychopaths, and foreigners knew how to win the favour of ruthless investors, while you were passed over and found no work to match your skills and creative powers. *Never forget* that art, which a high destiny has entrusted us Germans to nurture, has been pushed to the limit of insanity by foreign hands and misused as a means to express Marxist theories, while you were cast from the altar to which you devoted your life!

German composers! German musicians!

Never forget that the venerable values that have been handed down to us by our great German masters have been adulterated and pushed aside by a tangled web of *new slogans and doctrines*. *Never forget* that under the rule of the Jew Kestenberg[2] propaganda for *Marxist class-struggle music* was allowed in public with no other goal than the *destruction of the German soul!* But you had to put your instrument in the corner, and the applause of the corrupted masses was not bestowed upon you, because you had nothing in common with this witches' cauldron of new German music culture.

German artists! German radio listeners!

Never forget that for ten years *opportunists* were allowed to command the radio, which should be for the entire people, and these opportunists were imbued with neither their task nor their responsibility, yet they could pocket huge salaries only because they better understood how to bend their backs 'upwards' in a twisted manner than did you, who remain upright in your essence! *Never forget* what they dared to place before you as art with sugar-coated proclamations: *kitsch and slow poison of Jewish origin*, while you had to scrimp and save your last pennies for it!

All of you, German men and women, who are involved in the wider circle of German artistic life, be it through creative participation or through joyful reception: *never forget* what you had to suffer in silence as 'German' art in recent years, defencelessly given over to the scornful laughter of Muscovite and Jewish art-jobbers! For all of you a new day is dawning!

It has not been that long since *Adolf Hitler* took over the government, and already you feel the fresh wind heralding a better era, already you hear the pounding blow under which quakes the hollow, clay building that cultural Bolshevism has erected in our midst. Already the first stones are flying out of its brittle masonry.

2 Leo Kestenberg (1882–1962), pianist and music reformer; from 1918 sub-department head of music in the Prussian Ministry of Culture; dismissed by the Reich government in 1932; emigrated in 1933 to Prague and in 1938 to Palestine, where he was manager of the Palestine Orchestra and founder of the Music Teachers' Training College in Tel Aviv; author of works including *Musikerziehung und Musikpflege* (1921).

It is up to you to push some more and finish off this foreign pseudo-art of the post-war era!

It is up to you whether you want to stand in the shadows at this fateful hour, or whether you are willing to help restore the culture that befits the nature and talent of the German people.

It is up to you to decide if you are for yesterday or for tomorrow, for decline or for ascent, for Bolshevism or Germany!

Adolf Hitler is calling you! Adolf Hitler knows all of you, you the nameless and neglected! Adolf Hitler will lead you towards the new day!

Take hold of this grand work with us! No voice for the betrayers of culture!

Vote for the National Socialists! Vote List 1.

DOC. 6

Walter Gyssling describes riots and abuses in Munich on 9/10 March 1933[1]

Diary entry by Walter Gyssling[2] for 10 March 1933 (copy)

10 March. A night of horror lies behind us. Nothing else was ultimately to be expected. Whoever has heard the unbridled diatribes that were spoken yesterday evening in front of the Feldherrenhalle[3] is disgusted but not surprised. Esser,[4] Epp,[5] Röhm,[6] and whatever all the names of the 'leaders' are, have unhesitatingly poured oil on the flames. They bear the guilt for all the despicable crimes that took place last night. The workers' newspapers destroyed, the trade union premises attacked, hundreds of communist and social democrat leaders arrested. It is awful, but one is somehow used to it already, especially if one saw what happened the week after the Reichstag fire in Berlin. But that bloodthirsty criminals storm the apartments of peaceful, non-political citizens, that people are car-

---

1 Copy of the diary entry in Walter Gyssling, 'Mein Leben in Deutschland vor und nach Hitler' [My life in Germany before and after Hitler] (1940), pp. 99–101, Houghton Library, Cambridge, MA, Harvard University competition, 'My Life in Germany before and after 30 January 1933' (hereafter Harvard Competition), no. 86. Published in Walter Gyssling, *Mein Leben in Deutschland vor und nach 1933, und Der Anti-Nazi: Handbuch im Kampf gegen die NSDAP*, ed. Leonidas Hill (Bremen: Donat, 2003), pp. 150–153. This document has been translated from German.
2 Dr Walter Gyssling (1903–1980), journalist; career officer, then university studies; joined the Social Democratic Party of Germany (SPD) in 1929; leading member of the CV bureau for resistance to antisemitism, 1930–1933; fled to Basel in March 1933 to avoid arrest; author of *Der Anti-Nazi* (1931, reprint 2003).
3 Correctly: Feldherrnhalle (field commander's hall), a monumental loggia in Munich commissioned by King Ludwig I of Bavaria in 1841 to commemorate the Bavarian army. On 9 Nov. 1923 sixteen participants in the Beer Hall Putsch (as well as four policemen) were killed at the site in a clash with the Bavarian police.
4 Hermann Esser (1900–1981), journalist; joined the SPD in 1918 and the NSDAP in 1920; propaganda leader of the NSDAP, 1921–1923 and 1925–1926; took part in the Beer Hall Putsch, 1923; editor of the magazine *Illustrierter Beobachter*, 1926–1932; Bavarian state commissioner, then state minister without portfolio (head of the Press Office and State Chancellery), 1933–1935; head of tourism in the Reich Ministry of Public Enlightenment and Propaganda, 1935–1945; state secretary from 1939; interned in Nuremberg, 1945; classified by the civilian tribunal in Munich as a 'major offender' during denazification proceedings and sentenced to five years of hard labour, 1949; released in 1952.

ried off and roughed up, that nothing, nothing at all, is sacred to these gangs, that was never the case in Germany until now.

Today we are trying to at least get an overview of the night's events.

Just now a leader of the Bavarian People's Party informs us that the current minister of police, Dr Stützel,[7] was taken out of his apartment during the night by SA members, brought barefoot in his pyjamas to the Brown House,[8] and savagely beaten there. He probably would have ordered the police to march yesterday morning, had he foreseen his fate. Then a distraught friend comes and tells us that an acquaintance of his, a retailer who had never stood out politically, was assaulted in his apartment during the night by the SA. With the words 'we've starved for fourteen years and you, Jewish pig, have devoured the money', the beasts literally tore off one of his arms. The advertising director of a department store was beaten, taken to a remote forest, and tied naked to a tree with rope. Of a Jewish furniture dealer one hears only that, as a result of a night-time raid on his house by SA members, he now lies in the surgical ward with a fractured skull. I met the wife of a lawyer. Her husband has fled. Out of rage at this, she was viciously abused by intruding SA members. She can hardly walk. All her limbs are covered with welts and bruises. One arrest after another is being reported. Not only the leaders of the left-wing parties, but also numerous Jewish retailers were simply arrested on the basis of some kind of list of proscriptions. We go to the offices of a well-known Jewish society. What we see there is an image of meaningless destruction. Doors and windows smashed, telephones and furniture demolished by axe blows, everything thrown around. Pale and crying, the employees tell us about the attack. Whatever wasn't nailed down and bolted, files, books, typewriters, money, everything, was stolen. The looters did not even leave behind a single phone book or train timetable. There I also hear more details about the despicable fate of the venerable rabbi.[9] During the night, SA members took him to the Brown House, where he was greeted with the words 'here he comes, the crooked Jew-dog who will now be shot'. He was then led to the Oberwiesenfeld parade ground and placed blindfolded against a tree; an execution squad lined up and an officer commanded, 'Aim, fire!' But they did not fire. They merely wanted to give this dignified old man

---

5 Franz Xaver, Ritter von Epp (1868–1946), professional officer; military career, including postings in China and German South-West Africa, ultimately as major general, 1887–1923; commander of the Epp Freikorps, 1919; joined the NSDAP, 1928; Reichsstatthalter in Bavaria, 1933–1945; Reichsleiter of the Colonial Policy Office of the NSDAP, 1934–1944; leader of the Reich Colonial League, 1936–1945; interned, 1945–1946.

6 Ernst Röhm (1887–1934), professional officer; participated in the Beer Hall Putsch in 1923, then was dismissed from the Reichswehr; head of the SA, 1925 and 1930–1934; military instructor in Bolivia, 1928–1930; joined the NSDAP in 1930; Bavarian state minister, Reich minister without portfolio, president of the German Academic Exchange Service (DAAD), 1933–1934; murdered on 30 June 1934 for an alleged putsch attempt.

7 Dr Karl Stützel (1872–1944), lawyer; member of the Bavarian People's Party (BVP), 1918–1933; held posts including as assessor in Landshut, 1901–1914; district magistrate in Vilshofen, 1914–1918; Ministerialrat in the Bavarian Ministry of Social Welfare, 1918–1924; Bavarian minister of the interior, 1924–1933; initiator of the ban on the SA and the SS, 1932; imprisoned by the SA and removed from office, 1933.

8 Brown House: the Party designation for the NSDAP headquarters, which were located at 45 Brienner Straße in Munich from 1930 to 1945.

9 Probably Rabbi Leo Baerwald. On Baerwald, see Doc. 42, 13 May 1933.

'a little scare' and then let him go. Instead, another Jewish woman comes and tells about how National Socialists broke in her apartment in the night. Her husband and son were forced to sign a release with the following content: 'I, the Israelite J. L., hereby acknowledge that I am a traitor and agree to leave behind the assets that I have stolen from the German people and leave the country within four weeks.' Scarcely had they signed under the threat of drawn revolvers, when the SA leader explained to them that a Jew once demanded that Hitler be horsewhipped out of Germany. This utterance was now going to be avenged on them. Both were stripped naked and beaten with wire whips until they collapsed unconscious.

So it continues for hours. One shocking report after another. In the end I can't take it any more and leave. Yet I am not to have any peace. On the streets it is even worse. In front of my very eyes, berated and spat at by hysterical beasts, SA members chase a man with whips in broad daylight. He wears neither shoes nor socks, no jacket, no trousers, only a shirt and torn undergarments. A placard hangs around his neck with the inscription 'I the Jew Siegel will never again complain about the National Socialists'.[10] He is one of the most respected lawyers in Munich, who had gone to the police headquarters in order to intervene on behalf of an arrested friend. After he had first been cruelly beaten, he was then hounded through the streets in the condition described above.[11]

After today, I know what a pogrom is.

DOC. 7

On 14 March 1933 Hermann Badt offers the Deputy Minister President his resignation as Prussian representative to the Constitutional Court[1]

Letter from Ministerial Director Dr Hermann Badt,[2] Krummhübel im Riesengebirge, to the Deputy Minister President of Prussia, State Minister Dr Hirtsiefer,[3] Berlin, dated 14 March 1933

Honourable State Minister

You will understand that I have been pondering the question day and night whether it is in the interest of the Ministry of State for me to resume with Dr Brecht[4] the role of representative of the Prussian government at the Constitutional Court in Leipzig.[5]

---

10 Dr Michael Siegel (1882–1979), lawyer in Munich. He emigrated to Peru in 1940.
11 A photograph exists of the incident, published shortly thereafter in American, Argentinian, French, and English newspapers, in which the barefooted Siegel, badly abused by SA men and with cropped trouser legs, is wearing a placard around his neck with the inscription: 'I will never again complain to the police' (10 March 1933). Siegel had protested earlier at the Munich police headquarters against the imprisonment of a client in a concentration camp.

1 Jüdisches Museum Berlin, 2002-31-40. This document has been translated from German.
2 Dr Hermann Badt (1887–1946), lawyer; Zionist and social democrat; worked in the Prussian Ministry of the Interior, ultimately as ministerial director, 1919–1932; representative of the disempowered Prussian government in proceedings before the Constitutional Court (Staatsgerichtshof) in Leipzig regarding von Papen's coup, 1932; emigrated via Czechoslovakia to Palestine, where he founded a land settlement society in 1933.

Allow me to remind you that before the first hearing in October of last year you remarked in a session of the Ministry of State that under the present circumstances it would be a heavy burden for the Ministry of State if it were to be represented at this time by a Jew and Social Democrat. This was particularly called to your attention, honourable State Minister, by members of your party. Such signals supposedly came from the circles of the Reich Supreme Court as well.

At that time, I declared that I would as a matter of course not travel to Leipzig if any one of the ministers of state deemed this in the best interests of the matter. I would nevertheless offer the Ministry of State my full cooperation, in particular during the hearing, without being in any way offended. The ministers of state, however, at that time unanimously held the view that I should travel to Leipzig but should refrain from participating in the proceedings as much as possible. I believe that the now-available stenographic report of the hearing in Leipzig proves how much I have adhered to these instructions. Meanwhile, the situation has developed in such a way that I fully understand if, for example, the Ministry of State were now to decide that this time Mr Brecht alone should assume the representation of Prussia.

Furthermore, I would like to mention the following.

In the event that the Prussian Ministry of State were to decide that, given the narrow extent of its remaining powers, representation by three full-time delegates is no longer necessary, especially since for some time now one of the three positions has been earmarked in the budget to be cut in the future, as the youngest of the three delegates I consider myself obligated to vacate my post. Should the Ministry of State resolve to release me from duty with effect from 1 July this year and to grant me a leave of absence until then, this would be warranted by consideration of the fact that I will have served the Prussian state for a full quarter of a century on that day. I also agree, however, to being released from duty at an earlier date.

In the event of my release from duty, I request approval for a long-planned, one-year trip to study abroad. My place of residence will continue to be Berlin.

With deepest esteem and admiration

Your very devoted

3 Dr Heinrich Hirtsiefer (1876–1941), locksmith; until 1904 labourer for Krupp, then functionary of Christian trade unions; Prussian minister of national welfare, 1921 – March 1933; from 1925 also deputy minister president of Prussia; from Sept. to Oct. 1933 imprisoned in the Kemna and Börgermoor concentration camps.
4 Dr Arnold Brecht (1884–1977), lawyer; ministerial director in the Reich Ministry of the Interior 1921–1927; transferred to the Prussian Ministry of State, 1927; Prussia's representative before the Constitutional Court, 1932; imprisoned in 1933 following a speech directed against Hitler; then emigrated to the USA, where he was professor of political science; author of the memoirs *Aus nächster Nähe* (1966) and *Mit der Kraft des Geistes* (1967), among other works.
5 The Constitutional Court rejected a temporary injunction applied for by the Prussian government on 25 July 1932 against the enactment of the Reich President from 20 July 1932, which had appointed the Reich Chancellor as Reich commissioner for Prussia and disempowered the Prussian government (the so-called *Preußenschlag*). The Constitutional Court resolved on 25 Oct. 1932 that the appointment of a state commissioner was legal with reference to paragraph 2 of Article 48 of the constitution (considerable disturbance of public safety and order in the Reich), though not the dismissal of the state government, which thus initially remained nominally in office.

DOC. 8

On 15 March 1933 the Reich Minister of the Interior recommends that the immigration and naturalization of *Ostjuden* be prevented[1]

Circular decree of the Reich Ministry of the Interior (II B 5002/9 March), signed Frick,[2] to the state governments, in the case of Prussia: to the Reich Commissioner for the Prussian Ministry of the Interior, dated 15 March 1933 (copy)[3]

In order to introduce a consciously völkisch policy it is first of all necessary:

1. to ward off the immigration of foreigners who are Ostjuden;
2. to remove them, insofar as such foreigners are still residing unauthorized in this country;[4]
3. to refrain from naturalizing foreigners who are Ostjuden until further notice.[5]

To 1: I have asked the Reich Foreign Minister[6] to instruct the German representations abroad to categorically reject requests for the issuance of an entry visa for these foreigners, insofar as no compelling reasons exist in individual cases. In the latter case, the Interior departments will be contacted before a decision is made.

I request that the offices of the Foreigners' Police be notified and that they make it their duty to heighten awareness and crack down on immigration by foreigners who are Ostjuden.

---

1 BArch, R 43 II/134, fol. 14r–v. This document has been translated from German.
2 Dr Wilhelm Frick (1877–1946), lawyer; worked from 1903 in the Bavarian civil service; head of the political police in Munich, 1919–1921; head of the criminal police in Munich, 1923; imprisoned due to his participation in the Beer Hall Putsch, 1923–1924; removed from office and reappointed, 1924; joined the NSDAP in 1925; state minister of the interior and for education in Thuringia, 1930–1931; Reich minister of the interior, 1933–1943; Reich Protector of Bohemia and Moravia, 1943–1945; executed after receiving a death sentence at the Nuremberg trials, 1946.
3 On the basis of a suggestion by State Secretary Bang (Reich Ministry of Economics) submitted to Hitler on 6 March 1933, the head of the Reich Chancellery, Lammers, had requested Frick on 9 March 1933 to commence with 'preparations for a consciously völkisch legislation'. Lammers proposed (a) taking legislative action against the immigration of *Ostjuden*, (b) that all name changes carried out since Nov. 1918 be revoked, and (c) that a certain number of 'the immigrant and non-naturalized *Ostjuden*' be expelled. Lammers had added the third point to Bang's plans: letter from Bang to Lammers, dated 6 March 1933, and from Lammers to the Reich Minister of the Interior, dated 9 March 1933: ibid, fols. 10–12; published in Karl Heinz Minuth (ed.), *Akten der Reichskanzlei* (hereafter *AdR*), part 1, vol. 1 (Munich: Oldenbourg, 1983), pp. 182–183. Frick therefore passed on to Lammers and Bang the letter printed here, dated 15 March 1933: BArch, R 43 II/134, fol. 13.
4 Proposals for the expulsion of the *Ostjuden* were already being discussed in Prussia and Bavaria in the early 1920s: see Dirk Walter, *Antisemitische Kriminalität und Gewalt: Judenfeindschaft in der Weimarer Republik* (Bonn: Dietz, 1999), pp. 52–80.
5 According to point 8 of the NSDAP manifesto from 24 Feb. 1920, the immigration of all non-Germans was to be prevented and all non-Germans who had arrived in the country as immigrants since 1914 were to be forced to leave the country: Hofer (ed.), *Der Nationalsozialismus: Dokumente*, p. 29.
6 Reich foreign minister from 1932 to 1938 was Baron Konstantin von Neurath (1873–1956), diplomat; ambassador to Rome, 1921–1930, and London, 1930–1932; joined the NSDAP in 1937; Reich Protector of Bohemia and Moravia, 1939–1943; sentenced to fifteen years' imprisonment at the Nuremberg trials in 1946; released in 1954.

To 2: I most humbly request that extradition measures be taken for foreigners who are Ostjuden who reside unauthorized in the country, within the framework of the existing laws and treaties.

To 3: until further notice, I request that the naturalization of Ostjuden is desisted from. Further information will soon be made available regarding the convening of a conference on questions of naturalization.

[...]⁷

DOC. 9
Max Moses Polke reports on the persecution of Jewish judges and lawyers in Breslau between 11 and 17 March 1933¹

Submission by Max Moses Polke² to a Harvard University competition (1940)

[...]³

The next campaign took place on 11 March 1933, after the parliamentary elections of 5 March 1933 had not given the Nazis the expected absolute majority. I was among those who were immediately affected by this campaign and wrote the following about it to a friend in Palestine on 16 March 1933.

On 11 March, between 11 a.m. and 12, approximately a hundred Brownshirts invaded the premises of the Breslau Regional Court and searched the courtrooms and judges' chambers for Semites with the words 'Out with Jews and their descendants!' The work was diligently accomplished: a Jewish prosecutor and a Jewish judge were violently dragged out in the middle of a session, as were other Jewish judges from their chambers. The same fate befell a black-haired regional court judge who had never been Jewish. The same happened to the Jewish lawyers whom one met at trials. Finally, shouting the aforementioned call, the Nazis also invaded the lawyers' chambers and hit the first ones they encountered, although their batons were unfamiliar with racial differences. Severe injuries, I would like to remark, did not occur at this juncture. Only our friend Maximilian W. bore a bloody head wound from it, but is on the way to recovery. Naturally, the command 'Jews out' was widely obeyed. Some even hit the streets without their coat. A few supposedly even kept their robes on.

---

7 The text is followed by Frick's letters to the Reich Foreign Minister and the Reich Minister of Justice from the same day. The latter has the remark that for a discussion of the proposal 'to revoke all name changes of Jewish persons that have been carried out since November 1918', a 'consultation between departments [should] be convened as quickly as possible': BArch, R 43 II/134, fol. 14v.

1 Max Moses Polke, 'Mein Leben in Deutschland vor und nach dem 30. Januar 1933' [My life in Germany before and after 30 January 1933] (1940), pp. 58–63, Harvard Competition, no. 178. This document has been translated from German.

2 Max Moses Polke (b. 1895), lawyer and economist; practised law in Breslau from 1924; member of the Social Democratic Party of Germany (SPD); active in Breslau's Jewish Community; interned in a concentration camp after the pogrom of 1938; emigrated with his family to Palestine on 18 Dec. 1938; author of works including *Die deutschen Juden als nationale Minderheit* (1934).

3 The whole life story comprises 150 pages. In the preceding section the author describes his participation in the war, his university studies, and his work as a lawyer in Breslau.

Among the few remaining Aryans an acquaintance of mine, who related this to me, attempted to negotiate with the Browns. The latter invoked the authority of an order by Göring. Their ringleader, however, claimed not to have time to present this order. Those who remained were told to continue to ensure that the court remain Jew-free, otherwise they would also be shown the door. By way of negotiation, they ultimately arrived at the decision that a meeting of all judges and lawyers would be convened in the afternoon, excluding Semites but in the presence of representatives of the Browns. In this assembly it was resolved by a majority to instate a three-day moratorium on the administration of justice. Hence, from 13 to 15 March 1933 no meetings took place.

Whatever else was negotiated in these days and with whom is unknown to me; I only know fairly reliably that the executive of the German Association of Judges and the German Association of Lawyers visited Papen and that the latter influenced Hitler to call off the action. In any case, on Monday, 13 March 1933, the entire courthouse was occupied by SA rank and file, but no longer on Tuesday, 14 March 1933. In the Higher Regional Court, hearings even took place on that day, after it had only been occupied during the early hours of 13 March.

Today, the operations were supposed to proceed as usual, yet the newspapers published a WTB[4] report, which no one wants to admit to having arranged, according to which the only trials that will be conducted are those without the participation of any Jewish lawyers, whereas all others will be cancelled.[5] In addition, every lawyer found an appended letter, and it was communicated from telephone to telephone that one should preferably not go into the office, which some have done. Nevertheless, all meetings took place and verdicts were issued in absentia for the parties represented by Jewish lawyers. Aside from that, numerous conferences and consultations of the most diverse executive committees took place during the course of the day, the results of which are as yet unknown to me.

All Jewish lawyers and prosecutors have received a letter stating that the SA has occupied the regional court and does not permit Jewish civil servants to carry out their work. The recipient of said letter, it continues, is thus to be regarded as in fact unable to exercise his duties and suspended until further notice. The recipients of these letters can for the moment take a walk in the beautiful sunshine, and their salary has been sent punctually to their apartment. However, they fear that this vacation is the beginning of the end. All Semites are affected by this, even people whose grandfather was baptized, and all persons in question were identified with astonishing thoroughness, even though it is well known that personnel files are no longer allowed to contain information about religion. At any rate, I am not familiar with a single case in which a descendant of Jews was exempted.

By the way, it must be said that the senior civil servants, i.e. the judges, behaved responsibly and irreproachably during the entire incident, until they had to yield to the pressure. As for the mid-level officials and the court constables, I have been told that during the action against the Jews several could not suppress their malicious joy and at any rate did nothing to prevent it. The few Christian colleagues with whom I have spoken during the last few days could hardly suppress their delight over the anticipated increase in legal work for them.

---

4 Wolffsches Telegraphenbüro (Wolff Telegraph Office), founded in 1849 and renamed the Deutsches Nachrichtenbüro (German News Agency, dnb) in 1934.
5 The report could not be found.

The official letter mentioned in this correspondence from the Association of Breslau Regional Court Lawyers on 15 March 1933 was worded as follows:

To the members of the Association of Breslau Regional Court Lawyers.

Following a notification from the judicial administration, the sessions of the local court are to resume on Thursday, 16 March 1933.

Regarding the matters of the chambers of the regional court, most of the appointments have been cancelled until Saturday, the 18th of this month. The executive of the association has attempted to receive information from the judicial administration as to whether and in which way Jewish lawyers who appear at the court can and will be protected so that they can conduct their business unmolested, and has received the following response:

Congregating in front of the gates of the court buildings is to be prevented by the police. One police battalion is stationed at the main gate on the corner of Graupenstrasse and Stadtgraben. In the coming days, traffic should only proceed through this gate.

We have been informed that National Socialist patrols are expected to take place in the streets. For this reason, the president of the Higher Regional Court has let it be known that he advises Jewish lawyers to stay away from the court until further notice.

The Executive Board.

Thus, while efforts were made to enable Jewish lawyers to continue their activities, the president of the Higher Regional Court, Witte, advised the Jewish lawyers to stay away from the court. This was the very Witte[6] who recently, at the celebration for Privy Councillor Heilberg,[7] effusively congratulated the Jewish lawyer (see p. 52)[8] and had otherwise emphasized the value of good relations with such Jewish attorneys who held important political offices. About Witte's political attitude one is wont to say, 'No one knows what he believes.' Now he tries to gain favour with the new rulers. It was to no avail. As early as the end of April 1933, he was sent into statutory retirement.

The president of the Breslau Regional Court, Zint,[9] who had only been in office for a short time, behaved much more decently. As the Nazis occupied the courthouse and hoisted the swastika flag, he was hauled out and ordered to salute the flag. This he opposed, whereupon two SA members, as it was reported in the Nazi press, gave him assistance. On that very same day, Zint submitted his application for leave until his discharge and withdrew to a quiet place in the mountains. He had been badly disabled as a soldier on the front and was considered an outstanding lawyer. Everyone spoke of him with the greatest reverence.

---

6 Dr Max Witte (b. 1871), lawyer; director of the Regional Rourt in Gnesen, 1913, and in Hirschberg, 1920; president of the Breslau Regional Court, 1921; president of the Higher Regional Court in Königsberg, 1925, and in Breslau, 1927–1933.

7 Dr Adolf Heilberg (1858–1936), lawyer; practised law and worked as a notary in Breslau; pacifist; author of works including *Die privatrechtlichen Bestimmungen des Friedensvertrages* (1919).

8 This is a reference to part of the memoirs not printed here.

9 Dr Hans Zint (1882–1945), lawyer; director of the regional court in Danzig, 1921; president of the regional court in Stettin, 1930, and in Breslau, 1932; retired on the basis of the Aryan Paragraph of the Law for the Restoration of the Professional Civil Service of April 1933.

It is among the many unfortunate coincidences for Nazi opponents that the Silesian judicial administration was headed back then not by a man like Zint but by one like Witte, ready to sacrifice every other human being for the sake of his own personal advantage. On 17 March 1933 the following letter was sent by President Witte of the Higher Regional Court to all lawyers in Breslau:

To all lawyers licensed to practise in the courts of Breslau.

In the enclosure I am distributing a publication enclosed that will appear in the daily newspaper in Breslau at the instigation of the acting chief of police in Breslau.[10]

The guidelines mentioned herein contain the following content.

From all the Jewish lawyers in Breslau, seventeen will be selected to appear before the Breslau courts. These gentlemen will receive special police identification documents for the purpose of legitimation. All other Jewish lawyers will refrain from appearing in court. Aside from that, they are unrestricted in their occupation.

Regarding the identification documents, special notices will be sent to the gentlemen who have been selected.

I hereby reiterate the enclosed urgent request to all Jewish lawyers to adhere to these guidelines. I am confident that this will calm the populace and relax the general situation. However, this arrangement may also be in the interests of the persons concerned.

signed Witte.[11]

The enclosure[12] mentioned in the letter contains the report of a meeting from 16 March 1933 between the chief of police and representatives of the judicial administration, in other words Witte, the SA, and SS. In this way the alleged wish of the national populace to curtail the influence of Jewish judicial organs was voiced.[13] 'The representatives of the judicial administration', it literally says, 'have taken note of this statement.' In other words, they did not shy away from negotiating with men who unlawfully and violently shut down the business of the court, nor did they in any way oppose their illegal demand.[14]

---

10 Edmund Heines (1897–1934); member of the Freikorps, 1919–1920; joined the NSDAP and the SA in 1922; worked for the NSDAP from 1922; participated in the Beer Hall Putsch, 1923; imprisoned; again imprisoned because of a vigilante murder (*Fememord*), 1928–1929; deputy Gauleiter of Silesia and chief of police in Breslau, 1933–1934; murdered on 30 June 1934 during the action taken against the alleged coup by Ernst Röhm.

11 Circular from the president of the Breslau Higher Regional Court, dated 16 March 1933: Georg Weiss (ed.), *Einige Dokumente zur Rechtsstellung der Juden und zur Entziehung ihres Vermögens 1933–1945* (Berlin: n.pub., 1954), p. 12.

12 Ibid., pp. 12–13.

13 At a congress in Leipzig, the League of National Socialist German Lawyers had demanded that all German courts 'immediately purge' those civil servants 'of foreign race': *Vossische Zeitung* (evening edition), 17 March 1933, p. 2.

14 On 31 March 1933 the Reich commissioner for the Prussian Ministry of Justice, Hans Kerrl, then decreed the removal of Jewish judges and lawyers from Prussian courts: GStA PK, I HA, Rep. 84a/35, fols. 79–80; published in Herbert Michaelis and Ernst Schraepler (eds.), *Ursachen und Folgen: Vom deutschen Zusammenbruch 1918 und 1945 bis zur staatlichen Neuordnung Deutschlands in der Gegenwart. Eine Urkunden- und Dokumentensammlung zur Zeitgeschichte* (hereafter *UuF*), vol. 9: *Das Dritte Reich: Die Zertrümmerung des Parteienstaates und die Grundlegung der Diktatur* (Berlin: Wendler, 1964), pp. 391–392.

This led to the provision announced in the letter: 12 Jewish lawyers in the local and regional courts out of a total of 165, and 5 in the Higher Regional Court out of a total of 40, had to keep the appointments of the other Jewish colleagues until further notice. Immediately upon receipt of the letter, I spoke with my colleague Samuel Nothmann,[15] the spokesman of the Jewish lawyers, and I said to him that we must object to only 17 lawyers being active in court who furthermore have been selected by the judicial administration, in other words, who are no longer independent. None of the appointed should assume office. Then the judicial administration, together with the other bodies, would have to relent in order to prevent the courts from remaining completely paralysed. Nothmann replied: 'If at least 17 livelihoods can be saved, then we should not relinquish these as well.' Only those who had already been active on 1 July 1914, or who had participated in combat during the war, were among the 17 approved by the judicial administration. It was conspicuous, furthermore, that no Zionist was among them. [...][16]

DOC. 10
On 18 March 1933 the Combat League for German Culture calls on the Prussian Minister of Culture to exclude Jews from the cultural institutions of the Ruhr[1]

Letter by the Combat League for German Culture,[2] regional head North-West (Lag/o 14), Lagemann,[3] to the acting Prussian Minister of Culture, Rust,[4] dated 18 March 1933 (carbon copy)

Dear Minister,
I confirm my telephone conversation from today as follows.

1. *Collaboration between Combat League and Party*
The local branch of the Combat League of the North-West Regional District in Essen held a meeting yesterday together with the Essen Kreis of the NSDAP's Department of

---

15 Dr Samuel Nothmann (1880–1962), lawyer; practised law in Breslau; for a while trial representative of the city of Breslau; from 1919 active member of the Zionist movement; emigrated to Palestine in 1933.
16 In the following section of the account, the author describes events including the anti-Jewish legislation, his arrest during the Nov. 1938 pogrom, and his emigration to Palestine.

1 GStA PK, I HA, Rep. 90 B/9, fols. 3–5. This document has been translated from German.
2 This was an organization close to the NSDAP, founded on 4 Jan. 1928 as the National Socialist Society for German Culture and Science (Nationalsozialistische Gesellschaft für deutsche Kultur und Wissenschaft), and renamed in Oct. 1928 as the Combat League for German Culture (Kampfbund für deutsche Kultur). According to Alfred Rosenberg its goal was to combat 'bastardization and negrification'. After 1934 the Combat League operated under the name National Socialist Cultural Community (Nationalsozialistische Kulturgemeinde).
3 Paul Lagemann (1877–1936), engineer; started his career in urban, waterways, and rail construction; from 1918 director of the Rheinisch-Westfälische Bank für Grundbesitz AG; in the 1930s he ran an engineering office.
4 Bernhard Rust (1883–1945), teacher; joined the NSDAP in 1925; Gauleiter of Hanover, 1925–1940; compulsory retirement from the teaching profession, 1930; Reich commissioner for the Prussian Ministry of Science, Art, and Education, Feb. to April 1933; Reich minister for science, schooling, and education, 1934–1945; committed suicide in 1945.

National Education. The Director of the Gau of Essen, Department of National Education, and the Regional Directorate of the Combat League, with a few close colleagues and heads of regional specialist groups, also participated. Complete agreement was reached to the effect that now Party energies have been freed for cultural work after the triumphant election campaign, the NSDAP will henceforth stand completely behind the Combat League. Even the members of the Combat League had for the most part been hindered of late, by their intensive cooperation during the election campaign, from devoting themselves to the Combat League to the extent now possible. The correctness of the contractual relationship between the Reich Directorate of the KFDK[5] and the Reich Directorate of the NSDAP, Department of National Education, was recognized without reservation by the representatives of the Party. Accordingly, it is the mission of the NSDAP's Department of National Education to organize artistic or literary ventures only within the framework of its own party, whereas all public events of this type are a matter for the Combat League. It is unnecessary to go into the particulars of this question in this letter. To all intents and purposes, the cooperation ensures that the Combat League's specialist group heads have also become consultants to the Party. For a number of regional districts in my area, especially in the Gau of Westphalia North but also in Westphalia South, there has already been close collaboration for some time with the responsible Party offices. The cooperation, as decided yesterday for Essen, shall henceforth be carried out in a unified manner in the entire north-west region. Insofar as I cannot take care of this myself, I will send Dr Reismann-Grone[6] of Essen, whom you know, with this special assignment to the individual regional districts. For some time now the regional directorate has had at its disposal a staff of well-instructed and voluntary personnel, who are distributed among the individual areas of responsibility in line with our plan for the organization of the Reich, and are also equal to the administrative demands being made upon them.

A number of capable specialist group heads – I mention here only Party comrade and artist Willi Kelter[7] [of] Duisburg for the visual arts, who is also the Gau director for national education, Rich[ard] Euringer[8] for literature, Professor Aug[ust] Weweler[9] [of] Detmold for music, Dr Litterscheid[10] from the national newspaper for theatre – can guarantee, in my estimation, an irreproachable and appropriate cultural battle without any amateurism.

5 Kampfbund für deutsche Kultur: Combat League for German Culture.
6 Dr Theodor Reismann-Grone (1863–1949), historian and journalist; co-founder of the Pan-German League, 1890–1891; publisher of the *Rheinisch-Westfälische Zeitung*, 1895–1932; joined the NSDAP in 1930; mayor of Essen, 1933–1937; author of works including *Der Erdenkrieg und die Alldeutschen* (1919).
7 Will (Willi) Kelter (1899–1978), teacher and painter; joined the NSDAP in 1925; city councillor in Duisburg, 1929; director of the Westphalia-Ruhr regional office of the Reich Chamber of Visual Arts, 1933, and later a member of its presidential council and the Reich Senate for Culture.
8 Richard Euringer (1891–1953), writer; employee of the *Völkischer Beobachter* from 1931; joined the NSDAP in 1933; head of the city library, 1933–1937, and councillor in Essen, 1934–1937; military service, 1939–1945; detained in 1945; author of works including *Deutsche Passion* (1933) and *Als Flieger in zwei Kriegen* (1941).
9 August Benedikt Weweler (1868–1952), musician; head of the Regional Conservatory of Lippe, 1923–1931; joined the NSDAP and became the director of the Combat League for German Culture in Lippe in 1932; teacher at the Folkwang School in Essen, 1935; compositions include the opera *Dornröschen* (1903) and the anthem of the Lippe SA (1929).

2. Purging of artistic and cultural institutions

By the 20th of this month I will receive from all specialist group heads a list of the artistic and other forces to be purged initially in the north-west area. I already informed you on the telephone, honourable Minister, that the first conductor of the Essen Opera, the Jew Cohen,[11] must immediately resign from his position. We request permission to immediately approach the responsible authority in order to achieve by all means the prompt removal of this man. The baptized Jew Raabe[12] must likewise be removed from the Essen theatre. In Dortmund, the removal of the Jewish musical director and opera conductor Wolfes[13] would be a possibility, even if he is close friends with Pfitzner,[14] as well as that of the actor Weltner.[15] For Duisburg, I mention the name Hanns van Loewen.[16] I realize that this is only a small start and that, for example, at the Essen theatre at least ten to twelve personnel of Jewish or other foreign blood or of a corrupting communist disposition are hanging on, but they cannot be removed from one day to the next, unless one wishes to temporarily shut down the entire theatre scene. However, haste is necessary, because over the course of the next fourteen days the new engagements will be booked. I will also report in detail on the teachers at academic secondary schools, art schools, and others. I only mention here the Jewish schoolmaster at a local high school, Levy,[17] who has the most corrupting influence on the students.

3. State commissioner for German culture in Rhineland and Westphalia

I already emphasized on the telephone the urgent need to establish an authority upon which the Gau Directorate for National Education in Essen and the North-West Regional Directorate are in agreement. The region is so densely populated, with theatre upon theatre, school upon school, one museum next to another. Every larger or middle-sized city has one or more significant orchestra, and so on. There will soon be such a plethora of tasks at hand that a state commissioner, vested with extraordinary authority for several months, and supported by the specialist groups of the Combat League and the departments of national education supporting them, would be able to do exceedingly beneficial and urgently necessary work. We advise the entire Rhineland and Westphalia, the region of Lippe, and the Regierungsbezirk Osnabrück to respond to this commissioner. According to the organization of the Combat League this corresponds to the Rhine-Saar and

---

10 Dr Richard Litterscheid (1904–1995), musical educator; worked as a lecturer and journalist; author of works including *Hugo Wolf* (1939) and *Johannes Brahms in seinen Schriften und Briefen* (1943).
11 Frederic Cohen (1904–1967), musician; conductor of the city theatres of Münster and Würzburg; professor of music at the Folkwang School in Essen, 1928–1929; musical director of the Bayreuth Festival, 1930, and of the Municipal Opera House in Essen, from 1930; dismissed in 1933; emigrated to Britain and then to the USA in 1941, where he was a music professor at numerous colleges; later worked for various opera houses.
12 Hans Raabe (1887–1935), actor and director; committed suicide in Vienna in 1935.
13 Felix Wolfes (1892–1971), musician; conductor in Breslau and Essen, 1923–1931; musical director of the Dortmund Opera, 1931–1933; emigrated to France in 1933, then to the USA in 1938; employed at the Metropolitan Opera, New York, 1938–1947, and afterwards in Boston.
14 Probably Hans Pfitzner (1869–1949), composer and conductor.
15 Armin Weltner (1894–1990s); emigrated to Switzerland in 1933.
16 Hanns van Loewen: actually Dr Hans Löwenstein (b. 1901), opera singer.
17 Bertold Levy (b. 1906), teacher; emigrated to Sweden following his dismissal from the teaching profession.

North-West regional directorates. I emphasize that I have not yet consulted my neighbouring regional directorate on account of the urgency of the matter, and that I do not want in any way to disregard this department, with which I work on the best of terms.

The same proposal has already been submitted by local Party circles to Reich ministers Göbbels and Goering[18] under nomination of the art editor of the *Rheinische-Westfälische Zeitung* Dr Paul Joseph Cremers, the author of the *Battle of the Marne*, for this position.[19] In terms of his views, Dr Cremers is said to stand firmly with both feet on the ground of National Socialism and will surely represent a highly valuable force in the cultural battle. We would, however, like to make another suggestion with the consent of the Gau of Essen's Directorate for National Education. It concerns a champion of German art and German culture, well known for decades throughout this entire region, who is also a member of the NSDAP: Dr Reismann-Grone, of Essen. Incidentally, he has been the supervisor of Dr Cremers for many years at the *RWZ* and will surely collaborate with him at decisive moments.

4. Territorial division of the Combat League
We spoke briefly this morning, honourable Minister, about the size of the North-West regional zone. I repeat that this zone includes the political Gaue of Essen as well as Westphalia North and Westphalia South, that is, the entire province of Westphalia and Lippe-Detmold, as well as the Regierungsbezirk Osnabrück, by express wish of the Reich Directorate. This regional division was adopted by Mr Rosenberg[20] at the time as per my proposals, when the West German Directorate of Darmstadt was dissolved. I did this as a native of Essen and genuine authority on the local conditions in conscious opposition to the political division in regional surveys, because the provincial border of Rhineland Westphalia represents an inorganic dissection of a region that belongs together anyway by today's economic, housing, and, not least, cultural standards.

5. Enabling Act
You requested, honourable Minister, that I approach you again on Wednesday or Thursday of next week regarding the anticipated Enabling Act[21] and, should the situation arise, that I visit you. I am currently staying in Berlin on official business in any case and would appreciate a brief note as to when a personal meeting might take place.

---

18 The author means Joseph Goebbels and Hermann Göring.
19 Dr Paul Joseph Cremers (1897–1941), journalist; editor of the *Rheinisch-Westfälische Zeitung* (RWZ); author of numerous plays, including *Die Marneschlacht* (1932).
20 Alfred Rosenberg (1893–1946), architect and illustrator; joined the German Workers' Party (DAP) in 1919, the SA in 1921, and the NSDAP in 1925; took part in the Beer Hall Putsch in 1923; editor-in-chief, 1923–1924 and 1926–1937, and publisher, 1938–1945, of the *Völkischer Beobachter*; head of the Foreign Policy Office of the NSDAP, 1933–1945; plenipotentiary of the Führer for the supervision of the entire intellectual and ideological training and schooling of the NSDAP (Amt Rosenberg), 1934–1945; Reich minister for the occupied eastern territories, 1941–1945; executed in 1946 after receiving a death sentence at the Nuremberg trials; author of works including *Der Jude* (1918) and *The Myth of the 20th Century* (1982 [German edn, 1930]).
21 Law to Remedy the Distress of the People and the Reich (*Gesetz zur Behebung der Not von Volk und Reich*), 24 March 1933: *Reichsgesetzblatt*, 1933, I, p. 141.

I am sending a carbon copy of this letter to Reich Minister Goering, with whose ministry, as mentioned, I also spoke this morning, as well as Reich Minister for Public Enlightenment and Propaganda Dr Göbbels and the Reich Directorate of the Combat League in Munich.[22]

Heil Hitler

DOC. 11

On 20 March 1933 the German ambassador in the USA sends a telegraph to the Reich Foreign Office regarding press reports about the persecution of Jews in Germany[1]

Telegram (secret encryption) no. 115 from the German embassy in Washington, Prittwitz,[2] dispatched on 20 March 1933, 00:02 a.m., received by the Reich Foreign Office in Berlin on 21 March 1933, 8:30 a.m. (submitted to Reich minister)[3]

While direct reports from Berlin about German events are now appearing scattered throughout the local press, news coverage to this effect from Germany's neighbouring countries is, as already reported, on the rise. The latter is now increasingly assuming the character of the horror and persecution reports familiar from wartime. References to this effect appeared, for example, in today's *New York Times*,[4] with excerpts from the Paris report presented in no. 114.[5] Under the impact of this news coverage, the attitude towards Germany is steadily worsening. This sentiment is expressed in numerous protests, organized throughout the entire country, as well as in countless protest telegrams that are delivered here and to the consulate.

Fomented by antagonistic propaganda, an anti-German sentiment is emerging that is already adversely affecting our trade relations, especially the sale of goods and tourist travel. Further intensified by Einstein's behaviour,[6] commotion in Jewish circles is already downright hysterical and particularly acute in New York. The article published

---

22 Letter from Lagemann to Göring, 18 March 1933: GStA PK, I HA, Rep. 90 B/9, fol. 2.

1 PA AA, R 98 468. This document has been translated from German.
2 Dr Friedrich Wilhelm von Prittwitz und Gaffron (1884–1955), lawyer; worked from 1908 in the Reich Foreign Office; joined the German Democratic Party (DDP) in 1918; head of the Germany department of the Reich Foreign Office from 1918; ambassador to the USA from 1927; sent into retirement on 25 March 1933; later worked as an economic consultant in Berlin; after 1945 founding member of the Christian Social Union (CSU).
3 In the original there is an imprint of an internal distribution list of the Reich Foreign Office, as well as handwritten underlining.
4 The *New York Times* published a report from Paris which, on the basis of information from Americans coming from Germany, denounced the despotism and censorship prevalent in Germany, though especially the persecution and criminalization of the Jews: 'German Fugitives Tell of Atrocities at Hand of Nazis', *New York Times*, 20 March 1933, pp. 1–2.
5 This refers to the preceding telegram no. 114 to the Reich Foreign Office: PA AA, R 98 468.
6 At the beginning of March 1933, Dr Albert Einstein (1879–1955) had submitted a much-heeded statement to the International League against Antisemitism. In it he wrote that he only wanted to live in a country in which political freedom, tolerance, and equality of all citizens before the law were guaranteed; these conditions, he averred, were no longer being fulfilled in Germany.

yesterday by Feuchtwanger,⁷ and reported by WTB,⁸ which caused the greatest sensation, also had a most deleterious effect in the same direction.

No efforts have been spared here to counter the reports of persecution. Even in the State Department, efforts have been made that resulted in the declaration of Under Secretary of State Phillips⁹ from the 17th of this month,¹⁰ as provided by WTB.

To contain this increasingly dangerous and steadily spreading sentiment, it is urgently necessary to publish without delay an unambiguous and authoritative German statement on the protection of foreigners and persons of a different denomination, in order to pin down the false reports and exaggerations that are being disseminated by American correspondents over there to the press over here.

DOC. 12

On 24 March 1933 the mayor of Munich orders that municipal contracts no longer be awarded to Jews and foreigners[1]

Circular from the acting first mayor of Munich, Fiehler,[2] to all departments and offices, primary, vocational, and municipal secondary schools and academic secondary schools, the inspectorate of nurseries and after-school care centres, the singing school board, specialist consultants, school dental clinics, and full-time school doctors, dated 24 March 1933

Re: issuing of municipal work contracts and deliveries.[3]

Out of consideration for the incontrovertible, drastic plight of medium-sized craft, industry and retail enterprises, and in consideration of the fact that in recent years Marxist enterprises and large Jewish companies in particular (the latter far beyond the share owed to them based on the numerical proportion of the Jewish to the German population) have been awarded municipal work and delivery orders, I am ordering the follow-

---

7 Dr Lion Feuchtwanger(1884–1958), writer and theatre critic; lecture tour in the USA, 1933, then exile in France; internment, 1940, and flight via Portugal to the USA. Author of the novels *The Jew Süss* (1926 [German edn, 1925]), *The Judean War* (1932), and *Exil* (1940), among other works.

8 Wolffsches Telegraphenbüro: Wolff Telegraph Office; founded in 1849 and renamed in 1934 the Deutsches Nachrichtenbüro (German News Agency, dnb). In his article 'Hitler's War on Culture', Feuchtwanger had accused Germany of barbarism: *New York Herald Tribune Magazine*, section XI, 19 March 1933, pp. 1–2.

9 William Phillips (1878–1968), diplomat; under secretary of state, 1922–1924 and 1933–1936; ambassador to Rome, 1936–1941. Phillips advocated immigration restrictions and was outspokenly antisemitic: see Richard D. Breitman and Alan M. Kraut, *American Refugee Policy and European Jewry, 1933–1945* (Bloomington: Indiana University Press, 1987), pp. 36–37.

10 This declaration could not be found.

1 Stadtarchiv München, Personalamt/405 II. This document has been translated from German.

2 Karl Fiehler (1895–1969), businessman and civil servant; member of the Thule Society, 1919; joined the NSDAP and took part in the Beer Hall Putsch in 1923; sentenced to confinement in a fortress, which he spent with Hitler in Landsberg am Lech; honorary city councillor of Munich, 1924–1933; member of the Reichsleitung of the NSDAP, 1927; joined the SS in 1933; from 20 March 1933 acting first mayor and from 20 May 1933 to 1945 mayor of Munich; head of the NSDAP Main Office for Municipal Policy and chairman of the German Council of Municipalities, 1933–1945; imprisoned, 1945–1949, and thereafter manager of a construction company.

ing on the basis of Article 17 of the municipal code and until the adoption of a final resolution by a restructured city council:

Municipal work and delivery orders will as a matter of principle *not* be issued to department stores, wholesalers, and large-scale merchants or to cooperatives.

Orders will not be placed with *non-German* companies. *Non-German* companies are defined as all businesses that are exclusively or primarily owned or run by foreigners or *Jews*, or those that are to be regarded as enterprises built on *Marxist foundations*.

It is the duty of all responsible departments to undertake the *necessary precautions* when issuing work contracts. In *cases of doubt*, questions can be directed to the 'Combat League for Small and Medium-Sized Businesses, Munich, 14 Barer Straße'.

It is the absolute right of the small- and medium-sized sector of German descent and German consciousness, which is struggling for its livelihood, that the city of Munich use all means available for its preservation and advancement. This will happen most effectively if the city administration itself sets a good example.[4]

DOC. 13
On 25 March 1933 the metal trader Fritz Schünemann encourages the mayor of Munich not to sell scrap metal to Jewish firms[1]

Letter from Party comrade Fritz Schünemann,[2] proprietor of the firm von Schirach & Co.,[3] Munich, 156/II Nymphenburger Straße, to Karl Fiehler, acting first mayor, Munich, dated 25 March 1933 (copy)

Dear Mr Mayor,

Today I read with great interest your order in the *VB*[4] stating that the city administration may only issue work contracts to *German* companies. As proprietor of the above-mentioned purely German firm, which has existed for eleven years and was founded by the deceased Baron Friedrich von Schirach, I would like to encourage you to correspondingly apply this order also to *second-hand materials of all sorts*, such as *scrap metal and so on*, which municipal services such as the municipal tram service, the electricity works, the gas works, and so on sell on a continual basis.[5] My firm is indeed nearly always

---

3 Only a few days later, *The Times* reported on this decree: 'Discriminations against Jews in Bavaria', *The Times*, 27 March 1933, p. 11.
4 Fiehler altered this administrative circular on 6 April 1933. Instead of the Combat League, he cited the municipal trade office as the information centre for non-German firms. The city council of Munich approved this administrative circular, but retracted the exclusion of foreign firms: administrative circular from 6 April 1933 and bulletin from 15 May 1933, Stadtarchiv München, Personalamt/405 II.

1 Stadtarchiv München, Personalamt/405 II. This letter has been translated from German.
2 Fritz Schünemann (1884–1970), sales representative and metal wholesaler; joined the NSDAP in 1932; from 1938 advisory board member of a specialist subgroup within the Economic Group (*Wirtschaftsgruppe*) for Wholesale, Import, and Export Trade.
3 Von Schirach & Co. recycled scrap metal.
4 *Völkischer Beobachter*: the daily newspaper of the NSDAP.
5 The city did not respond until 24 June 1933, and only after Schünemann had spoken with Mayor Fiehler. He was informed that the municipal operations concerned with the selling of second-hand materials had been notified of the suggestion: letter from the city of Munich to the firm Schirach, dated 24 June 1933, Stadtarchiv München, Personalamt/405 II.

asked to place tenders, and it has repeatedly received second-hand materials, but Jewish companies have regularly been considered first and foremost. In this regard, I recently met with Mr Köhler from the Reich Directorate of the Economic Department. For thirty years I have held leading positions in both metal smelting works and metal wholesale, and I have always lamented that 90 per cent of metal wholesale trade and smelting are in *Jewish* hands, where precisely the ability of Germany to defend itself requires that the recycling of strategic metals be in *German hands*.

During the war, almost all management positions of the Kriegsmetall AG in Berlin were in *Jewish hands* and the consequence was that these circles only played into Jewish hands, with the result that now 90 per cent of the industry sector is under their control. I am readily prepared to altruistically make my services available, so that a correct recycling of scrap metal takes place in the interests of the national economy. I have enclosed copies of my qualifications, so that you will be convinced of my expertise. As a member of the Combat League for Small and Medium-Sized Businesses, I am also very much prepared to identify, together with my Christian colleagues in the city administration, the names of the few Christian metal traders who will provide a firm guarantee to the city administration that scrap metal will be recycled for the national economy. I myself represent two important plants, namely the Illerwerke AG smelting plant in Regensburg and the Federal Mining Administration in Vienna and Brixlegg (Tyrol), because south of the [River] Main not a single copper tank house exists, and the northern German firms are all in Jewish hands, with only very few exceptions.

Heil Hitler!

Your very devoted

DOC. 14

New York Times, 27 March 1933: article regarding preparations for mass protests in the USA against Hitler's anti-Jewish policies[1]

250,000 Jews here to protest today.

More Than 1,000,000 in All Parts of Nation Also Will Assail Hitler Policies. Jewish Congress[2] to Act. Four Demands to Be Presented to German Envoy Urging End of Anti-Semitism. Berlin Jews in Dissent. National Organization There Asks That Garden Mass Meeting Be Called Off.

More than 250,000 Jews in this city and 1,000,000 throughout the country will join in protest meetings today against the persecutions and discriminations practiced against Jews by the Hitler Government in Germany, while hundreds of thousands of Jews, in response to a call from their religious leaders, will spend the day in fasting and prayer that the persecutions may cease.

---

1 New York Times, 27 March 1933, p. 4. The original document is in English. This daily newspaper was founded in 1851 and is still in circulation today.
2 This refers to the American Jewish Congress (AJC).

The protest in this city will centre in a rally in Madison Square Garden to be addressed by leaders of Jewry and the Christian world. While more than 20,000 are expected to fill Madison Square Garden, overflow meetings will be held outside the Garden and in Columbus Circle. Meetings also will be held in Jewish temples and in halls throughout the city. At the same time, protest rallies will take place in more than 200 cities in all parts of the country.

The proceedings in Madison Square Garden will be heard through amplifiers by the crowds at the overflow meetings and will be broadcast throughout the nation and to thirteen foreign countries. The doors of the Garden will open at 6:30 P. M.

Rabbi Stephen S. Wise,[3] honorary president of the American Jewish Congress, organizer of the protest demonstration, will open the Garden meeting and will then introduce Bernard S. Deutsch[4] who, as president of the congress, will preside. Among the speakers will be former Governor Alfred E. Smith, Senator Robert F. Wagner, who will fly from Washington to be present; Bishop William T. Manning, Bishop John J. Dunn, representing Cardinal Hayes; Bishop Francis J. McConnell, Charles H. Tuttle and Mayor John P. O'Brien. Governor Lehman was to have spoken at the meeting, but he told The Associated Press at Albany last night that State business would not permit him to attend.[5] William Green, president of the American Federation of Labor, will voice the protest of 3,000,000 organized workers.[6]

Elaborate Police Arrangements.
Elaborate police arrangements for the Garden meeting and the overflow rallies have been made by Police Commissioner Mulrooney,[7] who will be in personal command of the 700 police, including mounted and motorcycle squads, detailed to the meetings. The speakers will be escorted to the meetings by motorcycle policemen.

Speaking before his congregation in Carnegie Hall yesterday, Rabbi Wise announced that following today's meetings, the American Jewish Congress will transmit to the German Government through Ambassador Wilhelm von Prittwitz four 'vital demands.'[8] The demands are:

'1. There must be an immediate cessation of all anti-Semitic activities and propaganda in Germany.

'2. The abandonment of the policy of racial discrimination against and of economic exclusion of Jews from the life of Germany.

'3. The protection of Jewish life and property.

---

3 Dr Stephen Samuel Wise (1874–1949), rabbi; delegate at the Second Zionist Congress in Basel, 1898; co-founder of the American Jewish Congress, 1917; president of the newly established World Jewish Congress, 1936–1949.
4 Bernard S. Deutsch (1883–1935), real estate agent and politician; president of the American Jewish Congress; president of the New York City Council, 1934–1935.
5 Herbert Henry Lehman (1878–1963), politician; governor of New York State, 1932–1942; member of the US Senate, 1949–1956.
6 William Green (1873–1952), coal miner; from 1924 until his death he was president of the American Federation of Labor; author of works including *Labor & Democracy* (1939).
7 Edward P. Mulrooney (1874–1960), police officer; active in the police service from 1895; police commissioner of New York, 1930–1933.
8 On the reaction of the German embassy, see Doc. 11, 20 March 1933.

'4. There shall be no expulsion of 'Ost-Juden'[9] Jews who have come into Germany since 1914.'[10]

'These are our demands,' Rabbi Wise said. 'If these demands be granted, as God knows they ought to be, there will be an end of every plan and undertaking of protest.'

As Dr. Wise spoke, the executive committee of the American Jewish Congress was in session in his study a few paces away. The meeting lasted for several hours.

Every seat in Carnegie Hall was taken as Rabbi Wise and Mr. S. Deutsch addressed the congregation. Hundreds were turned away. Mr. Deutsch read a statement in behalf of the congress.

Rabbi Wise emphasized that the protest movement against persecutions in Germany was not intended as a movement against Germany, and revealed that he had received a message from Berlin demanding that American Jews abandon their 'anti-German demonstrations.'

'I wish again to record my conviction that the Versailles peace treaties should have been revised long before this,' he declared; 'that the Allies in the last years have been guilty of deep wrongs against Germany, the German people, the German State, and that Germany has the right to demand that either the allied nations shall disarm, as they promised and covenanted that they would, or that Germany shall have the right to arm.

'Germany has the right and has had the right to demand certain things of the Allies which should have been granted long before this, and had they been granted, we might never have seen these days come upon Germany.'

Mass Meeting Brings Protest.

While Dr. Wise would not reveal the source of the message received by him from Berlin, it became known that Ernest Wallach,[11] vice president of the Central Association of German Citizens of Jewish Faith, had sent him a telegram on behalf of the president of the organization urging that tonight's rally in Madison Square Garden be called off. Copies of the telegram were sent by Mr. Wallach to Governor Lehman, Mr. Smith and others scheduled to appear at the Garden meeting. Mr. Wallach is now in the United States on business. In his message Mr. Wallach urged that if tonight's meetings cannot be called off that the speakers 'refrain from stirring the emotions of the audience against Germany.'[12]

The telegram said:

'The undersigned vice president of the Central Association of German Citizens of Jewish Faith has just received the following cable from the president of the association, Dr. Julius Brodnitz,[13] in Berlin:

---

9 German in the original: 'Eastern Jews'. See Glossary.
10 On such plans, see Doc. 8, 15 March 1933.
11 Correctly: Ernst Wallach (1878–1939), banker; senior partner, at Goldschmidt-Rothschild Bank in Berlin (until the takeover by the Reichs-Kredit-Gesellschaft AG), 1921–1933; member of the board at Dresdner Bank and other companies; deputy chairman of the Central Association of German Citizens of the Jewish Faith (CV), 1919–1937; emigrated to the USA in 1938.
12 On 25 March 1933 Göring urged representatives of Jewish organizations to do what they could to end anti-German propaganda in the USA: ministerial meeting on 29 March 1933, AdR, part 1, vol. 1, no. 78, p. 271.

'"We earnestly urge you to do all in your power in order that Monday's mass meeting be called off, or if such should, against our sincere hopes, not prove possible, to prevail upon the speakers of the evening to refrain from stirring the emotions of their audience against Germany. We can assure them that the German Government is permanently and successfully engaged in assuring peace and order to all citizens without discrimination."

'In conveying the contents of this telegram to you, as one of the principal speakers of tomorrow's event, I beg to identify myself with the appeal therein voiced by the elected representation of Germany's Jewish population and to earnestly bespeak you to aid us in preventing any action which is liable to encroach upon the prestige of our country and thereby seriously affect our most vital interests.'

Dr. Wise declared that the American Jewish Congress had not excited public opinion, but had 'merely sought to channelize the high indignation and the solemn protest of America into ways that shall be orderly and effective.' He then enumerated the demands to be made upon the German Government.

Denial Held 'Unconvincing.'

The statement of the American Jewish Congress, as read by Mr. Deutsch, follows:

'The denial of the Central Association of German Citizens of the Jewish Faith which was broadcast from Berlin on Friday is pitifully unconvincing.[14] We know from the sworn experiences of American citizens who were brutally assaulted and tortured by the Nazis because they were Jews, or looked like Jews, that it is a regular part of the Nazi technique to extort from the victims or survivors of their atrocities, under threat of further torture, or even death, a written denial that they had been mistreated or that anything untoward had happened to them. If these American citizens, knowing that the powerful government of the United States was behind them, nevertheless felt constrained to sign exculpating statements for their Nazi torturers under duress, how can we now credit any denial emanating from the terrorized Jews of Germany, whose civil rights and very lives are in peril and may be at stake.

'But if we read this forced denial itself carefully, we find in it its own repudiation – first, from what it denies; second, from what it eloquently fails to deny; and lastly, and most important, from what it specifically admits.

'It denies just three and only three specific charges, which are strictly limited as to time and place and description. The great particularity of the charges to which the denial is thus limited at once suggests that all the other charges with which the world has been ringing for the past two weeks are true and cannot be denied. The denial fails even to attempt to deny them.

'It fails to deny or even to explain why it is that such leaders of German Jewry and German intellectual life as Theodore Wolff, Alfred Kerr, Arnold Zweig, Bruno Walter

---

13 Julius Brodnitz (1866–1936), lawyer; practised law and worked as a notary in Berlin; member of the CV, 1900; president of the CV, 1920–1936; co-founder of the *C.V.-Zeitung* and the Philo publishing house; co-founder of the Reich Representation of German Jews, 1933; notary licence withdrawn, 1933.

14 On 25 March 1933 the *New York Times* published the front page article 'Jews in Reich Deny Atrocities'. The CV statement against anti-German propaganda from 24 March 1933 was quoted at length in the article: *New York Times*, 25 March 1933, pp. 1 and 10.

and dozens of others like them, besides hundreds and thousands of other German Jews of less prominence, have had to flee Germany for their lives and are now taking refuge in Prague, Switzerland, Holland, Belgium, France and even in Poland. It does not deny that many other German Jews, including great writers, physicians, business men and lawyers, whose only crime is that they are of the Jewish faith or race, are now languishing in German jails.

'It does not deny that the hospitals, universities and schools of Germany, and theatres, orchestras and banks have been, and are now, systematically being 'purged,' to use the Nazi phrase, of all Jewish personnel, no matter how eminent and world-famous or how lowly, to their economic ruin and to the shame and injury of German culture, science, art and finance. It does not deny that Jewish judges are being ruthlessly removed from the bench, notwithstanding their constitutional guarantee of tenure of office, and that Jewish lawyers are being driven from the bar. It does not deny that all Jewish civil servants of the State, whether in high or low position, have been, and are being, ruthlessly dismissed.

'The denial does not deny, as, indeed, it would be futile to deny in the teeth of the overwhelming evidence, the circumstantial tales of persecution and horror which the thousands of Jews and also Christian liberals who have just escaped out of Germany are telling – tales which have justly shocked the whole of civilized mankind. It does not deny and cannot deny that the persecution, suppression and even the total expulsion of the Jews from Germany has been for years the avowed policy and boasted program of the Nazis so soon as they attained power; that the Nazi Cabinet Minister[15] in charge of the police only last week announced derisively in a public speech that the police under his charge could not concern themselves with the protection of Jewish property,[16] and that Hitler himself, in his speech in Potsdam at the opening of the Reichstag, intimated that the Jews of Germany were outlaws and criminals, as pointed out editorially in *The New York Times* of Saturday (March 25).[17] With the heads of state making public announcements of this character, what bloody excesses may one not expect from their frenzied followers!

'Official' Threat Recalled.
'Finally, the statement of the Central Association does not deny and cannot deny the news of the very day on which the statement was published here, namely, that the Jews of the Palatinate, or Rhenish Bavaria, are all being rounded up by the police, with a threat of expulsion in the offing; that their funds in banks have been impounde[d], so as to make escape impossible in the meanwhile, and that the foreign correspondents were ominously told Saturday by 'an official Nazi source' that 'Chancellor Hitler will

---

15 This refers to Hermann Göring, who in his role as Prussian minister president was responsible for the Prussian police.
16 Göring gave a speech on 11 March 1933 in Essen regarding the upcoming local elections in Prussia: *Völkischer Beobachter* (northern German edition), 12/13 March 1933, p. 2.
17 Jews were not mentioned directly in Hitler's speech on the 'Day of Potsdam' on 21 March 1933: *Völkischer Beobachter*, 22 March 1933, pp. 1–2. The conclusions reproduced here were drawn from Hitler's speech and appeared in a cover story in the section 'Topics of the Times': *New York Times*, 25 March 1933, p. C 14.

take action to adjust the whole problem of Ostjuden who had taken refuge in Germany since 1914.'

'However, most significant of all are the admissions contained in the denial of the Central Association. The denial admits that there have been "acts of political revenge, also reprisals against Jews"; and it admits further that "the anti-Semitic aims in the various domains of life and business which are manifesting themselves fill us, indeed, with grave concern." The Central Association goes on to say, however, that that is "a German domestic affair." This we in turn deny, and deny most vehemently. It is not alone "a German domestic affair" that anti-Semitism in the various domains of life and business is the official policy and program of the German Government. Anti-Semitism in Germany is a challenge to civilization itself; and all civilized people and peoples have a right and a duty to protest against it. Whether the plan is to crush out the 600,000 members of the Jewish race in Germany by economic repression and a denial of civil rights or by bloodshed is equally a crime alike against God and humanity which calls for the condemnation of mankind and for the exertion of every possible means by the outside world to prevent it.'

Bernard H. Ridder,[18] editor of the Staats-Zeitung, who had been scheduled as one of the speakers at the Madison Square Garden meeting, will not address the gathering, it was said last night. A representative of Mr. Ridder explained that he had been unable to see eye to eye with the American Jewish Congress as to what he should say.

Mr. Ridder prepared a speech, the manuscript of which he submitted to the Congress, his representative said. That body did not regard it as satisfactory, and at Mr. Ridder's suggestion submitted an alternative speech. Mr. Ridder found that this contained stronger expressions than he desired to use, it was said, and consequently he rejected it.

A. H. Cohen,[19] executive director of the Congress, denied, however, that Mr. Ridder's speech had been rejected or that a substitute speech had been prepared. He said that so far as the officials of the Congress were aware, Mr. Ridder would speak at the meeting tonight.

All holders of tickets to the Madison Square Garden meeting tonight will be admitted until 7:30 P. M., after which time, conditions inside permitting, the doors will be thrown open to the general public. Holders of reserved seats are requested to use the Eighth Avenue entrance. All others will use the entrances at Forty-ninth and Fiftieth Streets.

The Jewish Theatrical Guild, meeting yesterday afternoon at the Morosco Theatre, passed a resolution protesting against the anti Semitic outrages. It also urged the Secretary of State to make representations to the government of Germany that the persecution be stopped. The meeting was attended by some 1,500 persons.

---

18 Bernard H. Ridder, owner and editor of the German-language American newspaper *New Yorker Staats-Zeitung*, which was founded in 1834.
19 Abraham H. Cohen (b. 1900); managing director of the Palestine Foundation Fund (Keren Hayesod), 1924–1927, and of the American Jewish Congress, 1932–1934.

DOC. 15

On 28 March 1933 the Frankfurt city administration orders the dismissal of its Jewish civil servants[1]

Order (urgent deadline) from the head of the municipal personnel department of the city of Frankfurt am Main, Lindner,[2] to all municipal offices as well as the chairmen of the supervisory boards of companies in which the city is a majority stakeholder, dated 28 March 1933

Re: dismissal or suspension from office of municipal civil servants and employees of the Jewish faith.

I. The delegated mayor[3] has ordered the following:[4]

As a defensive measure against vile propaganda spread mainly by Jews who have emigrated from Germany, which is harmful to the reputation of the Germans and the German economy, I decree the following:

1. Due to the necessity of cutting personnel costs and in accordance with section four, chapter I, § 1, par. 2, of the Prussian Cost-Cutting Regulation of 12 September 1931, all Jewish employees of the municipal administration, as well as of municipal companies in which the city is a majority stakeholder, shall be dismissed as soon as legally permissible, contingent on dismissal without notice in the event of corresponding legal authorization.

2. Furthermore, all Jewish civil servants will be suspended, until further notice, with immediate effect. In accordance with this, they should refrain from all further official duties.

Exceptions are permissible only in the event that the administrator in charge dutifully and most carefully examines the implementation of this measure and determines that the public interest or vital concerns of private persons would otherwise be at risk, and that a replacement cannot be found in time.

---

1 ISG Frankfurt, Magistratsakten/5039, fols. 5–6v. This document has been translated from German. Published in abridged form in Kommission zur Erforschung der Geschichte der Frankfurter Juden (ed.), *Dokumente zur Geschichte der Frankfurter Juden 1933–1945* (Frankfurt am Main: Kramer, 1963), pp. 65–66.

2 Karl Linder (1900–1979), civil servant; member of a Freikorps in 1919; joined the NSDAP in 1923; tax officer, 1923–1933; Gau treasurer, 1927–1929, and deputy Gauleiter of Hesse-Nassau-South, 1928–1932; city councillor in Frankfurt am Main, 1928–1930; Reichstag delegate, 1930–1945; Gauleiter of Hesse-Nassau-South, Oct. 1932 to Feb. 1933; mayor of Frankfurt, March 1933 to June 1937; member of the board of the German Council of Municipalities, 1933–1939; deputy Gauleiter of Hesse-Nassau, 1937–1945; went into hiding, 1945; incarcerated, 1950; denazification proceedings against him were dismissed.

3 The mayor was Dr Friedrich Krebs (1894–1961), lawyer; judge at the regional court, 1923–1925, and regional court judge in Frankfurt am Main, 1928–1933; member of the 'Völkischer Bloc' of the NSDAP from 1922; joined the NSDAP in 1929, NSDAP Kreisleiter from 1933 and mayor of Frankfurt, 1933–1945; chairman of the supervisory board of Deutsche Städte-Reklame GmbH; imprisoned, 1945–1948; classified as a 'lesser offender' during denazification proceedings; member of the Frankfurt City Council Assembly for the German Party until 1952; subsequently worked as a lawyer.

DOC. 15   28 March 1933   115

Should a replacement be necessary, only volunteers who have the same training as the civil servants or employees being replaced can be appointed, and this only under the guidance of the leadership of the corresponding National Socialist [NS] organizations (NS Teachers, NS Doctors, NS Lawyers, and the NS Civil Service Department, as well as the NSBO).

3. All departments are strictly forbidden to purchase merchandise at Jewish businesses of any kind. Violations will be punished severely.

4. All ongoing contracts with Jewish firms are to be cancelled as soon as legally permissible, contingent on dismissal without notice in the event of corresponding legal authorization.

II. (a) In pursuing the ordinances listed under numbers (1) and (2), all municipal departments and offices are requested during the course of tomorrow (29 March 1933) at the latest to produce a register of all Jewish civil servants working for the municipality, including first name and surname, official position, and date of entry into municipal employment, and to submit it here. The register should contain separate sections for each department. Within the individual departments, a distinction is to be made between

(aa) lifetime municipal civil servants,

(bb) temporary municipal civil servants,

(cc) adjunct civil servants (trainee civil servants) and candidates,

(dd) contracted employees,

(ee) adjunct contracted employees *with* the benefits of § 7 of the regulations for non-civil servants,

(ff) adjunct contracted employees *without* the benefits of § 7 of the regulations for non-civil servants,

(gg) salaried employees,

(hh) employees with special contracts.

The personnel records of said employees are also to be included.

(b) Furthermore, we ask that you inform us as to which *lifetime municipal civil servants* (see aa above) cannot, for the reasons listed under number 2, paragraph 2, of the delegated mayor's ordinance, be immediately suspended or dismissed.

(c) To the extent that replacements are available, we request to be informed of these cases during the course of tomorrow (29 March 1933), in order to make *volunteer* employees available as soon as possible in consultation with the appropriate National Socialist organizations.

III. With regard to Jewish teachers employed by the municipality, school officials are requested to take all steps necessary on their own initiative and to communicate the results as soon as possible.

IV. Department heads will be made responsible for the timely and complete execution of the above ordinance.

---

4 At 10:30 a.m. on 28 March 1933, Mayor Krebs had telephoned from Berlin and communicated the part of the ordinance that is in quotation marks here. The second part of was drafted by the municipal administration: note from 28 March 1933, ISG Frankfurt, Magistratsakten/5039, fols. 3–4.

V. Concerning the Jewish employees of companies in which the city is a majority stakeholder, the chairmen of the board are requested to immediately take all steps necessary and to communicate the results as soon as possible.

VI. In case of doubts or questions, please consult the municipal personnel department (telephone 1568).

VII. Concerning numbers (3) and (4) of the ordinance of the delegated mayor, it is duly requested that action is taken strictly in accordance with these orders and that all necessary steps are immediately taken.

DOC. 16

On 30 March 1933 the state commissioner for Berlin prohibits the municipal administration from placing announcements in the 'Jewish press'[1]

Circular from the State Commissioner for Berlin for Special Deployment (Na 2), signed Lippert,[2] Berlin, to the central administrations, the district authorities, and the municipal companies, dated 30 March 1933 (printed)

Ban on placing advertisements in the Jewish press

It has been noted that individual departments of the city administration, particularly individual district authorities, are still placing official announcements in the form of advertisements in the Jewish press and, however, seldom or never make use of the national press, particularly the National Socialist press.

We must work towards ensuring that in the future the Jewish press does not contain any official announcements of this type, especially since the boycott movement currently dictates such a course of action. The following are to be considered the main organs of the Jewish press: *Berliner Tageblatt, Die Vossische Zeitung, Die Morgenpost, Tempo*, and *8-Uhr-Abendblatt*.

1 'Verbot für die Aufgabe von Anzeigen in der jüdischen Presse', *Dienstblatt des Magistrats von Berlin*, 1933, part I/66, p. 122. This document has been translated from German. The bulletin published official notices from Berlin's city administration. It appeared from 1922 until 1944.
2 Dr Julius Lippert (1895–1956), journalist; joined the NSDAP in 1927 and the SA in 1933; editor-in-chief of the Nazi newspaper *Der Angriff*, 1927–1933; state commissioner for Berlin, March 1933–1936; president of the city council and mayor of Berlin, 1937–1940; later commander of the Propaganda Department Southeast; district commander of the Security Police in Arlon (Belgium), 1943–1945; in Allied custody, 1945; extradited to Belgium, 1946, and charged with war crimes in 1950; held in prison until 1952.

DOC. 17

Völkischer Beobachter, 30 March 1933: the NSDAP calls for an anti-Jewish boycott across Germany[1]

Call to action by the Reichsleitung of the NSDAP[2]
Boycott committees against Jewry in the entire Reich!
On 1 April at 10 a.m. sharp, boycott of all Jewish products, shops, doctors, lawyers – tens of thousands of mass meetings. The Jews have declared war on 65 million Germans, and so now they have to be struck at their most sensitive spot!

A call to action to the Party!
National Socialists! Party comrades!
After fourteen years of inner fragmentation, the German people have politically overcome their estates, classes, professions, and religious schisms, and have brought about an *uprising* that *ended the Marxist-Jewish spectre in a matter of moments*. In the weeks after 30 January, a unique national revolution took place in Germany. Despite long and deepest despondency, with complete calm and discipline the massed millions who stand behind the government of the national revolution *gave the new leadership of the Reich the legal protection needed in order to put through a root-and-branch reform of the German nation*. On 5 March the vast majority of the electorate placed its confidence in the new regime. *In this way, the completion of the national revolution has become a demand of the people.*

In all their pathetic cowardice, the Jewish-Marxist bigwigs have given up their [positions of] power. Despite all the outcry, not a single one of them dared to resist. For the most part they have *abandoned the masses they seduced* and *fled the country* with their bank accounts full of money. *It is only the unprecedented discipline and tranquillity in which the act of revolution occurred that allowed the profiteers and exploiters of our misfortune to go unharmed.* No one touched a hair on their heads. One needs only to compare this act of self-discipline of the national uprising in Germany with the Bolshevik revolution, which cost Russia 3 million lives, in order to see how thankful the guilty criminals should be to the forces of national uprising. One needs only to look at the *horrendous battles and the destruction during the revolution of these November men, their hostage*

---

1 'Aufruf der Reichsleitung der N.S.D.A.P.', *Völkischer Beobachter* (northern German edition), 30 March 1933, pp. 1–2. This document has been translated from German. Points 1–11 are published in Michaelis and Schraepler (eds.), *UuF*, vol. 9, pp. 387–388.
2 The call to action was presumably written by Goebbels at Hitler's suggestion. See diary entries for 27 and 28 March 1933 in Joseph Goebbels, *Die Tagebücher von Joseph Goebbels*, ed. Elke Fröhlich, part 1: *Aufzeichnungen 1923–1941*, vol. 2, no. 3 (Munich: Saur, 2006), pp. 156–157. On the cabinet meeting on 28 March 1933, see Minuth (ed.), *AdR*, part 1, vol. 1, no. 78, p. 271. The call to action from 28 March 1933 was first published in a summary on 29 March: *Völkischer Beobachter* (northern German edition), 29 March 1933, p. 2. On 30 March 1933 the Reich Representation of German Jews and the executive board of the Jewish Community of Berlin protested against this call to the Reich President, the Reich Chancellor and the Reich ministers: Landesarchivverwaltung Rheinland-Pfalz in association with the Landesarchiv Saarbrücken (ed.), *Dokumentation zur Geschichte der jüdischen Bevölkerung in Rheinland-Pfalz und im Saarland von 1800 bis 1945*, vol. 6 (Koblenz: Landesarchivverwaltung Rheinland-Pfalz, 1974), pp. 14–15. A protest appeared in the *C.V.-Zeitung* on 30 March 1933, p. 1.

shootings in 1918 and 1919, the mowing down of defenceless enemies, and one will again see the huge difference between this and the national uprising.

The men in charge have solemnly announced to the world that they want to live in peace with it. The German people give them loyal allegiance. Germany wants no world turmoil and no international complications. *But national revolutionary Germany is firmly resolved to put an end to internal mismanagement.* Since the domestic enemies of the nation have been rendered harmless by the people themselves, a situation has now arisen which we had long expected. The communist and Marxist criminals and their Jewish intellectual instigators have moved abroad, taking their vast funds with them. From there, they are now instigating an *unscrupulous and treasonous smear campaign against the German people as a whole.* Since it has become impossible for them to spread their lies here in Germany, they have taken up the same smearing of the young national uprising as they did at the beginning of the war against Germany. Only this time they are doing it from the capital cities of the former Entente.

Lies and calumnies of truly hair-raising perversity have been let loose on Germany. Horrendous tales of dismembered Jewish bodies, of gouged-out eyes and severed hands, are spread with the sole purpose of ostracizing the German people a second time – something they already succeeded in doing in 1914. Millions of innocent persons, whole peoples with whom Germany wants only to live in peace, are being agitated against us by these unscrupulous criminals. German commodities, the results of German work and production, are to be subjected to a boycott. So, Germany's hardship is too small for them – it must become even bigger. They tell lies about murdered Jewish women, about Jewish girls raped before their parents' eyes, about ravaged cemeteries. It is all just one big lie with the purpose of inciting a new world war. If one just stood by and watched this, one would be an accomplice to these crimes. The National Socialist Party will therefore take up the defensive struggle against this huge and heinous crime with means appropriate to punishing the guilty. For *the guilty* are among us, they live among us and abuse on a daily basis the right to hospitality granted to them by the German people. In times in which millions of us have nothing to live on, nothing to eat, in which hundreds of thousands of white-collar workers are lying destitute on the streets, these *Jewish intellectual literati* sit around among us and very much take advantage of this right to hospitality.

What would America do if America's Germans were to sin in this way against America as these Jews do against Germany? The national revolution has not touched a hair on their heads. They can go about their business now just as they did before. *However, corruption will be annihilated, no matter who commits it.* Belonging to the *Jewish race or to the Mosaic faith* is just as little a licence to commit crime as belonging to a Christian confession or to our own people. For decades Germany indiscriminately let every foreigner enter the country. Germany has 135 inhabitants per square kilometre. America has fewer than 15. Despite this, America set up quotas for immigration and even excluded whole peoples altogether. Germany, despite its own extreme hardship, did not take such measures for decades. A clique of Jewish literati, professors, and businessmen thanks us for this by inciting the world against us, while millions of our own Volksgenossen are unemployed and have gone to pieces. This will now stop! The Germany of the national revolution is not the Germany of the cowardly bourgeoisie.

We see the hardship and poverty of our own Volksgenossen and feel obliged to leave nothing unpursued that might prevent further harm to our people. The ones responsible for these lies and calumnies are the Jews among us. It is they who are the source of the hate campaign against us and the incitement with lies. It is in their power to reprehend liars in the rest of the world. Since they do not want to do this, we will ensure that the campaign of hate and lies is not directed against Germany, but rather against those responsible for this incitement. The incitement to boycott and the general incitement should not and will not strike the German people, but will strike the Jews themselves a thousand times harder.

For this reason, the following *directive* goes to all Party offices and Party organizations:

Point 1: In every local branch and every organizational structure of the NSDAP an *action committee is to be formed* to enable the practical and methodical execution of the boycott of Jewish shops, Jewish merchandise, Jewish doctors, and Jewish lawyers. The action committees are responsible for the boycott not affecting any innocent people, but striking the guilty all the harder.

Point 2: The action committees are responsible for the protection of foreigners, no matter what their confession, origin, and race may be. The boycott is a *purely defensive measure*, which is directed only against the *Jews in Germany*.

Point 3: The action committees are to immediately popularize the boycott by means of *propaganda and information*. The basic principle is: *a good German no longer buys from Jews* or allows them or their backers to offer them anything for sale. The boycott must be universal. It must be supported by the entire nation and must hit the Jews at their most sensitive spot.

Point 4: In cases of doubt, such businesses are not to be boycotted until the Central Committee in Munich gives a specific order to the contrary. The chairman of the *Central Committee* is Party comrade *Streicher*.[3]

Point 5: The action committees *will thoroughly scrutinize the newspapers* to ascertain to what extent they are involved in the information campaign of the German people against Jewish atrocity propaganda abroad. Whichever newspapers do not do this or do it only to a limited degree should be *immediately removed* from any house in which Germans live. No German man and no German business is to be permitted to advertise in such newspapers. They must be *subject to public condemnation*, since they are written for members of the Jewish race, but not for the German people.

Point 6: The action committees, *in cooperation with the Party's Factory Cell Organizations*, must bring information about the consequences of the Jewish atrocity propaganda for German work and thus for the *German worker* to the workplaces and inform the workers in particular about the necessity of the national boycott as a defensive measure for the protection of German labour.

Point 7: The work of the action committees must reach *even the smallest farming villages*, in order to strike out at the Jewish traders in rural areas. It is fundamentally important to always emphasize that these defensive measures have been forced upon us.

---

3 Julius Streicher (1886–1946), teacher; member of the German Socialist Party, 1919–1921; joined the NSDAP and the SA in 1922; took part in the Beer Hall Putsch in 1923; subsequently suspended from his teaching duties; founder and editor of the antisemitic weekly *Der Stürmer*, 1923–1944; Gauleiter of Northern Bavaria, 1925–1928; imprisoned for libel, 1926–1927; barred from teaching in 1928; Gauleiter of Franconia from 1929; imprisoned for antisemitic agitation, 1930; dismissed as Gauleiter on grounds of embezzlement, 1940; executed in 1946 after a death sentence at the Nuremberg trials.

Point 8: The boycott is not to begin in dribs and drabs, but rather *in one fell swoop. At present, all preparations* are to be made along these lines. *Directives* are to be issued *to the SA and the SS*, so that they are standing at their posts right from the first moment of the boycott, in order *to warn* the populace against entering Jewish shops and businesses.

The beginning of the boycott is to be *made known* by means of *posters and newspaper announcements*, also by means of *leaflets*, etc.[4]

The boycott will begin promptly on 1 April at 10 a.m. sharp. It will continue until a directive of the Party leadership is issued ordering its suspension.

Point 9: The action committees are to immediately *organize tens of thousands of mass demonstrations*, reaching even the smallest farming villages, which will call for the introduction of *quotas for the employment of Jews* in all professions *relative* to the percentage of Jews in the population at large. In order to increase the efficacy of the measure, this demand is to be initially restricted *to three areas*:

(a) German secondary schools and institutions of higher education,
(b) the medical profession,
(c) the legal profession.[5]

Point 10: The action committees have the further task of making sure that every German who has *connections abroad* makes use of these in letters, telegrams, and phone calls, informing their contacts of the truth, i.e. telling them that law and order has been maintained, that the German people have no greater wish than to go about their business in peace, and that this is a purely *defensive fight*.[6]

Point 11: *The action committees are responsible for making sure that this entire conflict takes place peacefully and with great discipline. No Jew is to be harmed personally in any way!* We will manage to end the atrocity propaganda by the sheer force of the planned measures alone.

It is more important than ever before that the *entire Party stands with one mind behind its leadership in blind obedience.*

National Socialists! You accomplished one miracle already by overrunning the November State[7] with a single attack. You will fulfil this task in exactly the same manner. World Jewry should know:

The government of the national revolution does not exist in a vacuum. It is the representative of the working people of Germany. Whoever attacks it attacks Germany as a whole. Whoever libels it libels the entire nation. Whoever fights against it has declared war on 65 million Germans!

We took care of Marxist agitation in Germany. They will not force us to our knees even by continuing from abroad these criminal acts of treason against the people.

---

4 See the draft poster produced by the Central Committee for the Defence against Jewish Atrocity and Boycott Propaganda, intended for publication in all Party newspapers: *Nationalsozialistische Partei-Korrespondenz*, no. 358, 30 March 1933, pp. 3–4.
5 Laws and regulations were passed on these three areas in April: Law on Admission to the Legal Profession, 7 April 1933; Regulation on the Admission of Doctors for Employment with the Health Insurance Companies, 22 April 1933; and Law against Overcrowding in German Schools and Institutions of Higher Education, 25 April 1933: *Reichsgesetzblatt*, 1933, I, pp. 188, 222, and 225.
6 On the implementation of this call to action, see the circular of the Association of German Engineering Institutions, Doc. 19, 30 March 1933.
7 Reference to the proclamation of the Weimar Republic on 9 Nov. 1918 and the agreement of an armistice two days later.

National Socialists! On Saturday at 10 o'clock on the dot, the Jews will find out with whom they have picked a fight!

National Socialist German Workers' Party. Party leadership.

DOC. 18

On 30 March 1933 the private tutor Johann Ackermann proposes a boycott of Jewish tutors in Munich[1]

Handwritten letter from Dr Ackermann,[2] Munich, 2 I Schommerstraße, to the Action Committee for the Defence against Jewish Atrocity and Boycott Propaganda for Munich-Upper Bavaria (received on 3 April 1933), Munich, dated 30 March 1933[3]

Dear Sirs,

In the interest of the large number of unemployed German private tutors, I most kindly request that you also take into consideration where feasible the boycott of all Jewish *private tutors*. I am aware of the following address: Dr K. Löwenstein,[4] Munich 13, 31 Elisabethstraße, who prepares students for their school-leaving examinations. There are a large number of other Jews who offer such preparatory courses.

May I also refer you in particular to the private business school of Dr Sabel on Kaufingerstraße.[5] I have heard that Dr Sabel's husband, who passed away, was also a Jew. It is only because Dr Sabel inherited from her husband and enjoyed the benefits of a *permanent* licence that she was able to run not only her own school, but also a number of other business schools. With her consistently high revenue she has also been able to acquire a number of houses here. In order to teach courses in a school of this kind, one would normally need a diploma in business education. However, in most cases someone with a diploma in business education seeking to teach such courses here is not granted the necessary licence. On the other hand, although she has no diploma at all, Dr Sabel has always enjoyed the benefits of a licence and has found ways of holding on to it. I am happy to inform the committee of these circumstances and would most kindly ask you to keep this communication *secret*.[6]

With a Party greeting

Dr Ackermann

Certified business school teacher

Currently a private tutor of preparatory courses for the school-leaving examinations.

---

1 BArch, NS 12/1027. This document has been translated from German.
2 Dr Johann Ackermann. No further information could be obtained on him.
3 Parts of the original are underlined by hand.
4 Dr Karl Löwenstein, private scholar in Munich.
5 The Rudolf Sabel Business School at 14 Kaufingerstraße, Munich, opened in 1900. It was modelled on the Sabel School for commercial training, which was founded by Dr Gottlob Sabel (1867–1911) in 1896 in Nuremberg.
6 The Boycott Committee of the NSDAP Gau of Munich-Upper Bavaria passed the letter on to the National Socialist Association of Teachers on 12 April 1933 for further consideration: ibid.

DOC. 19

On 30 March 1933 the Association of German Engineering Institutions calls on its member firms to combat 'international atrocity and boycott propaganda'[1]

Circular (series I, no. 13) from the Association of German Engineering Institutions (II/Dr.Kl/Hy, file ref.: Wp 289), executive member of the board of directors (signature illegible), Berlin, 35 Tiergartenstraße, to its member firms and for the information of members and the main board and professional associations, dated 30 March 1933

Re: international atrocity and boycott propaganda against Germany.

The atrocity and boycott propaganda that has recently been conducted by certain foreign newspapers is now appearing in private business correspondence. Owing to the repeated fraudulent claims of atrocities against citizens belonging to the Jewish religion in Germany, some of our member firms have had foreign contracts cancelled. Said foreign customers did not shy away from stating that they have no desire to award contracts to murderous German 'incendiaries'. This incitement, nurtured by a certain group of so-called intellectuals who fled Germany, is gleefully picked up by that part of the foreign press which for a long time, as far back as the war, made a point of accusing and insulting Germany in all manner possible. Their aim was not only to strike at Germany with a boycott of its products, but also to politically isolate Germany and harm its reputation abroad, with the purpose of reaching their own political goals.

The honour and reputation of the German nation require all of our industrial firms to aid us in decisively supporting the government of the Reich in its struggle against this fraudulent foreign reporting. It is an act of self-defence when the German government does not tolerate this boycott propaganda silently, but – if this foreign activity does not cease immediately – takes defensive measures. Official government statements have said as much.

Thus, it is the duty of every German engineering factory to speak out against the budding defamation of Germany abroad, and in letters, in telephone conversations, and in every other way possible to inform business partners about the actual state of affairs in Germany. They should also order their representatives to serve these goals to the utmost degree. It is especially important that the representatives also contact the foreign press in order to work for their part towards ending this incitement against Germany in the press.[2]

In order to support our member firms in raising awareness above and beyond their own measures, please find enclosed a statement from our association condemning this unqualified incitement against Germany, which is addressed to our foreign business partners and our representatives abroad. We request our member firms to immediately forward the statement to the offices in question and have attached ten copies to this end. We can provide as many additional copies of this statement as are needed, free of charge.[3]

---

1 Doc. in Clemens Berg (i.e. Max Kronenberg), 'Aus Deutschland vor und nach Hitler' [From Germany before and after Hitler] (26 March 1940), Harvard Competition, no. 123, appendix. This document has been translated from German.
2 See this demand in point 10 of the NSDAP call to action published the same morning: Doc. 17, 30 March 1933.

Furthermore, we request all member firms to inform us most promptly about all letters from abroad in which reference is made to the aforementioned atrocity and boycott incitement against Germany.

We will make use of this information with the relevant Reich authorities, in order that everything possible is done to protect German interests.

DOC. 20
Discussion between representatives of Jewish organizations on 31 March 1933 in Paris regarding the persecution of Jewish Germans[1]

Undated, unsigned minutes of a meeting on 31 March 1933[2]

Notes of Interview in Paris at which the following gentlemen were present:

Mr. Neville Laski,[3] President of the Board of Deputies[4] and one of the Joint Chairmen of the Joint Foreign Committee.[5]

Monsieur Israel Levi,[6] le Grand Rabbin of France.

Monsieur Oungre,[7] Director General of the ICA.

Monsieur Oungre,[8] Director General of HICEM.

Monsieur Golschak,[9] Director of Matters related to Unemployment in Belgium.

Monsieur Voss, a Dutch member of Parliament.

---

3 The statement enclosed with the letter is not printed here. The circular addresses the 'supposed atrocities of nationalist circles in Germany against Jewish citizens'. The foreign firms are requested to act so that 'the press in your country does not distort events in Germany, but instead portrays them objectively': Clemens Berg (i.e. Max Kronenberg), 'Aus Deutschland vor und nach Hitler', appendix.

1 Archives of the Leo Baeck Institute, New York, at the Jewish Museum Berlin, MF 129. The original document is in English.

2 The date can be established from a discussion that took place subsequently to this session: 'Notes of Conversation with Dr Kahn on Afternoon of Saturday (?), March 31, 1933': ibid.

3 Neville Jonas Laski (1890–1969), lawyer; president of the Board of Deputies of British Jews, 1933–1939; author of works including *Jewish Rights and Jewish Wrongs* (1939).

4 Board of Deputies of British Jews, founded in 1760 as the London Committee of Deputies of British Jews.

5 Joint Foreign Committee of the Board of Deputies of British Jews and the Anglo-Jewish Association. The Conjoint Foreign Committee, later Joint, was founded in 1878. The Anglo-Jewish Association was founded in 1871 with the aim of promoting Jewry.

6 Correctly: Dr Israël Lévi (1856–1939), rabbi; professor at the Séminaire Israélite of the University of Paris from 1892; chief rabbi of France, 1919–1938; author of works including *Histoire des Juifs de France* (1903).

7 Dr Louis Oungre (1880–1966), expert on colonization; co-initiator of the Joint-ICA Foundation, founded in 1924; in 1940 he emigrated from France to the USA; representative of the Alliance Israélite Universelle at the London Conference of Jewish Organizations in 1946.

8 Edouard Oungre was deputy director of the ICA and member of the HICEM board in the 1920s; representative of HIAS at the Evian Conference in 1938; head of HIAS for South America in 1942; he worked again for the ICA from 1945.

9 Probably Max Gottschalk (1889–1976), economist and social policy maker; plenipotentiary of the International Labour Office for Belgium and Luxembourg, 1923–1940; head of the Research Institute for Peace and Post-War Problems of the American Jewish Committee, 1940–1949; president of the Central Council for Jews in Belgium, 1956–1962.

Professor Cohen[10] of Holland.
Monsieur Dreyfus of Switzerland.
Professor Netter[11] and
Monsieur Bigart,[12] representing the Alliance.[13]

Dr. Bernard Kahn,[14] Director of Joint Reconstruction Fund, who had arrived from Germany the previous evening, attended the meeting. He stated that in his opinion, unless the three following points were dealt with, merely to put an end to the economic boycott was of no real value to the German Jewish community. His points, which I took down verbatim and read over to him, were as follows:

1. Take the question of administration out of the hands of the Brown Army and keep it in Government hands, for the trouble is not one of law but of action by a political party.

2. If the Government, as managers of the press, cannot stop the *Völkische Zeitung* and the *Angriff*,[15] there is no sense in any negotiations. These papers are making an explanation whether the Government want it or not. This is vital and definitive as a condition precedent. Stop the action of the Brown Army and police the country with the police force. Stop red provocation.

3. After [the fulfilment of point] one, there must be an assurance that no disenfranchisement or discrimination is contemplated. Dr. Kahn expressed doubt whether the German Government could be trusted.

After this statement Professor Netter said the following: 'Sommes nous décidés guèrre sans merci?'[16]

Dr. Kahn then said if you declare war on Germany, you each must take responsibility on yourselves. Hitler is a very weak man. Some ethos in him. He is in the hands of Goering and Goebbels. He cannot master his own army. He cannot hold them back. We must strengthen his hand. If the Government cannot concede the above three points, then anything can happen to the Jews and in that case nothing in the outside world is too strong. But any weapon used should be a non-Jewish weapon so far as possible.

---

10 Probably Dr David Cohen (1882–1967), historian; professor of ancient history in Leiden and Amsterdam; Zionist; founded the Committee for Special Jewish Interests (Comité voor Bijzondere Joodse Belangen) in 1933; also chairman of the Sub-Committee for Jewish Refugees; chairman of the enforced Jewish Council established by the Nazis in Amsterdam, 1941–1943; deported to Theresienstadt in 1943; convicted of collaboration by a Jewish civic court in 1947; sentence annulled in 1950.

11 Dr Arnold Netter (1855–1936), physician; professor at the University of Paris; vice president of the Alliance Israélite Universelle from 1905 and its president, 1935–1936; author of various medical works.

12 Jacques Bigart (1855–1934), lawyer; secretary general of the Alliance Israélite Universelle, 1892–1934; author of works including *L'Alliance Israélite, son action éducatrice* (1900).

13 The Alliance Israélite Universelle was founded in 1860 in France to defend Jewry.

14 Dr Bernhard Kahn (1876–1955), lawyer; secretary general of the Relief Association of German Jews, 1904–1921; chairman of the labour welfare office in Berlin, 1920; from 1924 to 1939 director general of the American Joint Reconstruction Fund and director of the European bureau of the American Jewish Joint Distribution Committee, initially in Berlin, later in Paris; emigrated to France in 1933 and to the USA in 1939.

15 Names of German newspapers.

16 French: 'Are we set on war without mercy?' Misspelt in the original.

The previous evening I had nearly two hours' discussion with Dr. Grönemann, Jewish lawyer and author from Berlin, aged about sixty-five.[17] He is a man who, from various sources, I have discovered to be of experience and standing. He expressed to me, independently of Dr. Kahn, exactly similar views.

Both Dr. Kahn and Dr. Grönemann, in answer to a specific question, stated that if they had to re-write the history of the previous fortnight's work, they would not, to use Dr. Grönemann's own expression, alter the dotting of an 'i' or the crossing of a 't'. Dr. Grönemann used two expressions which impressed me enormously. (a) He said that the German Government were feeding the people on panem et circenses[18] and that the circus was the Jew. (b) He said that in certain eventualities, regrettable though it was, he contemplated that their measures might produce a massacre, but that he thought in the end such a massacre might be to the advantage of the survivors. He used the expression 'sanguis martyrorum semen ecclesia'.[19]

I took certain other notes from a long conversation of several hours with Dr. Kahn following the more formal conference in the morning and I append these in a separate memorandum.[20]

DOC. 21
Henriette Necheles-Magnus describes expressions of solidarity during the anti-Jewish boycott on 1 April 1933 in Wandsbek[1]

Submission by Henriette Necheles-Magnus[2] to a Harvard University competition (1940)

[...][3] As I came to the office in the morning, I could already see from afar two burly SA men standing in front of my door. Pasted above the door was a large placard: a black background with a blazing yellow badge in the middle. I went to my clinic through the back door and sat down at my desk. First I had to console my crying house-sitter. I received the response: *We are so ashamed of our countrymen!* (her husband worked in

---

17 Probably Dr Sammy Gronemann (1875–1952), lawyer and writer; Zionist; practised law in Berlin from 1906; founding member in 1909 and then legal advisor of the Association for the Protection of German Writers; emigrated to France in 1933 and to Palestine in 1936; author of works including *Tohuwabohu* (1920).
18 Latin for 'bread and circuses'.
19 The dictum originates from Tertullian's *Apologeticus*, chapter 50: *Plures efficimur quotiens metimur a vobis; semen est sanguis Christianorum*. This is often also quoted as *Sanguis martyrum, semen Christianorum* ('the blood of martyrs, the seed of Christians').
20 This discussion addressed the problems of financing emigration and the impact that foreign reports covering the persecution of the Jews had on the Nazis: 'Notes of Conversation with Dr Kahn ... on March 31, 1933': Archives of the Leo Baeck Institute, New York, at the Jewish Museum Berlin, MF 129.
1 Henriette Necheles-Magnus, untitled text (25 March 1940), pp. 17–18, Harvard Competition, no. 163. This document has been translated from German.
2 Dr Henriette Necheles-Magnus (1898–1977), physician; worked as a doctor in hospitals in Wandsbek and Hamburg; ran her own practice from 1924 to 1935; emigrated to the USA in 1936.
3 The entire account comprises 29 pages. In the first part the author briefly describes her childhood and education as well as the work in her practice until 1933.

the shipyard). Across the street was a small egg shop that was run by a Jewish woman (her husband had died in the war), and in front of it again the two guardian angels. – At 9 a.m. the consulting hours began; at 9:10 the first patient arrived. Agitated, panting that someone would try to prevent her from going to see her doctor! 'Are we in the age of the persecution of Christians??' – At 9:20 there was a noise from outside the door: 'We want to see our doctor!!!' SA man: 'She isn't even there, she sneaked out!' In response, my girl goes to the door: 'The doctor is there. You aren't authorized to interrupt the consultation hours, you are only here to show that this is a Jewish doctor.' On and on it went, the patients kept coming with flowers, with small gifts: 'We want to show you what we think of these policies.' 'I'm not sick, doctor, I've come to see how you are doing.' A little piece of craftwork, the 'boycott blanket', still lies to this day in my room. A patient crocheted it for me during those days, to show her affection for me. –

In the afternoon it began to rain (in Hamburg, April rain is an ugly affair). Our protectors became surly and began to galumph in front of the door; the patients began to laugh and suggested to them that they go to a bar and play skat. Fortunately, it passed without any clashes, because outside the waiting room a few of my patients were real tough boys.[4] It was the same for my neighbour across the street; she said she had never sold so many single eggs as on this day, since these poor folk did not have enough money left over for more than one egg and somehow still wanted to give her a sense of alliance. Things did not go so smoothly or pass without incident everywhere. The proprietor of a clothes shop on our street tried to prevent the SA men from blocking the entrance (the rule was that the sentinels were only to stand there as a warning). He was drawn into a scuffle with the guards and of course he got the worst of it. There were no fatalities in our little town. All in all, the boycott was unpopular and was abandoned after one day, since the populace was still not accustomed to such a spectacle.

My pretty yellow badge was removed by a neighbour who was offended by it. He secretly scratched it off in the night ('The poor doctor!'). [...][5]

DOC. 22
The Times, 3 April 1933: article regarding the murder of the Jewish lawyer Schumm and other acts of violence on the day of the boycott[1]

Boycott of Jews. Scenes in Berlin. Business at a standstill. Lynching case at Kiel

From our own correspondent[2]

Berlin, April 2. What the Nazi *Völkischer Beobachter* calls 'the dress rehearsal for the permanent boycott of Jews' was ruthlessly enforced yesterday between 10 a.m. and midnight. It was completely effective, being withheld only from Jewish newspapers, banks,

---

4 The words 'tough boys' are in English in the German original.
5 In the next part of her account the author describes her preparations for emigration.

1 *The Times*, 3 April 1933, p. 14. The original document is in English. *The Times*, founded in 1785 as *The Daily Universal Register*, has been published in London under its current name as a daily newspaper since 1788. In the 1930s it had a circulation of 190,000. During the days prior to and following the boycott, *The Times* printed various articles on the persecution of German Jews.

and a few border-line undertakings. It was based on fear and force, and in general passed off quietly, though at Kiel it led to the first case of mob lynching.

The victim of this was a Jewish lawyer named Schumm,[3] who was killed by an angry mob in the police cell where he was confined. The *Völkischer Beobachter* states that one of three Nazi storm troopers was hit by shots fired through the door of Schumm's father's furniture shop as the Nazis took post outside it, and that after Schumm had been taken to the police station the police were unable to prevent the incursion of the mob.[4] The Catholic *Germania* gives a slightly different account. It says that there was an exchange of words between Schumm and one of the storm troopers which led to blows, and that a shot was then fired (the newspaper asks 'by whom?') which hit a Nazi named Asthalter.[5] The official statement attributes the shot to Schumm, who had come to Kiel to attend his sister's wedding. It says that Schumm and his father fled into the shop followed by storm troopers, who smashed their way in, arrested the whole family, and took them to police headquarters. The mob then demolished the furniture shop and went to police headquarters, where its members climbed the wall of the courtyard, forced their way into the cells, and killed Schumm.

Methods of Violence

The boycott completely paralysed Jewish business life. On the stroke of 10 uniformed Nazis took position outside every Jewish shop, store, café, or other undertaking. The order of the Nazi boycott leader, Herr Streicher, that there should be neither violence nor force, was not respected. In the small shops the Nazi picket – often wearing a revolver – usually stood with his legs planted astride in the doorway. Your Correspondent saw several people forcibly prevented from entering, or thrust violently away.

Mr. Albion Ross, an American citizen and the assistant correspondent of the Philadelphia *Public Ledger*, tried to enter the Wertheim stores in the Rosenthalerstrasse, where four Nazis were posted, but was thrust away, and one man followed him, struck him twice on the head, and called him '*Du verdammter Hundekopf*.'[6] Your Correspondent was at first denied entrance to a Jewish druggist's shop by a Nazi, who said, 'You cannot go in here,' and used force to prevent him entering, but gave way to the word 'foreigner.' A policeman not far away said that forcible hindrance was not allowed, but on being invited to go and see what was happening, answered that he would not mix himself up in such things.

Bodies of Nazis with paste-pots then appeared, and soon every Jewish shop bore on its window a placard exhorting Germans not to buy from the Jews. Similar posters were posted over the nameplates of Jewish doctors and lawyers, and pickets were placed outside the apartment-houses in which they live. In some cases the placards were hung over

2 The correspondent of *The Times* was Norman Ebbutt (1894–1968). He moved to Berlin in 1925 and headed the Berlin office of *The Times* from 1927 until his deportation in 1937.
3 The murdered Dr Friedrich Schumm (1901–1933) worked as a lawyer in Neidenburg in East Prussia.
4 See 'Bluttat eines Juden', *Völkischer Beobachter* (northern German edition), 2/3 April 1933, p. 1.
5 During a long stay in hospital, Asthalter recovered from the wound, which had penetrated his liver, and he was awarded the Blood Order medal. Wilhelm Asthalter (1910–1982), technical employee, joined the NSDAP in 1930 and the SS in 1931; later worked for the SD and was imprisoned in Belgium after 1945.
6 German in the original; roughly translates as 'You bloody dog.'

the shop door, and the Jewish inmates were prevented from opening it. Then Nazis with paint-pots appeared and soon the Jewish windows bore, in dripping red or white letters, the word 'Jew!' or such inscriptions as 'Purchases here entail danger to life,' 'Jerusalem,' and the like.

Empty Cafes

In the market halls the deserted stalls of Jewish traders bore placards with the words 'Closed as a protest against the Jewish atrocity propaganda at home and abroad – the Jewish proprietor of this business is responsible for the safety of this placard, which must be prominently shown.' Access to the University and the State Library was denied to Jews, visitors having to show their membership cards, which were taken from Jews.

At first there were rare attempts to keep Jewish businesses open, and in some cases the pickets took the 'no violence' order literally enough not to prevent people from entering. Determined people might thus penetrate into the hushed stillness of such vast emporia as that of Wertheim in the Leipzigerstrasse and the Kurfürstendamm, where scared waiters received the rare guests who had refused to be deterred with none too friendly an eye. By midday it was difficult to find a Jewish shop still open, and from the early afternoon onwards it was impossible. The great Kurfürstendamm, one of the main shopping thoroughfares of Berlin, was three parts dead; the boycott strikingly revealed how preponderant Jewish influence is in business life. The Kaufhaus des Westens and other great stores were closed; Nazi pickets stood impassively outside the Café Wien, Döbrin's,[7] and other great cafés, which had put the shutters up. Their closure and that of Jewish-owned cabarets left great gaps in the avenue of light which the Kurfürstendamm normally becomes after dusk.

Nazi Patrols

Police were rarely to be seen. In the afternoon groups of Nazis, with heavy weighted riding crops, strode about the Kurfürstendamm, and in one case were seen rushing into an apartment house, from a balcony of which missiles, as excitable rumour said, had been thrown at them. Your Correspondent saw two private citizens arrested by uniformed Nazis and led off, one of them to a Nazi 'home.'

Report brings a similar picture from most parts of the country. In Kassel part of a public place before a Jewish shop was fenced off with barbed wire, on which was fixed a placard with the words, 'Concentration camp for refractory citizens who make their purchase from Jews.' The enclosure contained a live donkey. Trains to the Czechoslovak frontier were searched on Friday night and many Jews are said to have been arrested.

In Berlin the Stock Exchange was surrounded by Nazis and entrance denied to Jews. The official quotations were fixed 'exclusively by Christian brokers,' of whom several wore Nazi uniform. There was a marked improvement, of mysterious origin, from the precipitous decline of recent days. The belief that the boycott might not be resumed, it was suggested, may have had something to do with this. Inquiry in competent circles, however, confirms the impression that this was in all probability not the case. There was no economic or political reason for the exuberant rise in values and it cannot be consid-

---

7 Correctly: Café Dobrin.

ered to give a true picture of the situation. Herr Streicher has stated that he expects it to be possible to avoid a resumption of the boycott, but the tone of the Nazi Press is less reassuring.

The attitude of the public towards the extraordinary scenes of yesterday seemed to be mainly passive. There is among the masses little spontaneous and active anti-Semitism, though there is a widespread feeling of dislike and distrust of certain alleged characteristics of a community which, as yesterday's events vividly showed, greatly predominates in business life, while forming less than 1 per cent of the population. One popular belief, formerly fed by the consistently hostile attitude of some Jewish newspapers to complainants in law suits relating to immoral offences, is that of the alleged exploitation of women in the entertainment industry, with its preponderantly Jewish influence; another prevalent belief is that workers in Jewish undertakings are ruthlessly treated. There is no spontaneous hostility to the hard-working small Jewish shopkeeper or trader.

The Berlin bank account of Dr. Einstein, who has now resigned from the Prussian Academy of Sciences, has been impounded, and the sum of 30,000 marks in securities or cash seized.[8]

DOC. 23

On 3 April 1933 Director Eugen Feuchtmann reports to the chairman of the board of directors of Johannes Jeserich AG on the forced resignation of two Jewish directors[1]

Letter from the board member of the public limited company Johannes Jeserich, Berlin,[2] unsigned [director Eugen Feuchtmann],[3] to the chairman of the board of directors, bank manager Ottomar Benz,[4] Deutsche Bank and Disconto-Gesellschaft in Berlin, dated 3 April 1933 (carbon copy)

Dear Doctor,

On Saturday 1 April, four agents of the NSDAP Factory Cell Organization appeared in our office and demanded the immediate dismissal of Jewish employees. This request was complied with by Director Fuld,[5] and Mr Adam and Mr Braun were subsequently

---

8 Albert Einstein, at the time in Belgium, had returned his Prussian nationality to the German consulate there. The tax office responsible for the Einsteins used this fact as a pretext for its actions: see GStA PK, I HA, Rep. 77/6061, fols. 5–16. On the discussion regarding the enforced denaturalization of Einstein, see Doc. 70, 14 August 1933.

1 BArch, R 8119 F, Nr. 14732 (microfiche P 2372), fols. 2–4. This document has been translated from German.
2 The chemical firm Johannes Jeserich in Berlin was founded in 1862. It was a civil engineering and construction materials company which manufactured products including varnish and asphalt, in Berlin and Hamburg, and also worked in road construction. The firm had branches in many German cities after 1933.
3 Feuchtmann was the author: ibid, fol. 7. Dr Eugen Feuchtmann (b. 1878), construction engineering graduate; retired government master builder; director of Johannes Jeserich AG.
4 Dr Ottomar Benz (1880–1960), banker and politician; mayor of Hildburghausen; Landrat of Kreis Sonneberg, Thuringia; finance minister in Thuringia, 1920–1921; from 1926 on the board of directors of Disconto-Gesellschaft, then director of the main branch in Berlin of Deutsche Bank and Disconto-Gesellschaft.
5 Lothar Fuld (1886–1938), director of Johannes Jeserich AG; committed suicide on 20 Nov. 1938.

dismissed. On Monday the 3rd of this month, the undersigned on the left[6] was called to a meeting by chief building inspector Leipold[7] (Mitte district authority) and informed in the presence of our authorized official, graduate engineer Erfurth, that the state commissioner for civil engineering of the city of Berlin, Government Master Builder Fuchs,[8] had rejected the proposal of the district authority for the issuance of larger contracts to our firm to build roads. The reason he gave for this was that ours is a Jewish company. Government Master Builder Leipold recommended that we promptly take steps to reverse this decision by releasing the two Jewish board members from the firm and at the same time informing the state commissioner of this course of action. Attempts were then made to gain an audience with the Gauleitung of the NSDAP, in order to learn more about the matter. The representative of the director of the Factory Cell Organization for the Gau of Berlin explained that the director would be unavailable until 4 o'clock and that the release of the Jewish directors was an absolute prerequisite for negotiations of any sort.

Having returned to the office, the chairman of the Factory Cell Organization of the NSDAP, Charlottenburg district, Mr Fengler, appeared before the undersigned on the left and informed him that the demand for the removal of Jewish employees made by the NSDAP Factory Cell representatives on Saturday also extended to the Jewish directors. The same information was also communicated to the undersigned on the right when he attempted to speak with his acquaintance State Secretary Daluege[9] about the matter.

The undersigned on the left has consulted in detail with his colleagues Director Fuld and Dr Stern,[10] with the result that both men have declared that they both intended to resign from the company with immediate effect and to discuss the handling of their personal affairs with the chairman.[11]

---

6 There are no signatures on the carbon copy of the original.
7 Artur Leipold (b. 1884), engineering graduate; chief buildings inspector for the municipal authorities, 1927; member of the German National People's Party (DNVP), 1927–1933; joined the SA in 1934 and the NSDAP in 1937.
8 Erwin Fuchs, engineering graduate; retired government master builder, 1933; city councillor in Berlin, 1933–1934.
9 Kurt Daluege (1897–1946), civil engineer; leader of the Upper Silesian Self-Defence force 1918–1920; joined the NSDAP in 1922; founded the SA Berlin and Northern Germany in 1926; worked as an engineer for the city of Berlin, 1927–1933; head of the Special Detachment Daluege in the Prussian Ministry of the Interior, 1933; chief of the Prussian Police, 11 May 1933 to 1936; chief of the Order Police, 1936–1945; deputy Reich Protector of Bohemia and Moravia, June 1942 to 1943; granted leave on grounds of ill health, 1943; executed in Prague in 1946.
10 Dr Ernst Stern (1892–1963), banker and journalist; from 1919 ministerial official; from 1924 worked for the Reichs-Kredit-Gesellschaft; in 1933 emigrated to London, where he worked as an economic advisor to Winston Churchill and various companies.
11 On 13 April 1933 the resignation of the board members Fuld and Stern was accepted during the advisory board meeting chaired by Benz, with the rationale that the firm would otherwise no longer receive public contracts. They were subsequently replaced by members of the NSDAP. In addition, members of the board of directors Ludwig Fuld (Mannheim), Dr Theodor Reis, Judicial Counsellor Theodor Marba, Dr Alfred Friedmann (all Berlin), and Judicial Counsellor Emil Krämer (Munich) had to resign from the board of directors because of their Jewish backgrounds. The firm was henceforth classed as Aryan: ibid, fols. 49 and 67–69.

Furthermore, the board, all salaried employees, and the majority of the staff have submitted a petition to the municipal authorities, which has been approved by Director Fuld and Dr Stern, and a copy of which is enclosed.[12]

By hereby informing you of what has transpired, we humbly entreat you to provide us with the instructions you deem appropriate, and recommend ourselves respectfully

DOC. 24
On 3 April 1933 patent lawyer Richard Wirth declares his solidarity with his Jewish colleagues[1]

Letter from Dr Richard Wirth,[2] Frankfurt am Main, to patent lawyers Dr G. Breitung, Berlin SW 11, 31 Bernburger Straße, E. Jordan, Berlin W 35, 16 Am Karlsbad, E. Heilmann, Berlin SW 61, 16 Waterlooufer, Mr P. Hapt, Berlin W 57, 46 Yorckstraße, and Dr R. Meldau, Berlin-Charlottenburg, Hochhaus am Knie, dated 3 April 1933 (copy)[3]

Dear colleagues,

As afforded and required of me solely by my unique position, I hereby wish to issue the following personal statement concerning developments within the Association of German Patent Lawyers.

I hereby declare my solidarity with our Jewish colleagues just as the Movement is intending or threatening to take the same steps as it has with respect to other Jewish lawyers.[4] I stand with my Jewish colleagues to the point of being expelled from this association, having my business restricted, or being removed from my post as a patent lawyer, accepting the unavoidable consequences for further employment, as provided by law.

Today it is perhaps necessary to add that my sense of justice alone has led me to take this step. It offends my sense of justice that an inevitable consequence of said development, whether desirable or not, would be that the work of Jewish colleagues would be carried out by Christian ones, though I do not wish to otherwise pass judgement on the difference between the exercise of patent law by Jewish and Christian lawyers.

---

12 The letter dated 3 April 1933 (not reproduced here) from the Factory Cell Organization of Johannes Jeserich AG, to Government Master Builder Fuchs of the Berlin municipal authorities contained the request – which subsequently received a positive response – that after the resignation of the Jewish members of the board of directors, the firm once again be considered for municipal building contracts in the future: ibid., fols. 5 and 9.

1 PA AA, R 98 472. This document has been translated from German.
2 Dr Richard Wirth (1865–1947), engineer and lawyer; member of Frankfurt am Main city council, 1894–1897, and head of the city council, 1897–1907; patent lawyer in Frankfurt; author of works including *Zur Rechtsfindung in Patentsachen* (1936).
3 The letter is one of two documents appended to a letter from Richard Wirth to Reich Foreign Minister Baron Konstantin von Neurath dated 11 April 1933: ibid.
4 On 12 April 1933 the *Völkischer Beobachter* reported that the National Socialist Association of Lawyers, to which National Socialist patent lawyers belonged, 'has taken steps in agreement with the Reich Patent Office' to regulate the licensing of Jewish patent lawyers in the same way as for other lawyers: *Völkischer Beobachter* (northern German edition), 12 April 1933, p. 2. According to the Law on Patent Lawyers issued on 22 April 1933, non-Aryans were no longer granted licences or their licences could be revoked: *Reichsgesetzblatt*, 1933, I, p. 217.

The conditions leading to the above declaration are solely occasioned by the complete lack of clarity in the matter, as a result of which none of the lists of candidates to the board has offered any kind of new political goal for this association, much less a response to the above-mentioned points. The requirement has already been met by the otherwise inherently contradictory aims found in the invitation from the first of this month issued by the circle associated with colleague Ullrich.

Another cause for my statement is that I do not know the extent to which our National Socialist colleagues are acting on their own or in the name of a body with legal authority today.

With collegial esteem

DOC. 25

On 4 April 1933 the *Jüdische Rundschau* calls for the development of a new Jewish self-assertiveness in response to the boycott[1]

[Robert Weltsch][2]

Wear the yellow patch with pride!
The 1st of April 1933 will remain an important day in the history of the German Jews, indeed in the history of the entire Jewish people. The events of this day not only have a political and economic but also a moral and psychological side to them. Much has been said in the newspapers about the political and economic context, though admittedly agitational concerns have frequently clouded factual insight. To speak of the *moral* dimension is *our* concern. For as much as the Jewish question is being discussed at this time, no one but ourselves can say what is going on in the soul of German Jews, what can be said of these events from the *Jewish* perspective. Today, Jews can only speak *as Jews*. Anything else is futile. The phantom of the so-called Jewish press has swept away. The fatal mistake made by many Jews in believing that Jewish interests could be represented under another guise has been dispelled. German Jewry was given a lesson on 1 April which is far more profound than even its acrimonious and currently triumphant opponents assume.

We are not the type to lament. We will let those Jews of a previous generation, who learned nothing and forgot everything, react to events of this magnitude with sentimental sententiousness. A *new tone* is required today in the discussion of Jewish affairs. We live in a new epoch; the national revolution of the German people is a glaringly visible signal that the old conceptual framework has collapsed. This might be painful for some, but in this world only he who keeps sight of reality can maintain himself. We are in the

---

1 'Tragt ihn mit Stolz, den gelben Fleck!', *Jüdische Rundschau*, 4 April 1933, pp. 131–132. Published in Robert Weltsch, *Tragt ihn mit Stolz, den gelben Fleck: Eine Aufsatzreihe der 'Jüdischen Rundschau' zur Lage der deutschen Juden* (Nördlingen: Greno, 1988), pp. 24–29. This document has been translated from German.
2 Robert Weltsch (1891–1982), journalist and writer; active in the Zionist student movement in Prague; editor of the *Jüdische Rundschau* in Berlin, 1919–1938; emigrated in Sept. 1938 to Jerusalem, where he was editor of the *Jüdische Weltrundschau*; correspondent for the newspaper *Ha'aretz* in London from 1946; member of the board of directors of the Leo Baeck Institute in London, 1955–1979.

midst of a violent transformation of spiritual, political, social, and economic life. *Our concern is: how are the Jews to react?*

The 1st of April 1933 can be a day of Jewish awakening and Jewish rebirth. If the Jews want that. If the Jews are mature and possess inner greatness. If the Jews are not as their opponents make them out.

Jewry, under attack, must *acknowledge what it is.*

Even on this day of most intense commotion, as the stormiest of emotions pervade our hearts in the face of an unprecedented display of universal ostracism of the entire Jewish population of a country of great culture, we must at least maintain one thing: *composure.* Even as we stand in astonishment before the events of these days, we must not despair and we must take stock of the situation without deceiving ourselves. These days, one would have to recommend that the text that stood at the cradle of Zionism, Theodor Herzl's 'Jewish State', *be distributed in hundreds of thousands of copies among Jews and non-Jews alike.*³ If a sense for greatness and nobility, for chivalry and justice, still prevails, then every National Socialist who reads this book would have to go numb at his own blind doing. But also every Jew who reads it would begin to understand, and would draw comfort and ennoblement from it. Theodor Herzl, the purity of whose name has been tainted before the entire German public these days because of a forged quote,⁴ wrote in the introduction to the aforementioned text:

> The Jewish question exists. It would be foolhardy to deny it. It is a misplaced remnant of the Middle Ages, of which even the cultured peoples of today could not to the best of their abilities rid themselves. Indeed, they displayed magnanimous willpower when they emancipated us. The Jewish question exists wherever Jews live in noticeable numbers ...
>
> *I believe that I understand antisemitism, which is in many ways a complicated movement. I contemplate this movement as a Jew, but without hatred and fear. I believe that I can discern what in antisemitism is a crude joke, base professional jealousy, inherited prejudice, religious intolerance – but also what in it is perceived self-defence. I consider the Jewish question to be neither a social nor a religious one, even when it is coloured in this way or another. It is a national question, and in order to solve it, we must above all make it a question of world politics to be settled by the council of cultured peoples.*

---

3 Theodor Herzl (1860–1904), journalist; co-founder of the Zionist World Organization, 1897; author of works including *A Jewish State* (1896).
4 This refers to the following passage of an appeal from 30 March 1933 signed by Streicher, 'Strike at the World Enemy': 'At the Zionist Congress in Basel, the Jews passed a resolution: "As soon as a non-Jewish state dares to take a stand against us, we must be in a position to pressure the neighbouring countries of that state to declare war against it. But if the neighbours were to join in opposing us as well, we must respond by unleashing a world war. We must force the non-Jewish heads of state to actively support this broadly conceived plan. To do this, we will use public opinion as pretext. This we have arranged using the so-called eighth great power, the press. With a few insignificant exceptions not worth mentioning, the press is entirely in our hands!" *Nationalsozialistische Partei-Korrespondenz*, 30 March 1933, p. 1. Reproduced as an editorial in the *Völkischer Beobachter* (northern German edition), 31 March 1933, p. 1. The appeal claims that this quote is taken from the seventh meeting of the Basel Zionist Congress. The passage does not appear in its protocol: Zionisten-Congress in Basel (29–31 August 1897), *Officielles Protocoll* (Vienna: Verlag des Vereines 'Erez Israel' 1898), pp. 189–192. In reality, the quote is taken from the fictive *Protocols of the Elders of Zion*. It can be found word for word in sections 3 and 5 of the 7th chapter, referred to as the minutes of a session: *The Jewish Peril: Protocols of the Learned Elders of Zion*, p. 25.

One would have to transcribe page upon page of this text from 1896 in order to demonstrate that: Theodor Herzl was the first Jew who was impartial enough to examine antisemitism as it relates to the Jewish question. And he recognized that an improvement could be made not through head-in-the-sand politics but only through the open treatment of the facts for all the world to see. He opposed nothing more passionately than that which is being imputed to him now, namely the idea that the Jews could create a secret world association or act in some way that could mistakenly awaken such notions among other peoples. In his essay 'Leroy-Beaulieu[5] on Antisemitism', he writes:

> We Zionists most explicitly and vehemently oppose every international association of Jews that, were they to be effective, would represent the much scorned state within a state and, because they are powerless and meaningless, only have disadvantages to offer ... Suffice it to say that we do not wish for an international association to solve the Jewish question, but an international discussion: that is, not coalitions, secret interventions, hidden paths, but *forthright discussion under the constant and complete control of public opinion.*

Even today, Jews raised in the spirit of Theodor Herzl do not wish to accuse but to understand. And to ask ourselves how we are at fault, how we have ourselves sinned. In trying times critical to their fate, the Jewish people have always first raised the question of their own guilt. Our most important prayer states: 'But *on account of our sins* we were exiled from our land.'[6] Only when we are critical of ourselves will we also be fair towards others.

The Jews bear a heavy burden of guilt, because they have not heeded the call of Theodor Herzl; indeed, they have partly ridiculed it. The Jews did not want to acknowledge that 'a Jewish question exists'. They believed it was only a matter of not being recognized as a Jew. Today we are accused of treason against the German people; the National Socialist press labels us the 'enemy of the nation', and we are defenceless against this claim.

It is not true that the Jews have betrayed Germany. If they have betrayed anything, then they have betrayed Jewry itself.

Because the Jew did not proudly parade his Jewishness, because he tried to avoid the Jewish question, he has made himself complicit in the debasement of Jewry. For all the acrimony that must overwhelm us when reading the National Socialist calls for a boycott and the unjust accusations, we can be grateful to the boycott committee for one thing. § 3 of the guidelines states:

Affected are ... of course businesses that are in the hands of members of the Jewish race. Religion plays no role. Tradespeople baptized as Catholics or Protestants or dissidents of the Jewish race are equally Jews in the sense of this ordinance.[7]

---

5 Anatole Leroy-Beaulieu (1842–1912), French orientalist and historian; protested against antisemitism and advocated equality for Russian Jews; author of *L'Antisémitisme* (1897).
6 From the so-called Mussaf prayer, a supplementary prayer said on Jewish holidays.
7 The quote is from the directives of the Central Committee for the Defence against Jewish Atrocity and Boycott Propaganda, dated 30 March 1933: *Völkischer Beobachter* (northern German edition), 31 March 1933, p. 2.

This is a lesson for all betrayers of Jewry. Whoever absconds from the community in order to improve his personal situation shall not reap the benefits of this betrayal. This statement against apostasy represents the first sign of clarification. The Jew who denies his Jewishness is no better fellow citizen than the one who openly avows it. Apostasy is an ignominy, but so long as the world around us placed a premium on it, it seemed to be advantageous. Now it is no longer an advantage. The Jew has been marked *as such*. He gets the yellow patch.

The fact that the boycott leadership has ordered that signs 'with the yellow patch against a black background' be affixed to boycotted stores is a powerful symbol. This measure was conceived as a branding, a defamation. We are accepting it and making a badge of honour out of it.

Many Jews had a difficult time on Saturday. Not through internal acknowledgement, not as a result of loyalty to one's own community, not out of pride for a great past and human achievement, but by virtue of the imprint on the red slip of paper and the yellow patch they suddenly stood there as Jews. The squads went from house to house, plastered over businesses and signs, painted over windows; the German Jews were pilloried for 24 hours, as it were. Besides other signs and inscriptions, one frequently saw on the windowpanes of storefront displays a large Magen David,[8] the Shield of King David. This is meant to be a defilement. *Jews, accept it, the Shield of David, and carry it with honour!*

For – and here begins our duty of self-reflection – if this shield is tainted today, it is not the fault of our enemies alone. There were many Jews who could not do enough for undignified self-mockery. Judaism was regarded as outdated, it was not taken seriously, one wanted to relieve oneself of this tragedy by smiling.

But there is already today a new type of free Jew, still unknown to the non-Jewish world.

Whenever today in the National Socialist and German nationalist press frequent references are made to the Jewish literary type and to the so-called Jewish press, whenever the Jews are made responsible for these factors, it must be reiterated time and time again that they are not representatives of Jewry, but have at most attempted to profit from Jews. In a time of bourgeois self-righteousness, these elements could count on applause from Jewish audiences as well, whenever they derided and trivialized Jews and Jewishness. How often they preached the ideals of an abstract cosmopolitanism to us Jewish nationalists, in order to destroy all deeper values of Judaism. Upright Jews were unfailingly indignant at the jokes and caricatures made by Jewish buffoons directed against Jews as much or even more so as they were against Germans or others. The Jewish public applauded its own debasement, and many attempted to use joining in with this ridicule as an alibi. Even now, in these hard times, many think that they can save themselves through desertion or by jumping on the bandwagon. The *Völkischer Beobachter* from 2 April reports with a smirk that the boycott leadership has been overrun by Jewish businesspeople hoping for exceptional treatment for themselves. Many, the *VB* claims, quickly had themselves baptized in order to be able to say that they were Christians.[9]

---

8 Six-pointed star; symbol of Judaism.
9 See 'Am Boykott-Tag im Berliner Aktions-Komitee: Massenandrang jüdischer Geschäftsleute – Tarnungen und "Umstellungen"' ('The Berlin Action Committee on Boycott Day: Huge Crowd of Jewish Merchants – Camouflage and "Conversions"'), *Völkischer Beobachter* (northern German edition), 2/3 April 1933, p. 2.

Fortunately, the depiction in the *VB* itself reveals that these were isolated incidents. But the time of pressure is not yet over: we are only at the beginning, and that is why this danger must be discussed.

For the danger, the greatest danger, threatening the Jews is that of a spoiling and crippling of character. The National Socialists claim in their speeches and rallies that they detest characterlessness above all else. In his last speech Dr Goebbels made fun of the transformation of the 'Jewish press', which, he says, has relearned so quickly that the editors of the *Angriff* must have turned green with envy.[10]

If National Socialism recognizes this as the state of affairs, then it must wish as a Jewish partner a Jewry that holds its honour in high esteem.

It cannot promote Jewish characterlessness in order to then stigmatize it. It cannot deny a Jew his honour who has openly avowed himself *as a Jew* and committed no crime. Whether this is indeed the case will soon be revealed: a quota has now been announced or already has been summarily introduced for certain professions. We will still have plenty to say about how seriously this measure affects German Jews morally and economically, but when the list is compiled of those *Jews* – for they will be selected as such for this purpose – who are allowed to pursue their occupation in accordance with the quota, the ones who openly and clearly avow their Jewishness may not be discriminated against. That is the logical consequence that would necessarily follow from the National Socialist view itself.

Thirty years ago, it was considered objectionable in educated circles to discuss the Jewish question. The Zionists were regarded as troublemakers with an *idée fixe*. Now the Jewish question is so relevant that every little child, every schoolboy, and the ordinary man on the street can speak of nothing else. On 1 April, the stamp 'Jew' was imprinted upon every Jew across Germany. According to the new guidelines from the boycott committee, a uniform designation for all businesses will be implemented in the event of a renewal of the boycott: for non-Jews the endorsement 'German business', for Jews simply the word 'Jew'. One knows who is a Jew. There is no more evading or hiding. The Jewish answer is clear. It is the short sentence spoken by Moses to the Egyptians:[11] *Iwri anochi.*[12] Yes, Jew. *Say yes to being a Jew.* That is the *moral significance* of present events. The time is too unsettled for discussions involving arguments. Let us hope that a calmer time will come, and that a movement which places all its pride in being honoured as the pacesetter of a national uprising will not enjoy humiliating others, even if they deem it necessary to fight them. But we Jews – we can defend our honour. We remember all those who for the last five thousand years have been named and stigmatized as Jews. We are reminded that we are Jews. We say yes, and wear it with pride.

---

10 The contents of Goebbels's speech could not be verified.
11 Corrected in the reprint to 'spoken by the prophet Jonah': Weltsch, *Tragt ihn mit Stolz*, p. 29.
12 Ancient Hebrew: I am a Hebrew. The passage from Jonah 1:9 in the Matthew Henry translation reads: 'And he said unto them, I *am* an Hebrew; and I fear the LORD, the God of heaven, which hath made the sea and the dry land.' Matthew Henry, *An Exposition of the Old and New Testaments: Wherein Each Chapter is Preceded by an Analysis of Its Contents, the Sense Given and Largely Illustrated, with Practical Remarks and Observations*, vol. 2 (New York: H. C. Sleight, 1833), p. 1259.

DOC. 26

On 5 April 1933 the student Heinrich Marx deliberates whether to remain in Berlin following the boycott or to leave[1]

Handwritten diary of Heinrich Marx,[2] entry for 5 April 1933

Wed. 5 April. The unrest, haste, and helplessness of these days and weeks hardly give one a moment for rest or reflection. I would often like to write entries for this book, but I lack the powers of concentration. Every evening we sit here at home or with acquaintances, discuss the situation, debate new ideas, consider this or that plan; lively discussions go back and forth about whether to leave or stay. Every time the result is the same, namely: wait. From the beginning I advocated that we persevere here in Berlin. I know the counterargument and I recognize that for those who fear for their lives it would be a false martyrdom to remain here. But one should bear in mind: leaving only makes sense if one is capable of breaking all ties, if one can reasonably expect to create a new life abroad, without in any way having to consider [having to] return to this country [with] this regime. Under a new one, however, one would be accepted only with great reserve. One should not allow oneself to be incited to panic. Everything should be carefully planned. – Nevertheless: what has transpired over the last few days has eliminated the last vestiges of composure among many people. The implementation of the boycott was the most depressing thing that I have had to endure in my whole life.

[...][3]

---

1 Heinrich Marx, 'Tagebuch II: 9. März 1933 bis November 1934', pp. 13–14, Deutsche Nationalbibliothek/Deutsches Exilarchiv 1933–1945, EB 96/160, Nachlass Henry Marx. This document has been translated from German.
2 Heinrich, later Henry, Marx (1911–1994), journalist; university studies in law and journalistic work in Berlin, 1929–1933; forced to terminate his studies in 1933; held internship in the banking house of the Arnold brothers in Berlin in 1934; incarcerated in a concentration camp in the summer of 1934; worked at the cigar factories of Heinrich Jacobi from Nov. 1934 to Jan. 1937; emigrated to the USA in 1937; editor of the *New Yorker Staats-Zeitung* and the *Herold*, 1937–1969; editor-in-chief of the Jewish weekly *Aufbau*, 1985–1994.
3 The entry breaks off here. Pages 15 and 16 of the diary are missing.

DOC. 27
The unimplemented draft of a law 'for the regulation of the status of the Jews', 6 April 1933[1]

Letter, signed Dr Rudolf Becker,[2] Berlin, from 6 April 1933, sent confidentially by Deputy of the Führer Heß[3] to Gauleiter Streicher, undated, with enclosure (carbon copy)[4]

Introduction to the Jew Law.

The attached draft of a law for the regulation of the status of the Jews, along with enclosures, is the product of a working group in conjunction with the undersigned, consisting of Oberregierungsrat Dr Diels (current head of the Political Police),[5] Dr Lippert (current state commissioner for Berlin), Dr Meier (director of the German Moving Pictures Syndicate),[6] Oberregierungsrat Dr Ziegler (Ministry of Propaganda),[7] Major Fischer (association head), and as specialists Dr Schulz[8] from the Prussian Statistical Office and the well-known writer and ethnologist Dr von Leers. The result of the workshops and independent work has been summarized by the undersigned with the haste necessitated

---

1 Staatsarchiv Nürnberg, Sammlung Streicher, Nr. 129. This document has been translated from German.
2 Dr Rudolf Becker (b. 1886), lawyer; from 1921 Ministerialrat in the Prussian Ministry of Finance, where he worked in 1931 in the first department of finance; head of the section for academic administration, 1939; Ministerialdirigent, 1940.
3 Rudolf Heß (1894–1987), retailer; member of the Thule Society; joined the NSDAP in 1920; participated in the Beer Hall Putsch in 1923 and consequently served a prison term in Landsberg am Lech; Hitler's private secretary; Deputy of the Führer, 1933–1941; sentenced to life imprisonment at the Nuremberg trials, 1946; committed suicide while in prison in 1987.
4 In the left-hand margin of the first page of the original is the handwritten note: 'Party comrade Streicher. I have arranged that you be invited to future meetings of this working group. Heß.' Becker later sent another copy of the document to Vicco von Bülow-Schwante in the Reich Foreign Office: PA AA, R 98 472. On the drafting of the law, see Uwe Dietrich Adam, *Judenpolitik im Dritten Reich* (Düsseldorf: Droste, 1972), pp. 33–38.
5 Dr Rudolf Diels (1900–1957), lawyer; head of department in the Prussian Ministry of the Interior, 1930; chief of the Gestapo Central Office (Gestapa), April 1933–April 1934; Regierungspräsident in Cologne, 1934–1936, and in Hanover, from 1936; SS-Oberführer, honorary rank, 1939; arrested in 1944 following the assassination attempt of 20 July; interned, 1945–1948.
6 Dr Alexander Meier, after 1951 Meier-Lenoir (1896–1961), lawyer; member of the German People's Party (DVP), 1929–1933; joined the NSDAP in 1933; employed from 1926 by the insurance firm Frankfurter Allgemeine Versicherungs-AG; from 1930 lawyer in Berlin and member of the board of Syndikat-Film GmbH; its general manager, 1933–1936; from 1943 lawyer and notary in Wiesbaden; after 1945 chairman of the Federal Association of Hesse for those Injured due to Foreign Occupation.
7 Dr Wilhelm Ziegler (1891–1962), historian; after 1933 section head in the Reich Ministry of Public Enlightenment and Propaganda (RMfVuP); honorary professor of modern history, politics, and the Jewish question at the University of Berlin, 1941; specialist for Jewish affairs (*Judenreferent*) in the literature department of the RMfVuP, 1943; state commissioner for the furtherance of the zone frontier districts (Staatskommissar für die Förderung der Zonengrenzkreise) in the Hessian State Chancellery, 1953–1956; author of works including *Die Judenfrage in der modernen Welt* (1937).
8 Dr Edgar Hans Schulz, author of works including *Judentum und Kriminalität* (1934) and (with Rudolf Frercks) *Warum Arierparagraph? Ein Beitrag zur Judenfrage* (1934). Footnote in the original: 'Contributed to the work "*Die Bevölkerungs- und Berufsstatistik der Juden im Deutschen Reich*" [Population and Occupational Classification of Jews in the German Reich], published in 1930.' The reference is to: Heinrich Silbergleit (ed.), *Die Bevölkerungs- und Berufsverhältnisse der Juden im Deutschen Reich*, part 1: *Freistaat Preußen, Tabellen* (Berlin: Akademie, 1930).

by the urgency of the circumstances. A few deviating suggestions by individual contributors on individual points had to be shelved for the sake of coherence, but the work itself led the participants to reach a broad consensus in practice on all essential points.

They were first and foremost concerned with carrying out practical work directly which could facilitate the rapid completion of an immediately effective and politically feasible law on Jews by the appointed ministers and leaders.[9] Wild tirades, as much as they are desired by internal German propaganda and correspond to justified feelings of vengeance, endanger the common goal: to take full advantage of the historically unique moment in order to cleanse the German people and to free it from an alien power, which has openly and secretly ruled it in its own house in ways that constituted an existential threat. On the other hand, excessive compromises and weakness of expression would not be understood by the people. It was our task to overcome this dilemma through the right arrangement of content and form. While formulating the content and drafting this law, the contributors were constantly aware of the great danger of world public opinion, which before, during, and after the war proved to be oft underestimated and, in truth, the most dangerous enemy of our people. The majority thus saw with some concern how a purely tactical and in many cases aimlessly waged feud against the Jews, with numerous localized, almost all too enjoyable isolated successes, but without the *decisive* and *long-term* general cleansing of the hundredfold camouflaged Jewish powers and influences, has met with a resistance in the world that endangers the decisive breakthrough. 'A man's greatness can be measured by his enemies' is German arrogance, not German strength conscious of its responsibility for the German past and future! That is why we are of the opinion that, in the face of an international Jewish power whose threat cannot be overestimated, it is necessary to create the legal foundation with quietly gathered strength and to make the appropriate administrative arrangements in order to force out both professed and surreptitious Jewry from all positions of authority overnight and throughout the entire spectrum of national character (spheres of culture), German administration (public and legal spheres), and the German economy (especially finance and the control of German land). Only actions that have been completed can surmount resistance! And this is particularly the case if these completed actions have been carried out *faultlessly*, in a clear and determined manner, yet free of the petty and vindictive torment of the soul of a slave, unbefitting of the German, indeed in recognition of the fact that, in practice, this overall cleansing of alien elements, which is crucial because the German psyche – weakened by thousands of its own afflictions – only has a limited capacity to absorb alien culture, may mete out a harsh and partially undeserved fate to these strangers, which should thus be mitigated if possible! For this reason, any injurious formulations have been avoided in the attempt to compensate for hardship, with a degree of pecuniary damage occurring as a result! We can be all the more uncompromising when it comes to what matters to us. It is a case of looking at the overall picture.

The colleagues of the undersigned remain imbued with the conviction that in the end the battle will be decided on the spiritual plane by greater moral strength. Yet the

---

9 It is unclear for whom this draft law was intended. Uwe Dietrich Adam surmises that Göring was the intended recipient. Uwe Dietrich Adam, 'An Overall Plan for Anti-Jewish Legislation in the Third Reich?', *Yad Vashem Studies*, vol. 11 (1976), pp. 33–55, here p. 39. However, from the document reproduced here one can presume that the intended recipient was Heß.

German's natural spiritual disinclination towards harsh violence may not lead to the misrecognition that Germany as a land of means has constantly had to endure a – previously insufficiently recognized – migration of eastern Jewry to the attractions of Western civilization, and that in the last century more Jews have stayed in Germany and come to power through Germany's own faults (growing materialism in the Wilhelmine period) than the German stomach can digest. For this reason, alongside the internal dethroning of Jewish powers through change and reflection, the healthy surgical cut, which removes or contains the superfluous, remains unavoidable.

Readers will have differing views about the particulars of the drafted law, in accordance with individual vitality, that it is biological optimism to think that one can do away with foreign entities without violence. But he who peruses the law should not forget that it is not a matter of what *he* thinks he is capable of, but of what one can in quiet contemplation expect the German people to digest mentally and spiritually right now! Some of its implementation can and must be left to administrative practice, but without a legal foundation it will remain mired in aimlessness and will fail in the long term owing to the good-naturedness and 'guilelessness' of the German people, on the one hand, and the repeated resistance from outside, on the other. Revolutions cannot be put on ice. That is why it is necessary to seize the moment and to definitely establish what is possible! – In order to provide an overview of the proliferation of Jewry, though this lags considerably behind their exercise of power, among the crucial occupations and functions of the German national corpus, which shows the legislator where to intervene and what the intervention requires, the enclosed 'Historical and Statistical Material for the Law on Jews' has been produced by Dr Schulz, whose preliminary academic work demonstrates his exceptional expertise in this area, in consultation with the undersigned.[10] An hour devoted to the attached tables is time well spent and fortifying. Further clarifications of the individual provisions of the draft law, which as the basic law of the German people intentionally refrains from juridical language, will, due to urgent necessity, follow tomorrow.

signed Dr Rudolf Becker.

Do not publish. [11]

Draft Law for the Regulation of the Status of the Jews. [12]

I. Jew, half-Jew, Jew spouse.

§ 1. A *Jew* as defined by this law is someone:

(a) who subscribes to the Mosaic faith,

(b) whose parents or all grandparents have subscribed to the Mosaic faith, even if they or some of them have later renounced the Mosaic faith,

(c) who is the offspring of those named under (a) and (b).[13]

---

10 The 'Amendments to "Historical and Statistical Material for the Law on Jews" VI–VIII' included commentaries and tables on the proportion of Jewish workers in different sectors of the economy according to the census of 1925, the edict of Friedrich Wilhelm III regarding the naturalization of Jews in Prussia from 11 March 1812, and a compilation of Prussian laws pertaining to Jewish emancipation passed between 1806 and 1883: PA AA, R 98 472.

11 Handwritten note by Rudolf Heß.

§ 2. *Half-Jews* as defined by this law are:

Children of marriages, one part of which is a Jew in the sense of § 1 of this law, insofar as they do not subscribe to the Jewish faith.[14]

Whoever is a half-Jew and marries a Jew or a half-Jew again becomes a Jew, as do his offspring, as defined by § 1.

§ 3. A *Jew spouse* as defined by this law is whoever is married to a Jew (male or female) in the sense of § 1, or is no longer married but has children from such a marriage.

II. Jew Registry.

§ 4. Every Jewish man or woman in the sense of § 1 of this law must be entered into the 'Jew Registry' provided by the police in his or her area of residence by 1 July 1933 at the latest.[15]

Those Jews who are not entitled to the rights of German citizenship are not subject to this obligation to register (see §§ 19 and 20).

Every half-Jew of the male or female sex in the sense of § 2 must be entered into the 'Half-Jew Registry' provided by the police in his or her area of residence by 1 July 1933.

Every Jew spouse of male or female sex in the sense of § 3 of this law must be entered into the 'Registry of Jew Spouses' provided by the police in his or her area of residence by 1 July 1933.

Registration is free of charge.

III. The 'Association of Jews in Germany'.

§ 5. All Jews as defined by § 1 of this law are upon registration automatically members of the 'Association of Jews in Germany'.[16]

The 'Association of Jews in Germany' is a corporation under public law.

Membership of the 'Association of Jews in Germany' can be verified by instigating legal proceedings. Legal proceedings can be brought against anyone whose affiliation with Jewry is determined in accordance with § 1.

§ 6. Every four years, the members of the 'Association of Jews in Germany' shall, in secret direct ballot and in accordance with the detailed instructions of the 'People's Warden' (see § 7), elect a 'Jewish Council'. The latter shall not comprise more than twenty-five persons. The elected must be confirmed by the 'People's Warden'.

---

12 For a critique of this draft law, see Doc. 48, May 1933.
13 On the various definitions of the concept of a 'Jew', see the Aryan Paragraph of the Law for the Restoration of the Professional Civil Service, Doc. 32, 11 April 1933, and the First Regulation to the Reich Citizenship Law, Doc. 210, 14 Nov. 1935.
14 On the definition of the so-called *Mischlinge* according to the Nuremberg Laws, see the First Regulation to the Reich Citizenship Law, Doc. 210, 14 Nov. 1935.
15 On the unsuccessful attempts by the Gestapo and the SD to set up similar registers, see Docs. 188, 17 August 1935, and 288, 12 July 1937.
16 The Tenth Regulation to the Reich Citizenship Law, (4 July 1939) compelled all Jews to become members of the Reich Association of Jews in Germany, which was controlled by the Reich Ministry of the Interior, specifically the Gestapo: *Reichsgesetzblatt*, 1939, I, p. 1097.

The 'People's Warden' is authorized to convene and dissolve the 'Jewish Council'. The 'Jewish Council' will establish its own by-laws; it will meet at least once annually. Its decisions are subject to approval by the 'People's Warden'.

The 'Jewish Council' can appoint commissions and individuals to fulfil its functions; their activities are to be monitored by the 'People's Warden'.

IV. The 'People's Warden'.

§ 7. The Reich Chancellor appoints the 'People's Warden' to safeguard the German people from the Jewish threat, to monitor the 'Association of Jews in Germany', to protect the Jews and safeguard their rights. He reports directly to the Reich Chancellor. He is responsible for the implementation of this law and its supplementary and executing provisions. In particular, he instigates the legal proceedings regarding the determination of Jewishness (see § 5).

The 'People's Warden' decides:

(a) on the amount of self-taxation by the 'Association of Jews in Germany',

(b) on the maintenance of schools and other institutions of the 'Association of the Jews in Germany',

(c) on those matters to be placed under the remit of the 'Association of Jews in Germany'.[17]

The 'People's Warden' is a political official of the Reich. In this capacity, he is not beholden to the trust of the 'Association of Jews in Germany'.

The 'People's Warden' possesses police authority over the members of the 'Association of Jews in Germany' in every region.

§ 8. The 'People's Warden' can:

(a) for the exercise of his office demand the submission of all official and commercial documents by the relevant authorities and persons at all times, have anyone interrogated, and

(b) require every Jew to register with the police,

(c) prohibit books and printed works by Jews,

(d) confiscate or prohibit the display of artworks in order to protect the German people from moral degradation,

(e) prohibit, entirely or temporarily, Jewish customs that endanger public peace and security,[18]

(f) prohibit provocative luxury, publicly unbecoming and pretentious displays of wealth, and ostentatious behaviour by Jews,

(g) dissolve Jewish clubs and associations.[19]

---

[17] In line with the proposal made here, the Gestapo had control over the Reich Association as of 1939: ibid.

[18] The Law and the Regulation on the Slaughter of Animals (21 April 1933) prohibited the slaughter of animals prescribed by Jewish tradition: *Reichsgesetzblatt*, 1933, I, pp. 203 and 212. See also the discussion in Berlin regarding the Feast of Tabernacles, Doc. 136, 21 Sept. 1934.

[19] On the dissolution of Jewish clubs by the Gestapo, see, for example, Doc. 148, 27 Dec. 1934.

§ 9. The 'People's Warden' can order all measures that appear necessary for the protection of German citizens from Jewish abuse of laws and economic power. To this end he can:

(a) issue public warnings about certain persons,

(b) prohibit the import of foreign Jewish printed materials from abroad,

(c) order punitive educational measures for Jewish youths whose behaviour endangers the morality of the people,

(d) establish institutes for the study of the Jewish question and impose a mandatory contribution on the 'Association of Jews in Germany' for their maintenance.

V. Legal status of Jewry.

§ 10. The members of the 'Association of Jews in Germany' enjoy the protection of the Reich via the German representations abroad.

§ 11. Members of the 'Association of Jews in Germany' are permitted to pursue a profession or a trade with the following restrictions:

(a) They are not allowed to serve as civil servants or employees of the Reich, state, or local authorities. Insofar as they hold such an office or perform such work at the time that this law enters into force, they are to be dismissed and granted an appropriate pension or a fair severance payment. The granting of a pension shall be waived if it is obvious that they have grossly abused their office to the detriment of the German people. This is to be decided by the proper disciplinary authorities.[20]

(b) They cannot be members of the Reichswehr or Reich Navy.[21] Nor shall they in the future be subject to mandatory military service; an alternative service is not incumbent upon them.[22] The provision of § 11(a) sentences 2–4 applies correspondingly.

(c) They cannot be directors of the Reichsbank, Golddiscontbank, Rentenbank-Kreditanstalt, Deutsche Genossenschaftskasse, Reichskreditgesellschaft, or of independent companies of the Reich, of the regions or of municipalities (e.g. Viag, Reichselektrowerke, gas and electricity plants, etc.). Furthermore, they cannot be directors or branch managers of large banks or such banking companies of which the public is a substantial stakeholder, nor can they be directors of land and real estate surveyors.

(d) They cannot be editors-in-chief or editors of German print periodicals, teachers at private schools (with the exception of Jewish schools), producers or directors of theatres, film institutes, or broadcasting companies, nor managers of publishing houses of cultural significance.

(e) The number of Jewish physicians, pharmacists, veterinarians, lawyers, legal consultants, and their employees, as well as the number of editors of German print periodicals

---

20 The stipulation was implemented the very next day with the Law for the Restoration of the Professional Civil Service: see Doc. 29, 7 April 1933.

21 On 28 Feb. 1934 the Reich minister of the army decreed that § 3 of the Law for the Restoration of the Professional Civil Service would apply to soldiers of the Reichswehr, thereby excluding Jews: ordinance published in Klaus-Jürgen Müller, *Das Heer und Hitler: Armee und nationalsozialistisches Regime 1933–1940* (Stuttgart: Deutsche Verlags-Anstalt, 1969), pp. 592–593.

22 The Military Service Law (21 May 1935) excluded Jews from active military service: *Reichsgesetzblatt*, 1935, I, pp. 609–614.

and of actors on German stages, shall not exceed the percentage of Jews in proportion to the entire number of inhabitants in any given locality.[23] Insofar as their number at the time that this law enters into effect surpasses the permitted maximum number, local representatives of the 'People's Warden' shall decide whom to remove after a hearing with the representatives of the professions and the 'Jewish Council'. They can be granted a transitional period of up to six months until their resignation and a one-time severance payment or one-time contribution towards an alternative source of livelihood in accordance with the detailed provisions. When terminating employment, hardships are to be avoided with consideration to age, family, and wealth, wherever possible. Those who are to remain are first and foremost such Jews who have served as soldiers at the front or otherwise rendered services to Germandom.[24]

§ 12. Jews are prohibited from working as proprietor, shareholder, or any other type of associate of a print periodical, a theatre, a film company, or a publishing house of cultural importance.

§ 13. The members of the 'Association of Jews in Germany' are neither actively nor passively entitled to vote in elections to the Reichstag, regional and municipal representative bodies, chambers of commerce, trade, agriculture or craft trades, or similar institutions of public life.[25]

They cannot be members of private German clubs.

§ 14. Children whose parents are both members of the 'Association of Jews in Germany' are prohibited from attending non-Jewish state or private schools. The 'Association of Jews in Germany' will be prompted by the 'People's Warden' to establish Jewish schools and academic secondary schools, which will be subject to supervision by the local school administration.[26]

§ 15. Marriages between Jews as defined by § 1 of this law and non-Jews can no longer legally take place.

Non-marital intercourse between Jews and non-Jews is prohibited and is punishable by no less than six months in prison. Jews who provoke such non-marital intercourse by misusing a relationship of dependency can be reported to the police by the 'People's Warden'.[27]

---

[23] The Law on Admission to the Legal Profession, passed the following day, 7 April 1933, allowed, for instance, the licences of Jewish lawyers to be revoked by 30 Sept. 1933. Newly trained lawyers of Jewish origin were no longer granted licences to practice: *Reichsgesetzblatt*, 1933, I, p. 188. The Regulation on the Admission of Doctors for Employment with the Health Insurance Companies allowed Jewish doctors to be excluded from work for insurance companies, while new admissions were prohibited: ibid., p. 222. In 1938 Jewish doctors and lawyers were, with few exceptions, banned from practising their profession: *Reichsgesetzblatt*, 1938, I, pp. 969 and 1403.

[24] These exceptions corresponded to the definitions in the Law for the Restoration of the Professional Civil Service of 7 April 1933: see Doc. 29, 7 April 1933.

[25] As a result of the First Regulation to the Reich Citizenship Law, Jews lost the right to vote and the right to hold public office: see Doc. 210, 14 Nov. 1935.

[26] On the attempt to separate Jewish and non-Jewish children in state schools, see the decree dated 10 Sept. 1935, Doc. 196.

[27] On this, see the discussion from 1934 and the Nuremberg Laws in Doc. 121, 5 June 1934, and Doc. 199, 15 Sept. 1935.

§ 16. Every member of the 'Association of Jews in Germany' is required to officially add the letter 'J' to his or her surname. Failure to do so is punishable as concealment of one's civil status.[28]

Writers must place a Star of David alongside their proper name or pen name in all publications.

The 'People's Warden' can order Jews to discard newly assumed names, or to reassume discarded names.[29] He can forbid their use of decidedly Germanic first names.[30]

§ 17. For 'half-Jews' as defined by § 2 and 'Jew spouses' as defined by § 3, the provisions of § 11(a), (b), and (d) and of § 12 correspondingly apply.

VI. Special provisions.

§ 18. The order of 'B'ne Brith'[31] is banned. Its property will be transferred to the state.[32]

§ 19. Naturalizations of Jews as defined by § 1 of this law granted after 2 August 1914 are null and void.[33] Fees paid by them are to be reimbursed. Insofar as they do not reattain foreign nationality through this nullification, they shall be deemed stateless.

§ 20. The *stateless* Jews residing in Germany must leave the German Reich within three months after this law comes into effect. The 'People's Warden' can extend the grace period to as much as six months upon application.[34]

The 'People's Warden' can deport *foreign* Jews residing in Germany from the territory of the German Reich within a period of three to six months.

The 'People's Warden' can, in accordance with the implementing provisions, award a one-off, reasonable resettlement payment to such persons deported, as compensation or to help them attain a new source of livelihood. The same is valid for the Jews deported by legal force, insofar as they have lost their nationality of the German Reich or of one of the German regions through the provisions of § 19.

---

[28] The passports of German Jews were marked with a 'J' from autumn 1938. The identity cards that Jews had to carry with them after Jan. 1939 contained the designation as an imprint.

[29] On the discussion of surnames, see fn. 7 of Doc. 8, 15 March 1933. Name changes were subsequently prohibited for Jews by the Law on Changes to Surnames and Forenames, 5 Jan. 1938: *Reichsgesetzblatt*, 1938, I, p. 9.

[30] On the discussion of the assignment of first names, see Docs. 178, 19 July 1935, and 184, 31 July 1935. In accordance with the Second Regulation on the Implementation of the Law on Changes to Surnames and Forenames, Jews had to bear the compulsory first names Sara or Israel as an official part of their name from 1 Jan. 1939: *Reichsgesetzblatt*, 1938, I, p. 1044.

[31] B'ne Brith, Bne Briss, or also B'nai B'rith (Children of the Covenant). The Independent Order of B'nai B'rith was founded in 1843 in New York by German Jews for the purpose of 'benevolence, brotherly love, and harmony'. The B'nai B'rith Grand Lodge was founded in Germany in 1882 and in 1933 had over 100 lodges with approximately 12,000 members. Their mission included the alleviation of general hardship, help for widows and orphans, and the patronage of science and the arts, as well as the moral support of their members.

[32] The B'nai B'rith lodge was dissolved in Germany on 19 April 1937 and expropriated by the Reich as an 'enemy of the state': see Doc. 274.

[33] For the discussion that took place in March 1933, see Doc. 8, 15 March 1933. See also the Law on the Revocation of Naturalization and the Deprivation of German Nationality, 14 July 1933: *Reichsgesetzblatt*, 1933, I, p. 480.

[34] See Doc. 8, 15 March 1933.

§ 21. No new naturalizations of stateless and foreign Jews are to occur.[35] Stateless and foreign Jews wishing to stay in Germany, insofar as this is not already denied them due to deportation, require the consent of the 'People's Warden'. Stateless Jews can only be granted a temporary residence permit. The residence permit of foreign Jews can be extended for six months at a time.

§ 22. The provisions of this law do not apply – with the following restrictions – to Jews, half-Jews, and Jew spouses as defined by §§ 1 to 3 of the law, who themselves and whose offspring have been recognized by the 'People's Warden' as fully legal German citizens.

Conditions for recognition are, in accordance with the provisions of implementation, outstanding service to the German people in times of war and peace and also that two German sponsors vouch for their German nature.

The maximum number of recognitions shall not exceed 8,000 altogether in the first two years after this law has entered into force and in subsequent years 50 per cent of the German excess of births over deaths.

Only the restrictions contained in § 11(a) and (b) apply to Jews recognized by the 'People's Warden' their offspring are also exempt from these restrictions.

DOC. 28

On 7 April 1933 the Reich Foreign Office opposes the granting of minority rights to Jews in Upper Silesia[1]

Memorandum, Reich Foreign Office, Berlin, Lieres,[2] dated 7 April 1933

A 'Jewish minority' is not recognized in Germany; nor has one been constituted for German Upper Silesia by the Geneva Convention. Article 66 of the Geneva Convention guarantees the protection of the ethnicity and religion of the inhabitants of the plebiscite territory, but does not grant any special minority rights[3] to the Jews in Western Upper Silesia.[4] The German regime will thus without further ado be able to reject any potential action by Mr Calonder[5] on the basis of Art. 585.[6]

Things are different with regard to the *Polish* minorities of Jewish faith in German Upper Silesia. However, since this could only apply to very isolated cases – the Prussian Ministry of the Interior is not aware of a single case of a member of the Polish minority

---

35 See the instructions of Reich Minister of the Interior Frick dated 15 March 1933, Doc. 8.

1 PA AA, R 83 033. This document has been translated from German.
2 Joachim Friedrich von Lieres und Wilkau (1886–1982), lawyer and economist; served in the Prussian judiciary from 1910; worked for the Reich Foreign Office from 1921; head of the Poland section of Department IV, 1933–1936; worked in the Political Department of the Reich Foreign Office, 1936–1938; after being sent into retirement worked as a farmer; in 1951 returned to the Foreign Office, including a period as head of the Restitution section in Department I (Personnel and Administration).
3 The Reich Foreign Office had to revise this view in the weeks that followed due to the stance of the League of Nations. The Council of the League of Nations regarded persecution of Jews in Upper Silesia as a violation of the status of minorities in accordance with the Geneva Convention on Upper Silesia of 15 May 1922, and discussed this publicly: see Doc. 46, 24 May 1933.

of Jewish faith – which Mr Calonder would be obliged to cite, his action appears unwarranted with respect to these persons as well.

Submitted herewith to Ministerial Director *Meyer*, with humble regards.[7]

DOC. 29
Law for the dismissal of Jewish and politically undesirable civil servants, 7 April 1933[1]

Law for the Restoration of the Professional Civil Service.[2]

7 April 1933.
The Reich government has passed the following law, which is hereby promulgated:[3]

§ 1

(1) For the purposes of restoring a national professional civil service and simplifying administration, civil servants can be dismissed from office in accordance with the following regulations, even if there are no grounds to do so under existing laws.

(2) Civil servants under the terms of this law are direct and indirect officials of the Reich, direct and indirect officials of the states, and officials of local governments and local government associations, officials of bodies governed by public law as well as institutions and enterprises of equal status (Third Regulation of the Reich President for the Security of the Economy and Finance dated 6 October 1931 – *Reichsgesetzblatt*, I, p. 537, part 3, chapter V, article I, § 15 (1)). The rules also apply to employees of social insurance providers who have the rights and duties of civil servants.

(3) Officials in temporary retirement also qualify as civil servants in accordance with this law.

---

4 The part of the plebiscite area of Upper Silesia that remained German after the partition between Germany and Poland in 1922.
5 Dr Felix Ludwig Calonder (1863–1952), lawyer; member of the Swiss Federal Council, 1913–1920; federal president of Switzerland, 1918; president of the German-Polish Conference on Upper Silesia from 1921 up to the treaty of 1922; chairman, 1922–1937, of the Joint Commission for Upper Silesia, which acted under a League of Nations mandate; afterwards employed in the private sector.
6 Article 585 of the Geneva Convention on Upper Silesia of 15 May 1922 granted the president of the Joint Commission for Upper Silesia the right to intervene with the responsible state representative in the event of a violation of the treaty. This representative was then obligated to inform his government: *Reichsgesetzblatt*, 1922, II, p. 519.
7 Richard Meyer (1883–1956), lawyer; served in the Prussian judiciary from 1906; worked at the Reich Foreign Office from 1913; member of the German delegation to the peace negotiations in Paris, 1919–1920; temporarily ambassador to Rome; head of Department IV of the Reich Foreign Office, 1931–1935; emigrated to Sweden in 1939.

1 *Reichsgesetzblatt*, 1933, I, pp. 175–177. This document has been translated from German.
2 *Gesetz zur Wiederherstellung des Berufsbeamtentums*. Acts to amend this law, also referred to as the Civil Service Law (*Berufsbeamtengesetz*), appeared on 23 June, 20 July, and 22 Sept. 1933 and on 22 March, 11 July, and 26 Sept. 1934, in addition to numerous implementing regulations: *Reichsgesetzblatt*, 1933, I, pp. 389, 518, and 655–656, and 1934, I, pp. 203, 604, and 845.
3 State Secretary Pfundtner announced on the radio on 13 April 1933 that the law would re-establish a 'national civil service' 'by ruthlessly purging' the public service of 'all alien elements': BArch, R 43 II/418a, fols. 17–18.

(4) The Reichsbank and the German Reich Railways are empowered to formulate corresponding directives.

§ 2

(1) Officials who entered the civil service after 9 November 1918 without possessing the required or usual prior training or other qualification for this career path are to be dismissed from service.[4] For a period of three months following dismissal, they are entitled to their previous remuneration.

(2) They shall have no claims to a temporary allowance, pension, or survivors' benefits and to the continuance of the official designation, title, uniform, and insignia.

(3) In case of need, especially if they are looking after destitute dependants, they may be granted a pension of up to one third of the respective basic salary of the post last held by them. This pension can be withdrawn at any time. There is no subsequent insurance in accordance with the social insurance under Reich law.

(4) The regulations of subsections 2 and 3 have corresponding application to persons as described in subsection 1 who entered retirement before this law came into effect.

§ 3

(1) Civil servants of non-Aryan descent are to be retired (§§ 8 ff.);[5] insofar as this concerns honorary officials, they are to be dismissed from service.[6]

(2) Subsection 1 does not apply to civil servants who have been officials since 1 August 1914 or who fought at the front during the World War for the German Reich or for its allies or whose fathers or sons were killed in the World War. Further exceptions may be permitted by the Reich Minister of the Interior in consultation with the appropriate Reich minister or by the supreme state authorities for civil servants abroad.

§ 4

Civil servants whose previous political activity provides no guarantee that they unreservedly support the national state at all times can be dismissed from service. For a three-month period following the dismissal, they will be paid their previous salary. Thereafter, they receive three-quarters of the pension (§ 8) and corresponding survivors' benefits.

§ 5

(1) Every civil servant must accept the transfer to another post of the same or an equivalent career path, including to a post of lower rank and scheduled salary – with

---

[4] To somewhat alleviate their position, dismissed officials obtained the right to give early notice on rented apartments that were no longer affordable: Law on the Termination of Rental Contracts by Persons Affected by the Law for the Restoration of the Professional Civil Service, 7 April 1933, *Reichsgesetzblatt*, 1933, I, pp. 187–188.

[5] This paragraph was subsequently applied in order to dismiss Jews not only in public administration but also in private organizations and associations.

[6] According to point 6 of the NSDAP manifesto from 24 Feb. 1920, 'every public office, regardless of what kind, whether of the Reich, state or municipality [is to] be held only by citizens': Hofer (ed.), *Der Nationalsozialismus: Dokumente*, p. 28.

remuneration of the standard removal expenses – if official needs so require. In the event of a transfer to a post of lower rank and expected salary, the official will retain the official title and salary of the previous post.

(2) The official can apply within one month to be retired instead of being transferred to a post of lower rank and scheduled salary (subsection 1).

§ 6

For the purposes of simplifying administration, civil servants can be retired, even if they remain fit for service. When officials are retired for this reason, they are not to be replaced.

§ 7

(1) The dismissal from a post, transfer to another office, or retirement is announced by the highest Reich or state authority, which ultimately renders a decision that is final and cannot be appealed.

(2) Decisions in accordance with §§ 2 to 6 must be served on 30 September 1933 at the latest. The time period can be shortened in consultation with the Reich Minister of the Interior, if the appropriate supreme Reich or state authority declares that the measures of this law have been implemented under its administration.

§ 8

Civil servants retired or dismissed in accordance with §§ 3 or 4 are not granted a pension unless they have completed at least a ten-year period of service; this also applies in cases where according to the existing regulations of the Reich and state legislation a pension is granted after a shorter period of service. §§ 36, 47, and 49 of the Reich Civil Service Law, the law of 4 July 1921 concerning an increased calculation for the service period accrued during the war (*Reichsgesetzblatt*, p. 825), and the corresponding regulations of the state laws remain unaffected.

§ 9

(1) For civil servants retired or dismissed in accordance with §§3 or 4, the calculation of the pensionable period of service, apart from the period of service that they have accrued in their last appointment, may only include one period in the service of the Reich, state, and local government according to the current regulations. The inclusion of this period of service is further only permissible if it is connected with the last post held according to prior training and career trajectory. Such a connection applies especially when the advancement of a civil servant from a lower career path to a higher one is to be regarded as due promotion. If the official would have obtained a higher pension in an earlier position duly obtained according to prior training and qualification with the later years of service being added, the more favourable arrangement applies to him.

(2) The calculation of the period of service in bodies governed by public law as well as institutions and enterprises of equal status is regulated by the implementation regulations.

(3) Stipulations and assurances concerning the pensionable period of service that impede the implementation of the regulations in subsection 1 cease to be valid.

(4) The Reich Minister of the Interior can, in consultation with the Reich Minister of Finance, offset hardship among civil servants of the Reich and bodies, institutions,

and enterprises governed by public law that are subject to Reich supervision. The supreme state authorities can offset hardship among other civil servants.

(5) Subsections 1 to 4 and § 8 also apply to officials who entered retirement or temporary retirement before this law came into effect and to whom §§ 2 to 4 could have been applied, had the officials still been in service when this law came into effect. The adjustment of the pensionable period of service and the pension or temporary allowance has to be made at the latest by 30 September 1933 with effect from 1 October 1933.

§ 10

(1) The guidelines used to establish for the salary level of civil servants are used as a basis for calculating the service remuneration and the pension. If decisions have not yet been made by the appropriate authorities concerning the application of the guidelines, they are to be issued promptly.

(2) If, according to the decision of the appropriate authorities concerning the application of the guidelines, civil servants have received higher remuneration than was due to them, they have to repay the additional sums received since 1 April 1932 to the fund from which the remuneration was granted. The objection that wealth is no longer accrued (§§ 812 ff. Civil Code) is excluded.

(3) Subsections 1 and 2 also apply to people who entered retirement within a year before this law came into force.

§ 11

(1) If employment outside the Reich, state, or local government service was included in determining a pay seniority level for civil servants who are discharged on the basis of §§ 3 or 4, then the pay seniority level is to be reassessed. Only work carried out in the Reich, state, or local government service or, in accordance with the implementation regulations, in the service of the bodies governed by public law as well as that of institutions and enterprises of equal status may be included. The Reich Minister of the Interior can, in consultation with the Reich Minister of Finance, allow exceptions, while the supreme state authorities can allow exceptions for other civil servants.

(2) If in accordance with subsection 1 a reassessment of the pay seniority level may be applicable, then in the case of those civil servants retired or dismissed according to §§ 3 or 4 the reassessment must be made when determining the pension.

(3) The same applies for the persons named in § 9 (5).

§ 12

(1) Those earnings of Reich ministers appointed since 9 November 1918 that are not calculated according to the regulations of §§ 16 to 24 of the Law on Reich Ministers from 27 March 1930 (*Reichsgesetzblatt*, I, p. 96) are to be adjusted. In making this adjustment, the named regulations of the Law on Reich Ministers are to be applied as if they had already been in force at the time when the Reich minister left office. Excess earnings received since 1 April 1932 are to be repaid accordingly. The objection that there is no longer personal gain (§§ 812 ff. Civil Code) is inadmissible.

(2) Paragraph 1 applies to members of a state government appointed since 9 November 1918 with the stipulation that the Law on Reich Ministers is replaced by the corresponding regulations of the state laws; however, earnings may only be paid up to the

level resulting from the application of the principles of §§ 16 to 24 of the Law on Reich Ministers.

(3) Adjustments to earnings are to be made by 31 December 1933.

(4) There will be no payments of arrears.

§ 13

The survivors' benefits are calculated in accordance with §§ 8 to 12.

§ 14

(1) The instigation of disciplinary proceedings against those civil servants retired or dismissed on the basis of this law remains permissible after their retirement or their dismissal on the grounds of misconduct during service with the aim of withdrawing the pension, survivors' benefits, title, uniform, and insignia. The instigation of disciplinary proceedings must take place on 31 December 1933 at the latest.

(2) Subsection 1 also applies to persons who retired within one year of this law coming into effect and to whom §§ 2 to 4 would have been applicable if these persons had still been in office when this law took effect.

§ 15

The rules concerning civil servants apply analogously to salaried employees and workers. The details are governed by the implementation regulations.

§ 16

Should undue hardship result from the implementation of this law, higher remuneration or temporary allowances can be granted in the framework of the general regulations. With regard to Reich officials, this decision is taken by the Reich Minister of the Interior in consultation with the Reich Minister of Finance, otherwise by the supreme state authorities.

§ 17

(1) The Reich Minister of the Interior issues in consultation with the Reich Minister of Finance the legal regulations and general administrative provisions necessary for implementing and executing this law.[7]

(2) If necessary, the supreme state authorities issue supplementary provisions. In so doing, they are to remain within the framework of the Reich regulations.

§ 18

Upon expiry of the deadlines fixed in this law, notwithstanding the measures formulated on the basis of this law, the general regulations applying to civil servants regain full validity.

---

[7] See the Implementing Regulation to the Law for the Restoration of the Professional Civil Service with the Aryan Paragraph, 11 April 1933, Doc. 32.

Berlin, 7 April 1933.
Reich Chancellor
Adolf Hitler
Reich Minister of the Interior
Frick
Reich Minister of Finance
Count Schwerin von Krosigk[8]

DOC. 30
On 8 April 1933 Cardinal Faulhaber writes to Alois Wurm about the latter's protest against the persecution of Jews[1]

Letter from Monsignor Cardinal Faulhaber,[2] Munich, to Reverend Alois Wurm,[3] Munich, 81 Königinstraße, dated 8 April 1933 (carbon copy with handwritten signature)[4]

Esteemed Doctor,

You should have directed your epistle about the current miserable state of the press to another address. The enclosed newspaper article, which I am returning, would have been well received if you had signed it with your name and thus assumed full responsibility.[5] I suppose that in the next issue of *Seele*[6] an ardent protest against the persecution of the Jews will appear in your name,[7] and the courage of the press would grow even stronger if there were a single person who had the courage to protest by having a leaflet printed in his name and circulating it on the streets.

These actions against the Jews are so very unchristian that every Christian, not merely every cleric, ought to speak out against them. For the higher Church authorities, [however,] there are far more important questions of our time; because schooling, the contin-

---

8 Count Johann Ludwig (Lutz) Schwerin von Krosigk (1887–1977), lawyer in the Prussian civil service from 1909; worked at the Reich Ministry of Finance from 1920, and headed that ministry's Budget Department from 1929; Reich minister of finance, 1932–1945; interned, 1945; sentenced to ten years' imprisonment in the Ministries (Wilhelmstrasse) Trial in Nuremberg, 1949; released in 1951.

1 Erzbischöfliches Archiv München, NL Faulhaber 8422. Published in Ludwig Volk (ed.), *Akten Kardinal Michael von Faulhabers*, vol. 1 (Mainz: Matthias Grünewald, 1975), p. 705. This document has been translated from German.

2 Michael von Faulhaber (1869–1952), Catholic theologian; professor of the Old Testament at Strasbourg University, 1903; bishop of Speyer, 1910; archbishop, 1917, and cardinal archbishop, 1921–1952, of Munich and Freising.

3 Dr Alois Wurm (1874–1968), Catholic theologian; founder and editor of the magazine *Seele*, 1919.

4 This is the response to a letter from Wurm: see Wurm's letter to Faulhaber, dated 5 April 1933, in Volk (ed.), *Akten Kardinal Michael von Faulhabers*, vol. 1, pp. 701–702.

5 Wurm had tried in vain to publish a critical article on the anti-Jewish boycott in a major (unidentified) Catholic newspaper. In his letter to Faulhaber he had complained that no Catholic newspaper had yet taken a stand against the persecution of the Jews; the 'Catholic people' thus remained 'without Catholic guidance' in the matter, which struck 'very many people as a Catholic failure': ibid.

6 The magazine *Seele* was published with the subtitle 'Monatsschrift im Dienste christlicher Lebensgestaltung' ('Monthly Journal in the Service of a Christian Lifestyle'), in Regensburg from 1919–1939.

ued existence of the Catholic associations, and sterilization[8] are even more important issues for Christianity in our homeland, especially as we may assume, and to some extent have already seen, that the Jews can help themselves and we therefore have no cause to give the government a reason to turn the Jew-baiting into Jesuit-baiting. I am receiving enquiries from various sides as to why the Church does not do anything to oppose the persecution of the Jews. I am rather taken aback by this, given that no one asked what could be done against agitation directed at Catholics or at the bishop. That is and remains the mystery of the Passion.

With devoted regards[9]

DOC. 31

On 10 April 1933 the Regional Contract Office for the State of Saxony proposes that Jewish firms no longer be permitted to supply the army, navy, or police[1]

Letter from the Regional Contract Office for the State of Saxony, signed p.p. (no signature), Dresden, to the Compensation Office of the States,[2] Berlin, dated 10 April 1933 (copy)[3]

A firm in our district has forwarded to us the following letter, which we hereby bring to your attention:

> Returning to the telephone conversation just conducted with your Mr Gärtner, may I inform you once again that the Liaison Staff of the NSDAP Reichsleitung in Berlin, following the customary negotiations with us, is contemplating the following directives:

---

[7] Alois Wurm subsequently published an article in his name, in which he clearly stated that every 'Christian [should] also embrace non-Christians and thus the Jews as well with true good will': God did not love that people the most who placed itself above others as the 'master race', but rather the people who most purely realized the 'concepts of justice and love': 'Christliche Gedanken zum nationalen Problem', Seele, vol. 15, no. 5 (1933), pp. 137–138.

[8] This refers to the preliminary discussions on the Law for the Prevention of Offspring with Hereditary Diseases, enacted on 14 July 1933: Reichsgesetzblatt, 1933, I, pp. 529–530.

[9] Wurm replied to Faulhaber on 9 April 1933 to the effect that an article in a major newspaper or a press reception given by a Church leader to establish a clear position on the part of the Church would suffice. His article had previously been rejected, he wrote, because the boycott was already over. Yet the article would certainly be published if Faulhaber were to give it his support: Volk (ed.), Akten Kardinal Michael von Faulhabers, vol. 1, pp. 706–707.

[1] BayHStA, MWi/6730, fols. 1–2. This document has been translated from German.

[2] The Compensation Office of the States (Ausgleichsstelle der Länder), in which the German state governments were represented, was established after the 1921 Military Service Act to regulate military procurement and delivery in order to ensure that the economic burden was shared between the states.

[3] On 11 April 1933 the Compensation Office of the States forwarded the letter printed here to the members of its management committee with the note that negotiations had taken place with the Reich Ministry of Finance concerning the exclusion of Jewish firms, and that the Reich Ministry of Finance would soon put forward uniform guidelines. Regardless of this, the letter continued, regional contract agencies should issue provisional guidelines 'as soon as possible': circular letter from the Compensation Office of the States, dated 11 April 1933: BayHStA, MWi/6730, fols. 3–4.

(1) Removal of all Jewish firms from the supplier lists of the Central Procurement Agency for the Army and the Navy, Berlin NW 40, 57 Lehrterstraße.

(2) The same applies to the supplier lists of the police administrations as well as state and municipal procurement offices.

(3) Access to the Central Procurement Agency in Berlin, the army uniform offices, and the police administration offices is prohibited to all Jewish representatives and suppliers.

(4) All officials of the aforementioned contract-awarding agencies are forbidden to allocate contracts to Jewish firms or to receive Jewish representatives in an official or an unofficial capacity.

(5) The Compensation Office of the States (regional contract offices) is to immediately notify the Central Procurement Agency for the Army and the Navy in Berlin and the police procurement agencies in their respective state of those Jewish firms in their state who have until now been invited to submit tenders and those supplier firms that have utilized Jewish representatives, directors, or salaried employees in contract negotiations.

In our opinion, the implementation of this directive would not only be an act of justice towards the old, tried-and-tested non-Jewish supplier firms but also make a fundamental contribution to restoring an untainted tendering business and preventing corruption scandals such as those related to the governing bailiff Schaale of the Dresden police.

The Economic Policy Department of the NSDAP Gauleitung just called us, and we recommended that they settle urgent matters directly with you as the regional contract office, namely via the Liaison Staff of the NSDAP Gauleitung, Dresden A1, 60 Grunaerstraße.

In so doing, we assume that we have acted in accordance with your wishes and we have explained that you welcome the aforementioned directive.

It is of the utmost importance to us that the regional contract offices in particular should gain more influence than hitherto over the contract-awarding agencies and that they are also granted above all greater controlling power.

We consider it appropriate that this matter is also taken care of by way of a proper discussion with the appropriate agencies, and we therefore request that those agencies make contact with the procurement agencies or with the Liaison Staff of the NSDAP Reichsleitung. We do not consider it possible for the regional contract agencies to be informed about the matter by individual firms.[4]

It is essential that it is also properly clarified what is meant by Jewish firms in view of the above statements made by the firm.

---

4 The Bavarian Regional Contract Agency also received similar demands from interested firms. The Reich Railways and the Reich Postal Service were already exercising 'restraint' in Bavaria vis-à-vis Jewish firms: memorandum of the Bavarian Regional Contract Agency from 27 April 1933, ibid., fol. 4.

DOC. 32

The Aryan Paragraph introduces the first legal definition of the term 'non-Aryan', 11 April 1933[1]

First Regulation on the Implementation of the Law for the Restoration of the Professional Civil Service.

11 April 1933.
Pursuant to § 17 of the Law for the Restoration of the Professional Civil Service dated 7 April 1933 (*Reichsgesetzblatt*, I, p. 175), the following is decreed:

Concerning § 2
1.
All civil servants who belong to the Communist Party or communist auxiliary or front organizations are unsuitable. They are therefore to be dismissed.

Concerning § 3
2.
(1) Any person descended from non-Aryan, especially Jewish, parents or grandparents is to be regarded as non-Aryan. It suffices if one parent or one grandparent is not Aryan. This is to be assumed particularly in the event that one parent or one grandparent was a member of the Jewish faith.[2]

(2) If a civil servant did not yet hold office as of 1 August 1914, he has to prove that he is of Aryan descent or a combat veteran, or the son or father of someone killed in action during the World War. The proof is to be adduced by the presentation of documents (parents' birth and marriage certificates, military papers).

(3) Should Aryan descent be questionable, an assessment is to be sought from the expert on racial research appointed by the Reich Ministry of the Interior.

Concerning § 4
3.
(1) In examining whether the conditions of § 4 sentence 1 are fulfilled, the civil servant's entire political activity, in particular since 9 November 1918, is to be taken into consideration.

(2) Every civil servant is obliged upon request to provide information to the highest Reich or state authority (§ 7) concerning the political parties to which he has previously

---

[1] 'Erste Verordnung zur Durchführung des Gesetzes zur Wiederherstellung des Berufsbeamtentums', *Reichsgesetzblatt*, 1933, I, p. 195. This document has been translated from German.
[2] This definition of the term 'Jew' was moderated by the First Regulation to the Reich Citizenship Law, according to which only a person 'who is descended from at least three grandparents who are full Jews by race' was considered to be a Jew: see Doc. 210, 14 Nov. 1935.

belonged. The Reich Banner Black-Red-Gold,[3] the Republican Association of Judges, and the League for Human Rights also qualify as political parties under this provision.

4.

All negotiations, documents, and official certificates required for the implementation of this law are free of charge and exempt from stamp duty.

Berlin, 11 April 1933.
Reich Minister of the Interior
Frick
Reich Minister of Finance
Count Schwerin von Krosigk

DOC. 33

The business representative Walter Hoffmann writes to Göring on 12 April 1933 to intervene following press reports in the USA concerning acts of violence on the day of the boycott[1]

Letter from Walter Hoffmann, New York, representative of Siemssen & Co. China Furs,[2] Shanghai, Tianjin (China), to Reich Minister Göring, dated 12 April 1933[3]

Dear Reich Minister,

I have taken the liberty of sending you the latest pictures from the New York newspaper *Daily News*. If these pictures are genuine one should feel ashamed to have once been a German and to have sacrificed four years of one's life on the battlefield. The damage being done to us here cannot yet be assessed. However, should these pictures be forged, then vigorous action should be taken against them. Far be it for me to criticize Germany in any way, for my former fatherland will have cause to take vigorous action, but ugly outrages such as those depicted should be resolutely avoided if Germany is interested in continuing to trade with the rest of the world.

Respectfully

---

[3] Formed by members of the Social Democratic Party of Germany (SPD), the German Catholic Centre Party, and the German Democratic Party (DDP) in 1924, the Reich Banner Black-Red-Gold derived its name from the German flag adopted in 1919, the colours of which were associated with liberal parliamentary democracy and the Weimar Republic. It came to be strongly associated with the SPD and to be viewed as its paramilitary force. It was banned throughout the Reich in March 1933.

[1] GStA PK, I HA, Rep. 90 B/30, fols. 1–3. This document has been translated from German.
[2] Siemssen & Co.: a German firm founded in 1848 in Canton, China.
[3] Enclosed with the letter were some photographs from the *Daily News* from 12 April 1933: two large photos on the front page show Jews in Chemnitz being forced to wash down the walls of a house, and a man being driven through the streets in a rubbish cart because he had refused to be humiliated in this way. In another photograph from the same issue, SA guards stand in front of a Berlin shop with the word 'Jew' smeared on its windows: ibid.

DOC. 34

On 15 April 1933 Karl Jarres writes to Theodor Lewald following the latter's resignation as president of the German Reich Committee for Physical Exercise[1]

Letter from Karl Jarres,[2] Duisburg-Hamborn, to retired State Secretary Dr Lewald,[3] Berlin W 10, 58 Kaiserin-Augusta-Straße, dated 15 April 1933 (draft, issued on 15 April 1933)

Esteemed Excellency,

Aside from the tribute paid to you, the last meeting of the Reich Committee[4] took an extremely disagreeable course. It would in fact have been better if the meeting of this large parliament, which entails substantial costs for the associations and federations already experiencing severe difficulties, had not taken place at this time. It was also highly unfortunate that we did not have authorization to communicate at the meeting the Reich government's secretly conveyed wish to refrain from any new elections, in particular the election of a new chairman. It was not until Mr Linnemann[5] belatedly obtained this authorization at my behest, and we were entitled to communicate this wish, that things calmed down, albeit far too late. My proposal to authorize some of the board members to hold negotiations with the Reich government in the presence of an NSDAP representative was accepted outright and evidently with a sense of relief. Personally, as will become known to you and as I hope you will understand, I suggested President Pauli[6]

---

1 Stadtarchiv Duisburg, 150/72. This document has been translated from German.
2 Dr Karl Rudolf Jarres (1874–1951), lawyer and politician; worked in municipal administrations from 1901; mayor of Duisburg, 1914–1923 and 1925–1933; Reich minister of the interior and vice chancellor, 1923–1925; member of the German People's Party (DVP); first deputy chairman of the German Reich Committee for Physical Exercise; committee member of various firms following his removal from office in 1933; chairman of the board of directors at Klöckner-Werke AG, 1942–1951.
3 Theodor Otto F. Lewald (1860–1947), civil servant and sports official; worked at the Reich Office (from 1919 Reich Ministry) of the Interior, 1891–1921; first chairman of the German Reich Committee for Physical Exercise, 1919–1933; from 1924 Germany's representative on the International Olympic Committee; in 1932 president of the organizing committee for the 1936 Olympic Games.
4 At the end of the Weimar Republic, the German Reich Committee for Physical Exercise, founded in 1917, comprised 38 gymnastics and sports associations with about 7 million members. On 25 March 1933 the Reich Committee's board members addressed a declaration of loyalty to the National Socialist government. In agreement with State Secretary Lammers (head of the Reich Chancellery) and State Secretary Pfundtner (Reich Ministry of the Interior) they convened an extraordinary general meeting of the Reich Committee for 12 April 1933 to discuss the 'incorporation' of the federation into the 'new Germany'. After anti-Jewish heckling, Lewald announced his resignation as chairman, at which point Jarres took over the chairmanship of the meeting. After Lewald was given an honourable farewell, the vote on the non-Aryans addressed here was taken. In May 1933 the Reich Sports Leader announced the dissolution of the Reich Committee, and in 1934 the German Reich League for Physical Exercise was founded to replace it.
5 Felix Linnemann (1882–1948), police officer; vice president, from 1919, and president, 1925–1945, of the German Football Association; also the second Reich Committee chairman; chief of the Criminal Police in Stettin, 1937–1939, and in Hanover, 1939–1945; joined the SS in 1940; interned in 1945.
6 Dr Heinrich Pauli (1874–1953), lawyer; from 1900 worked in the administration in Alsace; Regierungspräsident in Potsdam from 1920; from 1927 to 1936 president of the German Rowing Association, founded in 1883; head of the rowing section of the Reich League for Physical Exercise, 1936–1945.

as a representative, a proposal that was also gladly approved.[7] With the heavy demands made on me here, it is impossible for me to take part in these negotiations, which will probably take up a great deal of time. Besides, President Pauli is much better informed about the situation. He also deftly represented the matter of the associations at the turbulent meeting, something the other board representatives unfortunately failed to do.

To my regret, my proposal, which I discussed before the meeting with the appropriate gentlemen, namely to communicate at the meeting that the entire board will vacate its functions at the next general meeting, was not approved. I remain convinced that such a declaration would have eased the situation considerably.

Especially distressing was the majority wish to take a vote on the attendance rights of the not fully Aryan representatives.[8] I could not easily evade this request in the tumultuous form in which it was made, although in hindsight even an elusive last attempt seems possible. I deeply regretted this decision and am still very despondent about it today.

After the meeting I tried in vain to reach you at your apartment and at the Reich Committee offices. I would have dearly liked to discuss matters further with you and to have shaken your hand as a sign of my lasting high esteem. As this was not possible, I am making up for this today in writing. It was not only a matter close to my heart but also a special honour to express to you the Reich Committee's thanks and recognition after your masterful leadership and management over many years. The tumultuous applause that lasted several minutes served to show how these thanks and this recognition were in fact felt by the entire Reich Committee. This must, esteemed Excellency, provide some satisfaction for you amid all the unpleasantness that this time also brings you. Allow me once more to also express personally to you today my fervent thanks and my sincerest high esteem. In the history of German sport and German physical exercise, the name 'Lewald' will never be forgotten. I convey this to you with particular emotion in view of the fact that my modest participation in the Reich Committee's work and the general running of German sport is also probably no longer desired and is thus coming to an end. It was always a great pleasure for me to work with you.

With warm and respectful wishes I remain

Ever yours

[...][9]

---

[7] In addition to Pauli, both Linnemann and Edmund Neuendorff of the German Gymnastics Association were members of the delegation sent to the negotiations. On Neuendorff, see Doc. 61, 1 July 1933, and Doc. 80, 23 Sept. 1933.

[8] The meeting had been announced in the German Football League's publication *Der Kicker*. In addition to this notification, there appeared a declaration by the Southern German Football and Athletics Associations, including the Stuttgart Kickers, Bayern Munich, 1860 Munich, and Eintracht Frankfurt. According to a resolution from 9 April 1933, they were willing to collaborate with the 'national uprising' and in the course of 'this collaboration to draw all conclusions, especially in the question of removing Jews from sports associations': *Der Kicker: Mitteldeutschland*, no. 15, 11 April 1933, p. 56.

[9] The original also contains the following: '(2) To be filed. Reich Committee'.

DOC. 35

On 16 April 1933 Hertha Nathorff records her impressions of a meeting of the League of German Female Physicians in Berlin[1]

Diary of Hertha Nathorff,[2] entry for 16 April 1933 (typescript 1940)[3]

16 April 1933. Meeting of the League of German Female Physicians[4] – As I regularly do, I went over there today, since the most highly regarded and best-known colleagues in Berlin always met here. 'Funny mood today,' I thought, and so many strange faces. A colleague I didn't know said to me 'Surely you also belong to us?' and showed me the swastika on her coat collar. Before I could answer, she got up and fetched a gentleman to our meeting who said that he was obliged to demand the Gleichschaltung of the league in the name of the government. 'Gleichschaltung.' Another colleague – I know her; she was my predecessor at the Red Cross and at the time held rather left-wing views (she had in her time been discharged on grounds of ineptitude and other less than fine human qualities) – she stood up and said, 'I'd now like to invite the German colleagues into the room next door for a discussion –'. Our colleague S., a good Catholic, stood up and asked: 'What does that mean – the German colleagues?' – 'All those who are not Jews of course' was the answer. That's how it was said. Without a word we Jewish and half-Jewish physicians stood up, and with us some 'German' physicians – silently we left the room, pale, and deeply outraged. We then went to our colleague Erna B. to discuss what we should do. 'Unanimously announce that we're leaving the league,' said some. I am against this – I would happily allow them the honour of throwing us out, but I wouldn't willingly surrender my claim to membership. Now I want to see what will happen next. – I'm so distressed, so sad and despondent, and I'm ashamed for my 'German' colleagues!

1 Hertha Nathorff, 'Tagebuch 30.1.1933 – 9.5.1965', p. 12, ZfA, Lebensgeschichtliche Sammlung, Hertha Nathorff. Published in Hertha Nathorff, *Das Tagebuch der Hertha Nathorff: Berlin–New York. Aufzeichnungen 1933 bis 1945*, ed. Wolfgang Benz (Frankfurt am Main: Fischer, 1988), p. 40. This document has been translated from German.
2 Dr Hertha Nathorff (1895–1993), physician and psychotherapist; chief physician at the German Red Cross home for women and children in Berlin-Lichtenberg, 1922–1928; had her own practice in Berlin, 1923–1938; head of the first women's and families' advisory centre in Berlin, 1922–1933; board member of the Berlin Chamber of Physicians; emigrated in 1939 to Britain and in 1940 to the USA, where she worked as a psychotherapist from 1954.
3 Since parts of the original diary went missing during her emigration from Germany, Hertha Nathorff reconstructed it on the basis of salvaged notes and from memory. She submitted the typescript of the years 1933–1939 to Harvard University in 1940 for the competition 'Mein Leben in Deutschland vor und nach dem 30. Januar 1933' [My life in Germany before and after 30 January 1933].
4 The League of German Female Physicians was founded in 1924. Jewish colleagues were excluded in 1933, and the league was dissolved in 1936.

DOC. 36
Jüdische Rundschau, 25 April 1933: article on the suicide of a Jew with German nationalist convictions[1]

Personal tragedy

We received correspondence from Stuttgart: of the cases that reveal how current events are driving Jewish people to take their own lives,[2] there is one from *Stuttgart* worth mentioning given its accompanying circumstances. A young retailer, 31 years of age,[3] an enthusiastic supporter of German gymnastics and sport and squad leader of a gymnastics association, living a settled life, has shot himself dead. Among his papers was a marked news item on the decision by the German Gymnastics Association to introduce the Aryan Paragraph,[4] as well as the following letter addressed to his friends.

> My dear friends,
> I'm bidding you a final farewell! A *German* Jew could not bring himself to live with the awareness that he is regarded as a traitor to the fatherland by the movement by which nationalist Germany is hoping to be saved! I go without hatred or resentment. I cherish a deep wish – may reason soon call a halt to this! And because, until such a point, I am unable to do anything at all based on my way of thinking, I am attempting by virtue of my suicide to shake up my Christian friends. You might be able to recognize from this step I am taking how things look now for us German Jews. How much more gladly would I have given up my life for my fatherland! Do not mourn, but try to raise awareness of the situation, and help the truth to prevail.
> In that way you will do me the greatest honour!
> Your F...[5]

This case and this letter typify a phenomenon repeatedly observed during these days: in these times of severe turmoil, the Jew whose life revolves around the fact that he has *switched off* his Jewishness is more defenceless than someone who is somehow metaphysically bound to Judaism, whether by faith or by blood. F. wanted to die as a witness to his Germandom, but through his death he has, beyond his knowledge and wishes, also become a witness to the cause of Judaism.[6]

---

1 'Persönliche Tragödie', *Jüdische Rundschau*, 25 April 1933, p. 163. This document has been translated from German.
2 On the increase in suicides among German Jews, see Doc. 41, 9 May 1933.
3 Fritz Rosenfelder (1901–1933), retailer; partner in the firm Moritz Rosenfelder, 1932; sports coach of the gymnastics league in Bad Cannstatt.
4 On 8/9 April 1933 the main committee of the German Gymnastics Association voted to introduce the Aryan Paragraph. On the events in the German Gymnastics Association, see Doc. 61, 1 July 1933, and Doc. 80, 23 Sept. 1933.
5 Footnote in the original: 'At the request of the family, the name is to remain anonymous.'
6 *Der Stürmer* printed the suicide note on its front page under the heading 'Der tote Jude' ('The Dead Jew'), gave his full name, and commented on the suicide with the caption 'Fritz Rosenfelder is sensible and hangs himself': *Der Stürmer*, no. 30, July 1933, pp. 1–2.

DOC. 37

On 26 April 1933 Charlotte Gumpert informs Minni Steinhardt in Palestine about the political situation in Germany and conditions for emigrants[1]

Handwritten letter from Charlotte Gumpert,[2] Orselina-Locarno, to Minni Steinhardt,[3] Tel Aviv, dated 26 April 1933

Dear Minni, *answered*[4]

Thank you very much for your letter; it gave me great pleasure. If truth be told, it even moved me to tears in places. I'm terribly pleased that you are as far along as you are, and it went quickly enough. Although I'm firmly convinced that many more difficulties are to come (for example I'm sure the unusual summer heat will dish out its fair share), I nonetheless remain firmly convinced that it will certainly not become any more difficult or more unpleasant than in Berlin, but better. The time will come when we will all have cause to be grateful to Messrs Hitler, Göring and comrades!

I would now very much like to know, above all, whether you're getting your naturalization or settlement, or whatever it's called, for that is after all a very important point and also very urgent, as the demand will become very intense and entry will be restricted. I do find it sad that you're leaving most of your things behind, but after all it's probably sensible; only I would still be *sure to have the silver and linen* sent on with Jaques's[5] pictures. Many people are now coming over who could surely bring it to you. Aunt Martha can certainly take care of that. It is also a pity about the sideboard. Should you not try to sell it cheaply? It is what it is. Besides, I don't know whether you've used up all the money in your bank account. If not, have some money sent to you immediately. One is allowed to send 700 marks per passport every month. You must send the passport to Aunt Martha or the bank; the bank and any travel agent (Kurfürstendamm) can deal with the formalities. But I have no idea if you still have anything left.

Now to us. Martin[6] is doing very well. He is with Mrs von M. in Ascona and comes over every other day. He looks well but of course inwardly he cannot find peace. But despite that, he is finding the atmosphere of political freedom, the heavenly weather, and the beautiful scenery a great blessing. Nothing in the least has happened to him personally, and [his work in] Wedding was terminated only as of 1 July, but he says he

---

1 Jüdisches Museum Berlin, DOCS-95-27-613, fols. 1 4. This letter has been translated from German.
2 Charlotte Gumpert, née Blaschko (1898–1933), physician; married Martin Gumpert in 1923.
3 Minni Steinhardt (b. 1895), Martin Gumpert's sister; from 1922 she was married to Jacob Steinhardt (1887–1968), an artist of Polish descent who was a member of the group of artists in Berlin known as the Neue Secession. In 1933 the married couple emigrated to Palestine with their daughter Josefa (b. 1923). In Jerusalem, Jacob Steinhardt founded an art school in 1934, which he closed in 1948, after which he worked at the Bezalel Academy of Arts and Design, and was its director from 1954 to 1957.
4 Handwritten note by the recipient.
5 The author means Jacob Steinhardt.
6 Dr Martin Gumpert (1897–1955), dermatologist; head of the municipal outpatient clinic for sexually transmitted diseases in the Berlin district of Wedding, 1928–1933; he emigrated to the USA in 1936 and worked there as a doctor and a writer; author of medical history studies and poems, and of the autobiographical novel *Hölle im Paradies: Selbstdarstellung eines Arztes* [Hell in Paradise: Self-Portrayal of a Physician] (1939).

could no longer psychologically tolerate it. One cannot picture this after twenty-four hours in Switzerland. He'll stay here for about a couple of weeks and then go to Paris to look around for some potential opportunities there. It's impossible to settle in Switzerland as a physician. In France it's permitted; you just have to take the exam again! How is it in Palestine? A friend of Hermann's[7] wants to go there, but he's being advised against it by all his medical acquaintances because it is said to be inundated with physicians! Is that true? What about dermatology? Beauty care? Also, Martin had just developed a new, sensational, apparently highly effective treatment for gonorrhoea. Another *very nice* friend of Hermann's should have just arrived in Tel Aviv. I would like *to warmly recommend* him to you (especially in the event of any illness). He is called Nachmannsohn,[8] is a very clever fellow, an internist, Lichtwitz's assistant,[9] a wonderful soul (!); he already has a post in Tel Aviv at an outpatient clinic. So ask after him. His wife, who was very close friends in Hamburg with the Seikels (the poor things in Cologne!), is following with, I hear, a sweet baby in the autumn.

I'm still lying in bed and am starting to get rather impatient. Mother,[10] Nina,[11] and Miss Dora are living just below the sanatorium in a tiny boarding house; Nina is very happy. Otti and Helo Aarons have indeed gone to Zurich, but she quickly recovered her spirits. Hermann is convalescing here and is going to England at the end of May. He says to send you his best wishes and to tell Josepha that Joseph was also a very pious man! Unfortunately, we hear very little from the Seikels. They are undoubtedly very depressed and don't trust themselves to write. – On the whole the conditions in Germany are not quite as bad as you imagine over there. The mood is terrible of course and countless lives – not only Jewish ones – are being ruined, for the time being, however, Jews and among them mainly intellectuals. But it is calm, nothing is happening to anyone and after all it is a revolution. No one in my entire extended family seems to think of leaving apart from us. And in fact Martin for example would probably not have even had his statutory health insurance patients taken away because he was at the epidemic hospital. He would only have lost Wedding. But the mood is dreadful in fact, and imagine for example Nina hadn't been allowed to go to school! With the Ullsteins nothing has changed for the moment (!), not even any dismissals worth mentioning, but that is probably still to come.[12] In general it is relatively peaceful and I advise you to take the news-

---

7 Dr Hermann Karl Felix Blaschko (1900–1993), biochemist; did research under the supervision of Otto Meyerhof in the physiology department at the Kaiser Wilhelm Institute for Medical Research in Heidelberg, 1925–1932; emigrated in 1933 to Britain, where he worked at various universities.
8 Correctly: Dr David Nachmansohn (1899–1983), biochemist; worked with Blaschko at the Kaiser Wilhelm Institute in Heidelberg, 1926–1930; assistant then head of the chemistry laboratory at the Rudolf Virchow Hospital in Berlin, 1931–1933; emigrated to Palestine in 1933, then to France, and in 1938 to the USA, where he held professorships at universities including Yale.
9 Dr Leopold Lichtwitz (1876–1943), physician; director of the Rudolf Virchow Hospital in Berlin, 1931–1933; emigrated to the USA in 1933.
10 Johanna Blaschko, née Littauer (1873–1942); emigrated to Britain in 1939.
11 Daughter of Charlotte and Martin Gumpert.
12 The Ullstein publishing house in Berlin was founded in 1877. The major newspaper publisher was owned by a Jewish family and was Aryanized in 1934 by the NSDAP publisher Franz Eher Nachfolger in Munich, with Party and government playing an influential role. It was then renamed the Deutscher Verlag KG. The takeover was financed with public funds and organized by Deutsche Bank: Harold James, *The Deutsche Bank and the Nazi Economic War against the Jews: The Expropriation of Jewish-Owned Property* (Cambridge: Cambridge University Press, 2001), pp. 48–49.

paper reports and stories from people arriving with a pinch of salt and not to spread them around. It must always be kept in mind that one can do enormous damage to those remaining (and that is the vast majority)! And in reality it is also not as bad as it sounds to you, but exaggerated by the agitation of the many emigrants meeting each other! That was really my first impression from your letter and I really want to reassure you, also on account of Jak's sisters. Of course it is right that they're also going to Palestine and in your place I would try as quickly as possible to help them obtain a work permit for commercial activity, but I hardly think that there is any kind of immediate danger. Germany has politically isolated itself and made a fool of itself to such an extent that all efforts will now be made to maintain peace and order. Peritz[13] writes today from Joachimsthalerstraße that everything is taking its course and she seems to be very optimistic, even for her. Whether she is right remains to be seen. Eva Rothmann[14] was here for a few days, and extremely upset.[15] She doesn't want to go back and finds this difficult having just settled in. She and the good man have left for Rome, but she is coming back here in a fortnight and doesn't yet know what she will do then. – As I write, I keep hearing in the distance Nina's little voice from the garden across the street, where she is playing, which is a very pleasant bonus. For this too I am grateful to Mr Hitler! So write soon (to this same address) and best wishes for your move into the new apartment! And send some photographs! The more in detail you write, the happier I am. *Everything* interests me.

My warmest regards

Lotte

Have you looked up or rung Dora Zuckermann at all? Be sure to do so! She'll be able to help you, given her many connections. Ask around for her.

I am really moved that I can already write a proper address on the envelope and, what is more, your own! What does your apartment cost? Is life expensive there?

---

13 Dr Edith Peritz, physician; general practitioner in Berlin from 1928; elected to the Chamber of Physicians in 1931; chairwoman of the regional branch in Berlin Brandenburg; in 1933 her licence to treat statutory health insurance patients was revoked; she emigrated in 1936 to the USA and worked as a physician in New York. She was married to Dr Georg Peritz (1870–1936?), a neurologist and professor at Berlin University.

14 Dr Eva Rothmann (1897–1960), psychologist; received her doctorate in 1925 from the Psychological Institute at Frankfurt University; later worked as a neurologist with her own practice in Berlin; she emigrated in 1933 to Switzerland, then in 1935 to the USA, where she took her own life after long-term depression.

15 On 1 April 1933 the SA had stormed the hospital in the Berlin district of Moabit and taken Eva Rothmann's husband, Kurt Goldstein, prisoner. He was released on condition that he would permanently leave the country. The couple immediately fled to Switzerland and later emigrated to the USA. Dr Kurt Goldstein (1878–1965), physician; member of the Social Democratic Party of Germany (SPD); professor in Frankfurt am Main, 1918; director of the neurological department at Moabit hospital, 1930–1933; professor of neurology at Tufts Medical College, 1940–1945; afterwards practised privately and worked as a lecturer.

DOC. 38
Otto Marx reports on his arrest in Weiden and his imprisonment in Dachau concentration camp in March/April 1933[1]

Submission by Otto Marx[2] to a Harvard University competition (1940)

[...][3]

In 1914 I opened a menswear shop in Weiden, which provided a good living for my family and me. My wife and I came from long-established Jewish retailers' families whose ancestors had lived in Germany for around 300 years. We had loyal and devoted customers consisting mainly of labourers and farmers. The population in Weiden and the surrounding area was mainly Catholic, very pious and diligent churchgoers. In Weiden there are some large, important porcelain and glass factories, and also a textile shipping house, which alone employed 4,500 people. Unemployment was low in Weiden because of these factories. People had work and money and did not worry much about politics. Passions flared up somewhat whenever an election was called. The Catholic population were mainly in the Bavarian People's Party and the workers in the Social Democratic Party. There was also a Nazi Party there, but its membership was very small; its leader was a failed haulage contractor, a fanatical National Socialist, and a Jew-hater. This Nazi Party also often held meetings, had all kinds of outrageous speakers come from other places, who tried to incite people with antisemitic speeches in order to gain new supporters. The latter were to be found, and were mainly adventurers, people with failed lives and the dissatisfied, who were promised a better life if the Nazi Party came to power. In the circles we moved in, we noticed very little of that. We belonged to some associations and could go to restaurants, the cinema, and the theatre without being harassed or insulted by anyone. Our customers included intellectuals, senior teachers from academic secondary schools, and officials from the local and regional courts as well as the tax office. These people also socialized with us privately on most friendly terms and never noticed that we were Jews. I myself was friends for years with an official from the tax office and this was never overshadowed in any way by religious differences. The labourers and farmers among our customers were always nice and friendly to us and supported us in every way. But this all changed when Hitler came to power.

On 23 March 1933 police and SS entered my shop to conduct a search. They searched the entire premises, including all the books and anything that was not nailed down. When the search in the shop was over, they told me to come with them into the apartment on the second floor of the house. Here the same spectacle was repeated. They ransacked the entire apartment and turned everything upside down. The only thing they found was a membership card for the Democratic Party, of which I was a member. My wife had brought various silver items and sets of cutlery into the marriage. They packed

---

[1] Otto Marx, 'Mein Leben in Deutschland vor und nach dem 30. Januar 1933' [My life in Germany before and after 30 January 1933] (1940), pp. 2–5, Harvard Competition, no. 152. This document has been translated from German.
[2] Otto Marx (b. 1890), retailer; imprisoned in Dachau concentration camp, 12 April 1933 to 18 Nov. 1935; emigrated to the USA in June 1938.
[3] The report is 14 pages in total. In the first part Marx describes his childhood and schooldays.

these items into a suitcase. Then they took the suitcase and me to the police station and told my wife that I would be home again in half an hour. The suitcase with its contents was returned to my wife after a short time, but I was held there. I would also like to point out that the contents of the suitcase were left untouched and that surprisingly nothing was stolen from it, as is often the case in the Third Reich. This is due to the fact that the head of the police was an upright and decent man who had to carry out his duty as an official, but was in his heart opposed to the Nazi Movement. I was then taken by the police and SS to the regional court prison in Weiden. I was put in a small cell in which two of my fellow sufferers, also Jews, were already being held. The treatment in prison was good. Our relatives could bring us food and tobacco and also visit us. In addition, we were allowed to take some exercise for two hours every day in the open air in the prison yard under the supervision of the guards. My wife had meanwhile pulled out all the stops to get me released and had also made contact with an Aryan lawyer from Munich. This lawyer was himself a member of the SA and he made a personal visit to the government and the Political Police in Munich. On 11 April 1933 my wife visited me again in prison and told me that I would be released from protective custody the very same day. Not only had she been told this by Chief Inspector Gottinger,[4] but he also showed my wife the written order from the government in Munich for my release. I was also assured personally by the prison official that I would be released that day. During the night of 11 to 12 April, a great bustle of activity was noticeable in the prison. At 3 a.m. my cell doors were opened and I was told to get myself ready. When I appeared dressed in the yard, a large vehicle was already waiting there to transfer me along with twenty-eight other prisoners to the concentration camp at Dachau. We were now told how we were to behave during the journey and that they would immediately shoot at us at the slightest attempt to escape. The police and Nazis were armed to the teeth and would have used their weapons at the slightest incident. A stop was made near the town of Ingolstadt, and the prisoners were allowed to relieve themselves in the open air. I had an opportunity to talk with the head of the transport and I asked him what grounds there were for sending me to Dachau, given that I had never been politically active in my entire life. This was the same person who had returned the silver. He said verbatim, I am terribly sorry but I must carry out my orders. We arrested three Jews in Weiden; one of them has a serious heart condition, one is a Polish national, and the third is you. I received the order to bring at least one Jew with me and this fate has befallen you. But they don't have anything on you and in a few weeks you're sure to be back home again. Then the journey continued and at 12 noon we reached Dachau. The camp was a former munitions factory that had been in operation in the World War from 1914 to 1918.[5] It was surrounded by a wall approximately 4 metres high and inside the wall was a 2½ metre high barbed-wire fence that was electrically charged with a high voltage. A few weeks later three concrete towers, each with three heavy machine guns and searchlights, were built into this high wall so that any attempt to escape would have been futile. When we arrived in the camp we were led into the so-called shunt room and examined from head to toe with painful precision. Anyone who had a pocket knife or money had

4 Balthasar Gottinger (b. 1878), judicial inspector; lived in Weiden from 1902 to 1940.
5 Dachau concentration camp near Munich was built in March 1933 as the first official concentration camp in Germany.

it confiscated. A small proportion of the money was later returned to us. We did not receive prison clothing and shoes as nothing was yet available and the camp had not yet been fully built. Every prisoner received a number and I was given the number 346. I received a bitter foretaste even on this first day, for there was no restraint with slaps and blows, although I myself still got off lightly on that day. I was then assigned to a company and was placed in the second company. I would also like to point out that until my release on 18 November 1935 the camp comprised ten companies. Each company consisted of five platoons, each with 54 men, so that a full company was 270 men strong. Each man received a bed, made out of a straw sack, a headrest pad, two woollen blankets, blue checked sheets, [and] one white linen cloth, just like in the army. The bed had to be kept scrupulously clean and made every day as straight as a post. Anyone who made his bed incorrectly a few times received 25 heavy strokes of the stick.

The number of sick was extraordinarily low and there were no vermin. In addition, every man received one plate, one bowl, and some eating utensils. These items were kept in a rack and also had to be kept laboriously clean. Each company had one company leader. This was either a Scharführer or an ordinary SS man. Every morning the same man came and carried out a precise examination of beds and eating equipment. Pity the person who had something out of place. He was immediately hit in the face and after a few times he would receive a punishment beating. On the day of my arrival, on 12 April 1933 at 5 p.m., four SS people entered the prison camp and called up four young Jews aged between 19 and 24 years. These four prisoners were led into the woods behind the camp. The troop leader then gave the order 'march-march', which means jump, and the people were shot dead while supposedly trying to escape.[6] The next day a report was issued: four communists shot while trying to escape.[7] Incidents of this kind were the order of the day and I will explain them in more detail. In the first few days we suffered greatly from the rain and frost, as there was still no heating. The whole camp was fairly neglected and overgrown with weeds. Everything was now arranged in order to be prepared for the large influx that was coming. Meanwhile, 25 April 1933 had arrived, and this was to be a memorable day for me. On this day many transports arrived from all the Gaue. They included many Jews. There were terrible beatings and streams of blood flowed. The SS body of guards was in a bloody frenzy. I had hoped to get away from there unscathed but that evening I was taught a lesson. Around 7 p.m., two SS men entered my quarters and told me to go to the camp administrator. I reported to him and the administrator told me to go through the door there. I found myself in a detention cell. Four SS people then took up different positions around me, each holding a stick. They received me with the cry: 'bloody Jew', 'swine', and similarly foul expressions. In the room there was a wooden trestle and my tormentors ordered me to lie on it. I protested violently against this treatment, saying that I had served in the war for four years and fought for Germany. When I moved my arms to protect myself, the infamous mass murderer Hans Steinbrenner[8] drew his pistol, with the safety catch released, and put it to my temple. I then could only think of my wife and child and so I surrendered to my fate. They then took delight in beating me. They then incarcerated me for another hour

---

6 Those murdered were the economist Dr Rudolf Benario (1908–1933), the student Arthur Kahn (1911–1933), Ernst Goldmann, and Erwin Kahn.
7 See 'Flucht aus dem Konzentrationslager Dachau', *Neue Augsburger Zeitung*, 15 April 1933.

in the detention cell before letting me go. My scars remain a visible testimony to this event. This terrible beating broke both my thighs and I had to report for medical treatment. The physician at that time was the Jewish prisoner Dr Theodor Katz[9] from Nuremberg, who was later murdered there. While my wounds were being treated in the sick bay, the aforementioned Steinbrenner came in with the camp commandant, Wekkerle.[10] I could not see them, though the two of them were able to watch me from behind. I had festering wounds on both thighs and the physician was trying to remove the pus organisms with tweezers. I lay on the bench and did not move. The commandant asked Steinbrenner who this man was. Steinbrenner then gave my name and immediately said that I was a retailer by profession. At this time, a clothing and laundry room was being set up in the camp for the prisoners, with Steinbrenner in charge. I was now assigned to this work and had to begin the very same day in spite of my wounds. I furthermore received another Aryan prisoner as a companion. Only now did the time of suffering begin for us both. Directly next to our work room there were six detention cells. These were constantly occupied and there was beating all day long. My companion and I had to listen to everything. It would be too much if I tried to invoke all the cases that I still remember.

[...][11]

DOC. 39
On 3 May 1933 a resident of Bonn protests to Minister President Hermann Göring against the persecution of German Jews[1]

Handwritten letter from A. Müller, Bonn, to Minister President Hermann Göring (received by the Prussian Ministry of State on 4 May 1933, forwarded to the Prussian Ministry of the Interior, received on 7 May 1933), dated 3 May 1933

Esteemed Minister President,

The incomparably fine course taken by the May Day celebrations throughout Germany is a new and glorious chapter in the miraculous successes of our time-honoured Reich Chancellor. He has achieved so many fine and good things through the unification of the German people, once thought to be impossible, that it is unpleasant to contemplate

---

8 Hans Steinbrenner (1905–1964), retailer; guard at Dachau concentration camp, March–Nov. 1933; member of the SS; interned in May 1945 and sentenced to life imprisonment in 1952; released around 1962.
9 Dr Theodor D. Katz (1887–1933), physician; doctor for sexually transmitted diseases and skin disorders; worked among other places at the municipal hospital in Nuremberg; murdered in Dachau concentration camp on 8 Oct. 1933.
10 Correctly: Hilmar Wäckerle (1899–1941); commandant of Dachau concentration camp, April to June 1933; in the SS-Verfügungstruppe from 1934; SS-Standartenführer; killed in action during the war against the Soviet Union.
11 Marx goes on to describe his further imprisonment until 1935 and his life until his emigration from Germany in 1938.

1 GStA PK, I HA, Rep. 77, Tit. 416, Nr. 55, Bd. 2, fols. 67–68v. This document has been translated from German.

anything ever being any different again, but it is the very concern that this could indeed come to pass that inspires me to write the following lines.

I will be very brief; it is the *Jewish question*. I am a genuine 'Aryan' and also voted for the Nationalist Socialists, but (like most of my fellow countrymen) I cannot declare myself in agreement with the solution of the Jewish question.

The 'people' are not in fact aware of any Jewish question; it is only the authorities who unfortunately bring this matter to the people.

Jews were also persecuted during the Middle Ages, but that persecution at least had an ideal purpose, namely the boundless expansion of Christianity. Once the Jew became a 'Christian', the persecution ceased. Today, however, it is no longer the religion that is being tackled but the race. The Catholics reject this as unchristian; we are supposed to love *all* people, including other races, Negroes, Japanese, Chinese, and Jews; no distinction is to be made. With the Jewish race, though, there is also the specific consideration that Christianity is derived from Judaism. The Son of God did not assume human form among the old Germanic peoples but among the Jews. His mother, his foster father, and his relatives belonged to the Jewish nation. How is it then possible that a Christian hates the Jewish nation? The prayers at the mass of the Catholic Church, its priests' robes, and the 'commandments' are Jewish in origin. Thus, in short: we Catholics reject this hatred; enquire into Catholic spirituality sometime. As long as there is no reflection in this regard, there can be no complete unification of the German people.

Now to the practical aspect of the Jewish question:

The Jews are not allowed to become 'civil servants', they are permitted to study and practise 'learned professions' only to a limited degree, but no 'Aryan' may make use of their skills or buy anything from them; well, what are the people to live on then? They are not allowed to emigrate, or at least not take their wealth with them; and anyway the other countries would surely oppose the mass immigration, so what is to happen to them? Ultimately, they constitute a state within the state, just as they did in the worst periods of the Middle Ages, a condition that has certainly not proved successful.

This standpoint is unworthy of the German people and also incurs the hostility of other nations. If Jews have erred, they are to be punished, but most Jews in Germany are after all modest, thoroughly harmless people, whom we perhaps would not seek as our friends and for personal contacts, but who have perpetrated no crime other than just being Jews. That is unacceptable, and must be halted.

I request you, honourable Minister President, to ensure this.[2]

With the highest esteem

---

[2] The letter was filed on 10 May 1933 without any action having been taken: see handwritten note, ibid., fol. 67.

DOC. 40
On 6 May 1933 the National Socialist German Reich Estate Agents' League criticizes the approach taken by the Reich Association of German Estate Agents during the process of *Gleichschaltung*[1]

Letter, undated and unsigned (copy)[2]

'Attempt at Gleichschaltung in the Reich Association of German Estate Agents.'

On 6 May[3] of this year an extraordinary session of the Reich Association of German Estate Agents took place at the Kaiserhotel in Berlin.[4] At this estate agents' session the Gleichschaltung of this association was carried out in a classic example of the art of devious contortion. As we know, the Reich guidelines state that the executive committee should be composed of 51 per cent *senior, well-established* Party comrades and also the first chairman must be an *old, well-established* Party comrade, as should the management. And how has the association managed to adapt to these regulations? Just listen and marvel!

Instead of a *senior, well-established* Party comrade, a new untested Party comrade was elected as the first chairman, namely one Mr Friedrich Wilhelm Sohn.[5] On 29 April this Mr Friedrich Wilhelm Sohn resolved to announce his membership of the National Socialist Party. In response to reproaches from his own ranks, he explained: *it is better to join the Party because it is possible to be more effective from this position.* He also stated: *in every party programme there are individual points that one does not like and one such point in the case of the National Socialist is the Jewish question!* Generally Mr Sohn has an entirely positive attitude to the Jews and has declared that *if anything happens to the Jews, then he will leave immediately.*[6]

In issue 11 of the association's paper, the *Deutsche Immobilien-Zeitung*, dated 27 May 1933, the first chairman, Mr Friedrich Wilhelm Sohn, presented our league and members

---

1 GStA PK, I HA, Rep. 77, Tit. 307. This document has been translated from German.
2 The letter was enclosed as appendix I to a circular letter from the National Socialist German Reich Estate Agents' League from June 1933, which was sent to the Reich ministries and the regional ministries, as well as to all the police headquarters and chambers of commerce in Berlin and Munich: ibid.
3 The original is incorrectly dated 7 May. See the article by Dr Ahr, 'Der außerordentliche Maklertag am 6. Mai 1933', *Deutsche Immobilien-Zeitung: Zeitung des Reichsverbandes Deutscher Makler (RDM) für Immobilien, Hypotheken und Finanzierungen e. V.*, 13 May 1933, pp. 74–75.
4 The Reich Association of German Estate Agents (RDM) was founded in 1924 in Cologne as the professional body of the property industry.
5 Friedrich Wilhelm Sohn (b. 1875), estate agent; joined the NSDAP on 1 May 1933 and left it on 25 August 1933.
6 At the extraordinary session on 6 May 1933, a motion was put forward to forbid 'non-Aryan professional colleagues entry into the RDM and into the regional and local groups' and 'to exclude non-Aryan members'. However, chairman Sohn explained that it was not the intention of the government, the NSDAP, or the Berlin Chamber of Industry and Commerce to exclude 'non-Aryan members from the associations or federations'. Certainly, 'all executive committee and counsel posts were to be exclusively [filled] by Aryan gentlemen'. The motion was not discussed further: *Deutsche Immobilien-Zeitung*, 13 May 1933, pp. 74–75.

more or less as second-rate people, although most of our members, in fact the whole executive committee, have fought for the Party for the last ten or twelve years.[7]

The same method was used on the leadership. To comply with the Gleichschaltung guidelines, the former manager Dr Ahr[8] simply became a Party member on 29 April, and the other elected members of the executive committee Carl A. Schmid[9] and Hubert Schumann[10] also became members on 29 April. The few old Party members who were also elected to the executive committee are all based in rural areas, and so have no influence on leadership in Berlin. In addition, the first chairman, Mr Sohn, has also received sweeping powers from these executive committee members, so that he is, as of now, free to do what he pleases and when it pleases him.[11]

This Mr Sohn proclaims to the world that he is representing the interests of the profession of estate agents. We should be wary that a man who for years has presided over an up to 80 per cent Jewish association in Berlin and today even runs it for the whole Reich is setting himself up as the representative of estate agents' interests.

The association can never represent the interests of us National Socialist estate agents. These interests are only safeguarded by the *National Socialist German Reich Estate Agents' League based in Munich* and its subdivisions.

DOC. 41

On 9 May 1933 Heinrich Marx reflects on his personal situation in Berlin and on conditions in higher education institutions[1]

Handwritten diary of Heinrich Marx, entry for 9 May 1933

Tues, 9 May. Following on from the last entry: it turned out as I thought with my lecture. Last Wednesday Funk-Stunde[2] called to say that my lecture had been scheduled for 18 May. My comment that I am a 'non-Aryan' was followed by a prompt cancellation of

---

7 Sohn's article stated: 'At present in the real estate industry there is a proliferation of new groups and subgroups who call themselves purely National Socialist or Christian associations. In these new groups, a number of members have found a place that the Reich Association of German Estate Agents with its strong quality screening could not always provide': 'Blick auf's Ziel', *Deutsche Immobilien-Zeitung*, 27 May 1933, p. 81.
8 Dr Helmut Ahr (b. 1902), political scientist; legal advisor in Berlin, 1933; author of *Die Voraussetzungen der Arbeit* (1924).
9 Dr Carl Schmid, engineer in Berlin.
10 Hubert Schumann, estate agent (land holdings and mortgages) in Berlin.
11 Commenting on *Gleichschaltung*, Sohn stated: 'Since a Gleichschaltung in terms of prior Party membership is not possible in all organizations, Gleichschaltung is also considered by the relevant authorities to have been carried out if the executive committee is constituted of 51 per cent of NSDAP members who belong to the Party *after* 30 January 1933. Gleichschaltung does *not* mean: exclusion of Jewish members from the formations' associations': *Deutsche Immobilien-Zeitung*, 27 May 1933, p. 81.

1 Heinrich Marx, 'Tagebuch II: 9. March 1933 – November 1934', pp. 26–32, Deutsche Nationalbibliothek/Deutsches Exilarchiv 1933–1945, EB 96/160, Nachlass Henry Marx. This document has been translated from German.
2 A radio station in Berlin that was run from 1923 by the first German broadcasting company, Funkstunde AG Berlin.

the broadcast and now I will only get the fee. It doesn't bother me. A similar letter arrived yesterday from Breslau: a date cannot yet be set for the 'Verhinderte Dichter'.[3] So I will have to wait a while longer on that.

I was also still working with Schilling on the matter I mentioned;[4] we visited various correspondents, as well as Bojano, also Miss Lesser from the *Razon* (Buenos Aires),[5] René Lauret (*Temps*), Sefton Delmer (*Daily Express*), and Knickerbocker (*New York Evening Post*). Today we are also going to see Mowrer (*Chicago Daily News*). The discussions were invariably most interesting; whether of course anything comes of the whole matter is doubtful at any rate. All the same, the opportunity to make personal contact with these gentlemen is not completely insignificant. – Otherwise of course all personal undertakings are in abeyance. I have a completely different life now: whereas I used to sit in the library all day and always felt completely at ease there, now I'm increasingly reliant on my room and I'm doubly pleased that it is so cosy here. I read a great deal and try to fill some gaps here and there. So far I have withstood everything rather well, which was entirely as I expected on the basis of my own general attitude. At some moments I even feel full of vitality, free, and unfettered by any sentimentality and soppiness. (Which brings to mind [Theodor] Fontane's saying: 'A lack of emotions is better than false emotions.') To that extent I am feeling more at ease and better than before. Never before did I have, from my youthful perspective, so little understanding of the suicides that are happening every day. Never in a million years would I grant the enemy the supreme victory that he would achieve by extinguishing my existence. I absolutely must stand by what I have said and done. Anyone who thinks otherwise is lacking in honour or unworthy of a life that cannot always tread the old well-worn and peaceful paths. This time is the greatest test of character for the human being; it is doubtful how many will survive it and whether we will be among them. – The more politically left-wing the Jew was before, the less shaken he is by current events, amid all recognition of their seriousness and their danger. The nationalist Jew is now losing all support when he is repudiated by those who used to be *his* people. For me the question is framed in this way: while I've certainly been ousted from the cultural community, do I feel ousted? To that I can only answer: No! What I have is something that no one can take away from me; if I am prevented from gaining anything new, this does nothing to alter my attitude. Getting out of the dilemma in which I nevertheless find myself will not be so easy. – In the long term my current life will of course be impossible to maintain, however much my health recovers. Yet wherever I turn, difficulties mount: taking an exam here is pointless; gaining a doctorate, which costs a few thousand marks, is inadvisable, because after all it does not lead to any better prospects here. To begin something abroad: that is something I would consider very carefully.

---

3 Marx had already had to adapt the lecture and alter a section about Thomas Mann. See entry for 28 April 1933, Deutsche Nationalbibliothek/Deutsches Exilarchiv 1933–1945, EB 96/160, Nachlass Henry Marx.
4 Schilling was a friend of Marx's and was planning a radio feature about foreign correspondents: ibid.
5 Correctly: *La Razón*, a local newspaper distributed in the public transport system in Buenos Aires. It was founded in 1905.

The new student law has been issued;[6] last Saturday the Minister of Culture gave a speech at the university.[7] He was well aware that he had major obstacles to overcome from the professors; I doubt very much that he made any headway with this in his speech. The students are undertaking major actions against the un-German spirit, the culmination of which is to be an auto-da-fé at Opernplatz[8] at which 20,000 books will be burned.[9] Blacklists have been prepared, which are to be regarded as future guidelines for lending libraries and public libraries. The lists include every famous Jewish writer from Shalom Asch to Stefan Zweig.[10]

Apart from Franck[11] and Spranger[12] the following have resigned: Haber[13] with his assistants [Freund]lich[14] and Polanyi;[15] Liebermann, with a splendid declaration that

6 Law against Overcrowding in German Schools and Institutions of Higher Education, 25 April 1933: *Reichsgesetzblatt*, 1933, I, p. 225.
7 Minister of Culture Rust spoke on the subject 'Student and University'. He stated that as well as 'free academic research' the university also had the task of providing education, and the 'German youth is not to be guided by professors of another race, nor by those who deviate intellectually from the character of the German nation': 'Kultusminister Rust bei der feierlichen Proklamation des Studentenrechts', *Völkischer Beobachter* (northern German edition), 7/8 May 1933, p. 1.
8 Now Bebelplatz, Berlin.
9 The Deutsche Studentenschaft (German Students' Union) organized a national propaganda campaign that began with the publication of the twelve theses 'Against the Un-German Spirit' on 12 April 1933. The campaign ended on 10 May 1933 with the book burning in Berlin and other university towns.
10 On 6 May 1933 in Berlin students ransacked the Institute for Sexual Research run by Magnus Hirschfeld (1868–1935). Students confiscated literature of various types in Berlin lending libraries in accordance with 'blacklists' prepared in advance, and took it away in trucks.
11 Dr James Franck (1882–1964), physicist; from 1921 professor at the University of Göttingen; awarded the Nobel Prize, 1925; in 1933 resigned his professorship in protest against the National Socialist government and emigrated to the USA; afterwards held professorships at universities including Baltimore, Chicago, and Copenhagen; worked on the development of the atom bomb and cautioned against its deployment in the war against Japan.
12 Dr Eduard Spranger (1882–1963), philosopher; professor in Leipzig from 1912 and in Berlin 1920–1933; resigned in protest on 25 April 1933; from 1936 intermittently in Japan; imprisoned for several weeks in connection with the plot to assassinate Hitler on 20 July 1944; acting vice chancellor of Berlin University, 1945; professor in Tübingen, 1946–1952, and vice president of the German Research Foundation (DFG), 1951–1955.
13 Dr Fritz Haber (1868–1934), chemist; from 1906 professor at the Technical University of Karlsruhe; in 1908 he developed ammoniac synthesis, which was later used in the production of artificial fertilizers and explosives; from 1911 he established the first Kaiser Wilhelm Institute of Physical Chemistry and Electrochemistry in Berlin; during the First World War he took part in preparations for the deployment of gas in warfare; received the Nobel Prize for chemistry, 1919. On 30 April 1933 he requested that he be retired because of anti-Jewish policies, and emigrated to Britain.
14 Dr Herbert Max Finlay Freundlich (1880–1941), chemist; from 1911 non-tenured professor at the Technical University of Braunschweig; from 1916 granted leave to conduct important wartime gas-mask research at the Kaiser Wilhelm Institute of Physical Chemistry and Electrochemistry, where from 1919 to 1933 he was head of the department of applied physical chemistry and deputy director; professorship at Berlin University, 1923; on 20 April 1933 he made a request for retirement, then emigrated to London, and in 1938 to the USA, where he was professor at the University of Minnesota. He was the brother of Erwin Finlay Freundlich; on the latter, see Doc. 63, 18 July 1933.
15 Dr Michael Polanyi (1891–1976), physician and chemist; from 1920 worked at the Kaiser Wilhelm Institute for Fibre Chemistry in Berlin; head of department at the Kaiser Wilhelm Institute of Physical Chemistry and Electrochemistry, 1923–1933; on 21 April 1933 made a request for retirement and in July emigrated to Britain; from 1933 to 1948 professor in Manchester, where he went on to

was published yesterday in the *DAZ*.¹⁶ Otherwise there is more and more 'Gleichschaltung'. Worthy of mention is the action against the unions on 2 May. The great celebrations at Tempelhofer Feld [on 1 May] paved the way.¹⁷ –

[…]¹⁸

DOC. 42
On 13 May 1933 the Israelite Religious Community in Munich complains to the Reich Foreign Office about measures against Jewish associations in Munich¹

Letter from the board of the Israelite Religious Community in Munich, signed Baerwald,² rabbi, and Neumeyer,³ chairman, to the Reich Foreign Office, dated 13 May 1933 (copy)⁴

On the morning of 12 May 1933, officers of the Political and Criminal Police appeared in the welfare office of the Religious Community in Munich, in the offices and apartments of the chairmen of almost every Jewish association, and in some welfare establishments.

In house searches that sometimes went on for hours, officials confiscated files, correspondence, books of minutes, sums of money, savings bank books, and so on. They declared the associations to be dissolved and that the abolition of these associations by their chairmen was to be filed at the registry court. The association and its institutions would have to desist from all further activity. The association chairmen had to sign a pre-printed declaration indicating the expropriation of the association's assets with

---

hold a chair in social studies from 1948 to 1958; from 1958 senior research fellow in Oxford; active until 1968 on the Executive Committee of the Congress of Cultural Freedom; author of works including 'Tyranny and Freedom, Ancient and Modern', (1958).

16 The painter Max Liebermann (1847–1935) resigned from the Prussian Academy of the Arts and as its honorary president. The *Deutsche Allgemeine Zeitung* published his resignation statement, which contained the following explanation: 'Throughout my long life I have tried with all my abilities to serve German art: it is my conviction that art has nothing to do either with politics or with ancestry': *Deutsche Allgemeine Zeitung* (Greater Berlin edition), 8 May 1933 (evening), p. 6.

17 On 1 May, declared in 1933 as a public holiday in Germany (National Labour Day), there was a mass rally in Berlin at which Goebbels and Hitler gave speeches. The unions had also called for participation. On 2 May 1933 the premises of the Free Trade Unions were occupied throughout the Reich and many of their leaders were arrested.

18 A passage about keeping a diary follows.

1 PA AA, R 98 472. This letter has been translated from German.

2 Dr Leo Baerwald (1883–1970), rabbi; assistant rabbi in Munich, 1911–1918; military rabbi during the First World War, 1914–1917; rabbi of the Israelite Religious Community in Munich, 1918–1940; abducted by the SA, 1933; imprisoned in Dachau concentration camp, 1938; emigrated from Germany, 1940; rabbi in New York, 1940–1955.

3 Dr Alfred Neumeyer (1867–1944), lawyer; practised law in Munich; from 1895 public prosecutor and judge at various courts; judge at the Supreme Regional Court in Munich, 1929–1933; chairman of the Israelite Religious Community in Munich, 1920–1940; member of the executive board of the Central Association of German Citizens of the Jewish Faith (CV), 1932–1938; co-founder of the Reich Representation of German Jews, 1933; emigrated to Argentina, 1941.

4 Handwritten note from 24 May 1933 in the upper margin: 'Central Association of German Citizens of the Jewish Faith'.

reference to the Bavarian Law on the Expropriation of Goods used for Anti-national Purposes dated 4 April 1933.[5]

This measure was applied to around six synagogue and prayer hall associations, in particular the religious society of Ohel Jakob, the Association of Orthodox Jews in Munich, which runs a synagogue and a primary school, and about twenty charities and a number of general associations serving cultural interests, such as the Reich League of Jewish Combat Veterans, the Association for Jewish Museums, and some Jewish youth associations. Most of these associations are purely charitable and some of them have been operating for decades, two of them (the women's association and the study association) for over a hundred years.

The board and the rabbinate of the Religious Community can guarantee with the greatest certainty that not one single association has an anti-national attitude or has acted in any way in this direction.

Specifically, I would like to point out the desperate situation of the Youth Welfare Association, which runs a children's home at 7 Antonienstraße and was previously described by all the official agencies as an exemplary establishment. There are thirty-nine orphaned poor children at risk here, aged between three months and seventeen years. The chairwoman and judicial counsellor, Mrs Kitzinger,[6] was presented with a questionnaire about the association's assets. It was announced that everything was being confiscated. RM 713.80 was taken away. The filing cabinet was sealed. Under threat of preventive detention, the chairwoman was induced to refrain from all activity and to submit an application for the abolition of the association. This all took place with reference to the law dated 4 April 1933.

The apprentices' home at 3 Wagnerstraße, which houses fifteen to twenty pupils and apprentices, was also declared to be dissolved.

There is great turmoil in the Religious Community in Munich and throughout the country, because the community has been struck at the heart of its moral and religious life, namely in the welfare work and the practice of neighbourly love. The community has also been deeply offended by the assumption that its associations and institutions have supposedly acted in a way that is detrimental to the fatherland.

---

5 According to this law, issued on 4 April 1933, 'movable and fixed assets' could be expropriated for 'the general good at the request of the State Ministry of the Interior' if their intended purpose was irreconcilable with the 'state's national tasks' or conflicted with the 'strivings of the people's national will': *Gesetz- u. Verordnungsblatt für den Freistaat Bayern*, no. 10, 7 April 1933, p. 103.
6 Elisabeth Rachel Kitzinger (1881–1966), social worker; worked for Jewish youth welfare in Munich and for Jewish aid organizations, 1904–1939; emigrated to Palestine in 1939.

DOC. 43
Report by company representative Oskar Vangerow on the Jews and the mood in Poland, 16 May 1933[1]

Report by Oskar Vangerow, Breslau, dated 16 May 1933[2]

The situation in Poland

I made the following observations during a four-week journey throughout Poland that ended today:

As I was already able to ascertain in Yugoslavia before Easter, the centre of the all-Jewish boycott is in Cracow. At the beginning of April a prominent Jew in Zagreb told me that he had daily contact with Cracow. At the time the Jews were phoning daily to report their respective successes in short-selling in Reichsmarks. The *Illustrowany Kuryer Codzienny* is published in Cracow,[3] and according to the German consulate there it is 75 per cent Jewish-owned. The publication, considered to be well informed, is widely read throughout Poland, and many, including educated people, simply believe the lies about Germany that are dished up daily and cover three to five pages. All the horror stories that are going round are first published or at least reprinted by this newspaper.

The boycott and the outrages against German signs originate exclusively from Jewish circles. The causes are twofold; many Jews previously resident in Germany (there are said to be 14,000–16,000) have returned to Poland and have spread horror stories. You have a Jew showing up in the editorial department of a Jewish newspaper in Warsaw with his eyes closed and letting himself be photographed as a German Jew whose eyes have been gouged out. The second deeper cause of the rabble-rousing and the boycott was explained to me verbatim by a highly regarded Jew in Łódź: 'We Polish Jews have no interest at all in the 600,000 German Jews. They have always said that they don't want anything to do with us Polish Jews. But we are afraid that what is said to be happening in Germany might eventually happen to us in Poland and so we must discredit the country that is doing these things.' This frank explanation reveals the context of many partial statements by other Jews so as to form an accurate overall picture. It is obvious that Poland, with 10 per cent Jewish inhabitants, would – in the style of the Russian pogroms – treat the Jews differently to what has happened in Germany.

The Jews have managed to bring the current democratic government more or less into line. In the past, German goods were boycotted by the authorities; now the old slogan is being revived. But I have hardly met a single Christian Pole who has not immediately identified its Jewish origins and, amid the general anti-Jewish sentiment in

---

1 BArch, 62 Di 1, Film 1132/3846. This document has been translated from German.
2 The company Paul Vangerow GmbH delivered Oskar Vangerow's report on the same day to the Foreign Policy Office of the NSDAP in Berlin, with the observation that Vangerow had been travelling to Poland several times a year for eleven years and was therefore very familiar with conditions there. A request was made for anonymization in the event that the report was used in the press: letter from Paul Vangerow GmbH to the Foreign Policy Office of the NSDAP dated 16 May 1933, ibid. Paul Vangerow GmbH was founded in 1886 in Breslau. It handled the production of fine paper as well as the import and export of artists' materials.
3 'Illustrated Daily Courier': Polish newspaper published from 1910 to 1939.

Poland, renounced the government slogan. Only government offices are turning away the goods marked as German (but not in fact German goods).

The Jews themselves are carrying out the boycott more or less strictly, depending on their branch. There are some Jews who continue to buy while asking for this to be kept quiet, and others who, regardless of need, are strictly adhering to the boycott committee's instructions. Many physicians, irrespective of whether the patient suffers as a result, are therefore no longer prescribing German medication. It is correct that out of fear of indiscretions Jews are now avoiding appointments with Jewish representatives, just as they are now choosing Christian instead of Jewish hauliers.

In Germany it is anyway a fundamental mistake to believe that for Poland only a Jewish representative is possible and appropriate. Most of the trade that qualifies for import on the basis of its importance and creditworthiness is in Christian hands. But the Christian Pole buys more or less consistently only from the Christian representative, whereas the Jew still only asks about the item and the price, and never about race or religious belief.

I have tried to rebut the attacks from Jews everywhere I could, in conversations with customers, on trains, in restaurants, or in coffee houses. I have presented the *Völkischer Beobachter*, which is available when expressly requested in Poland, including in Warsaw, at large newspaper stands, as evidence that the German movement may not be considered from the narrow perspective of antisemitism.

I have tried in individual cases to get to the bottom of the horrific reports. Of fifty mistreated [Jews] it finally turned out after repeated questioning that only one had actually been seen. Thus, I was told that a Miss S. from Berlin (I am giving the name, address, and incident to the German consulate for the record and for further action) wrote in a letter to Cracow that her father and forty other Jews had been taken to the Berlin police headquarters. It is likely that in the meantime this Polish Jewess has been sentenced by a German court for spreading fake news abroad. Educated Jews have told me often enough that they do *not* believe the reports of atrocities but that certain ministerial speeches on the radio were indication enough of how the Jews are being mistreated in Germany. The speeches in the English House of Commons have done immense damage to Germany. Chamberlain was inundated with thank-you telegrams from Poland.

In general the Jews had no wish to be convinced of the contrary. The letters from German firms rebutting the horror reports have therefore completely failed.[4] A Hitler government, it is said, will always face constant opposition. It is telling that during the 1 May parade in Warsaw no anti-German signs were carried by any of the socialist groups, whereas the Jewish socialists, who marched separately, had added an anti-German inscription in Polish and Yiddish to almost every placard.

Two German newspapers are doing immense damage in Poland, with extracts often being reproduced in Polish newspapers. One is the *Rote Fahne*,[5] which is printed without fail and sent illegally every day to Poland from Berlin, and distributed here among communists. The other is the *Danziger Volksstimme*, which thanks to the incredible forbearance of the Danzig state government makes the wildest attacks on everything German

---

4 See the circular letter from the Association of German Engineering Institutions dated 30 March 1933, Doc. 19.
5 'The Red Flag': the newspaper of the Communist Party of Germany (KPD). It was founded in 1918 and appeared illegally in Germany after being banned in 1933.

(the masked hordes with brown shirts). The *Volksstimme* is being heavily propagated in Poland; countless free issues are dispatched. Polish restaurants that have no German newspapers on display only had these 'German' newspapers, probably also available for free.

Yet, as far as the Jewish question is concerned, only the Christian-Polish press fully understands the German movement.

On the national holiday, 3 May, in Poznań, no division attracted greetings and crowds anything like as strongly as the nationalist associations (fascist divisions).

Germany's course cannot be influenced by the boycott. But in the mainly Christian government it should not be difficult to bring the government boycott to an end and to prevent the excesses of Jewish agitation using the police, who are generally proactive. But external trade in particular should not be further aggravated on both sides by sanctions, but instead all forms of spitefulness should be avoided, in accordance with the German-Polish discussions that were very favourably received in Poland, in order to take the sting out of the Jewish boycott. A German-Polish agreement, for which preconditions perhaps exist or could easily be uncovered, can only benefit both Germany and Danzig.

DOC. 44

On 18 May 1933 Karl Landau asks retired Vienna senior municipal councillor Engelbert Siegl about employment opportunities[1]

Letter from Dr Karl Landau,[2] Berlin, 6 Xantenerstraße, to Dr Siegl,[3] Vienna, dated 18 May 1933

Esteemed Senior Municipal Councillor,

Dr Werner Hoppe[4] informs me that he told you about me in his letter of the 16th of this month.

In view of the fact that for certain reasons I must postpone my trip to Vienna for the time being, I am taking the liberty of expressing my wishes to you in this way.

In connection with the Gleichschaltung of the professional civil service in Germany I had to resign from the service of the Berlin Municipal Electrical Works[5] on the grounds of my non-Aryan descent.[6]

---

1 BArch, R 58/5102, fol. 8r–v. This document has been translated from German.
2 Dr Karl Landau (b. 1902); grew up in Austria; chief operating officer of the administrative division of the Berlin Municipal Electrical Works (BEWAG) from 10 April 1931 to 31 March 1933; then advisor at the electrical works in Łódź; later emigrated to Palestine, where he was executive board member of Vulcan Foundries Ltd in Haifa; director of Koor Industries & Crafts in Haifa and from 1947 managing director of the Palestine Portland Cement Works Nesher-Yagour.
3 Dr Engelbert Siegl (b. 1872), lawyer; worked for the city of Vienna from around 1895; from 1919 municipal councillor and from 1922 head official of Vienna's 9th district; retired senior municipal councillor, 1933.
4 Probably Dr Werner Hoppe (b. 1902), lawyer; from 1931 to 1939 local court judge and chairman of the labour court in the Berlin district of Mitte; joined the SA in 1933 and the NSDAP in 1937; fought in the war, 1939–1945; prisoner of war, 1945–1946; worked as a retailer, 1946–1949.
5 The company was founded in 1884. From 1915 it was in municipal ownership, from 1923 under the name Berlin Municipal Electrical Works (BEWAG).
6 Dismissal on the basis of § 3 of the Law for the Restoration of the Professional Civil Service: see Doc. 29, 7 April 1933, and Doc. 32, 11 April 1933.

In view of the current political situation in Germany I have now decided to seek employment outside the borders of the German Reich.

I am taking the liberty of enclosing for you copies of references and letters so that you can acquire a fuller picture of my knowledge and abilities.

As these letters show, in barely eight years of work I progressed from being a poor student trainee with no connections to my recent post, which has brought me recognition far beyond the context of my field of work. The current conditions in Germany are making it impossible for me to find a post here at present and I am taking the liberty of sending you, dear sir, this respectful plea, to ask whether you might be willing to help me find suitable employment in Austria.

On the basis of Mayor Dr Sahm's letter,[7] I ask you to keep in mind that, in addition to my main field of work, namely the electricity industry, I have also worked in other economic sectors in the city of Berlin. This has also given me the opportunity of being entrusted with the honourable task of addressing the professorial staff at Greifswald University on the subject of the city of Berlin and its economy.

Esteemed Senior Municipal Councillor, I ask you to grant me the opportunity of receiving a response from you before my journey to Vienna.

I remain with the highest regards

Your very devoted

DOC. 45

On 22 May 1933 the Polish Legation protests against attacks on Polish nationals in Germany[1]

Aide-memoire from the Reich Foreign Office with the Polish Legation (51a/143/33), Berlin, dated 22 May 1933 (copy)[2]

Aide-memoire.

In a series of interventions at the Reich Foreign Office in March, April, and the beginning of this month, the Polish Legation had the honour of addressing a number of cases of damage incurred by Polish nationals on Reich territory.

According to information from the Polish Legation, there are unfortunately still some cases where one can only conclude that the safety of persons of Polish nationality residing in Germany and their property is not adequately guaranteed.

---

7 Dr Heinrich Sahm (1877–1939), lawyer; worked from 1904 as a civil servant in several cities; president of the state government of the Free City of Danzig, 1919–1930; mayor of Berlin, 1931–1935; afterwards envoy in Oslo until 1938.

1 BArch, R 1501/125708, fols. 215–217. This document has been translated from German.
2 In the original there are handwritten revision marks. The list was sent by State Secretary von Bülow-Schwante (Reich Foreign Office) on 31 May 1933 to the Reich Ministry of the Interior with a request for verification: letter from the Reich Foreign Office to the Reich Ministry of the Interior/Prussian Ministry of the Interior, Rathenau, 31 May 1933, ibid., fol. 214. The Reich Ministry of the Interior (received 1 June 1933) classified the matter as urgent and planned an enquiry into the cases in Württemberg: handwritten note, 6 June, on the letter from the Reich Foreign Office to the Reich Ministry of the Interior dated 31 May 1933; see ibid.

On the 25th of last month the Polish national Mendel Selig Haber,[3] from Dortmund, disappeared. According to a notice that appeared in the section headed 'Bochum suburbs' in issue 99 of *Rote Erde* on the 28th of last month, Haber was taken to the SA guardhouse in Gehrte on the 27th of last month.[4] At present there are no reports on what then happened to him. A few days later Haber's body was found with gunshot wounds to the head, neck, and back in a side canal of the Dortmund–Ems canal. The corpse also showed numerous signs of severe maltreatment.

On 24th of last month in Bochum, Josef Schnitzer[5] was beaten up in an establishment at 17 Herrmannhöhe, during which he was severely brutally assaulted. On 3rd of the month in Düsseldorf, Chaskel Hofmann was arrested and severely maltreated in a vehicle. Prior to this, his wife and her sister Frieda Wachspress were beaten up in his apartment.

The legation is dealing in particular with the arrests and deportations of Polish nationals, likewise the question of Polish nationals' participation in annual markets and trade fairs.

Also, however, some cases have come to the Polish Legation's attention in which Polish nationals have been forced to close their shops. For example:

Moses Hersch Chimowicz, who was forced to close his footwear shops in Gronau in Westphalia and in Euskirchen.

Peter Gold[6] had to close his shop in Esslingen at the behest of the Association of Württemberg Footwear Retailers.

Plawner, Jakob, had to close his shoe shop 'Schuhhaus Neckar' in Cannstadt on 29th of last month.

Significant financial damage results from these decisions.

Uniformed men entered the garage of the Brecklinghaus store in Essen and demanded the surrender of vehicle no. I Y 36 483 belonging to Jakob Jedwab.[7] In an attempt to drive it out of the garage, the vehicle was seriously damaged.

Moses Schüller[8] in Cologne instructed the Kaufmann firm to sell a series of items. This firm instructed the Laussing haulage firm to collect these objects from Schüller's apartment. On 22nd of last month these items were confiscated by uniformed men,

---

3 Mendel Selig Haber (b. 1900/1901).
4 The article 'Neue jüdische Verkaufsmethoden' ('New Jewish Sales Methods') stated that a Polish Jew had been taken to the local SA guardhouse. The Jew was said to be a certain Max Haber, who had no papers and who had offered 'inferior items of underwear' in return for discount stamps from well-known firms. The inhabitants of Gehrte were warned against 'buying from swindlers of that kind as the value is not commensurate with the trash bought': *Rote Erde*, 28 April 1933, p. 16.
5 Joseph Schnitzer had a footwear store at 20 Königstraße with a branch at 22 Bongardstraße. He only lived in Bochum until 1933.
6 Peter Gold (1887–1937), retailer; from 1917 owner of a footwear store in Esslingen with branches in several locations; enforced closure of his shops in Esslingen, Göppingen, and Kirchheim, 1933; the company was struck off the register of companies in 1935; he died in 1937 as a result of injuries incurred during the First World War.
7 Jakob Jedwab (b. 1869), retailer in Essen. His sons Abraham (1893–1964) and Isidor-Julius (b. 1893) emigrated to France in 1933, and his daughter Ester emigrated to Britain in 1938 with her husband, Max Stern.
8 Moses Schüller, retailer, managing director of the firm Schüller and Rubruck, a light fittings factory at 72 Luxemburger Straße in Cologne.

supposedly at the demand of a certain Josef Machol, resident in Cologne, on the basis of a written instruction from the NSDAP, Gau Rhineland, SS Company 1/2/58 diary [entry] 43 or 33 from 29th of last month, at which point these items were handed over to Josef Machol.

On 8th of this month David Fajtlowicz in Bütow was forced to wash off propaganda written on walls.

In the cases cited, the Polish consular offices had immediately turned to the local authorities. For its part, the Polish Legation considers itself forced to reserve its right to take possible steps to compensate those harmed and considers itself again compelled to protest on account of the damage to the personal safety and property of Polish nationals in Germany.

On this occasion the Polish Legation has the honour of pointing out its repeated requests for an instruction that steps are taken by the appropriate German authorities to track down and punish the perpetrators, in order that similar incidents are avoided in future.

DOC. 46
Directive issued to the German delegation in Geneva on 24 May 1933 to prevent a discussion in the Council of the League of Nations on the persecution of Jews in German Upper Silesia[1]

Telegram no. 246 from the Reich Foreign Minister, von Neurath, to the German delegation, Geneva, dated 24 May 1933[2]

In response to telegram[s] 398, 402, 403.

At today's ministerial conference, attended by the Reich Minister of the Interior,[3] the Reich Minister of Justice, the Prussian Minister of Justice,[4] and State Secretary Grauert[5] as representative of the Prussian Minister President and Minister of Culture, agreement was reached concerning the following points:

(1) A Jewish debate in the Council of the League of Nations would be extremely undesirable and is to be avoided, if at all possible.

---

1 PA AA, R 83 033. This document has been translated from German.
2 In the left-hand margin: 'Note: Text approved by Ministerial Director Gaus. After dispatch for the kind attention of Dept. IV, Dept. V, Dept. VI.'
3 Wilhelm Frick was Reich minister of the interior and Franz Gürtner was Reich minister of justice.
4 Prussian minister of justice was Hanns Kerrl (1887–1941), judicial civil servant; joined the NSDAP in 1923; SA Gruppenführer, 1933; Reich commissioner at the Prussian Ministry of Justice, March 1933, then Prussian minister of justice until 17 June 1934 and thereafter Reich minister without portfolio; head of the Reich Office for Spatial Planning, 1935; Reich minister of church affairs, 1935–1941.
5 Ludwig Grauert (1891–1964), lawyer; until 1923 public prosecutor in Münster and Bochum, and afterwards managing director of the German Association of Steel Industrialists; joined the NSDAP in 1933; from 1933 state secretary in the Prussian Ministry of the Interior, then in the Reich Ministry of the Interior, responsible for the police; went into retirement, 1936; later member of the board of directors of the gas company Deutsche Continental-Gas-Gesellschaft in Dessau.

(2) You are authorized to issue a general declaration⁶ to the effect that the international agreements of the German Reich are of course not affected by German domestic laws and that, if any contraventions of the Geneva Convention provisions should have occurred in German Upper Silesia, these can only concern erroneous measures by subordinate bodies based on a misinterpretation of the law.⁷

(3) With reference to the Bernheim⁸ submission, it should be stated that it has not yet been possible to establish Bernheim's legitimation as a member of a minority. But even if he were to be a member of a minority, he would only be entitled to make his dismissal from a private post as a salaried employee the subject of a complaint on the basis of the Geneva Convention. He is under no circumstances authorized to issue complaints on the general question of the applicability of German laws in Upper Silesia, as these laws, in particular laws relating to civil servants, physicians, solicitors, and schools, do not concern him in any way.

I request that the issue of any further handling of the complaint under application of the above authorization be clarified before the meeting and that it be thereby ensured, if at all possible, that the agenda item will be dealt with by your statement without further discussion. The individual case of Bernheim would be correctly referred through local proceedings in accordance with Article 149 of the Geneva Convention.

Should this nevertheless still come up for discussion in the council⁹ after your statement, in which I ask you *not* to mention the Reich Chancellor's speech,¹⁰ and should the discussion in some way address domestic German legislation beyond Upper Silesia, then I ask you to oppose in the strongest terms any attempt to broach this subject.¹¹

---

6 Friedrich von Keller (1873–1960) represented the German Reich as envoy to the League of Nations.
7 On the actual conditions in Upper Silesia, see Doc. 67, 4 August 1933.
8 Franz Bernheim (1899–1990) had been dismissed as a salaried employee in a department store in Gleiwitz and had fled to Prague. On 17 May 1933 he directed a petition to the League of Nations, wherein he accused Germany of violating the 1922 Geneva Convention on Upper Silesia through its anti-Jewish laws there: document in French, PA AA, R 83 033. The petition had been prepared by representatives of the Comité des Délégations Juives: Philipp Graf, 'Die "Bernheim-Petition" 1933: Ein Fall jüdischer Diplomatiegeschichte', *Leipziger Beiträge zur jüdischen Geschichte und Kultur*, vol. 2 (2004), pp. 283–299.
9 The Council of the League of Nations in Geneva discussed the petition on 22, 26, and 30 May and on 6 June 1933.
10 On 17 May 1933 Hitler had declared in a speech on foreign policy in the Reichstag that he wanted to respect the national rights of other peoples.
11 In a report on the Bernheim petition commissioned by the council, dated 30 may 1933, the Irish diplomat Seán Lester (1888–1959) raised the criticism that the German legislation violated the Geneva Convention on Upper Silesia. He said that Germany must compensate the victims of the legislation that contravened the treaty. In accordance with instructions from the Reich Foreign Office, Friedrich von Keller vehemently rejected the report and questioned Bernheim's right to submit a petition. Several members of the council cautioned Germany against pursuing the criticism: 'Jewish Curbs Censured', *New York Times*, 31 May 1933, pp. 1 and 8.

DOC. 47

On 29 May 1933 the Jewish Community of Berlin complains to the state commissioner for Berlin about the city administration's anti-Jewish measures[1]

Letter from the board of the Jewish Community of Berlin (Dr B/SA/SK.), signed Stahl,[2] to the state commissioner for special purposes, Lippert, Berlin, dated 29 May 1933 (copy of a copy)[3]

We hereby take the liberty of respectfully presenting the following:

Over the past few weeks, municipal offices have issued a series of ordinances that constitute discrimination against Berlin's Jewish citizens as compared with the general population.

This does not so much concern ordinances made on the basis of the Law for the Restoration of a National Professional Civil Service,[4] but measures that are of profound importance in the area of welfare work and in business. We are convinced that, for these areas, also in the interests of the relevant state and municipal authorities, entirely different principles are involved from those that apply for the Civil Service Law, just as has been expressed, to our knowledge, for business life just in the last few days in the various publications of the Prussian Minister President and the Reich commissioner for the economy.

The Berlin Jewish Community, in which Berlin's Jews have been consolidated since 1671, therefore finds itself compelled to submit proposals and to request a review of the ordinances issued.

The community is working on the assumption that over the last 260 years Jewish citizens have made a significant contribution to the prosperity of the city of Berlin through their industriousness and public-spiritedness, and that their descendants, while they seek no privileges, should nevertheless remain protected from the harm caused by discrimination.

We would like to discuss in detail some of the ordinances issued, though we would like to note that the list is by no means exhaustive:

1. A public announcement from the Berlin procurement office, calling for tenders up to 30 April 1933, states the following:

> The approval process is to take place from 1 July 1933 onwards. Consideration will be given only to firms that have the support of the national government, whose owners and directors are citizens of German origin, and who provide only such goods that come from factories that fulfil the same requirements.

---

1 LAB, A Rep. 001-02/214, fols. 21–23. This document has been translated from German.
2 Heinrich Stahl (1868–1942), insurance salesman; board member of the Jewish Community of Berlin from 1931 and chairman of the board, 1933–1940; from 1939 deputy chairman of the Reich Association of Jews in Germany; in 1942 deported to Theresienstadt, where he died.
3 On 3 May 1933 Stahl had been commissioned by the board of the Jewish Community to negotiate 'with the responsible figures of the city of Berlin': minutes of the community's board meeting on 3 May 1933, Archives of the Leo Baeck Institute, New York, at the Jüdisches Museum Berlin, MF 587.
4 Correctly: Law for the Restoration of the Professional Civil Service.

Various other municipal agencies have proceeded in the same way. Since the middle of May this year, so we hear, the order forms of some district social welfare offices have been stamped with: 'This form is not valid for Jewish businesses.' Similarly, a letter along with a questionnaire from the municipal electricity office has been issued to us; this letter states the following:

> It is a condition of the approval that the applicant concurs with the national government, that the firm's owners and directors are citizens of German origin and that the materials and so on to be supplied by their firm come from factories that fulfil the same requirements.

The questionnaire also contains the following headings:
  (9) Does Jewish capital operate in the business?
If so: to what extent?
  (10) Is the proprietor or are the proprietors purely Aryan?

Through their wording and content, these measures are liable to lead to the commercial ruin of Jewish retailers and Jewish craftsmen. In particular we refer to the final clause of the ordinance from the procurement office, as well as the remark of identical meaning in the letter from the electricity office, which stipulates the condition that the firms consulted for their part also offer only goods that come from purely Aryan factories.

Those firms that supply their goods to the city of Berlin will not regard this as their only business connection; they are undoubtedly, also in the view of the procurement office, entitled to offer their goods, as far as possible on the free market as well as offering them to municipal agencies. But if these firms under the threat of losing the contract to supply municipal offices are enjoined not to buy from firms whose owners and directors are Jews, then the Jewish firms will be denied any direct and indirect sales opportunities not only with municipal agencies in Berlin, but in a large part of the rest of the business world.

The ordinance therefore represents a dramatic boycott measure which is likely to pose a serious risk to a great many livelihoods, especially in smaller and medium-sized operations.

2. Further affronts have emerged in the area of social welfare. The kitchens of our social welfare office in six districts have been stripped of their entitlement to accept municipal food stamps, and the nursery schools and after-school care of our social welfare agency and associated establishments have lost their wage subsidies.

These measures affect the poorest of the poor. Public kitchens are only used by these groups and for reasons of ritual most of the poor Jewish population is required to have its meals at our welfare kitchens. The same applies to nursery schools and after-school care, as well as for post-natal care, since the 'Jewish Home for Mothers and Infants' received an ordinance on 20 May that removed it with immediate effect from the list of homes engaged in post-natal care.

Our welfare organizations are also no longer in a position to present to the appropriate agencies the emerging doubts concerning such measures because Jewish members have been excluded from the municipal deputations and committees. We refer most respectfully to the implementing regulations of the Civil Service Law, which stipulate that the law does not apply to Jewish honorary officials who are appointed as such under legal prescriptions.

In the same way, it would only be fair to permit by means of local directives the contribution of a proportion of the population representing 4 per cent of the municipal population (calculated according to membership in our religious community).

3. According to legal provisions, swimming lessons are compulsory in primary-school education. However, access to the municipal swimming pool on Gartenstraße is denied to our primary schools and youth organizations. This measure not only makes it impossible to fulfil a legal obligation but is also likely to be detrimental to public health. The same judgement applies to the fact that Jewish adolescents are denied access to public sports grounds, gyms, and youth centres.

4. It is not economically but culturally significant that in the official guide to Berlin, distributed by the city of Berlin's Exhibitions, Fairs, and Tourist Office, all the local community's cultural institutions are no longer listed, although some of the institutes had previously been asked for more detailed information, and although several of the institutes, such as the New Synagogue and the Museum,[5] are of recognized artistic merit, and their absence will certainly be conspicuous to some of Berlin's visiting foreigners.[6]

5. Finally, on the basis of what appears to us to be an ambiguous ordinance, over the last few days the tendency has emerged within some administrative agencies to cancel the availability of rooms in municipal school buildings used by the Jewish Community's religious schools. At the objection of our school administration, however, some restraint has ensued pending the mayor's decision. We have addressed a special submission to the municipal authorities on this matter and most respectfully point out that this concerns supplementary or substitute religious teaching. We assume that it is in the interest of the city administration to also support the religious instruction of Jewish children as far as possible, and we confidently hope that the municipal authorities' decision will be made in such a way that religious teaching is not impeded.

We ask most respectfully for our objections to be examined and for us to be given the opportunity as far as possible to verbally present the substance of these and the other specific details of which we are also aware.[7]

---

5 This is a reference to the Jewish Museum in Berlin, which had opened on 24 Jan. 1933.
6 See Ausstellungs-, Messe- u. Fremdenverkehrs-Amt der Stadt Berlin (ed.), *Amtlicher Führer durch Berlin: Mit Plan der Innenstadt* (Berlin: abc, 1933).
7 Since the state commissioner referred the Jewish Community to the 'state supervisory authority', it presented its petition on 13 June to Prussian Minister President Göring. On 29 June 1933 the Jewish Community supplemented its submission with a list of further anti-Jewish measures. The Prussian Ministry of the Interior forwarded the petition to the municipal authorities for examination. The municipal offices concerned rejected the complaints by Jan. 1934. In April 1935 the municipal authorities abandoned the case file: LAB, A Rep. 001-02/214, fols. 19–65v.

DOC. 48

Nationalsozialistische Monatshefte, May 1933: article about the 'solution to the Jewish question'[1]

Dr Achim Gercke:[2]
(Expert on racial research at the Reich Ministry of the Interior.)

The solution to the Jewish question
The victory of the National Socialist revolution has also made the Jewish question a discernible problem to those who until now have not yet striven to reach a solution to the Jewish question or have never struggled to resolve it. Everyone has realized that the current situation is untenable; the free development and equal treatment of the Jews has become a competition 'unfairly' exploited by the Jews and has resulted in important positions within the German nation being handed over to those of a foreign race.

The consequence is that everyone wants to tackle this question, everyone is looking for a solution, everyone has a suggestion on their desk and puts forward a more or less good idea for discussion round the table. That was to be anticipated.

But solving such an important question is not quite as easy as is often assumed.

The legislative measures enacted by the government until now constitute a cleansing process that skilfully pursues retaliation against Judah's declaration of war. On the whole, the laws appear to be pointing the way in terms of raising awareness. This importance of the laws should not be underestimated. The entire nation is being enlightened on the Jewish question, and is coming to understand that the Volksgemeinschaft is a blood community and is registering for the first time the concept of race, and will be led away from the excessively theoretical treatment of the Jewish question and confronted with the actual solution.

Nevertheless, the preliminary laws that have already appeared do not provide any definitive solution to the Jewish question because the time is not yet ripe, although the regulations already point the way and in particular leave open all possible developments.

It would be premature these days in every respect to devise and present for public debate plans that seek to achieve more than is possible at present. Nevertheless a few principles must be highlighted so that thoughts which one would like and must allow to develop do not contain any flaws.

Fundamentally it must be decided whether or not one wishes to organizationally consolidate the Jews (and also the Jews' descendants) in Germany. Many plans that have come to light seek to incorporate the Jews into an association, in order to be able to

---

[1] 'Die Lösung der Judenfrage', *Nationalsozialistische Monatshefte*, vol. 4, no. 38 (May 1933), pp. 195–197. This document has been translated from German.
[2] Dr Achim Gercke (1902–1997), chemist and race researcher; worked in Göttingen on a register of all Jews in Germany, 1925; joined the NSDAP in 1926; in 1931 took away 70,000 index cards to Munich, where he became department head of the NSDAP Reichsleitung and director of the National Socialist Information Office in 1932; from 1933 expert on racial research in the Reich Ministry of the Interior; expulsion from the NSDAP and loss of all public functions in 1935 because of accusations of homosexuality; co-editor of the *Zeitschrift für Rassenkunde* (Journal for Racial Studies).

monitor the Jews, educate them, and retain influence over them.³ All these proposals are fundamentally wrong. If an association of Jews is created, e.g. under a Jewish governor, or even only a federation or a similar, harmless structure, the Jews gain a legal foothold in Germany for all eternity, a representative for their wishes, a tool for their plans, a legislative settlement for their secret links. In this way the impression at least is given that this concerns a national minority which is able to seek and will find protection under international law outside Germany. And one must not even appear to support this distortion of the Jewish question, particularly as it would be political madness to intertwine the domestic German resolution of the Jewish question with questions of foreign policy. All the proposals that seek a permanent status, a permanent arrangement for the Jews in Germany, fail to solve the Jewish question as they do not detach the Jews from Germany. And that is what it boils down to. If they are permitted forever to freeload off their host peoples, the Jews will remain a constant source of trouble that can readily provide the spark to reignite the open, destructive flame of Bolshevism, not to mention the fact that political uncertainty, the fragmentation of the people, and the threat to racial survival will be perpetually kept alive.⁴ Let us abandon such thoughts, whether they are born of inability to think or of evil intent, once and for all. In summary, it is only planned departure, migration, that can and must be controlled by the state.

Let us smash all organizational solidarity of the Jews in Germany and expel the dangerous Jewish agitators, who are hostile to the people and nonetheless have a tendency to form secret associations. In this way the Jews will be left with only the synagogue [and] the rabbi for protection and shelter. Let us then adopt the Zionists' plans and try to achieve an international agreement for the creation of a homeland for the Jews. Then we can solve the Jewish question not only for Germany but for Europe and the world. The whole world has an interest in the solution, in the removal of this source of unrest that is always the wellspring of Bolshevism. This we must clearly emphasize.

Perhaps the Jews can *become* a nation, a people. The precondition would be that Jewish labourers and craftspeople and Jewish settlers can emerge from the present Jewish population. If we regulate this process, then we create new foundations for resettlement. Scattering the Jews into the wind does not solve the Jewish question but exacerbates it; a planned resettlement, by contrast, is *the* possibility that presents itself to us.

Plans and programmes must have a future goal that does not merely consist in resolving a momentary, uncomfortable situation. What paves the way for a better future is the methodical approach to the solution of the Jewish question, not the organization of the Jews.

---

3 This passage was directed against the draft law dated 6 April 1933, which granted German Jews minority rights and thus potentially placed them under the protection of the League of Nations: see Doc. 27.
4 In the same issue Gercke published another article on the '*Mischling* question'. In it he wrote that a law prohibiting a mixed marriage did not solve the problem of 'racial intermixing': 'What is not legally permitted will happen illegally; what is impossible within marriage will take place illegitimately and outside marriage.' He furthermore criticized the Aryan Paragraph of the Law for the Restoration of the Professional Civil Service on the basis that an Aryan is 'someone with no Jewish ancestors at all': 'Grundsätzliches zur Mischlingsfrage', *Nationalsozialistische Monatshefte*, vol. 4, no. 38 (May 1933), pp. 197–202.

We have to build our state without the Jews; they can only remain stateless strangers and cannot obtain any legislative, juridical permanency. Only in this way will Ahasverus[5] be forced to take up his staff for the last time in order to then exchange it for an axe and spade.[6]

DOC. 49
On 11 June 1933 a representative of the American Jewish Joint Distribution Committee reports on a discussion with Leo Baeck in Berlin regarding the organization of the emigration of German Jews[1]

Memorandum (confidential), unsigned, Berlin, dated 11 June 1933, with undated enclosure

Interview with Dr. Baeck.[2]

Dr. Baeck was of the view that emigration must be the principal constructive activity. He gave me a short statement of his views, which is attached.[3] He fears that there may be another revolution in Germany this winter, it would have a bolshevist tendency. Many communists have joined the Nazis and if the economic position gets worse there may be an outbreak within the party.

No money should be sent to Germany from outside at present. The Jewish Communities can still cope with the relief problem within. It may be desirable that later help should be given to Jewish-Germans, particularly in the smaller places in order that they may maintain their organisation. It is of the greatest importance that the Community should not be allowed to collapse. He was concerned over lying propaganda which the German Government was carrying on and would probably pursue at the Economic Conference.[4] They were spreading false stories about Ostjuden and gross exaggeration of the number of Jewish officials. He thought this propaganda should be answered.

---

5 Ahasverus was a name given to the 'Wandering Jew' who, according to Christian legend, was doomed to live until the end of the world because he had taunted Jesus on the way to the Crucifixion.
6 The German Consulate General for South Africa informed the Reich Foreign Office on 29 August 1933 that the *Pretoria News* had published a Reuters report from Berlin about the Gercke memorandum: copy in BArch, R 1501/125708, fol. 604.

1 Archives of the Leo Baeck Institute, New York, at the Jüdisches Museum Berlin, MF 129. The interview section which goes down to point I., was written in English and has been reproduced according to the original, the remainder of the document has been translated from German.
2 Dr Leo Baeck (1873–1956), rabbi; reformist rabbi in Oppeln and Düsseldorf, 1897–1912; in Berlin, 1912–1943; lecturer at the School of Jewish Studies, 1913–1942; from 1922 chairman of the German Association of Rabbis; grand president of the German district of the B'nai B'rith Lodge; president of the Reich Representation of German Jews and the later Reich Association of Jews in Germany, 1933–1943; deported in 1943 to Theresienstadt concentration camp; emigrated to London after liberation; author of works including *Das Wesen des Judentums* (1922).
3 See the list of points printed at the end of the document.
4 A conference on the global economy began on 12 June 1933 in London and was attended by a representative from Germany.

With regard to the problem of the academic and intellectual persons, he was in communication with Dr. Dalton[5] in London and Dr. Frijda[6] in Holland. He was also in communication with an International Association for peace through the churches which was organising for the victims of German persecution.

He thought that emigration and relief schemes should not be restricted to professing Jews, but extended to persons who were partly of Jewish race and were persecuted as such.

The German Jews do not wish for minority rights but for the recovery of simple citizen rights.

They were having a meeting that day with the Reichsvertretung of the German Jews.[7] It was a Committee of five, of which he and Dr. Wolf,[8] a judge, were the Presidents. They represented the province organisations of the German Jews.[9]

1. Under the prevailing conditions, and in the case that this continues, there are in fact no prospects for the majority of German-Jewish youth, and psychologically there is no hope in this country to find a place to eke out an existence. A future for these people can only be found and indicated in other countries.

2. In the place of irregular attempts to flee, characteristic in the last months, there should be a systematic, organized emigration, which takes those eligible and suitable for the individual sectors to certain destinations. In connection with such emigration there can and will be prior professional retraining, where necessary. Only such a regulated emigration can prevent the undesirable consequences of fleeing.

3. The number of those who are designated for emigration can be estimated for the entire host territories at around 8,000 annually. A considerable number can find admission in Palestine, and even more so if parts of Transjordan are made accessible.

4. The regulation of emigration requires that the relief efforts are transferred from the philanthropic and charitable spheres to the level of supranational, international action. This task can be assigned either to the League of Nations, whose prestige and authority would be enhanced by this new role, or to a mandated government. The charitable organizations would retain their special aid duties.

5. Fulfilling this task requires that (a) an appointed office determines annually in all the countries in question in which cities and localities German Jews could find a place

---

5 Probably Baron Hugh Dalton (1887–1962), economist and politician; British minister of economic warfare, 1940–1942; president of the Board of Trade, 1942–1945; Chancellor of the Exchequer, 1945–1947.
6 Probably Herman Frijda (1870–1944), economist; deported to Auschwitz.
7 From April to June 1933 there was a Reich Representation of the Jewish Regional Associations, which, however, had little influence. Baeck was probably talking about this body. The Reich Representation of German Jews was not officially founded until 17 Sept. 1933. In it the regional unions of the Jewish religious communities and the three large Jewish organizations were represented: the Central Association of German Citizens of the Jewish Faith (CV), the Reich League of Jewish Combat Veterans, and the Zionist Federation for Germany. The Reich Representation was intended to combine the various strands of Jewry and represent them in public. It was headed by Leo Baeck.
8 Correctly: Dr Leo Wolff (1870–1958), lawyer; from 1910 local court judge in Berlin; chairman of the Jewish Community of Berlin, 1924–1927; member of the Central Association board; member of the Reich Representation board, 1933–1939; emigrated to Britain in 1939.
9 Below follows an undated statement from Baeck or the Reich Representation. It was composed in German and attached to the memorandum of the representative of the American Jewish Joint Distribution Committee (JDC).

of employment in specific professions; (b) the central organization of German Jews can regularly identify those persons who are morally, physically, and professionally suitable. A model for this is presented by the way in which immigration into Palestine has been regulated for some time.

6. The emigration of well-off persons who are suited to pursuing their own enterprises and determined to do so is left to individual initiative.[10]

DOC. 50
New York Times, 12 June 1933: report regarding a campaign to support German Jews[1]

Seeks to Aid Jews to Leave Germany.

B'rith Abraham Plans to Raise American Fund to Finance Emigration. Meets in Atlantic City. Joint Distribution Committee Reports $100,000 Received in Advance of Campaign.

Special to *The New York Times*. Atlantic City, N. J., June 11.

Jews throughout America were asked to help[2] finance the emigration of their German brethren to refuges in other lands by speakers here today at the annual convention of the Independent Order B'rith Abraham.[3] Only three courses are open to Hebrews in Germany, the 960 delegates were told by Abraham Herman,[4] New York President of the Hebrew Immigration Aid Society. 'These are economic extinction, emigration, or suicide,' Mr. Hermann said. He appealed for support in the work of transplanting refugees to the United States, South America and China, as well as to Palestine.

The situation under Hitler was the chief subject of today's addresses, including the annual report by Isadore Apfel, Grand Master of B'rith Abraham, and talks by Aaron J. Levy, New York State Supreme Court Justice, Judge Leon Sanders, and former Judge Gustave Hartman of New York, and Mayor Harry Bacharach of Atlantic City.

Grand Master Apfel declared 'the very existence of Jews in Germany is threatened by wild and barbaric hatred. Six hundred thousand Hebrews are being uprooted. Not only their possessions, but their lives are exposed to mob violence.'

Although the German Relief Campaign of the American Joint Distribution Committee is not scheduled to begin officially in this city until Wednesday evening, gifts totaling

---

10 In the records of the JDC, this document is followed by memoranda of discussions with Robert Weltsch from the newspaper *Jüdische Rundschau*, Dr Carl Melchior (economic aid), and Dr Tietz: Archives of the Leo Baeck Institute, New York, at the Jüdisches Museum Berlin, MF 129.

1 *New York Times*, 12 June 1933, p. 7. The original document is in English.
2 On 22 June 1933 the American Jewish Committee, the American Jewish Congress, and B'nai B'rith founded a joint committee to aid German Jews: Report of the American Jewish Congress dated 23 June 1933, Archives of the Leo Baeck Institute, New York, at the Jüdisches Museum Berlin, MF 57, reel 1.
3 Founded in 1887 as an offshoot of the Order B'rith Abraham; the latter was founded in 1859 in New York by German and Hungarian Jews.
4 Abraham Herman (1878–1947), pharmacist; director and board member of the Pennsylvania Exchange Bank; from 1926 president of the Hebrew Immigrant Aid Society; member of B'nai B'rith.

$100,000 were received during the last week,⁵ it was announced yesterday by Dudley D. Sicher,⁶ chairman of the New York drive.

This sum represents one-tenth of the $1,000,000 fund which New York Jews are endeavoring to raise as their quota of the $2,000,000 being sought for the relief of the Jews in Germany.

DOC. 51
On 12 June 1933 the Juvenile Court with Lay Judges in Frankfurt sentences Jewish youths for distributing political leaflets¹

Minutes of the hearing before the Juvenile Court with Lay Judges in Frankfurt am Main on 12 June 1933 (with verdict and enclosure)²

Public session of the *Juvenile* Court with Lay Judges. *Frankfurt am Main, 12 June 1933*³
In attendance:
*Local Court Judge Deschauer*⁴ as chairman,
Warehouse Keeper Konrad Buch
Retailer Hans Bamberger as lay judge,
Court Assessor Dr Weyrich as civil servant of the public prosecution,
Record by Krekels as clerk of the court.

Criminal case against
1. *Emil Carlebach*,⁵ born *10 July 1914 in Frankfurt am Main, resident there; 16 II Gaußstraße,*

---

5 The campaign was led by Felix M. Warburg and Rabbi Jonah B. Wise, national chairman of the American Jewish Joint Distribution Committee. The latter wrote a leaflet outlining the situation of those persecuted, the goals of the campaign, and to what end the funds would be used. The aid was used in Germany for poor relief and economic aid, construction of Jewish schools, and the demand for emigration: '600,000 Jews in Germany: What Is Their Fate?', *New York Times*, 12 June 1933, p. 7.
6 Dudley David Sicher (1876–1939), industrialist.

1 HHStAW, Abt. 461/15146, fols. 48–52 and 7a. Published in abridged form in Ernst Noam and Wolf-Arno Kropat (eds.), *Juden vor Gericht 1933–1945: Dokumente aus hessischen Justizakten* (Wiesbaden: Kommission für die Geschichte der Juden in Hessen, 1975), pp. 193–197. This document has been translated from German.
2 On the first page of the original there is an entry stamp from the Frankfurt public prosecutor's office dated 24 June 1933, as well as several handwritten notes and signatures.
3 All the points italicized in the main text were inserted in handwriting in the original.
4 Robert Deschauer (1878–1966), lawyer; juvenile court judge in Frankfurt from 1931.
5 Emil Carlebach (1914–2001), journalist; member of the Communist Party of Germany (KPD); spent three years in prison from 1934 after a special court sentenced him for high treason; afterwards imprisoned in a concentration camp until 1945; after 1945 co-founder of the *Frankfurter Rundschau* and the Association of Persecutees of the Nazi Regime (VVN); author of many books about the National Socialist period.

2. Paul Bloch,⁶ born 16 October 1911 in Zurich, resident in Frankfurt am Main, 2 Schützenstraße,

3. Ruth Cohnstaedt,⁷ born 17 June 1912 in Frankfurt am Main, resident there, 32 Hansa-Allee, for an offence against § 6 of the Regulation of the Reich President of 28 February 1933.⁸

When the case was called, *the* defendants appeared, *accompanied by their parents.*
The defendant named (1) with the solicitor Sandermayer.
The defendants with the solicitor Vogt
– The trial began with the summoning of the witnesses. The following appeared:
– Richard Rügen
– Karl Wolfram
– Fritz Hummel

The witnesses were informed about the subject under investigation and the persons accused. They were told about the meaning of the oath and specifically that the oath related to answering such questions that were put to the witness about his person and the circumstances otherwise provided for in § 68 of the Code of Criminal Procedure. They then left the courtroom for the time being.

The defendants, questioned about their personal circumstances, stated:
as on page 30 of the file
The decision of 26 May 1933 concerning the opening of the main trial was read aloud.
*The leaflet was read aloud.*⁹
The defendants were asked whether they wanted to respond to the accusation.
They stated:
concerning (1) I received the leaflet and distributed it together with the other two defendants.
concerning (2) I also received leaflets from a third person and went away with the others. It was said to be a dangerous matter.
concerning (3) arranged to meet Carlebach, met up with Bloch, arranged to meet in order to distribute leaflets.
The defendants' parents were given the opportunity to make a statement.
Neither side called any witnesses.

---

6 Paul Bloch (b. 1911), retailer; member of communist organizations from 1931; sentenced by the lay judges court in Frankfurt for storing leaflets, 1933; imprisoned until March 1934; in 1935 arrested again and sentenced by the Higher Regional Court in Kassel to seven years' penal servitude as leader of the Hesse-Frankfurt branch of the KPD; subsequently transferred to a concentration camp.
7 Ruth Cohnstaedt (b. 1912), retail apprentice.
8 According to the Regulation of the Reich President against Betrayal of the German People and Highly Treasonous Activities (28 Feb. 1933), the production and distribution of a printed publication, the content of which corresponded to the definition of high treason through 'incitement to violent struggle against the state's authority' or in another way (§§ 81–86 of the Criminal Code), could be punished by a sentence of between one month and three years in prison: *Reichsgesetzblatt*, 1933, I, p. 85.
9 See the attachment to this document below.

After each document was read aloud, the defendants were asked whether they wished to make a statement.

The public prosecutor and then the defendants – and the defence counsel – were given the floor for their remarks.

The public prosecutor requested:

in the case of the defendant Carlebach a prison sentence of three months
in the case of the defendant Bloch a prison sentence of three months
in the case of the defendant Cohnstaedt a prison sentence of six weeks
and repeal of the arrest warrant against all the defendants.

The defendant named in (2) and the defence counsels plead: *acquittal, possibly mild punishment.*

The defendants were informed that a conviction could also follow for a violation of the Press Law (§§ 6, 19) and that they should also focus their defence on this.

The defendants had the last word.

The ruling was announced *with an explanation of the rights of appeal* by reading aloud the operative part of the verdict and by verbal communication of the essential content of the grounds for the verdict:

For violating §§ 6, 19 of the Press Law the defendants are each sentenced to six weeks' imprisonment and shall meet the costs of the proceedings. The thirty days of custody will count towards the sentence.

The detention order is lifted.

Instead of the remaining twelve days in prison, fines of RM 100 each are stipulated for the defendants Carlebach and Cohnstaedt and RM 50 for the defendant Bloch in accordance with § 23b of the Criminal Code. For the defendant Bloch monthly instalments are decreased by RM 5.

Deschauer Krekels[10]

Grounds:

The main trial revealed the following based on the defendants' testimonies: the defendant Carlebach, 19 years of age, is the son of Jewish parents. The father is an independent retailer who runs a fashion accessories shop. After passing the school-leaving examination, the defendant began an apprenticeship in retail training at the Schiff company in Frankfurt, where he remains today.

The defendant Bloch, 21 years old, is also from a Jewish family. His father is deceased. He worked for the Mosse company for six years, but was dismissed on 1 May 1933. The defendant lives together with his mother, who has limited financial means, and contributes to the shared household from his earnings.

The defendant Cohnstaedt is the daughter of a Jewish editor and a Christian mother. She is a dissident. After passing the school-leaving examination, she initially studied law for two semesters, but then abandoned her studies. She lives with her parents.

None of the defendants has a criminal record.

On the evening of 12 May 1933 the defendant Carlebach met the defendant Cohnstaedt at Café Rothschild. According to the statement made by defendant Carlebach, a

---

10 In the original there is a stamp here: 'The judgement is legally binding. Frankfurt am Main, 21 June 1933.'

stranger gave him around thirty leaflets to distribute, which he placed unread into his pocket. The defendant Cohnstaedt noticed none of this.

On the same evening, the defendant Bloch entered the café; he also received around thirty leaflets from a stranger to be distributed and placed them unread into his pocket. He greeted the defendant Carlebach, whom he knew, and met by chance, and who introduced to him the co-defendant Cohnstaedt. Then Bloch sat down at the table with Carlebach and Cohnstaedt. In the course of the evening, Bloch and Carlebach agreed to distribute the leaflets together and asked the defendant Cohnstaedt to join in. It was then stated explicitly that the matter was extremely dangerous. The defendant Cohnstaedt agreed to participate, and the defendants left the café at around 12 o'clock and set off for the housing estate that lies in the opposite direction to their homes. Once there, Bloch and Carlebach dropped leaflets into the letterboxes. When three SA men arrived, the defendants ran away. Because of this, the SA men noticed them, arrested them, and handed them over the next morning to the police. The defendants have been in custody since 14 May.

The main proceedings were opened against the defendants for common violation of § 6 of the Regulation of the Reich President against Betrayal of the German People and Highly Treasonous Activities. This sanction presupposes that a printed document is distributed containing at the least a call or incitement to prepare a violent struggle against state authority. Thus, the *violent* struggle against state authority must in some way be outlined in the printed document. The distributed leaflet begins with 'Fellow NSBO member!'[11] and ends with 'RGO Greater Frankfurt'.[12] The leaflet constantly repeats the following, but in the most varied formulations: 'Fight in the NSBO; a national revolution can only be successfully carried out if we all fight together; join the front of the fighting proletariat; long live the struggle for a free, socialist Germany'.

However, there is nothing in the leaflet that constitutes a call to acts of violence. The purpose of the leaflet is to undermine the power of the National Socialist state using the insidious poison of doubt, but not in the open and direct manner of the unlawful but honest struggle. The unity of the German people, achieved by lengthy and relentless struggle, is to be destroyed and the course of destruction of state power is to be followed. However, this kind of cowardly and underhanded struggle is not punishable under the law. Therefore, a conviction could not be made on the basis of § 6 of the named regulation.

The leaflet is merely signed 'RGO Greater Frankfurt'. It was therefore necessary to establish whether the leaflet fulfils the provisions of § 6 of the Reich Press Law. The leaflet is a printed document in terms of this law, as it was produced by a copying process that permits mass reproduction (cf. Häntzschel, Reich Press Law § 2, note 2e). It must therefore state the name and place of residence of the printer and publisher. Both these pieces of information are missing; the information 'RGO Greater Frankfurt' does not suffice. Therefore, the accused were to be punished as co-perpetrators in accordance with §§ 6, 19 line 1 Press Law, § 47 of the Criminal Code, as they distributed the leaflet together in conscious and willing association.

11 Nationalsozialistische Betriebszellenorganisation: National Socialist Factory Cell Organization.
12 Revolutionäre Gewerkschafts-Opposition der KPD: Revolutionary Trade Union Opposition of the Communist Party of Germany; founded in 1930.

In the sentencing, the defendants' previous good repute and youth were considered as a mitigating factor. Two aspects favoured, on the other hand, an aggravation of the sentence: the sophisticated way in which the act was carried out and the danger the offence posed to the public.[13] In the execution of the deed, the defendants tried to make the matter seem like a gallant adventure and distributed the leaflets in a neighbourhood located in the opposite direction to where they lived. During and after their arrest, they admitted only to what could be proved even without their confession.[14] There was not the slightest sign of remorse, or even the recognition that it was not acceptable that they had violated the criminal laws out of discontentment with current conditions. On the contrary, the defendants are lawbreakers trying to fight the state in the most insidious manner, and do not want to resign themselves to the fact that the German people are governed exclusively by Germans. In view of these aggravating factors, the mitigating considerations were of no consequence. Since the state can be seriously damaged by the repeated distribution of this kind of leaflet, which endangers the people, the maximum admissible penalty was to be registered. The deduction of the period in custody is based on § 60 of the Criminal Code [and] the conversion of the remaining prison sentence into a fine according to § 25 of the Criminal Code. Since the defendant Bloch, unlike the other two affluent defendants, has lesser means, his fine was fixed at half of the fine registered against his two co-defendants, with permission to pay in instalments. The cost decision is based on § 463 of the Code of Criminal Procedure.

Deschauer[15]

NSBO[16]

Fellow NSBO member!

You joined the NSBO because you believed that your interests are represented by this organization!

And if you did not want to join of your own free will, you were forced into it by threats and blatant terror!

Colleagues, what can you demand from the NSBO:

Standard wages, increase in the pay scale, abolition of the volunteer system, the campaign against overtime, equal pay for female and male employees, a seven-hour day with no loss of pay and your specific operational requirements!

Demand from the NSBO that *members* of the *management* are not permitted to become NSBO members!

Fight in the NSBO against the exploitation of members, against high membership fees that you must pay without any services given in return. *Fight* against the many special payments, for example the demand that an entrance fee of 25 pfennigs must be paid during a roll call of members! Fight in the NSBO against the increase in the price of fat, oil, etc., which have already risen by 100 per cent without your salary having even increased by 1 per cent!

---

13 In the original the following phrase is crossed out: 'and the defendants' obstinacy'.
14 In the original the following sentence is crossed out: 'The two male defendants in particular showed themselves in the main trial to be thoroughly obstinate.'
15 The leaflet printed below is enclosed with the document.
16 In the original there is a large square here with NSBO inside it.

Keep asking your group leaders when the Treaty of Versailles and the Young Plan[17] are going to be torn up, and why Hitler only a few days ago recognized the treaties as legitimate! Ask who it benefits if lower-ranking Jewish workers and employees are dismissed at the NSBO's behest and no Christian colleagues then join the company?

Fellow NSBO members!

You must keep raising these issues, not alone but together with other like-minded fellow members!

Do not let yourself be put off; you have the right to make demands, you have the right to improvements!

Volksgemeinschaft – yes, indeed,

Community of all the oppressed, all workers, all salaried employees, small farmers, low-level civil servants, but not a *Volksgemeinschaft* with major agrarians, large-scale retailers, princes, and counts!

A *national* revolution is supposed to have taken place?

You are just as bound by the chains of Versailles as you were four months ago!

We are told that *national socialist* revolution has dawned!

Where is the socialism? Where is the expropriation of the bankers, stock exchange magnates, and coal barons?

You want national and social liberation from the yoke of capitalism! But this will never be carried out by Hitler or Göring, who themselves are tied to capital, who run around after Italy and Poland!

A national and social revolution can only be brought to victory by all of us together in *struggle*!

Join in the *struggle* against the national and international exploiters! Fight in the NSBO and you will realize who represents your interests.

You will realize why the *revolutionary organizations*, the Communist Party of Germany and the *RGO* are being suppressed, banned, and slandered! Because they are still leading the oppressed against the oppressors!

Do not lose heart!

If you have recognized the betrayal of the Nazi Party, join the front of the fighting proletariat!

Long live the battle for a free socialist Germany!

RGO Greater Frankfurt.

---

17 The Dawes Plan (1924–1930) and the Young Plan (1930–1932) regulated Germany's reparations payments after the First World War. They spread out the payments to alleviate their burden. It was not only the NSDAP that fiercely opposed the agreements on the grounds that the plans would make Germany dependent for a long time on foreign countries.

DOC. 52

The Reich Statistical Office reports on the regional distribution of Jews by faith according to the results of the census of 16 June 1933[1]

[...][2]

2. The distribution of Jews by faith in the German Reich

a. *The Jews by faith according to city and state*[3]

The bulk of Jews by faith live in large cities. In 1933 around 354,000 Jews by faith were counted here, i.e. 70.9 per cent of their total number, whereas only 30.4 per cent of the entire Reich population live in large cities. Jews by faith constitute in total 1.79 per cent of the population in large cities and thereby reach far more than double their share of the Reich population (0.77 per cent). In all other municipal size classes, they are proportionately more weakly represented than in the Reich average, and indeed the share of Jews by faith in the total population falls regularly with descending municipal size.

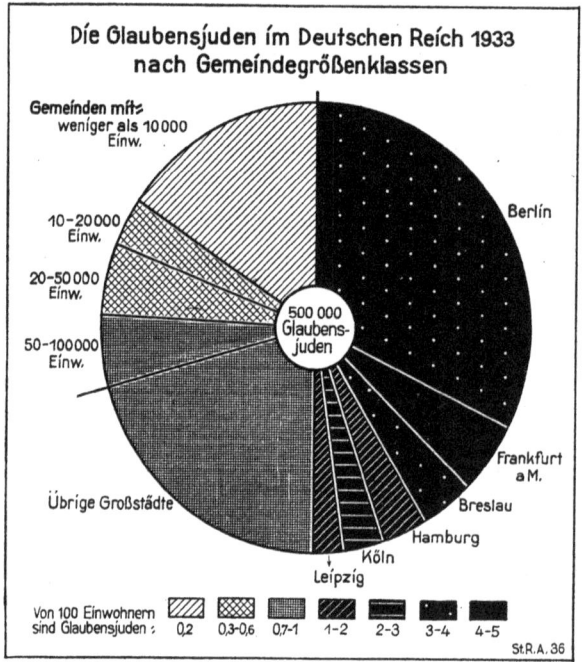

1 *Statistik des Deutschen Reichs*, vol. 451/5, *Volks-, Berufs- und Betriebszählung vom 16. Juni 1933. Volkszählung. Die Bevölkerung des Deutschen Reichs nach den Ergebnissen der Volkszählung 1933*, no. 5: *Die Glaubensjuden im Deutschen Reich*, Statistisches Reichsamt (Berlin: Verlag für Sozialpolitik, Wirtschaft und Statistik, 1936), pp. 9–10. This document has been translated from German.
2 Point 2 is preceded by an introduction and point 1, 'Die Glaubensjuden im Deutschen Reich und ihre zahlenmäßige Entwicklung seit der Emanzipation' (The Jews by faith in the German Reich and their development in numbers since their emancipation).
3 The pie chart is titled 'Jews by faith in the German Reich according to municipal size, 1933'. Viewed clockwise, it shows the proportion of Jews by faith in named cities and 'other cities', and in municipalities of sizes ranging from 10,000–100,000 residents (Einw.). The shading denotes the number of Jews by faith per 100 residents.

Jews by faith in the German Reich* in 1933 according to municipal size categories

Municipalities with ... inhabitants	Total population of the Reich		Jews by faith		Number of Jews by faith per 100 inhabitants
	Number	Percentage	Number	Percentage	
Under 10,000	33,039,382	50.6	77,168	15.5	0.23
10,000 to 20,000	3,930,115	6.0	17,172	3.4	0.44
20,000 to 50,000	5,028,133	7.7	25,714	5.1	0.51
50,000 to 100,000	3,418,495	5.3	25,508	5.1	0.75
100,000 to 200,000	3,430,297	5.3	31,091	6.2	0.91
200,000 to 500,000	5,776,234	8.9	50,824	10.2	0.88
Over 500,000 (excl. Berlin)	6,353,304	9.7	111,641	22.4	1.76
City of Berlin	4,242,501	6.5	160,564	32.1	3.78
Total	65,218,461	100	499,682	100	0.77
100,000 and more combined	19,802,336	30.4	354,120	70.9	1.79

* Without Saarland.

Only around one-sixth of Jews by faith live in municipalities with fewer than 10,000 residents, whereas more than half of the Reich population has been counted in the municipalities of this size class. The Jews by faith identified here live for the most part in rural communities and small towns of 2,000 to under 10,000 residents, and will therefore be referred to in the following as small town Jews by faith.

The big city element of Jewry comes even more to the fore if we look separately at the cities with 500,000 or more inhabitants. More than half of all Jews by faith counted in 1933 in the German Reich live in the 10 cities with more than half a million inhabitants, in which they constitute 2.57 per cent of the population.

Jews by faith in cities with 500,000 inhabitants or more

Cities	Inhabitants	Jews by faith		
		Number	Percentage of inhabitants	Percentage of Jews by faith in the Reich*
Berlin	4,242,501	160,564	3.78	32.1
Frankfurt a. M.	555,857	26,158	4.71	5.2
Breslau	625,198	20,202	3.23	4.1
Hamburg	1,129,307	16,885	1.50	3.4
Cologne	756,605	14,816	1.96	3.0
Leipzig	713,470	11,564	1.62	2.3
Munich	735,388	9,005	1.22	1.8
Essen	654,461	4,506	0.69	0.9
Dresden	642,143	4,397	0.68	0.9
Dortmund	540,875	4,108	0.76	0.8
In total	10,595,805	272,205	2.57	54.5

* Without Saarland.

Berlin, Frankfurt am Main and Breslau are decisive. In Berlin alone, around 160,000 Jews by faith, i.e. 32.1 per cent of their total number, were counted; their share in the population constitutes 3.78 per cent here. They are represented proportionately to an even greater extent in Frankfurt am Main with 4.71 per cent; by contrast, the proportion in Dresden and the industrial cities of Essen and Dortmund is less significant (0.68 or 0.69 and 0.76 per cent respectively).

This clustering of Jewry in a few large places is first and foremost a consequence of the increasing formation and concentration of the economy driven by the financial sector in the larger cities. Hence, since the introduction of free movement and free enterprise, the Jews by faith have left the small cities and gathered in ever greater numbers in the major cities. As the bar chart and the overview on the next page demonstrate,[4] the number of big city Jews by faith in the German Reich multiplied by more than five from 1871 to 1925.[5] In 1871 not quite one-fifth of all Jews by faith in the Reich (in today's borders) lived in major cities, in 1900 almost half, and twenty-five years later two-thirds.

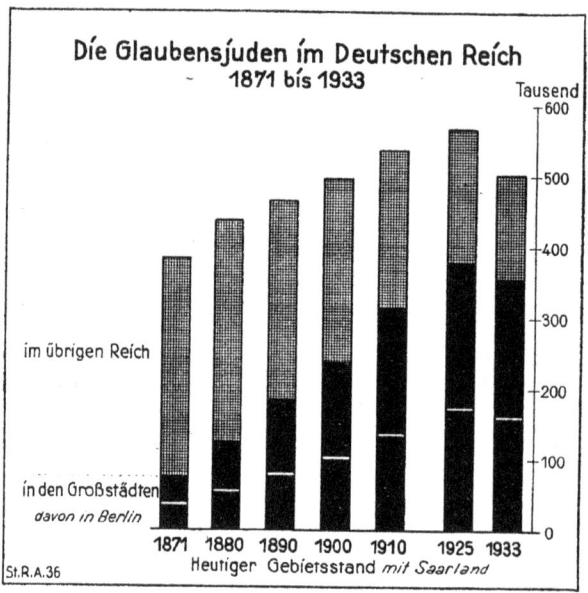

The strengthening of the big city element among Jews by faith continued during the eight years from 1925 to 1933. By contrast, the share of Jews by faith in the overall population of the major cities, as well as in the Reich in general, has continually declined since 1880, a consequence of their decreasing natural reproduction as well as their losses through persons leaving the religion and as a result of mixed marriages.

---

4 The author is referring to the bar chart that follows, titled 'Jews by faith in the German Reich, 1871–1933'. The black shading denotes Jews in cities, with the section below the white line representing Jews in Berlin. The grey shading denotes Jews elsewhere in the Reich. The dates refer to the 'current territorial status of the Reich, including Saarland'. The figures are given in thousands.

5 From 1875 to 1910, population censuses took place in the German Reich every five years, and thereafter only at irregular intervals, e.g. 1916, 1917, and 1919. The population censuses of 1925, 1933, and 1939 included both occupation and business censuses.

DOC. 53

The Reich Statistical Office reports on the occupational distribution of Jews by faith according to the results of the census of 16 June 1933[1]

V. *The occupational and social distribution of the Jews by faith in the German Reich*[2]

Almost half of the Jews by faith, like the overall population, belong to the working population.[3] *Among those without occupation,*[4] *in accordance with the ageing population among the Jews, there are proportionately more pensioners, rentiers, etc.*[5] *and wives but as a result of the lower number of children fewer 'other relatives'.*

More than three-fifths of the Jews by faith are in the trade and transport sector of the economy. Almost a quarter of the working population of Jewish faith work in industry and skilled crafts, but here too they are predominantly in economic sectors in which commercial activity plays a significant role (e.g. garment manufacture).

The distribution according to individual occupations shows that the Jews by faith favour certain academic and artistic as well as all the more important commercial professions, while they are only weakly represented in almost all the skilled craft and manual occupations.

The Jews are economically independent to a far greater extent than the Reich population; almost half of the Jewish working population are self-employed, compared with only a sixth of the working population overall. Those Jews who are employed by others are predominantly salaried employees, while the share of manual workers in contrast to the Reich population is extremely small.

1. *Distribution according to the working population and those without occupation*

The Jews by faith are employed to roughly the same extent as the Reich population overall; of around 500,000 Jews, around 240,000 or 48.1 per cent are employed, and of the Reich population, 49.5 per cent. Proportionately fewer Jewish women belong to the working population than women among the total population (27.4 per cent, as compared with 34.2 per cent). The proportion of retirees living on their own assets, also holders of an annuity, pensioners, benefit recipients, etc. is, at 12.2 per cent, considerably higher among the Jews by faith than the corresponding share of the Reich population (8.9 per cent). This is in

---

1 *Statistik des Deutschen Reichs*, vol. 451/5, *Volks-, Berufs- und Betriebszählung vom 16. Juni 1933. Volkszählung. Die Bevölkerung des Deutschen Reichs nach den Ergebnissen der Volkszählung 1933*, no. 5: *Die Glaubensjuden im Deutschen Reich*, compiled by the Statistisches Reichsamt (Berlin: Verlag für Sozialpolitik, Wirtschaft und Statistik, 1936), pp. 22–23. This document has been translated from German.

2 Footnote in the original: 'The professional and social organization of the Jews by faith has been carried out in the same way as that of the general population in the occupation census of 1933. The classification in the occupation census of 1933 is portrayed at length in volume 453 of *Statistik des Deutschen Reichs*, number 1; a brief overview can also be found on pp. 29–30 of this issue.'

3 'Working population' or, alternatively, 'economically active persons', are used to translate the term *Erwerbspersonen*, which in the *Statistik des Deutschen Reiches* comprises the two categories of *Erwerbstätige* (employed) and *Erwerbslose* (unemployed).

4 *Berufslose*: persons who do not count as part of the working population.

5 'Pensioners, rentiers, etc.': the German term is *berufslose Selbständige*, persons who are economically independent, but without occupation: a category comprising mainly rentiers living on their own assets and those in receipt of various categories of pensions and benefits.

line with the significant ageing of the population and the greater economic independence of the Jews. Women are particularly strongly represented among the pensioners, rentiers, etc. of the Jewish faith. Among the relatives without a main occupation, who are economically dependent on the working population or the pensioners, rentiers, etc. and are living in their households, the wives without a main occupation are slightly more strongly represented among the Jews than in the Reich population. The share of the 'other relatives without a main occupation', on the other hand, lags behind the Reich average as a result of the lower number of children among Jews.

The divergent age structure also causes several differences between native and immigrant Jews. The foreign and foreign-born Jews are more weakly represented than the average among the pensioners, rentiers, etc. but more strongly represented among the relatives without a main occupation, and especially among the 'other relatives'.

Larger differences in the composition of Jews by faith and the Reich population can be discerned in a further breakdown according to business and professional affiliation and social status:

2. Distribution according to employment in different types of business
(a) The working population according to economic sectors, selected economic groups, and branches

The Jews are especially active in trade. Around 147,300 or 61.3 per cent of the working population of Jews by faith are in the economic sector of trade and transport, compared with only 18.4 per cent of the total working population in the Reich. Of the total working population identified in this economic sector 2.48 per cent are of the Jewish faith, compared with the proportion of Jews in the total working population of only 0.74 per cent. In the 'public service and private services' sector – this concerns predominantly the private services – Jews by faith with a working population of around 30,000 or 1.11 per cent are also at the time of the census more strongly represented than corresponds to their share in the working population as a whole.

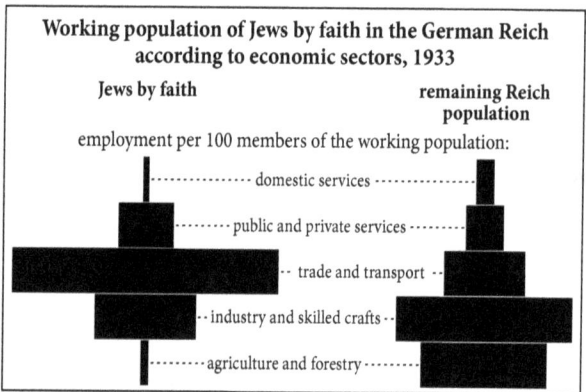

Working population of Jews by faith in the German Reich according to economic sectors, 1933

Jews by faith   remaining Reich population

employment per 100 members of the working population:
- domestic services
- public and private services
- trade and transport
- industry and skilled crafts
- agriculture and forestry

Some 12.5 per cent of the working population of Jews by faith belong to this economic sector, as compared with only 8.4 per cent of the total working population. Particularly low, and characteristic for the economic activity of Jewry in the German Reich, is the

Jews by faith in the German Reich,* 1933, according to occupation

Demographic group	Total population of the Reich		of which female		Jews by faith Total		% of the total population	of which female		Of whom Native		Immigrants†		% of Jews by faith
	Number	%	Number	%	Number	%		Number	%	Number	%	Number	%	
Working population of which in active employment	32,296,074	49.5	11,479,041	34.2	240,487	48.1	0.74	71,540	27.4	185,344	48.2	55,143	47.9	22.9
	26,441,056	40.5	10,336,455	30.8	206,826	41.4	0.78	60,444	23.2	161,490	42.0	45,336	39.4	21.9
Unemployed	5,855,018	9.0	1,142,586	3.4	33,661	6.7	0.57	11,096	4.2	23,854	6.2	9,807	8.5	29.1
Pensioners, rentiers, etc.	5,821,556	8.9	3,035,980	9.1	60,941	12.2	1.05	39,502	15.1	51,338	13.3	9,603	8.4	15.8
Relatives without a main occupation	27,100,831	41.6	19,017,878	56.7	198,254	39.7	0.73	149,893	57.5	147,995	38.5	50,259	43.7	25.4
Wives without a main occupation	9,900,947	15.2	9,900,947	29.5	84,482	16.9	0.85	84,482	32.4	63,878	16.6	20,604	17.9	24.4
Other relatives without a main occupation	17,199,884	26.4	9,116,931	27.2	113,772	22.8	0.66	65,411	25.1	84,117	21.9	29,655	25.8	26.1
Total	65,218,461	100	33,532,899	100	499,682	100	0.77	260,935	100	384,677	100	115,005	100	23.0

* Without Saarland. † See the explanation on p. 15.[6]

6 The explanation is not reproduced here. It refers to the total number of immigrant Jews by faith, which was estimated at approx. 115,000 people: *Die Glaubensjuden im Deutschen Reich*, p. 22.

Working population of Jews by faith in the German Reich,* 1933, by economic sector

Economic sectors	Total working population in the Reich				Working population of Jews by faith						Of whom			
	Total		of which female		Total			of which female		Native		Immigrants†		
	Number	%	Number	%	Number	%	% of the total population	Number	%	Number	%	Number	%	% of the Jews by faith
Agriculture and forestry	9,342,785	28.9	4,648,782	40.5	4,167	1.7	0.04	2,595	3.6	3,846	2.1	321	0.6	7.7
Industry and skilled crafts	13,052,982	40.4	2,758,802	24.0	55,655	23.1	0.43	15,663	21.9	40,175	21.7	15,480	28.1	27.8
Trade and transport	5,932,069	18.4	1,920,758	16.7	147,314	61.3	2.48	39,740	55.6	113,676	61.3	33,638	61.0	22.8
Public service and private services	2,698,656	8.4	901,063	7.9	29,974	12.5	1.11	10,249	14.3	24,820	13.4	5,154	9.3	17.2
Domestic services	1,269,582	3.9	1,249,636	10.9	3,377	1.4	0.27	3,293	4.6	2,827	1.5	550	1.0	16.3
Total working population	32,296,074	100	11,479,041	100	240,487	100	0.74	71,540	100	185,344	100	55,143	100	22.9

* Without Saarland. † See the explanation on p. 15.[7]

7 See fn. 3.

number of Jews by faith employed in agriculture and in domestic services. The Jews by faith also have a comparatively low presence in manufacturing industry and skilled crafts, compared with the total population (23.1 per cent and 40.4 per cent respectively).

The working population of Jews by faith with foreign nationality or birth, a total of around 55,000 persons, are at 28.1 per cent proportionately somewhat more strongly represented in industry and skilled crafts than the native Jews; they have barely any share at all, however, in agriculture and forestry.

If those economic sectors occupied more strongly by the Jews are broken down into economic groups and branches, the one-sided activity of Jewry in the German economy comes even more sharply to the fore.

Breaking down the economic sector occupied most strongly by the Jews in numerical and proportional terms, *trade and transport*, into economic groups demonstrates that the roughly 147,000 Jewish members of the working population are active almost exclusively in trade, while the transport economic groups are of almost no significance for the Jews. Around 137,000 persons are accounted for alone by the economic group of commercial trade and activities connected to trade, where they again find themselves for the most part in trade in merchandise and produce. Property trading, conveyancing etc. is the branch where Jews are most prevalent; here, almost every tenth person is of the Jewish faith.

The roughly 33,600 immigrant Jews by faith in the trade and transport sector constitute just under a quarter of the Jewish persons employed in this sector. The bulk of them (78.7 per cent) work in trade in goods and produce among them. Almost half of all Jews in peddling and street trading are immigrants (around 1,000 persons).

Within the economic sector of *industry and crafts*, garment manufacture, in which production is frequently largely connected with commercial activity, stands out with around 22,000 Jews by faith in the working population, i.e. 39.5 per cent of the Jews in the sector and 1.49 per cent of the working population counted in this group in general (see the overview on the next page).[8] Of these, around 14,800 persons alone work in the economic branch of tailoring, i.e. 1.71 per cent of all persons employed in this economic branch. Even higher, at 2.65 per cent, is the share of the Jews among hatters and milliners and, at 5.28 per cent, among the furriers (fur Jews), even if the absolute numbers here are small.

Of the roughly 10,600 Jews by faith working in the production of food, beverages and tobacco, around 6,000 work as butchers or in associated businesses; they constitute here 1.57 per cent of the working population overall. Alongside the production of goods, commercial activity also plays a significant role here.

An example of how Jews have frequently occupied managerial and intellectually leading positions is provided by the construction economic group: while the share of the Jews by faith in the entire group accounts for 0.14 per cent of the total working population, it rises to 1.37 per cent in the case of the architecture and surveying firms. In the remaining economic groups and branches of the industry and crafts sector, the Jews are proportionately and generally also numerically only weakly represented. In the case of the foreign and foreign-born Jews, the clothing trade especially plays a big role; this

---

8 The author is referring to the table after next, entitled 'Jews by faith in the working population in industry and skilled crafts according to selected economic groups and branches'.

Working population of Jews by faith in trade and transport, according to economic groups and selected branches

Economic group (EG)/ economic branch (EB)	Total working population in the Reich		Working population of Jews by faith			Of whom immigrants*		
	Number	%	Number	%	% of the total working population	Number	%	% of the Jews by faith
EG 41 Commercial trade and activities connected to trade	3,224,214	54.4	137,048	93.0	4.25	31,885	94.8	23.3
of which EB 411 Trade in goods and produce among them	2,725,945	46.0	114,659	77.8	4.21	26,480	78.7	23.1
EB 412 Peddling and street trading	55,077	0.9	2,196	1.5	3.99	1,034	3.1	47.1
EB 413 Publishing industry	127,250	2.2	1,831	1.2	1.44	448	1.3	24.5
EB 414 Property trading, conveyance etc.	180,290	3.0	17,100	11.6	9.48	3,620	10.8	21.2
EB 415 Haulage, storage and surveillance, leasing, market, and trade fair industry	135,652	2.3	1,262	0.9	0.93	303	0.9	24.0
EG 42 Banking, including stock market and insurance	393,082	6.6	6,272	4.3	1.6	769	2.3	12.3
of which EB 421 Banking and stock market	199,482	3.4	4,085	2.8	2.05	450	1.3	11.0
EB 422 Private insurance	107,881	1.8	1,908	1.3	1.77	295	0.9	15.5
EG 43 and 44 Transport	1,551,991	26.2	988	0.7	0.06	181	0.5	18.3
EG 45 Catering and innkeeping	762,782	12.8	3,006	2.0	0.39	803	2.4	26.7
Trade and transport economic sector overall	5,932,069	100	147,314	100	2.48	33,638	100	22.8

* See the explanation on p. 15.⁹

economic group comprises more than half of all the immigrant Jews active in industry and skilled crafts. Almost half of the roughly 30,000 strong Jewish population in the group comprising *public service and private services* (excluding domestic services) work in the administration, church, education, childcare, legal advice, etc. group. They can be found here above all in the legal and economic advice branch, where they comprise 3.27 per cent of the total working population; there is also a strong Jewish presence in

9 See fn. 3.

Working population of Jews by faith in industry and crafts according to selected economic groups and branches

Economic group (EG)/ economic branch (EB)	Total working population in the Reich		Working population of Jews by faith			Of whom immigrants*		
	Number	%	Number	%	% of the total working population	Number	%	% of the Jews by faith
EG 22 to 26 Metal industry	3,068,509	23.5	7,220	13.0	0.24	1,851	12.0	25.6
EG 27 Chemical industry	362,751	2.8	2,223	4.0	0.61	469	3.0	21.1
EG 28 Textile industry	1,118,715	8.6	3,517	6.3	0.31	756	4.9	21.5
EG 35 Food, beverages and tobacco trade	1,629,645	12.5	10,568	19.0	0.65	1,386	9.0	13.1
of which EB 354 Meat and fish industry	379,451	2.9	5,966	10.7	1.57	357	2.3	6.0
EG 36 Clothing trade	1,477,161	11.3	22,024	39.5	1.49	8,389	54.2	38.1
of which EB 361 Tailoring	865,029	6.6	14,823	26.7	1.71	5,476	35.4	36.9
EB 362 Furriery	32,829	0.2	1,735	3.1	5.28	1,226	7.9	70.7
EB 363 Cap makers, hatters and milliners	73,994	0.6	1,962	3.5	2.65	497	3.2	25.3
EB 366 Shoemaking and shoe industry	366,428	2.8	2,262	4.1	0.62	947	6.1	41.9
EG 37 Construction and related trades	2,002,803	15.4	2,771	5.0	0.14	781	5.0	28.2
of which EB 371 Architecture and surveying firms	31,765	0.3	436	0.8	1.37	125	0.8	28.7
EB 372 Civil engineering	1,948,366	14.9	2,291	4.1	0.12	646	4.2	28.2
Other economic groups in industry	3,393,398	25.9	7,332	13.2	0.22	1,845	11.9	25.2
E. sector 2/3 Industry and skilled crafts overall	13,052,982	100	55,655	100	0.43	15,480	100	27.8

* See the explanation on p. 15.[10]

the economic branch of fine arts, freelance writing, and academic activity, as well as the residential trade. In the economic branch of Reich, regional, municipal administration, and public administration of justice, a total of 1,827 persons of the Jewish faith in the working population were identified in June 1933, i.e. 0.22 per cent of the total working population in this economic branch.

Roughly 11,000 additional Jews were counted in the group comprising health and hygiene. More than eight-tenths are apportioned to the branch of nursing, sanatoriums,

---

10 See fn. 3.

Working population of Jews by faith in the public and private services economic sector, according to economic groups and selected branches

Economic group (EG)/ economic branch (EB)	Total working population in the Reich		Working population of Jews by faith			Of whom immigrants*		
	Number	%	Number	%	% of the total working population	Number	%	% of the Jews by faith
EG 51 Administration, church, education, childcare, legal advice, etc.	1,682,018	62.3	14,838	49.5	0.88	2,610	50.6	17.6
of which								
EB 513 Church, institutions for religious purposes	165,072	6.1	1,792	6.0	1.09	587	11.4	32.8
EB 514 Education, childcare, tuition	391,536	14.5	2,585	8.6	0.66	466	9.0	18.0
EB 515 Fine arts, freelance writing and academic activity	23,368	0.9	907	3.0	3.88	274	5.3	30.2
EB 516 Legal and economic advice etc.	191,035	7.1	6,249	20.9	3.27	698	13.5	11.2
EB 517 Residential trade (property management) etc.	67,505	2.5	1,478	4.9	2.19	437	8.5	29.6
EG 52 Health and hygiene	748,992	27.8	10,811	36.1	1.44	1,332	25.8	12.3
of which								
EB 521 Nursing, sanatoriums etc.	401,448	14.9	9,105	30.4	2.27	969	18.8	10.6
EB 522 Pharmacies	28,278	1.1	706	2.4	2.5	53	1.0	7.5
EG 53 Welfare services	104,512	3.9	1,307	4.3	1.25	215	4.2	16.4
EG 54 Theatre, moving pictures and film exposure, broadcasting, music business, sports and entertainment	163,134	6.0	3,018	10.1	1.85	997	19.4	33.0
E. sector 5 Public and private services (excluding domestic services) in total	2,698,656	100	29,974	100	1.11	5,154	100	17.2

* See the explanation on p. 15.[11]

11 See fn. 3.

etc. and here account for 2.27 per cent of the total working population. The in itself very low number of economically active Jews in the pharmacies branch accounts for 2.50 per cent of the total working population in this branch. Worthy of mention is, finally, the high share of Jews (1.85 per cent) in the group of theatre, moving pictures, etc. In the branches of churches, institutions for religious purposes, and fine arts, etc. and in the group of theatres, moving pictures, etc., the foreign and foreign-born Jews make up around a third of all Jews by faith counted here.

(b) Jews by faith in their entirety according to economic sectors
The distribution of the Jews by faith in their entirety according to economic sectors is determined, as with the overall population, in such a way that the relatives without a main occupation are assigned to their respective breadwinner. Aside from the working population, the pensioners, rentiers, etc. are also taken into account as such.

Jews by faith in the German Reich* according to economic sector, 1933

Economic sectors	Jews by faith in the working population and among the pensioners, rentiers, etc.				Total working population and pensioners, rentiers, etc. in the Reich	
	Excluding relatives		Including relatives		Excluding relatives	Including relatives
	Number	%	Number	%	%	%
Agriculture and forestry	4,167	1.4	5,124	1.0	24.5	21.0
Industry and crafts	55,655	18.5	95,472	19.1	34.2	38.8
Trade and transport	147,314	48.9	262,223	52.5	15.6	16.9
Public and private services	29,974	9.9	53,443	10.7	7.1	7.8
Domestic services	3,377	1.1	3,494	0.7	3.3	2.0
Pensioners, rentiers, etc.	60,941	20.2	79,926	16.0	15.3	13.5
Together	301,428	100	499,682	100	100	100

* Without Saarland.

First of all, the working population, together with their relatives with a main occupation, is organized as before according to five economic sectors. The pensioners, rentiers, etc. and their relatives without a main occupation remain; together, they make up a new, sixth economic sector. Through the addition of the pensioners, rentiers, etc. a corresponding shift in the proportions for the other sectors naturally occurs. It is striking, however, that the addition of the relatives without a main occupation affects the share of the individual economic sectors differently.

Whereas the share in the economic sectors of industry and crafts, trade and transport, and public and private services grows as a result of the addition of the relatives, it becomes less in agriculture, in domestic services and among pensioners, rentiers etc., which can also be observed in a similar fashion in the overall population. In the domestic services sector, it is mainly younger, single domestic staff and among the pensioners, rentiers, etc., frequently widows, older married couples living alone, etc. with a relatively low number of relatives without a main occupation. In agriculture, in which Jews work only in individual cases, there are also few relatives *without* a main occupation, since most of the relatives of self-supporting farmers work as assisting family members and are correspondingly included in the number of the working population.

3. Distribution of the working population according to occupation
Even more important than the question as to which type of *business* the Jews work in is the question of to which individual *occupations* they apply themselves. If we examine in which occupations Jews by faith accounted for more than 0.74 per cent of the total working population in mid-1933, i.e. were more strongly represented than corresponds to their share in the total working population, there emerges the ranking of the occupations preferred by the Jews, visible from the overview on p. 26 above.[12] The Jews have preferred to devote themselves primarily to certain academic professions (lawyers, doctors, dentists, pharmacists, judges and public prosecutors, university lecturers), furthermore artistic professions (directors, actors, visual artists, musicians, singers) and all important commercial professions. It can be observed that many Jews who have left the Jewish religious community and who could not be recorded in the census as 'Jews' are especially active in precisely these 'independent professions'. In fact, the Jewish infiltration of these professions, which are important for cultural life, will be considerably stronger than is expressed in the numbers for the Jews by faith. By contrast, almost all skilled craft and manual occupations are not among the professions favoured by the Jews; to the extent that individuals are represented, the close links with corresponding branches of trade (e.g. butcher – meat and cattle trade; furrier, hat and cap maker – fur trade; watchmaker – watch and precious metal trade) must be of decisive influence. Also revealing is a separate assessment of how many of the Jewish working population represented in the individual professions are immigrants from abroad (without the territories lost post-Versailles)[13] or possess foreign nationality. In occupations with a longer career path, especially the academic professions, the share of immigrants is generally far below the ascertained average of 22.9 per cent for the Jews by faith in the working population overall. In the commercial occupations, which decisively influence the overall picture, the share of immigrants among the travellers, sales representatives, vendors, accountants, etc. remains somewhat under the average, while among the 'remaining proprietors and tenants', who are also mostly active in trade, the average rate is somewhat exceeded. A distinctly immigrant occupation is that of the furrier; almost three-quarters of the roughly 1,200 furriers of the Jewish faith are from abroad. Approximately 30 per cent of the artistic professions and writers are immigrants, and the share of musicians and singers is as high as 38 per cent. Shares of 40 per cent and more immigrants can almost only be found, however, in occupations that require manual labour; the absolute numbers of Jews by faith among the working population in these professions are, however, generally small. The share of immigrants only sinks below the average in exceptional cases, e.g. among the butchers and glaziers.

---

12 Here there is an overview of selected occupations and their distribution within the working population and among working people of the Jewish faith; printed here as the next table.
13 This refers to the territories separated from the German Reich after the First World War.

Jews by faith in the working population in the German Reich,* 1933, according to selected occupations

Occupation	Total working population in the Reich		Working population of Jews by faith			Of whom immigrants**		
	Number	%	Number	%	% of the total working population	Number	%	% of the Jews by faith
Occupations with a share of more than 0.74 per cent of Jews by faith in the working population								
Lawyers and notaries	18,641	0.1	3,030	1.3	16.25	84	0.2	2.8
Estate agents and commissionaires	11,445	0.0	1,722	0.7	15.05	275	0.5	16.0
Patent lawyers	595	0.0	79	0.0	13.28	9	0.0	11.4
Doctors	51,067	0.2	5,557	2.3	10.88	451	0.8	8.1
Travellers, sales representatives, agents	265,105	0.8	24,386	10.2	9.20	5,160	9.4	21.2
Dentists	12,120	0.0	1,041	0.4	8.59	80	0.1	7.7
Property managers	3,481	0.0	297	0.1	8.53	147	0.3	49.5
Furriers	18,929	0.1	1,198	0.5	6.33	872	1.6	72.8
Directors and producers	1,070	0.0	60	0.0	5.61	18	0.0	30.0
Legal consultants	3,058	0.0	165	0.1	5.40	22	0.0	13.3
Other proprietors and tenants***	1,325,713	4.1	66,891	27.8	5.05	16,471	29.9	24.6
Editors and writers	17,277	0.1	872	0.4	5.05	280	0.5	32.1
Private tutors	10,730	0.0	461	0.2	4.30	146	0.3	31.7
Bookmakers	824	0.0	35	0.0	4.25	2	0.0	5.7
Managers, procurators	79,571	0.3	3,083	1.3	3.87	364	0.7	11.8
Pharmacists	18,220	0.1	657	0.3	3.61	52	0.1	7.9
Accountants, trustees etc.	14,293	0.0	515	0.2	3.60	80	0.1	15.5
Dancers, actors, artistes	23,694	0.1	703	0.3	2.97	225	0.4	32.0
Judges and public prosecutors	10,359	0.0	286	0.1	2.76	6	0.0	2.1
Brewers and distillers	2,339	0.0	62	0.0	2.65	2	0.0	3.2
University lecturers	7,272	0.0	192	0.1	2.64	42	0.1	21.9
Student teachers	14,683	0.0	367	0.2	2.50	18	0.0	4.9
Booksellers	14,733	0.0	361	0.2	2.45	73	0.1	20.2
Visual artists	14,750	0.1	360	0.1	2.44	104	0.2	28.9
Sales Personnel	537,426	1.7	12,835	5.3	2.39	2,597	4.7	20.2
Chemists, chemical technicians, laboratory workers	31,013	0.1	715	0.3	2.31	167	0.3	23.4
Other business and office employees***	1,336,690	4.1	30,167	12.6	2.26	6,126	11.1	20.3
Milliners	39,025	0.1	841	0.3	2.16	218	0.4	25.9
Dentists and dental technicians	30,981	0.1	653	0.3	2.11	206	0.4	31.5
Musicians, singers etc.	93,861	0.3	1,915	0.8	2.04	727	1.3	38.0
Other specialist and technical, as well as managerial employees***	318,158	1.0	5,605	2.3	1.76	1,042	1.9	18.6
Hatters, cap makers	10,695	0.0	186	0.1	1.74	105	0.2	56.5
Bookkeepers, correspondents, stenotypists, etc.	647,413	2.0	11,205	4.7	1.73	2,397	4.3	21.4
Photographers and film operators	20,766	0.1	335	0.1	1.61	86	0.2	25.7

Occupation	Total working population in the Reich		Working population of Jews by faith			Of whom immigrants*		
	Number	%	Number	%	% of the total working population	Number	%	% of the Jews by faith
Occupations with a share of more than 0.74 per cent of Jews by faith in the working population								
Veterinary surgeons	6,307	0.0	98	0.0	1.55	2	0.0	2.0
Butchers and sausage-makers	242,193	0.8	3,566	1.5	1.47	211	0.4	5.9
Opticians and watchmakers	36,629	0.1	484	0.2	1.32	251	0.5	51.9
Clerics (rabbis)	40,165	0.1	434	0.2	1.08	125	0.2	28.8
Glaziers	24,302	0.1	223	0.1	0.92	29	0.1	13.0
Teachers and head teachers	37,505	0.1	317	0.1	0.85	12	0.0	3.8
Tailors and needleworkers	822,555	2.6	6,939	2.9	0.84	3,332	6.0	48.0
Paperers, upholsterers, decorators	53,952	0.2	439	0.2	0.81	136	0.2	31.0
Home workers	158,178	0.5	1,273	0.5	0.80	675	1.2	53.0
Occupations with more than 1,000 but less than 0.74 per cent Jews by faith in the working population								
Other labourers***	3,744,990	11.6	4,019	1.7	0.11	1,457	2.6	36.2
Domestic staff	1,218,119	3.8	2,903	1.2	0.24	462	0.8	15.9
Engineers and technicians	202,574	0.6	1,443	0.6	0.71	467	0.9	32.4
Primary, secondary school and specialist teachers	251,102	0.8	1,323	0.6	0.53	221	0.4	16.7
Mechanics, plumbers, fitters	577,828	1.8	1,010	0.4	0.17	331	0.6	32.8
Other selected occupations								
Shoemakers	240,288	0.7	884	0.4	0.37	551	1.0	62.3
Locksmiths, girdle makers	839,877	2.6	648	0.3	0.08	187	0.3	28.9
Washers, ironers, pressers	77,403	0.2	330	0.1	0.43	138	0.3	41.8
Joiners (excluding patternmakers)	492,977	1.5	326	0.1	0.07	148	0.3	45.4
Masons, carpenters	752,247	2.3	95	0.1	0.01	26	0.1	27.4
Blacksmiths, braziers, etc.	342,329	1.1	65	0.0	0.02	23	0.0	35.4
Miners, pit foremen	455,396	1.4	52	0.0	0.01	30	0.1	57.7
Patternmakers, turners, cartwrights	143,972	0.5	32	0.0	0.02	19	0.0	59.4
Millers	40,154	0.1	19	0.0	0.05	7	0.0	36.8
Remaining occupations and assisting family members								
Remaining unlisted occupations	11,176,919	34.6	13,568	5.6	0.12	3,238	5.9	23.9
Assisting family members	5,312,116	16.4	23,160	9.6	0.44	4,411	8.0	19.0
Total working population	32,296,074	100	240,487	100	0.74	55,143	100	22.9

* Without Saarland. ** See explanation on p. 15.[14] *** See the 'Overview of the categorization in the occupation census', p. 30, on the right.[15]

14 See fn. 3.
15 Not reproduced; see fn. 1, p. 30.

Jews by faith in the working population in the German Reich,* 1933, according to their occupational status

Occupational status	Total working population in the Reich				Working population of Jews by faith						Namely				
	Total		of which female		Total		% of the total working population	of which female		Native			Immigrants†		% of Jews by faith in the working population
	Number	%	Number	%	Number	%		Number	%	Number	%	Number	%		
Self-employed in total of which	5,302,916	16.4	936,365	8.2	110,669	46.0	2.09	16,460	23.0	85,017	45.9	25,652	46.5		23.2
Proprietors and tenants	5,213,589	16.1	931,592	8.1	108,132	44.9	2.07	16,338	22.8	82,867	44.7	25,265	45.8		23.4
Salaried employees in management	61,262	0.2	3,970	0.1	2,338	1.0	3.82	115	0.2	1,976	1.1	362	0.7		15.5
Civil servants in management	28,065	0.1	803	0.0	199	0.1	0.71	7	0.0	174	0.1	25	0.0		12.6
Assisting family members	5,312,116	16.4	4,149,035	36.1	23,160	9.6	0.44	17,818	24.9	18,749	10.1	4,411	8.0		19.0
Civil servants (excl. those in management)	1,480,792	4.6	127,867	1.1	2,275	1.0	0.15	450	0.6	2,152	1.2	123	0.2		5.4
Salaried employees (excl. those in management)	4,032,345	12.5	1,566,754	13.7	80,559	33.5	2.00	27,611	38.6	63,662	34.3	16,897	30.7		21.0
Labourers	14,949,786	46.3	3,488,698	30.4	20,921	8.7	0.14	6,349	8.9	13,323	7.2	7,598	13.8		36.3
Domestic staff	1,218,119	3.8	1,210,322	10.5	2,903	1.2	0.24	2,852	4.0	2,441	1.3	462	0.8		15.9
Total working population	32,296,074	100	11,479,041	100	240,487	100	0.74	71,540	100	185,344	100	55,143	100		22.9

* Without Saarland. † See the explanation on p. 15.[16]

[16] See fn. 3.

DOC. 54

On 17 June 1933 the street vendor Luise Rupprecht asks the Breslau Chief of Police to expel a competing Jewish street vendor from the square[1]

Letter from the street grocer Luise Rupprecht, Breslau, to the chief of police in Breslau,[2] dated 17 June 1933 (copy)

Honourable Chief of Police,

As a small trader who owns a street stall on the corner of 2 Körnerstraße and II Elsasserstraße, I am turning to you with a heartfelt request for help.

For decades I have owned this small business and the three of us – my sister, her child, and I – have scraped our living from it.

It is surely common knowledge that we small traders do not have it easy, and pay fees and taxes from the few pennies we earn.

There is already a street stall like ours for every few houses, so each one of us has only a small number of customers.

For a few weeks now, directly across the street from me on Körnerstraße a handcart has been selling the same goods that I sell, fruit and vegetables, though with the difference that I offer German produce, whereas this street vendor only sells foreign produce.

The vendor is a young Jewish man,[3] or rather, there are usually two Jews standing by the cart. As a result of the obvious boycott that the Jews are carrying out against German businesses, the domestic employees in our area, who are in the service of Jewish masters, are being forced by the Jews to buy the essentials from this Jewish street trader, which in turn severely damages my business.

On top of this, it is probably not entirely hygienic that the Jewish vendor, before he drives his cart away in the evening, puts some of his goods in the basement apartment of the communist in front of whose front garden gate he has his stall.

In view of the many street stalls in our area, as well as the street trader who stands opposite Post Office 13 with fruit and vegetables, there is not the slightest need for, of all things, a Jewish and no doubt communist street trader of a foreign race to spoil for us Germans in our neighbourhood the few remaining opportunities to earn something.

As an honest old grocer I am therefore asking the Chief of Police most politely and sincerely for remedial action to remove the Jewish street vendor's stall right in front of my shop.

The obvious connection between the Jew and the resident of the basement at 9 Elsasserstraße, whom we know to be an enemy of the National Socialist state and National Socialism, with his special exit through the front garden to I Körnerstraße, seems especially noteworthy.

---

1 Archiwum Państwowe we Wrocławiu, Akta miasta Wrocław/22858, fols. 7r–v. This document has been translated from German.
2 The chief of police in Breslau from 1933 to 1934 was Edmund Heines.
3 The vendor was Nathalius Szikowitz, who ran his stall from 1 April 1933 at the site allocated to him by the city.

As chief of police, please help a poor woman to get rid of the unwanted Jewish competition who has established himself here without any need.[4]

With the greatest respect, I sign this as an old, hard-working German vendor

DOC. 55

Deutsche Allgemeine Zeitung, 19 June 1933: report concerning a speech by Berlin's mayor to American local politicians[1]

American local officials at town hall Berlin

The mayor's speech
At midday on Monday at the town hall, American local politicians attended a formal reception hosted by the mayor and the municipal authorities. In addition to the twenty-four Americans and Mayor Dr *Sahm*, the following were among those present at the reception: the state commissioners Dr Lippert, Hafemann,[2] Dr Maretzky,[3] Engel,[4] Dr Klein,[5] and

---

4 Together with three other traders, on 22 June 1933 Luise Rupprecht also asked the Combat League for Small and Medium-Sized Businesses for the 'removal' of the Jewish competitor. The chief of police and the Reich Association of Itinerant Traders of Germany in Breslau recommended to the city that the competitor's stall reservation be withdrawn. The municipal market administration had in fact already declared the reservation card invalid the previous day, although Szikowitz had invoked his minority protection as a citizen of the state of Danzig. Despite the Polish consul's intervention, he was allocated neither this site nor another site in Breslau: Archiwum Państwowe we Wrocławiu, Akta miasta Wrocław/22858, fols. 8–31.

1 *Deutsche Allgemeine Zeitung* (Greater Berlin, evening edition), 19 June 1933, p. 1. This document has been translated from German. The *Deutsche Allgemeine Zeitung* (*DAZ*) was published in Berlin from 1918, from 1922 to 1945 across Germany twice daily, and from 1944 once a day. In 1933 the paper had a circulation of 63,000.
2 Wilhelm Wolfgang Hafemann (1891–1945), lawyer; worked for the city of Berlin from 1919; joined the NSDAP in 1932; acting mayor of Berlin, 1933–1934; district mayor of Berlin-Kreuzberg, 1934–1935; classified as 'exonerated' during denazification proceedings in 1950.
3 Dr Oskar Maretzky (1881–1945), lawyer; mayor of the Berlin district of Lichtenberg, 1918–1920; member of the German National People's Party (DNVP), 1924–1933; acting mayor of Berlin, 1933–1935; acting head mayor of Berlin, 1935–1937; joined the NSDAP in 1937; thereafter worked in the private sector.
4 Johannes Engel (1894–1973), worker; lathe operator at Knorr-Bremse AG Berlin, 1925–1928; member of the German Social Party (DSP), 1922–1925; joined the NSDAP in 1927; city councillor in Berlin, 1929–1930; state commissioner, 1933–1934, and city councillor for transportation, 1934–1945, in Berlin; head of the Berlin tourist board, 1934–1945; member of the SS; deputy Gauleiter in Berlin, 1944.
5 Dr Wilhelm Klein (1887–1948), physician; state commissioner, 1933, and city medical officer, 1933–1936, in Berlin; author of works including *Wer ist erbgesund und wer ist erbkrank?* (1935).

Plath,⁶ as well as head of the city council, Spiewok,⁷ the chairman of the Reich Association of the German Press, Dr Dietrich,⁸ as representative of the Reich Foreign Office Ministerialrat Dr Dieckhoff,⁹ and the American chargé d'affaires *Gordon*,¹⁰ as well as the American consul general, Messersmith.¹¹

In the chamber, which was adorned only with the swastika flag, flanked by a black-white-red and a black and white flag, Mayor Dr *Sahm* began by giving a welcome speech to the American guests. He stated among other things the following:

> My dear colleagues! It gives me great pleasure to have this opportunity to show you at this moment in time, after the national German uprising, the German Reich's capital city and its institutions. You will be able to see with your own eyes the inaccuracy of all the news reports directed against the new Germany that are circulated abroad by interest groups. You have already had an opportunity and will have further opportunity in the next few days to get to know the city of Berlin and its people. On the one hand, you will be convinced of the scale of the *destitution* that was caused by the hardships of the post-war period under the yoke of a peace treaty that is suited to anything but the establishment of peace in the world. On the other hand, however, you will also have seen how the attitude and the faces of even the poorest among the population reflect feelings of redemption and a trusting and hopeful happiness.
>
> If you consider that not that long ago every third Berliner voted *Communist* and well over half of the Berlin population professed Marxism,¹² you must admit that the current attitude of Berlin's population provides the best evidence that the working population is not in some way suffering under the yoke of a harsh dictatorship, but on the contrary feels *released from long-standing servitude*.

---

6 Otto Plath (1879–1968), lawyer; district town councillor, deputy mayor, and head of the district youth and welfare office in the Berlin district of Steglitz, 1921–1933; state commissioner and head of the department for social welfare in the city of Berlin, 1933–1934; second mayor of Berlin, 1934–1945; joined the SA in 1933 and the NSDAP in 1937; classified as a 'lesser offender' during denazification proceedings in the Soviet occupation zone in 1948, and during proceedings in the Federal Republic in 1955 as not falling under any of the categories of incrimination.

7 Eduard Karl Spiewok (1892–1951), retailer; worked until 1933 for the electronics and electrical equipment company Allgemeine Elektrizitäts-Gesellschaft (AEG); joined the NSDAP and the SS, 1930; head of the Gau office for public welfare in Berlin, 1933–1936; director of the regional welfare office, 1934–1938, and of the municipal economics office, 1938–1945, in Berlin; fought in the war, 1943; prisoner of war in France, 1945–1946.

8 Otto Dietrich (1897–1952), political scientist; joined the NSDAP in 1929 and the SS in 1932; Reich press chief of the NSDAP; from 1938 state secretary in the Reich Ministry of Public Enlightenment and Propaganda; sentenced to seven years' imprisonment in the Ministries (Wilhelmstrasse) Trial in Nuremberg, 1949; released in 1950.

9 Hans-Heinrich Dieckhoff (1884–1952), diplomat; from 1912 in the diplomatic service; legation counsellor in Constantinople, 1916–1918; ambassador to the USA among other appointments, 1937–1938.

10 George A. Gordon (1885–1959), diplomat; US ambassador until 1933, then chargé d'affaires in Berlin; ambassador to Haiti, 1935–1937, and to the Netherlands, 1937–1940.

11 George S. Messersmith (1883–1960), diplomat; US consul general in Berlin, 1930–1934; US ambassador to Cuba, Mexico, and Argentina, 1937–1947.

12 In the Reichstag elections on 6 Nov. 1932, the Communist Party of Germany (KPD) received 31.02 per cent and the Social Democratic Party of Germany (SPD) 23.3 per cent of the vote in Berlin.

We attach importance not only to showing you those Berlin institutions that we are proud to describe as exemplary, but also to giving you a picture of the sins incurred by the previous system in Germany and Berlin. When you see the sites of dreadful dilapidation, the *breeding ground of Bolshevism*, alongside what German energy and organization, even in times of great adversity, have been able to achieve and maintain, then you must allow room for the conviction that the German people had a right to free themselves of those responsible for these ills and that by overcoming the Bolshevist destroyer of all culture it has merited *not the whole world's hatred but rather its gratitude.*

Please allow me to speak frankly about the *Jewish question,* which has also unduly inflamed passions in America. In the busiest neighbourhoods of Berlin you have seen the large Jewish department stores in full operation; you can find Jewish shops, Jewish physicians, Jewish bars and restaurants everywhere. Thus, you see that even here in Berlin the Jews, as everywhere in Germany, can go about their business peacefully and undisturbed. You will not have noticed any of the pogrom-like incidents that are so often the order of the day in other countries. The fact that even today so many Jews are interspersed in German public life and in the Reich's capital city, despite certain restrictions, reveals how clearly disproportionate the influence of Jewry must have been in Germany before the national uprising. Even today, after the introduction of a strict limitation on the admission of Jewish lawyers, for example, one third of all Berlin *lawyers* are still Jewish by race, although the proportion of Jews in the population is scarcely 2 per cent.[13] From this example you can see that the German people certainly had a right to limit the number of Jews in some professions to a normal level at a time when millions of Germans are on the streets without work or sustenance.

The German people have no greater wish than to live with all other peoples in *peace and friendship*. The National Socialist Movement, now running the state, has set itself the main task of restoring the German people's strength. Therefore, nothing can be further from its mind than the thought of a *war*, which even in the most favourable scenario would have to entail once again the irreplaceable loss of valuable national forces. The lessons of the World War have been too terrible for us all! What we expect, however, is that other nations will show some understanding for our distress and confirm our national right to exist, just as for us the national right of other nations to exist is a matter of course.

---

13 In Berlin the proportion of residents of the Jewish faith in 1933 was in fact 3.78 per cent: see the results of the census of 16 June 1933, Doc. 52.

DOC. 56
On 19 June 1933 Max Osborn writes to Minni Steinhardt about his plans to emigrate to Palestine[1]

Letter from Max Osborn,[2] Berlin-Schöneberg, 1 Nymphenburgerstraße, to Minni Steinhardt, Tel Aviv, dated 19 June 1933[3]

My dear lady,

Please accept my warmest, sincerest thanks for your kind and detailed letter of 10 June, which I was delighted to receive and to read. I cannot begin to tell you how happy it makes me to know that you are in good hands and your husband has been heartened by such good artistic prospects. It must be wonderful for you that you can build a new life in a free rural district that can truly fulfil your expectations and wishes. I am convinced that you will soon feel completely rooted there. You have your little daughter with you, which must be a great joy, and I was pleased to hear how the charming little one is settling into her new home. Our family has unfortunately been scattered, as our son has to travel a great deal and can hardly find any possibility of employment in Germany itself. My wife in particular is suffering greatly from this, just as she is also emotionally affected by my experience of having to leave the work I have been doing for so many decades.[4]

On the day your letter arrived, my old friend here Dr Karl Schwarz[5] told me that he has received and accepted an offer as director of the museum to be founded in Tel Aviv. He will soon be leaving for Palestine. I deeply regret that we are losing him here; he was such a competent director of the small Jewish Museum in Berlin that he will be sorely missed. That said, the local Jewish Community currently has such vast duties to fulfil that, in the long term, there will hardly be any money left for running the museum.[6] But I am happy for Schwarz that he is taking over such a fine and promising mission. For me personally the greatest opportunity that I might have been offered in Palestine has of course been taken away. Naturally, not for anything would I get in the dear Schwarz's way. He himself admittedly said in our last conversation, and he was most certainly sincere, that he will definitely invite me for a guest visit to Palestine in the foreseeable future. Aside from giving art history lectures there, I could in fact also give a literary

---

1 Jüdisches Museum Berlin, DOK-95-30-165, fols. 1–3. This document has been translated from German.
2 Dr Max Osborn (1870–1946), art historian; architecture and literary critic, 1918–1933; author of art history books and biographies; in 1933 co-founder of the Culture League of German Jews, and head of its art division; emigrated to Paris in 1938 and to New York in 1941.
3 In the original 'replied' is written by hand on the top left.
4 This probably refers to his work for the *Vossische Zeitung*.
5 Karl-Israel Schwarz (1885–1962), art historian; active Zionist; from 1920 editor at Gurlitt publishing house and contributor to the *Jüdisches Lexikon*; in 1926 curator, then director, of the Jewish Museum in Berlin; emigrated to Palestine in 1933; director of the Tel Aviv Museum, 1933–1937.
6 From the beginning of the persecution of Jews in 1933, the Jewish Community of Berlin noted a great demand for its advisory and aid organizations. Just one day after the boycott it increased the funds for the schools department, for financial aid, and for the Jewish welfare office by 120,000 Reichsmarks: minutes of the meeting of the community board on 2 April 1933, Archives of the Leo Baeck Institute, New York, at the Jüdisches Museum Berlin, MF 587.

lecture series and complement Schwarz's capabilities insofar as he thinks it appropriate. How would that work by the way: would it actually be possible to give lectures in German there? I have certainly heard that this would not be impossible. For instance, Professor Franz Oppenheimer[7] is said to have given lectures in German there for an entire semester. Is there a university by the way? And is it conceivable that there would be a place for me there? And, as I said, I could also imagine doing other work, such as running certain artistic and urban planning organizations. You mention the plan for an art school or applied arts school and ask who might be a suitable person to run it. Now, I would actually trust myself to do that, as well, and it would perhaps be no bad thing for such a post to be held by a non-artist, who does not compete with his own lecturers, but would take charge of directing and maintaining the whole institution. Well, you wanted to speak with Rosenthal at some point. Perhaps something will emerge in that direction. I do realize that the suggestion of appointing a man like me to run an art school might raise doubts in some quarters because it is believed that only an artist is suitable for it. This does not seem decisive to me; anyone who has concerned himself for so many decades, as I have, exclusively with art and artistic matters could bring no less important qualifications to such a post. Consider it with your husband and discuss the matter carefully with others as well. In any case I hope that we stay in touch. Perhaps fate will really bring us back together.

By the way, the museum is in Tel Aviv – so you will very soon come into contact with Schwarz. He has also firmly promised to take an interest in my son, who is not only an excellent pianist but also an outstanding and already experienced and successful music teacher and would certainly do excellent work at a conservatoire.[8] Do not forget that either, dear madam Minni. Actually, I care even more about that than about myself, for after all I have now gradually become a man who gladly gives way to youth.

Perhaps I will soon be hearing more news from you. We want to stay in touch after all, one way or the other!

With many warm greetings and wishes from my wife and me to you and your husband, and a little kiss for the young girl with elderly reverence.

Your warmly devoted

---

7 Franz Oppenheimer (1864–1943), physician; from 1886 to 1896 a practising physician, thereafter journalist and sociologist; acquainted with Theodor Herzl; prepared the 1903 World Zionist Congress in Basel; during the First World War worked at the Ministry of War; in 1919 was appointed to the first sociology professorship in Germany at the University of Frankfurt; became professor emeritus, 1929; emigrated to the USA via Japan, 1938.

8 Franz Joachim Osborn (1905–1955), pianist; emigrated to Britain in 1933.

DOC. 57
On 22 June 1933 the director of the Institute of Physics intervenes with the Breslau University administration on behalf of the lecturer Hedwig Kohn[1]

Letter from the director of the Institute of Physics at Breslau University, Schaefer,[2] to the trustee at the university and the Technical University in Breslau (received on 23 June 1933), dated 22 June 1933[3]

Noble Sir,

I would like to submit the following: when the questionnaires were sent out in April for the assistants to fill in, I was on leave and travelling abroad. Consequently, my substitute, Prof. Steubing,[4] was forced to fill in the section provided in the questionnaire about the political activity of the assistant in question. He has informed me that he limited himself to the observation that he knew nothing more. This circumstance prompts me to communicate the following as a supplement to the questionnaire in the case of the adjunct professor Dr Hedwig Kohn:[5]

(1) I have known Dr Kohn for over 23 years now. She wrote her doctoral thesis here at the institute, received her doctorate in 1913, and has held an assistant's post since 1914. I spent the entire period of the war with her – I was head of department at the Institute of Physics at the time – and in particular we experienced the 1918 revolution together. I can attest to the pain she felt inside during the Marxist revolution of 1918 and the deep outrage with which she viewed the events. Concerning her political views I can therefore state with certainty that she was and is thoroughly anti-Marxist. I would be grateful to you, noble sirs, if this could officially be noted as a supplement to the questionnaire.

(2) Dr Kohn represents a particular branch of physics, namely the examination of radiation, which my predecessors Lummer and Pringsheim made the domain of the Breslau Institute of Physics. In this field she has inspired the doctoral theses of five (Aryan) students, whom she is currently supervising. (I have not accepted any more non-Aryan students since I took up office in 1926.) If Dr Kohn were now to be removed as lecturer and assistant on the basis of § 3 of the Civil Service Law, the greatest damage would be incurred by her five students.[6] It would hardly be possible for these doctoral projects to continue under a different supervisor, since this requires such in-depth specialist knowledge as only Dr Kohn currently possesses. I feel obliged to explain this to you, noble sirs, as the students concerned have asked me to do this in their own interest.

---

1 GStA PK, I HA, Rep. 76, Va Sekt. 4, Tit. IV, Nr. 51, Bd. 1, fol. 87r-v. This document has been translated from German.
2 Dr Clemens Schaefer (1878–1968), physicist; professor in Marburg and Breslau; after 1945 in Cologne; author of works including *Einführung in die theoretische Physik* (2 vols, 1921).
3 Parts of the original have been underlined by hand. The letter was sent by the trustee to the Prussian Ministry of Science on 24 June 1933: GStA PK, I HA, Rep. 76, Va Sekt. 4, Tit. IV, Nr. 51, Bd. 1, fol. 88.
4 Dr Walter Steubing (1885–1965), physicist; professor of applied physics in Breslau, 1927; from 1948 professor in Hamburg; undertook research in the field of spectroscopy and atomic physics.
5 Dr Hedwig Kohn (1887–1965), physicist; assistant, 1914–1934, and from 1930 adjunct professor at the University of Breslau; conducted research at the Light Climatic Observatory in Arosa (Switzerland), 1935; in 1938 emigrated to Switzerland, and later to the USA, where she held a lectureship; professor at Wellesley College, MA, 1945–1952.
6 The clause is underlined in red in the original.

(3) If I may perhaps point out, it would be appropriate to simply allow Dr Kohn's assistantship to elapse – that would be another 1½ years. In this way, the goal stipulated by the Civil Service Law would be achieved and the damage to the students would also be avoided, as I would then ensure that she would not accept any new doctoral students.[7]

DOC. 58
On 22 June 1933 Professor James Goldschmidt protests to the Prussian Ministry of Science, Art, and Education against the withdrawal of his authorization to teach[1]

Letter from James Goldschmidt,[2] Berlin, to the Prussian Ministry of Science, Art, and Education, dated 22 June 1933[3]

Honourable Ministerialrat,

I was informed by a reliable source that the Minister once expressed the wish that if civil servants subordinated to him believe that they have been done an injustice they should turn to him in confidence. This fact, combined with the kind understanding that you have shown me until now and that has led to the repeal of my mandated forced leave, emboldens me to address my situation once again.

I was the *only one* of the Berlin law lecturers to be compulsorily suspended on 29 April. No plausible reason for this was then or is now apparent to me. Given that I became a professor on 23 August 1908, as planned, I undoubtedly fall into the category of exceptions in § 3(2) of the Civil Service Law. The stipulation from the Prussian Ministry of Justice that non-Aryans can no longer teach constitutional or criminal law in an academic setting is not only unjustified by the Civil Service Law but seems to be directed exclusively against me. In fact, to my knowledge, this summer many non-Aryans are lecturing in both constitutional and criminal law at Prussian universities. However, I would in fact have believed the opposite, that especially few objections could be raised against me personally from the standpoint of a national government. I am referring not only to my forty years of service, but also to my academic and political views. *I was the only German criminologist at the time to oppose the war guilt lie using the weapons of criminal law (Deutsche Juristen-Zeitung, 1922, column 402 ff.).*[4] I have expressed the same patriotic attitude throughout the entirety

---

7 Schaefer's endeavours were in vain. Hedwig Kohn was dismissed. On 7 Sept. 1933 her authorization to teach at the University of Breslau was revoked: GStA PK, I HA, Rep. 76, Va Sekt. 4, Tit. IV, Nr. 51, Bd. 1, fol. 92.

1 GStA PK, I HA, Rep. 76, Va Sekt. 2, Tit. IV, Nr. 45 A, fols. 53–54. This document has been translated from German.
2 Dr James Paul Goldschmidt (1874–1940), lawyer; professor of criminal law at Berlin University, 1908–1933; specialist in procedural law; visiting professor in Spain and in the USA, 1933–1936; emigrated to South America in 1938; author of works including *Der Prozess als Rechtslage: Eine Kritik des prozessualen Denkens* (1925).
3 The original contains handwritten underlining and a note: 'to be added to the questionnaires'.
4 Goldschmidt took issue in this article with Hermann Kantorowicz, who had stated in the magazine *Das Tagebuch* that Germany's war guilt was legally demonstrable. Goldschmidt put forward an argument against this view based on a legal theory and concluded by arguing that a united front in the war guilt question was urgently needed: 'Die Kriegsschuldfrage vor dem Forum der modernen Schuldlehre', *Deutsche Juristen-Zeitung*, vol. 27, nos. 13–14 (1922), pp. 402–405.

of my thirty-two years of teaching, to which every one of my numerous listeners and students will attest. I therefore find it all the more incomprehensible and painful that I am supposedly unworthy to teach criminal law in the nationalist state. I ask in the forthcoming resolutions for consideration of the suffering that I have experienced through what I believe to be unmerited treatment. In my petition of 30 April and my letter dated 11 June,[5] I stated that I am prepared to voluntarily sacrifice, though it has been asked of no one else, a part of my field of teaching on the condition that my teaching of procedural law in the faculty, of which I have been a member for thirty-two years and twice director, is not challenged. I have offered this sacrifice regardless of the impression that it must inevitably make abroad, especially in Italy, where I have many connections, and I nevertheless ask for this to be considered. But should my condition be untenable and, on the contrary, my transfer be ordered, then I may suppose it to be a matter of course that I will not be deprived of an area of teaching for which revocation there is no legal basis and to which I have contributed a lifetime's work, which, as the Reich Minister of Justice will confirm, has not been without use for reforming the national criminal law.[6]

I remain, honourable Ministerialrat,
Your gratefully devoted

DOC. 59
The board of the Talmud Torah School in Hamburg discusses the situation of Jewish schools at a meeting on 28 June 1933[1]

Memorandum from the board of the Talmud Torah School in Hamburg,[2] unsigned, dated 10 July 1933

School board meeting
  on Wednesday, 28 June, 8:15 in the evening.

The following gentlemen were present: Dr Hermann Samson, Dr Wilhelm Bodenheimer, the solicitor Bernhard David, John Gotthold, Jacob Katzenstein, Heinemann Schloss, Headmaster Spier, Walter Wolff, Dr Hugo Zuntz.

The following gentlemen sent their apologies: Jacob Heckscher, Hermann Philipp, Otto Ruben, Chief Rabbi Dr Spitzer.

---

5 At the end of April 1933 Goldschmidt had sought a repeal of the general suspension, accompanied with a request for a leave of absence from lecturing in criminal law. The latter had evidently been requested by him as a condition for the repeal of the suspension of 28 April 1933: Goldschmidt's letter dated 30 April 1933: GStA PK, I HA, Rep. 76, Va Sekt. 2, Tit. IV, Nr. 45 A, fol. 52. The letter dated 11 June 1933 is not in the file.
6 The evaluation sheet for § 3 of the Law for the Restoration of the Professional Civil Service contained the examiner's remark: '100 per cent non-Aryan, no front-line service; 1908 regular appointment as non-tenured professor'. The general examiner voted as follows: 'Not to be dismissed, to be transferred. 14 August': ibid., fol. 50. On 25 Sept. 1933 the Prussian Minister of Science informed Goldschmidt that he would be transferred to another university and added that a special order would be issued for the reassignment. But Goldschmidt later received the communication that he could not yet be granted a new professorship: ibid., fol. 61.

1 CAHJP, AHWTT/102. This document has been translated from German.

Dr Samson[3] opened the meeting and moved to postpone point 1 of the agenda, concerning the school's finances, to the next meeting because of Mr Heckscher's absence.

Dr Samson communicated that the tax office had recalled from the school a *revaluation loan* to the amount of RM 1,249.95 on 30 June 1934.

At Headmaster Spier's request,[4] the most urgent *maintenance work* was approved for execution during the summer holidays. This mainly involves painting the windows of the adjoining building.

Headmaster Spier reported on the matter of *non-Aryan pupils* in *state schools*. Whereas in Prussia the secondary Jewish schools to his knowledge are not in a position to accept pupils expelled from state schools as a result of the law,[5] there is no danger of this for Hamburg.

We are in a position to enrol all eligible pupils in the corresponding classes at our school without further ado. It is unlikely that any sixth-formers in Hamburg will be expelled from the state schools. In this respect, the headmaster pointed out that all measures undertaken on the Jewish side to bring about a legal settlement of Jewish matters can only be detrimental in view of the current overall situation. During his two stays in Berlin he expressed this opinion most forcibly to the appropriate Jewish associations, especially the *Reich Representation* of German Jews. The *interests of the Jewish secondary schools* will in future be put forward to all agencies by an 'interest group'.

The Jewish school in Altona had filed an application for *children from Altona* who attend our primary school to be referred back to Altona because the survival of the Altona school is in jeopardy due to the low number of pupils it now has. The school board cannot accept this application on grounds of equity.

This was followed by the conclusion of *voting matters*.

Two nominations have been received from the Association for the Promotion of the Talmud Torah School for the outgoing board members, Wilhelm Cohn and Jacob Heckscher. Nomination 1 is under the following names:

Dr Max M. Warburg, James Pels, Ernst Fink,

Nomination 2:

Jacob Heckscher, Jacob Goldschmidt, Dr Cäsar Heckscher.

---

2 The oldest Orthodox Jewish school in Germany, founded in 1805 in Hamburg. The Talmud Torah School was recognized in 1870 as a secondary school and in 1932 as an upper secondary school. Alongside a primary school, there was also an adult education centre, the upper secondary school, and remedial classes for pupils with learning difficulties. In 1937 the school had 800 pupils and 33 teachers. Like all Jewish schools, this school had to close in June 1942 following several forced relocations.

3 Dr Hermann Jacob Samson (b. 1860), lawyer; practised law in Hamburg, 1886–1938; board member of the German-Jewish Community in Hamburg, 1929–1930 and 1932–1933; he emigrated to London in 1939.

4 Dr Arthur Spier (1898–1985), teacher; headmaster of the Talmud Torah School in Hamburg, 1926–1940; organized the transports of German-Jewish children to Britain, 1938–1940; in 1940 he used a trip to the USA to emigrate.

5 The number of Jewish pupils and students in educational establishments had been limited by law according to the number of Jews in the general population in Germany: Law against Overcrowding in German Schools and Institutions of Higher Education, 25 April 1933, *Reichsgesetzblatt*, 1933, I, pp. 225–226.

On the basis of Dr Samson's conversation with Mr Warburg[6] on this matter, it was resolved to temporarily leave nomination 1 pending. From nomination 2, Mr Jacob *Heckscher* is unanimously *re-elected.*

This was followed by the consultation about forming nomination lists for the outgoing board members, David, Philipp, and Ruben. The committee jointly submitted the following suggestions:

(1) Bernhard David, Harry Wittmund, Dr Siegfried Streim,

(2) Hermann Philipp, Willy Stoppelmann, Marcus Bistritzky,

(3) Raphael Z. Bachrach, Simon Lederberger, Manfred Bauer.

Proposals 1 and 2 are endorsed as nomination lists without further discussion. Concerning proposal 3, some gentlemen expressed doubts about Mr Bachrach's nomination. These doubts are in no way directed against Mr Bachrach personally, but were raised in light of the fact that Mr Bachrach, according to the opinions expressed in the preliminary discussion, is to be elected to the board of the Talmud Torah School primarily as a representative of the Hamburg Community's liberal element. As a matter of principle, Dr Samson pointed out that all members of the Talmud Torah school board serve exclusively as such, and in no case as delegates of any party or movement. After an in-depth discussion it was decided to put the matter on the agenda for the next meeting given the absence of a number of board members at today's meeting.

Headmaster Spier reported on item 4 of the agenda to the effect that the pupils *Ernst Levy* and *Michael Rabinowitsch* were recently taken into custody at night by the police during a political meeting. The pupil Rabinowitsch was deported from Germany as a foreigner. The pupil Levy was released after sixteen days in custody. The following letter from the regional educational authority was received in the Levy matter:

> On the basis of the police file on the pupil *Ernst Levy,* 47 Klosterallee, the regional educational authority is convinced that no accusations could be levelled against the Talmud Torah Secondary School if it were not to allow Ernst Levy to continue attending the final year.
>
> On behalf of Oberdörffer,[7] superintendent of schools.

After a detailed discussion, it was resolved by all with one vote against (David) to advise the parents of pupil *Ernst Levy* to *withdraw* their son from school. It was further decided to expel Ernst Levy if the parents do not immediately act on this advice.

On the question of *youth associations* Headmaster Spier reported again on his reasons for forbidding the activity of our pupils in youth associations. On the basis of his various

---

6 Max Moritz Warburg (1867–1946), banker; shareholder in his father's banking house Warburg & Co. Hamburg, 1893–1938; member of the central committee of the Reichsbank, 1919–1924, and of its general council, 1924–1933; supervisory board member for various firms including HAPAG-Lloyd; from 1929 board member of the Central Association of German Citizens of the Jewish Faith (CV) and the Relief Association of German Jews. After 1933 he lost supervisory board seats, honorary positions, and business partners. He subsequently focused his efforts on Jewish issues and was an informal representative for German Jews in relations with state agencies, placing himself and his bank at the service of the emigration of Jews from Germany. After the introduction of the Nuremberg Laws in 1935, Warburg wrote a protest speech to be read aloud in all synagogues, but it was confiscated beforehand. He emigrated to the USA in 1938.

7 Dr Wilhelm Oberdörffer (1886–1965), scholar of English literature.

consultations with the regional educational authority, he does not consider it possible, despite discord on the side of some parents, to lift the ban. In order to offer the pupils a substitute, the school has organized its own *gymnastics classes* in those afternoons run by teachers from our school. These classes are attended by a large number of our pupils.

Mr Fritz Weinberger[8] had filed an application to enrol a *blind boy* in our school. The request was declined.

Similarly, the application by the *gymnastics teacher* Loni Priske[9] to organize gymnastics classes was rejected.

The pupil recently accepted by us on a trial basis, *Max Epstein*,[10] must be *removed from the school* again.

A request made by *Dr Heppmer* for a *reduction* of *school fees* for his two sons to a total of 30 marks per month was approved.

DOC. 60
A regional organization of the Central German Association of German Citizens of the Jewish Faith reports on the situation of Jews in Saxony and Saxony-Anhalt in June 1933[1]

Letter from the Central Association's regional organization in Central Germany (S.Gr. 274/33), unsigned, Leipzig, to the Central Association, Berlin, dated 6 July 1933[2]

Berlin head office
We are sending you below a report for the month of *June* from the regional organization of Central Germany:

The Reichsstatthalter for Saxony, Gauleiter Mutschmann,[3] gave a speech at Chemnitz town hall in which he turned on the Jews, as he also did in a speech in Dresden to business leaders.

The Saxon Minister of the Interior Fritsch[4] also expressed himself in highly antisemitic terms at a rally in the city hall in Glauchau.

Leipzig's chief of police banned a general meeting of the Central Association, in which the legal advisor for the regional organization wanted to speak about Jewish employers

---

8 Fritz Weinberger (b. 1887) lived in Hamburg until 1937, then in Leipzig.
9 Correctly: Leonie Briske, later Saulmann (b. 1903), gymnastics teacher; from 1941 in Berlin, from where she was deported at the beginning of Feb. 1943 to Auschwitz.
10 Max Epstein (1921–1982), son of David and Hella Epstein; emigrated to the USA in Feb. 1940.

1 RGVA, 721k-1-261, fols. 266–270. This document has been translated from German.
2 The original contains handwritten changes, revision marks, and stamps.
3 Martin Mutschmann (1879–1950), textile worker; from 1907 owner of a lace factory; joined the NSDAP in 1922; Gauleiter of Saxony, 1926–1945; Reichsstatthalter in Saxony, 1933–1945; managed government affairs in Saxony, 1935–1945; arrested, 1945; sentenced to death in Moscow in 1947 and executed in 1950.
4 Dr Karl Johann Erhard Fritsch (1901–1944), political scientist; member of the German-*Völkisch* Protection and Defiance League, 1919; joined the NSDAP in 1921; assumed various NSDAP functions, 1922–1928; from 1928 acting Gauleiter of Saxony; joined the SS in 1934; Saxony's minister of the interior, 1933–1944; deputy Reichsstatthalter in Saxony, 1938–1943.

and employees, on grounds of public security and order. In the legal advisor's[5] thorough consultation with Chief of Police Knoofe,[6] it was ascertained that the basis for the prohibition was the general tenseness of the situation and not due to our organization.

For a few days the situation of our fellow believers in Halberstadt was extremely alarming.[7] For this reason, the regional organization's legal advisor sent over Kamnitzer,[8] who had a detailed discussion with our friends there and asked them to refrain from any official intervention. The situation has now settled down. Furthermore, Kamnitzer was also sent to Magdeburg, where Dr Merzbach[9] had been taken into protective custody, while at the same time a search was carried out at his apartment, during which Central Association material was confiscated. After a short time, Dr Merzbach was released.

The president of the Chemnitz Regional Court had issued an ordinance to the effect that civil servants, salaried employees, and workers subordinated to him should not make purchases in Jewish, Marxist, and other shops hostile to the state. In response to a written intervention from the regional organization's board members, the regional court president von Miaskowski[10] explained that it was in no way his intention to equate all Jews with anti-state elements. His decree was to be understood to mean: 'in Jewish shops or Marxist and other shops hostile to the state'.

In Halle the National Socialist Association of Lawyers[11] issued statements on which Aryan firms continue to instruct Jewish solicitors to act on their behalf.

In Plauen the town council issued a directive prohibiting Jews from swimming in the municipal baths. We therefore directed an appeal to the Kreis governors in Zwickau.

In Zittau it was discovered that the Jewish cemetery had been desecrated. It was possible to identify the perpetrator as a labourer who had previously belonged to the Communist Party.

At the State Opera House in Dresden a Jewish conductor[12] and two répétiteurs were dismissed, while a further répétiteur and the Jewish members were lawfully dismissed.

---

5 Kurt Sabatzky: see fn. 13.
6 Correctly: Oskar Knofe (1888–1978?), career officer; military career, 1909–1920; from 1924 in the regional police; chief of police in Leipzig, 1933–1937; in 1937 transferred to Berlin, where he was colonel in the urban police; senior commander of the Order Police in Poznań, 1939–1942, and in Salzburg, 1942–1943; sentenced in Poland to eight years in prison, 1949; released in 1955.
7 This probably refers to the torture of Jewish men by National Socialists in the basement of a printing house in Halberstadt: see Hermann Schwab, *1933: Ein Tagebuch* (Zurich: Jüdischer Volksschriftenverlag, 1953), pp. 22–24.
8 The author probably means Dr Bernhard Kamnitzer (1890–1959), lawyer and politician; senator for finance in Danzig, 1929–1930, then worked as a lawyer; board member of the Central Association of Danzig Citizens of the Jewish Faith; following occupational ban and imprisonment, emigrated in 1938 to New York via Britain; after 1945 representative for restitution claims.
9 Dr Ernst Merzbach (1879–1952), lawyer; from 1906 practised law in Magdeburg; for many years representative of the Jewish Community; later chairman of the assembly representatives, chairman of the local branch of the Central Association of German Citizens of the Jewish Faith (CV) in Magdeburg, and until 1933 board member of the Prussian Regional Association of Jewish Communities; in 1938 his lawyer's licence was revoked and he emigrated to Chile.
10 Karl Woldemar Kurt von Miaskowski (b. 1869), lawyer; in 1920 regional court director; in 1934–1935 regional court president in Chemnitz and from 1935 in Leipzig; head of the League of National Socialist German Lawyers (Bund Nationalsozialistischer Deutscher Juristen, BNSDJ) in the Gau of Saxony.
11 The BNSDJ was founded in 1928 by Hans Frank. In 1936 it was succeeded by the National Socialist Association of Lawyers (Nationalsozialistischer Juristenbund).

The Jewish drama consultant had already long since been dismissed. Two principal singers were dismissed because of political unreliability.

The Saxon Ministry of Education organizes a race studies course for physicians. It was explained that if the course cannot take place due to a lack of participants, special measures would be taken against the physicians.

The Leipzig women's seminar had refused to accept a Jewish student. In response to our objection, the ministry instructed the municipal school authority that the student be accepted.

At a youth meeting of the Hitler Youth, at which the participation of schools was compulsory, it was declared that Negroes, Jews, and those of foreign races, even if they were German citizens, were not allowed to take part.

In Quedlinburg the Combat League for Small and Medium-Sized Businesses continued its boycott of a Jewish firm because it had flouted the league's wish for Jewish shops not to be allowed to display the term 'Pentecost sale' in the clearance sales before Pentecost by putting up a sign to that effect. A detailed consultation with our friends there took place in the presence of our legal advisor, Sabatzky.[13] By way of press reports at the end of June it was also announced that German housewives should take care to avoid being proclaimed as un-German and pilloried in the daily press in a publication under the heading 'In the pillory'.

We compelled members of the health insurance company of the 'Merkur' association in Nuremberg to protest to the management against their exclusion from the association and likewise against the levying of a special fee to remain in the association, as well as to appeal to the general assembly.

An ordinance from the local NSDAP branch in Chemnitz to the effect that Jews would have to make their cars available to the SA on demand, which was in place for several weeks, was revoked by the Party leadership.

Due to the encroachment on economic affairs related to the exclusion of market traders, as well as the extension of the boycott by municipal agencies, the chairman and legal advisor had a detailed discussion in the Ministry of Economics in Dresden with the personal advisor to the minister, Dr von Buch.[14] The Ministry of Economics was made aware of the illegalities, which it also at the time acknowledged. The ministry stated its intention to remedy the situation by means of a resolution from the Minister of the Interior. Dr von Buch requested that a position paper be drafted.

The syndicate had to undertake a large number of financial consultations.

---

12 General Music Director Fritz Busch (1890–1951) had directed the opera from 1922. Dismissed in 1933, he first emigrated to Zurich, then to Argentina, and later to Britain.
13 Kurt Sabatzky (1892–1955), journalist; legal advisor to the CV in Leipzig, 1922–1923; managing director of the CV in East Prussia, 1923–1932, and of the regional organization for Saxony and Anhalt in Leipzig, 1933–1938; member of the Reich League of Jewish Combat Veterans and B'nai B'rith; temporarily interned in Buchenwald concentration camp; managing director of the synagogue congregation in Essen, 1939; that year he emigrated to Britain, where he worked for Jewish organizations from 1943 onwards.
14 Dr Gustav Friedrich von Buch (b. 1883), lawyer; initially a member of the German National People's Party (DNVP), he joined the NSDAP in 1933; in the Saxon state service, finally as Ministerialrat, 1912–1939.

With reference to opportunities for physicians to settle abroad, enquiries were made at the Leipzig consuls general and at the consulates of Persia, China, and Japan.

At the instigation of the head office, enquiries were undertaken about contracts with the authorities and about trainee teachers living in the district. The local branches had to declare their current assets to the head office.

At a meeting of the Reich League of Jewish Combat Veterans in Leipzig, the former chairman Bravmann[15] launched a tirade against the Central Association, and, in fact, solely because at a general meeting at which Dr Hirschberg,[16] Sabatzky, and Dr Goldmann[17] gave papers the Central Association [had] not praised the merits of the local branch chairman of the Reich League of Jewish Combat Veterans. For his part, the chairman reprimanded Bravmann for having used this occasion as an opportunity to leave the Central Association.

We accorded legal protection to the employees dismissed from the firm Theodor Althoff owned by Rudolph Karstadt, Leipzig, because of their Jewish descent. They were represented at the labour court in Leipzig by Counsel Sabatzky. The court was successfully persuaded that dismissal without notice was indefensible. It ruled that the firm should pay the salary until the stipulated date for dismissal with notice and explained in the judgement that the firm would certainly have had the right to dispense with the plaintiff's services but that it was not released from its obligation to pay the salary until the legal dismissal date. The judgement was declared to be provisionally enforceable.[18]

---

15 The author probably means Salomon Stefan Bravmann (1887–1934).
16 This is probably Dr Alfred Hirschberg (1901–1971), journalist; worked in the management of the CV in Berlin, 1920–1938, from 1929 as legal advisor and from 1933 as director; editor-in-chief of the *CV-Zeitung*, 1933–1938; in 1939 he emigrated to Brazil via Britain.
17 Dr Felix Goldmann (1882–1934), rabbi; from 1907 rabbi in Oppeln; from 1917 community rabbi in Leipzig; board member of the CV; author of works including *Vom Wesen des Antisemitismus* (1925).
18 This concerned thirty employees. Sabatzky had argued before the court that these employees did not exercise any public functions, and therefore no analogy to the Law for the Restoration of the Professional Civil Service was admissible. The Reich Labour Court later followed the Leipzig judgement, though it regarded a justification for dismissal without notice to be present if the retention of Jewish employees led to an intolerable disturbance of operations for the employer in individual cases: Kurt Sabatzky, 'Meine Erinnerungen an den Nationalsozialismus' (1940), p. 37, Harvard Competition, no. 261.

DOC. 61

On 1 July 1933 Hans Kantorowitz refuses to leave the Berlin Gymnastics Association[1]

Letter from Hans F. Kantorowitz,[2] Berlin, 8 Lindenpromenade, to Naumann,[3] dated 1 July 1933[4]

Dear fellow gymnast *Naumann*,

First I would like to return to my letter addressed to you personally at the time regarding the BT[5] accident insurance, and note that to date I have not received a reply. I would be much obliged if you could send a short message.

I am taking this opportunity to give you the copy of a letter that I sent yesterday to the treasurer of the 'Fourth'.[6]

Today of all days the latest BT news bulletin arrived with its editorial, and believe me when I say that your words about the 'gymnast's sense of brotherhood', 'true comradeship', and 'for one's entire life' gave me a painful twinge.[7] I thought of the words: You can be certain of the nation's gratitude. How these words were upheld after the war! And how should I now experience the gymnast's loyalty and comradeship? Do you not feel the gaping contradiction between words and deeds?[8] Is there not an irreparable injustice happening here? My whole life I have championed with glowing enthusiasm 'all that is good and noble' in Jahn's[9] sense, not only in words but also in deeds that stand firm. By that I don't mean some kind of perfect high jump but the promotional and development work that I have done in countless places, far beyond the context of the BT. Indeed, I'd like to stress that this was done in full awareness of rendering a service to the nation to which I fully belong by birth, thought, and actions.

If my grandparents were not completely Aryan – I admit I am proud of them by the way, for I owe them a great deal – this is a mere coincidence that does not prevent me from believing myself to be as good and nationally minded a German as some others who, also by chance, are pure Aryan (or at least can prove it).

---

1 BArch, R 34/491. This document has been translated from German.
2 Hans F. Kantorowitz was athletics director for track and field. At the fifteenth German gymnastics tournament in Stuttgart in 1933 he came seventh in the men's pentathlon in sport class II. This is probably the same Hans Kantorowitz, also Kantorowicz (1900–1941), who was deported in Nov. 1941 to Kovno and shot dead there on 25 Nov. 1941.
3 Rupert Naumann (1885–1946?), editor; joined the Berlin Gymnastics Association (BT), 1905; BT deputy chief record keeper, 1925–1928; BT third chairman, 1930–1933, and first chairman, 1934–1936.
4 Parts of the original have been underlined by hand.
5 Berliner Turnerschaft: Berlin Gymnastics Association.
6 This letter is not in the file.
7 In his article Naumann had railed against a member who explained that his departure from the BT was due to antisemitic attitudes. He ended this part of the article with the sentence: 'A gymnast's sense of brotherhood [and] true comradeship must overcome this pettiness in a period that makes demands on the whole human being.' He also spoke in favour of National Socialism and against the 'ignoble peace' of Versailles: 'Streifzug durch die BT', *Nachrichtenblatt der Berliner Turnerschaft (Korporation)*, no. 7, 1 July 1933, pp. 107–108. Volume 49 of the news bulletin appeared in 1933.
8 In the original this sentence is underlined by hand.
9 Friedrich Ludwig Jahn (1778–1852), known as 'Turnvater Jahn' (father of gymnastics), gymnastics educator; started the nationalist German gymnastics movement during the Napoleonic Wars.

For my part, I am inclined to keep faith with my cause and that is why I have written the letter of which you find a copy enclosed.

I was good enough to do auxiliary and military service, and Dr Neuendorff[10] made me his assistant for his best-known work (*Handbook for Gymnastics, Games, and Sports*)[11] – and now I am supposed to leave? This guilt should be borne by others, not by me!

There is nothing left for me to do but watch and learn what German loyalty and comradeship mean between fellow gymnasts.

I know that the new sports commissioner[12] has not yet issued his final guidelines; I know that the participation of non-Aryans in the Olympic Games in Germany has been confirmed. The DT[13] would do better not to be too hasty with exclusions as long as there is still the possibility of amendments.[14] How can an Olympic candidate, for example, go on playing sports if he is removed from the clubs?

Yet these are only practical considerations; what weighs more heavily on me and probably also on my gymnast brothers (in the true sense of the word) is the question of what is becoming of German gymnasts' loyalty! Once it has happened, moral, specifically German values will surely be destroyed irretrievably, probably for no reason.

Dear fellow gymnast Naumann, do not close your mind to these suggestions! Given the high opinion I have of the men of the national uprising, I am convinced that reasonable advice and tips of this kind, too, will be met with understanding.[15]

Be well!

10 Dr Edmund Neuendorff (1875–1961), educator; director of the Prussian University for Physical Exercise, 1925–1932; from 1918 member of the German National People's Party (DNVP); joined the NSDAP in 1931 and the SA in 1933; head of the German Gymnastics Youth, 1921–1933; first chairman of the German Gymnastics Association (DT), 1933; head of the Institute for Physical Exercise at Berlin University, 1932–1934; director of the University of Physical Exercise in Prague, 1941–1945; after 1945 refugee priest in Bramsche; author of works including *Ewiges Turnen als Wegbereiter des Dritten Reiches* (1934).
11 Kantorowitz had written the contribution 'Aus der Welt des Springers' ('From the World of the Jumper') for the handbook edited by Edmund Neuendorff and titled *Die deutschen Leibesübungen: Großes Handbuch für Turnen, Spiel und Sport* (Essen: Schumann, 1927).
12 Hans von Tschammer und Osten (1887–1943), officer; joined the NSDAP and the SA in 1929; from 29 April 1933 Reich commissioner for sport in the Reich Ministry of the Interior; Reich sports leader, 1933–1943; head of the German Gymnastics Association from July 1933 until its dissolution in 1935; president of the National Olympic Committee, 1934–1943; head of the Reich Sports Office at the Reich Ministry of the Interior, 1936–1943; state secretary, 1938.
13 Deutsche Turnerschaft: German Gymnastics Association.
14 On 8/9 April 1933 the main committee of the German Gymnastics Association had resolved to introduce the Aryan Paragraph, at which point Naumann asked the approximately sixty Jewish BT members to leave.
15 Naumann expressed his doubts concerning the exclusion of prominent BT members to the chairman of the German Gymnastics Association, Neuendorff, on 11 Sept. 1933: see Doc. 80, 23 Sept. 1933.

DOC. 62

On 13 July 1933 Isaac Meyer writes to the Senckenberg Natural History Society in Frankfurt to justify his resignation[1]

Handwritten letter from I. Meyer,[2] Frankfurt am Main, to the Senckenberg Natural History Society,[3] for the attention of E. Marx,[4] Frankfurt am Main, dated 13 July 1933[5]

Dear Professor,

I confirm with deep gratitude the receipt of your esteemed letter from the 22nd of last month,[6] which was awaiting me on my return from a trip abroad. I now take the liberty of replying most respectfully as follows:

Your message stating that no changes have occurred in the collaboration between your members and friends, your visiting researchers and salaried employees, is a pleasing sign of an objective attitude in the relevant circles, particularly in current times. If I nevertheless ask for my letter of resignation to be regarded as accepted, I would like to bring the following to your attention in order to avoid any misunderstandings. I am a public official of the Frankfurt Jewish Community, which used to be a well-established body that led the way in all cultural domains. My earnings, aside from the cuts as a result of the various salary reduction regulations affecting all officials equally, have been reduced by 25 per cent because the Community is barely able to continue with its religious, cultural, and social tasks. This is supplemented by the catastrophe on an as yet immeasurable scale which has led to the financial ruin of thousands of Community members. For me personally, this state of affairs on the one hand entails a loss of income of almost 40 per cent since two days ago in light of the necessary cost-cutting. On the other hand, it entails an increased sense of obligation to help in any way possible my many co-religionists who, through no fault of their own, have fallen into destitution and misery, and the cancellation of other, less pressing duties – if only temporarily.

---

1 Archiv der Senckenberg Gesellschaft für Naturforschung, Nr. 449, fol. G23r-v. This document has been translated from German.
2 Isaac Meyer (1883–1938) was a public official of the Frankfurt Jewish Community; he was arrested during the 1938 November pogroms and died on 16 Nov. 1938 in Buchenwald concentration camp.
3 The Senckenberg Natural History Society (SNG) was founded in 1817 in remembrance of the physician and natural scientist Dr Johann Christian Senckenberg (1707–1772). It is now known as the Senckenberg Nature Research Society.
4 Dr Ernst Marx (1870–1951), physician; specialized in psychotherapy and psychiatry in Frankfurt, 1920–1938; he was the first director of the SNG.
5 The original is underlined by hand in several places.
6 When the resignations of mainly Jewish members amassed, Marx sent a circular letter on 22 June 1933 stating that the society did not want to accept the resignations: see undated draft by Rudolf Richter, Archiv der Senckenberg Gesellschaft für Naturforschung, Nr. 449, fol. G5. Since the letter had led to misunderstandings, the managing director approached the Jewish members with a circular letter on 25 June 1933: 'In answer to countless enquiries we state that the Senckenberg Society makes no distinctions between its members, but guarantees them all the same rights as before. […] Should you have left the Society under false assumptions, we ask you to reconsider the step you have taken and not to end your affiliation with the "Senckenberg" unnecessarily': Kommission zur Erforschung der Geschichte der Frankfurter Juden (ed.), *Dokumente zur Geschichte der Frankfurter Juden*, p. 88.

In the interest of your venerable and highly respected society, I hope that my case is an isolated one. However, should this not be so, and should resignations in greater numbers have the consequences indicated in your letter in certain circles of your employees, I would count myself free of any responsibility!

With the highest esteem

DOC. 63
On 18 July 1933 scientists at the Potsdam Observatory denounce their colleague Professor Erwin Finlay Freundlich as an 'anti-nationalist descendant of Jews'[1]

Letter from the National Socialist Civil Service Department, Observatories Department, Potsdam Kreis Branch, Gau Kurmark, Department Head Obst, and sent through official channels to the National Socialist Civil Service Department of the Gau Kurmark of the NSDAP, Berlin, 18 Dessauerstraße, dated 18 July 1933

Since 1 June 1920 Professor Erwin *Freundlich*[2] has worked as a Prussian civil servant at the Astrophysical Observatory, initially as observer and now as chief observer. Prof. Freundlich's father was a Jew. Before the war he signed, and signs again today, his name without proper authority as 'Finlay-Freundlich' by prefixing his surname with the family name of his maternal grandfather, a well-known English astronomer and discoverer of comets. During the war he did not use the English word 'Finlay' in his name, though he resumed this practice after the war.

At the beginning of 1932 the November parties'[3] Minister for Science, Art, and Education appointed Prof. Freundlich head of the Astrophysical Observatory-affiliated Einstein Institute, now the Institute of Solar Physics. At the same time, in deliberate humiliation of the thoroughly nationalist-minded director Prof. Ludendorff,[4] he was given – both in his management of the scientific work of the Einstein Institute and in administrative matters – an unusually far-reaching degree of autonomy that was otherwise uncommon for department heads.

Instead of defending the nationalist-minded director against the pretensions and intervention of his chief observer, the November government put the anti-nationalist Jewish descendant on a nearly equal footing with the director.

---

1 GStA PK, I HA, Rep. 76, Vc Sekt. 1, Tit. XI, Teil II, Nr. 6b, Bd. 10. This document has been translated from German.
2 Erwin Finlay Freundlich (1885–1964), astrophysicist; from 1921 to 1933 professor at the Astrophysical Observatory in Potsdam, where he worked with Einstein; emigrated to Turkey in 1933 and worked there as professor of astrophysics; moved to Prague in 1937 and to Britain in 1939; returned to Germany in 1956. He was the brother of Herbert Max Finlay Freundlich: on the latter, see Doc. 41, 9 May 1933, fn. 14.
3 This is a reference to those political parties who were associated with the armistice of Nov. 1918, the signing of the Treaty of Versailles in June 1919, and the subsequent Weimar Republic.
4 Hans Ludendorff (1873–1941), astrophysicist; began working at the Potsdam Observatory in 1898, first as assistant and then as observer; appointed professor in 1909; promoted to chief observer in 1915; appointed director of the Potsdam Observatory in 1921.

However, the National Socialist government has since largely reversed this policy of equivalent status. Yet that has not served to eradicate the un-Germanness of Prof. Freundlich. Enclosed is a statement by Chief Observer Prof. Münch[5] as evidence of his un-German behaviour.[6] I also have in my possession recent information in written form which was dispatched to me through official channels. This reveals that Mr Freundlich made remarks about the Führer of the National Socialist Movement that must deeply outrage every German Volksgenosse. All of the above has convinced the National Socialist Department for Observatories that Prof. Freundlich is – due to his anti-völkisch attitude – fit neither to be a civil servant in the new Reich nor least of all to hold a senior civil service post. It is doubtful that a dismissal in accordance with § 3 of the Law for the Restoration of the Professional Civil Service is applicable in the case of Prof. Freundlich. The department, however, deems a dismissal from service or at least a removal from his senior position to be necessary, for there is absolutely no guarantee that he will unreservedly and always support the national state. On the contrary, the department has gained the impression that he is quite spiteful towards the national movement.

The Department for Observatories therefore submits a request through official channels to the Kurmark[7] Gauleitung for the forwarding of the foregoing information to the appropriate officials.[8]

---

5 Wilhelm Münch (1879–1969), astrophysicist; from 1919 professor and chief observer at the Potsdam Observatory.

6 According to Münch, Freundlich made statements in 1920–1922 to the effect that Germany bore responsibility for the war and in 1932 that emphasizing 'nationalism' was a regression to a long-outdated era, and the only aim should be to create a European culture. Note regarding Münch's statement of 11 July 1933: GStA PK, I HA, Rep. 76, Vc Sekt. 1, Tit. XI, Teil II, Nr. 6b, Bd. 10.

7 German for 'electoral march' originally referred to the part of the Holy Roman Empire held by the margraves of Brandenburg but was later used as the name of one of the NSDAP Gaue. In 1940 it was renamed Mark Brandenburg.

8 Max Planck and Max von Laue interceded with the minister on behalf of Freundlich, who then accepted a position at the University of Istanbul and left Germany in Oct. 1933. Prior to this the ministry had decided to approve his compulsory retirement in accordance with § 3 of the Law for the Restoration of the Professional Civil Service. In Sept. 1933, however, the Reich Foreign Office and the Reich Ministry of the Interior intervened and proposed that Freundlich be granted a leave of absence for several years for foreign policy considerations, as they wanted him to establish an observatory for furthering German research in the Mediterranean region. Since he departed for Turkey before his leave of absence was approved, his salary was suspended on grounds of unauthorized absence from service. See letter from the Prussian Minister of Science to the director of the Astrophysical Observatory, dated 3 April 1934, ibid.

DOC. 64
On 26 July 1933 the German Council of Municipalities permits the city of Preußisch Friedland to partially exclude Jews from public baths[1]

Letter from the German Council of Municipalities (VIII 112/33), Managing Director Hopf,[2] Berlin, to the municipal authorities of Preußisch Friedland, dated 26 July 1933[3]

We acknowledge the receipt of your letter of the 6th of this month – 1724 –.

So far it has not come to our attention that special bathing and visiting times at municipal baths have been stipulated for the Jewish population.

We nevertheless see no legal obstacle to the municipal administration adopting such a resolution. As proprietor of the baths, it has the right to regulate visiting times and set special times for individual groups, as is often done not only for the different sexes but also for schools and associations. Since the bathing facility – if not operated *solely* for health purposes – is regarded as a commercial establishment of the municipality (see Stier-Somlo, *Handbuch des kommunalen Verfassungs- und Verwaltungsrechts in Preussen*, II 2, p. 196), it is not subject to the rules of public law applicable to public facilities, but rather its legal relations and usage policies are governed exclusively by the provisions of general civil law.

When drafting the resolution, it is necessary to specify in precise detail who is to be regarded as a Jew in accordance with the resolution, in order to ensure the proper implementation of the resolution.[4]

---

[1] BArch, R 36/2060, fol. 8. This document has been translated from German.
[2] Volkmar Hopf (1906–1997), lawyer; municipal councillor in Königsberg, 1932; joined the NSDAP in 1933; head of Dept I (Constitution, Administration, Police, Commerce) in the German Council of Municipalities, 1933; Landrat for Franzburg-Barth in Pomerania, 1934; Ministerialrat in the Federal Ministry of the Interior, 1951; president of the Federal Court of Auditors, 1964.
[3] The original contains handwritten amendments. The handwritten day of the month '12' was changed to '26'.
[4] The last sentence was added by hand.

DOC. 65
The executive board of the Hamburg Medical Association resigns in July 1933 because of an anti-Jewish amendment to the statutes[1]

Circular of the executive board of the Hamburg Medical Association,[2] signed Kümmell,[3] Marr,[4] Treplin,[5] Scholz, and Reye,[6] dated July 1933 (lithographic transfer)

The executive board of the Hamburg Medical Association would like to inform members of the following:

The authorized plenipotentiary of the Reich commissioner for the central medical associations, Dr W. Holzmann,[7] has made it compulsory for the executive board to incorporate the following provisions in the association's statutes:

1. Only Aryans can serve as regular members; non-Aryans can retain their membership as extraordinary members.

2. Only regular members are permitted to speak in lectures and debates.

3. Only regular members have voting rights in general meetings.

The executive board feels bound to the association's existing by-laws, according to which such an amendment to the statutes is not possible, and its members have therefore taken the decision to step down from their posts.

For the transitional period the executive board has placed Messrs *Treplin, Scholz,* and *Reye* in charge of managing the association's affairs.

---

1 BArch, R 1501/26401, fol. 146. This document has been translated from German.
2 The Hamburg Medical Association (Ärztlicher Verein Hamburg) was founded in 1816.
3 Probably Dr Richard Kümmell (b. 1880), physician; from 1915 professor of ophthalmology at the University of Hamburg.
4 Probably Dr Erich Marr (1896–1941), physician; from 1925 general practitioner in Hamburg.
5 Dr Lorenz Treplin (1875–1951), physician; from 1906 specialist in surgery; professor and head of the second surgical department at the Hamburg-Barmbek General Hospital, 1937.
6 Dr Edgar Reye (1882–1945), physician; specialist in internal medicine; professor and head physician at the Hamburg-Barmbek General Hospital, 1937.
7 Dr Willy Holzmann (1878–1949), neurologist; joined the NSDAP in 1923; founding member of the National Socialist Physicians' League, 1929; head of the Hamburg Gau office of the NSDAP's Racial Policy Office, 1933; honorary professor of racial studies at the University of Hamburg, 1933.

DOC. 66

In late July 1933 a member of Deutsche Bank's management board, Franz Urbig, reports on the dismissal of board members Theodor Frank and Oscar Wassermann[1]

Memorandum written by Franz Urbig[2] (3/Sch), Bühlerhöhe, late July 1933[3]

I. At the end of March this year the actions against our Jewish Volksgenossen were initiated, and one had to bear in mind that the Movement could also put Messrs Frank,[4] Solmssen,[5] and Wassermann[6] in jeopardy. This caused a certain amount of concern among board members, which was particularly directed towards Mr Wassermann, who appeared to be highly vulnerable as a result of his public support for Zionism and who at the same time drew criticism from inside the bank because of a debit balance of 2.6 million marks, guaranteed in equal amounts by Mr Felix Warburg[7] in New York and Mr Wassermann, that had been accumulated to promote Zionist objectives, and furthermore because of the debit balance of the company in London of Jakob Wassermann (brother of Oscar Wassermann), which began to falter several years ago.

It probably would have been unjustifiable for the executive committee of the supervisory board to ignore the newly established movement and its possible consequences. I therefore paid a call to Mr Schlitter[8] in his apartment on the evening of 31 March. The purpose of the very detailed conversation was to discuss with Mr Schlitter whether, in

---

1 BArch, R 8119 F, P 55, Inaktive ordentliche Vorstandsmitglieder, Allgemeines 8, fols. 8–25. Facsimile in Avraham Barkai, *Oscar Wassermann und die Deutsche Bank: Bankier in schwieriger Zeit* (Munich: Beck, 2005), pp. 157–174. This document has been translated from German.
2 Franz Urbig (1864–1944), banker; joined the Disconto-Gesellschaft in 1884; posts including manager of the branch in Tientsin, China, 1885–1897; appointed managing partner of the Disconto-Gesellschaft, 1902; chairman of the Monetary Committee of the Central Association of German Banks and Bankers, 1923; from 1927 engaged in preparations for the merger with Deutsche Bank; chairman of the supervisory board of the Deutsche Bank and Disconto-Gesellschaft, 1930–1942.
3 Urbig sent the memorandum to Schacht, von Siemens, Russell, Schlitter, de Weerth, Steinthal, Solmssen, Mosler, Wintermantel, Rummel, Schlieper, Boner, von Schinkel, and Kimmich, among others: undated memorandum from Franz Urbig: BArch, R 8119 F, P 55, Inaktive ordentliche Vorstandsmitglieder, Allgemeines 8, fol. 7. Carl von Siemens told Urbig verbally: 'It would have been a weakness if you had acted differently': undated memorandum from Urbig, ibid., fol. 28.
4 Dr Theodor Frank (1871–1953), banker; partner and member of the management board of the Disconto-Gesellschaft, 1922–1933; member of the management board of Deutsche Bank, 1929–1933; after being dismissed, still retained his seat on the supervisory board until 1938; subsequently emigrated to Belgium and later to Switzerland.
5 Dr Georg Adolf Solmssen (1869–1957), lawyer; from 1898 worked at the Prussian Ministry of Justice; joined the Berlin office of the Disconto-Gesellschaft in 1900; appointed director in 1904 and served 1911–1929 as managing partner of the Disconto-Gesellschaft; member of the management board of the Deutsche Bank and Disconto-Gesellschaft, 1929–1934, and retained a seat on the supervisory board until 1937; subsequently emigrated to Switzerland.
6 Oscar Wassermann (1869–1934), banker; member of the management board of Deutsche Bank, 1912–1933, and spokesman of the management board, 1923–1933.
7 Felix M. Warburg (1871–1937), banker; partner of the banking house Kuhn, Loeb & Co., New York; co-founder of the Jewish Agency for Palestine; chairman of the American Jewish Joint Distribution Committee, 1914–1932.
8 Dr Oscar Schlitter (1868–1939), retailer; member of the management board of Deutsche Bank, 1906–1932, and chairman of the supervisory board of the Deutsche Bank and Disconto-Gesellschaft, 1933–1939 (alternating annually with Franz Urbig).

the event that he also considered Mr Wassermann's position to be imperilled, it would not be better to drop him a hint in due time, so that he, on his own initiative, could pre-empt an otherwise potential incident from occurring. Mr Schlitter was not blind to the fact that there was a risk of Mr Wassermann being the target of attacks, but believed that Mr Wassermann could successfully withstand such threats using the clout still at his disposal. We parted that evening with the understanding that it was not yet necessary to drop Mr Wassermann a hint, but that, on the other hand, burying one's head in the sand was also not an option, and that instead it was necessary to seriously consider taking steps to clarify the situation.

On Saturday, 1 April, events occurred at the Central Association of German Banks and Bankers. Mr Bernstein[9] submitted his resignation, and Mr Solmssen was advised, in forthright terms, to relinquish the chairmanship. Both incidents appeared to be in accord with the goals advocated by Mr Schacht.[10] Deeply affected personally by what had happened, Mr Solmssen called on me on Sunday, 2 April. I advised strongly against anyone voluntarily stepping down, and Mr Solmssen then tried over the phone to persuade Mr Bernstein to withdraw his resignation, which he had since tendered in writing. After all, Mr Solmssen had now grown very uncertain about his personal situation, and it was very important to him to clarify the position. Upon his request, I telegraphed Mr Russell[11] that his presence was desired in Berlin as soon as possible, and I also cancelled my own arrangements to depart for Paris on the evening of 2 April to attend a meeting of the Caisse Commune.

On the morning of Wednesday, 5 April, a meeting was held between Mr Russell, Mr Schlitter, and me. In our discussion there was no longer a difference of opinion among us as to whether it was desirable to clarify the situation regarding the three gentlemen's continued service on the management board. Mr Frank and Mr Solmssen were, furthermore, fully in favour of taking action towards that end. The only open question was whether I should approach Mr Schacht directly. We eventually decided to first consult with Mr Friedrich[12] about the matter, because he participated in meetings of the bank's supervisory board in his capacity as a representative of the Reichsbank, and therefore had to be rightly considered a person of trust to whom one could turn in such a delicate affair. The discussion between Mr Friedrich and me took place at 12.30 p.m.,

---

9 Otto Bernstein (1877–1943), lawyer; until 1933 member of the management board of the Central Association of German Banks and Bankers and editor of the magazine *Bank-Archiv*; practised law until his licence was revoked in 1938; in Oct. 1942 was deported to Theresienstadt, where he died in Feb. 1943.

10 Hjalmar Schacht (1877–1970), banker; president of the Reichsbank, 1923–1930 and 1933–1939; Reich minister of economics, 1934–1937; until 1943 Reich minister without portfolio; in 1944 arrested in connection with the assassination plot of 20 July; acquitted at the Nuremberg trials, 1946; sentenced by a civilian tribunal to eight years in prison in 1947, but acquitted in 1948; founded the Deutsche Außenhandelsbank Schacht & Co. in Düsseldorf, 1953, and served as a financial advisor to countries including Egypt, Brazil, and Indonesia.

11 Dr Ernst Enno Russell (1869–1949), lawyer; from 1895 worked at the Disconto-Gesellschaft; partner at the Disconto-Gesellschaft, 1902–1929, and deputy chairman of the supervisory board of the Deutsche Bank and Disconto-Gesellschaft, 1929–1941.

12 Dr Carl Georg Friedrich (1873–1936), banker and lawyer; from 1897 worked for the Reichsbank; member of the management board of the Reichsbank and the supervisory board of Deutsche Golddiskontbank, 1919–1936.

and ended with Mr Friedrich expressing his intention with Mr Schacht to take up our concerns, which he regarded as entirely justified. To keep the management board apprised of the matter, I promptly informed Mr Mosler[13] of the discussion and its outcome.

On the afternoon of 5 April it was relayed to me by phone that Mr Schacht wished me, together with Mr Solmssen, to call on him, on Thursday, 6 April, at 5 p.m., to further discuss the matter brought to him by Mr Friedrich. I immediately informed Mr Russell and Mr Mosler of this request, which was somewhat noteworthy because of the desire to have Mr Solmssen accompany me. Mr Schlitter had in the meantime travelled out of town to attend meetings.

The first part of the discussion with Mr Schacht on 6 April concerned the Central Association. Mr Schacht removed all doubts that changes in the association's leadership were required, including the necessity of Mr Solmssen giving up the chairmanship and Mr Bernstein being replaced by another individual. He then made suggestions as to how the changes should be carried out. Mr Solmssen agreed to these suggestions. Mr Schacht thereupon broached the topic that I had discussed the day before with Mr Friedrich and explained that he had reserved for himself – with full approval of the relevant political officials – all measures that could possibly be taken within the banking industry. He said that this naturally also extends to personnel issues. He does not rule out that one or the other person might be affected by the changes, but said that in those cases where this occurs any rash action would be avoided, thus allowing for sufficient time to calmly arrange everything. There were no names mentioned. This was followed by factual remarks about the situation at the bank. During the first part of the discussion I abstained from making any remarks, and during the second part Mr Solmssen did the same.

I had a busy schedule on 7 April and therefore the day was free from any of the matters under consideration here. On the evening of Saturday, 8 April, I had a telephone conversation with Mr Schlitter. He expressed his irritation over the fact that, because Mr Solmssen had taken part in the discussion with Mr Schacht, the attempt to clarify the situation had taken a different course than he would have wished. He said that if Mr Wassermann's continued leadership should now become uncertain, the suspicion could arise that Mr Solmssen had used the opportunity to sacrifice Wassermann in order to save himself. He added that this put him in a very awkward position and that due to his long-standing collegial relationship with Mr Wassermann, he must now tell Mr Wassermann what had happened. I replied to Mr Schlitter that he had no reason to reproach himself or anyone else, because the discussion with Mr Schacht involving Mr Solmssen only dealt with the reorganization of the Central Association, and Mr Solmssen did not say a single word in the discussion about the matter of our concern. I added that there was in my opinion no objective duty to tell Mr Wassermann anything, but that I could nonetheless certainly understand his subjective judgement. I suggested that we discuss the matter again on Monday, 10 April, at the bank. This discussion took place at 10.30 a.m. and was very thorough. Mr Schlitter was unable to free himself from the feeling that he was obliged to tell Mr Wassermann what had happened, and following

---

13 Dr Eduard Mosler (1873–1939), lawyer; from 1911 member of the management team of the Disconto-Gesellschaft; later, member of the management board of the Deutsche Bank and Disconto-Gesellschaft and from 1934 to 1939 spokesman of the management board.

careful deliberation we decided that such a briefing could do no harm since no names had been mentioned.

Shortly thereafter, at about 12 noon, Mr Schlitter called on Mr Wassermann. Only Mr Schlitter knows exactly what was said during their discussion, which resulted in Mr Wassermann announcing his resignation to several colleagues even before the lunch break. Mr Wassermann did not appear at the management board's usual afternoon meeting, but was still at the bank. Although everyone had reckoned with the possibility that Mr Wassermann could be induced to step down from the management board, I saw upon my arrival at the meeting that the members of the management board were greatly affected by Mr Wassermann's resignation announcement. This made a strong impression on me, and at that very moment I felt that the board members would breathe easier if it were possible to persuade Mr Wassermann to remain at the bank. Influenced by this impression I went immediately to him. The outcome of our approximately one-and-a-half-hour discussion was not positive. I firmly advanced the standpoint that the executive committee not only had a right but also a duty to the leadership of the bank to clarify a matter of such importance, and said that I could accept responsibility for the action taken in good conscience. His reproach regarding not being told about the undertaking beforehand while his colleagues were briefed on the matter is without foundation, because we were greatly concerned about him, contrary to his own opinion, and would have thought it wrong to give him a chance to dissuade us of the necessity of the action. Mr Wassermann held fast to his explanation that after this incident it was not possible to restore trust between him and his colleagues, and that he therefore had no other choice than to resign from the management board, which, he added, would also cause a sensation abroad. I responded by telling Mr Wassermann that, in my opinion, he had no right to take this step on the basis of the events that had occurred, and that, above all things, neither side must speak of any kind of mistrust. I added that no one wanted him to resign, and that he should therefore take several days, or even several weeks, if he so wished, to carefully consider this matter. I also asked him, should he then still feel that he must stick to his decision, to consider choosing a manner much more suitable and less conspicuous to the public eye, namely resigning at the end of 1934 and announcing this step within a reasonable time before or after he turned 65 (4 April 1934).

On 11 April, just like almost every morning, Mr Schlitter and Mr Wassermann came to the bank together. Mr Schlitter was going on holiday the same day. Mr Wassermann did not say a word about the events of the previous day and wished Mr Schlitter a good trip. When I arrived at the bank shortly thereafter, I found on my desk a letter with the following content:

Dear Mr Urbig,

A few days ago I completed my 64th year. As per an earlier agreement, my duties at the bank are to terminate when I reach the age of 65. I therefore request permission to resign from the management board at the end of this business year. Should a suitable replacement be found beforehand, I would be prepared to step down from my position at any time before the year's end. Prior to or at the time of my departure, the bank may, of course, dispose of all my supervisory board posts as it sees fit, and I shall make sincere efforts towards ensuring that the bank's proposed successors to my posts are appointed. I do not foresee any difficulties in this regard, except in the case of the General Council of the Reichsbank.

With sincere admiration
Most humbly yours
O. Wassermann

I immediately informed the members of the management board of the letter's content and then went with Mr Russell, between 11 a.m. and 12 noon, to see Mr Wassermann again. We both tried to persuade him that his decision was an injustice to his colleagues and to the executive committee. The discussion was conducted without any irritability from either side and ended, though unsuccessfully, on cordial terms.

If Mr Wassermann had decided on 10 or 11 April not to follow through with his resignation, the entire affair would have been settled, and one could have waited calmly to see whether the bank would have come under any kind of pressure regarding personnel matters. Looking back today, it seems inconceivable to me that Mr Wassermann could so misjudge his own interests. Mr Wassermann's strengths were, and still are, his intellectual agility and his faculties of deliberation. Here both fell short, unless it was because he had overestimated himself.

II. If the events described thus far must be seen as a consequence of the efforts of the supervisory board's executive committee to provide clarification, then the events that now follow stemmed from the deliberations that occurred within the management board. In the night of 13 to 14 April Mr Wassermann fell ill. He had suffered heart spasms, and people close to him, his brother to be exact, described his condition as serious. As Mr Wassermann was 64 years old and had always been a heavy smoker, there was even less inclination at the bank to question this version of events. One expected Mr Wassermann to be confined to bed for a prolonged period of time and then, if everything went well, to remain off work for many weeks thereafter. Some doubt was expressed as to whether Mr Wassermann would ever recover his full strength. This line of thought logically led one to contemplate whether the illness that had set in was, though unexpected, the most natural solution to the resignation issue that he himself had precipitated. It was no less natural that this in turn raised the question of whether and how the bank could get along without Mr Wassermann, and the bank's management sought the answer to this question not only in present circumstances but also in past events, which they scrutinized carefully. This resulted in the following:

Following the resignation of Mr von Gwinner[14] and the death of Mr Mankiewitz,[15] the role of *primus inter pares* within the management board had fallen to Mr Wassermann, although he was neither the oldest nor the longest-serving board member. The only member who could have made a claim to this status was Mr Schlitter, but his responsibilities caused him to travel so much that he spent a good half of his time away from Berlin. This was the main reason why Mr Schlitter ungrudgingly relinquished the

---

14 Arthur von Gwinner (1856–1931), banker; member 1894–1919 and spokesman 1910–1919 of the management board of Deutsche Bank; member of the supervisory board of Deutsche Bank, 1919–1931.
15 Paul Mankiewitz (1857–1924), banker; member, 1898–1923, and spokesman, 1919–1923, of the management board of Deutsche Bank.

role to Mr Wassermann, who, moreover, was a born banker and had a masterful command of daily operations and the underwriting business. Mr Wassermann was also seen as the leader of the management board by the outside world, and he accentuated this fact in his social activities to a degree beyond what was necessary to represent the interests of the bank, yet even less commensurate with his financial means. The bank had grown very large, and responsibilities were divided among the management board members, who only convened for group discussions every Monday afternoon. These meetings lasted just a few hours, which did not provide sufficient time to discuss the more important business matters exhaustively. This then led individual board members to frequently talk over this or the other matter with Mr Wassermann in private. It demands a great sense of responsibility – either innate or acquired through rigorous training – to view things objectively at all times rather than to portray them as one would wish to see them, particularly in instances where something goes wrong. Such an endeavour is more likely to fail at a gathering of board members than in a one-to-one discussion. Another consequence of this situation was that it forced individual members of the management board to exercise a degree of independence to which they were not always equal, and which resulted in their losing that sense, so indispensable to a banker, for carefully assessing and limiting the risk that the bank can take. If a banker has independence, but lacks such self-discipline, then disaster ensues. This also happened here, for the losses that the bank incurred in the case of Ufa and Rheinische Kreditbank (von Stauss), and with regard to eastern trade (Bonn); a speculative account involving persons without a perfect record from within and outside the bank (Fehr); and the Schäfer affair (Kehl), all of which brought about the departure of the gentlemen involved, were alarmingly large and also damaged the bank's reputation. Where was the man who could not turn a blind eye to where such isolated cases were leading? Where was the hand that, while such things were still in the making, should have intervened decisively to stop the damage before it was too late? Where was the fist pounding on the table to bring back to reason those colleagues who had lost the sense of what risks were tolerable? Where was the *primus inter pares* who, less burdened by seats on supervisory boards, should have maintained with unfailing continuity an overview and influence over the whole and who in this respect inevitably felt morally responsible to the bank and his colleagues on the management board? Where was Mr Wassermann? The criticism expressed in connection with these questions was severe and, while acknowledging all of his abilities, spared neither Oscar Wassermann the banker nor Oscar Wassermann the person. It suddenly became clear that he had failed to invest sufficient energy in the much-needed task of disciplining management board members, and that the quality of boundless optimism that he possessed, along with his related attitude of stoic indifference, led him to believe that one could actually leave people and things to their own devices. Specific evidence of this belief was, for instance, Mr Wassermann's policy of never having anything forwarded to him while on lengthy holiday trips, on the grounds that if he were to die, things would have to go on without him.

From the thoughts that emerged during Mr Wassermann's period of illness, it became increasingly clear that one was leaning towards an affirmative answer to the question of whether it would not be better for the bank if he did not return to his leadership role. Whether Mr Wassermann was a Jew or a Christian no longer had anything to do with it. The question was now raised within the management board as to whether it would not be advisable to announce Mr Wassermann's resignation. In the discussion on 11 April, Mr Wassermann had given me discretion regarding the timing of the announcement. The ability to act towards this end was constrained by the fact that Mr Frank's departure from the bank was also being discussed due to the unfortunate outcome of his connections with Blumenstein, Richard Kahn, and Schapiro, and that on the day that Mr Wassermann's resignation was announced, Mr Frank's position would – according to the opinions that held sway at that time – become untenable. After the involuntary departures of Messrs von Stauss, Bonn, Fehr, and Kehl, and if now Mr Wassermann were also to leave, then the case of Mr Frank would acquire considerable psychological significance in terms of not permitting the accusation that the gentlemen from the leadership of the Disconto-Gesellschaft were inclined to pass a milder judgement on a colleague from their own ranks, despite the fact that his name was also connected with the loss-making transactions mentioned earlier. It was unthinkable to announce the resignation of both gentlemen without at the same time disclosing the new members joining the management board. Discussions that took place on this very important issue on 13 May were confirmed in the management board meeting on Monday, 15 May. On the day before, namely Sunday, 14 May, Mr Russell and I called on Mr Schlitter in order to re-examine the situation by means of a verbal exchange of views. We parted with an agreement that such an important change in the bank's leadership could not be announced without giving Mr Schacht, who was just about to return from a trip to America, an opportunity to comment on the matter, and that Mr Schlitter would assume the task of informing Mr Wassermann at the appropriate time.

This was the state of affairs when, in confirmation of the news I had since received of his vastly improved health, Mr Wassermann appeared at the bank on 18 May, greeted me and several other colleagues, and at once enquired if he should, as usual, perform the duties of spokesman of the management board at the general meeting on 1 June. He said that he felt by all means physically able to do so and had only asked so that he could prepare accordingly in case of an affirmative answer. This incident aroused surprise and, simultaneously, a sense of awkwardness among the members of the management board. Nevertheless, clarity was soon achieved regarding Mr Wassermann's enquiry. Since it was believed that Mr Wassermann still needed several weeks of rest and should seek out a place suitable for this purpose, it was prudent to have him refrain from performing duties and from even participating in the general assembly. He was informed of this opinion.

On 19 May I was not at the bank, but towards the evening I was requested by phone to attend a meeting at 9 a.m., which members of the management board and also Mr Schlitter attended. Mr Brunswig[16] reported that an acquaintance of his, a member of the NSDAP, had paid a friendly visit to tell him that a change in the bank's leadership was being called for. He further said that the demand was directed at Mr Wassermann and Mr Frank, and that if management did not at once decide to carry out this measure, it would face immediate pressure. The question arose as to what should be done.

---

16 Dr Peter Brunswig (1879–1953), lawyer; joined Deutsche Bank in 1904 and was a member of the management board, 1933–1934; from 1934 private banker and partner of the banking house C. G. Trinkaus in Düsseldorf; after 1945 member of the Joint German Financial Council (Gemeinsamer Deutscher Finanzrat) in Frankfurt am Main.

Mr Brunswig gave his report in a very emphatic and spirited manner, and the members of the management board were obviously inclined to be swayed by his conviction, making it necessary to act at once. I firmly refused, with the concurrence of Mr Schlitter, to allow myself to be pushed into a decision, and held the view that no one would be so bold as to pressure us. I also argued that if anyone, however, did follow through with it, then the responsibility would fall to the other party, and that until then we would have to carry this responsibility, as everything we do at this moment would surely be portrayed later as a voluntary act. The meeting ended at 11 a.m. with me expressing my willingness to brief Mr Dreyse[17] on the matter and obtain his opinion.

The events of 20 May can only be understood if one recalls the poisoned atmosphere that permeated this momentous day. In addition to the visit that Mr Brunswig had reported, the state secretary of the Reich Ministry of Transport (and/or Dr Fischer from the Reichskredit AG)[18] had called on Mr Solmssen early in the morning and demanded, reiterating requests already made to Mr Solmssen, that the Jewish members of the German-Atlantic Telegraph Company's supervisory board immediately step down from their posts, so that by-elections could be held at the general meeting scheduled to begin at 12 noon, which would thereupon enable a new chairman to replace Mr Solmssen. Although the state secretary, who had obviously covered himself by obtaining an order from the minister,[19] was rebuffed for now in the supervisory board meeting held prior to the general meeting, it was not possible to erase the distressing impression that this incident made upon the bank. At 1 p.m. I went to see Mr Dreyse. Our discussion lasted until shortly after 2 p.m. Mr Dreyse confirmed that no one had the right to put pressure on us, and that we should calmly dismiss anything that might come our way. As for the decisions that we freely took with regard to personnel issues, Mr Dreyse said, verbatim, that these were naturally 'our own affair'.

At 3 p.m. a new meeting took place between Mr Schlitter, me, and Messrs Blinzig,[20] Brunswig, Mosler, Schlieper,[21] and Solmssen from the management board. Mr Frank was not at the bank on that day. I reported on the outcome of my discussion with Mr Dreyse and stressed that, as a result, there was no reason to immediately announce the resignation of Mr Wassermann and thereby eliminate the option of justifying the

---

17 Friedrich Wilhelm Dreyse (1874–1943), banker; member of the management board of the Reichsbank, 1924–1939; vice president of the Reichsbank, 1926–1939; from 1936 deputy chairman of the Supervisory Office for Banking; deputy chairman of the supervisory board of Dresdner Bank, 1939–1943.
18 Christian Otto Fischer (b. 1882), lawyer; from 1925 member of the management board of the Reichs-Kredit-Gesellschaft; from 1933 president of the Association of German Banks and Bankers; from 1934 head of the Reich Group of Banks in the Reich Chamber of Economics.
19 Baron Paul von Eltz-Rübenach (1875–1943), engineer; from 1902 worked at the Railways Directorate Münster; from 1924 president of the Reich Railways Directorate Karlsruhe; Reich postmaster general and minister of transport, 1932–1937.
20 Alfred Blinzig (1869–1945), banker; joined Deutsche Bank in 1899; member of the management board of Deutsche Bank, 1920–1929, and of the Deutsche Bank and Disconto-Gesellschaft, 1929–1934; chairman of the supervisory board of Philipp Holzmann AG, 1932–1939.
21 Gustav Schlieper (1880–1937), banker; joined the Disconto-Gesellschaft in 1902; partner of the Disconto-Gesellschaft, 1914–1929, and member of the management board of the Deutsche Bank and Disconto-Gesellschaft, 1929–1937.

departure on the grounds of Mr Wassermann's ill health some time following the general meeting. The management board was of a different opinion. One reason it gave was that the departure of Mr Wassermann had already become a topic of conversation at the bank, while several members of the press had also already been informed. It furthermore said that the warning relayed to Mr Brunswig, which he in turn emphasized, ought by all means to be taken seriously. Even if the impact of pressure put on the bank were only to last two to three days, the management board continued, there was no way to foresee what the consequences would be. The resignation of both gentlemen, according to the management board, had to be announced at some point during 24 May, at the very latest. I interjected here that final action should not be taken until I had spoken with Mr Schacht, who was scheduled to return on 22 May. I added that if it was resolved that the departures were to be announced over the course of the next several days, I could not imagine asking Mr Schacht during my visit if he approved of the course of action, but only thought it possible to present him with a fait accompli. I also made it perfectly clear that although it was unlikely that Mr Schacht could be persuaded to make a particular statement, it was nonetheless conceivable that he might let his disapproval be known. What to do now? With the exception of Mr Blinzig, the members of the management board believed that Mr Schacht must be presented with a fait accompli. The discussion went back and forth and had reached its climax. I felt that it was absolutely imperative to reach complete unanimity on what must now be done or left undone. I therefore summarized the content of the discussion and stated that this convinced me that the affair had reached a stage where one must inform Mr Wassermann immediately that his and Mr Frank's resignations would be announced in the next several days. I also said that tomorrow (21 May) was Sunday and that on Monday (22 May) my discussion with Mr Schacht could possibly take place. I added that one owed this to Mr Wassermann, and asked if my view was shared. Owing to the question's crucial importance, I asked each gentleman individually; they all answered in the affirmative. With that, the decision had been taken and the direction for the discussion with Mr Schacht given. The meeting ended at around 4 p.m. At 5.30 p.m. Mr Schlitter and I then called on Mr Wassermann at his apartment to inform him of the decision. The discharge of this task proved to be psychologically burdensome for both of us, because we at once gained the conviction that the many days that had passed since 12 April had brought about a change in Mr Wassermann, and that he no longer reckoned with his departure.

Then, on 23 May at 11.30 a.m., I called on Mr Schacht to brief him on the events that had occurred, the ensuing developments, and the decisions consequently taken. Mr Schacht showed a great deal of understanding for everything and spoke of the difficult and thankless task that fell to me at the bank, in whose continued existence the Reichsbank had the greatest interest, but that I must see this task through. He then added that Mr Wassermann was arriving at 4 p.m. and that the information I had given him would naturally determine the course of their discussion.

On 29 May the following statement was then sent to the members of the main committee:

Mr Theodor Frank and Mr Oscar Wassermann have given the supervisory board notice that they do not wish to continue their contractual relationship beyond 31 December 1933. It is intended to put these gentlemen forward for election to the supervisory board at the proper time; they will remain associated with the bank by means of upholding interests on various supervisory boards. It is furthermore intended to put Dr Karl Kimmic[22] and Mr Fritz Wintermantel[23] forward for appointment to the management board.[24]

DOC. 67
On 4 August 1933 the Association of Synagogue Congregations of the province of Upper Silesia lodges a complaint with the Reich Foreign Office regarding discrimination against Jews[1]

Note issued by the Reich Foreign Office, signed Seel, with enclosure, dated 8 August 1933 (copy)[2]

On 4 August the following representatives from the committee of the Association of Synagogue Congregations of the province of Upper Silesia presented themselves:

1. Judicial Counsellor Dr Kochmann[3] from Gleiwitz,
2. Lawyer Dr Weißmann[4] from Beuthen,
3. Retailer Mr Behrend[5] from Beuthen.

They handed over the enclosed list of discriminations against Jews in Upper Silesia, which they considered to violate the Geneva Convention.[6]

The representatives of the Association of Synagogue Congregations also complained that intense antisemitic propaganda was being carried out in Upper Silesia, and that the relevant authorities were not taking sufficient action to counter such activities. In particular, they submitted a copy of the *Deutsche Ostfront*[7] and said that its supplement

---

22 Dr Karl Kimmich (1880–1945), banker; member of the management board, 1933–1942; spokesman of the management board, 1940–1942, and chairman of the supervisory board of the Deutsche Bank and Disconto-Gesellschaft, 1942–1945.

23 Fritz Wintermantel (1882–1953), banker; joined Deutsche Bank in 1902; member of the management board of Deutsche Bank, 1933–1945; chairman of the supervisory board of Orenstein & Koppel and Knorr-Bremse in Berlin; after 1945 management executive at the Rheinisch-Westfälische Bank in Düsseldorf.

24 Dating the withdrawal to 31 Dec. 1933 was a formality; after the events described here, Wassermann did not perform any more duties at Deutsche Bank: Barkai, *Oscar Wassermann*, p. 101.

1 PA AA, R 83 034. This document has been translated from German.
2 Enclosed, on pp. 7–10 of the original, are copies from the letter of the League of National Socialist German Lawyers, district leadership of Neiße, and the Gleiwitz-Mitte branch of the NSDAP, dated 10 July 1933.
3 Dr Arthur Kochmann (1864–1943), lawyer; from 1892 lawyer at the Gleiwitz Regional Court; from 1899 city councillor; from 1915 chairman of Gleiwitz synagogue congregation; from 1933 Upper Silesia's representative in the Reich Representation of German Jews; deported to Auschwitz, 1943.
4 Correctly: Dr Georg Weissmann (1885–1963), lawyer; practised law and worked as a notary in Beuthen; active Zionist; secretary of the action committee of Upper Silesian Jews, 1933–1937; disbarred, 1937; worked at the Palestine Office in Berlin, 1937–1939; in 1939 emigrated to Palestine, where he practised law.
5 Probably David Behrendt, member of the CV.
6 See also Doc. 28, 7 April 1933, and Doc. 46, 24 May 1933.
7 The newspaper *Die Deutsche Ostfront*, whose publisher in 1933 was Gauleiter Helmuth Brückner, was the National Socialist daily newspaper in Upper Silesia and was owned by the publishing company NS-Schlesien GmbH in Gleiwitz. It appeared from 1932–1936 and then merged with the NSDAP organ *Der oberschlesische Wanderer*.

Der Jude – now *Isidor* – constantly contained harsh attacks on Jews, portraying them as contemptible. They also said that Helmuth Brückner,[8] governor of the province, was the signed publisher of the *Ostfront*. According to the representatives, such publications presented an even greater danger when they were taken across the border en masse to Czechoslovakia, where they provided fuel for scaremongering.

In addition, they said that the boycott against the Jews was being extended, both openly and covertly, to every possible sphere, and presented as evidence a copy of a letter of the League of National Socialist German Lawyers, district leadership of Neiße, and the Gleiwitz-Mitte branch of the NSDAP, dated 10 July 1933.

The representatives noted that they had not seen any noteworthy influx from the Reich since the Aryan laws came into force, particularly not since the Geneva negotiations.[9] They added that thus far only a single application for admission had been submitted by the lawyer Dr Weißenberg,[10] a native of Upper Silesia who had formerly practised law in Breslau and had been struck from the list of lawyers there. The representatives of the Association of Synagogue Congregations said that they themselves were categorically of the view that the only persons who could lay claim to the minority rights in Upper Silesia, and thus to an exemption from the Aryan legislation, were those residents of Upper Silesia who were already living there when the exemption legislation came into force.

signed Seel.

Copy I C 6070/10.8.
I. *Discrimination of a general nature under public law.*
 1. Withdrawal of state subsidies for the district rabbinate of Upper Silesia and for religious instruction in the small municipalities.
 2. [Failure to] secure the claim to an equitable share of the total funding allocated in state and municipal budgets for the purposes of childcare and welfare (incl. subsidies for playgrounds and nurseries and for establishing new higher-level schools of our own); see Articles 69–70 of the Geneva Convention.
 3. Ban on the slaughtering of cattle and horses and poultry.[11]
 4. Prohibition of the use of municipal gymnasiums, tennis courts, etc. by Jewish gymnastics and sports associations.
 5. Withdrawal of reduced travel fares for Jewish youth associations.
 6. Denial of free schools and reduced tuition fees for Jewish pupils.

---

8 Helmuth Brückner (1896–1951), military officer; participated in the Beer Hall Putsch, 1923; joined the NSDAP in 1925; Gauleiter of Silesia, 1925–1934; Oberpräsident of the province of Lower Silesia, 1933 (responsible for Upper Silesia at the same time); expelled from the NSDAP and the SA in Dec. 1934; imprisoned until 1937 for homosexuality; arrested in Rostock, 1945; died in the Soviet Union.
9 See Doc. 46, 24 May 1933.
10 Probably Dr Kurt Weißenberg (b. 1880), lawyer; practised law in Beuthen, from where he was deported (date and destination unknown).
11 On the basis of an agreement between the National Socialist government and the Association of Synagogue Congregations in Upper Silesia, the part of Upper Silesia placed under the supervision of the League of Nations was exempted on 27 August 1934 from the slaughter ban that had been introduced by law in Germany on 21/22 April 1933. For more details on the slaughter ban, see the Law and Regulation on the Slaughter of Animals, *Reichsgesetzblatt*, 1933, I, pp. 203 and 212.

7. Announcement by the municipal authorities published in the *Beuthener Stadtblatt* forbidding:

(a) the purchase of Jewish books, under the threat of severe penalty,

(b) newspapers to accept advertisements from Jews, under the threat of the withdrawal of public announcements,

(c) the awarding of public contracts to Jews.

8. Introduction of special bathing times for 'non-Aryans' in the steam bath in Beuthen, Upper Silesia, and barring of Jews from using the outdoor swimming pool in Gleiwitz.

9. Confiscation of Jewish books, in particular the books by Grätz[12] and Dubnow[13] on Jewish history, the book *Die Juden in der Kunst*[14] by Schwarz, etc. in the bookshop in Beuthen, Upper Silesia, and occasional searches of all Upper Silesian bookshops for 'Marxist and Jewish literature'.

10. *Numerus clausus* for Upper Silesian students seeking university education, and the issue of admission to state examinations and further practical training (medical interns, etc.).

11. The *Ostfront*, particularly its Sunday supplement *Der Jude* and later *Isidor*, has carried with impunity countless articles insulting the Jewish religion and stirring up class hatred among the population.

12. Under the responsibility of A. W. Saala from the *Deutsche Ostfront* in Beuthen, Upper Silesia, the Combat League for Small and Medium-Sized Businesses, Kreisleitung of Beuthen, publishes a directory of Beuthen's Christian-German businesses that makes insulting remarks about Jews while also calling for the boycott of Jewish businesspeople, using language such as: 'Jews always sell trashy goods', 'Eating at Jewish restaurants will kill you', 'Anyone who buys from Jews is a scoundrel', 'Buy from Germans if you want to be treated fairly', 'Buy from Jews if you want to be swindled', 'What good is your German character if you buy from Jews', etc.

13. SA units gather in the streets and sing songs that aim to incite the population against the Jews.

14. Schools are required to introduce SA songbooks containing anti-Jewish songs, and pupils are required to purchase them.

15. The rules of procedure for meetings of the Beuthen City Council contained the provision that city councillors of foreign origin are allowed to speak only at the discretion of the head of the city council. It is not known whether this provision has been amended at the supervisory level.

16. Arbitrary shortening of religious lessons in the municipal Humboldt School in Beuthen and other municipal schools in Upper Silesia, e.g. in Hindenburg.

---

12 Heinrich Graetz (1817–1891), historian; professor at the University of Breslau; author of works including *Geschichte der Juden von den ältesten Zeiten bis zur Gegenwart* (1853–1878).

13 Simon Dubnow (1860–1941), historian; lived in St Petersburg, Odessa, Berlin (1922–1933), and Riga (1933–1941). After the German occupation, he lived in the Riga ghetto and was murdered in Dec. 1941; author of works including *Weltgeschichte des jüdischen Volkes* (1925–1929) and *Geschichte des Chassidismus* (1931).

14 Karl Schwarz, *Die Juden in der Kunst* (Berlin: Der Heine-Bund, 1928).

II. Civil servants.

1. Placing of judges and state and municipal civil servants on compulsory leave of absence.

2. Exclusion of Jews from posts as jurors, lay judges, and commercial judges, and from the labour and regional labour courts, as enumerators for the census, as arbitrators on state and municipal tax committees, etc.

3. Withdrawal of the mandates of assessors.

4. Prohibition of Aryan law clerks from carrying out their traineeships with non-Aryan lawyers.

5. Barring of Jewish assessors from serving as representatives of lawyers and notaries.

III. Liberal professions.

(a) Lawyers.

1. Boycott of lawyers on 1 April 1933.

2. Barring of Jewish lawyers from practising in the courts from 1 April to the end of May 1933.

3. Suspension of notaries.

4. Denial of *in forma pauperis*.

5. Boycott announcements by the *Ostfront* on 10 June 1933 in order to circumvent the German-Polish Convention.[15]

6. Dispatch of a circular of the Gleiwitz branch of the NSDAP to the Christian clients of Jewish lawyers.

(b) Physicians.

1. Dismissal of doctors and dentists employed in municipal welfare services and in the examination of war-disabled.

2. Dismissal of Jewish veterinarians employed by cities, municipalities, and public associations.

3. Dismissal of Jewish doctors employed by health insurance companies and miners' guilds, and general dismissal of doctors employed by health insurance companies. Wrongful dismissal carried out by individual health insurance companies, e.g. the Reich Railways health insurance fund.

4. Boycott of doctors, dentists, chemists, etc. on 29 March and 1 April 1933.

5. Barring of doctors from acting as experts before courts and other public authorities, and from providing expert advisory services, e.g. as done by the Reich Railways.

6. Midwives instructed by the medical commissioner in Gleiwitz to caution pregnant women approaching their due date against calling in Jewish doctors.

(c) Retailers and other liberal professions.

1. Boycott of Jewish shops on 29 March and 1 April 1933, and later in other towns (e.g. Kreuzburg, Gross-Strehlitz), as well as a silent boycott (Combat League).

2. Order issued by State Commissioner Heidtmann regarding the awarding of contracts to Jewish businesspeople, and boycott of businesses with non-Aryan owners by all Upper Silesian municipal administrations.

3. Exclusion from public contracts of those Christian craftsmen who buy from Jews.

---

15 This is probably a reference to the Geneva Convention on Upper Silesia (1922).

4. Identical order issued by the state and provincial building authorities.

5. Boycott of businesses by the Upper Silesian provincial administration and the Upper Silesian Chamber of Industry and Commerce.

6. Complete exclusion or discriminatory treatment of Jewish market traders in various Upper Silesian towns (Hindenburg, Tost, etc.).

7. Prohibition of tax deferral for Jews, and prohibition of the leasing of shops in municipal real estate (resolution of the Hindenburg City Council).

8. Exclusion of Jews from appointments as bankruptcy trustees, court experts, official receivers, curators of estates, tax appraisers, and auditing experts.

9. Exclusion of Jews from the tax consultant profession.

10. Exclusion of non-Aryans from all administrative posts, whether on executive boards, on the committees of retail associations, etc.

11. Exclusion of non-Aryans from membership in the Upper Silesian Chamber of Industry and Commerce in Oppeln as well as the Chamber of Skilled Crafts.

12. Denial of excise licences to Jewish restaurant owners.

13. Prohibition of welfare recipients from having medicines prepared in Jewish pharmacies.

14. Exclusion of Jewish singers and actors from the Upper Silesian Regional Theatre.

DOC. 68

On 11 August 1933 the Reich Representation of Jewish Regional Associations in Germany complains to the Reich Minister of Labour about occupational restrictions placed on physicians[1]

Letter from the Reich Representation of Jewish Regional Associations in Germany (signature illegible), Berlin, to the Reich Minister of Labour[2] (received on 12 August 1933), dated 11 August 1933[3]

Allow us to bring the following course of events to your attention:

On 12 July 1933, by resolution of the management board, the Physicians' Association of Chemnitz and the Surrounding Area issued the following restrictions, effective immediately:

1. Physicians of German origin and physicians of a foreign race are prohibited from standing in for each other.

2. Physicians of German origin are prohibited from referring patients to physicians of a foreign race or accepting referrals from them.

3. Physicians of German origin are prohibited from calling in physicians of a foreign race for consultation or from being called in by them.

---

1 BArch, R 1501/26401, fol. 160r–v. This document has been translated from German.
2 The Reich minister of labour was Franz Seldte (1882–1947), businessman; founder and head of the Stahlhelm, 1918; joined the NSDAP in 1933; Reich minister of labour, 1933–1945; arrested in 1945 and died in an American military prison in 1947.
3 The original contains several comments and handwritten underlining. The Reich Ministry of Labour (Zschimmer) sent the letter to the Reich Ministry of the Interior on 16 Sept. 1933: BArch, R 1501/26401, fol. 160r–v.

In the event of violation of this ban, a penalty will be levied amounting to 1.5 times the fee earned as a result of the violation.

In the *Deutsches Ärzteblatt*[4] of 29 July 1933 the chairman of the Hartmann League[5] and the Reich commissioner for the Central Medical Associations, Dr Wagner,[6] ordered all the regional groups of the medical associations to adopt these provisions. We are sending the text of the directive enclosed.[7]

We are of the opinion that these directives make it impossible for Jewish doctors to practise medicine fully and without restrictions. It is likewise made impossible for Jewish general practitioners to bring in non-Jewish specialists, as well as for non-Jewish general practitioners to bring in Jewish specialists. The same ban is placed on medical consultation. The decree thus causes almost as much harm to non-Jewish doctors as it does to Jewish ones.

According to the principles of the Civil Service Law, which in our view is to be applied by analogy to all laws as part of the reordering of occupational conditions, all persons remaining in employment are to be permitted to practise their profession without restrictions.

The aforementioned rules render this principle illusory.

Furthermore, these rules violate the framework agreements of the health insurance companies, which guarantee free choice among all the accredited physicians in the network.

Moreover, the decree also prevents the full exercise of the profession by private practitioners, a measure that runs counter to the government's guidelines regarding the unrestricted opportunity to exercise one's profession in the economy.

On behalf of all Jewish physicians, we therefore request suitable measures that will eliminate these serious encroachments on the professional activity of the Jewish physicians of Germany.[8]

With the highest esteem

---

4 The *Deutsches Ärzteblatt* was published in 1933 by the German League of Physicians' Associations (Deutscher Ärztevereinsbund) and the Association of Physicians in Germany (Verband der Ärzte Deutschlands). The weekly publication had been founded in 1872 as *Ärztliche Mitteilungen*, and was known as *Deutsches Ärzteblatt* from 1930 to 1945, as *Ärztliche Mitteilungen – Deutsches Ärzteblatt* from 1949 to 1963, and then again as *Deutsches Ärzteblatt*.

5 The Association of Physicians in Germany (also known as the Hartmannbund/Hartmann League) was founded as an advocacy group in 1900 on the initiative of the Leipzig physician Hermann Hartmann, and renamed the Hartmann League after his death in 1924.

6 Dr Gerhard Wagner (1888–1939), physician; joined the NSDAP in 1929; became head of the National Socialist Physicians' League in 1932; Reich commissioner for the Central Medical Associations, 1933; head of the Reich Chamber of Physicians and Reich Physicians' Leader, 1935.

7 The text of the directive is not printed here. Undated directive of the Reich commissioner, *Deutsches Ärzteblatt*, no. 5, 29 July 1933, p. 131.

8 On 12 Sept. 1933 the Reich Representation of German Jews added to its petition an example from Magdeburg: letter from the Reich Representation to the Reich Ministry of Labour dated 12 Sept. 1933, BArch, R 1501/26401, fol. 242. The Reich Ministry of the Interior finally asked Reich Physicians' Leader Wagner for an opinion and expressed 'grave doubts' as to the admissibility of the order issued by Wagner: letter from the Reich Ministry of the Interior to Wagner, 7 Oct. 1933, ibid., fols. 176–177. As a result of the criticism, Wagner moderated his order in a strictly confidential circular letter of 23 Oct. 1933. He was not rescinding his order, he said, but exceptions were permissible: ibid., fols. 251–252.

DOC. 69

The Prussian Ministry of Justice quashes criminal proceedings on 11 August 1933 in the case of the murder of a Jewish dentist[1]

Order from the Prussian Ministry of Justice, Krug,[2] dated 11 August 1933[3]

1. *Comment*

The criminal offence was committed before 16 July 1933 – page in the file –. The criminal act is related to the National Socialist revolution. On the basis of the decree of the Prussian Minister President[4] dated 22 July 1933 (J.M. I 4543) – JMBl.[5] p. 235 – in connection with the General Order of the Minister of Justice[6] from 25 July 1933 (I 4549) – JMBl. p. 236 – re pardons, the quashing of criminal proceedings seems necessary in light of the completion of the National Socialist revolution.

It concerns the killing of the Jewish dentist A. Meyer.[7] *M. is said to have been engaged in communist activities – p. 50 –, held meetings in which the elimination of § 218 of the Criminal Code*[8] *was debated – p. 50 – and had sexual intercourse with numerous Christian girls and boasted of the same – p. 52 –.*[9] The perpetrators, who have not yet been identified, are accordingly likely to have acted out of political considerations and the act is likely to have been committed in connection with the National Socialist revolution.[10]

2. To be submitted to the minister.[11]

---

1 GStA PK, I HA, Rep. 84a/53389, fol. 12. This document has been translated from German.
2 Dr Karl Krug (1902–1984), lawyer; joined the NSDAP in 1932; worked for the NSDAP in 1932–1933, first in the Culture Department of the NSDAP Gau of Electoral Hesse (Kurhessen), later as head of the Gau legal office there; from 1933 public prosecutor in the Central Public Prosecutor's Office of the Prussian Ministry of Justice in Berlin; later worked in the Reich Ministry of Justice; from 1938/39 Ministerialrat there; after 1945 lawyer in Düsseldorf and Cologne; editor of the journal *Deutsche Justiz*.
3 The original contains several handwritten annotations.
4 The Prussian minister president in 1933–1945 was Hermann Göring.
5 *Justizministerialblatt*: Ministry of Justice gazette.
6 The Prussian minister of justice in 1933–1934 was Hanns Kerrl.
7 Dr Alfred Meyer (1898–1933), dentist in Wuppertal-Barmen, had received threatening antisemitic telephone calls since March 1933, and the windowpanes of his surgery had been smashed. During several brutal raids on his home on the night of 2 April, his apartment was ransacked. On 16 May 1933 several SA men kidnapped and murdered Dr Meyer. His body, which was found the next day in the Bever Valley Reservoir near Hückeswagen, had two gunshot wounds and several stab wounds: ibid., fols. 13–40.
8 § 218 of the Criminal Code prohibited abortion.
9 All the charges were based on the statement of the neighbours, Mr and Mrs Fischer: ibid., fols. 50–53.
10 The paragraph in italics here is handwritten in the original.
11 Once Prussian Minister of Justice Kerrl had taken note of the case file, criminal proceedings were dropped on 12 August 1933: ibid., fol. 12.

DOC. 70
On 14 August 1933 the Reich Ministry of the Interior sends the Reich Foreign Office and the Prussian Minister of the Interior a preliminary list of persons to be deprived of citizenship[1]

Express letter from the Reich Ministry of the Interior (no. II B 5013/9.8.), signed Hering,[2] to (a) the Reich Foreign Office, Legation Counsellor von Kotze,[3] and to (b) the Prussian Ministry of the Interior, Ministerialrat Driest,[4] dated 14 August 1933, with a handwritten comment from the Reich Ministry of the Interior dated 16 August 1933 (copy)

Comment: I took part in the meeting. Apart from the Einstein case, to which the Reich Foreign Office raised objections,[5] *the list was approved. State Police Central Office made a few other suggestions, which should be borne in mind.*[6] *Further involvement of I A by II B is envisaged*

B[erlin], 16 August 1933

1. Department head
2. To be filed[7]

Re a: with reference to your letter of 9 August 1933 – Ref. D. 3496 –.[8]
Regarding: retraction of German nationality.

---

1 BArch, R 1501/125708, fols. 508–512. This document has been translated from German.
2 Hermann Hering (b. 1874), Ministerialdirigent in the Reich Ministry of the Interior; joined the NSDAP in 1941.
3 Hans Ulrich von Kotze (1891–1941), military officer; worked from 1921 in the Reich Foreign Office, from 1930 to 1932 in the administrative office of the League of Nations in Geneva, and from 1933 in the Culture Department of the Reich Foreign Office; envoy in Riga, 1938–1941; responsible for foreign policy matters in the office of the Reich plenipotentiary in Denmark, 1941.
4 Emil Driest (b. 1876), civil servant; in 1933 Ministerialrat in the Prussian Ministry of the Interior; from 1935 worked in Dept I (Constitution and Legislation) of the Reich Ministry of the Interior; not a member of the NSDAP.
5 At the urging of the Gestapo and the Reich Ministry of the Interior, Albert Einstein's name was on the preliminary list of suggested names. In the meeting, however, the Reich Foreign Office had voiced opposition to Einstein's immediate denaturalization because of fears that international reaction would be negative. He should either be quietly deprived of Prussian nationality, the ministry suggested, or denaturalized at a later time. Einstein was later placed on the second list by Minister of the Interior Frick, and his citizenship was retracted on 29 March 1934: Michael Hepp, *Die Ausbürgerung deutscher Staatsangehöriger 1933–1945 nach den im Reichsanzeiger veröffentlichten Listen*, 3 vols. (Munich: Saur, 1985–1988), pp. xxvi and 4; see also 'Einstein nicht mehr deutscher Staatsangehöriger', *Deutsche Allgemeine Zeitung*, 30 March 1934, p. 1.
6 The proposed list reproduced here contained (besides Einstein) fourteen other persons, including Dr Alfred Apfel (1882–1940); Elfriede Gohlke, known as Ruth Fischer (1895–1961); Albert Grzesinski (1879–1947); Wilhelm Pieck (1876–1960); Dr Bernhard Weiß (1880–1951); and Dr Kurt Tucholsky (1890–1935). The list, signed by State Secretary Pfundtner on 23 August 1933, was published in the *Deutscher Reichsanzeiger und Preußischer Staatsanzeiger*, no. 198, 25 August 1933. Thirty-three persons on 25 August 1933 were thus deprived of their German nationality for 'treasonous activity' and their assets were confiscated. The list is published in Hepp, *Die Ausbürgerung*, pp. 3–4.
7 In the original the italicized passage is handwritten.
8 The Reich Ministry of the Interior had sent out a circular letter on 22 July 1933 and requested suggestions for retraction of citizenship. The letter of the Reich Foreign Office mentioned here, dated 9 August 1933, presumably referred to this circular letter: Hepp, *Die Ausbürgerung*, p. xxvi.

In the case of the subjects of the Reich who are named in the enclosed list, available facts justify their loss of German nationality in accordance with § 2(1) of the Law on the Revocation of Naturalization and the Deprivation of German Nationality of 14 July 1933 (*Reichsgesetzblatt*, I, p. 480). Apart from the actual decision on retraction, it is advisable to decide at once the extent to which, in individual cases, use should be made of the possibility of seizing assets. In addition, the extent to which the loss of nationality should be extended to family members should be made clear (cf. § 2(4) loc. cit.).

I have the honour to invite you to a conference on the matter on *Wednesday 16 August 1933, 10.30 a.m.*, at the Reich Ministry of the Interior, room 220.

Addenda for the Prussian Ministry of the Interior: I would be grateful if the requisite information for the decision on extending the retraction of nationality to family members could be supplied as soon as possible.

Let me request that the Gestapo Central Office in Berlin be advised to take part in the conference.

By proxy
signed Hering

For II B 5013/9.8.
Subjects of the Reich who are under consideration for retraction of German nationality.
Bernhard, Georg,[9] honorary professor, formerly editor-in-chief of the *Vossische Zeitung*
Date and place of birth: 20 October 1875 in Berlin
Last place of residence: Berlin, 21 Kleiststraße
Nationality: Prussian
Current whereabouts: France (?)
Breitscheid, Rudolf,[10] Dr, formerly Reichstag delegate (SPD)
Date and place of birth: 2 November 1874 in Cologne
Last place of residence: Berlin W 30, 5 Haberlandstraße
Nationality: Prussian
Current whereabouts: presumably Paris (France)
Einstein, Albert, professor
Date and place of birth: 14 March 1879 in Ulm
Last place of residence: Berlin W 30, 5 Haberlandstraße
Nationality: Prussian
Current whereabouts: Coq s.M. (Belgium)

9 Georg Bernhard (1875–1944), journalist; member of the Social Democratic Party of Germany (SPD) until 1906; joined the German Democratic Party (DDP) in 1924; from 1908 managing director of the *Morgenpost* and *B.Z. am Mittag* in Berlin; editor-in-chief of the *Vossische Zeitung*, 1914–1930; board member of the Central Association of German Citizens of the Jewish Faith (CV); in 1933 emigrated to France, where he founded the *Pariser Tageblatt*; emigrated to the USA in 1941.
10 Dr Rudolf Breitscheid (1874–1944), economist and politician; SPD member from 1912, Independent Social Democratic Party of Germany (USPD) member from 1917 to 1922, then SPD member again; Reichstag delegate, 1920–1933; from 1931 in the SPD party executive; in 1933 emigrated to Switzerland, then to Paris; in 1941 extradited to Germany by the Vichy government; imprisoned and held in concentration camp, 1941–1944; died in Buchenwald concentration camp in 1944.

Falk, Alfred,[11] formerly secretary of the League for Human Rights
Head of the Republican Complaints Office
Date and place of birth: 4 February 1896 in Berlin
Last place of residence: 43 Kastanien-Allee, Hamelin
Current whereabouts: Strasbourg (France)
Feuchtwanger, Lion
Date and place of birth: ?
Last place of residence: ?
Nationality: ?
Current whereabouts: Switzerland
Foerster, Friedrich Wilhelm,[12] professor, PhD
Date and place of birth: 2 June 1869 in Berlin
Last place of residence: ?
Nationality: ?
Current whereabouts: Zurich, 2 Holtingerstraße (?)
Paris (France)
v. Gerlach, Helmuth,[13] editor of *Welt am Montag*
Contributor to *Weltbühne*
Date and place of birth: 2 February 1866 in Menschmotzelwitz, Kreis Wohlau
Last place of residence: Berlin-Wilmersdorf, 46 Brandenburgische Straße
Nationality: ?
Current whereabouts: April 1933, Vienna then Zurich (Switzerland)
Grossmann, Kurt,[14] formerly secretary of the League for Human Rights.
Date and place of birth: 21 May 1897 in Berlin
Last place of residence: Berlin-Charlottenburg, 86 Wilmersdorferstraße
Nationality: ?
Current whereabouts: Prague (Czechoslovakia)
Hansmann, Wilhelm,[15] formerly Landtag[16] delegate of the SPD,

---

11 Alfred Falk (1896–1951), journalist; conscientious objector; editor of the monthly *Der Krieg*, 1928–1930; emigrated to France in 1933.
12 Dr Friedrich Wilhelm Foerster (1869–1966), philosopher and publicist; university lecturer in philosophy in Zurich, 1899–1914; professor of philosophy in Vienna, 1913–1914; professor of education in Munich, 1914–1920; pacifist; author of works including *Mein Kampf gegen das militaristische und nationalistische Deutschland* (1920).
13 Helmuth Georg von Gerlach (1866–1935), journalist; from 1906 editor-in-chief of *Die Welt am Montag* in Berlin; co-founder of the German Democratic Party (DDP); board member of the League for International Law (Liga für Völkerrecht); in March 1933 emigrated via Austria to Paris; contributor to the *Pariser Tageblatt* and *Die neue Weltbühne*.
14 Kurt R. Grossmann (1897–1972), publicist; active in the German League for Human Rights; pacifist; member of the SPD; in 1933 emigrated to Prague, in 1938 to Paris, and in 1939 to the USA, where he was active in Jewish refugee relief work; author of works including *The Jewish Refugee* (with Arieh Tartakower, 1944).
15 Dr Wilhelm Hansmann (1886–1963), local politician; member of the SPD; Landrat in Kreis Hörde, from 1919, and in Kreis Ennepe-Ruhr, 1929–31; Landtag delegate in Prussia, 1928–1931; fled to the Saar in March 1933 after being maltreated; emigrated to France in 1935 and to Switzerland in 1942; chief municipal director in Dortmund, 1946–1954.
16 Regional diet, a representative state parliament operating during the Weimar Republic. The Landtag system was abolished under the Nazi regime.

Landrat, retired
Date and place of birth: 29 October 1886 in Eichlinghofen, Kreis Hörde
Last place of residence: Dortmund-Hörde, 13 Rathausstraße
Nationality: Prussian
Whereabouts: Luxembourg
Heckert, Friedrich,[17] formerly Reichstag delegate (KPD), party secretary
Date and place of birth: 28 March 1884 in Chemnitz
Last place of residence: Berlin, 24 Münzstraße
Nationality: Saxony
Current whereabouts: Moscow (Soviet Russia)
Hölz, Max,[18] technician
Date and place of birth: 14 October 1889 in Moritz near Riesa Sa[xony]
Nationality: Prussian
Has been living in Russia for years
Kerr, Alfred,[19] writer
Date and place of birth: 25 December 1867 in Breslau
Last place of residence: Berlin-Grunewald, 10 Douglasstraße
Nationality: Prussian
Current whereabouts: Zurich (Switzerland)
Mann, Heinrich[20]
Date and place of birth: ?
Last place of residence: Munich, 48 Leopoldstraße
Nationality: ?
Current whereabouts: ?
Münzenberg, Wilhelm,[21] writer, formerly Reichstag delegate (KPD)
Date and place of birth: 14 August 1889 in Erfurt
Last place of residence: Berlin, 9a In den Zelten
Nationality: ?
Current whereabouts: Paris, Saar, Prague, Basel

17 Dr Friedrich Heckert (1884–1936), mason and politician; joined the SPD in 1902 and the USPD in 1917; from 1920 leading member of the Communist Party of Germany (KPD); Saxon minister of economics, 1923; KPD representative to the Comintern in Moscow, 1932–1934.
18 Max Hölz (1889–1933), farm worker; joined the KPD in 1919; leader of insurgent labourer groups in the Vogtland region, 1920–1921; sentenced to life in prison in 1921 and released in 1928; emigrated in 1929 to the Soviet Union, where he died after an accident under suspicious circumstances; author of works including *Vom 'weißen Kreuz' zur Roten Fahne* (1927).
19 Alfred Kerr, correctly Kempner (1867–1948), theatre critic and writer; emigrated to France in 1933; author of various works, primarily travel accounts, poems, and essays.
20 Heinrich Mann (1871–1950), writer; emigrated to France in Feb. 1933 and from there to the USA in 1940. On Mann, see also Doc. 219, Dec. 1935.
21 Wilhelm (Willi) Münzenberg (1889–1940), politician and publicist; initially worked as unskilled labourer; established the Young Communist International, 1919; founded the Workers' International Relief in 1921 and the Anti-Imperialist League in 1927; edited, among other publications, the *Arbeiter-Illustrierte Zeitung*; from 1924 member of the KPD leadership; emigrated to Paris in 1933; expelled from the KPD in 1939; died in Oct. 1940 in unexplained circumstances.

Neumann, Heinz Werner,[22] editor
Date and place of birth: 6 July 1902 in Berlin
Last place of residence: Berlin-Charlottenburg, 4 Cauerstraße
Nationality: Prussian
Scheidemann,[23] Philipp, formerly head of the Reich government and mayor (retd) formerly Reichstag delegate
Date and place of birth: 26 July 1865, Kassel
Last place of residence: Berlin-Charlottenburg, 16 Sybelstraße
Nationality: Prussian
Current whereabouts: Carlsbad (Czechoslovakia)
Stampfer, Friedrich,[24] writer, formerly Reichstag delegate (SPD)
Date and place of birth: 8 September 1874 in Brno
Last place of residence: Berlin-Tempelhof, 18c Hohenzollernkorso
Nationality: ?
Current whereabouts: Prague (Czechoslovakia)
Toller, Ernst,[25] writer
Date and place of birth: 1 December 1893 in Samoczyn (Poznań)
Last place of residence: Berlin, 33a Wittelsbacherstraße
Nationality: Prussian
Current whereabouts: Switzerland
Wels, Otto[26]
Date and place of birth: 15 September 1873 in Berlin
Last place of residence: Berlin-Friedrichshagen, 23 Rahnsdorferstraße
Nationality: ?
Current whereabouts: Prague (Czechoslovakia)

[22] Heinz Werner Neumann (1902–1937), politician and publicist; from 1919 KPD member and from 1922 editor of *Die Rote Fahne*; in 1923, after organizing workers' uprisings, engaged in illegal activity; later fled to the Soviet Union, and returned in 1928; became editor-in-chief of *Die Rote Fahne* and the leading theoretician of the KPD; emigrated in 1933 to Switzerland and in 1935 to the Soviet Union, where he was arrested in 1937, sentenced to death, and shot.

[23] Philipp Scheidemann (1865–1939), politician; member of the Social Democratic Party of Germany (SPD); member of the Reichstag from 1903; proclaimed Germany a republic on 9. Nov. 1918; served as the first Chancellor of the Weimar Republic but resigned in June 1919 in protest against the terms of the Treaty of Versailles. Emigrated from Germany in 1933.

[24] Friedrich Stampfer (1874–1957), writer; editor-in-chief of the SPD organ *Vorwärts*, 1916–1933, and of *Neuer Vorwärts* in exile, 1933–1935; member of the SPD executive in exile, 1933–1940; emigrated to Prague in 1933, to Paris in 1938, and to the USA in 1940; returned to Germany in 1948.

[25] Ernst Toller (1893–1939), politician and writer; pacifist; USPD member; in 1919 sentenced to five years of fortress detention for participation in the Bavarian Council Republic; in 1933 emigrated to the USA, where he committed suicide; author of works including *Masse Mensch* (1921) and *Hoppla, wir leben* (1927).

[26] Otto Wels (1873–1939), paperhanger; from 1913 member of the SPD executive and from 1919 one of the SPD chairmen; opposed the Enabling Act in the Reichstag, 1933; emigrated to Prague in 1933 and to Paris in 1938; member of the SPD executive in exile, 1933–1939.

DOC. 71

Advertisement from mid August 1933 for the programme of the newly established Culture League of German Jews[1]

We call on you! Join the Culture League of German Jews (officially authorized organization for the cultivation of intellectual life within Judaism)	
What do we want? To give work, existence, a sense of purpose, and composure to hundreds of dismissed people condemned to resignation! To manifest the religious and ethnic solidarity of the Jews! From the commitment to Judaism in adversity, to build a proud consciousness for better times! To see and experience works of art! Hear and understand music! Harden the spirit on the spirit of the greats! To aspire to be a perceptive, modest part of the greater whole, committed with feelings and action to the community as an individual! This is how we understand the spirit of the *Culture League*. We all want and we all must join forces, to do so. *One* League – *one* Community – *one* Desire – *one* Religion	*The theatre* *will foster drama and opera* Overall artistic management: Dr *Kurt Singer* formerly director of the City Opera House, Berlin So far, the schedule includes: *Drama*

| Dramaturgical management:
Julius Bab
(deputy director of drama)

Director:
Oberregierungsrat Dr *Karl Loewenberg*
(formerly Theatre Frankfurt am Main)
Kurt Baumann

Guest productions:
Victor Barnowsky et al.
Lessing: Nathan the Wise
Shakespeare: As You Like It | Emil Bernhard: God's Hunt (premiere)

Molière: The Misanthrope

Beer-Hofmann: Jacob's Dream

Opera
Senior musical management: general musical director *Josef Rosenstock* (Mannheim) (deputy opera director)

Director: Dr Kurt Singer |

1 Advertisement in *Der Schild: Zeitschrift des Reichsbundes jüdischer Frontsoldaten e. V.*, 15 August 1933; in Clemens Berg (i.e. Max Kronenberg), 'Aus Deutschland vor und nach Hitler' [From Germany before and after Hitler] (26 March 1940), appendix, Harvard Competition, no. 123. This document has been translated from German. The Culture League of German Jews (Kulturbund Deutscher Juden) was founded in June 1933 in Berlin and officially authorized in July 1933. The Culture League (later the Jüdischer Kulturbund e.V./Jewish Culture League), led by Dr Kurt Singer, was intended to create work for Jewish artists. Following its example, culture leagues were later established in different localities, such as Bavaria: see Doc. 84, 10 Oct. 1933.

Honorary presidency:
Leo Baeck – Martin Buber – Ismar Elbogen – Arthur Eloesser – Georg Hermann – Leonid Kreutzer – Max Liebermann – Max Osborn – Franz Oppenheimer – Jacob Wassermann

League Chairman: Dr Kurt Singer, Director

Guest productions of prominent directors are envisaged
Mozart: The Marriage of Figaro
Beethoven: Fidelio
Donizetti: Don Pasquale
Mehul: Joseph in Egypt
Verdi: Rigoletto
Tchaikovsky: Golden Shoes (premiere)

Stage design and costumes:
Heinz Condell (previously stage designer in Hanover)
As guests: Prof. E. Stern and Walter Auerbach

Concerts

Floor managers:
Prof. Leonid Kreutzer
Dr *Herm.* Schildberger
Dr *Kurt Singer*

Conductors:
Michael Taube
General musical director
Josef Rosenstock et al.
Symphonic works and concerts of:
Handel, Haydn, Beethoven, Mozart, Schubert, Mendelssohn, Brahms, Mahler

Chamber music and chamber choir concerts

Composition evenings of present-day Jewish musicians with the assistance of renowned instrumental and singing soloists

(Please cut out and send!)
To the
Culture League of German Jews
Berlin-Charlottenburg 4, 56 Mommsenstr.
I herewith declare my admission to the *Culture League of German Jews* for the league year 1933/34 for the monthly membership fee of RM 2.50 (one-off subscription fee of RM 0.50). In return, the member has the right to attend three league events each month, namely one theatre production (drama or opera), one concert, and one presentation without further payment. Admittance to the events is *reserved for members*

Presentations:
Department of History: director Dr Leo Baeck
Presenters: Rabbi Dr Leo Baeck – Prof. Dr David Baumgart – Rabbi Dr Joachim Prinz – Prof. Dr Erwin Strauss.
Department of Literature and Theatre: director Julius Bab
Presenters: Julius Bab – Arthur Eloesser – Kurt Walter Goldschmidt – Lutz Weltmann
Recital evening: Ludwig Hardt – Edith Herrnstadt-Oettingen
Department of Art Studies: Dr Anneliese Landau – Dr Alfred Einstein
Department of Art History: Dr Max Osborn – Hedwig Fechheimer – Prof. E. Spiro

Name:	Interest group with the Jewish Adult
Address:	Education College
Telephone:	Further details and information material
(Please write clearly)	can be obtained from the
	League Bureau, Berlin-Charlottenburg 4,
	56 Mommsenstraße, J 1 Bismarck 471

DOC. 72

On 23 August 1933 Johannes Schräpel informs the Reich Minister of the Interior about the *Gleichschaltung* of the Association of Budgerigar Enthusiasts[1]

Letter from Johannes Schräpel,[2] head of the Association of Budgerigar Enthusiasts in the Hanover district of Linden, 3 Höpfnerstraße, to the Reich Ministry of the Interior, dated 23 August 1933 (original), with an undated statute attached (carbon copy)

As head of the VSH, the Association of Budgerigar Enthusiasts, registered in Hanover, I hereby inform you that the association began the process of Gleichschaltung on 29 June of this year in accordance with the wishes of the national government. The board consists 100 per cent of National Socialists.[3] The board members, who cannot obtain NSDAP membership because of the ban placed on admittance,[4] have made a declaration that they stand behind the national government and will apply for membership as soon as this is possible again.

The leadership concept is firmly anchored in our statutes. The board members are no longer elected but rather appointed by the leader, as are the local branch heads and staff members. We will unrelentingly remove from our ranks anyone who should attempt to act against the leadership and against the National Socialist idea. I am appending a copy of our statutes. As an employee of National Socialist daily newspapers, I further venture to enclose for you the offprint of an article signed with my name, which also demonstrates my strictly National Socialist way of thinking.[5]

An identical letter has been sent to the Prussian Minister of Culture, the Reich commissioner for sport, and the district leadership and Gauleitung of the NSDAP.

1 BArch, R 1501/125708, fols. 543 and 546. This document has been translated from German.
2 Johannes Schräpel (1899–1982), bookseller and writer; joined the NSDAP in 1937; member of the SA; author of works including *Ewigkeitssucher* (1919) and *Kommt die volkstümliche Biologie?* (1937).
3 According to an official club bulletin, the previous chairman, Gustav Hallgarten, had announced at the meeting his resignation for health reasons. In addition, the name 'Budgerigar Breeders' Association' (Verein der Wellensittichzüchter) was changed to 'Association of Budgerigar Enthusiasts' (Verband der Sittichliebhaber): see account in the newspaper clipping dated 8 July 1933, p. 129, BArch, R 1501/125708, fol. 545.
4 On 1 May 1933, the leadership of the NSDAP instituted a temporary ban on admittance to the Nazi Party in order to manage the influx of membership applications following the Reichstag elections in March 1933. See also Doc. 209, 1 Nov. 1935.
5 The article is not reproduced here.

Heil Hitler!
Jo. Schräpel,
head of the VSH.
[...]⁶

Statute

of the VSH: Association of Budgerigar Enthusiasts, registered in Hanover

§ 1. Name, registered office, purpose.

The association is known as the VSH: Association of Budgerigar Enthusiasts, and its office is registered in Hanover. The purpose of the association is to purchase articles needed for breeding, to purchase birds, to provide information internally and to the public, to establish mutual contacts, and to promote the parakeet as the most lovable caged bird.

§ 2. Joining and resigning from the association.

Individuals and clubs can become members. A member can resign from the association only at the end of a six-month period, after giving six weeks' notice. Foreigners can also join the VSH.

Non-Aryans cannot obtain membership in the VSH and also may not attend the gatherings of the members.

§ 3. Acquisition of membership.

Application for admittance must be made in writing and addressed to the vice chairman and executive secretary. Membership is acquired when a majority of the board has voted in favour of admittance. The board is not required to state the reasons for any rejection. The new member must be notified in writing and provided with a copy of the statute.

§ 4. Termination of membership.

Membership is terminated by voluntary resignation with notice, in accordance with § 2, or by expulsion. The latter must ensue if a member acts contrary to the interests of the association, fails to obey the decisions of the board, does not conform to the provisions of the statute, or is guilty of dishonourable conduct. It can ensue if a member fails to pay his dues for more than three months, brings lasting strife into the life of the association, or disregards the association's interests in any way. The decision on expulsion is made by the board.

No defamation is associated with expulsion; rather, it may take place solely for reasons of expediency.

§ 5. Business year.

The business year of the association begins on 1 January and ends on 31 December.
[...]⁷

---

6 Here the file contains two undated newspaper articles by Johannes Schräpel: in one, he welcomes the new National Socialist media landscape, while in the other he reports on changes within the Association of Budgerigar Enthusiasts; see fn. 3.

7 The carbon copy of the undated statute ends with § 5. In the file it is included as a supplement to a second copy of the statute dated 29 June 1933, which contains fourteen paragraphs, though the Aryan Paragraph is not among them: BArch, R 1501/125708, fols. 547–549.

DOC. 73
Special session of the board of directors of the Jewish Community of Berlin on 24 August 1933 to ensure kosher food in spite of the ban on shechitah[1]

Minutes, signed by Heinrich Stahl and Dr Breslauer,[2] of the meeting on 24 August 1933 held in the offices of the Prussian Regional Association of Jewish Communities, Berlin[3]

Subject to the subsequent approval of the Repr[esentatives'] Ass[embly], it is resolved that a sum of up to RM 5,000 should be made available for testing a shechitah device that conforms equally to the legal regulations and the ritual ones,[4] plus the costs of a trip to be made by Rabbi Dr Weinberg and the costs of obtaining expert opinions from professors.

The commission, consisting of the four rabbis present and Rabbi Dr *Hoffmann*,[5] Frankfurt am Main, in consultation with Mr *Schoyer*,[6] is to be authorized to control these funds.

Starting on 1 November 1933, kashrut[7] measures in the homes for the elderly and in hospitals are to be organized by dividing them among the institutions or by creating special facilities in the hospitals, in such a way that facilities that comply with the strictest ritual standards are available to all those for whom this is of great importance, along with facilities catering for those who place a greater importance on a more abundant supply of meat.[8] This decision is not to be implemented if the aforementioned commission of the five rabbis should be in a position to state, by the time specified, that there henceforth exists a shechitah procedure that complies with the legal regulations and may be used at least for the elderly and the sick in accordance with the commission's understanding of the ritual regulations.

---

1 Archives of the Leo Baeck Institute, New York, at the Jüdisches Museum Berlin, MF 587. This document has been translated from German.
2 Dr Walter Breslauer (1890–1981), lawyer; practised law in Berlin, 1919–1931; administrative director of the Jewish Community of Berlin, 1931–1936; he emigrated via Switzerland to Britain in 1936.
3 Present were (a) Stahl (chairman), Graetz, Dr Sandler for Dr Kollenscher, and also from the board Schoyer (at the start of the meeting), Rosenthal; (b) Dr Breslauer; and (c) as guests, rabbis Dr Freimann, Dr Jacobovits, Dr Unna, Mannheim, Dr Weinberg, Berlin; Dr Moses was absent, excused: ibid.
4 On 21 April 1933 the Law on the Slaughter of Animals and the Regulation on the Slaughter of Animals were made public, prohibiting the shechitah method of slaughtering warm-blooded animals according to Jewish law: *Reichsgesetzblatt*, 1933, I, pp. 203 and 212. The ritual requirement of shechitah in Judaism involves the slaughtering of animals by a specially trained shochet without stunning the animals first.
5 Jakob Hoffmann, later Jacob Hoffman (1881–1956), rabbi; initially worked in Austria, Moravia, and Bukovina, then from 1922 in Frankfurt am Main; member of the Prussian Regional Association of Jewish Communities; arrested by the Gestapo in 1937 and, as a Hungarian citizen, expelled from Germany. He emigrated to the USA in 1938 and to Israel in 1955.
6 Adolf Schoyer (1872–1961), businessman; co-owner of the Schoyer metal trading company in Berlin; Orthodox representative on the board of the Jewish Community of Berlin, later its deputy chairman, 1931–1938; emigrated to Britain in 1938; returned to Germany in 1945.
7 Religious dietary laws for Jews.
8 Since the ban on shechitah, there had been a shortage of kosher meat in Germany, which could be offset only to a limited extent with imports.

DOC. 74
On 25 August 1933 the Hamburg Mayor Vincent Krogmann notes a request by Jewish organizations for negotiations with the NSDAP[1]

Diary of Carl Vincent Krogmann[2] from 1933 (undated and unsigned copy)[3]

25 August 1933.

Mr Helfferich,[4] who asked me to sign a clemency appeal. –

Quite interestingly he told me that Mr Warburg[5] had approached him and informed him that he was speaking on behalf of all the Jewish associations and communities. He then asked whether there was a possibility of reaching some sort of agreement with the National Socialist German Workers' Party. He fully realized, he said, that the Jews can no longer work either in the administration or in leading positions in the large firms, but one ought to allow them some rights nonetheless. The hardship in Jewish circles is quite extraordinarily great, he said. In England, he added, large sums are indeed being collected, but if things continue in this way, the Jews here in Germany will all starve to death. England is attempting to settle Jews in Palestine again on a large scale, but that could never take place in anything but a limited manner. Mr Helfferich opined that one ought to try nonetheless at some point to bring about a face-to-face discussion with leading National Socialists. He believes that the Jews are now willing to make all kinds of compromises.

DOC. 75
On 6 September 1933 the Protestant Church of the Old Prussian Union introduces the Aryan Paragraph[1]

Church law on the legal status of the clergy and Church officials, 6 September 1933

The General Synod of the Protestant Church of the Old Prussian Union[2] has adopted the following Church law:

§ 1

1. Only someone who possesses the required prior training for his career path and who unreservedly supports the national state and the German Protestant Church

---

1 Staatsarchiv Hamburg, 622-1 Krogmann I, C 15/I 7. This document has been translated from German.
2 Carl Vincent Krogmann (1889–1978), businessman; commercial judge in Hamburg; joined the NSDAP in 1933; elected as mayor of Hamburg on 8 March 1933 on the recommendation of the NSDAP; mayor from Oct. 1933 to 1945; interned from 1945 to 1948; thereafter worked as a timber dealer.
3 The copy contains excerpts from the diary on the 'Jewish question' from 25 March 1933 to 2 Nov. 1933.
4 Emil Helfferich (1878–1972), businessman; worked in the Dutch East Indies, 1899–1927; chairman of the supervisory board of HAPAG-Lloyd in Hamburg from 1933.
5 Presumably Max Moritz Warburg: on another initiative by Warburg, see Doc. 291 from summer 1937.

1 'Kirchengesetz betreffend die Rechtsverhältnisse der Geistlichen und Kirchenbeamten', *Kirchliches Gesetz- und Verordnungsblatt*, vol. 57 (1933), pp. 142–145. This document has been translated from German.
2 Coalition of the eastern and western Protestant State Churches of Prussia with a common tradition of confession of faith.

may be appointed to serve as a clergyman or an official of the general Church administration.

2. Anyone who is of non-Aryan descent or is married to a person of non-Aryan descent may not be appointed to serve as a clergyman or an official of the general Church administration. Clergy or officials of Aryan descent who enter into marriage with a person of non-Aryan descent are to be dismissed.

The definition of a person of non-Aryan descent is based on the provisions of the laws of the Reich.[3]

§ 2

1. The clergyman can, after reaching the age of 65, be retired without any need to supply proof of unfitness for service.

2. The officials of the Church administration retire at the end of the quarter following the month in which they reach the age of 65.

3. The employment of the regional bishop and the leading Church officials is regulated by special law.

§ 3

1. Clergy or officials whose previous activity provides no guarantee that they unreservedly support the national state and the German Protestant Church at all times can be compulsory retired.

2. Clergy or officials of non-Aryan descent or who are married to a person of non-Aryan descent are to be retired.

3. Application of (2) can be disregarded if special service has been rendered to the development of the Church in the German spirit.

4. The provisions of (2) do not apply to clergy and officials who have been clergymen or officials of the Church, the Reich, a region of the Reich, or another public body since 1 August 1914, or who served at the front during the World War on behalf of the German Reich or its allies, or whose fathers or sons were killed during the World War.

§ 4

1. Every official must, if official needs so require, accept transfer to another post of the same or an equivalent career path, including to a post of lower rank or lower scheduled salary, with remuneration of the standard moving expenses. In the event of transfer to a post of lower rank or lower scheduled salary, the official retains his previous official title and the salary of the previous position.

2. The official can, within one month, request to be retired in lieu of transfer to a post of lower rank or lower scheduled salary.

§ 5

The transfer of clergy in the line of duty is regulated by special law.

§ 6

The clergyman who is acting in a spiritual supervisory capacity can be released from the duty of supervision if official needs so require.

---

3 This refers to the Aryan Paragraph of the Law for the Restoration of the Professional Civil Service: see Doc. 32, 11 April 1933.

§ 7

For the purpose of simplifying administration, officials can be retired even if they remain fit to serve. When officials are retired for this reason, their positions may not be filled again.

§ 8

1. Decisions regarding retirement, dismissal from office, and measures under §§ 3, 4, 6, 7 are made by the Church senate; these decisions are final and cannot be appealed.

2. Decisions in accordance with §§ 3 and 4 must be served by 30 June 1934 at the latest.

§ 9

The officials who are retired receive a pension in accordance with the rules applying to them.

§ 10

The provisions of §§ 1, 2(1), 3, 4, 7, 8(2), and 9 are correspondingly applicable to the officials of the Church communities, the other Church associations, and the educational establishments of the Church.

§ 11

The provisions of §§ 1 and 3 apply correspondingly to the members of the Church bodies as well as the holders of honorary Church offices.

§ 12

Should undue hardship result from the implementation of this law, higher remuneration or temporary allowances can be granted in the framework of the general provisions. The decision on this is made by the Church senate.

§ 13

The Church senate issues the regulations necessary for implementation of this law.

§ 14

The law takes effect upon promulgation.

Berlin, 6 September 1933.

The aforementioned law is promulgated herewith.

(Seal) The Church senate.

Dr Werner.[4]

---

[4] Dr Friedrich Werner (1897–1955), lawyer; joined the NSDAP in 1930; in 1933 specialist in church law in the Reich Directorate of German Christians, president of the Protestant High Consistory of Berlin, and president of the Old Prussian General Synod; co-founder in 1939 of the Institute for the Study and Elimination of the Jewish Influence on German Church Life in Eisenach; after 1945 lawyer in Düsseldorf.

DOC. 76
On 12 September 1933 Martin Bormann calls on the Gauleiter to stop local anti-Jewish measures[1]

Circular letter from the Deputy of the Führer/Chief of Staff, signed M. Bormann, Munich, to all NSDAP Gauleitungen, dated 12 September 1933 (copy)

The Deputy of the Führer has been informed that special measures against the Jews have been taken within the realms of various Gaue. In some Gaue, Jews have thus been generally forbidden to use public baths and in some cases denied access to localities, markets, etc. In addition, other arbitrary measures have been taken.

What was achieved thus far in the defensive action against Jewish encroachment is more than could be hoped for in view of the overall situation. Additional measures against Jewry beyond those taken thus far must at all costs be avoided for foreign policy reasons, and the measures listed in paragraph 1 are to be phased out wherever possible for the same reasons.

Furthermore, future announcements of measures against Jewry may only be issued with the express permission of the Reichsleitung.[2]

I ask that you take heed of the preceding without fail.
Heil!

DOC. 77
Juristische Wochenschrift, 16 September 1933: article on legal possibilities for the annulment of mixed marriages[1]

[Probationary Judge Wöhrmann, Münder am Deister]
The dissolution of marriages between Jews and Aryans.

As a result of the national revolution and the legislation of Hitler's cabinet, the race problem has been brought directly to the public. Aryan men with Jewish wives [and] Aryan women with Jewish husbands recognize the grave error they made in their marriage and are now seeking dissolution of the marriage. The question whether the established law affords the possibility of annulling such racially mixed marriages is to be answered in the affirmative.

---

1 BArch, NS 6/215, fol. 7. Published in Hans Mommsen and Susanne Willems (eds.), *Herrschaftsalltag im Dritten Reich: Studien und Texte* (Düsseldorf: Schwann, 1988), doc. 2, p. 429. This document has been translated from German.

2 On 13 Oct. 1933 Bormann, by order of Hitler, declared it impermissible to forbid civil servants to shop in 'department stores or in Jewish shops': BArch, NS 6/215, fol. 24.

1 'Die Auflösung der Ehe zwischen Juden und Ariern', *Juristische Wochenschrift*, no. 37, 16 Sept. 1933, p. 2041. This document has been translated from German. The *Juristische Wochenschrift* was launched in 1872 as the organ of the German Bar Association in Leipzig. From 1933 to 1939 it was the journal of the German Bar Association in the League of National Socialist German Lawyers (BNSDJ), during which time it was edited by Reich justice commissioner, state minister, and head of the BNSDJ Hans Frank. Since 1947 it has been known as the *Neue Juristische Wochenschrift*, and is published in association with the German Bar Association and the Federal Chamber of Lawyers in Munich and Frankfurt am Main.

Nowadays there can no longer be any doubt that our new national state has an interest in the annulment of such marriages. Reference may be made here to a few passages from Alfred Rosenberg's *Myth of the Twentieth Century*.[2] He says on p. 545 (1st printing, Part 3, IV, 3): 'Marriages between Germans and Jews must be forbidden, sexual intercourse between Germans and Jews must be punished, according to the gravity of the case, by confiscation of property, expulsion, jail, and death' p. 558 (Part 3, IV, 5): 'If a German woman voluntarily miscegenates with Negroes or Jews, then she is in no case entitled to legal protection, not even for her illegitimate and legitimate children who, in turn, shall not be entitled to the rights of German citizenship.'[3] What these words imply today is immediately clear to anyone who knows the paramount scientific importance of Rosenberg in National Socialism. Moreover, on 13 March 1930 the National Socialist parliamentary group in the Reichstag introduced the draft of a Law for the Protection of the German Nation (see Reichstag IV 1928, Printed Paper no. 1741; see also *Nationalsozialistische Monatshefte* 7, vol. 1, 1930, p. 310). In this draft law it is stated in § 5: 'Whoever contributes or threatens to contribute to the racial degradation and disintegration of the German people by mingling with members of the Jewish blood community will be sentenced to penal servitude for race defilement.' In the explanatory remarks pertaining to this draft law, the idea was expressed that defensive action against further mingling of Germans with members of the Jewish blood community must be pursued with all possible means in order to save our people from extinction.[4]

The established law alone affords the possibility of dissolving such marriages.

Admittedly, divorce on the grounds that one spouse is a Jew will not be possible, as divorce under § 1568 of the Civil Code requires fault, and this fault must have been committed during the marriage. The fact that one spouse is a Jew, however, never constitutes a fault. For the Jews are placed under the law of aliens in Germany not for reasons of morality but rather for reasons of racial hygiene.

On the other hand, the marriage can be challenged on the basis of § 1333 of the Civil Code. Whether the marriage is to be annulled because that person is a Jew depends on the personal attributes of the other spouse. These attributes are also such that would have prevented the Aryan spouse from entering into marriage, given knowledge of the situation with a sensible appraisal of the nature of the marriage. To be sure, it will be objected that the Aryan spouse did indeed know before the marriage that the other spouse was a Jew. This argument is not decisive, because until quite recently the general view among the people was that the Jew differs from the Aryan only in his religion, and only a very few Volksgenossen understood the interrelatedness of the race question and had knowledge of the significance of so-called race defilement. Only now, through the new government, through the new laws for the restoration of the professional civil service, through the laws on revoking the admission of Jews to the legal profession and the accreditation of Jews by health insurance companies, through the recent awareness of the militant agitation by Jews against emergent Germany, has every German become aware of the necessity of his own

---

2 Alfred Rosenberg, *Der Mythus des 20. Jahrhunderts. Eine Wertung der seelisch-geistigen Gestaltungskämpfe unserer Zeit* [The Myth of the Twentieth Century: an Evaluation of the Spiritual-Intellectual Confrontations of our Age] (1930). On the debate surrounding the book, see Doc. 182, 28 July 1935.
3 These are abridged versions of the passages in question. The page numbers cited are from the first German edition, published in 1930.
4 See § 15 on the prohibition of mixed marriages in the draft law of 6 April 1933, Doc. 27.

racial purity. If the Aryan spouse had recognized the significance of being Jewish, if he had known that in the Third Reich the children produced by him with the Jewish spouse would be subject to the law of aliens and would not enjoy the full rights of citizenship, then he would never have entered into the marriage.

The German spouse must be able to correct this error, of which he has only now become aware, for his own sake and that of his children, but also for the sake of the German people and its racial advancement.

DOC. 78
From the debate of the Congress of European Nationalities on 18 September 1933 on the persecution of Jews in Germany[1]

Third session.
18 September, afternoon.
President Dr Wilfan[2]

[...][3]

In accordance with my announcement this morning, it is now time for me to initiate the discussion about *'National dissimilation and the rights of nationalities'*. To do so, I would like to recall the remarks made in the opening speech on Saturday.[4] It is precisely the subject being addressed here and the difficulties that have arisen in its treatment that prove how wise it was that the congress leadership, since the beginning, since 1925,[5] with the approval of the congresses, has adhered to the principle that one should not get into

---

1 *Europäischer Nationalitäten-Kongress: Sitzungsbericht des Kongresses der organisierten Nationalen Gruppen in den Staaten Europas, Bern, 16. bis 19. September 1933* (Vienna/Leipzig: Braumüller, 1934), pp. 61–69. This document has been translated from German.
2 Dr Josip Wilfan (1878–1955), lawyer; from 1925 president of the Congress of European Nationalities; employee of the Institute for International Questions at the Ministry of Foreign Affairs in Belgrade, 1945–1947; representative of the Slovenian-Croatian minority in the Italian parliament.
3 Participating in the congress were representatives of the Bulgarian minorities from Yugoslavia and Romania; the German minorities from Estonia, Poland, Czechoslovakia, Hungary, and Romania; the Galician and Catalan minorities from Spain; the Yugoslavian minorities from Italy and Austria; the Lithuanian minority from Poland; the Ukrainian minorities from Czechoslovakia, Yugoslavia, and Romania; the Hungarian minorities from Czechoslovakia, Yugoslavia, and Poland; the Russian minorities from Estonia, Latvia, and Poland; the Belarusian minority from Poland; and the Czechoslovak minority from Poland. The representatives of the Jewish groups stayed away in protest: ibid., pp. v–vii.
4 In his opening speech Wilfan had described the persecution of Jews in Germany with terms such as dissimilation and 'national exclusivism'. At the same time, he emphasized that he himself favoured the 'clear division between lineages', meaning the rights and autonomy of national minorities, but could recognize no right to declare a people inferior. At the congress, he said, there could nonetheless be no specific discussion of the problem, for it was not current events but rather matters of enduring significance that were important: ibid., p. 10.
5 The Congress of European Nationalities was founded in 1925, largely on the initiative of the Baltic German Ewald Ammende, as a lobby organization for national minorities in Europe. The objective of the organization was to secure the protection and international acknowledgement of the minorities as natural or legal persons. From 1925 to 1938 annual conferences took place, bringing together the representatives of national minorities from every country in Europe. After 1933 the congress lost significance, because the withdrawal of the Jewish representatives and the stance of the representatives of the German expatriates meant that the deliberations were obstructed.

questions so specific that there is cause for sensitivity, for dissent or polarization, for irritation, and for conflict. We ourselves fail to correctly perceive the nature of our problem if we do not realise that it has a bearing on the deeply held convictions of broad circles, including in particular those of the nationalities we represent. We must realize this special nature of the problem and then draw the logical conclusion from it. With regret, I have just heard again today, from our midst, reproaches alleging that our discussion is too academic. Just imagine – and you already have practical evidence of it now – what the consequences will be if one attempts, in our discussions, to shift the difficult national problems, which essentially are on the psychological level, to the level of political reality. The result will be antagonism and conflict. It is an abstention that we must impose on ourselves, but one that will benefit the whole and be advantageous to the cause. Indeed, one day we too will vanish from the scene. Our work is intended not only for the present but also for the future. Anyone who is working for the future, for the long term, can quite easily do so academically as well and, in the process, can operate with concepts, solely with abstract concepts. For precisely therein lies the essence, which will retain its validity in future also.

In the matter of dissimilation, the following situation has come about: our Jewish colleagues – for whom I would like to testify right at the outset that they have always been at the forefront of our congress community both in terms of work and in manifesting the spirit of true solidarity – did not deem it possible that, when dealing with this issue, the position of the groups involved was not made concrete, that is, did not centre around the concrete situation. They further demanded that the congress itself not only speak out, in a resolution, on the essence of the question that has been opened by the events in Germany, but also venture to render judgement on the events themselves.[6] The congress leadership was unable to comply with the demand to the desired extent. Despite protracted negotiations, in which much goodwill was exhibited by both sides, no agreement was possible, and today we find ourselves in the position of having to note that our Jewish colleagues have stayed away from the congress this year.

They have explained their decision to withdraw in a letter addressed to me, which the authors would like me to read to the congress. Here I must explain from the outset that I will not read the entire letter aloud. It is self-evident that this letter will come to the attention of the broadest public by other means, especially through the press. But I do not regard it as compatible with our practice thus far that the president or any organ of the congress should contribute from this venue to the circulation of certain passages of this letter. The remaining contents, the crucial part in any event, I will venture to bring to the attention of the congress.

The letter is signed by Mr Leo Motzkin,[7] Dr H. Rosmarin, Dr Emil Margulies,[8] and Mr Farchi and it bears yesterday's date, but did not come into my possession until this morning. I will read aloud the following paragraphs:

---

6 Leo Motzkin, as representative of the Jewish minorities, had already written to President Wilfan before the opening of the congress, on 9 Sept. 1933, and made the appearance of the Jewish groups contingent on a debate concerning the persecution of the Jews in Germany and on the public decrial of the persecution: letter, ibid., p. 2.

7 Leo Motzkin (1867–1933), sociologist and politician; Zionist; participant in the First Zionist Congress in Basel in 1897; representative of the Jewish group and until 1933 one of the vice presidents of the Congress of Nationalities; executive member of the Comité des Délégations Juives.

Dear Mr President,

We have the honour of conveying the following statement to you by the authority of and in the name of all the Jewish groups that are members of the Congress of European Nationalities. As a result of the statement that was made in the opening session, without opposition, in the name of the German minority communities, a situation was created that not only places in question but also plainly negates the prerequisites for cooperation by the nationalities combined at this congress in joint work towards common goals.[9]

Before I continue reading, I would like to emphasize that this letter refers primarily to the statement read aloud in the Saturday session by Delegate Roth[10] in the name of the German groups.[11] I wish to establish at once that according to messages that have reached me, which are to be verified over the further course of the meeting by the responsible party, this statement has given rise to ambiguous interpretation. Its true meaning, however, was perhaps indeed delineated by me – if I may be so bold – in the statement I addressed it with, immediately after it was read out. I explicitly emphasized that this statement is not meant as a comment on the entire array of questions opened up by the events to which it relates. The statement, I said, fell short of satisfying those who plainly demand a full explanation. But from the standpoint of the congress, I have recognized the affirmative elements of this statement, in particular the avowal of the principles and ideals proclaimed by our congresses, with the participation of the German groups, for eight years. This profession of your principles is absolutely necessary, and perhaps even sufficient, for our work together. I repeat, this explanation is yet to be clarified and completed by the German side. The essential part of this explanation, with which I concurred, was at any rate the profession of our principles. To the extent that our Jewish colleagues may not have fully appreciated this positive aspect of the German statement, I might say that their letter springs from an erroneous or flawed assumption. But I also want to emphasize now that I understand the standpoint of our Jewish colleagues and am convinced that their emotional outlook, which resonates in this letter, is fully appreciated by the congress as well.

I will now skip over a few lines that plainly contravene our conference principle:

> In the German Reich, as a result of the state authority's intervention and the legislation, the problem of relations between the national majority and the citizens of other origin has taken on a configuration that is without precedent in the civilized world.

---

8 Dr Emil Margulies (1877–1943), lawyer; Jewish delegate from Czechoslovakia to the Congress of Nationalities; executive member of the Comité des Délégations Juives.

9 For the same reasons as in 1933, the Jewish groups also boycotted the meeting in subsequent years.

10 Dr Hans Otto Roth (1890–1953), politician and national church curator of the Protestant National Church of the Augsburg Confession in Romania.

11 As the representative of the Saxons of Transylvania, Roth had stated that the German minorities he represented rejected any assimilation: 'The exclusion of persons who are different, in particular racially different, from a popular culture, as could be observed in recent times, is something we regard in principle as justified': ibid., p. 26.

And I continue reading:

> The congress, in common accord, has denounced the assimilation of a national minority by state-sponsored or state-tolerated means of violence and inveiglement. We have never endorsed assimilation either, but we have regarded the efforts of a people to assimilate with another people, and the latter's reaction to and rejection of assimilation efforts, as matters that play out between one people and another and are settled between them. It seemed self-evident to us that minority representatives who for years have offered moral arguments to defend the rights of national minorities would condemn the encroachments of state authority in the rejection of assimilation, just as in the practice of assimilation.

Again, overly specific criticism follows:

> ... The actions of the German government, however, by no means constitute a rejection of the assimilation of one people to another, but rather are a deprivation of the Jews' rights in law and administration, a casting out of the Jews from emancipation and a defamation of them based on their origin, the defamation of their people – by the superior power of the state. It means not only a reduction or denial of minority rights but also a denial of human rights for persons of Jewish origin and thus a breach, indeed a systematic one, of the principles upon which the protection of the national minorities, including the German minorities, rests. A dangerous precedent, which, if allowed to go unchallenged, if accepted especially by the national minorities without passionate opposition and challenge, threatens the entire system of protection of minorities in Europe with collapse in the grip of a might-makes-right authority restrained by no legal principles.

And now follow these sentences, which I again recite verbatim:

> On the basis of many years of working together, we had hoped to find here this recognition of unavoidable solidarity in the defence of the rights of every minority, both the recognition and the expression of this recognition.
> Concerning the disenfranchisement, robbery, violation, and defamation of the German Jews, the statement from the German national groups submits only a word of approval of the 'dissimilation' of one people by the other. The statement explicitly endorses dissimilation in the way it has occurred in Germany: that is, the ousting of Jewish civil servants, the expulsion of Jews from the liberal professions, the taking away of livelihoods built up over long years of work, the denial of access to educational institutions, the public goading and defamation, in schools and among the youth as well, and the systematic boycotts based on hatred and envy and aiming at utter destruction.

And further:

> The statement that was submitted here in the name of the German ethnic groups is an affirmation ... of all these measures ... before the entire world. This affirmation is not mitigated but rather strengthened by the simultaneous avowal of the other principles of the congress of minorities, likewise by the addendum that the German groups consider it justifiable if the groups of persons thus disenfranchised, meaning

the Jews in this case, are 'anxious' to claim for themselves as well the rights defended by this congress, since the addendum acts rather to emphasize the right to forcible dissimilation, while

– here the aforementioned erroneous, overly narrow interpretation of the German statement especially manifests itself –

the Jews themselves are allowed only the aspiration to this right.
This statement makes it impossible for us to work together on the floor of the congress with those who profess these principles. We are therefore unable to take part in the deliberation of this congress.
We follow with sympathy the efforts of those who defend the ideals and principles of the congress, and we will have to make our subsequent resolutions dependent on the extent to which our friends, with whom we have worked so long in fellowship, succeed in restoring to the congress its original foundation, accord, and purpose.

As appears from this letter, the Jewish colleagues have not deemed it possible, given the German statement, to come here and participate in the further sessions of the congress. For those groups that are not directly involved, there now arises the question of what they have to say on the subject in this state of affairs. I personally see myself forced temporarily to divest myself of the office of the non-partisan chairman serving only his technical function and also to place myself in the role of those who now must take a stand on the problem.

We cannot go as far as our Jewish colleagues. We rely on the representatives of the German people in our midst, who despite the inevitable change of individuals still have been more often than not our companions for eight years now, have worked with us for eight years on hammering out a new law, on shaping a new mentality. But we wish to express openly what must be expressed at this time.

Peoples is the form in which we see the masses of humanity, particularly those that populate our continents, as entities which clearly stand out and differ from one another, survive generation after generation on the same soil, develop certain characteristic peculiarities of their own accord, from their collective life, and are brought together into a unit through the feeling and awareness of shared identity and a specific quality. We know that these peculiarities, the characteristic features of a people, can make themselves known in the most diverse areas and that, if we want to envision the image of a certain people, we need not always seek its specific quality only in the area of language or culture in the strictest sense. A people can be recognizable as a specific entity in the community of nations even if it appears to have merged, in the area of language, with another people to form one entity.

On the other hand, if we view Europe in our mind's eye and imagine the population types in purely physical terms, we even find distinct physical differences among the peoples. To use the fashionable term: racial differences. At the same time, however, we believe that the focus, the innermost core of a people, lies in its mental life, its feelings, its consciousness, its way of thinking. But how a people's concrete idea of itself must be shaped is something that surely no laws can prescribe. The question must be addressed to the very people concerned, and outsiders have no alternative but to go by a people's self-understanding and self-perception. If a people – in conceptual terms, I see this as the characteristic feature of recent development – acquires a sharper, narrower perception of itself, of its own nature, according to which not all those previously considered to belong to this people are still counted among it (I refer to natural membership, which has purely statistical relevance, not to legal membership, which is based on the status of citizenship), then nothing must be done to oppose this. It is a tragedy if individuals suddenly hear the majority of the people telling them: 'We no longer count you among us, we no longer acknowledge you as belonging to us.' Yet, in this non-acceptance, in this refusal on the part of certain individuals or groups to affiliate with a specific people or a distinct national character there is something that actually comes close to what our congresses have been representing for eight years now as one of our highest postulates. For what is the consequence of the narrowing, the closer specification, of the idea a people conceives of its own character, and the resulting exclusion of elements that were previously considered part of the people in question? The consequence is the negation of the preceding process, which had led to the previous expansion of the concept of the people concerned; the attempt to trim back the development: essentially to nothing other than the rejection of an assimilation that had taken place. Now what is it that our congresses have been fighting for, perhaps first and foremost, for eight years, if not precisely the rejection of assimilation? We refuse to become assimilated, we protest against the national majorities' misuse of the power given to them in their states to discolour, alter, and distort the national character of the so-called national minorities, the population segments of other nations that live in the same state with them, and to adapt this national character to that of the majority, the constitutive people. To this extent, therefore, there is, as I have said – I hesitate, because the expression really does not seem correct to me – something in the concept of dissimilation that comes close to our endeavours.

Now, as a congress, or at least as the totality of all the national groups participating in it that are not directly involved in this specific case, let us consider the fundamental problem and, while looking away from the present, as it were, and imagining the problem as one possible only in future, ask ourselves: if something similar ever happens somewhere at some point, how should one face that challenge as a matter of principle? We must be clear not about the change in concept, which is inherently a purely abstract one, or the change in a certain people's perception of its characteristic features, but rather about the practical consequences resulting from such a change and the methods permissible for implementing these consequences, the appropriate course of action. Here, to answer this question – and I believe we are probably all united in this and you all agree with me, some of you explicitly, others silently, and perhaps with a reserve that we incidentally wish to recognize and respect – here, the following is now to be said. First, that one ought not to speak of dissimilation or even expulsion. That sounds harsh, gives rise to misunderstandings, falls short of the mark. Second, however, that such separation, such parting of elements that had been joined thus far, should nonetheless be brought about in a way that causes no preventable harm and pain, and that, above all, human dignity and the right of the individual to life and liberty are not violated. These things I hope I may be permitted to say in the name of those groups which are not directly involved in the matter despite its great topicality. Incidentally, I am now developing somewhat further the same ideas that I already hinted at in my opening speech.

We will, I believe, all be able to agree on the wording of a resolution, which will in fact be merely a resolution in principle – my friend Szüllö[12] would say: an academic one. But in our situation, it is the only practicable way. We will all be able to agree on a resolution that expresses our fundamental demand for the eventuality of national dissimilation. With regard to the question about which one could quarrel, as to whether the underlying change is to be welcomed or repudiated, we do not wish to express ourselves. All the more decisively, on the other hand, we wish to state that if it comes to a separation of a people, to a removal of a part that already seemed to have coalesced with the whole of the people, then the principles that have been proclaimed by our congresses, and which we all avow, must remain untouched and unviolated – if I have not already said too much on the subject, I believe at least that I have nothing more to say on it now. The thoughts I have just expressed are ones I venture to present in the form of a draft resolution. I ask that you pass this resolution. It reads as follows: 'In the event of the introduction and implementation of national dissimilation, the freedoms and rights that the Congresses of European Nationalities have advocated in their declarations and decisions from the beginning must remain unimpaired.' In this text I would like to call our attention to the word 'introduction', which at least hints at the fact that our fundamental demand refers to the process in question in its full magnitude.[13]

---

12 Dr Géza von Szüllö (1873–1957), from 1925 delegate in the Czechoslovak parliament, where he represented the Hungarian minority.
13 During the voting on the resolution, Professor Mikhail Kurchinsky (Kurchinskii) (1876–1939), a university professor in Dorpat and a representative of the Russian group in Estonia's parliament, made the following statement on behalf of the Russian groups from Estonia and Poland, the Lithuanian group from Poland, the Catalan group, and all the Hungarian groups: 'The wave of decidedly antisemitic measures now observable in some countries is something we view as at odds with general human rights and the ideals of our Congresses': cited in ibid., p. 70. The resolution proposed in Wilfan's speech passed with small changes, with the Hungarian groups abstaining from the vote: see reproduction of the resolution, ibid., p. 98.

DOC. 79

Junge Kirche: report, dated 20 September 1933, by the Faculty of Theology at the University of Marburg opposing a limitation of the rights of non-Aryan Christians[1]

The Aryan Paragraph in the Church. Expert opinion of the Faculty of Theology at the University of Marburg

Faculty of Theology of the University   Marburg, 20 September 1933

The following petition was submitted to the Faculty of Theology:

The clergy and clerical and secular delegates of the Church Congress of Electoral Hesse from the three Upper Hesse church districts of the Protestant Church in Hesse-Kassel, assembled in Marburg, ask the esteemed Faculties of Theology in Marburg and Erlangen[2] for formal and responsible instruction of German Protestant Christians as to whether the law on the terms of employment for clergy and officials of the Church administration, passed in recent days by the General Synod of the Church of the Old Prussian Union and envisaged for the entire German Protestant Church – containing the Aryan Paragraph[3] – is in keeping with or is contrary to the teaching of Holy Scripture, the gospel of Jesus Christ and the teaching of the Apostles, the character of the sacraments, baptism, and Holy Communion, the ecumenical creeds and the teaching of the Reformation regarding salvation through Jesus Christ, the Church and its ministry, baptism and Holy Communion, as well as the preamble to the constitution of the German Protestant Church.

Marburg, 11 September 1933   signed *Schmidmann*, Deanery Pastor.[4]

After consultation the faculty decided unanimously in its meeting on 19 September to issue the following response and, contemporaneously with its delivery to the signatories of the petition, to make it known to the German Protestant Church governments, the faculties of theology, the members of the German Protestant National Synod, and the Church press.

The Church law on the legal status of the clergy and Church officials, which has been adopted by the General Synod of the Protestant Church of the Old Prussian Union and

---

1 'Der Arierparagraph in der Kirche: Gutachten der Theologischen Fakultät der Universität Marburg', *Junge Kirche*, no. 14, 28 Sept. 1933, pp. 166–171. Also published in Kurt Dietrich Schmidt (ed.), *Die Bekenntnisse und grundsätzlichen Äußerungen zur Kirchenfrage des Jahres 1933* (Göttingen: Vandenhoeck & Ruprecht, 1934), pp. 178–182. This document has been translated from German. *Junge Kirche* was published from 1933 as the newsletter of the Reformed Youth Movement in the Confessing Church, from Oct. as a twice-monthly periodical for Reformation Christianity.
2 In their expert opinion issued on 25 Sept. 1933, the theologians at the University of Erlangen took the approach that the Church should demand that the 'Jewish Christians' relinquish Church offices because the German people now believed the Jews to have an alien national character: published in Schmidt (ed.), *Die Bekenntnisse*, pp. 182–186.
3 See Doc. 75, 6 Sept. 1933.
4 Gottfried Schmidmann (1874–1954), clergyman; 1902–1932 pastor in Kassel and Caldern (Kreis Marburg); 1931–1949 deanery pastor, then superintendent and dean in the church district of Marburg; senior pastor in Marburg, 1932–1949; from 1945 chairman of Christian Emergency Aid.

the regional synods of several other German regional churches, and is likely to be requested for the entire German Protestant Church at the upcoming German Protestant National Synod, contains the following *fundamental provisions* transferred from the new Reich Civil Service Law:

§ 1(1). *Only someone who possesses the required prior training for his career path and who unreservedly supports the national state and the German Protestant Church may be appointed to serve as a clergyman or an official of the general Church administration.*

(2). *Anyone who is of non-Aryan descent or is married to a person of non-Aryan descent may not be appointed to serve as a clergyman or an official of the general Church administration. Clergy or officials of Aryan descent who enter into marriage with a person of non-Aryan descent are to be dismissed. The definition of a person of non-Aryan descent is based on the provisions of the laws of the Reich.*

§ 3(1). *Clergy or officials whose previous activity provides no guarantee that they unreservedly support the national state and the German Protestant Church at all times can be retired.*

(2). *Clergy or officials of non-Aryan descent or who are married to a person of non-Aryan descent are to be retired.*

§ 8(1). *Decisions regarding retirement, dismissal from office ... are made by the regional church government;*[5] *these decisions are final and are not subject to appeal.*

§ 11. *The provisions of §§ 1 and 3 apply correspondingly to the members of the Church bodies as well as the holders of honorary Church offices.*

The exceptional cases envisaged in § 3(3) and (4), in which application of § 3(2) is to be refrained from,[6] can be disregarded here as not relating to the principle, although they reveal an uncertainty of the legislator regarding his own principles and simultaneously indicate the political origin and character that is foreign to the specific quality of the Church.

The faculty considers both of the cited fundamental provisions of §§ 1 and 3 or 11 to be incompatible with the nature of the Christian Church, as it is defined by the solely applicable authority of Holy Scripture and the gospel of Jesus Christ and attested to by the creeds of the Reformation. At the same time, it points out that the concordat concluded by the German Reich with the Holy See regarding the legal status of the Catholic Church in Germany contains nothing that corresponds to these regulations.[7]

The first of the aforementioned provisions (§ 1(1), § 3(1)) threatens the independence of the clergy in their preaching and pastoral care and the officials of the Church in their discharge of official duties, an independence that is linked to God's Word and the believing conscience, and puts them in danger of subordinating their personal responsibility to

---

5 The original law referred to the Church senate, but in this report, the term regional church government is used instead.
6 Footnote in the original: '(3). Use of (2) can be disregarded if special service has been rendered to the development of the Church in the German spirit. (4) The provisions of (2) do *not* apply to clergy and officials who have been clergymen or officials of the Church, the Reich, a region of the Reich, or another public body since 1 August 1914, or who were engaged in the World War on behalf of the German Reich or its allies, or whose fathers or sons were killed in action in the World War.'
7 This is a reference to the Reich Concordat of 20 July 1933.

submission to subjective and temporary, political or ecclesio-political preferences of superior authorities, Church groups or even authorities outside the Church. *The danger is all the greater since the command of the law can be broadened indefinitely and since a legally regulated procedure of taking evidence is precluded for its application (§ 8(1)).* As Christians, it is self-evident that the Protestant clergy and Church officials stand up for the Church and the state of their nation; the obligation to do so is determined in their obedience to God's Word. But it is subject to the proviso inalienably founded in this very obedience, that the mission of the Church is not political and that this mission if need be can also obligate one to take critical positions, appropriately expressed, regarding processes in Church and state life. A law in the Church of the Reformation can only protect the freedom for genuine and unabbreviated accomplishment of its spiritual mission precisely for the sake of resisting the politicization of the spiritual. In cases of seemingly intolerable conflict, resolution is required in a proceeding that is protected from false accusations and arbitrary decisions. Well-known historical experiences warn most emphatically, also in the interest of the state, against any politicization of the Church's message and of Church service.

The second of the aforementioned fundamental provisions (§ 1(2), § 3(2)) makes Church members of non-Aryan origin into Church members with lesser rights and lesser dignity, inasmuch as both they and the Church members of Aryan descent married to them are denied eligibility to hold office in the Christian community as a matter of principle.

That the message of Jesus Christ as the saviour of the world is directed to all peoples and thus to all races as well, and that accordingly all who believe this message and are baptized in it belong to Christ's Church, is indisputable.[8] *The members of the Church are brothers among themselves.* The concept of brother excludes any inequality of rights as well as, in general, any avoidable separation in worldly circumstances. In principle it does not matter whether separation and inequality of rights are implemented in such a way that special Jewish Christian communities are formed or that the Jewish Christians are barred from the offices of the one Christian community. The Christian Church knows no other division than that formed by denominations within Christianity on the one hand and by countries and peoples on the other hand. The latter division applies only in the sense that communities based on language establish themselves for obvious reasons, and communities based on citizenship form for political and legal reasons, though without barring individuals or communities who speak another language or are citizens of another state from Church membership as a matter of principle. According to both the prevailing legislation of the established church and the provisions of international law, the requirement that members of the clergy must be citizens [of that state] in order to hold Church office is also merely a rule of thumb that allows exceptions. Throughout its entire history the Church, like the state and ecclesiastical law of all peoples, has until now not understood the term Jew in the sense of race but exclusively

---

8 Footnote in the original: "'Of a truth I perceive that God is no respecter of persons: but in every nation he that feareth him, and worketh righteousness, is accepted with him.' Acts 10:34–5. "There is neither Jew nor Greek, there is neither bond nor free, there is neither male nor female: for ye are all one in Christ Jesus." Galatians 3:28.'

according to denomination, that is, according to the definition whereby the Jew does not acknowledge Jesus as the Messiah sent by God. The Jew who sees in the law and the prophets of his people the prophecy of Christ, and who converts and is baptized, is for the *Church* no longer a Jew, and limitations on civil rights for the baptized Jew have never been advocated by the *Church*. Even if a *state*, in an appraisal of racial factors that was far from people's minds in earlier times, now finds such restrictions necessary for national political reasons, they can claim no validity in the sphere of the Church as such, for the Church is a community of those who believe in Christ and are baptized in his name, and nothing more; it would cease to be this in the full sense if it allowed any other characteristic of its community to justify distinctions. The Church cannot abandon its oneness as the oneness of the body of Christ, in which all believers are baptized through one Spirit.[9] It knows no grounds for separation other than apostasy and heresy, unless and until it is unable to overcome these with proof of the spirit and the power.

One must not say that this oneness is valid only for the Church invisible, while in the Church visible the barriers that otherwise separate men must be esteemed and preserved. The Church visible must, to the extent of what is possible in this world, create itself in the image of the invisible one, if belief in it is a genuine truth for the Church. 'Spots and wrinkles' may be borne on its body as indissoluble signs of earthly weakness (Eph. 5:27). To deliberately mutilate this body is a sin against the spirit that is given to the Church. To tolerate in the Church any imperfection other than because of weakness – and it will not be claimed that the disenfranchisement of the Christians of Jewish origin in the German Protestant Church is so intended – means to make a virtue of the necessity of the lack of faith and love and negates the gospel of the kingdom of God and the vindication of the sinner through grace in faith.

One must not further argue that race and national character are not to be ignored by the Church but rather respected as orders of creation. Certainly, the fact that the Church fumbled at this point in its entire previous history would be no reason not to follow better information all the more decisively now. Meanwhile, the reference to the order of creation in this context is erroneous. In its preaching and pastoral care the Church may not have always coped with the serious question and task that race and national character indeed pose to it. It may have yielded, frequently more than was proper, to these natural and historical forces, and occasionally also have heeded them less than was required – the fact that it has granted them no special rights in the Church constitution is in accordance with the true order of creation, correctly perceived in faith, which is nothing other than God's sole sovereignty over all whom he has created, and his redemptive judgement on sin, under which all are confined. The Church falls short on the essentials of its message in dealing with race and national character, which it must serve in each case, when it recognizes race and national character as circumstances that substantiate or preclude membership or rights in the community. The fostering of race and national character as articles of creation is possible in the Church only by the Church incorporating them and proclaiming to everyone the calling of his distinctiveness as well as the

---

9 Footnote in the original: "'For by one Spirit are we all baptized into one body, whether we be Jews or Gentiles, whether we be bond or free, and have been all made to drink into one Spirit.' 1 Cor. 12:13.'

encumbrance of his separation. Otherwise, veneration of the created takes the place of veneration of the creator.

The quite isolated *examples of small church communities outside Europe* with racial restriction of church membership, as encountered in Asia, Africa, and America (which, incidentally, have nothing to do with the distinction between Jews and Aryans), are to be evaluated as backward or recidivist formations, in which the Christian gospel and its claim are ruptured. Equally out of place here is a reference to the *Jewish Christian communities in the church of Christian antiquity*. First, they were not racially defined communities but rather Christians who felt a need to combine the belief in Jesus as the Christ with the attitude of Old Testament law. Above all, however, they did not come into being because the Christian communities of the Greco-Roman world excluded the Christian Jews, but because sections of the Christian Jews set themselves apart from the Christian communities. If one recognizes the Apostle Paul as 'the chosen vessel' of the Lord Jesus Christ (Acts 9:15), then it is a violation of his gospel, which is also Luther's gospel, at its core to acknowledge or introduce such separations. Indeed it must also be noted here that Christians of Jewish origin, as at every time and in every people, have been called upon in our fatherland as well to render blessed service to the Christian community until the most recent times. Suffice it to mention the theologian *August Neander*, the composer of hymns *Philipp Spitta*, and the painter *Wilhelm Steinhausen*. In the theological work of Neander, the spiritual songs of Spitta, and the art of Steinhausen, no one will discern an un-German trait. Rather, they all are representatives of the specifically German form of Protestant piety, and prove that the character bestowed upon it and binding it is by no means endangered by the preservation of Christian unity in faith and love.

Anyone who is unwilling to join the apostles and reformers in recognizing complete unity between Jewish and non-Jewish Christians in the Church, as it is most impressively developed in the New Testament by the Epistle to the Ephesians, and to make it an absolute reality in the constitution of the Church, deludes himself when he confesses that he accepts the Scriptures as God's Word and Jesus as God's son and Lord of all. It is indisputable that God makes His word known in the world through Jews, not only in the Old Testament but also in the New, and has chosen His son from among the Jews. The attempts to discern an Aryan in Jesus lack all historical foundation and are ineffective in addition, since his gospel presupposes the law and prophets of the Jews as God's revelation, and in any event his apostles were Jews. To deny soteriological significance to his birth from the tribe of David by referring to his divine sonship means to misunderstand completely the *sensus fidei* of divine sonship. To make the crucifixion of Jesus by the Jewish people a reason for disenfranchising Christians of Jewish origin is Pharisaic aberration. With all that, salvific history, which God allowed to occur, is made by men who are ashamed of it, and the service of the spirits of the time is raised up alongside that of Christ.

The first article of the constitution of the German Protestant Church of 11 July 1933 reads as follows: 'The inviolable foundation of the German Protestant Church is the gospel of Jesus Christ as it is attested for us in Holy Scripture and brought to light again in the Confessions of the Reformation. The full powers that the Church needs for its mission are hereby determined and delimited.' If these sentences are to be taken seriously in theological terms, then a political or ecclesio-political shackling of the Church's preaching is incompatible with them, as is likewise a restriction of the rights of non-Aryan Christians in the Church.[10]

The Faculty of Theology at the University of Marburg. The Dean: D. von Soden.[11]

DOC. 80
The chairman of the German Gymnastics Association writes to Rupert Naumann on 23 September 1933 in response to his concerns about banning all Jews from the Berlin Gymnastics Association[1]

Letter from the chairman of the German Gymnastics Association[2] (N./Schl.), Edmund Neuendorff, Berlin-Charlottenburg, to R. Naumann, Berlin Gymnastics Association, dated 23 September 1933

Concerning the letter of 11 September 1933.[3]
Re: Aryan §.
My dear fellow gymnast Naumann,
I completely understand your distress. I have always been völkisch, I belonged to the Völkisch League[4] before the war. And nonetheless I am a human being. In that respect

---

[10] Martin Niemöller (1892–1984), along with Dietrich Bonhoeffer (1906–1945), who was later executed, composed a 'Statement from Opposition Pastors', in which they termed the Aryan Paragraph in the Church Civil Service Law an injustice: draft, 7 Sept. 1933, in Dietrich Bonhoeffer, *Dietrich Bonhoeffer Werke*, ed. Eberhard Bethge et al., vol. 12: *Berlin 1932–1933*, ed. Carsten Nicolaisen and Ernst-Albert Scharffenorth (Munich: Chr. Kaiser, 1997), p. 123. At the end of Sept. 1933 Bonhoeffer also wrote to the National Synod of the Protestant Church and protested against the demotion of individual community members to the status of second-class Christians. He asked the synod to take a stance against the Aryan Paragraphs introduced by several regional churches following the example of the Old Prussian Union: see draft petition, 24 August 1933, ibid., pp. 135–136.

[11] Baron D. Hans von Soden (1881–1945), Protestant theologian; professor in Breslau in 1918 and in Marburg in 1924; forcibly retired in 1934 under § 6 of the Law for the Restoration of the Professional Civil Service, but reinstated as professor on 27 Oct.; member of the Pastors' Emergency League and the Confessing Church.

[1] BArch, R 34/491. Published in Reinhard Rürup (ed.), *1936: Die Olympischen Spiele und der Nationalsozialismus: Eine Dokumentation* (Berlin: Argon, 1996), p. 38. This document has been translated from German.

[2] In 1933 the German Gymnastics Association had around 1.6 million members, who were organized in 16,000 clubs.

[3] On 11 Sept. 1933 Naumann had asked Neuendorff for advice concerning the 'Aryan question' in his organization. Naumann reported that he had first enforced the Aryan Paragraph based on the Law for the Restoration of the Professional Civil Service at the behest of the German Gymnastics Association and then, by order, a stricter regulation for the Berlin Gymnastics Association. Only very few of the sixty Jewish members resigned voluntarily, he said, and he ordered many to be removed from the membership roster. Regarding the membership of some persons, however, he said there was a question whether one should make concessions based on 'human sentiments': BArch, R 34/491. See also Doc. 61, 1 July 1933.

[4] This is presumably a reference to the German-*Völkisch* League (Deutschvölkischer Bund); it merged with other associations in 1919 to form the German-*Völkisch* Protection and Defiance League (Deutschvölkischer Schutz- und Trutzbund).

I feel exactly as you do, and I am not at all ashamed of reading with painful regret the list of men whose names you recited for me.

Hans Kantorowicz:[5] I have not seen him for years, but I always held him in high esteem as a lively, decent, and fine fellow. I have never heard that his grandfather was a Jew.

Alfred Flatow:[6] old, world-class gymnast, I have known him for years and have followed the progress of his fortunes in life.

Ladewig:[7] he has actually never completely denied his Jewishness, but he has undoubtedly rendered services to the DT.[8]

Paul Strassmann:[9] I know him and am aware of his love for the DT.

I do not know *Kurt Liebenthal,*[10] *Kurt Simon,* or *Sally Ephraim,*[11] but I can imagine that on the basis of what you write it may be hard enough for you to take responsibility for their expulsion from the DT. And yet it must happen! Nothing can be done about it. Three things bring me to advise you urgently to act very resolutely and firmly and consistently here.

First, concern for the other Jews who had to be expelled comes into consideration. After all, we cannot differentiate between first, second, and third classes of Jews. Basically, that cannot be right, least of all for those who are themselves affected.

Second, however, and this is the main point, the German idea applies to us. Germany has suffered so infinitely much from the Jews in the last decades. German culture, German public life, German morals have been so greatly disfigured by the Jews, German politics so dreadfully mistreated by them, that we must quite firmly draw a line under the past there, by all means. What we have experienced must never happen again. And if that is what we want, we must not start with half measures, we must continue quite clearly and firmly on our way. It is my innermost conviction, infinitely difficult though it may be in the individual case, because I thoroughly understand that even a Jew can be a fine person. But he must disappear from our national public life, and the DT is a piece of this national life and should become even more so in the future.

---

5 Correctly: Hans Kantorowitz. See Doc. 61, 1 July 1933.
6 Alfred Flatow (1869–1942), athlete and gymnastics teacher; from 1887 member of the Berlin Gymnastics Association; Olympic gold medallist in 1896 in individual and team gymnastics; in 1900 deputy senior gymnastics warden of the Berlin Gymnastics Association; emigrated to the Netherlands in 1938; deported in Oct. 1942 to Theresienstadt concentration camp, where he died in Dec. 1942; author of works including *Der Weitsprung* (1909).
7 Hans Carl Ladewig (b. 1886), practised law in Berlin; head of the youth committee of the Berlin Gymnastics Association for many years; barred from practising law in 1937 and emigrated to Italy in 1938.
8 Deutsche Turnerschaft: German Gymnastics Association.
9 Correctly: Dr Paul Ferdinand Straßmann (1866–1938), physician; owner and director of the Straßmann Women's Hospital in Berlin, 1900–1933; prominent member of the Berlin Gymnastics Association for decades and a promoter of women's sport in particular; from 1918 professor in Berlin; in 1936 his licence to teach was revoked; he emigrated to Switzerland, where he committed suicide in 1938.
10 Probably: Dr Kurt Liebenthal (b. 1894), lawyer; deported to Auschwitz in late June 1943 and last recorded there in Sept. 1943 in the prisoner infirmary at the Buna-Monowitz camp.
11 Sally Ephraim (b. 1880), lived in Berlin from 1907; youth leader in the Berlin Gymnastics Association; deported to Auschwitz in mid-Feb. 1943.

Finally, however, there is a *third additional factor*: in the negotiations with the *German Gymnastics Association* we have expressed clearly and unambiguously that we want to remove all Jews from the DT. If we fail to do so in Berlin, the clamour will resume at once and then we will harm the entire DT and its völkisch reputation for the sake of these few Jews.

To sum up: however painful it may be to you, my advice is to abide by the regulations and expel even the former members whom you have named.[12]

Keep well and Heil Hitler!

DOC. 81

On 25 September 1933 the Reich Ministry of Economics criticizes the banning of Jewish dealers from trade fairs and markets[1]

Circular decree from the Reich Ministry of Economics (HG 13 046/33), p.p. signed Wienbeck,[2] to the governments of the states, for Prussia: to the Minister of Economics and Labour, for Lübeck: to Department II Finance and Economics, dated 25 September 1933 (copy)

Re: market trading.

I. Numerous petitions that have reached me from the most diverse parts of the territory of the Reich indicate that non-Aryan dealers are increasingly being banned from trade fairs and annual and weekly markets through measures taken by the local police or market police authorities. In this connection, it can often be established that a distinction is made between foreign non-Aryans and non-Aryans who hold Reich nationality, probably owing to the commitments that result from trade agreements, and that the exclusion measures are limited to non-Aryans who hold Reich nationality. I regard such measures as objectively undesirable and legally questionable. I venture to point out that under §§ 64 and 65 of the Reich Commercial Code, attendance at trade fairs and annual and weekly markets, as well as buying and selling at these events, is open to all Reich nationals and foreigners with equal authorization. As a result, discrimination between Aryan and non-Aryan or not purely Aryan firms or traders is not compatible with the principle still prevailing: freedom of market access and trade.

II. Further, it is to be pointed out that trade fairs and markets that existed for many decades have been cancelled, in many cases without compelling grounds. Since for a considerable number of traders the loss of a market can mean serious harm, in especially

---

12 In response to this letter, on 18 Oct. 1933 Naumann called for the resignation of the remaining Jewish members; Paul Straßmann and Hans Kantorowitz were among those who protested. Since Kantorowitz did not withdraw, Naumann had his name struck off the membership list on 10 Nov. 1933. On 14 Nov., Naumann reported to Neuendorff that the Berlin Gymnastics Association no longer had any non-Aryan members: BArch, R 34/491.

1 BArch, R 3101/13862, fol. 275r–v. This document has been translated from German.
2 Dr Erich Wienbeck (1876–1949), economist; legal advisor for the Hanover Chamber of Crafts, 1903–1933; member of the German National People's Party (DNVP); in 1933 worked as the ministerial director in the Prussian Ministry of Economics and Labour and as Reich commissioner for medium-sized businesses; worked in the Reich and Prussian Ministry of Economics from 1935 to 1938.

grave cases even the loss of livelihood, it seems to me imperative, in the interests of economic reconstruction, to limit the cancellation of trade fairs and markets to instances in which it is unavoidable for compelling reasons (such as the event being dropped or falling on the same date as other events). With reference to part II of my circular letter of 1 September 1933 – HG 12 083/33³ – and my circular letter of 8 September 1933 – HG 11 093/33⁴ – I therefore respectfully request that you undertake to ensure that these points of view are borne in mind by the subsidiary bodies.⁵

DOC. 82
On 5 October 1933 the billboard-advertising company Städte-Reklame GmbH asks the Trustee of Labour in Hesse for an opinion on putting up advertising for Jewish firms¹

Letter from Städte-Reklame GmbH, Frankfurt am Main (Dr B/S.), senior management, to the Trustee of Labour for the economic region of Hesse, Lüer,² Frankfurt am Main, dated 5 October 1933 (copy)³

Our billboard-advertising company, with its subsidiaries, operates in approximately 260 German cities. In all these places, without exception, we have the sole right of utilization, so that any enterprise that wants to put up posters can do so only by using our firm. Accordingly, if we exclude an enterprise from placarding, it is unable to advertise by displaying posters on public streets and squares. Until now, therefore, in keeping with legal norms, we have assumed a certain responsibility to contract with our clients, that is, we have felt obligated to execute every proposal, except in cases of clients that were notoriously slow to pay or posters that were in violation of the law or of good morals.

Now the question has been raised whether, under the altered economic and political circumstances, our firm is entitled to turn down assignments from companies that,

---

3 This was the circular decree issued by the Reich Ministry of Economics prohibiting the boycott of craft enterprises: *Ministerialblatt der Preußischen Verwaltung*, 1933, pp. 1115–1118; Joseph Walk (ed.), *Das Sonderrecht für die Juden im NS-Staat: Eine Sammlung der gesetzlichen Maßnahmen – Inhalt und Bedeutung* (Heidelberg/Karlsruhe: Müller Juristischer, 1981), p. 50.
4 On 8 Sept. 1933 the Reich Ministry of Economics had forwarded to the regional governments a letter responding to an enquiry from the Association of Chambers of Industry and Commerce from 27 July 1933. In it, the Reich Ministry of Economics made it plain that 'discrimination between Aryan and non-Aryan firms for the purpose of boycott must have negative economic consequences': Reich Ministry of Economics circular decree of 8 Sept. 1933, BArch, R 3101/13863, fol. 6. Published in Kurt Pätzold (ed.), *Verfolgung, Vertreibung, Vernichtung: Dokumente des faschistischen Antisemitismus 1933–1942* (Leipzig: Reclam, 1983), p. 58.
5 See the circular decree of the Prussian Minister of Economics and Labour of 13 Oct. 1933 with a copy of the Reich Ministry of Economic decree: BLHA, Rep. 60/641, fol. 13.

1 LAB, Rep. 142/7, 4-1-5/22. This document has been translated from German.
2 Dr Carl Lüer (1897–1969), businessman and economist; joined the NSDAP in 1927; city councillor in Frankfurt am Main, 1929–1933; Trustee of Labour in Hesse, 1933–1934; president of the Rhine-Main Chamber of Industry and Commerce, 1933–1942; board member of Dresdner Bank, 1938–1941; chairman of the board of Adam Opel AG, 1941–1943; interned after 1945; later worked in the private sector.
3 The letter printed here was forwarded to the German Council of Municipalities in Berlin (received on 7 Oct. 1933) with a request for a statement: ibid.

owing to their structure or the character of their owners, are not consistent with present-day political and economic policy views. Falling into this category are:

(1) Jewish firms,
(2) department stores,
(3) cooperative societies,
(4) foreign companies (such as Bata).[4]

We have discussed this question, considering its fundamental significance, in our supervisory board, 80 per cent of which consists of leading National Socialists.[5] While some of the supervisory board members take the view that our company must, by refusing such jobs, contribute to the support of the economic policy of the NSDAP, others are of the opinion that a sudden elimination of these companies from billboard advertising means a serious disruption of economic development, and that commissions from such firms should be carried out at tariff rates in the same volume as before.

It was further decided to submit the matter to the Trustees of Labour and the German Council of Municipalities, since from the standpoint of the provision of employment the Trustees of Labour must have a special interest in this question, which is of significance not only for our firm but for all advertising companies. We are submitting the matter also because we have learned from notices in newspapers that the Trustees of Labour have recently lifted so-called advertising bans in several cases.

Regarding the foreign companies listed under (4), we take the liberty of noting that an advertisement of a foreign footwear retailer such as Bata is to be regarded at first glance as harmful to small- and medium-sized business interests. It must not be forgotten, however, that the exclusion of such a firm from the German advertising market could possibly provoke reactions by foreign countries. For this reason, this question too requires calm assessment of the arguments for and against it.

We would be grateful to you if you would inform us as soon as possible of your opinion on this set of questions, or if you could bring about a decision on the part of the proper authorities. We have had quite a large number of copies of this letter made, as we assume that you will address this question to the other Trustees of Labour as well or perhaps relevant government and Party bodies.

We request that you arrange for the requisite number of copies to be picked up at our office.

With German regards!

---

4 Czech shoe concern with branches in various countries.
5 The senior management of Städte-Reklame GmbH had already stated in late March 1933 that it had no longer employed 'any Jews for many years': letter from Städte-Reklame GmbH to the City of Frankfurt am Main, 29 March 1933, ISG Frankfurt, Magistratsakten/5039, fol. 219.

DOC. 83

On 9 October 1933 the dismissed civil servant Johanna Rosenthal asks the Berlin Main Post Office Headquarters to grant her a pension on compassionate grounds[1]

Letter, unsigned [Johanna Rosenthal],[2] Berlin, to the Berlin Main Post Office Headquarters, dated 9 October 1933 (draft)[3]

On 22 September 1933 I received news of my compulsory retirement informing me that … (add exact wording)[4] no pension is due to me. The prohibition of my further employment as a civil servant because of my non-Aryan origin is a heavy blow to me. I am not aware of having contravened my official duties in any way. I always endeavoured to perform the functions assigned to me to the best of my ability and to keep myself fully fit for my duties. The fact that in fourteen years I have taken so few days off due to illness demonstrates how rarely I neglected my duties. I have always avoided political ambitions. In addition, I was not a member of any political party.

The degree to which the members of my family felt they were Germans may be seen from the following information:

My father served in Prussia from 1875 to 1878. Two of my brothers were conscripted for military service in 1914. One fought on the Western Front and was wounded twice. Both brothers are now unemployed. As much as the ban on further employment has shaken me, it is in fact the realization that I am disqualified from being granted a pension that plunges me into profound despair. My 81-year-old father and I are facing ruin as a result.

Therefore, I venture to submit to the Main Post Office Headquarters my request for the granting of a pension on compassionate grounds.[5]

---

1 DHM, 20 024 583. This document has been translated from German.
2 Johanna Rosenthal (1900–1944), civil servant; post office employee, 1920–1933, and later permanent civil servant; deported to Theresienstadt in June 1943 and from there to Auschwitz in Oct. 1944.
3 The 9 is added by hand. As the reply from the Main Post Office Headquarters indicates, the letter was actually posted on this day: DHM, 20 024 586.
4 Note by Rosenthal for the later final version.
5 On 15 Dec. 1933 the Berlin Main Post Office Headquarters granted Johanna Rosenthal a temporary allowance in the amount of 821.89 Reichsmarks annually for three years, with the addendum: 'The pension has been awarded to you only to ease the transition to other circumstances. You cannot anticipate permanent support. You are therefore strongly advised to make a serious effort to obtain alternative employment': ibid.

DOC. 84

On 10 October 1933 conductor Erich Erck applies to the Bavarian State Minister for Education and Culture for the authorization of a Jewish Culture League[1]

Letter from Erich Erck,[2] Munich 13, 12 Blütenstraße, to the State Minister for Education and Culture[3] (received on 26 October 1933), Munich, dated 10 October 1933[4]

Re: application for authorization of a 'Jewish Culture League in Bavaria' as a priority initiative of the Winter Relief social welfare programme.

With three enclosures.[5]

As a result of the implementation of the guidelines that were applied in all possible areas of public life in accordance with the directives of the Law for the Restoration of the Professional Civil Service, it is practically impossible for a large number of Jewish artists and academics to continue practising their professions.

In the vast majority of cases, these are persons for whom integration into other professions is out of the question in the long term in view of the present economic situation, or altogether impossible on account of their advanced age. The distress in these Jewish circles is extraordinarily great; almost without exception, those concerned are already a burden on the public welfare system.

Therefore, at the urging of influential Jewish circles in the Reich capital, the Prussian Ministry of Science, Art, and Education, considering the existing state of emergency, issued a decree of 13 July 1933 authorizing the establishment of a 'Culture League of German Jews' in Berlin. This league has already been brought into being and is operating very successfully. It arranges theatre performances, concerts, and lectures with Jewish artists or university teachers exclusively for Jewish audiences, and in this way it gives those in need the possibility of obtaining gainful employment in their professional field.

In Munich and Bavaria too, great distress prevails among Jewish artists and academics, whereby it appears that here in particular those affected are particularly reliant on public welfare.

The Israelite Religious Community of Munich has therefore awarded a contract to me, as a Jewish artist and former front-line officer, by virtue of my knowledge of the practical and social circumstances in this area, instructing me to devise a plan which, in analogous application of the example given by the Berlin 'Culture League of German Jews', yields an opportunity to provide work and a livelihood to the Jewish artists and academics in Munich and Bavaria in the sense of the generous Winter Relief initiative introduced by the Reich government.

---

1 BayHStA, MK 15 382. This document has been translated from German.
2 Erich Eisner (1897–1956), also known by his stage name of Erich Erck, musician; director at various theatres, 1923–1933; in 1933 founded the Jewish Culture League in Bavaria; in Nov. 1938 was imprisoned in Dachau concentration camp; in 1939 emigrated first to Britain, then to Bolivia, where he taught music teachers in Sucre until being commissioned to establish a state symphony orchestra in La Paz in 1944.
3 From 1933 to 1935 the state minister was Hans Schemm (1891–1935).
4 The original contains several handwritten annotations and underlining.
5 The enclosures are not reproduced here.

In the enclosure, I submit a draft version of 'Guidelines for a Jewish Culture League in Bavaria'.⁶ The plan closely follows the model of the arrangement established in Berlin, but exhibits a few necessary differences corresponding to the prevailing circumstances here. A far more modest framework is envisaged for the undertaking planned in Munich and Bavaria. Mainly, only lectures and concerts can be given consideration here; stage performances are nonetheless under consideration in a few isolated cases. It was also necessary here to abstain from creating a subscription scheme, since in the current onerous economic situation in Jewish circles, which are also far smaller here, only a few individuals would be in a position to join such an organization permanently, and consequently it could not provide the necessary financial basis for the undertaking. The draft thus involves ticket sales to Jewish booking agencies for the Jewish public, as has always been customary for Jewish events until now. There are no plans for advertisements in the daily press or public posters. The list attached to the draft, showing the events and project groups planned for the time being, clearly sets out the intended operation of the 'Jewish Culture League in Bavaria'.

To bring about the authorization of the entire plan, I submitted a corresponding application to the Theatre Department of the Munich Police Headquarters on 18 September 1933, in the expectation that it would be forwarded from there to the Bavarian Ministry of State for Education and Culture. However, it was passed on to the Political Police that same day, and to the best of my knowledge it has not been forwarded by this office.

As the enclosures to the present letter make clear, the nature of the planned undertaking is not only completely apolitical but instead exclusively cultural and social. In contrast to the Berlin undertaking, no association is contemplated for Munich and Bavaria, just a working committee. In addition, the fact that in Berlin the Prussian Ministry of Science, Art, and Education addressed the matter and granted permission indicates that political aspects can be entirely ruled out. As a result, the responsibility of the Bavarian Ministry of State for Education and Culture for the present application ought to be assumed in every respect.

In view of the pressing state of emergency explained above and the necessity of quick remedial action, I therefore address to the State Minister, pursuant to my assigned task, the respectful request that authorization be granted for the creation of the 'Jewish Culture League in Bavaria', with acceptance of the enclosed draft and the schedule of activities, as set forth there in detail.⁷

With the greatest esteem

---

6 The guidelines stated: 'The purpose of the League is, first, to provide work and material assistance to needy Jewish artists and members of the intellectual professions, and second, to promote Jewish community life.' Sections for 'lectures and project groups', 'music and theatre', and 'visual arts' were to be created, and events for exclusively Jewish audiences were to be organized. The necessary funds were supposed to be supplied by the Israelite Religious Community of Munich and private donors: undated draft version of the guidelines, BayHStA, MK 15 382.

7 The Bavarian Ministry of State for Education and Culture approved the application on 16 Jan. 1934: see letter of the Jewish Culture League in Bavaria to the Munich Police Headquarters dated 6 Feb. 1934, BayHStA, MK 15 382.

DOC. 85

On 19 October 1933 the Reich Association of Christian German Citizens of Non-Aryan or Not Pure Aryan Descent writes to the government to offer its support[1]

Letter from the Reich Association of Christian German Citizens of Non-Aryan or Not Pure Aryan Descent,[2] vice chairman, signed Günther Alexander-Katz,[3] to State Secretary Pfundtner[4] (Reich Ministry of the Interior), dated 19 October 1933 (copy)[5]

Dear State Secretary,

With reference to the visit of members of our working committee, Mr Max Lenz and Mr Fred-Egon Schlenger, with Oberregierungsräten Win[...]en and von Brose[6] from the office of the vice chancellor[7] and to the conversation Mr von Brose had with you, we take the liberty of presenting to you the following.

The Reich Association of Christian German Citizens of Non-Aryan or Not Pure Aryan Descent, which was recently entered in the Register of Associations following the approval of the chief of police, represents the affiliation of non-Aryans and persons not of pure Aryan descent who are Christians and have always been nationally minded. At the same time, our cause involves not only our present members but also, above all, the hundreds of thousands of Christian non-Aryans and their families. All these are Volksgenossen who, in some cases for generations, have felt themselves to be only Germans

---

1 BArch, R 43 II/602, fol. 17. This document has been translated from German.
2 The association (Reichsverband christlich-deutscher Staatsbürger nichtarischer oder nicht rein arischer Abstammung) was founded in Berlin on 20 July 1933 and was known from autumn 1934 as the Reich Association of Non-Aryan Christians (Reichsverband der nichtarischen Christen e. V.). The chairmanship was held first by Gustav Friedrich and then, from 1934, by Richard Wolff. The association, with local branches in several large cities, looked after the Christians who were stigmatized as non-Aryans and helped to place them in jobs. In response to pressure from the authorities, the association was renamed as the St Paul's Covenant, Association of Non-Aryan Christians (Paulus-Bund, Vereinigung nichtarischer Christen) in 1936. From March 1937, on official instructions, only *Mischlinge* were allowed to be members, and the name was changed again, to the 1937 Association (Vereinigung 1937).
3 Dr Günther Alexander-Katz (b. 1891), lawyer; practised law and worked as a notary in Berlin; in 1933 temporarily banned from representing clients; from April 1933 again authorized to represent clients in legal proceedings; lived in a mixed marriage; after 1945 in Rhineland-Palatinate.
4 Johannes (Hans) Pfundtner (1881–1945), lawyer; after the First World War, worked first in the Reich Ministry of Economics; lawyer and notary, 1925–1933; joined the NSDAP in 1932; state secretary in the Reich Ministry of the Interior, 1933–1943; retired in 1943; committed suicide in 1945; editor of the journals *Das neue deutsche Reichsrecht* and *Die Verwaltungsakademie*.
5 Parts of the original have been underlined by hand.
6 Correctly: Herbert von Bose (1893–1934), career officer; began his career in the military; from 1924 head of the German Overseas Service; from 1929 head of the press office of the government of Prussia; in 1933 assistant to Vice Chancellor Franz von Papen; murdered on 30 June 1934 during the operation against the alleged coup by Ernst Röhm.
7 Franz von Papen (1879–1969), career officer; military career, 1891–1919; stationed in Turkey in the First World War; member of the Catholic Centre Party, 1920–1932; member of the German National People's Party (DNVP), 1932–1933; joined the NSDAP in 1939; in 1932 appointed Reich chancellor then Reich commissioner for Prussia; vice chancellor, 1933–1934; ambassador to Vienna, 1934–1938, and Ankara, 1939–1944; in 1946 acquitted at the trial of the major war criminals in Nuremberg; classified as a 'major offender' during denazification proceedings in 1947 and sentenced to eight years in a labour camp; granted amnesty in 1949.

and acted as such. They would gladly, with their whole selves, support the cause of national Germany today as well, at any time, once they are convinced that they are not being excluded by the government in the pooling of all national forces. To free these Christian German non-Aryans in the coming Reichstag election from the conflict of conscience into which they were driven as a result of the gravest emotional and economic distress, we would like to learn how we should rationalize this support for the national government, support that appears self-evident to us, the Reich leadership of the Association.

We venture most respectfully to request the conversation with you that was announced to us by the office of the vice chancellor. We can be reached by telephone on the number B 4 7422.

It would be most valuable to us if, during this conversation, we could learn the official stance of the government with regard to this problem, so that we are in a position to reply in accordance with the government's wishes to the numerous pressing enquiries from our circle of members and friends.[8]

With German regards!

DOC. 86
On 24 October 1933 the Reich leader of the German Medical Association urges the Association of Statutory Health Insurance Physicians to use lists of non-Aryan doctors discreetly[1]

Circular letter from the Reich leader of the German Medical Association, Wagner, Munich, to the plenipotentiaries and heads of the regional and provincial offices of the Association of Statutory Health Insurance Physicians of Germany, dated 24 October 1933[2]

Strictly confidential!

In my circular letter of 2 September 1933 (A 94 of the Hartmann League),[3] I instructed, for disclosure to the private health insurance companies, that only a list of those non-Aryan doctors be compiled to whom the exemption clauses do not apply, that is, only the non-Aryan doctors who are barred from working in practices operated by health insurance companies or are not approvable for licence.

---

8 On 21 Oct. 1933 Max Lenz spoke by telephone with Ministerialrat Franz Medicus (1890–1967) of the Reich Ministry of the Interior. He asked for advice from Hitler or Frick as to whether the association should pledge its support to the national government before the election or not. It was, he said, a matter of hundreds of thousands of votes that could be lost: Lenz to Medicus on 21 Oct. 1933, BArch, R 43 II/602, fol. 18. The Reich Chancellery replied with the non-binding advice that all those eligible to vote should support the Reich government on 12 Nov. 1933. Promises could not be made to the voters, it was said: letter from the state secretary (Reich Chancellery) to Max Lenz, 2 Nov. 1933, BArch, R 43 II/602, fol. 19.

1 BArch, R 1501/26401, fol. 250r–v. This document has been translated from German.
2 In the circular letter Gerhard Wagner responded to complaints about which the Reich Ministry of the Interior had informed him: see letter from the Reich Directorate of the National Socialist Physicians' League to the Reich Ministry of the Interior, dated 6 Oct. 1933, ibid., fol. 384.
3 Association of Physicians in Germany. See also Doc. 68, 11 August 1933, fn. 5.

As a consequence of my directives regarding the regulation of cooperative work by stand-ins, referral, and consultation (*Deutsches Ärzteblatt* 1933, page 131 and page 218),[4] lists of Aryan and non-Aryan doctors have understandably been compiled in many instances. The preparation of these lists will be unavoidable as long as I keep my regulation in effect. *These* lists are intended only for internal use by the physicians among themselves, as they refer only to stand-ins, referral, and consultation between one doctor and another. I can retain these directives only if my plenipotentiaries proceed in a liberal and far-sighted manner. For this purpose, I refer to my circular letter of 23 October 1933.[5] I request that you not place on the list of non-Aryans, or more correctly on the list of doctors affected by my order regarding the regulation of cooperative work by doctors in replacement, referral, and consultation, all those for whom exceptions can be appropriate for specific reasons. In my circular letter of 2 September 1933 I have already pointed out that an unmasking of the doctors to whom the exemption clauses of the Civil Service Law apply and who have only one Jewish grandparent is to be avoided in particular.

Should rigorous procedures continue to be followed despite this letter and my letter of 23 October 1933, there is a danger that I will have to countermand my orders for the preparation of lists at the instruction of the Reich government. I anticipate that a judicious handling of my orders will prevent this danger.

DOC. 87

Deutsches Philologen-Blatt, 1 November 1933: article on the introduction of racial studies in schools[1]

[Düsseldorf, R. Rein][2]
Suggestions for teaching racial studies.
From the experiences of a biologist.

To do justice to the spirit of racial research, lessons in racial studies must be spread over several subject areas. In biology, the foundation for the study of race is first laid through genetics, eugenics, and population policy, but as for racial studies proper, basically only the anthropological part is dealt with in terms of genetics, anatomy, and physiology, with the psychological properties of race only briefly hinted at. On the other hand, the subjects of *German, history, geography, music,* and *visual arts* have the important task of

---

4 Directives of the commissioner dated 29 July and 10 August 1933: see also Doc. 68, 11 August 1933.
5 Circular letter from Wagner, dated 23 Oct. 1933; BArch, R 1501/26401, fols. 251–252, and Doc. 68, 11 August 1933.

1 'Vorschläge für den Unterricht in der Rassenkunde', *Deutsches Philologen-Blatt*, vol. 41, no. 44 (1933), 1 Nov. 1933, pp. 502–503. This document has been translated from German. The *Deutsches Philologen-Blatt* was published from 1892 as *Korrespondenz-Blatt für die Philologenvereine Deutschlands* in Gelsenkirchen, from 1900 as *Korrespondenz-Blatt für den akademisch gebildeten Lehrerstand*, and from 1912 to 1935 as *Deutsches Philologen-Blatt* in Leipzig. In 1933 the journal was edited by the teacher Erich Hassel.
2 Dr Richard Rein (1883–1956), teacher; from 1920 head of the State Main Office for the Instruction in Natural Sciences, Düsseldorf branch; joined the NSDAP in 1933; author of works including *Vererbungslehre, Rassenpflege, Urgeschichte* (edition for schools, 1934).

using the facts of their fields to bring to school pupils' awareness the characteristics and differences in the psychological structure of the races.

Biology.
Year ten.
The cell and its parts, significance of the cell nucleus, chromatin and achromatin, behaviour of the chromosomes during cell division. The chromosomes as carriers of characteristics. The essence of fertilization as seen in examples from the plant kingdom and the lower animals. *Laws of heredity.* Laws of uniformity, independent assortment, segregation, dominance. The discovery of the laws of heredity by Gregor Mendel, their rediscovery around 1900. Chromosomes and Mendelian laws, genotype and phenotype. Which characteristics segregate? Significance for plant and animal breeding and for the inheritance of human physical and psychological characteristics. *Eugenics (racial hygiene),* dominant and recessive traits of valuable and inferior characteristics, deformities, diseases. People with grave hereditary defects should not marry! Health certificates, tasks of the civil registry offices, ancestral charts, genealogies, family history, *racial studies.* The concept of race as illustrated by examples from the plant and animal kingdoms. 'Human race as a group of persons who are hereditarily identical in principle.' Dominant and recessive racial attributes. The Nordic, Mediterranean, Eastern, Dinaric, East Baltic, Phalian races as parts of the German people. The alien and inferior racial components within the German people. Jewish question. Physical and psychological peculiarities. Mission of the Nordic race (in connection with German and history). Decrease in the Nordic racial proportion: de-Nordification; countermeasure: Nordification.

Year thirteen.
Repeat, intensify, and expand the year ten curriculum. Phenomena of fertilization in plants, animals, and humans. Behaviour of the chromosomes during meiosis of generative cells. Mathematical formulation of the *laws of heredity.* Monohybrids, dihybrids, polyhybrids. Sex chromosomes, determination of gender, linkage of factors, localization of genetic carriers, crossing over, research methods; backcrossing. Dominant and recessive inheritance as seen in examples and exercises. Heritability or non-heritability of acquired characteristics? Mutations. – *Human genetics.* National degeneration and regeneration. Population policy. Genealogy. Law for the Prevention of Offspring with Hereditary Diseases. Sterilization, castration, racial studies. Concept of race and its relationship to language, ethnicity, nationality, religion. Physical and psychological attributes of the races represented in Germany. Historical causes of de-Nordification. Self-help of the Nordic race and state measures for Nordification. Choice of spouse, law relating to inheritance of farms and forestland, immigration law, settlement efforts, etc. (in connection with history and German).

History.
History will be oriented to racial biology in general in future, in order to bring the values of blood and soil to life in young people. From prehistory through all the subsequent millennia up to the present, the significance of race must be given due consideration, since it 'represents the primeval soil from which grows the entire root character of both the individual and of nations' (see also the statements in the *ZentrBl.,* pp. 197–198).[3]

Geography.
Years five and six.
Representative images from the German homeland, used to illustrate the distribution of the German race in specific examples (for example, Friesland: Nordic man; Alpine landscape: Dinaric man).
Year seven.
The peoples of Europe are to be characterized by the percentages of the six main races in their makeup. For example, southern France: Mediterranean race; Russia: Eastern Balts and Mongols; Scandinavia: the Nordic man.
Years eight and nine.
The leadership of the Nordic race in the history of discovery and colonization; its significance in the present-day civilized world on earth.
Year ten.
Deepening of the fundamental racial concepts introduced at lower levels.
Advanced level.
The human races of the Ice Age and their presumed evolution into the present-day races. Distribution of the races over the earth, particularly of the European races throughout Europe, composition of the present-day peoples based on their racial components, dependence of civilization on the distribution of the races. The Nordic race as a factor of value among Germandom abroad and in colonization.

German.
The literature to be dealt with in school must be re-examined or newly compiled from the standpoint of its value for race and nationhood. In the lower classes, for example, suitable reading passages must be used to convey to the youth the characteristic psychological traits of the German races; further, a sense of family and the study of genealogy must be fostered. Essay topics are to be assigned accordingly. The mentality of the various races is to be demonstrated by reference to the difference between German literature and that produced by other races.

Music.
Fostering of German folk song!
The musical creations of the European peoples in their links to the psychological structure of the European races (German and Norwegian music as expression of the Nordic emotional moods; Russian music as expression of the Nordic-Mongol mix in the soul of the Eastern Balt; Bohemian, Thuringian, Silesian folk songs as musicality of the Eastern race; music [of] Tyrolean folk festivals as product of Dinaric national characteristics; Italian and French music in part attributable to the Mediterranean race; assessment of music by Jewish composers).

Art
In the visual arts, understanding, enthusiasm, and joy in the creations of the Aryan-Nordic race must be deliberately awakened, from the Hellenes via the Renaissance to

---

3 This publication could not be found.

the modern day. The products of art created by other races should be used to illustrate that such art may be singular, but is not congenial to us. Figures in art and styles are to be dealt with correspondingly. In this way, the anticipation of a new artistic Renaissance of Aryan-Nordic man is also awakened (cf. the speech on culture by Adolf Hitler in Nuremberg in the *D. Phil-Blatt*, no. 37).[4]

DOC. 88
Völkischer Beobachter, 15 November 1933: article on the demand of the 'German Christians' that 'Jewish Christians' are excluded from the Protestant Church[1]

Resolution of the 'German Christians'[2]
Berlin, 14 November. The members of the *religious movement 'German Christians'* in the Gau of *Greater Berlin*, assembled in the Berlin Sportpalast on 13 November, have resolved the following:[3]

1. As National Socialist fighters, we are accustomed not to abandon the struggle that comes with the shaping of a great idea in favour of a lazy peace. The ecclesio-political struggle cannot be over for us until the mistrust existing in many places between clergy and communities has been *removed everywhere*, a mistrust that has been created by the open and covert resistance of the pastors, the majority of whom are still hostile towards us or approach us without understanding. A lasting peace can be created here only by *transferring or dismissing all the pastors who are either not willing or not able to play a leading role in the religious renewal of our people and the completion of the German Reformation through the spirit of National Socialism.*

2. We will not allow to be forced upon us any leaders whom we must inwardly reject because we lack proper confidence in both their National Socialism and their German faith. In the ecclesiastical field we can recognize the Führer principle, if at all, only with regard to the external system.

3. We expect our regional church to *implement, immediately and without watering it down,* the Aryan Paragraph, in accordance with the Church law adopted by the General

---

4 The reference is to Hitler's programmatic speech at the Nuremberg rally on 1 Sept. 1933 about the 'renewal of cultural life'. In it, he emphasized the significance of race for the shaping of culture and the value assigned by the National Socialist state to the fostering of culture: see report 'Nürnberg', *Deutsches Philologen-Blatt*, vol. 41, no. 37 (1933), 13 Sept. 1933, pp. 414–416.

1 'Entschließung der "Deutschen Christen"', *Völkischer Beobachter* (northern German edition), 15 Nov. 1933, p. 7. This document has been translated from German.

2 In 1932 Pastor Joachim Hossenfelder (1899–1976) founded the religious movement 'German Christians' (Deutsche Christen) within the Protestant Church. The goals of the movement, which was close to the NSDAP, were to break up the regional churches, to create a Reich church, and to exclude Jews. It won the church elections in summer 1933 and soon counted 1 million members. Its radical demands, however, caused many members to leave the movement again. In the following years the 'German Christians' split into several groups.

3 The *Vossische Zeitung* reported on the meeting, stating that after addresses by Joachim Hossenfelder, now a bishop, and the chairman of the 'German Christians' in Berlin, Dr Reinhold Krause, the resolution was passed. Krause, in his speech, had called for the 'uncompromising removal of all

Synod,[4] and further to consolidate all Protestant Christians of foreign blood into separate communities of their own kind and to arrange for the *founding of a Jewish Christian church*.

4. We expect our regional church, as a German people's church, to free itself from all that is un-German in the divine service and confession of faith, in particular from the Old Testament and its Jewish moral code of retribution.

5. We demand that a German people's church earnestly undertake the propagation of the simple good news, cleansed of all Oriental distortion, and of a heroic Jesus figure as the basis of an appropriate Christianity in which the broken servant's soul is replaced by the proud man who, as the child of God, feels an obligation to the divine element in himself and in his people.

6. We confess that to us, the only true divine service is service to our Volksgenossen, and as a community of struggle we feel obligated by our God to help build a *watchful and authentic, völkisch Church*, in which we see the completion of the German Reformation of Martin Luther, and which alone fulfils the claim to totality of the National Socialist state.

DOC. 89

On 15 November 1933 the trader Louis Skalawski complains to the Reich Minister of Economics about being barred from a Berlin market[1]

Letter from Louis Skalawski,[2] Berlin, 15 Weimarerstraße, to the Reich Minister of Economics (received 6 December 1933), dated 15 November 1933[3]

My distress compels me to submit the request below to the Reich Minister of Economics: for six years I had a stall on Mondays and Thursdays at the market in the Berlin district of Charlottenburg, *Suarezstrasse*. This stall was taken away from me in August of this year because I am not Aryan.

My repeated personal requests and written petitions to the market inspectorate were unsuccessful. In my written petition from 15 November of this year,[4] I had referred to the edicts of the Reich Minister of Economics from 25 September 1933, HG. 13 046/33,[5] and the Prussian Minister of Economics and Labour from 13 October 1933, III. A. 4461.

---

that is ethnically foreign' in the German people's church: 'Deutsche Christen für Arierparagraph', *Vossische Zeitung*, 14 Nov. 1933, newspaper clipping in Archiv des Diakonischen Werkes der Evangelischen Kirche Deutschlands, CA, AC-S/66, Materialsammlung der Apologetischen Zentrale.

4 See Doc. 75, 6 Sept. 1933.

1 BArch, R 3101/13862, fol. 106r–v. This document has been translated from German.
2 Louis Skalawski (b. 1879), businessman; deported from Berlin to Auschwitz in March 1943.
3 Parts of the original have been underlined by hand.
4 Since the letter from Skalawski is dated 15 Nov. 1933, the date of the petition mentioned is likely to be 15 Oct. 1933.
5 In this circular decree the Reich Minister of Economics had ordered that it was not permissible to treat Aryan and non-Aryan traders differently under the commercial code in force: ibid., fol. 275r–v.

L.,[6] re market trading and requested consideration once again, whereupon City Councillor Sommer[7] of the Charlottenburg district authority, market inspectorate, stated that he could not give consideration to me because I am not Aryan.

I ask most respectfully for a review of the circumstances and request that you issue instructions for the continued provision of a stall to me at the market on Suarezstrasse.

I am 54 years old, my wife is 54 years old, and we have three children to support in our household. Thus far it has been possible for me to earn the most meagre livelihood for my family only by trading in goods at the weekly markets. At the market on Suarezstrasse I already had regular customers, and loss of this market two days a week has put me in the greatest distress and left me unable to earn a livelihood. In addition, I have been in arrears with the rent for our flat for weeks now, so that the landlord is threatening me with an action for eviction unless I can pay the arrears by the 15th of this month.

I was born [in] Gniezno, province of Posen, as a citizen of the German Reich, and lost my livelihood there when the province of Posen fell to Poland. In the process, my two plots of land in Gniezno were liquidated. As a result I have lost all my assets, have no means to rent a shop, and am left only with the possibility of earning my living by selling goods at the weekly market, with precisely the stall at the market on Suarezstrasse being the determining factor.

During the World War, I was conscripted to serve in the army and was detailed to work in Berlin as a plumber. I ask most respectfully for consideration because I am a refugee from the Ostmark and damaged by expropriation, and because I have no other means of subsistence.

In anticipation of a prompt and favourable reply, I remain yours respectfully

---

6 Circular decree issued by the Prussian Minister of Economics and Labour, with copy of the Reich Ministry of Economics decree of 25 Sept. 1933, BLHA, Rep. 60/641, fol. 13.
7 Karl Sommer (1906–1982), career officer; military career, 1923–1928; joined the SA in 1929 and the NSDAP in 1930; co-founder of the National Socialist People's Welfare; worked for the city of Berlin from 1931; district councillor and city councillor in Berlin-Charlottenburg from 1933; interned in 1945.

DOC. 90
On 4 December 1933 the municipal school inspector of Berlin forbids teachers to marry Jewish partners[1]

Announcement of the acting municipal school inspector p.p. Meinshausen,[2] Berlin, dated 4 December 1933, concerning a decree issued by the Oberpräsident of the province of Brandenburg and Berlin/ Schools Department (II A/B 12 100 Bbg./9 November 1933), p.p. Hassenstein,[3] dated 11 November 1933 (printed)

Marriage to persons of non-Aryan origin.
(For all school categories)
Under § 1a(3) of the Reich Civil Service Law in the version of the law of 30 June 1933 (*Reichsgesetzblatt*, p. 433), anyone who is not of Aryan descent or is married to a person of non-Aryan descent may not be appointed a civil servant of the Reich. Reich civil servants of Aryan descent who enter into marriage with a person of non-Aryan descent must be dismissed. Guidelines issued by the Reich Minister of the Interior determine who is to be considered a person of non-Aryan descent. The provisions of § 1a of the Reich Civil Service Law apply correspondingly to the Civil Service Law of the states, communities, etc.

Under the guidelines of 8 August 1933 concerning § 1a(3) of the Reich Civil Service Law (see *Reichsgesetzblatt*, p. 575), which also apply to the Civil Service Law of the states, anyone who is to be appointed a civil servant must prove that he and his spouse are of Aryan descent. Every civil servant who intends to enter into marriage must prove that the person whom he wishes to marry is of Aryan descent. The proof of Aryan descent must be brought by submitting documents (birth certificate, marriage certificate of parents).

I therefore request that teachers (male and female) be instructed that, when announcing a marriage, they must simultaneously present the designated documents as proof of the Aryan descent of the person with whom the marriage is to be contracted.

---

1 'Eheschließung mit Personen nicht arischer Abstammung', *Dienstblatt des Magistrats von Berlin*, 1933, part VIII/472, p. 288. This document has been translated from German.
2 Dr Hans Meinshausen (1889–1948), teacher; joined the NSDAP in 1929 and the SA in 1940; deputy Gauleiter of Berlin, 1930–1933; state commissioner for schools and municipal school inspector in Berlin, 1933–1944; acting mayor of Görlitz, 1944–1945; sentenced to death in Görlitz in 1948 and executed in Dresden.
3 Fritz Hassenstein (b. 1873), teacher and theologian; rector at the Protestant primary school and preacher in Seeburg, East Prussia, 1901–1904; employed by state schools, 1904–1934; as Regierungsdirektor worked for the state commissioner for Berlin as head of the Department of Primary and Secondary Schools in 1934–1937; in 1940 section head for the hospital chaplaincy in the Protestant Church Community of Berlin and section head of the Berlin City Synodal Association.

DOC. 91

New York Times, 24 December 1933: article on the work of the High Commissioner of the League of Nations and aid for Jewish refugees[1]

J. G. M'Donald[2] puts exiles at 60,000.

League Commissioner for the Reich Refugees Says Here Their Number Is Growing. Tells Need for Funds. Appeals for Cooperation in Task of Finding Homes for Jews Ousted by Nazis.

The machinery set up to coordinate the work of aiding refugees from Germany to find a new place in the world was discussed in detail by James G. MacDonald, high commissioner for refugees coming from Germany, in a statement prepared at the request of *The New York Times* and issued shortly after his arrival last night on the United States liner Manhattan.

Commissioner MacDonald, who was appointed by the Council of the League of Nations, said the latest estimates of the total number of refugees that reached him placed the figure at about 60,000 and pointed out that 'it is likely that the number of refugees from Germany will continue to increase.'

'It is for all of us, Jews and non-Jews alike, who believe in the fundamental principles of equality before the law and of racial toleration, so painfully won through the ages,' he declared, 'to work together to make this instrumentality contribute in the fullest possible measure to the settlement of the refugees in new homes where they will have opportunities to build a new life for themselves and to enrich materially and culturally their new homelands.'

MacDonald's Statement.

His statement follows:

The problem created by the refugees coming from Germany is in its implications world-wide. It involves principles vital to civilized peoples everywhere. It can be solved only by the cooperation of many governments and private organizations in different parts of the world. The present proportions of the work, though large, are an inadequate measure of the possible needs. It is this present and potential task which, as Lord Cecil[3] put it, constitutes 'a great challenge – a challenge to the principles of our civilization which have governed the world increasingly for nearly 2,000 years. We must either respond to that challenge or, as it seems to me, the civilization we enjoy will receive a terrible blow.'

---

1 *New York Times*, 24 Dec. 1933, p. 10. The original document is in English.
2 Correctly: James G. McDonald (1886–1964), politician; chairman of the Foreign Policy Association, 1919–1933; High Commissioner of the League of Nations for Refugees Coming from Germany, 1933–1935; US ambassador to Israel, 1949–1951. On his resignation as high commissioner, see Doc. 221, 7 Jan. 1936.
3 Lord Robert Cecil (1864–1958), lawyer and politician; from 1906 Member of Parliament; co-founder of the League of Nations; from 1918 head of the British League of Nations section; from 1927 organized a private campaign for the League of Nations and for peace; awarded the Nobel Peace Prize in 1937.

According to the latest estimates to reach the High Commissioner (the figures are still tentative), the total number of refugees from Germany is about 60,000. Classified on a religious basis, about 51,000 refugees, or 86 per cent, are Jews. The other 14 per cent are non-Jews – Catholics, members of various Protestant denominations, or not classified as members of any religious group. Contrary to the popular opinion, not all of the refugees from Germany are Germans; a considerable proportion are non-Germans. It is estimated that more than 16,000 are of Polish or of other than German nationality, or are stateless – that is without any clearly defined or recognized nationality.

The distribution of refugees is now estimated as follows:

France	25,000
Palestine	6,500
Poland	6,000
Czechoslovakia	5,000
Holland	5,000
England	3,000
Belgium	2,500
Switzerland	2,500
Scandinavia	1,500
Austria	800
Saar and Luxembourg	500
Italy	500
Other countries, including Spain and the United States	1,000

Magnitude of the Problem.

Other refugee situations since the World War have involved larger numbers of persons, but none has presented more inherent difficulties or has been thrust upon the world at a time of more acute and general economic crisis. Moreover, it is likely that the number of refugees from Germany will continue to increase. Some of the most intelligent and sober students of the present situation are of the opinion that unless the plight of the Jews in Germany is radically ameliorated it may become necessary for tens of thousands of the younger generation to be settled elsewhere. This would be a task which would test to the uttermost the resources of the private organizations and persons interested as well as the absorptive capacities of the receiving countries. Happily there is still the possibility that this mass migration may not have to be carried out. Meantime the actual task has borne heavily upon certain countries.

In general the countries neighboring on Germany adopted, at the beginning of the flight of the refugees, a policy of the open door and generous hospitality. Czechoslovakia and Poland received several thousands of refugees. In the latter country many of these were Polish nationals. Denmark, Belgium and Holland also received refugees in large numbers in proportion to their size. But it was France which became the temporary home of by far the largest numbers.

The French Government, priding itself on its tradition of hospitality to the oppressed, put no obstacles in the way to the stream of refugees that crossed the Belgian frontier or passed through the Saar into France. French citizens, acting chiefly through Le Comité National de Secours aux Réfugiés,[4] have raised and expended for the care of these refugees nearly ten million French francs. The larger proportion of this total was raised from

French collections. The balance was contributed by American and British relief agencies. Now the French Government feels that it has to reconsider its policy, and the officers of the Comité National have renewed their urgent appeals for enlarged financial contributions.

Large Sums Are Needed.
The data available for the Jewish refugees in France and elsewhere are much more accurate than those for the non-Jewish refugees. The efforts by private Jewish organizations and communities have been unremitting.[5] Large sums have already been expended to meet the immediate needs of the refugees and much larger amounts will probably be raised by these organizations for the retraining and settlement of their coreligionists. It would be unfair, however, not to underline that the Jewish efforts have by no means been limited to Jewish refugees. Protestants, Catholics and refugees of no religious faith at all, have been and are in many instances being relieved by Jewish charity.

Unfortunately only a few non-Jewish organizations and individuals have manifested active interest in the non-Jewish refugees. The result is that the work among this group has been less well organized and less adequately financed. However, excellent work is being done by non-sectarian organizations – for example, those devoted to finding positions for intellectuals and professional men and women; and the trade unions and the labor organizations have made unremitting efforts to support those who particularly look to them for help. But it is quite clear that much more than has been done must be done by non-Jews if the Christian and non-sectarian refugees are [to be] adequately cared for and if the whole problem is to be solved.

At the assembly of the League of Nations last September[6] there was a singular unanimity of feeling among the representatives of countries bordering on Germany that the refugee problem could no longer be handled adequately merely by the private organizations. It was this conviction which led the representative of the Dutch Government to present and press his proposal for the creation of the office of a High Commissioner to help coordinate the efforts of the private organizations and of the governments.

It was at first planned that this office should be an organ of the League of Nations, responsible to the Council of the League and financed by the League. But the office as finally set up was made autonomous. The Council of the League named the High Commissioner,[7] invited fifteen countries to name representatives to constitute the governing body, and advanced the sum of 25,000 Swiss francs as a loan for the initial administrative expenses. These things done, the new institution was left to organize itself and to determine the scope of its activities.

The High Commissioner was named on Oct. 26. The first meeting of the governing body was held within six weeks of that appointment. The site of the office of the High Commission was fixed at Lausanne. Representatives of twelve of the countries invited were present, as follows:

---

4 The Comité National de Secours aux Réfugiés was founded in June 1933 and existed until 1935.
5 See Doc. 50, 12 June 1933.
6 The fourteenth regular session of the Assembly of the League of Nations took place from 23 Sept. to 11 Oct. 1933 in Geneva.
7 James G. McDonald was appointed high commissioner: see fn. 2.

Professor *Bourquin*, Belgium.
Dr. *Lobkowicz*, Czechoslovakia.
Dr. *Borberg*, Denmark.
Senator *Berenger*, France.
Viscount *Cecil of Chelwood*, Great Britain.
Senator *Majoni*, Italy.
Dr. *Doude von Troostwijk*, Netherlands.
Dr. *Chodzko*, Poland.
Dr. *Westman*, Sweden.
Dr. *Rothmund*, Switzerland.
Professor *Chamberlain*, United States.
Ambassador *Guani*, Uruguay.

Lord Cecil, the British representative, was elected chairman. His acceptance of this post greatly encouraged all of those associated with the work. Ambassador Guani, representative of Uruguay, was named vice chairman. These two officials and the representatives of Holland, Switzerland and France, together with the High Commissioner, make up the Permanent Committee of the High Commission. This committee acts in effect as an executive for the larger body.

Organization and Policy.
The sessions of the governing body during its four-day meeting were devoted to questions of organization and of general policy. The relationship between the governing body and the High Commissioner was outlined. Provision was also made for effective cooperation with the governing body by interested private organizations. To this end an advisory council was created. Nine Jewish, and an equal number of non-Jewish organizations, were invited to name representatives on it.

The former were:
The American Jewish Joint Distribution Committee.
The Jewish Colonization Association.
The Jewish Agency for Palestine.[8]
The Group of Organizations of the American Jewish Community.
The Group of Organizations of the French Jewish Community.
The Group of Organizations of the Anglo-Jewish Community.
The Group of Organizations of the Polish Jewish Community.
The Group of Organizations of the Dutch Jewish Community.
Le Comité des délégations juives, comprising representatives from the Jewish communities of Central and Eastern Europe, Greece and Italy.

The organizations other than Jewish were:
Caritas Catholica.
Joint representation of the Universal Christian Council for Life and Work and the European Office for Inter-church Aid.
The Society of Friends.

---

8 A representation of Jews set up by Britain in accordance with Art. 4 of the League of Nations Mandate. The representative was to advise the Mandate government on economic, social, and other matters concerning the interests of the Jewish population of Palestine.

The International Federation of Trade Unions.

An international employers' organization (no specific organization has yet been suggested).

Le Comité de placement des Intellectuels Réfugiés.

Joint representation of the Emergency Committee in Aid of Displaced German Scholars, the Academic Assistance Council and the International Student Service.

Save the Children International Union.

Le Comité National (Français) de Secours aux Réfugiés.

It is expected that the Advisory Council will be convened regularly in advance of meetings of the governing body, in order that its suggestions may be available for consideration by the governmental representatives.

A smaller advisory body, called the 'bureau', was also set up, composed of representatives of those organizations which in the judgment of the High Commissioner 'can best assist him in the work of relief and reconstruction.' On this bureau the following were invited to name representatives:

The Jewish Colonization Association.

The American Jewish Joint Distribution Committee.

The Jewish Agency for Palestine.

Caritas Catholica.

One representative for the Universal Christian Council for Life and Work, and the European Office for Inter-Church Aid.

One representative for the Academic Assistance Council, the Emergency Committee for Displaced German Scholars, Le Comité de placement des Intellectuels Réfugiés and the International Student Service.

Opportunity to Give [Help to] Jews.

It is anticipated that the bureau will be convened before each meeting of the permanent committee of the governing body and that it will work closely with the governmental representatives. In these ways it is hoped that the private organizations will have a full opportunity to present their views at every stage of the High Commission's activities. There can be no doubt that only through such close coordination of private initiative and governmental cooperation can the High Commissioner's office be made to function effectively.

The governing body at its Lausanne meeting did not undertake to delimit except in very broad terms the work to be undertaken by the High Commissioner. It is conceived, however, that the High Commissioner's office should not undertake direct work of relief, that instead the dealings with individual refugees should be left to the private organizations already functioning or to others which might be set up. For the High Commissioner's office itself to undertake case work would necessitate the building up of a large and expensive staff, with representatives in numerous centres, and would involve considerable overlapping and duplicating with existing organizations – precisely the condition which the High Commissioner is expected to lessen.

In general the High Commissioner's office would seem to have two broad functions: first, the work of coordination; second, the conduct of negotiations with governments.

In his opening address to the governing body the High Commissioner interpreted the first of these functions as follows:

'The need for coordinating the varied activities of the many organizations now serving the refugees is clear. The responsible heads of the larger of such organizations have already expressed to the High Commissioner their cordial desire to cooperate with him in efforts to secure a more effective division of labor and of responsibility. But beyond this there is also the need for a larger measure of coordination in the formulation of a comprehensive program, not so much for relief as for the retraining and placement of the refugees in communities in different parts of the world.'

Funds for Reconstruction.
Such a program of reconstruction will require very large funds. To secure these the governing body, it is hoped, will give its moral support to the financial appeals launched on behalf of the comprehensive programs when these are formulated.

The other major portion of the High Commissioner's task – negotiations with governments – will have to do, presumably, with such technical questions as travel and identification papers for the refugees and their property rights, and in general with the privileges now accorded or to be accorded to the refugees in the countries where they now are or to which they might be expected to emigrate. This latter subject is the more important because of the magnitude of the financial and economic crisis through which the world is passing.

Many countries which in other and more promising circumstances would have welcomed the refugees as immigrants have felt compelled, reluctantly no doubt, to restrict or almost to exclude newcomers. It will therefore be the task of the High Commissioner, in cooperation with the organizations experienced in this work, to fit some of the refugees for absorption in the life of the countries where they now are, and to search the world for places where others can go to begin their life anew.

Thus far in our efforts at Lausanne we have created a machine. It is for all of us, Jews and non-Jews alike, who believe in the fundamental principles of equality before the law and of racial toleration, so painfully won through the ages, to work together to make this instrumentality contribute in the fullest possible measure to the settlement of the refugees in new homes where they will have opportunities to build a new life for themselves and to enrich materially and culturally their new homelands.

DOC. 92
On 29 December 1933 Fritz Wolfes asks the mayor of Hanover to lease a sports hall to the Jewish Gymnastics Association[1]

Letter from Fritz Wolfes,[2] Hanover, 312 Podbielskistraße, to Mayor Menge,[3] Hanover, dated 29 December 1933

Dear Mayor,

A resident of Hanover, who has been one for thirty years, someone from the great multitude who holds no office, has achieved no distinction, lacks contacts and has no commission, someone who is something 'special' only in that he is a Jew, requests that you grant him two minutes of your attention:

We Jews are barred from all sports associations.[4] We have taken note of that. We are not begging for admission but rather founding a Jewish gymnastics association. But we have no sports hall, no gymnastics apparatus. Why is the city unwilling to lease them to us? We are not asking for preferential treatment; instead, we want to pay a fair price. The city sells us water, gas, electricity. We are allowed to use the tram system and railway. We swim in the city facilities; why are we not allowed to do gymnastics there? – I try to grasp many an aspect of the present-day views, regarding the theory of race as well, but this refusal is something I do not understand!! If twenty Japanese were to lease a sports hall, nothing would stand in the way of it. Other cities where the Jewish question played a substantial role as recently as a few months ago have abandoned the stance of refusal. Should our peaceful Hanover not be able to do the same? It is not our intention to engage in anti-German or Marxist propaganda. We intend to treat the city's property, which was acquired with our money too, with care. Let acceptable requirements be imposed on us if need be, but fulfil this wish for us! Your Honour, let us not waste too many words on it. I ask for your valued response, with the reasons for it, if at all possible. Whatever the answer may be, I will comply, but one request: Do not pass on this letter 'on account of the area of competence concerned' to …[5]

---

1 Stadtarchiv Hannover, Hauptregistratur 15/441. This document has been translated from German.
2 Fritz Wolfes (b. 1894), businessman in Hanover; emigrated to the USA in Oct. 1938.
3 Dr Arthur Menge (1884–1965), lawyer; senator of the city of Hanover, 1914–1918, then director of the city's tram system; mayor of Hanover, 1925–1937; sentenced to three years in prison in Feb. 1945 in connection with the attempt to assassinate Hitler on 20 July 1944.
4 Jewish athletes had been excluded from the German Gymnastics Association, the German Swimming Association, and the German Rowing Association in April and May 1933: Lion Feuchtwanger (ed.), *Der Gelbe Fleck: Die Ausrottung von 500 000 deutschen Juden* (Paris: Carrefour, 1936), pp. 188–189. On the Berlin Gymnastics Association and the German Gymnastics Association, see Doc. 61, 1 July 1933, and Doc. 80, 23 Sept. 1933.
5 The mayor passed on the letter to the department in charge of sports, whose director asked Wolfes in a telephone conversation for the names of the cities where Jews were allowed to continue using facilities. With a request for confidentiality, Wolfes then named the following to him, based on information from the Reich League of Jewish Combat Veterans: Aachen, Beuthen, Chemnitz, Düsseldorf, Emmendingen, Erfurt, Felsberg, Fürth, Geilenkirchen, Magdeburg, and Opole: letter from Wolfes to Löhdefink, 15 Jan. 1934, Stadtarchiv Hannover, Hauptregistratur 15/441. On 29 June 1934 the Jewish Gymnastics and Sports Association Bar Kokhba Hanover sent the mayor an additional petition regarding the leasing of a sports field: Stadtarchiv Hannover, Hauptregistratur 20/315.

Here the Führer principle is in place. *Make a decision!* Then I will have no doubt how the decision turns out.

With the highest esteem

DOC. 93
Ernst Hofmann reports on mistreatment at the hands of SS and SA men, 1933[1]

Letter, signed Ernst Hofmann, 1933 (copy)[2]

'Non-organized' isolated acts of violence and arrests

Fourteen days before the official boycott, the shop of a friend of mine in a small town was closed down by SS men. In his distress, he turned to me and asked me to help him, so that he could reopen his shop. I decided to venture into the lion's den with him. We immediately drove to the Gauleitung in the nearby provincial capital. The officials in charge could not be reached straight away, and [so] I decided to wait in front of the building with my friend. Besides us, between sixty and seventy people were standing about there, some in uniform, some in plain clothes, and they seemed to be there by special arrangement.

While we were waiting, I heard a few people whispering to each other: 'Well, we'll get the Jew in a minute.' Since no one could suspect me of being a 'non-Aryan', I asked the man who wanted to get the Jew exactly who was supposed to be arrested. Then he asked me whether I had been ordered to be there, and I answered in the affirmative, although I did not know what was actually going on. Then he told me the following: 'Well, you know the Jew, the professor, who treated us so badly during the war? We're going now with two trucks to I., to chain him up and drive him through the Harz Mountains, (?) then he'll get a thrashing and be put in prison.' Naturally I was quite outraged at this and had already worked out my plan to prevent a defenceless man from being handed over to these renegades. I said to my friend that we still had time to have a cup of coffee, and I promptly went to a nearby phone box, where I placed a call to Professor X in B. and urged him to disappear at once, because the Nazis intended to arrest him. It all went off without a hitch. In five minutes Prof. X. was in the car, on his way to an unknown destination. Once I knew that the prof. was safe, I took care of the matter for my friend, so that he could reopen his shop in the afternoon. We now drove in the same direction as the two vehicles full of SS and SA men and overtook them along the way.

In B., I arranged to meet the professor's wife in the waiting room, to relate my experiences to her in detail. Later I heard that, at the hospital, people had torn the swastika flags to pieces. The professor, thank God, was long gone.

The next day, when I tried to go into a boycotted shop, I was denied entry, and at the same time a secret policeman appeared and told me I was under suspicion of being an informer and would be arrested at the slightest further suspicion. I thanked the hero for the warning and vanished from town for a few weeks.

---

1 Wiener Library, P.II.c., no. 987. This document has been translated from German.
2 The document was composed in Amsterdam in 1933 and submitted to the Wiener Library in London in 1959 for its collection of eyewitness reports: Wiener Library, P.II.c., no. 987.

One evening I was sitting with a few business friends in a restaurant, which several SA & SS men also frequented regularly. In the cloakroom I was jostled by one of them, who told me in threatening tones that he had a score to settle with me. Since I knew the danger, I now tried to get out of the restaurant quickly and left the town with my friends, in the hope that I would now be left in peace by this sinister fellow. How great was my surprise, however, an hour later when I saw this hero of the Third Reich in front of my building, rushing at me and trying to grapple with me. I tried to defend myself as well as I could and did not inconsiderable damage to his head with my house key. I lost a few teeth in this brawl. I now retired for the night and thought the matter was over. Now, however, there began something unheard of in normal times. Around 2 a.m., three SS men turned up and searched the entire building until I was caught in pyjamas and dragged away, barely dressed, to the police station. Then I was locked in a cell where otherwise only vagrants and people picked up at night are kept. After I had spent an hour there, two SS men with rubber truncheons appeared, tore my clothes off my body and ill-treated me until I could no longer move a single limb and was only barely conscious. I was left to lie in this condition until 8 a.m., and then two new people abused me in the same manner. After half an hour, I was also forced to drink a large mug of castor oil. Towards 11 a.m. I was told that I could now go home, but how great was my surprise when there was a pushcart standing in the street, hundreds of SA men and a big crowd, and I was forced to get into the pushcart. After initial resistance, I lay down in the cart, jumped back up, was thrown back again with brutal force, and since I could do nothing, I surrendered to my fate and, accompanied by 100 SA men, was hauled for about an hour through the city to the prison. Hundreds of people watched this sad spectacle with disapproving looks.

At the prison, I was immediately put into hospital because I looked like a zebra, my whole body was black and blue, but the treatment as well as the food was good. After two weeks I was released because I made a declaration that I would disappear from X. That same night I left Germany, for which I had fought for four years on the Western Front.

DOC. 94
Pariser Tageblatt, 4 January 1934: commentary on the cancellation of the boxing match between Max Schmeling and King Levinsky[1]

Schmeling[2] is not permitted to box against a Jew. A ban by the German government

A Paris daily evening newspaper reports that the fight between Max Schmeling and King Levinsky[3] scheduled for 18 February in Chicago was cancelled because the German government did not allow Schmeling to compete against the Jew Levinsky. It is further reported that King Levinsky has stated that he would like to square up to Hitler. Wishful thinking, but unfortunately unfulfillable.

---

1 'Schmeling darf gegen keinen Juden boxen: Ein Verbot der deutschen Regierung', *Pariser Tageblatt*, 4 Jan. 1934, p. 1. This document has been translated from German. The exile newspaper, headed by Georg Bernhard, was published from Dec. 1933 to June 1936. The circulation totalled 14,000 copies in 1935. The successor was the *Pariser Tageszeitung*, published from 1936 to 1939.

If the news is accurate, Schmeling might be the aggrieved party. In all probability, the way to the world championship is through a Jew, whether it be Max Baer[4] or Levinsky, for this inferior, feeble race is actually not poorly represented in boxing. Schmeling and Heuser[5] have had to learn that through experience.[6] If Berlin wants to preserve Schmeling's status as a national hero by preventing him at all costs from losing to a Jew again, then he can be declared default world champion by the grace of Germany. That costs nothing. One laugh more or less is of no significance.

DOC. 95

On 4 January 1934 businessman Julius Fromm protests against the planned retraction of his German citizenship[1]

Letter from Julius Fromm,[2] unsigned, Berlin-Schlachtensee, 4 Rolandstraße, to the chief of police in the Reich capital Berlin,[3] dated 4 January 1934 (copy)[4]

I ask permission of the *chief of police* to present the following:

In connection with the implementation of the Law on the Deprivation of German Nationality, dated 14 July 1933,[5] I have been summoned to furnish my particulars to the police station in charge. I take the liberty, in what follows, to lay out the reasons to the

---

2 Max Schmeling (1905–2005) was initially a labourer and then a professional boxer from 1924 to 1948; he was heavyweight champion of the world, 1930–1932, and in 1936 defeated the American boxer Joe Louis, in a match celebrated by the National Socialist propaganda machine; in 1938 he lost to Joe Louis in a world championship match; after 1948 he worked as a businessman.
3 King Levinsky, born Harris Krakau (1910–1991), American professional boxer.
4 Maximilian Adelbert Baer (1909–1959), American professional boxer; heavyweight champion of the world, 1934–1935.
5 Adolf Heuser (1907–1988), professional boxer from 1929; twice European champion.
6 Schmeling lost to Max Baer in New York in 1933 by a technical knockout; the same year Heuser challenged world light heavyweight champion Maxie Rosenbloom (1903–1976) and lost.

1 BLHA, Pr.Br. Rep. 2A, I St Einbürgerung, Julius Fromm, fols 50–57. This document has been translated from German.
2 Israel, later Julius, Fromm (1883–1945), businessman; born in Konin (Russian Poland), he emigrated to Berlin in 1893; initially an outworker; in 1914 he founded the company Israel Fromm, which was renamed Fromms Act in 1916 (made rubber products and condoms); German citizen as of 1920; the company was Aryanized in 1938, and Fromm emigrated to Britain in Oct. of that year.
3 Berlin's chief of police was Magnus Levetzow (1871–1939), marine officer; naval career, 1889–1920, finishing as a rear admiral; worked in the Junkers company, 1925–1928; joined the NSDAP, 1932; Berlin chief of police, 1933–1935; thereafter worked in the private sector.
4 The original is underlined by hand in several places.
5 In accordance with the Law on the Revocation of Naturalization and the Deprivation of German Nationality (14 July 1933), cases of naturalization dating from the period between 9 Nov. 1918 and 30 Jan. 1933 were examined with the help of a special questionnaire. In most cases, they were revoked: *Reichsgesetzblatt*, 1933, I, p. 480. On the earlier history of the expatriation of *Ostjuden*, see Doc. 8, 15 March 1933.

chief of police for my assumption that the aforementioned law, including its implementing regulations of 26 July 1933, does not apply to me.⁶

I came to Germany as a child in 1893 and have resided without interruption since then in Berlin. My schooling was in Berlin at a German school. I *only* speak the *German* language and was raised *exclusively* in the *German* spirit and in *German* culture, and have *always* remained true to them in both word and deed. This is not unknown. I do not have, nor have I ever had, any personal, familial, or political relationships to the country of birth of my father, dead now these thirty-six years. I am happily married to a native of Berlin who *since birth* has had Prussian nationality. My wife's family has resided in Berlin for generations. My father-in-law was also Aryan and German in the truest sense of the word. The three boys⁷ resulting from our marriage attended school in Berlin and were *exclusively* raised in the *German* spirit and in *German* culture by their German-disposed parents. I founded my industrial company in Berlin, and I – at the outset its sole employee and worker simultaneously – have promoted it from its humble beginnings to its current prominence. Thus, through my *German* manner and my *German* industriousness, I have properly and honestly become one of the biggest taxpayers of my district of Zehlendorf-Schlachtensee. Until May 1933 I was the sole proprietor of my company: *Fromms Act, Julius Fromm, Rubber Works, Berlin-Köpenick*. It was then transformed into a 'private limited company'. Naturally, I still own the main part of the company shares even after this change. The company, which has roughly 500 workers, employees, and salesmen on its books, has thus far *not* dismissed anyone despite a substantial decline in revenues as a result of the general economic crisis. On the contrary, in a recognized social-minded approach, and without mean-spirited economic considerations, the company has maintained its stock of workers and employees, only about 1 per cent of whom were non-Aryans in early 1933.

The company produces surgical and sanitary rubber products. The reputation and prestige of the company, which – without immodesty – enjoys an excellent international reputation, are common knowledge. The company has exported and continues to export a large range of German products abroad and has *always* done its part to further Germany's national trade and payments balance, and thus also to help raise Germany's foreign currency holdings. The stimulation of exports that is now being encouraged with all possible means, and the wide-ranging organizational measures linked to it, currently confronts me with challenges and tasks that are of the greatest importance. The company maintains factories in three different locations: Berlin-Köpenick, Berlin-Friedrichshagen, and Danzig. The main factory and central administration are located in Berlin-Köpenick. Without the least arrogance, one can assert that the company, through its technical and architectural achievements and its equipment and facilities, which are of the highest social and sanitary standards, is *known far beyond the bounds of Berlin*. Foreign customers and specialists have frequently described it as one of the sights to see

---

6 The implementing regulation cited '*völkisch*-nationalist' principles and Eastern Jewish heritage of the naturalized citizens as criteria for revocation: Implementing Regulation to the Law on the Revocation of Naturalization and the Deprivation of German Nationality, 26 July 1933, *Reichsgesetzblatt*, 1933, I, pp. 538–539.
7 Max Fromm (1907–1969), actor; emigrated to France in 1933. Herbert Fromm (1911–1961), retailer, and Edgar Fromm (1919–1999), emigrated to Britain in 1934 and 1938, respectively.

in Germany, and even in the world. *This is my German life's work.* My pride in this, which even down to the last detail is the result of my life's work, which exudes *German* achievement of the highest order, can be most clearly seen in the convincing testament of *my German* mindset: by visiting, surveying, and auditing the company itself.

Even in the current period of crisis, and following the Führer's encouragement, the company distributed Christmas bonuses to all its employees. The attached original of a letter from the chairman of the workers' council and *long-standing* member of the NSDAP Weinold, dated 11 December 1933 (i.e. *before* the written summons this letter is in reference to), is informative as regards how my workforce relates to me. Mrs Margarete Puls, Berlin-Köpenick, 38/39 Friedrichshagener Straße, who has worked in my company for twenty-one years, operational manager Alfred Hausding (member of the NSDAP), the two managing directors of the company (both members of the NSDAP), but also all the other workers and employees – without exception – will bear witness for me. The police station and the Criminal Police in Berlin-Köpenick, as well as the current mayor of Berlin-Köpenick, will also attest to my patriotic and social stance and that it is supportive of the national economy. The 'Kreisleitung of the NSDAP in Berlin East, Pettenkoferstraße' and the 'local branch of the NSDAP in Berlin-Hirschgarten' will likewise do me justice on this matter.[8]

Regarding my person, I would like to leave its further discussion to third parties. I would like to bring your attention to the contents of the attached documents. These draw on objective evidence of figures and departments within the national movement. Not only have I *quite naturally* and *at all* times fulfilled my duty to country and Volksgemeinschaft, but moreover I have allowed public and general charities to share in the fruits of my labour to a *far greater than usual extent*, as one can see. Thus, on the very first day after the call for donations to the Winter Relief by the Berlin organization, I immediately placed RM 10,000 at its disposal. Under Brüning's government, I already supported the Working Committee of the 'Reich Labour Community for German Labour Service Obligation', the receipt for which is attached, whereby I knowingly intended to support an equal and unconditional *obligation* for all Volksgenossen, to replace an unsatisfactory voluntarism.

Without intending to brag, I feel compelled to point out the measures I have taken to combat atrocity propaganda abroad. In this context, I dispatched *twenty* telegrams, with confirmations, as well as *seventeen* letters to authorities in the Saar region, Danzig, and foreign countries on 30 March 1933, as documented in the material and letters attached. As indicated in the additional enclosures, these measures on my part were met with success; this can be seen in the report published in the *Aussiger Tagblatt* (Czechoslovakia) no. 76 from 31 March 1933, as well as the written response from the Canadian company 'The Swedish Linen Industry' in Regina, Saskatoon, dated 20 April 1933, the Athens newspaper, and many others.[9]

---

8 In response to a query the manager of the NSDAP Gau Factory Cell Division of Greater Berlin wrote to the Regierungspräsident in Potsdam on 19 Jan. 1934, stating that Fromm's company, which at the time had 550 employees and workers, was 'exemplary both in the operational as well as in the social sense'. He wrote that if Fromm were to be expatriated, there was a danger that many jobs would be lost: BLHA, Pr.Br. Rep. 2A, I St Einbürgerung, Julius Fromm, fols. 62–63.

9 These enclosures are not in the file.

Regarding my attitude during the *pre-war* and *wartime* eras, I include a copy of my request to Berlin's chief of police, dated 7 September 1914; the original and the proceedings relating to it should be available in the files of the authorities. It should be clear therein why I did *not* strive for naturalization *earlier*: I was barely aware of my Russian nationality at the time! When, in September 1914, I applied to be admitted into the Prussian Federation in order to serve in the German army, my request (see the attached document) was denied on 25 November 1914.[10] At the time, I was told that it was out of the question that I could perform active military service due to my weak physical constitution. I was advised to make a renewed application for Prussian nationality following the 'soon anticipated' end of the war. I hereupon devoted myself to patriotic homeland service and committed myself (according to enclosure 26 089) to duty in the 'voluntary fatherland service' in November 1915. Other enclosures provide information on my unceasing commitment to Germany, as proved by my active duty in Berlin's 'Citizens' Militia'[11] in 1918/1919.[12]

I consciously and openly decided that my own interests would be best served at all times by putting them *behind* the good of the business community, the good of the people, and the good of the fatherland.

During the war, I invested my *entire* savings in war bonds, and my sons have obtained certificates of recognition for the collection of war bond subscriptions. In accordance with the corresponding documentation and certificates of recognition, I have delivered all gold currency and furthermore all gold that I myself was able to collect – against a 50 per cent higher goods invoice to *my own* detriment – to the authorities out of a sense of patriotic duty. Wherever possible, I was also extensively active for the Red Cross during the war. Among other things, I organized the distribution of care packages among German soldiers.

For about the last twenty years, I have been a member of the 'Invalidendank', as well as the 'Kolonialkriegerdank'[13] and other similar organizations. I was also a member of the politically neutral 'German Committee – With Hindenburg for Volk and Reich'.[14] When this committee was dissolved in June 1933, its president, His Serene Highness Prince Otto of Salm-Horstmar, honoured and recognized in the enclosed letter my work and my commitment to the good of people and country.

It saddens me greatly that I am forced to disclose acts undertaken as a matter of course as an honest German in order to demonstrate that the requirements of the Denaturalization Law and its implementing regulations, dated 26 July 1933, do not, in fact, apply. I am not able to believe that, in view of *my* deep-rootedness in Germandom and the life's work of my company, I could fall foul of the effects of this law without any consideration. There is no doubt that the company founded and run by me, which has supported the German national economy not least by employing several hundred workers, and which in every way serves it by its significant export of German goods, would be severely endangered, if not entirely destroyed, by my expatriation.

---

10 See the draft of the letter from the chief of police to Israel Fromm, dated 25 Nov. 1914: ibid., fol. 7.
11 Citizens' militias (Einwohnerwehren) were paramilitary groups subordinate to the Reichswehr.
12 These enclosures are not in the file.
13 Patriotic welfare associations.
14 The group backed Franz von Papen in the 1932 Reichstag elections.

Thus, I allow myself to express the plea that my German citizenship be maintained not only out of mercy, for I am aware of having been raised *German* in the best sense and to always have lived and worked in a *German* manner.

As references, I would like to offer the *Pan-German*[15] legal advisor Dr Paul Stuermer, Berlin-Charlottenburg 2, 80 Knesebeckstraße,[16] who has known me for about twenty years. He was also executive member of the board of directors of the 'German Committee – With Hindenburg for Volk and Reich' until its dissolution. Furthermore, I would also like to name the civil engineer Fritz Schmitt, Berlin-Charlottenburg, 6 Clausewitzstraße.[17]

I will produce a more extensive list of persons capable of providing supporting statements, if requested.

With a request for a decision[18] – not least in the hope of receiving the quickest possible remedy to the paralysis caused to my work and company due to severe emotional distress – I sign
wholly devoted

DOC. 96

Der National-Sozialistische Erzieher, **13 January 1934: article on 'racial separation'**[1]

Setting things straight between what is German and what is Jewish!
By Professor M. Staemmler[2]
We consider it entirely unnecessary to have to demonstrate the inferiority of Jewish traits. They are a Near Eastern and Oriental people and we are an overwhelmingly

---

15 Member of the Pan-German League (Alldeutscher Verband), a nationalist and antisemitic organization, founded in 1890 as the General German League (Allgemeiner Deutscher Verband) and known as the Pan-German League from 1894.
16 Stuermer sent a letter to the Regierungspräsident in Potsdam, dated 7 Jan. 1934, in which he advised against expatriating Fromm 'out of patriotic considerations', citing Fromm's beliefs and character and his diligence as an industrialist: BLHA, Pr.Br. Rep. 2A, I St Einbürgerung, Julius Fromm, fols. 58–60.
17 On 24 Jan. 1934 chief engineer Schmitt submitted a positive report on the factory of the Julius Fromm company in the Berlin district of Köpenick: ibid., fols. 68–69.
18 In Dec. 1933 the government in Potsdam called on Berlin's chief of police to examine Fromm's case. After completing its investigations, the Potsdam government handed the case on to the Prussian Ministry of the Interior with the recommendation to make an exception in this case and not to revoke naturalization. On 21 April 1934 the Prussian Ministry of the Interior decided in favour of this recommendation and against revocation: ibid., fols. 47 and 99.

1 'Reiner Tisch zwischen deutsch und jüdisch!', *Der National-Sozialistische Erzieher*, 13 Jan. 1934, p. 29. This document has been translated from German. *Der National-Sozialistische Erzieher* was a weekly newspaper published from 1933 in various regional editions. The text here is from an edition produced by the National Socialist Association of Teachers, Westphalia-Lippe, published in Iserlohn.
2 Dr Martin Staemmler (1890–1974), physician; joined the NSDAP in 1931 and became section head in the NSDAP Racial Policy Office; professor in Leipzig and Kiel, 1933–1935, then in Breslau, 1935–1945; vice chancellor of the University of Breslau, 1938–1942; director of the Pathology-Bacteriology Institute at Aachen Municipal Hospitals, 1950–1960; author of works including *Rassenpflege im völkischen Staat* (1933); co-editor of the journal *Volk und Rasse*.

Nordic people. They are thus quite different from us. We are proud of our race, they are proud of theirs. But as we are not speaking here of maintaining racial purity in the Near East or in Palestine but rather of racial purity in Germany, for us the admixture of Jews is an alien and unwelcome element. That they are mentally and psychologically completely different from us, particularly in their emotional life, can be understood by every German who reads newspapers, magazines, and books with German eyes. One does not even have to stoop to the level of the *Berliner Tageblatt*, the *Frankfurter Zeitung*, the Ullstein press, or the so-called *Lustige Blätter*.[3] Nearly all newspapers were under Jewish influence until only a few months ago, an influence which, though disguised, one could recognize. The fact that this Jewish control over public opinion has now been eliminated should be seen as one of the most significant successes of the National Socialist revolution. It fulfils point 23 of the 1920 Party programme, according to which all editors and newspaper employees must be Volksgenossen.[4]

Much as the Negro and the Chinese are quite different from us both outwardly and inwardly, so, too, is the Jew. For all I care, the Jew can even believe he is something better. Yet we don't want universal people but rather German people. And the characteristic type of the German is debased by Jewish admixture. For that reason we say: separate the races!

But why not blend and absorb?

The characteristics of a pure race are internally compatible. They fit together. There is an internal harmony between them. This came about through an existential struggle that lasted millennia, and everything that did not fit, everything disharmonious, was eradicated until what remained was only what was harmonious. Thus an image of a race was created whose characteristics fit together internally. This is true for all pure races. To some extent, this is also true for peoples who are a mix of races. But if quite alien elements are mixed into this more or less balanced condition, then hereditary elements that do not fit with one another will be churned together. Much as it clearly would not be nice to see a pug with the legs of a greyhound, or have a greyhound with the head of a bulldog, inner psychological dispositions would come together that do not fit with one another. Those who are 'between races' belong to none of them; they do not know what they are. They hold to nothing, they are internally torn, and are often the leaders of the inferior race against the superior race.

Jews in Germany have often said, and demonstrated, that they feel themselves to be Jews, so it is not necessary to even mention such testimonials. Had they felt themselves to be fully German, they would have prevented (and they, in particular, could have particularly well prevented it!) thousands of Ostjuden from arriving in Germany as immigrants or becoming naturalized. Of these no one, no German, can assert that they have been a benefit for our people. If the so-called German Jews had felt themselves to be German, they themselves would have demanded that these exploiters be kept at arm's length. But they took them in, pampered them, and then let them leave again, along with their plunder. That created a clear precedent. Here, too, one could hear: 'All Israel vouches for one another.'

---

3 A satirical magazine founded by Alexander Moszkowski.
4 NSDAP programme dated 24 Feb. 1920: Hofer (ed.), *Der Nationalsozialismus: Dokumente*, p. 30.

And these people are supposed to become naturalized, we are to take them in, make them Germans? A völkisch state could never want this; otherwise it abandons its status as a völkisch state. So for that reason we need to set things straight between what is German and what is non-German!

But first a preliminary note, even though it should, in fact, be superfluous today.[5] We are speaking here not of Jews by faith but rather of Jews by race. Even if a person is baptized and third or fourth generation, even if he is a good Catholic and belongs to the Catholic Centre Party, he remains a Jew. One should finally stop speaking of 'Christian' shops; one should finally cease comparing Jews and Christians. In our country there are Germans and there are Jews. The Jew can never be German even if he has been baptized as a Protestant or a Catholic.

Our goal is thus the separation of the races![6]

DOC. 97
Juristische Wochenschrift, 13 January 1934: article on two Reich Labour Court rulings concerning the dismissal of Jewish employees[1]

B. Labour Courts.
Reich Labour Court.
Reported by Dr W. Oppermann,[2] lawyer, Dresden.
1. § 626 Civil Code. The fact that an employee is Jewish does not in itself entitle an employer to immediately terminate a contract of employment, irrespective of circumstance. The assessment of such cases requires a considered view of the current situation, not a rash approach influenced by political events.[3]

I. In 1925 the plaintiff acquired the business Deutsches Schuhwarenhaus, a long-established shoe shop in C., from its previous owner, Max G. It continued operating, now under the name 'Deutsches Schuhwarenhaus, Owner Fritz K'. The business acquired footwear from the H.P. manufacturing company in B., which was solely owned by Privy Commercial Councillor Hans P. in B. In 1929 an agreement was reached between the

---

5 Though Staemmler uses the term 'preliminary note', this passage is followed not by any further text but rather only news items.
6 At the second Reich Conference of the National Socialist Physicians' League in Leipzig in 1932, Staemmler had called for a legal prohibition of marriages between 'Germans and Jews': cited in Käthe Frankenthal, 'Ärzteschaft und Faschismus', *Der sozialistische Arzt*, vol. 8, no. 6 (1932), pp. 101–107, here p. 105; facsimile in Stephan Leibfried and Florian Tennstedt, *Berufsverbote und Sozialpolitik 1933: Die Auswirkungen der nationalsozialistischen Machtergreifung auf die Krankenkassenverwaltung und die Kassenärzte* (Bremen: Universität Bremen, 1979), pp. 203–209.

1 *Juristische Wochenschrift*, 13 Jan. 1934, pp. 121–122. This document has been translated from German.
2 Dr Hermann Walther Oppermann (1876–1942), lawyer; practised law in Dresden; author of works including *Studien zum Arbeitsgerichtsprozeß* (1929).
3 Footnote in the original: 'On 1. See Rohlfing, "Rechtsfragen aus der Zugehörigkeit zur jüdischen Rasse im Arbeitsrecht": JW [*Jüdische Wochenschrift*]. 1933, [pp.] 2098–2099, and the decisions of the Berlin Labour Court authorities to be found there. D.S.'

H.P. company and the plaintiff to restructure the store in C. into a private limited company. All company shares were later transferred to Privy Councillor P., and the plaintiff was appointed general manager of the company.

The boycott of Jewish businesses ordered on 1 April 1933 impacted on the sales outlet of the Deutsches Schuhwarenhaus in C. in such a way that SA men appeared at the store during the morning following the start of the boycott set for 10 a.m., and stated that it was necessary to close the store because the boycott regulations also applied to it. Though the plaintiff explained that all shares in this enterprise were in the hands of the non-Jewish Privy Councillor P., the SA men did not alter their demand, and the store, like Jewish establishments, was ordered to shut. Further efforts on the part of the plaintiff and steps taken by the employee sent to C. that day by the defendant meant it was possible to reopen the store in the course of the afternoon, before the time set for the general boycott had expired.

On 2 April 1933 the plaintiff received a letter from the defendant dated 1 April 1933, according to which, following the plaintiff's dismissal as general manager following a shareholder resolution of 14 March 1933, his contract was now being terminated without notice because the store had been subject to the boycott and this boycotting had evidently taken place due to the person of the plaintiff. The plaintiff challenged his dismissal as unjustified but the defendant, in subsequent elucidations, upheld the dismissal.

The plaintiff contends that his contractually guaranteed remuneration should be paid as compensation for the loss of his contracted position.

He argues that the defendant used current anti-Jewish sentiment as a pretext to remove the plaintiff. Under the circumstances of this particular case, one could not claim that the plaintiff's position as manager of the store in C. had become untenable on account of his Jewishness, with the result that the defendant, so as not to suffer unreasonable losses of assets, had had to remove the Jewish plaintiff. Local conditions in C. were such that one could in no way speak of widespread public antisemitic sentiment. The public had not adopted a hostile attitude towards Jewish stores per se. The enterprise, under the name Fritz K. Deutsches Schuhwarenhaus, had been doing business for many years and was well established. Both its former owner, G., and the plaintiff were widely known to be Jews, but none of the customers, and these came from a broad range of social milieus, had taken offence at the Jewishness of the owners. The public would surely have continued to shop at this store in C. had the plaintiff continued to work there. The store would certainly not have suffered any loss of customers on account of the plaintiff. The defendant would have had no reason to expect any losses if the plaintiff continued to work at the store, particularly as, according to official statements, no subsequent impositions of a boycott of any kind were to be expected. The defendant, who tried to depict the Jewishness of the plaintiff as a reason for the public to take offence, only removed the name of the plaintiff, known in C. to be a Jew, from the store's name on 23 May 1933, and thus apparently had previously had no concern whatsoever that having the Jewish plaintiff's name as part of the store's name could make a negative impression on a customer or on any other body.

The alleged participation of the plaintiff in a disturbance was nothing more than a remark, in itself harmless, made to an SA man personally known to the plaintiff who was observing the customers going in and out of Sch., a Jewish business. The plaintiff, however, had been taken into protective custody in the evening, and on the following morning had simply been released following police questioning, as he could not be accused of any offence whatsoever. Evidently, the defendant had been searching for completely unfounded excuses just to remove the plaintiff from his position.

Both lower courts ruled against the defendant. The appeal was unsuccessful.

Certainly, the fact that an employee is of non-Aryan descent can be grounds for dismissal. But it is not automatically grounds in itself per se. It always depends on the circumstances of the individual case. The changed views and circumstances that have come to the fore as a result of the national uprising and renewal should largely be taken into account. A justified reason for summary dismissal, in particular, can be assumed if the retention of the employee in the employer's enterprise would give reason to expect detriment or even just the threat of such, to such a degree that the employer cannot be reasonably expected to retain the employee until the end of his established employment relation as per the contract.

The appeals court did not let these legal assessments go unrecognized. It examined the circumstances of the case closely, and found it unproven that, had the plaintiff continued to work in this store in a managerial capacity, the store would have had to fear a downturn. From the position the defendant took, as explained, the appeals court instead inferred that the defendant herself basically did not have any serious worries that the store would have suffered significant losses after 1 April 1933 on account of the Jewishness of the plaintiff. Since, according to public statements, a repeat of a boycott could not reasonably be expected, and, in the case of local business trade, the store in C. had a clientele that to this point had taken no offence at the Jewishness of the plaintiff, it was not clear that the enterprise of the defendant in C. would have had to encounter much greater difficulties if the defendant openly portrayed the store as an entirely German enterprise, in the event that the defendant had retained the plaintiff as manager. As a war veteran, the plaintiff had proved himself in such a manner that local customers, who otherwise might have little sympathy for Jews, would not deny him personal respect and would not have denied him employment at a long-standing store. To conclude, as the discussion of the development of the relationship between the disputing parties has demonstrated, when considering the relations of the parties to one another in light of the significance of the general situation at present, one should not disregard the aspects of the personal relationship between the parties in particular that may favour a contractual relationship being maintained, perhaps even at the risk of the defendant incurring a certain loss of assets.

(Reich Labour Court, decision dated 28 Oct. 1933, RAG 220/33. – Frankfurt an der Oder.)

II. The defendant, then still known as the 'German Pharmacists' Association', employed the plaintiff, son of a Jewish father and a mother of German blood, as a clerk to carry out advertising and other work as specified in a contract between them dated 12 October 1931. In a letter dated 1 April 1933, the defendant summarily dismissed the plaintiff, making reference to the government's regulation against so-called atrocity propaganda.[4]

---

4 This is probably a reference to the Regulation of the Reich President for the Defence against Treacherous Attacks on the Government of the National Uprising (the so-called *Heimtückegesetz*), 21 March 1933: *Reichsgesetzblatt*, 1933, I, p. 135.

The plaintiff regards the dismissal as inadmissible and is suing for continued payment of his wages.

Both lower courts rejected the claim. The appeals court reversed and remanded the case.

Fundamentally, one should assume, even given the changed attitudes the nationalist state and the German people in general have taken towards the Jews, that a statement stipulating that every employee of non-Aryan descent can be summarily dismissed should not be recognized in the realm of economic life. Laws and regulations issued by the Reich government with respect to the employment of non-Aryans refer to career civil servants, salaried employees and workers in public enterprises, lawyers, patent lawyers, physicians, dentists and dental technicians, commercial judges, lay judges, jurors, employment judges, tax advisors, and the like, all of them persons who provide public services or who are in positions of public trust. Corresponding legal measures do not exist with respect to employees in private firms, and their employment is thus not in itself subject to any restriction. However, this does not mean that the non-Aryan descent of an employee, given the fundamentally altered attitudes of the present time, *could not* provide significant grounds for the immediate termination of an employment contract, if, namely, the employer, in particular circumstances, cannot be reasonably expected to extend the contractual relationship to the end of the statutory period for giving notice. The new attitude of the German people to Jewry, rooted in the national uprising, is so fundamentally different to that of the past that it will not fail to have an impact on the area of private contract law. Yet this impact can always only be seen in the context of a given case, and only then can one judge whether and to what extent the race question fundamentally stands in the way of maintaining a contract of employment. What is required here is a considered view of the current situation, not a rash approach influenced by political events.

In its letters dated 1 April 1933 the German Pharmacists' Association justified the immediate dismissal of the plaintiff with reference to fighting Jewish atrocity propaganda abroad. In the lawsuit the defendant did not stick to this justification, and in light of the quite transitory, one-time character of this industrial action, which culminated primarily in the boycotting of Jewish stores, it was also manifestly unfounded. However, the justification, which deems the disputed judgement for dismissing the plaintiff to be radical, gives reason to doubt whether the appeals court proceeded in a legally sound manner in examining the key grounds given for that dismissal. One may wholly ignore the question whether the contractual position of the plaintiff was in fact managerial, as the lower court assumes. The contested judgement justifies the impossibility of continued employment of the plaintiff by the defendant only with reference to the danger of unrest or disturbance among the members [of the German Pharmacists' Association] and potential conflicts with official authorities, and evidently makes the assumption that the mere subjective suspicion of such a danger on the part of the defendant is sufficient grounds for dismissal. Such an assumption would be legally erroneous. Any assessment of the significance of grounds given for dismissal must, after all, consider whether circumstances exist, not solely in the view of the person serving notice of dismissal, but also in reality, according to which the employer can be reasonably expected to continue employing the person concerned. This scrutiny must therefore begin with the question as to whether the subjective opinion leading to the dismissal also has a substantial objec-

tive basis. A question in this direction is not evident in the appeal court's documents. A new examination based on the considerations noted is therefore required.
(Reich Labour Court, decision of 25 Nov. 1933, RAG 224/33. – Berlin.)

DOC. 98
Letter dated 26 January 1934 from a German to the Foreign Policy Office of the NSDAP, describing her impressions from a trip to Poland[1]

Letter, unsigned, dated 26 January 1934[2]

Report on a visit to my Polish city of birth, Łódź.
I spent four weeks in Poland before Christmas, specifically in my native city of Łódź. In November 1918 my husband picked me up in Łódź, and we left the city together with the German troops. It has now been fifteen years since I was last there and I was keen to find out what the conditions are like today. I have seen and heard a number of things, and take the liberty today of sending you a modest report of my observations.

On 16 November 1933 I met up with a young Swiss gentleman in Breslau who is studying in Stuttgart and whose parents live in Łódź. Our destination was the same, namely to celebrate his parents' silver wedding anniversary, an event to which I too had been invited. We had barely crossed the border at Drachenberg-Rawicz when we had our first experience, namely with a Jew from Germany on his way to Warsaw who had boarded our train in Poznań. He made an exhausted impression, and in a quiet, weary voice related how he had been beaten and kicked in Germany; his whole body was black and blue. We were speechless. But then my young Swiss companion jumped up and quite energetically refused to believe this fairy tale and said it was quite strange that one only ever heard this kind of outrageous news once one was over the border. One saw nothing of the sort in Germany, for we ourselves also came from Germany. The Jew did not respond, remained quietly in his corner, and then left. We were annoyed that we had so precipitously broken off the Jew's tale and not asked for his particulars, for he had said that he had relatives in Berlin. When, after some time, the Jew returned, we wanted to make up for this omission so that we could report on it back in Germany. My young companion politely asked the Jew to please tell us more about his experiences, but he would have nothing of it! He didn't want to talk any more whatsoever about politics, he shouted. We were Germans and remained Germans, and he, the Jew, was a Pole and remained a Pole. He hollered this twice, so loudly that I thought there would be a fearful row and matters would go badly for us. It was our good fortune that a Pole had joined us in our compartment while the Jew was absent; we told him about what the Jew had said and let him know that it was all a pack of lies. We told the Pole how exemplary and wonderful it was now in Germany, how proud we were of our Germany and of the man who now held Germany's destiny in his hands. We also told him about the great love our people had for their Chancellor. This Pole immediately took matters into his own

---
1 BArch, 62 Di 1, 1132/3846. This document has been translated from German.
2 Parts of the original are underlined by hand. The document is located in a file of the Foreign Policy Office of the NSDAP, a body established on 1 April 1933 and headed by Alfred Rosenberg.

hands & simply chased the Jew, with his suitcase, out of our compartment, threatening to report him to the police. Then the Pole confided that at heart he too was a friend of Hitler even though he was a Pole, but what was right must remain right. He added that only very few people knew his genuine feelings, for one had to be very careful about this in Poland. But I was nevertheless relieved when we had to change to the Łódź train in Kutno, for the affair could have turned a little nasty for me as a German. After all, we were already on Polish soil and, for the moment, a Jew here has more rights than a German. I was told later that 50 per cent of the Polish government are Jews, and I was also told that Marshal Piłsudski[3] has a Jew for a wife and that as a result the Jews always speak of him as 'their brother-in-law'. I told an old friend in Łódź about my experience on the train. He replied that one often heard such things; it was nothing new to him. This friend is a German Pole, has owned Fritsch's *Handbook of the Jewish Question*[4] for thirty years now, and even then, before the war, had given it to all his friends and acquaintances to read. Nowadays, Fritsch's book lies on his writing desk next to 'his house Bible', as he calls it, by which he means *Mein Kampf*! In his life, my friend has always had considerable business dealings with Jews, and because he has impeccable command of the Jewish jargon, Jews often took him for one of their own and told him things that they would never have related to a Christian. He knows the danger posed by the Jews through and through and said to me: 'I hope for God's sake that the German government doesn't get cold feet regarding the Jewish question and never gives up the fight!'

The voices raised against Jews in Polish officers' circles are becoming ever louder. A Polish officer told me that were it in his power, there would be twice-daily prayers for Adolf Hitler in all the churches. Many similar sentiments exist in Poland. But they can't be voiced aloud. One can genuinely feel sorry for all my friends, former Reich Germans and German-Russians now forced to be Poles, as they have to exercise such restraint in what they say. When they speak of our Reich Chancellor, they refer to him as 'Uncle Adolf', and Dr Goebbels is 'Uncle Doctor', so that outsiders will not know of whom they speak. Day after day they sit by the radio, at times with tears in their eyes, and they affirm again and again how they have followed and experienced all the events in Germany. I had travelled to Łódź with the intention of making my friends there into Hitler supporters, but lo and behold they were all already enthusiastic supporters in their hearts. With some we sang the 'Deutschlandlied',[5] very quietly so that one couldn't hear it outside, but we did so with raised arms. I was so moved that tears ran down my cheeks. The Germans in Łódź have still got their German grammar school, now 25 years old. It was built using private funds provided by the Germans, and continues to be maintained today, with difficulty, from private funds. I participated in the 25th anniversary celebrations. But

3 Józef Klemens Piłsudski (1867–1935), career officer; provisional Polish head of state, 1918–1922; after 1920 marshal of Poland; established an authoritarian regime in 1926; prime minister, 1926–1928 and 1930, and simultaneously minister of military affairs, 1926–1935.
4 Theodor Fritsch (ed.), *Handbuch der Judenfrage: Die wichtigsten Tatsachen zur Beurteilung des jüdischen Volkes*. Fritsch (1852–1933) first published this work in 1887 as *Antisemiten-Katechismus* and after 1896 as *Handbuch der Judenfrage*. The 49th edition appeared in 1944.
5 'Song of Germany'. The words are from a poem written in 1841 by August Heinrich Hoffmann von Fallersleben (1798–1874) and entitled 'Das Lied der Deutschen'. The third stanza is now the German national anthem.

even in this school they are not permitted to be fully German. One was not even above spying on the children so as to discover the disposition of their parents. But all this has only served to cement the Germans there even more closely together; they couldn't hear enough from me about our Führer! They pray, too, for our much beloved Chancellor. The books – *Horst Wessel*, *Mein Kampf*, *With Hitler on the Road to Power* and others – are bought by German children when they go on organized vacation trips to Germany and are then smuggled back into Poland. After the children returned last summer from such a trip, they excitedly talked about the SA men they had met who had shown and explained many things to them. One or another boy surreptitiously brought back a swastika, which he wore hidden under his tie. – They all asked me to convey my greetings to the Führer, to Dr Goebbels, to Germany, to the SA, and to the German Rhine river. When the international football match between Germany and Poland was held in Berlin before Christmas, many Germans and people favourably disposed to Germany had hoped to travel there for the occasion. It was made known beforehand that special trains would be sent to Berlin and those who wanted to attend the match should volunteer, as they would not have to pay the passport fees of 500 zloty, the equivalent of about 250 marks. The very first day about 10,000 people volunteered to go to Berlin; the government quickly withdrew its offer and determined that only 200 people would be allowed to travel. In Warsaw they doubtless thought it better to have 200 Hitler supporters return than tens of thousands. And that was what happened! Most of the sports fans came back full of enthusiasm and reported much that was good and nice about Germany, how well they were received, and how friendly Dr Goebbels had been. They brought newspapers and books, which were soon clandestinely passed on to be read by others. In the family where I stayed (Swiss nationals), one can find a comprehensive National Socialist library, augmented by the son every time he visits from Stuttgart. The father, who has lived for over thirty years in Łódź, has subscribed for at least ten years and through a German bookstore in Łódź to the *Völkischer Beobachter*. He also receives the *IB*[6] and the *NS-Funk*.[7] A simply wonderful spirit pervades this house. Most Germans, if at all possible, send money to Germany for the Winter Relief.[8] Foodstuffs & clothing are very cheap in Łódź, and yet very few can buy anything, as they have so little money. Poverty and need are very great, as industry is in tatters. On the street, one is besieged by beggars every few steps, even by Jews, which I had never experienced before. Many of my friends and acquaintances, too, suffer under these hardships and find it difficult to meet their daily needs. For now, they have no hope that the situation will improve and see the future bleakly. – The radio is now their best friend because through it they are connected to Germany, and can feel happy inside for at least a few hours. Very few can now afford to travel to Germany because the passport fees are very steep. Over Christmas, my Swiss friends visited their son in Germany; they wanted for once to celebrate a genuine German Christmas in the Third Reich. They told me that right after I

---

6 Probably the *Illustrierter Beobachter*, which appeared from 1926 to 1945. This illustrated weekly was published in Munich by the NSDAP publishing house Franz Eher.
7 The newspaper *NS-Funk* was published by the Reich Chamber of Radio in Berlin and Munich and appeared in 1933–1939. From 1930 to 1933 it appeared as a weekly under the title *Der Deutsche Sender* and was published by the Reich Association of German Radio Licence Holders.
8 An annual charitable drive launched in 1931 to provide poorer Germans with food, clothes, coal, and other items to help them through the winter.

left for Łódź, a Polish neighbour had come to them to warn them to be more careful about what they did and did not do. A Polish secret agent had stopped by and made detailed enquiries. Four of us from Germany were at the silver anniversary, and I think it appeared suspicious that there were so many German visitors. The Germans are even spied on to discover whether they speak Polish or German at home: everything is grounds for suspicion. I myself thank God that I turned my back on Łódź right at the end of the war. I brought my mother and sister to Germany eight years ago. My mother lives with me, and my sister, currently applying for German nationality, lives in Breslau. I have named no names in my report so that my friends in Łódź will be spared further problems, for they are already in such a bad way. I enclose a (newspaper) description of the 25th anniversary of the German grammar school in Łódź.[9] The interior of this wonderful building was completely destroyed last year on Palm Sunday. The windows and the glass panes in the doors were completely shattered. None of the wonderful pictures on the walls were left intact, inkpots were thrown against the walls, door curtains and window curtains were ripped down, and tables, chairs, books, and files were thrown into the courtyard and burned. Two lovely pianos and a harmonium were thrown into the courtyard from the first floor and smashed up there. All this was the work of a few young communists and a horde of young Jewish louts. The police arrived only once everything had been destroyed. The parents came with their children the next day, and they were literally walking on shards of glass. It was a sad sight: the children cried aloud for their beautiful school, and the parents had tears in their eyes too. Yet even this event has only served to cement the Germans in Łódź even more tightly together. And now I have a major request that I feel very strongly about.

When Dr Goebbels or another member of the Reich government speaks again on the radio, could he please direct a few brief words to the *Germans abroad*, send his greetings and thank them for their faithful devotion? The Germans in Poland would then feel their inner connection to Germany, it would certainly give them great joy, and it would be a ray of light in their difficult situation. –

Our Führer wrote in his book *Mein Kampf*:

> Only he who through his own experience knows what it means to be a German without being allowed to belong to the dear fatherland will be able to comprehend the deep longing that burns at all times in the hearts of the children who are separated from the motherland. This longing tortures those it has seized and denies them contentedness and happiness until the doors of the father's house open and the common blood finds peace and quiet again in the common Reich.[10]

I request that this letter not be published, and emphasize again that I do not want to create any difficulties for my friends.

I only hope that my report is forwarded to our Chancellor so that he learns what loyal friends he has abroad.

---

9 The newspaper clipping has not been preserved in the file.
10 Adolf Hitler, *Mein Kampf*, trans. from German (New York: Reynal & Hitchcock, 1941 [German edn, 1925–1926]), p. 161.

DOC. 99
Memorandum dated January 1934 on the situation of the Jewish population, sent by the Reich Representation of German Jews to the Reich government[1]

Submitted to the Reich government by the Reich Representation of German Jews[2]
Berlin, January 1934.
Printed as manuscript no. 16 by the Reich Representation of German Jews.
Printer: Max Lichtwitz, Berlin.

Even as the Reich government appeals to the entire German nation to renew the fatherland, both emotional and objective hardships weigh on German Jews – who are rooted in Germany and in German culture. Jewish descent and fellowship, to which generation after generation has committed itself with a pride born of heritage, have been deprecated and reviled. Jewish persons whose conduct no one questions are dismissed from office, and expelled from profession and position, their families all too often cast into deep economic misery. If German Jews have sacrifices imposed upon them for reasons of state, then patriotic devotion and Jewish dignity would demand their silence. But speaking out becomes a duty when it is a matter of the continued existence of German Jewry and when the basis for our religious community is threatened with collapse; when measures are directed against German Jews, it not only hurts them but runs counter to Germany's welfare.

For this reason, the *Reich Representation of German Jews*, in which Jewish communities and their regional associations work together, and which enjoys the trust and confidence of German Jewry's large organizations,[3] submits the following to the government of the Reich.

I.
Through legislation passed this year, Jews, aside from some well-known exceptions, have basically been excluded from the administration of justice, from offices in the Reich, the state, municipalities, and other public corporations. This has been justified by the argument that in a Reich being newly constructed on a racial basis, Jews may not exercise or hold state powers. In addition, the share of Jews in all academic professions has been substantially reduced or even eliminated. By contrast, in employment, the Reich government, which works to support and calm the German economy, has ignored the Aryan principle in its legislation. If the Aryan principle were to be extended to commercial life, it would not just rob German Jews of the possibility of economic existence. Goods produced in the German economy, and valuable domestic and international trade relationships connected to individuals, would also suffer severe harm. Yet numerous decrees

---

1 BArch, R 3001/5107, fol. 27. This document has been translated from German. The memorandum is seventy-eight pages long, including the cover page. Apart from the table of contents for appendix I, the text that follows this introduction and the appendices is not reproduced here: Appendix I, Measures taken against the Jews in economic life; Appendix II, Obstructions to vocational training in agriculture and crafts. Several examples, as well as Appendix III (no title). The introduction is published in Kulka (ed.), *Deutsches Judentum*, vol. 1, pp. 117–122.
2 This memorandum, along with the request for a personal meeting, was also sent to State Secretary Lammers: letter from the Reich Representation to Lammers on 19 Jan. 1934, in Kulka (ed.), *Deutsches Judentum*, vol. 1, p. 118.
3 Footnote in the original: 'Central Association of German Citizens of the Jewish Faith, Reich League of Jewish Combat Veterans, Zionist Federation for Germany.'

issued by Reich and state authorities, by Party agencies and municipalities, and by professional associations of all kinds have made the *economic activities of Jews as employees and employers* difficult. In some parts of the country and some economic sectors it has become near-impossible to work. We provide some examples of this in Appendix I. They are only a small subset from the last months, but even they provide a clear picture. They show how German Jews, their places already largely taken away from them through legislation, are boycotted in those free professions where they are still permitted to work. Now efforts are under way to exclude them from or drive them out of trade and industry, crafts and agriculture.

Not just impoverishment but pauperization must be the result of such intrusion into the economy. It is unmistakable that this development has already begun. The taxable capacity of German Jews is dwindling, and the Jewish communities directly affected can barely meet the burdens increasingly placed on them to provide religious, social, and cultural welfare. If nothing changes, the collapse of these communities can scarcely be avoided. As this cannot be in the interest of the new Reich, we turn to the Reich government for relief. It will be able to reconcile the demands of the new state with the living conditions of German Jews. The precondition is that in the future the unequal treatment of Aryans and Jews in the labour force should stop. Every effort to displace or hinder gainfully employed Jews should stop, regardless of the direction from which this pressure comes.

II.

Closely connected to this matter is the question as to which profession those Jews should choose who are now already unemployed. Aside from those made redundant by the economic crisis, two groups in particular are the focus: first, those working persons who have been removed from their freelance professions or from their employment as a result of legislation or private boycotts; second, the young persons who now, the more they are blocked from pursuing academic studies, are increasingly demanding imminent training in a trade or profession. We are aware that the occupational profile of German Jews, their preponderance in the academic professions and in larger cities, has been unhealthy. Knowing this, Jewish youths have been trying for years to rectify this grievance, which arose partially out of a particular historical development. Significant preparatory work has been done to set in motion a comprehensive *occupational restructuring* of German Jews. The desire of Jewish youth to engage in physical labour of all kinds exists. But by the same token, willingness must also exist to integrate them into occupational groups where they have hitherto been under-represented relative to their share in the population. Here, too, we ask for governmental assistance. We enclose an *Appendix II*. It shows how the trade and agricultural professions attempt to bar access to training and keep Jewish people from being integrated. Despite all our educational efforts, Jewish youth would be in despair if they did not have the prospect of future work. We therefore expect that *fundamentally, no profession should be closed to Jews and that in the restructuring overseen by Reich agencies in the areas of crafts and labour, agriculture and forestry, Jews will also be able to enjoy training and integration.*

III.

Even if this happens, which we hope, many Jewish people, given the constraints of the current situation, will have to emigrate. It is true that for a century, the Jewish part of the population of the German Reich has been dwindling. One can point to the two largest German states: in Prussia, Jews made up 1.2 per cent of the population in 1816, but by 1925, they only constituted 1.06 per cent. In 1818 Jews still accounted for 1.45 per cent in Bavaria, but by 1925, this had fallen to 0.66 per cent. The situation in the largest cities is no different. Berlin had 5.14 per cent Jews in 1895, but only 4.29 per cent in 1925. Hamburg had 4.4 per cent Jews in 1866, but by 1925 this had fallen to 1.73 per cent. Since then, the number of Jews has fallen still further.

Even so, one may assume that many German Jews will no longer be able to find any living space in Germany and will have to emigrate. Both German and Jewish reputations require that this emigration take place in an orderly and planned manner. This presupposes that appropriate occupational training takes place in Germany first, and that, with the help of the German authorities and of Jewish organizations, emigration will be to those countries ready to accept and in need of the correspondingly trained workers. If this occurs, the immigrant in his new location will maintain an attachment to the country in which his parents and ancestors lived and in which he was educated and trained. Family ties and cultural connections will then establish valuable economic links to the old country. If the immigrant knows his trade, the respect for German skills will increase abroad. If, on the other hand, he becomes a burden to immigrant welfare associations, condescension towards the alms receiver will be all too readily paired with a disdainful aversion towards the country from which he came. We therefore ask the Reich government *to support the work that we and organizations responsible for emigration to Palestine and other countries undertake in the area of emigration.*

IV.
Emotional burdens weigh on us even more heavily than all our economic needs. The racial premise on which the National Socialist state is built assumes the idea of the otherness of its Jewish component. But no community that prides itself on honour and dignity can accept an accusation of inferiority. We German Jews have had to experience the efforts to defame us in Germany. In *Appendix III* we have collected a few examples, but everyone knows many more. We know that government authorities and senior Party echelons have condemned and deplored the raw and insulting form such assertions have taken. Our pride as German Jews, particularly with respect to our children, prevents us from expressing in detail what we feel about them. But we do wish to point to one thing because it has a political significance: Jews live in those countries with which Germany must compete for international standing. No atrocity propaganda affects them more than hearing about its highly respected lineage and faith being defamed in German newspapers and demonstrations. The hurt is all the deeper when it is not just an occasional faux pas in the heat of a political campaign but rather premeditated and repeated statements, and this at a time when the community seems stable, when it comes from inside a state with the power and means to oversee and guide public opinion.

From whatever perspective one regards this question, we believe we can express the expectation *that in future every defamation of the Jewish community and its lineage be prohibited.*

In submitting this exposition, we are well aware of just how many tasks currently occupy the Reich government. We have therefore limited ourselves to those matters that can be delayed the least, also for the sake of the German state. To draw attention to these matters is not just our duty towards our own communities but just as much a duty to the Reich government. We do so in the knowledge of having served the German fatherland by so doing.

January 1934.
Reich Representation of German Jews
Berlin-Charlottenburg, 158 Kantstr.

Appendix I
Measures taken against the Jews in economic life

Table of contents.
1. Legislative measures.
2. Occupational restrictions placed on Jewish lawyers admitted to the bar.
3. Measures taken against Jewish physicians.
4. Exclusion of Jewish artists.
5. Exclusion of Jewish press photographers.
6. Against Jewish accountants.
7. Discrimination of Jewish firms in contracts with the authorities.
8. Subsistence vouchers may not be taken from Jewish firms as payment.
9. Vouchers for benefit recipients may not be accepted from Jewish firms.
10. Jewish radio dealers may not sell the 'people's [radio] receiver'.[4]
11. Festive costume for members of the German Labour Front. Exclusion of Jewish firms.
12. Public credit institutions cancel the credits of Jewish debtors.
13. Advertising ban.
14. Aryan supplier directories.
15. Call to boycott Jewish firms.
16. Civil servants are prohibited from buying from Jews.
17. Party members are prohibited from buying from Jews.
18. A general prohibition on buying from Jews.
19. Those who shop in Jewish stores are pilloried.
20. Jews are prohibited from entering localities.
21. Exclusion of Jews from the agricultural trade.
22. Measures taken against Jews in the flour trade.
23. Exclusion of Jews from the barley trade.
24. Elimination of Jews from the hops trade.
25. Measures taken against Jews in the tobacco trade.
26. Dairy cooperatives are against fostering business connections with Jews.
27. Elimination of Jews from the livestock trade.
28. Exclusion of Jewish livestock dealers from stockyards and livestock markets.
29. Exclusion of Jewish market vendors. Discrimination in admittance.

---

4 The People's Radio (Volksempfänger) refers to a series of simple and affordable radio models developed by order of Joseph Goebbels from 1933 to facilitate public access to the radio and thereby significantly increase exposure to National Socialist propaganda.

DOC. 100
The Gestapo Central Office informs the Prussian Minister of the Interior about a meeting of the Central Association of German Citizens of the Jewish Faith held in Deutsch-Krone on 4 February 1934[1]

Letter from the Gestapo Central Office (II F 2 259/8) (signature illegible), in Berlin, to the Prussian Minister of the Interior (received 28 February 1934), dated 19 February 1934

Re: activities of Jewish associations

On 4 February a general meeting of the 'Central Association of German Citizens of the Jewish Faith' took place in the anteroom of the synagogue in Deutsch-Krone. It was opened and chaired by the representative of the Jewish Community of Deutsch-Krone, the retailer Leo Schönfeld, who was born on 23 October 1874 in Deutsch-Krone and still resides there. The meeting was attended by about a hundred Jews. After making some introductory remarks, Schönfeld gave the floor to a certain Ernst *Behrend*[2] from the Central Association's main office in Berlin. Behrend began his remarks by explaining to the attendees the aims and objectives of the 'Central Association of German Citizens of the Jewish Faith', stressing that it was the largest Jewish association in Germany and had brought forth outstanding men in business and in public life. He commented that although the national revolution had had a decisive impact on Jewish conditions, there was absolutely no reason to despair. He stated that the truth of the matter was that a large portion of the Jewish population had drifted away from the traditions of their forefathers, who had made their living as honest craftsmen, farmers, and farm labourers, and added that if one or the other Jewish commercial counsellor would look back three generations, they would discover that their forefathers had still been honest craftsmen at that time. These financiers, according to Behrend, did not make up as large a portion of the Jewish population as stated in public reports. As evidence he referred to the head of the Winter Relief Agency in Berlin, Staatsrat[3] Spiewok, who had determined that 40 per cent of the 142,000 Jews living in Berlin relied on assistance from the Winter Relief Agency. Behrend went on to quote from an article[4] by Dr Wilhelm

---

1 GStA PK, I HA, Rep. 77, Abt. II, Tit. 4043, Nr. 477, fol. 2r–v. This document has been translated from German.
2 Correctly: Ernst Josef Behrendt (1884–1944), trade union official; from 1919 member of the executive board of the German Democratic Party (DDP); district secretary of the Federation of Salaried Employees' Unions in Upper Silesia; from 1923 city councillor in Beuthen and member of the executive board of the CV; head of the emigration department of the Relief Association in Berlin, 1938; deported to Theresienstadt, 1943; in 1944 transferred to Auschwitz, then to Dachau concentration camp, where he died at the end of the year.
3 Correctly: Stadtrat (city councillor).
4 In his article 'Zur Judenfrage' ('On the Jewish question') Grau provided an overview of the history of the Jews from the Middle Ages via the time of emancipation to the National Socialist era. He advocated using the 'race principle' to solve the 'Jewish question' in the National Socialist state. According to Grau, a solution to this question that included *Mischlinge* and combat veterans would not be possible without causing hardships for the individuals concerned: *Völkischer Beobachter* (northern German edition), 21–22 Jan. 1934, p. 5.

Grau[5] on German Jews and their participation in the economic life of the German people, which appeared in the *Völkischer Beobachter* on 26 January 1934.[6] Behrend emphasized that in view of the economic conditions abroad, he could not recommend emigration to anyone. In this context he gave an account of the political and economic life of Jews and Arabs in Palestine, which, according to his statements, was not a good one. He added that if the 'Zionist Federation' repeatedly relied on the fact that Palestine was a territory that belonged to the Jews and had to be given back, this was indeed understandable from a religious perspective. However, the economic and political conditions in Palestine did not allow for such a possibility. In his closing remarks, Behrend said that the Jewish population would have to accept the prevailing conditions and could devote themselves to occupations in agriculture and the skilled crafts or other occupational opportunities, while adding that it was anticipated that the life prospects of Jews would be regulated by legislation.

DOC. 101

On 5 February 1934 Rabbi Wahrmann reports on the mounting social and pastoral problems in his Silesian district[1]

Memorandum, unsigned [Wahrmann],[2] dated 5 February 1934

Report on my activities in the second half of 1933

1. *General activities.*

Broadly speaking, the restructuring of Jewish life brought about by last year's state legislation did not take place until the second half of the year. The activities in the reporting period were therefore heavily influenced by this process, which played a crucial role in determining the nature and tempo of the work. An ageing population and low birth rates had already threatened the existence of small communities in previous years, and now, on top of that, heavy migration is putting the survival of many small communities in real jeopardy. It is not only the shortfall of tax receipts that is critical, but also equally the diminishing numbers, which is leading to the disappearance of community life. The reasons for the exodus are in most cases purely economic in nature, but in a number of cases the motivation also includes a spiritual component. The Jew in a small community who regards himself as isolated and lonely feels more secure in the midst of a large community. Older people in particular want to spend their twilight years at the centre

---

5 Dr Wilhelm Grau (1910–2000), historian; from 1936 edited the section entitled 'History of the Jewish question' in the *Historische Zeitschrift*; managing director of the research department for the Jewish question at the Reich Institute for History of the New Germany in Munich, 1936–1938; joined the NSDAP in 1937; director of the Institute for Research into the Jewish Question in Frankfurt am Main, 1940–1942; served in the Wehrmacht from 1942; after 1945 owner of a printing company.

6 The article in fact appeared a week earlier: *Völkischer Beobachter* (northern German edition), 21–22 Jan. 1934, p. 5.

1 CAHJP, P 33/29. This document has been translated from German.

2 Dr Nachum Wahrmann (1895–1961), rabbi; district rabbi in Oels, 1929–1939; lecturer in the Talmud and history at the Jewish-Theological Seminar in Breslau, 1933–1938; co-founder of *Germania Judaica*; in 1939 emigrated to Palestine, where he worked as a teacher until 1953.

of vibrant Jewish life. I viewed the primary objective over my activities of the past half year as alleviating, as far as possible, the sense of isolation felt by Jewish people in small communities while also strengthening their spirit.

2. In Oels.
Migration has also had a very significant impact here. The community has lost 20 per cent of its members and just as much tax capacity. But despite this, Jewish community life has not suffered in any way. I still give religious instruction two afternoons [a week], and since November I have additionally taught a two-hour course for adults (modern Hebrew). Several out-of-town members from neighbouring communities also take part in this course, which has been very well attended and has met with considerable interest. On Saturday afternoons in the synagogue I have just introduced regular youth meetings devoted to fostering the synagogal and domestic liturgy. I have also taken pains to perform, in regular contact with the executive board and charitable associations, all other cultural and social work in the community (lectures, winter relief, etc.).

3. In the district.
The work in the district was carried out in the same manner as during the first half-year. A hindrance over the past few months was the fact that although the synagogues in many of the communities lacked heating, the community members did not want to move to a public meeting place, and it was often necessary to refrain from using private rooms for fear of malicious gossip. As a result, many events could not take place, and visiting these communities must be limited to meetings with the executive board and special counselling sessions.

4. Pastoral care in institutions.
I continued with my visits to the Leubus Provincial State Hospital and Nursing Home. At the instruction of the Prussian Regional Association for several months now these visits have taken place only twice a month, which I think is insufficient, considering the large number of patients (average number of attendees at the worship services is twenty). For several months during the reporting period I made weekly visits to the Oels prison.

5. Inspection of religious instruction.
During the reporting period the following changes occurred in the district: our cantor Mr Pakula has moved permanently to Gross-Wartenberg and gives the religious instruction there. Mr P. also teaches in Strehlen and Frankenstein. Mr Zarek[3] has now taken over the teaching duties in Bernstadt for good. He is also giving instruction in Festenberg again. Mr Wagschal,[4] Breslau, has replaced Miss Ehrlich as the instructor in the Neumarkt school district, and Rabbi Brilling[5] has replaced Mr Czollek as the instructor

---

3 Probably Hermann Zarek (b. 1906); he later emigrated to Belgium.
4 Wilhelm Wagschal (1906–1980); lived in Breslau and emigrated to Palestine in 1939.
5 Dr Bernhard Brilling (1906–1987), rabbi and historian; from 1927 archivist of Breslau's Jewish Community; from Nov. 1938 to Jan. 1939 imprisoned in Buchenwald concentration camp; emigrated to Palestine in 1939, then worked as an archivist in Tel Aviv; returned to Germany in 1957; awarded a doctorate in 1958; worked as a research assistant and in 1979 became professor at the University of Münster.

in Trebnitz and Trachenberg. Since Mr Badler,[6] Fraustadt, now has a district ticket that includes travel as far as Wohlau, I recently suggested to the Association of Synagogue Congregations of the province of Lower Silesia, Breslau, that he be assigned the instruction in Steinau and Kohlau, which would enable savings to be made in fees and travel expenses. The complete prohibition of shechita[7] has significantly freed up Mr Badler's schedule, and he can therefore take over these teaching duties with no difficulty. During the reporting period I inspected Mr Badler (Neusalz, Fraustadt, and Guhrau) and Mr Pakula (Gross-Wartenberg). The inspection has not yet been concluded. Upon completion I will send in the inspection forms.

6. Overview.

My activities during the reporting period extended to the following localities: Bernstadt, Festenberg, Fraustadt, Guhrau, Leubus, Militsch, Namslau, Neumarkt, Neusalz, Oels, Sagan, Sprottau, Steinau, Trebnitz, and Ulbersdorf, and were structured as follows: 26 sermons, 7 lectures, 1 speech, 28 meetings and community assemblies, 4 inspections of religious instruction, 5 official pastoral acts, 101 pastoral counselling sessions, 27 official trips, 6 institution visits, and 343 letters to communities, associations, and civil servants.

DOC. 102

On 7 February 1934 the Dresden Chamber of Industry and Commerce calls on the Saxon Ministry of Economics to exclude Jews from serving as sworn experts[1]

Letter from the Dresden Chamber of Industry and Commerce (B/Be. 5941/33), signed Bohlmann[2] and Queck,[3] to the Saxon Ministry of Economics, Dresden, dated 7 February 1934 (copy)

Re: non-Aryans serving as sworn experts.
While a regulation of the Ministry of Justice stipulates that non-Aryan court-sworn experts must be forced to step down from their appointments if they do not resign voluntarily, the Reich Ministry of Economics has unfortunately still not issued instructions regarding the dismissal of non-Aryan sworn experts and samplers on the basis of § 36 of the Commercial Code. This makes it possible, for example, that of the approximately 1,000 experts serving in the Chamber of Industry and Commerce, some 250 are still non-Aryans. At the 'Berlin Court of Arbitration (Higher Court of Arbitration) of the German Land Trade League', the Berlin Chamber of Industry and Commerce has even adopted the following provisions:

---

6 Elias Badler (b. 1890); lived in Liegnitz in 1939.
7 Method of slaughtering permitted animals and poultry in accordance with Jewish law. It was prohibited in Germany in April 1933. On the impact of the ban, see Doc. 73, 24 August 1933.

1 Sächsisches Staatsarchiv, Hauptstaatsarchiv Dresden, Außenministerium/1723, fols. 63–64. This document has been translated from German.
2 Probably Dr Johannes Bohlmann, lawyer; legal advisor in Dresden; owner of the company Bohlmann & Co., which specialized in business consulting.
3 Dr Johannes F. Queck (1890–1966); deputy legal advisor, 1934; managing director of the Dresden Chamber of Industry and Commerce, 1940.

If both parties in a dispute are non-Aryans, the Court of Arbitration is to consist of an Aryan chairman and two non-Aryan associate judges; if one of the disputing parties is a non-Aryan, then upon request one of the two [associate judges] must be a non-Aryan. The same applies to the Higher Court of Arbitration.

Such a provision does nothing less than propagate the use of non-Aryan arbitrators and prevents the administration of justice in the National Socialist spirit; it also plainly contravenes a recent decree of the Reich Ministry of Justice regarding the barring of non-Aryan arbitrators[4] from practice (details concerning this can be found in the *Berliner Börsenzeitung*, issue 47, 28 January 1934).[5]

A non-Aryan sworn sampler, for example, has drawn on this state of affairs in not stepping down voluntarily from his appointment after we lodged a request; he refused to resign. We have no other leverage against him because of § 53 of the Commercial Code, since we have nothing on him and he is also a combat veteran. Nonetheless, it does not seem right that non-Aryans can continue to serve as experts.

We therefore ask that action be taken to ensure that guidelines regarding the removal of non-Aryan sworn experts from their appointments are promptly issued by the Reich Ministry of Economics, and furthermore that such provisions of the arbitration court described above cease to apply.[6]

Heil Hitler!

DOC. 103

On 9 February 1934 the Central Germany Branch of the Central Association of German Citizens of the Jewish Faith (CV) reports on the representation of the interests of Jewish salaried employees[1]

Letter from the CV's Central Germany Branch (S/B 491/92/34), Sabatzky, Leipzig, to the CV's main office (received on 10 February 1934), Berlin, and to the *C.V.-Zeitung* (requesting publication),[2] dated 9 February 1934[3]

On 6 February the CV's unemployed persons group hosted a lecture evening 'the Jewish salaried employee in the new state'. The group's representative, Hans *Blankenstein*,[4] chaired the meeting. Counsel Kurt *Sabatzky* took the floor first, calling attention to the

---

4 On 23 Jan. 1934 the Reich Ministry of Justice decreed that parties to court proceedings may reject an arbitrator of non-Aryan descent on the basis of § 1032(3) of the Code of Civil Procedure: cited in Walk (ed.), *Das Sonderrecht für die Juden im NS-Staat*, p. 69.
5 The Reich Ministry of Justice's decision to bar non-Aryan arbitrators was taken at the suggestion of the Reich Foreign Office: see 'Der Reichsjustizminister zur Ausschaltung nichtarischer Schiedsrichter', *Berliner Börsen-Zeitung*, 28 Jan. 1934, p. 4.
6 From 1937 the chambers of industry and commerce no longer appointed Jews to serve as experts. Directive of the German Chamber of Industry and Commerce, 15 April 1937: Walk (ed.), *Das Sonderrecht für die Juden im NS-Staat*, p. 188.

1 RGVA, 721k-1-265. This document has been translated from German.
2 See *C.V.-Zeitung*, 15 Feb. 1934, p. 6.
3 The original contains several annotations, such as 'to be filed'.
4 Hans Blankenstein (b. 1903); resided in Leipzig, from where he was deported on 10 May 1942 to the town of Bełżyce, near Lublin.

expulsion of Jewish salaried employees from business enterprises and from trade unions. The speaker stressed emphatically that the CV had made the greatest possible efforts to alleviate the associated hardships. He added that in the case of those employees who had been summarily dismissed, the CV had succeeded in securing millions of marks in salaries through the judgements handed down by labour courts.[5] The next speaker, the retired labour court judge Dr Bruno Mannes, gave an overview of the new labour law. He called attention to the new provisions for enterprises, and stressed that an Aryan Paragraph has not been included in the new labour law.[6] He reported that the Jewish employer is the leader of the Council of Trust to the same extent as the non-Jewish employer. He went on to say that it was necessary to work towards ensuring that Jewish salaried employees soon received recognized representation, which should also be able to operate social relief funds.

DOC. 104

On 13 February 1934 the hotelier Hanns Kilian complains to the municipality of Garmisch about the denunciation of an Austrian performer as a Jew[1]

Letter from Hanns Kilian[2] to the municipality of Garmisch, dated 13 February 1934 (copy)

Subject: letter from Dr Max Vollkommer,[3] Munich, dated 14 January.

I refer to the discussion with your magistrate Mr Holzschuh and comment, as requested, on the letter that Dr Vollkommer addressed to Minister Esser on 14 January about the incident that took place on 30 December in the Alpenhof Park Casino.

I would like to state that it does not correspond to the facts that the performer engaged at the time, Ridi Grün, behaved – as alleged by the writer of the letter – in any way that was offensive or brash. Ridi Grün only performed Viennese folk and operetta songs whose quality and propriety have found favour all over the world through the style and simplicity of their delivery, and this also enabled her to secure the utmost success with large audiences in attendance.

When I engage performers through the agency and the booking department of the Munich office, it is unfortunately not possible for me to ascertain if these performers are of Jewish descent or not, and it would be to the credit of Dr Vollkommer if he saw to it that the booking office did not give any assignments to Jewish personnel.

In any event, if Ridi Grün is in fact a Jewess (I do not know and am unfortunately unable to verify this), then I must emphatically reject the allegation that she had the audacity to disparage the German people in my hotel through her performance. At any rate, I do not know anything about such a thing.

---

5 See the passage about the successful representation of the dismissed Karstadt employees before the labour court in Doc. 60, June 1933.
6 This is a reference to the Law for the Regulation of National Labour, 20 Jan. 1934: *Reichsgesetzblatt*, 1934, I, pp. 45–56.

1 BArch, NS 23/158. This document has been translated from German.
2 Hanns Kilian (1905–1981), sportsman and businessman; successful bobsledder; took part in the Beer Hall Putsch, 1923; owner and manager of the Alpenhof; SA-Sturmbannführer and leader of the Garmisch branch of the National Socialist Motor Corps, 1934; president of the German Bobsleigh and Luge Federation from 1952.

In my opinion, it would have been more useful, and better all round, if Dr Vollkommer – since he, after all, knew who I was – had told me that night what he thought, instead of bringing this matter to the attention of Minister Esser. I imagine that the minister is inundated with quite different and more important tasks, and it is thus inappropriate to bother him with such matters.

I would be very grateful to Dr Vollkommer if he could advise me on where to find good and genuine German performers for my weekly events, for at the ball hosted by the German Stage on 7 February, I unfortunately observed that the performers were poorly received, and that the master of ceremonies engaged for the evening, Carl Maria Braun, delivered such unbelievable remarks (dirty jokes and wisecracks of the worst kind) that my guests were outraged.

I think that if such a mistake is made by the head of the Combat League for German Culture, Dr Heinz, by way of the section head for theatre in the Propaganda Department, Mr Schneider Franke[4] from Munich, who books the performers through the Society for Literature and the Performing Arts, then Dr Vollkommer's accusation must be unreasonable.

It is easy for guests from Garmisch-Partenkirchen to hurl criticism and insults, as these people understand neither the business nor how difficult it is to satisfy all tastes, which, as is well known, vary widely. However, when something inappropriate actually does happen, it is unfortunately not possible to legislate for this beforehand.

In any event, I can assure the municipality of Garmisch that I have endeavoured, and will continue to endeavour, to run my hotel according to the principles of the 'New Germany', and ask you to give credence to my assurance.

Heil Hitler

signed Hanns Kilian

NB. As I learned from Mr R. Kunig,[5] the long-standing operetta tenor for Munich's Gärtnerplatz Theatre, which performed in our hotel yesterday, Ms Ridi Grün is not a Jewess, according to a statement he made. This was also confirmed by my establishment's master of ceremonies, Otto Clemente, who asked Ms Ridi Grün last summer if she was a Jewess, to which she replied in the negative. This therefore excuses me from Dr Vollkommer's accusation, and I would like to leave to him the task of establishing whether the said performer is a Jewess or not.[6] Dr Vollkommer probably mistook her Viennese accent for Jewish jargon.

---

3 Probably Dr Max Vollkommer (1894–1985), physician; resident of Munich; joined the NSDAP in 1931. Acting 'in advocacy of the aims of our Movement', Dr Max Vollkommer, an SA-Obersturmführer and Party member, had informed the Bavarian state minister without portfolio, Hermann Esser, that on 30 Dec. 1933, at a dance event at the Alpenhof hotel, an 'offensive, brash Jew' had sung the 'Lied vom Hünen' ('Song of the Giant') in a way that could be interpreted as a 'disparagement of Germany': ibid.
4 Probably Josef Rudolf Schneider Franke, writer; author of works including *Der Goldene Käfig* (1937).
5 Rudolf Bonifaz Kunig (1894–1951), actor in Munich.
6 Though the Austrian Ridi Maria Grün, a resident of Vienna, only learned of the denunciation later, she lodged a complaint on 25 April 1934 with the Supreme SA Command in Munich. She rejected the accusation that she was a Jew. Because she felt she had suffered 'considerable damage', she demanded that Vollkommer be brought to account, and threatened to bring the matter to Hitler's attention: BArch, NS 23/158.

DOC. 105
On 18 February 1934 a Jewish pupil and her parents write to a teacher who emigrated to Palestine[1]

Letter from Ruth,[2] Becky, and Iwan Moses,[3] Hamburg, to Lilli Traumann,[4] Tel Aviv, dated 18 February 1934

Dear sweet, sweet Miss Traumann,

We thank you warmly for the nice, long letter. On Monday we visited the harbour. We walked on the wobbly bridge and watched a man feed the seagulls. We also saw large ships, launches, tugboats, and barges. On the way back we went to the Bismarck Monument and climbed up on it. Afterwards we walked down a very, very long and steep hill. We were then supposed to go down all the way to the bottom, where Miss Traumann was.[5] We said that there were not enough steps but we had to come down anyway. From there we went to school[6] and from school to home.

I had so much looked forward to going to Eretz,[7] but my parents said that it won't be possible any time soon; we are all very sad about this. I celebrated the 'New Year of the Trees'[8] quite nicely in Bar Kokhba.[9] Each child received a riddle to solve and a Jaffa orange, as well as a young tree to take care of.

Miss Traumann, can all of the children that you meet over there already speak Hebrew?

Best wishes from your pupil Ruth Moses

Dear Miss Traumann,

could it be that you like it so much there that you have decided not to come back? You haven't seen our relatives, have you? A cousin of mine (surname Landshut), whose

---

1 Published in Behörde für Schule, Jugend und Berufsbildung, Amt für Schule, Hamburg (ed.), 'Aus Kindern werden Briefe': Dokumente zum Schicksal jüdischer Kinder und Jugendlicher in der NS-Zeit (Hamburg: Freie und Hansestadt Hamburg, Amt für Schule, 1999), p. 8. This document has been translated from German.
2 Ruth Moses (1925–1941?) was deported from Hamburg to Minsk on 8 Nov. 1941.
3 Becky and Iwan Moses were the parents of Ruth Moses. Iwan Moses, born in Hamburg in 1888, initially worked as a bookbinder and later became works manager. Rifka (Becky) Moses, born in Constantinople in 1896, and her husband were deported along with their daughter on 8 Nov. 1941 from Hamburg to Minsk, where they were probably murdered.
4 Lilli Traumann (b. 1903), teacher; from 1926 teacher at the Israelitische Töchterschule (Israelite Girls' School) in Hamburg; a staunch Zionist; she emigrated in 1933 to Palestine, where she published Hebrew teaching material for the children of German immigrants.
5 After Lilli Traumann's emigration her sister Susi took over the teaching of third-year pupils. Susi S. Traumann (b. 1911), teacher, emigrated to Britain in March 1939.
6 Hamburg's Israelite Girls' School at 35 Karolinenstraße was founded in 1884 and recognized as a secondary school in 1930; like all Jewish schools, it had to close in June 1942.
7 Hebrew for 'land'. Here it refers to Palestine.
8 Tu B'Shevat; the fifteenth day of the Hebrew month of Shevat. This day, which has been marked since the Mishnaic period, is important for religious commandments related to fruits. In the sixteenth century, the rabbi Yitzchak Luria invested the festival with a Kabbalistic symbolism that includes the consumption of fruits native to the 'land of Israel'. Within Zionist culture in Palestine the day became a symbol of national renewal and is still marked today, with trees being planted throughout the country.

daughters also attended our class at Mr Gärnter's a number of times, arrived in Haifa several weeks ago now. They are all more fortunate than we are! The prospect of our coming is nil.

With warmest regards from your Becky and Iwan Moses.

DOC. 106
Report on the performance of the school puppet show *Till Ülespegel* in late February 1934 in Cologne-Ehrenfeld[1]

Handwritten entry by Josef Rieger in the 'Ehrenfeld Secondary School Chronicle', dated 23 March 1934[2]

Now to the show performed by Class II[3]

At the end of February 1934 we, the Hänneschen players[4] from [Class] II, performed *Till Ülespegel*,[5] a piece we had written ourselves. We received lots of applause, for the show went off exceptionally well. We captured some of the successful scenes in pictures. Here is the first one:

[...][6]

The tooth of time.[7]

Here one sees Till Eulenspiegel buying the tooth of time from the Jew Moses. The Jew sold Till all sorts of old stuff from his junk shop: feathers from the cranes of Ibycus, blue smoke, the ribbon of love, the flying Dutchman, the box of misfortune, and the tooth of time. The Jew sold a watch spring as the feathers from the cranes of Ibycus, and a garter as the ribbon of love.[8] On the left is the smart aleck who bought all the wonderful things without any money. Next to him is the Jew's son Itzig, who far surpasses his father (in the centre) when it comes to uncleanliness. On the right we see Hänneschen, who, of course, must always be present. The Jew Moses drew the most laughter. When the curtain fell at the conclusion of the first act, the players received an enormous round of applause.

---

9 This is a reference to the Bar Kokhba Association. The name, generally used for Jewish gymnastics and sports associations, comes from the leader who headed the last revolt of the Jews against the Romans.

1 'Schülerchronik der Mittelschule Ehrenfeld 1930–1934', pp. 93–95 (copy in the Trapp Privatarchiv); a facsimile of the first part is in Joachim Trapp, *Kölner Schulen in der NS-Zeit* (Cologne: Böhlau, 1994), p. 75. This document has been translated from German.

2 The chronicle, which begins in 1930 with a foreword by the headmaster, contains entries by pupils, photographs, and newspaper clippings detailing school events, holidays, and outings from the years 1930–1934.

3 Class II of the Municipal Secondary School for Boys, Cologne-Ehrenfeld, Gravenreuthstraße (now Municipal Secondary School, 1 Dechenstraße, Eichendorff School).

4 The 'Hänneschen-Spiel' is a traditional puppet show in Cologne.

5 Spelling as in the original. Till Eulenspiegel ('Master Till Owlglass') is a mythical character featured in a collection of Middle High German stories about a jester who travelled on adventures throughout Germany during the Middle Ages.

6 The photograph is missing in the original.

7 The German expression *Zahn der Zeit* literally means 'the ravages of time'.

8 The German names of the objects sold – *Uhrfeder* (watch spring) and *Strumpfband* (garter) – translate literally as 'watch feather' and 'stocking ribbon', respectively.

In the second act, Till was at the University of Cologne and wanted to put his knowledge to the test. The vice chancellor assailed him with questions to which no one knows the answers. Till, however, answered them all quickly and succinctly. To the question of how big the halls of heaven are, Till replied: 'Simply go up and take their measure; they are surely not all that small, for that big head of yours fits through the doors!' Incensed and offended by this, the vice chancellor jumped up to throw him out of the room. But Till refused to be thrown out, and left instead after a bout of fisticuffs in which Hänneschen, Tünnes, and Schäl[9] fought alongside him to give the students a pummelling.

[...][10]

At the master tailor's shop.

In the second photograph we see Till at the shop belonging to Speimanes, the master tailor. In the corners, loafing about, are Speimanes's two journeymen. On the left is Eulenspiegel. Then comes the master tailor, who is negotiating with a Frenchman about a new suit. Naturally, Hänneschen must be present. He can again be seen on the right. Eulenspiegel is to be given the apprentice examination by Speimanes. But Till threw the sleeves on to the jacket when Speimanes told him what to do, even though he knew that by 'throw' the master tailor had meant 'sew'. We then see Till calling on Mayor Adenauer.[11]

Till was supposed to paint the mayor's ancestors and took his payment in advance. But instead of painting pictures he took a nap. When Adenauer asked to see the paintings, Till pointed to the white wall and tried to deceive him into believing that Charlemagne, the Duke of Brunswick, and Philip of Swabia could be seen there. Adenauer, who felt that he had been swindled, called the police and wanted to have Till arrested. However, as in all Hänneschen pieces, everything turned out well. Eulenspiegel sang a nice song for 25 guilders, and everyone joyfully danced along. When the curtain fell this time, lively applause broke out from the audience.

Now we turn to those for whom the applause was intended. We see them in the third photograph.

[...][12]

The players.

From left to right, we see standing Niederwipper, who played the role of the Jew Moses very well. Rieger was the voice of the Berlin journeyman and the mayor. Jansen did an excellent job as Schäl. Seated is Neideck, who was our master prompter. Zimmermann, who played Eulenspiegel, received much applause from the audience. Knips played the Cologne journeyman. Trapp, our Hänneschen, cracked so many jokes that even we players had to laugh along with the audience.

The show has come and gone. But these photographs will reveal something of our work to future pupils.

9 Hänneschen, Schäl, Tünnes, and Speimanes, mentioned in the next paragraph, are characters in Cologne's traditional Hänneschen puppet theatre.
10 A photograph is missing here in the original.
11 Konrad Adenauer (1876–1967), lawyer; joined the Catholic Centre Party in 1906; mayor of Cologne, 1917–1933; imprisoned in connection with the attempted assassination of Hitler on 20 July 1944, but escaped from the concentration camp; mayor of Cologne, 1945; chairman of the Christian Democratic Union (CDU) in the Rhineland, 1946; first chancellor of the Federal Republic of Germany, in office 1949–1963.
12 The photograph is missing in the original.

DOC. 107

On 27 February 1934 State Secretary Herbert Backe voices misgivings to the Gestapo Central Office over the retraining of Jews for agricultural occupations[1]

Letter from the Reich Ministry of Food and Agriculture, p.p. H. Backe[2] (Section Head Dr Lorenz[3] IV/5–656), to the Gestapo Central Office (II F 258/ O. U. 4./34), with a copy to the Reich Minister of Labour,[4] the President of the Reich Institute for Labour Placement and Unemployment Insurance,[5] and the Reich Minister of Propaganda, attn Dr Taubert,[6] dated 24 February 1934 (draft, finalized on 27 February 1934)[7]

In response to your letter – the report – from 13 February 1934.[8]

I have *in all respects* serious misgivings about the intended policy *concerning* the issue of retraining Jews with no relevant experience to become farmers and craftsmen.

---

1 BArch, R 3601/2130, fols. 68–69. This document has been translated from German.
2 Herbert Backe (1896–1947), agronomist; joined the SA in 1922 and the NSDAP in 1926; from 1933 state secretary in the Reich Ministry of Food and Agriculture; from 1936 leader of the administrative group for food of the Plenipotentiary for the Four-Year Plan; head of the Reich Ministry of Food and Agriculture and SS-Obergruppenführer, 1942; Reich minister and Reich Farmers' Leader, 1944; committed suicide while in custody in Nuremberg, 1947: author of works including *Um die Nahrungsfreiheit Europas: Weltwirtschaft oder Großraum* (1942).
3 Dr Erwin Lorenz (b. 1894), economist; joined the NSDAP in 1932; editor of the *Pommersche Zeitung*, 1932–1933; section head in the Reich Ministry of Public Enlightenment and Propaganda, 1933, then in the Reich Ministry of Food and Agriculture, 1933–1941; Reich government commissioner for the Deutsche Rentenbank-Kreditanstalt 1942.
4 Franz Seldte was Reich minister of labour from 1933 to 1945.
5 The president of the Reich Institute was Dr Friedrich Syrup (1881–1945), engineer, lawyer, and political scientist; in the Prussian civil service from 1905; president of the Reich Office for Labour Placement, 1920–1927, and of the Reich Institute for Labour Placement and Unemployment Insurance, 1927–1932 and 1933–1938; Reich minister of labour, 1932–1933; responsible for labour deployment in the Office of the Four-Year Plan, 1936–1942; state secretary in the Reich Ministry of Labour, 1939–1942; died in Soviet custody at Sachsenhausen special camp, 1945.
6 Dr Eberhard Taubert (1907–1976), lawyer; joined the NSDAP in 1931; section head in the Reich Ministry of Public Enlightenment and Propaganda, responsible for anti-Jewish propaganda, among other duties, 1933–1935; judge of the First Senate of the People's Court, 1938; scriptwriter of *Der ewige Jude* (The Eternal Jew), 1940; head of the Propaganda/2 section, 1941, and of the Eastern Area general section, 1942, in the Reich Ministry of Public Enlightenment and Propaganda; after 1950, consultant on psychological warfare for the German armed forces.
7 The original contains several handwritten corrections, which are reproduced here in italics. These were made by at least two different authors, one of whom was Herbert Backe.
8 The Gestapo Central Office (Gestapa) had informed the Reich Ministry of Food and Agriculture on 13 Feb. 1934 that the number of Jews being retrained for agricultural occupations was increasing. There were 163 Jews reportedly receiving training, mostly from the Zionist youth organization Hehalutz and ORT (Society for Trades and Agricultural Labour), in nine municipalities in the Frankfurt an der Oder administrative district alone. The Gestapa felt there was no reason to object to retraining Jews in closed camps for the purpose of preparing them for emigration; however, it was opposed to finding employment for Jewish re-trainees in the free economy because they would take jobs away from 'German agricultural workers'. The Gestapa announced its plan to issue a corresponding regulation and asked the Ministry for an opinion by 5 March 1934: express letter from the Gestapa to Reich Minister of Food and Agriculture Darré, dated 13 Feb. 1934 (copy): BArch, R 3601/2130, fol. 87.

I have repeatedly heard complaints *that* the employment of urban labourers as agricultural workers in rural areas has caused contagious diseases, including but not limited to syphilis, to spread from the city to the countryside. *The President of the Reich Institute for Labour Placement and Unemployment Insurance has already arranged for subordinate offices to be instructed to procure jobs only for those agricultural workers who possess a health certificate.* In addition to the threat that the urban labourers pose to the health of the rural population, the migration of a considerable number of Jews with no relevant experience to rural areas would pose an even great*er* danger to the preservation of racial purity. The cash allowance of RM 30–60 that is paid and the prospect of *almost* free labour will *give some farmers who find themselves in a particularly poor economic situation a certain incentive* to hire such workers. In light of the few diversions available in the countryside, the cramped domestic settings of *the village residents* and the often *confined* housing conditions, the danger *of blood mixing* – despite the rural population's aversion to the Jewish race – must not be underestimated.

We will not be able to eliminate this danger by retraining Jewish labourers in closed camps. In the long run, it will prove impossible to prevent the internees in the camps from visiting the neighbouring villages, establishing relations, *engaging in trading activities*, frequenting the pubs, attending dances, etc.

I therefore implore you, not only *in individual cases*, but *categorically* in every last case, to prevent these *Jewish efforts that, under the cloak of retraining, aim to bring about racial poisoning.*

The Reich Minister of Labour and the President of the Reich Institute for Labour Placement and Unemployment Insurance have received a copy of this letter.

I ask you kindly to advise me of your decision.[9]

DOC. 108

On 4 March 1934 Gertrud Baumgart writes to Paula Tobias about the women's movement and about the Jewish question as a vital issue for Europe[1]

Letter from Gertrud Baumgart,[2] Heidelberg, 7 Werrgasse, to Paula Tobias,[3] dated 4 March 1934 (copy)[4]

Dear Doctor Tobias,

I do apologize for making you wait so long! I took the lines you wrote with me on a lecture tour in central Germany so that I could answer you as soon as I had some free time on my hands, but now I have returned home without having replied to your letter. I found your remarks, particularly your enclosures,[5] extremely interesting, and this

---

9 On the subsequent discussion, see Doc. 122 13 June 1934 and the meeting in the Reich Ministry of Labour concerning the 'retraining of Jews in closed camps' on 27 Nov. 1934: BArch, R 3601/2130, fols. 58–59.

1 The document is in Harvard Competition, no. 235 (Paula Tobias), appendix, fols. 46–48. This document has been translated from German.
2 Dr Gertrud Baumgart (1880–1962), writer; joined the NSDAP in 1932 and the National Socialist Women's League in 1934; author of works including *Die altgermanische Frau und wir* (1935).

shows that I have before me a highly educated person with character traits and intellectual faculties of a rare kind, who did more during the war years and the years that followed, and in a more selfless fashion, than many a German woman.[6] I understand perfectly that the discriminatory treatment you suffer today has come about through no fault of your own, and that you feel it to be an incomprehensible hardship. I deeply regret these hardships that hit individual people so undeservedly.

I, of course, hold a fundamentally different view regarding the Aryan Paragraph. I do not see in it any kind of personal value judgement and identify within it a fourfold meaning: (1) A means to help establish racial thinking in marriage. This is an old concept that has been advocated for decades, as you certainly know, and the Jews of the Old Testament perhaps espoused it with even greater zeal. Germany lies at the heart of Europe; because of its open borders, its historical development, and the wars that raged on its soil, it more than any other country was subjected to the mixing of peoples and races, and more than any other it lost its sense of racial purity. Every mixed marriage *must* shift race consciousness towards one or the other side; you will concede that because you yourself have entered into a racially pure marriage. The second meaning is cultural in nature. There is no denying that today this is coupled with the social; we are suffering from overpopulation and unemployment, many professions are overfilled with non-Aryans, and you have very nobly acknowledged this aspect yourself. On the other hand, you take issue, on page 2 of enclosure 6, with the dismissal of men from the civil service who did not belong to the 'Party'. You write that 'it has to do with Germany, not a party'.[7] Only someone outside our Movement can deliver such a judgement. It is never just about a party; it constitutes a world view that permeates all of life, in all of its expressions, in private as well as public life. Precisely in this totality or, to avoid that catchword, in this intensity and extent of the idea, its strength and universality, lies that which is new, world-transcending, and constructively necessary for establishing the new Reich. Our task consists of training the people to adopt this view; it therefore seems that only *the* men and women who take up and adhere to this idea are fit to hold positions in our state leadership and in our public offices. Numerous mistakes have been made when

---

3 Dr Paula Tobias (1886–1970), physician; practising paediatrician in Bevern near Holzminden an der Weser and other towns; emigrated to the United States at the end of 1935. On Paula Tobias see also Doc. 167 (24 May 1935) regarding the protest she lodged in 1935 against the new Military Service Act.
4 After reading Baumgart's book *Frauenbewegung: Gestern und heute* (Women's Movement: Then and Now), Paula Tobias wrote to Baumgart on 11 Jan. 1934 criticizing her for failing to mention how organizations in the women's movement used the Aryan Paragraph: Harvard Competition, no. 235 (Paula Tobias), appendix, fol. 43.
5 Enclosures 1–6 consist of copies of two letters from 1915, a lecture from the war years on nutrition, a lecture from 1926 on venereal diseases, a poem entitled 'Auf dem Feld der Ehre' ('On the field of honour') from the nineteenth century, and an article from the *Deutsche Allgemeine Zeitung* from 1933: no. 235 (Paula Tobias), appendix, fols. 15–41.
6 During the First World War and immediately afterwards, Paula Tobias was, while her husband was performing military duty, the only physician in her county to provide medical care to the population. She also tended to the medical needs of soldiers, for which she was awarded the Iron Cross, Second Class: ibid., appendix.
7 The passage quoted here by Baumgart is not from Tobias, but is a paraphrase from the article 'Gespräche in Deutschland' by Dr Wolfgang Köhler (*Deutsche Allgemeine Zeitung*, 28 April 1933). Enclosure 6 (copy), Harvard Competition, no. 235 (Paula Tobias), appendix, fols. 39–41.

filling positions, and 'the political opportunists, the 110 per cent National Socialists' who do us the most harm and have driven out many an able man (and woman) are a phenomenon that, as you are aware, is being tackled with urgency by even the highest level of authority.

However, something else is at play here. You belong to a very ancient and sophisticated culture. Ours, on the other hand, is young, perhaps more volatile, and full of ideas and seeds, while yours is entirely completed and unchanging.

This *had to* lead to a contradiction, to an obstruction of one by the other. It is difficult to give the common people an understanding of the different ways of thinking and feeling that have been expressed continuously in the tension found in our cultural life, and I concede that the ideas formulated have been oversimplified, but that is inherent in the recurring process of conveying a concept to the masses. The more highly developed person interprets the ideas in his own individual way. One must also concede that there are in fact marked character differences that led to friction, particularly with the Teutons. I remind you, for example, of the Semites' pronounced streak of acquisitiveness, which was the source – albeit not the only source – of serious conflict. One of the roots of antisemitism is the dissimilar natures of the two races, which must not be overlooked. The third factor is political, i.e. the need to set boundaries and to regulate the political influence according to the inner laws of our people and their life necessities. I am aware that many Jews have very nationalist feelings, and I naturally count you among these, but they have a different outlook on things than we National Socialists do; I almost believe that they have to have such an outlook, and this should not be understood as a reproach. In addition to this, there is another factor which is closely related to the previous one, but which also applies to Jews who have an extraordinarily high status intellectually and morally. This is an experience that I have often had, even with a Jewish friend of mine who died prematurely. At the World Conference of the International Jewish Women's League, the league's president expressed this dichotomy in the following way (she was American): 'My people, the Jews; my country, America.' We are bound by our blood not only to one another but also to the soil from which we sprang; beyond this we have no further earthly ties. The Jew is bound internationally by his race. This may constitute a weakness vis-à-vis his native land, excluding a blood affiliation to the country, a rootedness to the soil, something many Jews also admit. However, on the other hand, in this fact lies a strength, a great power in relation to us, as recent events and the entire last chapter of our history have demonstrated. Some individuals may realize this only to a limited extent or not at all, but this idea is powerfully present in many people, particularly those who are idealistically minded. In Marxism and Bolshevism this idea threatened to ruin us. And from this standpoint, I see the Jewish question as nothing less than a fateful issue for Germany. I am convinced that Europe will not settle down until the Jewish question is radically solved, and the only solution that I can personally imagine is gathering together this highly gifted and dispersed people.

You ask me why I did not touch on the problem in my short work.[8] I had begun working on a chapter that dealt with the issue, but I then put it aside because it would have become personal, and my cause, including the Jewish question, has nothing to do

---

8 Gertrud Baumgart, *Frauenbewegung: Gestern und heute* (Heidelberg: C. Winter, 1933).

with personal attacks. The women's movement has had within its ranks very fine non-Aryan women, to whom we owe a great deal, particularly Alice Salomon,[9] while the work of many other non-Aryan women has not been a boon.

We expect our new state to continue the life work of Helene Lange[10] and her fellow campaigners, and to incorporate the strength of women into the Volksgemeinschaft. Our duty as women now rests on a coherent ideological foundation, and I consider severing ties as necessary for the reasons stated above, although it was a painful experience for many, and even involved a sacrifice from the innocent. Should I revive bitterness in a work that was meant to serve the cause of peace? Developments will relentlessly run their course without any assistance from me. I would have a difficult time deciding to comment on this issue publicly and would have to be compelled to do so by others, but only if my views could contribute to clarification and reconciliation. But I am uncertain as to whether it would succeed or not.

With kind regards.[11]

DOC. 109

Deutsche Justiz, 23 March 1934: article disagrees with a court decision precluding 'racial differences' as grounds for applying to annul a marriage[1]

[Massfeller][2]
Civil law

When does the period for applying to annul a mixed marriage expire if the significance of the race question was already recognized in 1926? (Decision of the Higher Regional Court of 8 February 1934 – 13 U. 7677/33 –.)

The plaintiff is a subject of the German Reich and is of Aryan race. In 1918 he entered into marriage with the defendant, who, as he was aware, was a Jew in terms of race and

---

9 Dr Alice Salomon (1872–1948), social education worker; founded the Social School for Women in Berlin in 1908 and served as its director until 1925; head of the German Academy for Social and Pedagogical Women's Work, 1925–1933; emigrated to the United States in 1937.

10 Helene Lange (1848–1930), teacher and politician; founded the magazine *Die Frau*, 1893; awarded an honorary doctorate by the University of Tübingen, 1923; author of works including *Die Frauenbewegung in ihren modernen Problemen* (1908).

11 Paula Tobias sent a detailed reply on 27 March 1934. Here she argued that it was not a question of her personal circumstances, but rather that she was protesting against the condemnation of all Jews in Germany as inferior: Harvard Competition, no. 235 (Paula Tobias), appendix, fols. 49–53.

1 'Burgerliches Recht', *Deutsche Justiz: Rechtspflege und Rechtspolitik* (1934), pp. 395–396. This document has been translated from German. The periodical, with the subtitle 'Amtliches Blatt der deutschen Rechtspflege' (Official Paper of the German Judicial Administration), appeared from 1933 to 1945. Reich Minister of Justice Franz Gürtner was its publisher in 1934, while state secretaries Schlegelberger and Freisler served as its editors. One of its forerunners was the *Archiv für Rechtspflege*, which was founded in 1853.

2 Franz Massfeller (1902–1966), lawyer; in the Prussian judicial service from 1928; worked in the Prussian Ministry of Justice from 1932; later responsible for family law in the Reich Ministry of Justice; never joined the NSDAP; fought in the war from 1943; Ministerialrat for family law in the Federal German Ministry of Justice, 1950–1964.

religion. The plaintiff's application to annul the marriage based on the racial differences of the parties was unsuccessful.[3]

On these grounds:
According to the plaintiff's statements, he became increasingly conscious of the different nature of the defendant from 1924 or 1925 onwards. Even if this awakening or increasing of consciousness had at that time not yet gone so far as to bring about an awareness of the circumstance, characterized by the plaintiff as an error, specifically as an error related to a personal quality of the defendant, this awareness grew more and more evident in the subsequent period, and the differences in the defendant's nature resulting from her race became ever more clear to him, so that ultimately there were no more points of contact between him and the defendant. No later than this time, the plaintiff recognized the error according to § 1339 of the Civil Code. Yet even if one were to assume to the benefit of the plaintiff that he has still, today, not yet gained certain knowledge about the nature of the race question, this is in any event to be established as the time at which he separated from the defendant. This circumstance occurred in 1926. For the plaintiff states that, from that moment on, the different nature of the defendant became so disagreeable to him that he decided to separate from her. But if this is the case, then this separation is precisely what led to the awareness of the error, the same error regarding the race-based character of the defendant that the plaintiff claimed he committed when he entered into the marriage. If, however, this awareness of the error had existed as early as 1926, by 1933 the period for claiming annulment had long since expired.

Commentary: the question of whether awareness of the significance of racial differences can serve as grounds for applying to annul a mixed marriage has been repeatedly debated in case law and legal literature. Arguments for and against the question have been thoroughly expounded (see also *Deutsche Justiz*, 1933, p. 635). Thus, no comment will be made here on this issue. The Higher Regional Court also does not concern itself with this substantive legal question in the decision under review. As several judgements have since been delivered by [other] higher regional courts,[4] it is to be assumed that the Reich Supreme Court will take up this issue in the foreseeable future.[5]

The Higher Regional Court's ruling is therefore of particular interest since according to the factual determinations the plaintiff possessed awareness of the significance of the race question as early as 1926, whereas this awareness could only be assumed as of spring 1933 in the decisions that have since been handed down. The Higher Regional Court

---

3 See Doc. 121 for the discussion on racial differences as an argument for the dissolution of so-called mixed marriages in the meeting convened by the Reich Ministry of Justice on 5 June 1934 to prepare such legislation.
4 On 2 March 1934 the Karlsruhe Higher Regional Court (file ref. II 208/33) had reversed the decision of the Heidelberg Regional Court and allowed a 'mixed marriage' to be challenged on the grounds that the plaintiff had been mistaken about the nature and significance of race when entering into marriage: 'Burgerliches Recht', *Deutsche Justiz: Rechtspflege und Rechtspolitik* (1934), pp. 384–385.
5 The Reich Supreme Court decided on 12 June 1934 to apply § 1333 of the Civil Code as follows: it disallowed, on the one hand, the challenge on the grounds of an error, but on the other hand it did not rule out such challenges altogether: *Entscheidungen des Reichsgerichts in Zivilsachen*, vol. 145 (Berlin/Leipzig: Walter de Gruyter, 1935), pp. 1–2.

dismisses the action because in 1933 the period laid down in § 1339(1) of the Civil Code had long since expired. It is obvious that this decision cannot satisfy our sense of justice. If the Higher Regional Court's decision were correct, then those who had already come several years ago to a clear estimate of the nature and the significance of the races through their investigation of race questions or through early instruction, and thus felt compelled to terminate their marital partnership with a member of a different race, would be legally required to remain married; for there can be no doubt that an application for annulment instituted prior to 1933 would have been unsuccessful. In contrast, all those upon whom the significance of race had to be clearly impressed once National Socialism triumphed in Germany and the National Socialist state introduced legislation would be able to rectify their earlier mistake. This outcome *cannot* be correct. A review of the legal situation shows that the Higher Regional Court failed to consider two points that are essential to the decision.

In the case of § 1333 of the Civil Code, the six-month period laid down in § 1339(1) starts at the point when the marital partner discovers the error. However, the concept of discovering the error makes no requirement that the plaintiff be convinced that the grounds for annulment would be sufficiently acknowledged by the court. If, for this reason, he lets the period expire without taking action, he forfeits the right to apply for annulment. On the other hand, § 1333 of the Civil Code only makes sense if one brings forward the commencement of the period to the moment when case law first begins to recognize the error as a ground for annulment as a result of the fundamental shift in moral and cultural views. Thus, the period during which an application for annulment may be instituted can in any event not have started until spring 1933. One also arrives at the same outcome on the basis of an analogous application of § 1339(3) of the Civil Code, which was unfortunately not even mentioned once by the Higher Regional Court. In accordance with § 203 of the Civil Code, which was declared to be applicable here, the period is suspended for as long as the entitled party is prevented by *force majeure* from prosecuting his rights. If it is the purpose of § 203 of the Civil Code that those who, despite exercising the highest possible prudence and diligence, cannot prosecute their rights should not forfeit these through the expiry of the period, one must then conclude that in any event a corresponding application of § 203 of the Civil Code is required in the case under review. For the individual who was well acquainted with the significance of the race question it was in effect a kind of *force majeure* that the awareness he had gained had not yet penetrated into the consciousness of the people. It was only possible for him to prosecute his rights after the awakening of the people's consciousness.

The charge should therefore not have been dismissed on the grounds cited by the Higher Regional Court.[6]

---

6 On 12 June 1934 the Reich Supreme Court issued a similar ruling on § 1339 of the Civil Code: it held that the period for claiming annulment had – in contradistinction to the view of the Higher Regional Court – not expired: ibid., pp. 8–9.

DOC. 110

On 23 March 1934 the Reich League of Jewish Combat Veterans protests to Reich President Hindenburg over the exclusion of Jewish soldiers from the German armed forces[1]

Letter from the Reich League of Jewish Combat Veterans, Berlin, signed Löwenstein, retired captain on the reserve list,[2] national chairman, to Reich President and Field Marshal von Hindenburg, dated 23 March 1934

Esteemed Reich President and Field Marshal,

On the occasion of the decree that brings the Law for the Restoration of the Professional Civil Service of 7 April 1933 into force in the Reichswehr and thus excludes our young Jewish generation from military service,[3] I respectfully request Your Excellency to allow me to communicate the following on behalf of former Jewish soldiers.

The Reich League of Jewish Combat Veterans, of which I am the chairman, takes the view that German Jews, who for generations have been rooted in their German homeland, always have to be mindful of their duty and their right to this ancestral German homeland of ours. For us, this also means an honourable integration into the Nationalist Socialist German state. We believe that such integration is possible, even within the framework of National Socialist legislation. We regard this honourable conciliation and integration as vitally important not only for us, but also for Germany and its internal and external consolidation.

We are also of the opinion, however, that no community can lastingly endure being divorced from the supreme duty and supreme right to its ancestral homeland, namely that of being trained to defend the homeland and being ready to give everything for it. This applies to us German Jews just as it does to any other branch of the German nation. Depriving our young generation of this military instruction would condemn it to go to waste. But Germany must wish that each and every community on its soil does not fall into atrophy, but instead develops its moral energies for the maximum benefit of our German homeland.

We German Jews have been called upon to fulfil this honourable duty of military service since there has been a compulsory service, a general people's army in Germany, since the Wars of Liberation. We have always proved ourselves in the fulfilment of this honourable duty, and of everything that attests to this assertion I have elected to highlight here only a single piece of evidence:

---

1 BArch, R 43 II/602, fols. 89–92. This document has been translated from German.
2 Dr Leo Löwenstein (1879–1956), chemist and physicist; worked in the Prussian Ministry of War, 1918; chairman of the Reich League of Jewish Combat Veterans, 1919–1938; deported to Theresienstadt, 1943; emigrated to Sweden, 1946.
3 Decree issued by the Reich Minister of the Army on 28 Feb. 1934 pertaining to the application of § 3 of the Law for the Restoration of the Professional Civil Service to soldiers of the Reichswehr. Published in Müller, *Das Heer und Hitler*, pp. 592–593.

A detailed memorandum prepared in 1847 by the Prussian Minister of the Interior regarding the military obligations of Jews, which was submitted at the time to the united parliament, states in its summary of the reports of the individual Prussian high commands the following about the Jews in the Wars of Liberation:

> If one summarizes the content of these enquiries one must, in the light of experience, arrive at the conclusion that the Jews of the Prussian Army do not in general differ noticeably from the soldiers of the Christian population, that they have proved themselves in times of war to be the equal of the rest of the Prussians, and in times of peace in no way inferior to the rest of the troops; furthermore, Jewish religious matters in particular were at no time a hindrance to military service.

Some 100,000 German Jews also served in the military during the World War. At least 12,000 lost their lives; now, a decade after the end of the war, we have been able to reproduce the names of 10,275 of these soldiers in our book of remembrance,[4] so that they can be checked at any time at the Central Information Bureau in Spandau in the casualty lists that we have specified. One can say that the German Jews saw the same number of men killed in action during the World War as the social, economic, etc. milieu from which they came. Reference must also be made here to the war-related and other services rendered by German Jews for military campaigns, which can also be regarded as a very significant contribution. We can therefore justifiably assert, even from a purely military standpoint, that excluding German Jews from the general duty to serve in the armed forces would weaken Germany's military strength.

We former Jewish soldiers therefore lodge a protest against the exclusion of our young Jewish generation from service in the German armed forces, the most honourable duty and the most honourable right to our ancestral German homeland, and against the exclusion that amounts to the defamation of our youth and thus also of our military honour.[5]

I respectfully beg Your Excellency to graciously accept today my assurance, and that of my comrades, of boundless devotion and gratitude, as well as the pledge of unwavering loyalty to the Reich and homeland made to Your Excellency repeatedly, both verbally and in writing, and I remain,

Your Excellency
Most obediently yours

---

4 Reichsbund jüdischer Frontsoldaten (ed.), *Die jüdischen Gefallenen des deutschen Heeres, der deutschen Marine und der deutschen Schutztruppen 1914–1918: Ein Gedenkbuch* (Berlin: Der Schild, 1932).
5 The protest proved unsuccessful. Some seventy members of the Reichswehr were dismissed: Müller, *Das Heer und Hitler*, p. 79. General conscription was introduced in May 1935, but Jews were excluded: see Doc. 167, 24 May 1935.

DOC. 111

Frankfurter Zeitung, 28 March 1934: article about the ongoing elimination of Jews from the economy[1]

Non-Aryans in the economy.
Trends and their limits.
Since the autumn of 1933, the legislation put forward by the National Socialist state to address race questions has taken a particular direction. The *Aryan Paragraph* has been widely applied to civil servants; to occupations with a civil service character; to salaried employees and workers of state, municipal, and other public enterprises; to cultural professions (such as journalistic and artistic activities); and finally to those members of what were previously known as the 'liberal professions' – lawyers and doctors approved by health insurance companies. The rule has not always been formally applied in the same manner to all areas: in the case of lawyers, for example, objective and easily objectively identifiable characteristics determine whether non-Aryans are able to practise the profession; in other areas decisions are made on a case-by-case basis. The basic tendency, however, is the same everywhere. It consists on the whole of barring non-Aryans from a rather broad range of occupational areas due to the particular importance that the new state attributes to such areas when it comes to developing the people's political and ideological views. To a greater or lesser extent, numerous *exemptions* have been made in all of these areas, exemptions that are, it must be said, almost uniformly temporary in nature, since those remaining in their positions and occupations were, in the overwhelming majority of cases, allowed to do so because of their long-time service or because they were combat veterans. The individuals belonging to these categories will gradually pass away. Young non-Aryans can *no longer* be able to pursue their vocation in these fields.

As non-Aryans were heavily represented in the free and artistic professions, for example, a relatively large number of them have been affected by the new arrangement; others, mostly the majority of *physicians,* are today faced with the particularly difficult situation, from a practical standpoint, that the legal permission to practise fails to put them on an equal footing with their Aryan colleagues because of certain codes of professional ethics. Be that as it may, materially speaking (the non-material aspects are not considered here), it is of crucial importance for the development of the race problem in Germany as to whether, and to what extent, there will remain any areas *at all* in which non-Aryans can freely – 'free' in the sense of being afforded an equal status with all other citizens – pursue an occupation.

With respect to these points, the Reich government and the ministries involved have in the past few months repeatedly issued statements indicating that the private sector should *not* fall under the scope of the Aryan Paragraph. As early as September 1933 the *Reich Minister of Economics* voiced his opposition to the boycott of non-Aryan companies in a letter to the Association of Chambers of Industry and Commerce.[2] In November the *Reich Minister of Labour* brought to the attention of the Trustees [of Labour]

---

1 'Nichtarier in der Wirtschaft', *Frankfurter Zeitung*, 28 March 1934, p. 3. This document has been translated from German. Founded in 1856 as the *Frankfurter Geschäftsbericht*, the liberal-oriented newspaper was published under the name *Frankfurter Zeitung* from 1866. It was banned in 1943.

the fact that non-Aryan employees also enjoy the protection of the government. In this letter he referred again not only to the Reich Minister of Economics and the Prussian Minister of the Interior, but also to the express finding of the *Reich Minister for Public Enlightenment and Propaganda* that Jews were not subject to any exceptional laws whatsoever in the economic sectors.[3] Since the beginning of the year the *Reich Minister of the Interior* has three times (in an essay,[4] in a letter to public authorities,[5] and in a speech to diplomats[6]) declared his opposition to extending the principles of the race legislation to the economy. In the letter to the highest government authorities he states that it would not be expedient, and would even be *a cause for concern*, if the principles of the so-called Aryan Paragraph in the Reich Law for the Restoration of the Professional Civil Service, which has often served as a model, were extended to areas for which they were not at all intended. This applies in particular, he continues, as the National Socialist government has stressed repeatedly, to the private sector. He goes on to request that incursions into this area be firmly and resolutely *opposed*.

It therefore appears that the lines have been clearly drawn. This was certainly not done in this particular manner without the Reich government giving careful consideration to this issue, bearing in mind both the economy as well as the living conditions remaining for non-Aryans. But the task of spreading the awareness of this policy *among the people themselves* is obviously being met with a great deal of resistance and restraint. The question of whether one can operate a commercial enterprise is not determined by laws and regulations alone, but equally by whether the conviction prevails among consumers that one is *allowed* to shop there, or by the degree to which the owner retains the right to determine his own business policies in the context of the existing legal restrictions, and even by the extent to which an enterprise can practically undertake advertising. But what is more: even the most forceful Trustee [of Labour] would have difficulty protecting an employee's job in the long run *against* the unified will of fellow workers.

Because of the enormous transformation that has taken place in all aspects of German life, the issues that arise here are too diverse to provide a full description of their

---

2 Reich Ministry of Economics circular decree containing a letter from the Reich Ministry of Economics to the Association of Chambers of Industry and Commerce, dated 8 Sept. 1933: BArch, R 3101/13863, fol. 6.

3 The Reich Ministry of Labour circular decree (III b 14 872/33) stated that action was to be taken against attempts by factory representatives and other officials to dismiss Jewish employees or prohibit their employment. It also stated that Jews were not subject to special laws in the economic sphere: Walk (ed.), *Das Sonderrecht für die Juden im NS-Staat*, p. 62.

4 In his essay 'Die Rassenfrage in der deutschen Gesetzgebung' ('The Race Question in German Legislation'), Reich Minister Frick offered a justification for the 'race laws', but criticized the fact that the principles of the Law for the Restoration of the Professional Civil Service were being applied to areas for which they were not intended. He also wrote that these principles could not be used as grounds for dismissing Jewish non-management employees from department stores: *Deutsche Juristen-Zeitung*, no. 1, 1 Jan. 1934, pp. 1–6.

5 In his circular decree of 17 Jan. 1934, Frick highlighted the necessity of the 'Aryan legislation', but said that 'certain limits' must be observed in its application: BArch, R 3101/13862, fols. 485–486.

6 Frick gave a speech to the diplomatic corps on 5 Feb. 1934: Gunter Neliba, *Wilhelm Frick: Der Legalist des Unrechtsstaates. Eine politische Biographie* (Paderborn: Schöningh, 1992), pp. 170–171.

scope. It is only possible to give examples. The most timely issue is that of *non-Aryan heads of enterprises*. The Reich government has, as we all know, made clear in an official public announcement that non-Aryans as well as Aryans can serve as heads of enterprises. The Trustee of Labour for Bavaria also promptly issued a statement, countering the widely known declaration of the Gauleitung of the NSBO/DAF[7] in *Central Franconia*, saying that 'it is out of the question for Jews to serve as heads of enterprises'.[8] This deals with the negative aspects, but what about the positive? According to the new labour law, all members of an enterprise are to stand together as a community of trust. But under some circumstances this is a question of the particular stance taken by the local leadership. In fact, many matters today that were previously matters of law have actually become *leadership issues*.

That brings us to *another issue*: the economic and socio-political *associations*. Although they do not have the right to oblige every member of the profession or trade to join, many of these nevertheless seek, and justifiably so, the widest possible incorporation of all relevantly employed persons. In the pursuit of this goal tremendous progress has been achieved in terms of sheer numbers. When it comes to practising a profession or trade, the significance of whether or not the person in question belongs to the association representing the respective branch of the economy may vary widely in individual cases. These run the entire gamut of distinctions, from a severe hindrance of one's economic activity to the unimpeded practice of the same. Needless to say, the National Socialists have laid claim to the leadership of these organizations, as they have done everywhere else, but it is not really plausible that such associations would go so far as to introduce the Aryan Paragraph for their members. The Central League of German Trade Representatives' Associations has now reported a temporary halt to its dissolution and transfer measures, which would have affected the league's non-Aryan members, because of the new Law for the Preparation of the Organic Development of the Economy. In an opposite move, the Reich Association of German Estate Agents just announced that it intends to introduce the Aryan Paragraph.[9] It seems obvious that there is a particular need for harmonization. One will certainly seek to find some way to manifest economic opportunities for non-Aryans in the *statutes of the economic and socio-political associations*.

A third issue is the question of *doing business with Jewish companies* and making purchases in Jewish shops. This appears to be a rather delicate matter in some small towns, and most likely there are quite considerable differences between the various regions in Germany. There has also been much talk of the 'Spring Offensive of German Crafts, Trade, and Commerce', which is taking place from 23 March to 7 April under the motto 'Community Action Serves Reconstruction'. It has been emphasized that this campaign should serve to strengthen the concept of individual achievement and not advance racial principles in the economy. If our information is accurate, local authorities have, where possible, corrected misguided views on this matter. According to the NSK[10]

---

7 Nationalsozialistische Betriebszellenorganisation: National Socialist Factory Cell Organization/ Deutsche Arbeitsfront: German Labour Front.
8 It was not possible to verify this statement.
9 On the debate in the Reich Association of German Estate Agents, see Doc. 40, 6 May 1933.
10 Nationalsozialistische Partei-Korrespondenz: National Socialist Party Correspondence.

the organizers of the campaign have *expressly prohibited* any form of anti-Jewish boycott propaganda. Effectively disseminating the required information to all parties involved is itself apparently no easy task, especially considering that in such cases the local press often shows absolutely no inclination to cooperate. Drastic and publicly visible actions against non-Aryan businesses and shops are perhaps not always the most decisive methods in this respect either. In many instances a personal appeal combined with a certain measure of control can have a significant impact, particularly in smaller towns.[11] It is indeed the case that as the people continue to concern themselves with race questions, it is also necessary to give comprehensive instruction on the limits of the desired course of action if *spontaneous* trends that go beyond the intended restriction of the Aryan *laws* to non-economic areas are not to emerge. Such trends seem to make it almost impossible today for non-Aryans to accommodate the frequently voiced demand that they distribute themselves more evenly throughout the different professions and trades. In fact, only recently some press organs publicly warned of the consequences of allowing non-Aryans to work as apprentices in the agricultural sector.[12] Strong protests were also made about recent attempts by Jews 'to get hold of apprenticeships for their offspring in crafts and commerce'. From these arguments it is difficult to make out how young German non-Aryans could or should go about organizing their lives. How the living environment for German non-Aryans will eventually be determined by these factors depends on the extent to which the state, which plays a leading role in so many areas of personal conduct, gives the trends mentioned above room to manoeuvre *outside* the [law] – or takes steps to limit their impact.

DOC. 112
Printed form of the NSDAP Kreisleitung in Ansbach, dated March 1934 for submitting a declaration of honour to sever all contact with Jews[1]

Standard letter from March 1934 (printed)[2]

To the NSDAP Kreisleitung in Ansbach-Feuchtwangen.
Ansbach.
I hereby *declare on my word of honour* that from now on and in the future I shall never conduct any kind of business with a Jew or an associate of a Jew, or engage the services of an intermediary to do the same. I shall never enter a Jewish shop, and will turn away any Jew who sets foot on my property or enters my apartment.

---

11 See Doc. 112, March 1934.
12 On the discussion between the Gestapo and the Reich Ministry of Food and Agriculture, see Doc. 107, 27 Feb. 1934.

1 NACP, RG 59, 87/1 Confidential U.S. State Department Central Files. Germany, Internal affairs, 1930–1941, MF 22, frame 241. This document has been translated from German.
2 The original contains the following note at the top: 'Enclosure no. 1 to dispatch no. 1539, dated 21 April 1934'. James P. Moffitt, the US consul in Stuttgart, forwarded the form and its English translation in his letter, dated 21 April 1934, to the US Secretary of State as proof of discrimination against Jews in Germany. Moffitt had received the form from a visa applicant: ibid., frames 237–243.

I shall consult neither a Jewish physician nor a Jewish lawyer.

I shall also ensure that no one in my family, or among my relatives or acquaintances, visits a Jew.

I am aware that I have the opportunity to consult a list containing the names of Jews and Jewish businesses in Kreis Ansbach-Feuchtwangen.[3]

I am furthermore aware that if I fail to keep this pledge or if I try to circumvent it, I shall be expelled immediately from the Party – the SA – the municipal council – the National Socialist organization (strike out any that do not apply), and that I may be branded, both verbally and in writing, a man who has broken his word of honour and is a scoundrel.

(Place) ...., ... March 1934

(Signature) ....

DOC. 113

Die Neue Welt, 5 April 1934: news reports about anti-Jewish riots in Gunzenhausen and the increasing Nationalist Socialist propaganda against 'race defilement'[1]

The pogrom in Gunzenhausen

A news report from Prague: the JTA[2] in Prague has received from a *completely reliable* source an account of extraordinarily tragic events in *Gunzenhausen* in the Regierungsbezirk Central Franconia in Bavaria, thus in the immediate sphere of influence of Hitler's closest friend Gauleiter *Julius Streicher*, who exactly a year ago led the Jewish boycott antics in Germany that became notorious around the world, and who is now preparing to repeat last year's events.

Several days ago[3] *the Jewish population of Gunzenhausen was the target of a grave attack, which resulted in the death of two Jews and injury to several others. One Jew was so terribly beaten that he took advantage of the moment when he was left alone to commit suicide by hanging. A second Jew, who had been badly beaten before managing to escape, was shortly thereafter found dead with four knife wounds around the heart. Not a single one of the aggressors was arrested, while eleven Jews who had been attacked were taken into 'protective custody'.*

Another news report states:

The *signal for the beginning of the pogrom* was given during a wild scene at a local inn. A *Jewish guest* who entered the establishment was roughed up by the Christian guests and thrown out into the street. The patrons from the inn, joined by National Socialists who had taken part in the *Jewish boycott antics* of the past several days, now proceeded to *indiscriminately attack* Jewish *houses*. The residents, even women, were

---

3 Enclosed in Moffitt's letter was also the list entitled 'Juden und Judenfirmen in Ansbach' (Jews and Jewish businesses in Ansbach): ibid., frames 239–240.

1 'Der Pogrom in Gunzenhausen', *Die Neue Welt: Revue*, 5 April 1934, p. 1. This document has been translated from German. The weekly newspaper *Die Neue Welt: Revue* appeared in the years 1927–1938 in Vienna. Its publisher was the Zionist Robert Stricker (1879–1944).

2 Jewish Telegraphic Agency. See Glossary.

3 The riots, in which several hundred people took part, occurred on 25 March 1934.

brutally *dragged* out onto the streets and *mercilessly beaten*. There are doubts as to whether the 20-year-old[4] Jew Rosenfeld,[5] who was found *hanged* on a garden fence after being subjected to horrible torture, committed suicide as the *official* version would have it. Rosenfeld certainly no longer had the strength to commit suicide. It is assumed instead that he *was hanged by his tormentors*. The man who was found *dead* on the street with *four knife wounds* in his heart has been identified as Rosenau,[6] a 60-year-old Jewish citizen of Gunzenhausen. Although the local authorities promised a thorough investigation of the murders,[7] both of the victims were *quickly buried* at the instruction of the authorities on Tuesday, 27 March, without a *court autopsy* being performed.[8] The Jewish citizens of Gunzenhausen who suffered injuries are receiving medical treatment. All Jewish residents, insofar as they have not fled, live in an atmosphere of absolute panic.

The *boycott antics* have since spread throughout Central Franconia. Bakers and grocers in Neustadt an der Aich have been forbidden to sell *bread to Jews*, causing the Jewish population to go hungry. In the same city Jewish shopkeepers have been *forced* to put up placards in their shops bearing the following inscription: 'Streicher is right, the *Jews are the Germans' misfortune!*'

It is only too understandable that increasingly severe riots are taking place against Jews in Hitler's Germany. The prediction that the antisemitic agitation of the swastika-bearers would become less bloodthirsty after seizing power has *proved to be false*. The literature supported and recommended by Hitler's government is becoming increasingly vile, and the charges made against the Jews have moved into the realm of the absurd. For example, Dr Kurt Plischke's book *Der Jude als Rassenschänder*, which was recently published by the official NS Druck und Verlag[9] and also warmly recommended by none other than Reich Minister of Propaganda *Goebbels*, contains the following passages:[10]

---

4 This should read 'the 30-year-old'.
5 Correctly: Jakob Rosenfelder (1904–1934), retailer.
6 Max Rosenau (1869–1934); lived on a private income.
7 In June 1934 the Ansbach Regional Court conducted a trial for serious breach of the peace. It sentencend nineteen of the twenty-four defendants to several months in prison for the acts of violence in Gunzenhausen. All those convicted initially remained at large. After the trial the SA officer Kurt Bär (1912–1941), who as the principal defendant had been sentenced to eighteen months in prison, on 15 July 1934 – before beginning his prison sentence – shot and killed the innkeeper Simon Straus and seriously injured Straus's son. Only then did the police take Bär into custody. The case was then brought to appeal in August 1934. As the court assumed that the Jews had committed suicide, all of the defendants were acquitted except Kurt Bär: BayHStA, StK 6410; *New York Times*, 19 July 1934, p. 11; and Gunnar Beutner, 'Das Pogrom von Gunzenhausen 1934: Anfänge des NS-Terrors in Westmittelfranken', in Heike Tagsold (ed.), *'Was brauchen wir einen Befehl, wenn es gegen die Juden geht?' Das Pogrom von Gunzenhausen 1934* (Nuremberg: ANTOGO, 2006), pp. 7–30.
8 Rosenfelder was probably murdered. Rosenau took his own life out of fear of the SA, which had stormed his house. For an analysis of the circumstances surrounding their deaths, see Peter Zinke, 'Der Strick mit dem Knoten: Suizid oder Mord bei Max Rosenau und Jakob Rosenfelder?' in Tagsold (ed.), *'Was brauchen wir einen Befehl'*, pp. 31–44.
9 Correctly: NS-Druck und Verlag; National Socialist publishing house.
10 Kurt Plischke, *Der Jude als Rasseschänder: Eine Anklage gegen Juda und eine Mahnung an die deutschen Frauen und Mädchen* [The Jew as Race Defiler: An Indictment of Judah and a Warning to German Women and Girls] (Berlin: NS-Druck und Verlag, 1934).

The Jew has an insatiable craving to *defile non-Jewish women and girls* and drag them down into the mire of his base sentiments.

Among the various peoples, the Jewish race is the *main carrier of venereal diseases*, which should come as no surprise considering their *bestial-sensual* disposition and their dissipated way of life.

The *traffic in girls* is almost *exclusively* in Jewish hands.

It is necessary to enact a race protection law for the German people. It must make the crime of race defilement punishable, as it once was, by death – and namely *death by hanging*.

An article in *Der Führer*, the *official gazette* of the NSDAP in the Gau of Baden, reported the following:

Kreisleiter Epp[11] sharply criticized *Jewish race defilers* during a meeting of civil servants. He announced that he would not shy away from publicly denouncing *by name* those Volksgenossen who have strayed from their nature and associate with Jews. In the foreseeable future the National Socialist state will naturally create the legal foundation required to fight *Jewish lechers*. It is essential to enlighten every last Volksgenosse about the Jewish and race questions, so that they recognize Jews as the *mortal enemy* of national life and avoid them *like the plague*.

DOC. 114

On 10 April 1934 the Groß-Karben gendarmerie reports on the public humiliation of a woman on the grounds of race defilement[1]

Letter from the Regional Gendarmerie District Friedberg, Groß-Karben Post (diary no. 489), Gendarmerie sergeant (signature illegible) to the Gendarmerie District of Friedberg (diary no. 1137, received on 11 April 1934), dated 10 April 1934

Re: political events.
On 22 March 1934, during an unexpected inspection by the district leader, it was confidentially reported by Mr Flach,[2] the mayor of Gross-Karben, that Heinrich Becker's wife Anni, née Bohlert, was having a secret love affair with the Jew Sally *Braun*,[3] a resident of Gross-Karben.

---

11 Emil Epp (b. 1890), driver; joined the NSDAP and the SA in 1930 and the SS in 1931; NSDAP Kreisleiter in Bruchsal, 1931–1945; classified as a 'major offender' by the Bruchsal denazification tribunal in 1948, and sentenced to five years in a labour camp; sentence reduced on appeal in 1950 to three years and five months in a labour camp and deemed to have been served already on grounds that he had been in custody since 1945.

1 HStAD, G 15 Friedberg Q 188, fols. 35–36. An abridged excerpt is published in Otto Dov Kulka and Eberhard Jäckel (eds.), *The Jews in the Secret Nazi Reports on Popular Opinion in Germany, 1933–1945*, trans. William Templer (New Haven, CT/London: Yale University Press, 2010 [German edn, 2004]), enclosed CD, no. 107. This document has been translated from German.

The district leader and the undersigned thereupon questioned Mrs Becker, who confessed to having sexual intercourse with Braun. Then Sally Braun was interrogated at once on the subject. He openly admitted to having intercourse with Mrs Becker for two years. Over the course of his interrogation, he stated, among other things, that a certain Julius Ross[4] – a Jew – had also had sexual intercourse with Mrs Becker. After the Jews and Mrs Becker had been formally interrogated on the subject, both Jews – *Braun* and *Ross* – were taken into protective custody and admitted to the local court prison in Friedberg. On Saturday 31 March 1934, both Jews were transferred to Osthofen.[5]

When news of Mrs Becker's conduct became known in Gross-Karben, she was then, on 24 March 1934, paraded through the streets of Gross-Karben by eight members of the SA. Two members of the SA each carried a sign reading the words 'Jews' sweetheart'. It was not possible to identify who had actually ordered the action. It was only established that the members of the SA had come to SA-Truppführer Heinrich Lanz[6] of Gross-Karben and asked him if he would summon Mrs Becker to come out onto the street. Thereupon Lanz proceeded to go to the Beckers' apartment. When he arrived there, Mrs Becker was lying in bed and claimed to be ill. Truppführer Lanz therefore left without having achieved his purpose. Meanwhile, a Sturmführer in the SA Reserves, Alfred *Gross*[7] of Gross-Karben, had appeared on the scene. When he saw that Lanz was incapable of dealing with the matter successfully, he entered the Beckers' apartment and instructed Mrs Becker to get up and go out onto the street, and she then complied. As the members of the SA were leading Mrs Becker down Ludwigsstrasse, Sturmführer Gross took a photograph.

When Heinrich Becker, Mrs Becker's husband, learned of the incident, he went to the Hessian district authority in Friedberg, where he lodged a complaint and claimed, among other things, that Mr Gross intended to publish the photograph.

Assessor König ordered the confiscation of any photographs. Thereupon, the undersigned called upon Sturmführer Gross, who, however, more or less refused to hand over the photograph. A telephone discussion was then conducted with the regiment, which ordered any photographs not to be handed over, while at the same time giving an assurance that they would not be published. The undersigned therefore refrained from confiscating any photographs from Sturmführer Gross.

Otherwise, no further incidents worth mentioning have occurred in this part of the district.

---

2 Heinrich Daniel Flach (b. 1901), structural engineer; joined the NSDAP in 1931; head of the local NSDAP branch and mayor of Groß-Karben, 1933–1941; interned, 1945; classified as a 'major offender' by the Darmstadt denazification tribunal in 1948, but his classification was subsequently reduced to 'offender (activist)' by the Gießen appellate tribunal.
3 Sally Braun (1887–1960), retailer; imprisoned in Osthofen concentration camp on 22 April 1934.
4 Julius Ross (1897–1941); later resident in Frankfurt am Main; in Nov. 1941 he was deported from there to Kovno, where he was murdered.
5 Osthofen concentration camp was set up by the SS and SA near Worms in March 1933. The camp was legalized at the beginning of May 1933 by order of the state commissioner for the police in Hesse, Werner Best. It operated until July 1934.
6 Heinrich Lanz (b. 1902), farmer; joined the NSDAP in 1931 and the SA in 1933; classified as a 'lesser offender' by the Friedberg denazification tribunal in 1948.
7 Alfred Gross (b. 1890), engineer; joined the NSDAP in 1933; lived in Groß-Karben until 1935, then in Klein-Karben, and from 1939 in Marbach, Baden.

DOC. 115

A clipping from the *Pariser Tageblatt* along with a letter from the Reich Minister of Labour to the Deputy of the Führer, dated 25 April 1934, about the exclusion of non-Aryan business managers from the 1 May celebrations[1]

Newspaper clipping, undated, accompanied with a short note from the Reich Chancellery[2]

Tageblatt
Paris[3]
Confidential circular. Regarding non-Aryan business leaders
The question of whether non-Aryan business managers are permitted to be 'leaders' of their enterprises is being vigorously debated in Germany at present. While Reich Minister of Economics Schmitt[4] has stated that they should by all means be granted this right, the Gauleiter and the leaders of the 'German Labour Front' are giving orders that non-Aryans should be pressurized into not exercising 'leadership'. Evidence of how the Third Reich is playing a double game – keeping up appearances to the outside world, while behind closed doors blackmailing anyone they please into submission – is this original letter, which came into our hands by accident.

The Reich Minister of Labour
Berlin, 25 April 1934.
Dear Mr Hess,
I share your view that in order to avoid anything detrimental happening it is not desirable for non-Aryan business managers to take part in the parade celebrating national labour on 1 May. I have therefore made clear through the Fifth Regulation to the Implementation of the Law for the Regulation of National Labour dated 13 April 1934 (*Reichsgesetzblatt*, I, p. 310) that the swearing-in ceremony of the Council of Trust foreseen in the law will not be performed jointly at the celebration on 1 May, but will instead be held separately at each enterprise. It can accordingly be expected that non-Aryan managers will not take part in the parade. So far I have also made regular efforts to notify individual enterprises that their participation is unnecessary. It would only be possible through radio or the press to inform all non-Aryan managers that their participation in the parade is not desired. I think it would be imprudent to arrange for an announcement through these channels.

The deputy of the head of the enterprise can also conduct the swearing-in ceremony foreseen in § 10 of the Labour Regulation Law[5] in those instances in which the ceremony being performed by non-Aryan managers could present difficulties. I have already pointed out this possibility to anyone making enquiries.

1 BArch, R 43 II/1268, fol. 108. This document has been translated from German.
2 The original consists of an A4 sheet of paper to which is attached a newspaper clipping containing handwritten notes and several sections underlined by hand. The article is from *Pariser Tageblatt*, 3 May 1934, p. 2.
3 This is written by hand. Followed by newspaper clipping.
4 Dr Kurt Schmitt (1886–1950), lawyer; chairman of the managing board of the Allianz AG insurance company, 1921–1933; joined the NSDAP, 1933; Reich minister of economics, 1933–1934; then returned to the private sector.

I have also informed the Association of Chambers of Industry and Commerce and the Labour Front accordingly.

Heil Hitler!

Your very devoted

signed Franz *Seldte*.

To the Deputy of the Führer of the National Socialist German Workers' Party, Reich Minister Hess, Munich, 45 Briennerstraße.

(1) The Reich Chancellor has been informed.[6]
(2) Ministerialrat Dr Killy[7] and R.Arb.[8]

DOC. 116

Report, dated April 1934, by the Gestapo Central Office in Berlin on the surveillance of Jewish organizations and their activities in Germany[1]

Draft memorandum, unsigned, dated April 1934 (copy)[2]

The Jews in Germany.[3]

I. *General information.*

Jewish associational life, which had already been highly developed early on, has received a significant boost from the exclusion of Jews from the Reich civil service and public

---

5 Law for the Regulation of National Labour: § 10 of this law stipulated that members of the Council of Trust were to 'festively pledge before the workforce on the day of national labour (1 May)' that they would 'set aside selfish interests and serve only the welfare of the enterprise and the community of all Volksgenossen, and be an example for members of the enterprise through the manner in which they conduct their lives and fulfil their duties': Law for the Regulation of National Labour, 20 Jan. 1934, *Reichsgesetzblatt*, 1934, I, pp. 45–56.
6 Stamped notation.
7 Dr Leo Killy (1885–1954), naval officer and lawyer; worked in customs from 1925; served in the Reich Ministry of Finance, 1929–1930, and in the Reich Chancellery, 1933–1944.
8 Point 2 was added by hand. The abbreviation 'R.Arb.' stands for Reichsarbeitsministerium (Reich Ministry of Labour). See the response by the Reich Minister of Labour in his letter to the state secretary in the Reich Chancellery dated 9 June 1934, regarding the participation of non-Aryan heads of enterprises in the 1 May celebrations, BArch, R 43 II/1268, fol. 110r–v.
1 RGVA, 501k-1-18. Published in abridged form in Kulka and Jäckel (eds.), *The Jews in the Secret Nazi Reports*, doc. 32, pp. 31–37. This document has been retranslated from the original German.
2 The month and year were added by hand in the original, which also contains handwritten revisions and underlining. The document is located in the archives of the Gestapo in Berlin and came from section 2 B (religious associations, Jewish organizations, and Freemasonry).
3 This document is the earliest known report by the Gestapo Central Office (Gestapa) in Berlin on the Jewish question. Soon thereafter, the SD compiled a comprehensive report on this topic in which it stated that the emigration of Jews should be encouraged by imposing 'restrictions on [their] livelihood', as the goal was the 'complete emigration of the Jews'. The SD criticized the Gestapa for proposing the establishment of Jewish umbrella organizations by arguing that this would work against the political objective of creating divisions among the Jews; RGVA, 501k-1-18. Published in Michael Wildt (ed.), *Die Judenpolitik des SD 1935 bis 1938: Eine Dokumentation* (Munich: Oldenbourg, 1995), pp. 66–69.

corporations, as well as from the suppression of their influence in economic and private life. Existing associations have recorded a constant growth in members, and new associations, particularly ones of an inner-Jewish political and economic nature, have been founded. The result is very lively activity in the associational milieu, which places heavy demands on the organs of the Gestapo due to the necessary surveillance and monitoring.

Until now the Gestapo Central Office has consciously refrained from bringing the numerous, often vehemently antagonistic associations into line, for the internal disunity of the Jews is the best ally in preventing the influence of Jews within the realm of domestic politics.

II. *Organizations and associations of the Jews.*

The only, and therefore most dangerous, organization in which all Jewish factions are represented is the Independent Order of B'nai B'rith, which has already been reported on in detail in issue no. 5 of the Notifications. Nearly all rabbis and all leaders of other Jewish organizations are members of this lodge. There is no part of Jewish life or the Jewish organizational system whose leadership positions are not occupied by brothers of the grand lodge. The order is under constant monitoring and surveillance by the Gestapo so that any potentially subversive activities can be nipped in the bud.

Moreover, the political stance of Jews in Germany is dominated by two schools of thought, namely Zionism and German Judaism (assimilation).

(a) Zionism

Zionism, which aims at the emigration of Jews from Germany and the creation of a Jewish state in Palestine, is advocated by the following organizations in Germany:

The Zionist Association for Germany. This aims to bring together all Jews in order to strengthen self-awareness and ethnic consciousness. Its primary objective is the purposeful promotion of the settlement of Palestine with Jewish farmers, craftsmen, and tradesmen. The Palestine Office, which handles questions related to emigration, is affiliated with it.

The State Zionist Organization. This is Jewish-fascist minded and advocates a Jewish state on both sides of the Jordan under Jewish administration, with the removal of the British Mandate government. Through its support for Jewish emigration to Palestine, it aims to displace the anti-Jewish Arabs from Palestine and make them a minority. The State Zionist Organization recently joined the Association of German Zionists-Revisionists.

The youth group of the State Zionist Organization changed its name from 'Brith Trumpeldor' to 'Herzlia' in the wake of the radical transition of the state.

The Independent Mizrachi Organization of Germany. This is the Zionist organization of Orthodox Jews and sees in Palestine not only the land of the Jewish nation, but also the land of the Jewish religion. It publishes the periodical *Zion, Monatsblatt für Lehre, Volk und Land*. The organization has been significantly weakened by emigration and today has approximately 1,500 members within its twenty local branches.

The Hehalutz (Pioneer).[4] This is a particularly active Zionist youth movement with numerous associations and local branches in Prussia. Its principal activity is the re-

---

[4] Zionist youth organization, founded in 1917 with the aim of preparing young Jews for emigration to Palestine: see also Glossary.

deployment of Jewish youth who lack a livelihood and their transfer to occupations in agriculture and the skilled crafts. For the purpose of the subsequently planned youth emigration, the Hehalutz promotes the learning of the modern Hebrew language. The movement numbers approximately 15,000 members in Germany. It has strong international ties and runs a leader's seminar in Berlin.

Sub-organizations of the 'Hehalutz' are the '*Hashomer* Hatzair' and the '*Werkleute*'.

The Agudas Israel.[5] This is the association of the strictest orthodoxy. The Agudas Israel has a branch association in Germany with headquarters in Frankfurt am Main and operates special women's and youth groups. This movement also advocates the development of Palestine, but by the rabbis instead of the Zionists: 'Palestine should be and remain the land of the Bible.' The German leadership of Agudas has repeatedly spoken out against the boycott propaganda against Germany. Foreign Jews refer to its leaders as 'agents of Hitler'.

The Keren Kayemeth Leisrael Jewish National Fund. This affiliate organization of the Zionist Association collects money and other assets under the motto 'Land in Palestine for Jewish youth'. The land purchased in Palestine with the donations is to remain the inalienable property of the Jews (national property). The Keren Kayemeth Leisrael is involved only in activities that promote colonization, independent of all religious, political, and socio-political ambitions. It supports penniless emigrants to Palestine while they undergo training in Germany. The organization has approximately 7,000 members.

The transfer to Palestine of the money collected by the KKL occurs on a case-by-case basis upon approval of the Reich Ministry of Economics and the president of the State Tax Office in Berlin.

The Keren Hayesod Jewish Palestine Foundation Fund.[6] The KH is a sub-organization of the Jewish Agency for Palestine. It has tasked itself with raising funds for the emigration of Jews irrespective of their affiliation with the Zionist or assimilationist schools of thought. It sees its primary aim as removing the development of Palestine from the narrow party framework, particularly arousing the interest of non-Zionists in Palestine.

The export of the collected money is governed by an economic agreement and a regulation of the Reich Ministry of Economics. The export of this money is linked to the purchase of German goods so as to favourably influence the foreign trade balance of the Reich.

The Ort Society, German Section. This is an affiliate organization of the large World Ort Union, which concerns itself with the problem of vocational retraining and with the promotion of crafts, industry, and agriculture among the Jews for the purpose of their emigration to Palestine.

The German Maccabi Circle. This is under the control of the Zionist Association and serves as the umbrella organization for the various Zionist youth associations, particularly the sports organizations. It seeks equal status with German sports. Its most important sub-organizations are the Bar Kokhba gymnastics and sports clubs and the Jewish Boxing Club.

---

5 Union of Israel: world organization of Orthodox Jewry, founded in 1912 in Katowice. Its head office was in Vienna in 1936.
6 Raised funds for Jewish development work in Palestine; founded in 1920; based in Jerusalem from 1926.

(b) German Judaism (assimilation)

German Judaism advocates that Jews should remain in Germany and regain equal status with German citizens. The best-known and largest assimilationist organizations are:

The Central Association of German Citizens of the Jewish Faith. This aims to bring together German Jews irrespective of religious or political leanings in order to strengthen them in the defence of their civil and social equality and in the nurturing of their German-mindedness. The CV has 14 regional offices and approximately 500 local branches in Germany. It publishes the *C.V.-Zeitung*. Among the economic organizations belonging to it are the CV specialist group 'Travelling Merchants' and Fairground traders, as well as the CV Unemployed Persons Group and the CV Sales Representatives' Committee.

The Reich League of Jewish Combat Veterans (RjF). The league's objectives are similar to those of the CV, and it originally recruited its members from front-line soldiers of the Jewish race. The vigorous growth of the league and the admittance of young non-front-line soldiers necessitated a division into the league proper, the sports sections, and welfare for war victims.

The RjF sees its task as that of securing living space in Germany for every German Jew and of giving him the opportunity to openly and freely express and act on his Jewish convictions. It counts approximately 2,500 former Jewish soldiers as regular members in 16 regional associations and 365 local branches. The league's newspaper is *Der Schild*. Its youth organization is the League of German Jewish Youth.

The Reich Association of Christian German Citizens of Non-Aryan or Not Pure Aryan Descent. This association aims to promote the interests of its members, independent of political and commercial objectives. According to statements made by its founder and first chairman, the Reich Association seeks to have the Aryan Paragraph amended so that its members can again hold civil service posts.

The Association of National German Jews. This small, very active association occupies a special position among Jewish organizations. It emphasizes the 'national German will' of its members and seeks to draw a strict distinction between German Jews and foreign Jews. Its leader is the lawyer and former captain of the reserves *Naumann*.[7] Because of the emphasis placed on the nationalist idea, the association is vigorously opposed by all other Jewish organizations.

'The Reich Representation of German Jews' was formed in the autumn of 1933, with its headquarters in Berlin, as the umbrella organization of the Jewish associations. Nearly all Jewish associations are represented in it. The 'Reich Representation' is, however, vigorously opposed by the National German Jews because the previously dominant assimilationist influence has been greatly impaired by the ascendancy of the Zionist groups. On the other hand, these organizations are criticized for inadequately representing the Zionist idea, which has prompted the recent founding of 'Jewish Action' as a rival group.[8]

---

[7] Dr Max Naumann (1875–1939), lawyer; until 1938 notary and practised law in Berlin; member of the German People's Party (DVP); chairman of the Association of National German Jews from its founding in 1921 to its disbandment on 18 Nov. 1935; publisher of the magazine *Der nationaldeutsche Jude* ('The National German Jew'), 1922–1934; from 18 Nov. 1935 imprisoned by the Gestapo; released on 14 Dec. 1935 after attempting suicide.

III. *Activities of the Jews.*

(a) In politics.

If today Jews still, on rare occasions, make their subversive views outwardly apparent, then Jewish organizational activity of a subversive nature has of late no longer been observed. The number of cases in which Jews have publicly displayed their subversive views has fallen off sharply thanks to the alertness and vigorous action of the Gestapo.

To the extent that political issues were even discussed, lively meeting activity had a neutral character. No attacks on the National Socialist Movement and the new state have been recorded. As is apparent in nearly all larger meetings, the Jews make efforts not to conspicuously present themselves in the new state as adversaries. The assimilationist movements in particular deny any association with international Jewry.

Even if an *open* antagonism of domestic German Jewry towards the new state is not apparent, this, however, should not hide the fact that the Jew will always be an enemy of the National Socialist state in terms of his inner attitude. His liberal-international world view cannot be reconciled with the National Socialist way of thinking. He will repeatedly attempt, in a deft and covert manner, to gain influence in domestic German affairs and to breed discord in the National Socialist Volksgemeinschaft.

(b) In the economy.

Since circumstances in Germany have hindered or prevented the Jewish population from continuing their economic activities, the Jews are attempting to move these activities abroad. The NSDAP's call for the public to refrain from patronizing Jewish shops has forced many Jewish shop-owners, particularly those in rural districts, to close their businesses. This fact, along with the aspirations of Zionism, has resulted in broad circles of the Jewish population applying themselves to an occupation in the skilled crafts.

The fall in business experienced by Jewish department stores in the cities, which continued until the end of 1933, has now almost been offset by a renewed influx of shoppers. It is mainly the unemployed, the impoverished middle class, and the rural population who obtain what they need from these stores. Unfortunately, it has also been possible to identify civil servants and even members of the SA, SS, and PO[9] as customers of the department stores. This renewed influx of shoppers in the department stores and the discount stores is mainly attributable to the fact that certain items are sold more cheaply here than in the Aryan stores.

In addition to enlightening the masses once again about the danger that department stores pose for German economic development, the appropriate Reich officials will be tasked with employing suitable measures to make it clear to the business world that the decline in business was caused first and foremost by an unsound pricing practice that sought to generate disproportionately high profits on small items. Once the principle gains acceptance in the retail trade that sales prices can be cut through a combination of smaller profit margins and lower general charges, the less well-off will also stay away from the department stores and thereby help to alleviate the baneful influence of large department stores on the retail industry.

---

8 In the original the following was crossed out by hand: 'which also lays claim to be *the* Reich Representation of German Jews, but prioritizes the Zionist idea'.

9 Parteiorganisation: the NSDAP's party administration.

The Jew continues to wield influence in the cattle trade. In the near future the Gestapo Central Office will therefore submit proposals to the appropriate Reich authorities for strengthening the cattle marketing cooperatives in order to also curtail the dominance of the Jews here.

In some cases it was possible to ascertain that Jewish business owners had appointed Aryan business owners in order to lend the enterprise a Christian character in the eyes of the outside world, and that Jewish employers had deftly attempted to stir up division and subversion among personnel. Another means employed by the Jews to fight National Socialism is the dismissal of employees with National Socialist convictions, allegedly due to a shortage of work. Here the Gestapo has also made provisions to respond to such machinations with the utmost severity.

The directives of the Reich Ministry of Economics and the Reich Ministry of Labour concerning the equal status of Aryans and non-Aryans in the economy[10] have given rise to the belief within the Jewish community that every threat to them in their economic life has now been overcome. They even entertain the hope that, on the basis of these directives, they will be able to regain their economic influence. As a result of this, large segments of the population who believed in complete liberation from the Jews are making the assumption that the Jew, in contradiction to the programme of the NSDAP, will remain forever anchored in German economic life. For this reason, a part of the working class in particular is alarmed because it cannot understand how it is possible for Jews to continue to be economic leaders. In addition, the decree issued by the Reich Minister of the Interior regarding the non-application of the Aryan legislation to the private sector has provided the Jewish organizations, particularly the assimilationists, with powerful propaganda material whose effects are visible in the undesirable rise of Jewish elements, especially the increased number of returning Jewish migrants.

Owing to the vocational redeployment of Jews, there have recently been an increasing number of cases in which Jewish youth are being retrained in rural areas to become farmers and craftsmen. In the Regierungsbezirk Frankfurt an der Oder there are currently, in 9 municipalities alone, 163 Jews engaged in retraining in agricultural enterprises, and in Kreis Simmern there have so far been 5 Jews engaged in such retraining programmes. Similar undertakings have also been reported from the districts of the State Police offices in Aurich, Königsberg, and Allenstein. The placement of persons to be retrained is coordinated mainly by the ORT Society for Trades and Agricultural Labour, the *Hehalutz*, and the Land and Crafts organization.

Before the National Socialist revolution, Jews who had emigrated from Russia during that period were already retrained by the local branch, particularly in labour camps in Lithuania, in order to provide them with settled employment in countries outside Russia, mainly Palestine. With the tackling of the Jewish question in Germany, vocational reintegration also became necessary here for Jews dismissed from their previous employment and for those who could not expect vocational advancement in Germany. As long as retraining to become farmers or craftsmen in countries outside Germany or in

---

10 See the letter of the Reich Ministry of Economics to the Association of Chambers of Industry and Commerce, dated 8 Sept. 1933, and the circular decree of the Reich Ministry of Labour, dated 24 Nov. 1933, in BArch, 3101/13863, fol. 6; also Walk (ed.), *Das Sonderrecht für die Juden im NS-Staat*, p. 62.

closed camps is carried out with the aim of facilitating the emigration of the retrained persons from Germany, to Palestine in particular, there are unlikely to be any fundamental concerns that could be an obstacle. In those instances where retraining in closed camps causes the local police to take into consideration the maintenance of public security and order, it must be left to the discretion of the competent authorities whether a different decision is warranted in individual cases.[11] There are unlikely to be any concerns at the political level.

The placement of the persons to be retrained in the private sector, particularly on individual farms, is, however, undesirable. Since previous experience shows that the organizations coordinating the retraining pay the farmers or craftsmen who take on the retraining a monthly subsidy of RM 30–60 on average, these are all the more inclined to undertake the training as, in addition to the monetary benefits, they also acquire a helper. The result will be the inevitable displacement of German farmhands and labourers from employment.

If this procedure leads accordingly to a sabotaging of the Reich government's measures in the field of work creation, the employment of numerous Jews in rural areas also creates significant unrest and agitation among the population, which can cause unpleasant riots and provide new material for the atrocity propaganda that continues to circulate abroad. Retraining within the private sector must therefore be prevented wherever possible.

There have also recently been attempts, led by the Land and Crafts organization, to retrain Jews to become agricultural workers and craftsmen, with the aim of creating new employment opportunities for the retrained persons – through the provision of loans or the purchasing or leasing of land – in *Germany itself*. Since such efforts are not in keeping with the measures being taken by the Reich government to establish a native class of German farmers and craftsmen, they are to be discouraged.

In order to bring about a general policy for dealing with these issues, the Gestapo Central Office has submitted proposals to the appropriate Reich ministries so that in this regard uniform measures may be expected in the foreseeable future.

(c) In the cultural sphere.

Until recently there existed in Prussia a large number of Jewish culture leagues, whose surveillance by the authorities was only possible with great difficulty. In consultation with the state commissioner for Prussian theatre,[12] the Gestapo Central Office has harmonized Jewish cultural endeavours in such a way that the Culture League of German Jews, together with its local branches, is to be regarded as the authoritative organization in this area.[13] The Culture League is obliged to meet certain conditions when establishing new

---

11 On the inter-ministerial discussions in 1934, see Doc. 107, 27 Feb. 1934, and Doc. 122, 13 June 1934.
12 Hans Hinkel was the state commissioner in the Prussian Ministry of Science, Art, and Education, and head of the Prussian Theatre Commission.
13 In the summer of 1935 the regional culture leagues merged to form the Reich Association of Jewish Culture Leagues (Reichsverband der jüdischen Kulturbünde) under the supervision of the Reich Ministry of Public Enlightenment and Propaganda; see the guidelines of the Gestapa (II 1 B 2 – 67 217/J 706/35) dated 13 August 1935, published in Michaelis and Schraepler (eds.), *UuF*, vol. 11: *Das Dritte Reich: Innere Gleichschaltung. Der Staat und die Kirchen. Antikominternpakt – Achse Rom-Berlin. Der Weg ins großdeutsche Reich* (Berlin: Wendler, 1966), pp. 155–156.

local branches and has to submit all of its programmes to the Prussian Theatre Commission for approval. This has therefore enabled the appropriate officials to monitor and control all Jewish cultural movements.

Jewish performers are now rarely engaged by German theatres.

As a result of the ever-growing cultural consolidation, Jews are seldom seen any more at general concert and theatre performances. When in public, they generally frequent only restaurants run by Jewish proprietors. In Berlin, on 8 March 1934, members of the NSDAP disrupted the premiere of the British film *Catherine the Great*, in which the Jewish film actress Elisabeth *Bergner*[14] appears. This incident has given the Jewish agitation press abroad fresh cause to print malicious statements about the new Germany, but in the wake of this episode the serious foreign daily press has also threatened to boycott German films.

(d) In sports.

Sports, like all other branches of Jewish communal life, have also received a tremendous boost. Here the youth groups of the Reich League of Jewish Combat Veterans are particularly active. In some cases it was observed that the Jews even engaged in military and open country sports. Since these activities are incompatible with state interests, the Gestapo Central Office has made provisions to ensure that such occurrences are prevented in the future.

Attempts have also been made by various youth leagues and hiking groups to have their members dress in standardized clothing, occasionally even in brown uniforms. Such attempts have naturally caused a big stir among SA and SS members. In order to prevent clashes, the Gestapo Central Office has proposed to the Reich Youth Leader[15] that general rules should be established on this issue. Specific directives may be expected in the near future.[16]

IV. Emigration.

The measures taken against the Jews since the seizure of power with respect to economic affairs have primarily led to Jews making efforts to migrate. In particular, there has been an upsurge in the numbers of Jews leaving the countryside and the small towns for the large cities, with a contributing factor being that the Jews thought they could go into hiding in the big cities. However, the Jews have emigrated abroad in much larger numbers.

This flood of Jewish emigrants has mainly poured into *Palestine* over the course of the last year. According to present reports, approximately 13,000 Jews have immigrated to Palestine since the start of the emigration up to the beginning of March 1934. As, however, the British Mandate government does not intend to increase the immigration quota, the flow of Jews to Palestine is currently held in check.

The European emigration destinations also have a limited capacity to absorb immigrants. Since the economic situation in these countries does not offer livelihood oppor-

---

14 Elisabeth Bergner (1897–1986), actress; member of the Communist Party of Austria (KPÖ); from 1921 performed at Berlin theatres, including for the director Max Reinhardt, and in films; emigrated to Britain in 1932 and to the United States in 1940.
15 Baldur von Schirach (1907–1974) was the Reich Youth Leader of the NSDAP from 1931 to 1940.
16 On 2 August 1934 the Gestapo prohibited members of Jewish youth associations from wearing uniforms: see Doc. 130.

tunities to Jews, a growing number of immigrants are complaining about the bad conditions, thus causing prospective emigrants to postpone emigration or abandon it completely. This has led not only to a sharp drop in emigration, but also, especially recently, to the return migration of emigrants to Germany.

A committee on which the former British undersecretary of state for war and well-known Germanophobe Lord *Marley*[17] serves was recently established under the direction of Felix *Warburg* in London, for the purpose of settling German Jews in the Soviet-Russian region of Birobidzhan.[18] In negotiations with the Soviet government, the committee is said to have obtained permission in 1934 for 3,500 Jewish families, a total of 15,000 souls, to settle each year in Birobidzhan. According to observations to date, only 200 families and 481 individuals, altogether 1,209 souls, have been brought to the territory in the first quarter of the year. It remains to be seen whether the emigration opportunities in this completely uncultivated region with its unfavourable climate can be successfully exploited.

Since the neighbouring European countries take a disapproving stance towards Jewish immigration and the bleak situation of Jewish emigrants in these countries offers their fellow believers who remain in Germany little incentive to settle there, the Jewish Agency has made efforts to create settlement opportunities for Jewish emigrants in non-European countries. Here it has allegedly succeeded, through negotiations with the French government, in enabling the migration of approximately 100,000 Jews to the French Mandated Territory of Syria. In view of the readiness that exists in Syria, the Jewish Agency has initiated the purchase of large stretches of land on the Palestine–Syria border.

The natural resource-rich and still undeveloped Republic of *Ecuador* has also urged Jewish emigrants to settle within its territory. In addition, Abyssinia is willing to take in emigrants.

V. Boycott propaganda.

Those Jews who have fled or emigrated from Germany continue their systematic agitation against Germany. The main centres of the agitation activity are in nearly all neighbouring countries. The boycott propaganda is being conducted with particular intensity from England, Holland, and America. It is reported from *London* that the Jewish circles there are still placing their hope in the economic boycott of Germany. They are of the opinion that Germany will be destroyed within a year if this boycott is stringently carried out by all Jews of the world and associations amicably disposed to them. The Jewish associations of England accordingly resolved to boycott German goods. They thereupon convened delegates from all countries to London and gave the responsibility for enforcing the boycott to the Israelite Council. A proposal for economic sanctions against Germany was also submitted to the League of Nations.

The British government itself has refused to declare its solidarity with these decisions, but, on the other hand, it has not taken any steps to stop these machinations. The

---

17 Lord Marley, born Dudley Leigh Aman, first Baron Marley (1884–1952), politician; Labour member of the British parliament; supported the emigration of Eastern European Jews and ORT.
18 Since the 1920s Birobidzhan, in the far eastern part of the Soviet Union, had been designated an official territory for Jewish colonization; in 1934 it was declared a 'Jewish autonomous oblast'.

Paris-based Committee for the Defence of Persecuted Jews (*Comité de défense des Juifs persécutés en Allemagne*), which is under the protectorate of Édouard Herriot[19] and headed by the notorious lawyer *Mo-Giafferi*,[20] and which is to be regarded as the centre of all the boycott efforts taken against Germany from Paris, recently decided, in accord with the London committee, to also enlist the interest of the Soviet Union for its efforts and to win it over to participate or even support the boycott battles. The Soviet representation, however, declared that the Soviet-Russian government would have to refuse to take part in the boycott against Germany for reasons of party doctrine.

The Jewish organizations in *Belgium* scheduled and conducted a week-long boycott, and reports from Latvia also tell of intensive promotion of the boycott movement against Germany.

A conference was held in *Warsaw* organized by the United Jewish Relief Committee for Refugee Aid, the United Committee for the Boycott of Hitler's Germany, and the Jewish representatives of the largest Polish cities.[21] At the conference the following resolution, among others, was adopted.

The conference notes:

1. In spite of assurances from official German elements, the systematic campaign to expel German Jewry from all areas of economic, political, and cultural life continues.

2. The ruling party of Hitler is conducting an extraordinarily comprehensive antisemitic campaign in various European countries and in America.

3. Public opinion in the world has not yet learned the full scope of the imminent danger faced by civilization as a consequence of Hitler's barbarism and its developments.

The conference called on Polish Jewry to continue with all its energy to wage the political fight against Hitlerism in the international arena. In recognition of the expediency of the boycott campaign as Jewish society's most effective weapon in the fight against Hitlerism, the conference demanded that the popularization of the campaign be intensified in the broader segments of the Jewish population and solidary collaboration established with the Anti-Hitler Committee.

In *Holland* the Boycott Committee, behind which is the Social Democratic Workers' Party of Holland, is distributing an exhaustive register of all the goods manufactured in Germany with an appeal to refrain from buying the goods listed. Emigrant-run agitation newspapers, which are common in Holland in particular, have naturally taken up the boycott issue initiated by Dutch Jews, and are further stirring up this economic conflict through reports of atrocities.

In *America* the Non-Sectarian Anti-Nazi League to Champion Human Rights was recently established under the direction of the Jew Samuel *Untermeyer*,[22] and has proclaimed a worldwide boycott of German goods, German ships, and German transport companies.

---

19 Édouard Herriot (1872–1957), French writer and politician; mayor of Lyons, 1905–1940 and 1945–1947; served as minister and prime minister; president of the Chamber of Deputies, 1936–1940; imprisoned in Germany, 1944–1945; president of the French National Assembly, 1947–1954.

20 Correctly: Vincent de Moro-Giafferi (1878–1956), French lawyer; served as one of the defence counsels of the Bulgarian communist Dimitrov at the Reichstag fire trial in Leipzig in 1933, and defended Herschel Grynszpan in Paris in 1938.

21 This is probably a reference to the Warsaw Conference that took place on 30 March 1934.

It needs no special enquiry [to conclude] that this economic campaign waged by international world Jewry against the new Germany entails large risks. Every attack, even the smallest, against the Jews in Germany is picked up by the Jewish world press and blatantly exaggerated in order to stir up the economic war. German antisemitic newspapers are collected by the boycott committees and put on display at the world stock exchanges in Amsterdam, London, and New York in order to thereby influence the money market to Germany's disadvantage.

National Socialist Germany's fight against international Jewry and Jewish high finance is still in its infancy. Since it is a purely economic fight, it cannot be waged with physical instruments of power as in the fight against communist and reactionary elements. Measures taken against Jewry in Germany that are not covered by state authority must be avoided by any means, since they only provide the boycott press with new material.

Only objective and truthful educational work in countries outside Germany can deprive the Jewish boycott movement of its weapons. Promising measures in this area have already been initiated.

In addition to the surveillance and monitoring of the Jews in Germany and the prevention of unlawful attacks against the Jews, it will be a priority task of the Gestapo to keep a close eye on the boycott movement and propaganda abroad, in order, in consultation with the appropriate Reich ministry, to counter it by shedding as much light on the issue as possible.

DOC. 117
Völkischer Beobachter, 11 May 1934: excerpt from a speech by Josef Goebbels criticizing detractors, the Jews, the churches, and the foreign press[1]

Dr Goebbels launches the fight against the 'rear-echelon heroes'

The NSDAP is bringing a great wave of rallies to the people. Dr Goebbels inaugurated this campaign on Friday with a huge rally in the *Sportpalast* in Berlin, thus signalling that the time has come to wage a fight for enlightenment throughout the German Gaue and *in every last village* against defeatist attitudes and fault-finding, against rumour-mongers and agitators.

Reich Minister Dr Goebbels's speech included the following remarks:

There are people who cannot stand themselves, and who even get annoyed when they look in the mirror. They find fault with anything and everything. They *spoil* their own lives as well as the lives of others. One cannot discuss with them great things, because their hearts are far too weak and far too lacking in passion to grasp great things.

---

22 Samuel Untermeyer (1858–1940), lawyer and politician in the United States; vice president of the American Jewish Congress; co-founder and first president of the Non-Sectarian Anti-Nazi League, 1933; president of the World Jewish Economic Federation.

1 'Dr. Goebbels eröffnet den Kampf gegen die "Etappenhelden"', *Völkischer Beobachter* (northern German edition), 13/14 May 1934, pp. 1–2. This document has been translated from German.

They used to grumble about the parties; now they grumble that there are no longer any parties. They used to grumble about governments changing so often; today they grumble that this government has stayed in power so long.

They used to find the newspapers too nuanced; now they find them too monotonous. They used to grumble about political violence causing such and such a number of deaths every night; now they grumble that nothing ever happens.

Germany has become too boring for them; they are doing too well, and to bear good fortune with evenness of mind is no easy task.

For some time we have not concerned ourselves with these people; *now they will get to know us!*

We will not do it, as we are very well capable of doing, through the power of the state; instead we appeal *to our allies – the people.*

If today the defeatists believe that, because of our silence, they can rise to speak, then they have been wrong about us. Because those who helped us with the work of reconstruction know how difficult it was and thus arrive at a fair judgement. Only those who made no contribution to the reconstruction sing a different tune. They are not aware of the situation that existed when we came to power. So we will now deal with them. National Socialism can take pride in reducing unemployment by half without abandoning in any way its ideological principles. If nearly 4 million more people are employed this summer than two years ago, then it is only natural that *raw materials* are required in order to employ these people. It is also natural that we *import* such *raw materials* and that we must pay for these imported raw materials and that, because we are employing so many more people, our foreign currency holdings will decrease. One should not throw in the towel immediately when events such as these make themselves felt; instead it is the duty of every German to help overcome this crisis. It is absolutely criminal when some individuals in this country go around discouraging people who are already struggling. If part of the outside world still imposes an anonymous boycott on us and refuses to buy German goods, *then we know very well that this can be traced back to our Jewish fellow citizens.* It is not possible for me to rescind the Jewish legislation domestically because the Jews abroad are boycotting us; instead we must get through this crisis. The Jews might think they are doing their fellow Jews in Germany a service. They are doing the worst thing that they could possibly do, for they should not believe that if they really carried the boycott to the lengths needed to actually endanger our economic situation, it would mean that we would let the Jews leave freely.

If Germany is forced to declare to the world that it is no longer in a position to pay its debts and transfer interest, then the blame does not lie with us. It was not we who incurred the debts, but rather the governments who preceded us. We have shied away from nothing to liberate the German people from these vermin. The National Socialist government has spared no effort to redress the severe crisis that it inherited from its predecessors.

If we silently adopted the legacy of Marxism, if we went too easy on the supporters of the Marxist concept of the state, then this was perhaps a grave mistake. It might possibly have been better if we had not dealt so generously with them.

We have spared our opponent and have quietly addressed the terrible legacy that was left to us. For this we can *expect to gain the confidence* of the nation. We have spared the Jews. But if they think that this allows them to return to the German theatres to present art to the German people, if they think they can return to the editorial bureaus to write German newspapers, if they stroll again along Kurfürstendamm as if absolutely nothing had happened, let these words serve as a final warning to them.[2]

They are to conduct themselves in Germany in a manner that is appropriate for *guests.*

If those who are behind the hostile reaction to us now try to continue the fight against National Socialism indirectly through the churches, then we will be ready to challenge whatever threatens us.

It is not the churches that are waging this battle against us, but rather a very small clique.

If they were concerned about Christianity, then they would have had thousands of opportunities since 1918 to demonstrate what Christianity is capable of doing. All of these militant men of God are invited to accompany me on a visit to the poor in Wedding and Neukölln.[3] We will then stand before these poor people and ask them *what they believe to be more Christianlike: that one argued about dogmas this past winter or that one gave these poor people bread and helped them stay warm.* These militant men of God should not delude themselves as to what the German people think about them. The German people have long grown tired of their incessant squabbling. They are only angered by dogmatic efforts that seek to replace political turmoil with religious turmoil. If these servants of God try to tarnish our great historical past, if they claim that our forefathers were mindless barbarians, then the people have a right to refuse indignantly to tolerate such practices. What would the church dignitaries say if we started poking around in their papal history, where, according to accounts, events have not always conformed to the Christian code of ethics.

When the foreign press declared in response to the announcement of our wave of rallies that the prestige of National Socialism had weakened in Germany and that one was therefore forced to resort to this measure, then I can only say:

One should not judge others by one's own standards. It would be desirable for all governments to be as firmly established as ours.

Many a foreign minister could congratulate himself if he had such a long term ahead of him as we have ahead of us. The German people can only dismiss this allegation with a pitying smile. We make this appeal to the people because it is our *inner* need, because it is our joy and because we want to once again stand amid the [National Socialist] Movement and the people. All attempts to sabotage this Movement will be smashed. It will relieve the government of the obligation to take action against the defeatists and the saboteurs. Millions of voices will cry out:

Enough is enough; our patience has reached its limit! Our patience shall be abused no longer! The Movement now appeals to the nation, and this appeal will not go unheeded! When the Movement appeals to the nation, the nation will stand by it.

---

2 On reactions among the Jewish population to this part of Goebbels's speech, see Doc. 133, 29 August 1934.
3 Working-class districts in Berlin; traditionally strongholds of the Communist Party. Wedding, known as Red Wedding, was the site of violent clashes between communist and Nazi militants in the 1920s.

DOC. 118

On 26 May 1934 the Regierungspräsident of Frankfurt an der Oder issues a statement to the Prussian Minister of Finance justifying the confiscation of Hugo Simon's estate [1]

Statement by the Regierungspräsident (I Pol. – B.S.1.), Frankfurt an der Oder, signed p.p. (no signature), to the Prussian Minister of Finance, dated 26 May 1934 (copy regarding II G 1501/104 to be filed)[2]

Re: confiscation of the Schweizerhaus country estate in Seelow, Kreis Lebus, belonging to the banker Hugo *Simon*.[3]
Reference: decree of 23 April 1934 – II G 1501/104 –.
Report prepared by: Regierungsrat *Möbus*.[4]
Six enclosures.[5]

By means of the order dated 5 October 1933 and in accordance with the laws issued on 26 May and 14 July 1933,[6] I have seized and confiscated for the benefit of the Prussian state the Schweizerhaus estate in Seelow, Kreis Lebus, belonging to the Jewish banker *Simon*, and consisting of approximately 230 acres of land, one fruit orchard, one chicken farm, and the corresponding farm buildings, as well as the livestock and deadstock. The confiscation order was published in the *Deutscher Reichsanzeiger*, no. 236, of 9 October 1933.

Simon is co-owner of the banking house Bett, Simon & Co. in Berlin and was known to be very wealthy, which allowed him to purchase landed property in Seelow, Kreis Lebus, for the development of which he spent extraordinary sums over the years. In addition to running an exemplary agricultural enterprise with a pig farm that is just as exemplary, a large chicken farm, and a large fruit orchard managed according to the latest principles and consisting of approximately 20,000 trees, Simon also has for hobby purposes a modern apiary, as well as raccoon and budgerigar breeding farms. To set up and manage these operations, part of which can be described as extravagant, Simon has enlisted the services of recognized experts, some of whom are still working on the estate. The seizure and confiscation occurred because Simon, who fled to France immediately after the National Socialist government came to power, was for a while minister of

---

1 GStA PK, I HA, Rep. 151 I A/8083. This document has been translated from German.
2 The original contains minor handwritten amendments. On 16 April 1933 Simon filed a disciplinary complaint through his lawyer against the Regierungspräsident: ibid.
3 Hugo Simon (1880–1950), banker and politician; member of the Social Democratic Party of Germany (SPD) and pacifist; in 1918–1919 undersecretary in the Prussian Ministry of Finance, then briefly minister of finance; member of the supervisory boards of various companies and member of the executive boards of several art associations; emigrated to Paris in 1933 and to Brazil in 1940.
4 Johannes Möbus (b. 1895), lawyer; joined the NSDAP, the SA, and the SS in 1932; head of the State Police Office and the Department for Citizenship Affairs and Blood Protection Legislation of the Frankfurt an der Oder government, 1934–1936; Oberregierungsrat, 1936; from 1937 served at the disciplinary court for officials of the Reich Ministry of the Interior in Frankfurt an der Oder.
5 The enclosures mentioned here are not in the file.
6 This is a reference to the Law Concerning the Confiscation of Communist Property (*Gesetz über die Einziehung kommunistischen Vermögens*), 26 May 1933 and the Law Concerning the Confiscation of Subversive Property (*Gesetz über die Einziehung staats- und volksfeindlichen Vermögens*), 14 July 1933: *Reichsgesetzblatt*, 1933, I, pp. 293 and 479.

finance in Prussia's Marxist government and a member of the SPD, and because after his departure from government service until shortly before 30 January 1933 he continued to maintain close ties with high-standing Marxist figures, who visited him frequently at his country estate in Seelow. His regular guests included the previous ministers Braun, Severing, and Greszinsky,[7] as well as the Marxist leaders Bernhardt,[8] Weiß,[9] and Dr Breitscheid. The notorious pacifist and fanatical opponent of the National Socialist Movement Hellmuth von Gerlach, publisher of *Welt am Montag*, was also among the guests at the Schweizerhaus country estate.

Of the aforementioned persons, Hellmuth von Gerlach, Bernhard Weiß, Greszinski, and Dr Breitscheid have since been denaturalized because of their subversive activities abroad.[10] Simon is currently sojourning in southern France, and in the exact same areas in which the denaturalized enemies of the states mentioned above are now located. It can therefore be assumed with a great degree of certainty that Simon is continuing to maintain ties with these emigrants, with whom he feels connected not only socially and because of their shared interest in hunting – as he would like us to believe – but also quite obviously ideologically and because of their hatred against all that is National Socialist.

If Simon claims that his guests also included figures who could not be categorized as leftist, then this only proves that he was clever enough to seek wider views on the political and economic situation. It would at least contradict common wisdom if no 'political discussions of any kind' had taken place 'on the estate, either directly or indirectly'. I do not hesitate to characterize this statement of Simon as a deliberate falsehood. It is also untrue that his senior employees 'had already had rightist political leanings for years'. In fact, the most relevant ones, agronomists Zörner and Volz, did not join the NSDAP and the SS, respectively, until the last days of April and the beginning of July 1933 – that is, only after Simon had long fled. Zörner is still considered politically unreliable today.

It is incorrect that the confiscation was carried out to a certain extent as a result of pressure from the NSDAP Kreisleiter Friedrich. The Landrat also resolutely denies mentioning to Saara the lawyer that the confiscation was necessary in order to prevent the illegal confiscation by the Kreisleiter of the NSDAP. Kreisleiter Friedrich approached the Landrat with the request to arrange for the Simon residence in Seelow to be made available to the girls' class of the Seelow agricultural school. This request by the Kreisleiter was, however, not the reason behind the decision to confiscate the entire property. The actual ground for the confiscation on the basis of the aforementioned circumstances, an action which was considered as early as April 1933 but not legally possible until the promulgation of the law on 26 May 1933, was instead the disclosure of the fact that after Simon fled to Amsterdam, he encumbered his property with a land charge of

---

7 Correctly: Albert Grzesinski (1879–1947), labour official; from 1903 trade union and SPD functionary; chief of police in Berlin, 1925–1926 and 1930–1932; Prussian minister of the interior, 1926–1930; emigrated to France in 1933 and to the United States in 1937.

8 The author means Georg Bernhard.

9 Dr Bernhard Weiß (1880–1951), lawyer; served on the Berlin police force from 1918; deputy chief of police of Berlin, 1928–1932; fled to Britain in 1933. During the Weimar Republic, Weiß was subjected to overt antisemitic harassment, particularly by Goebbels, which he successfully contested in court.

10 On the denaturalization of Breitscheid and von Gerlach in the summer of 1933, see Doc. 70, 14 August 1933.

RM 400,000 for the benefit of the banking house Bett, Simon & Co. (formerly Karsch, Simon & Co.), known in Berlin as a 'red establishment', whereby the suspicion seemed warranted that this charge exceeded the actual value of the property, thus allowing funds to be transferred abroad.

I request that *the complaint be rejected.*

The seizure and confiscation of the property is, in my opinion, factually as well as legally well founded. Reversing the confiscation would have extraordinary consequences for state policy because among the population of Seelow and its district, which is overwhelmingly National Socialist minded and which had expected and enthusiastically welcomed the measures taken, it would cause an irreversible loss of confidence in the leadership of the National Socialist state. Not to mention the fact that the utilization of the Simon property in accordance with the aims of the regional farmers' leader, who intends to found a model establishment there, is expected to commence forthwith.

With respect to the great political and economic significance of the affair, please allow me to suggest an inspection of the Simon estate supervised by the Landrat and in consultation with the official in my office handling the case, who is also familiar with the local conditions.

The files concerning the confiscation of the Simon estates are currently at the Gestapo Central Office in Berlin, which had requested them as per the decree of 28 March 1934 – II A – S 3/33 –.[11]

DOC. 119
Excerpt from the Sopade report for May/June 1934 about reactions to the persecution of Jews in Germany[1]

Sopade report on Germany, May/June 1934, Prague, dated 26 June 1934 (typescript)

The mood among the well-educated
The following is an excerpt from a report on a trip through Germany (*Neuer Vorwärts*, 10 June):[2]

> The attitude of the propertied middle class and senior employees in the private sector, as well as many members of the liberal professions and many intellectuals, has

---

[11] On 4 October 1934 the Gestapo Central Office (Gestapa) informed the Prussian Minister of Finance that it could not establish any facts that would have justified a confiscation in accordance with the laws of 26 May and 14 July 1933. In order to retroactively provide a legal basis, it recommended that the Reich Ministry of the Interior swiftly denaturalize Simon. The case was still pending as late as 1937 because the Reich Foreign Office had not approved the application: GStA PK, I HA, Rep. 151 I A/8083.

[1] AdsD, 'Deutschland-Berichte der Sopade', May/June 1934, part A 16–18. Published in Klaus Behnken (ed.), *Deutschland-Berichte der Sozialdemokratischen Partei Deutschlands (Sopade) 1934–1940*, 7 vols. (Frankfurt am Main: Zweitausendeins, 1980), vol. 1, pp. 115–117. This document has been translated from German.

[2] See 'Die Stimmung in Deutschland: Bericht von einer Reise', *Neuer Vorwärts*, 10 June 1934, supplement, p. 1.

changed again. The first two groups in particular are keeping their eyes on the economy; they see the whole picture and not just a part of it. They have contacts abroad and a sufficient knowledge of economics to understand the origins of the shrinking currency reserves and the financial calamity. They have a home that allows them to have discussions with larger numbers of people. In addition, they recognize and hate the loutish behaviour of the Party, and fear that there is a danger of a sudden turn – to Bolshevism, as they say, but to complete chaos would be more accurate.

There are several concurring reports about the situation and mood among the liberal professions:

First report:

Most Jewish physicians in the large cities can no longer complain about a lack of patients. Their waiting rooms are full of demonstrators.[3] But their incomes have fallen because of their being barred almost everywhere from working in health insurance practices. Even the practices of seriously war-disabled doctors are damaged. The relations between Aryan physicians and their Jewish colleagues are no longer in such a sad state as in the first months of the Hitler regime. Some Aryan physicians are making an effort to refer patients to capable Jewish specialists.

Second report:

Just a few months ago the lawyers and judges were still currying favour with the National Socialists, but now a great many are attempting to dissociate themselves from them. The law concerning the People's Court in particular is scaring off a considerable number.[4] Many interpret the brutalization of the judicial system as a sign that the Nazis are finished. Political discussions are again taking place in the lawyers' chambers. The lawyers organized in the NSDAP are so overburdened with Party assignments that they very often give more general cases to non-National Socialist lawyers at the last minute. Surprisingly, the Jewish colleague is no longer treated with contempt and often makes up the left wing of the rival German nationalist lawyers.

Third report:

The lawyers are very ill-humoured. The extraordinary decline in their caseload, in some instances by half to three quarters or even more, has pauperized the profession. The reason for the decline in their professional activity can be attributed to the fact that the legal protection of debtors against enforcement has been significantly strengthened, which thus discourages people from pursuing litigation in numerous cases. One must also take into account the fact that many plaintiffs fear the use of extralegal measures by the SA and choose not to initiate legal proceedings out of

---

3 As in the original (*Demonstranten*); possibly a reference to patients showing solidarity with Jewish physicians.
4 The People's Court (Volksgerichtshof) was established by the Law Amending Criminal Law and Criminal Procedure (24 April 1934) in order to impose harsher sentences for cases of high treason (Art. III, § 1): *Reichsgesetzblatt*, 1934, I, pp. 341–348.

caution. Added to this is, of course, the general adverse state of affairs in the economy itself.

Lawyers, and civil servants in the judiciary, are particularly unhappy about the regulation issued several days ago that grants the National Socialist legal bureaus as equal status to tribunals with respect to arbitrating in property disputes and settlement proceedings. These Nazi bureaus are authorized to declare undisclosed settlements and agreements to be enforceable with immediate effect.[5] This will probably take a further field of activity away from the lawyers, while judicial officials, who take great pride in their profession, will have to compete with Nazi laymen. The Jewish lawyers still licensed to practise in Saxony, who, as is generally known, are struggling under difficult conditions to secure their livelihood, were hit particularly hard by a ministerial decree concerning the appointment of lawyers to poor litigants, which effectively takes *in forma pauperis* cases away from them, thus depriving them of one of their main sources of income.[6]

From the universities in Halle and Leipzig:

Since Easter a significant change of mood has taken place at the universities. The students are becoming monarchistic. Their antisemitism is waning. Many students are seeking social contact with the Jews. But the Jewish students are still very intimidated. Some of them would do well to show more courage.

A change of mood is also gradually taking hold among the *civil servants*. 'Most of the civil servants are not Nazis at heart; some are simply grudgingly tagging along' (from the Rhineland). 'The civil servants are temporizing, but refrain from showing any overt sympathy for the regime; the Hitler salute is being sabotaged in some cases. The recent hiring of SA officials has created a great deal of ill feeling' (from Hamburg). 'In philologists' circles one is furious about being brought into line with the primary school teachers in the National Socialist Association of Teachers' (from Saxony). A report from Berlin states:

Political training evenings are regularly held for Reichsbank officials in indoor tennis centres. Cards are handed out to monitor attendence, and the stubs are not torn off until after the event is over. The officials are offended by the poor quality of the lectures. One speaker recently concluded with these exact words: 'Our big mouth has helped us up to now, and will continue to do so in the future.' They call that political training! One can imagine the effect this has on the civil servants.

---

5 This regulation could not be found.
6 Regarding the appointment of lawyers to poor litigants, the decree of the Saxon Ministry of Justice (565 a I 1/34) of 27 April 1934 stated that a relationship of trust was not present if the lawyer and the poor litigant were of different races: *Sächsisches Justizministerialblatt*, vol. 68 (1934), pp. 51–52.

DOC. 120

On 2 June 1934 Legation Counsellor Hermann von Stutterheim reports on a discussion with Leo Löwenstein, the chairman of the Reich League of Jewish Combat Veterans[1]

Memorandum (on R.k. 4682) from the Reich Chancellery, Legation Counsellor von Stutterheim,[2] dated 2 June 1934[3]

1. *Memorandum*

The national chairman of the Reich League of Jewish Combat Veterans called on me by appointment yesterday morning in order to explain at length the general views and aims of the league, and to present a series of requests which he desired to resubmit to the state secretary.[4]

Dr Löwenstein stated that the Reich League of Jewish Combat Veterans and the affiliated youth organization have approximately 45,000–50,000 members and therefore constitute, when the league members' families are counted, a very significant part of the Jewish population in Germany. He said that the principle of the Reich League has been, not just recently but for several years now, to achieve an unconditional national stance that firmly rejects all international ties, particularly all connections to the goals of the Zionist movement. In addition, according to him, its main principles are to adopt the military fitness of the youth and the rootedness of league members to German soil. Here he emphasized that the Reich League of Jewish Combat Veterans does not seek on its own accord to mix with the Aryan population in any way, but rather its members wish absolutely and unanimously to keep to themselves, though it is resolved for its part, in absolute recognition of the goals of the National Socialist state, to devote its energies and its labours to the German fatherland.

Dr Löwenstein is convinced that the aims pursued by the Reich League of Jewish Combat Veterans can be achieved in a better and purer way in today's state than in the Marxist state under Jewish domination, the latter of which, according to him, was always firmly rejected by the league.

He said that on this basis the Reich League of Jewish Combat Veterans wishes to put forward the following concrete requests:

1. It is requested that members of the youth organization of the Reich League of Jewish Combat Veterans be allowed to take part in voluntary labour service in closed work camps, as is the case with non-Jewish young men.

---

1 BArch, R 43 II/602, fols. 69–70. Published in Klaus J. Herrmann, *Das Dritte Reich und die deutschjüdischen Organisationen 1933–1934* (Cologne: Heymanns, 1969), pp. 135–136. This document has been translated from German.
2 Hermann von Stutterheim (1887–1959), lawyer; served in the Braunschweig civil service, 1924–1934; from 1 March 1934 personal aide to the state secretary in the Reich Chancellery.
3 The original contains handwritten annotations and amendments.
4 In 1933 Leo Löwenstein had already presented his 'proposals on resolving the Jewish question within the National Socialist state' to State Secretary Lammers. On 16 May 1934 he again asked to meet Lammers. Stutterheim turned down this request because of Lammers's overloaded schedule, but offered on 17 May to meet with Löwenstein himself: BArch, R 43 II/602, fols. 66–67.

2. Permission is sought to train and instruct the Jewish youth within the Jewish sports associations, which are affiliated with the Reich League of Jewish Combat Veterans, for the purpose of attaining military fitness.

3. It is desired that the Reich League be permitted to have its members establish settlements in the same manner as has occurred already in the vicinity of Cottbus. Some years ago the league purchased a relatively large estate near Cottbus from a Jewish owner and had several of its members establish settlements there in commercial plant nurseries with an average size of ten acres, an undertaking that could be regarded as quite a success.[5] The Reich League aims, along these lines, to establish further settlements on property that it intends to purchase from Jewish owners.

In addition to these three main requests, there were two further requests.

Firstly, to permit Jews, if not right away, then at some later time, to once again serve in the military, whereby it is not sought, according to Dr Löwenstein, that Jewish soldiers should also hold officer positions. Instead he said that the Reich League's sole concern is that the young people of Jewish religion and race are trained for military defence in the Reichswehr.[6]

Furthermore, the Reich League is very keen on Jews being allowed to become members of the Reich Federation for Air Raid Protection; this is a request that can perhaps be fulfilled sooner.

Dr Löwenstein thereupon presented me with a copy of a petition addressed to the Reich Chancellor on 6 May 1933, which was not yet in our local files, as well as with an article about the invention of sound measurement from the seventh issue of *Heerestechnik* from 1928, which reveals that Dr Löwenstein was the person who invented and introduced the use of sound measurement in the army during the war.

I replied to Dr Löwenstein that I would apprise the state secretary of his statements. However, I told him that I thought it was unlikely that the state secretary would be in a position to effectively address his specific requests. Here I pointed out to Dr Löwenstein that at the very least it was highly doubtful at the present time whether an official or public consideration of the issues he raised would be really advisable and consistent with the interests and objectives of the Reich League. Dr Löwenstein said that he indeed appreciated my thoughts, but nevertheless wished to inform the state secretary in detail about the issues he had presented.[7]

---

[5] This is probably a reference to the Groß-Gaglow training centre near Cottbus, which was established in 1928.

[6] The Reich Minister of the Army had issued a decree on 28 Feb. 1934 applying § 3 of the Law for the Restoration of the Professional Civil Service to soldiers of the Reichswehr, which thereby excluded Jews from military service. Decree published in Müller, *Das Heer und Hitler*, pp. 592–593.

[7] Stutterheim informed State Secretary Lammers on the same day and confirmed this to Löwenstein two days later: BArch, R 43 II/602, fol. 71.

DOC. 121

Report by Vice President Fritz Grau during a session of the Criminal Law Commission on 5 June 1934 about 'race protection' and the social segregation of the Jews[1]

Minutes of the Criminal Law Commission,[2] 37th session, dated 5 June 1934 (draft)[3]

Race protection

[...][4]

Rapporteur Vice President *Grau*:[5]

In the current era of international tensions, it is not very easy to come to a conclusion about provisions in criminal law for race protection in Germany. For we know what political and economic difficulties were created by the non-binding suggestions made in the Prussian position paper,[6] and it cannot be doubted that our current foreign policy situation does not allow present desires in this direction to be completely fulfilled in legislation, especially in the penal code.

If one wants to know whether to include anything at all about race protection in a new penal code, then as you, too, Reich Minister,[7] have already emphasized, one first needs to make clear which penal code would be regarded as appropriate, if our hands were not tied, as is now unfortunately the case. Only then can we decide which statements of fact are to be disregarded in the present circumstances and which statements of fact, despite the present difficulties, perhaps might be included in a penal code.

---

1 BArch, R 22/852, fols. 75 and 79–84. This document has been translated from German.
2 The official Criminal Law Commission began its work on 27 Nov. 1933. Reich Minister of Justice Gürtner presented the Reich government with a 'draft for a German penal code' on 2 Dec. 1936 for its approval, but this draft was not approved. On the work of the commission, see Franz Gürtner (ed.), *Das kommende deutsche Strafrecht. Allgemeiner Teil: Bericht über die Arbeit der amtlichen Strafrechtskommission* (Berlin: Vahlen, 1934), and Franz Gürtner (ed.), *Das kommende deutsche Strafrecht. Besonderer Teil: Bericht der amtlichen Strafrechtskommission* (Berlin: Vahlen, 1935).
3 The complete minutes can be found in BArch, R 22/852, fols. 75 to 317. A reprint of the final version can be found in Jürgen Regge and Werner Schubert (eds.), *Quellen zur Reform des Straf- und Strafprozeßrechts, II. Abteilung: NS-Zeit (1933–1939) – Strafgesetzbuch*, vol. 2: *Protokolle der Strafrechtskommission des Reichsjustizministeriums* (Berlin: De Gruyter, 1988), pp. 223–348.
4 According to the handwritten attendance list, the following persons were present: Reich Minister of Justice Dr Franz Gürtner, Rapporteur Vice President Fritz Grau, Rapporteur Professor Eduard Kohlrausch (Berlin), Oberregierungsrat Dr Johann von Dohnanyi, Oberregierungsrat Dr Bernhard Lösener, State Secretary Dr Roland Freisler, Chief Judge Professor Karl Klee (Berlin), Professor Georg Dahm (Kiel), Ministerialrat Dr Möbius, Professor Count Wenzel Gleispach (Berlin), Professor Edmund Mezger (Munich), Ministerial Director Ernst Schäfer, Professor Johannes Nagler (Breslau), Regional Court Director Dr Gerhard Lorenz (Leipzig), Senior Prosecutor Dr Werner Reimer (Berlin), Ministerial Director Dr Alfred Dürr, and Ministerialrat Dr Leopold Schäfer.
5 Fritz Grau (1890–1975), lawyer; public prosecutor in Kassel, 1923; regional court president in Düsseldorf, 1930; joined the NSDAP and the SA, 1933, and the SS, 1938; active until 1934 in the Prussian Ministry of Justice, then in the Reich Ministry of Justice; co-editor of *Das deutsche Strafrecht*, vol. 1 (1941).
6 A position paper by the Prussian Minister of Justice Kerrl dating from the summer of 1933, which contained a proposal to penalize the occurrence of 'race treason': see Hanns Kerrl (ed.), *Nationalsozialistisches Strafrecht: Denkschrift des Preußischen Justizministers* (Berlin: R. v. Decker, 1933).
7 The reference here is to Reich Minister of Justice Gürnter, present at the meeting.

If we, as already noted, disregard foreign policy considerations, then we must start from the following position: the Party programme states that only those of German descent can be citizens and that alien races are to be treated under the law of hospitality. The programme thus wants to create the new German state on a racial basis. Much has happened over this past year to accomplish this objective. A first effort was made to eradicate alien race elements from the racial corpus by denying them influence; they were pushed out of political leadership positions and removed from other influential posts and professions. Here I draw attention to the Law for the Restoration of the Professional Civil Service, the revision of the Reich Civil Service Law, and to provisions and regulations limiting the number of Jewish lawyers as well as that of Jewish students. By means of the law of 14 July 1933, a successful effort was made to expatriate at least some of those naturalized foreign race elements who had arrived as immigrants from the East, in all too large numbers, during the last fourteen years and to strip them of German nationality.[8]

In addition to these negative measures, there are also numerous positive measures regarding the cultivation of the race. I recall the eugenic measures, the whole complex of questions surrounding the Regulation on the Granting of Marriage Loans, the Law for the Prevention of Offspring with Hereditary Diseases, and the revision of the penal code with respect to the emasculation of dangerous sex offenders. I have in mind social measures, particularly the Reich Hereditary Farm Law, which strove, and to a large extent was successful, to bring the German people back to their racial origins, namely to the peasantry, and to anchor them there again.[9] I call attention to the Law against the Abuse of Marriage and Adoption, which again underscored the holiness and purity of the family, and which concerned the need to annul adoptions or marriages of convenience that took place for purely commercial reasons.[10]

All these measures have, without question, moved us a step further, but they have not achieved and could not achieve a genuine isolation of the foreign race elements in Germany from those of German descent. For foreign policy reasons, such a law could not be passed – a law that would have legally prevented any sexual mixing between those of German descent and those of an alien race.

Now one can perhaps say – and here I come to the second question posed by the Reich Minister – that this goal could also be gradually achieved without an explicit law, through education and information. Other peoples, one could argue, have basically accomplished this goal through societal segregation. Yet this is surely only partially true. Among the other peoples – I am thinking here primarily of North America, which even has laws of this kind – there is a different problem, namely of keeping the members of coloured races at arm's length, a problem that plays virtually no role here in Germany. In our case, the problem is quite sharply delineated and concerns the Jews and how to

---

8 The Law on the Revocation of Naturalization and the Deprivation of German Nationality (14 July 1933) made it possible to revoke naturalizations granted between 9 Nov. 1918 and 30 Jan. 1933: *Reichsgesetzblatt*, 1933, I, p. 480.
9 Reich Hereditary Farm Law (*Reichserbhofgesetz*), 29 Sept. 1933, *Reichsgesetzblatt*, 1933, I, p. 685.
10 Law against the Abuse of Marriage and Adoption (*Gesetz gegen Mißbräuche bei der Eheschließung und bei der Annahme an Kindesstatt*), 23 Nov. 1933, in *Reichsgesetzblatt*, 1933, I, p. 980.

permanently keep them away, as they without a doubt represent an alien body among the German people. It is my conviction that this goal will not be achieved alone via the path of societal separation and segregation as long as the Jews in Germany continue to possess such extraordinary economic power. As long as they continue to hold such sway over the economy of our German fatherland as at present, as long as they still have the nicest cars, the prettiest motor boats, as long as they play a significant role in all the amusement and recreation parks, and everywhere where things are costly, then I do not believe one can genuinely separate them from the German racial corpus without the help of a law. This can only occur by means of positive legal measures that prohibit and severely penalize any sexual mixing of a Jew with a German.[11]

If one wishes to carry out the Party programme, there is thus a need to create a legal barrier to marriage, and on this basis, place every kind of sexual mixing between Jews and those of German descent under penal law, with the ultimate goal, in accordance with the Party programme, to denaturalize the Jews and place them under the law of hospitality. For there can be no doubt that all measures regarding race breeding will remain unsuccessful and useless as long as Jews continue to be permitted to contaminate members of our race. The Jews are a wholly outrageous mix of oriental races, and as history shows, wherever this mix goes, it pulls peoples down to its level and destroys the races.

The core aspects of race protection, the prevention of marriage, the legal prohibition of race mixing, and denaturalization, can certainly not be accomplished at the moment, and now the third question posed by the Reich Minister arises. If one puts these core issues aside, is it expedient and is there still a need now, if I can put it this way, to grant ancillary race protection in the penal code?

Aside from sexual mixing, the Prussian position paper foresees three offences: first, the violation of racial honour. It wants to punish those Germans who shamelessly and in gross breach of public feeling entertain open social contacts with members of the coloured races. I would like to recall that it was precisely this offence that led to foreign policy difficulties of a particular kind. Consciously or unconsciously, it was overlooked that this offence was very limited in that the shameless social contacts with members of coloured races have to be public. Nevertheless, precisely this offence has led to démarches by diplomats representing coloured races and already created difficulties solely on the basis of the suggestions made in the position paper.

The two other offences foreseen in the position paper consist of a blanket provision under which individuals make themselves liable for prosecution if they violate other legal provisions for maintaining or improving the purity of the community of German blood. A further blanket provision stipulates that any opposition, if of ill intent, to measures passed by the Reich or in the German states to enlighten the German people about maintaining and improving their community by blood will be subject to punishment. I would

---

11 In the original the following paragraph is crossed out: 'As long as Jews can continue, under the law, to marry German women, such a separation seems to me to hardly be possible without legislative measures.'

like to recall that this last offence is already partly contained in our § 169, in its current version, in which we have penalized every open call to oppose laws, governmental regulations, or even mere recommendations made by the government.[12] If genuine race protection, as the Party programme foresees it,[13] were to become part of the penal code, then I would not refer to this general offence but would instead clearly and completely regulate race protection here. I would suggest, beyond prohibiting sexual mixing, that every act of sabotage against public enlightenment on the race question be criminalized, along with all violations of laws and decrees passed that intend to refine the race and keep it pure.

If one assumes that, with respect to criminal prosecution, the core question of race protection cannot currently be resolved, then one can also doubt that any ancillary points ought be put in the penal code, and whether it would be more practical in this case to say nothing at all in the penal code about race protection. This question, as noted, is closely connected to politics, and cannot be conclusively decided from here. My personal inclination, under the present circumstances,[14] is for the time being to put nothing at all about race protection in the penal code, because I tell myself that what is most important to keep the race pure cannot be included. It will be left to subsequent legislation[15] to regulate the applicable criminal law with respect to race protection in a complete and satisfactory manner.[16]

DOC. 122
On 13 June 1934 State Secretary Hans Pfundtner writes to the Reich Minister of Agriculture proposing the creation of closed camps for the agricultural retraining of Jews[1]

Letter from the Reich Ministry of the Interior (IV 5012/11.5), p.p. Pfundtner, to the Reich Ministry of Food and Agriculture (received on 14 June 1934), dated 13 June 1934[2]

Re: the agricultural retraining of Jews.[3]
Your letter dated 5 May 1934 – IV/5. 1589–.[4]

In response to the questions in your letter to the Gestapo Central Office on 27 February 1934 – IV/5. 656[5] – I would most humbly like to note the following.

If the Jewish question is to be settled, then no suitable means to encourage the emigration of Jews living in Germany should be ruled out from the outset. It is not beneficial

---

12 In the original the following sentence is crossed out: 'In the area of race protection, this especially would be of particular importance.'
13 Crossed out in the original: 'starting from the core problem and extending to these ancillary points'.
14 Crossed out in the original: 'and, painful as it is for me to suggest it'.
15 See Doc. 199, 15 Sept. 1935.
16 This last sentence was added by hand.

1 BArch, R 3601/2130, fols. 96–97. This document has been translated from German.
2 The original contains handwritten underlining along with editorial notes from several authors, presumably including State Secretary Herbert Backe.

to the domestic or international standing of the Reich government if, on the one hand, it declares that the Aryan legislation was only intended to break the unbearable influence Jews have on running the state and on German cultural life, and maintains that every Jew can pursue his profession unhindered, when, on the other hand, Jews or those of Jewish descent are pushed out of, or prevented from being trained in virtually every occupation by the estates and professional organizations that control them. But it would be even less sustainable, in my view, if the Reich government were also to follow this path.[6]

Regarding the matter in hand, one should also add the following:

The Jews, with good reason, have been repeatedly accused of having a limited inclination to do physical and, in particular, agricultural labour. This fact, one also admitted by insightful Jews themselves, is simultaneously also a hindrance to the envisaged emigration, as academic and other professions involving intellectual work are already hopelessly oversubscribed in all the potential destination countries. It is therefore not only understandable but, from the standpoint of the German government, also to be welcomed if the Jews in Germany now seriously intend to retrain their primarily intellectually oriented brethren in agricultural work, the only area which still promises success.[7] The sooner and more energetically this plan can be realized, the better it is for both parties. If the government wanted to demand that this retraining be undertaken abroad, then the plan would fail for the foreseeable future. Given the situation in the new state, one need not fear that after their retraining Jews would not emigrate but would instead wish to remain within the German Reich as farmers.[8]

Moreover, an outright rejection of the plan would undoubtedly, and in this case justifiably, add renewed fuel to the global propaganda against Germany. It would not be understood why, if the Jews are being accused of a one-sided intellectualism, they are nonetheless prohibited from making the first serious attempt to reorientate themselves, using their *own* means and in recognition of the truth of this accusation.[9] One also should not underestimate the indirect practical consequences of this reorientation. I expect that this will lead to a certain easing of the Jewish question in Germany, a question which, as it stands, is still far from being brought to a definitive conclusion, as would

---

3 The Gestapo Central Office (Gestapa) also received a copy of the letter on 14 June 1934 from the Reichsstatthalter of Prussia: RGVA, 500k-1-178, fol. 88. Reinhard Heydrich stated his position to the Reich Ministry of the Interior on 16 June 1934 and to the Reichsstatthalter of Prussia on 14 Sept. 1934. He had no objections if the training camps would make emigration, particularly to Palestine, easier. In April 1934, 2,154 Jews were counted in such camps: letter from the Gestapa (II 1 B 2 43 431/1179) to Göring, 14 Sept. 1934, GStA PK, I HA, Rep. 90 P/58, H. 1, fols. 68–70. See also the meeting in the Reich Ministry of Labour on 27 Nov. 1934 on the 'retraining of Jews in closed camps': BArch, R 3601/2130, fols. 58–59.

4 On 5 May 1934, the Reich Ministry of Food and Agriculture had sent its own letter of 27 Feb. 1934 to the Reich Ministry of the Interior, as the latter was in charge of this matter: BArch, R 3601/2130, fol. 72r–v.

5 See Doc. 107, 27 Feb. 1934.

6 Handwritten note in the left hand margin of the original: 'precondition is maintaining the purity of the race'.

7 Handwritten note, in red, in the left hand margin of the original: 'help!'

8 Handwritten note in the margin of this paragraph: 'they pollute the race beforehand!'

9 Handwritten note at the bottom of the page: 'Can the racial orientation be altered?'

be desirable. I would consider it irresponsible if such a vent, which could also be of great use to the government, were not opened as a way of releasing the existing tensions.

Of the two options available for carrying out the plan, I am in agreement with you that individual training is not appropriate. By contrast, both I and the Gestapo Central Office have no serious objections to carrying out the retraining in closed camps. The negative consequences you fear with respect to this solution could, in my view, be prevented, if necessary by the use of state force. Given the ongoing education of the population, this danger also does not seem as great as it was just a few years ago. Finally, with respect to this point, one should note that the dangers you refer to already exist, and in fact to a considerably larger extent. The Jews envisaged for the retraining camps do not represent a new influx from without but instead already live in Germany, and are currently forcibly unemployed. They therefore have far more opportunity and incentive to act in detrimental ways than if they were in closed camps, tired and distracted by strenuous physical labour, spending their days until emigration with the prospect of having a way out of their existing situation.

I intend, therefore, to pursue the idea of agricultural retraining in camps, and would be thankful for your prompt response to my remarks.

I enclose a copy of my letter.[10]

DOC. 123

On 14 June 1934 the Gestapo Central Office orders the seizure of the assets of the League of Jewish Employees in Prussia[1]

Circular decree issued by the Gestapo Central Office in Berlin (B. Nr. 21806 – I 1 B), p.p. signed Dr Bode, to all Regierungspräsidenten in Prussia, dated 14 June 1934 (copy)[2]

Re: the seizure of assets belonging to enemies of the state and the people.

The following order has been issued and takes effect as of today.

On the basis of § 1 of the Law Concerning the Confiscation of Communist Property, 26 May 1933 (*Reichsgesetzblatt*, I, p. 293), in conjunction with the Law Concerning the Confiscation of Subversive Property, 14 July 1933 (*Reichsgesetzblatt*, I, p. 479) and the Prussian Implementation Regulation, 31 May 1933 (GS. p. 207),[3] all the assets of the League of Jewish Employees and its subsidiaries and auxiliary organizations, including written materials and office supplies, will be confiscated to the benefit of the Prussian state.[4]

---

10 This enclosed letter is not in the file.

1 BArch, R 58 II/276, fol. 4. This document has been translated from German.

2 The copy of the circular decree reprinted here was prepared by the Regierungspräsident in Cologne (I.J.p.6[10] 537/34), p.p. Dr Möller, and sent to the State Police office in Cologne, division for the municipal district of Cologne, the mayor of Bonn, and the Landräte of the Regierungsbezirk of Cologne on 21 June 1934.

3 These laws both allowed for the targeted expropriation of German Jews and Jewish organizations from 1933 onwards.

The editors of the *Reichs- und Staatsanzeiger* have been instructed to print the confiscation order in the next issue.

I sincerely request that further action to this effect be taken at the level of the Regierungsbezirke.

DOC. 124
On 14 June 1934 Julius Plaut asks Hamburg's Reichsstatthalter, Karl Kaufmann, to retract his dismissal[1]

Letter from Julius Plaut,[2] Hamburg 22, 5 Volksdorferstraße, to Reichsstatthalter Karl Kaufmann,[3] Hamburg, dated 14 June 1934[4]

Dear Reichsstatthalter,

I most politely request that you rescind my dismissal from the public welfare services issued on 17 May 1934, as I have been unjustly targeted by two zealous National Socialists, namely the salaried employees Mrs Hecker and Mr Walter Schultze.

I was born a Jew, but converted to Christianity in 1912 with complete conviction and I write articles on religious topics.[5] In 1914 I was employed as a medical orderly by the city of Hamburg, and I was drafted into the army in March 1915. After the war I was employed once again in the civil service. Following a year and a half break, I was re-employed in the civil service in 1924, and I was employed as an orderly in the Friedrichsberg State Hospital from then onwards. As the work there proved to be too difficult because of my military service injuries, I was transferred to the Welfare Department in August 1931. I was employed as a medical orderly in Welfare Office 7. I grew especially fond of this post because it was beneficial to my health. At the beginning of this year, I was unexpectedly, and for reasons unbeknown to me, transferred to the archives on Rentzelstraße. Miss Kuchel, my block leader at 72 Richardstraße, can only tell you, dear Reichsstatthalter, good things about me. The same holds true for the head of Archive 3, Mrs Meyer. Unfortunately, the latter became ill, and since then I have been subjected to

---

4 In Saxony the League of Jewish Employees had already been dissolved on 18 April 1934 and its assets seized: *Sächsisches Verwaltungsblatt*, part 1, *Verordnungsblatt*, 1934, no. 32, p. 138.

1 Staatsarchiv Hamburg, 113–10 I, 1934 Ma I/200. This document has been translated from German.
2 Julius Plaut (1889–1960), medical orderly; began working for the city of Hamburg in 1912. Plaut was married to the non-Jew Erna Grimmsmann and had two children, Günther (b. 1925) and Renate (b. 1927). He survived in Hamburg.
3 Karl Kaufmann (1900–1969), agricultural labourer; in several Freikorps formations, 1918–1923; joined the NSDAP in 1921 and the SS in 1933; took part in the Beer Hall Putsch in 1923; labourer, 1923–1925; Gauleiter in the Ruhr, 1926–1929, and in Hamburg, 1929–1945; Reichsstatthalter in Hamburg, 1933–1945; imprisoned several times after 1945, sentenced in 1948, released in 1949; wholesaler in Hamburg after 1953.
4 Parts of the original are underlined by hand.
5 Since the 1920s Julius Plaut had published a series of small works with the Christian publishing firm J. Maar, including *Wie ein Jüngling aus Israel den Heiland fand* [How a young Man from Israel found the Saviour] (1928) and *Junge Helden und Heldinnen. Jugend heraus!* [Young Heroes and Heroines: Youth go Forth!] (1933).

the venom of colleague Schultze, who is an SA man. His behaviour towards me has left much to be desired. He talked almost incessantly about politics with his colleague Prill, another SA man, and complained about the civil servants from the previous government; it was in this respect that he showed no consideration for me. Despite the low temperatures – it was often only one degree outside – he opened the window every day and did not close it again. I remained silent, despite the fact that I sat next to the window and suffered from the cold, and the noise of the trains rolling past made it quite difficult for me to talk on the phone. I also ignored his gibes against the Jews, which were aimed at me. One day, when these two colleagues had left the room, I forgot to push down the lever of the telephone, which I did not realize until these two colleagues returned to the room. I could hear in Schultze's comments that he thought I had done so on purpose, but I remained silent. In the meantime, I answered the telephone twice. Then a civil servant came into our room and complained that he hadn't been able to get a connection to our office. Mr Schultze then stood up and told me right to my face that I had purposely neglected to push the lever and that he had been keeping an eye on me for several days for this reason. But I can attest with a clear conscience to the fact that this was not the case. After I had kept my mouth shut the entire day and taken everything quietly, I could not keep quiet any longer. I retorted to Mr Schultze that he was a liar and that his behaviour was more like that of a communist than that of a National Socialist, and that I had also fought for him and shed my blood. Schultze replied in return: 'You Jew, you did not fight for Germany, but for your Jews!' When I countered that I am a Christian, he said: 'For me, race is all there is!' If Schultze claims that I called him a 'criminal', I can swear before God that this is not the truth. On the last day that I worked in Archive 3, Schultze whistled the song 'Haven't you seen little Cohn?' in my presence.[6] He also stirred up so much hatred in colleague Prill, who is otherwise a peace-loving, quiet, and amiable man, and whom I often praised to my dear wife, that he was no longer willing to give me information or even greet me.

I would also like to add that since I was transferred to the archives, I have been hounded by a Mrs Hecker who is known to the authorities and among colleagues as an extremely intolerant National Socialist because of the Hitler salute, which I believed, and still believe, is my duty to give. She once told me directly to my face that I had no right to do so and that she would make sure that I would be dismissed. All my colleagues in the archives can attest to what I have just put forth and to the fact that I am a quiet and peace-loving person. The department head of the archives as well as my boss in Archive 6 can also confirm this. Some of my colleagues will also be able to confirm that Mrs Hecker had stirred up hatred against me and influenced Schultze, too.

As a result of the commotion and everything that I had to endure from Schultze, I got diarrhoea and became so ill that my doctor had to prescribe four weeks of recuperation in the Haus Hessenkopf convalescent home near Goslar. While I was there, my letter of dismissal was brought home to my wife. In response to my query to the personnel department, I was first told that every employer had the right to terminate an employ-

---

6 The couplet by Julius Einödshofer (1863–1930) 'Haben Sie nicht den kleinen Cohn gesehen?' comes from the operetta *Seine Kleine* and was a big hit in 1902. With the help of small figurines, jokes, and postcards, an anti-Jewish stereotype became associated with the figure of 'little Cohn'.

ment contract at will, and, in response to my objection that this was not a sufficient reason, I was told that I was too difficult to work with. I have always done my duty to the best of my knowledge and according to my conscience, and I have always sought to act and live in a Christian way. Everyone who comes into contact with me can attest to this, and my writings prove this as well.

I performed military service in the war from March 1915 until December 1918, and fought for Germany once on the Eastern Front and twice on the Western Front. On the Eastern Front, I intercepted Russian spies at the listening post, which I can credibly demonstrate by means of a poem that I wrote. A shot grazed my carotid artery, and it was only thanks to God's mercy that I did not bleed to death. A piece of shrapnel became lodged in my left ankle, and I still suffer greatly from the effects of this injury every time the weather changes. Furthermore, I also caught dysentery during the war, which resulted in the development of a duodenal ulcer in 1926. In the years that followed up to the end of 1930, I suffered from diarrhoea up to twelve times a day, which really took its toll on my entire nervous system. In 1930 I was almost always ill. Alongside the ulcer, I also developed a blistering rash on my buttocks that spread over my entire body and from which I still suffer today. It was also recognized that I became anaemic as a result of all the diarrhoea. Previously, I had already been recognized as a severely disabled veteran, and afterwards this was reduced to 30 per cent. I am also in the possession of a civil servant certificate and I was designated for such employment positions.

I have a Christian-born wife and two children aged almost 9 and 6½ years to feed. I would also like to add that I do not look Jewish and therefore no one could take offence at my appearance. Finally, I would like to reaffirm once again that I have always conscientiously done my duty towards the state and my superiors. I therefore ask you, Reichsstatthalter, to ensure justice in the name of the Führer and to order that my dismissal be rescinded.[7]

With German regards,

Your very devoted

---

7 The Hamburg Welfare Office did not retract its dismissal issued in May 1934 for the reason that Plaut had supposedly had 'repeated disputes' with colleagues: Frank Bajohr, 'Aryanisation' in Hamburg: The Economic Exclusion of Jews and the Confiscation of their Property in Nazi Germany (New York/Oxford: Berghahn, 2002), p. 63.

DOC. 125

Haynt, 15 June 1934: article on the establishment of an 'antisemitic international' in Nuremberg[1]

Dr Azriel Karlebach[2]
The Antisemitic International

1. Just two years ago I commented here in a note:

> Hitler will come to power. Only that is not the worst of it. We have already experienced Haman's rule and we have already seen Jews dancing on their own graves.[3] The worst is not the oppression of individual Jews, the beatings, the imprisonment, the pogroms – the worst is: out of antisemitism, out of a suppressed instinct that people used to be ashamed of, Hitler has created an ideology.
> The danger is not that people will attack Jews (because that remains a constant local phenomenon). The danger is that hitting Jews will become a religion. The 'liberal prejudice' that a Jew is also a human being will be swept away, an end will be put to all inhibitions (which come from a good conscience, shame, and fear), which until now curbed the antisemitic feeling that lives in every non-Jew.

And that's all that is needed, one merely has to give a base human instinct the garb of an idea, and there are no longer any limits. Then it will, if not today then tomorrow, stop being a specifically German movement; it will become a universal movement. Then the epidemic will, then it must, make the leap to all countries.

Because all countries will be populated by people in whose hearts the antisemitic instinct lives. It lives in all hearts – inhibited and restrained by civilization's traditions and morals. Take the fence away – and you have a finished pogrom. But if you create an idea out of the bestiality of antisemitism – you have an antisemitic 'International'.

2. Today we already have it, the Antisemitic International. I have lived long enough to see it, thank God. Mr Streicher, the publisher of the *Stürmer* and the head of government in the German province of Franconia, has called together all antisemites for a conference at his residence.[4] At this convention the Fifth International is set to be founded, the International to annihilate the Jews.

---

1 *Haynt*, 15 June 1934, p. 3. This document has been translated from Yiddish. The Polish Zionist daily newspaper *Haynt* was published from 1908 to 1939 in Warsaw.
2 Dr Azriel Karlebach, also Carlebach (1908–1956), journalist; from 1929 editor of the *Israelitisches Familienblatt* in Hamburg; emigrated to Poland in 1933 where he worked for the newspaper *Haynt*; in 1934 he emigrated to Britain and in 1936 to Palestine, where he was later editor of the daily newspaper *Yediot Aharonot* and founder of the newspaper *Ma'ariv*.
3 According to the Book of Esther in the Old Testament, Vizier Haman tried to exterminate the Jews. Since then his name has been a symbol in Judaism for brutal rulers who are ultimately defeated.
4 The existence of such an invitation could not be verified. An editorial in *Der Stürmer*, 'Der Antisemitismus ergreift alle Völker' ('Antisemitism takes hold of all nations'), paid tribute to antisemitic movements and parties in various European countries: *Der Stürmer*, June 1934, pp. 1–2.

In truth – this is an historic hour. Not only because we are witnessing the birth of an International, one that will be no less significant than the First and Second[5] – not only for that reason is this a historic hour. It is also historic because in the entire large Jewish book of tears and to this day no such calamity has been recorded. There have previously been worse persecutions than that of today. But no antisemitic international, no universal front, no united organized attack as will be prepared at the upcoming congress has yet existed.

Among the attendees will be: the Narowtses from Poland,[6] the Iron Guard from Romania,[7] the Coty people from France,[8] the Mosley people from England,[9] the Germans from America, the Legionnaires from Lithuania and Latvia,[10] the Arabs from Syria and EI,[11] etc. They are all from countries where both today and in the Middle Ages a hatred of Jews has already been 'demonstrated'. But it was a local hatred, an individual event. Now, with the creation of an antisemitic international, the movement is entering a completely new phase.

3. On the one hand it will be stronger than we are, stronger than our defences. As long as antisemitism remained a hooliganism of local hooligans, we could defeat the movement with an appeal to calm and order, to humanity, to the *starost*,[12] and to the police. The nature of the situation is thus: one can catch a single thief, an individual criminal, because his main act reflects only his personal criminality.

And even when a mass movement arose in one country, one could appeal to neighbouring or to foreign countries. One was able to discriminate against the troublemakers who disturbed the calm and order as one would with those from culturally undeveloped countries, such as Romania, Tunis,[13] etc.

But as antisemitism becomes an international movement and the individual hooligan a representative of a worldwide struggle, just as, not to equate these things, a worker is a representative of the class struggle – at that point the person involved in the pogrom stops being an individual criminal and becomes a fighter. And then if one convinces a policeman to imprison him, that does not mean that he receives his justly deserved punishment as a knifeman, but that he suffers in prison for an idea.

And if the antisemite is a man of ideas international in outlook, it naturally does not help to appeal to a neighbouring country, to a League of Nations, etc. Then we cannot

---

5 The First International was the International Workingmen's Association, an organization of labour groups founded in 1864. The Second International was subsequently formed from socialist and social-democratic organizations and parties in 1889. The Third International was an association of communist parties founded after the Russian Revolution and the Fourth International made up of Trotzkyist organizations.
6 From the Polish *narodowiec* (nationalist).
7 Garda de Fier: ultranationalist movement in Romania, founded in 1927 by Corneliu Zelea Codreanu (1899–1938), initially under the name Legion of the Archangel Michael.
8 Solidarité Française: a radical right-wing movement founded in 1933 by the industrialist François Coty (1874–1934).
9 British Union of Fascists: founded in 1932 by Oswald Mosley (1896–1980).
10 The existence of this group could not be verified.
11 Eretz Israel; Hebrew for 'the Land of Israel'.
12 Polish district official.
13 Probably Tunisia.

defeat him with political acts. He is as good as the others; he occupies an honourable, officially recognized place among the representatives of ideas. He is stronger than we are.¹⁴

4. On the other hand he will be weaker than he was. Because when an antisemite becomes an internationalist he loses the strength of his principles and the main 'virtue' that he had with his people: his nationalism. Just as he becomes an internationalist, as he should be, just as he sees a problem from a broader European viewpoint, according to the interests of *all* countries – he is no longer a patriot. Yet he manages to sneak into the hearts, into the parliaments, as if he were the truest and most spirited patriot and nationalist.

Besides – as soon as he is an international antisemite, he says – it's a lie. Because, for example, the German antisemites are as interested in French Jewish lawyers, in truth, as they are in last week's news. The Polish farmer isn't interested in the Jews in America; rather, he is willing to accept a large loan from them. He does not actually hate the foreign Jew; he just hates the Jewish cattle-dealer in his shtetl.¹⁵ He does not want to get rid of the Jewish lawyers in Regensburg – he only wants to get rid of the cattle-dealers here, his debtors. Furthermore: in the event that he hates a country, he would want there to be *more* Jews there, especially influential Jews. The struggle against '*global catastrophe*' does not and cannot interest him.

But if he goes now and pretends that it does interest him, if he organizes internationally, he afflicts himself with all the considerations and difficulties one faces in every international. Then he must deal with the 'antisemitic interests' in a faraway country, with the situation of the Jews, with anti-Jewish villains, and with foreign circumstances. Then he cannot interfere with the policies of the second state through his 'actions', he cannot take loans from foreign Jews, he cannot, on his own responsibility, make separate negotiations with 'his' Jews, and he is, on the other hand, also obliged to support, with blood and money, an anti-Jewish struggle in a foreign country that does not concern him.

Internationalism breaks apart. (If anyone knows that, then it is we Jews, the dispersed and scattered.) At an international table one can – nowadays – disagree. This delegate cannot accept this resolution and that decision contradicts the local interests of *that* delegate.

An international machine does not budge. It is, in our nationalist age, a pretence and nothing more. It is a kind of Second International, a kind of alliance – deserted and empty.¹⁶ It weakens the momentum and the breadth that every single participant would

---

14 *Der Stürmer* responded to the *Haynt* article in Nov. 1934 with an article titled 'Jüdischer Schrecken vor der antisemitischen Internationale: Ein Jude schüttet sein verängstigtes Herz aus' ('Jewish Fear of the Antisemitic International: A Jew Pours out his Frightened Heart'). In the introductory comments to the printed translation of the first three paragraphs of Karlebach's text, *Der Stürmer* wrote that the Antisemitic International was necessary in order to hinder Jewish world domination: *Der Stürmer*, no. 46, Nov. 1934, no page number.
15 The term shtetl refers to predominantly Yiddish-speaking Jewish market towns in Eastern Europe.
16 The Second International broke up at the beginning of the First World War due to the pro-war stance of important member parties, including the Social Democratic Party of Germany and the British Labour Party.

have in his own country, in his own home. It burdens and encumbers him with a manifold, multicoloured perspective of 'all of Europe'. It tells him to be 'tactical' it does not allow him any emotional release.

Because it is an old truth: if you want to paralyse an idealist's momentum, then give his idea an international.

5. Since a conference of antisemites is thus taking place next week in Nuremberg, we wish it every success from the bottom of our hearts.

May it succeed 100 per cent in its mission. May it internationalize every single antisemite in the whole world. May they all have the slogan 'the Jew enemies of all countries' in their mouths. For only such a leash can choke and strangle.

Yes, from next week on, the internationally expanding antisemitism will be more conspicuous and exaggerated.

But also – less dangerous.

DOC. 126
On 23 June 1934 Kurt Rathenau informs his brother Fritz about the catastrophic situation of his company Ernst Rosenberg & Co. in Berlin[1]

Letter from Kurt Rathenau,[2] Berlin W 62, 40 Bayreutherstraße, to Fritz Rathenau,[3] Berlin, dated 23 June 1934

Dear Fritz,

With respect to our repeated conversations regarding the restructuring of my company,[4] I am sending you, as requested, a memorandum on the status of the company and the measures envisaged.[5]

The aim is to come to a *private bankruptcy arrangement*, which has already been accepted by the major creditors. The negotiations with the company Georg Fromberg & Co., Berlin,[6] are still pending, and they might be delayed for a couple of days due to the death of the co-owner, Mr Fehr, yesterday.

1 Jüdisches Museum Berlin, 2001-106-904, fol. 1. This document has been translated from German.
2 Dr Kurt Rathenau (1880–1942), retailer; co-owner of Ernst Rosenberg & Co. In June 1942 he was deported to Minsk, where he was murdered.
3 Dr Fritz Rathenau (1875–1949), lawyer; worked in the Prussian Ministry of the Interior, 1920–1933; transferred to the Prussian Building and Finance Headquarters in 1933 and dismissed in 1935; emigrated in 1939 to the Netherlands, from where he was deported to Theresienstadt in 1943; lived in the Netherlands after 1945.
4 The company Ernst Rosenberg & Co., Berlin, had specialized in the sale of machines for manufacturing electrical cables.
5 The reasons for the poor financial situation of the company can be ascertained from the enclosure sent with the letter of 23 June 1934: 'Since the devaluation of the £ and the $, the export business has shrunk considerably, as is well known, and it has been decreasing sharply over the last fifteen months. As we are a non-Aryan business, we are barred from supplying the authorities as we did before. These factors have escalated the situation': Jüdisches Museum Berlin, 2001-106-904, fol. 2.
6 The company Georg Fromberg & Co. was a Berlin banking business that developed from the Berlin bank Ehrecke, Fromberg & Co., which had been established in the nineteenth century.

The settlement issue would not be so pressing if it were not for the fact that the matter of the office rent and an outstanding payment (bill for goods) need to be dealt with immediately. The landlord has exercised his lien rights and seized part of the furnishings.

Approximately 1,500 Reichsmarks are needed by 1 July in order to settle these matters, as well as the removal costs incurred.

I ask you, dear Fritz, since you and Sophie[7] have said that you are willing to help me, to send your sons the memorandum and obtain their consent to release some money from the inheritance in order to come to my aid.

You know, dear Fritz, how unbelievably heavy these matters weigh upon me and how happy I would be to be able to breathe freely again and devote all my energy to a new kind of work.

With best regards

DOC. 127
Petition to the Regional Tax Office in Silesia dated 4 July 1934 requesting exemption from the Reich Flight Tax for Erich Frank, appointed professor at the University of Istanbul[1]

Letter from Hans Lachmann,[2] lawyer, Breslau, 9 Freiburger Straße, to the president of the Regional Tax Office in Silesia, Breslau, dated 4 July 1934 (copy of S 1915 A – 488 III preuß. FM)

Re: Reich Flight Tax case[3] Professor Erich *Frank*,[4] Breslau – S 1915 – F7 –1/2–

In response to the statement from the tax office in South Breslau[5] the following should be noted:

It cannot be disputed that in the following case the pursuance of certain private economic interests is closely tied to that of general German interests. According to the rulings handed down by the Reich Fiscal Court, this fact alone, however, cannot adequately negate the existence of the legal premise that such emigration is in the interests of Ger-

---

7 Sophie Rathenau, née Dannenbaum (1882–1973), had been married to Fritz Rathenau since 1904.

1 GStA PK, I HA, Rep. 76, Va Sect. 4 Tit. IV, Nr. 51, Bd. 1, fol. 537. This letter has been translated from German.
2 Dr Hans Lachmann (1892–1981), lawyer; practised law in Breslau; emigrated first to Belgium and then in June 1938 to New York.
3 The Reich Flight Tax had been levied in Germany since 1931 in order to make it more difficult to transfer capital out of the country. Subjects of the Reich who left the country had to pay a quarter of their assets as a 'flight tax', provided that they had assets exceeding 200,000 Reichsmarks or a yearly income of more than 20,000 Reichsmarks. From 1933 the National Socialist state applied this tax in particular to Jewish emigrants. On the increased use of the tax against Jews by individual tax offices, see the memorandum of the tax office in Mannheim dated 30 Nov. 1935, BArch, R 2/5973, fols. 67–72v. Published in abridged form in Martin Friedenberger, Klaus-Dieter Gössel, and Eberhard Schönknecht (eds.), *Die Reichsfinanzverwaltung im Nationalsozialismus: Darstellung und Dokumente* (Bremen: Temmen, 2002), doc. 8, pp. 35–37. On the revenue from the tax, see Doc. 280, 16 May 1937.
4 Dr Erich Frank (1884–1957), physician; from 1918 lecturer in pathological physiology at the University of Breslau, where he was awarded a professorship in 1921; emigrated to Turkey in the autumn of 1933; professor in Istanbul, 1933–1957.
5 The statement is not in the file.

many. The tax office has overlooked the fact that there is no application process for a university professor; the petitioner never applied for a professorship at the University of Istanbul, but rather he was appointed to the post by the Turkish government on the basis of his recognized scientific achievements.

If the tax office claims that the petitioner, owing to his non-Aryan descent, can never be called upon to promote the nature and character of the German state or to advance its culture, then the rulings of the Reich Fiscal Court must be held up against these claims. In the judgement dated 12 April 1934 (*Reichssteuerblatt*, p. 591) the Reich Fiscal Court determined that the decision as to whether emigration lies in the interests of Germany with respect to non-Aryans as well as taxpayers of German descent can only be made on a case-by-case basis.[6]

We ask once again that the Reich Foreign Office in Berlin be consulted (cf. last paragraph of the petition dated 5 June 1934).[7]

Most respectfully

DOC. 128
Margot Littauer describes her everyday school life in Breslau in mid 1934[1]

Submission by Margot Littauer[2] to a Harvard University competition (1940)

[…][3]

At school a number of things now began to change nonetheless. The first indication was the choice of topics for German essays – for example, '1 May – Day of National Labour'.[4]

---

6 Lachmann sent another letter on 17 July 1934 in which he explained that the economic situation of the petitioner was worse in Istanbul than in Breslau; he further stated that he would have taken on the appointment previously and that his assets amounted to only 22,000 Reichsmarks, an amount that was just over the tax exemption limit. The president of the Regional Tax Office in Silesia rejected the petition on 20 July 1934: GStA PK, I HA, Rep. 76, Va Sect. 4 Tit. IV, Nr. 51, Bd. 1, fols. 539–541.

7 Through the Reich Ministry of Finance, the Prussian Ministry of Science was also asked to comment on the matter. The latter summoned expert opinions from the University of Breslau in Sept. 1934 and from different NSDAP offices as to whether Frank's intended position was in the interests of Germany. Two of the opinions fell in favour of the petition and two opposed the exemption from the Reich Flight Tax obligation. The Prussian Ministry of Science returned the case file to the Reich Ministry of Finance on 23 Oct. 1934 without endorsing the petition: ibid., fols. 542–548.

1 Margot Littauer, 'Mein Leben in Deutschland vor und nach dem 30. Januar 1933' [My life in Germany before and after 30 January 1933] (1940), pp. 17–19; Harvard Competition, no. 142. This document has been translated from German.

2 Margot Littauer (b. 1918) lived in Königsberg, Prussia, 1919–1931, and then in Breslau; from 1935 she worked as a maid and doctor's receptionist; she emigrated to Palestine in 1939.

3 The entire account, posted from Tel Aviv, consists of 34 pages. Littauer first describes her childhood in Königsberg and Breslau, the political situation before 1933, and how she took care of her mother, who had a heart condition, after her father's death in 1934.

4 Shortly after coming to power in 1933, the National Socialist government declared 1 May as the 'Day of National Work' (Tag der nationalen Arbeit) and made it a public holiday. Through propagandistic events and parades held on 1 May 1933 the National Socialist regime aimed to garner support from the working classes and eliminate the power of the trade unions. On 2 May 1933, trade union offices were occupied by the SA and leading trade unionists were arrested.

We, the Jewish girls, must have sat there fairly baffled. Suddenly a shout rang out from a member of the League of German Girls: 'Are the Jewish girls supposed to write about this with the rest of us?' The teacher, completely uncomprehending, shrugged his shoulders and said: 'Well, of course.' So there was nothing else for it but to begin writing about the topic. But from just what angle should we approach the subject? If we praised May Day, they would certainly say: 'Jewish bootlickers' if we wrote something to the contrary, one could only imagine the outcome. So I decided to give an objective account of 1 May in the National Socialist state, to the best of my ability. Naturally, the essay seemed quite stilted – I had included a few phrases from the newspaper in addition – because it was really impossible for me to try writing the essay in an unselfconscious way. We sat there fairly helplessly, looked at each other, and shrugged our shoulders. On one occasion the teacher saw this shoulder-shrugging – again, with a complete lack of comprehension! Finally, I handed in the ill-fated exercise book. On the way to the teacher's desk, I felt downright foolish. After the essay-writing period no one said anything; it seemed as if it had been unimportant and already forgotten. I was well aware that the essay could not be any good, but this time nobody needed to reproach me. The next day we had German class again. At the beginning of the class the German teacher, as was his custom, stood before the front row of desks, leaned on the middle desk until his knuckles turned quite white, and said: 'Yesterday, strangely enough, someone asked whether the Jewish girls should take part in writing the essay, and I was rather surprised at the question, since I did not regard it as so very relevant; but now that it has been raised, let's clarify it and, furthermore, establish our position on the Jewish question.'

No one made a sound in the classroom. Finally the teacher asked the girl who had posed the question the day before, and whom he liked: 'So, Eva Lotte, what were you thinking when you asked the question?' Eva Lotte was quite smitten with this spectacle. She liked to showcase herself and was always trying to be the centre of attention. So she now felt she was in her element here. She presented her reasons in quite a sensible way, and made it clear to us that the topic was not suitable for the entire class to work on at the same time. She declared that we could not have approached it in either a positive or a negative fashion. But when she added that it signified a debasement of the topic and the 1 May holiday in general if these things were addressed by non-Germans, non-Aryans, the teacher intervened and said that, as everyone was well aware, the last thing he had intended was to discredit May Day and thus a National Socialist institution. But since the Jewish pupils were still included in the school setting, he added, it was necessary for them to find a form of presentation that could be appropriate for them and their special case. He had believed every one of the Jewish girls had sufficient tact for the assignment, he said, and incidentally they had absolutely proved his opinion correct, which we Jewish girls, at least, interpreted as great praise. Slowly, the discussion began to move from the question of tact into a more general direction; it was kept within very polite, well-fenced boundaries. In this discussion I spoke up only once, to rebut a factual charge made by the teacher. He had pointed out that in medieval times the Jews had dedicated themselves too greatly to trade. Even so, we Jewish girls were grateful for his having avoided the usual catchword 'usurers'. I thus attempted to explain to him that, first, the Jews were not allowed to engage in any other occupation in the Middle Ages, whether that of a craftsman or that of a farmer. The guilds had the strictest bans on the admission of Jews to their professional associations. As a result, the Jews were initially restricted to a one-sided focus on commerce and trade occupations. In addition, Christians were forbidden to charge interest, and instead the Jews were forced to lend money on interest. The fact that the issue of interest had been exploited by the National Socialists and described as 'usurious interest' had to do with a change in the meaning of the word 'usury', which in the medieval period had been merely a term for 'use' of money at an ordinary interest rate and only later became a term for lending at an unreasonably high interest rate. But in five sentences, of course, it was impossible to put the teacher right; as one could always see, he was too firmly rooted in the theories of Jews 'sucking people dry'. Even so, my remarks made a certain impression on him, since he still seemed open to rational arguments and most likely personally had never had any bad experiences with Jews. But the supporters of the teacher were a small minority, and the class was coming to an end. After the dramatic statement by one girl, 'So, then, there's nothing left for the Jews but to turn on the gas,' the teacher concluded with the following comments: 'I am thus in favour of opposing the Jews dispassionately and removing them from among us. They are indeed foreign to us, and they obstruct our nationhood.'

And we had debated for two hours to reach that conclusion! We really had not been allowed at all to deal with the fundamental things that could have touched on National Socialism. And so we heard one day, candid and unvarnished, the opinion of our 'teacher and educator' concerning us. We probably should be grateful to him for being so accommodating, for wanting, unlike many others, to oppose us merely 'dispassionately'.

[...]5

---

5 Subsequently, Margot Littauer describes how she worked in Königsberg, beginning on 1 Oct. 1935, as a doctor's receptionist for Dr Littauer, a general practitioner, and with his help completed the school-leaving exam. She married him in 1938. After the revocation of his medical licence, they emigrated to Palestine in quick succession in 1939.

DOC. 129
Internationales Ärztliches Bulletin, July/August 1934: article about the murder of Erich Mühsam in Oranienburg concentration camp[1]

Murder of Erich Mühsam[2]

In the first week of July in Hitler's Germany, corpses of leaders from all levels, noblemen, political assassins, Catholic journalists, and persons shot in error were piled up.[3] In the prisons and concentration camps, too, where tens of thousands of German workers and members of the liberal professions have been exposed to the National Socialists' brutality for 18 months, this week of free licence to murder wrought havoc. The German news agency spread the report that *Erich Mühsam*, the intrepid fighter, poet, and bard of freedom, had put an end to his life by hanging himself. Everyone who knew this honest man knew that Erich *Mühsam* would never do his jailers the favour of taking his own life. Now his widow, Mrs *Zensl Mühsam*,[4] who managed to reach Prague in recent days, has described at a press conference the whole ordeal of the various concentration camps. Arrested immediately after the Reichstag fire, Mühsam was brutally mistreated in an unimaginable manner in the so-called 'Jew companies' of the infamous camps at Sonnenburg, Oranienburg, and Brandenburg, kicked to the ground and beaten with rubber truncheons and fists. On 9 July 1934 he was told by [SS] Sturmbannführer Erhardt:[5] 'How much longer are you intending to walk around in this world? If you don't commit suicide within the next two days, someone will lend a hand!' Erich Mühsam rejected suicide with utter determination. On the evening of the same day, someone made it happen. The corpse exhibited marks on the neck, showing that Mühsam was obviously dragged by a rope, and in such a way that his head was broken open by striking the ground, because the back of the head was smashed. On the death certificate, too, suicide

---

1 'Erich Mühsams Ermordung', *Internationales Ärztliches Bulletin*, Prague, 1934, nos. 7/8, pp. 119–120 (published in *Beiträge zur nationalsozialistischen Gesundheits- und Sozialpolitik*, vol. 7, Berlin, 1989). This document has been translated from German. The *Bulletin* was published as the central organ of the International Association of Socialist Physicians from 1934 to 1939, first in Prague and then in Paris.

2 Erich Mühsam (1878–1934), writer, anarchist, and anti-war activist; arrested in 1919 for involvement in the Bavarian Council Republic; active in Red Aid, 1925–1929; publisher of *Fanal: Anarchistische Monatsschrift*, 1926–1933; from late Feb. 1933 imprisoned in various jails and concentration camps, and from Jan. 1934 in Oranienburg concentration camp, where he was murdered on 10 July 1934; author of works including *Wüste, Krater, Wolken: Gedichte* (1914) and *Staatsräson: Ein Denkmal für Sacco und Vanzetti* (1928).

3 During an SA leadership conference on 30 June 1934, Hitler had the head of the SA, Ernst Röhm, and other members of the SA's leadership murdered by the SS. Simultaneously, intra-party opponents, including 'old fighters' of the NSDAP, fell victim to the purge, as did political opponents from the conservative ranks, including the last Reich Chancellor of the Weimar Republic, Kurt von Schleicher. On 2 July 1934 the Reich government retroactively justified the operation, also known as the 'Night of the Long Knives', by declaring it a neccessary response to the 'national' emergency posed by the coup allegedly planned by Röhm.

4 Correctly: Kreszentia Mühsam (1884–1962). Married to Erich Mühsam since 1915, she emigrated after his death to the Soviet Union. There she was imprisoned in camps for years; she left the country for the German Democratic Republic in 1955.

5 Probably Hermann Erhardt; joined the NSDAP on 12 Feb. 1933.

was not recorded as the cause of death, because no doctor was willing to sign his name to it. Mrs Mühsam, whose news understandably caused a sensation at the press conference and in the newspapers of every country, justifiably demanded a post-mortem examination of the body. It must be the concern of the world public to do its duty, over and above reporting, and compel the release of the many threatened activists.

With [the death of] *Erich Mühsam*, who had countless friends in every political and cultural camp in the world, and in the circle of socialist physicians, in speech and writing, worked time and again for the liberation and humane treatment of political prisoners, a magnificent fighter and noble human being has been destroyed. He showed his defiance and indomitable courage in his life and in his songs:

> Then a blow with the rifle butt puts him on his back,
> And, dying, he threatens the Whites:
> Though I myself am lost, you cannot
> Wrest my conviction from me:
> I will die, but the Revolution
> Will live on nonetheless!

DOC. 130

On 2 August 1934 the Gestapo prohibits members of Jewish youth organizations from wearing uniforms and participating in military sports training[1]

Circular issued by the Inspector of the Gestapo (II 1 B. 2 23 929/672 /R. 5), p.p. signed Patschowski,[2] to all State Police offices and for information only to all Oberpräsidenten and Regierungspräsidenten, dated 2 August 1934

Working Guideline 5
regarding *Jewish youth organizations*, with reference to the decree II 1 16 426 of 29 May 1934.

I have surmised from the reports coming from numerous State Police offices that the united appearance of Jewish youth organizations in matching uniforms has caused major unrest within Party organization circles and among the population in general, which has even led to clashes in some instances.

Given the fact that Jewish youth organizations for the most part also engage in sporting activities and the German Olympic Committee has granted Jewish sport organizations equal rights of participation in the Olympic Games held in Germany, I would like to refrain from issuing a general prohibition of Jewish youth organizations at the present time. Owing to considerations of a national political nature, I also consider it inexpedient to subsume the fragmented Jewish youth groups into one umbrella organization, because such a legal compulsion might in fact work to reduce the fragmentation among the youth groups.

1 RGVA, 501k-1-17, fols. 22–24. This document has been translated from German.
2 Dr Günther Patschowski, known as of 1937 as Günther Palten (b. 1903), lawyer; practised law in Breslau; joined the NSDAP in 1931 and the SS in 1932; state prosecutor in Breslau, 1932–1933; joined the police administration, 1933; deputy to the chief of police in Gleiwitz, 1935–1938; Regierungspräsident in Bromberg, 1939–1941; Regierungspräsident in Linz, 1941–1945; SS-Brigadeführer, 1944.

However, in order to prevent further confrontations between Jewish youth groups and Party organizations, in consultation with the Reich Youth Leadership, I call for Jewish youth groups to be prohibited from wearing matching clothing (outfits, uniforms, etc.) in public, by means of a State Police directive drawn up on the basis of § 1 of the Regulation of the Reich President for the Protection of People and State issued on 28 February 1933 (*Reichsgesetzblatt*, I, p. 83) and §§ 14 and 58 of the Police Administration Law issued on 1 June 1931 (*Gesetzsammlung*, p. 77). Clothing prohibited under this directive also includes associational attire or pieces of clothing that are part of a uniform, as well as any insignia that may be hidden under civilian clothing (such as coats) and any other kind of uniform clothing that can be considered as a replacement for the former associational attire.

Furthermore, I request that the carrying or displaying of flags, banners, or pennants in public be prohibited.

Field or military exercises of any kind, as well as group parades or marches, especially marches in military-type gear, are also to be prohibited. In contrast, athletic or national sports activities, as well as casual walks and excursions or hikes on a small scale, as long as they do not have any kind of demonstrative character, do not fall under this prohibition. Marching in rank and file, on the other hand, is not permitted.

Finally, the sale and distribution of press materials of any kind, especially leaflets, is to be prohibited.

In the event that this directive is not followed, a fine may be imposed and, in the event of this being unobtainable, a prison sentence may be imposed. This State Police directive does not have any bearing on criminal prosecution according to the respective penal provisions. In the directive it must also be noted that offenders may be taken into protective custody and that any prohibited uniform clothing or insignia worn, as well as any prohibited flags, banners, or pennants carried and prohibited press materials and leaflets distributed, may be confiscated.

I expect to receive a report on what has been ordered by 25 August 1934. A copy of the issued directive is to be enclosed.[3]

DOC. 131

Verordnungsblatt der Obersten SA-Führung: on 16 August 1934 the Deputy of the Führer, Rudolf Heß, prohibits NSDAP members from consorting with Jews[1]

10. Re: consorting with Jews[2]
Directive.

Notifications have indicated that Party comrades have failed to demonstrate the necessary restraint in dealings with the Jews.

---

[3] Corresponding State Police directives were subsequently issued in Prussia as well as in other regions, for example in the Prussian Regierungsbezirk Münster on 11 August 1934 and in the state of Saxony on 30 Nov. 1934: ibid., fols. 38–39v, and Sächsisches Staatsarchiv Leipzig, Polizeipräsidium/ 5007, fol. 173.

[1] *Verordnungsblatt der Obersten SA-Führung*, no. 34, 24 Sept. 1934, p. 3. This document has been translated from German. The *Verordnungsblatt der Obersten SA-Führung*, the regulations gazette of the SA leadership, was published from 1931 to 1944.

Irrespective of the status and opportunities afforded to Jews living in Germany by the current laws, I prohibit all Party comrades from the following:

(1) representing Jews against Party comrades before the courts etc.;
(2) advocating for Jews in state and other public offices;
(3) issuing certificates of any kind for Jews;
(4) accepting any funds that the Jews wish to donate for Party purposes;
(5) consorting with Jews in public or in restaurants or bars;
(6) wearing Party insignia during the hours in which they are working as employees in Jewish businesses.

The Party has had to make enormous sacrifices in the struggle against the hegemony of the destructive Jewish spirit directed against the people of Germany and it must therefore declare that it is undignified for Party comrades to stand for those who have brought unspeakable misfortune on our German people, at a time in which millions of German Volksgenossen are still living in misery.

Violations against this directive will be subject to Party court proceedings.[3]

Munich, 16 August 1934 signed Heß

DOC. 132

On 29 August 1934 the Tenants' Protection Association in Frankfurt proposes that the mayor rename certain streets and squares[1]

Letter from the Frankfurt am Main Tenants' Protection Association, in the Reich League of German Tenants' Associations (Rtr/Ko. 1698), serving Regierungsrat, Association Chairman Ritter,[2] to the mayor of the city of Frankfurt am Main, Dr Krebs (received on 31 August 1934), dated 29 August 1934[3]

Re: *suggestion*

The board of the Frankfurt am Main Tenants' Protection Association would like to propose to you, dear Mayor, that the square in front of the main station, which does not actually have a name, be named in honour of the late field marshal and Reich President.[4] It is precisely this square in front of the train station that may be judged as the most suitable and has earned such a name, because it is a tourist hub and, after all, every citizen of Frankfurt crosses this square from time to time.

---

2 The previous and following points in the *Verordnungsblatt* deal with different topics. Clause 9 addresses the work of SA physicians in the Party; clause 12 deals with complaints: ibid.
3 A week after the directive was published in the *Verordnungsblatt*, the SA leadership declared that the directive also applied to all members of the SA who were not Party members: ibid., no. 35, 1 Oct. 1934.
1 ISG Frankfurt, Magistratsakten/6294. This document has been translated from German.
2 Dr Karl Ludwig Ritter (b. 1888), career officer; military career, 1908–1920; Regierungsrat, 1922; chairman of the Tenants' Protection Association in Frankfurt am Main, 1924–1934; classified as a 'follower' by the Frankfurt denazification tribunal, 1949.
3 The original is underlined by hand in several places and contains a stamp from the mayor: 'to be sent to the building office for comment and a reply to be submitted in writing by 15 September 1934'. Another stamp reads: 'Municipal Building Office received on 5 September 1934'.
4 Reich President Paul von Hindenburg had died on 2 August 1934.

As the late Reich President was an honorary citizen of the city of Frankfurt am Main, this is now the right moment.

We would also like to take this opportunity to further propose that streets and squares named after non-Aryans gradually be renamed. First and foremost, Börneplatz and Börnestrasse come to mind. Street names could be chosen in celebration of the [fiftieth] anniversary of the beginnings of our colonial past. For example, such names could include Windhoukplatz[5] or Lüderitzstrasse or the like.[6]

Heil Hitler!

DOC. 133
On 29 August 1934 the Reich Office for Emigration Affairs provides information concerning the state and problems of Jewish emigration from Germany in the second quarter of the year[1]

Report by the Reich Office for Emigration Affairs[2] (ref. no. A 1002/28 August), signed Schmidt,[3] Berlin, 2 Fürst Bismarckstraße, dated 29 August 1934 (copy IV 6101 II/29 August)

Re: status of emigration developments in the second calendar quarter of 1934 (II/34).
Author: Ministerialrat Dr Müller.[4]
Co-author: Regierungsrat Flemke.[5]

The work of the emigrant advisory offices has *slightly increased* when compared with the first calendar quarter of 1934 (I/34). The number of those seeking advice was 20,437, as against 20,325 in I/34 (up 0.45 per cent). The total number of enquiries fell from 26,625 in I/34 to 26,434 in the reporting quarter.

---

5 Correctly: Windhoek.
6 The original contains a handwritten comment from the author: 'Perhaps you could appoint an office to review all the names of streets and squares.' The mayor of Frankfurt responded on 17 Sept. 1934 that the renaming of a square after Hindenburg would be looked into and that the renaming of 'Jewish street names' would be kept in mind: ISG Frankfurt, Magistratsakten/6294.

1 BayHStA, StK 6266. This document has been translated from German.
2 The Reich Office for Emigration Affairs (Reichsstelle für das Auswanderungswesen) in Berlin, with branches in various German cities, was established in 1902 as the central information office for emigrants. Known as the Reich Migration Office from 1919 to 1924 and the Reich Office for Emigration Affairs from 1924 to 1945, its work fell under the remit of the Reich Ministry of the Interior.
3 Dr Schmidt, who until his death in 1939 was director of the Reich Office for Emigration Affairs.
4 Dr Adolf Müller (1886–1974), lawyer and administrator; member of the German Democratic Party (DDP), 1923–1929; worked at the Bavarian Regional Statistical Office from 1914, at the Reich Statistical Office, 1919–1921, and at the Reich Ministry of Food and Agriculture, 1921–1922; economic advisor for the occupied Rhineland regions at the Reich Ministry of the Interior; deputy director of the Reich Office for Emigration Affairs, 1933–1944; after 1945 founder of the People's Social Commission for Hesse-Palatinate.
5 Hugo Flemke (b. 1886), teacher and farmer; head of the foreign department of the Aid Association for Returning German Migrants (Fürsorgeverein für deutsche Rückwanderer), 1909–1917; Regierungsrat in the Reich Office for Emigration Matters, 1918–1944; from 1924 editor of the Reich Office news bulletin.

Of those seeking advice, 40.4 per cent *originated* from Prussia, with approximately one quarter from Berlin and almost one fifth from the Rhineland. Bavaria accounted for 12.84 per cent, and 41.82 per cent were from the rest of the Reich. Of these, 15.14 per cent were from Württemberg and 6.80 per cent from Baden, i.e. more than half. Foreign countries accounted for 4.94 per cent of those seeking advice.

The total number of those seeking advice is only *marginally higher* than that of the same reporting quarter in 1933 and approximately *one tenth higher* than in II/32.

While a reduction in the Jewish urge to emigrate was reported for IV/33 and I/34, in the second calendar quarter of 1934 there was a new *resurgence in the Jewish* desire to emigrate. There are various reasons for this increase, which was reported in particular by the advisory offices in Berlin, Munich, Frankfurt, and Hamburg.

The Aryan legislation of the past year had initially concerned all Jews who were in the civil service or whose economic existence was in some way dependent on the public purse, but not purely commercial circles, in which civil service regulations do not apply. But these circles were also gradually affected by the shift in the mindset of the German people, albeit more slowly, in that the population more strongly rejected financial ties with the Jew. This was also shown in the decline in professional activity of those Jewish doctors and lawyers who were still permitted to practise after the new legislation. The Berlin advisory office experienced an unusually high onslaught of Jewish visitors towards the end of May. It believes that this increased urge to emigrate on the part of Berlin's Jews can also be attributed to the speech made by the Reich Minister of Public Enlightenment and Propaganda at the Sportpalast on 11 May this year.[6]

The continuing positive response in many of the Jews' destination countries also resulted in an intensification of the tendency to emigrate. In particular, the German Jews' connections to those who had emigrated to Palestine, South Africa, and North America became closer. Relatives and friends followed their set of relations and acquaintances. Jewish parents primarily sought accommodation for their children abroad and remained behind in Germany themselves.

In a few places, it was estimated that the tendency of Jews to emigrate had increased by approximately one third in relation to the previous quarter.

Whereas at the beginning Jewish emigration was often very hasty, it now took place in an organized and considered way despite increased demand. Everything was prepared down to the last detail among the Jews' excellent connections, and with considerable help from relatives and acquaintances in the destination countries. Changes of profession were very frequent. Farmers and trained craftsmen, who are poorly represented among the Jews, had easier and better possibilities of advancement than those who belonged to the merchant class and the liberal professions.

A very large number of retraining opportunities for professions with better prospects emerged both in Germany and in the neighbouring countries. Prosperous circles also took up these opportunities for longer-term training.

Jewish organizations in all parts of the world made particular efforts to reduce the tensions that had arisen to various degrees as a result of the immigration of their racial comrades, and were generally successful in this endeavour. Thus, in the new destination

---

6 See Doc. 117, 11 May 1934.

countries the view was spread most emphatically that the influx of the Jews, especially from Germany, would not represent a burden but instead an economic advantage through the creation of increased job opportunities.

The Jewish organizations faced particular difficulties in placing Jewish intellectuals. But here, too, good results are reported. Thus far, 600–700 university lecturers and over 1,500 students from a total of 7,000 students said to have left German universities are thought to have gone abroad. Jewish organizations have attempted to distribute the profuse number of academics, members of liberal professions, and students as widely as possible.

Palestine has *again* become main destination country of the Jewish emigrants. The economic renewal in Palestine continued in the reporting quarter. Many new plantations were set up. A strong progression in industrial plants was reported. The construction industry was still unable to meet the demand for accommodation. A severe lack of Jewish workers was reported in the Jewish press, with the result that many Arab workers had to be used not only for the work in the cities but also in the Jewish plantations.

The advisors frequently reported an increase in advisory work compared to the provision of expert services. The issuing of *foreign currency certificates*, however, created a great deal of work for the advisory offices.

According to the report from the advisory office in Frankfurt am Main, the transfer of funds through special account I at the end of July was such that approximately 65 per cent of the authorized sum was approved after four months for withdrawal in Palestine, and the remainder after 5 and a half to 6 months, and in fact with a loss of 5 to 6 per cent, of which 1 per cent could be paid in Reichsmarks to Paltreu.[7]

The advisory offices in Berlin, Munich, Cologne, Hamburg, Breslau, and Dresden issued in the second calendar quarter of 1934 a total of 1,709 (as against 1,119 in I/34) certificates, and 20.3 million Reichsmarks (as against 11.5 million Reichsmarks in I/34) were approved for release – that is on average approximately 11,900 Reichsmarks per emigrant (compared to 10,200 Reichsmarks in I/34).

The advisory offices repeatedly point out the stark contrast between Jewish and Aryan would-be emigrants. Notable among the Jews is the great wealth and among the Aryans the scant means available for establishing a new life abroad. Among a large proportion of the Aryan would-be emigrants even the funds for travel costs are unavailable, so that pursuit of their emigration plans has had to be abandoned due to a lack of means. Jewish emigrants, however, aside from taking with them considerable funds for establishing a new life, are in many cases still leaving substantial funds behind in Germany.

Suitable would-be emigrants for Terra Nova near Castro could in many cases be referred in addition to the *Association for Settlement Abroad*.[8]

Considered by *continent*, the following picture of the requests emerged: *America*, with its 29.7 per cent of enquiries, had to record a stronger decline compared with the period I/34 in favour of *Asia*, whose share rose from 9.74 to 11.69 per cent. The number of enquiries concerning *Europe* with 27.95 per cent, *Africa* with 7.02 per cent, and *Australia* with 0.71 per cent remained almost unchanged as compared with I/34.

Of the 7,852 information documents (as against 8,848 in I/34) that were retrieved concerning living and settlement conditions on the *American continent*, the USA ac-

---

7 Palestine Trust Agency to Advise German Jews (Paltreu). See Glossary.
8 Probably the Terra Nova settlement in southern Brazil.

counted for 2,202 (as against 1,576 in I/34) and Canada, 262 (324); the Central American countries, 207 (224), with Haiti and the Dominican Republic, 19 (7), and Cuba and Puerto Rico, 7 (15); the South American countries, 5,181 (6,724), with Brazil, 3,533 (4,815), Argentina, 579 (644), Paraguay, 325 (311), Chile, 206 (227), Uruguay, 81 (76), Colombia, 78 (95), Bolivia, 54 (106), Venezuela, 44 (70), Peru, 36 (54), and Ecuador, 20 (33).

The increase in demand *regarding the United States* is to be attributed to the easing of the conditions of entry clearance for Jews.[9] Only in a few cases were Aryan German Reich nationals also able to take advantage of this easing.

The Frankfurt advisory office indicated in particular that a significant number of students or young academics who had passed their final university examination had submitted enquiries concerning the United States. The examination board for doctors at New York University wrote in a letter that the only appreciable difficulty for German x doctors in obtaining permission to open a practice in New York State lay with the immigration authorities. A person who has immigrated in accordance with the regulations, holds a degree from a recognized German university, and has been active in practice for at least five years could receive recognition of his German degree in New York State without a further examination. A student at Reed College in Portland, Oregon, indicated to his friend the possibility of cheap study if one lives very frugally. The student would be able to earn something on the side at most American universities.

The family, friendship, and good business connections between the old prosperous Jews of German nationality and the inhabitants of the United States, the Jew-friendly attitude of the American government, and the size of the country offered, despite the general depression, many earning opportunities to immigrants with some capital. Here the excellently run Jewish aid organizations have played a role. It is therefore easy to explain why the United States has become the main destination country of Jewish emigrants after Palestine.

The decline in *requests concerning Brazil*, which remains the most requested destination country, is presumably to be attributed to communications in the press regarding the quota allocation of immigrants. Moreover, Jewish would-be emigrants, in particular emigrants who had experienced disappointment in the European destination countries of France, Belgium, and Holland, had enquired in the reported quarter more frequently than before regarding Brazil. As previously, however, Brazil, Paraguay, and northern Argentina were the destination countries sought almost exclusively by Aryans.

Of the *European* target countries, concerning which 7,388 information documents were issued, the *Netherlands*, as in I/34, held first place, with 1,276 (4.83 per cent) of all requests. The majority of the emigrants to the Netherlands were domestic employees whose job prospects had significantly improved here because the previously strong supply from Germany had declined.

The requests *concerning France* (973) remained at almost the same level as in the previous quarters. Jewish emigrants gave visible expression to their great disappointment in France, where the position of immigrants without means continually worsened

---

9 This statement cannot be readily confirmed. The USA pursued a restrictive immigration policy from the mid 1920s, with annually set immigrant quotas per native country. The emigrants had to demonstrate capital or securities to receive an entry visa. The quotas that applied for Germany could initially thus not even be completely met. It was not until 1938 that the USA interpreted the regulations somewhat more generously for Jewish refugees.

as a result of the lack of assistance that had originally been plentiful, by travelling on to Palestine, North America, and South Africa, and also in smaller numbers to Brazil. Some of them also required the approval of foreign currency.

The requests *concerning England* (950, as against 955 in I/34) remained at the level observed for several reporting quarters. The requests concerning Belgium (257), Norway (74), and Finland (48) had increased very little; those concerning Sweden (176), Denmark (125), and Luxembourg (71) had decreased insubstantially.

The number of requests concerning *Central and Southern Europe* (3,050, as against 3,064 in I/34) had only slightly altered. Italy, Switzerland, Czechoslovakia, and German-Austria were slightly higher in demand than in the previous quarter.

The enquiries concerning *Eastern Europe* (388, as against 378 in I/34) had remained almost the same. Russia (66) and Estonia (5) were down; Poland (158), Lithuania (80), and the Memel territory (79) were rather more strongly sought after.

The number of enquiries *concerning Asia* increased from 2,594 (9.74 per cent in I/34) to 3,089 (11.69 per cent).

The strong increase is exclusively due to the increase in enquiries concerning Palestine, from 1,795 (6.74 per cent) to 2,425 (9.17 per cent of all enquiries). The remaining Asiatic countries are requested to a similar extent as compared with I/34.

Of the 1,856 *enquiries concerning Africa*, 989 were accounted for by South Africa (and indeed 562 by British South Africa and 427 by the former *German South-West Africa*). In South Africa the Jews showed the same eagerness to help their racial comrades as in America, although there were fewer family connections there. The Jewish aid organizations came to the fore here and offered extensive help for obtaining work opportunities. For the former *German East Africa* almost the same interest was shown as in the previous quarter. The number of enquiries was 443 as opposed to 474.

The information documents concerning *former German Cameroon* rose from 44 in I/34 to 77.

The number of enquiries concerning *Australia* including *New Zealand and Oceania* amounted to 187, as against 180 in I/34.

The enquiries concerning *non-specified* countries amounted to 3,056 (11.56 per cent of all enquiries) as against 2,885 (10.84 per cent) in I/34.

The sequence of persons seeking advice according to their professional affiliation has altered only very slightly with regard to the previous quarter. Those belonging to the agriculture and forestry occupational group have moved from third to fourth place.

The actual *overseas emigration* of Germans via German ports amounted in the second calendar quarter of 1934 to 2,953 persons, as against 2,441 persons in I/34 and 1,990 persons in II/34.[10]

The numbers that travelled through the following ports were:

	via Bremen	via Hamburg	in total
April	357	590	947
May	526	587	1,113
June	444	449	893
II/34 in total	1,327	1,626	2,953.

10 As in the original. The figure probably relates to the period II/33.

DOC. 134

On 31 August 1934 Reichsstatthalter Fritz Sauckel urges Hitler and Heß to expropriate the Simson Arms Factory in Suhl[1]

Letter (strictly confidential) from the Reichsstatthalter in Thuringia (ST.S. Nr. 2526/34), Sauckel,[2] Weimar, to the Reich Chancellor and the Deputy of the Führer, dated 31 August 1934[3]

The Simson Works[4] in Suhl are of the greatest importance to the German Reich because of their exclusive licensing under the Treaty of Versailles for army deliveries, and remain so to this day because of their monopoly position.[5] The proprietors, the Simson Jews, are among the most noxious representatives of their race. They have demonstrably defrauded, if not in fact cheated, the German Reich, the Reich Ministry of the Army, and therefore the German taxpayer of many, many millions by unparalleled and disgraceful price speculation. In the course of the national revolution it proved possible to largely eliminate these Jews, who are prepared to engage in any form of corruption, from business operations. It now appears that the Simson brothers are getting the upper hand again and trying to regain their old positions of power. May I emphasize that a criminal procedure is pending against both Jews, which is, however, being severely obstructed because the so-called main culprit (the managing director), Bätz, is based in Switzerland, while the Jews dispute having anything to do with the indictable actions and shift everything on to the goy in Switzerland. However, it was ascertained incontestably by telephone monitoring that they are still very much in contact with him and that they are carrying out all kinds of secret manoeuvres in order to regain their old influence.

I therefore request the Deputy of the Führer to receive and listen to the police superintendent of Thuringia, Gomlich,[6] who has thoroughly investigated this entire affair,[7]

---

1 BArch, R 43 II/358a, fol. 16r–v. This document has been translated from German.
2 Ernst Friedrich (Fritz) Sauckel (1894–1946), sailor; joined the SA in 1922, the NSDAP in 1923, and the SS in 1934; NSDAP Gauleiter of Thuringia, 1927–1945; in 1932–1933 minister president and minister of the interior and in 1933–1945 Reichsstatthalter of Thuringia; general plenipotentiary for labour deployment, 1942–1945; executed in 1946 after receiving a death sentence at the Nuremberg trials.
3 Parts of the original are underlined by hand. The letter addressed to Hitler dated 31 August 1934 was forwarded by Lammers on 6 Sept. 1934 to Rudolf Heß, with the suggestion that he ask Hitler if he might pursue the matter in accordance with Sauckel's wishes. Reich Minister of the Army von Blomberg also received a copy: ibid., fol. 17r v.
4 The Simson firm was founded in 1856 by Löb and Moses Simson in Suhl. It produced charcoal steel from which it manufactured high-quality weapons; later it also made bicycles, cars, and motorbikes.
5 Due to the armaments restrictions laid down in the Treaty of Versailles, since the First World War only the Simson firm had been allowed to produce small armaments for the army in Germany. In 1925 the Reichswehr granted it the monopoly throughout the Reich for the manufacture of light machine guns.
6 Correctly: Hellmuth Gommlich (1891–1945), naval officer and policeman; police inspector in Bremen, 1921–1924; head of a guard detachment at North German Lloyd, 1924–1926; worked for the Criminal Police in Weimar, 1926–1930; head of the police office in Zella-Mehlis, 1930–1934; joined the SS and the SD in 1934; head of police department III in the Thuringian Ministry of the Interior, 1935–1938; Landrat in Meiningen, 1938–1945; committed suicide along with his family in 1945.
7 Gommlich had personally received the confidential assignment from Sauckel in 1933 to investigate the Simson firm in order to Aryanize it. He carried out house searches and instigated audits to try to find material that would justify an expropriation. An initial trial on the grounds of deception and defrauding the Reich failed in 1934 in Meiningen.

and a few of my colleagues, who have detailed knowledge of the whole matter. It would also be politically intolerable for us if the Jews, the Simson brothers, who previously actually cultivated communism in their business, were able to resume their old position of economic power.[8]

Heil Hitler!

DOC. 135

On 16 September 1934 the historian Willy Cohn describes a visit to a Zionist Hachsharah camp[1]

Handwritten diary of Willy Cohn,[2] entry for 16 September 1934

Klein Silsterwitz,[3] 16 Sept. 1934

At the Proskauer home with the *halutzim*.[4] The meeting at the lodge to mourn departed members was very short yesterday evening, and Posner's speech only so-so. The individual deceased members were merely commemorated by name. Among the pictures decorated with mourning bands was one of Franz. It made me feel very melancholy.

Got up at 6 o'clock this morning, went to the post office with Trudi[5] and Ruth,[6] from there by the number 14 to the station; left at 7:48 on a train that doesn't stop until Zobten, then went by bus to Klein Silsterwitz.

We feel very comfortable here among the *haverim*.[7] The kibbutz currently has twelve people: ten boys and two girls; however, the girls and a few of the boys are not here today! Discussed with them the problems facing them in the world: Hachsharah, the

---

8 In 1934 control of the firm was compulsorily removed from the Simson family at the instigation of the Army Ordnance Department, and the company was turned into a limited partnership. The Reichswehr received the majority of the shares. The name of the firm was changed to Berlin-Suhler Waffen- und Fahrzeugwerke Simson & Co., and car production was discontinued in favour of armaments. Faced with a new criminal proceeding in Jena, the Simson family surrendered the firm on 28 Nov. 1935 and emigrated to the USA in 1936. By May 1936 the firm had been turned into the Reich-owned Wilhelm Gustloff Foundation: BArch, R 43 II/358a, fols. 25–26, 38–39, 44–45, 55, and 85. Concerning the intervening plans for the takeover of the Simson Works by the Flick Corporation, see Doc. 165, 22 May 1935.

1 Willy Cohn, 'Tagebuch Breslau, August–Oktober 1934', fols. 58–60; CAHJP, P 88/59. Abridged English translation in Willy Cohn, *No Justice in Germany: The Breslau Diaries, 1933–1941*, ed. Norbert Conrads, trans. Kenneth Kronenberg (Stanford, CA: Stanford University Press, 2012 [German edn, 2006]), p. 43. This diary entry has been retranslated from the original German.

2 Dr Wilhelm (Willy) Cohn (1888–1941), teacher and historian; Zionist and member of the Social Democratic Party of Germany (SPD). From 1919 until his compulsory retirement in 1933 he taught at a grammar school in Breslau, and from 1933 he earned his living from lecture tours on Jewish history. His plans to emigrate to Palestine failed, and at the end of Nov. 1941 he was deported to Kovno, where he was murdered.

3 A place in Kreis Breslau.

4 Plural of *halutz*, Hebrew for 'pioneer'. The term was used in Zionist discourse to refer to people who were or who trained to be agricultural labourers in settlements in Palestine.

5 Gertrud Karoline Cohn, née Rothmann (1901–1941), secretary. She was Willy Cohn's second wife. In Nov. 1941 she was deported with her husband and two youngest daughters to Kovno, where she was murdered.

6 Ruth Cohn, later Atzmon (b. 1924), the eldest daughter from Cohn's marriage to Gertrud Rothmann; emigrated in 1939 with the Youth Aliyah first to Denmark and then via Stockholm, Helsinki, Moscow, Odessa, and Istanbul to Palestine, where she arrived at the end of Dec. 1940.

sexual question, and their relationship to their surroundings here. Their windows were recently smashed in, and shots were fired. Problems with the SA school. Talk centres exclusively on the Jewish farm. But they have good relations with most of the villagers; they also sell some of the produce in the village! Double the amount of ground is being cultivated this year! One of the *haverim* from last year died of polio in Eretz![8] Altogether splendid people here, with the serious desire for a new life! Our hope for a revival of Judaism!

DOC. 136

On 21 September 1934 the state commissioner for Berlin makes arrangements on the occasion of the Jewish Feast of Tabernacles[1]

Letter from the state commissioner (St.K. I,2 -533/34), Lippert, Berlin, to the mayor of the Tiergarten district, the chief of police, and the mayor of Berlin, dated 21 September 1934 (draft, sent on 21 September)[2]

(1) To the mayor of the Tiergarten district.

In response to the question submitted to me by Jewish residents concerning the setting up of booths in order to celebrate their Feast of Tabernacles.[3]

Formal permission from the building control authorities is not required for these booths, which are made using primitive means and only intended to last for a few days. Besides, I take the fundamental standpoint that the practice of religious customs is open to every resident of the capital, Berlin. A precondition here is that residents who hold different views are not offended, and peace and order are not disturbed in any way. It is recommended that these points are emphasized strongly to the applicants.

(2) To the chief of police in Berlin.

Copy of (1) for your kind attention. I consider it possible that, on the part of the population, action will be taken against the Jews regarding the practice of their Feast of Tabernacles customs, unless they for their part exercise the caution that I am advising. I am therefore taking the liberty of drawing your attention to the matter.

(3) To the mayor *here*.

Copy for your kind attention, in case the same question is posed in other districts.

---

7 Plural of *haver*; used in modern Hebrew to mean 'comrade' in political organizations and 'member' (of a board or association).
8 Hebrew for 'land'; in pre-Holocaust Zionist discourse an abbreviation for Eretz-Israel/Palestine.

1 BLHA, Rep. 60/471, fol. 8. This document has been translated from German.
2 The original contains several handwritten revisions.
3 The Feast of Tabernacles (Sukkot or Succoth) is a Jewish festival commemorating the sheltering of the Israelites in the wilderness after the exodus from Egypt; celebrated for seven (and outside the Holy Land for eight) days (15–22/23 Tishri; usually in the second half of September or the beginning of October). It is marked by the erection of small booths (sukkot) made of natural materials in which, according to the Halakha (Jewish religious code), one should eat and sleep throughout the festival.

DOC. 137

Der National-Sozialistische Erzieher, 13 October 1934: draft syllabus regarding the treatment of the Jewish question on so-called State Youth Days[1]

Draft syllabus for the State Youth Day[2]

Week	Subject matter	Link to the Jew	Reading material
1st – 4th	Germany in the pre-war era. Class struggle, profit, strikes.	The Jew makes himself at home!	From Hauptmann's *The Weavers*.
5th – 8th	From agrarian state to industrial state. Colonies.	The farmer in the clutches of the Jew!	Depictions from the colonies. From Hermann Löns.
9th – 12th	Conspiracy against Germany. Encirclement. Barrage around Germany.	The Jew rules! Societies at war.	Beumelburg: 'Barrage...'[3] Life of Hindenburg. Wartime letters.
13th – 16th	German struggle – German want. Blockade! Death by starvation!	The Jew becomes prosperous! Exploitation of German want.	Manke: *Espionage on the Western Front*.[4] Depictions of the war.
17th – 20th	The stab in the back.[5] Collapse.	Jews as leaders of the November revolts.[6]	Pièrre des Granges: *In the Enemy's Country*.[7] Bruno Brehm: *That Was the End*.[8]

---

1 'Entwurf eines Lehrplanes zum Staatsjugendtag', *Der National-Sozialistische Erzieher: Gauamtliche Wochenzeitschrift des NSLB Gau Westfalen-Süd*, 13 Oct. 1934, p. 578. Published under a different heading in Helmut Eschwege (ed.), *Kennzeichen J: Bilder, Dokumente, Berichte zur Geschichte der Verbrechen des Hitlerfaschismus an den deutschen Juden 1933–1945* ([East] Berlin: VEB Verlag der Wissenschaften, 1981), p. 57. This document has been translated from German.

2 At the beginning of Oct. 1934, Reich Minister of Education Rust initiated the State Youth Day. Members of the Deutsches Jungvolk (German Youth) and the Hitler Youth were given Saturdays off school in order to receive tuition in national policy, while lessons took place as usual for all other schoolchildren: 'Durchführung des Staatsjugendtages', *Deutsches Philologen-Blatt*, vol. 42, no. 32 (1934), p. 349.

3 Werner Beumelburg (1899–1963), journalist and writer; from 1933 member and secretary of the German Academy for Literature; author of works including *Sperrfeuer um Deutschland* (1929) and *Deutschland in Ketten* (1930).

4 Correctly: Friedrich Monka, *Spionage an der Westfront: Aus den Aufzeichnungen eines ehemaligen Mitgliedes des deutschen Geheimdienstes im Weltkrieg 1914/18* (1930).

5 Following Germany's defeat in the First World War, antisemitic and anti-socialist conspiracy theories known as stab-in-the-back myths that placed the blame for defeat on saboteurs at home gained in popularity. This greatly destabilized and delegitimized the Weimar Republic and was one factor contributing to the rise of the National Socialist Party.

6 A series of uprisings initiated by war-weary sailors, soldiers, and labourers which demanded an end to the First World War, the abdication of the Kaiser, and the establishment of a democratic republic.

7 Correctly: Pierre Desgranges, *In the Enemy's Country* (1931). Desgranges wrote under the pseudonym Joseph Crozier.

8 Dr Bruno Brehm (1892–1974), Austrian writer; editor of the magazine *Der getreue Eckart*, 1938–1945; author of works including *That Was the End* (1932).

Draft syllabus for the State Youth Day

Week	Subject matter	Link to the Jew	Reading material
21st – 24th	Germany's calvary! Erzberger's[9] crimes! Versailles.	Ostjuden as immigrants. Judah's triumph!	Volkmann: *Revolution over Germany*.[10] Feder: *The Jews*.[11] Newspaper: *Der Stürmer*.
25th – 28th	Adolf Hitler. National Socialism.	Judah's foe!	*Mein Kampf*. Dietrich Eckart.[12]
29th – 32nd	Bleeding frontiers. Enslavement of Germany. Freikorps. Schlageter.[13]	The Jew capitalizes on German misfortune. Bonds. (Dawes, Young.[14])	Beumelburg: *Germany in Chains*. Wehner: *Pilgrimage to Paris*.[15] Schlageter, a German hero.
33rd – 36th	National Socialism in the struggle against the underworld and criminality.	Jews, instigators of murder. The Jewish press.	Horst Wessel.[16]
37th – 40th	Up with the German Youth! The victory of faith.	The final struggle against Judah.	Herbert Norkus.[17] Reich Party Congress.

9 Matthias Erzberger (1875–1921); German politician who negotiated and signed the ceasefire agreement ending the First World War and supported the ratification of the Versailles Treaty, drawing the ire of right-wing radicals who labelled him a 'November criminal' and a 'traitor of the Volk'.

10 Erich Otto Volkmann (1879–1938), career officer; worked from 1920 in the Reich Archives; author of works including *Revolution über Deutschland* (1930).

11 Gottfried Feder (1883–1941), civil engineer; joined the NSDAP in 1920 and became an employee of the *Völkischer Beobachter*; took part in the Beer Hall Putsch, 1923; editor of several magazines, 1927–1933; state secretary in the Reich Ministry of Economics, 1933–1934; professor of settlement studies at the Berlin-Charlottenburg Technical College, 1934; author of works including *The Programme of the N.S.D.A.P. and Its General Conceptions* (1932) and *Die Juden* (1933).

12 Dietrich Eckart (1868–1923), writer; editor-in-chief of the *Völkischer Beobachter*, 1921; author of *Der Bolschewismus von Moses bis Lenin: Zwiegespräch zwischen Adolf Hitler und mir* (1924). Hitler dedicated the first part of volume one of *Mein Kampf* to Eckart.

13 Albert Leo Schlageter (1894–1923), agricultural labourer; fought in several Freikorps; sentenced to death for bomb attacks by a French court during the occupation of the Ruhr in 1923, and executed.

14 The Dawes Plan (1924–1930) and the Young Plan (1930–1932) regulated Germany's reparations payments after the First World War. They spread out the payments to alleviate the burden. It was not only the NSDAP that fiercely opposed the agreements on the grounds that the plans would make Germany dependent for a long time on foreign countries.

15 Josef Magnus Wehner (1891–1973), writer; joined the NSDAP in 1933; author of works including *Die Wallfahrt nach Paris: Eine patriotische Phantasie* (1932).

16 Horst Wessel (1907–1930), member of the SA and the NSDAP, frequently involved in street brawls with communist groups. His 1929 poem, 'Raise the Flag!' ("Die Fahne hoch!"), published in *Der Angriff*, was popularized as the 'Horst-Wessel Song' and became an anthem of the Nazi Party. Albrecht Höhler (1898–1933), a member of the Red Freedom Fighters League, attacked him on 14 January 1930, and Wessel subsequently died of his wounds, sparking a propaganda campaign and Horst Wessel cult, which portrayed him as a martyr of the Nazi revolution.

17 Herbert Norkus (1917–1932), stabbed to death by political opponents as a member of the Hitler Youth in Berlin.

DOC. 138

On 13 October 1934 the Regional Farmers' Leader for Saxony-Anhalt writes to the Reich Farmers' Leader to justify the removal of Jews from the local economy[1]

Letter from the Reich Food Estate, Regional Farming Community for Saxony-Anhalt, regional farmers' leader (7611/34), Eggeling,[2] Halle an der Saale, to the Reich farmers' leader,[3] Administrative Office (received on 15 October 1934), Berlin, dated 13 October 1934[4]

Re: complaint by Meyer-Brüggemann,[5] Salzwedel.[6]
Your letter dated 8 Oct. 1934 – B.C. 5832/34.[7]

I provide the aforementioned report as follows:

It is correct that the Meyer-Brüggemann firm is old and also enjoys a certain standing in liberalist circles. Nevertheless, according to our definition Meyer-Brüggemann is in fact a Jew,[8] and the Kreis Farmers' Leader[9] and the Kreisleiter[10] are only doing their duty when they force this Jew out of his leading economic and social positions. Meyer-

---

1 BArch, R 16/144. This document has been translated from German.
2 Joachim Eggeling (1884–1945), career officer and farmer; military career, 1904–1919; farmer, 1922; joined the NSDAP in 1925 and the SS in 1936; regional farmers' leader for Saxony-Anhalt, 1933–1937; deputy Gauleiter of Magdeburg-Anhalt, 1933–1937; Gauleiter of Halle-Merseburg, 1937–1945; Oberpräsident in Merseburg, 1944–1945.
3 Richard Walther Darré (1895–1953), farmer; member of the Artaman League, 1924–1933; joined the NSDAP in 1930 and the SS in 1931; chief of the Race and Settlement Main Office of the SS, 1932–1938; Reich Farmers' Leader, 1933–1942; Reich minister of food and agriculture, 1933–1942; internment, 1945; sentenced to seven years' imprisonment at the Ministries (Wilhelmstrasse) Trial in Nuremberg, 1947; released in 1950; author of works including *Das Bauerntum als Lebensquell der nordischen Rasse* (1929).
4 The date in the original is written with the Germanized month name: 13 Gilbhard 1934. In the original there is also an entry stamp for the Main Department I from 25 Oct. 1934, and handwritten underlining.
5 Johannes Meyer-Brüggemann (1871–1957), retailer; worked in his father's banking and goods manufacturing company M. Nelke Wwe. in Salzwedel from 1895; from 1912 owner of the company; town councillor in Salzwedel, 1919–1933; until 1935 advisor to the Reich Potash Office in Berlin; Landrat of Kreis Salzwedel, 1945; town councillor in Salzwedel, 1946–1949.
6 The complaint is not in the file. From the available correspondence it is clear that on 10 July 1934 Meyer-Brüggemann had addressed a complaint to the Reich Ministry of Food and Agriculture which had been passed on to the Reich Farmers' Leader. In it Meyer-Brüggemann protested that Kreis Farmers' Leader Gagelmann had influenced the decisions of the shareholders' meeting of the sugar factory by threatening violence. Shortly before that, Hermann Bacharach had levelled similar accusations at Gagelmann: BArch, R 16/144.
7 The Reich Farmers' Leader had forwarded the complaint to the Regional Farming Community of Saxony-Anhalt on 8 Oct. 1934: ibid.
8 Johannes Meyer-Brüggemann had a Jewish grandfather. On the persecution of his family, see Ernst Block, '*Wir waren eine glückliche Familie*': *Zur Geschichte und den Schicksalen der Juden in Salzwedel/Altmark* (Salzwedenl: Renner & Meineke, 1998), pp. 77–83.
9 The Kreis Farmers' Leader in Salzwedel from 1933 was Wilhelm Gagelmann (b. 1885).
10 The NSDAP Kreisleiter of Salzwedel was Dr Gerhard Törne (b. 1892), physician; doctor in Lüchow from 1927 and in Salzwedel from 1929; joined the NSDAP in 1930; acting mayor of Salzwedel, April–Sept. 1933; head of the Association of Germans from Russia, 1934; later moved to Austria; had a practice in Freudenstadt from 1952.

Brüggemann is not being obstructed in carrying out his business, but a National Socialist farmer cannot be expected to tolerate him in any position of leadership.

It was therefore a mistake that the German Land Trade League appointed him as Reich expert advisor. It certainly only did this because it did not know about Meyer-Brüggemann's Jewish ancestry. The Main Department IV therefore has also refused to entrust him with any kind of functions.

The sugar industry is known to have been run along purely liberalistic lines until now and it was the duty of the Kreis Farmers' Leader to establish a National Socialist leadership here. Kreis Farmers' Leader Gagelmann has acted in accordance with his duty here, and has implemented the Gleichschaltung of the board of directors and the managing board of the Salzwedel sugar factory and secured the National Socialist leadership along the lines of the Reich Food Estate. There is a general lamentation about this across the whole spectrum of responses in Salzwedel, especially in 'economic' circles. To me this only goes to prove that his course of action was correct and I defend it completely insofar as he has not proceeded in a criminal way here. If the Kreis farmers' leader is attempting to remove Meyer-Brüggemann from the leadership of the Chamber of Industry and Commerce, then he is likewise doing his duty.

Furthermore, Volksgenossen with National Socialist views must be able to entrust their account to a bank that is under Aryan and National Socialist leadership. Meyer-Brüggemann is adequately protected by the laws against unfair competition and so on. If the Kreis Farmers' Leader acts in conflict with these, Meyer-Brüggemann may hold him to account before the appropriate courts.

Likewise, a Jew does not bring special renown to the veterans' associations and the marksmen's guild, and I can understand it if the National Socialists are trying to remove him from the leadership.

It is inappropriate to see this as a personal insult, because in all these cases it concerns a National Socialist principle and not a proceeding against the person of Meyer-Brüggemann.

I regard the claim that the complaints regarding the Salzwedel reaction never went beyond Dessau as an attack on the Gauleiter,[11] and I must therefore request that the material be made available to him, in order to give him the possibility of taking appropriate measures against the concealed criticism of suppressing justified complaints.

As for the claim that the Kreisleiter and the Kreis Farmers' Leader are weeds in Hitler's wheat, I ask them both to utterly reject the claim as it is expressed in Meyer-Brüggemann's letter, for by keeping silent about the supposed author of this statement he makes himself responsible for it.

Finally, I would like to remark that the Kreis Farmers' Leader in Salzwedel has conducted and is still conducting an extraordinarily difficult battle against reactionary tendencies. He has prevailed with outstanding energy despite all false accusations and difficulties and therefore deserves my fullest recognition. I also ask the relevant Berlin offices to support him in this struggle.

---

11 The NSDAP Gauleiter of Magdeburg-Anhalt from 1934 to 1935 was Wilhelm Friedrich Loeper (1883–1935), career officer; joined the NSDAP in 1925.

I do not need to comment on the personal attacks against the Kreis Farmers' Leader, since these do not belong here and also cannot incriminate Gagelmann. The attacks on the Kreisleiter are not my concern.

Heil Hitler!

DOC. 139
On 16 October 1934 the Regierungspräsident in Liegnitz reports to the Prussian Minister of the Interior about an incident in Görlitz in connection with a 'Jewish department store' hoisting a swastika flag[1]

Letter (secret) from the Regierungspräsident[2] (I D 5 (36) Nr. 353 II/34), author Regierungsrat Palme,[3] on behalf of (signature illegible), Liegnitz, to the Prussian Ministry of the Interior (received 19 October 1934), dated 16 October 1934[4]

Re: Jews hoisting swastika flags.

Case file: my report (incident report) from the 2nd of this month – I D 5 (36) no. 353/34.[5]

As already communicated in the report (incident report) from the 2nd of this month, on 29 September of this year the Zum Strauß department store (Karstadt corporation) in Görlitz had hoisted the swastika flag alongside the black-white-red flag on the occasion of the harvest festival. This swastika flag was then – apparently at the behest of the NSDAP local branch leader – taken down by Party members.[6]

Although the general agitation among the populace caused by the hoisting of the swastika on a Jewish department store is understandable, the displaying of the black-white-red flag and the swastika flag is in line with the regulations for the hoisting of

---

1 GStA PK, I HA, Rep. 77, Div. II, Tit. 4043, Nr. 477, fol. 26. This document has been translated from German.
2 The Regierungspräsident in Liegnitz in the years 1933–1936 was Herbert Suesmann (b. 1885), lawyer; joined the NSDAP in 1933; enforced retirement in 1936; Landrat representative in Calau, 1943–1944.
3 Erich Palme (b. 1891), lawyer; joined the NSDAP in 1932 and the SS in 1933; political advisor on police matters in the Liegnitz government, 1930–1934, and in the Schleswig government, 1934–1935; worked at the police headquarters in Mönchengladbach-Rheydt, 1935–1937; deputy chief of police there, 1937; advisor to the chairman of the Berlin City Council, 1937–1940; fought in the war, 1940–1943; worked in the office of the Oberpräsident in Hanover, 1943–1944, and in 1944 in Schneidemühl.
4 There are several handwritten revisions in the original.
5 On 2 Oct. 1934 the Regierungspräsident in Liegnitz had briefed the Reich Ministry of the Interior and the Prussian Ministry of the Interior on the incidents described here: ibid., fols. 24–25.
6 The head of the local branch, Witte, had earlier assured the police that any attempt to take down the flag would be prevented, but he then himself ordered it to be taken down. Subsequently, there were apparently also calls to boycott the department store: ibid.

flags. It should be borne in mind that the general population had been called upon to display the flags during the harvest festival.

I ask you to consider whether it might not be advisable to make some provision by a general directive so that this kind of incident cannot occur in the future.[7]

DOC. 140
On 29 October 1934 SA member Werner Siemroth denounces his Hamburg employer for employing Jews[1]

Letter from Werner Siemroth,[2] Hamburg, to SA Company 14/45, Hamburg, dated 29 October 1934

Report.

The undersigned, SA member *Siemroth*, Werner, Company 14/45, in the SA since 1 November 1933, reports the following to Company 14/45 for transmission to the appropriate authority.

Since 1929 I have been employed at the firm Nebel & Sander,[3] 2 Wagnerstr., as a salesman. In May this year the firm was taken over by a Mr Hagenow[4] from the previous owner, *Krug*[5] (a Jew), and it is now called 'Joachim Hagenow'.[6] Following this takeover, signs appeared in the windows: 'Now a purely German company'. This enabled Hagenow to accept payment in the form of subsistence vouchers for marriage loans etc.[7] To all appearances, however, the firm is *not* a 'purely German company', since of the shop's fifteen employees, five are *Jews*! (including two apprentices). Hagenow is *in the Motor SA*[8] and apparently only a frontman in the business, because in all commercial matters

---

7 There is a handwritten note in the original stating that it is not suitable to pass on to the minister and that government intervention would be inappropriate, as well as the note 'to be filed, 24 Oct.' On 12 Feb. 1935, however, the Gestapo Central Office (Gestapa) issued a decree referring explicitly to the 'hoisting of the Reich flags' on 'Jewish department stores' as well. The circular decree (II 1 B 2-61250/J 195/35) prohibited Jews from displaying the swastika flag and the black-white-red flag: BArch, R 58/276, fol. 12. § 4 (1) of the Law for the Protection of German Blood and German Honour, dated 15 Sept. 1935, prohibited Jews from hoisting the Reich and national flags and displaying the Reich colours: see Doc. 199, 15 Sept. 1935.
1 Staatsarchiv Hamburg, 614-215/B 202. This document has been translated from German.
2 Werner Siemroth (b. 1910), commercial employee in Hamburg.
3 The company was founded in 1919 in Hamburg as a general partnership, and later had various branches there.
4 Joachim Hagenow, retailer in Hamburg.
5 Georg Krug (b. 1906), retailer in Hamburg; managed a branch of the company Nebel & Sander in Barmbek from 20 May 1933 to May 1934; emigrated to Barcelona at the end of 1934.
6 Joachim Hagenow took over the branch in May 1934.
7 From June 1933 young families could receive interest-free marriage loans up to a value of 1,000 Reichsmarks, provided that they were classified as Aryan and 'hereditarily healthy' and the wife did not work. These loans were granted by the state in the form of vouchers for furniture and household goods: Regulation Implementing the Regulation on the Granting of Marriage Loans, 20 June 1933, *Reichsgesetzblatt*, 1933, I, pp. 377–379.
8 The Motor-SA, founded in 1931, was incorporated into the National Socialist Motor Corps in 1933.

Hagenow is guided by Krug's 'suggestions'. Krug, who is the manager, always gives Jewish business representatives special consideration.

Hagenow told me: 'You are approaching your tenth working year and would then earn 166 Reichsmarks, which I cannot pay you. As a colleague I advise you to look around for another position.' He cannot pay me, an SA member, the 166 Reichsmarks but the two *Jewish* employees, who are also in their tenth working year, he can! – On 1 November 1934 I'll start work at a company in Wandsbek.

Swastika flags are always put up on special occasions but SA Sturmmann Hagenow's business practices flout all National Socialist principles, and it is imperative that they be investigated.

Heil Hitler!

DOC. 141

On 12 November 1934 the Central Association of German Citizens of the Jewish Faith informs the Reich Ministry of Economics about the hindrance to Jewish traders in town markets[1]

Letter from the CV, Chairman Brodnitz and Counsel Reichmann,[2] Berlin, to the Reich Ministry of Economics (received 13 November 1934), dated 12 November 1934, and two enclosures with copies of various letters[3]

Re: Market trading
We hereby submit to the Ministry:

(1) a number of decisions by market authorities, in particular in Hesse, which have been issued to Jewish day traders;

(2) statements concerning these decisions by the local authorities and government agencies contacted.

In our view the content of all the enclosures contravenes the provisions concerning market trade issued by the Reich Minister of Economics (28 September 1933, H. G. 13 046/33) and the Prussian Minister for Economics and Labour (13 October 1933, J. Nr. III A 4461 L.)[4] because Jewish traders – contrary to the tenet that the Aryan principle is not to be applied in the economic sector – are being admitted to the market either not at all or only under difficult conditions.

We would be obliged if measures were taken to ensure in the localities and districts in question that Jewish market traders are treated in a way that conforms to the Ministry's regulations.

Brodnitz Reichmann[5]
Chairman. Counsel.

---

1 BArch, R 3101/13862, fols. 384–389. This document has been translated from German.
2 Dr Hans Reichmann (1900–1964), lawyer; practised law, 1929–1933; counsel and chairman of the Central Association of German Citizens of the Jewish Faith (CV), 1927–1938; imprisoned in a concentration camp following the November pogroms of 1938; in 1939 emigrated to Britain, where he was general secretary of the United Restitution Organization at its administrative central offices in London, 1955–1964; co-founder of the Leo Baeck Institute, London.
3 The original contains handwritten revisions and underlining.

Enclosures

Re: enclosure 1
Hesse Mayor's Office, Lauterbach, 1 June 1934
Re: annual fair on 6 June 1934.
In response to your enquiry of 29 May this year, we hereby inform you that Jewish businesses have no access to the annual fair on the 6th of this month.
signed [signature]

Gross-Gerau/Hesse
The autumn market in Groß-Gerau will take place on 8–10 September 1934. Places for fairground rides (only the best businesses), sideshows, and stalls are assigned on the basis of proposals in writing. The market is restricted to authorized traders. Non-Aryans are not permitted. – Proposals should be sent by 8 August to: Mayor's Office, Gross-Gerau.

Hungen/Upper Hesse
Hungen, 8 October 1934
In response to your postcard of 3 September 1934, we hereby inform you that you can have a stall of the desired size for the All Saints' Day market (1 November 1934) on condition that you are of Aryan descent.
Mayor's Office, Hungen
signed Fend[6]

Mayor's Office, Ortenberg/Hesse
Ortenberg, 10 October 1934
From your enquiry dated 3 September of this year we have seen that you wish to obtain a pitch for your hosiery stall for this year's Annual Agricultural Fair, which will take place from 28 October to 1 November.
If you are of Aryan descent, you can expect to be allocated a pitch accordingly. However, you must take part in the draw to allocate pitches, which will take place on Monday, 29 October, from 9 to 11 o'clock in the morning. We ask you to be present at this draw or to commission someone to represent you.
With German regards
Mayor's Office Ortenberg, Hesse
signed [signature]

Grünberg/Upper Hesse
Mayor's Office, Grünberg, Hesse
Grünberg, 11 October 1934

---

4 On both circular decrees, see Doc. 89, 15 Nov. 1933.
5 The signatures are handwritten in the original.
6 Correctly: Julius Fendt (1869–1939), retailer and leather tradesman; worked as a retailer in Frankfurt am Main, Vienna, and Berlin, 1889–1896; took over his parents' business in Hungen, 1896; no party affiliation; mayor of the town of Hungen, 1904–1934; afterwards in retirement.

In response to your enquiry from the 10th of this month, I hereby inform you that this year's St Gall Fair is a *Jew-free market*. I therefore regret to inform you that you cannot be admitted to the market.

Should you not possess German nationality, I ask to be informed accordingly.

Mayor's Office, Grünberg, Hesse

signed [signature]

Re: enclosure 1

Edenkoben/Pfalz

Before we grant permission for you to book our market, would you please inform us whether you are of Aryan descent. Jewish businesses are not admitted here.

Edenkoben, 28 July 1934

Municipal police station

signed [signature]

The mayor as local police authority

Pyritz, 30 August 1934

Re: stall at the autumn market on 12 September 1934.

You can be allocated a stall if you are *Aryan*.

I must refuse to grant any stalls to non-Aryans, since the admission of such persons entails the risk of a disturbance of public order and security here.

Should the condition stated in paragraph 1 not apply to you, I ask you to stay clear of the autumn market here on 12 September 1934 in order to prevent unnecessary expenses.

signed Floret

Angermünde, 26 September 1934

A place will be allocated to you upon arrival. You will only be admitted if you are of Aryan descent. The allocation of places will take place on 17 October 1934 at 6 o'clock in the evening or on 18 October 1934 at 7 o'clock in the morning.

Heil Hitler!

signed [signature]

From the *Hakenkreuz-Banner*, evening edition, 2 October 1934

German businesspeople, crockery traders, Chinese, and Jews.

... This is the order of shops at the sales fair that will be opened on Saturday at the same time as the exhibition fair on Adolf-Hitler-Ufer, for which the provision has again been retained that the Jews may not set up their stalls between the Aryan traders. As was the case at the spring fair, the Aryan tradespeople will come first at the *front* near the fire station, followed by the crockery traders. The Jews will add their stalls only at the back between the crockery traders and the Adolf-Hitlerbrücke. They will now be joined at the autumn market by some Chinese people, who have also expressed an interest in places.

Enclosure 2

Copy. No. II 2225

Government of Schwaben and Neuburg, Chamber of the Interior

Augsburg, 14 June 1934
Address: Augsburg 1, PO Box
Cash office. Account no. 8713
Postal Cheque Office Munich
Re: annual trade fair in Nördlingen on 2–11 June 1934.
The Nördlingen City Council refused to admit non-Aryan businesses to the annual market for 1934 on the basis of resolutions from April and June 1934. The grounds for this decision were that no responsibility could be assumed for the preservation of order and security if non-Aryan businesses were admitted, and also that no more admissions could be made due to lack of space. As the annual market is now over and the city council has held out the prospect of repealing the resolution concerning the exclusion of non-Aryan businesses in the coming years, we believe we should rule out any unwelcome consequences.
    p.p. signed Dr Schwaab[7]

Mayor of the Kreis capital Konstanz
Konstanz, 28 August 1934
Re: Konstanz trade fair
Your application was discussed at the city council meeting on 27 August 1934. An arrangement in your favour could no longer be made for the forthcoming September trade fair in view of the time that has already elapsed, as the places have already been allocated. However, a new arrangement will therefore be made in time for the Konradi trade fair at the end of November and you will be notified.
    signed Gruner,[8] city councillor

Mayor of the Kreis capital Konstanz
Konstanz, 8 September 1934
Konstanz trade fair.
Further to my letter of 28 August 1934
Subject to there being sufficient places and punctual application, there are no objections to the admission of non-Aryan or not pure Aryan tradespeople against whom there is nothing politically incriminating. However, stalls in the assigned trading area may only be allocated to non-Aryan or not pure Aryan traders should such stalls be or become available. No liability can be taken, though, for the personal safety of the person admitted or for the safety of their goods. The city council reserves the right of exclusion in such cases where this appears to be necessary to avoid any threats from a general security policing perspective.

7 Dr Otto Schwaab (1878–1949), lawyer; served in the Bavarian civil service, 1905–1919; worked in the Lower Bavarian government, 1919–1922, and in the Swabian government, 1927–1945, lastly as deputy Regierungspräsident; joined the NSDAP and the SA in 1934; classified as a 'follower' during denazification proceedings in Augsburg in 1948.
8 Carl Gruner (1876–1967), engineer; director of a public limited company for mechanical engineering in Konstanz, 1922–1929; dissolved this firm and became a self-employed engineer, 1929–1933; joined the NSDAP in 1929; from 1933 city councillor and head of the engineering plant Technische Werke Konstanz; removed from office by the French military government in May 1945; thereafter in retirement.

The applications are to be submitted as before to the trade fair supervisor (city revenue office). We have notified the trade fair supervisor accordingly.

signed C. Gruner, city councillor

Copy.

Government of Upper Bavaria
Chamber of the Interior
Munich, 10 September 1934
Munich
Re: exclusion of non-Aryans from the Auer Fair.[9]
Concerning the letters of 2 July and 20 August 1934
Enclosure: one specialist journal, *Der Komet*.[10]

According to report no. 1527/III 34 of 29 July 1934, Munich's city council has never passed a resolution stating that non-Aryan market traders are to be refused access to the Munich fairs. In the allocation of places, however, Aryan applicants are granted precedence over non-Aryans. As all the places were claimed by Aryan applicants, non-Aryans were unsuccessful. If City Councillor Ruhrmann[11] is said to have stated at the opening of the fair that it conformed to legal provisions and the spirit of the time if non-Aryans had been excluded this year, the fact remains that there is no city council resolution to that effect.

signed Gareis[12]

DOC. 142

On 22 November 1934 Heinrich Himmler asks Hitler to oblige the Federation of Bavarian Regimental Officers' Associations to expel its Jewish members[1]

Letter from the Commander of the Political Police of the States and Inspector of the Prussian Gestapo (II 1 B 2–62940/ 1685.), signed H. Himmler, to the Führer and Reich Chancellor, dated 22 November 1934 (copy of Reich Chancellery 10 496)

Re: Federation of Bavarian Regimental Officers' Associations.

According to a communication I received from the Bavarian Political Police, the Federation of Bavarian Regimental Officers' Associations is still, even now, taken a position on

---

9 Auer Dult: a traditional market in Munich, established in 1905, that is held three times a year.
10 The journal issue was not enclosed. *Der Komet* was a specialist journal for the travel industry and market trading, and the official organ of the German Association of Fairground Traders. The journal has appeared since 1883 and is based in Pirmasens, in the German state of Rhineland-Palatinate.
11 Probably Otto Fuhrmann (1880–1967), Munich city councillor, 1933–1945; municipal sanitation supervisor of slaughterhouses.
12 Heinrich Gareis (1878–1951), lawyer; worked from 1909 in the Bavarian civil service; head of the police in Nuremberg-Fürth, 1921–1933; in charge of government affairs, 1934–1940, and Regierungspräsident in Upper Bavaria, 1940–1943; joined the NSDAP in 1937 and the SS in 1938; interned, 1945–1947; classified as a 'follower' during denazification proceedings in Munich in 1948.

1 BArch, R 43 II/602, fols. 154–155. This document has been translated from German.

the question of Jewish membership that must be deemed inadmissible in the National Socialist state.

Thus, in a report dated 28 March 1934 the federation commented as follows on the Jewish question:

> Officers who are members of both our federation and the Reich Veterans' League are in a dilemma regarding the Jewish question, because the Reich Veterans' League has excluded non-Aryans from their veterans' associations.[2] Our federation is unable to reach a compromise. The assembly approves the standpoint taken by our federation for years, whereby Jews who acquired federation membership in the first three years of its existence remain our comrades. Jews who applied to join only later or are still applying can no longer be accepted, since they have demonstrated by their earlier absence that they did not feel connected with us during the most difficult period. We will not abandon this standpoint until we are ordered to take a different one.

The continued presence of Jewish members in the Federation of Bavarian Regimental Officers' Associations is entirely inappropriate in this day and age, and liable to discredit the Movement and its programme in the eyes of the public.

I request instructions as to whether the Federation of Bavarian Regimental Officers' Associations should be told to immediately expel its Jewish members or whether there will be orders for its dissolution on the basis of its previous standpoint on this question.[3]

---

[2] In late Sept./early Oct. 1933 the president of the Reich Veterans' League, also known as the Kyffhäuser League, had ordered the expulsion of Jewish members from the veterans' associations belonging to the league: *C.V.-Zeitung*, 4 Oct. 1933, p. 1.

[3] On 11 Dec. 1934 Lammers replied that Hitler desired neither the expulsion of the federation's Jewish members nor the federation's dissolution, because 'the question of the Jewish members of the federation [will] reach its own solution in time': BArch, R 43 II/602, fol. 153.

DOC. 143

On 26 November 1934 an NSDAP member sends an anonymous letter to the ministries in Berlin in protest against the ongoing boycott of Jewish shops in Braunschweig[1]

Letter, unsigned, Braunschweig, to the Reich Chancellery, the Reich Ministry of Economics, the Reich Ministry of the Army, the Reich Ministry of the Interior, and Braunschweig's regional government, dated 26 November 1934 (copy)[2]

On behalf of the employees of Jewish firms in Braunschweig I *urgently* request *your assistance* and your *support*.

As an old Party comrade, who in the early struggles for power remained loyal to and constantly ready to serve for his Führer Adolf Hitler, I accuse the Braunschweig government and the Braunschweig Minister President Klagges[3] of sabotaging the Reich government. I accuse the leader of the local NS-Hago group of frivolously tolerating and endorsing interventions in the Braunschweig economy, and the Braunschweig police and along with the chief of police of failing to prevent gatherings in front of Jewish shop windows and the occupation of the entrances of Jewish company premises.

I have repeatedly learned from the press that any open boycott of Jewish companies is to be avoided and that you have most firmly rejected any kind of interference by any organizations in German economic life. But what do you intend to do when, despite your instructions, wreckers of our National Socialist idea and world view who call themselves National Socialists take measures that are liable only to incite unrest among the Braunschweig population?

Five hundred employees of Jewish firms in Braunschweig are worried about their livelihood. Five hundred employees and their families think day in, day out, that their managers' shop windows may be smashed in again by irresponsible elements, as in the past year under the leadership of City Councillor Ammen,[4] when around sixty large shop windowpanes were shattered to pieces. Should employees of the Jewish companies and Party comrades oppose these provocateurs and take the law into their own hands? Should they be traitors in a matter for which so many of our Party comrades in Jewish businesses have fought, in order to be scorned by those who have only discovered their National Socialism since the revolution? Should they show these parasites what our Führer demands from a true National Socialist?

---

1 BArch, R 43 II/602, fols. 162–164. This document has been translated from German.
2 In the original there is handwritten underlining in several places. The letter was sent on to the Reich Chancellery from the Gestapo Central Office (Gestapa) in Berlin on 17 Dec. 1934 with the comment that the details were highly exaggerated and that the riots in Braunschweig were immediately quashed after the police had been notified. It had not been possible to identify the author of the letter: ibid., fol. 161.
3 Dietrich Klagges (1891–1971), teacher; joined the NSDAP in 1925 and the SS in 1934; state minister for the interior and for education, 1931–1945, and minister president of Braunschweig, 1933–1935; sentenced to life imprisonment in Braunschweig in 1950; released in 1957.
4 Correctly: Wahrhold Ammon (b. 1906), bookseller; NSDAP member; lived until 1932 in Nuremberg; city councillor, 1934, and director of the municipal tourism association in Braunschweig, 1934–1935; later returned to Nuremberg.

Positive and open criticism of the local leaders' measures is forbidden. But where are we to turn to obtain rights and justice in the matter of our Party comrades working in Jewish companies? The Labour Front, the courts, and the regional government have not been responsive to our requests. In the utmost distress and greatest urgency, we turn to you.

I hereby report on some incidents that occurred between 10 and 24 November 1934. A survey among the employees of the Jewish companies would not only confirm the truth of the events but also bring to light some things that are only possible *in Braunschweig, our Führer's problem child*. You will see from the nature of the description that I am reporting to you facts that cannot be objectively refuted. Members of NS-Hago, including

- the owner of Café Hintze, Hulfäutchenplatz
- the owner of the company Schmidt, Vor der Burg
- the shoemaker Wesche, Schützenstraße
- the retailer Faustmann, Hutfiltern
- the Kreisleiter of NS-Hago, Deuter
- the local group leader of NS-Hago, Brinkmann
- the owner of the company Schuhkönig, Sack
- the master painter and Sturmführer Bauermeister, Parkstr.

took up positions in front of the Adolf Frank department store, Schuhstraße, one of the most reputable department stores in our city, on several afternoons during the aforementioned fortnight and insulted the emerging shoppers in the foulest terms, so that a majority of the customers did not dare to shop there during the main shopping hours. *Members of our armed forces had their insignia torn off*; at the whim of an NS-Hago member *forestry trainees* had to present their identification papers to a *police officer on duty*. Airmen from our military flying school were not permitted to enter the shop. Working men were scorned. Old ladies were barred entry. The NS-Hago people used red oil-paint and caustic acids to mark on the shop windows that the shop was in Jewish hands. But that is not all. On Saturday 24 November 1934, when the provocateurs gathered in front of the shop and assumed a threatening attitude, the owners were forced to close the shop early. Peaceful shoppers, who were aware of no wrongdoing, were met with bellowing sarcastic remarks such as *Buy German Christmas tree decorations at the Christian Frank's*.

All these dirty attacks on customers of Jewish stores, to whom we owe our livelihood and therefore our very existence, began after the rally with the leader of Franconia, Julius Streicher, who stressed in his speech that he would not follow the Reich government's ordinances in relation to shops and would do what he wanted.[5]

The employees of Jewish firms are at the end of their tether. The daily worry about their existence is wearing them down. Every day they must be prepared for the Jewish shops to be closed under pressure from unprincipled denunciators. They are powerless against these capricious intrusions, which enjoy legal protection. Is there no longer any justice in our new German Reich?

---

[5] Streicher had given a speech on the 'race question' to an audience of thousands in the Braunschweig civic hall on 7 Nov. 1934: *Braunschweiger Neueste Nachrichten*, 9 Nov. 1934, Stadtarchiv Braunschweig, Z 5, Film 91.

As a Party comrade I have no cause to forward this letter to the foreign press. As a member of a Volksgemeinschaft, however, I urge that this appalling injustice be expiated. If you bring any boycott of Jewish shops to an end, then you will have cooperated in the great goal that our Führer has set himself of creating and *preserving* jobs for all Volksgenossen.

Heil Hitler

An old Party comrade.

DOC. 144

New York Times, 4 December 1934: report on Germany's pledge to take heed of the rights of Jews for one year in the event of a reincorporation of the Saar territory[1]

Jews Urged to Be Hopeful.
By the Jewish Telegraphic Agency.

Rome, Dec. 3 – Because of the insistence of the League of Nations Germany has agreed to a special paragraph in the Saar agreement,[2] guaranteeing the rights of the Jews, Julio Lopez Olivan,[3] the Spanish delegate on the Saar committee appointed by the League of Nations, declared today.[4]

Disclosing that the guarantee is valid for one year only and that Germany refused to accept a longer term proposed by the Saar committee, Señor Lopez Olivan, advised that the Jews of the world should not be too pessimistic about the fate of Saar Jewry.

'There is no ground for excessive pessimism with regard to the situation of the Jews in the Saar,' he said.

Diplomatic circles here were somewhat surprised to learn that Germany had agreed to assure full equality for the Jews in the Saar. This concession was taken as a sign that the French Government had made the question of Jewish rights one of its major conditions.[5]

---

1 *New York Times*, 4 Dec. 1934, p. 12. The original document is in English.
2 On 3 Dec. 1934 an agreement on matters relating to the reincorporation of the Saar territory was concluded between France and Germany in Rome: *Reichsgesetzblatt*, 1935, II, pp. 126–130. In a supplementary declaration issued the same day, Foreign Minister von Neurath guaranteed the League of Nations that for the period of one year the inhabitants of the Saar territory, regardless of their 'language, race, or religion', would not experience a worsening of their situation and would be handled in accordance with the laws prevailing in the Saarland: ibid., p. 125.
3 Julio Lopez Olivan, (1891–1964), lawyer and diplomat; worked at the Permanent Court of International Justice in The Hague, 1936–1945.
4 The Treaty of Versailles placed the Saar territory under a mandate of the League of Nations and stipulated that fifteen years later its inhabitants were to decide on whether the territory would be returned to Germany, whether it would be incorporated into France, or whether the status quo would be maintained. Following the plebiscite in favour of a return to Germany, the Saar territory was unified with Germany on 1 March 1935.
5 From the end of the First World War, France exerted control over the Saar territory under the mandate of the League of Nations. On 31 August 1934 the French foreign minister had declared that in the event of an incorporation of the territory into France, the Jews would be granted full civil rights. International Jewish organizations appealed in Geneva to the state representatives in the League of Nations to issue a guarantee in favour of the Jews: *Pariser Tageblatt*, 18 Sept. 1934, p. 1.

DOC. 145

Juristische Wochenschrift, 7 December 1934: the Hanau Labour Court overturns the dismissal of a Jewish employee[1]

Labour courts

Hanau

84. § 57 ArbOG.[2] *Unreasonably harsh dismissal of a non-Aryan employee from an Aryan company.*

On 24 June 1934 the defendant purchased the clothes-manufacturing business previously run by company B. The owners of the defendant company are Aryans, whereas the owners of company B were not. The plaintiff has been working at the latter firm since 1 July 1924. He runs the carpets and curtains department. He is non-Aryan, but married to an Aryan. He has a 5-year-old child. He was a front-line soldier in the First World War and a prisoner of war.

On 31 October 1934 the defendant dismissed him from his post without any reasons being stated, with effect from 31 March 1935. He appealed against this dismissal to the Council of Trust within the prescribed time limit and filed a suit, likewise within the prescribed time limit, after a retraction of the dismissal had not been obtained.

The grievance based on §§ 56 ff. ArbOG is justified. The dismissal of the plaintiff is unreasonably harsh and not caused by the firm's circumstances.

Up to the time of the dismissal, the defendant evidently did not object to the fact that the plaintiff is non-Aryan. This is already clear from the fact that he was the only non-Aryan out of sixty-five employees to be kept on after 24 June 1934 and not dismissed. According to the personal account of one of the co-owners of the defendant firm and the plaintiff during the main proceedings, it can also be discerned that the plaintiff and the owners of the defendant's firm have had an excellent working relationship. Both have mutually declared on several occasions that they work well together and there are no personal disagreements of any kind. There are also no notable disagreements between the other staff members and the plaintiff. Moreover, the customers cannot have been irked by the fact that the plaintiff is non-Aryan, for otherwise the turnover in the plaintiff's department would have dwindled rather than increased, as it incontestably has, and the defendant could have raised the point that customers had protested against the plaintiff's presence. The defendant was, however, unable to attest to this.

In view of the above, the defendant was certainly to be expected to continue employing the plaintiff, who will in any case continue to work at the company of the defendant

---

1 *Juristische Wochenschrift*, 8 and 15 June 1935, p. 1732. Published in Noam and Kropat (eds.), *Juden vor Gericht*, pp. 87–88. This document has been translated from German.
2 *Gesetz zur Ordnung der nationalen Arbeit*: Law for the Regulation of National Labour. §§ 56 and 57 on protection from dismissal allowed the possibility of appealing dismissal after working at a firm for one year. The law made provision for the reinstatement or compensation of the plaintiff in the event that his or her dismissal was overturned by the court. Law for the Regulation of National Labour, 20 Jan. 1934: *Reichsgesetzblatt*, 1934, I, pp. 45–56, here p. 52.

until 31 March 1935, and his dismissal does not therefore result from the conditions of the firm or by his own person.³

The dismissal is, however, unreasonably harsh. After all, the plaintiff is a front-line soldier, a fact which alone in view of the general consideration given to such soldiers – think of the non-Aryan civil servants who serve as front-line soldiers – is to be taken particularly into account. He is married and has a young child for whom he must provide. Finally, special consideration is also to be given to the fact that as an older non-Aryan employee he will encounter great difficulty in finding a position corresponding to his income thus far.

Therefore, the repeal of dismissal and the continued employment of the plaintiff under the terms of work to date were to be recognized in accordance with § 57 ArbOG. In the event of refusal, an appropriate compensation was to be awarded to the plaintiff. Under consideration of the provision of § 58 of the law and in view of the fact that the plaintiff has since earned RM 320 gross per month, the sum of RM 1,000 gross seemed appropriate.

(Labour Court Hanau, judgement of 7 December 1934, A C 114/34)

DOC. 146
Discussion at the Staff of the Deputy of the Führer in Munich on 20 December 1934 regarding 'special legislation on Jews'¹

Note, unsigned, dated 20 December 1934 (draft)²

*Outcome of the discussion on racial policy at the Brown House, Munich, on 20 December 1934.*³

The handling of Aryan legislation to date has had a number of extremely detrimental effects on foreign and domestic policy:

In foreign policy, this can be seen in that the concept of 'Aryan' and 'non-Aryan' appears to have resulted in large population groups of different races being equated with and placed on the same footing as Jewry in the German state.

In terms of domestic politics, it can be seen from the fact that, first, beyond the (very incomplete) elimination of the Jews from a series of professions there are no clear principles for the further elimination of Jewry from Germany itself and, second, not

---

3 The regional labour court in Frankfurt am Main reached a different decision in another case on 5 March 1935: since the defendant had dismissed the plaintiff to avoid commercial damage with regard to a threatened boycott, the motives were deemed to be neither illegal nor unethical: Noam and Kropat (eds.), *Juden vor Gericht*, pp. 93–96.

1 BArch, R 1509/35, fols. 51–54. This document has been translated from German.

2 The original contains handwritten underlining and revisions. The transcript was made by Walter Groß and Gerhard Wagner, and the last paragraph was written by Wagner and Dr Bartels without the knowledge of the other participants. The note was sent without the handwritten additions, for example under 1(a) and (b), as well as points 6 and 7: letter from the Staff Office/Reich Farmers' Leader to the Reichsführer SS/Race and Settlement Main Office dated 15 March 1935, with note from 20 Dec. 1934, BArch, NS 2/143, fols. 15–18. In mid Jan. 1935 Himmler (Reichsführer SS), Heydrich (Gestapo Central Office, Gestapa), and Darré in his capacity as chief of the Race and Settlement Main Office of the SS also received the note regarding the meeting: ibid., fols. 19–31.

only does the treatment of Jew Mischlinge by the state and the Party occur according to various principles, but also within the state and Party agencies the treatment is not uniform.

It therefore seems necessary to create specific Jewish legislation alongside the general racial legislation in order to consciously separate Jewry from other non-Aryan population groups in terms of status, and in this way to regain the possibility of adopting the necessarily stringent measures against Jewry both in law and in propaganda. The present approach of placing Jews and non-Aryans on an equal footing for domestic and foreign policy reasons largely rules out this possibility.

This legislative settlement of the Jewish question will have to distinguish politically between (I) the definitive and total elimination of the Jews from the German national community, and (II) the treatment of the Jew Mischlinge.

I. A Jew is a person who has two Jewish parents. According to these definitions, a Jew is also a person who has one Jewish parent or one Jewish grandparent.[4]

The following legal provisions are to be applied to this group:

(1) A ban on marriage with persons of German descent.

(a) A Jewish person who has extra-marital sexual intercourse with a non-Jewish person is subject to punishment.[5]

For the Jew, penitentiary; for her, prison

(b) defilement – death[6]

(2) A ban on holding public office.[7]

(3) The preclusion from serving as a company manager according to the Law for the Regulation of National Labour of 2 May 1934.[8]

(4) A ban on owning land or soil that can be used for agriculture and forestry.

(5) A ban on employing German female domestic staff.[9]

(6) In terms of criminal prosecution

service for Mischlinge

(7) Special education[10]

---

3 Reich Physicians' Leader Wagner had invited the staff of the Deputy of the Führer to the meeting: BArch, NS 2/143, fol. 38. Ministerialrat Bartels, Ministerial Director Dr Schultze, Dr Groß, Dr Gercke, SS-Standartenführer Rechenbach, SS Sturmbannführer Brandt (Race and Settlement Main Office), and SS-Untersturmführer Mayer (Race and Settlement Office) attended the meeting, which was chaired by SS-Obergruppenführer Buch and SS-Obergruppenführer Wagner: ibid., fols. 15–18.
4 This definition follows the Aryan Paragraph of the Law for the Restoration of the Professional Civil Service: see Doc. 32, 11 April 1933.
5 Demands 1 and 1(a) were achieved with the Law for the Protection of German Blood and German Honour, 15 Sept. 1935: see Doc. 199.
6 The words from 'Jew' to 'death' were inserted by hand.
7 This demand was met with the First Regulation to the Reich Citizenship Law, 14 Nov. 1935: see Doc. 210.
8 The Law for the Regulation of National Labour was in fact passed on 20 Jan. 1934: see Doc. 145, 7 Dec. 1934, fn. 2.
9 This demand was realized with the Law for the Protection of German Blood and German Honour, 15 Sept. 1935: see Doc. 199.
10 The words from '6' to 'Special education' were inserted by hand.

Germany considers the Jewish question to be resolved definitively only once a complete spatial separation between the Jewish people and the German people has been achieved. For this reason, Germany therefore supports every endeavour that aims to cause the Jews to migrate from Germany and to take up residence in their own settlement area.

II. For the treatment of Jew Mischlinge, the same provisions apply as to the Jews. Insofar as these Mischlinge forego having any offspring, they can retain public positions and continue to possess land suitable for agriculture and forestry as long as they prove themselves. The prohibition of marriage with a German person and of extramarital sexual relations with a German person nonetheless also apply to them. Children of such Mischlinge who were conceived after the enactment of the law fall under the provisions of paragraph I.

(1) Jew Mischlinge are people whose ancestors alive on 1 January 1800 were descended from parents who were not christened at birth.

(2) The Führer alone decides on cases where it is necessary to deviate from this underlying position. Petitions to the Führer in this connection can only be addressed to a special court yet to be established, which then submits them to the Führer.

The proposed regulation will clearly differentiate Jewry from Volksgemeinschaften made up of other races.

The concept 'Aryan' is to be understood as applying to members of those population groups that originate from the closed racial nuclei that have formed in our Lebensraum in the narrower sense.

The German racial community and Volksgemeinschaft have emerged from this Aryan group. The furtherance of this German community must have priority. However, absolutely no distinction may be drawn between the value of the descendants of the individual basic races in this German racial community.

DOC. 147

On 22 December 1934 the management of the Hermann Tietz department store informs the Reich Ministry of Economics about an antisemitic pamphlet[1]

Letter from the management of Hermann Tietz & Co.,[2] Munich, to the Reich Ministry of Economics, for the attention of Oberregierungsrat Michel[3] (received on 27 December 1934), dated 22 December 1934, with enclosure (copy)[4]

Dear Oberregierungsrat,

Enclosed is a copy of a leaflet that was distributed in *Freimann*, a suburb of Munich. With German regards!
Hermann Tietz & Co.
[...][5]

Enclosure
German Volksgenossen
We still have 550,000 Jews in Germany today; only 50,000 have gone where they belong. The important commercial districts in Munich are still teeming with Jewish businesses and trashy department stores. Volksgenossen, be honest, has an item that you bought more cheaply than elsewhere at Epa[6] or Uhlfelder[7] or in a similar crook operation actually lasted?! No, it looked fancy on the outside but in reality was nothing but lies and deception – it was more expensive than what you would get from a real Aryan businessman! For the entire Jewish business approach is built on deception and lies. The Jew is actually *obligated* by *his law*, the Shulchan Aruh,[8] to deceive wherever possible *all non-Jews, all goys – and that means you, German Volksgenossen.*

This law also says that every non-Jew – that is you, German Volksgenossen – is to be regarded as an animal and therefore only has a human form to be able to serve the 'chosen' Jewish people. In fact *all goys* – that means you, German Volksgenossen – are called pigs under this law. And as such you run to the Jew in his shops. Is that really

1 BArch, R 3101/13862, fols. 313–314v. This document has been translated from German.
2 Hermann Tietz & Co.: in 1882 Hermann Tietz (1837–1907) founded his first company in Gera. The department stores he opened in Berlin from 1900 became well known. In 1930 the Tietz family owned fifty eight department stores, including the famous Kaufhaus des Westens (KaDeWe) in Berlin. The corporation was Aryanized in 1934 and renamed the 'Hertle Waren- und Kaufhaus-GmbH'.
3 Dr Elmar Michel (1897–1977), lawyer; section head in the Reich Ministry of Economics, 1925–1940; joined the NSDAP in 1940; head of the economic division at the administrative headquarters of the military commander in France, 1940–1944; responsible in this capacity for the removal of Jews from the French economy; prisoner of war, 1945–1949; ministerial director in the Federal Ministry of Economics from 1953; acquitted by a French military tribunal, 1954; chairman of the board of directors at Salamander AG, 1968–1973.
4 In the original there are several revisions.
5 The signatures are illegible.
6 Einheitspreis AG: a chain of department stores.
7 Kaufhaus Heinrich Uhlfelder GmbH: department store.
8 Correctly: *Shulchan Aruch*; Hebrew for 'set table'. Together with its commentaries, this is the most widely accepted compilation of Jewish law (Halakha), formulated by Rabbi Joseph Karo in Safed, Palestine, in 1563, and first published in book form in Venice in 1564–1565.

what you want to be?! You must surely have enough pride to refrain from demeaning yourselves as the Jew's pigs? *Shame on you if you have continued to frequent Jewish shops and don't do it again! The Jew should see that we Germans have come to our senses!*

So don't buy in the city centre from the Jews:

not at Epa, Uhlfelder, Wohlworth, Tietz, Oberpollinger (department stores)

not at Bach, Bamberger & Hertz, Spielmann, Goldene 19 (gentlemen's clothing)

not at Eichengrün, Weinberger & Bissinger (fabrics)

not at Speier, Spier, Deutsch-Amerik. Schuhges. München, Schuhwaren-Haus Brück, Kleinmann Schuhe [footwear]

not at Loewenthal, Rotschild, Lewkowitz (ladies' hats)

not at Josephson, Mühlhäuser, Schulhoff, Rosa Klauber, Gerstle & Löffler (ladies' fashions)

not at Schlicht (chocolates)

not at Strumpfsachs (stockings)

not at Sigurd (bicycles)

not at Pauson (household goods and kitchenware)

but instead buy in the city centre at German shops

at Knagge & Peitz (Färbergraben), Lodenfrey (Maffaistrasse), Neubert & Ebert (both Sendlingerstr.): *gentlemen's clothing*

at Rieger (Sonnenstr.), Tiarks, Stalf (both Kaufingerstr.), Horn (Sonnenstr.), Indanthrenhaus (Marienplatz), Kübler (Kaufingerstr.): *ladies' fashions*

at Deininger, Heene (both Neuhauserstr.), Roman Mayr (Kaufingerstr.), Indanthrenhaus: *ladies' and gentlemen's underclothing*

at Horn, Indanthrenhaus, Kübler: *clothing and underclothing fabrics*

at Knagge & Peitz, Lodenfrey: *gentlemen's fabrics*

at Diegel (Stachus), Mössbauer (Marienplatz), Hartlmaier (Rosental, corner of Pettenbeckstr.), Salamander (Weinstr., Neuhauserstr.), Fuchsberger (Sendlingerstr.), Maier (Theatinerstr.), Ried (Fürstenstr.): *shoes*

at Schleich (Rosental), Eid (Neuhauserstr.): *ladies' hats*

at Schmidt (Neuhauserstr.), Wiedling (Maffaistr.), Obletter (Stachus): *toys*

at Zuckerbär, Schokoladenbuck: *chocolates*

at Traphöner (Zweibrückenstr.): *bicycles.*

And in *Schwabing* do *not* buy from the Jew Gottlieb; instead buy in *German* shops:

at Posega, Kellner (both Danziger Freiheit): *underclothing*

at Geigl (Feilitzschstr.), Felber (Marktstr./corner of Haimhauserstr.): *shoes*

at Winter (Herzogstr.): *household goods and kitchenware*

at Kröninger (Marktstr.), Schwarz (Herzogstr.): *hardware*

at Schubert (Feilitzschstr.), Lun, Silberbauer (both Leopoldstr.): *canned goods.*

Give special consideration when shopping to all the smaller shops not named here, for these are very rarely Jewish; the Jew does big business. But above all *buy everything you can get in Freimann in Freimann* itself because in Freimann we have no Jewish firms, only German businesspeople who have to struggle for their living in this small suburb.

Every Party member, every SA and SS man, every Hitler youth and every BDM[9] girl, in particular all members of the National Socialist Women's League and the entire German Labour Front, the NSKOV,[10] and disabled German workers, caught buying at Jewish shops is to be denounced by name on all four Party noticeboards in Freimann, so that everyone knows who has degraded himself as a pig to the Jews.

Heil Hitler!

The leadership of the Freimann local branch of the NSDAP

DOC. 148

On 27 December 1934 the Gestapo Central Office dissolves the Association of German Motor Car Owners for having Jewish members[1]

Decree issued by the Gestapo Central Office (Gestapa) (II 1 B 2 64 964/1871), signed Heydrich,[2] Berlin, to the Association of German Motor Car Owners, Berlin 50, 4 Tauentzienstraße, dated 27 December 1934, in a circular to all State Police offices, dated 27 December 1934 (copy)[3]

On the basis of § 1 of the Regulation of the Reich President for the Protection of the People and the State of 28 February 1933 (*Reichsgesetzblatt*, I, p. 83) in connection with § 14 of the Police Administration Law of 1 June 1931, I hereby dissolve the Association of German Motor Car Owners (AAD)[4] with immediate effect and ban it from all further activity. I request notification within four weeks that the dissolution of all the branch organizations has been carried out.

Grounds:

The AAD, the majority of whose members are non-Aryans, has set itself tasks that are already being discharged by Autoklub 1927,[5] which is alone permitted by the Gestapo Central Office to admit non-Aryan car owners. The organization's activities, which have repeatedly given rise to complaints, cannot be tolerated in the interests of the state.

9 Bund Deutscher Mädel: League of German Girls.
10 Nationalsozialistische Kriegsopferversorgung: National Socialist Welfare for War Victims.

1 BArch, R 58/276, fol. 9. This document has been translated from German.
2 Reinhard Heydrich (1904–1942), career officer; naval career, 1922–1931; joined the NSDAP and the SS in 1931; from 1932 chief of the SD; from 1933/1934 he supervised the centralization of the Political Police in all states; from 1934 chief of the Gestapo Central Office (Gestapa) in Berlin, which was initially responsible only for Prussia; chief of the Security Police and the SD, 1936–1942; head of the Reich Security Main Office, 1939–1942; from Sept. 1941 also deputy Reich Protector of Bohemia and Moravia; died on 4 June 1942 as a result of injuries sustained during an attempt to assassinate him in Prague.
3 The copy printed here was sent with an accompanying letter from the State Police office for the Regierungsbezirk Cologne, signed Dr Möller, to the State Police office, division for the municipal Kreis of Cologne, the mayor in Bonn, and the Landräte of the Regierungsbezirk, dated 9 Jan. 1935: ibid.
4 Arbeitsgemeinschaft der Automobilbesitzer Deutschlands.
5 Originally the German Reich Auto Club, in 1934 renamed Auto-Club 1927, and restricted to Jewish car owners. It had 1,842 members in 1934 and 3,069 by 1935, as the German Automobile Club founded in 1933 had expelled all non-Aryan members in 1935. In 1936 the Gestapo ordered that the Auto-Club 1927 be renamed Jewish Auto-Club. It was then dissolved at the end of 1938.

DOC. 149
Pariser Tageblatt, 30 December 1934: article regarding a conference of East Prussian communities on the decline and destitution of the Jewish population[1]

Twenty-five per cent of East Prussian Jews emigrated. Critical situation in the communities[2]

Königsberg, 29 December. In a meeting of the Provincial Federation of East Prussian Communities, attended by the communities of Königsberg, Allenstein, Bartenstein, Braunsberg, Elbing, Goldap, Insterburg, Marienwerder, Osterode, Rastenburg, Tilsit, and Zinten, Rabbi Dr Lewin[3] (Königsberg) gave an overview of population movements in the East Prussian communities based on detailed statistics. In the whole of East Prussia, resident Jewry has gone down by approximately 22 per cent in the year 1933 compared with 1925.[4] To this are added the foreign Jews who have moved away.

Whereas in 1931 there were still fifty-three public officials working in sixty-three communities, in 1934 there are now only twenty-nine public officials in fifty-six communities. The kind of catastrophic conditions that prevail in some communities was demonstrated by a reference to Elbing, where in six years only one single Jewish child has been born. It was proudly emphasized in some communities that they have avoided a decline in the population figures by means of business owners taking on Jewish men and women as commercial employees.

But what was repeatedly emphasized as especially sad was that the community members' capacity to pay taxes has declined to a much more critical degree than the actual number of community members, and that in many communities it could be ascertained that it is precisely the members with the highest economic potential who have left the community. The meeting demonstrated a heartening optimism and an all-round willingness to work, in spite of all the pressures and difficulties.

---

1 '25 Prozent der ostpreussischen Juden ausgewandert: Kritische Lage der Gemeinden', *Pariser Tageblatt*, 30 Dec. 1934, p. 2. This document has been translated from German.
2 This refers to the Jewish communities.
3 Dr Reinhold Lewin (1888–1943), rabbi; from 1912 in Leipzig, from 1921 to 1938 in Königsberg, Prussia, and from 1938 in Breslau; from there he was deported in March 1943 to Auschwitz and murdered.
4 In the June 1933 census it was ascertained that the number of Jews by faith in East Prussia had decreased from 11,960 in 1925 to 8,838. In Königsberg alone the number of Jews by faith had fallen from 4,061 to 3,170: *Statistik des Deutschen Reichs*, vol. 451/3: *Volks-, Berufs- und Betriebszählung vom 16. Juni 1933* (Berlin: Verlag für Sozialpolitik, Wirtschaft und Statistik, 1936), pp. 32–33.

DOC. 150
The Aid Committee of Hamburg's United Jewish Organizations reports on financial aid, emigration assistance, and professional training provided in 1933 and 1934[1]

Aid and reconstruction in Hamburg

[...][2]

III. Report for the period from April 1933 to the end of December 1934
From the outset, our basic tenet was that our work should be limited to constructive aid and reconstruction; general welfare had to remain a matter for the community and public provision. From this perspective, the three following areas of activity very soon emerged:
1. Financial aid
2. Migration
3. Occupational restructuring and vocational education

1. Financial aid
Our work began with *financial and occupational advice*. This initially concerned the perplexed and helpless masses. It was often initially a matter of calming people who had been psychologically thrown off balance, then by talking to them in an understanding way in order to gain a clearer picture of their aptitudes, opportunities, and wishes, and finally to refer them to the relevant specialist worker who then had to deal with them further.

We were given some valuable assistance in this preliminary work by *the Jewish Vocational Advisory and Placement Board*. Their long-standing experience was extremely useful for our work, particularly with regard to occupational restructuring, something that these advice sessions revealed to be necessary.

We were expected not only to provide material support but also in particular to open up the possibility of a new life through our advice. But this entailed a huge responsibility that required detailed legal and financial knowledge in an entirely new area. In these particular advice sessions we were supported in an effective way by the *Central Association of German Citizens of the Jewish Faith*, the *Reich League of Jewish Combat Veterans*, and the *Hamburg Zionist Association*. This involved finding personnel in every area who could clarify every case on the basis of their particular specialist knowledge. A series of men and women made themselves available for this task, for which they deserve our thanks.

---

1 Hilfsausschuss der Vereinigten Jüdischen Organisationen in Hamburg (ed.), *Hilfe und Aufbau in Hamburg: April 1933 bis Dezember 1934* (Hamburg: Hilfsausschuss der Vereinigten Jüdischen Organisationen in Hamburg, 1935), pp. 11–26. This document has been translated from German.
2 In the original the report printed here follows a preface and sections I, 'Division of work and overview', and II, 'Fellow workers'.

Financial provision and the granting of loans

In most cases, more than advice was needed, as these were almost always people who had been wrenched out of their previous occupation and whose own resources, as well as their family's, were exhausted. Here, as far as possible, given our limited funds, help had to be provided in the form of money. Financial aid was generally not granted until all other options were exhausted, such as recourse to help from relatives and friends and general social provision. But in every case we only granted support if there was a prospect of ensuring that an endangered life could be spared or rebuilt by granting a strictly *one-off* sum. Almost all the support was provided in the form of a loan. In individual cases the amount was paid out by the *loan office*, to which we had made a substantial sum available for this purpose. – The lawyers and doctors who had been dismissed from their posts were given advice and financial aid in collaboration with *aid for lawyers and aid for doctors*. The colleagues who still had posts had each created a special fund for this purpose. The many artists who had become destitute were supported by our *aid for artists*. Through the Jewish Society of Arts and Sciences, it became possible to make a sphere of activity available again to a number of artists.[3] Although the surge of people not knowing where to turn has abated, individual cases have accordingly become more complicated. Whoever turns to us now for the first time will have already struggled hard for a long time, and greater effort and aid are needed to get such individuals back on their feet; they are also at a disadvantage in relation to those who decided on a change earlier.

2. *Migration*

This concerned people who partly for ideological reasons, but mainly for purely economic ones, were convinced that their future could not be in Germany. It was our task above all to prevent unplanned emigration. Support was given only to those who had a justified hope of an improved existence abroad. The emigration occurred in three directions:

(a) migration to Palestine;
(b) migration to other countries;
(c) return migration to their native countries in the case of foreign Jews resident in Germany.

The number of emigrants supported by us came to a total of 1,256 persons.

(a) The Palestine migration accounted for a significant proportion of these. Approximately 20 per cent, i.e. around 250 persons, emigrated from our region with our assistance. Palestine is the only country that is prepared for a substantial immigration of Jews and offers the possibility of integrating the immigrants completely into the economy. Furthermore, the targeted preparatory training in agriculture and the skilled crafts (Hachsharah), which is obligatory for those in possession of immigration certificates, is extremely well organized as a result of decades of experience. Our help was implemented in conjunction with the relevant organizations: *the Hamburg Zionist Association, the*

---

[3] The Jewish Society of Arts and Sciences in Hamburg was founded at the beginning of 1934. Organizationally speaking, it was comparable to the pre-existing culture leagues of Berlin, Frankfurt, and Cologne, but it initially operated purely as a subscribers' organization. It did not receive a theatre licence until 18 July 1935, shortly before it was renamed the Hamburg Culture League.

Hamburg branch of the Palestine Office of Berlin, the Jewish Agency for Palestine, and the *Hachsharah Association, Hamburg*, whose own funds were not adequate for the number of applicants, which increases daily. This mainly concerned travel grants that amounted on average to 92.40 Reichsmarks per certificate recipient.

The number of people emigrating to Palestine is still rising and the number of claims submitted to us is constantly increasing.

(b) Migration to the remaining countries and
(c) return migration.

The picture of this general emigration has fundamentally changed over what is now almost two years. The initially large number of those who wanted to emigrate during the initial agitation without justified prospects for a new life has become increasingly small. But whereas at first we helped numerous people to get to France, Holland, England, and other neighbouring European countries, these countries are now almost entirely closed to immigration. It is now mainly overseas countries that remain. However, immigration into these countries requires a complete reorientation; the travel costs are also considerably higher, so that only a few decide to emigrate overseas. Today, this is more about individual cases in which the emigrant has relatives in the country concerned or has especially good connections, or in which there are favourable conditions for his particular professional training.

The advice and funding were made available in the closest collaboration with the *Relief Association of German Jews*. For many of the foreign Jews resident here who had lost the possibility to work in Germany, their native country was open to return migration. – With our support, 880 persons emigrated from our region, as well as 126 persons who were transported back to their native countries.

Emigration to	*Persons*	*Percentage*
United States of America	156	17.73
Mexico	10	1.14
Canada	27	3.07
Cuba	2	0.23
Argentina	56	6.36
Brazil	89	10.11
Uruguay	31	3.52
Paraguay	4	0.45
Chile	8	0.90
Colombia	6	0.67
Santo Domingo	2	0.23
Guatemala	2	0.23
Costa Rica	12	1.37
Peru	2	0.23
Ecuador	3	0.34
Venezuela	12	1.37
Nicaragua	2	0.23
South Africa	19	2.16
Australia	2	0.23
China	1	0.12

Emigration to	Persons	Percentage
England	60	6.82
France	94	10.68
Holland	65	7.38
Belgium	38	4.32
Switzerland	19	2.16
Italy	21	2.38
Denmark	26	2.95
Sweden	8	0.90
Czechoslovakia	14	1.60
Poland	9	1.01
Latvia	2	0.23
Bulgaria	2	0.23
Spain and Portugal	64	7.28
Greece	1	0.12
Yugoslavia	8	0.90
Turkey	2	0.23
Syria	1	0.12
	880	100
Return migration		
Austria	14	11.10
Hungary	8	6.35
Poland	75	59.50
Czechoslovakia	9	7.15
Romania	7	5.55
Soviet Russia	7	5.55
Holland	6	4.80
	126	100

3. Occupational restructuring and vocational education

During consultations with the many discharged civil servants, doctors, lawyers, students, and commercial employees, it had become clear to us that we need to create training establishments in order to retrain these people.

What is to become of our Jewish youth? An academic career is closed to them; young people have recognized that they must turn to practical occupations. We were entirely convinced of the need for a standardized occupational structure. Thus, for occupational restructuring and vocational education in predominantly practical occupations, independent training establishments had to be created in agriculture, horticulture, and skilled crafts, as well as courses in tailoring and housekeeping. Provision was also made for the training of nautical staff[4] (see cover picture[5]). We barely had any experience in

---

[4] See Doc. 164, 8 May 1935.

[5] The cover picture shows young people on a tugboat of the Fair Play shipping company. The publication contains several photographs documenting the training of young people and adults in the various workshops in skilled crafts as well as in agricultural work.

this area; methods and forms of occupational restructuring and vocational education had to be tried out. Experience shows here that it would be misguided to pursue a one-sided vocational restructuring and thereby neglect the training of young retail staff.

The need for restructuring led to the establishment of the *Wilhelminenhöhe School for Settlers*, which had originally been created by the Reich League of Jewish Settlements. Garden and house were provided to us by the community; a greenhouse was built. Under a gardener's direction, the inhospitable land that was still partly wooded was cleared, furrowed, and worked into terraces. Vegetables were grown on a field made available to us. Fifty young men and women were given practical and theoretical horticultural training over the course of a year; the girls in particular were instructed in household management. At Wilhelminenhöhe itself we learned a great deal from this experience. At first we believed that the people trained here would find the possibility of work perhaps in Germany or France, and we therefore focused on thorough horticultural training, with theoretical teaching, as well as courses in English, French, and Hebrew. It soon became clear that our students can only make practical use of their training abroad, essentially in Palestine.

In devising the craftsmanship courses, it was clear to us from the outset that only a first-class apprenticeship can enable future Jewish craftspeople to obtain a sustainable existence in practical work.

In the *carpenter retraining programme*, 8–10 Weidenallee, fifteen young people in each of two parallel courses were trained in a one-year programme by a master workman and two assistants. In the *sewing and tailoring retraining programme*, 70 Heimhuderstraße, fifteen young girls and women in each of two parallel courses were also taught by a senior master workwoman and a trained seamstress. In closest collaboration with the Jewish Vocational Advisory and Placement Board, as well as Hehalutz, we supported and guided some 100 young people who were preparing themselves for *individual posts in crafts, agriculture, or housekeeping* in Palestine (Hachsharah). They live in the *bathe halutz*,[6] in which they are prepared for all kinds of living conditions in Palestine. A shipping company thankfully made its facilities available for nautical training.[7] As it was not possible by Easter 1934 to provide apprenticeship placements for all the young school-leavers, establishments were created in joint collaboration with the heads of the Talmud Torah School[8] and the girls' school of the German-Israelite Community, which enabled young people to prepare for their future professions. For the young men, *preliminary courses in carpentry, 8–10 Weidenallee*, and *metalworking, 8–10 Weidenallee*, were created. Workshops equipped for the purpose admitted thirty young people. Because of this preliminary training it has proved possible to place the young people in appropriate apprenticeships over the past year. For the female school-leavers, a *household management school, 70 Heimhuderstraße*, was established with a syllabus matching that of state schools and a one-year course of training. Administration and teaching are in the hands of recognized experts. The syllabus encompasses all the practical and theoretical subjects in the area of household management. The household management training year is regarded as preparation for occupations in the household or in a business, and also as the

---

6 *Bathe* comes from *bet* and is Hebrew for 'house' the reference here is to pioneers' houses.
7 The reference is to the Fair Play shipping company. See Doc. 164, 8 May 1935.
8 On the Talmud Torah School, see Doc. 59, 28 June 1933.

foundation for training as a nursery school teacher, playgroup teacher, housekeeper, or nurse.

In this important area of activity, the significance and scope of which increase daily, the demands placed on us are especially great. We financed the setting up and running of the training establishments. Since the people undergoing professional reorientation and the vocational trainees were mostly poor, we also had to support their training, at least in part. In the past 1¾ years the number of those we supported amounted to 381, of whom the individual received an average subsidy of 203 Reichsmarks.

When developments during the course of 1933 made it necessary to manage the new major areas of activity described above, completely new means of funding had to be found because the communities' funds were not sufficient for these new tasks. Foreign Jews have generously shown their readiness to help. Of course, this help could only be utilized when the German Jews spontaneously demonstrated the greatest willingness to make sacrifices. This idea led to the centralization of all the German Jews' financial resources in the Central Committee for Relief and Reconstruction.[9] Inside Germany, every community first had to squeeze the maximum out of itself, carry out active self-help measures in its area, and attest its solidarity by supporting less capable communities before it could claim the central funds. A vivid expression of this reciprocal help is the fact that from the outset 25 per cent of the contributions made here for central funds were passed on to Berlin; by contrast, the Central Committee supported us in the erection of training establishments and bore up to two thirds of the total costs of the occupational restructuring and vocational education. The Relief Association of German Jews and the Palestine Office of the Jewish Agency contribute significantly to the expenditure in their area of emigration. The Relief Association of German Jews bears approximately two thirds of the costs and the Palestine Office a large proportion that is determined case by case. All expenses in the area of economic aid had to be paid from the regional funds of the advisory office. Here we were given some supplementary help by the Welfare Committee of the German-Israelite Community, Aid for Small and Medium-sized Businesses, the Welfare Committee of the Lodges, the Henry and Emma Budge Foundation, the Lazarus Gumpel Foundation, the Elfriede Salomon Foundation, and other Jewish foundations in Hamburg.

To ensure the raising of funds, it was agreed with the Central Committee that only the advisory office should have the right to collect in Hamburg – with the exception of Keren Hayesod. This measure has a dual advantage: on the one hand, the methodical deployment of all charitable forces, and on the other, getting the most out of the readiness for sacrifice by indicating that many small collections are covered by a single real sacrifice. – In addition, the community's Winter Relief Agency had to remain in place because otherwise the community's purely charitable tasks could not be carried out. But the advisory office contributed appropriately to the outcome of the community's Winter Relief Agency. It also received a subsidy from the community.

---

9 The Central Committee of the German Jews for Relief and Reconstruction (Zentralausschuss der deutschen Juden für Hilfe und Aufbau) was founded in April 1933 as the central institution of Jewish welfare work. Among the organizations involved were the Central Association of German Citizens of the Jewish Faith (CV), the Zionist Federation for Germany, and the Relief Association of Jews in Germany. In 1935 it was incorporated into the Reich Representation of Jews in Germany.

The collection for the aid committee was carried out in two ways. First, by appealing for generous annual donations; second, by means of the monthly running contributions based on the blue contribution cards. For two years, from April 1933 to April 1935, it was possible to secure funds for the aid committee's tasks.

While the work has been reduced to individual sub-areas, where difficulties required urgent resolution, on the whole, especially in vocational education, occupational restructuring, migration to Palestine, and above all economic aid, the range of tasks has grown rather than diminished. Future work can only be carried out – despite all the difficulties and burdens with which the individual has to struggle in his immediate sphere – if everyone expresses his bond with the community by sharing in this work to the full extent of his capacities in the same way or even more than before!

DOC. 151
Martin Andermann describes the political and social changes that took place in the city of Königsberg in 1934[1]

Submission by Martin Andermann[2] to a Harvard University competition (1940)[3]

[…][4]

When I transferred my practice to Königsberg in January 1934, I had been away from my native town for almost twelve years. Although I had repeatedly gone home during the holidays or for short visits, I had rarely spent longer than two weeks there. I was fond of the town, and while it had also become somewhat alien to me in those twelve years, I was not unhappy to be home again. Of course, much had changed in the meantime. The circle into which I returned was a society that vegetated outside the actual life of the town. At every turn, much more strongly than in Berlin, it could be felt and seen that as a Jew one could only lead the life of a pariah. Apart from one café that belonged to a Swiss man who dared to defy the SA's stipulations thanks to his foreign nationality, there were large signs up in all the restaurants and inns: Jews not welcome. We could no longer go to the theatre, no longer go to concerts. Almost all the theatrical and musical events were [now] put on by the organization 'Strength through Joy', and a completely new audience had emerged that probably never used to go to the opera or concerts. But now people were ordered to go, as with everything else, and this also applied to enjoyment. I happen to know something about these things because we had an Aryan acquaintance who was employed at the Königsberg opera house. We doctors no longer

---

1 Martin Andermann, 'Mein Leben in Deutschland vor und nach dem 30. January 1933' [My life in Germany before and after 30 January 1933] (1 April 1940), pp. 108b–114; Harvard Competition, no. 6. This document has been translated from German.
2 Martin Andermann (b. 1904), physician; worked as a doctor in Berlin from 1933 and from 1934 in Königsberg, Prussia; emigrated via Switzerland to the USA in April 1937.
3 The original contains handwritten amendments.
4 This submission comprises 119 pages in total. The author firstly describes his childhood, then his medical studies in Heidelberg, Marburg, Freiburg, and Berlin, and finally his work as a doctor in a Berlin hospital up to 1933.

had permission to attend the meetings of the doctors' association, so Jewish doctors arranged further training courses among themselves.

I could list endless further details: they would all signify the same thing – the exclusion, the virtual ghetto in which we had to live. But ultimately we got used to it until it almost became a matter of course. When I later went abroad, I found it hard to get used to being allowed to take a seat in just any café. When I think back to those years, life was certainly difficult. Nevertheless, there were also many things that were beautiful. It was after all only natural that the Jewish families who relied on each other had more dealings with each other than before. A certain kindness and warmth arose that was fostered by the shared misery and persistent fear in which we lived. So many emigrated, as well, and those who stayed behind drew ever closer together. We began to value much more highly the things that were still possible, that were not forbidden, and were much more grateful for many things that were taken for granted before. My wife and I delighted in many of the scenic charms of Königsberg; we were happy that we were allowed to go for a walk unhindered, or that we could go to the sea, our wonderful Baltic Sea that I went without for so long. Of course, we could not go into bars and had to stay outside everywhere, but we could still go for walks and enjoy with greater intensity all the beauty that was not 'forbidden to Jews'. We were glad that no one forbade us to buy books or to reread the books that we owned. My old father, whose legal practice had also been severely restricted – he later had to abandon it completely – always said: now at least I have time to read everything I always wanted to read and never could. But we were especially grateful for visits from non-Jewish former or even new friends. For we knew that there were no longer any conventional visits. There were after all so many who only too eagerly showed that they would rather no longer know us. We were acutely aware that a non-Jew who visited us was taking a considerable risk, and that he did it to prove to us that he accepted the danger involved in assuring us of his respect and allegiance. We did not need to say much; we knew even without words that the other person was sincere because otherwise he would not have come. We were also grateful when sometimes a former friend or fellow student answered a letter in a warm and understanding way. How much all those things that we had previously not known how to value had now come to mean. A Jewish friend told me once that when he came home he was always happy to find everything still as he loved it: his furniture to which he was attached, his books and everything. For, he continued, how long will all this still exist; how long will we be able to maintain even the most limited existence? One Jewish patient told me: 'It's actually undignified, but believe me, the more the Nazis act against us and the more urgent it is to think about emigrating, the more I love Germany, love East Prussia, the town and everything.' Before, this woman said, 'I was happy when I travelled to Italy with my husband. But now in Italy I only think: if only I were back home, for who knows how many times I'll still be able to return home.'

I do not know if a similar change also occurred in non-Jewish circles. My relations with non-Jews became increasingly rare. I can only report on so few things, observations on the margins, as it were. After all, the non-Jews [also] lived an entirely different life; politics and the state with its demands on every individual overshadowed everything. The processions, festivals, marches, parades, and duties never stopped. They penetrated into the family and tore it to pieces. A school friend of my sister's came to us from time to time and poured her heart out: her husband, a grammar school teacher, was a former students' association member, monarchist, conservative. The boy – the only son – 18 years old, was a zealous Nazi. The family was in danger of breaking apart, father and son no longer got along, the mother stood helplessly between them. She feared for their livelihood because the father's intransigence had already damaged his position considerably; 'he can never keep his mouth shut', she complained. Our seamstress, a simple woman, aired her outrage every time she was with us. Her two sons were rarely at home any more. She was a widow, had struggled to bring up the boys, they were in the Hitler Youth all day, and there they were incited against everything, against their own mothers, against religion, and against everything.

A Catholic primary school teacher, also a childhood friend of my sister, was among those who almost adopted a stance of open opposition. She often distributed circular letters from the bishops and was a resolute combatant against the regime. But all these people were older and belonged to the pre-war generation. They thought differently, but they were also generally regarded by the young as the dying generation. Our friend's 18-year-old son, as the mother said, considered 'everything right and necessary', and was zealous and devoted to the new ideas. I once met a former schoolfellow, who was about my age, in the tram. He was a Christian, but after his father's premature death he had grown up with Jewish friends, who had become his second parents. As no one was present, I ventured to say a few words to him. I knew that he had had very left-wing tendencies and for many years had played a role in the German Wandervogelbewegung.[5] Now he was a dentist for the Hitler Youth and also seemed to be highly active in other ways in this organization. I asked whether he did not find it hard because the current trends were after all very different from those of the old Wandervogelbewegung. 'Oh no,' he said, 'on the contrary, fundamentally it is all very similar. With us in the Hitler Youth', he said, laughing, 'the word "Socialism" is incidentally written in huge capital letters.' I noticed that he found the entire conversation with me in the tram unpleasant and so I said goodbye. I had gained the impression that the man took a truly positive and hopeful view of the new Germany. When I had an opportunity to talk with non-Jews one-to-one, I often encountered the following way of looking at the problem: you just can't understand it, I would then hear. We are Germans, our place is here, whatever may happen. Opposition is futile, we must join the Party, join the Movement – that is the only way; that is the only way we can prepare what will later replace the current state. I encountered the most extreme case of this kind in a social worker. As a particularly straightforward person, with a deep aversion to the Party, but one who felt very German, she was in a particularly difficult position. All social work posts went through the Party; she did not want to join, and was therefore having difficulties finding any job. Her brother was a priest in the Confessing Church,[6] and she was close to this movement.

---

5 The Wandervogelbewegung was a German youth movement that emerged at the end of the nineteenth century and attempted to develop a lifestyle that was close to nature and specifically for young people. It gave rise to various youth associations with differing political orientations.
6 In the original: 'Bekenntniskirche' probably refers to the Bekennende Kirche (Confessing Church). See Glossary.

By chance, the leader of the National Socialist Women's League[7] got to know this girl, immediately saw her intelligence, and very much wanted to have her as a colleague. Finally, she gave in. She was trusted and given increasingly large tasks; she was sent as a delegate to one of those officers' academies for 'ideological training', and finally she was commissioned to give lecture tours in rural areas to publicize the Party's social work to women. I saw her one evening at the house of some Jewish friends, where she had secretly crept in late in the evening. She was in deep conflict and it was having a visible effect on her. 'Should I not seize the opportunity to work to the best of my ability, where this possibility is presented to me?' she asked. 'Can I not do much more to overcome the National Socialist Movement from the inside than by opposing it from the outside? You have no idea', she said, 'what types of colleague we have there. Some of them are only in it to be there at the right time, when it all "starts to work out". – A non-Jewish artist we were friendly with, who had given concerts with a Jewish artist for many years, was faced with the question of whether he wanted to leave Germany together with this Jew or to separate and remain in Germany. He found it difficult but he ultimately chose the latter, since he simply belonged in Germany. Everywhere I came into contact with non-Jews, one thing seemed clear to me: people were troubled, full of questions, had to make decisions that deeply affected them. As a result, I always had the strong feeling as though, behind the façade of this marching Germany that had undergone Gleichschaltung, each individual's life was being lived with an intensity that had never existed before. The intense pressure, the danger, the ever-present possibility that something terrible could happen – such as the Röhm purge[8] in 1934 – meant that every single individual action in life was heightened. Nothing was simple or self-evident any more. Just as it was a feat if a non-Jew visited an old Jewish friend – he might be publicly denounced in the *Stürmer* [newspaper] – it was also a feat if the priest of the Confessing Church dared to preach despite having been forbidden to do so. It was even more of a feat if, next time he was prevented from speaking in the church, the same Königsberg priest began to preach on the square in front of the church and the community surrounded him so that no one could arrest him. It was a feat if our seamstress went to hear this outlawed priest on the square. Previously, her Christianity might have been something that she took for granted and was not all that particular about. Now her right to be a Christian in the way she wanted was being contested, and this ordinary woman began to wonder whether that was right, and what her belief was all about, anyway. It was like that with everyone. The grocer or baker in the East Prussian town whom the SA had forbidden to sell bread to Jews took it to his old Jewish customer at night, secretly, across the rooftops, and whereas previously he would not have given much thought to the matter of selling bread day in, day out, now he thought about it, and it took courage to sell it to people who had been expelled from society.

[...][9]

---

7 The National Socialist Women's League (Nationalsozialistische Frauenschaft) was founded in 1931 as the official NSDAP women's organization. It later had 2.3 million members.
8 Also known as the Night of the Long Knives: see Glossary.
9 In the next part of the report the author describes events including his emigration.

DOC. 152
On 4 January 1935 Hamburg's health and relief authority writes to SA-Oberführer Heusser to insist on the necessity of buying from Jewish traders[1]

Letter from the president of the Health and Relief Authority in Hamburg, Friedrich Ofterdinger,[2] to the SA-Brigade 12 (received on 7 January 1935), for the attention of SA-Oberführer Heusser, Hamburg, 44 Gr. Theaterstraße, dated 4 January 1935[3]

Dear Mr Heuser,[4]

I am returning to you enclosed a decree issued by the relief authority, of which you sent me a copy, concerning the payment for purchases from Jewish traders made by welfare recipients.[5] The decree of the relief authority has been issued by Vice President Martini[6] following consultation with me and meets with my approval. The reasons are as follows: the majority of second-hand dealers in Hamburg are Jewish by race. Above all else, in the purchase of items of clothing, which in the interests of the state must be as cheap as possible, the recipients with the appropriate vouchers are directed to traders. Insofar as there is an Aryan tradesperson in the city district, attention is drawn to this fact. But it frequently happens that the recipients, either out of ignorance or because an Aryan tradesperson is simply not available, go to Jewish traders.

Some time ago Jewish tradespeople's invoices were repeatedly left unpaid by welfare offices because of their race, as a result of which the traders of course turned to the purchaser, namely the recipient. There were endless difficulties. I then instructed that of course not only purchases from the half a dozen Aryan traders had to be paid for but also those from the Jewish ones. It is regrettable in itself that in some respects we are reliant on Jewish dealers and that it is not possible to manage entirely without these people. No Aryan yet seems to have been born for this filthy business; on the other hand, it is not an indifferent matter for the authorities whether we buy a worn but good suit for 15 Reichsmarks from the second-hand dealer or for 30 Reichsmarks in an Aryan clothing shop.

1 Staatsarchiv Hamburg, 614-215/B 202. This document has been translated from German.
2 Dr Friedrich Ofterdinger (1896–1946), physician; doctor in Hamburg, 1926–1933; joined the NSDAP in 1929; Gau inspector, 1933; member of the Hamburg state government and director of the Hamburg Health and Relief Authority, 1933–1945; also responsible for education matters, 1933 and 1942–1944; died in an internment camp, 1946.
3 The original contains handwritten revisions.
4 Correctly: Oskar Heusser (b. 1895), policeman; joined the NSDAP and the SA in 1929 and the SS in 1939; leader of the SA-Brigade 12 in Hamburg, 1933–1935; self-employed estate agent, 1931–1933; in the urban police in Hamburg, 1936–1939; worked in the Order Police Main Office in the Reich Ministry of the Interior, 1939–1944; commander of the urban police in Leipzig, 1944–1945; in 1949 classified as a 'follower' during denazification proceedings.
5 The enclosure is not in the files. This is likely to be the circular letter from the relief authority dated 14 Nov. 1933. It stated that welfare recipients would be reimbursed for the sum of allowed goods even if the trader from whom they had bought these was non-Aryan: Uwe Lohalm, *Fürsorge und Verfolgung: Öffentliche Wohlfahrstverwaltung und nationalsozialistische Judenpolitik in Hamburg 1933 bis 1942* (Hamburg: Ergebnisse, 1998), p. 17.
6 Oskar Martini (1884–1980), lawyer; president of the Welfare Authority in Hamburg, 1920–1933; vice president of the Health and Relief Authority with responsibility for relief matters, 1933–1936; president of the Relief Authority, 1936–1938; head of the Social Security authority in Hamburg, 1938–1945; joined the NSDAP in 1937; from May to Oct. 1945 head of Hamburg social services; classified as a 'follower' in denazification proceedings.

I hope that the number of those supported by welfare declines sufficiently in the foreseeable future and that the state budget consolidates itself, so that in this matter we no longer have to count every penny three times before we approve it.

Much more problematic than these things is the fact that with large items we are simply not in a position to completely exclude Jewish firms or Jewish middlemen. Unfortunately, these firms often cannot be recognized or avoided. I am thinking of Beiersdorf,[7] manufacturer of many medicines, bandage materials, and so on (Leukoplast) that are not manufactured by other firms. (Leukoplast can, however, be replaced by Germania-plast, made by Blanck, Bonn.)

Heil Hitler!

DOC. 153
On 19 January 1935 the SS-Standortführer in Berlin prohibits SS men and their families from having private contact with Jews[1]

Circular order from the SS-Standortführer in Berlin (diary no. 0242/35), signed Breithaupt,[2] 9 Prinz-Albrecht-Straße, to the Main District East with all units, dated 19 January 1935 (copy)

Garrison order

Every three months, the following is to be announced:

1. It is forbidden for SS members:
(a) to buy in department stores and Jewish shops,
(b) to engage Jewish lawyers,
(c) to be treated by Jewish doctors.

It is every person's duty to extend this ban also to family members (parents, wives, siblings, children, and so on).

In cases of doubt, an enquiry should be directed to the Reichsleitung of the NSDAP, Reichsleiter for Organizational Affairs, NS-Hago Main Office, Central Office of the Executive (Archives), Berlin SW 11, Saarlandstrasse, Europahaus, second floor, room 267, tel. A.1. 7731.

Violation of point 1 will result in expulsion from the SS.

Reference is made to the special directive of the Reichsführer SS, Dept. III no. 12 234/34 dated 5 November 1934.[3]

---

7 Beiersdorf AG, Hamburg, was founded in 1882. It manufactured well-known branded products. As a 'Jewish firm' it was subject to significant antisemitic propaganda after 1933, especially by rival companies. Following the resignation of Jewish members of the board of directors and supervisory board, the firm was considered to be a 'Christian company' from the end of April 1933: Bajohr, 'Aryanisation', pp. 22–26.

1 BArch, NS 31/89. This document has been translated from German.
2 Franz Breithaupt (1880–1945), career soldier and businessman; director of the German Gymnastics Association until 1931; joined the NSDAP and the SA in 1931, and the SS in 1932; adjutant of the Reichsführer SS, 1932–1942; SS-Standortführer in Berlin, 1934–1942; chief of police in Breslau, 1942; chief of the Main Office SS Courts, 1942–1945.
3 This directive could not be found.

2. (a) The SS member must adopt the greatest simplicity and reserve regardless of whether he is in uniform or civilian dress.

It is forbidden to visit bars and inns of a similar kind in uniform.

In cases of doubt in relation to the above inns, the SS Garrison Command in Berlin will provide information.

2. (b) SS members must demonstrate their exemplary behaviour at all times, especially on public transport. In overcrowded conditions, the SS member gives up his seat for a *woman* – without exception.

DOC. 154
Report by the Gestapo Central Office in Berlin on the situation of Germany's Jews in December 1934 and January 1935[1]

Situation report by the Gestapo Central Office (Gestapa) (II 1 B 2), unsigned, dated 19 February 1935

Jews
The work of the Jews in organizations, which was interrupted during the Christmas period on account of their business activity, has recommenced and become more extensive.

The outcome of the Saar referendum has not been without repercussions for the various currents of opinion within Jewry.[2]

Hence, the Jews inclining towards Zionism regard the surprising result of the referendum as an incentive to strengthen their propaganda aimed at emigration to Palestine.

The dismay caused to Jews who identify as German patriots by the outcome of the referendum has quickly given way again to strong optimism. Alongside the Central Association of German Citizens of the Jewish Faith, the Reich League of Jewish Combat Veterans in particular campaigns for adherence to Germandom and for remaining in Germany. It thereby repeatedly draws on the assertion that the sacrifice of 12,000 Jewish soldiers in the World War has granted entitlement to this and tries to win young people over from the Zionist movement. In the endeavour to retain their supporters, the German patriots among the Jews recently went so far as to discuss practical measures for planning a future in Germany. In order to obstruct this organization's activity as far as possible and to encourage the Zionist trend, I have issued a decree instructing all State Police offices that Jewish meetings at which adherence to Germandom and remaining in Germany are to be discussed are to be banned until further notice.[3]

No new Jewish organizations have been established in the reporting period. A Jewish youth group 'Black Pennant', which was modelled on the Hitler Youth and supposed to

---

1 RGVA, 501k-1-18, fols. 63–69. Published in Kulka and Jäckel (eds.), *The Jews in the Secret Nazi Reports*, enclosed CD, no. 551. This document has been translated from German.
2 In the Saar territory, over 90 per cent of participants in a national referendum on 13 Jan. 1935 voted for reincorporation into Germany. The referendum was envisaged by the Treaty of Versailles, which had placed the Saar under French control after 1920: see Doc. 144, 4 Dec. 1934.
3 Circular decree issued by the Gestapo Central Office (Gestapa) (II 1 B 2–6093/J 191/35), dated 10 Feb. 1935, BArch, R 58/276, fol. 11. Published in Kurt Pätzold (ed.), *Verfolgung, Vertreibung, Vernichtung: Dokumente des faschistischen Antisemitismus 1933–1942* (Leipzig: Reclam, 1983), p. 90.

be a non-political youth organization, has disbanded at the suggestion of the Reich Youth Leader.

Despite the limited number of certificates [issued], the emigration of Jews to Palestine has not come to a standstill. According to the provisional result of the count, around 10,000 Jews emigrated from Germany to Palestine in 1934, including 436 from Berlin alone in December 1934. In January 1935, 200 Jews emigrated from Berlin and 150 Jews from the Reich.

The high figure attributed to Berlin is explained by the fact that the emigrant transports are generally assembled here. Complaints reveal that the Jews seem to be abandoning the restraint that was previously shown. The surprisingly brisk Christmas trade has contributed considerably to an increase in their self-confidence. In many cases the irresponsible behaviour of Party comrades, who allow their National Socialist honour and German name to showcase Jewish enterprises, is also to blame for this.

The defiant appearance of the Jews gives the Aryan population greater cause to take things into their own hands. The defensive boycott measures instigated by the population are mainly ineffective and liable to damage the reputation of the authorities who have to follow the instructions of the Reich Ministry of Economics and cause conflicts between the state and the [National Socialist] Movement.

I have asked the Deputy of the Führer to issue a decree banning Party organizations again from having any dealings with Jews and forbidding members of the organizations to make purchases in Jewish shops and department stores.[4]

In many parts of Germany the cattle trade is still almost exclusively in the hands of Jewish cattle traders who are reappearing with great audacity and obtrusiveness. The Aryan cattle trade cannot compete with them because it cannot draw on sufficient capital.

The authorities grant permission to bring in horses from Belgium almost exclusively to Jews, which appears to have caused a considerable stir even in the foreign neighbouring regions abroad bordering on Germany.

The fact that the Reich Sports Leader has placed no restriction on sporting activity has given a particular boost to the Jewish sports movement.[5] The reasons behind this decision are unclear to the population and give rise to misunderstandings, especially as the Jewish sports associations are still permitted to use community facilities (playing fields, gyms, swimming pools).

With reference to the successful activity of Jewish pilots in the World War, the Jews have of late attempted to interest their youth in glider piloting and to form glider pilot groups. I have asked the Reich Sports Leader to prevent the formation of glider pilot groups.

---

4 On 11 April 1935 the Deputy of the Führer, Rudolf Heß, issued the corresponding internal Party directive no. 63/35 on NSDAP members' dealings with Jews: Hans Mommsen and Susanne Willems (eds.), *Herrschaftsalltag im Dritten Reich: Studien und Texte* (Düsseldorf: Schwann, 1988), pp. 430–431.
5 In two directives dated 15 and 17 Sept. 1934, the Reich Sports Leader drew up guidelines for the sports practice of Jews and non-Aryans. In the first directive the Jewish organizations Schild and Maccabi were officially recognized. The second directive stated that the Deputy of the Führer's prohibition on dealings with Jews dated 16 August 1934 did not apply to sports or to preparatory courses for the Olympic Games: Walk (ed.), *Das Sonderrecht für die Juden im NS-Staat*, p. 92.

On the occasion of the celebration of the Saar victory, many Jewish shops and Jews' apartments had hoisted the swastika flag, thereby causing unrest in the population. As Jews do not belong to the German Volksgemeinschaft according to National Socialist tenets, I consider it inappropriate for them to display the swastika flag. Neither can they be allowed to hoist the black-white-red flag. I have instructed the State Police offices under my control to implement these principles in an appropriate form.[6]

Among the Jews who were resident in the Saar, the result of the Saar referendum has caused huge consternation. Approximately one third of them, including 50 per cent of the wealthiest, are said to have already gone abroad, and those who have stayed behind do not feel especially safe there. The unrest is especially great because the two large organizations who describe belonging to the German fatherland as the basis of their activity, the Central Association of German Citizens of the Jewish Faith and the Reich League of Jewish Combat Veterans, had overtly campaigned for the status quo in the referendum campaign. The leaders of these organizations therefore moved, presenting French passports, to France or Luxembourg immediately after the referendum.

According to a report in Luxembourg, 80 per cent of the emigrants who have settled in Luxembourg are from very wealthy Jewish families. As well as their rabble-rousing activity there they continue to further their organizations that originate from the period of the Marxist government, such as the League for Human Rights. In public the provocative appearance of the émigrés has increased the prevalence of a distinctly negative attitude towards the Jews, first because it is becoming noticeable that the Jew has understood how to monopolize trade in the host country to an overwhelming degree; in addition, the fear must be entertained that the Jewish families, while having sufficient capital reserves at present, will in the future, once they have distributed their capital among their offspring, have to try and earn their own living and will then also attempt to infiltrate the economic activities of the host country.

Recently, it has been observed that Jewish artists when performing in public attempt to address more strongly the government's measures and Germany's political and economic situation, and use mimicry and inflection to express a deliberately undermining critique in front of the audience, which consists mainly of non-Aryans. A further provocation to the state authorities has occurred when police intervention in the case of unwelcome collaboration between Aryan and non-Aryan performers has led to ovations for the non-Aryan performers.

I have instructed the State Police offices to remain vigilant so that non-Aryan artists refrain in their performances from any reference to domestic German affairs and, in cases of contravention, to have them put into protective custody on the basis that the interference of non-Aryans in German matters will in no way be tolerated. Where it is to be feared that joint performances of Aryan and non-Aryan artists will cause provocation, the non-Aryans are to be immediately prohibited from appearing.[7]

As was communicated to me in confidence, according to a new Jewish plan, descendants of Jews from Germany are due to be taken for a period to America, from where

---

6 See circular decree of the Gestapo Central Office (Gestapa) (II 1 B 2–61250/J 195/35), dated 12 Feb. 1935: BArch, R 58/276, fol. 12. On the origins of the decree, see also Doc. 139, 16 Oct. 1934.
7 See the circular decree of the Gestapa (II 1 B 2–60038/J 257/35), 25 Feb. 1935: BArch, R 58/276, fol. 15.

they are to return to Germany as American citizens following linguistic training and adoption by American Jews. The purpose of this journey is to protect these Jewish offspring from being seized by the German authorities on their return. Recently, two transports of Jewish children aged between 10 and 14 years left for New York. Investigations into the accuracy of the claim with regard to the adoption are still under way.

DOC. 155
On 17 March 1935 the NSDAP member Walter Tanke denounces participants in a 'Jew-friendly' church gathering to the Stettin Gestapo[1]

Letter from Walter Tanke,[2] Altdamm, to the Gestapo in Stettin (diary no. 746/35, received on 18 March 1935), dated 17 March 1935[3]

Report from Party comrade Walter Tanke, Altdamm,[4] Party membership no. 452 947

On Saturday, 16 March 1935, at 8 o'clock in the evening I attended the meeting of the church community of the regional church in the assembly hall of the town school in Altdamm.

Nearly 100 people were gathered. The attendees were mainly women of all ages. The men included some officials from the railway, postal service, and municipal authorities. It became clear from the speaker's contribution that the church community is internationally minded and Jew-friendly. He also explained that the religious Jews will some day judge over us Christians before the judge in heaven. He further emphasized that the Antichrist has been making trouble on earth for two and a half years. He said that a false prophet is driving these people to the Antichrist.

Present were: Party comrade Wilhelm Vogel, Altdamm, 39 Langestr. Party comrade Walter Borchardt, 43 Stargarderstr. Vg.[5] Domrös and siblings (town hall). Vg. Hoppe and sister, Vgn.[6] Gransow, Vg. Callies, the school caretaker Borchardt.

Party comrade Borchardt and Vg. Domrös and siblings are members of the church community and sing in its choir.

The speaker at the meeting was Vg. Korschelt from Daber.

---

1 RGVA, 503k-3-81, fol. 3. This document has been translated from German.
2 Walter Tanke (b. 1895), trader; joined the NSDAP in 1931.
3 The original contains minor handwritten corrections and a note: 'Party comrade [illegible] was also here'.
4 Altdamm (Kreis Randow) became a part of Stettin in 1939.
5 *Volksgenosse*: '(male) ethnic comrade'.
6 *Volksgenossin*: '(female) ethnic comrade'.

DOC. 156
On 22 March 1935 the Catholic Church establishes the Aid Committee for Catholic Non-Aryans[1]

Minutes of the meeting, unsigned, of 22 March 1935 (carbon copy)[2]

Minutes of the inaugural meeting of the Aid Committee for Catholic Non-Aryans, which took place at the Wohlfahrtshaus in Berlin on 22 March 1935 at the invitation of His Excellency, the Most Reverend Bishop Dr Berning.[3]

I. Background

After practical aid work had already begun in 1933, on the initiative of the German bishops and the German Caritas Association, to provide help with emigration or re-employment in new occupations to Catholic non-Aryans resigning from official posts as a consequence of the new legislation,[4] and after the St Raphael Society[5] in particular had begun special, partly successful aid work with regard to emigrating Catholic non-Aryans, it became clear that appropriate social assistance should, if possible, be extended for many different reasons. In particular, this was due to the consideration that non-Aryan or partially Aryan children and young people present special challenges in relation to both their education and their future livelihood.

To the initiative of the aforementioned people was added the proposal of the affected circles themselves, in particular Dr H. W. Friedemann[6] in Heidelberg. All who took part agreed from the outset that aid must operate within the bounds of the relevant German legislation and its resulting circumstances, and that they wished to carry out the intended aid operation with the knowledge of the German bishops. His Excellency Bishop Dr Wilhelm Berning had not only addressed this question in his capacity as president of the St Raphael Society but also regarded the future of the Catholic non-Aryan youth as his special concern in his capacity as chairman of the Catholic schools organization. Furthermore, appeals for help from Catholic non-Aryan circles were constantly being sent to him and his episcopal official representatives. Personally, he also regarded it as his particular task, as the bishop entrusted by the Pope with the welfare of German-speaking Catholics abroad, to help emigrating Catholic non-Aryans to preserve their native German mother tongue and their sense of home and feeling for German culture abroad.

---

1 EAF, Akten des Erzbischöflichen Ordinariats, B2/NS-51, fols. 315–319. Published in Kommission für Zeitgeschichte (ed.), *Akten deutscher Bischöfe über die Lage der Kirche 1933–1945*, vol. 2: *1934–1935*, ed. Bernhard Stasiewski (Mainz: Matthias Grünewald, 1976), doc. 129, pp. 129–136. These footnotes partly follow the annotations in *Akten deutscher Bischöfe*. This document has been translated from German.
2 The original contains handwritten underlining.
3 Dr Wilhelm Berning (1877–1955), Catholic theologian; from 1901 schoolmaster in Meppen; from 1914 bishop of Osnabrück and from 1949 archbishop; author of works including *Katholische Kirche und deutsches Volkstum* (1934).
4 See the Law for the Restoration of the Professional Civil Service, 7 April 1933, Doc. 29.
5 The St Raphael Society for the Protection of Catholic German Emigrants was founded in 1871 in Mainz. The director was the bishop of Osnabruck. The society was banned on 25 June 1941.
6 Dr Heinrich Walter Friedemann (1872–1945), writer and director in Heidelberg.

His Excellency Bishop Dr Wilhelm Berning began negotiations with the Reich Ministry of the Interior as the body responsible for non-Aryan legislation. The ministry showed fundamental goodwill towards the future of Catholic non-Aryan children in relation to their schooling, and so on; indeed, a favourable decision had already been made. Since March 1934 the relevant questions had passed into the jurisdiction of the Reich Ministry of Education. HE Bishop Dr Berning then began negotiations with this body on the question of whether schools might be founded specifically for non-Aryan Catholic children who wanted to settle abroad. In December 1934 the Ministry of Education stated that a decision would be issued concerning this question. In the meantime the Reich Association of Christian German Citizens of Non-Aryan or Not Pure Aryan Descent[7] had continued its work, and it is questionable whether or not Catholic circles should resolve this issue in the interests of educating the Catholic non-Aryan youth within this association or rather on a purely ecclesiastical and denominational basis. On the Protestant side, Pastor Lindemann endeavoured to establish a Protestant aid committee. Pastor Lindemann unfortunately died before his efforts with the Protestant Bishop Adler at the time in Münster could prove successful.

In the meantime, HE Bishop Dr Berning received further proposals from the St Raphael Society, Dr Friedemann, Director Joerger,[8] [and] Secretary Höfler[9] from the Caritas Association to set up an aid committee for special Catholic tasks. However, HE Bishop Dr Berning wanted to wait for the decision of the state offices, especially in this matter. On 11 March 1935 a statement was then issued by the Reich Ministry of Education. The most reverend bishop was informed by the Reich Minister of Education that the Reich Ministry of Education had entered into discussion with the Reich Foreign Office on the matter of creating overseas schools for Christian non-Aryans, and also that there were no fundamental objections from the Reich Ministry of Education. Regarding the details of the implementation, a further discussion was anticipated with the section head in the Reich Foreign Office and the main petitioner. A final decision, it was added, could only be issued at the conclusion of these ongoing negotiations. – HE Bishop Dr Berning believed that the time had now come to arrange a discussion about founding an aid committee for Catholic non-Aryans, and he invited to this discussion President Dr Kreutz,[10] Prelate Wienken,[11] Director Joerger, Dr Krone[12] of Caritasnotwerk,[13] Dr Friedemann, and Dr Groesser[14] of the St Raphael Society. As President Dr Kreutz and Director Joerger could no longer take up the last-minute invitation,

---

7 On the Reich Association, see Doc. 85, 19 Oct. 1933.
8 Kuno Joerger (1893–1958), Catholic theologian; secretary general of the German Caritas Association, 1921–1958.
9 Heinrich Höfler (1897–1963), journalist; from 1931 Caritas director at the headquarters of the German Caritas Association in Freiburg im Breisgau, and editor of the journal *Caritas*; imprisoned by the Gestapo in Berlin, 1944–1945; from 1949 Bundestag delegate for the Christian Democratic Union of Germany (CDU).
10 Dr Benedikt Kreutz (1879–1949), Catholic theologian and political scientist; president of the German Caritas Association, 1921–1949.
11 Heinrich Wienken (1883–1961), Catholic theologian; chaplain in Münster, 1909, and in Berlin, from 1912; director of the Berlin branch of Caritas, 1922–1946; bishop from 1937 and head of the Episcopal Commissariat at the Fulda Bishops' Conference, 1937–1951; representative of the Catholic Church to the government of the German Democratic Republic, 1949–1951; bishop in Meißen, 1951–1957.

they commissioned Prelate Wienken to represent them. Apart from the two aforementioned gentlemen who were absent, all the other persons named took part in the discussion.

II. Course of the discussion
HE Bishop Dr Berning began by describing the developments outlined above, and placed particular emphasis on the fundamental questions concerning the accommodation of Catholic non-Aryan youth. As representative of the Church and Catholic Germandom, he saw the task as being how one can preserve for these young people their Catholic belief and their German cultural roots. The youth must be grouped together for a life abroad. Without special retraining, the grouping has no purpose. If nothing were done, the youth would be embittered against their homeland and also suffer damage to their feelings for German culture and Christianity. The training must strive to help this youth to feel that Christian love transcends racial differences and that Germandom can be preserved, even when no possible future can be found in their homeland because of existing laws and it is therefore necessary to emigrate.

On practical matters, HE Bishop Dr Berning stated that there were monasteries already willing to provide boarding schools for the training of Catholic non-Aryan girls in order to prepare them for all suitable purposes, including childcare, nursing, and so on. Such possibilities would also have to be found for boys. The young men would have to be trained for manual crafts, trade, farm work, and so on. If the Catholic non-Aryan young people are trained in this way, they can move abroad, where a place must be established so that they will find their future in a non-Aryan Catholic settlement (understood in a broader sense). In other words it would probably be of no use placing them in older settlements where there are Aryan Catholics and where disputes about racial matters could disrupt peaceful developments. It is therefore a Christian duty of care, for which the relevant organizations of the Catholic Church and the circles involved must assume responsibility. For this reason, he had invited to the discussion the German Caritas Association, Caritasnotwerk, the St Raphael Society, and a representative of the Catholic non-Aryans themselves.

In the detailed consultation afterwards, the following subjects were discussed and the decisions indicated were reached.

Dr H. W. Friedemann expressed heartfelt thanks on behalf of the Catholic non-Aryans to the Most Reverend Bishop Dr Berning as representative of the Catholic Church for his words and the plans presented, and expressed his belief that Catholic non-Aryans

---

12 Dr Heinrich Krone (1895–1989), teacher; secretary general of the Catholic Centre Party, 1922–1933; executive director of Caritasnotwerk, 1934; arrested in 1944 in connection with the attempt to assassinate Hitler on 20 July; chairman of the CDU/CSU parliamentary group in the German Bundestag, 1955–1961.
13 The Caritasnotwerk was a relief agency established in 1934 by the German branch of the Catholic charity Caritas to provide help to Catholics who, because of their political beliefs, had lost their jobs under the National Socialist regime as well as non-Aryan Catholics. The Notwerk acted as a kind of job agency, finding employment opportunities for those in need.
14 Dr Max Größer (1887–1940), philosopher; from 1921 worked for the St Raphael Society in Hamburg; executive director of the Reich Federation for Catholic Germans Living Abroad, 1927–1930; secretary general of the St Raphael Society, 1930–1940.

were now aware that as Catholics they could rely on the brotherly love of their fellow believers and that this would be a solace and encouragement to them in their difficulties. Dr Friedemann in particular gave thanks that this was not to be small-scale aid work for individual non-Aryans who had fallen into destitution but that the focus would essentially be on the question of retraining and resettling the young generation.

The number of non-Aryans concerned was estimated. The NSDAP's Race Office[15] estimates the number of Jews today still at 490,000 and believes that the number of non-Aryans is many times higher. The assumption of the Reich Association of Christian German Citizens of Non-Aryan or Not Pure Aryan Descent that there are only 200,000 Christian non-Aryans is dismissed as improbable because the calculation made on the basis of Christian Jewish marriages and conversions upon marriage can in no way be considered correct. The number of Catholic non-Aryans is certainly unlikely to exceed 500,000. A more precise calculation of the numbers could perhaps be facilitated by contacting experts employed at the Reich Ministry of the Interior (Lossen, Burwig).[16]

The Aid Committee for Catholic Non-Aryans would in any case be concerned only with Catholic and not with Protestant non-Aryans. It is to be anticipated that the Protestant Church both wants to and will be able to resolve the tasks with which it is faced.

Relevant work in other circles. This is carried out first by the 'Reich Association',[17] which was founded in Berlin on 23 August 1933 and has its offices in Berlin W 15, 40 Uhlandstraße. The chairman is Dr Richard Wolff,[18] former editor-in-chief of the Reich government's news reports. The federation is thought to have 3,400 to 4,000 members and publishes a four-page 'Bulletin of the Reich Association of Non-Aryan Christians', now in its second year. It expects a membership fee of 3 Reichsmarks and a monthly contribution of 2 Reichsmarks; from the unemployed it expects a contribution of 50 pfennigs. This Reich Association has all kinds of enemies because it is said to have no programme and to be content with minor work placement services and social events. It also provides information on special cultural events, hosting lecture evenings, theatrical and musical events, sport clubs, and educational and legal advice sessions. In its bulletin, as in its office, the federation particularly publicizes job offers, job searches, marriage announcements, fire sales of used goods, and so on. The federation has around ten local branches so far in major cities in Germany. The chairman, Dr R. Wolff, has published a short work entitled *We Non-Aryan Christians*, 44 pages, printed by R. Schenker, Frankfurt an der Oder. This work presents the author's speeches.[19] The Aryan gynaecologist Dr Fieseler[20] in Berlin, 200 Kaiserallee, has tackled (at the suggestion of a Mrs Hamburger) the question of the education of non-Aryan children and published some 'proposals

---

15 This refers to the NSDAP's Racial Policy Office.
16 In fact, the Reich Ministry of the Interior based its own assumptions on the inflated estimates of the NSDAP's Racial Policy Office. See Doc. 159, 3 April 1935.
17 Reich Federation of Christian German Citizens of Non-Aryan or Not Pure Aryan Descent.
18 Dr Richard Wolff (1885–1958), historian; worked in the press department of the Reich government, 1926–1933; from 1934 chairman of the Reich Federation of Non-Aryan Christians.
19 Published in 1934 under the title *Wir nichtarischen Christen: Drei Reden vom Vorsitzenden des Reichsverbandes der nichtarischen Christen*.
20 Correctly: Dr Karl August Fiessler.

for setting up overseas schools for Christian German non-Aryan young people'. He also put in the first request to the Reich Ministry of Education.

The special aid work started by the St Raphael Society at the beginning of 1934, which at first succeeded in providing help in England, the Netherlands, Belgium, France, Spain, Italy, and Austria, especially to immigrant German Catholic non-Aryans, some of whom it was able to place in employment, has also helped Catholic non-Aryans in the usual way to immigrate to Italy, France, the Netherlands, Spain, and North and South America, and was helpful to them in their adaptation to a new life. Most recently, it succeeded in arranging free holiday stays in England and Switzerland. The individual German dioceses made this aid work possible through one-off subsidies that raised a total of 3,090 Reichsmarks.

Organization of the aid. The aid committee to be founded for Catholic non-Aryans is only to be provisional. There is as yet no definitive answer on the number of members and their profile. Thought is also being given to the possibility of a larger committee. No information will be communicated to the public for the time being about the establishment of the aid committee. The decision of the Reich authorities must first be awaited. *A provisional division of labour* should be structured based on the following:

(a) *Dr Friedemann* will try to obtain names and addresses of Catholic non-Aryans, in particular parents who are interested in the schooling of their children.

(b) *Dr Krone* will investigate the possibility of how adult Catholic non-Aryans in this country can be helped to reorientate themselves professionally or to obtain a secure accredited post, especially in the case of people for whom there is no question of emigrating.

(c) *The St Raphael Society* will continue its work and in particular make assessments of where and how a non-Aryan German settlement could be established abroad.

The office of the aid committee is first to be opened at Caritasnotwerk in Berlin, at 13–14 Oranienburgerstraße. Dr Krone has already informed the German Caritas Association that he is willing to provisionally run the secretariat of the aid committee. This office would then carry out all relevant tasks once the Reich Ministry of Education has reached its decision. Among other things, by means of official church gazettes, priests' offices, and Catholic schools, enquiries about the non-Aryan Catholic circles in question would have to be made, as well as precise proposals concerning the young people's schooling in this country, which would then be presented to the Reich Ministry of Education, and so on.

The difficult question of funding still has to be resolved. We are mainly thinking of voluntary subsidies and donations from Catholic Aryans and especially from wealthy Catholic non-Aryans. Whether and to what extent the Reich can bear the costs of settlement abroad still remains to be seen. The proposal to capitalize benefits also paid to non-Aryans (unemployment and welfare benefits) is unlikely to be adopted. Contributions from members of an association of Catholic non-Aryans, the provision of usual advice sheets for a fee, regular contributions, and advance payments by parents for their children who are to be schooled and settled abroad could help with the financing. HE Bishop Dr Berning suggests that the German Caritas Association initially provide some funds for the start of the work, the office, and so on. Prelate Wienken has taken on the task of presenting this request from the Reverend Bishop Dr Berning at the next central meeting of the Caritas Association. At this meeting, the aid committee's plans could also be put forward and discussed.

Members of the aid committee: His Excellency Bishop Dr Berning declared – in his capacity as Catholic bishop, as president of the St Raphael Society, and as the person commissioned by the Pope with the religious care of German-speaking Catholics abroad – the Aid Committee for Catholic Non-Aryans to be established, assumed the chairmanship himself, and appointed as provisional members of the aid committee:

Prelate Wienken and *Director Joerger* of the German Caritas Association,
Dr Krone of Caritasnotwerk,
Dr H. W. Friedemann as representative of Catholic non-Aryans,
Dr Groesser of the St Raphael Society.

Some consideration was given to also appointing a *women's representative* (Catholic German Women's League), the *industrialist Weissenfels*,[21] director, Heidelberg-Wieblingen. The founding of an enlarged committee for eligible individuals, such as the editor Höfler as representative of the Catholic church press, Dr Hackelsberger,[22] wealthy non-Aryan Catholics, wealthy Aryan Catholics, non-Aryans with school-age children, and so on, was also postponed.

Work of the aid committee in Germany. It is assumed that one can help adult non-Aryans in Germany only in specific cases, as Dr Krone will attempt to do, but that no special establishments can be created for non-Aryans. The main task in the homeland will therefore relate to preparing exact plans as to how the grouping and schooling of the non-Aryan youth and their settlement abroad are to be considered in practical terms. These plans will be presented to the Reich Ministry of Education. Following approval, the work can then commence.

Type of settlement. The question of settlement abroad arises for Catholic non-Aryans who want to and can emigrate, and above all for young people. The settlement is to be understood in the broader sense, in such a way that it concerns not only farmers but also manual workers, traders, and a very small number of intellectual workers. We should emphasize to the authorities what use can accrue to the Reich through import and export from such a settlement. Such experience as exists for the emigration to Palestine, its financing, the modes of asset transfer, and so on can perhaps somehow be utilized.[23] Setting up a holding company, a settler bank, or a trustee account in Germany must still be discussed. Suitable people from industry must be brought in for this difficult matter. With reference to the potential countries for settlement abroad, Dr Friedemann indicated that in Nablus in Palestine some landholdings of the Catholic archbishop of Jerusalem

---

21 Correctly: Weissenberg from Wieblingen.
22 Dr Albert Hackelsberger (1893–1940), retailer and lawyer; managing director of the firm J. Weck & Co., 1925–1938; deputy chairman of the Catholic Centre Party, 1933; member of the General Council of Economics, 1933–1938; arrested in 1938 for treason against the people and currency offences.
23 This refers to the Haavara Agreement. See Glossary.

had been available for settlement but have unfortunately already been allocated. He favoured individual small outposts in Palestine, so that the Holy Land should not be entirely lost to the Jews. He also mentioned Lebanon, a free republic in Syria, where further possibilities could emerge. The Australian government is also said to be making available 500,000 km² in the north of the region for the purpose of settlement. Finally, he mentioned South Africa. Dr Zintgraff[24] believes that cheap landholdings in South Africa could even now still be acquired from Prime Minister Hertzog.[25]

Concluding the discussion, HE Berning thanked those who had attended, asked Prelate Wienken to present the matter at the Central Council of the Caritas Association, and held out the prospect of further meetings of the current aid committee at a later date.

DOC. 157
On 22 March 1935 the Central Association of German Citizens of the Jewish Faith reports on anti-Jewish incidents in Mecklenburg communities[1]

Letter (urgent!) from the CV regional federation in north-western Germany, Hamburg (signature illegible), to the CV, Berlin, dated 22 March 1935[2]

Re: Mecklenburg.
We would like to present you below with a fuller picture of the difficulties that have emerged in specific locations in Mecklenburg.

1. Crivitz. Our representative there informs us that in all the meetings of the Party and its sub-organizations, agitation is being stirred up most violently against him and the business he is running there, and that the inhabitants of Crivitz are being told to stop buying from our friend.

2. Neubukow. As in Crivitz, the representative in Neubukow informs us that in every Party meeting the boycott is still being preached repeatedly, and that NSDAP members are being threatened with expulsion if they contravene it.

3. Lübz. From this place our friend informs us that, in view of the new circumstances, he felt compelled in 1934 to sell his business to an Aryan.

4. Stavenhagen. As already communicated to you by the head of the Israelite Community in Stavenhagen, the local branch leader states at every Party meeting that it is forbidden to buy in Jewish shops. The turnover of the few Jewish shops in Stavenhagen has fallen dramatically as customers do not dare to buy from our friends.

---

24 Probably Dr Alfred Zintgraff (1878–1944), lawyer; editor of *Beiträge zur auslandskundlichen und außenpolitischen Schulung der Kameradschaften der NSDStB* (1938).
25 James Barry Munnik Hertzog (1866–1942), lawyer and politician; prime minister of the Union of South Africa, 1924–1939.

1 RGVA, 721k-1-258, fols. 56–58. This document has been translated from German.
2 The original contains handwritten revisions, underlining, and a stamp.

5. *Wismar.* This regional group also reports that because of the general mood being generated in the press and through prohibitions on purchasing, there has been a substantial drop in turnover.

6. *Ludwigslust.* After this town had long been spared any boycott, the owner of the only Jewish shop here found herself forced by the new attempts to organize a boycott to suddenly sell her shop, which had been in the same family for 108 years. In addition, her loan from the savings bank in the town of Ludwigslust was cancelled for no reason.

7. *Neustrelitz.* More intense antisemitic agitation has recently begun to be generated. When the coal vouchers for the Winter Relief were distributed, every person in need was told that anyone who took the vouchers to the Jew would be excluded from a further delivery by the Winter Relief. – The shop windows of most of the Jewish shops have been smeared with the word 'Jew', for which a caustic fluid was used. – Our representative, who runs a coal business, is being spied on, and those who buy his goods are threatened, if they continue to buy from him, with being boycotted themselves and with a termination of state deliveries. A similar measure has already been carried out at most of the master bakers'.

8. *Schwaan.* Here too extraordinarily active antisemitic propaganda is being spread. At all public meetings the leaders of the individual political organizations emphasize most emphatically that no one must buy from the Jew any longer. – In particular the Jewish doctor who lives in Schwaan, Dr Marcus,[3] is being confronted with considerable difficulties in every conceivable way.[4]

9. *Parchim.* The retail shops here are facing extraordinary difficulties as customers are afraid to enter the Jewish shops. On the second Sunday before Christmas, the Kreisleiter of the NSDAP stood opposite the Ehrlich department store during the main shopping time. Right up to Christmas a uniformed SA man stood in the same position. Furthermore, the Jewish question has been discussed at the most recent Party meetings.

10. *Schwerin.* With some non-Aryans already having given up their shops in the past year, now some more fellow believers have been forced to close their businesses. It is clear from the attached newspaper clippings[5] how anti-Jewish agitation is being generated at every meeting, and those who still buy in Jewish shops are being denounced as traitors. In particular, the Jewish shops can no longer rely on having civil servants among their customers, as the latter are being threatened with transfer for disciplinary reasons and dismissal from the service. This has even reached a point in Schwerin where people who stand in front of Jewish shops are being told: 'If you want to be a German, then move

---

3 Dr Paul Marcus (b. 1887), physician; from 1911 assistant doctor in places including Dresden and Darmstadt; from 1922 he had a practice in Schwaan (Kreis Güstrow); probably emigrated in 1935.
4 It is likely that these difficulties originated with Wilhelm Dopheide, a doctor who had his practice in Schwaan until Nov. 1934; later Kreis physician and head of the public health authority in Hagenow. See also Doc. 241, 30 July 1936.
5 These clippings were not found with the original document.

on and don't stand here.' The owner of a larger goldware shop found the enclosed anonymous card in his post office box.[6] It should be kept in mind that this shop has existed since 1888, enjoys the best reputation, and still employs around twenty staff today.

The names of the Jewish shops are displayed on the noticeboards of the Schwerin barracks as well as in the state theatre. As reported, however, further action is said to be in preparation against non-Aryan shops.

During attempts to organize a boycott over the Christmas 1934 period, Jewish firms were officially refused police protection. The police expressly declared that they had been instructed by a higher authority not to intervene.

Furthermore, a while ago notes were stuck on the windows of the Jewish shops reading: 'Anyone who buys from the Jew is a traitor to the people.'

A loan company in Schwerin that has been operating for some twenty-two years suddenly had its loan cancelled by the bank. The bank immediately obtained a title, so the matter was heard before the regional court in Schwerin. However, the regional court took the view that coercive measures of that kind should be refrained from. The Jewish businessman who had given the bank the best collateral was saved from ruin by the court's opinion.

11. Waren, Hagenow, Rostock, Penzlin, Dargun, Neubrandenburg, Grabow. On the basis of the communications that have reached us, our friends there have no cause to complain about difficulties.

In summary, we observe that after significant antisemitic endeavours had previously become noticeable throughout Mecklenburg, a more intense boycott movement has recently started. Our friends' economic situation had already worsened extraordinarily in the last two years, forcing many to leave the Mecklenburg region, mostly to build a new life in the cities. Also very recently in some cases commercial sales of long-established firms, some of which have been in the same family for centuries, have been reported to us. The economic circumstances and productivity have declined to such an extent because of the recent wave of antisemitism that in many cases a collapse can be expected very soon.

As well as the decline in turnover of sometimes almost 75 per cent, which in many cases has necessitated the dismissal of employees, there is a marked decline in the number of residents, especially in the small communities that flourished in previous years and decades, a decline that amounts to up to 50 per cent of the community members. Apart from school-age children, there are no young people in active employment in almost any community, even in the largest, Rostock. Almost 100 per cent of these young people have migrated abroad or to the cities.

---

6 This card was not found with the original document.

DOC. 158
On 23 March 1935 the gendarmerie informs the regional council in Hünfeld about an attack on visitors to the Rhina Synagogue[1]

Letter from the Wehrda gendarmerie control area, Kreis Hünfeld, Regierungsbezirk Kassel, Gendarmerie Sergeant Wolf and Gendarmerie Sergeant on Probation Schulz,[2] Neukirchen, to the regional council (received on 24 March 1935), dated 23 March 1935[3]

On 22 March 1935, at 7:20 p.m., at our apartment, we received a telephone message that an attack had taken place at the synagogue. Gendarmerie Sergeant Wolf and I immediately went to Rhina, where we ascertained that at around 6:45 p.m., after the Jewish religious service had ended, when the first people were leaving the synagogue through the main door that opens on to the street, suddenly around fifteen to twenty people in disguise, wearing black masks and equipped with rubber truncheons, forced their way into the synagogue and attacked the Jewish men at random. The following people were slightly or seriously injured: Nathan Nußbaum, Jakob Katzenstein, Sally Klebe,[4] Isaak Katzenstein,[5] Moses Blumenthal,[6] Samuel Buxbaum, Hermann Wetterhahn,[7] Jakob Klebe,[8] Issak Oppenheim,[9] Moses Bacharach,[10] and Siegfried Oppenheim.[11] It was also ascertained that the people who broke into the synagogue drove through Rhina in a grey truck with a closed grey tarpaulin at 6:30 p.m. from the direction of Rothenkirchen, and took up a position right next to the synagogue and in the direction of Schletzenrod. Paper had also been stuck over both the number plates on the truck so that no number could be identified. The truck's driver stood by the vehicle on the street, while the disguised and masked people stayed hidden until the first Jews came out of the synagogue. At the sound of a whistle, the disguised people are said to have jumped out of the truck and forced their way into the synagogue, which had now opened its doors. This entire incident in the synagogue lasted around three or four minutes, after which the masked people climbed into the truck that was standing ready immediately nearby and drove on in the direction of Schletzenrod.

---

1 HHStAW, Abt. 483/6752, fol. 20r–v. Published in Kulka and Jäckel (eds.), *The Jews in the Secret Nazi Reports*, enclosed CD, no. 753. This document has been translated from German.
2 Robert Schulz (b. 1900), policeman; senior constable in the Berlin urban police, 1932–1934; gendarmerie sergeant at the Landrat office in Hünfeld, 1934–1945; joined the NSDAP in 1937.
3 Parts of the original have been underlined by hand.
4 Sally Klebe (b. 1871).
5 Isaak Katzenstein (1890–1961), son-in-law of Moses Bacharach; emigrated to the USA.
6 Moses Blumenthal (1874–1962), baker; in 1940 moved to Frankfurt am Main and emigrated from there to the USA.
7 Hermann Wetterhahn (1902–1979), butcher and cattle trader; emigrated to the USA in 1937.
8 Jakob Klebe (b. 1881), cattle trader; deported from Frankfurt to Theresienstadt in August 1942.
9 Isaak Oppenheim (1889–1978); in 1939 moved to Frankfurt am Main and emigrated from there with his family to the USA.
10 Moses Bacharach (b. 1860), cattle trader; emigrated to the USA in 1939 with his daughter Bella, his son-in-law Isaak Katzenstein, and his grandson Manfred.
11 Siegfried Oppenheim (probably 1909–1998), son of Isaak Oppenheim; in 1939 moved with him to Frankfurt am Main, and emigrated from there to the USA.

In the investigations carried out so far, nothing could be ascertained either about the perpetrators of the incident or the truck. According to the general suspicions of the Jewish people, who did not want to say anything for fear of further outrages and mistreatment, the supposed perpetrators are thought to be from Rothenkirchen or neighbouring localities in Kreis Hünfeld. After the perpetrators had fled and left the community of Rhina, on the same evening at 11:00 p.m. several windowpanes were broken at the following people's homes: Sally Klebe, Samuel Viktor II, the widow Bella Nußbaum, Moritz Viktor I.[12] The culprits who broke the windowpanes are likely to be found in the village of Rhina. Among others we met on the street were Nikolaus Hergert and Adam Manns, who both live in Rhina, and are known by the undersigned from all the actions previously carried out in Rhina. In two cases we were told in the strictest confidence by the Jew Max Blumenthal[13] that during the past week his current employee in the bakery, Nikolaus Hergert, said that soon or in the first few days of the week, people in black would come to assault Max Nußbaum and other Jews. Blumenthal also admitted that in this regard he had informed the other Jews about the approaching attack. Sally Nußbaum[14] also told us in confidence that on the evening in question (22 March 1935), after the attack had taken place, he had stood in his yard and had asked the electrician living opposite him, Philipp Will, who was also standing in the street, whether he was the local group leader or something similar from the Party, and what he had to say about the incident, whether he condoned the action, to which Will replied, 'No!' This conversation that took place between him and Will was overheard by Nikolaus Hergert, who was standing with a bicycle in the street, at which point Hergert called out to Will, 'Why are you even answering the Jew, what is he doing here, if you (Jew) don't clear off, I'll throw the bike in your face.' The investigations are ongoing.

12 Moritz Viktor (b. 1903), retailer.
13 Emanuel (Max) Blumenthal (b. 1905); baker; probably emigrated.
14 Sally Nussbaum (1905–1959); later emigrated to the USA.

DOC. 159
On 3 April 1935 the Reich Ministry of the Interior informs the Office of the Wehrmacht Adjutant to the Führer and Reich Chancellor about the estimated number of Jews in the German Reich[1]

Letter from the Reich and Prussian Ministry of the Interior (A 2841/5012), p.p. signed Pfundtner, to the adjutant of the Wehrmacht to the Führer and Reich Chancellor, for the attention of Major Hoßbach,[2] Berlin, dated 3 April 1935, dispatched by the Reich and Prussian Ministry of the Interior (IA 2841/5012), on behalf of the state secretary, signed Dr Buttmann,[3] to the Reich ministers (received by the Reich Ministry of Education, 24 April 1935 – Z III a 1526), Göring, the Prussian Minister of Finance, the Reich Statistical Office (Burgdörfer),[4] the Reich Office for Emigration Affairs, the Reich Office for Kinship Research,[5] the Gestapo Central Office (Gestapa), and the Racial Policy Office of the NSDAP[6] on 23 April 1935 (copy)[7]

Re: the number of full, half-, and quarter-Jews in the German Reich.[8]
With adequate precision, the number of full Jews can be determined and also those who only profess the Mosaic faith. This is based on the data from the Reich Statistical Office according to the national census of 16 June 1933,[9] in which the distribution of the populace by religion was determined, though not by race. The figure came to *499,682 Mosaic Jews* (0.77 per cent of the total population).

Added to these are the Mosaic Jews of the Saar who were not counted at the time. There is a figure of 19 July 1927 counting 4,038 such persons in the Saar territory. In mid 1933 around 503,900 religious Jews were therefore living in the German Reich including

---

1 BArch, R 4901/11787, fol. 4r–v. This document has been translated from German.
2 Friedrich Hoßbach (1894–1980), career officer; chief of the central section of the General Staff and Wehrmacht adjutant to Hitler, 1934–1938; general, 1943, and commander of the 4th Army, 1945.
3 Dr Rudolf Buttmann (1885–1947), lawyer; co-founder of the German National People's Party (DNVP), 1919; joined the NSDAP in 1925; head of the cultural policy department in the Reich Ministry of the Interior, 1933–1935; general manager of the Bavarian state library, 1935–1945; author of works including *Nationalsozialistische Staatsauffassung* (1933).
4 Dr Friedrich Burgdörfer (1890–1967), statistician; departmental head in the Reich Statistical Office, 1925–1939; director of the Regional Statistical Office in Bavaria, 1939–1945, responsible for the special registration of German Jews in the censuses of 1933 and 1939; honorary member of the German Statistical Society, 1960; author of works including *Sterben die weißen Völker?* (1934).
5 The Reich Office for Kinship Research (Reichsstelle für Sippenforschung) was in existence from 1935 to 1939 and was headed by the historian Dr Kurt Mayer. Its precursor in the years 1933–1935 was the 'Expert for Race Research at the Reich Ministry of the Interior'. The Reich Kinship Authority (Reichssippenamt) emerged in 1939 from the Reich Office for Kinship Research.
6 From 1934 the NSDAP's Racial Policy Office (Rassenpolitisches Amt der NSDAP) was under the authority of the Deputy of the Führer and was run by Dr Walter Groß. It was devoted to 'demographic and racial political questions' as well as corresponding training and propaganda.
7 In the original there are several handwritten revisions, including the note 'presented on 20 May'. The copy referred to here was sent to all offices and departments within the Reich Ministry of Education on 17 May 1935: BArch, R 4901/11787, fol. 4.
8 The estimates were used in the preparatory discussion on the new Military Service Law, which in May 1935 excluded non-Aryans from military service: *Reichsgesetzblatt*, 1935, I, pp. 609–614.
9 See the statistics from the census of 16 June 1933, Docs. 52 and 53.

the Saar. This figure has since decreased further by an estimated 30,000 as a result of emigration.[10] The number of *religious Jews* living in the Reich today is therefore around 475,000.

The number of full Jews who are not of the Jewish faith (baptized and non-affiliated), as well as the number of German-Jewish Mischlinge of the first and second degree (i.e. with a Jewish parent or a Jewish grandparent), can currently only be estimated due to a lack of any census or possibility of carrying one out. The estimate is based on the findings of the Reich Ministry of the Interior, the Reich Office for Kinship Research, and the Racial Policy Office of the NSDAP in their activities to bring about racial separation. Even these *estimates*, for which there are *only few actual indications* (exclusion of non-Aryans from the civil service and from the NSDAP), widely diverge.

The average of these estimates reveals the following:

Full Jews not of the Jewish faith	300,000
(according to the register of Jewish baptisms held by the Reich Office for Kinship Research)	
Jewish-German Mischlinge, first and second degree	750,000
Non-Aryans in total:	
Full Jews (Mosaic)	475,000
Full Jews (non-Mosaic)	300,000
Mischlinge, first and second degree	750,000
	1,525,000
	= approx. 1½ million

(2.3 per cent of the total population).

In the 1933 census, the number of religious Jews (499,682) was divided into:
Persons of the male gender   238,747 (47.78 per cent)
Persons of the female gender   260,935 (52.22 per cent)

These subdivisions by gender can only cautiously be taken as a basis for the total number of Jews and Mischlinge, as it is uncertain whether this distribution of the sexes operates in the same way in the progeny of mixed marriages as it does in the progeny of marriages between full-blooded Jews. If this is taken as a basis, the total number of non-Aryans (c. 1½ million) ascertained would contain:

728,645 persons of the male gender (c. 728,500)

The number of these who are of the military-service age of between 18 and 45 years can be estimated for Prussia in the year 1925 using the statistical data from the book *Die Bevölkerungs- und Berufsverhältnisse der Juden im deutschen Reich*[11] (Akademieverlag, Berlin, 1930). At that time, 45 per cent of the male Jewish population of Prussia were between the ages of 18 and 45.

The application of this percentage to 728,500 male non-Aryans results in the following for the present day:

---

10 In fact, twice as many Jews had permanently left Germany during the first two years of National Socialist rule.
11 The Demographic and Occupational Situation of the Jews in the German Reich.

Jews and Mischlinge of military-service age 327,825 (i.e. c.328,000)
Summary:

Full Jews of the Mosaic faith	475,000
Full Jews not of the Mosaic faith	300,000
Mischlinge, first and second degree	750,000
	1,525,000
	around 1½ million.
Of whom males	728,500
Of whom men aged between 18 and 45 years	328,000

To be deducted around 20,000 foreigners.
Thus remaining: *308,000.*

DOC. 160
On 8 April 1935 the Central Association of German Citizens of the Jewish Faith protests to Mayor Goerdeler against the boycott of Jewish doctors in Leipzig[1]

Letter from the CV Regional Federation for Central Germany, Sabatzky, Leipzig, to Mayor Dr Goerdeler[2] (received on 9 April 1935, administrative office), Leipzig, dated 8 April 1935[3]

Re: *complaints about Mayor Haake*[4] *etc.*
According to notifications received by us, in a departmental meeting that took place on 18 March 1935 in the Alberthalle, Mayor Haake said something along these lines: 'When looking through the health insurance accounts of the municipal civil servants, I noticed that many civil servants still go to non-Aryan doctors. We have nothing against these gentlemen, but it is immoral if a civil servant goes to a Jewish doctor!'[5]

It has further emerged that a series of municipal civil servants were summoned to their supervisors and that they were told that any of them visiting a Jewish doctor would be reported to the personnel office.

Furthermore, the health insurance company stated that municipal civil servants are not to go to Jewish doctors. This is an entirely illegal boycott that is in no way admissible because, firstly, Jews are in fact permitted to practise as doctors even in the National Socialist state, and any boycott is in itself prohibited, and, secondly, it is precisely defined

---

1 Stadtarchiv Leipzig, Kap. I/122, fol. 3r–v. This document has been translated from German.
2 Dr Carl Friedrich Goerdeler (1884–1945), lawyer and politician; second mayor in Königsberg, Prussia, from 1920; member of the German National People's Party (DNVP) until 1931; mayor of Leipzig, 1930–1937; Reich commissioner for price control, 1931–1932 and 1934–1935; resigned as mayor, 1937; then consultant for Bosch AG; conspirator in the assassination plot of 20 July 1944 (earmarked as future chancellor in the event of Hitler's demise); executed on 2 Feb. 1945.
3 The original contains handwritten underlining, Goerdeler's signature, and a signed note by him dated 13 April 1935 to 'Mayor Haake'.
4 Rudolf Haake (1903–1945), businessman; joined the NSDAP in 1922; NSDAP city councillor in Leipzig, 1930–1933; editor of the NSDAP newspaper *Der Freiheitskampf*, 1931–1932; mayor in Leipzig, 1933–1943, and deputy mayor, 1935–1937; acting mayor, 1937; mayor, 1938–1939; compulsory retirement, 1943.
5 In the original the second half of the quotation has been underlined by hand, probably by Goerdeler.

in the 1934 Regulation on the Admission of Doctors which circle of Jewish doctors may be consulted, namely that of the old doctors and combat veterans, by members of all health insurance funds, therefore also the municipal civil servants' health insurers.

We most respectfully ask the Mayor to ensure that the boycott of Jewish doctors declared by Mayor Haake and the subordinate departments, as well as the health insurance company for civil servants, is immediately repealed.

DOC. 161
Jüdische Rundschau, April 1935: speech by Rabbi Joachim Prinz concerning the social and cultural isolation of the Jewish population[1]

Living without neighbours

Attempt at a first analysis. Ghetto 1935 (from a speech: 'The Jewish Situation – Today') by Joachim Prinz.[2]

The following extract from a major lecture provides only an analysis without including the attempted resolution that is undertaken in the lecture itself.

It is now beginning to penetrate our consciousness that we are living in a ghetto. This ghetto is of course different in many ways, conceptually and materially, from what we previously understood by it. This is precisely why an analysis of the ghetto as an *internal* and an *external* state, but precisely in terms of these inner characteristics and conceptual definitions, appears to be a valuable and important task to explain the current situation.

The inner state that we call a 'ghetto' is revealed in a fact for which there are of course only *moral* yardsticks, which develop inside and therefore have no general application. These are therefore yardsticks that differ by degree according to each individual person's sensitivity and what he expects from life. But whatever the case may be, based on our feelings and our expectations of life, we define a ghetto as the fact *that as Jews in Germany we are living in a country where in many places we are assured that our very existence is burdensome to the German people*. If we summarize everything that has happened to us in the last two years in legislative acts, official announcements, important speeches, and essential measures, it amounts to a ghetto: regardless of our wishes, our goodwill, our capabilities, and everything that we do or do not do, many people in this country feel that we are a burden on their national life. They often say that the nature of our race, the existence of our spirit, the presence of our religion, the physiognomy of our faces, and our customs of living make the population unhappy. There is no 'standpoint' on such value judgements. They can only be acknowledged, but they cannot possibly be registered as a fact that 'has nothing to do with me'. It has already so often been

---

1 'Das Leben ohne Nachbarn', *Jüdische Rundschau*, 17 April 1935, p. 3. This document has been translated from German.
2 Dr Joachim Prinz (1902–1988), rabbi; liberal rabbi in Berlin, 1926–1937; after 1933 arrested on several occasions for his speeches against the Nazi regime; emigrated in 1937 to the USA, where he was vice president of the American Jewish Congress after the war and its president, 1958–1962; author of works including *Wir Juden* (1934) and *Das Leben im Ghetto* (1937).

said that love concerns the beloved, and the opposite of love also concerns us, insofar as it makes us an object. Those who can simply acknowledge and then add 'what has it to do with me?' are happy indeed. But this happiness comes from a superficial mindset and a deficient sense of honour and decency. No argument should be made for this 'happiness'. It is an ignoble and false happiness. We others regard it as *unhappiness* and as we have not been able to conform to the will of the German people, which feels us to be a burden, as quickly as possible and unhesitatingly, because many Jews have remained here out of consideration for the economic situation of the population itself but also on account of inner processes in ourselves, and, as around 100,000 people in number, we are becoming aware of the *inner ghetto* that remaining here produces in us. Of course we would have to be cleared if we were put on trial for inferior moral quality. It is not this that prolonged our stay, but *our life remains a ghetto life, life in the awareness of being for many millions a 'guest' whose life, and in fact whose mere existence, is according to the host a constraint on his light, air, and joy.*

To this inner state that we call a 'ghetto', others are being added. The ghetto of the Middle Ages was closed in the evening. The gate would shut harshly and cruelly. The bolts were carefully drawn; people left the 'world' and entered the ghetto. Today it is the other way round. When our front door shuts behind us, *we leave the ghetto and enter our home.* That is a fundamental difference. The ghetto is no longer a *geographically defined district*, at least not in the sense known in the Middle Ages. The ghetto is the 'world'. For us, outside is the ghetto. In the marketplaces, on the country roads, in the restaurants, the ghetto is everywhere. It has an emblem. The emblem means: neighbourless. *The Jew's lot is to be neighbourless.* Perhaps this is a unique phenomenon in the world, and who knows how long it can be endured: life without neighbours. Everywhere in life there are people who are neighbourly. This is not a friend but someone who is willing to lead his life *with* another, not to make it difficult for him, to take a friendly view of his efforts and activities. That is missing. Jews in the large cities do not feel it in that way, but the Jews in small towns, who live at the market square without neighbours, whose children go to school without neighbouring children, feel the isolation that is entailed by neighbourlessness, which is crueller than anything else, and it is perhaps the harshest fate for human community that anyone can encounter. We would not find it all so painful if we did not have the feeling that we once *did have* neighbours.

There is something else that should be added. We are living in a very strange cultural situation. Anyone with eyes to see can recognize it and everything that we do around all that is in fact illusory. But anyone who considers the Jews' cultural situation in Germany even only from above and flakes off just a tiny bit of the varnish that extends over an apparently massive painting knows that all this is merely the *torso* of a shocking barrenness and a gaping wound. When we reflect that we no longer have any legitimate place in German cultural activity, not so much by our own doing, but by the doing of that culture, then everything that we 'do' culturally turns out that way. We play Beethoven, Bach, and Mozart, we return to Goethe and Hölderlin, we listen longingly to the great revelations of these sacred Germans. That is a good thing, and there is always something beautiful and captivating about going back to old things. But what a spectacle, what a tragedy for people who live in a time without living *in it. We have no contemporary status* in present-day German life. We are also culturally uprooted and we have been handed a plumb line that we drop into the course of German and European cultural events, and we sharply divide the great literature of old, to which we devote ourselves, from the literature, painting, and music of today, in which we may not indulge. The fact, for example, that we may not perform the work of any contemporary German dramatist on our stages, the fact that no large German orchestra would play the melodies or creations of a Jew living today, and the huge barriers to creative work faced by our painters condemn our cultural situation to a *pseudo-life that is cruelly remote from reality*. There is no establishment, no association, no cultural federation that can help with this. For there is no 'temporary culture'! I do not know how long it is possible to live in this way. I do not know how long young people can live in this way. Memories can certainly help in surviving a harsh season, and the experiences of old, from the time in which Jews could at least make some kind of legitimate claim to shared collaboration and creation, in which Gustav Mahler composed music and Gundolf[3] interpreted Goethe, are the vast and beautiful treasure-house that can be entered, if we wish. But *we* still have it. Our young people do not have it. That is a question. It is not an answer. *There is no answer.*

As well as the cultural situation, another part of the ghetto, our ghetto of 1935, is something difficult to describe and that outlines our *life in the German landscape*. There is no need to give stirring speeches about it. We only need to walk through the German countryside once a day, now in spring, when everything is coming back to life, and fresh green is covering the meadows, the streams are shining like silver in the mountains, the trees are blossoming, and the woods are young and fresh on the mountains. That is all we need, and we feel it with all certainty and an elemental force that is as strong as an axiom: that we are bound to this landscape, bound for all time, and the longing of many Jews who leave Germany for karstic Palestine, the longing for the rustling forests and the luxuriant meadows, is genuine and robust. We were born into this landscape. I do not want to say anything about the mysticism or myth of a landscape. I do not know the limits of this domain. But leaving all that aside, the bond is great, strong, and genuine. And yet over the last two years it has been transformed. For there is no landscape without people. That is nothing but a chimera, a shadow, a picture, a board on the wall. Landscape, real landscape, is made up of people and their lives, their thoughts, their reactions, their feelings, and their ways of living. There is no bond with the bare landscape alone, without any people, and beyond mere aesthetics landscape is never devoid of people. But if that is so, then the face of the landscape in which we are living is gradually beginning to change. For where on earth could the bond remain undisturbed when this landscape is full of posts. Barriers, signs that forbid me as someone living in this landscape to enter it. For me that becomes a stake in the flesh of the landscape and its body is fatally wounded. For knowing that landscapes in the mountains, on the plains, and by the sea, small villages, and towns do not wish the Jew to enter, and therefore do not wish me to enter, this is not only something that causes sorrow. That would be too little; in fact *this also transforms the landscape itself, its objective image, its appearance, not only my feelings*. And mountains, rivers, trees, and meadows begin to grimace at us, in a transformation that was never anticipated nor believed. By this unmasking of a landscape that is also ours, our ghetto state is revealed once again.

---

3 Dr Friedrich Gundolf, actually Gundelfinger (1880–1931), literary historian and writer; professor of German literary history in Heidelberg from 1920; author of works including *Goethe* (1916).

The walls of the 1935 ghetto are certainly also in the fabric of measures and laws. But it is good if we can see these invisible walls that belong to the culture, the landscape, and the inner reactions. It is good for us and the others to know what that actually means: the 1935 ghetto.

This is all stated here without any resentment or any accusatory tone. We are far too aware of the scale of historical turmoil to react to this fate with futile complaints. We know only one thing: the form of existence described cannot be the representative form of Jewish life. And we know that in the same era that has brought us this unexpected transformation of our life, there is a *new* form of Jewish life and a transformation of the Jewish person in the land of Jewish birth and Jewish rebirth.

DOC. 162

Berliner Tageblatt, 20 April 1935: article on the call of the German Council of Municipalities to abolish municipal financial subsidies for Jewish schools[1]

Financial subsidies for Jewish schools. The Council of Municipalities desires new regulations[2]

Doubts have arisen within some of the German municipalities about the continuing validity of the older educational legal provisions requiring the providers of municipal educational support to make cost subsidies for Jewish schools and Jewish religion lessons. The view is being put forward that it is for the Jewish communities or school associations to raise the necessary funds. The argument against this is that *the existing legal provisions concerning the municipal duty to contribute have not yet been overturned*, but still formally apply. In Prussia, there was no legal requirement to provide the public funds previously allocated for Jewish religion lessons.

In a complaint lodged by the synagogue congregation against the city of Hanover, the city's district administrative court denied the admissibility of the administrative dispute proceedings, because the Jewish religious school for which a further grant of the community financial subsidy is requested cannot be regarded as one of the schools that serves universal compulsory school attendance in accordance with the legal provisions. But the complaint was also rejected because the legal provisions on which the claim is based stipulate that in the absence of an amicable agreement *the amount of the subsidy is to be set by the minister.*

As the court states, it was not considered that the minister only decides about the amount of the subsidies; rather, the entire decision is transferred over to him.

The Council of Municipalities, which conveys this decision, attaches to this the expectation that, regarding both the Jewish primary school system and the provision of Jewish religious instruction, a fundamental new arrangement should be found by law.

---

1 'Beihilfen für jüdische Schulen', *Berliner Tageblatt* (morning edition), 20 April 1935, p. 4. This document has been translated from German.
2 Correctly: German Council of Municipalities.

DOC. 163

On 2 May 1935 Victor Klemperer describes his dismissal as professor
of Romance languages at the Dresden Institute of Technology[1]

Handwritten diary of Victor Klemperer,[2] entry for 2 May 1935

2 May, Thursday

I eagerly awaited Monday because I was going to find out whether students from the PI,[3] which had started on 24 April, were coming to me. No one came. There was no need to be excessively gloomy about it, since Janentzky[4] has apparently seen no sign of the 200 new PI students either. They have evidently been told: 'The institute is going to be detached from the university, so don't waste your time with the lectures there.'

So I gave my lecture to the student from Leipzig and to Susi Hildebrandt,[5] the one with the hare and the lecture on Petrarch.[6] Lore Isakowitz[7] also turned up and asked me for books – she now wants to obtain a diploma at the Department of Oriental Languages in Berlin – which I promised her for Tuesday. On Tuesday morning, without any previous notification, two sheets came by post: (a) on the basis of § 6 of the Law for the Restoration of the Professional Civil Service ... I have recommended your dismissal.[8] Notice of dismissal enclosed. The acting director of the Ministry of Education; (b) 'In the name of the Reich', the notice itself, signed in a child's hand: Martin Mutschmann.[9]

1 Victor Klemperer, 'Tagebuchaufzeichnungen', Nr. 136-1-3/036/00189-037/00190; SLUB, Abt. Sammlungen, Ref. Handschriften/Seltene Drucke, Mscr.Dresd.App.2003, Nachlass Klemperer, Victor (1881–1960). English translation in Victor Klemperer, *I Shall Bear Witness: The Diaries of Victor Klemperer, 1933–1941*, trans. Martin Chalmers (London: Weidenfeld & Nicolson, 1998 [German edn, 1995]), pp. 146–147. This document has been retranslated from the original German.
2 Dr Victor Klemperer (1881–1960), scholar in Romance languages; journalist and writer in Berlin, 1905–1912; professor of Romance languages at the Dresden Institute of Technology, 1920–1935; assigned to a 'Jew house' (*Judenhaus*), 1940; forced labourer from 1943; joined the Communist Party of Germany (KPD) in 1945; professor in Greifswald, Halle, and Berlin, 1947–1960; author of works including *Die französische Literatur von Napoleon bis zur Gegenwart* (4 vols., 1925–1931) and *The Language of the Third Reich: LTI, Lingua Tertii Imperii: A Philologist's Notebook* (1947).
3 Pedagogical Institute of the Dresden Institute of Technology.
4 Dr Christian Janentzky (1886–1968), scholar in German studies; professor at the Dresden Institute of Technology, 1922–1952.
5 Susi Hildebrandt, daughter of a non-Jewish industrialist from Niedersedlitz. She studied with Victor Klemperer and stayed in touch with him even after his dismissal.
6 Klemperer probably means the Dante lecture he had given in the previous term, for which this female student thanked him with a hare that had been shot by her father: see diary entry for 21 Feb. 1935 in Klemperer, *I Shall Bear Witness*, p. 138.
7 Lore Petzal, née Isakowitz (b. 1915), daughter of a dentist, came from Dresden. Her family became friends with Klemperer. She emigrated with her parents to Britain in 1936 and for several years worked for the sociologist Karl Mannheim (1893–1947), who had emigrated to Britain in 1933.
8 In accordance with § 6, civil servants could be forced to retire 'to simplify the administration': see the Law for the Restoration of the Professional Civil Service, Doc. 29, 7 April 1933.
9 Mutschmann was an NSDAP Gauleiter and Reichsstatthalter of Saxony.

I rang the university; no one there had a clue. Göpfert,[10] the commissioner, does not bother to ask the rector's office for advice. At first I felt alternately numb and slightly romantic; now there is only bitterness and wretchedness.

My situation will be very difficult. I shall still receive my salary until the end of July, the 800 M, which I agonize over, and after that a pension, which will amount to approximately 400 M. On Tuesday afternoon I went to Blumenfeld,[11] who has meanwhile finally received the offer of a professorship in Lima, and he gave me the addresses of the aid agencies. It was snowing on Wednesday, the 'Festival of National Labour'.[12] I wrote correspondence for hours. Three identical letters to the Emergency Association of German Scholars Abroad, Zurich, to the Academic Assistance Council, London, to the Emergency Committee in Aid of German Scholars, New York City.[13] In addition cries for help (I wrote 'SOS') to Dember[14] in Istanbul and to Vossler:[15] Spitzer[16] is leaving Istanbul for the USA (but his comments to Dember about me were not very flattering). I emphasized everywhere that I can give lectures on both German literature and comparative literature (my lectureship in Naples, the fact that I deputized for Walzel[17] at examinations, etc.), that I can give lectures in French and Italian immediately (!), in Spanish within a short time (!), that I 'read' English and if necessary could also speak it in a couple of months.

10 Arthur Göpfert (b. 1902), teacher; head of the local NSDAP branch and town councillor in Glauchau, 1923; Gau chairman of the National Socialist Association of Teachers in Saxony and head of the Gau office for education, 1930–1945; Ministerialrat, 1933; head of Saxony's Ministry for Education, 1935–1945.

11 Dr Walter Georg Blumenfeld (1882–1967), electrical engineer and psychologist; professor at the Pedagogical Institute of the Dresden Institute of Technology, 1924–1934; in 1936 he emigrated to Peru, where he was professor and director of the Institute for Educational Psychology at the University of San Marco in Lima.

12 The National Socialist government declared 1 May as the 'Day of National Work' (Tag der nationalen Arbeit) and made it a national holiday shortly after coming to power in 1933. Through propagandistic events and parades held on 1 May 1933 the National Socialist regime aimed to garner support from the working classes and eliminate the power of the trade unions. Indeed, on 2 May 1933, trade union offices were occupied by the SA and leading trade unionists were arrested.

13 All three organizations had been founded in 1933 to support academics who were being persecuted for their religion or political beliefs. As well as liaising between emigrants and academic institutions with interest in them, all the aid organizations endeavoured to provide additional funds to establish non-tenured posts for emigrants.

14 Dr Harry Dember (1882–1943), physicist; professor at the Dresden Institute of Technology; emigrated in 1933 to Turkey, where he was professor in Istanbul; he later emigrated to the USA. Dember was one of over thirty professors and assistants for whom the Emergency Association of German Scholars Abroad was able to find posts in Istanbul in 1933: Cem Dalaman, 'Die Türkei in ihrer Modernisierungsphase als Fluchtland für deutsche Exilanten', doctoral thesis, Berlin, 1998, pp. 100–105: http://www.diss.fu-berlin.de/diss/receive/FUDISS_thesis_000000000526 (2001).

15 Dr Karl Vossler (1872–1949), novelist; professor in Würzburg, 1909, and in Munich, 1911; vice chancellor at the University of Munich after 1945.

16 Dr Leo Spitzer (1887–1960), novelist; professor in Marburg, 1925–1930; vice chancellor of the Department of Romance Studies at the University of Cologne, 1930–1933; in 1933 he emigrated to Turkey, where he was professor in Istanbul; moved to the USA in 1936.

17 Dr Oskar Walzel (1864–1944), Germanist; professor of modern German literature at the University of Bern, 1897, at the Dresden Institute of Technology, 1907, and at the University of Bonn, 1921–1933; author of works including *Die deutsche Romantik* (1908).

But what good is all this activity? For one thing, the prospect of a post is very small, since the German surge has been under way for a good two years and is unpopular. For another and above all: what post could I take? According to Eva,[18] who has recently been suffering a great deal again – repeated dental treatment, root inflammation, general nervous strain – she would be a prisoner in any boarding house or furnished or city apartment, and it is true; she needs a house and garden. And she would on no account give up this house permanently. Therefore, I would only be able to accept an especially well-paid post. The likelihood of that is no greater than of winning the top prize in the lottery. […][19]

DOC. 164
On 8 May 1935 Naftali Unger briefs the Palestine Shipping Company on the difficulties in obtaining training positions for Jewish youth on ships[1]

Letter from Naftali Unger (N/G),[2] unsigned, currently in Givat Brenner,[3] post office in Rehovot, to the Palestine Shipping Comp. Ltd,[4] for the attention of First Officer Mr Rosenthal,[5] Haifa, dated 8 May 1935 (carbon copy)

Dear Mr Rosenthal,

Many thanks for your letter of 10 April 1935,[6] which I received only today because it was sent on to me from Germany.

I believe that we are not so very far apart in our endeavours. But I would like to set out for you briefly how I have reached my current standpoint, in order that these things are settled. I expect to be in Haifa in fourteen days and I hope that we will then have the opportunity of talking to each other at greater length.

---

18 Eva Klemperer, née Schlemmer (1882–1951), pianist; married Victor Klemperer in 1906. As she was not Jewish, his marriage to her afforded Klemperer a degree of protection from persecution.
19 The remainder of the diary entry for this day concerns the Klemperers' financial troubles.

1 IGdJ, Archiv 14-027. This document has been translated from German.
2 Naftali Unger (1908–1987) was a Zionist and travelled to and from Germany between 1933 and 1934 to help organize the hashcharah on behalf of the Union of Hebrew Labourers in Eretz Israel (Histadrut), a Jewish trade union organization established in 1920. Together with Lucy Borchardt he tried to promote the training of young Jewish people on ships.
3 A Zionist kibbutz in Palestine, founded in 1928 and named after the Zionist writer Joseph Chaim Brenner (1881–1921), who died in Haifa during an Arab uprising.
4 The Palestine Shipping Company Ltd was founded in 1934.
5 Hans Rosenthal, previously first officer of a large Bremen shipping company; he then became captain of the *Atid* ship of the Hamburg Fair Play shipping company, later the Atid-Navigation Company Ltd, Haifa. At the beginning of 1935 he moved to the Palestine Shipping Company Ltd and became an officer on the ship *Tel Aviv*.
6 In this letter, Rosenthal responded to Unger's criticism of Rosenthal's move from the *Atid* to the *Tel Aviv*. He emphasized that his aim was to establish Jewish shipping: Rosenthal's letter to Unger, 10 April 1935, IGdJ, Archiv 14-027.

As you know, it is only through the 'Fair Play'[7] that we have been able to place our young people in nautical professions.[8] The Fair Play shipping company gained no financial benefits from this training. On the contrary, it entailed expenditure for them and, much more importantly, they experienced extreme difficulties with the authorities as a result. I know this from my own experience, because three weeks ago I was still in contact with the employment office in Hamburg and the Fair Play made every effort to communicate with the employment office in Hamburg, with the trustee of the work, and with the Maritime Office so that we should have the possibility of placing our young people on your ships.

Long before the *Tel-Aviv* was to go to Palestine, I promptly made direct contact with the first procurator, Mr Gumprich, so that he might also give us the opportunity to bring people for training to the Bernstein Shipping Company. This promise was made to me, and I committed myself to send the Bernstein Shipping Company a CV, photograph, and medical certificate with every application, as well as copies of references with our own evaluation. I fulfilled this obligation and submitted four applications to the Bernstein Shipping Company. I received no response regarding these four applications. The company did not even consider it necessary to return to me the documents provided. I then made contact with the counsel, Dr Gottschalk,[9] who promised me that he would speak to Mr Arnold Bernstein[10] himself. He did so and he informed me that I could speak to Mr Arnold Bernstein, who was coming to Hamburg for a few days at the time. In the conversation I had with Mr Bernstein, he told me that he could not take responsibility for now placing young Jewish people on German ships. When I explained to him that it does not make a difference to our young people, and that we ourselves have placed people with shipping companies that have no kind of Palestine interests (e.g. Julius Schindler),[11] he referred me to Captain Jochimsen. I then made contact with Captain Jochimsen and stated that I was also willing to send the same documents for every individual application. And I did it this time with only one application, at which point I received a refusal in response. In the reply I was told that they are subordinate to the German Labour Front in their employment of people, and that they cannot employ anyone of whom they have not previously obtained a personal impression. In response to the first claim, I would like to say that the German Labour Front exercises no influence on the employment of people, especially since in this case it concerns additional work, i.e. the employment of other people was not prejudiced by it. In answer to the second

---

7 The Fairplay Schleppdampfschiffs-Reederei Richard Borchard GmbH (Fairplay Towage), Hamburg, founded in 1905, still exists today. The owner and managing director was Lucy Borchardt, later Borchard (1877–1967). In 1933 she also founded the shipping company Atid (Hebrew for 'future') for the sea route from Europe to Palestine. She emigrated to London in 1938.
8 See the reference made in the report of the Aid Committee of the United Jewish Organizations in Hamburg for 1933 and 1934, Doc. 150.
9 Gottschalk worked as a lawyer for the Palestine Shipping Company Ltd.
10 Arnold Bernstein (1888–1971), shipowner; founded a trading company in Hamburg in 1911; from 1919 a shipowner, first in the transatlantic freight business, then in the passenger business; he emigrated to the USA in 1933; in 1937 he was arrested during a stay in Germany for currency offences and imprisoned until 1939, when he returned to the USA.
11 The Julius Schindler Shipping Company was founded in 1922 as an independent sister company of the Julius Schindler Oil Works. Julius Schindler had emigrated to France via Switzerland in 1930. The business was run by Robert Schindler.

reason that was given, I would like to ask you what the company thinks about our having a boy sitting somewhere in Cologne or Munich who wants to become a mariner, calling him to Hamburg just for an interview, only to then potentially send him home again. I believe that the documents submitted must be sufficient (in fact, they sufficed for the other shipping companies as well).

With this kind of attitude, I believe the shipping company cannot make any special claim to be called Jewish, for a Jewish sea voyage can only be made by *sailors* and not Jewish stewards, musicians, and so on, and if these Jewish sailors are not yet there at the moment, while I fully understand that the safety of a ship must [not] be put at risk by a crew that is not first-rate, the company should have attempted to enlist this young nautical talent. It still has this opportunity if it employs people on the North Atlantic Line (Antwerp–New York). That is what I insisted on being done. I have placed no value at all on it putting especially large numbers of Jewish people on to the *Tel-Aviv* ship because I knew in advance that there people are given positions that will mainly only bring them into contact with passengers. The few people from Hehalutz who were employed were actually only placed in such positions. (The people from Hehalutz were not employed with our help, and we have not even been able to approve these posts as Hachsharah.)

All these endeavours have failed. Nevertheless, I have not yet declared myself satisfied and have turned once more to the Bernstein Shipping Company with the help of the Palestine Office in Berlin. The Palestine Office received the assurance that the Arnold Bernstein Company is willing to employ 'six young Germans of the Jewish faith' on the North Atlantic Line. A further application that I sent in has remained unanswered even after three weeks. I have since left Hamburg and cannot tell you how matters have developed since.[12]

As I have already told you above, I wanted to inform you of all this in writing beforehand so that we do not waste unnecessary time talking about things that have happened, and we will have the opportunity to gain an understanding of how we can undertake something in this matter in order to advance Jewish shipping. I hope that our conversation will succeed in bringing this about.

In the meantime I send expressions of the highest esteem and shalom

---

12 Unger's attempt to persuade the Bernstein Shipping Company to introduce a seafaring Hachsharah failed.

DOC. 165
Discussion between the German Army Ordnance Department and the Flick Corporation on 22 May 1935 concerning the Aryanization of the Simson Arms Factory in Suhl[1]

Memorandum by the Flick Corporation[2] management (St/Ga.), Steinbrinck,[3] [Berlin], 23 May 1935

Re: Simson/Suhl.

On 22 May we were visited by Oberstleutnant Dr Zeidelhack[4] of the HWA[5] with regard to the Simson/Suhl matter and he communicated the following:

He came by order of Lieutenant General Liese,[6] Colonel Leeb,[7] and probably also Lieutenant General von Reichenau,[8] and in consultation with the Prussian Ministry of the Interior, Mr Keppler,[9] and Reichsführer SS Himmler in order to ascertain from the Mittelstahl/Flick Group whether we were prepared to take over Simson/Suhl.[10] Things

---

1 IfZ-Archives, MA 1555-39, NI-5337. This document has been translated from German.
2 Industrial and manufacturing conglomerate founded by Friedrich Flick in Germany in the early 1920s and operating in the coal and steel industries. Its management enjoyed close ties to Himmler and Göring and Aryanized many Jewish firms. During the Second World War, the corporation made extensive use of slave labour, which resulted in the post-war prosecution of Friedrich Flick and five leading officials in the Nuremberg Trials. After serving three years of a seven-year prison sentence, Flick returned to the coal and steel industry and amassed another fortune.
3 Otto Steinbrinck (1888–1949), career officer; from 1925 an employee in Flick's private secretary's office; later board member of several companies; joined the NSDAP and the SS in 1933; chief executive of the Flick Corporation, 1937–1939; chief executive for the steel industry in Luxembourg, France, and Belgium, later also of the Reich Coal Association for Mining and the Coal Industry, 1940–1942; sentenced to five years' imprisonment at the Nuremberg Flick Trial, 1947.
4 Dr Johann Martin Zeidelhack (1891–1955); lived in Munich; Oberregierungsrat in the Reichswehr Ministry, 1929; chief executive of the Army Ordnance Department at Montan GmbH, 1934; returned to Munich in 1944; classified as a 'follower' during denazification proceedings in Munich in 1947.
5 Heereswaffenamt: Army Ordnance Department, the central office for the technical development and production of arms, ammunition, and equipment for the German Army.
6 Kurt Liese (1882–1945), career officer; chief of the Army Ordnance Department, 1933–1938; general of the infantry, 1937.
7 Baronet Wilhelm von Leeb (1876–1956), career officer; commander of Wehrkreis VII and regional commandant in Bavaria, 1930–1933; commander of Reichswehr Group II, 1933–1938; commander of Army Group C (West), 1939, and of Army Group North, 1941; field marshal, 1942; sentenced at the Nuremberg High Command Trial in 1948.
8 Walter von Reichenau (1884–1942), career officer; from 1929 in the Reich Ministry of the Army and chief of staff to the inspector of signals; from 1934 chief of the Wehrmacht Office in the Reich Ministry of War; field marshal, 1940; commander of the 6th Army and later of Army Group South, 1941.
9 Wilhelm Keppler (1882–1960), engineer; joined the NSDAP in 1927 and the SS in 1933; from 1931 Hitler's economic advisor; commissioner for economic matters in the Reich Chancellery, 1933; advisor to Göring (Plenipotentiary for the Four-Year Plan), 1936; state secretary for special deployment in the Reich Foreign Office and Reich plenipotentiary for Austria, 1938; SS-Obergruppenführer, 1942; sentenced at the Nuremberg Ministries Trial to ten years' imprisonment, 1949; released in 1951.

had developed in such a way in the last few days that Mr Arthur Simson[11] had given his written declaration of consent to the sale of the works. He was willing in principle to sell his firm with all the equipment. It was a precondition that the purchaser was acceptable and would continue his firm's 100-year tradition with regard to keeping the workforce, constant operation of the works, and so on. Zeidelhack added that the four named Reich offices, namely the Reich Ministry of the Army, the Prussian Ministry of the Interior, the Reichsführer SS, and the Führer's Plenipotentiary for Economic Matters, desired that our group should take over the Berlin-Suhl arms factory from the current owners, the Simson family. If we were willing to do this, Arthur Simson would be released to commence negotiations. – With regard to further discussions it was envisaged that of the four named Reich offices the Reich Ministry of the Army be authorized to determine the form and conduct of these negotiations. It is being considered that under Keppler's chairmanship a discussion will then be convened that will include Mr Flick, the lawyer Koch, the trustee Hoffmann, Arthur Simson, and representatives of the Reich Ministry of the Army. The intention is to advance the negotiations very quickly, as the matter must be settled by 23 June at the latest.

Dr Z. indicated that the wish expressed by the four Reich offices for our company is especially significant and demonstrates the strong confidence placed in the Flick group. Some new prospective buyers had also emerged in the last few days: Klöckner[12] and Hermann Röchling.[13] But they [the Reich offices] preferred to conduct the negotiations with us.

Mr Flick[14] officially declared that he and the Mitteldeutsche Stahlwerke or the Maxhütte are prepared in principle to conform to the wishes of the Reich offices that they take over the factory, although there were still a series of preliminary questions to be resolved:

(1) the question of the price,
(2) the question of the company's future activity, and
(3) the question of raw materials.

---

10 The Flick Corporation had been interested in the Simson Works since autumn 1934. Following Arthur Simson's arrest, the corporation was told by the Army Ordnance Department and the Reich Chancellery that the negotiated sale price of 9 million Reichsmarks could be further reduced under the current circumstances. Memo of the Flick Corporation, dated 9 May 1935: ibid., NI-5335. Published in abridged form in Eschwege (ed.), *Kennzeichen J*, pp. 51–53.
11 Arthur Simson (1882–1969), entrepreneur; shareholder and technical director of the Suhl arms factory of Simson & Co.; resigned from the board at the end of 1934, under pressure; arrested for alleged treason; emigrated to Switzerland in 1936 and later to the USA.
12 Peter Klöckner (1863–1940), businessman; founded the ironmongery firm Klöckner and Co. in Duisburg in 1906, which was later expanded to form the Klöckner Works AG.
13 Hermann Röchling (1872–1955), entrepreneur; from 1898 managing partner of the firm Gebrüder Röchling (bank and wholesaling in iron and coal) and technical director of the Röchling iron- and steelworks in Völklingen an der Saar.
14 Friedrich Flick (1883–1972), entrepreneur and head of the Flick Corporation; from 1913 commercial director of the ironworks company Eisenindustrie zu Menden und Schwerte AG; board member and majority shareholder of Charlottenhütte AG, 1915; founder of the Mitteldeutsche Stahlwerke (Central German Steel Works), 1926; later owner of one of the most important mining companies in the German Reich; joined the NSDAP in 1937; sentenced to seven years in prison and expropriation at the Nuremberg Flick Trial in 1947; early release in 1950; subsequently rebuilt the Flick Corporation.

Concerning the *price question*, according to a communication from Dr Z., Mr Arthur Simson is said to have stated that Mr Flick himself had offered RM 10 million for Suhl. Dr Z. was informed that the purchase price of RM 8–9 million had been quoted by the HWA. In the earlier negotiations conducted by Dr Bruhn, a generally worded proposal that half would be given as a down payment and the remainder could stand as a loan over several years had been accepted in principle by Simson. Following the discussion with Colonel Büchs in October 1934, we had then considered the idea of making a down payment of RM 3 million, with RM 6 million remaining to be distributed over six to ten years. There had also been a brief conversation along these lines with Koch or Dr Bruhn, but we had not made a specific offer.

With reference to *future activity*, Dr Z. stated that Keppler also took the view that there was a possibility of setting the condition that Suhl be commissioned for approximately 60 per cent of the total requirement of light machine guns, in order to ensure the activity of the works. The company's monetary position was currently favourable. In the previous year, a sum of RM 1,580,000 had been earned and for the most part distributed. The investment programme, which was to be decided shortly, anticipated expenditure of RM 1.3 million, to be completed by 1 October 1936.

It was said that the question of the *raw materials* base (assembling an electrical steelworks and corrugated roller works in Unterwellenborn) could also be raised by us.

Greater difficulties are undoubtedly still being caused by the personnel question, in particular the debate with the government of Thuringia, as well as with the trustee Hoffmann.

The current management consists of an engineer, Heinen, who entered the company management at the behest of the HWA, and the businessman Berkutz, who has a detailed knowledge of the situation.

The discussion ended with Mr Flick instructing Dr Zeidelhack to officially declare Mr Flick's willingness to begin negotiations with Mr Keppler and the other offices in question. For further consideration of the matter a discussion was envisaged with General Liese for Monday 27 May.[15]

---

15 At the suggestion of Thuringia's Gauleiter Sauckel, however, with Hitler's approval the company was converted into the Reich-owned Wilhelm Gustloff Foundation by May 1936: see Doc. 134, 31 August 1934.

DOC. 166
Werdauer Zeitung, 23 May 1935: report concerning an antisemitic speech at a meeting of the Women's Office of the German Labour Front[1]

Educational meeting of the DAF (Women's Office) on the Jewish question[2]

At a meeting of the Women's Office of the Zwickau DAF held in the clubhouse yesterday, the member of the local Party branch *Pleißner*[3] made some lengthy remarks setting out the line on the Jewish question, which deserve to be brought to the general public's attention.

Starting with international Jewry's latest dispersal tactics, which in both the Cairo[4] and the Bern[5] trials sought to introduce a kind of disruptive fire into the people's political awakening, he described Jewry's corrosive influence on the existence of their host peoples. In ancient times, as in the most recent period, the chosen people has known how to subjugate its host politically and economically and, while itself always remaining in the background, to conduct a systematic war of attrition on its race by every means and in all domains. Almost 80,000 Jews were smuggled into Germany via the Breslau passport-counterfeiting centre of one Dr Rathenau.[6] 'And he summoned his people into the land …' Antisemitism is not a religious struggle, as the Talmud is not comparable with other religious constitutions; its precepts are in fact purely ethnic race laws.

If one wanted to follow them in controlling the world's peoples, then one had to take their particular world view – and thus their strength – from them and internationalize them. In this way, the intellectual was ensnared by the international Freemasonry lodges and the German worker by Marxism, and mentally and racially uprooted, and in this way the German people was robbed of its leadership concept during the course of the 100 years of the liberalist age. Behind the political murders of Sarajevo[7] and Yekaterinburg,[8] behind the degeneration of German art, behind the contamination of morality and conventions, behind the desecration of everything sacred, there was constantly one force – international world Jewry. Via the theatre, the cinema, the press that fell into their hands, the soul of the German people was systematically and incessantly poisoned.

---

1 Newspaper cutting from the *Werdauer Zeitung*, 23 May 1935; Sächsisches Staatsarchiv, Hauptstaatsarchiv Dresden, Nachrichtenstelle der Sächsischen Staatskanzlei/583, fol. 53. This document has been translated from German.
2 Deutsche Arbeitsfront: German Labour Front. The original contains some handwritten underlining and a stamp: 'Property of the Intelligence Bureau of the State Chancellery. Circulated on 25 May 1935.'
3 Paul Pleißner, bookkeeper; in 1934 he was the leader of the NSDAP local branch group in Zwickau-Eckersbach, and plenipotentiary for settlement in Zwickau in 1940–1941.
4 In 1933 Jews in Cairo filed a civil case for compensation against the German Club on the grounds of moral damage caused to Jewry after the club had distributed a propaganda sheet on the Jewish boycott from the German Foreign Office to Egyptian businesspeople. The case was dismissed in 1934.
5 In Bern a court had classified *The Protocols of the Elders of Zion* as a forgery and plagiarism on 14 May 1935 and ordered the publishers to pay a fine.
6 No reference to this could be found.
7 The assassination of the heir to the Austro-Hungarian throne, Archduke Franz Ferdinand, and his wife in Sarajevo on 28 June 1914 sparked the First World War.
8 Tsar Nicholas II and his family were murdered in Yekaterinburg (Russia) in mid July 1918.

The Jews forced their way into the ranks of the German nobility with their daughters' gold, destroying the purity of the blood and producing bastards.

The battle of race against race – that is what the Jewish law teaches: if you want to control your people, then go and corrupt its women. This began with the Marxist teachers, the youth organizations, the glorification of birth outside marriage, and the 'human right to abortion'. The goal was the disintegration of the German family as the strongest bulwark against racial extinction. The German woman in particular as guardian of most of our national wealth was enticed into the department store, where she bought cheap and shoddy frippery without realizing that these prices were paid for with the ruin of productive German people, as she herself was, to whom Jewish capitalism had left no other choice than bankruptcy. But the Jew also had to poison the woman physically by driving her into his arms through destitution or destroyed concepts of education. Antisemitism is not, as it is echoed beyond the frontiers by Semites and Semigrants, the scandal of the twentieth century – it is the end of an unceasing chain of desecration of German women's honour!

In our nation, whose buried soul has now been revealed again through the struggle of National Socialism, the person of a different race possesses only visiting rights, and that is only as long as he behaves respectably. The cleansing of the German nation is also in the racial domain a struggle for each individual soul. Never again may those who have betrayed Germany's work and the German worker gain influence over the shaping of German destiny and the work of building Germany. They have taken away leadership and purpose from our people; National Socialism has given them both back.

Every farmer is familiar with the racial characteristics of his domestic pets, every dog trainer destroys the bitch once it is racially corrupted, every intellectual is proud of the pedigree of his luxury dog – it is only allowing the human being as the highest of creatures the obligation to preserve the purity of his race that many refuse to acknowledge. The Third Reich will only be attained when every German person also thinks in National Socialist terms in racial matters, behaves accordingly, and commits himself to the great German community of fate!

At the end of the presentation, which was received with applause, local administrator and Party comrade Ilse[9] thanked the speaker and announced that the struggle would in future be taken into workplaces. In commemoration of the great speech by the Chancellor,[10] he brought the meeting to a close with a 'Sieg Heil' to our people's Führer.

---

9 Rudolf Ilse (1906–1940); joined the SA in 1925 and the NSDAP in 1926; from 1934 leader of the DAF local administration and the National Socialist Factory Cell Organization local branch in Werdau; city councilman in Werdau, 1935–1940.
10 This probably refers to the speech given by Hitler to the Reichstag on 21 May 1935 regarding the reintroduction of conscription in Germany: *Völkischer Beobachter* (northern German edition), 22 May 1935, pp. 1–4. See also Doc. 167, 24 May 1935.

DOC. 167

On 24 May 1935 Paula Tobias protests to the Reich Ministry of the Army about the discrimination against her sons caused by the new Military Law[1]

Letter, signed Paula Tobias, Bevern, Kreis Holzminden, Weser, to the Reich Ministry of the Army in Berlin, dated 24 May 1935 (copy)

To the Ministry of the Army, Berlin,

I ask you to read the enclosed papers[2] and to let me know why our children are being equated in the Military Law with those who were punished by the courts with severe shaming punishments.[3] We have done and sacrificed everything, completely as a matter of course for our German fatherland, and never with any thought of a reward. But that in return for this our children are being made to resemble the most common criminals – this we have not deserved. For us 'German loyalty' has never been an empty phrase. We have upheld it and still uphold it, even when it is being broken for us today and we are laughed at for nonetheless continuing to uphold it. For us, as for Hindenburg, loyalty is the mark of honour and, as for him, so it will remain until the last moment. For Hindenburg there was no other viewpoint than the testing demonstrated by deeds in war. When today his legacy, the combat veteran's cross on the black-white-red ribbon, reaches us at the same moment that we are forbidden to fly the black-red-white flag that we have always flown justifiably in the eyes of the whole local population, that is also embarrassing for Aryan Germans, especially for old soldiers.[4] To be sure, the fact that, contrary to the hopes we continue to cherish, the Wehrmacht is also now ostracizing us can no more take our honour than any of the previous measures have done.[5] We know today that despite all difficulties it is easier to suffer injustice than to cause injustice, and realizing this enables us to maintain our stance. But would it not be better for *all* and first and foremost for Germany, which is alone what ultimately matters, if this injustice did not take place?

---

1 Document in Paula Tobias, 'Mein Leben in Deutschland vor und nach dem 30. Januar 1933' [My life in Germany before and after 30 January 1933] (March 1940), p. 75; Harvard Competition, no. 235. This document has been translated from German.
2 These papers are not enclosed with the original.
3 § 15 of the Military Service Law of 21 May 1935 stipulated 'Aryan descent' as a prerequisite for active military service and for a career as an officer, and prohibited members of the Wehrmacht from marrying persons 'of non-Aryan descent': *Reichsgesetzblatt*, 1935, I, pp. 609–614, here p. 611.
4 With a circular decree (II 1 B 2–61250/J 195/35) dated 12 Feb. 1935, the Gestapo Central Office (Gestapa) had forbidden Jews to display the swastika and the black-white-red flags: BArch, R 58/276, fol. 12.
5 As early as 25 March 1935, shortly after the government had enacted the Law for the Establishment of the Wehrmacht, Leo Baeck wrote a letter to Reich Minister of the Army von Blomberg on behalf of the Reich Representation of German Jews to demand equal participation in military service. It was issued by the CV as a circular letter. See *Pariser Tageblatt*, 13 April 1935, p. 2.

DOC. 168
On 26 May 1935 the lawyer Leopold Weinmann urges the Reich Ministry of the Interior to take action against the instigators of anti-Jewish violence in Munich[1]

Letter from Dr Weinmann,[2] Munich, 31 Neuhauserstraße, to the Reich Ministry of the Interior (received on the morning of 28 May 1935), dated 26 May 1935[3]

Allow me in the public interest to draw the attention of the Reich Ministry of the Interior to the intolerable conditions that currently prevail in Munich. It should be common knowledge that for some time now during the night the shop windows of Jewish businesses in Munich have been repeatedly besmirched and smashed by irresponsible elements.

On 18 May 1935, a Saturday afternoon, during the riots that broke out because of the Caritas[4] collection, Jewish shop-owners were for the first time also subjected to abuse and forced to close their shops.[5]

On 25 May 1935, again a Saturday afternoon – obviously the best business period of the week is being systematically targeted by these elements – the criminal activities reached their peak. A number of Jewish shops on Neuhauserstrasse, such as the Kloster pharmacy – owned by Eugen Fröhlich[6] – the Orliansky fur shop, Salberg, the Koch music shop, the Jakob company, and others were again forced to close, as were some on other streets. Employees of individual firms such as Salberg were, I was told, called 'Jew people' by thugs who pushed their way in, and were severely mistreated because they did not comply with the demand to close the shop. Completely uninvolved passers-by who expressed their horror at this activity were likewise mistreated in the roughest manner. I am aware that one old gentleman, who was rightly appalled by the acts of violence, was struck down and so seriously injured that he could not get up again.

I live in the premises that belong to the aforementioned Mr Fröhlich at 31 Neuhauserstrasse. At 3 o'clock in the afternoon I was about to enter the building, accompanied by my wife, when the incidents described occurred. When I, like many other bystanders, expressed my horror at this activity, I was abused and threatened by a gang of lads who were evidently the instigators of the attacks on Mr Fröhlich's shop and those adjacent. After I had entered the house and locked the front door, four or five of these thugs tried to break down the doors and force their way into the house. I immediately notified the riot squad by telephone from my apartment; they arrived very quickly and soon restored peace and order. Whether any arrests were made I do not know.[7] During the aforementioned onslaught on the front door, the inset pane of glass was smashed.

---

1 BArch, R 1501/127079-35, fols. 95-98. This document has been translated from German.
2 Dr Leopold Weinmann (1884-1936), lawyer; practised law in Munich; he took his own life in 1936.
3 The original contains handwritten underlining and revisions.
4 Roman Catholic charitable organization, founded in 1897 in Germany and with branches all over the world.
5 On the events that occurred during the Caritas collection, see the letter from the Reichsstatthalter in Bavaria, Franz von Epp, to the Reich and Prussian Ministry of the Interior, dated 27 May 1935, BArch, R 1501/127079-35, fols. 107-112.
6 Eugen Fröhlich (1874-1942), businessman; emigrated to London in 1939.
7 On the riots, see the report of the Munich police headquarters from 26 May 1935, BayHStA, StK 106 411, published in Kulka and Jäckel (eds.), *The Jews in the Secret Nazi Reports*, enclosed CD, no. 862.

These conditions are intolerable. It cannot possibly be tolerated that in a cultural and cosmopolitan city such as Munich, Wild West scenes should occur on a systematic and regular basis. This is severely damaging not only to the internal standing of the state's authority but also to the cultural standing of the Reich abroad, in the rest of the civilised world. This unlawful activity also brings economic disadvantages to the business world *in general*. For understandably the public's desire to buy completely disappears as a result of such tumultuous scenes. Aryan shop-owners have also noted this fact and expressed their outrage. Even the outcome of the street collection arranged last Saturday may have been very unfavourably influenced by the events described. Right at the beginning of the Munich tourist season this economic damage is all the more substantial when criminals cause trouble, with breaches of the peace, domestic break-ins, physical injuries, and assaults in broad daylight in the streets of Munich.

It is therefore requested in the general interest that the authorities prevent any repetition of these events by means of vigorous intervention, and severely punish the culprits, insofar as they can be identified.[8]

DOC. 169
A mother's complaint about her 15-year-old son's participation in nocturnal activities of the Hitler Youth against Jews in Munich (around 26 May 1935)[1]

Note, undated and unsigned[2]

A clarification on the point: *combatting the Jews.*

A mother of a Hitler Youth boy who belongs to Bann[3] 37 on Hörwarthstraße reports the following:

During the night of 11 to 12 May I had to get up because of a minor ailment. It was 11:30 p.m. When I went into the kitchen, my 15-year-old boy was just getting dressed. When I asked what he was doing, he told me that they had a roll call at 12. I suspected this was a dream and wanted to send him back to bed. Yet he firmly refused and insisted on doing his duty. Shortly afterwards he left the apartment, where another 14-year-old was waiting for him outside on the steps. I heard my boy being asked whether he had

---

8 Gauleiter Wagner announced to the press on 26 May 1935 that criminal elements had formed terrorist groups in order to 'promote the antisemitic movement'. Those responsible for the riots of the past fortnight were to be taken to court: 'Gegen Terrorgruppen in München – Eine Bekanntmachung der Polizeidirektion München', *Münchner Neueste Nachrichten, Stadtnachrichten und General-Anzeiger*, 27 May 1933, p. 9. On 28 May 1935 the SS, which played a significant part in the riots, was instructed by the SS garrison command in Munich to maintain the 'tightest discipline': letter from the SS Main District South (Munich) to the State Minister Adolf Wagner, 29 May 1935, BayHStA, StK 5618.

1 BArch, R 1501/127079–35, fol. 106. This document has been translated from German.
2 The document is located in the same file as the preceding Doc. 168, dated 26 May 1935. It is one of four enclosures sent with the letter from the Chancery of the Archdiocese of Munich and Freising to the Reich Ministry of the Interior, dated 27 May 1935: ibid., fol. 99.
3 A Hitler Youth unit for an entire district, consisting of 2,400 to 3,600 members; equivalent to a military regiment.

any caustic paint on him. When the boy came home (5 o'clock in the morning) I immediately asked him why he needed caustic paint. After some hesitation he admitted to me that they had to stick things on the Jews' shop windows and smear them. From every troop, each of which has about 500 members, the 40 best were chosen for this action. At 3 o'clock in the morning additional pieces of paper were collected on Königsplatz, although the action was already nearly finished. A few lads were arrested by the police, but soon had to be released. Apparently, the police had not been notified of the action.

To my great surprise, my boy told me that they were under strict instructions not to tell their parents anything about the roll call and the action. My son, in his youthful ignorance, also told me with glee that this had been his finest roll call. As his mother I was outraged by these incidents because they completely undermine parental authority. In their earliest youth, children are being removed from any parental control and incited to behave illegally.

DOC. 170

On 28 May 1935 the Gestapo Central Office demands that the Reich Minister of Justice prevent marriages between Jews and non-Jews[1]

Letter from the Gestapo Central Office (Gestapa) Berlin (II 1 B 2 – J 562/35), p.p. Dr Best,[2] to the Reich Minister of Justice (received on 18 June 1935), dated 28 May 1935[3]

Re: Jewish mixed marriages.

Aryan Volksgenossen who have entered into marriage with a member of the Jewish race are lost to the German Volksgemeinschaft. In view of the fact that their offspring will not be of pure blood, they cannot according to National Socialist tenets be granted the same rights as Aryan Volksgenossen.

Following a ruling by the Reich Supreme Court, the annulment of marriages between Aryans and non-Aryans on grounds of racial incompatibility is now practically impossible, since the disclosure of the National Socialist programme has virtually ruled out the likelihood of an error regarding racial affiliation as a personal characteristic.[4]

1 BArch, R 3001/459, fols. 109–110. This document has been translated from German.
2 Dr Werner Best (1903–1989), lawyer; probationary judge at local courts in Hesse from 1929; joined the NSDAP in 1930 and the SS in 1931; appointed state commissioner for the police in Hesse in 1933; deputy head of the Gestapo in 1935; head of Office I in the Reich Security Main Office, 1939–1940; head of the administrative staff for the military commander in France, 1940–1942; Reich plenipotentiary in Denmark, 1942–1945; sentenced to death in Copenhagen in 1948 but released under an amnesty in 1951; later worked as a lawyer and legal advisor to the Free Democratic Party (FDP) in North Rhine-Westphalia.
3 The original document contains several handwritten comments concerning the letter's resubmission, including 'legal provisions currently under consideration' and 'after 2 weeks, 6.7.'.
4 While the Reich Supreme Court had dismissed an annulment suit filed by a non-Jewish spouse who had married in 1930, it had also declared that annulment would be permissible in exceptional cases where the 'spouse of German blood' had not been aware that his or her marital partner was of Jewish descent at the time of marriage: *Entscheidungen des Reichsgerichts in Zivilsachen*, vol. 145, p. 1. See also Doc. 109, 23 March 1934, fn. 5.

In any case, in the interest of preserving the purity of the race, it seems imperative to prevent marriages between Aryans and non-Aryans. Despite the extensive educational work undertaken in this field, large sections of the German population apparently have not yet realized the full perniciousness of the Jewish race. Due to this ignorance, many mixed marriages are still contracted today. Until the matter is regulated by law, however, the relevant authorities are not able to intervene.

In many cases the State Police have succeeded in preventing such marriages at the last moment by summoning the Aryan partner and informing them in detail of the disadvantages the marriage would entail, including for any offspring. In the majority of such cases, the marriage had evidently been planned in complete ignorance of the consequences.

However, the activity of the State Police in this respect can only have limited effectiveness as long as they are not informed of all such cases reported to the registry offices.

For this reason, I have proposed to the Reich Minister of the Interior to instruct the registrar to report all cases of intended marriage between Aryans and non-Aryans to the local State Police offices so that the latter can take action to prevent the contracting of mixed marriages by issuing a summons and providing relevant information.[5]

May I express my sincere hope that legal provisions will soon be made to eliminate the current difficulties concerning this question of extreme importance for maintaining the purity of the race.[6]

DOC. 171
In a letter of 29 May 1935 Professor Johann Plesch responds to the Kaiser Wilhelm Society's demand for additional contributions[1]

Letter from Professor Johann Plesch,[2] unsigned, London, to the secretary of the Kaiser Wilhelm Society for the Advancement of Science, Berlin C2, dated 29 May 1935 (copy)

Dear Mr Secretary

When I felt compelled to leave Germany in May 1933, I cancelled all my engagements and memberships in the country. All my belongings were confiscated by the authorities, so my books and correspondence are no longer at my disposal, nor is my membership badge.[3]

---

5 Such marriages were banned by a decree dated 27 July 1935 issued by the Reich Ministry of the Interior to the registry offices: see Doc. 181, 27 July 1935.
6 The legal provisions finally came in the form of the Law for the Protection of German Blood and German Honour of 15 Sept. 1935. See Doc. 199.

1 Jüdisches Museum Berlin, DOK-86-25-328. This document has been translated from German.
2 Dr Johann Plesch (1878–1957), physician; a member of the Kaiser Wilhelm Society for the Advancement of Science from 1926; emigrated to London in May 1933. Having overcome considerable difficulties, he was finally able to return to his profession after gaining an additional qualification from Britain. He later emigrated to the USA. See ibid. and Archiv der Max-Planck-Gesellschaft, Abt. I, Rep. 1 A B Mitglieder, Johann Plesch (3002-18).
3 On 4 April 1935 the Kaiser Wilhelm Society had instructed Plesch to return his membership badge and pay retrospective membership fees for a further two years: see Jüdisches Museum Berlin, DOK-86-25-326.

Since the whole affair is as yet unresolved, I kindly ask you to postpone regulating the [contributions] issue until the authorities have come to a conclusion. I am not in a position to name a date for this as I cannot and am not permitted to exert any influence on the course of things, but please be assured that I will take the first opportunity to settle the matter, which has always been close to my heart, as best and expediently as I can.

With all my best wishes for the survival and success of the Society, I remain with the highest esteem

DOC. 172
Der Stürmer, May 1935: the mayor of Meißen is insulted as a 'slave to Jews' in a purported letter to the editor[1]

What happened at Meißen town hall

Dear Stürmer,[2]

I have known you for a very, very long time. I was occupied with you back when you still had to be 'duplicated' and I realized then that you certainly used cast-iron words – hard but true. Yes, when people laughed at us and dismissed us as fools, you were a constant friend and companion to me. More than a dozen years have passed now. You have not tired of drawing strength from the uphill struggle, and still today you speak out again and again with the same voice. The victory is yours, too!

I must point out how important your words will also remain in future: in our local town hall (public relief office, general welfare, room 22) a notice was stuck on the inside of the door for some weeks where everybody who came into the room could see it and couldn't avoid reading the familiar motto: '*Anyone who buys from Jews is a traitor to the people!*' We, your old friends, are happy to see things like that. After all, it's true. But just imagine, it didn't suit some Jew slave and people's traitor who felt slighted by it. He had nothing better to do than to report what he had seen to the Jews.

One day a letter arrived from the '*Central Association of German Citizens of the Jewish Faith* (i.e. Jewish race, eds.[3]) *in Leipzig*', a copy of which I have enclosed. It reads:

> S/B 656/35.
> To the Mayor[4] of the City of Meißen.
> Re: boycott.
> It has come to our knowledge that a notice is attached to the door of the welfare office in room no. 22 of the town hall, showing a caricature of a Jew surrounded by the words 'He who buys from Jews is a traitor to the people.' A sign of this kind, especially

---

1 'Was sich im Meißener Rathaus zutrug', *Der Stürmer*, no. 21, May 1935, p. 5. This document has been translated from German.
2 *Der Stürmer* often published its own articles as purported letters to the editor.
3 The editors of *Der Stürmer*.
4 The mayor of Meißen from 1927 to 1935 was Dr Walther Busch (1877–1954), lawyer; mayor of Sommerfeld (Lower Lusatia), 1916–1927; joined the NSDAP in 1933; retired on 30 May 1935 – probably in response to these allegations.

on official premises, most certainly contravenes the Reich government's regulations, according to which there is no Aryan Paragraph in the economy, and pursuant to which all boycotts are forbidden. We most respectfully ask the Mayor of the City of Meißen to order the removal of this illegal sign.
  Central Association of German Citizens of the Jewish Faith
  Regional Group for Central Germany. Signature.

The note on the door of the public relief office/general welfare in Meißen then disappeared. But we say to the Jew slave and his cronies: the final chapter has not been written yet. He who laughs last laughs longest.
  G. R.
  We cannot believe that the mayor of the city of Meißen ordered the sign to be removed on account of a letter from the Leipzig Jews. We know of no German mayor who would take orders from Jews or need Jews to remind him of the Reich laws or explain Reich government regulations to him.

DOC. 173

Antisemitic polemic by Adolf Stein on Jews in Berlin, dated 4 July 1935[1]

[Rumpelstilzchen][2]
Looking around – Small town conversations – Are we city slickers? – At the Berliner Theatre – Our new Jewish minority right – The former Palais Simon – A rash of verses.

[...][3]
  So I happen to pass the former Ferdinand Bonn's Berliner Theatre on Charlottenstraße. What's all this, why are there people flocking there? I thought it had closed down. At least no performances are announced in the press. I let myself drift with the crowd into the lobby. Am I in Galicia or Armenia? True, there are brassy blondes here, while the men are almost all dark, but the brass is fake. Lo and behold, the place is full of – Jews! I gradually work out the deal. The theatre is, I learn from notices, leased by the Jewish Culture League, which stages private performances for members only.[4] The only Aryan to gain admittance is a monitoring officer of the Gestapo. He has to make sure that no hate propaganda against the Reich or suchlike is disseminated. Banned pieces can be staged, though. It's all the same to us what kind of 'culture' youngsters not of our

---

1 Rumpelstilzchen, *Nee aber sowas! Rumpelstilzchen*, vol. 15 (1934/1935) (Berlin: Brunnen, 1935), pp. 259–266. This document has been translated from German.
2 Translates as Rumpelstiltskin: pseudonym of Adolf Stein (1870–1948?), officer and journalist; on the editorial board of the German News Service in the Hugenberg media group from 1920. From the 1920s, Stein published Berlin polemics under the pseudonym Rumpelstilzchen in the daily newspaper *Tägliche Rundschau* and in annual anthologies published by the Brunnen publishing house, Berlin.
3 The excerpt reproduced here is preceded by observations on small-town life and on Berlin being an amalgamation of small towns.
4 On the Jewish Culture League, see Doc. 71, mid August 1933, Doc. 116, April 1934, and Glossary.

stock are exposed to. Fritz Kortner[5] and Elisabeth Bergner can act in peace here.[6] The Culture League also organizes concerts and lectures by classy people for classy people. In complete freedom! The minority right created by the new regime in this way is exemplary. We don't want to be enslaved or infected by the alien culture but we don't intend to Germanize these people either. We don't force them to attend German schools like other people force diaspora Germans to attend their schools. We don't prescribe them German names either; oh, quite the opposite. May they educate and amuse themselves however they like!

An Englishman currently living in Berlin drivels on about what he has read in the *Manchester Guardian* about the persecution of Jews in Berlin.[7] Oh, please!

Companies such as Julius Berger[8] are doing splendidly from their participation in the construction of new military and government buildings. The Reich Railways still awards Hirsch Kupfer[9] and other companies in the metal industry major contracts. Mr Stefan Zweig wrote the libretto to Richard Strauss's latest opera *Die schweigsame Frau*. Nobody has considered dismissing Professor Herxheimer[10] or other medical staff of his ilk.

The poet and theatre director von Dingelstedt,[11] a liberal type born in 1814, cried the following verses to the German people, long before anybody had even heard of antisemitism: 'Wherever you turn you will find Jews / Everywhere God's chosen people; / Come, lock them again in the Jewish alleys, / Before they lock you in the Christian quarters!'

But even the Third Reich, patient as the Germans tend to be, is not reinstalling ghettos that are closed off in the evenings but leaves the Jews their freedom of movement, commercial activity, and culture as they see fit, and protects their property and honour

---

5 Fritz Kortner (1892–1970), actor; performed in various theatres in Mannheim, Berlin, Vienna, and Hamburg from 1910; based in Berlin from 1919; emigrated to Vienna in 1933, to Britain in 1934, and to the USA in 1937; returned to Germany in 1947.
6 The Gestapo Central Office (Gestapa) issued a circular order (II 1 B 2–60038/J 257/35) stating that the government did not welcome Jewish artists performing to non-Jewish audiences. Performances were to be banned without hesitation if there was any hint of provocation: BArch, R 58/276, fol. 15.
7 Around the time this was written, the British daily newspaper the *Manchester Guardian* ran several reports from its correspondents in Germany on the persecution of Jews, including 'Berlin – Boycott of Jews Called Off' and 'Persecution in Germany': *Manchester Guardian*, 27 and 29 June 1935. The newspaper was temporarily banned a number of times in Nazi Germany in response to negative reporting, for example from 1 April to 10 August 1933, and with lasting effect from 23 Sept. 1936.
8 Julius Berger (1862–1944), entrepreneur; owner of a construction company founded in Bromberg in 1890; based in Berlin from 1910; involved in the construction of the Berlin underground railway and the Baghdad railway; his company, Julius Berger Tiefbau AG, was Aryanized after 1933; in 1944 Berger was deported to Theresienstadt, where he died.
9 The reference is to the copper and brass manufacturer Hirsch Kupfer- und Messingwerke AG Eberswalde. The company was Aryanized in 1937. Siegmund Hirsch (1885–1981), co-founder of one of Germany's first Hachsharah training camps in Eberswalde, was its managing director, 1918–1931; he emigrated to Palestine in 1933 and to the USA in 1952.
10 Dr Karl Herxheimer (1861–1942), physician; worked as a physician from 1887 and as director of the municipal dermatology clinic in Frankfurt am Main from 1894; held a professorship at the university clinic for skin and venereal diseases in Frankfurt, 1914–1929; appointed its director in 1930; his licence was revoked in 1936; deported in September 1942 to Theresienstadt, where he died that December.
11 Franz von Dingelstedt (1814–1881), writer; director of theatres in Weimar, Munich, and Vienna.

like that of every foreigner within our borders. Indeed, there are many among them who acknowledge the previous sins of their race, are grateful for being tolerated, and consider their hasty émigrés foolish. One can live just as well or even better in Berlin than in Paris or Prague or London or even Tel Aviv. But these folks are aware that their time at the top is over and that they would be brought back down to earth with a hefty jolt if they presumed to take the kind of role in public life that they were able to play in the Barmat–Sklarek–Kerr–Tucholsky[12] era.

There is one secret that I haven't been able to get to the bottom of. There is a gaping hole in the wall to the right of the booking office in the lobby of the Berliner Theatre. A slanting stone has been placed over it, inscribed only with a date: 15 May 1935.[13] I have no idea what significance the date has for the Jewish Culture League.

But I know one thing: that sooner or later all the people of the earth will acknowledge that the minority right that the National Socialists have granted the Jews is the best solution to the question for the time being.

Of course my English acquaintance is right when he says that here and there people have lost their fortunes. But that already happened long ago to hundreds of thousands of Germans. Ups and downs like that happen everywhere. Even the former Viennese billionaire Castiglioni, now a naturalized 'Italian', who after the November Revolution acquired items on the cheap such as Kaiser Wilhelm's special train, is 'only' a millionaire now. Similarly, a number of palaces have been vacated, such as that of the former newspaper baron Mosse,[14] who managed to get himself out of the country with his millions but left his properties as bankruptcy assets in Germany, including the Schenkendorf manor house. The luxurious conversion of this property alone cost 1 million marks. The famous fountain with the dancing Three Graces stood in the grand courtyard of his city palace on Voßstraße, a feast for the eyes of all passers-by, but which has now disappeared. The home of the speculator Simon,[15] appointed minister of finance in 1918, has also changed hands. After the uprising – led by the so-called People's Naval Division and Lord Chamberlain Count von Platen – the man [Simon] gained possession of the Kabinett wines in the royal wine cellar. Then there was merry carousing in his villa crammed with artworks and antiquities in the Tiergarten district. The coffered ceiling above the

---

12 In antisemitic circles, the names of the businessmen Barmat and Sklarek were synonymous with corruption and economic crime; those of the writers Kerr and Tucholsky stood for 'subversive' journalism in the Weimar Republic. Julius Barmat (1887–1938), who had been born in the Russian Empire, lived in the Netherlands from 1906, and settled in Berlin in 1919, was arrested in Dec. 1924 and charged with fraud. Several leading members of the Social Democratic Party of Germany (SPD) were implicated in the scandal. The fraud charges could not be proved, but Barmat was convicted of bribery in March 1928 and sentenced to eleven months in prison. His brother Henry Barmat (b. 1892) was sentenced to five months in prison.
13 This should probably read 15 May 1934, the day on which theatres in Germany were placed under the supervision of the Ministry of Propaganda: Theatre Law, 15 May 1934, *Reichsgesetzblatt*, 1934, I, pp. 411–413.
14 Hans Lachmann-Mosse (1885–1944), lawyer and publisher; from 1920 co-owner of the Rudolf Mosse publishing house; publisher of several Berlin daily newspapers as well as the Jewish-interest newspaper *Allgemeine Zeitung des Judentums* and, from 1922 to 1933, the *C.V.-Zeitung*; board member of the Jewish Reform Community Berlin; after bankruptcy and the Aryanization of publishing rights in 1933, he emigrated to France and, in 1940, to the USA.
15 The reference is to Hugo Simon. On the expropriation of his country estate, see Doc. 118, 26 May 1934.

stairs is decorated with ancient Roman-style images and mottos, including the famous 'carpe diem' (seize the day) extended to 'carpe diem et noctem' (and the night). Today this palazzo, minus its art treasures, is owned by the Karl Schurz Association,[16] which uses it as a venue for its meetings, to receive American friends and also to host occasional discussions between Germans and Americans, such as recently on the gripping subject: freedom of the press.

What is old collapses, times change, and new life blossoms in the ruins, as we used to like to say. [...][17]

DOC. 174
Meeraner Zeitung, 12 July 1935: article on cases of so-called race defilement[1]

Positive racial protection now![2]

NSK. Almost daily one finds newspaper reports informing the readers of the arrest of Jews who have committed sexual crimes. Most recently, the case of the Jew Hirschland,[3] who ran a private business school in Magdeburg where he outrageously violated German girls, caused a justified stir.[4] According to a report in the *Frankfurter Zeitung*, a Jewish physician, Dr Brück,[5] was arrested in Karlshafen an der Weser for raping and sexually abusing female patients who had consulted him in confidence, in some cases using hypnosis to suppress their free will.[6] According to another report in the *Frankfurter Zeitung*,

---

16 The Carl-Schurz-Vereinigung (here spelled: 'Karl-Schurz-Vereinigung') was founded in 1926 by members of the Reichstag in Berlin. It was named after Carl Schurz (1829–1906), an active participant in the 1848/1849 revolution in Baden, who subsequently went into exile in the USA, where he rose to become an influential politician.

17 These lines are followed by a section on the nightly practice of mounting advertisements on businesses and shopfronts.

1 Excerpt from the *Meeraner Zeitung*, 12 July 1935: 'Jetzt positiver Rasseschutz!' Sächsisches Staatsarchiv, Hauptstaatsarchiv Dresden, Nachrichtenstelle der Sächsischen Staatskanzlei/583, fol. 97. The *Meeraner Zeitung* appeared from 1897 as a daily newspaper in Meerane (Saxony). This document has been translated from German.

2 This article in the *Meeraner Zeitung* is an unabridged and verbatim reproduction from the National Socialist Party Correspondence news service: NSK, Folge 158, 10 July 1935, p. 6.

3 Albert Hirschland (1896–1943), business graduate; director of a private business school in Magdeburg, 1928–1935. In 1935 Hirschland was given a ten-year prison sentence in Brandenburg and later deported to Auschwitz, where he died in Feb. 1943.

4 A special issue of *Der Stürmer* entitled 'Albert Hirschland: Der Rasseschänder von Magdeburg' ('Albert Hirschland: the Race Defiler of Magdeburg') covered the case in detail in August 1935. The author Karl Holz reported on the sentencing of Hirschland and Fritz Voß, managing director of the Rheingold shoe shop in Magdeburg, for race defilement. Both were sentenced by a Magdeburg court to time in prison followed by preventive custody: *Der Stürmer*, special issue 2, August 1935, pp. 1–4.

5 Dr Paul-Richard Brück (1893–1943), physician; doctor in Karlshafen (Hesse-Nassau), 1920–1934; arrested after being reported to the police for allegedly attempting to sexually abuse female patients in July 1935 in Kassel; sentenced to nine years in prison in Nov. 1935; deported in 1942 to Auschwitz, where he died in Jan. 1943.

6 The *Völkischer Beobachter* also reported on Brück's arrest by the Gestapo: *Völkischer Beobachter* (northern German edition), 7 July 1935, p. 9.

Manfred Eckstein,[7] a Jewish butcher's apprentice from Darmstadt aged only 15 and a half, was sentenced to three years' imprisonment for committing sexual crimes against a 9-year-old girl.[8] The latest incident in the series of Jewish crimes of this nature to come to light within a few days was the arrest reported in the *Völkischer Beobachter* of the Düsseldorf Rabbi Mannheimer[9] for the rape of his housemaid.[10]

A truly eye-opening inventory of scandalous Jewish deeds, which is by no means exhaustive, as countless more cases are never disclosed to the public!

The official report by the press office of the Darmstadt Higher Regional Court states in the case of the butcher Eckstein, among other things, that the usual concessions for juvenile offenders, such as the conditional suspension of sentences, were not made as 'by this act he has clearly proved his only partially stated belief that although he may not violate Jewish children, he may abuse German children'. In other words, Eckstein has stated that his 'religion' permits him to sexually assault non-Jewish children.

The Jews had hitherto denied any 'religious precepts' of this nature even though the relevant Talmud commandment had been disclosed by the tireless educational work and thorough research into Jewish writings conducted in National Socialist circles. But from the wording of the official announcement, it clearly emerges that Eckstein admitted the existence of a commandment against abuse and acted in accordance with his 'religion'.

Even to Volksgenossen who were not previously aware, the incidents described above surely show that the defilement of German women and girls and hence the contamination of German blood is being systematically conducted in accordance with the dictates of Jewish doctrine. Jewish offenders are wilfully and knowingly – as specified in the murder section of the penal code governing the terms of the death sentence – committing one capital crime after another against the German people. None of these desecrated women will ever be able to give birth to truly racially pure children, not to mention the contamination of their souls. Steps must be taken against these acts committed by Jews with every means available under the state of emergency to prevent further harm. It would therefore be desirable if Jews were initially prohibited, under pain of death, from:

(1) taking non-Jews as tenants,
(2) employing non-Jewish household staff,
(3) serving non-Jewish clients as physicians or lawyers.

---

7 In May 1935 Manfred Eckstein (b. 1919) was sentenced to three years in prison by a juvenile court with lay judges in Groß-Gerau, and on 31 Dec. 1937 he was released on parole. In mid June 1938 the police arrested Eckstein during the 'Asozialenaktion', a campaign against those branded 'asocial', on the grounds of being a previously convicted Jew. He was detained in Sachsenhausen concentration camp until 15 August 1938. He emigrated to Colombia in Sept. 1938.
8 No further information on this conviction could be found. The *Völkischer Beobachter* reported that Eckstein had been sentenced on the grounds of attempted rape in connection with having committed the crime of child abuse: *Völkischer Beobachter* (northern German edition), 7 July 1935, p. 9.
9 Emil Mannheimer (1899–1948), teacher and cantor in the Cleves Jewish Community from 1934; sentenced to eight months in prison for 'assaulting' a servant girl in 1935; emigrated with his family to Palestine in 1936. His sentence was revoked after 1945.
10 Under the heading 'Sittliche Verbrechen' (Sexual crimes), the *Völkischer Beobachter* reported that Mannheimer had been arrested on charges of sexual misconduct: *Völkischer Beobachter* (northern German edition), 8 July 1935, p. 4.

The German people have hitherto looked on these activities of national defilement with a generosity that has been poorly repaid by the Jews. Our patience is spent! If the Jewish 'religion' commands the rape of non-Jews, as shown by the Jew Eckstein's admission, may the National Socialist-created state forbid Jews any dealings or relations with non-Jews under pain of the most severe punishments. In 'free' North America, race defilers are hanged! Wn.[11]

DOC. 175
On 13 July 1935 the Regierungspräsident in Düsseldorf asks the Reich Minister of the Interior for instructions regarding the handling of Polish Jews by the Police for Foreign Nationals[1]

Letter from the Regierungspräsident in Düsseldorf (P. 5201/12.7), signed Schmid,[2] to the Reich and Prussian Minister of the Interior, dated 13 July 1935 (copy)[3]

Re: the handling of Polish nationals by the Police for Foreign Nationals.

Following the national uprising,[4] the chief of police in Düsseldorf[5] undertook a detailed review of all cases of residence permits previously issued to Polish nationals (Ostjuden) who entered German national territory after the war and established permanent residency with or without the consent of the German consular authorities. He sometimes used the failure to pay taxes, which had been determined in previous years, as the basis for denying residency, or he denied applications for the renewal of a residence permit on this basis. I have dismissed any complaints directed to me about such decisions – apart from a few cases of particular hardship – because it seems to me that the actions of the chief of police should be supported, given the fact that the immigrant eastern foreigners were excessively indulged by previous governments.

In several instances, however, the Polish consulate in Essen has raised pressing counterarguments against these police measures against foreign nationals and expressly requested me on 6 July 1935 to take action to ensure an improvement in the treatment of Polish nationals by the police headquarters in Düsseldorf.

---

11 Probably the initials of the author.
1 PA AA, R 82778. This document has been translated from German.
2 Carl Christian Schmid (1886–1955), lawyer; mayor of Düsseldorf, 1920–1923; from 1933 Regierungspräsident of Düsseldorf; resigned in Nov. 1938 after demonstrations against him because of his Jewish wife.
3 The letter was sent from the Reich Ministry of the Interior, signed Hering, to the Reich Foreign Office on 29 July 1935 with the comment 'confirmation requested' to the effect 'that the current status of German–Polish relations does not necessitate any mitigation in the handling of Ostjuden by the Police for Foreigners': PA AA, R 82778.
4 This is a reference to the entry to power of the National Socialist government in Germany in Jan. 1933.
5 The chief of police in Düsseldorf from 1933 to 1940 was Friedrich (Fritz) Weitzel (1904–1940); trained as a metalworker; joined the NSDAP in 1923, the SA in 1924, and the SS in 1926; worked as a mechanic in Frankfurt am Main, 1927–1929; SS-Oberführer in the West, 1930–1932; Higher SS and Police Leader (HSSPF) assigned to, among others, the Oberpräsident of Westphalia, 1938–1940; from 1940 HSSPF assigned to the Reich commissioner for the occupied Norwegian territories.

I request instructions as to whether there should be any mitigation in the way in which the Police for Foreign Nationals deals with the aforementioned eastern foreigners in light of the current state of German–Polish relations.[6]

DOC. 176

Neue Zürcher Zeitung: article dated 16 July 1935 about anti-Jewish violence on Kurfürstendamm associated with the screening of an antisemitic film from Sweden[1]

Antisemitic riots in West Berlin

Berlin, 16 July (Telephoned in by our local correspondent) Yesterday evening, antisemitic riots broke out on *Kurfürstendamm* and its neighbouring streets in the west of Berlin. A strong SA presence was attending a screening of the Swedish film *Pettersson and Bendel*[2] at the UFA Theatre, where whistles had been heard the night before (supposedly coming from the Jewish side).[3] On Kurfürstendamm, minor traffic congestion was observed as well as small crowds acting menacingly towards Jews who were passing by or going to coffee houses. A group of fifty young people in white shirts gathered in front of the theatre. Together with the SA men who streamed out of the film, they stopped in front of the elegant *Café Bristol*, which is favoured by 'Aryan' and Jewish patrons alike. The demonstrators smashed one of the windows and began to violently remove the Jews from the premises. Most of the *Jews* retreated in haste. Others who chose not to accept the raid in silence or even tried to fight back were dealt with roughly. Faces were slapped, ribcages were punched, and bits and pieces of smashed chairs flew across the marble tables. Crowds grew on the streets, mostly composed of curious onlookers who were satisfied with a merely passive role. Finally, two trucks of riot *police* arrived who sealed off the streets and convinced the demonstrators to move on.

Similar scenes occurred later at Café Dobrin, also located on Kurfürstendamm, which was closed after it was emptied of all its patrons. The endlessly repeated cry 'The

---

6 This entire paragraph is underlined by hand.

1 'Antisemitische Ausschreitungen im Berliner Westen', *Neue Zürcher Zeitung* (evening edition), 16 July 1935, p. 2. This document has been translated from German.

2 In 1933 Per-Axel Branner filmed *Pettersson & Bendel*, based on the novel of the same name by Waldemar Hammenhög. The film tells the story of Bendel, a retailer from Galicia, who founds a company in Stockholm together with the unemployed Swede Pettersson. It contrasts the figure of the business-savvy *Ostjude* Bendel against the honest Aryan Pettersson. In July 1935 the film was classified as politically valuable on account of its antisemitic content.

3 Joseph Goebbels commented: 'Telegram from Berlin. Jews demonstrate against an antisemitic film. The Führer has had enough. He wants to dismiss Levetzow soon and issue an ultimatum to Frick. It is really quite hair-raising. Now heads are going to roll soon.' Diary entry for 15 July 1935, in Joseph Goebbels, *Die Tagebücher von Joseph Goebbels*, ed. Elke Fröhlich, part 1: *Aufzeichnungen 1923–1941*, vol. 3, no. 1 (Munich: Saur, 2005), p. 262. Levetzow was replaced as chief of police shortly thereafter by Count Wolf-Heinrich von Helldorf (1896–1944), farmer; joined the NSDAP in 1930 and the SA in 1931; chief of police in Potsdam (1933–1935) and in Berlin (1935–1944); executed in 1944 as a conspirator in the 20 July assassination plot against Hitler.

Jews are our misfortune'⁴ echoed on the streets. Several Jewish *shops* were *demolished*. Some figures, hardly discernible in the glow of the street lamps, fled down the road in absolute terror. In fear, one Jew climbed over the iron fence enclosing the tram tracks and ran away in the direction of oncoming trams. The sellers of the *Stürmer* appeared amid the tumult with thick bundles of the pogrom paper and turned a good profit. Little by little, the police dispersed the crowds and ensured that normal traffic was restored. By half past midnight, the commotion had been brought to a halt.

Agitated demonstrations also took place on the same evening in front of a Jewish pharmacy in the Berlin suburb of *Reinickendorf*. They were apparently prompted by the temporary detention of two National Socialists who had called for a boycott against the shop's owner.⁵

DOC. 177
On 17 July 1935 the head of the Regional Welfare Office in Berlin reduces welfare benefits for newly arriving Jews in need[1]

Memorandum from the mayor of Berlin, Regional Welfare and Child Support Office (Lawohl 1), p.p. Spiewok, dated 17 July 1935 (copy)[2]

Re: support for new arrivals in need.

According to § 33 of the Reich Guidelines on the Prerequisites, Nature, and Extent of Public Welfare,[3] in Berlin, as a community in a state of emergency, welfare benefits for new arrivals can be limited, under strictest evaluation of neediness, to those measures absolutely essential for maintaining a minimal standard of living or institutional housing if public welfare is refused.[4] The regulations of 10 March 1934 – Lawohl 1 – stipulated that, in principle, new arrivals are to be offered housing in public shelters. However, at the same time, the arrivals are also supposed to be informed of the fact that, should they prefer, a monetary allowance to the amount specified by the regulations can be paid in lieu of the aforementioned housing.

---

4 German: *Die Juden sind unser Unglück*, a long-standing antisemitic slogan, coined by the historian Heinrich von Treitschke in 1879, which was printed at the foot of the front page of every edition of the *Stürmer* after 1927.

5 Reports on the events can be found on page two of the *Neue Zürcher Zeitung* from both 18 and 19 July 1935. A report appeared in the *Pariser Tageblatt* under the title 'Blutiger Pogrom am Kurfürstendamm' ('Bloody Pogrom on Kurfürstendamm'): *Pariser Tageblatt*, 16 July 1935, p. 1. On press coverage in Norway and Britain, see the letter of the German ambassador in Oslo addressed to the Reich Foreign Office dated 20 July 1935 and the letter from the German embassy in London to the Reich Foreign Office dated 29 July 1935, PA AA, R 121 224. Joseph Goebbels commented: 'The foreign press drones on about a "pogrom".' Diary entry for 19 July 1935, Goebbels, *Die Tagebücher von Joseph Goebbels*, part 1, vol. 3, no. 1, p. 263.

1 LAB, Rep. 214, Acc. 794, Nr. 13. This document has been translated from German.
2 The original contains the handwritten note: 'Regulation see files 101/10/9. B. 9.11.38'.
3 *Reichsgrundsätze über Voraussetzung, Art und Maß der öffentlichen Fürsorge*, 1 August 1931: *Reichsgesetzblatt*, 1931, I, pp. 441–445.
4 § 33 cited here had been added by the Fourth Regulation to the Amendment of the Reich Guidelines on the Prerequisites, Nature, and Extent of Public Welfare, 10 Feb. 1934: ibid., 1934, I, pp. 99–100.

But, as has been observed recently, there has been an extremely strong influx of non-Aryan elements coming to Berlin. As this influx is entirely undesirable,[5] I request you to refrain from making *any* use of the option of reduced monetary support and instead to refer newly arriving non-Aryans, if need is demonstrated, to the municipal shelters *without exception*. The exceptions listed in clause 3 of the aforementioned regulations under b to 1 do not apply to these non-Aryans.[6]

DOC. 178
On 19 July 1935 Reich Minister of the Interior Frick informs Hitler about the practice of changing Jewish names[1]

Letter from the Reich and Prussian Minister of the Interior (I B I B.J.6 V), Frick, to Hitler, dated 19 July 1935, with enclosure[2]

My Führer,

In his letter dated 20 May 1935 (I p 16 445) the Reich Minister of Justice has already commented in detail on the piece in the *Stürmer* entitled 'Why the Jew Wants to Change His Name'.[3] I would like to add just one further point: in accordance with the practice that has been followed without exception in Prussia since the seizure of power, name changes have been expressly prohibited for non-Aryan individuals by the circular decree dated 25 June 1934 (*MBliV*,[4] p. 885). Only *offensive* Jewish names (such as Cohn, Levy, Isaksohn) may be changed to *other Jewish* names. Requests of this kind have yet to be submitted. A copy of the guidelines that apply to the changing of Jewish names is enclosed.[5] These guidelines have been decreed mandatory for the entire Reich as per my

---

5 A day later, on 18 July, the SS organ *Das Schwarze Korps* publicly demanded an 'immigration stop for Jews' see also the report in the *Pariser Tageblatt*, 19 July 1935, p. 2.
6 Berlin's decision to break with the principle of welfare for poor Jews 'ordinarily resident' was commented on approvingly in the *Völkischer Beobachter*: 'Warnung vor dem Zuzug bedürftiger Nichtarier nach Berlin', *Völkischer Beobachter* (Berlin edition), 1 August 1935, p. 18. The Gestapo Central Office (Gestapa), however, feared that this new regulation would lead to an increased influx to other municipalities. For this reason on 16 August 1935 Reich Minister of Economics Schacht was moved to decree a general prohibition against the immigration of Jews into major cities: BArch, R 58/6409, fols. 6–7.

1 BArch, R 43 II/602, fols. 181–182v. This document has been translated from German.
2 The original contains handwritten underlining and annotations from the Reich Chancellery.
3 *Der Stürmer* had criticized the fact that David Isak from Nuremberg wanted to change his name to Rudolf Fritsch. It claimed that this was not merely a matter of the usual kind of deception, but also that it made a mockery of the antisemitic movement because the name 'Fritsch' belonged only to the antisemite and author of the *Handbuch der Judenfrage* (Handbook on the Jewish Question) Theodor Fritsch: *Der Stürmer*, no. 17, April 1935, p. 2.
4 *Ministerialblatt der inneren Verwaltung*: Ministerial gazette for the internal administration.
5 See below.

circular decree dated 26 December 1934 addressed to all state governments. The changing of Jewish names in order to hide Jewish descent has thus been eliminated.[6]

Heil my Führer!

Frick[7]

Copy of enclosure to I B (I B.J.6 V).

VII. Jewish names

(1) If individuals of Aryan descent bear Jewish names, requests to change these names will be granted. In principle, only the same new name will be approved for members of the same family. Which names are to be considered Jewish will be determined by general public consensus. Without a doubt, there are numerous last names that are German in their origin, but which are generally held to be Jewish names in the eyes of the people (e.g. Hirsch, Goldschmidt, etc.). There are also numerous biblical names that are likewise thought to be typical Jewish names, but that are used not only by Jews but also non-Jews (Salomon, Israel, Moses, etc.). Generally speaking, those names that derive from the place of origin (Krotoschiner, Hamburger, Darmstädter, etc.) are also considered to be Jewish names. In contrast, names used by Jews but more commonly by Christians (Meyer etc.) are not to be included in this context.

(2) Requests by individuals of non-Aryan descent to change their names will on principle not be approved because such a name change would disguise the non-Aryan descent of the person bearing the name. Conversion to Christianity does not merit a name change either.

(3) Only offensive Jewish names that, based on experience, provoke jibes or arouse aversion directed at the bearer can be changed in the same manner as the objectionable names of other name-bearers, but only another Jewish name will be approved (Cohn, Levy, Isaaksohn, etc.).

---

6 On name changes, see also Doc. 184, 31 July 1935. On 14 August 1935 the Reich and Prussian Minister of the Interior sent the Deputy of the Führer and the Reich Ministry of Justice a draft law on the changing of first and last names for Jews: Hartmannsgruber (ed.), *AdR*, part 2, vol. 2 (Munich: Oldenbourg, 1999), pp. 736–738. Although the Reich Ministry of Justice was positively inclined towards the plans, the matter was no longer considered urgent following the enactment of the Nuremberg Laws: draft proposal by Globke for Frick dated 18 April 1936, in Hartmannsgruber (ed.), *AdR*, part 3, pp. 264–266.

7 Handwritten signature.

DOC. 179

On 20 July 1935 Mr and Mrs Lau complain to the newspaper *Das Schwarze Korps* about Jews in a Berlin allotment garden area[1]

Letter from Fritz and Elly Lau,[2] Berlin SW 29, 18 Lilienthalstraße, to *Das Schwarze Korps*,[3] Berlin SW 11, 9 Prinz-Albrecht-Straße, dated 20 July 1935[4]

Across from our apartment is the 'Hasenheide Park Shooting Range', entrance on Lilienthalstraße. Garden plots are leased in this area. The person in charge is Police Inspector Krüger – Police Services, Columbiastraße.

When we moved here in October 1932, my wife was in poor health and I obtained permits for short walks for my family in accordance with the enclosed,[5] which was not made at all easy for me, however. The next year I did without the permits.

But then I observed that the garden owners had made things quite nice for themselves there and felt extremely comfortable. What appalled us, however, was the fact that there were, and still are today, also *Jews* among them and that the Jewish children are good friends with the civil servants' children. Someone recently asked us why it wasn't possible to obtain a garden patch over there. We are not seeking to assist the person concerned, but we are repeatedly incensed that we see *Jews* coming out of the area while Aryan applicants are told that the plots are granted *only* to *civil servants*.

It will surely be easy for you to conduct an examination of the garden owners, and we believe we know the name of one Jew, 'Buttermilch'. But there is also another family that makes itself very much at home, with a dog named 'Sonja'. Can these Jews still be civil servants? We cannot believe that they are, because we have never yet seen them give a Hitler salute. Instead, we have noticed that they shirk from saluting the flag.

Since 1 April 1935 there has been an SS man living at the shooting range, and we believed that this nuisance would be redressed, but unfortunately we have heard nothing about it to date. We ask that you also give consideration to this matter.

Heil Hitler!

---

1 BArch, R 58/6409, fol. 54. This document has been translated from German.
2 Fritz Lau, retailer in Berlin, and his wife, Elly.
3 The weekly newspaper began publication in March 1935 as the organ of the Reichsleiter of the SS, edited by Gunter d'Alquen. It started with a circulation of 70,000 copies.
4 Written on the document in large letters: 'S.D.'
5 The enclosure is not in the file.

DOC. 180

On 24 July 1935 the Central Association of German Citizens of the Jewish Faith informs the Reich Minister of the Interior about acts of violence in East Prussia, Mecklenburg, Hesse, Westphalia, and Berlin[1]

Letter from the CV Berlin, unsigned, to the Reich and Prussian Minister of the Interior, dated 24 July 1935 (carbon copy)[2]

We would like to draw the attention of the Reich and Prussian Minister of the Interior to a number of incidents, which are merely examples and therefore cannot by any means be considered as a complete list, that attest to the general situation in which Jewish state subjects find themselves in different regions, especially in parts of East Prussia, Mecklenburg, and Berlin.

I. For weeks, in approximately thirty localities in East Prussia, the houses of Jewish residents have been repeatedly defaced with insulting and degrading remarks written in oil paint, and corresponding notices have been pasted on them. Customers patronizing Jewish businesses are being photographed, and their pictures are being displayed publicly in newspaper display cases, sometimes with names and addresses provided. Shoppers are being addressed by sentries posted in front of the shops and their names are being recorded. Occasionally, young people have even pushed their way into Jewish shops to stop customers from making purchases. In many places the affected Jewish business owners have barely been able to earn 10 per cent of their usual daily income for about five weeks now.

When on 10 July 1935 a Jewish businessman in *Osterode* tried to reprimand an adolescent who was pasting such notices on his property, he was overpowered in his own shop by boys aged 12 to 14 years, led by two 18- to 19-year-olds, and thrown to the floor, before a placard was hung around his neck that read 'This dirty Jew struck a German boy', and he was kicked while being led through the city for about an hour. When the boys tried to force the Jewish businessman into a jog after this hour-long march, the police took the man into protective custody.

Afterwards, the troop of boys pushed its way into the office of the steam mill run by the Guttstein brothers, ransacked the correspondence, and pasted signs on all the office furniture, doors, windows, etc. inside the building. Without any cause, the troop tore the owner himself out of his business premises and also dragged him through the town before the police took him into protective custody. Subsequently, the Jewish shops were forced to close.

These incidents and a complete paralysis of business in Jewish shops during the five weeks that preceded, owing to boycott sentries, picture-taking, and the actual physical blocking of customers attempting to make purchases, prompted a number of Jewish residents of Osterode to leave their home town in haste.

The East Prussian authorities have been informed of the incidents verbally and in writing. As the head office for East Prussia, the State Police office in Königsberg has

---

1 RGVA, 721k-1-258, fols. 248–253. This document has been translated from German.
2 At the end of the document, 'enclosure' has been added in handwriting, but no enclosure is included in the file.

issued an official statement on a window-breaking incident in Gerdauen in the enclosed issue 202 of the *Preussische Zeitung* from 23 July.³

II. In *Parchim*/Mecklenburg, an incident that took place in front of the house of the Jewish couple A. resulted in the most severe measures against all Jewish residents. According to the testimony provided in the police report by the couple's Aryan maid R., she had poured a glass of water out of her window on the evening of 16 July in response to harassment coming from members of the Wehrmacht. The contrary account that it was not water but rather urine that was poured prompted a crowd to assemble in front of the house, and a number of Jewish residents were also paraded through the town; ultimately, almost the entire Jewish community, with the exception of just a few women and children, was taken into custody. The shop of Mr A. was also defaced at the same time in allusion to the incident. Those arrested were set free shortly thereafter; the couple A. were released last of all on 19 July. On the advice of the authorities, the Jewish residents stayed away from Parchim and kept their shops closed until 22 July. Shortly after reopening on 22 July, the windows of the individual stores were smashed and plastered with warning notices advising all Jewish residents to leave Parchim again as soon as possible. On 23 July the police called on the owners to keep their businesses closed. At the moment, the Jews who have been living in Parchim for generations do not dare to remain in their home town.

In Bad *Arendsee*, the windows of the Jewish Hausmann Foundation were shattered during the night of 20 to 21 July. (The foundation's premises themselves were then taken over.)⁴

Around the same time, in Neustadt *Glewe*/Mecklenburg, the windows of the offices of the Adler & Oppenheimer leather factory, which employs approximately 2,000 workers, were smashed.

III. On 22 July a formation of about 100 men from the Labour Service marched in file through the towns of *Elsoss*⁵ and *Paecklhausen*⁶ in Kreis Wittgenstein/Westphalia in front of the homes of Jewish residents and began chanting as the houses were then bombarded with stones.

IV. In *Wächtersbach* in Kreis Gelnhausen, the Jewish livestock dealers who had come to attend the livestock market on 17 July were beaten and chased from the market by a group of about forty non-locals. Some of them sought refuge in nearby houses, while others were followed all the way to the train station. The reinforced gendarmerie did not intervene, but the likewise reinforced railway security put a stop to any further

---

3 The enclosure could not be found.
4 From 1931 the Hausmann Foundation in Arendsee (now part of Kühlungsborn) was located in a villa built in 1912 belonging to the Jewish judicial counsellor Wilhelm Hausmann (1856–1921) and his wife, Margarete (1863–1929), from Berlin. Before her death, Margarete Hausmann had stipulated that her beneficiary, the Higher Institute for Jewish Studies in Berlin, use the villa as a retreat for academics of the Jewish faith. According to her wishes, the institute established the Academic Society of the Hausmann Foundation in Arendsee. The foundation's villa was Aryanized in 1937 and then used by the Goebbels Foundation for Stage Artists.
5 This is presumably a reference to the town of Elsoff.
6 This is presumably a reference to the town of Beddelhausen.

persecution in the grounds of the train station. A similar occurrence also took place at the livestock market in *Fulda* in July.

V. In *Berlin*, Jewish shops along entire streets were repeatedly defaced with insulting phrases written in oil paint and had notices stuck all over them.[7] A number of large display windows were smashed. During the evening Jewish passers-by were harassed on the streets, and Jewish schoolchildren were forced to abandon their holiday camps in the immediate vicinity of Berlin.

The following incidents have occurred in the last few days alone:

(1) The front section of the house of worship on Prinzregentenstrasse was completely defiled with insults.

(2) The glass store fronts of the Jewish company Herz-Licht were smashed on 22 July.

(3) The patrons of a Jewish restaurant on Woltersdorfer Schleuse were ejected by intruders and prevented from paying their bills.

(4) The same thing then took place in the Jewish-owned Café Hansa on Flensburgerstrasse night after night. The intruders went after the patrons, shouting 'The Nazis are coming' every time. In order to avoid further demolition, the owner had to close down his café on 20 July.

In response to the persistence of such incidents, other Jewish restaurants have also closed down entirely for the time being.[8]

As the legal certainty of the Jewish residents in the regions and cities noted above has been threatened to the extreme, we request prompt measures that are designed to put an end to such unlawful incidents.[9]

DOC. 181

In anticipation of a future law, Reich Minister of the Interior Frick bans marriages between Jews and non-Jews on 27 July 1935[1]

Circular from the Reich and Prussian Minister of the Interior (I B 3 /245), signed Frick, to the state governments and, in the case of Prussia, to the registrars and their supervisory authorities, dated 27 July 1935 (copy for Deputy of the Führer Heß in Munich)[2]

The Reich government intends to legislate on the question of marriages between Aryans and non-Aryans in the near future. In order to avoid any impairment to the effectiveness of this law caused by marriages concluded before it is issued, I have determined the following:

---

[7] Boycotts of Jewish-owned businesses had been taking place since mid June 1935: GStA PK, I HA, Rep. 90 P, Lageberichte Provinz Brandenburg 2.2, fols. 182–235, here fols. 224–228.

[8] See also the report of Berlin's chief of police from 30 July 1935 in Kulka and Jäckel (eds.), *The Jews in the Secret Nazi Reports*, enclosed CD, no. 934.

[9] See a similar letter from the Central Association of German Citizens of the Jewish Faith (CV) to the Gestapo Central Office (Gestapa) dated 30 July 1935: RGVA, 721k-1-258.

[1] BArch, R 58 II/6401, fol. 10. This document has been translated from German.

For all cases of marriage in which it is known or can be proved that one of the parties involved is a full Aryan and the other is a full Jew, registrars must delay the reading of the banns or the marriage itself until further notice.

If one of the parties involved in such a case is a foreigner, then I am to be informed directly and provided with the case files as soon as possible.

In all other cases, the general rules are to be followed.³

DOC. 182
Anti-Jewish prejudices within the Confessing Church: a letter from schoolmistress Elisabeth Schmitz to Walter Künneth, 28 July 1935¹

Letter, unsigned [Elisabeth Schmitz],² currently of Hanau am Main, 16 Corniceliusstraße, to Dr [Walter Künneth],³ dated 28 July 1935 (carbon copy)

Dear Doctor,

I do not know whether you remember me. We met last year at the home of Renate Ludwig⁴ on her birthday.

I am deliberately placing this personal remark at the top because it will be very difficult for me to write this letter without great bitterness. I want to attempt to do so, but you make it almost impossible.

---

2 The decree was published with minor alterations to the wording using the date of the previous day (RMdI I B 3/195): *Ministerialblatt der inneren Verwaltung*, 1935, p. 980c. The decree resulted from a meeting held on 18 July 1935 in the Reich Ministry of Justice: see Bormann's letter to the Deputy of the Führer from 2 August 1931, BArch, R 58 II/6401, fols. 9–10.

3 The text of the decree was published in the *Juristische Rundschau* under the title 'Zur Frage der Mischehe: Eine grundsätzliche Regelung bevorstehend' ('On the Question of Mixed Marriages: General Ruling Imminent'): *Juristische Rundschau*, 13 August 1935, p. 8.

1 Archiv des Diakonischen Werkes der Evangelischen Kirche Deutschlands, CA/AC 26, fols. 5–7. This document has been translated from German.

2 With respect to the authorship of the unsigned carbon copy, see an identically worded draft (signed Elisabeth Schmitz) in the collection of sections of the literary estate of Elisabeth Schmitz in Hanau, Privatarchiv Gerhard Lüdecke. Dr Elisabeth Schmitz (1893–1977), historian and secondary school teacher; school teacher in Berlin, 1923–1938; from 1929 secondary school teacher; retired at her own request following the pogroms of Nov. 1938; from 1928 worked in the Protestant Church in a voluntary capacity; from 1934 a member of the Confessing Church; worked in Hanau as a teacher from 1946 to 1958.

3 Because the file contains only letters from and to Walter Künneth, the unnamed addressee is presumably Dr Walter Künneth (1901–1997), Protestant theologian; from 1926 lecturer at the Centre for Apologetics, a department of the Central Committee for Inland Mission in Berlin, and from 1932 its director; in May 1933, together with Martin Niemöller, founded the Young Reformation Movement; member of the Confessing Church; after the ban on the Centre for Apologetics in 1937, one of his posts was as a pastor in Starnberg and Erlangen; from 1946 professor of theology in Erlangen; in 1966 received the Grand Cross of the Order of Merit of the Federal Republic of Germany.

4 Dr Renate Ludwig (1905–1976), Protestant theologian; section head at the Centre for Apologetics in Berlin, 1933–1938; editor of the journal *Wort und Tat*; from 1936 vicar in Berlin; member of the Confessing Church; after 1945 senior secondary school teacher in Baden-Württemberg.

The issue at hand is your statements about Jewry in your book about the *Myth*.[5]

You speak about our German Jews of today in words none other than those favoured at present, 'decadent world Jewry', 'asphalt Jewry',[6] etc., and you actually manage to assert that Jews of the post-Christian era are ultimately exclusively self-seeking, misuse the peoples of the world,[7] and are becoming the 'germ carriers' of the 'contamination of the peoples'![8] That is, you only know the distorted image of Jewry; at least you speak *only* about this. That is exactly the same as when someone characterizes the DC[9] today and then holds that *they* represent Christianity. All that is 'pretence', is 'myth', and has very little to do with historical truth.

Because it really is common knowledge, there is no point in first clarifying here what German science alone owes to the Jews – the natural sciences, mathematics, medicine – how many endowments in museums and, what is more, donations for public welfare have been made by Jews. I do not know whether that is 'subversive'. But how are we to look the bereaved families of the 12,000 Jews killed in action in the war (out of 550,000 Jews in Germany) in the eye, and the many thousands of Jewish combat veterans, if we make such statements and thus take from them the ultimate thing a human being possesses on this earth: honour? Even the Jews on the front lines had to defend themselves against defamatory statements. 'I am happy to be able now to bear witness to the sacred truth of our idea in bloody earnest, and love for the German fatherland blazes in us more intensely than ever. The fact that, alas, back at home the dishonourable voices of defamation have not yet fallen silent is incapable of daunting us. This only makes us sad, terribly sad. What more do they want, besides our blood?' (*War Letters of German Jews Killed in Action*, p. 54).[10]

If Jewish nationalism, too, flourishes today in a world that is overheated with nationalism – is it any wonder? But if the majority of German Jews still proclaim their loyalty to Germany today, after two and a half years of the gravest persecution, with life and death at stake – it *is* almost a miracle.

Was it a 'lack of a heroic cast of mind'[11] when, during the persecutions of the Middle Ages, Jews threw themselves and *their children* into the flames to prevent them from renouncing their faith? But is it heroic then that the *entire* Jewish Community of Nuremberg was massacred on two occasions, or that 66 million are setting upon half a million today?

I said above that it will be very hard for me not to write with great bitterness, and I must openly admit that since the shock of the boycott of 1 April 1933, nothing has upset

---

5 In March 1935, in response to Alfred Rosenberg's *Mythus des 20. Jahrhunderts* (The Myth of the Twentieth Century), Künneth had published a book entitled *Antwort auf den Mythus: Die Entscheidung zwischen dem nordischen Mythus und dem biblischen Christus* [Response to the Myth: the decision between the Nordic Myth and the Biblical Christ] (Berlin: Wichern, 1935).
6 See Künneth, *Antwort auf den Mythus*, p. 67. In antisemitic writings the German word 'Asphalt' became a synonym for big cities and Jews and referred to the rootlessness of the urban population and its separation from the natural soil.
7 Ibid., p. 68.
8 Ibid., p. 69.
9 Deutsche Christen: German Christians.
10 The *Kriegsbriefe gefallener deutscher Juden* was published in 1935 by the Reich League of Jewish Combat Veterans.
11 See Künneth, *Antwort auf den Mythus*, p. 69.

and appalled me as much as these passages in your book. Anyone who writes such things today must know that he thus places himself on a level with a certain element of the press that is prevalent today. And when such things and – as I am aware, of course – even far worse ones are printed nowadays in the *Schwarzes Chor*[12] and the *Stürmer*, I cannot change it, and it is no concern of mine. But when this takes place in the Confessing Church, it does concern me, and I consider myself – permit me to say this – obligated in the eyes of God, on the basis of my responsibility as a member of the Church and my responsibility for people who are near and dear to me, to protest against it with the utmost seriousness.

Again and again, when I read your sentences, it seems to me that you have no real knowledge of the actual present-day situation of German Jews or non-Aryans, as one by rights would have to say. Only in this way can I understand how it is possible to write such things today. Indeed, you know that in the worst centre of persecution, in the area surrounding Nuremberg, posters calling for a pogrom had already been put up, so that even Mr Streicher had to take action against the 'lack of discipline' (!). In a small town in Electoral Hesse (also Protestant, like the area around Nuremberg!), a Jew was literally kicked to death. Anyone who writes today that the Jews are the people of the curse[13] and germ carriers of the contamination of the peoples has to know what he is doing.

How do you know, actually, that 'preserving the purity of the blood' is a duty? Responsible-minded geneticists are far from certain of that, since plant and animal experiments, in scientific terms, are still in the very early stages, and far from having anything conclusive to say about human races.

If you agree with Rosenberg about the 'accursed nature' of the Jew,[14] you thus affirm the racial linkage of this 'accursed nature', for how else could Rosenberg be on solid ground? And if one holds this notion together with the 'duty of preserving the purity of the blood',[15] one cannot quite understand the effrontery with which the church then undertakes its mission to the Jews. Should our members of the Protestant community all be condemned to celibacy? Or should they marry confessional Jews? Or are you espousing a separate Jewish Christian Church?

I want to say something personal, just very briefly. I live together with a friend who is a Jewess by birth.[16] In her family I have found the most consciously and unswervingly loyal Germans I have ever known. And now, for two and a half years, day after day, I have experienced together with them the grievous heartaches and physical torments that are the result of these times. I see the outward destruction of their livelihood in both the close and the extended family circle; I see everywhere, in the homes of acquaintances, the dispersal of the family to the four corners of the earth; I see the disloyalty and cowardice, for miles around, of the 'Aryan friends'. I know of the suicides and the many

---

12 This is a reference to the SS organ *Das Schwarze Korps*.
13 See Künneth, *Antwort auf den Mythus*, pp. 68–69.
14 Ibid., p. 68.
15 Ibid., pp. 189 and 199.
16 Dr Martha Kassel, later Seefeld (1880–1952), physician; medical practitioner, 1912–1933. In 1933 her authorization by the public health insurance funds was revoked, and she emigrated in 1938 to Argentina, where she worked on a farm, and then to the USA in 1946. Elisabeth Schmitz had taken Martha Kassel into her home in 1933.

deaths that are the result of this persecution 'without bloodshed' I see the misery and despair – and I see the dreadful guilt of the other side, the side on which we stand.

My friend was baptized long ago, but as a result of her profound disappointment she has not yet found the way to the Confessing Church. Repeatedly I am confronted with bitter questions and accusations: why does the Church do nothing? Why does it allow this nameless injustice to take place? How can it make, time and time again, declarations of faith in the National Socialist state, which are political declarations, after all, and thus direct its efforts against the lives of a part of its own members? Why does it fail to protect at least the children? Should all that, which is simply incompatible with the humaneness that is scorned today, be compatible with Christianity? And time and again, I hear: the Catholic Church at least takes care of its members, hires non-Aryan doctors and nurses, for example – the Protestant Church's Inland Mission has Aryan Paragraphs! From within the ranks of non-Aryan Christians, I have been told that they feel abandoned by the Protestant Church and ecumenical Christianity. They need not worry about their Catholic members, I was told; they will not go under, because the church is taking care of them. About the stance of the Protestant Church, however, one can only say: Lord, forgive them, for they know not what they do. – The [Protestant] Church makes it bitterly hard for one to defend it.[17] Luckily, I locked up your book straight away, so that my friend does not find it. I dare not think what the result would otherwise be.

That is the most important part of what I have to say. Should it have nonetheless been said too harshly in places, please accept my apology. For you and for me, it is a question of the matter at hand.

Your book is regarded as *the* response of the Protestant Church to the *Myth*, indeed as the reply of the Confessing Church, especially considering that it was published with the foreword by Marahrens.[18] It is bad for the Confessing Church that it is so. Therefore it is my urgent, heartfelt, and very earnest request that you submit these passages to a comprehensive reworking before a new edition of your book is published.

---

17 This last sentence and other passages are found in identical or similar wording in the fifteen-page position paper written by Schmitz before Sept. 1935, 'Zur Lage der deutschen Nichtarier' ('On the Situation of German non-Aryans'). From 1933 she had collected information and reports concerning discrimination against German Jews. She distributed 200 copies of the paper to influential figures in the Confessing Church in order to encourage an official Church statement opposing the persecution, though without success. The position paper is published in Hannelore Erhart, Ilse Meseberg-Haubold, and Dietgard Meyer, *Katharina Staritz, 1903–1953: Dokumentation*, vol. 1: *1903–1942* (Neukirchen-Vluyn: Neukirchener, 1999), pp. 220–246, here p. 245.
18 August Marahrens (1875–1950), Protestant theologian; dean of Einbeck, 1920; Lutheran regional bishop of Hanover, 1925–1947; president of the Lutheran World Convention, 1935–1945.

DOC. 183
On 31 July 1935 the Gestapo Central Office reports to Reinhard Heydrich on new plans for discriminating against the Jewish population in Berlin[1]

Letter from the Gestapo Central Office (II 1 B 2 – J 895/35) to its head, SS-Gruppenführer Heydrich, by internal mail, dated 31 July 1935 (draft, sent out on 2 August 1935)[2]

In light of the anti-Jewish rallies on Kurfürstendamm and in other Berlin neighbourhoods, a discussion took place on 30 July in the office of Vice President Steeg[3] in the Berlin City Hall, in which, besides the mayor of Berlin, representatives of the Gestapo Central Office, police headquarters, Berlin's State Police Office, the Gauleitung, and the SA Troop of Berlin-Brandenburg participated. The purpose of the discussion was to find suitable ways and means to combat the Jews in Berlin effectively without public demonstrations or individual actions.[4]

Overall, the discussion had the following outcome:

(1) Jewish businesses.
The new establishment of Jewish businesses is to be prevented in the future by having the question of demand subjected to a strict examination by the city's administrative court. The Berlin municipal administration intends to issue guidelines for this in the future, according to which the granting of the permit to Jews is to be denied in principle.

In the case of existing Jewish shops, the Law for the Protection of Retail Trade is to be interpreted in a restrictive way. In particular, it is to be used to prevent Jews from enlarging their business premises. In the process, difficulties are also to be made by the Building Inspection Authorities, in the form of appropriate requirements.

It is of extraordinary importance that in the future the existing Jewish businesses be immediately recognized as such by the purchasing public. The final arrangement is to be implemented by the NS-Hago[5] in conjunction with the Reich government. It was proposed that the Aryan – non-Jewish – businesses be marked with a corresponding sign. The NS-Hago and individual National Socialist organizations are to work closely together to determine whether the business is an Aryan one. In addition, it was agreed that education inside and outside the National Socialist organizations would continue in increased measure, in order to prevent the population from purchasing in Jewish shops.

---

1 RGVA, 500k-1-379, fols. 51–52. This document has been translated from German.
2 The original contains handwritten amendments and annotations.
3 Ludwig Steeg (1894–1945), administrative civil servant, from 1919 employed by the City of Berlin; joined the NSDAP in 1933; member of the SS; representative of State Commissioner Lippert, 1933; mayor of Berlin, 1937; acting mayor of Berlin and chairman of the city council, 1940–1945, and then mayor, 1945; died in Soviet internment in 1945.
4 See the order of the new Chief of Police von Helldorf prohibiting individual actions: 'Gegen Einzelaktionen': *Völkischer Beobachter* (northern German edition), 28 July 1935, p. 2.
5 NS-Handwerks-, Handels- und Gewerbe-Organisation: National Socialist Organization of Crafts, Trade, and Commerce.

As a measure against Jewish ice-cream parlours, which have notably been the object of anti-Jewish demonstrations, it has already been ordered that, in the future, every ice-cream parlour must have a lavatory facility. By corresponding stringent application of this regulation to Jewish ice-cream parlours, one hopes to bring about the closure of the same, particularly as, in many cases, compliance with the order is impossible for reasons of space.

(2) Jewish property and real estate management.
Houses and land owned by Jews are to be subjected to close examination in the future, to determine whether Building Inspection Authorities requirements (repairs and the like) can be imposed. In addition, the Gau of Berlin should, through appropriate monitoring, make efforts to ensure that when a comparison between Aryan and non-Aryan tenants reveals that Aryan tenants are being charged too much rent, a regulation favouring the Aryan tenants is introduced.

(3) Bathing by Jews at municipal public bathing beaches.
Out of consideration for the 1936 Olympics, for the time being no signs are to be put up at the city's open-air pools forbidding Jews the use of the pools. The operation of the pools, however, will be monitored by patrols, which – provided with special identification – are entitled to direct Jews to leave the open-air pool immediately, in the event of improper conduct. In the case of municipal indoor pools, however, Jews are to be turned away as soon as they reach the till.[6]

(4) Contracts with Jews.
A thorough investigation should be made to determine whether and by which office public contracts have still been awarded to Jewish firms.

(5) Marriage between Aryans and Jews.
The Berlin marriage registrars have already been instructed to no longer perform such marriages.[7]

Further discussions about the fight against Jewry in Berlin are scheduled to take place in the near future.

---

[6] The mayor of Berlin had prohibited Jews from access to all municipal baths in July 1935: Behnken (ed.), *Deutschland-Berichte der Sozialdemokratischen Partei Deutschlands*, no. 7, July 1935, p. 800. From mid July 1935 there was a campaign in the newspapers calling for restrictions on Jews' use of municipal bathing facilities: see *Völkischer Beobachter* (northern German edition), 19, 20, 24, and 27 July 1935.

[7] See Doc. 181, 27 July 1935.

DOC. 184

On 31 July 1935 the German Labour Front writes to the SD Main Office to propose name changes for Jews[1]

Letter from the German Labour Front Central Bureau/Information Office (letter no. 5347/35/khe), SS-Sturmbannführer (signature illegible), Berlin, to the SD Main Office of the Reichsführer SS (received on 2 August 1935), dated 31 July 1935, and with unsigned enclosure from 24 July 1935

Re: necessity of name change for Jews.
Reference: none.
The Information Office received a paper in the form of a file memorandum dealing with the necessity of the name change for Jews. In it, the proposal is made that:
  (1) the Jews bear only Jewish given names,
  (2) their Aryan names be changed back to Jewish names,
  (3) they be allowed to employ only Jewish domestic servants rather than Christian ones.
  The paper in question goes to the SD Main Office to be processed further if required.[2]
  Heil Hitler!
  [...][3]
  SS-Sturmbannführer.
  p.p.
  [...][4]
  SS-Obersturmführer.

Enclosure.
File memorandum.
Name change for Jews.
It has always been the principle of the Jews to adopt famous names in order to extract advantages from them. There are thousands of examples, so let only the more important ones be mentioned here.
  After [Gotthold Ephraim] Lessing had become famous as a writer and poet, a vast number of Jews adopted the name Lessing. The German Lessing family, from which the writer came, can prove that one ancestor was a pastor in the region of Chemnitz in the sixteenth century. At the time of the socialist Jewish government in Germany in the period 1919–1930, one of the Jewish Lessings in Hanover had been appointed professor. His forebears were named Moses Aron and Simon Heilbronn. The latter died on 3 June 1775. The behaviour of this Professor Theodor Lessing,[5] who fled to a foreign country when the National Socialists came to power, has confirmed, through its baseness, that he is of Jewish ancestry and descent.

1 BArch, R 58/6409, fols. 32–35. This document has been translated from German.
2 On the discussion about name changes, see also Doc. 178, 19 July 1935.
3 The signature is illegible.
4 The signature is illegible.
5 Dr Theodor Lessing (1872–1933), physician, philosopher, and writer; professor of philosophy in Hanover from 1923; in 1933 emigrated to Marienbad, where he was the victim of a political assassination on 20 August; author of dramas, poems, and philosophical works.

The situation is similar for the name Reuter. Our great writer of Low German[6] gave his authentically German name a fine reputation for centuries. Then, unfortunately, the name Reuter was again adopted by Jews. Thus, the original name of the man who founded the Reuter's Telegram Company[7] in London in 1851 was Josephat. In 1845 he established a firm, Stargard and Reuter, in Berlin, and at that time he discarded the name Josephat. Then a German prince – venal, like many of his kind – ennobled the Jew Josephat-Reuter, in return for a fee, in 1871, conferring on him the title 'Baron Paul Julius von Reuter'.[8] Unfortunately, German princes have completely fallen short in this respect for centuries and have always been willing, in exchange for Jewish money, to betray German national traditions. Luckily, this behaviour has had dire consequences for them. These incompetent noble families were robbed of their authority by the Jews themselves, partly by Napoleon, who arose from France's Jewish revolution of 1789, and partly by Germany's Jewish revolution of 1918, after the aristocratic families had proved themselves incapable of representing true German interests.

There is no need to cite further details. Suffice it to mention the epidemic of Germanic given names in Jewish families that broke out in Richard Wagner's day: Siegfried, Siegmund, etc. have become nothing but Jewish names. Why are Jews not prohibited now by statutory provision from bearing Aryan forenames, and why are they not forced to bear Jewish forenames, of which a relatively rich and lovely collection exists, of course, in the Old Testament? Ample choice is available, and for every Jewish character trait, too, a corresponding given name can be easily supplied. Every child, too, should by all means have several Jewish given names.

A further step, but one that absolutely ought to follow, would be to force the Jews to change their Christian surnames back to their original Jewish names, particularly if the relevant Aryan families so request it. However, it is also sufficient if the Jews are permitted to have only Jewish given names and no Aryan ones.

Jews cannot object to this, because they describe themselves as the chosen people, and because it must therefore be an honour for them that one can immediately recognize this 'chosenness' from their very name.

In this connection, let it be recalled that in the Middle Ages individual cities very often enacted laws forbidding the Jews to keep Christian domestic servants, because abuses of manifold sorts had repeatedly come to light. A law in this regard is absolutely essential.[9] It would also be thoroughly justifiable in every respect, because those Jews who complain that other Jews have lost their positions in Germany will then have available to them the splendid opportunity to take the jobs in domestic service that become vacant in the homes of their racial comrades. Why should Jews be unable to provide positions as domestic servants as well? Admittedly, they themselves usually place no value on such servants, because they are too untidy and slipshod. Under Jewish guidance, however, they will surely improve their performance.

24 July 1935.

---

6 Fritz Reuter (1810–1874).
7 Forerunner of the worldwide news agency Reuters.
8 Baron Paul Julius von Reuter (1816–1899).
9 The Law for the Protection of German Blood and German Honour, enacted in Nuremberg on 15 Sept. 1935, contained such a regulation in § 3: see Doc. 199, 15 Sept. 1935.

DOC. 185

Das Schwarze Korps, 7 August 1935: article calling on the population to arrest Jews[1]

[Dr W. Zarnack, Reich Office Head][2]
What everyone must know: when may I arrest someone?[3]

In broad sections of the German Volk, a *lack of clarity* still prevails regarding the legal prerequisites for a provisional arrest. Recent events have shown that clarification thereof is *urgently* called for.

Paragraph 127 of the Code of Criminal Procedure stipulates:

'If someone is caught in the act or pursued, then, if there is a suspicion that he may abscond, or if his identity cannot be immediately established, anyone is authorized to place him under provisional arrest, even in the absence of an arrest warrant from a judge.'

Accordingly, two cases are distinguishable:

(1) catching in the act and suspicion of absconding, or

(2) catching in the act and inability to immediately establish the identity of the person in question.

The prerequisite *in each case* is the presence of a culpable act. Whether this act is a crime or a misdemeanour, or even just a petty offence, is irrelevant.

A Jew who, abusing his right to hospitality, appears in public with a German woman, a Jew who obtrusively performs contortions of his limbs in a public dance hall, or a Jew who behaves in a boisterous and conspicuous manner in German public baths causes a public nuisance and thereby threatens the external existence of public order.

Unless laws against more serious crimes have been violated, he will be punished for disorderly conduct according to § 360(11) of the Criminal Code.

An explanation of what constitutes disorderly conduct is not provided by the law itself. The label is also not relevant. On the basis of case law in the German courts, a violation of § 360(11) of the Criminal Code is always present if someone knowingly commits an act that is a substantial violation of accepted standards and is likely to disrupt the order based on these standards.

After the reawakening of the soul of the German people, punishment is *to be extended to such cases in which the inner feelings of the German individual are grossly violated* and this inner disquiet results in the endangerment of public order.

A deliberate act occurs not only when the disturber intentionally seeks to produce the disruptive effect, but also when he is unaware that his conduct will unduly annoy the German Volksgenossen, which he must recognize upon proper reflection.

---

1 'Was jeder wissen muß. Wann darf ich jemanden festnehmen?', *Das Schwarze Korps*, issue 23, 7 August 1935, p. 5. This document has been translated from German.

2 Wolfgang Zarnack (b. 1902), lawyer; member of the Freikorps Reinhard, 1919; joined the NSDAP and the SA in 1923; SA officer on the staff of the Supreme SA Command East, 1930; office head in the legal department of the Reichsleitung of the NSDAP; after 1945 worked as a lawyer, including serving as defence counsel in trials dealing with National Socialist crimes.

3 The article was forwarded the next day as a circular letter to the Regierungspräsidenten, Landräte, and mayors, as well as the NSDAP Kreisleiter, district propaganda chiefs, and local branch heads: circular letter from the NSDAP Reichsleitung for Propaganda, signed Hugo Fischer, 8 August 1935, Sächsisches Staatsarchiv, Hauptstaatsarchiv Dresden, 13 471 NS-Archiv des MfS, ZA VI 3852 Akte 12.

Any Volksgenosse who catches a Jew in the act of committing a culpable offence under § 360(11) of the Criminal Code, or pursues him immediately after the completion of the act, *is authorized to place him under arrest* and, if he resists, to employ force, provided that he cannot give sufficient proof of his identity, perhaps by presenting official identification papers, or if, despite establishment of his identity, there is a suspicion that he will abscond. *Tying him up is permissible only in the most extreme cases.* According to case law, an error regarding the legal power to arrest excludes the liability of the person making the arrest. This person thus cannot be prosecuted for unlawful detention.

If the individual affected resists arrest, he is acting *unlawfully*. If, while offering resistance, he causes a physical injury, he is *guilty of an offence*. The man who has been arrested *cannot* invoke self-defence, since the provisional arrest is lawful under the conditions cited, and thus no unlawful assault justifying self-defence is present.

It is urgently necessary for every German Volksgenosse to commit to memory the prerequisites for a provisional arrest, so that he does not violate a law, but also so that he can intervene uncompromisingly and with a clear conscience whenever he sees a violation of the honour of the German people.

The person arrested is thereupon to be presented without delay to the local magistrate of the district in which the arrest occurred. But it is also sufficient to take him to the nearest police authority.

The person arrested must then answer to his statutory judge.[4]

DOC. 186

On 8 August 1935 the Gestapo informs the Reich Foreign Office about the public humiliation of a woman in Beuthen[1]

Express letter (delivered by special motorcycle courier) from the Prussian Gestapo, the deputy chief and inspector (1 B 2–67665/J 911/35), by order of Best, to the Reich Foreign Office in Berlin (received on 9 August 1935), dated 8 August 1935

Concerning the letter of 30 July 1935 – P 5725 –
Re: events in Beuthen, Upper Silesia.
On 22 July 1935 two irresponsible persons requested the hairdresser Lotte *Teichgräber*, whose relationship with a Jew had caused the greatest uproar among the population, to come out of her place of work. On the street, after cutting off some of her hair, they smeared her with tar. A sign was hung round her neck, reading 'I am the race defiler Teichgräber'. The crowd that had assembled in the meantime was planning to march Teichgräber through the town. As a result of the intervention of the local police authorities, this plan was thwarted by arresting Teichgräber a few minutes later for her own protection and taking her to the hospital in Gleiwitz to clean off the tar.

---

4 On 9 August 1935 the *Daily Telegraph* in London reported on the call for civilians to arrest Jews. The article was published in *Meldung des Deutschen Nachrichtenbüros*, no. 219, 9 August 1935 (morning), p. 5, BArch, R 43 II/602, fol. 185.

1 PA AA, R 121 224. This document has been translated from German.

Those who were ascertained to be the main perpetrators were immediately taken into protective custody and will be sent to a concentration camp.

Teichgräber is a German citizen and has at no time resided in Poland. In this respect, therefore, the report in the *Daily Herald* is inaccurate.[2]

I have once again made it the specific duty of the authorities reporting to me to comply in the most scrupulous way with the Geneva Convention[3] and have instructed them to use the most severe measures to bring to justice every person, regardless of status, who should contravene the provisions of the Geneva Convention. As an identical instruction has also been issued to the officials of the local formations of the Party, precautions have thus been taken to ensure that similar incidents do not occur again in the future.

DOC. 187
On 15 August 1935 the head of the NSDAP Gau organization in East Prussia demands that the Landrat in Marienwerder be excluded from the Party[1]

Letter from the head of the NSDAP Gau organization,[2] unsigned, in Königsberg, to Party comrade Bethke,[3] vice president in the Governor's Office in Königsberg, dated 15 August 1935 (carbon copy)[4]

From a report by Kreisleiter Haffmann[5] in Marienwerder, I gather the following:

Landrat Wuttke,[6] Marienwerder, has recently clashed severely with the National Socialist will. District court proceedings for exclusion of Landrat Wuttke are under way, based on the following incidents:

(1) Without informing the SA, he has had police authorities remove the anti-Jewish banners that had been put up by the SA.

---

2 This announcement could not be found. *Le Temps* reported somewhat differently on the incident: a young Polish woman, Mademoiselle Feingreber, was hounded through the town by supporters of Hitler on account of her engagement to a Jew. After the incident she was admitted to hospital following a nervous breakdown. She then sued for 150,000 francs in damages: *Le Temps* (Paris), 31 July 1935.
3 The Geneva Convention on Upper Silesia: *Reichsgesetzblatt*, 1922, II, p. 519. See also Doc. 28, 7 April 1933, and Doc. 46, 24 May 1933.
1 GStA PK, XX HA, Rep. 240/B 12 b Gauleitung, fol. 37. This document has been translated from German.
2 Paul Dargel (b. 1903), retailer; timber dealer, 1919–1930; NSDAP head of the Gau office, 1932; head of the Gau organization in East Prussia, 1933–1945; Regierungspräsident in Zichenau (Ciechanów), 1940–1945; permanent representative of the Reich commissioner in Ukraine, 1942–1944; lived in Hanover after 1945.
3 Dr Hermann Bethke (1900–1940), lawyer; Regierungsassessor employed by the government in Königsberg, Prussia, 1927–1932; section head and head of the Gau legal office, 1929, and head of the Gau office of the NSDAP Gauleitung in East Prussia, 1933; from 1933 deputy in the Oberpräsident's office in the province of East Prussia; acting Regierungspräsident in Zichenau, 1939–1940.
4 In the original, 'Oberpr.' (= Oberpräsident's office) is written by hand at the top.
5 Arthur Haffmann (b. 1899), farmer; member of the Völkisch Freedom Movement; joined the NSDAP in 1931; from 1933 NSDAP Gau inspector and Kreisleiter in Marienwerder and in Angerburg.
6 Bernhard Wuttke (b. 1902), civil servant; worked in the Landrat's office in Bersenbrück, 1928–1930, and for the government in Gumbinnen, 1930–1932; joined the NSDAP in 1933; Landrat in Marienwerder, 1933–1939, and in Jägerndorf from 1939.

(2) He has removed from office a Red Cross nurse who had been working very much along National Socialist lines in the Polish-threatened region around Tiefenau. In my opinion, he did so only because the matron, who is anything but a National Socialist, was unwilling to tolerate this National Socialist work.

(3) Landrat Wuttke has had the gendarmerie investigate whether Party member Neumann, the head of the District Women's League, who is also the deputy head of the District Office for People's Welfare, has campaigned for the German Faith Movement in the course of her work in the district.

As a result of the outrageous behaviour of Landrat Wuttke, I no longer consider him worthy of being a National Socialist Party comrade.[7]

Heil Hitler!

DOC. 188

On 17 August 1935 the Gestapo Central Office orders the State Police offices to provide material for a central 'Jewish registry'[1]

Circular decree from the head of the Gestapo Central Office (II 1 B 2-68327/J 995/35), Reinhard Heydrich, to all State Police offices, dated 17 August 1935 (copy)

For the purpose of registering the Jews in Germany, a Jewish registry is to be compiled.[2] In order to create a basis for this, all Jewish organizations located in the region of the local office are to be required to submit membership lists in triplicate, as per the enclosed sample.[3]

These membership lists must reflect the current status as of 1 October 1935. To obtain them, however, *only* the local associations and groups can be approached; *under no circumstances* are the regional associations to be approached. The organizations are to be made aware that false statements will lead to dissolution. Supervision along these lines is the responsibility of the local office.

The membership lists received are to be collected and sent to me in two copies by 1 November at the latest. The third copy will remain with the local office for assessment and for the creation of a district registry.

The changes that arise are then to be reported, without special prompting, using the first day of every quarter as the reference date, in a supplementary list, also in triplicate. This list must contain:

---

7 Vice President Bethke subsequently wrote to NSDAP Kreisleiter Haffmann on 10 Sept. 1935 that the matter would be better handled informally with the Gauleitung and governor's office rather than through a Party court proceeding. All appearance of a conflict between Party and state was to be avoided: GStA PK, XX HA, Rep. 240/B 12 b Gauleitung, fol. 42. The differences were resolved during a conversation with the vice president: letter from Bethke to the Gauleitung, 30 Dec. 1935, ibid., fol. 64r–v.

1 BArch, R 58/276, fols. 22–23. This document has been translated from German.
2 On the registration of the Jews, see Doc. 252, 12 Oct. 1936; Doc. 283, 28 May 1937; and Doc. 288, 12 July 1937.
3 The sample index card enclosed with the circular decree is not printed here.

(1) withdrawals, broken down into:
(a) those resulting from resignation,
(b) those resulting from death,
(c) those resulting from emigration;
(2) the new additions.

These supplementary lists are then to be sent to me at the latest on the first day of the month following the first day of the respective quarter. Apart from that, the same provisions apply as for the first submission. In the event of 'no change', this must also be reported in each and every case.

DOC. 189

Ministers' conference on 20 August 1935 concerning the next steps in anti-Jewish policy[1]

Memorandum from the Gestapo Central Office (II 1 B 2), unsigned, dated 20 August 1935 (draft)[2]

Report on the conference held on 20 August 1935 in the Reich Ministry of Economics to discuss the practical solution to the Jewish question.[3]

Reichsbank President Dr Schacht presided over the meeting. [...][4]

Reichsbank President Schacht opened the meeting[5] and stated that the Jewish question is beginning to disrupt the economy, so that he has serious doubts regarding the accomplishment of the tasks he is responsible for. This situation, Dr Schacht explained, forces him to ask the heads of the other ministries to firstly give a general outline of their intentions and wishes with regard to the Jewish question, because the present anarchic

1 RGVA, 500k-1-379, fols. 75–85. This document has been translated from German.
2 The original contains handwritten changes and notes, including: 'SD', 'prepared and enclosed on 30 August, removed on 31 August 1935, Fir'. The draft was prepared on two typewriters.
3 On 13 August 1935 Schacht had invited all the departments to the conference on the grounds that the heightened struggle against Jewry was also affecting Aryan businessmen and workers, as well as the overall economic interests of the German people. In an express letter dated 15 August 1935, Schacht changed the meeting to a top-level conference because the issues to be addressed were of such significance for financial and economic policy: BArch, R 41/24, fols. 73–74. See Hartmannsgruber (ed.), *AdR*, part 2, vol. 2, p. 742, fn. 1.
4 The list of participants appears at this point in the original: Reich Minister of the Interior Frick, Reich Minister of Justice Gürtner, Prussian Minister of Finance Popitz, State Minister Gauleiter Adolf Wagner, State Secretary von Bülow (Reich Foreign Office), State Secretary Krohn (Reich Ministry of Labour), State Secretary Backe (Reich Ministry of Food and Agriculture), Reichsleiter Groß (Racial Policy Office of the NSDAP), Ministerial Director Haegert (Reich Ministry of Public Enlightenment and Propaganda), and SS-Gruppenführer Heydrich (Gestapa), as well as additional unnamed representatives of the Reich Ministry of the Interior, Reich Ministry of Justice, Ministry of Transport, Reich Foreign Office, staff of the Deputy of the Führer, Advertising Council for the German Economy, Reich commissioner for banking, and SD.
5 Additional transcripts of the meeting exist: Notes by Lösener (Reich Ministry of the Interior), BArch, R 1501/5513, fols. 3–4. Published in Hartmannsgruber (ed.), *AdR*, part 2, vol. 2, pp. 742–746. See also: Notes by Legation Counsellor Röhrecke (Reich Foreign Office), 21 August 1935, *Akten zur deutschen auswärtigen Politik 1918–1945*, series C: *1933–1937*, vol. 4, no. 1: *1. April bis 13. September 1935* (Göttingen: Vandenhoeck & Ruprecht, 1975), pp. 559–561.

state of affairs is making it impossible to resolve the economic issues incumbent upon him.

Next, Dr Schacht, citing several specific examples, went into the difficulties that the present way of handling the Jewish question is causing for the economic reconstruction of the Reich. He pointed out, among other things, that foreign diplomats have repeatedly been verbally harassed while in a Jewish-owned department store in the eastern part of the Reich, and that this very department store is one of the best providers of foreign currency. Gauleiter Streicher's demand that Jewish representatives of German firms abroad be recalled, he said, is an impossible one. These firms have been advised to get rid of their Jewish agents. However, this is utterly impossible, he said, because all world trade is in Jewish hands, so that when a Jewish representative abroad is eliminated, the foreign customer base is almost always lost to the German business, and these customers, along with the representatives who have been let go, switch over to the Jewish competitors.

Dr Schacht very sharply opposed the anti-vaccination articles in the newspaper edited by Gauleiter Streicher, *Volksgesundung aus Blut und Boden*,[6] and in so doing pointed out in particular that the German chemicals industry has suffered a colossal loss as a result of this publication. In addition, he said, it is madness to disparage the reputation of a prominent German scholar by making the bogus claim that this scholar (Dr Robert Koch)[7] was married to a woman who was half-Jewish.[8] The anti-Jewish riots, Dr Schacht continued, have also had a serious effect on business at the East Prussian Trade Fair. Also incomprehensible to him, he said, is the bathing ban on Jews that has been decreed in Leipzig.[9] If one expects commissions for German industry from the Jews at the fair, one must, after all, at least give them an opportunity to bathe somewhere.

Dr Schacht further explained that it is not just buying from Jews but also selling to Jews that is prohibited. This also includes selling groceries to Jews. 'I do not hesitate', Dr Schacht continued, 'to describe such a course of action as barbarity of the worst sort.'

'The antisemitic excesses have not only led to numerous suspensions of payments by Jewish businesses but have also resulted in a most alarming way in the redundancies among Aryan personnel. The German Labour Front has even threatened workers who dared to buy more cheaply from Jews with the loss of their jobs. This Jewish campaign is now spreading to the department stores as well, no matter if they are in Jewish or in Aryan hands. Here one can no longer speak of a struggle over world views; rather, only the crass competitive intentions of the NS-Hago are present here.'

---

6 The journal *Deutsche Volksgesundheit aus Blut und Boden: Gesundheitserziehung auf rassischer Grundlage*, edited by the Combat League for German Health Care and Racial Hygiene, was published twice a month in Nuremberg from Jan. 1933 to March 1935 and covered public health issues from a racial perspective. It advocated naturopathy and homeopathy, as well as the 'preservation of the purity of German blood', which it regarded as a central measure of healthcare policy.
7 Dr Robert Koch (1843–1910), physician and bacteriologist; awarded the Nobel Prize for Medicine in 1905.
8 The article Schacht criticized is 'Der Jude als Seuchenstifter: Wie Robert Koch beschnitten wurde' ('The Jew as Creator of Epidemics: How Robert Koch was Circumcised'), *Deutsche Volksgesundheit aus Blut und Boden*, no. 7, 1 April 1935, pp. 5–8.
9 Reich Economic Advisor Köhler had already intervened in opposition to the ban on use of public baths enacted by the city: see memorandum from the mayor of Leipzig, Haake, dated 8 August 1935, Stadtarchiv Leipzig, Ch. I/122, fol. 15.

Dr Schacht further stated that, contrary to the existing regulations of the Reich, the municipal authorities are switching over to neither awarding contracts to Jewish firms nor making purchases from them. In Riesa, he said, the local municipal authorities have ordered their officials not to buy in Jewish shops any longer, otherwise the most severe disciplinary punishments will be imposed on them. However, such an approach is simply grotesque, Schacht said, if one considers that central departments of the Reich, in particular the Reich Railways Administration, continually do business with Jewish firms because, above all, the timber trade is almost exclusively in Jewish hands.

Discussing the effects of such [anti-]Jewish measures on foreign countries, Dr Schacht emphasized that French buyers have cancelled a large order placed with the Salamander firm.[10] In addition, he said, it is virtually impossible to market German goods in South Africa. In a great many cases, he added, foreign purchasing agents have travelled on to Czechoslovakia because the anti-Jewish posters in Germany are not to their liking. English spa guests have left German spas in large numbers on account of the campaign against the Jews, and a large American central purchasing office recently transferred its headquarters from Berlin to Prague.

The effect of the antisemitic upsurge on the economy is catastrophic, he said. In addition, the negotiations that the Reich is now conducting with foreign countries are made far more difficult by it. Export today is based to only a small extent on the private initiative of the individual businessman, because the Reich Ministry of Economics has directly intervened in almost every instance as a result of the foreign exchange situation. The excesses brought about by irresponsible parties result in a refusal by foreign countries to deal with representatives of the Reich itself. In addition, the generosity of foreign countries, in particular advance deliveries, changes to contracts, and exchanges of goods, is severely threatened by the campaign against the Jews. In the case of the trade agreement negotiations with South America, the ministers of four countries are Jews who, citing the conditions prevailing in Germany, are reluctant to enter into further talks. In Poland, all trade is in Jewish hands. The upcoming negotiations with the United States will most probably fail, he said, given the mood that has been produced in America by the antisemitic riots. He, Dr Schacht, must therefore reserve the right to hold responsible for these effects the individuals who orchestrated these excesses.

Then Dr Schacht expressed his personal opinion, saying that he is of the opinion that the principles of the National Socialist programme are indeed correct and must be carried out without fail. 'I have', Dr Schacht explained, 'lived with Jews for thirty years and have taken their money from them for thirty years, but not vice versa. The present methods are nonetheless unsustainable. A system must be established amid the present methods, and until this system is put into practice, no other action should be taken.'

After that, Dr Schacht requested the representatives of the relevant departments in attendance to make their desires known and explain to him their thoughts regarding a legal regulation of the Jewish question, so that this question can be resolved as soon as possible through a regulation issued by the Reich government.

---

10 Shoe company founded by Jakob Sigle in Kornwestheim, Württemberg, in 1885.

Reich Minister Dr Frick stated that the Jewish question will be resolved slowly but surely in a completely legal way – and specifically, this will occur along the lines of the Party programme, to the effect that the Jewish alien body will be totally eliminated from the German people. The Jewish question, however, can never be solved by unauthorized actions on an individual basis, he said, for such measures merely delay the success of the National Socialists' reconstruction work. Reich Minister Dr Frick then declared that the Führer, through the Deputy of the Führer, has ordered that individual actions against Jews by members of the NSDAP and its organizations must cease without fail. Demonstrations against Jews may indeed be justified in a given case, but here there exists the great danger that dark elements will gain the upper hand and that then things will come to pass that the Party never intended, and for which it can never take responsibility. Therefore, he said, he has prepared a directive for all the regional governments and the Gestapo, according to which any individual action against Jews must cease, and anyone who takes part in such activity or incites it will be considered a provocateur and rebel. Action must be ruthlessly taken against such elements, and illegalities are to be prevented by the harshest means available to the police.[11] Besides the riots, he said, there are also other anti-Jewish boycott measures at present. These too ought to be prevented at all costs. In addition, there are laws already in preparation that are suitable for keeping Jewish influence under control. For example, the racial law is about to be finalized, and other measures, on which he did not want to elaborate at this juncture, are in the offing.

On government authorities awarding contracts to Jews, Dr Frick noted that the principle of parity of Aryans and non-Aryans in the economic sphere has so often been violated in practice that a new regulation of this matter must follow. But in the economy, too, the power of Jewry must slowly but organically and consistently be driven back, as has been done in the civil service and the arts. Therefore, he said, he cannot concur with the view of the Reichsbank President that there should be no Jewish question in the area of the economy. The stemming of Jewish influence in the economy must, however, come about in a legal way.

It is incomprehensible to him, he said, how news reports can damage the chemical industry to such an extent. These are actions that no level-headed person understands. The Führer, too, has come out sharply against such a course of action. As far as the bans on bathing are concerned, it is difficult to manage this question across the board. In an international trade city such as Leipzig, a bathing ban for Jews is certainly inappropriate. Putting up signs with messages along the lines of 'Jews are unwelcome here' or 'Jews enter this place at their own risk' can be arranged only in the closest concert with the Party. He will therefore turn to the Führer for clarification here. If the state, in this instance, were to ruthlessly require the removal of the signs, this would engender an insoluble conflict with the Party, which is impossible, given the unity of state and Party. In this matter, therefore, there must be the closest accord with the Party offices.

---

11 Circular decree (secret) from the Reich and Prussian Ministry of the Interior (III P 3710/59), Frick, to all regional governments and the Reich commissioner for the reintegration of the Saarland, dated 20 August 1935, expressing opposition to individual actions against Jews: BArch, R 1501/5513, fol. 2. Published in Landesarchivverwaltung Rheinland-Pfalz (ed.), *Dokumentation zur Geschichte der jüdischen Bevölkerung*, pp. 54–55.

State Minister Gauleiter Wagner[12] declared that there is unanimity of opinion that what has occurred of late with regard to the Jewish question in the Reich must be impossible in future. The Jewish question, which has always played a major role in the idea of National Socialism, *must* be resolved. The reason for the recent excesses, he said, is that there has not only been divergence between Party and state concerning the handling of the Jewish question; even in the individual departments in the Reich, conflicting opinions have been advocated. Our Volksgenossen, he said, have thoroughly endorsed the removal of the Jews from the civil service, the arts, and the universities. That is not all that is necessary, however. The Party thus demands that headway be made with the solution to the Jewish question in the economy as well. Because there has been no visible success in this area thus far, however, our Volksgenossen have taken matters into their own hands. The Reichsbank President rightly stated that the solution to this question must come about in a legal way. The legislator must take into account the opinion of the people. Should he fail to do so, illegal actions would be the inevitable result. Thus far, the Party and the Reich have emphasized only negative aspects, that is, the prohibition of riots. This negative activity, however, will not suffice in future. Rather, the Reich cabinet must make up its mind about what can be done in the area of the Jewish question, and what must expediently be done. If the public sees that at least something is being attempted in this area, the excesses will stop right away. It is wrong, however, if the legislature waits as long as it now has done, because it then undermines the authority of the state. It is therefore necessary for the legislation to anticipate the developments. He thus proposed the following:

(1) to ensure that the Jew is deprived of the potential to open new businesses,

(2) to instruct the public authorities to award their contracts mainly to Volksgenossen,

(3) to give preference to German rather than Jewish businesses in the allocation of foreign exchange.

It is self-evident, he said, that the entire solution to this question cannot come about all at once, but our Volksgenossen must at least see that endeavours are being made to move forward step by step. The Party is ready to play an active part in all issues that are likely to stem the Jewish influence in the field of the economy, even if only in small sectors. The Party, he continued, wishes the Reich to assume absolute leadership in this matter, and if the Reich makes an attempt to do so, it will have the Party's fullest support.

Dr Schacht welcomed these proposals and acknowledged that the Party does not wish to exert any pressure with respect to economic questions. Regarding proposal (1), he pointed out that, to all intents and purposes, there have been hardly any new businesses opened by Jews, and proposal (2) is already being put into practice. With respect to showing preference to Aryan businesses in the allocation of foreign exchange, however, Dr Schacht expressed doubts, saying that his experiences indicate that it is the Jew who brings in the most and cheapest foreign currency, and that Aryan businesses understand

---

12 Adolf Wagner (1890–1944), mining engineer; joined the NSDAP in 1922; took part in the Beer Hall Putsch in 1923; Gauleiter of Munich and Upper Bavaria, 1929–1944; from 1933 Bavarian minister of the interior and deputy minister president; from 1942 no longer carried out his duties because of illness.

foreignexchange speculation just as well as the Jews do. He declared himself nonetheless willing to subject proposals (1) and (2) to legislative scrutiny.¹³

*Minister of Finance Popitz*¹⁴ then pointed to the *Stürmer* agitation regarding State Lottery collectors and stated that the Prussian-South German Class Lottery has put the regulations of the Civil Service Law into effect in their entirety among its ticket sellers. Of 650 Jewish lottery collectors, only 16 are still in office today. The actions of the *Stürmer* are therefore not only completely unjustified but also apt to block a source of considerable income for the state. Minister Popitz then spoke out against the boycott measures that have been introduced in Prussian public baths and have led to an exodus of Jewish and foreign bathers in particular. Next, he pointed out that the Jewish boycott also has a substantial influence on state finances, in that sales in Jewish shops have decreased appreciably, so that these businesses are no longer able to pay their taxes and duties. He then protested against the general posting of signs such as 'Jews are not welcome here' and 'You enter this place at your own risk'. Such signs are childish, he said, if Jews are already living in the place in question. Here, a clear regulation must soon be made.

*Reich Minister of Justice Dr Gürtner*¹⁵ stated that the Racial Law will soon be promulgated.¹⁶ The solution, he said, will be found in the fact that when there is an intended marriage between a Jew and an Aryan, the Jewish race is to be regarded as a hindrance to the marriage. This regulation is to apply to full Jews and half-Jews. In addition, Reich Minister Gürtner pointed out that, by promulgation of a law, a line must be drawn with respect to the present lawless goings-on. It is regrettable, he said, that the state authority has already been undermined to the extent that definitive statements by leading figures are described by subordinate offices as being on paper only, while everyone regards himself as entitled to interpret the true meaning of the legislative order at his own discretion. 'There is', Reich Minister Dr Gürtner stated, 'no order that anyone believes to have the absolute weight of a mandate behind it.' It is essential that this matter is rectified.

*State Secretary von Bülow*¹⁷ requested urgently that the press should not publish the decree issued by Reich Minister Dr Frick.¹⁸ This decree, he said, would be interpreted by world Jewry as a success. Detrimental effects have also resulted from posting the sign 'German shop', because in so doing the question of how one must behave towards foreign shop-owners has arisen. A handicapping of foreign shopkeepers contravenes inter-

---

13 These points are not mentioned in the draft law of 9 Oct. 1935 that was presented by the Reich Ministry of the Interior in consultation with the Reich Ministry of Economics. See Doc. 205, 9 Oct. 1935.
14 Dr Johannes Popitz (1884–1945), lawyer; in 1914–1919 worked in the Prussian Ministry of the Interior and in 1919–1929 in the Prussian Ministry of Finance, where he was state secretary from 1925; became Reich minister in 1932 and acting head of the Prussian Ministry of Finance; from 1933 Prussian minister of finance; member of the NSDAP; in 1944 sentenced as complicit in the plot to assassinate Hitler on 20 July and executed in Berlin in Feb. 1945.
15 Dr Franz Gürtner (1881–1941), lawyer; from 1909 worked in the Bavarian Ministry of Justice; Bavarian minister of justice, 1922–1932; brought about the lifting of the ban on the NSDAP; Reich minister of justice, 1932–1941; joined the NSDAP in 1937; edited works including *Das kommende deutsche Strafrecht* (1934).
16 See Doc. 199, 15 Sept. 1935.

national agreements in most instances and results in serious disadvantages for German shops abroad. State Secretary von Bülow further pointed out that the rioting, in numerous instances, has affected foreigners who are not even Jews. Such incidents, he said, are apt to place the success of the Olympic Games in doubt. He therefore suggested that the posting of anti-Jewish signs in particular, with the Olympic Games in mind, could be regulated to the effect that such signs would be prohibited at places frequented by people attending the Olympics.

The representative of the Ministry of Transport pointed out that the anti-Jewish actions have resulted in a major loss of earnings in the field of transportation. For example, earnings have declined by 7 per cent in comparison with 1934. The shipping companies alone have thus far recorded a deficit of 1.5 million dollars.[19]

State Secretary Krohn[20] noted that the boycott is also affecting the labour force. In particular, numerous lay-offs have already been recorded as a result of the drop in Jewish business. Under the Law for the Regulation of National Labour, Jews are, even today, allowed to serve as works managers. This arrangement will continue, he added. Admittedly, he said, it is impossible for the Aryan personnel to set aside their pledge of loyalty to the Jewish works manager. To this end, therefore, an amendment of the law must take place in the near future.

State Secretary *Backe* pointed out that precisely in the fields in which there is a shortage of goods, Jews easily can be and will be eliminated. However, he said, he considers it questionable to regulate such a measure publicly, and suggested instead that this matter be handled silently, along the lines he proposes.

The representative of the minister of propaganda, Ministerial Director *Haegert*,[21] said that the antisemitic upsurge has been produced by the brazen behaviour of the Jews, who presumed to be rude even to the wife of a Reich minister on Kurfürstendamm. He, too, he said, is of the opinion that violent individual actions must be avoided. Nonetheless, he asked that the interpretation of such individual actions not be overly broadened, but rather

17 Dr Bernhard Wilhelm von Bülow (1885–1936), lawyer; in 1912–1919 and from 1923 worked in the Reich Foreign Office, where he was head of the Special Section for the League of Nations and, from 1930, state secretary.
18 See fn. 11.
19 As a result, a decree of the Reich Minister of Transport of 30 August 1935 stated that the use of public transport was for the time being not subject to any restrictions for Jews: BArch, R 3101/13862, fols. 542–543.
20 Dr Johannes Krohn (1884–1974), lawyer; worked from 1920 in the Reich Ministry of Labour, where he became head of the Department of Social Insurance and Social Welfare in 1932; from 1933 state secretary; from 1941 Reich commissioner for the handling of enemy assets in the Reich Ministry of Justice; chairman of the Federal Committee of Physicians and Health Insurance Companies, 1955–1968.
21 Wilhelm Haegert (1907–1994), lawyer; Freikorps member, 1923; joined the NSDAP and the SA in 1929; in 1931 became head of the Legal Protection Department of the Gau of Berlin; chief of staff of the NSDAP Reichsleitung for Propaganda; from 1933 head of Department II (Propaganda) in the Reich Ministry of Public Enlightenment and Propaganda; vice president of the Reich Literature Chamber, 1941; worked as a lawyer after 1945 in Berlin.

that those actions that are necessary for political propaganda reasons be allowed. In addition, he expressed his opinion to the effect that the riots will dwindle if our Volksgenossen see that the government is now seizing the initiative in the area of the Jewish question.

After that, much time in the discussion was taken up by the question of whether individual communities are allowed to put up antisemitic posters if such an ordinance is issued by the responsible bodies of the communities concerned. Here, the views of the Reich Ministry of Finance, Ministry of Transport, and Reich Ministry of Justice were on one side, and those of the Party on the other side. While the representatives of the Reich authorities pointed out that the Jewish policy guidelines might be determined by the Reich alone, with due regard given to the Führer principle, Gauleiter Wagner noted that it is incompatible with the National Socialist idea to suppress the justified antisemitic viewpoint of individual communities. After lengthy debate, agreement was achieved to the extent that the Reich will of course not prevent an anti-Jewish approach by individual communities if this is consonant with the overall objective.

In conclusion, SS-Gruppenführer Heydrich took the floor and stated that, as things stand now, the Gestapo always comes off badly, because it is obliged, if necessary, to proceed against Party comrades. Such a state of affairs, however, can be corrected in a practical way if two fundamental things are taken into account:

(1) legislative measures of the state that bring closer, step by step, the goal of stamping out the influence of the Jews, upon the instruction of the Führer, and

(2) a comprehensive political and ideological schooling and training of Party members and Volksgenossen with respect to the Jewish question, in combination with cast-iron Party discipline.

From the experience of the Political Police as an intelligence gathering point for the relevant Reich departments, SS-Gruppenführer Heydrich then urged that:

(1) beyond the banning of mixed marriages, race defilement also be punished as a crime;[22]

(2) the purchase and lease of land by Jews be prohibited, in acknowledgement of the fact that land is available only to Volksgenossen;

(3) legislation concerning the rights of Volksgenossen and citizens be proclaimed at once, applying a legal exemption for the Jews;[23]

(4) the Jews' freedom of movement be curtailed to the extent that they are prohibited, as much as possible, from moving into the large cities.

Whether and to what extent these proposals can be carried out in practice, [SS] Gruppenführer Heydrich stated, must, of course, be left to the relevant departments.[24]

Reichsbank President Dr Schacht welcomed these statements and added that he is in full agreement with the contents of items 1 to 3 and will subject them to legal scrutiny, but he considers item 4 worrying, if it were to amount in effect to a ghetto, but endorsed in principle the ban on taking up residence in large cities.

---

22 This demand was met by the so-called Law for the Protection of German Blood and German Honour, 15 Sept. 1935: see Doc. 199.
23 This demand was met by the Reich Citizenship Law, 15 Sept. 1935: see Doc. 198.
24 On the demands of the Gestapo Central Office (Gestapa), see Doc. 195, 9 Sept. 1935.

Towards 18.30, Reichsbank President Dr Schacht called the conference to a close, noting that additional discussions will follow shortly regarding the implementation of the practical responses to the questions addressed.[25]

DOC. 190

On 22 August 1935 Walter Kühne's section in the Reich Ministry of Finance airs proposals for tax discrimination against Jews[1]

Memorandum from the Reich Ministry of Finance, section headed by Kühne,[2] Berlin, dated 22 August 1935[3]

Re: tax treatment of non-Aryans.[4]

A. *Wealth tax.*

1. *Public* corporations are not subject to the wealth tax (sole exception: public credit institutions). Accordingly, the Jewish religious associations, which under national law are indeed public corporations everywhere, cannot be subjected to the wealth tax. There are two ways of imposing the wealth tax on them:

(a) by amending the wealth tax in such a way that the Jewish religious associations are singled out as being liable for tax; such an exemption for *one* taxpayer would be flawed;

(b) by withdrawing the status of public corporation through a measure taken by the Reich Ministry of the Interior. Such a measure would probably be in keeping with the times anyway. It would automatically result in imposition of the wealth tax on the religious association.[5]

2. Enterprises that pursue solely and directly charitable, benevolent, or church-related aims are not subject to the wealth tax. The terms 'charitable', 'benevolent', and

---

25 On 23 Sept. 1935 Reich Minister of the Interior Frick and Reichsbank President Schacht discussed restrictions for Jews in the economy: memorandum dated 23 Sept. 1935, in Hartmannsgruber (ed.), *AdR*, part 2, vol. 2, pp. 800–802.

1 BArch, R 2/56014, fols. 9–14. This document has been translated from German.
2 Dr Walter Kühne (1892–1962), lawyer; worked in 1921–1923 for the Berlin-Steglitz Tax Office and in 1923–1938 at the Reich Ministry of Finance, where he was a specialist in taxes and assets; head of the Cologne Regional Tax Office, 1938–1945; in 1949–1952 at the Federal Ministry of Finance, Special Division for Equalization of Burdens (*Lastenausgleich*), finally as Ministerialdirigent; president of the Federal Equalization of Burdens Office, 1953–1957.
3 The original contains several handwritten annotations.
4 The memorandum can be traced back to the directive issued by the Reich Ministry of Finance after the top-level conference on 20 August 1935 in the Reich Ministry of Economics, stating that opportunities for tax discrimination should be examined in all departments. See also the memorandum from Blümich's section regarding measures against non-Aryans in the area of income tax, 22 August 1935, BArch, R 2/56014, fols. 2–3. Abridged version in Friedenberger, Gössel, and Schönknecht (eds.), *Die Reichsfinanzverwaltung*, doc. 104, p. 263.
5 The Income Tax Section of the Reich Ministry of Finance had also proposed this measure: see ibid. In March 1938 Jewish communities lost their status as public corporations and the associated tax advantages: Law on the Legal Status of the Jewish Religious Communities, 28 March 1938, *Reichsgesetzblatt*, 1938, I, p. 338.

'church-related' are explained in greater detail in §§ 17 and 19 of the Tax Adjustment Law.[6] Accordingly, the question of whether an aim is *charitable* is to be evaluated on the basis of the opinions of the national community. *Church-related* aims are solely those pursued in order to promote a *Christian* religious association under public law. Accordingly, enterprises that benefit the Jewish race exclusively are not granted exemption from the perspective of charitable or church-related aims. With regard to *benevolent* aims, however, there is a grey area. These are, under § 18 of the Tax Adjustment Law, those that are focused on supporting 'needy persons who are located *in this country* or needy German Volksgenossen who are located *abroad*'. The wording of this suggests that the purely Jewish so-called 'charitable foundations' (such as Jewish institutions for the blind) also fall under it. One could challenge this only with reference to § 1 of the Tax Adjustment Law, under which the tax laws are to be construed on the basis of National Socialist ideology.[7] The same applies to corporation tax.

3. Housing and residential associations that are specifically recognized are exempt from the wealth tax under § 4 of the Implementing Regulations to the Wealth Tax Law.[8] Can the exemption be linked to the requirement that no Jews should live in the residences of the associations that benefit? The same applies to corporation tax.

4. Under §§ 5 to 7 of the Implementing Regulations to the Wealth Tax Law, pension and benevolent funds of a certain kind, if they have legal capacity, are exempted from the wealth tax. Can this exemption be rescinded for cases in which the fund belongs to a non-Aryan operation or in which non-Aryans are included among the individuals who are to benefit from the payments of the fund? The same applies to corporation tax.

5. Under §§ 62 and 74 of the Reich Valuation Law,[9] the debts are to be deducted from the assets. These also include tax debts. Even if Jewish religious associations lose their legal status as public corporations and become private associations, the overdue association contributions would be deductible unless there is a special regulation.

6. Should the intercorporate privilege[10] be denied to corporations that are in Jewish hands? The same applies to corporation tax.

7. Insurance policies are exempt from the wealth tax if their value does not exceed RM 5,000, or if they were concluded in relation to an employment or service contract. One might consider giving this advantage only to Aryans or limiting it to cases in which the insurance company is purely Aryan.

8. Cars, motor yachts, and sailing yachts are exempt from the wealth tax regardless of their value, if they are manufactured in this country. One might consider declaring these items always to be taxable if owned by non-Aryans, or making the tax exemption subject to the items' being manufactured not only in this country but also by Aryan companies.

---

6 *Steueranpassungsgesetz*, 16 Oct. 1934, *Reichsgesetzblatt*, 1934, I, pp. 925–941.
7 § 1: see ibid., p. 925. In the amended version of the Tax Adjustment Law (1 Dec. 1936), in § 18(1) the words 'needy persons in this country or needy German Volksgenossen abroad' are replaced with the words 'needy German Volksgenossen': *Reichsgesetzblatt*, 1936, I, p. 977.
8 Wealth Tax Law (*Vermögensteuergesetz*), 16 Oct. 1934, Implementing Regulations, *Reichsgesetzblatt*, 1934, I, p. 1056.
9 *Reichsbewertungsgesetz*, 16 Oct. 1934, *Reichsgesetzblatt*, 1934, I, p. 1035.
10 An intercorporate tax privilege is a benefit for corporations that are participants in other taxable enterprises. In order to prevent multiple taxation, they do not have to pay any commercial tax or wealth tax on earnings from such participations under certain conditions.

B. Inheritance (or gift) tax.

1. Spouses are not subject to inheritance tax if, at the time the tax liability arises, children from the marriage or equivalent persons are alive. One might consider treating the accrual to the non-Aryan spouse in accordance with § 17a(3) of the Inheritance Tax Law issued in 1934. Under this provision there is no tax exemption for the spouse in instances where only limited tax liability exists.[11]

2. If full tax exemption for the acquisition by the spouse does not arise, he or she benefits from a tax exemption of 30,000 Reichsmarks. The acquisition by the children and equivalent persons benefits from the same tax exemption. Grandchildren and other descendants are entitled to a tax-free sum of 10,000 Reichsmarks. These advantages do not apply, and only a taxation limit of 500 Reichsmarks is possible, in instances where only the limited tax liability applies. One might consider treating the non-Aryan spouses, children, and grandchildren in general according to this limitation. One would have to reconsider the extent to which the utilization of individual tax exemptions from among the numerous ones available under § 18 of the Inheritance Tax Law might be excluded for non-Aryan applicants. In particular, the exemptions for donations to domestic churches, church-related, charitable, and non-profit foundations, and other special-purpose assets, and to pension and other benevolent funds (§ 18 Nos. 15, 18, 19, Inheritance Tax Law) are to be taken into consideration. In this regard, reference is made to the statements under A, items 2 and 4.

C. Property tax.

1. In accordance with the Property Tax Framework Law, the Jewish houses of worship are exempt from property tax. The Property Tax Framework Law has been introduced only in Mecklenburg.[12] The same legal situation, however, will exist under the provisions of almost all the states. One might consider rescinding the property tax exemption for synagogues. The valuation of such buildings, however, would cause certain difficulties.[13]

2. Under the Property Tax Framework Law, public burial sites are exempt from property tax. The same thing should probably apply to all the states under the property tax regulation. One might consider excluding Jewish burial sites.

---

11 Inheritance Tax Law in the version of the law dated 16 Oct. 1934: *Reichsgesetzblatt*, 1934, I, p. 1056.

12 The Property Tax Framework Law constituted Chapter II of the third part of the Regulation of the Reich President for the Protection of the Economy and Finance, 1 Dec. 1930. § 3 stipulated that taxable items used by religious associations under public law were exempt from the property tax: *Reichsgesetzblatt*, 1930, I, p. 517, here p. 532. At the request of the states, the law's entry into force was postponed by a regulation of 17 Feb. 1932; only in Mecklenburg-Schwerin did the law come into effect on 1 April 1932: *Reichsgesetzblatt*, 1932, I, p. 73.

13 In Baden the Minister of Finance and Economics rescinded by administrative order 'the exemption of the synagogues from the property and special buildings tax' as of 1 April 1936. This was mentioned in a letter from the Baden State Chancellery to the Reich Minister of Church Affairs, dated 7 July 1937: Paul Sauer (ed.), *Dokumente über die Verfolgung der jüdischen Bürger in Baden-Württemberg durch das nationalsozialistische Regime 1933–1945*, vol. 1 (Stuttgart: W. Kohlhammer, 1966), pp. 312–313.

Regarding (1) and (2) the State of Hesse has enacted a law on the property tax this year, which already constitutes action in this field.¹⁴

D. *Newly constructed residential buildings.*
Under the Second Law for the Reduction of Unemployment, small apartments and private residential buildings constructed after 31 March 1934 are exempt, under certain conditions, from the wealth tax, income tax, state property tax, and half of the municipal property tax.¹⁵

Questions:
(a) Small apartments: is the exemption of small apartments to be denied if either the owner is a non-Aryan or the tenants are non-Aryans?
(b) Private residential buildings: is the exemption of private residential buildings to be denied if the owner is a non-Aryan?

Note on A to D:
It must be pointed out that every measure requiring the verification of the Aryan status of individuals for tax purposes represents a complication of the tax law. The more numerous the cases become in which such verification would have to be undertaken, the more concerns arise. Besides, it would have to be decided to what extent the verification is to be carried out, in particular if every person in question would have to present baptismal certificates all the way back to their grandparents.

DOC. 191

On 25 August 1935 the historian Willy Cohn reports on the situation of an acquaintance living in a mixed marriage¹

Handwritten diary of Willy Cohn, entry for 25 August 1935

Breslau, Sunday. Yesterday morning gave Kleemann a lesson; I was so weakened that I had to spend much of the day lying down. In the morning dictated correspondence to Trudi, letters to both boys.² There was also satisfactory news from Wölfl.³ He is diligent, as always. Went with Trudi to the post office, before that to the barber's, then sat on a bench with Trudi and talked about books. In the afternoon, lay down until 6 and also read the *Jüdische Rundschau*. Heartening, the reports from the Zionist Congress.⁴ Ger-

---

14 In Hesse the word 'Christian' was added before the words 'religious associations' in Articles 2 and 3 of the Law Regarding the Property Tax and Special Buildings Tax for Properties Serving Religious Purposes, 11 Nov. 1935. The law entered into force retroactively as of 1 April 1935: *Hessisches Regierungsblatt*, no. 18, 21 Nov. 1935, p. 189.
15 *Zweites Gesetz zur Verminderung der Arbeitslosigkeit*, 21 Sept. 1933, *Reichsgesetzblatt*, 1933, I, p. 651.

1 Willy Cohn, 'Tagebuch Breslau August 1935', fols. 49–52; CAHJP, P 88/65. Abridged English translation in: Cohn, *No Justice in Germany*, p. 80. This document has been retranslated from the original German.
2 The reference is to Willy's sons from his first marriage. Wolfgang had been studying in Paris since 1933, while Ernst (b. 1919) had emigrated to Palestine in 1935 with a youth certificate.
3 Nickname for Wolfgang Cohn.

many, of course, was not represented among the diplomats in attendance at the congress. Especially insightful was the speech by the member of the Swiss National Council, who compared the Jews' fight for freedom to that of the Germans!⁵ And the reports from Germany stand in such screaming contrast to that. Everywhere, new verbal abuse of our people and strangulation of all living space.⁶

If there are still Jews in Germany who lack the sense of honour to perceive this, because they still have some earnings, it is indeed a disgrace!

In the evening, went for a walk with Trudi. First sat in the Sauerbrunn,⁷ then ran into my former colleague Lebeck with his wife. What these people who live in a racially mixed marriage, and their children, have to endure even goes beyond our lot. Because he has a wife of Jewish origin, he himself is not even permitted to teach German in the lower year groups. He anticipates that when the Jewish pupils are removed from the school,⁸ he too will be released. His children have no idea at all where they belong, and they are stripped of every possibility for the future. He himself is spied upon from all sides.

How many destinies have been destroyed in this way! All this is inhumanly cruel!

Around 10 p.m. we were back home. Slept well, but nonetheless I'm always very listless in the morning. Today I'm also doing a guided tour through the Jewish Museum.

DOC. 192

In late August/early September 1935 a citizen of Leipzig writes to Mayor Haake with suggestions for the further marginalization of the city's Jews¹

Undated letter from E. Müller with undated newspaper clipping²

'Benches for Aryan Spa Guests' in Poland

dnb³ Warsaw, 7 July. The awakening racial consciousness of the Polish people is asserting itself in all areas of public life. After the attempt by numerous associations and professional organizations to introduce the Aryan Paragraph, a directive from the spa management

---

4 The Nineteenth Zionist Congress was held in Lucerne from 20 August to 3 Sept. 1935. The *Jüdische Rundschau* devoted six pages to its opening: *Jüdische Rundschau*, 23 August 1935, pp. 1–6.
5 In the speech published in the *Jüdische Rundschau*, the member of the National Council referred to the Swiss people, not to the Germans: ibid., p. 3. National Council member Dr Heinrich Walther (1862–1954) had praised Theodor Herzl as a great visionary in his speech. At the end of his opening address, he emphasized that, as the Swiss had fought for their freedom for centuries, they understood and supported the 'longing of another people for liberation': ibid.
6 In the same issue, under the heading 'Ausschlüsse und Verbote' ('Exclusions and Bans'), the *Jüdische Rundschau* reported on anti-Jewish measures in more than twenty different places: ibid., p. 11.
7 A park in Breslau.
8 Only two weeks later, Reich Minister of Education Rust issued his decree concerning the segregation of Jewish school pupils from non-Jewish ones: see Doc. 196, 10 Sept. 1935.

1 Stadtarchiv Leipzig, Chap. I/122, fol. 26. This document has been translated from German.
2 The approximate dating of the document to sometime between 27 August and 9 Sept. 1935 is based on its place in the chronologically organized file.
3 Deutsches Nachrichtenbüro: German News Agency.

in *Szczewnica*,[4] a very well-known resort town in Poland, has aroused great alarm in Jewish circles. In the spa park, the spa management has reserved a number of *benches 'exclusively for Aryan resort guests'*. The Jews regard this innovation as the first step towards the introduction of recreation areas in Poland that are 'free of Jews'.[5]

[Dear Mayor] Haake,[6]

Forgive me, a Volksgenosse, for encroaching on your valuable working hours, but as you are well known as *energetic* and *understanding* and as a tireless fighter for the goals of our Führer, I am turning to you personally on behalf of all concerned.

The enclosed report, which I took from an East Prussian newspaper, reminded me of the nuisance caused in the *Rosental*[7] by the local *Jews*, who still believe that they can lay claim to special rights. Everyone complains that the majority of the benches are appropriated by the sons and daughters of Israel, who do not waver and give way when 'Aryans' want to sit down, so a secret struggle always flares up between the two groups, with the ultimate outcome being that the insolent and hard-boiled 'Yids' are victorious. Granted, the Jews are also taxpayers and the Rosental is a public park, but the assumption of rights must not go so far that the Jews feel 'at home' there.

The situation is the same on the sports fields, for example, the grounds of the 1867 Gymnastics and Athletics Field. On fine summer days, Jews sit with their relatives in the little garden of the small lunchroom and 'bask' in the sun. But if the city baths are off limits to them, it ought to be impossible for them to make themselves at home elsewhere. Like everywhere here in Leipzig, one finds that friendliness to the Jews is still quite widespread. Many housewives thus complain, for example, that Jews are served far more cordially in various shops on *Frankfurterstraße* and *Waldstraße*. I myself have frequently had to make the same observation. Even though I myself am a 'feisty sort' and do not put up in any way with abuses from this 'race' and duly rebuff them at once, the majority of our Volksgenossen, unfortunately, are still not thus forearmed and hence complain at an inappropriate moment or not at all. In any event, those who live in the same building as Jews also complain about their impertinent behaviour. Would it not be possible to assign these people only certain buildings to live in and thereby create a ghetto, as was customary in the Middle Ages, where they would then be completely among themselves?

Although I am not a Party member, I am one of those Volksgenossen who stand steadfastly by our Führer, and for this reason, too, I am outraged by the 'manners' of the Hebrews.

Heil Hitler!

---

4 Correctly: Szczawnica.
5 This is the text of a newspaper clipping that has been stuck to the top left-hand corner of the letter.
6 In the original, the salutation is partially obscured by the newspaper clipping.
7 A city park in Leipzig.

DOC. 193

On 7 September 1935 the Reich Railways ask its agencies to take action against the posting of anti-Jewish signs on Reich Railways premises[1]

Circular letter from the German Reich Railways, Central Administration (47 Lg), director general, signed Dorpmüller,[2] to the Reich Railways divisions, for information to the Reich Railways Central Accounting Office, Berlin, dated 7 September 1935 (copy)[3]

Copy for information and attention. Accordingly, signs with the wording 'Jews Not Welcome' or similar content that are directed against the use of public transport facilities by Jews are not to be tolerated in Reich Railways areas. If NSDAP offices order such signs to be put up and threaten to take measures in the event of non-compliance with the order, we request that you contact the appropriate NSDAP Gauleiter, making reference to the Reich Railways' legal duty of transport and to the above-mentioned decree of the Reich and Prussian Minister of Transport,[4] and work towards a retraction of these instructions and towards ensuring that no job discrimination occurs against persons involved in the operation of travel services.

Addendum for the Reich Railways Division of Stettin:

The report from 27 August 1935 (13 Lg 12 Lgw) is hereby settled.[5]

---

1 BArch, R 3101/13862, fol. 542. This document has been translated from German.
2 Doctor of Engineering h.c. Julius Heinrich Dorpmüller (1869–1945); railway and highway engineer in Germany and China, 1893–1917; president of the Reich Railways divisions of Oppeln and Essen, 1922–1926; director general of the German Reich Railways, 1926–1945; in 1933 chairman of the advisory board of the firm Reichsautobahnen (Reich Motorways); Reich minister of transport, 1937–1945.
3 This document was sent to the head of the Economic Group for the Catering and Hospitality Industry, with reference to a letter of 14 August 1935 (IIf/3032/35 Kro/Ho). The copy comes from the Reich Ministry of Economics (received on 4 Oct. 1935) and contains several handwritten annotations.
4 The decree reproduced earlier in the original, though not printed here, was issued by Reich Minister of Transport Baron Paul von Eltz-Rübenach on 30 August 1935 in response to an official letter from the Reich Railways dated 23 August 1935. It stated that so long as Jews were not legally prohibited from using public transport and the associated services (station bars and restaurants, sales kiosks), all travellers, without distinction of race and nationality, would be granted unrestricted access to the facilities intended for them: BArch, R 3101/13862, fol. 542. Hitler was informed of the circular: note, dated 5 Sept. 1935 on the original Reich Minister of Transport circular dated 30 August 1935 (copy for the head of the Reich Chancellery), BArch, R 43 II/602, fol. 189.
5 This report could not be found.

DOC. 194

On 7 September 1935 a colleague assembles material for Reichsbank President Hjalmar Schacht concerning future burdens on the economy due to Jewish emigration[1]

Reichsbank memorandum for Hjalmar Schacht, submitted by W., on 7 September 1935[2]

A mass emigration of Jews represents a serious bloodletting of the German economic organism.[3]

It is not possible to have mass emigration without substantial amounts of capital being taken away. Impoverished Jews find no accommodation in other countries. We have therefore been forced to make substantial foreign exchange sacrifices for the emigration of the Jews. In 1932 all the foreign exchange offices in the Reich made RM 2.2 million available to seventy-eight emigrating families. In 1933 and 1934 the desire to emigrate rose to unprecedented levels. Despite the tightening of the foreign exchange situation, in these two years the foreign exchange offices had to make RM 118 million available to a total of 13,000 families. Of that amount, around two thirds were in actual foreign currency, with around one third available by means of bank clearing, removal of goods, and other forms of substitute transfer. Experience shows that more than 90 per cent of it was accounted for by non-Aryans.

It is well known that considerably more than 13,000 Jewish families have emigrated. *The headcount for the Jewish emigrants is estimated at around 75,000.* These multitudes are unlikely to have gone abroad without means. Sizeable amounts of Jewish assets must have been illegally shifted into foreign countries. There are plenty of ways. In practical terms, it is scarcely possible to prevent a Jew from selling his merchandise to someone abroad, emigrating, and collecting the money due him once he is outside the country. It is difficult to prevent Jews from taking mark notes or securities over the border in the dead of night. We also cannot place an official auditor at the side of every Jewish firm, to be on guard lest it try to assemble a fortune abroad by issuing false invoices and the like. In addition, Jewish emigration burdens us with a sizeable new foreign debt. All the credit balances left behind in this country by the emigrants turn into debts owed abroad by the German economy, and some day they must be converted into cash, so long as we refrain from a general expropriation of the emigrants' assets.

---

1 BArch, R 2501/6992, fols. 300–302. This document has been translated from German.
2 The original contains a handwritten addition: 'Respectfully submitted to the President. W 7.9.'
3 This draft was used as preparation for a speech by Schacht, which in a revised version of 14 August 1935 contained statements on general questions, the foreign exchange situation and its repercussions for foreign indebtedness, the effect of Jewish emigration on the economy, the import of goods required under trade policy, and the repercussions of antisemitic propaganda for the big banks: material dated 7 Sept. 1935 for the address at the Nuremberg rally, BArch, R 2501/6992, fol. 261. Schacht spoke twice at Nuremberg. In his first speech, at the Third Annual Congress of the German Labour Front on 14 Sept. 1935, he evidently did not deal with the topic discussed here: *Völkischer Beobachter* (northern German edition), 15 Sept. 1935, pp. 7–9. In a speech to the Gauleiter and Gau economic advisors, by his own admission, he criticized 'Party attacks' on Jews. It remains unclear whether he used the text printed here in the speech: Hjalmar Schacht, *76 Jahre meines Lebens* (Bad Wörishofen: Kindler und Schiermeister, 1953), pp. 443–444.

And what has been accomplished by this sacrifice? The emigration of approximately 75,000 Jews, while six times that number of full Jews still live in Germany, not to mention the 75, 50, and 25 per cent non-Aryans.

This much is clear: the toughened policy against the Jews will bring about a new wave of Jewish emigration and thus a considerable deterioration of the foreign exchange balance, even if we decline all direct allocation of foreign exchange. That means a corresponding complication of the procurement of raw materials. The German economy is unable today to sustain a forced emigration of the Jews. Economic self-preservation therefore demands authoritatively that we take things easier with regard to the Jewish question. Tidy solutions will not be economically sustainable until we sense an appreciable easing of the burden on our foreign-exchange balance. The entire Jewish question will have been significantly simplified by then. As a result of the marked emigration of young workers, around half of the full Jews living in Germany today are already over the age of 45. The Jewish question in Germany would perhaps be resolvable over the course of one or two generations in this way, by means of the emigration of young workers.

DOC. 195

On 9 September 1935 the Gestapo Central Office outlines to Reich Minister Walther Darré its own proposals for the 'solution of the Jewish question'[1]

Letter from the Gestapo Central Office (II 1 B 2-68224/J 1057/35), p.p. Dr Best, to the Reich and Prussian Minister of Food and Agriculture (received on 14 September 1935), dated 9 September 1935[2]

Re: proposals for the solution to the Jewish question.[3]

With reference to the departmental conference in the Reich Ministry of Economics on 20 August 1935,[4] allow me to submit my proposals now in written form.

In my opinion, the Jewish question cannot be solved by the use of force, maltreatment of individuals, damage to personal property, or other individual actions. Its settlement appears possible only by curbing, step by step, the influence of the Jews in the course of the organic reconstruction of the Reich and by having the Party and the press concurrently begin intensified public enlightenment measures.

Just as the influence of the Jews has been almost totally eliminated in the administration, the civil service, the arts, and cultural affairs, it must be curtailed in all other branches of public life. In view of the excesses of the recent past, I consider it essential that the principle of equality be renounced precisely in the area of private enterprise too, and I am convinced that the individual actions in the country will subside at the moment

---

1 BArch, R 3601/1860, fols. 105–110. This document has been translated from German.
2 The letter was also received via express mail the same day by the Reich Ministry of Justice, the Reich Ministry of Economics, the Reich Ministry of the Interior, the Reich Ministry of Public Enlightenment and Propaganda, Göring, the Deputy of the Führer, and the Plenipotentiary of the Führer for Economic Matters, W. Keppler: published in Wildt (ed.), *Die Judenpolitik des SD*, doc. 3, pp. 70–73.
3 The original contains a handwritten note by Reich Minister Walther Darré: 'Pace and extent of the suppression of Jewry is to be decided solely by the Führer, 25/9 Darré'.
4 On this see Doc. 189, 20 August 1935.

when our Volksgenossen see that the dominant position in the economy thus far occupied by the Jews has been destroyed.

Considering that the Jews, according to National Socialist principles, are not classified as part of the German Volksgemeinschaft, I regard their placement under the law for resident aliens as essential. This measure alone would offer sufficient opportunity to hinder them from open competition in the economy, end their freedom of movement, and separate them from the German Volksgemeinschaft.

However, should the placement of the Jews under the law for resident aliens be impracticable for particular reasons, allow me to put forward the following proposals for the legal regulation of this question:

(1) To stem the further influx of Jews to the big cities, an amendment of the Law on Freedom of Movement[5] is necessary, one that makes it difficult for them to change their place of residence within the country. In the amendment, it would have to be pointed out that this measure is in no way intended to result in the creation of a ghetto. It would serve merely to prevent a concentration of the Jewish element in the large cities. Owing to the possibility of better concealment there, this element constitutes a danger and a lasting source of unrest.

(2) Prohibition of mixed marriages between Germans and Jews. Until recently, Volksgenossen have evinced an intention to marry Jews, in misapprehension of the racial problem and despite the grave consequences that arise for them from this decision. A prohibition on mixed marriage could serve to preserve racially valuable parts of the Volksgemeinschaft.[6]

(3) In connection with the banning of mixed marriages, a legal regulation that provides for the punishment of extramarital sexual intercourse between Germans and Jews appears necessary.

If, when marriage between Germans and Jews is contemplated, Jewish ethnicity is regarded as an impediment to marriage, the contracting of marriage is essentially ruled out. However, after marriage has been prevented, the partners often try to live together without marrying, in order to circumvent the ban on mixed marriages. Through a legal order that makes extramarital sexual intercourse between them a punishable offence – race defilement – the police authorities would be given a lever for effectively preventing extramarital relationships between Jewish men and German women and girls who are lost to their own kind.

(4) Public-sector contracts ought not to be awarded to Jews.

Experience has shown that cash-rich Jewish firms, even when there are obvious financial losses in the solicitation of contracts from the public sector, seek to undercut

---

[5] The Law on Freedom of Movement dated back to 1867 and permitted members of the North German Confederation to move about freely and establish their residence within the confederation. This law was taken over as a law of the German Empire after its constitution came into effect on 1 Jan. 1871.
[6] This demand and the one that follows were met by the Law for the Protection of German Blood and German Honour passed on 15 Sept. 1935: see Doc. 199.

their Aryan competitors and to strengthen their position in the economy through such rock-bottom bids. To protect the German economy, legal measures are needed, ones that prohibit the authorities from awarding contracts by proxy to Jewish firms and disguised Jewish firms.

(5) To the extent that licences are required for commercial undertakings, in principle, they ought not to be granted to Jews in coming years. Existing licences ought to be reviewed and a strict standard applied to determine whether the Jewish owners still comply with the licensing regulations with respect to personnel and substance. If necessary, proceedings for withdrawal of the licence would have to be instituted. Also, through corresponding legal regulation, one would have to ensure that the Jews are forbidden from opening new commercial undertakings not requiring a licence, for example, shops. In particular, I regard as very dangerous the granting to Jews of trade licences for travelling salesmen in the present large number, because the Jews, as intellectual opponents of the state, spread atrocity reports when they visit their customers in the rural countryside.

(6) In principle, owning and dealing in land, as well as the right to its use, must be left solely to our Volksgenossen. Because the Jews are not part of the Volksgemeinschaft, they must be eliminated as completely as possible from the leasing or purchasing of land or plots of land. The acquisition of land by Jews through a legal transaction and lease or rental, therefore, would have to be prohibited.

During the years of inflation, a substantial part of the property in big cities passed into Jewish ownership. Many of these Jewish landlords are in foreign countries, where the rent, undiminished, is transferred to them, while their properties deteriorate. I thus consider it necessary to direct the attention of the building authorities to this state of affairs and to campaign for a regulation that makes possible the drastic renovation, if not the dispossession, of these properties at the expense of the Jews living abroad, so that Volksgenossen are accommodated in conditions fit for human habitation.

(7) If placement under the law for resident aliens does not seem practicable, I regard as necessary at least a change to the Passport Announcement, explicitly ordering that issuance of a passport be denied in principle to all Jews, on grounds of political unreliability. Exceptions to this might be made only if it is proved that they use the passport for trips that are in the interest of the German economy.[7] This passport would have to be furnished with a special, conspicuous distinguishing mark for the external identification of the holder's race.[8]

---

[7] A decree issued by the Karlsruhe Gestapo on 11 Sept. 1935 stipulated that Jews would henceforth only be issued with passports for travel abroad when this was economically necessary, and such passports would have limited validity: Sauer (ed.), *Dokumente über die Verfolgung*, part 2 (Stuttgart: W. Kohlhammer, 1966), doc. 353, p. 108. With the circular decree of 16 Nov. 1937, the Reichsführer SS introduced a ban throughout the Reich on Jews being issued with passports for travel abroad, except in cases of emigration or trips in the economic interest of Germany: Walk (ed.), *Das Sonderrecht für die Juden im NS-Staat*, p. 205.

[8] With the implementation of the Regulation on Passports for Jews (5 Oct. 1938), Jews' passports were marked with a 'J': *Reichsgesetzblatt*, 1938, I, p. 1342.

I view this regulation as necessary because the Jews, especially in recent times, have applied in large numbers for passports, the issuance of which was permissible under the existing provisions. They used the passports for trips abroad, during which they moved money illegally and contributed substantially to the spreading of atrocity reports.

I believe that legislation along the lines of these observations can definitely be expected to result in a calming of the German economy, and the framing of such arrangements in legal terms would be gratefully received among our Volksgenossen as a meaningful step towards the settlement of the Jewish question. This attack on the dominant position of the Jews in the economy would, on the other hand, serve to guide them towards Zionism and effectively encourage them to emigrate.

DOC. 196
On 10 September 1935 the German News Agency comments on the decree of Reich Minister Bernhard Rust ordering the creation of separate schools for Jewish children[1]

Mitteilungen des Deutschen Nachrichtenbüros G.m.b.H, printed as a manuscript, from the afternoon edition, vol. 2, Berlin, 1935, no. 1372, dated Tuesday 10 September 1935

Establishment of Jewish Schools in Germany.

Berlin, 10 September. Reich Minister *Rust* has made an energetic start on a long-standing National Socialist demand by issuing a decree concerning the separation of races in state schools. In the decree, surveys to determine the race of the school pupils are prescribed as preparation for the creation of Jewish schools as of Easter 1936.[2]

This decree, drafted in close concert with the NSDAP Racial Policy Office, establishes another important phase in the racial legislation of the new Germany and proves that Germany is by no means inclined, as foreign press commentaries allege, to give up its fundamental racial viewpoint. Our objective, the total separation of Jewry from the German sphere of life, is unalterably clear and has already been implemented in various areas (civil service legislation, hereditary farm law, etc.).

In order to accomplish this objective in primary schools, the *grouping together* of those *non-Aryan schoolchildren* who belong to the Jewish religion in separate Jewish primary schools has already been promoted vigorously. Specifically, with state approval, a sizeable number of *private Jewish primary schools* have been newly created since 1934.[3]

The *decisive* aspect, however, is not *belonging* to the Jewish religion but rather *to the Jewish race*. The Jewish pupil, a pupil of a foreign race, constitutes an alien element in the classroom community of Aryan pupils and teachers. His existence is an extraordinary

---

1 BArch, R 43 II/602, fol. 190r–v. This document has been translated from German.
2 Circular decree from the Reich Minister of Education (file ref. E II e Nr. 1953/35) to the education authorities of the states (with the exception of Prussia), 10 Sept. 1935, *Reichsministerialblatt*, no. 27, 16 Sept. 1935.
3 Such as the Kaliski Private School in Berlin: see Doc. 306, 9 Nov. 1937.

impediment to the German-minded National Socialist teaching and renders impossible the requisite rapport, founded on race, between teacher, pupil, and subject matter. The new decree of Reich Minister of Education Rust therefore aspires to *implement a total separation of races* in the primary schools, regardless of the religious affiliation of the racially foreign Jewish pupils, and also to reconstitute the Jewish schools. For both groups he fulfils what is a self-evident requirement from a völkisch perspective: *community of race between teacher and pupil.*

The decree of the Reich Minister of Education communicates the following information:

> A key prerequisite for all fruitful educational work is racial conformity between teacher and pupil. Children of Jewish descent constitute a serious impediment to the homogeneity of the classroom community and the smooth implementation of National Socialist youth education in the general state schools. The spot checks made thus far, at my order, in a few parts of Prussia have shown that the state primary schools are still attended to a significant extent by Jewish pupils. This is chiefly the case in the larger cities; however, in the rural countryside as well, there are areas that are heavily populated by Jews to a greater or lesser extent. Schools that lead beyond the goal of primary education, too, despite the admission restrictions imposed by the law of 24 April 1933 (*Reichsgesetzblatt*, I, p. 225),[4] are still attended by a share of Jewish pupils that is disproportionately high in some places. Serious inhibitions for the development of the National Socialist school system result from this. The establishment of state and private Jewish schools has, of course, led in several places to a certain separation of those Jewish schoolchildren who are of the Jewish faith. Separation based on religion, however, is not sufficient for a National Socialist school system. The creation of National Socialist classroom communities, as a foundation for youth education based on the idea of the German national character, is possible only if a clear separation of the children according to race is undertaken.
>
> I thus intend, starting with the 1936 school year, to implement a separation, as complete as possible, of pupils who are subjects of the Reich in all school types.
>
> In the case of the schools providing compulsory education, considering the attendance requirement still in effect even for non-Aryans, a referral to private primary schools is not feasible. Instead, the establishment of state primary schools for Jews will be necessary. All those pupils who have one or two Jewish parents will be concentrated in these schools. With respect to the racial separation to be performed in the school system, I intend to leave aside the so-called quarter-Jews, who have one Jewish grandparent.
>
> The prerequisite for the creation of a state Jewish primary school is the existence, within a community or within a defined area (municipal or regional area), with due regard to reasonable ways to get to school, of a number of Jewish children that is sufficient for proper schooling. At the same time, if necessary, several or all age groups must be combined in one primary school classroom. The number of twenty children is to be used as an adequate guideline figure for proper schooling.
>
> To gain an overview of the extent to which the creation of state Jewish primary schools is necessary or possible, I request that, for all age groups in all the state and

---

4 The reference is to the Law against Overcrowding in German Schools and Institutions of Higher Education, 25 April 1933.

private primary schools in your area of supervision, the race of the children currently attending the schools be recorded.[5]

With regard to the schools not classified as schools providing compulsory education, I am considering a modification of the provisions made by the Law against Overcrowding, dated 24 April 1933, with a view to introducing a stricter separation.
(signed) *Rust.*

The decree shows how painstakingly and conscientiously the state is proceeding in the field of its racial legislation, to avoid unnecessary hardships and yet accomplish its objective, a völkisch community cleansed of alien elements. This community can be based only on the common genetic predispositions of blood and race and must already be realized in the educational community of the school. With the present decree, the Reich Minister of Education has made a major contribution to this, one that provides, along with the previous decrees, the foundation for German school reform. It is to be hoped that all state and Party offices will do their part to help accomplish the goal set by Reich Minister of Education Rust, so that as of Easter 1936 as complete a separation as possible is carried out between German and Jewish children in the state primary school system.[6]

DOC. 197
On 11 September 1935 the State Political Police departments are requested to report Jews to the Regional Tax Authorities prior to their emigration[1]

Circular decree of the Commander of the State Political Police/Prussian Gestapo, the deputy chief and inspector[2] (II 1 B – 2746/35), issued to all Gestapo offices and State Political Police departments, dated 11 September 1935 (copy)

Re: the Central Intelligence Bureau of the Berlin Regional Tax Authorities.
The president of the Berlin Regional Tax Authorities reiterates that a Central Intelligence Bureau has been set up within his agency. It deals in particular with measures *against* all sorts of tax fraud, capital flight, manipulation of assets, and the like.

Considering that Jews whose emigration was not made known in time to the Regional Tax Authorities have recently caused financial harm to the Reich through tax evasion etc., the president of the Regional Tax Authorities requests that every instance in which it becomes known that Jews, especially Jewish businessmen, are preparing to emigrate be reported to the Central Intelligence Bureau at once, along with personal particulars and the exact address of the individual under suspicion.

---

5 Rust's decree included several sections containing the instructions for registering the pupils and a discussion of the funding of the Jewish primary schools, which were not reproduced in the German News Agency report: *Reichsministerialblatt*, no. 27, 16 Sept. 1935.
6 Although separate school classes or schools for Jewish pupils were subsequently set up in several cities, the decree was not fully implemented until 1938.

1 BArch, R 58/276, fol. 27. This document has been translated from German.
2 Heinrich Himmler.

The Central Intelligence Bureau must make the data submitted to it accessible to the relevant regional tax offices and support them in their work, wherever possible, on the basis of other materials that extend beyond the scope of the particular case. If the material accruing spans several regional tax offices, the Central Intelligence Bureau must establish the requisite relationships and connections, and ensure the necessary cooperation.

The business premises of the Central Intelligence Bureau are situated in the Berlin Regional Tax Authorities, Berlin NW 40, 144 Alt-Moabit.[3] In especially urgent cases, a telephone call to C 5 6601 will suffice.

DOC. 198
The Reich Citizenship Law, proclaimed in Nuremberg on 15 September 1935, turns German Jews into second-class citizens[1]

Reich Citizenship Law.
15 September 1935.[2]

The Reichstag has unanimously passed the following law,[3] which is promulgated herewith:

§ 1

(1) A subject of the state is someone who belongs to the protective union of the German Reich and who in consequence has specific obligations towards it.

(2) The status of subject of the state is acquired in accordance with the provisions of the Reich and State Citizenship Law.

§ 2

(1) Only a subject of the state who is of German or kindred blood, and who proves by his conduct that he is willing and fit to serve the German people and Reich faithfully, is a Reich citizen.

---

3 The Berlin Tax Office in Moabit-West was later responsible for the expropriation of Jewish assets throughout the territory of the Reich.

1 'Reichsbürgergesetz', *Reichsgesetzblatt*, 1935, I, p. 1146. This document has been translated from German.

2 During the Party rally on 14 Sept. 1935, the National Socialist leadership discussed the ministerial draft bills that had been submitted. Goebbels noted, 'Führer has me called to his side again. [...] Frick and Heß still there. Talking over the laws. New citizenship law that strips Jews of the status of Reich citizens, flag law, which elevates the swastika to the status of sole national flag. Law pertaining to Jews, ban on marriages of Jews to Germans, in addition a number of other tightened provisions. We are still fine-tuning them. But this should do the job: and bring the Movement into line': entry for 15 Sept. 1935, in Goebbels, *Die Tagebücher von Joseph Goebbels*, part 1, vol. 3, no. 1, p. 294. See undated drafts for the Nuremberg Laws, BArch, R 1501/5495, fols. 3–132.

3 Following an introduction by Hitler, Reichstag Speaker Göring read out the Reich Citizenship Law and the Law for the Protection of German Blood and German Honour to the Reichstag, which had been specially summoned to Nuremberg. The Reichstag delegates approved the laws: *Deutsche Allgemeine Zeitung*, 16 Sept. 1935, p. 2.

(2) The right to be a Reich citizen is acquired by the granting of the Reich citizenship certificate.

(3) The Reich citizen is the sole holder of full political rights in accordance with the law.

§ 3

The Reich Minister of the Interior, in consultation with the Deputy of the Führer, issues the legal and administrative provisions necessary to implement and supplement the law.

Nuremberg, 15 September 1935, at the Reich Party Meeting of Freedom.
 The Führer and Reich Chancellor
 Adolf Hitler
 The Reich Minister of the Interior
 Frick

DOC. 199
The 'Blood Protection Law', promulgated in Nuremberg on 15 September 1935, prohibits marriage and extramarital sexual relations between Jews and non-Jews[1]

Law for the Protection of German Blood and German Honour.[2]
Dated 15 September 1935.

Steeped in the knowledge that the purity of German blood is the prerequisite for the continued existence of the German people, and inspired by the indomitable will to safeguard the German nation for all time to come, the Reichstag has unanimously adopted the following law, which is promulgated herewith:

§ 1

(1) Marriages between Jews and subjects of the state of German or kindred blood are prohibited. Marriages contracted in violation of this prohibition are invalid, even if they have been contracted abroad in order to circumvent this law.

(2) Proceedings for annulment can be instituted only by the public prosecutor.

§ 2

Extramarital relations between Jews and subjects of the state of German or kindred blood are prohibited.

§ 3

Jews are not permitted to employ female subjects of the state of German or kindred blood under the age of 45 in their households.

§ 4

(1) Jews are forbidden to hoist the Reich and national flag and to display the Reich colours.

---

1 'Gesetz zum Schutz des deutschen Blutes und der deutschen Ehre', *Reichsgesetzblatt*, 1935, I, pp. 1146–1147. This document has been translated from German.
2 See also the comments on the Reich Citizenship Law of 15 Sept. 1935, Doc. 198. On the background to the law, see Cornelia Essner, *Die 'Nürnberger Gesetze' oder die Verwaltung des Rassenwahns, 1933–1945* (Paderborn: Schöningh, 2002), pp. 113–140.

(2) They are permitted, however, to display the Jewish colours. The exercise of this right is protected by the state.

§ 5

(1) Anyone who contravenes the prohibition in § 1 will be punished with penal servitude.

(2) A man who contravenes the prohibition in § 2 will be punished with a jail term or penal servitude.

(3) Anyone who contravenes the provisions in §§ 3 or 4 will be punished with a jail term of up to one year or payment of a fine, or both.

§ 6

The Reich Minister of the Interior, in consultation with the Deputy of the Führer and the Reich Minister of Justice, issues the legal and administrative provisions necessary for the implementation and amendment of the law.

§ 7

The law takes effect on the day after its promulgation; § 3, however, will not become effective until 1 January 1936.

Nuremberg, 15 September 1935, at the Reich Party Congress of Freedom.

The Führer and Reich Chancellor
Adolf Hitler
The Reich Minister of the Interior
Frick
The Reich Minister of Justice
Dr Gürtner
The Deputy of the Führer
R. Heß
Reich Minister without Portfolio

DOC. 200

On 22 September 1935 State Secretary Wilhelm Stuckart explains drafts of the First and Second Regulations to the Reich Citizenship Law to Reich Physicians' Leader Gerhard Wagner[1]

Letter from the Reich and Prussian Minister of the Interior, signed Stuckart,[2] to Reich Physicians' Leader and Main Office Head Dr Wagner, Munich, Brown House, dated 22 September 1935 (carbon copy)

In the enclosure, I am sending the new version of the First and Second Regulations to the Reich Citizenship Law and the First Implementing Regulation to the Law for the Protection of German Blood and German Honour.[3] Simultaneously I confirm the receipt of the official letter from the liaison staff, dated 21 September 1935, which contains the decisions of the Führer concerning these three regulations.[4]

I have negotiated with Reich Minister of Justice Dr Gürtner and State Secretary Dr Freisler[5] concerning the issues that were raised in (4) of this letter with regard to the Jewish lawyers and doctors. Both gentlemen are in agreement with the Reich Minister of the Interior and with me that it is not expedient to reduce the number of lawyers etc. to the proportional share of Jews in the population, for instance, in the future Regulations for Lawyers. In addition, Reich Minister of the Interior Dr Frick is of the opinion that it is not expedient to resolve the issue for the doctors in the Regulations for Doctors, and that this will be better accomplished in a Second Regulation to the Reich Citizenship Law. Accordingly, I am enclosing the draft of a Second Regulation to the Reich Citizenship Law that has met with the approval of the Reich Minister of Justice and the Reich Minister of the Interior. With regard to the final section of this regulation, I note that the occupations affected by this section involve counsel before the administrative courts who, in Prussia, for example, have the occupational title 'administrative law counsellors'.

With respect to the question raised in (6) of the letter, as to whether the Reich Foreign Office considers the further provision for the protection of the purity of German blood to be sustainable, I have, in the absence of Reich Foreign Minister von Neurath and State Secretary von Bülow, dealt with heads of department Gaus[6] and Köppke[7] of the Reich

---

1 BArch, R 1501/5513, fols. 15–21. This document has been translated from German.
2 Dr Wilhelm Stuckart (1902–1953), lawyer; joined the NSDAP in 1922 and the SS in 1936; from June 1933 state secretary in the Prussian Ministry of Education, and from 1935 state secretary in the Reich Ministry of the Interior (responsible for Department I, Constitution and Legislation); in 1942 attended the Wannsee Conference; interned, 1945–1949; convicted in 1949 in the Ministries (Wilhelmstrasse) Trial in Nuremberg (sentenced to time served); classified as a 'follower' during denazification proceedings in 1950.
3 The latter is not in the file. On the two laws, see Docs. 198 and 199, 15 Sept. 1935.
4 This letter could not be found.
5 Dr Roland Freisler (1893–1945), lawyer; member of the *Völkisch*-Social Bloc, 1923–1924; joined the NSDAP in 1925, then performed functions in the NSDAP Gauleitung in Hesse-Nassau; lawyer in Carlsbad, 1923–1924, and in Kassel, 1924–1933; city councillor in Kassel, 1924–1933; state secretary in the Prussian Ministry of Justice, 1933–1934, and in the Reich Ministry of Justice, 1934–1942; president of the People's Court, 1942–1945; author of works including *Nationalsozialistisches Recht und Rechtsdenken* (1938).

Foreign Office. Both, as the department heads at the Reich Foreign Office, have stated that they have no objections, insofar as foreign policy is concerned, to including the relevant provision in the Blood Protection Regulation.

During the discussions with Reich Ministers Dr Frick and Dr Gürtner, the following new areas of doubt arose, which I have tried to clarify in the enclosed new drafts of the First Regulation to the Blood Protection Law.[8] The issues are as follows.

(a) The concept of the German-Jewish Mischling was previously not fixed. Admittedly, the term 'Jew' was defined in the First Regulation to the Reich Citizenship Law, and, on the one hand, a boundary was thus drawn between Jews within the meaning of the Reich Citizenship Law and German-Jewish Mischlinge. But on the other hand, there was no fixing of the boundary between subjects of the state of German blood and state subjects who are German-Jewish Mischlinge. In my view, it is expedient and practicable to draw this boundary in the case of the quarter-Jews, so that quarter-Jews and Mischlinge with a stronger blood admixture all the way up to three-quarter-Jews are exclusively German-Jewish Mischlinge within the meaning of the law. The legal formulation of this notion is effected in I (3) of the Blood Protection Regulation.

The definition of the German-Jewish Mischling necessitated an amendment in the wording of the impediment to marriage for German-Jewish Mischlinge, as occurred under III.

(b) Further, it emerged that the term 'Jew' in § 3(3) of the First Regulation to the Reich Citizenship Law, with the inclusion of the three-quarter-Jews, was not sharply delimited by the wording 'more than two grandparents' vis-à-vis the other German-Jewish Mischlinge. As a result of the wording 'more than two', considerable difficulties in defining the term inevitably arose in practice. More precise delimitation and technically easier definition in practice have been achieved in the latest version by defining the term 'Jew' in the First Regulation to the Reich Citizenship Law in this way: 'A Jew is someone who is descended from at least three grandparents who are full Jews by race.' This definition means that all Mischlinge with 75 per cent or more Jewish blood are correctly and easily identifiable as Jews, but that all German-Jewish Mischlinge with less than 75 per cent Jewish blood are non-Jews within the meaning of the law.

(c) The provision that marriage shall also not be contracted if it is anticipated that the offspring will endanger the purity of German blood could have led to a situation in which although the marriage registrar would have declined to marry a full Aryan and a German-Jewish Mischling under the specific provisions for Jews and German-Jewish Mischlinge, he would have refused to do so on grounds of the threat to the purity of

---

6 Dr Friedrich Gaus (1881–1955), lawyer; from 1907 worked at the Reich Foreign Office, including postings in Genoa and Constantinople, 1910–1912; head of the legal department in the Reich Foreign Office, 1923–1943.
7 Correctly: Dr Gerhard Köpke (1873–1953), lawyer; from 1896 worked in the Prussian judicial service and from 1903 in the Reich Foreign Office, where he was head of the legal department, 1921–1923, and head of the department for Western and South-Eastern Europe and deputy of the state secretary, 1923–1935; compulsory retirement, 1935; later worked in the private sector.
8 These new drafts are not in the file. See the First Implementing Regulation to the Law for the Protection of German Blood and German Honour, 14 Nov. 1935, *Reichsgesetzblatt*, 1935, I, pp. 1334–1336.

German blood. Therefore, it had to be stated that the impediments to marriage due to the Jewish blood element are exhaustively regulated in § 1 of the law and Nos. 2 and 3 of this regulation. Hence the provision under IV of the Blood Protection Law.

(d) Provision No. 5 of the Blood Protection Law in the most recent version was, without the addition of the last sentence, further subject to the objection that, at least for the time being, it left it to the marriage registrar to judge whether it is to be expected that offspring will endanger the purity of German blood. The marriage registrar, on the basis of his entire preparatory training, is not qualified to make that assessment.

For this reason, to establish clarity here once and for all, and to avoid leaving the registrar to judge whether the purity of German blood is at threat, the provision was adopted that proof of the absence of this danger can be supplied only by the certificate of fitness for marriage, issued by the public health authority. The adoption of this provision fulfils an urgent requirement of the Reich Minister of Justice. I also consider it unavoidable in the interest of practice. No concerns need to be raised on this account, because the certificate of fitness for marriage, in accordance with its principle, will be introduced only through the Law for the Protection of Hereditary Health; it is certainly to be expected that this law will be adopted at the cabinet meeting on 18 October.[9] Cases of doubt that appear during the period between the entry into force of the Blood Protection Law and the entry into force of the Hereditary Health Law can, after detailed instruction through a corresponding decree, be handled by the public health authorities in the form of temporary certificates of fitness for marriage even before the Hereditary Health Law comes into force.

(e) Concerning the definition of a Jewish household, the Reich Minister of the Interior now proposes the following wording:

'A household is Jewish if a Jewish man is the head of the household or a member of it.'

As a result of this wording, the single Jewish woman is not affected, provided no male Jew lives in her household. This qualification can be justified by the purpose of the Blood Protection Law, which is intended as a safeguard against the mixing of blood. The danger of a mixing of blood does not exist if a single Jewish woman (with no Jewish males in the household) has a housemaid of German blood. As is already being seen, one must expect a very large number of applications from single Jewish women who wish to retain their female domestic staff. The qualified wording would therefore presumably signify a substantial easing of the burden on the authorities, without weakening the effect of the law.

I request that you present the three newly worded regulations, on behalf of the Reich Minister of the Interior, to the Führer and Reich Chancellor for a decision.[10] In order to clarify any remaining doubts, I will arrive at Munich Central Station on 24 September at 8:04 a.m. and will be available until the beginning of the conference. I would be grateful if a car could fetch me from Central Station.

Heil Hitler!

signed St[11]

---

9 See the Law for the Protection of the Hereditary Health of the German People (Marital Health Law) (*Gesetz zum Schutz der Erbgesundheit des deutschen Volkes [Ehegesundheitsgesetz]*), 18 Oct. 1935; *Reichsgesetzblatt*, 1935, I, p. 1246.

10 On the further discussion see, for example, the comment by Pfundtner, dated 8 Oct. 1935: BArch, R 1501/5513, fols. 132–134.

First Regulation to the Reich Citizenship Law. Sixth version

Dated .... 22 September[12]

On the basis of § 3 of the Reich Citizenship Law of 15 September 1935 (*Reichsgesetzblatt*, I, p. 1146), the following is decreed:

§ 1

Until further regulations concerning Reich citizenship certificates are issued, subjects of the state of German and kindred blood who hold the right to vote in Reichstag elections when the Reich Citizenship Law takes effect are to be regarded for the time being as Reich citizens.

§ 2

Only the Reich citizen, as the holder of full political rights, can exercise the right to vote in political affairs and hold public office. The Reich Minister of the Interior or the agency authorized by him can grant exemptions during the transitional period with regard to admission to public office. The affairs of religious associations are not affected.

§ 3

(1) A Jew cannot be a Reich citizen. He is not entitled to the right to vote in political affairs; he cannot hold public office.

(2) Jewish civil servants will retire when the law comes into force. The employment of teachers at Jewish state schools will remain unaffected pending the reorganization of the Jewish school system. § 2(3) will apply.

(3) A Jew is someone who is descended from at least three grandparents who are full Jews according to race. A grandparent is automatically considered to be a full Jew if he has been a member of the Jewish religious community.

(4) Insofar as Reich laws or directives of the National Socialist German Workers' Party and its organizations include more stringent requirements for purity of blood, they remain unaffected. Other requirements that go beyond the provision of this regulation may be imposed only in consultation with the Reich Minister of the Interior and the Deputy of the Führer. The existing requirements of this kind cease to apply on 1 January 1936, unless they have been approved by the Reich Minister of the Interior in consultation with the Deputy of the Führer; application for approval is to be submitted to the Reich Minister of the Interior.

§ 4

Exemptions from the provisions of this regulation can be granted by the Reich Minister of the Interior in consultation with the Deputy of the Führer.

§ 5

This regulation comes into force on 30 September 1935.[13]

Berlin, ...

The Reich Minister of the Interior.

The Deputy of the Führer.

---

11 In the original, the abbreviated signature is handwritten.
12 In the original, the date has been added by hand.
13 The final version of the First Regulation to the Reich Citizenship Law, dated 14 Nov. 1935, was somewhat more detailed than the draft reproduced here, but the content was essentially the same: see Doc. 210, 14 Nov. 1935.

Second Regulation to the Reich Citizenship Law. Fourth version

Dated ....22 September[14]

On the basis of § 3 of the Reich Citizenship Law of 15 September 1935 (*Reichsgesetzblatt*, I, p. 1146), the following is decreed:

§ 1

(1) The provision of § 3(1) of the First Regulation to the Reich Citizenship Law regarding the holding of public office applies also to the positions of notaries outside the civil service, chief physicians at state hospitals, and independent medical officers.

(2) Jewish notaries outside the civil service will resign their positions when the law comes into force. Jewish chief physicians at state hospitals and Jewish independent medical officers will resign from their positions no later than 31 December 1935.

(3) The number of Jewish lawyers, patent lawyers, litigation agents, and physicians must be brought into line with the Jewish share of the overall population of the German Reich. To this end, the Reich Minister of Justice can revoke the certification of Jewish lawyers, patent lawyers, and litigation agents, and the Reich Minister of the Interior can revoke the licence to practise of Jewish physicians.[15]

(4) (3) applies also to professions that under state law are equivalent to lawyers.[16]

§ 2

This regulation comes into force on 30 September 1935.[17]

Berlin, ...

The Reich Minister of the Interior

The Deputy of the Führer

The Reich Minister of Justice.

---

14 In the original, the date has been added by hand.
15 This is not in the published final version of the regulation. From 13 Dec. 1935 on, however, according to the Reich Physicians' Law, a new licence to practise medicine could be denied to Jews if the percentage of Jewish doctors exceeded the percentage of Jews in the overall population: *Reichsgesetzblatt*, 1935, I, p. 1433.
16 This is not in the published final version of the regulation. A cabinet bill forwarded by Reich Minister of Justice Gürtner on 4 Dec. 1935 with a corresponding amendment to the Regulations for Lawyers was not passed: Hartmannsgruber (ed.), *AdR*, part 2, vol. 2, doc. 282.
17 The Second Regulation to the Reich Citizenship Law was enacted on 21 Dec. 1935, and it contained, as in the draft – although in greater detail – provisions regarding the exclusion of Jewish civil servants, including notaries, doctors, professors, and teachers from the civil service and public institutions. § 1(1) and (2) of the draft are to be found in the regulation as §§ 5(1) and 6(1), respectively; (3) and (4), however, which dealt with a limitation on the proportion of lawyers and other professionals in accordance with the share of Jews in the Reich's population, were not adopted in the regulation: *Reichsgesetzblatt*, 1935, I, p. 1524.

DOC. 201

Jüdische Rundschau, 24 September 1935: statement by the Reich Representation of Jews in Germany regarding the Nuremberg Laws[1]

Declaration by the Reich Representation
The Reich Representation of Jews in Germany announces the following:

I.
The laws passed by the Reichstag in Nuremberg have affected the Jews in Germany in the gravest way. They are supposed to create a basis, however, on which a tolerable relationship between the German and Jewish peoples is possible.[2] The Reich Representation of Jews in Germany is willing to contribute all its efforts to this aim. The precondition for a tolerable relationship is the hope that the Jews and Jewish communities in Germany will preserve the moral and economic possibility of existence through the discontinuance of their defamation and boycotting.

The regulation of the life of the Jews in Germany requires government recognition of an autonomous Jewish leadership. The Reich Representation of Jews in Germany is the body called upon for this purpose. It has the backing, with very few exceptions, of all the Jews and Jewish communities, in particular all the regional associations and all the large communities, as well as the independent Jewish organizations: the Zionist Federation for Germany, the Central Association of Jews in Germany (CV), the Reich League of Jewish Combat Veterans, the Association for Liberal Judaism, the Organized Orthodox Community, the League of Jewish Women, [and] the Reich Committee for Jewish Youth Organizations.

The most pressing tasks of the Reich Representation, to which it will attend with full commitment, energetically pursuing the path it has taken thus far, are:

1. The separate Jewish *school system* must serve to educate the youth as upstanding Jews, centred in their faith, who draw the strength to meet the heavy demands life will make of them from conscious attachment to the Jewish community, from work for the Jewish present and faith in the Jewish future. Beyond the transmission of knowledge, the Jewish school must serve the purpose of systematic preparation for future occupations. With regard to the capacity to migrate, particularly to Palestine, emphasis will be placed on the introduction to manual labour and the study of the Hebrew language. The education and vocational training of young women must focus on preparing them to fulfil their duties as upholders of the family and mothers of the next generation.

---

1 'Erklärung der Reichsvertretung', *Jüdische Rundschau*, 24 Sept. 1935, pp. 1–2. The statement was also published in *C.V.-Zeitung*, 26 Sept. 1935, p. 1. This document has been translated from German.
2 The German News Agency had reported on 16 Sept. 1935 that Hitler, at a celebration during the Nuremberg rally, had emphasized the significance of the new laws and pointed out 'that this National Socialist legislation opens up the only possibility of entering into a tolerable relationship with the Jews living in Germany': *Deutsche Allgemeine Zeitung*, 16 Sept. 1935, p. 2.

An independent cultural structure must provide opportunities for employment to Jews who are artistically and culturally creative, and must serve the separate cultural life of the Jews in Germany.³

2. The increased *need to migrate* must be met with planning on a large scale that includes, first and foremost, *Palestine*, but also all other countries in question and pays special attention to the youth. This includes efforts to increase the opportunities for emigration, *training* in occupations suitable for emigrants, especially agriculture and the skilled crafts and trades, creating possibilities for mobilizing and liquidating the assets of those who are economically independent, expanding existing transfer possibilities and creating new ones.

3. Support and care of the needy, sick, and elderly must be ensured through additional systematic expansion of the Jewish *social welfare* provided by the communities to supplement government welfare services.⁴

4. An impoverished community is not equal to these manifold and difficult tasks. The Reich Representation will try by all available means to safeguard the economic strength of the Jews by seeking to *preserve* the existing *means of earning a living*. Those who are economically weak must be strengthened by the further organization of *economic assistance measures* such as employment agencies, economic advice, and personal or real-estate loans.

5. *The lively progress in the building of Jewish Palestine gives us strength in the present and hope for the future.* In order to involve the Jews in Germany in this development to an even greater extent than before, the Reich Representation as such is joining the *United Jewish Appeal (Keren Hayesod)*, and it calls most emphatically on the Jewish communities and associations to follow its example. The Reich Representation declares itself willing to *establish the organizational link between the institutions of the Jews in Germany and the United Jewish Appeal in Palestine.*

In full awareness of the magnitude of the responsibility and the gravity of the task, the Reich Representation calls on all Jewish men and women and all of Jewish youth to display unity, a Jewish attitude, the strictest self-discipline, and the greatest willingness to make sacrifices.

II.

In accordance with a proposal made in the executive committee of the Reich Representation, the Reich Representation, regional associations, and communities are asked to take, without delay and in close cooperation, *the organizational and personnel measures* that are required in the Jewish institutions to ensure a vigorous and consistent implementation of the new work programme by all Jewish entities.

---

3 The Reich Representation was reacting here to the guidelines issued on 13 August 1935 by Reinhard Heydrich (Gestapa) for the activity of the Reich Association of Jewish Culture Leagues in Germany, which, for one thing, combined the culture leagues into a single Reich organization and, for another, placed them under Gestapo control and banned them from performing in non-Jewish public life: published in *UuF*, vol. 11: *Das Dritte Reich: Innere Gleichschaltung. Der Staat und die Kirchen. Antikominternpakt – Achse Rom–Berlin. Der Weg ins Großdeutsche Reich* (Berlin: Wendler, 1966), pp. 155–156.

The following have given their *explicit approval* to the aforementioned decisions of the executive committee of the Reich Representation:

Prussian Regional Association of Jewish Communities, by Counsellor of the Higher Regional Court Judge Wolff and Dr Alfred Klee; Association of Bavarian Israelite Communities, by Supreme Regional Court Judge Dr Neumeyer, Munich; Saxon Association of Israelite Communities, by Wilhelm Breslauer, Leipzig; Regional Association of Israelite Religious Communities of Hesse, by Commercial Counsellor Mayer, Mainz; Supreme Council of the Jewish Religious Community of Württemberg, by Leopold Levi, Stuttgart; Supreme Council of Jews in Baden, by Prof. Stein, Karlsruhe; the Community Representation of the Hanseatic Towns, by the lawyer David, Hamburg, and Dr Manasse, Altona; Supreme Council of the Jewish Regional Community of Mecklenburg-Schwerin, by Dr Josephy, Rostock; Jewish Community of Berlin, by Director Stahl; Jewish Community of Breslau, by Mr Lachs; Jewish Community of Frankfurt am Main, by Judicial Counsellor Blau; Jewish Community of Cologne, by Dr Callmann; Jewish Community of Mannheim, by Rabbi Dr Grünewald; Jewish Community of Essen, by Dr Hirschland; Jewish Community of Nuremberg, by Commercial Counsellor Rosenzweig; Jewish Community of Königsberg, by Privy Councillor Falkenheim; Zionist Federation for Germany, by Dr Moses; Central Association of Jews in Germany (CV), by Judicial Counsellor Brodnitz; Reich League of Jewish Combat Veterans, by Dr Leo Löwenstein; Association for Liberal Judaism, by the lawyer Stern; the Organized Orthodox Community, by Rabbi Dr Hoffmann, Frankfurt am Main; League of Jewish Women, by Mrs Ottilie Schönewald; Relief Association of German Jews, by Max Warburg; Palestine Office of the Jewish Agency, by Dr Franz Meyer; Reich Committee for Jewish Youth Organizations, by Dr Friedrich Brodnitz.

4 Many Jews were impoverished as a result of unemployment and Aryanization and became dependent on public welfare. Municipal welfare offices, however, began to cut back on welfare services for needy Jews. Since, in addition, elderly or ill family members of emigrants often had to stay behind in Germany, an expansion of Jewish welfare for their care seemed urgently required.

DOC. 202

Comments from 25 September 1935 concerning a presentation by the head of the NSDAP's Racial Policy Office, Walter Groß, about Hitler's new approach to the Jewish question[1]

Memorandum (secret), signed Schlösser,[2] undated (copy)[3]

Report by [SS] Sturmmann Dr Schlösser, charged with the conduct of business, on the conference at the Racial Policy Office on 25 September 1935 concerning the regulatory statutes to the 'Nuremberg Laws'.

The remarks, of which an account will be given below, were made by Reichsleiter Dr Groß,[4] by special order of the Führer, before the heads of the Gau offices of the Racial Policy Office,[5] 'in order that there is available in each Gau, at least one expert besides the head of the Gau office, who is completely conversant with the fundamentals of the new direction in the handling of the Jewish question'. Reichsleiter Dr Groß explained that the ultimate goal of the entire racial policy of the Third Reich was to eliminate everything Jewish, in the sense of the purging of a foreign body. In the process, effectively only these groups of persons were actually distinguished: (1) 'Aryans' (2) Jews and persons of Jewish blood.

For members of the Party organizations and for hereditary farmers, proof of descent to 1800 was required. For members of the civil service, the Civil Service Law regulated this matter somewhat more leniently with the so-called 'Aryan certificate dating back to the grandparents'.

Over the past year, as a result of the renewed intensification of anti-Jewish propaganda, other large organizations such as the Students' Union and the Labour Front had adopted the strict standard of the Party for their members. An often very strident and not always adroitly presented antisemitic propaganda (here Dr Groß had some very sharp words concerning Streicher's work) has, in Groß's opinion, harmed a gradual progression and brought about an immediate and fundamental new decision. This fundamental revision, particularly with respect to the Mischling question, which requires of us all a very considerable change in thinking, can be traced back to the personal intervention and decision of the Führer. Briefly, the substance of the new policy is as follows: a fundamental divide, one that can no longer be bridged, will be made between

---

1 BArch, NS 2/143, fols. 4–8. This document has been translated from German.
2 Probably Dr Ludwig Schlösser (1906–1973), natural scientist; joined the SS in 1933 and the NSDAP in 1937; from 1933 head of education in the biology of human populations and racial studies at the Race and Settlement Main Office (RuSHA) in Munich; from 1935 to 1936 worked at the RuSHA in Berlin and from 1936 in the staff office of the Reich Farmers' Leader; served in the war; interned in 1945.
3 The original contains several handwritten alterations.
4 Dr Walter Groß (1904–1945), physician; joined the NSDAP in 1925; from 1929 to 1932 worked at Braunschweig Regional Hospital; from 1932 member of the leadership of the National Socialist Physicians' League; from 1933 to 1941 plenipotentiary for race policy on the staff of the Deputy of the Führer; from 1934 to 1945 head of the Racial Policy Office of the NSDAP; in 1938 honorary professor of racial studies at the University of Berlin; author of works including *Die rassenpolitischen Voraussetzungen zur Lösung der Judenfrage* (1943).
5 This refers to the office heads of the Racial Policy Offices in the NSDAP Gau administrations.

full Jews (in racial terms) and Germans. In the process, the Jews obtain the rights and duties of a national minority. Extramarital intercourse across this divide will be punished in both directions only in the case of the man. It is hoped that the pressure of a possibility of blackmailing the woman, who goes unpunished, will result in a serious decrease in this disreputable sexual intercourse.

The greatest difficulty arose concerning the handling of the Mischling question, which will now be resolved in a completely different way. The Führer had developed the notion that there are ways to solve every Mischling question: (1) expulsion or emigration under state pressure, (2) sterilization, and (3) assimilation, that is, absorption of the Mischling substance by the major race. On this occasion the Führer said that his whole policy thus far consisted in always choosing the lesser of several evils, and that he must proceed in this way in deciding on this question too. The Führer has ordered that the Mischling question be settled by means of assimilation over the course of a few generations. At this point he also stated that, in the event of war, he is 'prepared to accept all consequences' on all fronts. In future, three groups of persons will be distinguished in Germany: Germans, German-Jewish Mischlinge, and Jews. Like the Germans, the German-Jewish Mischlinge, to whom the half- and quarter-Jews belong, will receive the temporary Reich citizenship certificate on 1 October. If a quarter- or half-Jew wishes to marry, he requires legal permission to take this step. He can either marry a Jew, the result being that he automatically becomes part of the Jewish minority and loses the temporary certificate of Reich citizenship, or he can marry a German girl, and then, along with this consent for marriage, which is granted in most cases, he will automatically receive the permanent certificate of Reich citizenship. However, he does not hereby obtain the full rights of a citizen of the German Reich, for example, because the restrictions of the Professional Civil Service Law still apply to him. He nonetheless has the certainty that his children will not be subject to these special provisions. Marriage between German-Jewish Mischlinge is prohibited as a matter of principle. This would lead to the creation of a Mischling caste, which is precisely what must be prevented. On this occasion, Groß said, the Führer stated that he has no interest in adding the valuable characteristics of our race to the specifically Jewish aptitudes, that is, in 'Nordicizing' the Jews.

The reasons that led the Führer to undertake such a fundamental adjustment are the following, along domestic and foreign policy lines: all our work is focused on the sole objective of making Germany strong, mighty, and powerful so that, in the coming decisions that it must face, it is the strongest power and can therefore determine its own destiny. Everything that has even the most remote chance of endangering this objective and the work must disappear. The Führer said that in this regard it is intolerable that a large disenfranchised class of Mischlinge, who do not know where they belong, should exist. Such a class obstructs the coherence and capacity of a people. An additional reason cited by the Führer for this position, based on foreign and economic policy considerations, is to be found in the ideas of Reich Minister Dr Schacht.

Schacht explained that the majority of our export trade, through which we obtain foreign currency for the arms build-up (copper, nickel, cobalt), is in the hands of half-Jews. If one were to disenfranchise the half-Jew totally with the new legislation, our export trade would be severely damaged as a result, and that is something we cannot afford to happen. Schacht, according to Groß, said, 'what use is the best idealism of the old guard if they have nothing to eat?' (Reich Minister of the Army von Blomberg[6] supported Dr Schacht in his comments), and gave individual examples that illustrated his stance. He said, among other things, that some Jew, the agent of a large German insurance company in Cairo, brought him in 5 million in foreign exchange through his work, which at the moment is more valuable than all the utopias of any idealists.[7] The Führer then went on to say that it is not important to pursue utopias at the moment, but that what matters is to directly face the reality of the political situation. If a decision has been made in favour of an arms build-up and combat readiness, and he has indeed made such a decision, then all other things must be subordinated to this goal. It was mentioned in this regard by Dr Groß that all antisemitic propaganda, for example, in the form of the *Stürmer*, would thus have to be classified as 'treason'.

For all propaganda and educational work, there now arise fundamentally new tasks, the difficulty of which should by no means be underestimated.

It goes without saying that the change in course being taken here may under no circumstances be shown and emphasized in propaganda work. Rather, it must be specifically pointed out that by separating the full Jew from the German a fundamentally new path is being taken. This new attitude has the additional consequence that all propaganda and defamation of the German-Jewish Mischling, that is, the half- and quarter-Jew, will have to cease. In addition, in accordance with the will of the Führer, the boycotting of Jewish shops (whose owners are full Jews) must also cease. In future, these shops will be marked as Jewish ones. The Führer wishes those Jews who belong to the national Jewish minority to be left with a means of livelihood, so that they do not become a burden on the public welfare system. The Führer wants no promotion of Zionism and increased emigration of the 550,000 members of the Jewish minority. According to Groß, the Führer is even said to be prepared, in some circumstances, to permit a slight relaxation of the legislation pertaining to Jews in matters of the Reich Chamber of Culture[8] (a statement that nonetheless appears highly doubtful to this reporter and which he reproduces here only with this caveat). By specific order of the Führer, Groß announces with great urgency that it must be pointed out that these new implementing regulations signify a fundamentally new policy direction rather than a 'tactical manoeuvre'.

Several points arise in response to these statements by Groß.

First of all, the figures for the population of Jews and Jewish Mischlinge in Germany on which these measures were based are new ones. It was claimed that there are 550,000 full Jews, 200,000 half-Jews, and 100,000 quarter-Jews. These numbers were not well known and were established by Director Burgdörfer of the Reich Office of Statistics only

---

6 Werner von Blomberg (1878–1946), career officer; from 1897 military career; in 1925 head of army training; from 1933 Reich minister of the army; Reich minister of war and commander-in-chief of the Wehrmacht, 1935; in 1936 field marshal; in 1938, under political pressure, forced to resign as minister and retire from the Wehrmacht; died in US custody in Nuremberg in 1946.
7 On Schacht's ideas, see Doc. 189, 20 August 1935, and Doc. 194, 7 Sept. 1935.
8 The Reich Chamber of Culture (Reichskulturkammer) was established by a law issued on 22 Sept. 1933. Membership in one of the newly created seven individual chambers, including the Reich Chamber of Music, the Reich Chamber of Film, and the Reich Chamber of Literature, was the prerequisite for working in a branch of culture. Non-acceptance or exclusion meant being virtually banned from a profession. Jews were generally not admitted as members: *Reichsgesetzblatt*, 1933, I, pp. 661–662.

two days before the formulation of the laws in Nuremberg.⁹ Until then, no office anywhere in the Reich had solid numerical data on this issue. This task actually would have fallen to the Racial Policy Office. Let me remind you as well that on the occasion of the Aryan legislation of the Reichswehr, one was working, with respect to the Führer, on the basis of 'absolutely solid figures' of 2 million Jews and Jewish Mischlinge and a loss of 90,000 recruits annually.¹⁰ It is indeed hard to determine the origin of these figures. When contrasting the two figures in this way, one cannot rid oneself of a sense of unease. The obvious helplessness with which these new measures of the Führer are met even within the Racial Policy Office might be made clear by the fact that Groß, replying to a question about the management of propaganda in these matters, said that one must certainly point to the humanity of these measures, a path that could perhaps make sense in foreign policy terms but would be unlikely to find much sympathy domestically and among staunch Party comrades. At the same time, it must also be stated that the head of the Racial Policy Office did not take part in the decisive meetings preceding the legislation, as he himself has said. With regard to this entire statement by Groß, I would like to note the following, from the standpoint of someone involved in racial policy in the context of the SS: if our practical work in the SS is not affected by this fundamental revision of the Jewish question, it is nonetheless vitally necessary that the personnel of the Racial Policy Office, which is supposed to do general-staff work, harbour no doubt of any kind about the fundamental change of course that the Führer has ordered regarding this question and the motivations that inevitably led to this. Above all, it must be clear that the path being taken here to a conclusive arrangement is not intended to be a tactical manoeuvre or a superficial concession. Once we have fully acquainted ourselves with this matter, which we will all surely find difficult to grasp at first, and once we are entirely clear about the reasons that led the Führer to this arrangement, we will retain the inner momentum to awaken an appreciation of the necessity of these measures.

Because Groß, in his remarks, let a comment slip in from which one had to infer that an easing of the requirements for proof of descent back to 1800 is within the realm of possibility for Party comrades too, the SS and the hereditary farmers remain more or less the only racially valuable intact bodies in the Reich. This fact inevitably results in the urgent necessity of close cooperation between the SS and the Reich Food Estate. And specifically [it is necessary] that this cooperation does not get bogged down in superficial organizational matters, but rather that it must, in the not so distant future, achieve an SS whose focus rests specifically in farming-related matters. Even at the risk of saying something unpleasant, I wish to point here unambiguously to this as yet unresolved question, which I believe to be the vital one for the future of the SS.

The SS should become the kinship association of the racially most valuable part of our people, with the self-evident sine qua non of a soldierly attitude and a clear ideological orientation. Clearly defined tasks of breeding, which should absolutely safeguard and increase for the future the best blood of our people, are in the interests of this kinship

---

9 This could not be verified. The same figures, however, are found in the report by Dr Hermann Vellguth concerning the origins of the Nuremberg Laws, dated 26 Sept. 1935: RGVA, 500k-1-343, fols. 47–48.
10 On this see the letter of the Reich Minister of the Interior to the Office of the Wehrmacht Adjutant to the Führer and Reich Chancellor, 3 April 1935, Doc. 159.

association. The Race and Settlement Main Office of the SS[11] was created for the sole purpose of serving this end. Now, however, it is a fact that more than four fifths of the current members of the SS are non-rural people. (Here, the rural craftsmen and agricultural workers living in a relationship of tenancy are, in addition to the farmers, counted as part of the rural population bound to the soil.) But it is incontrovertible that breeding work cannot be done with people who no longer lead a way of life thus bound to the soil. More than 90 per cent of urban families die out after three to four generations at the most. But in the present context, this means, seen plainly, that at the moment the work of the Race and Settlement Main Office of the SS is for the most part following the wrong course. For what does it matter, in the long run, for the blood history of our people if we succeed, by using all the tools of a wise education – here too, one is still quite far from the attainable goal – to get racially valuable but disengaged city dwellers to marry properly, along our lines, if we nevertheless know that these urban families will have died out within a short space of time. If one looks at a map of the distribution of the garrisons of SS formations, it is obvious that the SS is least heavily represented in the areas where we have the racially most valuable human material and the healthiest population of farmers. Ways must therefore be found to tackle this problem. There are obvious difficulties in this regard. The soldierly Führer rightly says that in open rural areas it is extremely hard to produce a hard-hitting and militarily viable [SS] formation. For the sake of the great goal, however, ways must be found to circumvent these difficulties. Here reference must be made again to an idea of SS-Standartenführer Dr Rechenbach,[12] who proposed a fundamental change to the SS service of the formations for racially valuable rural areas. Instead of roll calls twice a week, only one or two roll calls per month should be scheduled during periods of more intense farming activity. Later, after the harvest season, the young SS men should be placed together for three to four weeks in strict camp communities and screened. During the winter, well-structured ideological educational work must begin, along the lines of our broad objectives. If it is possible to work along these lines on a large scale, despite the justified misgivings of the military officers in rural areas, the significance will be twofold. First, through the SS, we will include a large part of the racially valuable part of our people that is still bound to a fixed way of life. In addition, however, the following is of particular importance: the goal of renewing our religious life from a racial standpoint has of course been in the background for generations. This renewal can only come about via the racially valuable and bound rural man, who can be won over only very slowly, but once he has been won over, he will stand by this renewal firmly. It cannot come about, however, via the urban

---

11 The Race and Settlement Office of the SS (Rasse- und Siedlungsamt der SS, RAS), established in 1932, was headed by Walther Darré. From 1935, upgraded to the Race and Settlement Main Office of the SS (Rasse- und Siedlungshauptamt der SS, RuSHA), it provided education on 'racial questions' and was used for 'racial vetting' of SS members and their wives. Later, it was also responsible for the 'Germanization' of the population in the occupied territories.
12 Dr Horst Rechenbach (1895–1968), farmer; from 1932 to 1933 deputy head of the Race and Settlement Office; from 1933 also main department head in the staff office of the Reich Farmers' Leader; in 1940 plenipotentiary for settlement on the staff of General Fromm at the High Command of the Wehrmacht; from 1943 head of the NSDAP Reich Office for the Rural Population; after 1945 taught at private agricultural schools.

man (for example, the [German] Faith Movement), who readily agrees but is far less able to live out a new belief system.

Put in exaggerated terms – and I am well aware of the danger of such exaggerations – for the future of the SS, this means either rural militia, promotion of the idea of breeding, and truly meaningful work by the Race and Settlement Office, or urban military preparedness and relinquishment of the idea of breeding. In the latter case, the work of the Race and Settlement Office would be a misguided effort.

On the whole, for our educational work in the SS, this new regulation of the Jewish question means an even sharper and clearer differentiation of our specific tasks and a renewed obligation to serve our objectives with even more earnest and thorough action. In future it will be particularly important to give prominence to the physical and mental profile of the Nordic man as we wish him to be, in ever-fresh and exemplary ways, using pictures and words. This task will be all the more urgent because the admission of stronger, dominant alien racial elements via the assimilation that has been ordered constitutes a renewed racial burden for our people, even if it might only be a burden in appearance.

DOC. 203
On 25 September 1935 the head of the Department of National Health in the Reich Ministry of the Interior uses Mendel's principles of heredity to justify the prohibition of marriage between Jews and non-Jews[1]

Memorandum, Reich Ministry of the Interior/Department of National Health, Dr Gütt,[2] dated 25 September 1935

I. Principles of Mendel's law of heredity

The genetic constitution of the individual is a mosaic made up of numerous units of heredity, which combine in the progeny on a 50–50 basis with the units of heredity of the other partner. Each one of these genes (units of heredity), however, retains its unique character over the course of the generations. If one mixes two different races with one another, the individual units of heredity can never completely disappear as a result of this commingling. Rather, each hereditary characteristic as such will appear in the offspring in a proportion that can be calculated in advance, based on Mendel's law of heredity. For example, the probability that a specific genetic endowment of a grandparent will appear in the grandchild is one in four.

Certain genetic factors that combine with one another come out on top: that is, they put their stamp on the hybrid (dominant). The genetic factor that is thereby concealed

---

1 BArch, R 1501/5513, fols. 33–39. This document has been translated from German.
2 Dr Arthur Gütt (1891–1949), physician; in medical practice from 1918; joined the NSDAP in 1932; SS-Obersturmbannführer, 1933; head of the Office for Population Policy and the Study of Genetic Health on the staff of the Reichsführer SS, 1935; in the Reich Ministry of the Interior from 1933; head of the Department of National Health there from 1934; dismissed from the Reich Ministry of the Interior in 1939 following internal conflicts; briefly interned in 1945; co-editor of the journal *Volk und Rasse*; editor of the *Handbuch der Erbkrankheiten* [Handbook of Genetic Disorders] (1940).

(recessive), however, is not lost. Instead, it will make its presence felt later, in further mixing, when the conjunction of hereditary factors produces a combination that contains only the recessive trait.

Every genetic trait must be considered separately with regard to the application of Mendel's First Law of Genetics (segregation). This implies that offspring of later generations need not have individual units of heredity, but that, on the other hand, as a result of the many possibilities for combination, phenotypes can appear that were not present in the original forms.

Sketch for p. 1.
Mixing of two different gene pairs (black/white; wire-haired/smooth-haired), where black and wire-haired are dominant traits.

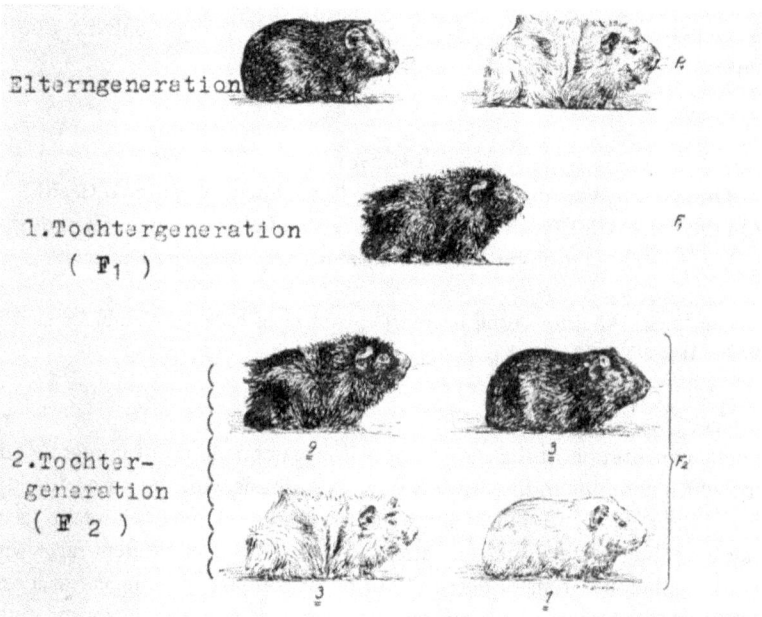

The accompanying sketch shows the inheritance when two pairs of traits (black/white; smooth-haired/wire-haired) are mixed.[3] Because black is dominant over white, as is wire-haired over smooth-haired, in the first filial generation (F 1) only black wire-haired animals result. If these are mixed among themselves, the second filial generation contains diversified animals, specifically nine with black wiry hair; three with black smooth hair; three with white wiry hair; and one with white smooth hair. This last animal is true-bred, as it exhibits only the recessive, concealable traits. In addition, of the nine black wire-haired animals, one must be true-bred black and one true-bred wire-haired,

---

[3] The captions read (from top to bottom): 'parental generation', 'first filial generation (F1)', and 'second filial generation (F2)'.

while the rest of these animals also inherit genes for the recessive traits in the genotype, which are concealed only by the dominant traits they exhibit.

II. Application of Mendel's law to humans
With regard to the application of these facts to humans, there appear to be certain difficulties, as one can only ever apply the pattern of Mendel's law to individual hereditary units of the human when there is a mix of a hereditary unit, as with the red and white four o'clock plant.

If, for example, a white person is mixed with a Negro, mulattos result. If the mulattos are now further mixed with whites, quadroons are produced.

No one here has yet seen a pure white person result from such a conjunction. The coloured blood always remains perceptible in some way.

Through Fischer's studies of the bastards of Rehoboth,[4] however, we know unequivocally that the individual characteristics of humans follow Mendel's laws of heredity. This has since been proved a thousand times over, for example, also for the inheritance of pathological traits.

The phenomenon of the mulatto mix can be simply explained by the fact that in humans we must expect thousands and tens of thousands of characteristics, each of which segregates on its own (Mendel's law). Because the combination of the genes (germ layers) that determine the individual characteristics follows the laws of probability, it can be readily calculated that the probability of the formation of a pure white human when backcrossed with a mulatto is so low that it should not be entertained in practice.

III. Jew problem
For the racial mixing of persons of German blood and Jews, the following results:

1. By *mixing quarter- and half-Jews with persons of German blood,* complete disappearance of the Jewish characteristics cannot be achieved. Persons of pure German blood thus cannot result from additional cross-breeding with either half-Jews or quarter-Jews.

2. However, one can easily achieve the result that the Jewish properties are repeatedly broken down, so that, in this sense, one can speak of a dilution that increases with each generation, provided no backcrossing with Jews or Mischlinge occurs again. *After many generations, therefore, the pure German type is at least approximately achieved, though the Jewish element, of course, will nonetheless remain perceptible in one characteristic or another.*

Therefore, unless one wants to perpetuate, besides the Jews, a new German-Jewish Mischling race, one must resolve to cause the Mischlinge to merge into the German or the Jewish people. From a biological standpoint, there is no completely satisfactory solution here at all.

If one chooses the path of merging the German-Jewish Mischlinge into the German people, this can take place quickly or slowly, depending on the measures taken.

If one wishes to accelerate the absorption:

(a) one will have to allow quarter-Jews to marry persons of German blood without restriction, but prohibit this to full Jews or Jewish Mischlinge;

---

[4] Eugen Fischer, *Die Rehobother Bastards und das Bastardisierungsproblem beim Menschen* (Jena: Gustav Fischer, 1913).

(b) for half-Jews, who exhibit 50 per cent Jewish characteristics, an alternative arrangement is advisable.

1. Half-Jews may be permitted to marry persons of German blood only after a screening on the basis of a special permit.

2. Half-Jews must be forbidden to marry Jewish Mischlinge.

3. Half-Jews who, in accordance with (1), have not received a permit to marry persons of German blood and who are also denied recognition as citizens of the Reich are thus automatically to be declared members of the Jewish portion of the population. The same applies to those half-Jews who are granted a permit to marry Jews or who are married to Jews.

4. Only female half-Jews could be allowed to decide for themselves whether to voluntarily commit to the Jewish portion of the population, but they would thereby have to be treated as full Jews with respect to the legislation.

5. In the case of all other half-Jews, with the exception of the females mentioned under (4), however, the state must reserve the right to screen them and determine their affiliation.

As far as possible, this screening must take place within the framework of the Reich Citizenship Law on the basis of the following principles:

1. The assessment of individual half-Jews is to be carried out on the basis of outward appearance, disposition, and mental or other capacities.

2. During the screening, one will have to reject descendants of Ostjuden, Jews with a strongly Jewish appearance, Jews with a hereditary defect, and all those who have a bad reputation or even criminal tendencies. Finally, once world opinion and feelings in Germany are calmer, one will also be able to consider granting approval for voluntary sterilization upon application by a half-Jew.

In the reverse case, in which slow absorption is deemed more advantageous, one will have to permit the German-Jewish Mischlinge to marry each other. In the process, the following must be taken into account:

In these cases too, permission to marry each other could only be granted to the German-Jewish Mischlinge:

(a) if they both obtain the right of Reich citizenship;

(b) if they would, where applicable, also be permitted to marry persons of German blood.

At the same time, however, one must expect that half-Jews would continue to be born in the coming generations too, and that the absorption of the German-Jewish Mischlinge would thus be delayed for generations to come.

Concluding remarks

As a matter of principle, one must stand by the idea that the alliance of especially high-value persons of German blood with German-Jewish Mischlinge is not advisable. There can thus be no question of the state encouraging marriage between persons of German blood and German-Jewish Mischlinge. Instead, there must be an effort to ensure either that they remain single and, if at all possible, have no children, or that these Mischlinge enter into alliances solely with the more insensitive portion of the German population.

DOC. 204

On 27 September 1935 the Swiss ambassador in Berlin reports on the increased number of applications for immigration permits by German Jews[1]

Letter from the ambassador of Switzerland (151-E 2001 (D) 2/110), E. Feer,[2] in Berlin, to the head of the Foreign Relations Section of the Political Department, M. de Stoutz,[3] dated 27 September 1935

In a letter dated the 23rd of this month, I briefly informed you of my fears regarding an overly liberal granting of residence permits to German subjects who wish to leave Germany because of their religious denomination or political attitude.[4] In the meantime I have instructed the officials of this embassy whom this mainly concerns that they should continue to pay attention to this problem, an extremely serious one for Switzerland, and inform me in future about cases that are of particular interest.

In this regard, I would like to point out that, particularly since the enactment of the German Law for the Protection of German Blood and German Honour,[5] naturally no day goes by without enquiries coming in from Reich subjects asking about the possibility of resettling in Switzerland. The passport department of the embassy observes in this respect that it is striking that only in the rarest instances are the requests for issuance of the residence permit directly submitted at the embassy. The interested parties, after receiving information, often make comments to the effect that it seems expedient to them to travel to Switzerland themselves and personally conduct the negotiations for issuance of a short-term residence permit there. Unfortunately, the number of cases in which this procedure has led to a successful outcome is beyond the knowledge of the embassy. It must nonetheless be stated that it happens repeatedly that interested parties obtain residence permits from cantonal or even municipal authorities and, on that basis, apply to the embassy for issuance of the requisite certificate for toll-free import of their personal effects. If the residence permit comes from a cantonal office, the certificate must be issued in accordance with the existing regulations. It is self-evident that persons who, on the basis of a short-term residence permit, move to Switzerland with their furniture are probably likely only in very rare instances to leave our country again after expiration of the permit. In most cases the authorities probably refrain from forcing them to

---

1 Commission nationale pour la publication de documents diplomatiques suisses, *Documents Diplomatiques Suisses. Diplomatische Dokumente der Schweiz. Documenti Diplomatici Svizzeri 1848–1945*, vol. 11: *1934–1936*, ed. Mauro Cerutti, Jean-Claude Favez, and Michèle Fleury-Seemüller (Bern: Benteli, 1989), no. 151, pp. 455–456. This document has been translated from German.
2 Dr Eduard Albert Feer (1894–1983), lawyer and economist; in 1925 commercial attaché of the Swiss embassy in Berlin; legation counsellor of the Swiss embassy in Berlin, 1931–1936, and in Washington, 1936–1945, then envoy in Buenos Aires; from 1950 in Brazil.
3 Maxime de Stoutz (1880–1969), diplomat; from 1907 posted in London, later in Tokyo and Paris; envoy in Madrid, 1925–1932; head of the Department for Foreign Affairs of the Swiss Political Department, 1932–1937; envoy in Brussels, 1937–1940 and 1944–1945; from 1938 also in Luxembourg and from 1940 to 1941 in Rome.
4 In his letter Feer wrote: 'Observed from Berlin, in any event, this surge of people seems somewhat alarming; let us not expose ourselves to the risk of having a Jewish problem in Switzerland a decade from now as well': ibid., p. 455, note 1.
5 *Gesetz zum Schutz des deutschen Blutes und der deutschen Ehre*: see Doc. 199, 15 Sept. 1935.

leave the country, as this would likely mean a much greater hardship than if one had not let them in to begin with.

In connection with the enquiries about issuance of residence permits, information is almost routinely sought concerning the period of time in which one can become naturalized in Switzerland. Here too it must be said that the interested parties believe they can attain their objective more quickly than by taking the legally prescribed avenue, if they simply direct their request to the correct recipient in Switzerland. One visitor claimed point-blank that, 'according to his sources', he would not have to wait six years before becoming a Swiss citizen.

The obvious question is whether, particularly in the case of the Jews, it is just Jewish offices in Switzerland that are advising their fellow Jews. This would be a great mistake on the part of the Swiss Jews, however, because, if an antisemitic tendency should also arise in Switzerland, certainly no distinction will be made between Swiss and international Jews.

But, quite apart from the Jews, it is really incomprehensible to me that one continues to issue residence permits in apparently not inconsiderable numbers to gainfully employed German subjects, while the emigration of Swiss citizens to Germany is almost totally prevented in practice.

With the present letter, therefore, I would like to reiterate that I am following the development of this problem with concern, for which I cannot be blamed if one knows the extent to which the embassy must occupy itself with safeguarding the interests of its Jewish subjects, of whom only a very few have any connections to our homeland besides the passport.

I must leave it to the appropriate authorities whether, in light of the present situation, a tighter control, if necessary by limiting the powers of the cantons, should be introduced regarding German subjects who want to settle in Switzerland.[6] In any event I consider it my duty to call your attention once again to these dangers, which absolutely demand the greatest restraint with respect to the granting of short-term residence by the cantons and also the naturalization of non-assimilable foreigners.

Let the enclosed copy of a letter to the embassy from Mr Kurt Werner in Kassel serve as an indication of the mentality of the interested parties.[7] With all due understanding for the extremely difficult situation of the Jews in Germany, we cannot, with the best will in the world, grant asylum in our country to all these people for humanitarian reasons.

---

6 At a conference in early Oct. 1935, the police authorities in Switzerland agreed to reject immigration requests from Germany. At the same time, the Swiss consulates in Germany were also supposed to turn down applications because of the threat of 'being overwhelmed by immigrants': see letter from H. Rothmund to Feer dated 17 Oct. 1935, Commission nationale pour la publication de documents diplomatiques suisses, *Documents Diplomatiques Suisses*, p. 457.

7 The letter is not enclosed.

DOC. 205

On 9 October 1935 State Secretary Wilhelm Stuckart informs Reich Minister of the Interior Wilhelm Frick about the planned law for restricting the economic activity of Jews[1]

Memorandum of Department I of the Reich and Prussian Ministry of the Interior, signed Stuckart, for Frick, dated 9 October 1935 (copy for State Secretary Pfundtner)

To the Minister, respectfully, through official channels.

I submit enclosed the reworked draft of a law regulating the economic activity of Jews.[2]

The Reich Ministry of Economics, the Ministry of Propaganda, and the Advertising Council for the German Economy attach particular importance to the addition of (2) to § 1. The intention is thus to make sure that the designation envisaged in (1) of § 1 really is the only one. All three offices fear that unless the possibility of further forms of marking for identification purposes is not excluded, an additional form of marking would be retained in individual Gaue, meaning that the markings used by the state and the marking used by the Party might perhaps again diverge widely. A real calming of sentiments and of industry can be expected only if the method of marking envisaged in the law remains the only one available.

Article II has been added. Jews are to be excluded from work as private detectives because experience has shown that espionage can be conducted through private detective agencies. The fact that Jews can no longer be marriage brokers by profession follows from the ban on marriage between Jews and Aryans. The security industry should be closed to Jews, to prevent them from potentially maintaining a force of hundreds of armed men in certain circumstances. It should be possible to deny Jews the trade licence for travelling salesmen, in order to limit the Jews' fomenting of unrest, an activity frequently connected with door-to-door selling. However, the Jews should not be entirely prevented from operating as itinerant traders, because otherwise they would be deprived of an additional occupational opportunity.[3]

---

1 BArch, R 1501/5513, fols. 135–140. This document has been translated from German.
2 The draft law can be traced back to a discussion, initiated by Reich Minister of the Interior Frick, between him and Reichsbank President Schacht on 23 Sept. 1935 concerning restrictions for Jews in the economy. State secretaries Pfundtner and Stuckart (both from the Reich Ministry of the Interior) and State Secretary Posse and Ministerial Director Pohl (both from the Reich Ministry of Economics) had also taken part in the discussion: memorandum, dated 23 Sept. 1935, published in Hartmannsgruber (ed.), *AdR*, part 2, vol. 2, pp. 800–802. Most of the measures discussed were included in a first draft of a law regulating economic activity by Jews dated 27 Sept. 1935: BArch, R 1501/5513, fols. 93–96. On 7 Oct. 1935 there was a further discussion, led by Stuckart, about the draft, with representatives of the Reich Ministry of Economics, Reich Ministry of Justice, Reich Ministry of Public Enlightenment and Propaganda, and Reich Foreign Office: BArch, R 3001/10228, fols. 520–522.
3 In a circular decree dated 28 Dec. 1935 Reich Minister of Economics Schacht attempted to stop the police authorities from increasingly rejecting applications by Jews for trade licences for travelling salesmen: LAB, Rep. 142/7, 1-11-1/Nr. 13.

Article III – formerly Article II – has also been revised. The substantive changes concern Jewish works managers or Jews entrusted with acting as managers swearing an oath on 1 May. In my view, there is no internal reason for not administering an obligatory oath to the Jewish works manager. If Jews should be drafted in case of emergency, I have no doubt that they, as German subjects, would also be required to take an oath of allegiance at that time. The regulation now contained in Article III provides that the Jewish works manager, as chairman of the Council of Trust, cannot administer the oath to the members of the Council of Trust. Instead, this oath must be administered by the Trustee of Labour or someone delegated by him, though as the Jewish works manager still belongs to the Council of Trust, he must take this oath as well.[4]

Incorporated into Article IV, 'Branch establishment by Jews', in order to make circumvention of the ban on residence impossible, is the provision that Jews are also prohibited from establishing a commercial branch office in communities with fewer than 20,000 inhabitants.[5] Sentence 2 of § 8 does not represent a factual change but rather merely introduces the technically correct term for those state authorities that can approve exceptions.

Finally, among the concluding provisions of Article V, § 12 has been added. It empowers the Reich Minister of Economics, in consultation with the Reich Minister of the Interior etc., to set the guidelines for *all* commercial enterprises according to which such enterprises are to be considered Jewish or non-Jewish.

signed Stuckart

9 October 1935
Draft law regulating the economic activity of Jews.
Date ....
The Reich government has passed the following law, which is promulgated herewith:

Article I
Marking of retail shops.

§ 1

(1) Retail shops that are owned by or *actually run by*[6] Jews are to be marked as such. The designation must be effected through an addition to the firm's name or the name of the tradesperson, in Hebrew letters, in domestic business operations.

(2) Other forms of marking by which retail shops are directly or indirectly identified as Jewish or non-Jewish are prohibited.

(3) In cases of doubt, the decision is made by the higher administrative authority, and, upon appeal, by the Reich Minister of Economics in consultation with the Reich Minister of the Interior and the Reich ministers involved in the particular case.

---

4 On this see Doc. 115, 25 April 1934, and Doc. 314, 7 Dec. 1937.
5 This can be traced back to a demand made by the Gestapo Central Office (Gestapa). See Doc. 189, 20 August 1935, and Doc. 195, 9 Sept. 1935.
6 Corrected by hand; originally 'significantly influenced'.

§ 2

(1) If the owner, or in the case of corporate bodies the legal representative, fails to fulfil the obligations of marking (§ 1) despite being called upon to do so by the police, he will be punished by a fine.

(2) The police can have the marking carried out at his [the owner's] expense.

(3) Anyone who removes a designation affixed by the police will be punished by imprisonment for up to one year or a fine or both.

Article II
Amendments to the Commercial Code.

§ 3

(1) Jews are prohibited from practising the following trades or professions:
(a) providing information about financial circumstances or personal matters;
(b) acting as marriage brokers, unless the marriages are Jewish ones.
(2) Jews are to be denied permission to work in the security industry.
(3) Jews can be refused issuance of the trade licence for travelling salesmen.

§ 4

Corresponding to the obligations applicable to other tradespersons, public limited companies and private limited companies also must, pursuant to the requirements of § 15a(1) of the Commercial Code, display the name of their firm at the entrance to their business premises in clearly legible lettering.

§ 5

The Reich Minister of Economics is empowered to revise the Commercial Code in accordance with these amendments.

Article III
Administration of the oath to members of the Council of Trust.

§ 6

The solemn oath of the members of the Council of Trust – § 10(1) of the Law for the Regulation of National Labour of 20 January 1934 (*Reichsgesetzblatt*, I, p. 45) and § 8(1) of the Law on the Regulation of Labour in Public Administrations and Enterprises of 23 March 1934 (*Reichsgesetzblatt*, I, p. 220) – cannot be administered by a Jew.

§ 7

If the works manager is a Jew and has not entrusted a person of German or kindred blood with representing him, or if a Jew has been entrusted with representing the works manager, the Trustee of Labour himself must administer the oath of the Council of Trust or have it administered by a person delegated by him.

Article IV
Branch establishment by Jews.

§ 8

Jews are forbidden from moving into communities of fewer than 20,000 residents to establish a residence or to reside there permanently; the same applies to the establishment of a commercial branch office. Exemptions can be granted by the state authority specified in § 33(1) of the First Implementing Regulation to the German Municipal Code of 22 March 1935 (*Reichsgesetzblatt*, I, p. 393).

Article V

Final provisions.

§ 9

If there are doubts as to whether a person is a Jew, the higher administrative authority decides.

§ 10

Exemptions from the provisions of this law can, in the cases of Articles I and II, be granted by the Reich Minister of Economics in consultation with the Reich Minister of the Interior, and, in the case of Article III, by the Reich Minister of Labour in consultation with the Reich Minister of the Interior.

§ 11

Intergovernmental treaties remain unaffected.

§ 12

The Reich Minister of Economics is authorized, in consultation with the Reich Minister of the Interior and the Reich ministers involved in the specific case, to set the guidelines according to which commercial enterprises are to be considered Jewish or non-Jewish.

§ 13

The Reich Minister of Economics issues the legal and administrative provisions otherwise required for implementation and supplementation of Articles I and II in consultation with the Reich Minister of the Interior, and for Article III in consultation with the Reich Minister of Labour.

§ 14

The law takes effect on 1 January 1936, with the exception of Article IV, which takes effect the day following its proclamation.[7]

Berlin, ...

The Führer and Reich Chancellor
The Reich Minister of the Interior
The Reich Minister of Economics
The Reich Minister of Labour[8]

---

7 This law was not enacted. In addition to the points mentioned here in the draft, bans on the approval of new Jewish shops, the granting of licences to Jews for operations requiring a licence, and training of Jewish apprentices in commerce and the skilled crafts and trades had also been debated. Also discussed were the non-admission or dismissal of Jewish employees in chambers of industry and commerce, chambers of crafts, and trade and industry organizations, as well as the exclusion of Jews from markets, from the awarding of public contracts, and from the purchase of land: memorandum of the Reichsbank, dated 7 Sept. 1935, BArch, R 2501/6992, fols. 321–323.

8 This was added to the original by hand.

DOC. 206
Frankfurter Zeitung, 11 October 1935: report on a statement made by the Racial Policy Office of the NSDAP about mystical tendencies in 'racial theory'[1]

Against the theory of impregnation.
Statement by an employee of the Racial Policy Office of the NSDAP.

Professor Dr *Löffler*,[2] director of the Racial Biology Institute at the University of Königsberg and an employee of the Racial Policy Office of the NSDAP, made available to the 'News Agency of German Newspaper Publishers' statements 'opposing superstition in the racial question'. In these remarks Professor Löffler notes, among other things, that, unfortunately, even today Volksgenossen who have thoroughly recognized the importance of race and the essence of heredity frequently cause harm involuntarily, by mixing rigorous research on race and heredity with mystical and superstitious attempts at explanation. As a result they do harm to the ideology of the National Socialist Movement, if nothing else. In particular the speaker opposes the theory of *telegony* (inheriting the characteristics of a previous mate of the female parent) or *impregnation* (saturation), which resurfaced quite recently. The theory claims that a non-Jewish woman who at one time had intimate relations with a Jew can give birth only to children with Jewish elements, even if the father is a non-Jew. The existence of this alleged telegony or impregnation is mostly asserted on the basis of instinctive opposition to intimate relations between non-Jewish women and Jewish men. The professor says that these assertions, however, as has been proved by animal experiments conducted by distinguished researchers here and abroad, do *not stand up* to rigorous *scientific verification*.

All the genetic material inherited by a living being who has been created by reproduction is transmitted solely through the combination of the paternal nucleus with the maternal nucleus of the germ cell. The speaker adds that if telegony is accepted as fact, no man, for example, would dare to marry a divorced or widowed woman, if he had to be aware that in his children he would rediscover the first husband's hereditary characteristics, surely undesirable ones in some instances. The very fact that women thus far have never reported telegony with regard to the children from a second or third marriage should give one pause for thought. Chaos with respect to population policy and racial policy would ensue if today we were still to allow constructs of mystical ideas and farfetched theories about thoroughly explainable phenomena to be spread with impunity in public as racial doctrine. It is an entirely different matter, of course, whether, for example, women who surrender to race defilement of their own accord, perhaps even out of vile profit-seeking, are actually worth so much that one would desire offspring from them.

The statements of Professor *Löffler* are to be published verbatim in a scientific medical journal in the near future.

---

1 'Gegen die Lehre von der Imprägnation', *Frankfurter Zeitung*, 11 Oct. 1935, p. 2. This document has been translated from German.
2 Correctly: Dr Lothar Loeffler (1901–1983), physician; joined the NSDAP and the SA in 1932; professor of racial biology at the University of Königsberg in Prussia, 1934–1942, and professor of genetics and racial biology in Vienna, 1942–1945; lectureships at the University of Hanover, 1954–1959 and 1968–1972.

DOC. 207

On 16 October 1935 Reich Minister of the Interior Wilhelm Frick protests to Robert Ley against the marking of non-Jewish shops by the German Labour Front in Saxony[1]

Letter from the Reich and Prussian Minister of the Interior (I A 11 562/5012), signed Frick, to Robert Ley, head of the Reich organization of the German Labour Front (DAF),[2] dated 16 October 1935 (copy)

Re: marking of German shops.

As I am informed, a large-scale public operation has been under way in Leipzig since the 10th of this month, conducted by the administration of the German Labour Front in the Gau of Saxony, with the purpose of marking all the German shops with a DAF placard so that they can be outwardly and clearly distinguished from the Jewish ones. I note most respectfully that, in accordance with an express order by the Führer and Reich Chancellor at the last Reich Party Congress, the Reich Minister of the Interior is in sole charge of the entire remit of the Jewish question. It is thus not permissible under any circumstances for public campaigns of any kind to be directed against the Jews without my knowledge and consent. Moreover, the marking of retail shops is already the subject of a draft law that will soon be submitted to the Reich cabinet.[3] An independent approach by other offices is contrary to the will of the Führer and Reich Chancellor and endangers the purpose of the upcoming economic laws against the Jews, because it dissipates energies and gives the outward impression of insufficient internal unity of Party and state.

I therefore urgently request that these and any other similar actions still envisaged with regard to the Jewish question be halted with the greatest possible speed.

I would appreciate being informed soon about the measures taken.[4]

---

[1] BArch, R 1501/127079-35, fol. 226. This letter has been translated from German.
[2] Dr Robert Ley (1890-1945), chemist; worked at Bayer and IG Farben, 1921-1927; joined the NSDAP and the SA in 1925; NSDAP Gauleiter for Rhineland-South, 1925-1931; jailed and fined several times for antisemitic agitation; from 1933 Reichsleiter of the German Labour Front; indicted at the Nuremberg trials in 1945; committed suicide the same year.
[3] On the draft law see Doc. 205, 9 Oct. 1935.
[4] After the Reich Ministry of Economics had also intervened, Ley evidently issued a decree on 24 Oct. 1935 prohibiting all marking and labelling of non-Aryan shops and referring to imminent Reich regulations: see letter from the Reich Ministry of Economics to Ley dated 2 Nov. 1935, BArch, R 2/14518, fols. 22-23.

DOC. 208

On 27 October 1935 NSDAP member Peters urges Mayor Krogmann to dismiss Jewish collectors from the Hamburg State Lottery[1]

Handwritten letter from H. Peters, Hamburg, to Mayor Krogmann, Hamburg, dated 27 October 1935[2]

Dear Mayor and Party Comrade,

As is well known, the propaganda campaign conducted by the Party throughout the Reich with respect to the Jewish question has had great success.

However, to their greatest amazement, countless Party comrades in Hamburg note that, in the case of the Hamburg state, the Jewish question has failed to make an impression. The Hamburg State Lottery thus continues to operate today as the Marxist regime did at one time, hand in hand with the Jewish collectors (90 per cent are Jews), in the closest business relationship.

In contrast, the Prussian State Lottery immediately dismissed eighty Jewish collectors when the National Socialists took power. To cleanse its sphere of business completely of Jewish elements, it totally eliminated the remaining eighteen Jewish collectors, who were even combat veterans, in accordance with the current major enlightenment drive of the state.[3]

This great state campaign against the Jews had such an effect on the Jewish collectors of the Hamburg State Lottery that not a single Jewish collector expected to continue being entrusted with the distribution of lottery tickets.

For example, the Jewish collector Ichenhäuser[4] arranged for his collection business to be signed over to his employees. This measure, however, is only a cover, a way to retain his lucrative business in future. The Jewish collector Dammann,[5] in addition to others, has already sold his collection business. This offers the best proof of how successfully the campaign has affected the Jews. The collection business is not being taken away even from such a thoroughly international Jew as the collector Julius Heckscher.[6] Yet it is well known to the Hamburg authorities (tax, finance, foreignexchange offices) that during the capital flight under Marxist rule he moved his place of residence to Geneva for one year. Then he returned, only to move his residence back to Geneva for 1½ years again, right after the NSDAP government assumed power. Once he knew that even the Hamburg NSDAP government remained friendly to the Jews, he came back here for good.

The Jewish collectors are downright amused at the great one-sided affection shown to them by the Hamburg state.

---

[1] Staatsarchiv Hamburg, 113-3, III/7. This letter has been translated from German.
[2] Several sections of the original are underlined by hand.
[3] The Prussian-South German Class Lottery had quickly implemented the provisions of the Law on the Restoration of the Professional Civil Service of April 1933: see Doc. 189, 20 August 1935.
[4] Emil Ichenhäuser (b. 1874), collector for the State Lottery in Hamburg; emigrated to the Netherlands in June 1939 and was deported from there to Minsk in April 1943.
[5] Paul M. Dammann (b. 1893), businessman; Dammann Bank and Lottery Company; worked as collector for the Hamburg State Lottery until 1933/1934; emigrated to Africa in 1936.
[6] Julius Heckscher (1866–1938), lottery collector. Heckscher was married to Maria, née Frank. They had four children. Maria Heckscher emigrated to Britain in May 1939.

While everything is being done by the state and the Party to prevent and eliminate the concentration of Jewish elements, such concentration is being literally promoted by the Hamburg state and the Hamburg State Lottery.

This is a stab in the back of the NSDAP, which brings every Party comrade and good German to the point of embitterment and outrage, and contributes to a situation where Germany is quietly being undermined again.[7] There is still time (before the new lottery draw is launched) to put an end to this un-German behaviour and toadying to the Jews that is being encouraged by the Hamburg state and the Hamburg State Lottery. We old Party comrades do not want to have fought and bled so that international capitalist Jewish circles can continue to run their lucrative business and use the German people as an object of exploitation. It is therefore a dictate of the moment that here, too, a Gleichschaltung with the Prussian Class Lottery or removal of the Jewish collectors from the Hamburg State Lottery must take place and that there must be an immediate halt to the practice of favouring Jews over old Party comrades.

With German regards

Heil Hitler

DOC. 209

On 1 November 1935 the Branch Group for Private Health Insurance asks the relevant Economic Group for permission to exclude Jewish policyholders[1]

Letter from the Branch Group for Private Health Insurance of the Economic Group for Private Insurance, part of the Reich Group for Insurance, director, signed Bökenkamp,[2] executive office, signed Dr Balzer,[3] Berlin, to the Economic Group for Private Insurance, dated 1 November 1935 (copy)[4]

Re: insuring of Jews.

Now that the Reich government has clearly expressed its attitude towards the Jewish question through the so-called Nuremberg Laws, we consider it our duty also to make our own attempt to solve this question for our area. Two aspects come under consideration, specifically:

(1) elimination of medical care provided by Jewish doctors,

(2) a ban on acceptance of Jews.

---

7 In the original, this paragraph is marked by hand in the left-hand margin.

1 BArch, R 3101/17169, fols. 147–149. This letter has been translated from German.
2 Presumably Hans Bökenkamp, senior engineer in Berlin.
3 Dr Albrecht Balzer (1899–1980), economist; worked for banks, insurance companies, and associations, 1921–1934; joined the NSDAP and the SS in 1933; executive director of the Branch Group for Private Health Insurance, 1935–1939, and, from 1940, of the Economic Group for Life and Health Insurance; in 1962 director of the Association of Private Health Insurance Companies.
4 The letter was forwarded by the Economic Group for Private Insurance to the Reich Ministry of Economics on 14 Nov. 1935 for information: BArch, R 3101/17169, fol. 145.

In our letter dated 18 October 1935 we already took the liberty of asking you to ensure that the regulatory statutes for the Nuremberg Laws result in the elimination of the provision of medical care by non-Aryan physicians.[5]

Today we request in addition that you obtain authorization from the Reich Minister of Economics for us to order a ban on acceptance for all Jews interested in obtaining insurance, which will be binding for all members of the Branch Group.

We believe we require special authorization for this purpose, because in your letter of 21 October 1935 you inform us of a circular letter from the Reich Economic Chamber that prohibits economic organizations from effecting changes in the position of Jews in economic life until a universal legal regulation has been made.[6]

The provision of the Jews living in Germany with insurance coverage is in no way threatened by the measure we envisage, because two purely Jewish companies are already members of the Branch Group, and another eight companies are registered with the Reich Supervisory Office for Private Insurance alone.

To our knowledge, ten purely Jewish health insurance companies are thus operating in the German Reich. Specifically, they are:

(1) the Israelite Women's Health Insurance Company, Frankfurt am Main
(2) the Israelite Men's Health Insurance Company, Frankfurt am Main
(3) the Israelite Women's Benevolent Association for Sick Women and Women in Childbed, Bühl i. B.[7]
(4) the Israelite Men's Medical Care Association in Karlsruhe
(5) the Israelite Men's Medical Care Association in Breisach
(6) the Israelite Women's Medical Care Association in Breisach
(7) the Israelite Nursing Care Association for the Elderly, Mainz
(8) the Israelite Medical Care Association for Women and Girls, Mainz
(9) the Israelite Men's Health Insurance Company, Offenbach am Main
(10) the Israelite Women's Health Insurance Company.

In addition, it is to be assumed that there exist a number of other Jewish companies throughout the territory of the Reich. Jews living in Germany wishing to obtain health insurance cover thus have sufficient opportunity here to meet their insurance needs.

We also ask that you inform us whether you concur with our attempt to transfer the persons of Jewish race still insured with our members to these Jewish companies listed above, in order that the health insurance portfolio of German companies is free of Jews. The opportunity for this should likewise be affirmed by all means, because if just two of the most influential Jewish companies were to expand to the whole Reich, they alone would be able to take on the Jews currently insured with German companies. If you delegate to us the authority to take this initiative, we would make contact to this effect with the Jewish members of the Branch Group.

The implementation of the measures would merely legalize a state of affairs that has already been created by the actions of our members. That is to say, quite a number of German companies have already officially incorporated into their policy conditions or

---

5 See letter dated 18 Oct. 1935: BArch, R 3101/17169, fols. 150–151.
6 The letter is not in the file.
7 Bühl in Baden.

statutes the stipulation that Jews cannot be accepted. Many other companies have issued internal instructions to their insurance canvassers that prohibit such acceptance. Only a very small proportion still take the view today that they must insure all individuals who are not subject to compulsory insurance, regardless of their race. Our planned initiative, therefore, should undoubtedly be welcomed by the vast majority of our members and, for the others, it would have an educational effect, which, from the Party's perspective, is absolutely within the scope of duties of the Branch Group's management. Besides, the Reich government, of its own accord, has already reached a similar decision, forbidding Jewish children to attend German schools as of next year and creating separate educational establishments for them.[8] We believe, therefore, that the requests described above are also in accordance with legislative intent.[9]

We would appreciate a swift response.

Heil Hitler!

DOC. 210

The First Regulation to the Reich Citizenship Law of 14 November 1935 defines the term 'Jew'[1]

First Regulation to the Reich Citizenship Law.[2]
Issued on 14 November 1935.

On the basis of § 3 of the Reich Citizenship Law of 15 September 1935 (*Reichsgesetzblatt*, I, p. 1146), the following is decreed:

§ 1

(1) Until further regulations concerning Reich citizenship certificates are issued, subjects of the state of German or related blood who held the right to vote in Reichstag elections when the Reich Citizenship Law came into effect, or who are granted provisional Reich citizenship by the Reich Minister of the Interior in consultation with the Deputy of the Führer, are regarded as Reich citizens for the time being.

(2) The Reich Minister of the Interior, in consultation with the Deputy of the Führer, can withdraw provisional citizenship.

---

8 See Doc. 196, 10 Sept. 1935.
9 The Economic Group replied to the Branch Group on 14 Nov. 1935 to the effect that until the issuance of appropriate laws, for which one must wait for a definition of the term 'Jew', subsidiary entities would have to abstain from taking new measures: BArch, R 3101/17169, fol. 152. Enclosed with the letter was a Reich Ministry of Economics decree dated 4 Nov. 1935, in which the prohibition of such measures was established: Walk (ed.), *Das Sonderrecht für die Juden im NS-Staat*, p. 138.

1 *Reichsgesetzblatt*, 1935, I, pp. 1333–1334. This document has been translated from German.
2 On the discussion regarding the implementing regulations to the Reich Citizenship Law, see the draft of the First Regulation, dated 22 Sept., and the memorandum from Gütt, dated 25 Sept. 1935 (Doc. 200 and Doc. 203), as well as the entries for 1 Oct., 26 Oct., 7 Nov., and 15 Nov. 1935 in Goebbels, *Die Tagebücher von Joseph Goebbels*, part 1, vol. 3, no. 1 (Munich: Saur, 2005), pp. 301, 317, 324, and 329.

§ 2

(1) The regulations in § 1 also apply to the Jewish Mischlinge who are subjects of the state.

(2) A Jewish Mischling is someone who is descended from one or two grandparents who are full Jews according to race, provided that he is not considered to be a Jew under § 5(2). A grandparent is automatically considered to be a full Jew if he has been a member of the Jewish religious community.

§ 3

Only the Reich citizen, as the holder of full political rights, can exercise the right to vote in political affairs and to hold public office. The Reich Minister of the Interior, or the agency empowered by him, can grant exceptions during the transitional period with regard to occupying public offices. The affairs of the religious organizations are not affected.

§ 4

(1) A Jew cannot be a citizen of the Reich. He is not entitled to the right to vote in political affairs; he cannot hold public office.

(2) Jewish civil servants will retire as of 31 December 1935. If these civil servants fought at the front for the German Reich or its allies in the World War, they will receive as a pension, until they reach retirement age, the full pensionable pay that they last received; however, they will not advance in seniority. After reaching retirement age, their pension will be recalculated in accordance with the last-received pensionable pay.

(3) The affairs of religious organizations are not affected.

(4) The employment of teachers at Jewish state schools remains unaffected, pending the reorganization of the Jewish school system.

§ 5

(1) A Jew is someone who is descended from at least three grandparents who are full Jews according to race. § 2(2) sentence 2 applies.[3]

(2) Also regarded as a Jew is the Mischling who is a subject of the state descended from two grandparents who were full Jews:

(a) who belonged to the Jewish religious community at the time this law was enacted or subsequently joined this community

(b) who was married to a Jew at the time this law was enacted or subsequently married such a person

(c) who is the offspring of a marriage to a Jew within the meaning of (1) that was contracted after the Law for the Protection of German Blood and German Honour became effective on 15 September 1935 (*Reichsgesetzblatt*, I, p. 1146)

(d) who is the offspring of extramarital relations with a Jew within the meaning of (1) and was born out of wedlock after 31 July 1936.

---

3 Under the Aryan Paragraph of the First Implementing Regulation to the Law for the Restoration of the Professional Civil Service (7 April 1933), one Jewish grandparent was sufficient to qualify someone as a Jew in the National Socialist state: see Doc. 32, 11 April 1933.

§ 6

(1) Insofar as Reich laws or directives of the National Socialist German Workers' Party and its organizations include requirements for purity of blood that go beyond the scope of § 5, they remain unaffected.

(2) Other requirements for purity of blood that go beyond the scope of § 5 may be imposed only with the approval of the Reich Minister of the Interior and the Deputy of the Führer. Insofar as requirements of this kind already exist, they will become void as of 1 January 1936, unless they have been approved by the Reich Minister of the Interior in consultation with the Deputy of the Führer. The application for approval is to be submitted to the Reich Minister of the Interior.

§ 7

The Führer and Reich Chancellor can grant exemptions from the provisions of the implementing regulations.

Berlin, 14 November 1935.
The Führer and Reich Chancellor
Adolf Hitler
The Reich Minister of the Interior
Frick
The Deputy of the Führer
R. Heß
Reich Minister without Portfolio

DOC. 211
On 16 November 1935 Albert Herzfeld reports on the compulsory dismissal of his non-Jewish household help[1]

Handwritten diary of Albert Herzfeld,[2] entry for 16 November 1935

16 November 1935 Today there were no further explanations in the newspapers, but it is clear to Elsa[3] and also to Annemarie[4] that we must let our maid Hedwig go by 1 January, although there was no mention of this date in the laws yesterday. It was mentioned,

---

1 Albert Herzfeld, 'Tagebuch', pp. 14–17; Stadtarchiv Düsseldorf, XXII H 61. Published in Albert Herzfeld, *Ein nichtarischer Deutscher: Die Tagebücher des Albert Herzfeld 1935–1939*, ed. Hugo Weidenhaupt (Düsseldorf: Triltsch, 1982), pp. 19–21. This diary entry has been translated from German.

2 Albert Herzfeld (1865–1943), painter; worked until 1905 in his father's textile firm, then as a painter in Düsseldorf; forbidden to paint in 1938 by the president of the Reich Chamber of Fine Arts; in 1942 deported from Düsseldorf to Theresienstadt, where he died in 1943.

3 Elsa Herzfeld, née Volkmar (1882–1944); deported to Theresienstadt with her husband, Albert, in 1942 and from there to Auschwitz-Birkenau in May 1944.

4 Daughter of Albert and Elsa Herzfeld. Dr Annemarie Herzfeld (b. 1903), lawyer; dismissed from her traineeship as a junior lawyer in 1933; secretarial work, 1934–1938; deported to Minsk in Nov. 1941.

however, in the Reichstag session in Nuremberg on 15 September. I am still of the opinion, and this supposedly appeared in foreign newspapers too, that the deadline is to be pushed forward by three months, first, because places cannot be found in such a short time for the number of servants who become available, jobless and unemployed, and, second, the maids themselves are not at all happy about this measure because they all, without exception, have been working happily and for decades in Jewish households. In my long life, I have never yet heard of a case in which the honour of an Aryan maid in a Jewish home has been offended in any way by a non-Aryan male. Hedwig was quite despondent when Elsa told her that she has to let her go, because she never imagined that she would have to leave our service before her marriage. She feels extremely comfortable in our home and like a member of our family. We also strongly regret her leaving. – Today there is a big announcement in the newspapers about the wearing of decorations.[5] Only decorations for which one can present pertinent documentation may be worn. Now, about forty years ago, when I switched to the home guard, I received the Reserve Force Service Award, and the bestowal of this decoration was also recorded at that time, in accordance with the rules, in my military documents. I handed over the originals of these documents, with the record of the award, to the district commandant's office in Minden in Westphalia in 1914, when I entered the army. At the same time, I handed over the original certificate of my qualification as a reserve officer in the Provincial Cavalry, issued in September 1887 by Guard Dragoon Regiment II in Berlin. But I never got them back. Likewise, I have written confirmation that I was awarded the so-called Orange Medal, bestowed in large numbers on the 100th birthday of old Kaiser Wilhelm I,[6] which I received only because I was on active duty under Wilhelm I, and had taken part in an eight-week military exercise under Friedrich III and another one under Wilhelm II. I no longer have written confirmation of that either, but I do still have the original medal. Then I also have the Kyffhäuser Medal and the Iron Cross Second Class, for which I do possess certificates. However, about a week ago, a policeman, on behalf of the chief of police and with his congratulations, presented me with the Honour Cross with Swords for Combatants in the 1914/18 War, and naturally it was accompanied by a certificate. Now it is downright comical that in the same week I am presented with the Honour Cross and at the same time legally deprived of citizenship status. It reminds me that on 19 August of this year the Paintbox Artists' Association,[7] of which I have been a full member for thirty years, congratulated me on my 70th birthday in a very kind letter from the chairman, Otto Ackermann;[8] sent a member of the board and several old members to my home to congratulate me in person; and also sent me a basket splendidly decorated with flowers and containing twelve bottles of fine wine. Six weeks later, the

---

5 This refers to the Implementing Regulation to the Law on Titles, Medals, and Decorations, 14 Nov. 1935. It stipulated that awards for faithful service were no longer to be bestowed on Jews: *Reichsgesetzblatt*, 1935, I, pp. 1341–1347.
6 Orange Medal: this refers to the Kaiser Wilhelm Memorial Medal, established on 22 March 1897. The nickname derives from the colour of the ribbon.
7 The Paintbox (Malkasten) Artists' Association was founded in Düsseldorf in 1848 as an association for social gatherings of artists. Later, non-artists were also permitted to join. Herzfeld was temporarily a member of the board and the auditor of the association.
8 Otto Ackermann (1872–1953), landscape painter in Düsseldorf.

association removed me, along with the other eight non-Aryan members, from its membership rolls. – It is very difficult to preserve one's equanimity! Besides, this removal from the membership list is quite illegal and just as unpleasant and embarrassing for the board as for me, because according to the statutes, only a member who has been found guilty of an offence can have his membership revoked, and this is not the case for either me or those who share my fate. – This afternoon I was visiting my thoroughly Aryan friends Dr and Mrs K. Bischoff,[9] and the latest regulations were the main topic of conversation for all. I have never yet met anyone who is in agreement, even in the slightest, with these measures and anti-Jewish laws. – You poor 12,000 who were killed in action, some of whom volunteered to serve in the war, are to be pitied! I wonder whether you will be thrown out of Valhalla.[10] And the poor old parents who have sacrificed their sons to the fatherland are now no longer allowed to have Aryan household help! Sometimes I put my head in my hands and do not understand the logic.

DOC. 212
Pariser Tageblatt, 25 November 1935: editorial regarding the absurdity of the definition of race according to the Nuremberg Laws[1]

Nuremberg trinkets.[2] Legally unenforceable bans on marriage
  by Dr Ernst Frankenstein[3]

The *Pariser Tageblatt* has already reproduced in detail the implementing provisions to the Nuremberg Jewish Laws of the Third Reich.[4] We have also already availed ourselves of the opportunity provided by publication of the texts to criticize these implementing

---

9 Dr Karl Wilhelm Bischoff (b. 1875), physician; worked from 1905 as a gynaecologist in Düsseldorf; arrested by the Gestapo in 1939 and sentenced in 1940 to eight months in prison; proceedings for professional misconduct were stayed by the Rhineland Medical District Court in late 1940, but Bischoff was struck off the Register of Physicians.
10 A great hall or palace in Nordic mythology where the god Odin receives half of the soldiers who die in battle to dine with him as heroes for eternity. The other half feast with the goddess Freyja in Fólkvangr.

1 'Nürnberger Tand. Juristisch undurchführbare Eheverbote von Dr. jur. Ernst Frankenstein', *Pariser Tageblatt*, 25 Nov. 1935, pp. 1–2. Excerpts published in *UuF*, vol. 11, pp. 177–179. This document has been translated from German.
2 A reference to the saying 'Nürnberger Tand geht durch alle Land' (Nuremberg trinkets pass throughout the land), which itself referred to the city's heyday between 1470 and 1530, when Nuremberg's products were traded throughout the world.
3 Dr Ernst Frankenstein (1881–1959), lawyer; practised law in Berlin; he emigrated to Paris in 1933 and in 1936 to London; author of works including *Internationales Privatrecht (Grenzrecht)* (vols. 1–4, 1926–1935) and *Justice for My People: The Jewish Case* (1943).
4 See 'Vier Kategorien 'Nichtarier'. Die Ausfuehrungsbestimmungen zu den Nuernberger Judengesetzen erlassen – Die Vorschriften ueber die Eheschliessung – Regelung der Beamten- und Dienstbotenfrage', *Pariser Tageblatt*, 16 Nov. 1935, p. 1, and 'Wie die Nuernberger Gesetze angewendet werden. Die ersten Ausfuehrungsbestimmungen – Sondervorschriften fuer *Mischlinge* – Pensionierung der letzten juedischen Beamten – Aufnordung von Nichtariern – Der gemilderte Hausangestelltenparagraph', ibid., 17 Nov. 1935, p. 2.

provisions, which only make the laws even more curious. Nonetheless, the following expert comments by the universally esteemed specialist in the problems of international civil law ought still to be of great interest to our readers.

It has taken two months for the implementing regulations to the Law for the Protection of German Blood and German Honour to appear.[5] One may thus assume that they not only were drawn up with great care but also take into account the numerous objections that have already been raised to the wording of the law. The impression created by the regulation is all the stronger. It certainly confirms very clearly that, despite intense efforts, the concept of race has not been successfully defined.

What is prohibited is marriage between German subjects of the state of German or related blood and Jews. What constitutes a Jew is defined by § 5 of the First Regulation to the Reich Citizenship Law: 'A Jew is someone who is descended from at least three grandparents who are full Jews according to race. A grandparent is automatically considered to be a full Jew if he has been a member of the Jewish religious community.' Therefore, race is determined not by a biological characteristic but rather by the legal concept of membership of a religious community. But that is, as the phrase '*automatically* considered to be a full Jew' shows, only one instance in which one can belong to the Jewish race. And the other instances?

Here the lawmaker falls short. He is unable to define the concept of the Jewish race. Admittedly, he works with the concept of descent from Jewish grandparents who are 'full Jews according to race', but can explain this comprehensive term only by using a less comprehensive one, that is, by referring to those who 'are automatically considered to be full Jews'. The law does not state who is not 'automatically considered to be a full Jew' based on membership in the Jewish religious community but is nonetheless a full Jew. Here there is a yawning gap that cannot be filled.

Whether grandparents who have been raised in a different religion or with no religion by their Jewish parents are 'full Jews according to race', the law does not and cannot say, because the concept of race in the legal sense simply does not exist. For the third generation, the law swaps the concept of race for the concept of religious affiliation but is unwilling to acknowledge it, and thereby enters an insoluble contradiction. One must either abandon the concept of race on which the world view of the present-day German lawmaker rests, or one must define it in a way that is legally comprehensible, which is impossible.

This internal contradiction is exposed in every detail. For example, under § 5 of the Regulation to the Reich Citizenship Law, the 'Jewish Mischling' who descended from two Jewish grandparents, who also belonged to the Jewish religious community when the law was enacted or subsequently joined this community, is considered a Jew. While race is thus obviously something biological to which one is inescapably subject, for the 'Jewish Mischling', being a member of the Jewish race (more precisely, being a Jew) depends on whether he professes membership in the Jewish religious community, that is, on his will. Conversely, in the case of the Aryan who has converted and joined the Jewish religious community or is converting, it is not his denomination, not his will, that is decisive, but rather the biological factor of race. *This Jew is not a Jew.*

---

5 This refers to the First Regulation to the Reich Citizenship Law, 14 Nov. 1935: see Doc. 210.

Indeed, there is more. If the Jewish son of a Jewish father and a non-Jewish mother marries a non-Jewish (Aryan) woman who converts to Judaism, and raises his children in Orthodox Judaism, these Jewish children, whose male ancestors were always Jews, are not Jews. They are 'Jewish Mischlinge', who under § 2 of the implementing regulation are even forbidden to marry Jews, because only one of their grandparents was a full Jew.

These observations suffice. The concept of the Jew, against whom the ban on marriage is aimed, is a pseudo-concept that eludes all definition. The fundamental concept of 'grandparents who were full Jews' is not universally defined at all, but rather is defined for only one of its cases of application (belonging to the Jewish religion), while the other cases of application remain open. Among the offspring, however, someone who professes the Jewish religion is a 'Jew' one moment and not a 'Jew' the next, and even finds himself forbidden to marry members of his own faith.

The confusion of concepts rises to the point of complete absurdity in the provision of § 4, which prohibits marriage between Jewish Mischlinge who have only one full Jew as a grandparent. In other words: the Orthodox Jews mentioned in the example above may marry only Jews who are of pure Aryan descent ...

No, the implementing regulations have not improved the law. They continue to permit marriage between German subjects of the state 'of German or related blood' and Negroes and mulattos, but fall short when they try to define the 'Jew' whom one is not allowed to marry. One can call someone who belongs to the Jewish religious community a Jew. One can also extend the term to the previous members of this community and to the non-Jewish descendants. But one cannot create a concept of the Jewish race that, as an umbrella concept, includes both the narrower concept of adherents of the Jewish religion and an undefined unknown. No one can say what, under the law, a 'fully Jewish grandparent according to race' who does not belong to the Jewish religious community is. And yet, this is what the regulation requires.

A work of legislation that uses something unknown and indeterminable as an initial concept may be interesting. For the application of law outside the country of origin, it is out of the question, because it lacks the most important prerequisite of the law: determinability of its concepts.

DOC. 213
Travel report dated 29 November 1935 about the dramatic situation of the Jewish population after the enactment of the Nuremberg Laws[1]

Letter from S. R., Geneva, dated 29 November 1935, no addressee (copy)[2]

I. General situation.

When stating the reasons for the laws pertaining to Jews that were issued in September of this year, the German Reich Chancellor explained that these laws are intended to produce a tolerable relationship between Germans and Jews. Regardless of whether this statement was in earnest, it must be said that since the enactment of the Nuremberg

---

1 CZA, S 7/16. This document has been translated from German.
2 Parts of the original are marked and underlined by hand.

Laws the situation of the Jews has been growing more difficult every day, in particular because even while the laws were being issued, the release of implementing regulations for them was being announced. Approximately four weeks after Nuremberg, Reich Minister of the Interior Frick stated in a speech that the future implementing regulations would also restrict the position of Jews in the economy.[3] However, the state of affairs that has come about in the meantime is becoming more untenable every day. The Jews live in a state of the greatest uncertainty and nervous turmoil. Personal and business arrangements can scarcely be made, and the rumours concerning the implementing regulations change from day to day. One moment it is said that they are to ease the economy, and the next that they are soon to bring about a total exclusion [of the Jews].

The implementing regulations that have appeared thus far for a part of the Nuremberg Laws have altered nothing about this state of affairs, because they leave the economic questions untouched and merely define the set of persons now to be viewed as Jewish.

Further, a certain clarity has been achieved regarding the question of employing Aryan household help in Jewish homes. Here it is assumed that these implementing regulations are known and that there is thus no need to go into their content in any greater detail. In this context, however, the problem of employing Aryan girls in Jewish households must be briefly touched upon. Even if it is clear, of course, that this question does not ultimately have such great significance, it must not be overlooked that it does have a certain influence on the situation of the Jews, to the extent that it is symptomatic of the difficulties to which Jews are subjected in Germany today, even in their daily and quite personal lives. The domestic servant question indeed has significance not only for the propertied circles of persons who can still afford household help today but also for a very considerable number of persons with little or no means. As a result of the altered circumstances since April 1933, the number of Jewish women holding jobs has substantially increased, particularly where the family was especially hard hit by the exclusion of the breadwinner from his occupation. A great many wives of lawyers, civil servants, writers, and artists have, in the course of the past few years, made enormous efforts in an attempt to feed the family by doing jobs of a great many kinds. They were able to do this so long as their children and their household were looked after by a maid. Now, when the Aryan maids are being dismissed, the entire family is gravely affected, because the woman of the house, who is simultaneously the provider for her family, can no longer devote herself to her occupation. This has severe repercussions for the existence of many families. The difficulties are particularly great for elderly people who are no longer able to manage the housekeeping alone and are dependent on outside help. The result of this state of affairs is that a reorganization of the entire way of life becomes mandatory, leases for apartments must be terminated, families move in together, and the overall standard of living will have to be further reduced, even where people were already feeling the pinch.

Especially difficult is the situation of Jewish schoolchildren. Of approximately 45,000 children, around 17,000 have been placed thus far in Jewish schools; the rest

---

3 This refers to the original plans of the National Socialist leadership to also incorporate economic measures against Jews into the implementing regulations. These plans were, however, dropped by late Oct. 1935: on the plans see also the draft law of 9 Oct. 1935, Doc. 205.

attend state schools. At the same time as the Nuremberg Laws came out, there also appeared a decree by Minister of Culture Rust announcing the removal of the Jewish children from state schools and the concentration of them in Jewish schools by 1 April 1936.[4] The implementing regulations for this school law have not yet been made public. Therefore, a total lack of clarity prevails as to how these new Jewish schools will be constituted and who will maintain them. The extent of the state's contribution towards expenses has not yet been determined, and the proposed influence to be exercised by the state over the curricula and selection of teachers is not known. It is certain, however, that the creation of these new Jewish schools is immensely problematic, if only because there is simply a lack of the requisite teaching staff for the supervision of such a large number of children. But the fact that the Jewish pupils are to be removed has led a great many head teachers to entertain a certain ambition to make their school free of Jews as quickly as possible, that is, even before the legally established deadline of 1 April 1936. This is being attempted in a great variety of ways. The Jewish children are being tormented and mistreated by teachers and other children, the *Stürmer* has become habitual reading matter at numerous schools, and Jewish children are being used to demonstrate various racial characteristics, in accordance with the *Stürmer*. At one school (in Dessau) the headmaster has simply suspended the children from attending school until April 1936. When the parents protested, the suspension was withdrawn, but the children are regarded merely as visiting pupils; that is, they are not tested and are discriminated against in class, as far as possible. The results of this state of affairs are downright disastrous for the children. They are suffering almost incurable psychological damage and becoming unstable and insecure, and their achievements, in terms of what they are learning, are also declining markedly.

For a great many families, in the past few months, the new worry of housing has been added to the general anxiety, concerns with keeping the household going without help, and worries about the children. Most flats put up in the last fifteen years were built with the help of public funds. They are owned by so-called building societies, which are non-commercial associations. These not-for-profit residential building societies are controlled by the local authorities. The local authorities, like all public entities, are staffed exclusively by National Socialists. In increasingly large numbers, the leases of Jewish tenants in these buildings are being terminated. Because these are mostly cheap apartments, in which members of the middle class and salaried classes live, a new and immensely difficult problem arises, aggravated particularly by the fact that today even the private owners of blocks of flats are refusing in increasing numbers to accept Jewish tenants. The buildings still in Jewish ownership cannot be used as a substitute here, because they are usually inhabited by Aryan tenants, and the Jewish owner must be wary of cancelling the leases of these residents. On 1 January and 1 April, the dates on which apartment leases expire, the awful problem of homelessness is looming for thousands of families. This also applies in the big cities of Berlin,[5] Hamburg, Cologne, and Frankfurt, where the Jews, in comparison with the state of affairs in the medium-sized and small towns, were able until now to live in more bearable circumstances.

4 On this decree see Doc. 196, 10 Sept. 1935.
5 During this phase, several Berlin city building societies and housing associations terminated the leases of Jewish tenants in small flats as of 1 Jan. or 1 April 1936: see letter of Acting Mayor Steeg, 14 March 1936, LAB, A Rep. 09/31419.

In the small and medium-sized towns, the so-called passive boycott is increasingly common; that is, a growing number of food shops, coal purveyors, and craftsmen are refusing to supply Jews with the requisite goods for their daily needs or to complete orders for them. In many cities this is so widespread that it is even extremely difficult to provide children with milk.

These few remarks, in which I deliberately omitted especially difficult individual cases and avoided exaggeration, are merely intended to characterize the general state of affairs. Below is a report on various individual problems.

II. Economic life.
General uncertainty as a result of the absence of the implementing regulations mentioned above is having an increasingly detrimental effect on the economic situation. There are an increasing number of Jewish owners of relatively large shops and enterprises who see themselves forced through circumstances to sell their businesses or factories. Hardly a day passes without several significant shops and factories passing into Aryan hands. The drive to dispose of Jewish shops and enterprises has become almost a psychosis among well-to-do Jews. The growing general difficulties in the economy give rise to the resolve to sell as quickly as possible, because everyone must fear that the increasing deterioration of the economic situation must inevitably inhibit the number of Aryan buyers who are able to pay. On the basis of impeccable reports, it can be stated that the sales of businesses yield barely more than 30 per cent to at most 45 per cent of their actual value, which means that an enormous reduction in Jewish assets occurs as a result.

The extensive sale of Jewish enterprises signifies not only a decline in assets but simultaneously the loss of jobs for Jewish employees and workers of all kinds, because the first action taken by the Aryan purchasers of Jewish firms is to remove and dismiss the Jewish employees. Because Jewish workers, as a result of the developments of the past few years, are now employed only in Jewish companies, the progressive Aryanization of the economy produces an increase in Jewish unemployment. Those affected have no prospect of ever finding a job or line of work in Germany again, because the labour market for Jewish workers continues to shrink with the elimination of the Jewish businessmen.

Another cause for the sale of Jewish firms is the attempted elimination of Jews from the economy through administrative channels. Almost all public institutions, such as state offices, the Reich Railways, the Reich Postal Service, municipalities, local gasworks and power utilities, trams, and large banks, have decided to stop awarding contracts to businesses that belong to Jews or that maintain business relations with Jews. Civil servants are forbidden to buy from Jews. The delivery book that has been introduced for the skilled crafts and trades enables the German Labour Front to determine which shops the craftsmen buy their materials from. Wherever Jewish suppliers are identified, the craftsman is barred from obtaining public contracts. In some places the skilled construction workers, for example, have already decided that where the contracting entity itself obtains the materials (bathtubs, conduit pipes, electric lamps), they will refuse to work if these items are bought in Jewish shops.

This all signifies enormous pressure on the Jewish businessmen and provides cause for the accelerated sale and liquidation of their businesses.

Jewish booksellers and Jewish cinema owners have been informed by their professional associations that permission to continue their businesses will be revoked, probably by 31 December, and they are therefore being advised to arrange for the transfer of these businesses into Aryan hands as quickly as possible.⁶

After the dismissal of all civil servants, including the war veterans who had previously been kept on, the last managing directors of the banks and large insurance companies are now being let go as well.

The cancellation of the mortgages on Jewish landholdings is proceeding, and the number of Jewish properties being forced into public auction is increasing. There is a lack of financial capacity in Jewish companies that would be in a position to intervene here and help by taking on the mortgages. Assistance for Jewish landholdings is becoming a difficult problem generally, as the economic implementing regulations for the Nuremberg Laws will evidently contain a ban on land acquisition by Jews, which is also to be concluded from the fact that the courts are already rejecting deed registrations for Jews who buy plots of land.⁷ The decrease in Jewish landownership must inevitably also affect the housing conditions of the Jews, as was suggested above in the remarks made under I.

Even the few Jews who work in agriculture are being harshly oppressed. For quite some time now, the measures of the Ministry of Food have provided for the elimination of Jews from trade in farm produce, but even agricultural production is being hampered by the fact that, during the harvest, the Jews are denied the local help that has been customary for decades. They were given no workers to bring in the crops, they were denied use of the threshing machine, and almost everywhere they are prohibited from renting horses and carts, which are necessary for harvesting. The result is that the plight of these landowning Jews, who live mainly in Hesse, Franconia, and Wuerttemberg, has become so untenable that in many instances they are leaving all their property behind and fleeing to the neighbouring towns.

In the past few days, even the few Jewish brokers who are accredited with the stock exchanges have been ousted, forbidden to practise their occupation.⁸ Admittedly, this measure now only affects approximately thirty families, but it is symptomatic of how even the last remaining Jew is being excluded from an occupation in which Jews once were very numerous.

III. The liberal professions.
The displacement of Jews from the liberal professions is continuing. These days, consultations about a further exclusion of Jewish lawyers are taking place. Even though the general plight of the Bar is being cited as justification for these measures, the exclusionary measures appearing in the next few days will affect solely the Jewish lawyers. Moreover, the head of the National Socialist Association of Lawyers, Dr Frank,⁹ pointed out in a speech several days ago that the corollary of the Nuremberg Laws is the judiciary being

---

6 On 17 Oct. 1935 the Reich Film Chamber had demanded that all Jewish cinema owners in Germany sell their businesses by 10 Dec. 1935; after that date their licences expired: Feuchtwanger (ed.), *Der Gelbe Fleck*, p. 153.

7 As representative of the Gestapo Central Office (Gestapa), Werner Best had indeed called for corresponding provisions, but such paragraphs were not present in the draft regulations that pertained to the economy: see Doc. 195, 9 Sept. 1935, and Doc. 205, 9 Oct. 1935.

8 On 14 Nov. 1935 Reich Minister of Economics Schacht had ordered that accreditation of Jewish brokers be withdrawn as of 22 Nov. 1935: see 'Keine jüdischen Kursmakler mehr', *Jüdische Rundschau*, 26 Nov. 1935, p. 4.

totally cleansed of Jews.¹⁰ Hundreds of older Jewish lawyers, who even now are struggling for their livelihood, face these measures with grave trepidation.

For doctors, too, further exclusions from the health insurance companies are planned. If this does not happen immediately, as demanded by many National Socialists, then it is because a certain amount of time is needed to groom the young generation of German doctors, and, besides, the newly created Wehrmacht also has a significant demand for doctors. Nonetheless, on the basis of reliable information, further measures against Jewish physicians are to follow.¹¹ How insecure the doctors themselves believe their situation to be can be seen from the fact that, following news of the suspension of physician licensing in Palestine, around 400 Jewish doctors have left Germany in the space of a few weeks, including some who still had a very good practice to date.¹²

IV. Cultural activity.
The problems in the area of cultural activity are also increasing. The ban on selling Jewish newspapers on the street or at kiosks does extremely grave damage to the economic situation of the Jewish press.¹³ The editorial difficulties, too, are growing. The increasingly severe censorship forces editorial staff to be extremely cautious; insignificant remarks result in long-term bans. For example, publication of the *C.V.-Zeitung* was suspended for three months, and later the *Israelitisches Familienblatt* for three months as well.¹⁴ It is clear that such a long shutdown results in such great material damage that resumption of the newspapers' publication after a further ban is seriously called into question. On 21 November, Mr Hinkel, the National Socialist commissioner for Jewish cultural affairs,¹⁵ announced in a widely publicized statement that the Jewish cultural

---

9 Dr Hans Frank (1900–1946), lawyer; in 1919 board member of the Thule Society and member of the German Workers' Party (DAP); joined the NSDAP and the SA in 1923 and took part in the Beer Hall Putsch the same year; legal representation of the NSDAP, 1927–1933; Reich leader of the National Socialist Association of Lawyers, 1928–1942; state commissioner, then Bavarian state minister of justice, 1933–1934; Reich minister without portfolio, 1934–1945; Governor General in occupied Poland, 1939–1945; sentenced to death and executed in 1946 at the Nuremberg trials.
10 This was presumably the speech at the conference of the Reich Branch Group of Lawyers at the National Socialist Association of Lawyers in Berlin on 23 Nov. 1935. There, Frank had characterized the removal of all Jews and 'unworthy elements' from the Bar as an imperative of National Socialism: *Völkischer Beobachter* (northern German edition), 24 Nov. 1935, p. 2.
11 A change to the Reich Physicians' Regulation of 13 Dec. 1935 meant that it was prohibited to issue new licences to Jews to practise medicine if their representation in the medical profession exceeded the percentage of Jews in the general population: *Reichsgesetzblatt*, 1935, I, p. 1433.
12 In 1935 the British Mandate government had introduced a *numerus clausus* for doctors in Palestine, as a result of which the issuing of licences was greatly decreased. Many physicians from Germany subsequently tried to reach Palestine before the effective date of this regulation.
13 On 6 Sept. 1935 the president of the Reich Press Chamber had ordered a ban on sales of Jewish newspapers in street trade: *Völkischer Beobachter* (northern German edition), 8 Sept. 1935, p. 5.
14 The *C.V.-Zeitung* was prohibited from 20 June to 26 Sept. 1935 and the *Israelitisches Familienblatt* from mid August to early Nov. 1935.
15 Hans Hinkel (1900–1960), journalist; joined the NSDAP in 1921 and the SS in 1931; took part in the Beer Hall Putsch, 1923; editor of several National Socialist newspapers, 1924–1933; state commissioner in the Prussian Ministry of Culture, 1933–1934; special representative for supervision of the cultural activities of non-Aryans in the Reich Ministry of Public Enlightenment and Propaganda, 1935–1938; specialist for Jewish affairs there, 1938–1941; secretary general of the Reich Chamber of Culture, 1941–1944; Reich grand Director of Film, 1944–1945; extradited to Poland in 1947; released to the Federal Republic of Germany in 1952.

associations have more than 100,000 members and that 650 Jewish artists are employed. Apart from the fact that these figures are greatly exaggerated, one must note that the plight of the Jewish artists, actors, and musicians, as well as sculptors and painters, is extraordinarily grave. Only a portion of the performing artists and musicians can be employed at all, and they barely appear more than two or three times a month and do not even earn as much as is needed to support themselves for a week. Even the cultural associations, which have a fixed ensemble, are engaged in a difficult struggle for their existence, because the number of Jews who can still afford membership in cultural associations is dwindling.

The news from Germany from the National Socialists about the cultural freedom of the Jews and the employment opportunities for Jewish artists thus constitutes sweeping exaggerations.

V. Situation of foreign Jews.
In addition, the situation of the foreign Jews living in Germany, who are still quite numerous, is increasingly difficult. Besides the general anti-Jewish measures in every sphere of life, foreign Jews are also subjected to particular forms of oppression. Because of the legal requirements in effect, foreigners need special permission if they intend to work as blue- or white-collar employees. Previously, foreigners who lived in Germany for more than ten years automatically received permission to take any job. These regulations are now much harsher and are being implemented in the strictest, most rigorous manner. Increasingly common are cases in which Jewish foreign nationals who were born in Germany or have lived here for twenty years and more are not being granted a work permit. As a result, they are forced to remain unemployed and to have recourse to public assistance. Such assistance, however, is denied to them on the grounds that they are not available to the labour market because they cannot accept work without a permit, and this permit is not granted to them. So this means that the people are first put out of work, and then they are denied assistance, after which they are expelled from the country because they cannot support themselves independently. These cases are piling up in alarming numbers. Likewise the cases in which individuals who have lived in Germany for decades are being denied, for trivial reasons, extensions of their residence permits for Germany. Expulsions and punishment for non-compliance with these expulsions are piling up on an enormous scale. Similarly, the difficulties and harassment of foreigners who are dependent on public assistance are increasing, and more and more city administrations are proceeding to deny all assistance to Jewish foreigners. Especially hard hit by these measures are the stateless foreigners, as not even the basic consular protection is available to them. Among these stateless foreigners are thousands of people who once held German citizenship but have been deprived of it. The situation of these people is becoming downright tragic. They have no means of livelihood, benefit from no protection of any kind whatsoever, and are unable to leave Germany because, owing to their statelessness, in addition to the general difficulties of emigration, they can hardly obtain an entry permit for any country.

Even those very large numbers of foreigners who thus far earned their living as travelling salesmen and pedlars are experiencing incredible hardship, because their permit for doing business has been revoked.[16] Thousands of Jewish families that have managed thus far to survive independently, though scraping by, are thus forced to have recourse to public assistance. Such assistance is denied to them, as in the case of the unemployed, and their expulsion is ordered.

VI. Emigration.

The circumstances sketched only briefly here have resulted in an enormous increase in the Jews' need to emigrate, and now it is not only the younger and less well-to-do people who are deciding to leave. The very well-off and still well-established families also find themselves forced into emigration. There is no group within German Jewry that is not convinced today that emigration is the only way to save themselves. The Palestine offices are so overrun with people eager to emigrate that they can scarcely cope with the numbers of people pouring in. The Relief Association of German Jews, which handles emigration to all other countries, also has such a large number of would-be emigrants to advise that it must substantially enlarge its organization and set up around fifteen regional offices.

There is an increased need to emigrate, but in contrast there are only a few possibilities for emigration. The number of immigration certificates still available in the present year cannot be assessed yet,[17] and the possibilities for emigration to other countries are very slight. The JCA[18] has now launched an attempt at colonization in Argentina with twenty Jewish families, and the transport carrying these specially selected people ought to be leaving for Argentina in the next few days. It is due to be followed in a few weeks by a group of sixty young people, also destined for agricultural settlement in Argentina. It is to be hoped that, if these attempts prove successful, larger numbers of emigrants can go to Argentina. In view of the enormous number of would-be emigrants, however, these small possibilities signify only a very modest degree of relief. Unless new and ample opportunities for immigration are made accessible soon, it is to be feared that the countries bordering on Germany will be swamped by new waves of refugees. The Jewish organizations are indeed trying to calm the agitated, overly nervous, and fearful people and warn them against impulsive flight to another country. Given the catastrophic deterioration of conditions, however, these warnings will have no effect in the long run.

VII. Concluding remarks.

Fear, uncertainty, and trepidation characterize the state of the Jews in Germany today. Economic decline and the increased number of people in need demand of the Jewish communities the greatest effort and greatest sacrifices if they are to raise the enormous resources required as assistance. The growth in the number of well-to-do and affluent emigrants, who previously contributed to the maintenance of the Jewish communities, means an extraordinary weakening of the capabilities of the communities. A community that grows poorer every day is facing these new, heavy burdens. There are already numerous communities that are unable to meet the simplest needs of religious and social life, communities that consist exclusively of indigent persons who can continue to support themselves only thanks to the benefits they receive from the central Jewish bodies.[19]

---

16 On the revocation of trade licences for travelling salesmen, see the circular decree of the Reich Ministry of Economics dated 28 Dec. 1935, LAB, Rep. 142/7, 1-11-1/Nr. 13.
17 The author means immigration certificates for Palestine: see Glossary.
18 Jewish Colonization Association.
19 On the situation of religious communities in Silesia see Doc. 101, 5 Feb. 1934, and Doc. 272, 16 April 1937.

DOC. 214
On 12 December 1935 Reich Minister of Justice Franz Gürtner discusses with Hitler the removal of Jews from the liberal professions[1]

Memorandum of Reich Minister of Justice Gürtner, dated 12 December 1935[2]

Reception in the Chancellor's office at 12:30 p.m.

I.

I asked the Chancellor what his intention is with respect to the implementation of the Jewish legislation in the liberal professions. The judicial authorities, I said, have a stake in this issue on account of the lawyers and will submit a law to amend the Regulations for Lawyers at the next cabinet session.[3] For this reason, I added, I was asking him to inform me of his intentions.

In my view, I said, three solutions are possible:

(a) legal cancellation of all licensing in one go;

(b) delegation of authority to cancel the licences, in which case one must be clear in advance on the way in which this authority is to be used;

(c) solution of the problem by natural means, that is, by letting them die out. The Chancellor asked me whether that is possible in twenty years. I explained to him that this would be mathematically the maximum time; in reality a much shorter period of time would come into consideration.

In reply the Chancellor declared that at the moment it does not seem expedient to him to take approach (a) or (b). He does not wish, he said, for any measures at all to be taken now in the area of the liberal professions.

II. To State Secretary Schlegelberger,[4] for his attention.

---

[1] BArch, R 3001/8521, fol. 275. Published in Hartmannsgruber (ed.), AdR, part 2, vol. 2, p. 986. This document has been translated from German.

[2] The original contains handwritten initials. The deputy Reich lawyers' leader, Dr Walter Raeke (b. 1878), had asked the Reich Ministry of Justice on 6 Dec. 1935 to include a *numerus clausus* for Jews in the new Regulations for Lawyers as well as the option to revoke the licence to practise law: BArch, R 3001/8521, fols. 378–379.

[3] On 4 Dec. 1935 Reich Minister Gürtner had already sent a cabinet draft with a change to the Regulations for Lawyers, providing for retraction of licences to practise if the proportion of Jewish lawyers exceeded the proportion of Jews in the population as a whole: ibid., fols. 346–347. See also Hartmannsgruber (ed.), AdR, part 2, vol. 2, doc. 282.

[4] Dr Franz Schlegelberger (1876–1970), lawyer; from 1901 in the judicial service; from 1931 state secretary at the Reich Ministry of Justice; joined the NSDAP in 1938; temporarily charged with the conduct of affairs as Reich minister of justice, 1941 to August 1942; sentenced to life imprisonment in 1947 at the Nuremberg Judges' Trial; released in 1950.

DOC. 215
A leading official in the Reich Ministry of Education reports on the top-level conference on 12 December 1935 regarding the continuation of anti-Jewish policies[1]

Memorandum of the Reich Minister of Education, unsigned, dated 12 December 1935 (copy regarding E II e 2883/35)

(1) *Memorandum*

I[2] was present at today's top-level conference on the Jewish question.[3] It was attended by a great many people, all the ministers or their deputies.

With regard to the questions that concern us, Reich Minister *Frick* and State Secretary *Stuckart* stated the following: Jews (here and below, this always means people who are Jews under the Nuremberg Laws, that is, full and three-quarter-Jews) must be removed from the primary schools and put in separate state schools. Mischlinge must be accommodated in the normal state schools, that is, not in the Jewish schools, because they are to be treated as Germans.

The Jews must be removed from the academic secondary schools too. It is to be left to the Jews to create private academic secondary schools for themselves. Of the existing laws, it was stated only that they must be brought into line with the new definition of a Jew.

With respect to the institutions of higher education, it was stated that Mischlinge must be admitted to them with no restrictions. Reich Physicians' Leader *Wagner*, in attendance as the representative of the Deputy of the Führer, raised the subject of the Reich Organization of German Students[4] and demanded that it must likewise accept Mischlinge. Selection is entirely a matter for the National Socialist Association of Students, to which our minister has indeed already delegated the political education of the students.

I protested against this decisively and with lengthy substantiation. Minister *Frick*, however, aligned himself with the same standpoint [as Wagner].

I explained that we are already working on an application to retain the Party regulations for the Reich Organization of Students. Not being a member of the German Students' Union, after all, does not prevent anyone from studying at a university.

With regard to the institutions of higher education for teacher training and similar institutions that serve exclusively to train future teachers or civil servants, admission of

---

1 BArch, R 4901/11787, fol. 30. This document has been translated from German.
2 This presumably refers to Ministerial Director Siegmund Kunisch (1900–1978), from 1934 to 1936 acting state secretary in the Reich Ministry of Education.
3 There is no written record of the full conference. From another memorandum, the following additional decisions can be derived: in a new version of the Regulations for Lawyers, nothing needed to be said about the licensing of Jewish lawyers. Licence to practise for Jewish physicians could be revoked if their percentage in the legal profession exceeded the percentage of Jews in the general population; memorandum of Schlegelberger, BArch, R 3001/8521, fols. 272–279. One day after the conference, on 13 Dec. 1935, the new licensing of Jews was prohibited by means of a change to the Regulations for Lawyers with this rationale: *Reichsgesetzblatt*, 1935, I, p. 1433.
4 Correctly: Reich Organization of Students at German Universities and Technical Colleges.

Mischlinge was demanded, even though Mischlinge cannot be hired as teachers and civil servants.

With regard to the farm service year, there was consensus that membership in the Hitler Youth on the part of individuals for whom farm service is mandatory and on the part of farm service leaders makes it necessary to apply the Party principles.

DOC. 216
On 14 December 1935 the city of Radeberg reports to the Saxon State Minister for Economics and Labour on the boycott of Jewish businesses[1]

Letter from the deputy mayor of Radeberg (XI A VII regarding I 3b: J 68), signed Gubitz,[2] to the State Minister for Economics and Labour,[3] Dresden, dated 14 December 1935 (copy)

Re: *Jewish businesses in Radeberg.*
In response to the regulation of 7 December 1935, while returning the two petitions[4] from the lawyer Dr Neumark[5] of Dresden to the Reich Ministry of Economics, I report the following on the basis of my records and the police investigations in particular:

The principals listed in the petition of 11 September 1935, Franz *Schaefer* (the owner of the business is his wife, Rosa Schaefer, née Ikenberg),[6] Franz *Hofstein*, Martin (not Max) *Liegner*,[7] and Franz *Herzfeld*,[8] are the owners of the four Jewish shops that are well-known here and located in the main street.[9]

During the night of 20 July 1935, the words 'Jew' and 'race defiler' were painted on the display windows of these four shops and the pavement in front of them with paint made of whiting and soluble glass. The proprietor Rosa Schaefer, née Ikenberg, reported this to the police early in the morning, before six o'clock, and identified the culprit as

1 Sächsisches Staatsarchiv, Hauptstaatsarchiv Dresden, Außenministerium/1723, fols. 145–147. This document has been translated from German.
2 Paul Gubitz (b. 1886) was a police sergeant in 1920, then deputy mayor from June 1935 to March 1936 and mayor of Radeberg from 1936 to 1945.
3 In 1935–1943 the Saxon state minister for economics and labour was Georg Lenk (1888–1945), businessman; joined the NSDAP in 1930 and the SS in 1934.
4 Neither the regulation nor the petitions could be found. Presumably the regulation mentioned is the ministerial instruction that a report on the events described in the petitions be submitted to the Reich Ministry of Economics.
5 Dr Ernst Josef Neumark (b. 1888), lawyer; practised law in Dresden, 1925–1938, then worked as a 'legal consultant' (*Rechtskonsulent*).
6 Rosa Schaefer (b. 1889); lived in Dresden; was deported from there to Auschwitz in early March 1943.
7 Martin Liegner (b. 1883), retailer; moved to Radeberg from Dresden, and opened a knitwear shop in Radeberg in 1931.
8 Probably Franz Herzfeld (b. 1902). He was later a prisoner in Buchenwald concentration camp and was released on 25 April 1939.
9 All the shopkeepers gave up their businesses as a result of public pressure and left Radeberg. In a final step in summer 1938, the Ikenberg firm was Aryanized by the draper Rudolph Martin: Bund der Antifaschisten, Region Dresden, and Helfried Wehner (eds.), *Radeberger Land unterm Hakenkreuz: Fakten und Ereignisse aus unserer Stadt und umliegenden Orten während des 'Dritten Reiches'* (n.p.: privately published, n.d. [c.1999]), p. 55.

the pharmacist Rudolf *Dauster*, who lives at 28 Pulsnitzer Straße here and was born in Breslau on 11 March 1911. She learned the name of the perpetrator from the local watchman of the German Protection and Security Service, Max *Anders*.[10] When questioned, Dauster admitted having carried out the act of his own volition and solely out of personal conviction, as an antisemite. Dauster is not a member of the NSDAP. From October 1933 to 1934 he was in the Labour Service. Dauster was most explicitly cautioned by me in person on 27 July 1935, in my official capacity.

On the night of 26 July, the word 'Jew' was again painted on the display windows of these Jewish shops and the pavement in front of the shop doors. Police investigations to ascertain the perpetrators were, however, unsuccessful.

The local group of the NSDAP in Radeberg, with my permission, put up a fairly large display case near the town hall on 17 August 1935 to display the journal *Der Stürmer*. The case contains the inscriptions: 'The Jew triumphs with the lie and dies with the truth. Anyone who buys from Jews is a traitor to the people.' In a small section of this case the Party also put up for a time, *without* any special heading, like a 'corner of shame', photographs of the four Jewish shops. It is also true that several times customers were photographed upon leaving one of the four Jewish shops, and the photos were displayed in the aforementioned case. I have been unable to find a reason for the police to intervene in this matter.

It is also true that the leadership of the local NSDAP group and the local leadership of the German Labour Front have distributed to the Party members and the trade union members, respectively, notes to the effect that Jewish shops are absolutely to be avoided. I too have forbidden my civil servants, salaried employees, and other members of staff to buy from Jewish shops. I still keep this ban in force to the present day. On the other hand, however, it is not true that guards regularly stand, or stood, in front of these shops to discourage customers.

On the basis of a circular issued by the Kreisleitung of the Dresden NSDAP, dated 6 August 1935, according to which all anti-Jewish propaganda involving the hanging of bills, posters, and banners must disappear,[11] we have refrained here too from everything that would have contravened this order and those of the government offices.

According to the records of the local tax office, the four shops in question have generated the following sales in the past few months:

		Schaefer RM	Hofstein RM	Liegner RM	Herzfeld RM
April	1935	11,579 RM	12,529 RM	1,778 RM	1,515 RM
May	”	10,992 ”	13,637 ”	1,296 ”	1,790 ”
June	”	11,431 ”	12,328 ”	1,860 ”	1,933 ”
July	”	8,951 ”	10,473 ”	1,248 ”	1,400 ”
Aug.	”	8,312 ”	10,455 ”	938 ”	1,047 ”
Sept.	”	4,945 ”	4,686 ”	410 ”	430 ”
Oct.	”	6,627 ”	7,591 ”	593 ”	502 ”
Nov.	”	8,125 ”	8,200 ”	675 ”	530 ”

10 Max Anders (b. c.1891) was the caretaker at the Pestalozzi School in 1927 and a watchman in Radeberg in 1937.
11 This circular could not be found.

These figures indicate that sales, in terms of amount, were somewhat lower in the months of July and August than in the previous months, but that Dr Neumark's claim that sales have declined by two thirds is greatly exaggerated. The fact that sales dropped still lower in September cannot be attributed to any boycott measures, which did not in fact take place.

I do not want to fail to mention that the Jewish businessman Martin Liegner had to be placed in protective custody on 24 September of this year because of his subversive attitude, and at the order of the Gestapo central office for Saxony in Dresden he was in the Sachsenburg concentration camp until 8 November 1935.[12]

DOC. 217

On 17 December 1935 ministry representatives discuss the economic and financial advantages and disadvantages of Jewish emigration[1]

Reich Ministry of Finance memorandum (F 4380–1061 I A), unsigned, dated 17 December 1935 (copy)[2]

Memorandum of session:
By way of introduction Ministerial Director Wohlthat[3] emphasized that the objective could not be to reach a decision as to whether and how *Jewish emigration* should be promoted. Rather, the purpose of the meeting was to look for ways in which a furthering of Jewish emigration is possible in general, and to examine their pros and cons from a purely economic perspective. With respect to the problem of Jewish emigration, he said that the Reich Ministry of Economics intended to submit to the Führer an account of the purely economic perspectives and to request a conclusive decision.[4]

The statements by the representative of the Deputy of the Führer and the representative of the Reich Minister of the Interior concerning the previous decisions of the Führer on the question of Jewish emigration were inconsistent. Admittedly, both agreed that the Führer did not want to hear that pressure was being put on the Jews to emigrate. However, while the representative of the Reich Minister of the Interior said that, to his knowledge, the most recent expression of the Führer's opinion was to the effect that the Jews within

---

12 Sachsenburg concentration camp was in operation from June 1933 to mid 1937. It was set up in a factory building below Sachsenburg Castle near Frankenberg in Saxony.

1 BArch, R 2/56014, fols. 60–64. This document has been translated from German.
2 The original contains several handwritten corrections and notes, including 'Groth's section', 'Zülow', and, in the left-hand margin: 'to be filed under "Jew" in III a'.
3 Helmuth Wohlthat (1893–1982), economist; worked as a retailer (import/export), 1920–1933; worked in the Reich Ministry of Economics, where he was head of the Reich Office for Foreign Exchange Control, 1934–1938; in the Office of the Plenipotentiary for the Four-Year Plan (BVP), 1938–1945; joined the NSDAP in 1940; representative of the BVP at the Central Bank of the Netherlands in Amsterdam, 1940–1941; head of the German Delegation for Economic Negotiations in Japan, 1941–1945; returned to Germany in 1947; worked in the private sector, 1947–1973.
4 On this see the account of the Economic and Statistical Department of the Reichsbank for Hjalmar Schacht, 22 Jan. 1936, regarding the effects of the anti-Jewish measures on the economy: BArch, R 2501/6789, fols. 181–190, published in Hartmannsgruber (ed.), *AdR*, part 3, pp. 67–73.

the economy should be bothered as little as possible or not at all, the representative of the Deputy of the Führer stated that the Führer had made up his mind that the Jews should first be induced to emigrate by opening up ways for them to take along their assets, and that ultimately pressure should be exerted on them to emigrate, once a viable way has been found to enable them to take along their assets, even if it means losses for them. He said that the Führer had declared himself in agreement with this approach.

In the opinion of the Reich Minister of Economics, the ways in which the emigrants may be able to take part of their assets abroad soon or over time are as follows:

(1) the preferential use of the abandoned blocked mark accounts of emigrants[5] for purposes of travel or for consignments of goods; however, because the emigrants lose around two thirds to three quarters of their assets, the Reich Flight Tax will not be charged;

(2) payment of purchases of goods for one's own use or on one's own account with one's own blocked mark account for emigrants up to 50 per cent of the invoiced amount; however, only when it is a matter of *additional* purchases of goods, if there are no clearing agreements, and if there is a guarantee that the emigrant will not sell the exported goods abroad below cost and thus violate the normal German export regulations;

(3) establishment of foreign distribution outlets, provided the emigrant remains a participant on an equity basis in domestic firms, and provided asset transfers by means of artificially suppressed export prices are prevented by involving reliable individuals in the domestic operations (authorization of the establishment of foreign manufacturing sites seems impossible for reasons of trade policy);

(4) use of emigrants' assets for domestic financing of large, long-term export orders, which otherwise encounters difficulties; relinquishment of a portion of the accruing foreign exchange and thus facilitation of the taking out of long-term loans abroad by the emigrants;

(5) redemption of Jewish holdings in domestic firms by foreign owners of blocked marks;

(6) offsetting of the assets of re-migrants and immigrants against emigrants' blocked mark assets.

The method described in no. 4 seems to be really attractive and possibly promising as well. However, in the opinion of the Reich Minister of Economics, an office in Germany must be created to undertake the liquidation of the Jewish assets. Then medium-sized and small assets could also be included. Negotiations regarding the creation of such an office are said to be already in progress.

According to statements by the Reich Ministry of Economics, the approach described in no. 2 has little prospect of success, because the question of additionality presents great difficulties and, above all, there is said to be a high risk of upsetting foreign markets. This assessment is significant because it relates to the approach that the Deputy of the Führer primarily has in mind and has also presented to the Führer on the basis of an actual case.

---

5 On the basis of the foreign exchange regulations, emigrating Jews were not allowed to take their remaining money abroad, even after payment of all taxes and fees. They had to leave it behind in the Reich, in a 'blocked mark account for emigrants' (Auswanderersperrmark-Konto). The blocked marks could be exchanged for foreign currency only at a substantial loss, which increased over time.

In the most general sense – always based on the economic standpoint – the following objections were stated with respect to enforced Jewish emigration:

(1) Only the Jew with assets decides to emigrate, but not the poor Jew, who ultimately becomes Germany's burden.

(2) When wealthy Jews emigrate, Germany loses taxpayers. This also makes it harder to forego the charging of the Reich Flight Tax.

(3) The emigration of the Jews is preceded by the conversion of their assets into cash. The result is that property markets, stock markets, etc. are kept under pressure for quite some time to come.

(4) Every asset transfer, however sophisticated, to a foreign country delays the reduction of the foreign debt, and under some circumstances even causes it to increase.

(5) Jewish emigration does not necessarily result in the transfer of Jewish assets into Aryan hands. Rather, in many instances foreign Jews will step into the place of the emigrating Jews, particularly if foreign blocked mark accounts are to be released.

Finally, another possibility was mentioned: promoting the emigration of *young* Jews by supporting occupational restructuring for new occupations. One option is the training of young Jews as farmers or craftsmen. The Reich Minister of Food has spoken out against training as farmers for reasons of racial policy.[6] The members of the skilled crafts and trades have opposed training them as craftsmen, particularly because of the call to prioritize Jews by providing accelerated training courses.

Briefly discussed at the end was also the cancellation of passports, with the aim of denying Jews the possibility of shifting their assets into a foreign country. The official from the Reich Ministry of Economics spoke out against the cancellation of passports, because economic ties to foreign countries would be disrupted as a result of this measure.[7]

---

6 See Doc. 107, 27 Feb. 1934.
7 The Gestapo Central Office (II 1 B 2 – J. 23/36) subsequently decided on 25 March 1936 that the passports of Jews could not be cancelled on the basis of their Jewishness alone, and that the issuance of passports, identity papers, and trade licences for travelling salesmen could not be refused on such grounds. But at the same time, extra caution was required with respect to Jews: Walk (ed.), *Das Sonderrecht für die Juden im NS-Staat*, p. 158.

DOC. 218

On 19 December 1935 the Gestapo Central Office in Berlin announces how the concept of 'prohibited individual actions' against Jews is to be interpreted[1]

Circular decree of the Gestapo Central Office (II 1 B 2 77 318 J J 1057/35 E), p.p. signed Dr Best, to all State Police offices, dated 19 December 1935 (copy)[2]

Re: individual actions against Jews.

In connection with the repeatedly declared ban on all individual actions with regard to the Jewish question, there have been enquiries in numerous instances as to what is meant by 'individual actions'.

Now the Reich and Prussian Minister of the Interior, in concert with the Reich and Prussian Minister of Economics and the Deputy of the Führer, has taken a stand on this issue and described as individual actions all measures that are not based on an explicit order of the Reich government or the Reichsleitung of the NSDAP.[3]

I request that circulation of this understanding in the offices be ensured, and I point out that the definition of an individual action is not met if the corresponding measures directed against Jews have been ordered or authorized by the Gestapo Central Office or the commander of the Political Police as the central authority of the Political Police.

DOC. 219

***Die neue Weltbühne*, December 1935: Heinrich Mann protests against the persecution of Jews in Germany[1]**

The Germans and Their Jews
by Heinrich Mann

The German Jews are being systematically destroyed; there is no longer any doubt about this. Circumspect older Jews said two years ago: 'We live, after all, in a state under the rule of law' – which they wished to regard as immutable protection against the impending excesses of emotion and propaganda. At the time, the first pogroms had already

---

1 BLHA, Pr.Br.Rep. 2 A I Pol/1919, fol. 291. This document has been translated from German.
2 Parts of the original have been underlined by hand. The circular decree of the Gestapo Central Office (Gestapa) was conveyed to the Landräte on 7 Jan. 1936 via a circular decree of the Potsdam State Police Head Office: ibid., fol. 291. On 19 Dec. 1935, it was also sent as a decree of the commander of the State Political Police departments, with the same file reference, to the State Political Police departments: BArch, R 58/276, fol. 34.
3 See the correspondence between the Reich Minister of Economics, the Reich Minister of the Interior, and the Deputy of the Führer, dated Oct. 1935: published in Kommission zur Erforschung der Geschichte der Frankfurter Juden (ed.), *Dokumente zur Geschichte der Frankfurter Juden*, p. 27.

1 'Die Deutschen und ihre Juden', *Die neue Weltbühne*, 1935, no. 49, pp. 1532–1536. Published in Heinrich Mann, *Es kommt der Tag: Deutsches Lesebuch*, ed. Peter-Paul Schneider (Frankfurt am Main: Fischer Taschenbuch, 1992 [1936]), pp. 39–46. This document has been translated from German. *Die neue Weltbühne: Wochenschrift für Politik, Kunst und Wirtschaft* was the successor to *Die Weltbühne*, which was banned in Germany in March 1933. *Die neue Weltbühne* was published in Prague from June 1933 and then in Paris from 1938 to 1939.

taken place. Because calm subsequently ensued, one could persuade oneself that the law, rather than the soul of the people and its drives, was nonetheless the stronger component. Now, no one believes that any more. It has been demonstrated that the National Socialist interest stands above the law, and that it makes laws. What is right has now become whatever 'serves the German people', even the most vicious thing, even the most infamous thing.

It has come to the point where the Jews probably look back at the initial acts of violence as an idyllic period. They were sometimes knocked to the ground, sometimes mocked and driven through the streets with signs on their chests. Their shops were boycotted on a daily basis and looted in an unprecedented manner: all of that was still bearable. They could put it down to the turbulent circumstances, to the 'Movement' in general. Even the 'Movement' needs the norm in the long run, rather than arbitrariness. Indeed, and since then it is precisely arbitrariness that has become the norm. Pogroms and boycotts have been introduced into regular social relations; they now have their proper purpose both in human intercourse and in business life. The Jew who in 1935 has to deal with an Aryan businessman, so to speak, regarding the sale of his business would greatly prefer to deal with the Aryan rabble, so to speak, of 1933. The rabble smashed the place and stole the cash box; but one can get over that. An insightful Jew, as they often are, sees that as the exuberant mood of a crowd, a crowd that would be pleasing to him, indeed, an object of his melancholy admiration, did it not wish to choose precisely him as its victim. But the Aryan businessman in 1935 acts deliberately, rather than in a frenzy of an alcoholic or a nationalistic nature. There can be no question of that in the case of the Aryan businessman who wants to take the Jew's business from him at one twentieth of its value. Admittedly, he expresses himself in the way that a normal negotiator would have spoken at any time; all over the world, such deals are introduced with similar words. The Aryan businessman's suit and manners are likewise in keeping with practice and convention – which enhances the illusion. Because from the very first word and even before, the Jew has been well aware that it is not equals who are having a civilized debate here: rather, a rape is being committed, an expropriation is taking place, and the consent of the seller is being extorted with non-businesslike instruments of power. They are not the instruments of power of the individual Aryan businessman – at most one can ask from where does he get the audacity; two years ago he would not have believed anyone who predicted to him this scene and his role in it. But the entity that is really acting through him is his association, an organization whose objective is the forcible buying up of Jewish businesses – behind it, menacingly, stands the Party or the state; one can say both, they are the same thing.

For the space of a few short weeks, the Jews had perhaps hoped that the 'Jewish legislation' would specify and place limits on the injustice allowed against them. There is Jewish legislation: this is how the state under the rule of law looks now. No, even the Jewish laws say nothing about the Jews' recent, actual experiences, for example, about the forced buying up of their businesses. A law about that will perhaps be passed later, once the practice has been in existence long enough and no longer upsets anyone. The Jewish legislation intentionally lags behind the events. First, every time, comes a new breach of the law; it is tolerated, penetrates into customs and practices; then, at a propitious moment, follows its justification by a law. The world must be heavily engrossed elsewhere at that moment and must not take a closer look. At the time when the first

Jewish laws were promulgated in Nuremberg, Mussolini gave more offence to the world than they did.[2] Besides, the laws affected only the civil rights of Jews, which indeed were reduced to nothing; to all intents and purposes, however, they had already reached that point well before. The position of the Jews in the economy, however, has not yet been legally affected even now; until recently, it was even officially declared to be unaffected. In the meantime, the Jews are being dispossessed by so-called Aryans, one at a time, assisted by the Party and the state. 'Race defilement', too, was for a long time merely the pretext for targeted excesses, before the state duly expressed it in paragraphs. The National Socialist state had itself brought up the concept of race defilement and provided its followers with a new pursuit, mob law against race defilement. Then the state intervenes and takes over the legal punishment. Recently the population has been encouraged not to provide anything edible to Jews. Because of the food shortage it seems that the right has been reserved to elevate to the status of public law the complete, merciless starvation of the Jews.

That would be the last step. They are no longer citizens, and have no right to freedom of choice in matters of sexual relations; in reality they have also lost their freedom of movement, because every public place individually greets them with the 'Not welcome' sign. Security of ownership has been eliminated for them alone; at least, it is happening overtly only to them for the time being. Physical safety is no longer guaranteed to them: anyone who attacks them acts in self-defence; their dangerous nature is regarded as proved by their mere existence. Their money is locked up, and substantial withdrawals from Jewish assets are monitored. They can leave the country only as beggars, and cannot even do that, because every country already has enough beggars. At first glance, the lot of these people seems beyond all comparison, their attitude towards life well-nigh unimaginable. But it is by no means so. Their experiences are definitely on the German path, and what is Jewish is, in an abbreviated, concentrated sense: German.

The German Jews are, minus the fact that they are also Jews, as German as all the others – and are more so than quite a few Germans who are not in the deep middle stratum of the nation, as they are. They are nothing but petit bourgeois and assiduous disciples of the German nature, if not simply its unwitting products. They are aware of no other nature than the German one, have felt bonded to no other kind of people on earth but the German one. The categories of German thought, no less than all the platitudes and characteristic features of the German community: the Jews are completely caught up in these. For a long time, they had neither the inclination nor the calling to cultivate idiosyncrasies. What is singular, in relation to Europe, is the Germans themselves, and their Jews were singular along with them. Endowment with greater gifts – let us suppose that the Jews are often thus endowed – has never yet stamped anyone as a national exception. Intellectualism in general is a social fact; it is only that. It can be just as little 'racially contrary' as 'racially appropriate'. It is regrettable enough that truths such as these still have to be stated.

If the German Jews were less German, they would have been able to prove this especially to the Third Reich – by resisting its attacks. One could not expect that to work, you say? There were too few of them? But the Romanian Jews, for example, are no more

---

2 The Italian army had invaded Abyssinia (now Ethiopia) on 3 Oct. 1935.

numerous; they have merely grown up amid customs that have nothing German about them, customs that are determined neither by devotion to law nor by faith in the state. A Romanian Jew said to a German Jew: 'The amount you put up with puts us to shame. Pogroms take place in our country. But when the people force their way into my house, into my yard, I shout: Stop! Or else everything will explode, including me and you.' – 'All a bluff,' was the German Jew's first thought upon hearing this tale. 'Nothing would have blown up.' But the Romanian said: 'On the contrary. Everything.' Now, this is an exotic way of approaching life; it would be unfair to expect it of everyone. In German offices, at German regulars' tables in pubs, it has not flourished as of yesterday. The German Jews had not had time to adopt it when it would have been useful. The National Socialists found them in a well-behaved state of defencelessness, like all the other Germans, incidentally. And that is exactly why the Third Reich exists.

The fate of the German Jews is terrible; if one tracks its sequel, however, then one has the fate of the Germans, their inseparable companions. The regulatory statutes of the 'Jewish laws' are exactly as pedantic and scrupulous as everything that passes through the hands of the German petit bourgeois, especially when it comes to gruesomeness. Long ago, the details of the regulation on witch trials also left nothing to chance: it prescribed how the fingernails of the women had to be constituted for them to be burned as witches. That is German, only German, the specificity with regard to what is heinous. In the same way the composition of the blood is now graded, three quarters Jewish, half Jewish, one quarter Jewish blood, and each variety is subject to special orders or prohibitions. Those who are one-quarter Jews are allowed to marry only Aryans – as if the breeder could predict what the result will be. But after everybody is pedantically ranked, a single master appears and reserves the right to grant 'exemptions'. The single master can make a Jew no longer a Jew. His discretion overturns nature; it prevails over the 'race' for the sake of which the law was allegedly enacted.³ That is German, only German, the ruse and the disloyalty in the face of sworn principles.

That is how all Germans, by no means only Jews, are dealt with. The multitude that has become the object of the Jewish legislation does not by any means consist exclusively of Jews: an 'Aryan' man is imprisoned for sexual relations with Jewish women. The limits of the 'racial' have already been exceeded. As with regard to the deprivation of civil rights, as with respect to the arbitrary expropriations. The great majority of Germans are subject to laws that are scarcely less harsh than the 'Jewish laws'. But they are less harsh to some extent. One could therefore think that the 'Jewish laws' have been made only as compensation to the Germans for their own bondage. Some 12 million full citizens play the role of a master caste in Germany; 54 million, including the Jews, are subject to them. The assets put aside by the 54 million are at the command of those who are building palaces for themselves and maintaining bodyguards, but their years of apprenticeship and journeying once were spent in institutions for the unfit and asylums for those who have gone off the rails. The Germans, who find it more difficult each day to feed themselves, are being told that guns are more important than butter. 'World domination': that is the sort of notion used to console a down-at-heel society of Germans

---

3 The reference is to §7 of the First Regulation to the Reich Citizenship Law, 14 Nov. 1935: 'The Führer and Reich Chancellor can grant exemptions from the provisions of the implementing regulations': see Doc. 210, 14 Nov. 1935.

who have not managed to rule even themselves, and this is precisely why they have fallen into such hands.

Indeed, the Germans are going the way of their Jews, and incidentally recognize themselves in the Jews. They themselves are subjugated, without rights, close to extreme poverty and driven towards devastating catastrophes – a fairly large number of them go far enough in their moral degeneracy to take revenge for this on people who are even more tormented. And that was precisely the intention of their tutors. The Jews must suffer immense misfortunes because the other Germans suffer many misfortunes. All of them together have reached that point – not abruptly, not from one day to the next, but rather arranged in detail and systematically by a group, oh, at first it was no more than a heap of vermin. But the group gathered and took shape – it is not a social class; several classes have contributed to it. The group that now rules brings together everything about the Germans that is thoroughly bad and undeniably hostile to life. The ruling vermin and their 12 million full citizens: the vermin were able to come to power – inevitably did so, because instincts hostile to life have been inculcated in Germany, more than elsewhere, over long centuries of an unfortunate history. Now suffer! Your Jews are leading the way for you; they have gone significantly beyond you in terms of suffering. The mountain of suffering that they inhabit, however, merges into the surrounding land and, though higher at some points and lower at others, is the same everywhere.

DOC. 220

In early January 1936 the Jewish Telegraphic Agency provides information on plans to finance the mass emigration of Jews from Germany[1]

Report plan to raise $15,000,000 in 4 years for mass exodus of Reich Jews

London, Jan. 6.[2] (JTA) – The reported plan[3] to transfer between 100,000 and 250,000 Jews from Germany to Palestine and British territories involved the raising of $15,000,000, the Jewish Telegraphic Agency learned today.

Three British Jews, it was also learned, have already pledged $500,000 each toward the fund. They include Viscount Bearsted,[4] head of the Shell oil interests, and Simon Marks,[5] department store magnate and vice-president of the English Zionist Organization.

---

1 *Jewish Telegraphic Agency: Latest Cable Dispatches*, vol. 1, no. 128, 7 Jan. 1936, pp. 5–6. Doc. in AJA, The World Jewish Congress Collection Series A: Central Files, 1919–1975, Subseries 1: Organizational History and Activities, 1919–1970, box A3, file 4, International bank plan for Reich fund withdrawal, 1935. The original document is in English.
2 The handwritten '6' replaced the typed '4'.
3 See fn. 7.
4 Sir Walter Horace Samuel, 2nd Viscount Bearsted (1882–1948), British businessman; influential representative of British Jewry; participated with Sir Herbert Samuel in the negotiations on plans to transfer assets; chairman of the Shell Transport and Trading Company.
5 Sir Simon Marks (1888–1964), businessman; president of the British Keren Hayesod; vice president of the Zionist Federation of Great Britain and Ireland.

Sir Herbert Samuel,[6] former High Commissioner of Palestine, confirmed to the Jewish Telegraphic Agency today that he is sailing January 15 for New York with Viscount Bearsted and Mr. Marks on the Majestic.

Reich officials aware of plan for transfer of Jews; refuse details
Berlin, Jan. 4. (JTA) – Government circles told the Jewish Telegraphic Agency today that they were aware of the plan reported abroad for transferring between 100,000 and 250,000 Jews from Germany to Palestine and British territories with the financial backing of British and American Jews.

The officials refused, however, either to vouchsafe details of the plan or to reveal their attitude towards it.

The plan is assumed here to have arisen from earlier proposals, reported by the Jewish Telegraphic Agency on November 26, 1935,[7] for setting up an international bank with headquarters in London to enable Jews emigrating from Germany to withdraw their money.

Report Reich would demand 50 % commission on goods exported under plan
Berlin, Jan. 7. (JTA) – Reports of the impending visit of three British-Jewish leaders to the United States have aroused considerable interest here, but it was indicated to the Jewish Telegraphic Agency in the most authoritative government quarters that the trip will be fruitful only if Germany receives fifty percent commission in foreign currency on the goods that it would permit German Jews to export under the emigration plan.

It was made clear in the same circles that the conditions enumerated in the New York Times do not come from the German Government. (The Times stated that the German consent to mass emigration of Jews would be dependent on the obtaining of British consent to settling Jews in Palestine and British territories,[8] on setting up of a transfer agreement similar to that between Germany and Palestine and on provision of a fund to finance the German exports involved in the second condition.)

The entire project for removing between 100,000 and 250,000 Jews from Germany comes from German-Jewish banking circles interested in assisting mass Jewish emigration through an extended transfer agreement and the establishment of an international Jewish bank for discounting credits received by the emigrants through the transfer, it was stated.

This project has been submitted to Minister of Economics Hjalmar Schacht and is now in his hands.[9]

---

6 Sir (Viscount) Herbert Louis Samuel (1870–1963), politician and diplomat; British home secretary, 1916 and 1931–1932; high commissioner of Palestine, 1920–1925; president of the Council for German Jewry; leader of the Liberal Party in the House of Lords, 1944–1955.
7 'Report International Bank is planned to aid German Jews withdraw funds from Reich': *Jewish Telegraphic Agency: Latest Cable Dispatches*, vol. 1, no. 94, 26 Nov. 1935, pp. 1–2, in AJA, The World Jewish Congress Collection Series A: Central Files, 1919–1975, Subseries 1: Organizational History and Activities, 1919–1970, box A3, file 4, International bank plan for Reich fund withdrawal, 1935.
8 This refers to the so-called Haavara Agreement. See Glossary.
9 For more on the position of the Reichsbank and its president, Schacht, on the question of foreign exchange and mass emigration, see Doc. 194, 7 Sept. 1935.

DOC. 221

Danziger Echo, 7 January 1936: article on the resignation of the High Commissioner of the League of Nations over the persecution of Jews in Germany[1]

The League of Nations must intervene. / The High Commissioner cannot perform his duties of office

High Commissioner *James McDonald*, appointed two years ago by the League of Nations to safeguard the interests of the refugees from Germany, has resigned from his League of Nations office, and on this occasion has written an official letter to the Secretariat of the League of Nations that is *an absolute denunciation of the racial policy of the Third Reich* and ends in a plea to the League of Nations and the powers to intercede with the German government on behalf of the Jews who are threatened with extermination.[2] In the circles of the League of Nations, James McDonald's farewell letter has caused a real stir.

The letter, which we quote below, with the omission of numerous passages, begins with McDonald's appointment to head the office for German refugees, which, as was well known, had *not* been organized as a League of Nations office. The concern at that time, in autumn 1933, was to provide *for approximately 80,000 Jewish and non-Jewish refugees coming from Germany*, of whom around 15,000 could not yet be placed. *Today*, he writes, one is confronted with the fact that as a result of the race laws, which affected 450,000 Jews and tens of thousands of Christian 'non-Aryans', *a new wave of refugees from Germany will spill across the borders. But among them are also a great many martyrs of the Christian denominations*. As a result of the Nuremberg Laws, one portentous fact faces the community of states: more than half a million persons, against whom no charge can be made except that they are not 'Nordic', are facing destruction. Tens of thousands are anxiously seeking ways to flee abroad. McDonald writes that the Jewish and Christian private organizations can certainly be expected to contribute to the solution of the problem if the governments, acting through the League, enable such a solution. But the problem cannot be solved simply by taking in those people who are fleeing from the Reich. Efforts must first be made *to remove or mitigate the causes that create German refugees*. That was not part of the work of the High Commissioner's office. This can only be *a political task, which is assumed by the League of Nations itself.*

---

1 'Der Völkerbund soll eingreifen', *Danziger Echo*, 7 Jan. 1936, p. 1. This document has been translated from German. This Jewish weekly for economics, culture, and politics began publication in 1934. It was prohibited by the Danzig Senate in 1936 because of its reporting on the persecution of Jews in Germany.
2 The High Commissioner for Refugees coming from Germany, James G. McDonald, resigned in late 1935. With his resignation letter of 27 Dec. 1935 to the Secretary General of the League of Nations he enclosed thirty-seven pages of documents about the persecution of the German Jews. The letter and the documents were made public by the League of Nations: James G. McDonald, *Lettre de démission adressée au Secrétaire général de la Société des Nations: Avec une annexe contenant l'analyse des mesures prises en Allemagne contre les 'non-Aryens' et de leurs effets sur la question des réfugiés* (Geneva: n.pub., 1936). See also Henry Friedlander and Sybil Milton (ed.), *Archives of the Holocaust: An International Collection of Selected Documents*, vol. 7 (New York: Garland, 1990), doc. 53, pp. 241–286.

James McDonald goes on to state that Jews and non-Aryans are being relentlessly excluded from all public offices, from the exercise of the liberal professions, and from any part in the cultural and intellectual life of Germany. Ostracized from any social relations with 'Aryans', they are subjected to every kind of humiliation. Neither sex nor age exempts them from discrimination. Even the children do not escape segregation. In official orders from the Party, 'Aryan' children are incited to hate the Jews.

James McDonald states in his letter that the Jews in Germany, condemned to segregation in a legal and social ghetto, are finding it increasingly hard to earn a living. Indeed *more than half of the Jews remaining in Germany have already been deprived of their livelihood.* This has already exhausted the resources of the Jewish philanthropic institutions in Germany. The victims are being driven to such anguish and despair that it is to be expected that *new waves of refugees* will come crashing over the borders. As so often during its history, he adds, Germany has made the Jewish people into a scapegoat despite the *continuous loyalty of the Jews to the state.* In Imperial Germany, Jews had helped to unify Germany and to make it strong. Jewish youth sacrificed itself for the fatherland no less than other young people. Jewish scholars and businessmen were instrumental in enabling Germany to prolong the struggle. Under the [Weimar] Republic they helped to save Germany from some of the worst effects of defeat and to establish ties to the rest of the world. Nonetheless, he continues, though less than a one-hundredth part of the total population, they are held responsible for the defeat and all the other adversity. Apart from the Upper Silesia Convention of May 1922,[3] McDonald writes, Germany does not appear to be expressly bound by a treaty obligation providing for equal citizenship of racial, religious, or linguistic minorities. But the principle of *respect for the rights of minorities* has entered into an *obligation of the public law of Europe* and was recognized in some of the most important international instruments of the nineteenth century. May I refer [he writes] to the provisions of the Congress of Vienna,[4] the Congress of Berlin in 1878,[5] and finally to the Peace Conference of 1919.[6] During the Peace Conference, the German delegation declared spontaneously that 'Germany for her part was resolved to grant minorities of alien origin equal rights and treatment.' From the moment of her admission to the League, Germany even took the lead in fulfilling the principles of international protection of minorities.

The League of Nations and its member states, McDonald declares, must, *in the name of humanity and international law,* make a forceful appeal to the German government and bring Germany to respect the internationally valid principles. All the facts outlined

---

3 Also known as the Geneva Convention of 15 May 1922, this treaty on the protection of minorities granted equal rights for Poles and Polish Jews living in the German part of Upper Silesia.

4 The Congress of Vienna was held in 1814–1815 following the Napoleonic Wars and the abdication of Napoleon I with the aim of redistributing territory in order to restore the balance of power among the major European nations.

5 Dominated by the German chancellor, Otto von Bismarck, the Congress of Berlin was held from June to July 1878 following the conclusion of the Russo-Turkish War. It revised the Treaty of San Stefano, thereby nullifying most of Russia's gains under this peace settlement. Germany grew closer to Austria-Hungary and more distanced from Russia as a result of the Congress, laying the foundation for the system of alliances prior to the First World War.

6 Conference held from 1919 to 1920 in the wake of the First World War, which resulted in the establishment of the League of Nations and the signing of the Treaty of Versailles, the Treaty of Saint-Germain, and the Treaty of Neuilly.

above would serve as the basis for an emphatic appeal which all states, whether members of the League of Nations or not, should make to the German government, an appeal based on the principles of humanity and international peace.

Should this appeal, against all expectations of reason and pity, meet with no response, the problems caused by the threatened situation of the Jews, the Christian 'non-Aryans', the Protestants, and the Catholics cannot be solved merely by philanthropic action. A decision will have to be made to tackle all this persecution at its source, for it will constitute *a continuous threat to international peace* and harm the legitimate interests of other states, particularly the neighbouring states of Germany that have taken in the refugees. The League, as an association of states, must itself examine this matter of common concern for the states. The League of Nations Covenant explicitly empowers the Council and the Assembly to deal with any matter which affects world peace or to interfere otherwise in the activity of the League of Nations. According to McDonald, the most vital condition of international peace and security, however, is *the protection of the individual from religious and racial intolerance*. The League must intercede where it is a matter of averting an impending human tragedy.

High Commissioner James McDonald closes his letter to the Secretariat of the League of Nations with the following words:

> Since I am convinced that desperate suffering in the countries adjacent to Germany and an even more terrible human calamity within Germany's borders are inevitable unless present tendencies in the Reich are checked or reversed, I cannot remain silent. When the domestic policy of a state threatens to demoralize and exile hundreds of thousands of people, considerations of diplomatic courtesy must yield to those of common humanity. I should be recreant if I did not call attention to the actual situation, and plead that world opinion, acting through the League and its member states, move to avert the existing and impending tragedies.

High Commissioner McDonald encloses with his letter *a factual report*, which cites official documents dealing with the situation of the Jews in Germany. McDonald refers to them as '*harrowing human documents*'.

DOC. 222
Der Stürmer: letter from a National Socialist Christian warning the churches against baptizing Jews en masse, January 1936[1]

Letter from Berlin
Documents that give one pause for thought. Mass conversions of Jews to the Catholic Church. Sense and purpose of baptizing Jews. A Berlin National Socialist's cry for help

Dear *Stürmer*,

Hundreds of thousands of workers live in the capital of the Reich. Most of them are not members of the NSDAP. Because of the ban on membership, they were no longer able to join the Movement. Nonetheless, they are *true National Socialists*. They know that the Party membership book and badge alone cannot create a Party member. It is beliefs and character that are the decisive factors. Hundreds of thousands of Berlin workers prove by their actions that they have become National Socialists. I was one of those who no longer had a chance to join the Movement. As a good Catholic, I was a member of the [Catholic] Centre Party, as was simply the custom previously. It was not easy for me to understand the reasoning of an *Adolf Hitler*. I was still too encumbered by the ideas of a man of the Centre. Today I have freed myself. I have abandoned all the confused trains of thought. Today I stand by the swastika unconditionally and – I know it to be so – for all time. I count myself among those who, through their deeds and their steadfast loyalty to the Führer, *want to merit* the honorary title of 'National Socialist'.

National Socialism and Christianity
Since 1933 I have read the *Stürmer* on a regular basis. But I do not 'read' the *Stürmer*, I *study* it. I study it every week. From the first page to the last. And I owe it exclusively to the *Stürmer* that I have now understood the foundation of the National Socialist world view, the *race question*. There are Volksgenossen who claim that National Socialism is anti-religious. The swastika and the cross of Christ can never be unified, they say. Anyone who asserts such things has either been struck blind or is a liar. I am a National Socialist. At the same time, however, I am also a good Christian. And I know that a National Socialist can simultaneously be a good Christian, assuming, of course, that he does not equate Christianity with *politicizing Catholicism*. No! True Christianity has nothing in common with politicizing confessionalism.

Jews in the Catholic mass
I go to church almost every Sunday. I have done so since I was a boy. And as a mature man, too, I have the need to tarry in God's house. I must acknowledge, however, that I am no longer as dedicated as was once the case. Sunday after Sunday I am forced to observe something that increasingly spoils church attendance for me. Previously, we German churchgoers were exclusively *among our own kind*. But now that has changed. Whether I kneel in a stall or stand in a corner of the church, I repeatedly see people in my vicinity who do not belong there with us. *They are Jews! Baptized Jews!* And their

---

[1] 'Brief aus Berlin', *Der Stürmer*, no. 3, Jan. 1936, p. 7. This document has been translated from German.

numbers are growing! Month after month there are more of them. When I attended High Mass on the day after Christmas, I even stood right among a *cluster of Jews*.

Devotions are over and done with!
Whenever I see a *Jew* in a Christian church, my devotion is over. However hard I try to compose myself, it does no good. My thoughts wander up to *Calvary*. I see *Christ* hanging on the cross. And the Christ-killers who mocked the Son of Man have the same faces as the Jews standing around me. My thoughts wander over to *Russia*. I see the Jewish subhumans burning the churches to ashes and murdering the priests. My thoughts occupy themselves with the Jews' secret book of laws, the *Talmud*. And I read the sayings in the Talmud, which go as follows:

'*Christ is a son of a whore. He was conceived by a menstruating mother. He was born of fornication.*'

I think of the abundance of baptized Jews who have brought nothing but ignominy and disgrace to our Church. I think of the statements of prominent baptized Jews who openly declare that the conversion of a Jew to Christianity is only a *means to an end*. I recall the words of the Jew Öttinger,[2] who said: '*I am a Jew by birth. And I became a Christian only so that it would be less dangerous for me to remain a Jew.*'[3]

Finally, however, my thoughts move on to the *Stürmer*. And I see before my eyes all the articles that have warned the churches against the Jew and his *pseudo*-conversion to the Christian faith. I see before me the drawing of the artist *Fips*,[4] which, under the title 'The Jews' Baptism', has this caption: 'We get wet, we become Catholic, but we still stay Jews!'

Mass conversions of Jews
Since the Nuremberg Reichstag[5] the Jews' changeover to the Christian denominations has reached a dramatic level. We Berliners in particular can observe this. I myself know of Jews who formerly belonged for years to the *organizations of the godless*. With unparalleled shamelessness, they spat upon and decried everything associated with our religion. And now? Now they have become 'Christians' overnight. 'Christians', who today slip *rosaries* through their fingers as skilfully as they once rolled up their phylacteries. Who recite the *Ave Maria* with the same 'reverence' they once displayed when mumbling their blasphemous *Talmud sayings*. Every Sunday I see them, these miserable liars, at my side in church. Their rubbery lips whisper prayers. Their crooked fingers make the sign of the cross. One can see that they are not yet entirely confident in their motions. A pity

---

2 Correctly: Eduard Maria Oettinger (1808–1872), journalist and writer; editor of several journals, including satirical magazines, and author of numerous novels and novellas.
3 In the original, Oettinger wrote, in response to Richard Wagner's diatribe 'Das Judenthum in der Musik' (Judaism in Music) (1869): 'Above all the writer must say first, before penning these lines, that he, a Jew by birth, had become a Catholic Christian solely in order to have the right to safely remain a Jew': Eduard M. Oettinger, *Offenes Billet-doux an den berühmten Hepp-Hepp-Schreier und Juden-Fresser Herrn Wilhelm Richard Wagner* (Dresden: Wolf, 1869), pp. 5–6.
4 Pseudonym of Philipp Rupprecht (1900–1975), illustrator and interior designer; cartoonist for *Der Stürmer*, 1925–1945; sentenced to forced labour after 1945 and released in 1950.
5 This refers to the anti-Jewish laws passed by the Reichstag in Nuremberg in Sept. 1935: see Docs. 198 and 199, 15 Sept. 1935.

that I am not familiar with the Jewish ritual. I am convinced that otherwise I could frequently see how the Jews lapse into their customary *synagogue practices*. And repeatedly I think: 'Lord, if only I were a mind reader! If I only knew what is going on in these brains while the mouth lisps Catholic prayers and the Jewish hands work on the rosary in an apelike manner!'

A first warning
Dear *Stürmer*! Now I have given vent to my feelings for once. Now I have said for once what has been troubling me for a long time. I said it because I wish my Church, and my true co-religionists, well. And I beg you, dear *Stürmer*, pass all of this on to your millions of readers! How often you have warned the German people against pan-Judaism. How much the nation owes to you! *And therefore, warn the Christian churches today. Warn them repeatedly against baptizing Jews. I know there will some day come a time when people in denominational circles too will applaud you and say: 'The* Stürmer *was right.'* H. K.

DOC. 223
From the Sopade reports of January 1936 regarding reactions in Germany to the Nuremberg Laws[1]

Sopade report on Germany, January 1936, Prague (typescript)

The following reports on the effects of this National Socialist *educational work* are not altogether uniform. Nonetheless, the majority concur in the assessment that although Streicher's methods meet with general rejection, the antisemitic propaganda is not without influence upon the attitude of the population towards the Jews. That a 'Jewish question' exists is the general understanding.

Saxony, Report 1: The Jew-baiting by the Party, however, is still being pursued with the greatest energy and spite. The authorities and the schools are tirelessly active along the same lines, and one office seeks to outdo the other with ever-new anti-Jewish ideas in order to demonstrate its proficiency to those higher up. But it is also reported that a substantial part of the population is already convinced of the correctness of National Socialist racial theory and regards its application to the German people as a historical necessity, however regrettable the harsh consequences for the individual Jew or Aryan may unfortunately be.

Report 2: Antisemitism has undeniably gained a foothold among broad segments of the populace. If people nonetheless buy from Jews, it is not to help the Jews but rather to vex the Nazis. The general antisemitic psychosis affects even rational people, even our comrades. All are staunch opponents of the excesses, but there is support for breaking, once and for all, the dominant position of the Jews and allotting to them a specific sphere

---

[1] AdsD, 'Deutschland-Berichte der Sopade', vol. 3, no. 1, Jan. 1936, part A 17–21. Published in Behnken (ed.), *Deutschland-Berichte der Sozialdemokratischen Partei Deutschlands*, vol. 3, pp. 24–27. This document has been translated from German.

of activity. Streicher is repudiated everywhere, but for the most part there is agreement with Hitler's plan to force the Jews out of the most important positions. The workers say: in the Republic and in the Party too, the Jews have grown strong.

Report 3: The opinion of the population with regard to the Jewish question is that the Jews may be allowed to live in Germany for the future, but that they should no longer occupy any top positions in the state. The German people should be governed by Germans. In the case of the attitude towards Jews in the labour movement, however, the situation is different. There is no opposition to letting Jews also take leading roles in the labour movement. After all, Jews are human beings too. The majority of the population is not in agreement with the Jewish boycott, and the Nazis have realized this as well, on their own, and have now discontinued this form of crackdown on Jews.

Report 4: Most people describe the laws pertaining to Jews as nonsense. Sympathy for the Jews is far more commonly encountered than approval for the laws. In the working classes, antisemitism has not established a foothold, perhaps precisely because Leipzig has had more experience than other cities with Jews as employers and has no bad memories of that experience. People are beginning to realize what antisemitism means. A middle-class teacher watched the Swedish antisemitic film[2] and opined: 'If one recalls all the traits of individual rotten head teachers and combines and universalizes these traits, then one can pillory the head teacher just the same as the Jew.' Critical thinking about the racial mania is perceptibly on the increase.

Central Germany. A Jewish travelling salesman reports:

> On my many trips, no difficulties have been raised for me yet. The population either does not participate in the Jew-baiting at all or does so only under duress. The businessmen, too, inwardly reject the Jewish boycott. A few examples:
> In X, I entered a hotel in the company of some Jewish friends. We were greeted in the friendliest manner and asked what we would like. We answered that we wanted to have breakfast, but unfortunately had overlooked the sign 'Jews not welcome' and were therefore offering our profuse apologies. 'But please, gentlemen, don't be deterred, the sign is of no consequence, we are required to display it,' was the reply we received. Naturally, we left the establishment.
> In Y, I went to a well-known restaurant. I ordered a beer and asked for the menu. Suddenly I caught sight of the ominous sign 'Jews not welcome'. I immediately summoned the waiter and apologized most politely, saying that I had not noticed the sign. The waiter, visibly astonished, explained that the sign meant nothing, I could by all means dine there, they had no choice but to display the sign. I stated, however, that the sign was indeed binding for me, paid for my beer and left the establishment.
> I have quite often experienced such things. Even confirmed National Socialists frequently do not act on the Party slogan.

Silesia, Report 1: Jew-baiting continues to be practised, but with no particular success among the population. Only the loudest Nazi extremists comply with the demand not

---

2 This is a reference to the film *Pettersson & Bendel*, which had been the motivation for the anti-Jewish excesses in Berlin in July 1935: see Doc. 176, 16 July 1935.

to patronize Jewish shops. There are people who take a look at the *Stürmer* display case and then go shopping in a Jewish store.

Report 2: Next to a fairly large quarry in X is a public house owned by a Jewish woman. Almost the entire workforce frequents this pub. Not long ago the representative of the 'stone and earth' industry organization put up a placard prohibiting dealings with this establishment. The workmen go there nonetheless, because they unanimously take the view that it is their private affair.

Bavaria: The struggle against Jews and Catholics has abated again. People's opinions vary a great deal here, too. There are quite a few who, though not National Socialists, are nonetheless in agreement, within certain limits, with curtailing the rights of Jews and separating them from the German people. This opinion is held by many socialists, too. Admittedly, they are not in agreement with the harsh methods that the Nazis use, but they still say: 'It doesn't do any harm to the majority of the Jews.'

Hesse: The population of this region is not antisemitic. However, one must bear in mind that since time immemorial the Jews in southern Germany have occupied a different position than in other parts of the country. In this region, there is also no discussion among the workers about the position of Jews in politics. In general, however, the people are so vulgarized that they do not sense the human baseness of antisemitism. Only the middle classes, who have an intellectual tradition, constitute an exception.

Berlin, Report 1: Jew-baiting too is not without influence on popular opinion. Very slowly, opinions that once were rejected are being filtered in there. First one reads the *Stürmer* out of sheer curiosity, but then in the end some parts of it do stick. Nevertheless, it has to be said: it says a great deal for the German people that, despite the years of Jew-baiting, Jews are still able to live in Germany at all. If the German people were not inherently good-natured, the propaganda would have inevitably led to the Jews' simply being beaten to death in the street.

Report 2: In general, one can say that the racial issue has not become prevalent as a world view. The *Stürmer* is not taken seriously by anybody. The Jew-baiting has admittedly had certain psychological effects, but they are not solely detrimental for the Jews. There are also cases in which the Jews seem to educated people to be martyrs, so that in addition to the general antisemitism, there are signs here and there of a distinct philo-semitism.

At the same time, one must keep in mind that antisemitism on the whole is no longer in fashion among the intellectuals: first, because the invective against the Jews is too coarse and crude and, second, because antisemitism in general is too simplistic a matter to retain the attention and interest of the intellectuals.

Report 3: I have the impression that antisemitism has reached its peak. Certainly, there may still be additional legislative measures in the process of implementing the Nuremberg Laws, but purely rowdy antisemitism has passed its zenith. If one considers that even now, despite years of agitation against the Jews, only a fraction of the people participates in this Jew-baiting and that most people even boycott the Jewish boycott itself, then one must simply note how little the antisemitic slogans have had the desired effect among the people. On the other hand, one must consider that the German people have always been inwardly antisemitic. This moderate antisemitism, even today, is still on firm ground in the groups that reject rowdy antisemitism. The German nationalists, for example, who are in opposition to the regime, do indeed repudiate the antisemitism of the *Stürmer*, but essentially have no objections to the Nuremberg Laws. When one talks with them about the Jewish question, they also regard a 'solution' of this problem as necessary, although with methods other than those used by the Nazis. In a general way, one can state that the National Socialists have actually managed to deepen the rift between the people and the Jews. The feeling that the Jews are a different race is common today.

The extent to which the antisemitic excesses are condemned among National Socialist circles themselves is difficult to determine. It is the same with this question as with all the others. The loud-mouthed radicals set the tone, and the quiet ones go unnoticed. As things are today, they are hardly likely to have the courage to say anything. Nonetheless, even today one can still hear from Jewish doctors that Party members continue to go to them for treatment.

DOC. 224

On 4 February 1936 the Regierungspräsident in Potsdam informs Gauleiter Wilhelm Kube of his planned circular directive concerning the Jewish question[1]

Letter (secret) from the Regierungspräsident in Potsdam[2] (I Pol. gh. 903) to the Gauleiter and Oberpräsident of Brandenburg province, Prussian Staatsrat Wilhelm Kube,[3] Berlin, dated 4 February 1936 (draft)[4]

Re: issuance of a circular directive concerning the Jewish question. Without enactment.
Reporting secretary: Government Assessor *Radmann*[5]
The legislation on Jews has temporarily been concluded with the issuance of the implementing provisions and regulatory statutes for the Nuremberg Laws. However, the details of the future treatment of the Jews are not yet settled by the legislation. A number

---

1 BLHA, Pr.Br.Rep. 2 A I Pol/1919, fols. 281–283v. This document has been translated from German.
2 The Regierungspräsident in Potsdam was Dr Ernst Fromm (1881–1971), political scientist; joined the NSDAP in 1932; worked in the Reich Ministry for the Occupied Territories, 1923–1930; in the Reich Ministry of the Interior, 1930–1933; from 1933 Regierungspräsident in Potsdam; forced into non-active service in 1937; from 1943 in the administration of the Oschersleben Regional Council Office.
3 Wilhelm Kube (1887–1943), journalist; member of the German National People's Party (DNVP), 1919–1923; joined the NSDAP in 1927 or 1928 and the SS in 1933; Gauleiter in the Prussian Ostmark, 1927–1933; Oberpräsident of the Prussian province of Brandenburg and Gauleiter in the Kurmark, 1933–1936; in 1936 lost all his offices; general commissioner for Belarus, 1941–1943; assassinated by partisans.
4 The original contains handwritten changes and annotations. The original date, 29 Dec. 1935, has been crossed out and replaced by the handwritten date '4 Feb. 1936'. In the left-hand margin is a handwritten note: 'completed and sent Sch 4 Feb.', 'resubmission 2 March 1936'. The circular decree of the Regierungspräsident in Potsdam was issued on 3 March 1936 to chiefs of police, Landräte, mayors, and local police administrators: ibid., fols. 307–308v.
5 Probably Helmuth Radmann (b. 1908), lawyer; joined the NSDAP in 1932; in 1932 junior lawyer in Beuthen; lived in Breslau, 1933–1935, in Potsdam, 1935–1937, and, after 1937, in Berlin.

of Landräte in my district have already submitted reports in advance with regard to local measures for a solution to the Jewish question.⁶ The issues covered above all concern decisions by individual municipalities regarding future legal relations and on the dealings of their inhabitants with Jews. Through a circular decree enclosed with this draft, I intend to take a stand on the abuses that they and I observed in the area of public enlightenment concerning the Jewish question.

However, considering the cardinal importance of the matter, and to ensure that it is treated uniformly in the entire Gau Kurmark, I request that you comment on my draft.

I would appreciate your forwarding the approved directive also to all the Gau's Party offices in question, because the decisions of the municipalities have frequently been prompted precisely by the Party offices.

The circular directive dated 22 August 1935 (I Pol.g.705 geh.) that is cited in my draft has made the authorities responsible to me aware only of the Secret Circular Decree of the Reich and Prussian Minister of the Interior dated 20 August 1935, (III P.3710/59 XIII g)⁷ concerning the prohibition of individual actions against Jews.⁸

2. As an annex to 1, the following draft is to be prepared:
Draft.
As a result of the Nuremberg Laws and the implementing rules and regulatory statutes issued for them, the Jewish question has been conclusively regulated for the moment. I am using this as an opportunity, with reference to my circular directive of 22 August 1935 (I Pol.g.705 geh.), once again to remind, with all due urgency, all the offices involved of the ban on all individual actions against Jews. Recent experiences have demonstrated the limited value – or, more properly, the worthlessness – of independent actions by individuals to combat the harmful influence of the Jews. The position of the vermin has remained unaltered in the main. The Jew, by contrast, has used the harm allegedly done to him in order to arouse sympathy by referring to it and, in the end, to promote himself in this way.⁹

---

6 These reports could not be found.
7 See the circular decree of Reich and Prussian Minister of the Interior Frick dated 20 August 1935, BArch, R 1501/5513, fol. 2. Published in Landesarchivverwaltung Rheinland-Pfalz (ed.), *Dokumentation zur Geschichte der jüdischen Bevölkerung*, pp. 54–55.
8 The following paragraph is deleted in the original: 'In drafting my circular directive I have taken into account the decree of the Reich and Prussian Minister of Economics dated 12 December 1935 (IV 26 037/35), presented together with a report dated 22 December 1935 (I Po g. 3040) and, attached to it, a copy of the written statement of the Deputy of the Führer, the Reich and Prussian Minister of the Interior, and the Reich and Prussian Minister of Economics regarding the definition of individual actions against Jews. Accordingly, I intend, as expressed in my directive, to obtain the approval of the Reich and Prussian Minister of the Interior for any resolutions by the municipalities of my district that have become necessary with regard to the Jewish question. Measures against any form of informative notice opposing Jews (*Stürmer* display cases) are, in my opinion, not to be anticipated, also because of the comments obtained by the Reich and Prussian Minister of Economics and the view he himself holds concerning individual actions. Additional instructions about these notices are therefore still necessary.' At the bottom of the page, handwritten: 'A carbon copy for use by the Gauleitung is enclosed.'
9 In the original, the following paragraph has been crossed out: 'Observations concerning the defence against Jewry being made by the Volksgemeinschaft in many instances in the municipalities of my district lead me to note the following, in addition to what has been said above.'

A number of municipalities in my district believed they needed to vent the existing conscious and instinctive rejection of the Jews by German Volksgenossen by issuing resolutions with regard to the restriction of legal relations and the dealings of their citizens with Jews. The resolutions frequently go beyond the bounds imposed on the local administration by the law. To give one example, they deny the Jews a building licence and a permit for residential development, the issuance or denial of which is in reality a matter for the state authorities. The release and publication of the resolutions must, in addition – and therein, in particular, are to be seen the objections to them – arouse in everyone not familiar with the true circumstances the impression that the Jew in Germany, independently of the racial laws, is heavily burdened by restraints, in contrast to the German citizen. In actual fact, however, the Jews' ability to live decently in Germany is by no means impaired, even after the new legislation. In particular, they continue to have the opportunity they wish to freely pursue a gainful occupation. The announcement of such resolutions, therefore, serves only to give rise at home and abroad to completely mistaken views of the situation of Jewry in Germany and to provide welcome material for world Jewry's agitation against Germany.

Consequently, I cannot endorse formal and fundamental municipal decisions about the future treatment of the Jews, and I forbid the municipalities of my district, with immediate effect, to pass additional resolutions regarding the Jewish question without my explicit, previously obtained permission. Of course, that is not intended to rule out a solution to individual questions that has become necessary. For example, I am aware of the detrimental effects that use of municipal public baths by Jews can have. But I request that, in accordance with what was stated above, my consent be obtained in such cases before passage of a resolution, with a detailed report.[10] Superfluous and avoidable publication of any authorized resolutions must not occur.

The anti-German propaganda of the Jews also forces me – here I address particularly the municipalities with large numbers of tourists – to warn against the now common erection of signs etc. with informative contents regarding the Jewish question in streets and on squares with a high volume of traffic.[11] The foreigner visiting Germany has been exposed in advance to constant and unbounded anti-German agitation by the Jewish press, and in many instances he feels compelled to see the public display of what are, in his understanding, 'intolerant' sentiments. The anti-German propaganda cleverly exploits that, and the supposed successes of educational work among the German people take a back seat, by and large, to the loss of pro-German views abroad.

In my opinion, it will also be out of the question, apart from the concern for tourism, to put up signboards with informative contents, which necessarily often include quite unpleasant material drawn from sexual life, in the immediate vicinity of schools and other places frequented by young people. As a result, in a surely unintended but nonetheless harmful secondary effect, adolescents will very regrettably reach impressions that can only have harmful effects at this stage of their development.

---

10 In the original, a sentence has been crossed out: 'If necessary, I will give a report in high places.'
11 In the original, a sentence has been crossed out: 'The successes of the untiring work in the area of educating the German people about the Jewish danger, particularly by the purposefully crusading newspaper *Der Stürmer*, are undeniable.'

Putting up signs with alarming contents, such as 'Entry here is life-threatening for Jews', must be avoided, of course, as has already been repeatedly announced in individual cases.

Precisely during this year, on account of the Olympic Games, proper handling of the Jewish question along the lines of the aforementioned instructions acquires the utmost significance, specifically in the Potsdam administrative district. Not only is the Olympic village located there, but the district will also be visited by large numbers of members of all the nations on short excursions. The foreign visitors include not only Jews but also, above all, numerous non-Jews who, if not exactly sympathizers with Jews, are nonetheless not opponents in principle and who are still uncomprehending as yet with regard to the German racial legislation. The feelings of all these foreign participants in and spectators at the Olympic Games must not be offended, for reasons of politeness to Germany's guests alone, by posters, placards, and boycott measures that have an irritating effect in terms of foreign policy.

Generally and in principle it must always be kept in mind that the Jewish question, to the extent that it has not already been legally settled in accordance with the wishes of the Third Reich, now under development, cannot be solved decisively and lastingly by more or less non-legal weapons. Rather, it can be solved only through the exertion of educational influence upon German Volksgenossen and through increasing practice, as a result of this influence, of self-discipline and restraint by all German Volksgenossen with regard to the Jews. All educational measures for this purpose must not exceed certain boundaries, and thus cease to have an educational influence upon German Volksgenossen and begin instead to signify an impermissible duress, levelled publicly and more or less directly against the Jews.

DOC. 225
On 5 February 1936 the Reich Minister of the Interior orders that anti-Jewish excesses occasioned by the assassination of Wilhelm Gustloff in Davos must be prevented[1]

Circular decree of the Reich and Prussian Ministry of the Interior (III P 3710/459) issued to the Reichsstatthalter, the Reich commissioner for the reintegration of the Saarland,[2] the regional governments, in the case of Prussia to the Oberpräsidenten and to all police authorities, dated 5 February 1936[3]

Re: prevention of excesses occasioned by the murder of Gustloff, NSDAP group leader for Switzerland.[4]

With reference to my decree for the prevention of excesses from 20 August 1935 (III P 3710/59),[5] I order, in consultation with Deputy of the Führer Rudolf Hess, that individual actions against Jews that are motivated by the murder of the leader of the

---

1 BArch, R 58/276, fol. 36. This document has been translated from German.
2 In 1935–1936 the Reich commissioner for the reintegration of the Saarland was Josef Bürckel (1895–1944), primary school teacher; joined the NSDAP in 1921; NSDAP Gauleiter from 1926 of Rhineland-Palatinate and from 1933 also of the Saarland, which was still administered by France; Reich commissioner for the Saarland, 1936–1940, and Reich commissioner for the reunification of Austria with the German Reich, 1938–1940; head of the civil administration in Lorraine, 1940–1944; committed suicide in 1944.

NSDAP regional branch in Switzerland, Wilhelm Gustloff, in Davos must under no circumstances take place.[6] I request that steps be taken against any such actions and that public safety and order be maintained. If excesses should occur, I am to be informed promptly by telephone or telegraph.

DOC. 226
On 13 February 1936 the sales representative Bernhard Eidmann complains to the retailer Ludwig Bertram about the selling of goods from Jewish firms in Aryan shops[1]

Letter from Bernhard Eidmann,[2] Berlin-Zehlendorf, 61 Eckener-Allee, currently in Erlangen, to the Ludwig Bertram Company,[3] Gera, Thuringia, dated 13 February 1936 (copy)[4]

During my visit yesterday, Wednesday, you, Mr Bertram, made a remark to your wife that I told you I must perceive as a grave insult. Nevertheless, you used no occasion to apologize. I cannot stand for this insult and am hereby demanding that you give me an appropriate explanation.

I entered your shop with the question: 'Am I in a German shop here?' The lady greeting me, your wife, said in reply, with obvious indignation, 'But of course.' To this I responded that I had taken the liberty of asking this question only because the Eres banner[5] was still hanging outside, something that generally is still to be seen only in Jewish shops. Your wife replied that this was indeed not the case. Other and bigger firms,

---

3 Communicated here by radio message from Berlin (K 8 126) on 5 Feb. 1936 to all district offices, chiefs of police, and police headquarters (recorded by the Freiburg im Breisgau police service on 6 Feb. 1936; received at the Baden District Office in Schopfheim on 7 Feb. 1936).
4 Wilhelm Gustloff (1895–1936), banker; joined the NSDAP in 1929; from 1932 head of the regional branch of the NSDAP Foreign Organization in Switzerland.
5 Circular decree of the Reich and Prussian Minister of the Interior (III P 3710/59), Frick, dated 20 August 1935: BArch, R 1501/5513, fol. 2. Published in Landesarchivverwaltung Rheinland-Pfalz (ed.), *Dokumentation zur Geschichte der jüdischen Bevölkerung*, pp. 54–55.
6 Wilhelm Gustloff was assassinated in Davos on 4 Feb. 1936 by the student David Frankfurter (1909–1982). Frankfurter handed himself in to the authorities and was sentenced to eighteen years in prison by the Graubünden Cantonal Court in Chur in Dec. 1936. He was pardoned in 1945 and emigrated to Palestine.
1 Staatsarchiv Hamburg, 131–6, Nr. 106. This document has been translated from German.
2 Bernhard Eidmann (b. 1886), retailer; worked as a salaried employee, then a manager, at several textile firms, 1903–1924; from 1925 owner of the Bernhard Eidmann Textile Department Store in Berlin, the Leo Taverne Men's Clothing Factory in Stettin, and the Rockmann Brothers' Firm in Leipzig; simultaneously worked as a sales representative for Szillath & Co. in Berlin.
3 Ludwig Theodor Bertram (1874–1941), retailer; owner of an eponymous textile firm in Gera.
4 The letter reproduced here, part of a correspondence, is included in a file of the Hamburg State Chancellery with a case file on the Rappolt company in Hamburg. Ludwig Bertram had forwarded this correspondence confidentially to the Rappolt company on 27 April 1936 for the latter's attention.
5 The banners advertised the textiles manufactured by the Rappolt company (Eres = R.S. = Rappolt & Söhne) under the 'Eres' seal of quality. Rappolt & Söhne, a Hamburg textiles firm founded in the mid nineteenth century, had 610 employees and 200 outworkers during the National Socialist period. It was Aryanized in 1938 and given a new name, Eres KG (Eres Kommanditgesellschaft Hamburg).

too, she said, still carry Eres articles, and it is for them at some point to lead the way in giving up their Jewish connections, for example Hollenkamp. My reply that Hollenkamp is indeed no longer working with Eres, or at least no longer has any Eres advertising on the front of its shop (in Erfurt, in place of the word Eres, the outer curve in the banner has been replaced by a red disc), was passed on by your wife to you, as a result of which I had the honour of entering into conversation with you. The first thing you said was that you could only describe the behaviour of Hollenkamp and also that of your friend Zelle in Leipzig as cowardly. You see no reason to give up the thirty-six-year connection with Rappolt, you said, especially as you are personally a good friend of the owners (or owner). In addition, there is no substitute for Rappolt. Its goods and services are unique, you said. Against this, I argued that this is no longer the case. I said I could give proof of this assertion of mine, however, only by presenting the range of goods and the delivery of flawless, first-class articles. To do so, however, your kind approval would first be required, and I asked you for this approval. You refused that, too, with the comment that as a matter of principle you do not allow meddling in your business affairs. You buy only where you think it right to buy, you said; you do not mix politics and business. By way of contrast, I permitted myself to make a polite reference to the fact that wearing the SS badge is not in keeping with the public display of the Eres placard. Against this, you asserted that you had been asked at the time to join the SS as a contributing member (if I am not mistaken, you even said you had been put under pressure). You gave in, you said, and became a member to declare your solidarity with the new Movement. But that is a private matter, you said, it has nothing to do with business.

I made the effort, as you are an older gentleman, around ten to twenty years older than me, to refrain from remonstrating that in general such *outward* markings are worn *in the shop* for the very specific purpose of using them to attract or retain customers who attach importance to buying German goods in German shops. You yourself obviously sensed the contradiction to your assertion that you wish to keep politics and business separate, and I limited myself to urging you to be cautious about making such statements as you now had made in some number, because they are no longer in keeping with the general present-day opinion. If I, for example, were to report the conversation word for word to my firm and it were to pass on this report to the Adefa,[6] either the SS badge or the Eres placard would probably vanish within a few days. You disputed this and said, literally: 'For all I care, you can report all of this to your firm. On no account do I allow myself to be lectured, and I will not allow any interference with my business arrangements.' In addition you said, word for word: 'I am also an antisemite. I occasionally read the *Stürmer*. But this policy has nothing to do with business. My father advised me forty years ago, "Keep politics out of business".' Least of all, you said, were you willing to have the gentlemen from the Adefa meddling in your business. In reply, I said that what you call politics can, in my view, hardly be kept separate from business nowadays. Even if one is not an antisemite, one can, as a German retailer, take the view that it is an important task to eliminate the existing situation, or at least the one that has existed until now, whereby Jews dominate the ready-to-wear clothing sector. That is both the

---

6 The Association of German-Aryan Clothing Manufacturers (Adefa) was founded in 1933. It represented around 500 firms and the products of the member companies were labelled 'Adefa – the mark of goods made by Aryan hands'.

Adefa's task and mine, I said, and I allowed myself to express the opinion that it is your task as well, particularly as a member of a PO.[7]

After continuing the conversation, which consisted in the main of repeating what was said above, I wanted to bring my visit to an end, and I asked you to confirm that you were in agreement with the report to my firm. You reiterated your consent but then inconsistently addressed your wife as follows: 'There, you see these German sales representatives again, the way they want to use blackmail to do business.'

I refused to tolerate these words placed in quotation marks, *these German* sales representatives and the mention of blackmail, and told you that I could not put up with this insult. Nevertheless, you refrained from offering an apology, although the conversation on my part had been conducted in the most conciliatory fashion and most polite tone. Neither my firm nor I have any need to generate business success by emphasizing our Germandom, much less by blackmail. We place our honour on bringing in business through performance. I am all the more unable to stand for the insult that was uttered. As emphasized at the beginning, I now ask that you give an appropriate explanation.[8]

With German regards!

DOC. 227

On 3 March 1936 the Karlsruhe Regional Tax Office reports to the Reich Minister of Finance on cooperation with the Gestapo in monitoring Jews[1]

Letter from the director of the Karlsruhe Regional Tax Office, p.p. (Schneider),[2] reporting secretary Oberregierungsrat Brandt, to Reich Ministry of Finance/Department III, Berlin (received on 4 March 1936), dated 3 March 1936[3]

Case file: Decree of 23 January [19]36 0 2011–5 III/0 1729–998 II[4]
Annex: 1 carbon copy of the report.
1 copy.[5]

At most tax offices and central customs offices in my district, observations have not been made to the effect that persons liable to tax – in particular, non-Aryan persons –

---

7 Parteiorganisation: Party organization (NSDAP).
8 Bertram replied on 18 Feb. 1936 stating he refused to tolerate being interrogated by a sales representative concerning his badge, origins, and suppliers. In addition, he said Eidmann had no right to threaten to report him to the Adefa: ibid.

1 BArch, R 2/5978, fols. 34–38. This document has been translated from German.
2 Ludwig Eduard Schneider (1873–1941); from 1920 Oberregierungsrat in the Karlsruhe Regional Tax Office; director of that office, 1933–1938; joined the NSDAP in 1938; retired in 1938 and was reinstated as a tax officer in the Stockach Tax Office, 1939–1941.
3 The original contains several handwritten notes.
4 On 23 Jan. 1936 the Reich Minister of Finance had asked the regional tax offices to report by 1 March 1936 on experiences 'during the emigration of non-Aryan persons': ibid., fol. 9. See, in the same file, the reports of the regional tax offices, such as the letter from the head of the Berlin Regional Tax Office to the Reich Ministry of Finance on 27 Feb. 1936: ibid., fols. 12–17v. Published in Friedenberger, Gössel, and Schönknecht (eds.), *Die Reichsfinanzverwaltung*, doc. 11, pp. 42–43. For a summary of the reports see BArch, R 2/5978, fols. 34–38, fols. 96–106.
5 BArch, R 2/5978, fols. 34–38, fols. 67–72v.

are withdrawing their bank deposits or post office giro assets or attempting to sell their furniture, land, machinery, and the like, with the assumed intention of fleeing to another country. To the extent that such assessments were made, I have prompted the offices to inform the Gestapo office in Karlsruhe, 25 Gartenstraße, and the customs investigation office in Freiburg im Breisgau of this.

The cooperation between the Gestapo, Gestapo offices,[6] tax and central customs offices, foreign currency office, and customs investigation office in Freiburg (including branch offices) in the monitoring of foreigners and persons suspected of planning to emigrate is running smoothly, in the main. In a number of instances, the tax offices and the customs investigation office have been informed by the Gestapo offices (particularly the passport offices) and the Gestapo of persons who are suspected of planning to emigrate, so that the measures necessary for securing the taxes, especially the Reich Flight Tax, could be taken. Some of the tax offices also work together with various other offices, for example post offices, notaries' offices, chambers of commerce, NSDAP Kreisleitungen, the [German] Labour Front, emigration information centres, etc.

Fiscal monitoring of emigrating non-Aryan persons in the district of the Karlsruhe Regional Tax Office is the responsibility in particular of the Tax Investigation Service, with the Customs Investigation Service called in where required. The notifications received in the tax offices concerning emigrants or persons suspected of planning to emigrate are generally forwarded to the Tax Investigation Service for tax review and monitoring of the taxable persons in question. In order to achieve maximum cooperation between the Tax Investigation Service and the Customs Investigation Service, I have instructed the tax and customs investigation officials to keep one another informed, as far as possible, about the measures to be used against tax dodgers.

The number of non-Aryan persons, particularly persons suspected of intending to flee, is small in most tax office districts of my district, so that comprehensive arrangements for full taxation of these individuals were thus far not necessary for these districts. By contrast, the number of such persons in the large cities (Mannheim, Karlsruhe, Freiburg, Heidelberg, Pforzheim) is quite substantial.

The number of non-Aryan persons (5,000) as well as emigrants and persons suspected of planning to emigrate is particularly large in Mannheim. In order to tax these persons fully and prevent them from fleeing to a foreign country, the Mannheim City Tax Office has centralized the processing of all Reich Flight Tax matters and all tax-related and other issues associated with emigration in *one* particular office – the Reich Flight Tax Office. With regard to the establishment of this office and the measures of the Mannheim City Tax Office for monitoring non-Aryan persons and collecting the Reich Flight Tax and other taxes, allow me to refer to the report by this office, dated 30 November [19]35 (o 2011/X), a copy of which is enclosed.[7]

Central processing of the Reich Flight Tax and all matters associated with emigration in the Mannheim City Tax Office has proved quite successful. As a result, all these tasks

---

6 The author means the Gestapo Central Office (Gestapa) in Berlin and the regional Gestapo offices.
7 Memorandum of the Mannheim Tax Office, 30 Nov. 1935, BArch, R 2/5973, fols. 67–72v. Published in abridged form in Friedenberger, Gössel, and Schönknecht (eds.), *Die Reichsfinanzverwaltung*, doc. 8, pp. 35–37.

are handled in a uniform manner in the tax office, and the civil servants can work through them thoroughly. I have therefore recommended that the remaining tax offices proceed in a similar manner if a relatively large number of non-Aryans are present in their district.

In the case of the Freiburg City Tax Office, too, a special office for processing the Reich Flight Tax and matters associated with the emigration of non-Aryan persons was created in December 1935. It works closely together with a number of other offices (passport offices, police headquarters, Gestapo, Criminal Police, customs investigation office, NSDAP Kreisleitung, Labour Front, Land Registry, etc.). In late November and early December 1935 the passport office at police headquarters in Freiburg instructed police officers to immediately restrict to Germany itself the validity of the passports of all non-Aryans living in Freiburg. This was done by collecting and securing the passports or by deleting the endorsement for foreign travel. As a result of these measures, it was made impossible for approximately 1,000 non-Aryans to make an escape abroad, take their assets there, or manage assets there that had previously been shifted abroad without this coming to the knowledge of the tax authorities.

For non-Aryans who for some reason (export activity, travel activity, visits to family and relatives in cases of illness or death, etc.) want to travel abroad and therefore appear at the passport office to extend the validity of their domestic passport to foreign countries, before permission to travel abroad is issued the provision of a certificate of non-objection by the Freiburg City Tax Office has been arranged.

Through finding out about the allocation of a foreign-travel passport, the tax office has the opportunity to obtain information about the purpose of the trip abroad or even to draw conclusions as to what the taxable person might do there. The tax office (Freiburg City) has granted the certificate of non-objection without further ado only in instances involving small incomes and assets, as well as honest taxpayers, whose assessments can be assumed to be in order and who had no tax arrears. In all other cases, the issuance of the certificate of non-objection has been made contingent on the securing of any Reich Flight Tax due and, if applicable, other taxes too. Particularly in the case of taxable persons with sizeable assets or persons known to be tax cheats or taxable persons who have applied for a foreign-travel passport for their entire family, or whose assets are liquid, the tax office has required the deposit or securing of a part of their assets.

The Central Office for Reich Flight Tax in the Freiburg City Tax Office also has the task, within the tax office, of supervising all cases that are to be taxed and evaluated until they are finalized and, where necessary, the task of processing them itself.

The other larger offices proceed in a similar manner.

The central customs offices, district customs commissioners, and customs investigation office (including branches) also participate, although to a lesser extent, in the monitoring of emigrants and persons suspected of planning to emigrate. In so doing, in many instances (excluding the tax offices and the Tax Investigation Service) they work closely with the district offices, gendarmerie, and Gestapo. Because the Toll Investigation Service as a rule intervenes only when liquid assets are acquired, deposited with banks, and moved to border towns, or where currency customs offences are concerned, a heavier burdening of the Customs Investigation Service by this activity has thus far not occurred.

On the other hand, the Tax Investigation Service is kept extremely busy by such work, and is in some instances extraordinarily overburdened, particularly in Mannheim.

Among the observations and proposals of the offices, the following should be of interest as well:

(a) *Exporters.* Recently the Jews have been arguing in numerous instances that they must travel abroad for export purposes. Investigations have revealed that the alleged exporters are frequently persons who until now have never engaged in export at all or have done very little export business. In the case of other exporters, it has become apparent that they have substantial receivables abroad, and are granting overly long terms of payment etc., so that the suspicion cannot be denied that this is a matter of moving capital to a foreign country. Currently one tax office is involved in negotiations with the relevant Reichsbank office for the purpose of seeking a way to uncover these movements of capital in good time. The office that has made these observations deems it advisable to subject the export value declarations submitted to the Reichsbank to a more painstaking review than before, and particularly to compare the terms of payment with the credit time-limits that are customary in the individual industries and, when there are substantial failures to meet deadlines, to make the exporters aware of the obligation to deliver with respect to their foreign currency. If the exporters cause problems in the process, this should be sufficient reason to issue a security order.

(b) *Bank deposits etc.* It has repeatedly been the case that non-Aryan persons have withdrawn substantial bank balances shortly before their emigration. In the opinion of the office in whose district this observation was made, a way should be found to require that the banks inform the tax office immediately in such cases. Perhaps the bank commissioner can give universal instructions to the banks in this respect.

(c) *Purchase of foreign securities.* Recently there have been an increasing number of cases in which non-Aryan persons have invested their capital in foreign securities. This is probably attributable to the fact that foreign securities, unlike German ones, can be converted into cash abroad at more favourable rates.

(d) *Cash surrender of insurance policies.* It was determined in numerous instances that non-Aryan persons, shortly before emigrating, cancelled their insurance policies, purchased in this country, in exchange for the cash surrender value. A way should be found that makes it possible to oblige the insurance companies to notify the tax office before paying the cash surrender value to non-Aryan policyholders.

(e) *Withdrawal of passports for foreign travel.* To prevent flight by non-Aryan persons, one office urges that the passports for foreign travel of all these individuals be withdrawn, provided they are not persons who must frequently travel abroad to conclude economically desirable and lucrative business deals.

(f) *Retention of large sums of money by non-Aryan persons.* One tax office, when performing a tax review of non-Aryan persons, determined in two instances that these individuals, regardless of the loss of interest, had kept relatively large sums of cash in a bank deposit safe for quite some time, obviously with the intention of having cash on hand immediately, in an emergency.

A carbon copy of the report is attached.

DOC. 228

On 3 March 1936 the German Council of Municipalities lets the mayor of Stuttgart introduce restrictions on Jews in municipal public baths[1]

Letter (very urgent!) from the German Council of Municipalities (I 1454/36), the executive president, p.p. signed Schlempp,[2] to the mayor of Stuttgart,[3] dated 3 March 1936 (copy)

Re: Jews in municipal public baths
Concerning the letter of 21 February 1936 (7-E/941/22)[4]
With respect to the use of municipal baths by Jews, the German Council of Municipalities has addressed a petition to the Reich and Prussian Minister of the Interior. The decision on this request is still pending.[5] The stance of the German Council of Municipalities will become apparent to you from the excerpt from the petition enclosed in the attachment.[6]

As is well known, the Reich offices concerned have pronounced a ban on all individual actions with regard to the Jewish question. In connection with this, the Reich and Prussian Minister of Economics announced on 12 December 1935 that both the Deputy of the Führer and the Reich and Prussian Minister of the Interior had agreed with his view, according to which individual action should be interpreted as meaning all measures directed against Jews that are not based on an explicit order of the Reich government or the Reichsleitung of the NSDAP.[7]

The German Council of Municipalities, however, is of the opinion that this ban on individual actions does not hinder the individual municipalities from separately regulating the use of bathing facilities by Jews. This view is also shared by the officials in charge of the Reich and Prussian Ministry of the Interior. The spatial and temporal restriction of use for Jews is based on a provision of Reich law (§ 17 DGO[8]) and on the implementation guidelines for § 17 subparagraph 2. Accordingly, the municipalities can more closely regulate the prerequisites, terms, and manner of use. The temporal and spatial separation of Jews during use of bathing facilities belonging to the municipality, therefore, is not a measure that requires an explicit order from the Reich government. Such treatment also

---

1 BArch, R 36/2060, fol. 34r–v. This document has been translated from German.
2 Dr Hans Schlempp (b. 1907), lawyer; joined the NSDAP in 1932; until at least 1941 represented President Jeserich in Department I of the German Council of Municipalities and headed the Organizational Section; co-author of *Deutsches Kommunalrecht* (1939–1943) and author of *Die hessischen Landkreise* (1958).
3 The mayor of Stuttgart was Dr Karl Strölin (1890–1963), career officer and political scientist; joined the NSDAP in 1923; from 1923 worked for Stuttgart city council; city councillor, 1931–1933, and mayor of Stuttgart, 1933–1945; after 1945 was interned temporarily, and later classified during denazification proceedings as a 'lesser offender'.
4 This letter is not in the file.
5 With a decree (V a 12 518/36) issued on 2 April 1936, the Reich Ministry of the Interior authorized a segregation of Jews an non-Jews in municipal baths, but at the same time prohibited the harassment of Jews: see the decree issued by the Baden Ministry of the Interior to the district offices, 27 May 1936, published in Sauer (ed.), *Dokumente über die Verfolgung*, vol. 1, pp. 87–88.
6 This excerpt is not in the file.
7 See Doc. 218, 19 Dec. 1935.
8 § 17(1) of the German Municipal Code of 30 Jan. 1935 read as follows: 'The inhabitants, under the existing provisions in this regard, are entitled to use the public facilities of the municipality and are obligated to bear the municipal expenses': *Reichsgesetzblatt*, 1935, I, p. 51.

does not mean the exclusion of Jews from use in general. The German Council of Municipalities unfortunately does not possess exhaustive materials regarding the arrangements made by the larger cities in detail. However, especially as the position of the Reich and Prussian Minister of the Interior regarding my petition has not yet been made known, I will give consideration to arranging for a survey. As far as is known here from the files, Frankfurt am Main, for example, plans to make a separate municipal bathing beach available to non-Aryans for the summer months and to exclude them from the other municipal bathing beaches.[9] Likewise, Stettin has completely prohibited the use of certain municipal swimming baths by Jews and in general has allowed Jews to use bathing facilities only on a set day each week.[10]

DOC. 229
The Beck publishing house pitches its annotated edition of the Nuremberg Laws to the National Socialist Association of Teachers on 5 March 1936[1]

Letter from the C. H. Beck publishing house, Munich and Berlin, (signature illegible), Munich, 9 Wilhelmstraße, to the National Socialist Association of Teachers, Main Office for Educators[2] (received on 6 March 1936), Bayreuth, 20 Ludwigstraße, dated 5 March 1936[3]

After thorough preliminary work, the first volume of the *Commentary on the German Race Laws* by State Secretary Dr Stuckart of the Reich Ministry of the Interior and Oberregierungsrat Dr Globke of the Reich Ministry of the Interior has just appeared:[4]

Reich Citizenship Law, Blood Protection Law,[5] *and Marital Health Law*,[6] along with all the implementing regulations and the pertinent laws and regulations, XII, 287 pages. Clothbound, RM 5.80.

---

9 On the discussion in Frankfurt am Main, see Kommission zur Erforschung der Geschichte der Frankfurter Juden (ed.), *Dokumente zur Geschichte der Frankfurter Juden*, pp. 360–361.
10 The German Council of Municipalities sent almost identically worded letters in 1936 and 1937 to several cities that wanted to introduce restrictions for Jews in various municipal facilities; BArch, R 36/2060, fol. 34r–v.
1 BArch, NS 12/1458. This document has been translated from German.
2 In Sept. 1934 the NSDAP set up a Main Office for Educators in the Reich Administration of the National Socialist Association of Teachers (NSLB). It was headed by Reich Administrator Hans Schemm (1891–1935), after March 1933 also Bavarian minister of culture. After Schemm died in an accident in 1935, he was succeeded that year as chief of the Main Office by Fritz Wächtler (1891–1945), who was also Gauleiter of the Bavarian Ostmark.
3 The original contains the receipt stamp of the NSLB with handwritten sign-offs.
4 Dr Hans Globke (1898–1973), lawyer; joined the Catholic Centre Party in 1922; from 1925 deputy chief of police in Aachen; in 1929 Regierungsrat in the Prussian Ministry of the Interior; from 1932 specialist for citizenship questions in the Reich Ministry of the Interior, and Ministerialrat there in 1938; during denazification proceedings after 1945, classified as a 'follower' joined the Christian Democratic Union (CDU); in 1949 Ministerialdirigent in the Federal Chancellery; state secretary there, 1953–1963.
5 For the texts of the Reich Citizenship Law and the Law for the Protection of German Blood and German Honour, see Docs. 198 and 199, 15 Sept. 1935.
6 Law for the Protection of the Hereditary Health of the German People (Marital Health Law), 18 Oct. 1935, *Reichsgesetzblatt*, 1935, I, p. 1246.

The commentary by Stuckart and Globke gains its special significance from the fact that in it the three closely related fundamental race laws are annotated *in a consistent way* by two *authors who were officially involved* in the realization of the racial legislation. The work opens with an academically thorough and useful 'Introduction', which provides a detailed rationale of the National Socialist racial legislation. In the annotations all the uncertain points and specifics and processing of the implementing regulations and decrees are explained in detail. Each law and each implementing regulation is explained separately, and the interrelationship is made clear by numerous references. In addition, the pertinent provisions from forty-one laws and regulations and thirteen major decrees are reproduced verbatim. The user of the work, therefore, has *all the legislative material* to hand.

At a later date, following the passage of each, the *Reich Subjects Law, Kinship Office Law*, etc.[7] will also appear in similar editions – self-contained and available for purchase separately.

The commentary by Stuckart and Globke will perform a valuable service for the Party offices as an authentic interpretation of the new race laws. By enclosing an inspection copy, we take the liberty of recommending the purchase of the work.

Heil Hitler!

DOC. 230

On 12 March 1936 the emigration advisor for the Jewish Community in Leipzig reports on those seeking advice and their financial situations[1]

Report, undated and unsigned (copy)

Excerpt from the report of the emigration advisor in *Leipzig*, Dr A. *Wachtel*,[2] dated 12 March 1936

The advisory office for Leipzig began its work on 1 February 1936. Unfortunately, there was no existing institution within the community that it could rely upon. The office itself had to be set up first and furnishings acquired, etc. This initially inhibited the actual advisory work.

Although I had at first informed only the Leipzig Community of my consultation hours, the stream of visitors was quite considerable. Ever since the existence of the office was announced in the Jewish papers, people from outside Leipzig have been making enquiries, especially by letter. In February 130 letters were sent out, including many addressed to the Relief Association with several enclosures. The influx of enquiries will surely increase dramatically as soon as the consultation hours are announced, as is currently planned. Without a doubt, there is a need for such an advisory office, especially because many do not have the money to travel elsewhere.

---

7 Both laws were discussed for a long time but never brought to completion.

1 CZA, S 7/357. This document has been translated from German.
2 Dr Alex Siegfried Wachtel (b. 1881), lawyer; until 1933 regional court judge in Gotha; lived from 1936 in Leipzig, where he was head of the local office of the Relief Association of Jews in Germany; emigrated to the Netherlands in Feb. 1939; deported from Westerbork to Theresienstadt in Jan. 1944 and then sent to Auschwitz in Oct. 1944.

Profile of those seeking advice.

(a) *Nationality.*

To begin with, the Ostjuden *within the Leipzig Community* comprise a considerable contingent. The poor economic situation in the Brühl[3] has left many destitute. In addition, *a large number of pedlars have no longer been granted a trading licence*, while *others have lost their work permits* or *been stripped of their residence permits.* A particularly *large number* are *stateless*, often because they have not fulfilled their military service requirements in Romania and Poland. A considerable number were Polish nationals. *A large proportion literally have nothing left.* They have not been able to save anything and they are no longer permitted to trade. They are a burden on the Leipzig Community, which will probably soon be in a state of emergency. How these people, especially the many young people who have learned nothing but trading and cannot speak any languages other than German and Yiddish, can and should be helped is a question that cannot be resolved at the moment. It puts a heavy strain on our advisory work. The feeling of complete helplessness is often very depressing.

(b) *Profession.*

The vast majority of those seeking advice are involved in trade or sales or are commercial employees.

Craftsmen include cobblers, tailors, and furriers. Among the cobblers and tailors, many are older people who were self-employed up to now, but have now lost their former Aryan customers and have not been able to find enough customers within the Jewish community to replace this lost business. Furriers and fur workers have become penniless thanks to the decline in the fur business in general. Unfortunately, there is not much hope of being able to bring them to the new larger centres of the fur trade such as London and New York, even though many are proficient experts.

An increasing number of enquiries are arriving from tradesmen and the owners of small textile shops in the countryside, who are plagued by a miserable existence, especially in the Rhön Mountains, for example. These people are at their wits' end. Living in the small towns is torture, and their businesses have been boycotted almost entirely. Here a field might be available to shift these people into agriculture because they often engage in farming on the side. They would have been able to liquidate some property, but now they also have nothing left.

(c) *Age.*

As far as I can tell, people of all ages have come, up to about 60 years old and in a few cases older, but a larger number appear to be young people who either have lost their jobs or are about to lose them. The limited immigration quota for Palestine has prompted many who were already part of a Hachsharah or still belong to one to explore other emigration options.

Agriculture.

In my opinion, there are a certain number of livestock traders, butchers, and textile traders in the countryside who would be suitable for family settlements.[4] A rough estimate is that there are about forty to fifty such families in my district. I plan to travel through the countryside over the next few months to get a more accurate picture, but I am pretty sure that they are mainly young people. I'm guessing, without any guarantee, that there are about seventy to a hundred of them.

Assets.
Most of those making enquiries unfortunately have no assets.

It is high time that all the responsible offices, especially those abroad, recognize that the hardship and suffering is increasing and that any further delay will make it even more difficult to overcome these problems and, eventually, impossible to do so, thus unleashing immense suffering if something drastic does not happen soon.
bis dat, qui cito dat.[5]

DOC. 231

The Potsdam government circumvents a directive issued by Reich Minister of Justice Franz Gürtner on the purchase of plots of land by Jews (around 26 April 1936)[1]

Directive (no. IV b 3493) issued by Reich Minister of Justice Gürtner, addressed to the president of the Higher Regional Court in Cologne,[2] dated 14 March 1936, with an undated note from the Potsdam government[3]

Re: the purchase of plots of land by Jews.[4]
With regard to the local case dated 13 December 1935 (IV 23/579)[5] I would like to inform you, President of the Higher Regional Court, of the following in consultation with the Deputy of the Führer and the Reich Minister of the Interior.

---

3 A street in the centre of Leipzig. Until the Second World War, the Brühl was a world-famous centre for fur processing and trade.
4 This refers to plans to send families to agricultural settlements in other countries.
5 Latin: 'he gives twice who gives promptly'.

1 BLHA, Pr.Br.Rep. 2 A I Pol/1919, fols. 225–226. Copy of the directive issued by the Reich Minister of Justice dated 14 March 1936 in Landesarchivverwaltung Rheinland-Pfalz (ed.), *Dokumentation zur Geschichte der jüdischen Bevölkerung*, p. 80. This document has been translated from German.
2 The president of the Higher Regional Court in Cologne from 1933 to 1943 was Dr Alexander Bergmann (1878–1965).
3 The directive of the Reich Minister of Justice was passed on via the circular decree issued by the Reich and Prussian Minister of the Interior (I A 5831/5012), p.p. Dr Stuckart, addressed to the Reichsstatthalter, the Reich commissioner for the reintegration of the Saarland, the regional governments, the Oberpräsidenten, the State commissioner for the Reich capital Berlin, and the Regierungspräsidenten, with carbon copies for the lower state administrative offices (for Prussia: the Landräte; for Bavaria: the directors of the district authorities etc.), dated 21 April 1936. The original was received by the Potsdam government on 26 April 1933 and contains handwritten notes and instances of underlining.
4 In the left-hand margin, a handwritten addition reads: 'An addition is required before it is forwarded to the Landräte at least to the effect that high-profile cases should be reported to the Reich Minister of Justice in advance.' In the right-hand margin: 'For the version for the Landräte.'
5 This case file could not be found. On the issue of the purchase of property by Jews, see also the earlier demand by the Gestapo Central Office (Gestapa) on 9 Sept. 1935 to prohibit such transactions, Doc. 195.

The Nuremberg legislation has only established legal guidelines on the Jewish question – apart from the matter of the Mischlinge – in terms of constitutional and marriage law. The economic rights of the Jews have yet to be codified in law. The legal regulation of these matters is exclusively a matter for the supreme organs of the state, just as they alone had the authority to deal with the problems related to constitutional and marriage law. It cannot be the task of individual offices across the country to resolve this aspect of the Jewish question in lieu of the supreme organs of state. The economic activities of the Jews are governed only by the existing[6] laws. As the current legislation does not outline any limitations on the purchase of plots by Jews, no legal foundation exists for either prohibiting the sale of a piece of land or for declaring such a sale as invalid because the purchasing party is a Jew.

Please inform the regional and local courts as well as the notaries in your district accordingly.

signed Dr Gürtner.

The sale of plots of land to Jews[7]

(1) Statement on the contents of the directive and our *decision. A ruling will follow*

(2) In general, the purchase of plots of land by Jews does not require authorization, but there are other means available:

(a) exertion of influence over the seller and the purchaser

(b) no sales by *communities*!

(3) The sale of agricultural land over 5 acres requires authorization in accordance with the regulation of 1918. As a rule, such requests can therefore be denied!

---

[6] This word is underlined by hand. Next to this sentence there is a mark and '!' in the margin.
[7] Handwritten note from the Potsdam government (I, 5).

DOC. 232
Slaughterhouse director Karl Boerner terminates business relations with Gustav Schroeder in Waren (Müritz) on 30 May 1936[1]

Letter, signed Dr Boerner,[2] slaughterhouse director, Waren, to G. W. Schroeder,[3] Waren, Rosenstraße, dated 30 May 1936 (copy)

You have put me in the extremely embarrassing situation, although you have not done anything to me personally, of having to cut off all your relations with me and my family. The Party has officially notified me that you continue to do business with the Jew Leopold[4] and that you sell his wares. It is even assumed that the wire brushes for the slaughterhouse and the waterworks came from these Jewish hands.

As the municipal slaughterhouse director, it is impossible for me or anyone in my family to maintain relations of any kind with you. As you know, such relations with Jews are viewed by the Party as treason against the people and as Jewish bondage. I also have to return the brushes already purchased because the town, of course, cannot buy Jewish goods. Your initial claim that the brushes came from Röbel is no longer believed to be credible.

It is extremely embarrassing for me to have to write such a letter to you. But I am not doing so for personal reasons. Yet, the facts of the matter are so clear and it is absolutely essential for me, as an employee, to stick to these facts as long as you are not able to rebut the official Party accusations made against you. Personally, I can only add that I would simply have no understanding for any decision of yours to maintain such relations. These kinds of things simply cannot be kept hidden. There are no advantages that can outweigh the disadvantages brought by such relations.

I naturally assume that you will be able to understand the embarrassing nature of this matter as well as the absolute necessity of my letter.

With best wishes for your future[5]

---

1 RGVA, 721k-1-258. This document has been translated from German.
2 Dr Karl Boerner (1883–1965), veterinarian; from around 1933 until at least 1941 slaughterhouse director in Waren (Müritz); after 1945 in Stalinstadt (Eisenhüttenstadt).
3 Gustav Wilhelm Schroeder (1883–1943), retailer; owner of a car dealership in Waren (Müritz) from 1913; committed suicide in August 1943.
4 Joseph Arnold Leopold (1876–1945), retailer; owner of a hardware store in Waren; head of the Jewish Community in Waren, 1920–1937. He moved to Berlin with his wife Karoline (b. 1884) in 1937. Both were deported from Berlin to Theresienstadt at the end of Oct. 1942. Joseph Leopold died in the camp on 19 May 1945.
5 On the lower edge of the page there is a handwritten note: 'Leop[old] is a severely disabled veteran!'

DOC. 233

On 17 June 1936 the Regierungspräsident in Königsberg writes to the Reich Minister of the Interior to outline an amendment to the charter of the Driesen Foundation discriminating against Jews[1]

Letter from the Regierungspräsident[2] in Königsberg in Prussia (no. I A 46 K.1.d.1), p.p. (illegible signature), addressed to the Reich and Prussian Minister of the Interior, dated 17 June 1936[3]

Re: amendments to the charter of the Driesen Foundation in Königsberg (Prussia) – introduction of the Aryan principle.

Enclosures: (1) Proposal of the mayor of Königsberg (Prussia)[4] dated 24 October 1935, with minutes dated 26 September 1935 and two copies of the new charter dated 15 October 1935.

(2) The currently valid charter dated 28 February 1934.

(3) The last will and testament of the businessman Driesen dated 8 April 1880, with the charter of the foundation dated 16 January 1884.

(4) One booklet of files.

Rapporteur: Regierungsrat von Cardinal and Regierungsrat Urbanus as legal advisors.[5]

In his last will and testament dated 8 April 1880, the Jewish retailer Adolf *Driesen* of Königsberg (Prussia), who died on 1 January 1881, appointed a foundation for the poor in Königsberg (Prussia), to be established according to the detailed stipulations of his testament, as his sole heir. He appointed the city council of Königsberg as the executor of his last will and testament. The establishment of the foundation on the basis of the foundation charter dated 16 January 1884 was approved by supreme decree on 18 April 1884. At the same time, the foundation was granted the rights of a legal entity. It is therefore an independent foundation. The purpose of the foundation was – apart from the construction of 'free houses' – the construction of a 'care home'. This care home is to provide life-long asylum and a livelihood as independent as possible for people of both sexes who have become unemployed through no fault of their own, regardless of their professed faith (p. 16 under C in the enclosed last will and testament). According to § 10(2), page 17 of the last will and testament, preference is to be given to needy relatives of the testator over 40 years of age, regardless of the conditions for eligibility that otherwise apply for non-relatives.

On page 18, paragraph 3 of the last will and testament, the stipulations continue:

---

1 BArch, R 1501 II/127202, fols. 97–99v. This document has been translated from German.
2 The Regierungspräsident was Werner Friedrich (1886–1966), lawyer; Regierungspräsident in Königsberg in Prussia, 1932–1936; sent into provisional retirement in July 1936; then acting executive head of the Schleswig-Holstein Savings Banks Association; at the Court of Auditors of the German Reich, 1939.
3 The original contains annotations as well as a receipt stamp: 'Oberpräsident 18 June 1936 Königsberg, Prussia.'
4 The mayor of Königsberg from 1933 to 1945 was Dr Hellmuth Will (1900–1982), lawyer.
5 The enclosures are not published here.

In view of the fact that I myself profess the Mosaic faith, and significantly fewer institutions with a purpose similar to that of the care home to be constructed at my behest exist for those who share my faith in the local town in comparison to the other citizens of the city of Königsberg, I specify that preferably one third of the available spaces be reserved for married as well as single members of the local synagogue congregation, and simultaneously, I grant the respective chairman of the synagogue congregation the right of nomination.

This stipulation in the testament – the reservation of a third of the care home spaces for Jews – was written into the original charter of the foundation dated 16 January 1884 under § 3 and retained in later amendments of the charter (especially as in § 3 of the currently valid charter dated 28 February 1934, Encl. 2).

At the moment, the foundation owns four houses – namely the houses numbered 6, 7, 10/11, and 12/13 on Yorkstraße in Königsberg. Forty-four foundation apartments are accommodated within them – twenty-two for married couples and twenty-two for unmarried individuals. In keeping with the charter, a third of each are preferentially reserved for Jews.

On 26 September 1935 the board of trustees of the foundation, chaired by the representative of the mayor of Königsberg, voted to amend the charter and simultaneously submitted a new version of the charter to me for approval (Encl. 1). Among the amendments written into the new charter, the last sentence of § 3 stipulates that 'non-Aryans are not to be admitted'.

This stipulation emerged out of consideration for the fact that, given the clear racial divisions that the National Socialist state ever more strongly draws between German Volksgenossen and Jews, it would be an intolerable situation to bestow upon German Volksgenossen as well as Jews the benefit of free accommodation in foundation housing together.

The fact that the assets with which the Driesen Foundation was created were donated by a member of the Jewish race cannot be permitted to override these considerations (report of the mayor of the town of Königsberg dated 19 October 1935 in enclosures booklet 4).

The adoption of the Aryan principle in the charter of the foundation contradicts the directive set out by the benefactor for the establishment of the foundation and approved by the state to the effect that one third of the foundation-sponsored spaces are to be reserved for Jews.

According to § 38 Part II Title 19 of the General Laws [for the Prussian States], the regulatory authority must ensure that 'regulations expressly or implicitly approved by the state are followed and that there are no infiltrations that run contrary to the ultimate purpose of such foundations'. The purpose of the foundation is to provide accommodation not only for German Volksgenossen – Aryans – but also needy Jews in the foundation's houses.

According to this still currently valid stipulation, as the regulatory authority, I believe that I am obligated to refrain from granting my approval for the complete exclusion of non-Aryans from the benefits of the foundation as per the decision of the board of trustees. On the other hand, however, it must be recognized that since the death of the benefactor, the clear distinction between Aryan Volksgenossen and Jews implemented by the new National Socialist state has led to changed circumstances as referred to in § 41 II 19 of the General Law and § 1 of the law of 10 July 1924 (*GS*, p. 575),⁶ which would seem to justify the amendment of the existing foundation charter in this respect.

In order to reconcile these considerations with the intentions of the benefactor as far as possible, I intend to suggest to the board of trustees of the foundation that the final sentence in § 3 of the new charter, which reads 'Non-Aryans are not to be admitted', should be replaced with the following stipulation:

> One third of the existing spaces are to remain reserved for individuals of the Jewish faith who belong to the local synagogue congregation, as long as Aryan foundation residents do not have to live together with Jews in the same house. The board of the synagogue congregation in Königsberg is to retain the right to nominate these individuals.
>
> Among the Jewish applicants, preference is to be given to relatives of the benefactor of over 40 years of age, even if they do not belong to the local synagogue congregation and are not residents of the city of Königsberg. The synagogue congregation's right of nomination does not apply in the case of relatives of the benefactor.

As already noted above, according to the deed of foundation, preference is to go to needy relatives of the benefactor, regardless of the stipulations that apply to non-relatives. Accordingly, they also have a right to be granted housing even if the third of the spaces reserved for Jews are already occupied, but a space is free among the non-reserved portion.

In the history of the foundation since its establishment in 1884, none of the relatives of the benefactor have made use of these privileges thus far. Therefore, it seems sufficient – as provided for in my suggestion – to account for the relatives of the benefactor among the third of the spaces reserved for Jews. A spatial separation between Jewish and Aryan residents of the foundation can be achieved to a great extent by assigning one of the four foundation buildings, the house at 6 Yorkstraße, to the Jewish foundation residents.

This would allow twelve Jewish households with six two-room apartments and six one-room apartments to be kept completely separated from the other households.

The garden behind the house at no. 6 could be separated from the other gardens by a fence. The cost of a fence would be approximately RM 200. No further costs would be incurred.

Given that is a fundamental issue, I ask for a decision as to whether you approve my intention to refrain from approving the complete exclusion of Jews from the benefits of the foundation and to propose to the board of directors instead of the complete exclusion of non-Aryans an amendment to the currently valid charter regarding the segregation of the foundation's beneficiaries as outlined above.⁷

---

6 Law on Changes to Foundations, 10 July 1924: *Preußische Gesetzsammlung*, 1924, no. 42, 18 July 1924, pp. 575–576.

7 The Reich and Prussian Minister of the Interior replied to the Regierungspräsident on 10 August 1937 to the effect that there were no objections to his suggestion: letter (draft) from the Reich and Prussian Minister of the Interior to the Regierungspräsident in Königsberg (sent on 10 August 1937), BArch, R 1501 II/127202, fol. 109r–v.

DOC. 234
Historische Zeitschrift: the establishment of the column
'History of the Jewish Question', spring 1936[1]

History of the Jewish Question[2]
by Wilhelm Grau

Preface: in this issue of the HZ, for the first time ever, an academic forum has been established for the history of the Jewish question, which is to be continued from time to time in future issues. A forum on this topic is also an innovation among the other German historical journals. The fact that the appearance of these pages might still seem to be unusual is the most bitter justification that can be cited on the occasion of their launch.

One of the most pressing tasks to be addressed by these reports is the academic critique of all important studies on the Jewish question in history and especially within German history. It is not only the universal perspective of the HZ but also the nature of the problem itself that makes it impossible for us to restrict the territorial scope to the German-speaking lands at all times. Likewise, it is just as impossible to divide the subject matter according to the sub-disciplines of historical scholarship – Semitic philology, philosophical history, theological history, literary history, economic history, legal history, racial theory – because they are all involved but must be united by general political history. The Jewish question is a political problem today just as it has always been. The sooner and more often we can supplement this criticism with our own small- and large-scale research, the more impressive our intention with this forum will become: to unearth the truth cognitively and unleash intellectual and spiritual powers to serve in the interests of this truth.

On Jewish involvement in Bolshevism.
Although the general opinion prevails that the Jews played a decisive role in the Bolshevik revolution and in the creation of the Bolshevik state – see, for example, the remarkable book by the Englishman Hilaire *Belloc, The Jews*, Munich 1927,[3] and Hermann Fehst, *Bolshevism and Jewry*, Berlin 1934[4] – a recently published academic study by Abraham

---

1 'Geschichte der Judenfrage', *Historische Zeitschrift* (HZ) (1936), vol. 153, pp. 336–343. This document has been translated from German. The *HZ*, founded in 1859 by Heinrich von Sybel, was edited from 1894 to 1935 by Friedrich Meinecke and from autumn 1935 until the last war issue in 1943 (vol. 168) by Karl Alexander von Müller.
2 The first issue of the *HZ*, for which Karl Alexander von Müller was responsible, contained not only the newly established column 'History of the Jewish Question' but also an introductory programmatic declaration by the editor in which he made a commitment to the study of history in the 'new era', as well as the speech given by the future president Dr Walter Frank (1905–1945) in honour of the inauguration of the new Reich Institute for History of the New Germany on 19 Oct. 1935, entitled 'Guild and Nation' (*Zunft und Nation*). Frank outlined the institute's research programme as follows: (1) the influence of Western ideas in Germany between the French Revolution and the Revolution of 1848; (2) the efforts to establish a national church in the nineteenth century; (3) the history of German philosophy; (4) the history of the Jewish question from 1789 to 1933: *HZ* (1936), vol. 153, pp. 1–23. The *Völkischer Beobachter* reprinted von Müller's declaration in its entirety; *Völkischer Beobachter* (northern German edition), 29 Nov. 1935, p. 5.
3 Originally published by Constable & Co., London, in 1922.
4 *Bolschewismus und Judentum: Das jüdische Element in der Führerschaft des Bolschewismus* (Berlin/Leipzig: Eckart-Kampf, 1934).

Heller[5] (*The Situation of the Jews in Russia from the March 1917 Revolution to the Present*, Publications of the Society for the Promotion of Jewish Studies, vol. 39, M. & H. Marcus, Breslau 1935, xii and 128 pp.[6]) aims to demonstrate emphatically on the basis of 'authentic sources' and with the help of statistical tables 'how the war of destruction against the Jews of Russia', even after the fall of the tsarist regime, 'continues to progress' (p. v). Indeed, the book gives the impression that, despite the declaration of emancipation for the Jews that suddenly came about with the revolution of 1917, Russian antisemitism has not been halted. But the author often mistakenly mixes up inner-Jewish struggles and anti-Jewish measures in his account. As a Zionist nationalist Jew he vehemently opposes the schemes of Jewish Bolsheviks, who threaten the congregational life of the Zionists, and aim to destroy Jewish rituals and the Hebrew language. As a Jew he chastises any antisemitic impulses, even if they are quite obviously anti-Bolshevik in nature, and conceals the diabolical links between the Jews and Bolshevism. What can be said when an academic work categorically dismisses the leading role of *Jewish* elements within the Bolshevik movement with the sentence that these Bolshevik Jews acted 'not as Jews, but rather as "pure internationalists" in non-Jewish circles', and that it would therefore be a 'historical injustice' to call them Jews (p. 7)? Should Trotsky not be regarded as a Jew because, 'when reading' his autobiography, 'a layperson [yes, that's right!] might get the impression' that 'Trotsky is the son of a Russian landowner rather than of a Jewish-traditional settler' because Trotsky does not give his parents' names, because he only mentions his Jewish schooldays – which lasted for a few months – cursorily, because 'nationalist fervour and prejudices are rationally incomprehensible' to him, and because his Marxist upbringing had imbued him with an 'active internationalism' (p. 7)?[7] In the tsarist empire, the Jews were considered to be a 'foreign population' (p. 1). But the Russian Jews, including the Zionists, who one would think were surely just as aware of their 'foreignness' as their Basel Programme,[8] which aimed to 'establish a home for the Jewish

---

5 Dr Abraham Heller (b. 1911), historian; began his university studies in 1929 at the Higher Institute for Jewish Studies in Berlin and at the University of Berlin, where he completed his PhD in 1934; in 1935 he emigrated via Vilnius to Palestine, where he was a grammar school teacher of history and Bible studies until 1973; author of works including *Who Has a Right to This Country?* (Hebrew, 1969).
6 Abraham Heller, *Die Lage der Juden in Rußland von der Märzrevolution 1917 bis zur Gegenwart*, Schriften der Gesellschaft zur Förderung der Wissenschaft des Judentums, vol. 39 (Breslau: Marcus, 1935). A reprint of this book was published in 1992. On the book, see Ingo Loose, 'Verfemt und vergessen: Abraham Hellers Dissertation "Die Lage der Juden in Rußland von der Märzrevolution 1917 bis zur Gegenwart" an der Berliner Universität 1934–1992', *Jahrbuch für Antisemitismusforschung*, vol. 14 (2005), pp. 219–241.
7 Footnote in the original: 'See the Jewish view on the apostasy from Judaism: "According to religious law, any child born to a Jewish mother is and remains a Jew. In the eyes of the law the baptized Jew is therefore only considered to have violated religious law." (*Jüdisches Lexikon*, V, 884). The primacy of the right of blood is therefore clearly acknowledged. Trotsky was not baptized. Whether he had violated Jewish religious law as a "pure internationalist" would first have to be proved. If we assume that Trotsky's world view was in direct opposition to Jewish *religious law*, this would still not indicate that Trotsky's character and way of thinking were foreign to the Jewish *nature*. After all, Jewish descent also manifests itself beyond the boundaries of Jewish religious law.'
8 The First Zionist Congress, chaired by Theodor Herzl, took place in August 1897 in Basel. The congress passed the Basel Programme containing the principal demand expressed in the passage quoted in the text above.

people in *Palestine* secured under public law' (p. 101), sought to achieve civic equality in *Russia*. 'The Jewish problem seemed impossible to solve as an isolated issue in the tsarist empire. It was an inseparable part of the entire complex of the absolutist state and could only be dealt with within the general framework of the state superstructure. On the basis of this conviction, many Jews took an active part in the revolutionary movements in Russia' (pp. 1–2).

Therefore, not only the 'pure internationalists' but also the Zionist Jews contributed to the fall of the Tsar and the establishment of Bolshevik rule. This historic culpability is also not mitigated by the fact that the Jewish parties had their doubts after the overthrow because the Bolshevik economic policies (war communism) hit the private capitalist structure of Russian Jewry hard. These economic impairments, as well as all the damage that the Jews of Russia suffered in the stormy days of the revolution and the civil war that ensued, are outlined in minute detail by the author. We search in vain for any reference to the suffering that Jewish leaders brought upon the Russian people and the peoples of this world. When looked at more closely, however, much of the misfortune that befell the large nationalist Jewish population in Russia was the result of an *inner-Jewish factional dispute* over the principle of assimilation on the one hand and the world of Zionist thought on the other. 'The main fighters against the Hebrew educational system in the Soviet Union are the assimilated Jewish Bolsheviks' (p. 114; cf. p. 115).

However, these struggles are neither specifically Russian nor Bolshevik. Since the days of Mendelssohn and David Friedländer, they have been part and parcel of the history of the Jews in *all* countries. Consequently, the author is not able to successfully illustrate the existence of a specifically *anti-Bolshevik* position among the Jewish population. While it is stated that the Zionist party 'consistently refused to bend to communism' (p. 104), 'communism' quite clearly means Jewish communists who sought to push through their ideas of assimilation with the help of their political position of power, in keeping with their conviction that 'the Jewish people have been condemned by history to assimilation' (p. 115).

Likewise, one cannot speak of a specifically anti-Jewish stance within Bolshevism. In Russia, Jews have the right to their own schools, councils, courts, and administrative autonomy in the areas in which they constitute the majority (p. 123). They have retained the colloquial language of the majority of the Jewish population, Yiddish (Jewish-German dialect), as a state-recognized language. The Jews are not only connected to the Bolshevik revolution and the emergent Soviet state through *individual*, very influential leaders, but rather they also contribute to this communist rule in an exceptional way in a sociological sense.

The total number of Jews in Russia in 1926 was 2,672,398, which amounted to 1.8 per cent of the entire Russian population (p. 65). In 1926 the number of Jewish communists in Russia was 44,300, which amounted to 4 per cent of all communists. In 1922 the Jewish percentage even amounted to 5.2 per cent (p. 107). The book does not say how high this percentage was in 1917/18. According to Heller, this 'relatively high number of Jewish communists' can only 'be explained by the fact the Jews are an urban population' (p. 108).

The symbiosis between the Jews and Bolshevism becomes even more apparent if we take into account the changes in the social structure of Russian Jewry. Whereas the '*state employees*' category hardly ever appeared in the social organism of the Jews in the tsarist empire, it accounts for 23.4 per cent of all Russian Jews in the Soviet state.[9] With this percentage, the state employees account for the largest single social group within Russian Jewry.

The Jewish occupational statistics for 1926 have the following range (see p. 74):[10]

State employees	23.4 %
Craftsmen and outworkers	19.5 %
Workers	14.8 %
Traders	11.8 %
Unemployed	9.3 %
Farmers	9.1 %
Liberal professions	1.6 %
Miscellaneous professions	10.5 %

It is particularly interesting that in Moscow 50.1 per cent and in Leningrad 40.1 per cent of all Jews[11] are state employees. The Jewish state employees now account for 8 per cent of all civil servants and state employees in the Soviet Union as a whole. In certain areas this already considerable percentage is doubled or tripled. In the USSR, 16.8 per cent of all state employees are Jews; in the BSSR, 25.5 per cent are Jews.[12]

What does Heller, the vehement opponent of assimilation and Bolshevism, have to say about this record number of Jews in the Bolshevik state apparatus?

> This disproportionate percentage of Jews in the civil service can be explained on the one hand by the fact that the Russian, the Ukrainian (83.0 per cent), and the Belorussian (85.1 per cent) people are first and foremost an agrarian people. This can also be explained on the other hand by the complete urbanization of the Jewish population. Above all, the Bolshevik government also had to rely from the outset on the intellectually vigorous Jewish elements because the earlier civil service could not be trusted because it still clung too tightly to the old regime. Furthermore, the Russian intelligentsia sabotaged the Soviet power almost completely until 1921. A significant portion of the assimilated Jewish intelligentsia, by contrast, which played an eminent role in the revolutionary parties, was viewed by the new rulers as a good instrument to have within their government apparatus. Yet another portion of the Jewish intelligentsia (or, rather, semi-intelligentsia), which was principally opposed to Bolshevism, was pushed into the civil service through the loss of employment opportunities that came about with the advent of the new Bolshevik order. (p. 77)

Heller, therefore, finds no fault with the high number of Jewish civil servants and he dismisses all the political and ideological reasons that could account for this. We choke over his words that 'the Bolshevik government *relied* from the outset on the intellectually vigorous Jewish element'. It was not because they felt and acted as Jewish Marxists that so many Jews became Russian civil servants, but rather because they were 'intellectually vigorous' and because they were '*forced into*' the Bolshevik civil service. The fact that

---

[9] The author means all *employed* Jews.
[10] Grau structured this table somewhat differently from Heller. Heller, for example, had counted workers and craftsmen as 34.3 per cent: Heller, *Die Lage der Juden in Rußland*, p. 74.
[11] The author means all *employed* Jews.
[12] USSR: Ukrainian Soviet Socialist Republic; BSSR: Belorussian Soviet Socialist Republic.

'the new rulers', who saw the Jews as a good instrument for their governmental apparatus, were themselves Jews is not taken into account by Heller in any way. Likewise, Heller fails to mention that millions of Russians also lost their employment prospects but did not become civil servants in the Bolshevik state.

Let us keep in mind that the Bolshevik ideology rests on the teachings of the Jew Karl Marx. Alongside Lenin, the highly visible command posts within the Russian Revolution were held almost entirely by Jewish Bolsheviks: Trotsky-Bronstein, Radek-Sobelsohn, Joffe, Kopp, Kamenev-Finkelstein,[13] Scheinmann, Sokolnikov-Brilliant, Zinoviev-Radomylsky.

A quarter of all Russian Jews are now officials, mostly in leadership positions, in the service of the Bolshevik state.

The Soviet resettlement policies treated the Jews preferentially over all other peoples of the Russian empire: 'No other people in Russia received such sprawling and well-established pieces of land as the Jewish farmers on the Crimean peninsula' (Theodor Seibert, *Red Russia*, Munich 1932, p. 43;[14] similarly, though more cautiously, Heller, p. 95).

In the factional political struggles within the Party, the rise of Stalin forced many of the important Jewish Bolsheviks of the Lenin era into the opposition. Nonetheless, even today there is still an extraordinary number of Jewish Bolsheviks. 'The People's Commissariats are teeming with them. In the ministries of trade, foreign affairs, and education, Jews are still absolutely dominant' (Seibert, p. 47).

No one contests all these facts. And yet the rule of the Jews in Bolshevik Russia is supposed to be nothing but a 'legend' and a 'delusion' (Seibert, pp. 45 and 47). And Heller claims that the 'Bolshevik convictions of the Jews' are only 'used as a smokescreen' for antisemitic riots (p. 38)!

Certainly, Bolshevism is not synonymous with Judaism and Judaism is not synonymous with Bolshevism. Not every Bolshevik is a Jew and not every Jew is a Bolshevik. But the intellectual affinity between these two powers is obvious. The moral, political, and sociological contribution of the Jews to Bolshevism is incontestable, and it is only the open manifestation of this intellectual and spiritual commonality. Whoever does not concede this point, despite the clear language of historical facts, will never be able to comprehend the phenomenon of Russian antagonism against the Jews.

Like all Jewish historians, Heller is stunned and at a loss when it comes to explaining the elementary fabric of antisemitism. It brings him to deduce the formula: malignancy, lack of culture, tsarist reaction.

A demoralized and defeated people, at the end of a long war, thrown into despair by the most horrible revolution in the history of the world, rose up in Ukraine against Bolshevism with the last ounce of its resolve. A Ukrainian proclamation from this time (6 September 1917) calls for action against the enemy within the country: 'People of Russia, wake up! Just a short time ago, the sun shone in Kiev and the Russian Tsar deigned to come here. Now the Jews are everywhere! We want to cast off this yoke; we cannot bear it any longer! They will destroy the motherland. Down with the Jews! Russian people unite! Give us back the Tsar' (quoted in Heller p. 27). Civil war came: the

---

13 Kamenev was actually born Rozenfeld. The author was perhaps confusing Kamenev with the Russian revolutionary and Soviet diplomat Maxim Litvinov (1876–1951), who was born Wallach-Finkelstein.
14 *Das Rote Rußland: Staat, Geist und Alltag der Bolschewiki* (Munich: Knorr & Hirth, 1932).

Red Army against the White. In this war, Jews were murdered, robbed, plundered. Pogroms! Many innocent women and children were included. Deeply regrettable! But the great historical power of right and justice in this *war* was on the side of the anti-Bolshevik. The Jews in Ukraine felt a connection with the Bolsheviks in Moscow and Leningrad, in opposition to Ukrainian nationalism. It was the Jews who, 'for reasons of caution', as Heller says (p. 30), balked at the decisive anti-Bolshevik act of the secession of Ukraine from Russia. And thus the tribunal raged harshly, but justly.

A historian who wants to stick to the truth cannot describe Jewish suffering one-sidedly. A much mightier and deeper torrent of blood was shed than that of all the Jews that Heller so carefully calculates, a torrent in which the most noble and most valuable blood of the Russian people and the tsarist family itself flowed, whose origins lie in the bestial call to murder also coming from Bolshevik Jews.

For the most part, antisemitism in Russia also bears an anti-Bolshevik character. But then it also appeared for a while within the Communist Party itself, in which anti-Jewish statements especially coming from the provinces and the lower ranks made their presence felt as an expression of social and political, and certainly also racial, instincts. The harsh measures initiated by the *central* Bolshevik powers against such manifestations are evidence of the fact that this 'communist' antisemitism was mostly interpreted as a critique of and a form of opposition to Bolshevism (p. 127).

There are many other details that could be cited in contradiction of Heller's work. But the point here was only to show that the 'authentic sources' that Heller presents lead a historical observer in a completely different direction from that to which Heller tries to lead these 'authentic sources'. The biased intentions and the insufficient theses of this book are so striking that one can only wonder how Heller earned his PhD[15] in October 1935 from the Faculty of Philosophy of the University of Berlin with this study supervised by Professor Hoetzsch[16] and Professor Vasmer.[17]

[...][18]

---

15 Heller had submitted his doctoral thesis to the Philosophy Faculty of the University of Berlin in Feb. 1934 and passed his viva in July 1934. The thesis was published in Oct. 1935. When the newly appointed dean of the faculty, Ludwig Bieberbach, became aware of Heller's thesis as a result of the sample copies provided, he refused to issue the PhD certificate. On the basis of the review by Wilhelm Grau reprinted here and another expert opinion, Bieberbach instigated a university resolution on 10 March 1936 against the acceptance of the PhD. Heller was therefore not considered to have obtained his doctorate. It was not until 1992 that he received his doctoral degree certificate in Israel: UA-HUB, Phil. Fak. 791 (Promotionsakte Abraham Heller), vols. 1 and 2.

16 Dr Otto Hoetzsch (1876–1946), historian; joined the German National People's Party (DNVP) in 1918; editor of the *Zeitschrift für osteuropäische Geschichte* [Journal of East European history], 1911–1914; foreign affairs columnist for daily newspapers, 1914–1924; as a Reichstag delegate for the DNVP he called for a ban on the immigration of Jews from Eastern Europe in 1919; from 1920 professor of Eastern European history and cultural studies at the University of Berlin; compulsory retirement in 1935.

17 Dr Max Vasmer (1886–1962), scholar of Slavonic studies; professor of comparative linguistics in Saratov, Dorpat, and Leipzig, 1917–1925; from 1925 professor of Slavic Studies at the University of Berlin; visiting professor at Columbia University, 1938–1939; after 1948 professor at the Free University in Berlin; editor of the *Russisches Etymologisches Wörterbuch* [Russian etymological dictionary], 4 vols., 1950–1958.

18 The column 'History of the Jewish Question' continued with another review of Ismar Elbogen's *Geschichte der Juden in Deutschland* [History of the Jews in Germany] as well as a collective review of Jewish journals: HZ, (1936), vol. 153, pp. 343–349.

DOC. 235

Pariser Tageszeitung, 23 June 1936: article about conditions for the German Jews shortly before the Olympic Games in Berlin[1]

A paradise for blackmailers
The ordeal of the German Jews continues

London, 22 June. *Over the last few months, there has been little about the situation of the Jews in Germany in the foreign press. The evident reason for this is that in light of the upcoming Olympic Games the press in Germany was directed to refrain from reporting much on the anti-Jewish movement within the Party and the anti-Jewish measures taken by the authorities. The following exposition by one of the special reporters of the Jewish Telegraphic Agency indicates, however, that the ordeal of the some 480,000 Jews still living in Germany[2] under the regime of the Nuremberg Laws has not abated and has even escalated in many respects, and that a new anti-Jewish campaign is feared in the wake of the Olympic Games. This portrayal is based on thorough observations over an extended time period.*

Lately even less than usual has been trickling out of the country regarding actual conditions for the Jews in Germany. This is partly due to the fact that, with respect to the upcoming Olympic Games, larger campaigns that would catch foreign attention have been avoided. Furthermore, the net cast by the Gestapo is closing in, which has made it more difficult to pass along any news. Nonetheless, while travelling through Germany it is still possible to make a few observations that are not widely known. First of all, the zealousness of the subsidiary organs of the Party has not abated, especially in regard to the Jewish question. Every regional chief rules over this issue as he wishes, and the economic existence of several thousand Jews depends less on the regulations issued by the Reich Ministry of Economics than on the fanaticism of the hundreds and hundreds of subordinate leaders and their subordinate leaders.

In the shadow of the Nuremberg Laws
In nearly all medium-sized and small towns, the general situation of the Jews still living there has worsened. The shadow of the Nuremberg Laws is an enormous burden hanging over the whole of Germany, but in particular over small and medium-sized towns. With these laws, and especially the one concerning race defilement, Germany has become a classic country for blackmailers. The nature of the things involved, as well as a certain coyness about airing the intimacies of sexual life in public, has thus far prevented a detailed discussion of the matter.

Only a very small proportion of the resulting judicial convictions have been given a few lines in press reports in Germany and other countries. From these reports, it can be ascertained that there has been a volley of prison sentences. But no one speaks of all the

---

1 'Ein Paradies für Erpresser', *Pariser Tageszeitung*, 23 June 1936, p. 2. This article has been translated from German. The *Pariser Tageszeitung* was the successor newspaper to the *Pariser Tageblatt*. It was published from June 1936 to Feb. 1940 in Paris. Georg Bernhard was editor-in-chief from 1936 to 1938.
2 The actual number of Jews by faith was estimated at 409,000 at this time: see Doc. 240, 24 July 1936.

tragedies in the realm of the most secret things in human life, which remain hidden in the much greater number of cases that have not been made public. Nor does anyone speak of the ensuing economic ruin of those involved or of the destruction of human relationships, which, for reasons that cannot always be simply dismissed with a wave of the hand, have not always been considered legitimate.

The impoverishment of Jewish intellectuals
Economic conditions for the Jews naturally differ depending on location and profession. In general, their situation is similar to that of their professional colleagues, but it is much worse in many respects. In the legal profession, which at one time offered good prospects for Jews, the overall situation is bad. One single number says it all: in Berlin the number of ordinary court cases, which was about 64,000 in 1932, shrank to just 14,000 in 1935! For the most part the Jewish lawyers today have virtually no cases. There are no more Jewish civil servants or Jewish notaries. Migration among Jewish doctors is particularly high because they, in contrast to others such as lawyers, still have opportunities at their disposal, despite all the impediments to advancement in the world. In some specialist areas, a certain shortage of Jewish doctors has already set in.

Across the broad spectrum of artistic and literary activity, the existing Jewish organizations, the newspapers, and the Culture League of German Jews naturally cannot provide enough work and sustenance for all those capable and in need. From now on, it must be expected that migration will increase among these professions.

Growing desire for emigration
But, for someone who has not been in Germany for a while and now has the opportunity to once again observe the general state of mind of the Jewish community, there is a profound difference between what one could surmise before the issuance of the Nuremberg Laws and the agitation that was unleashed among the German Jews preceding its enactment: the desire to emigrate has grown to an extraordinary extent. Previously the somewhat quieter periods between the individual waves of radicalism immediately prompted a corresponding optimism within Jewish circles, but now it is generally believed that the will of the National Socialist Movement to annihilate German Jewry and, if it had the power, all the Jews in the world continues unabated, and that this is only toned down where the internal domestic situation and the dictates of foreign policy make limitations seem unavoidable.

Today it has become clear to the majority of the German Jews that National Socialism will only permit a small portion of German Jewry, completely proletarianized and stripped of all its rights, to live in Germany, provided that economic conditions in the country or international intervention do not force a different course. It is therefore a disastrous mistake to think that Jewish emigration from Germany has already come to an end. Rather, what is true, and what the world needs to confront, whether it wants to or not, is that when a new wave of intensification commences, the number of emigrations will undoubtedly increase beyond that of 1933 and 1934.

The situation in Upper Silesia
There is a problem in Upper Silesia. The Geneva Convention [on Upper Silesia] itself was concluded for a period of only fifteen years. As a result of the negotiations at the

General Assembly of the League of Nations in 1933 prompted by the petition from Bernheim, Germany was forced to acknowledge that the Jews in German Upper Silesia are entitled to rights as a minority.[3] The state of affairs that emerged out of this acknowledgement is so entirely different from that in the rest of Germany that the approximately 20,000 Jews in Upper Silesia anxiously wonder what legal status will prevail after 15 June 1937.[4] The entire set of Aryan legislation has not been introduced in Upper Silesia. There are still Jewish judges, civil servants, and notaries, and the Nuremberg Laws do not apply. In short, a kind of 'nature reserve' has been created, which, according to the statements coming from the dominant German side, should be eliminated as soon as possible. But this will not be so easy, given the acquired rights to which the Jews of Upper Silesia are entitled, especially because Germany has a much greater interest than Poland in preserving the protection afforded to minorities in general in this territory.

The terrible number of suicides
Lastly, a psychological aspect still needs mentioning. For a fourth year now, the German Jews have been subject to a series of exceptional laws that compare unfavourably with those of the Middle Ages. The profound indignities that continue to be inflicted upon them have also left their mark on those actually resolved to hold out in Germany as long as it is at all possible. They have made a conscious decision to stay at the front. But the links to the area behind the front and to the rear echelons have largely disappeared. The vast majority of the Jews living in Germany have no idea about what is happening in the world other than the impressions conveyed in the newspapers, which are strongly censored, as we well know. But the Jewish newspapers too, whose sphere of influence has become quite limited because of the repeated intervention of the Ministry of Propaganda, cannot even hint to readers that, despite everything, there is still movement within the entire civilized world on the issue of Germany's Jewish legislation. It is only possible for a small minority to take trips outside the country. This present lack of a connection with the outside world exacerbates the feeling of despair that has overcome many of the Jews in Germany. The horrible number of suicides, for which statistics cannot even be provided, speaks eloquently and irrefutably of this.[5]

---

3 See Doc. 46, 24 May 1933.
4 See Doc. 292, 11 August 1937.
5 On the problem of suicides, see Doc. 36, 25 April 1933, and Doc. 41, 9 May 1933.

DOC. 236

On 1 July 1936 Albert Herzfeld reports on his expulsion from the Reich Association of German Artists and on being banned from practising his profession as an artist[1]

Handwritten diary of Albert Herzfeld, entry for 1 July 1936

1 July 1936. After not writing anything for weeks, today I need to give a chronological rundown of my correspondence with the Reich Association of German Artists and the Reich Chamber. On *24 Aug. 1933* I received a questionnaire from Baron Erich von Perfall,[2] who was at the time the chairman of the old Association for the Organization of Art Exhibitions, to which I have belonged for many years. The questionnaire contained all kinds of private questions, including one that asked for 'confession (also earlier confession)', which I filled out correctly. In my folder regarding this matter, I find that I apparently did not receive this questionnaire until January 1934, because according to the copy of my letter before me, I first sent this questionnaire to the Reich Cartel of Visual Artists, Gau of Westphalia-Lower Rhine, Düsseldorf, Wilhelm-Marx-Haus, on 1 February 1934, accompanied by a longer letter in which I noted that I belonged to a completely nationalist family that – on both my father's side and that of my mother – had been in Germany for over 200 years, and that despite my 49 years of age at the time, I signed up to join the army on the first day of mobilization, but that I was not accepted because of my age. I tried another seven times and finally, after the eighth attempt, I was advised to sign up with the infantry as a former deputy master sentinel of the cavalry. I did this immediately and was called up on 1 November 1914 to Minden in Westphalia and promoted to the rank of lieutenant on the Kaiser's birthday in 1915. I went to the front as a company leader in autumn 1915; there I fell severely ill with dysentery, and was then sent along to several military posts until 1 December 1916. I possess the Iron Cross Second Class (I also later received the combatant insignia) and the final letters of reference from my commanding officers. At the same time, I also submitted RM 1 as a registration fee and two passport photos. In response I received a letter several months later in Nov. 1934 from the president of the Reich Chamber of Visual Arts with the request to provide evidence by 10 December 1934 proving that I fought at the front during the war. I answered promptly with a long letter on 25 November 1934 and showed the local director of the Reich Chamber, Mr Siekmeyer,[3] my military pass from the field, and also submitted another confirmation of my national convictions, as Mr Siekmeyer had strongly advised me to do. In response, on 29 November 1934, I received a request to pay the annual membership fee of 12 marks, which I answered on the same day, noting that I was not aware of any outstanding amount and that I had yet to receive any confirmation as to whether I was a member of the Reich Chamber or not, as I was told on 28 November 1934 that my admission to the Reich Chamber had to be 'reviewed'. I then

---

1 Albert Herzfeld, 'Tagebuch', pp. 133–139; Stadtarchiv Düsseldorf, XXII H 61. Published in Herzfeld, *Ein nichtarischer Deutscher*, pp. 63–66. This diary entry has been translated from German.
2 Baron Erich von Perfall (1882–1961), landscape painter in Düsseldorf; for a time the first chairman of the Paintbox (Malkasten) Artists' Association.
3 Emil Siekmeyer (1891–1967), painter; joined the NSDAP in 1933; employed from 1931 to 1934 as a painter and from 1934 to 1945 as a clerk by the city of Düsseldorf.

received a signed mimeographed letter from the regional head, the local director of the academy Prof. Grund,[4] on 15 May 1935, with the request to pay my annual membership fee on time. I wrote a longer letter in response on 7 June 1935 in which I explained that I had still not received a response to my detailed letter of application and I once again asked to be admitted and promised to pay the amount immediately thereafter. On 11 June 1936, i.e. a year later, I then received a registered letter from the president of the Reich Chamber that informed me that the results of the review indicated that due to reasons related to my personal character, I did not possess the necessary disposition and reliability to take part in the advancement of German culture for the [German] people and the Reich. Furthermore, in the wording of the letter itself: 'You therefore do not fulfil the requirements for membership of the Reich Chamber of Visual Arts. – On the basis of § 10 of the First Regulation to the Implementation of the Reich Chamber [of Culture] Law of 1 November 1933 (*Reichsgesetzblatt*, I, p. 797) I reject your admission to the Reich Chamber of Visual Arts and prohibit the further practice of your profession as a painter. Per proxy signed Hoffmann.'

This naturally hit me like a thunderbolt. At the instigation of my colleague Pagenstecher,[5] who has a way with words and had already given me advice in my correspondence with the artists' chamber, I then went to the local lawyer Hengeler[6] and presented my case to him. He then drafted a letter to the president for me in which I asked him to disclose the applicable legal regulations. But I never actually sent the letter because I had already contacted the Reich Association of [Non-]Aryan Christians in Berlin to request potential admission to this association. A representative of the association wrote to me on 19 June 1936 that he would be pleased to accept me as a member because I was well known to him and that he already had a group of 'visual artists' within the culture department led by him (Dr Spiess) under the direction of State Commissioner Hinkel, and that he had already organized an art exhibition. On 21 June [19]36 I sent this association a copy of my previous correspondence with the Reich Association. In response, I received a letter on 27 June in which a G. Lewaldt informed me that by power of the order of State Commissioner Hinkel, the members of the Reich Association of Non-Aryan Artists were permitted to practise their professions as long as they only made their works available to non-Aryans and foreigners and only sold them to these people, where applicable. I replied to this letter on 29 June 1936 with a question as to whether I would first have to ask potential buyers about their descent even if they approached me *without* any prior offer from me. Then I enclosed a copy of the letter drawn up for me by the lawyer Mr Hengeler and asked whether or not I should send off the reply. At the same time, I remitted the initial membership fee for the association as well as the quarterly fee, and also enclosed the completed questionnaire about my personal details etc. This morning I received a reply to this letter, signed by Lewaldt and dated 30 June 1936, that read: 'In response to your letter from the 29th of this month, I must inform you that you must unfortunately accept the inconvenience of having to ask people interested in your

---

4 Dr Peter Grund (1892–1966), architect; professor and director of the State Academy of Art in Düsseldorf, 1933–1937; regional head of the Reich Chamber of Visual Arts in Düsseldorf.
5 Wolfgang Pagenstecher (1880–1953), painter and heraldist; designed the coat of arms of North Rhine-Westphalia after the Second World War.
6 Hans Hengeler (b. 1902), lawyer.

paintings, unless they are foreigners, about their descent. Apart from that, I *sincerely* (emphasis by Lewaldt) recommend that you do not respond at all to the letter of exclusion from the president of the Reich Chamber of Visual Arts, in order that you do not attract any kind of special attention. With association regards!' – And this is what has happened to a now 71-year-old combat veteran! – They have now taken from me all that I have left in the world and I have no rights to do anything about it! A distant observer would never be able to comprehend the injustice that has befallen me (and also presumably thousands of other so-called non-Aryans), and in later decades, no one will be able to understand this treatment of loyal citizens. The time will come in which the disgrace inflicted upon us will be recognized as such.

DOC. 237
On 9 July 1936 the government of Silesia plans to make it compulsory for Landräte and mayors to compile a civil registry of the Jews[1]

Draft of a regulation by the Regierungspräsident in Breslau to the Landräte and mayors, dated 9 July 1936 (copy)[2]

The Association for the History of Silesia is publishing a new directory of the church registers of both confessions in Silesia under the editorship of the director of the State Archives,[3] because the directory of Jungnitz-Eberlein that was published in 1902, which is now completely outdated, is already out of print, and this evidence is essential for any research into genealogy and kinship.[4]

The inclusion of the civil registry of Jews has proved to be necessary for the new directory of church registers because it can be very useful for official purposes alongside the necessary determination of who is of German blood, in accordance with the Reich Citizenship Law of 15 September 1935 and the Law for the Protection of German Blood and German Honour of 15 September 1935 (*Reichsgesetzblatt*, I, p. 1146), including the corresponding implementation regulations. Moreover, in the absence of other documents, a certain degree of evidence for Aryan descent can be deduced from the fact that a given person or family is not listed in the Jewish civil registry.

---

1 Archiwum Państwowe we Wrocławiu, Rejencja Wrocław, I/7639, fols. 3–4. This document has been translated from German.
2 Parts of the original have been underlined by hand and there is a handwritten note at the end of the text: '1.) Circumcision Register 2.) Divorce Register'.
3 Dr Erich Randt (1887–1948), teacher and archivist; archivist in the State Archives in Breslau, 1921–1930; director of the Prussian State Archives in Stettin and then the State Archives in Breslau, 1930–1935; joined the NSDAP in 1937; head of the German archival administration in the General Government in Cracow, 1939–1944; director of the Privy State Archives in Berlin, 1944–1945; from 1947 plenipotentiary of the Polish Military Mission for Archival Matters in the East.
4 *Die älteren Personenstandsregister Schlesiens*, edited by State Archivist Erich Randt in cooperation with Hellmut Eberlein, was published in 1938 by the Verlag für Sippenforschung und Wappenkunde (Publishing House for Kinship Research and Heraldry) in Görlitz.

The edict of 11 March 1812[5] in conjunction with the instruction of 26 June 1812 (*Kamptz Annalen*, vol. V, p. 364) stipulated for the first time that an orderly civil register be kept for the Jews. The Jews were obliged to take on firmly defined surnames and allow themselves to be registered in a citizens' list. The civil registries were maintained in the cities by the local police authorities and by the Landräte throughout the countryside. A duplicate of these registries was to be provided to the government. In 1847 the responsibility for the maintenance of the registries was transferred to the courts and, in 1874, to the registry offices.

It is requested that all remaining citizens' lists and civil registries of the Jews be recorded in detail according to the attached example by 31 August 1936. The titles are to be checked carefully against the contents of the registry. It should also be noted that these registries were often kept under other names, such as circumcision registry etc., no longer used today. This also includes divorce registries and the like. Should Jewish directories from the period *before* 1812 exist, then naturally it is also urgently necessary to index them as well. Should church registries or duplicates from church registries dating from prior to 1874 still exist, these should also be noted at the end of the list.

---

5 The 'Edict Concerning the Civil Status of the Jews in the Prussian State' from 11 March 1812, signed by Friedrich Wilhelm III, declared the Jews to be residents and citizens of Prussia. They were also permitted to hold office in academia, schools, and local administration. It was intended that their admission to other offices as well as their military service duties be regulated at a later date.

DOC. 238

On 16 July 1936 the Reich Circle for Propaganda and Public Enlightenment issues recommendations for the conduct of the SA towards foreigners and Jews during the Olympic Games[1]

Notification from the director of the Reich Circle for Propaganda and Public Enlightenment,[2] Tießler,[3] Munich, 16 July 1936, for the SA, communicated via a circular from the Supreme SA Command (F 1 a Nr. 11 159), chief of the Command Office, p.p. Michaelis,[4] Munich, for disclosure to the officers, NCOs, and men of the SA, dated 22 July 1936 (printed)[5]

First communiqué of the Reich Circle for National Socialist Propaganda and Public Enlightenment.

On Saturday 11 July 1935, the world received fresh evidence attesting to the new Germany's love of peace. The German-Austrian Agreement is another step towards securing peace in Europe and the world.[6] This new proof of peaceful intentions is so convincing that even the most malicious opponent could hardly make any objections to it. And yet we still have the task of convincing the rest of the world that peace, order, and security reign in Germany and that the German people desire peace with all their hearts.

A once-in-a-lifetime opportunity to show this to the entire world is the upcoming Olympic Games.[7] Representatives of almost all the states in the world are coming to Germany as athletes or spectators, and they will report on what they found in Germany when they return to their own countries.

It is therefore the task of every single German to bear in mind in the coming weeks that the impression that the visitors to the Olympic Games take home also depends on every last German Volksgenosse. Especially now, every person has to realize that he is also a propagandist for the new Germany. Therefore, it is also the special task of the SA

---

1 BArch, NS 23/556. This document has been translated from German.
2 The Reich Circle for National Socialist Propaganda and Public Enlightenment was under the command of the Chief of Staff of the NSDAP Reichsleitung for Propaganda. Established by Walter Tießler in 1934, it had the task of coordinating the propaganda of all the organizations of the NSDAP and their affiliated associations.
3 Walter Tießler (b. 1903), Party official; joined the NSDAP in 1922; Kreisleiter from 1925; part of the Halle Gauleitung for Propaganda from 1926; employed in the Munich Reichsleitung for Propaganda from 1934; head of the Reich Circle for National Socialist Propaganda and Public Enlightenment, 1934–1944; department head in the staff of the Deputy of the Führer from 1940, liaison office to Goebbels; liaison of the Party Chancellery to Governor General Frank, 1944.
4 Rudolf Michaelis (1902–1945), engineer; joined the NSDAP in 1923; member of the 'Black Reichswehr', illegal paramilitary formations that existed alongside the Reichswehr; SA-Brigadeführer and department head of the Supreme SA Command, 1934; chief of the Office for Physical Training in the Supreme SA Command, 1937–1938; SA-Gruppenführer, 1938; fought in the war from 1940.
5 The original bears the circulation stamp of the Judicial and Legal Office of the Supreme SA Command and handwritten processing notes.
6 On 11 July 1936 the German Reich assured Austria that it would respect its sovereignty. A joint communiqué to this effect was issued. In a secret 'gentlemen's agreement', Austria promised, among other things, to align its foreign policy with that of the Third Reich; facsimiles of both documents are in Gabriele Volsansky, *Pakt auf Zeit: Das Deutsch-Österreichische Juli-Abkommen 1936* (Vienna: Böhlau, 2001), pp. 285–292.
7 The 11th Olympic Summer Games took place from 1 to 16 August 1936 in Berlin.

to point out among acquaintances in a subtle yet emphatic way just how important the coming weeks are for the future of Germany and its further development. During these weeks of the Olympic Games, we want to prove to the rest of the world that it is a lie, despite what has been repeatedly claimed abroad, that the persecution of the Jews is part of the agenda in Germany. The Olympic visitors should learn the truth that every foreigner in Germany, including the Jews, can live unmolested. For this reason, we need to avoid anything that might give rise to a false impression. Therefore, even songs from the struggle before the National Socialist entry to power, which might potentially give a false impression in this regard, should not be sung because the foreigners do not know that these are just old fighting songs and they might read the text of these songs in a different light, which might lead them to make false assumptions.

In particular, it must be clear to each and every German Volksgenosse that not only should all foreigners be treated with courtesy as a matter of course, but also that even if a foreigner does not necessarily behave properly, no Volksgenosse has the right to take matters into his own hands. Instead, he should contact the police if the case is serious. In this context, we would like to remind you once again of the appeal made by the Reichsleiter for Propaganda:

> According to the will of the Führer, Germany has made preparations for the 1936 Olympic Games like hardly any country before. The hundreds of thousands of foreign guests should be received in an appropriate manner and experience German hospitality at its very best. I am certain that every German will uphold his honour in taking pains to be courteous towards the foreign visitors, all of whom stand under the protection of the German Reich, and, if one of them should require help, in offering assistance in word and deed.[8]

DOC. 239

On 21 July 1936 the historian Willy Cohn criticizes the behaviour of Eastern European Jews during a convalescent stay[1]

Handwritten diary of Willy Cohn, entry for 21 July 1936

21 July 1936. Kudowa,[2] Tuesday – evening. Today after our evening meal I lay down for two hours without really being able to rest. – When I break my usual routine somewhat, I notice immediately when it comes to my sleep. The afternoon post did not bring anything special – at the fountain relatively early. Reading room. – A great revolution in Spain; it is still not clear what will come out of it. – These conflicts between the two opposing ideologies are cropping up everywhere. – Otherwise the papers are full of the Olympic Games. –

---

8 The appeal could not be found.

1 Willy Cohn, 'Tagebuch Kudowa-Breslau Juli-August 1936', fols. 22–26; CAHJP, P 88/71. Abbreviated English translation in Cohn, *No Justice in Germany*, p. 339. This document has been retranslated from the original German.

2 Spa town in Silesia.

I walked slowly along the Weidenweg, and today I trusted myself to go a bit further again; met the former mayor Schindler,[3] who was working in his garden. He is not doing well financially; he'll now have to sell his library. – Stopped at the Tavern in the Meadow, which I had enjoyed visiting last year. It belongs to the sister-in-law of the local poet Anna Bernard,[4] whom I have known for a very long time; we talked pleasantly for an hour; she told me a lot about what she is currently working on. – She knows how to describe the people of Glatz wonderfully. – For a while Mr Kohn from Schweidnitz came by, who knows her from his time in Neiße. – Then walked home slowly. – Took my usual walk after supper and watched the trains depart. – It cooled down very quickly; nature wrapped itself in wisps of fog. – It was quite lonely up there today. –

I am slowly beginning to get stronger; I am also very satisfied with my stay here; but the only thing is that it is not peaceful enough in the house. – Many among our eastern brethren are less than pleasant. – Their behaviour leaves much to be desired. – The way they spoil their children is the worst. Above all, they have not at all grasped that they ought not to be attracting attention. – Today I told an old lady, whom I already know from last year, that she should stop wearing eye make-up. –

You can just imagine that when such people show up in great crowds that even in such a place the anti-Jewish sentiments grow, too. – They might be good people, but the outside observer cannot tell; they are judged according to the way they come across, and that is unpleasant – through and through. Sad enough that one has to come to such a conclusion.

DOC. 240
Jüdische Rundschau, 24 July 1936: article on the number and destinations of Jewish emigrants[1]

Numbers that speak[2]
Emigration from Germany, 1933–36

The Reich Representation of Jews in Germany announces: together with the *Relief Association* of German Jews and the *Palestine Office*, the *Migration Committee of the Reich Representation* has conducted an assessment of the materials available to date on emigration statistics for Jews in Germany. The purpose of this assessment is to come up with a uniform quantitative basis for the discussion of migration issues and migration plan-

---

3 Probably Dr Karl Schindler (1905–1986), literary scholar.
4 Anna Bernard (1865–1938), writer; author of works including *Am Landestor* (1924).

1 'Ziffern, die sprechen', *Jüdische Rundschau*, 24 July 1936, p. 3. This article has been translated from German.
2 The article reprinted here was also published in *Der Schild*, the newspaper of the Reich League of Jewish Combat Veterans on 24 July 1936 under the headline 'Die jüdische Bevölkerungsziffer Deutschlands: Starker Rückgang durch Auswanderung' (The Jewish Population Figures in Germany: Sharp Decline as a Result of Emigration). It is based on the report 'Eine Untersuchung des Wanderungsausschusses der Reichsvertretung. Zur Problematik der Auswanderungsstatistik und -planung' (An enquiry by the Migration Committee of the Reich Representation: the problems of emigration statistics and Planning), 21 July 1936, published in Kulka (ed.), *Deutsches Judentum*, vol. 1, pp. 289–292.

ning, and thereby resolve anything that is unclear or any differences among the private publications that have appeared to date. The results of this assessment are an *estimate*, made in light of the lack of completely sufficient detailed documents, as well as in consideration of all the significant factors pertaining to migration.[3] For migration to Palestine it is based on the statistical publications of the Jewish Agency [for Palestine], and for migration to all other countries it is based on the number of those emigrants who migrated with the help of Jewish organizations. The number of those emigrants who emigrated *without the support* of the Jewish organizations and therefore without being registered was determined on the basis of *estimates*. The *ratio between independent and supported emigration* has fluctuated greatly over the last few years. It can be assumed that the numbers for this independent emigration have been at least as high as those for supported emigration, and even sometimes double that of supported emigration.

An analysis of the period between 1 February 1933 and 1 April 1936 according to the intended emigration destination in the different countries provides the following *general overview*:

European migration
The number of emigrants to Western Europe in 1933 is estimated at 36,000, of whom the following have migrated:

back to Eastern countries	3,000
further to Palestine	3,000
further overseas	8,000
	= 14,000

which means that the total of those who remained in Western
European countries is   22,000

These 22,000 emigrants remaining in Europe are distributed as follows:

Western Europe (Belgium, England, France, Netherlands)	15,600
Central and south-eastern Europe (Switzerland, Austria, Italy, Czechoslovakia, Yugoslavia)	3,000
Nordic countries	1,000
South-western Europe (Spain, Portugal)	2,000
Other European countries	400

Return migration (from Germany)
Jewish foreign nationals to their homelands, especially to
Eastern Europe (Poland, border states, the Balkans)   18,000
Palestine migration   31,000

---

3 The Reich Representation of Jews in Germany only had information on the members of Jewish communities and not about people who had left the communities or converted but were still persecuted as Jews in accordance with Nazi legislation.

Overseas migration

United States of America	9,500
Brazil	4,500
Argentina	2,000
Chile	600
Other South and Central American countries	2,000
South Africa	3,000
Other overseas countries	400
	22,000
	93,000

According to the census of 16 June 1933, the number of Jews by faith in Germany was 499,682.

The *number of Jews by faith in Germany* on 1 April 1936 can be estimated at *409,000*, taking into account *all* emigration since 1 February 1933, which occurred in part prior to the effective date of the census, as well as the natural population decline due to the *surplus of deaths over births.*[4]

The figures correspond, as our readers will remember, to those given by Dr Michael Traub[5] in his presentation at the last regional council meeting of the *ZVfD*.[6] A more detailed discussion and commentary on the sources on which the above-mentioned publication was also based can be found in a booklet by Dr Traub which is due out soon from the publishing house of the *Jüdische Rundschau.*[7]

---

[4] The report at hand was reproduced almost verbatim in the work report of the Reich Representation for 1936. The figures for the second half of the year were finalized: 'Arbeitsbericht des Zentralausschusses für Hilfe und Aufbau bei der Reichsvertretung für das Jahr 1936' (Berlin, 1937), pp. 14–23, ZfA, Arbeitsberichte, MF 2.

[5] Dr Michael Traub (1891–1946), lawyer; Zionist and chairman of the Keren Hayesod in Germany; author of works including *Jüdische Wanderungen* (1922) and *Realpolitik und konstruktive Selbsthilfe der Keren Hajessod* (1936).

[6] Zionistische Vereinigung für Deutschland: Zionist Federation for Germany.

[7] See Michael Traub, *Die jüdische Auswanderung aus Deutschland: Westeuropa, Übersee, Palästina* (Berlin: Jüdische Rundschau, 1936).

DOC. 241
On 30 July 1936 Medical Officer Wilhelm Dopheide from Hagenow justifies his boycott of Dr Hans Sommerfeld to the Mecklenburg Ministry of State[1]

Letter from the Public Health Authority of Kreis Hagenow, Medical Officer Dopheide,[2] Hagenow, currently St Andreasberg in the Harz, addressed to the Mecklenburg Ministry of State, Department of Medical Affairs, Schwerin, dated 30 July 1936[3]

Sometime in mid June 1935, a Volksgenosse came to me to ask that I examine him, or rather take an X-ray, for the army. It was explained to him that this was not possible because the Public Health Authority did not yet have an X-ray machine. He was told to contact the relevant office and ask whether he could have the X-ray done there. After about thirty minutes, he came back: 'My physician told me that it has to be done here, just as it has always been done.' After he was told once again that this was not possible for purely technical reasons, he answered: 'But my physician said so.' 'Who is that then?' 'Dr Sommerfeld.'[4] – 'Really. Did you know, by the way, that Dr Sommerfeld is a Jewish physician? I only wanted to tell you because, after all, you want to join the military.' – The next morning, Dr S. called me in agitation: 'Why would you say such a thing?' 'As a National Socialist, it is my duty to enlighten my Volksgenossen.' 'That is boycotting. I have already suffered enough injury. You don't seem to know that I am a severely war-disabled veteran.' – 'No, actually I didn't know that. For this reason, though, I will do you a favour and, in the future, I will not tell people so directly. Will that be sufficient?' – 'Yes.' –

Afterwards, as the independent medical examiner for the health insurance companies in the district of Hagenow, I noticed repeatedly that a striking number of Volksgenossen let themselves be treated by Dr S., and I took advantage of the opportunity in all the cases in which I felt it was justified to let these people know that Dr S. is a non-German physician.

When, for example, an ill person wearing the insignia of the German Labour Front came, I asked him whether he had worn this insignia when he had been to see the doctor.

---

1 LHAS, 5.12-7/1, Nr. 9918a. This letter has been translated from German.
2 Dr Wilhelm Dopheide (1901–1970), physician; initially a doctor in Schwaan (Kreis Bad Doberan); joined the NSDAP in 1933; from 1935 Kreis medical counsellor, Kreis physician, and head of the Public Health Authority in Hagenow; head of the Department of Health in the Galicia District in the General Government, 1941–1944; deputy head of the Public Health Authority in Parchim, 1944–1945; interned, 1945–1947; then physician at the Von Bodelschwingh Institutes and later head of the Public Health Authority in Hagen.
3 The letter printed here supplemented a first report submitted by Dopheide, dated 18 July 1936, which the Ministry of State had deemed insufficient. The ministry had requested the report after Sommerfeld had complained that the medical officer had boycotted him and called upon others to boycott him as well. Sommerfeld claimed that Dopheide had threatened midwives in public: 'Whoever works with Jewish doctors will be kicked out.' Sommerfeld had already protested twice to the Deputy of the Führer against the harassment of the medical officer, which had been taking place since 1935: ibid.
4 Dr Hans Adolf Sommerfeld (1894–1965), physician; from 1922 general practitioner in Hagenow; revocation of his licence to practise medicine, 1938; lived in a mixed marriage; later moved to Hamburg.

When he then answered 'Yes', I asked him whether he thought it was fitting to wear the insignia with the swastika in the house of a Jewish physician.

Or, when a midwife from my district let twins be delivered by Dr S., I asked her quite frankly whether she thought it was fitting for a Jewish physician to enter a house in which the children belonged to an organization that bore the name of the Führer. (To my knowledge, one of the children has a scholarship for Neukloster.[5]) Or, when the members of the Hitler Youth came from Dr S., I felt it was my duty as the physician of the Hitler Youth to tell these comrades that Dr S. is a Jew.

But I always emphasized that everyone was free to seek out whichever physician they preferred and I only pointed out that they needed to know the consequences, especially if they belonged to one of the Party organizations. But I regarded it as my duty to draw their attention to the fact that Dr S. was not a German physician.

I also occasionally spoke about the cultivation of heredity and race in the Third Reich at an extended members' assembly of the Party in Hagenow and – after consulting with the Kreisleiter, so as to avoid being accused of acting independently – also about the Nuremberg Laws, among other subjects: a Jew is someone who … For us National Socialists, a Jew is always a Jew, regardless of whether he is baptized as a Catholic or a Protestant. I have always emphasized that I have enlightened people in my role as a member of the Party or as a physician of the Hitler Youth or as an administrative official in the Party.

DOC. 242
On 31 July 1936 Martin Gumpert writes to his sister in Palestine about the problem of transferring money and assets when emigrating to the USA[1]

Handwritten letter from Martin Gumpert, Camp Mount Soy, Roscoe, NY dated 1 September 1936, Hotel Bedford, 118 East 40th Street, New York City,[2] to Minni Steinhardt, Jerusalem, dated 31 July 1936

Dear Minni,

I have just received a letter from my mother-in-law from Hotel Penegal at the Mendel Pass[3] where she is currently staying with Nina.[4] She writes that she received a distressed letter from you because I had not replied to your letters. I cannot recall not having responded to your letters, if I received them.

She writes that you would like Jak's[5] paintings, 'ancestral portraits', books, and gifts for Josefa.[6]

---

5 This refers to the Neukloster Teacher Training College.

1 Jüdisches Museum Berlin, DOK-95-27-518, fols. 1–4. This document has been translated from German.
2 Martin Gumpert had evidently just emigrated to the United States and was still being held in the Mount Soy immigration camp in the state of New York. On Gumpert, see Doc. 37, 26 April 1933.
3 This refers to the Grand Hotel Penegal at the Mendel Pass near Bolzano.
4 Daughter of Martin Gumpert.
5 The author means Jacob Steinhardt's: see Doc. 37, 26 April 1933.
6 Daughter of Minni and Jacob Steinhardt, who had emigrated with them to Palestine.

I have let out my apartment in Berlin furnished until 1 October, and then it will be liquidated. I can only have a few things brought over here because their value in comparison to the transport costs is far too low.

Jak's paintings, two of them, one of which you gave to me as a wedding gift, will be at your disposal. I want to have my books brought over, if at all possible, but I will write to my mother-in-law to tell her that she should keep a few books for you after the apartment is liquidated.

I don't really know what kind of 'ancestral portraits' you would like to have – there are just a few old family pictures.

With gifts for Josefa, you probably mean a few gold pieces. It was 30 marks in gold and 20 or 25 dollars in gold that Aunt Martha gave me three years ago for safekeeping. I had to register the gold dollars at the Reichsbank according to a law against treason.[7] As ten years of penal servitude are imposed for unauthorized possession, and since our house has often been searched, I could not take the risk. I wrote to the Reichsbank stating that the money was only given to me for safekeeping for someone else and the Reichsbank replied that I had to hand it in immediately. In exchange, I received 42 – or 64 – [Reichsmarks] (4.20 = $1). The money is stored in my locked cupboard. I have no idea how I can get this transferred to you. I myself emigrated with 10 marks and am living on borrowed money. The best thing to do is probably to try to bring it here undetected with my moving allowance. But please *do not* write anything about money or gold to my mother-in-law because she has a pathological, although not unjustified, fear of any kind of money transfer stories. It was and is impossible to give the gold to someone to bring. It is really too much to ask of someone to take on that responsibility. You all seem to have no idea what it means to risk your life for something like that. I have paid the costs for the maintenance of the graves over the last few years and paid for two years in advance. We will have to send the money later on.

I find the state of affairs in Europe to be extremely concerning and I won't be able to rest until I have Nina with me. As soon as I return, I want to set her emigration in motion. But, please do not write anything about this back to Germany, either.

By the way, my mother-in-law writes that she does not think that the Liliens, whose plans are still very uncertain, will be able to bring you these things anytime soon. She says they were not very friendly.

I did not receive your letter.

I hope that I will soon receive genuine news from you, as it is quite difficult to get a picture of what things are actually like in Palestine. Have you met Dr Heinz Ludwig?

Warm regards to you all

---

7 This refers to the Law against Betrayal of the German National Economy of 12 June 1933, which stipulated that the possession of foreign currencies and financial assets abroad had to be registered: *Reichsgesetzblatt*, 1933, I, p. 360.

DOC. 243

On 14 August 1936 the Jewish Social Service and Youth Welfare Office in Berlin asks the Foreign Currency Department of the Regional Tax Office to authorize support for a Jewish refugee family[1]

Letter from the Jewish Community of Berlin/Jewish Social Service and Youth Welfare Office (Jug D/K), p.p. Mendelsohn,[2] to the Foreign Currency Department of the Regional Tax Office in Berlin (received on 17 September 1936), Neue Königstraße, dated 14 August 1936[3]

We have been contacted by Mrs Feiga *Gayer*, currently living at 4 Veteranenstr., c/o Bilbel, born 14 February 1900[4] in Bialostock, Poland.[5] She has fled Spain with her two children, Sally,[6] born 7 July 1928, and Leo, born 20 July 1929, and requests lodging for her two children.[7] She has no suitable place to live for herself and her children, so that we had to take it upon ourselves to place the children on 13 August cr.[8] in our Ahavah Home,[9] 14–15 Auguststr.

We ask for authorization to be able to support Mrs Gayer as well as her two children through money and payment in kind from the resources available to us, all of which can only be used in Germany. In this case, we ask in particular for authorization of the resources to provide lodging for the children.[10]

DOC. 244

On 30 August 1936 State Secretary Hans Pfundtner complains to the Bavarian Minister President about Jewish spa guests in Bad Kissingen[1]

Handwritten letter from the state secretary in the Reich and Prussian Ministry of the Interior, Pfundtner, currently resident in Kissingen, to the Bavarian Minister President,[2] dated 30 August 1936[3]

Dear esteemed Minister President,

With my sincere thanks for your friendly letter dated the 21st of this month,[4] I am pleased to inform you that I have been staying at the public spa hotel for four days and feel quite well again here in Kissingen. Two things, however, have the potential to detract

---

1 BLHA, Rep. 36 A/2661, fol. 12. This document has been translated from German.
2 Presumably Dr Bruno Mendelsohn (1888–1942), lawyer; legal practitioner and notary in Berlin; worked for the Jewish Community of Berlin from 1933; head of the financial assistance office; murdered in Dec. 1942 while a hostage.
3 The original contains handwritten annotations.
4 Correctly: 1901.
5 Correctly: Białystok.
6 Correctly: Salomon.
7 Feiga Gayer, née Zonstein, was deported with her two sons from Berlin to Minsk in June 1942 and presumably murdered there on arrival.
8 Latin 'currentis' – here it means the current year.
9 Hebrew for 'love' – here the Association for Children and Youth Homes in Berlin.
10 Handwritten note in the left margin: 'amount?'

1 BayHStA, MF 67 937. This document has been translated from German.

from this local sojourn. The one thing is the automobile and motorcycle traffic around the spa hotel at the moment, especially the lorries, which clatter like machine guns often late into the night and then again in the morning. I believe it is time to think once again about a bypass road for this traffic, so that at least the actual spa and the spa gardens are reasonably free of noise. Even now it would be possible, in my opinion, to reduce the excessive noise from the rattling and honking, especially during the night, through a police regulation or a police ordinance.

The second thing is the many Jews! For years I haven't seen so many Jews together in one place as there are here right now in Kissingen.[5] At many places, for example at the saltern, there are downright 'masses' of them. I believe that the town and spa administration really do have to do something about this, especially as the Olympic Games are now over. With all due tolerance for gravely ill patients, Kissingen does not by any means need to become a Jewish spa town!

Many thanks for the kindness you have bestowed upon me once again, especially in relation to hunting! As it stands now, I will attend only part of the Party congress![6] Afterwards, I want to go by car to Upper Bavaria (Garmisch) with my wife. When we pass through Munich, I also want to take a look at the Nymphenburg porcelain factory, among other things! I hope to see you again soon!

With the best regards and compliments from year to year and
Heil Hitler,
Your very devoted[7]

---

2 The Minister President was Ludwig Siebert (1874–1942), lawyer; civil servant in Bavaria from 1897; mayor of Rothenburg ob der Tauber, 1908–1919, and of Lindau, 1919–1933; member of the Bavarian People's Party (BVP); joined the NSDAP in 1931; Bavarian minister of finance and minister president, 1933–1942.
3 Parts of the original are underlined by hand. The letter is written on the stationery of the state secretary of the Reich and Prussian Ministry of the Interior.
4 The letter is not in the file.
5 Bad Kissingen had already made international headlines in 1934 because of a boycott against Jewish spa guests. In 1935 the Bavarian authorities discussed the alleged 'flooding' of the spa by Jews, which a registration of the visitors showed to be far from reality: see the correspondence of the State Ministry of the Interior from autumn 1934 and 1935: ibid.
6 The NSDAP rally took place in Nuremberg from 8 to 14 Sept. 1936.
7 Siebert responded on 2 Sept. 1937 to the effect that he would take care of the traffic noise issue. He noted that he was surprised, however, by Pfundtner's claims about the Jews because among the 4,200 visitors in the year prior, there were only 80 Jews, most of whom were foreigners and therefore desirable as a source of foreign currency. Siebert wrote that he would look into the matter as he likewise had no interest in a 'Jewified Kissingen': ibid. Pfundtner issued a decree in July 1937 to segregate Jews in spa resorts: see Doc. 289, 24 July 1937.

DOC. 245
On 2 September 1936 Mally Dienemann reports on antisemitism in Offenbach am Main[1]

Diary of Mally Dienemann,[2] entry for 2 September 1936 (copy)

We were having breakfast. Across from us is the grammar school (the only institution in the city devoted to classical education). From its windows resounded: 'Jew pigs, Jew pigs!' Max[3] said it left him unmoved. It shocked me very much.

Yesterday I went to the tram stop. There we saw a sign that read: 'Assembly point during air attacks is the school.' Tomorrow Gaby is supposed to go on a hike with her class! The children plan to stop for a bite to eat at a hotel on Feldberg (a mountain in Taunus). A placard on the wall of the hotel proclaims: 'Jews not welcome'. What should the child do now? She's the only Jew taking part in the outing. Max and her teacher Professor Peters think that she should go on the outing. It's a tour of the observatory. But all along the way she will be thinking: 'What's going to happen?' She will never be at ease again.

DOC. 246
On 16 September 1936 the Reich Ministry of Economics informs the Reich Minister of Food about the complaints of Jewish grain-trading companies[1]

Letter from the Reich and Prussian Ministry of Economics (I 1035/36 C XI), signed Dr Soltau,[2] to the Reich Ministry of Food and Agriculture (received on 18 September 1936), dated 16 September 1936[3]

Re: participation of Jewish companies in the trade in grain etc.
I enclose for your kind attention excerpts from copies of two petitions submitted by large Jewish grain-trading companies to the Reich commissioner at the Berlin Stock

---

1 Copy of the diary entry in: Mally Dienemann, 'Mein Leben in Deutschland vor und nach dem 30 Januar 1933' [My life in Germany before and after 30 January 1933], 15 March 1940, p. 23a; Harvard Competition, no. 50. This document has been translated from German.
2 Mally Dienemann (1883–1963), wife of Rabbi Dr Max Dienemann, lived in Ratibor in Upper Silesia, then Offenbach am Main; emigrated initially to London on 30 Dec. 1938, and then to Palestine.
3 Dr Max Dienemann (1875–1939), writer and rabbi; rabbi in Offenbach am Main, 1919–1938; from 1931 to 1933 co-editor of *Der Morgen* and representative for Germany on the executive board of the World Union for Progressive Judaism; temporarily imprisoned in a Gestapo jail and in Buchenwald concentration camp, 1938; emigrated to Britain in 1938 and to Palestine in 1939; author of several books on religious-philosophical themes.

1 BArch, R 3601/1859, fols. 44–50. This document has been translated from German.
2 Dr Fritz Soltau (b. 1886), statistician and economist; from 1919 to 1940 section head for statistics in the Reich Ministry of Economics, where from 1926 he served as Ministerialrat in the Department for Monetary, Banking, Securities, and Insurance Systems and Economic Financing; spent 1945–1946 in internment; head of the Department for Agricultural Statistics of the Statistical Office for the British Zone, 1946–1948; deputy head of the Statistical Office of the United Economic Area in Wiesbaden, 1948; head of department in the German Federal Statistical Office, 1949–1952.
3 Parts of the original have been underlined and annotated by hand.

Exchange. I would desire to know whether these are the consequences of a systematic course of action initiated with your approval against Jewish grain-trading companies or just unilateral measures taken by individual grain trade associations. Furthermore, I would also like to bring the petitions to your attention because a sudden suppression and liquidation of capital-rich Jewish wholesale enterprises could, under some circumstances, lead to disruptions in bringing the harvest to the market if a sufficient substitute for them is not available. The same would apply to the management of import and export activities.[4]

p.p.
signed Dr Soltau

Copy pertaining to no. I 1035/36 C XI.
Berlin, 31 August 1936.
My company was entered into the local commercial register in 1853. It is the longest-standing member of the Berlin commodity exchange. My grandfather and my father served on the exchange's board of directors, just as I did until 1933.[5]

Of my salaried employees, most of whom have been with me for more than ten years, three quarters are Aryan and one quarter non-Aryan.

After the upheaval, several of my lines of business were taken from me; for example, commercial transactions with agricultural producers (see circular of the District Farmers' Leader Belbe)[6] and the oats and feedstuff business with local livestock farmers and feed traders, because the Reich Office for Grains assigned me hardly any feedstuffs. I therefore remain active only in the malting barley and seed businesses.

Now I am being hindered in these areas to such an extent that if this policy is not stopped I will soon be forced to close my business.

I. The Kurmark Wheat Trade Association.
This association issues warnings to traders and cooperatives who conduct trade in commodities with non-Aryans. Should, for example, non-Aryans be listed on the orders for goods, the association would considerably delay the exchange for permits to purchase. This threat is effective because the farmer who wants to dispatch his barley, and needs the money, cannot wait. The association will also carry out this threat. It wrote the following to the Max Gagelmann company, of Meyenburg, which had sold me a wagon of malted barley:

> I have made note that you have sold 15 tonnes of malted barley to the non-Aryan company Simon Boehm, of Berlin. I regret to inform you that I am unable to release

---

4 In response to a request from the Reich Ministry of Food and Agriculture (RMEuL), the Central Association of the German Grain Trade wrote on 13 Oct. 1936 that the 'liquidation of a number of Jewish grain-trading companies' would not pose any danger for the grain trade because the sector was 'oversupplied' domestically: ibid., fol. 59. The Reich Office for Grains, Feedstuffs, and Other Agricultural Products replied to the RMEuL on 10 Oct. 1936 that its decision to refuse to accept several deliveries was not because the Boehm company was Jewish: ibid., fols. 65–67.
5 The author of the letter, Simon Boehm, ran a business in Berlin providing banking services and trading in grain, malt, fertilizer, animal feed, and seed.
6 The circular mentioned here is not in the file.

the goods to you because at present I do not have any permits to purchase at my disposal.

With regard to this, Gagelmann wrote:

> What I told you right after concluding the contract has now happened. I am on the blacklist and am still stuck with my barley.

The Gustav Noeske & Kirstein company, of Schneidemühl, a major supplier with which I have continuously worked for years and years, saw itself forced by this and similar agencies to turn away non-Aryan purchasers.

This information was passed on to me by the Arno Vieth company.

On 29 August Arno Vieth[7] informed me on the telephone that the Haase & Schrodt company, of Frankfurt an der Oder, had refused to accept the offer I had made for barley because the Kurmark Wheat Trade Association had forbidden it from trading with non-Aryans; should Haase & Schrodt violate the prohibition, it would not receive a licence to deal in bran or feedstuffs.

Today, Ernst Nehring & Co., of Deutsch-Krone, informed me that although it had sold me 15 tonnes of barley, it was unable to obtain the permits for purchase and must therefore rescind the contract.

At the end of last week the Kurmark Wheat Trade Association rang the largest German brewery – Schultheiss-Patzenhofer[8] – and forbade it to buy from non-Aryans. I have long-standing relations with Schultheiss-Patzenhofer; I trade very substantial quantities with this brewery. Should the association succeed in having me barred from trading with Schultheiss-Patzenhofer, then it would hardly be possible for me to conduct a reasonable business any longer.

The largest industrial consumer of barley in Germany – Kathreiner GmbH[9] – has refused to allow me to purchase from non-Aryan firms, because it is worried about its allotment for next year.

In order to circumvent the difficulties that arise from the fact that local agents at many traders and cooperatives are insisting on Aryan buyers out of fear of the wheat trade associations, I came to an agreement with the grain retailer Alfred Freytag,[10] with whom I have had contact for many years, that he would make the purchases on my behalf in such cases. F. thereupon received on 29 August the letter from the Kurmark [Association], a copy of which is enclosed.[11] The managing director, Mr Schlemmermeyer, then told F. that as long as he stooped to serve as a front for a non-Aryan company he would receive neither a licence to conduct retail trade nor an allocation of feedstuffs.

---

7 Probably Arno Vieth, a retailer based in the Berlin district of Adlershof.
8 Founded in 1843 as the Schultheiss Brewery. After merging with the Patzenhofer Brewery in 1920, it was known as the Schultheiss-Patzenhofer Brewery; from 1938 it operated under the name Schultheiss Brewery.
9 Franz Kathreiner founded the company in 1829. Starting in 1870 it was run under the name Franz Kathreiners Nachfolger and dealt in coffee, tea, spices, tropical fruits, sugar, edible oils, and spirits. From 1890 the company also produced malted coffee.
10 Probably Alfred Freytag, a retailer based in Berlin.
11 The letter mentioned here is not in the file.

He added that there was one thing he could not hold against F.: if he sold to Simon Boehm barley that was offered to him and that he could *either not sell to breweries at all or only sell at unfavourable terms.* This, however, could only occur two to three times a year!

II. A civil servant at the Central Association of the German Wheat Trade has forbidden the Central Union of Agricultural Cooperatives of Lower Silesia and the Silesian Farmers' Trading Company in Breslau from doing business with non-Aryans. Both companies rank among the largest barley suppliers in Silesia. During the last season I purchased more than a quarter of my Silesian barley needs from them alone.

An official at the Central Union of Agricultural Cooperatives told us on the phone a few days ago how much the directors of his firm regret that they are no longer permitted to trade with Simon Boehm.

III. Pomerania.
As agent Gutzeit, co-owner of the Johannes Wenzel company, has reported, traders in Pomerania have also been warned not to do business with non-Aryans. The Central Union of Agricultural Cooperatives of Pomerania trades in Berlin only with Aryan firms.

Landhandel GmbH, Ratzebuhr (Pomerania), sold me barley on 25 August through the mediation of agent Arno Vieth. The seller informed me today that it did not want to fulfil [the contract] because I am a non-Aryan.

IV. Dresden.
The enclosed card from the Arno Schlesier company in Dresden[12] shows that these threats about not exchanging for permits the orders for goods have also been effected elsewhere.

V. Reich Office for Grain, Monopoly Office for Seeds.
This Monopoly Office is treating me unfairly with regard to the allocation of rapeseed, oilseed, mustard, and poppy seed. I have been allotted a total of 260 centners of mustard over the last twelve months. For these oilseeds, which mainly come from Poland, I was for a while the largest importer from Poland. There were cases where I concluded contracts with Polish suppliers with whom I am on friendly terms for prices that were agreeable to the Monopoly Office, and was then forced by the Monopoly Office to cede the contracts to Aryan companies.

In light of the above, the following is clear: if no immediate aid is provided to alleviate the measures identified above, I will be forced to liquidate my business and dismiss my employees. It would be impossible and pointless to carry on my work if I am boycotted at the buying and selling end, namely by authorities who have the power to impose their will on agricultural dealers by refusing to issue licences to trade and by denying the allotment of feedstuffs.

---

12 The card mentioned here is not in the file.

Excerpted *copy pertaining to no. I 1035/36 C XI.*

For approximately fourteen days our company,[13] because it is non-Aryan, has been hindered in carrying out its business activities to such an extent that we will be forced to dismiss our employees unless a stop is put to these hindrances very soon.

We point out that our company has been in business since 1857 and at present still has twenty-one salaried employees, of whom two thirds are Aryan. We refrain from providing further details about our company because our earlier activity is known to the president and the members of the executive board.

The hindrances of which we speak have emanated this year from the buying side. Although we are besieged by our regular purchasers to submit offers, we are unable to do so because we are not provided with any goods.

We know that the wheat trade associations in East Prussia, Prussian Saxony, and Hanover have long forbidden agricultural traders from doing business with non-Aryan companies. This year the wheat trade associations in Pomerania, Silesia, Kurmark, and the Free State of Saxony have followed suit, so that we are practically no longer able to purchase goods in any significant quantities.

The hindrance arises as a result of the grain trade associations applying pressure on the agricultural trade. They [the traders] are warned and told that if they continue to do business with non-Aryan companies, they will be excluded from the allotment of those feedstuffs that are intended for distribution, and that they run the risk of no longer receiving permission to deal in bran. Thus the agents, one after the other, receive instructions to no longer take orders where non-Aryans are the purchasers.

Our business is therefore in danger of coming to a complete standstill due to the lack of purchasing opportunities. Because of the huge burden of expense that we have to bear, it is impossible to continue operations under these circumstances.

To illustrate our remarks, here is a quote from a letter that a wheat trade association wrote to an Aryan company:

> Returning to your letter of the 17th of this month, I would like to inform you that I am not in a position to grant you a licence to purchase bran for the purpose of resale.
> The reliability that I require for the granting of a bran licence extends not only to the bran contracts you have executed, but rather to your entire business dealings. You may want to review your entire contracts in that respect.

We can claim to have performed an important function in the German grain trade in an irreproachable manner, and to have the confidence of our colleagues in the profession not only domestically but far beyond the borders of Germany.

---

13 The name could not be found.

DOC. 247

On 28 September 1936 Alex Löwenstein gives Rosalie Gehrike in Berlin an account of his new life in Argentina[1]

Letter from Alex Löwenstein,[2] Buenos Aires, to Rosalie Gehrike,[3] Berlin, dated 28 September 1936

Dear Röschen,

By now you will have received our letter [sent] with the *Cap Arcona*. The main purpose of today's letter is to send you, dear Röschen, the Reich Insurance papers. After overcoming a number of difficulties, yesterday I received the necessary papers from the German consulate. In the meantime I have learned that the money is also paid out here; however, it is supposed to take several months. Could you look into how long it takes? We do not need the money urgently, but when we have it, it will be all the better. On the form that Gretel[4] has signed you still need to write in the insurance card number. Also enquire if you can get an acknowledgement of receipt for the submitted documents in order to facilitate the filing of subsequent complaints. My father has since written to me that he has the cards, and he will have already given them to you by now. That concludes the Reich Insurance matter.

In the last eight days nothing else has happened here. We hope that you are in good health; we can report the same about ourselves. My father and brother-in-law now also plan to carry out everything expeditiously, selling their houses, etc., in order to soon take the same path as many others. I wonder how everything will turn out. I'm particularly happy that I will soon see my dear father again; he worries so much about everything. Here things are taken more lightly than in Europe. People with worries sleep here just as soundly as those with no worries. It's not possible to put all of these things on paper, for everything here is different. The people here live more freely and more at ease; everyone does what he thinks is right. You don't have to register with the police. Ever since I've been here no one has asked for my papers, but every policeman knows exactly where you live. That requires, of course, a fair amount of competence. Now the weather is finally settled and nice and warm, but my dear Gretel always feels cold; that's something I know all too well. Please give Mr Borchheim my regards and let him know my new address; I shall write to him again soon. Tell him that I constantly receive mail from distant relatives, which takes up a great deal of my time. The things people want to know! Someone asked if it's possible to swim here, as if there wasn't any water here; if one wears high heels or shoes, and much more. Each week I receive mail from people whom I have to think hard about to remember who they are. If I have the time, I answer each and every question. One person sent me a letter in Spanish, asking if he'd be able to find employment here as a musician and if I would run an ad for him; he also enclosed copies

---

1 Jüdisches Museum Berlin, DOK-94-1-4008, fol. 4v. This document has been translated from German.
2 Alex Löwenstein emigrated to Argentina in the mid 1930s; his wife Margarete Löwenstein, née Cyrus, followed in 1936. Both had previously been salaried employees at the company N. Israel in Berlin. On the company, see Doc. 298, 3 Oct. 1937.
3 Rosalie Gehrike (b. 1910), née Elsner, worked as a non-Jewish salaried employee at the company N. Israel in Berlin.
4 This is a reference to Margarete Löwenstein.

of his references. We have often laughed about this; what matters here are not references, but what you can do. Well, emigrating is not as easy as you might think. I had a more difficult time of it; no one gave me any help, and when I was painting barrels no one asked me what I had done before. Everything is in constant motion; people do not bother about others' affairs if you do your work. There is a period of notice only after you have been in the job three months; before then you can be dismissed on any given day. That's just America. You must already be having very autumnal weather by now. Here the leaves on most trees stay green throughout winter, and the palm trees are, of course, always green. Yesterday I worked the whole day in Devoto;[5] I had to reclose all the crates according to regulations. I simply ate out there because it's not worthwhile going back into the city. But I was glad afterwards that I had finished the work. So, dear Röschen, I have told you enough for today; send us confirmation soon that you have received the papers, write to us again very soon, and to you the warmest of greetings from

your *Alex*.

DOC. 248
Meeting of state secretaries in the Reich Ministry of the Interior on 29 September 1936 about the further course of anti-Jewish policy[1]

Reich Ministry of the Interior memorandum (secret), signed Stuckart (copy)[2]

Memorandum about the discussion on 29 September 1936
Participating in the discussion were:
  for the Reich and Prussian Ministry of the Interior
  State Secretary Dr Stuckart
  Ministerialrat Dr Lösener[3]
  Regierungsassessor Dr Schiedermair
  for the Reich Ministry of Economics
  State Secretary Dr Posse
  Ministerialrat Dr Hoppe
  Regierungsassessor Dr Humbert
  for the Deputy of the Führer
  Ministerial Director Sommer
  Head of Reich Office Dr Blome.

---

5 Villa Devoto: a district in the north of Buenos Aires.

1 BArch, R 1501/5514, fols. 199–211. Published in Hartmannsgruber (ed.), *AdR*, part 3, pp. 525–532. This document has been translated from German.
2 The original contains several handwritten notations and sign-offs. A handwritten note on the bottom left suggests that the copy was intended for State Secretary Pfundtner.
3 Dr Bernhard Lösener (1890–1952), lawyer; initially worked in the Customs and Tax Administration; joined the NSDAP in 1930; employed from April 1933 to the end of 1942 in the Reich Ministry of the Interior; from mid 1933 race specialist for Jewish affairs there in Department I (Constitution and Legislation); from 1943 at the Reich Administrative Court; from 1944 to 1945 in custody in connection with the 20 July attempt to assassinate Hitler; worked in the Cologne Regional Tax Office, 1949–1952.

State Secretary Dr Stuckart stated by way of introduction that the purpose of the discussion was preparation for a top-level meeting about *Jewish policy*.[4] To regulate the economic position of the Jews, he said, it is necessary to ascertain the fundamental direction of overall Jewish policy and thus the uniformity of all measures related to Jewish policy. The economic position of the Jews must now be clarified in order to guard against the danger that the Jews might gain new economic positions in Germany. In his letter of 28 July 1936 President Schacht has already formulated[5] the questions that come into consideration as possibilities for Jewish policy. To begin with, therefore, it is a matter of debating which of the avenues discussed therein should be taken.

Ministerial Director Sommer[6] stated that from the standpoint of the NSDAP, in accordance with the Party programme, the Jewish question cannot be viewed as resolved until there is no longer a single Jew in Germany. This ultimate goal is fixed. The current solution can be regarded only as a partial one in achieving this goal. Therefore, it can be only a matter of specifying the extent and pace of the individual measures.

State Secretary Dr Posse[7] declared that if it is a matter of carrying out the Party programme, economic matters should also be adapted to this goal. That is possible; however, the stages would have to be determined.

According to the current state of affairs, to all intents and purposes various different laws are valid. The state's basic principle is to allow the Jews freedom to pursue economic activity. The implementation of this principle is not uniform. The principle is not implemented especially in those administrations that follow the Party line more closely, as for example in the areas under the remit of the Ministry of Propaganda or the Ministry of Food. On the other hand, the Jews were inevitably pushed into economic activity as a result of their exclusion from many professions in general. What matters to the Ministry of Economics is to obtain a clear legal position. Therefore, above all, a harmonization of the views that exist at present must take place.

State Secretary Dr Stuckart pointed out that no difference of opinion can exist with regard to the ultimate objective of Jewish policy: it is total emigration, because, for the state as well, the Party programme is binding. The goal, however, can be reached only in stages. The guideline and standard for the pace of emigration must be, in each case, the greatest possible utility for the German people. The emigration must be effected in accordance with what is practical in each case. It is necessary to align all measures to this objective. The *furtherance of the emigration of the Jews* arises from the goal itself as a *baseline* for all measures. All measures in the area of Jewish policy ought to be targeted to this goal. Economic activity by Jews should be authorized only in the context of earning their own livelihood, but without their economic and political situation resulting

---

4 No verification of this top-level meeting could be found.
5 This letter could not be found.
6 Walther Sommer (1893–1946), lawyer; joined the NSDAP in 1928 and was a member of the SS, 1936 to 1942; from 1925 to 1934 worked in the Thuringian Ministry of the Interior, lastly as Ministerialrat; on the staff of the Deputy of the Führer, where he headed the Constitutional Law Department, 1934; from 1941 president of the Reich Administrative Court; resigned in 1942 to pre-empt removal from office; sentenced to death and executed in 1946 in the Soviet Union.
7 Dr Hans Ernst Posse (1886–1965), lawyer; from 1924 ministerial director and head of the Customs and Trade Policy Department in the Reich Ministry of Economics; from 1935 state secretary in the Reich Ministry of Economics.

in them losing their will to emigrate. In the final analysis, one must also consider the implementation of emigration by force.

Accordingly, the fact must be stated that there will continue to be Jews in Germany for the time being. In this regard, therefore, one must clarify the question of whether and to what extent the Jews should be segregated from the German people and granted some kind of self-administration. For cultural and religious activities, this question has already been answered in the affirmative. The establishment of a separate Jewish school system is already in progress.⁸ One should not go beyond this sphere, however, and in particular should not grant the Jews any self-administration in the area of social policy, because the solidarity and cohesion of the Jews would be promoted as a result. From the standpoint of domestic politics, that could only be undesirable and, above all, would eclipse the desire among the Jews to emigrate.

State Secretary Dr Posse declared that one should permit the Jews an opportunity for activity in Germany until emigration is possible, and not take the path of assigning the Jews to pauper relief. He said that on 24 August 1936 English banks submitted to the Ministry of Economics a plan that aims to enable the Jews to emigrate from Germany with the help of foreign capital.⁹ In connection with this plan, it may become necessary to allow the Jews a certain degree of economic independence as well, because only those German Jews who possess either capital or some kind of preparatory training can expect to be admitted by another country. Therefore, one will at least have to allow the Jews to set up the necessary schools.

Ministerial Director Sommer pointed out that wealthy Jews in general will not leave of their own free will. One therefore must not leave open to the Jews a considerable degree of opportunities for economic activity. On the other hand, one should also prevent the formation of a Jewish proletariat. Also, one cannot avoid allowing the Jews, in addition to cultural and religious activities and the school system, a number of self-administrative bodies, such as the Jewish League of Combat Veterans, Jewish associations for the blind, facilities for Jewish social welfare, and the like.

It is also necessary to give the Jews the opportunity for agricultural training. The Minister of Food would probably have to abandon the adverse position he has adopted on this question thus far.¹⁰ As for the rest, there would also be no objections to schools for industrial or technical training.¹¹

State Secretary Dr Posse concurred.

---

8 On 10 Sept. 1935 Reich Minister of Education Rust had ordered the segregation of Jewish school pupils from non-Jewish ones in state schools: see Doc. 196. Because many Jewish pupils were now assigned to Jewish institutions, these had to be enlarged or new schools established. Owing to shortages of money or space, however, the mandated segregation could not be implemented everywhere until 1938.
9 On the origins of this plan, see the Jewish Telegraphic Agency reports from early Jan. 1936, Doc. 220.
10 On this discussion, see Doc. 107, 27 Feb. 1934, and Doc. 122, 13 June 1934. As late as May 1936 the Reich Ministry of Food had even rejected separate training of Jews overseen by an Aryan supervisor; memorandum of Section IV/8 dated 19 May 1936, BArch, R 3601/1845, fols. 34–37.
11 On 13 July 1936 the Reich Ministry of Education had ordered that technical schools providing training in skilled crafts and agriculture for Jews could be established only if the Jews were trained with an eye to their emigration. The organization and activity of these schools were to be subject to the strictest supervision: Walk (ed.), *Das Sonderrecht für die Juden im NS-Staat*, pp. 167–168.

State Secretary Dr Stuckart stated in summary: Schools and other establishments that prepare Jews for emigration should be tolerated. Nonetheless, it must be ensured that emigration actually takes place. This guarantee is especially necessary for the area of trade and industry. In the area of agriculture, a certain guarantee for emigration is present, since in Germany a Jew is unlikely to have the prospect of agricultural employment on a permanent basis.

State Secretary Dr Stuckart then raised the question of the target country for Jewish emigration. It must be made clear to what destination the flow of Jewish emigrants should be directed. At the same time, it must be pointed out that the German Jews in general will be superior to the inhabitants of the target country, especially in the South American countries. It is therefore inevitable that the Jews will soon gain influence there and form an anti-German economic class. For this reason, the emigration of the Jews to Palestine has been the main focus thus far.

Head of Reich Office Dr Blome[12] was of the opinion that the primary rule must be the emigration of the Jews under all circumstances. One should not pursue an emigration policy focused solely on Palestine.

State Secretary Dr Posse pointed out that if the emigration of the Jews is made possible with the help of foreign money, it will not be possible to exert influence on the choice of country.

State Secretary Dr Stuckart stated in conclusion that the emigration of the Jews must of course be encouraged without regard to the target country, but that *German* resources could be brought to bear primarily for Palestine.[13]

In reply to the question of whether an appeal should not be made to the press, so that especially pointed reports about anti-Jewish goings-on, for example in Palestine, do not cause the Jews to lose interest in emigration, Ministerial Director Sommer stated that one cannot take offence at other people if they refuse to accept the Jews. An attempt to influence the press does not seem appropriate.

The discussion of the question of the treatment in the economy of Jewish Mischlinge and persons intermarried with Jews resulted in consensus that all measures be limited to Jews (§ 5 of the First Regulation to the Reich Citizenship Law).[14] The Jewish *Mischlinge and persons intermarried with Jews* are to be equated with respect to economic affairs with persons of German blood.

The discussion of the questions contained in the letter of the Reich Ministry of the Interior dated 3 June 1936[15] produced the following result.[16]

---

12 Dr Kurt Blome (1897–1969), physician; took part in the Kapp Putsch in 1920; joined the NSDAP in 1922 and the SA in 1931; physician in Rostock, 1924–1934; from 1934 worked in the NSDAP Main Office for Public Health; deputy Reich Physicians' Leader and assistant head of the National Socialist Association of Physicians and the NSDAP Main Office for Public Health, 1939–1945; plenipotentiary for biological weapons research, 1942–1945; in 1948 acquitted in the Nuremberg Doctors' Trial; from 1948 physician in Dortmund.
13 This is a reference to the Haavara Agreement.
14 See the First Regulation to the Reich Citizenship Law, 14 Nov. 1935, Doc. 210.
15 This letter could not be found.
16 On the following restrictions on trade and industry, see the Draft Law on the Status of the Jews in the Economy, 9 Oct. 1935, Doc. 205.

(1) Jews are to be excluded from the credit agency business, security industry, marriage bureaus (with the exception of agencies that arrange Jewish marriages), arms trade, and itinerant trade.[17]

Ministerial Director Sommer urged that Jewish *travel agencies* should no longer be tolerated either, because these agencies aim to channel the flood of travellers to countries in which an attempt would be made to exert an anti-German influence upon German travellers.

State Secretary Posse agreed to arrange for an examination of the question.

The decision on this question was reserved for the top-level meeting.

(2) Regarding the question of excluding Jews from *property transactions*, State Secretary Dr Posse pointed out that this branch of trade is still largely in Jewish hands, in Berlin approximately 90 per cent of it. Therefore the real estate business would inevitably be profoundly shaken by the complete exclusion of the Jews.

Consensus was reached that those Jews who now engage in property trading are to be left in place for the time being. At the same time, however, one must examine the question of how to bring about, with the passage of time, the disappearance of Jewish brokerage firms that are currently run in the form of a company. (The introduction of the requirement to obtain permission for new company members or for the company in the event of a change in the composition of the management board or the supervisory board is under consideration.)

In future, however, Jewish estate agents are no longer to receive accreditation (obligation to hold a licence).[18]

(3) Regarding the question of arms manufacture, Ministerial Director Sommer declared that it is not acceptable for Jewish firms to manufacture arms and thus to profit from the German arms build-up. Jews are thus to be forbidden to manufacture weapons. This goal can be reached via the following measures:

(a) exclusion of Jews from the management board and supervisory board of all firms that engage in arms production;

(b) mandatory restructuring of the Jewish equity participation in these firms into bonds yielding interest of no more than 4 per cent.

The decision on this question was reserved for the top-level meeting.

However, to begin with, the Ministry of Economics is to examine which firms are to be considered for this.[19]

---

17 This was mainly effected by the Law on the Amendment of the Commercial Code for the German Reich of 6 July 1938: *Reichsgesetzblatt*, 1938, I, p. 823. Following the passage of the Law on Operating a Travel Agency of 26 Jan. 1937, the licence for a travel agent could already be revoked in the event of 'unreliability' on the part of the tradesperson: *Reichsgesetzblatt*, 1937, I, p. 31.

18 In 1938, Jews were prohibited from dealing in real estate and brokering real estate contracts: Law on the Amendment of the Commercial Code for the German Reich, 6 July 1938, *Reichsgesetzblatt*, 1938, I, p. 823.

19 On the expropriation of the Simson Suhl arms factory, see Doc. 134, 31 August 1934, and Doc. 165, 22 May 1935. On 14 March 1938 Jews were legally prohibited from producing and selling arms on a commercial basis: *Reichsgesetzblatt*, 1938, I, p. 265.

(4) Consensus was reached on the necessity of excluding, alongside the Jews, the Jewish Mischlinge from cultural *creativity*, though it does not seem justifiable to also exclude Jewish Mischlinge from activity in the cultural *industry*, as is currently being done by the Ministry of Propaganda. This ministry will therefore have to be approached in order to effect a change in the practice followed thus far.

(5) *Ministerialrat Dr Hoppe*[20] pointed out that it will not be acceptable to prohibit the individual businessman, as a Party comrade, from maintaining business relations with Jews,[21] since there are still certain branches of trade and industry that are entirely or almost entirely in Jewish hands. In practice, it is thus not possible to satisfy demand by dealing with non-Jewish firms. In addition, such a ban would inevitably cause grave damage to Germany's foreign trade, quite apart from the fact that in the case of foreign firms it is generally not possible to determine whether a firm is Jewish or non-Jewish.

After extensive discussion of the question, consensus was reached that restrictions for Party members and civil servants in commercial transactions with Jews and Jewish firms should apply only to *consumers*, but not to internal commercial transactions or to the entire export/import area.

In general, *selling* to Jews should be permissible.

(6) Concerning the group of persons who are to be subjected to restrictions, there was consensus that it should include the members of the NSDAP, of the Party organizations, of the Wehrmacht, and of the Labour Service, but not the members of the affiliated associations.

On the question of extending the prohibition to civil servants, Ministerialrat Dr Hoppe advised that President Schacht will presumably object to such a prohibition for his area of jurisdiction.

State Secretary Dr Stuckart commented on this, saying that, above all, reasons of civil service policy point to the need for the prohibition. The civil servant is regarded as a representative of the state. It will not do, therefore, for him to be permitted to make purchases in Jewish businesses.

State Secretary Dr Posse suggested a differentiation of the term civil servant here. It was viewed as practicable to limit the prohibition to persons who are civil servants within the meaning of the term civil servant under constitutional law, and specifically to refrain from extending it to salaried employees and workers in the public sector.[22]

---

20 Dr Alfred Hoppe (b. 1882), lawyer; local court judge in the Berlin district of Köpenick, 1915–1920; from 1920 section head, later Ministerialrat, in the Reich Ministry of Economics; until 1933 Reich commissioner for small and medium-sized businesses; joined the NSDAP in 1932; member of the supervisory board of the Deutsche Bau- und Bodenbank in Berlin.

21 This refers to Directive no. 63/35 on commercial dealings between NSDAP members and Jews, issued by Deputy of the Führer Rudolf Heß on 11 April 1935: published in Hans Mommsen and Susanne Willems (eds.), *Herrschaftsalltag im Dritten Reich: Studien und Texte* (Düsseldorf: Patmos, 1988), pp. 430–431.

22 In practice, salaried employees and workers in the public sector were already included in such prohibitions in many places: see Doc. 97, 13 Jan. 1934.

(7) *State Secretary Dr Posse* raised the question of whether an objection should be made when Jewish representatives work for a German firm abroad. Such cases are generally investigated by the Foreign Organization of the NSDAP, which requires the firms to dismiss their Jewish representatives. In practice, however, the dismissal of the Jewish representatives usually entails substantial disruptions of German foreign trade and thus of the volume of foreign exchange.

The result of this discussion was that as a rule no objection will be made when a Jewish representative is working for a German firm abroad.

The regulation of individual cases will be at the discretion of the Ministry of Economics. In Austria, however – wherever possible – no Jewish representatives are to act for German firms.

(8) The discussion of the question as to what extent the public sector should be allowed to enter into business dealings with Jews, above all to award public contracts to Jews, resulted in the decision that a strict prohibition cannot be implemented at present. Regulation must take the line of allowing public contracts to be awarded to Jewish firms only *in case of emergency.* Even this principle would signify a substantial toughening of the guidelines prevailing thus far.[23]

The principles that guide the NSDAP in awarding its contracts must continue to be left to its discretion; however, the concept of the Jewish business must be the same for the Party and the state.

(9) There was consensus that Jewish firms must be forbidden to hoist the Reich and national flag.[24] It should be recognized, of course, that the German personnel of a Jewish enterprise will usually have an interest in displaying flags at their place of business and also a certain right to do so. Consideration of the personnel, however, must occur not in connection with the flag question, but rather in determining what defines a Jewish business.

(10) Accordingly, it was recognized that there is a pressing need to make clear which enterprises are to be regarded as Jewish ones. For the main part, three questions arose in the process:

(a) Which substantive provisions should be implemented? – The draft submitted by the Reich Ministry of the Interior will be able to serve as a basis.[25] No fundamental objections to this draft were raised.

---

[23] In summer 1933 the Reich Ministry of Economics (RWM) initially prohibited discrimination against Jewish firms with respect to public contracts. Aryan firms could nevertheless be given preference: see the RWM decree, with a letter to the Association of Chambers of Industry and Commerce dated 8 Sept. 1933: BArch, R 3101/13863, fol. 6. Then, on 1 March 1938, the RWM excluded Jewish firms from the awarding of public contracts: Sauer (ed.), *Dokumente über die Verfolgung*, vol. 1, pp. 195–197.

[24] § 4(1) of the Law for the Protection of German Blood and German Honour (15 Sept. 1935) forbade Jews to 'hoist the Reich and national flag and to show the Reich colours': see Doc. 199, 15 Sept. 1935.

[25] This draft was not found.

(b) Which bodies should be assigned to make decisions? Here, too, the regulation envisaged in the draft of the Reich Ministry of the Interior is to serve as a basis. A Party office will have to be involved in the decision. The question of whether a special representative can be positioned in each Gau for this decision-making should be examined.

(c) In what form should the provisions be issued? A regulation pursuant to the Reich Citizenship Law would undoubtedly create a great stir. Therefore, one must give thought to casting the provisions merely in the form of a decree. This decree, admittedly, would have no legal force. If, however, there is complete agreement among the departments involved and if the provisions are utilized in a uniform manner by the government agencies and the Party offices, then the outcome achieved thereby could be practically the same as that achieved by a regulation. It is primarily a matter of eliminating the anxiety in economic life caused by the lack of clarity regarding the concept of the Jewish business. A decree could also serve this purpose.[26]

A decision on this question was reserved for the top-level meeting.

(11) The Jewish businesses have not been designated as such, by order of the Führer. Consideration must therefore be paid to the introduction of a uniform designation for all non-Jewish businesses. A special sign should possibly be created for this purpose, a sign that can also be used by Jewish Mischlinge and, in particular, also by foreigners. The sign can, for example, be mounted where, according to the provisions of the Commercial Code, the name of the proprietor of the business must be placed. One cannot avoid having some kind of designation, because if certain categories of persons are forbidden to make purchases in Jewish businesses, then these persons must also have the possibility to determine whether, in a given case, a business is Jewish or not.

This type of designation is by its nature limited to retail outlets. For the other Jewish enterprises the plan to compile a special directory should be pursued, because of the need to obtain information quickly and reliably about the individual businesses, in particular with regard to the matter of awarding public contracts and enforcing the ban on flags.

The details are yet to be determined.

---

26 The Third Regulation to the Reich Citizenship Law (14 June 1938) decreed that a business undertaking was Jewish if the owner was a Jew under § 5 of the First Regulation to the Reich Citizenship Law: *Reichsgesetzblatt*, 1938, I, p. 627.

DOC. 249

On 6 October 1936 the German embassy in Warsaw reports to the Reich Foreign Office on Polish initiatives concerning Jewish emigration[1]

Letter from the German embassy in Warsaw (PI 11/ 10.36), (signature illegible), to the Reich Foreign Office (received on the morning of 7 October 1936), dated 6 October 1936[2]

A follow-up to the report from August of this year (P I IIa/ 8.36)[3]
Re: Poland's raising of the colonial question and the emigrant question at the League of Nations.
The speech that Vice Minister Rose[4] gave in Geneva on Poland's aspirations with respect to the issue of the redistribution of raw materials and the resolution of the overpopulation problem has been thoroughly commended by the Polish press of all shades. The *Iskra* news agency, which is closely affiliated with the Foreign Ministry, states that Poland's demands in the colonial and emigrant questions at present have top priority in Polish foreign policy. It also comments that Poland must gain access to raw materials and have guaranteed opportunities for a colonizing emigration. According to the agency, Poland has to sort out the huge problem of its industrialization, and seeks to resolve the question of its access to raw materials and overseas expansion by means of international cooperation. The agency also maintains that since Poland has just about the largest surplus population in the world, it is forced to pursue further industrialization, for which it needs the corresponding raw materials.

The National Democratic press covers in particularly great detail the statements made by Vice Minister Rose on the Jewish question, and demands that the League of Nations come to the aid of Poland on the issue of Jewish emigration.[5] This press also argues that it is of vital importance to the Polish people that the Jews living here retain the possibility to emigrate.

The Polish proposal in Geneva is certainly to be attributed first and foremost to the fact that the emigration of 20,000 Polish Jews to Palestine each year, as has been customary hitherto, has been thrown into jeopardy by political conditions there.[6] The Polish government may also have felt obliged to take an active approach on the Jewish question because of the increasingly virulent antisemitism, particularly among the rural population. The further development of the Jewish problem could, however, assume an even greater foreign policy significance because leading political circles, including Foreign

---

[1] BArch, R 901/68371, fols. 8–10. This document has been translated from German.
[2] The original contains the note 'Duplicate has been submitted to the director. Office W.' as well as several handwritten notes and instances of underlining.
[3] In this report the embassy had given an account of the latest debates in Poland on issues related to emigration and population policy. Three topics played a major role here: the question of Polish emigration in general, Polish colonial aspirations, and Jewish emigration from Poland: report by the German embassy in Warsaw (P I 11a/8.36) dated 21 August 1936, ibid., fols. 1–6.
[4] Adam Karol Rose (1895–1951), economist; Polish envoy to the International Labour Office in Geneva, 1921–1922; head of the Economics Section in the Ministry of Agriculture and Agrarian Reform, 1930–1936; deputy minister of industry and trade, 1936–1939; Polish envoy to the Economics Commission of the League of Nations, 1936; unofficial envoy to France for the Polish government in exile, 1940; lived in exile in Geneva, 1942–1945; advisor to the Polish vice minister of foreign trade and shipping, 1945–1949; lived in exile in Paris, 1949–1951.

Minister Beck[7] in particular, as I have learned from a reliable source, seek, with help from the League of Nations, to prevail upon the Soviet government to take in a large portion of the Polish Jews.

I regard as inaccurate, however, the opinion, which is also held by the local British ambassador, that Poland's only reason for raising the colonial question is to address the difficulties in Palestine. The explanations that Mr Komarnicki[8] gave to Mr Krauel[9] in Geneva (see report from 30 September of this year, Pol. V 3786),[10] according to which Poland has absolutely no intention whatsoever of laying claim to parts of Germany's former colonial possessions, are also not confirmed by my observations here. The Polish desire for national prestige necessitates the acquisition of colonies. The Colonial and Maritime League, which has more than 500,000 members and works hand in hand with the government, has for months already been laying the propaganda groundwork for the raising of Polish colonial demands. In July alone some 200 meetings were held at which it was stated openly that Poland has a legal right to acquire Germany's erstwhile colonial possessions since the former parts of Prussia would have been entitled to a proportional share. If today the Polish representative in Geneva attempts to base the Polish demands on the need to find an outlet for the Jewish surplus population, then in my opinion there can be no doubt that Poland is ultimately using the colonial question to pursue wider objectives, and that Beck intended his proposal in Geneva to serve as a means to weigh in at the right time on all possibilities for progress in this regard.

5 Rose had based his proposal at the League of Nations on the unusually high proportion of Jews in the overall population and the 'unhealthy' economic structure of Polish Jewry. He stated that Poland's urban population totalled 10 million people, of whom 3.5 million were Jews by faith, employed mostly in trade. According to Rose, more than 1 million Jews were without any income. He maintained that emigration was the only possible solution. In another speech, Delegate Komarnicki (see fn. 8) said that Poland could neither finance this emigration nor permit Jews to take their own financial resources with them: letter from the German embassy in Warsaw to the Reich Foreign Office, dated 13 Oct. 1936, ibid., fols. 12–16. According to the Polish census of 1931, 3,136,000 inhabitants professed to be adherents to Judaism: *Mały rocznik statystyczny polski, wrzesień 1939 – czerwiec 1941* (Warsaw: Główny Urząd Statystyczny, 1990 [1941]), p. 10.
6 This is a reference to the unrest and violent conflict between Arabs and Jews in 1936.
7 Józef Beck (1894–1944), officer and diplomat; Polish military attaché in Paris, 1922–1925; chief of staff to Polish minister of military affairs, 1926–1930; state secretary in the Ministry of Foreign Affairs, 1930–1932; Polish foreign minister, 1932–1939; close associate of Marshal Piłsudski.
8 Probably Tytus Komarnicki (1896–1967), diplomat; from 1924 served in the Polish diplomatic service; Polish delegate to the League of Nations, 1934–1938.
9 Wolfgang Krauel (1888–1977), lawyer; from 1914 worked in the Prussian judicial service; served in the Reich Foreign Office, 1922–1944; from 1928 legation counsellor and from 1932 consul in Geneva; joined the NSDAP in 1939; took up residence in Switzerland, 1944, and was denaturalized; from 1951 served as consul in Brazil for the German Federal Foreign Office.
10 The report mentioned here is not in the file.

DOC. 250
Amtsblatt der Preußischen Regierung zu Königsberg: regulation issued by the Oberpräsident on 7 October 1936 regarding name changes for towns[1]

Regulations and announcements of the Oberpräsident.

542. Decision

in accordance with § 10 in conjunction with § 117(3) of the German Municipal Code of 30 January 1935.[2]

The name of the municipality of Judendorf, Kreis Prussian Holland, is hereby changed to 'Hermannswalde',[3] and the name of the residential quarter of Juden belonging to the municipality of Kalthof, district of Prussian Holland, to 'Buchental'.[4]

Königsberg (Prussia), 7 October 1936.

The Oberpräsident of the Province of East Prussia.[5]

DOC. 251
Pariser Tageszeitung, 11 October 1936: article about the expulsion of German Jews from economic life[1]

Plundering of businesses and property is being organized
New period of Jewish persecution

A special correspondent of the Jewish Telegraphic Agency, who has been travelling through Germany these past several weeks, has found that concerns about the recent Nuremberg rally of the NSDAP ushering in a new period of Jewish persecution in Germany have indeed materialized. In many larger and smaller provincial towns, local National Socialist leaders called on the Jewish owners of enterprises employing a substantial number of workers to

---

1 *Amtsblatt der Preußischen Regierung zu Königsberg* [Official gazette of the Prussian government in Königsberg], 24 Oct. 1936, p. 285. This document has been translated from German.
2 § 10 stipulated: 'The municipalities maintain their current names. After a hearing of the municipality, the Reichsstatthalter issues a pronouncement changing the name of the municipality and he assigns names to newly established municipalities. The same applies to the special assignment of names to parts of municipalities.' Paragraph 3 of § 117 transferred the duties of the Reichsstatthalter in Prussia to the Oberpräsident: German Municipal Code, 30 Jan. 1935; *Reichsgesetzblatt*, 1935, I, pp. 49–50.
3 The original name of the municipality translates literally as 'Jew Village', the new name literally as 'Hermann's Wood'.
4 The original name of the residential quarter translates literally simply as 'Jews', the new name literally as 'Beech Valley'.
5 Erich Koch (1896–1986), railway official; member of the von Killinger Freikorps, 1918; worked for the Reich Railways, 1919–1926; joined the NSDAP in 1922; NSDAP Gauleiter of East Prussia, 1928–1945; Oberpräsident of the province of East Prussia, 1933–1945; Reich commissioner for Ukraine, 1941–1944; in 1950 extradited to Poland, where in 1959 he received a death sentence, which was then commuted to life imprisonment; author of *Aufbau im Osten* (1934).

1 'Geschäfts- und Immobilien-Raub wird organisiert', *Pariser Tageszeitung*, 11 Oct. 1936, p. 2. This document has been translated from German.

turn over their businesses to Aryans. They also threatened to take the most severe measures in the event of refusal. A number of Jewish shop and factory owners were even arrested by the Gestapo without prior warning.

This action has been initiated by the German Labour Front, whose officials are visiting the owners and heads of Jewish enterprises one by one and urging them to hand over their shops and factories. The officials give as an explanation that while the Nuremberg rally was taking place, the instruction was issued to all members of the Labour Front to renew their campaign against Jewish commercial and industrial enterprises, including the stationing of boycott guards in front of each Jewish shop. The most severe disciplinary action and other methods of pressure will be taken against Aryans who get ideas about making purchases in Jewish shops. Before, however, this new boycott action is fully under way, the Labour Front officials are to call upon Jewish commercial and industrial enterprises to 'quietly' liquidate their activities and relinquish their shops and factories to Aryans.

Among the Jewish businessmen who have already been arrested is the managing director of the Bielefeld-based Katz and Michel textile factory,[2] Sigmund Heymann.[3] Gestapo officials arrested him on the grounds that he 'had ridiculed the German Labour Front by having the factory, which employs more than 100 workers, close one and a half hours earlier than usual on the Jewish Day of Atonement'.[4] In reality, however, the arrest constituted a means of applying pressure in order to bring about the transfer of this company into Aryan hands.[5] The Berlin newspaper *Der Angriff* expressed its satisfaction with the arrest of Heymann, who had allegedly had the 'audacity' to remain seated in the presence of the Labour Front officials.[6]

Parallel to the new action against the Jews engaged in commerce and industry, the campaign to exclude Jews from the grocery trade has been renewed, taking advantage of the ill feeling occasioned by the growing food shortage. In the past two weeks the Reich Office for Food Supply has forced more than 2,000 Jewish meat, fat, and egg traders to liquidate their businesses. In Berlin alone, more than fifty Jewish grain companies, some of which had been in business for over a century, were forced into liquidation.[7] In rural areas Jewish grocers were barred from supplying meat, butter, fats, and eggs to the retail trade.

---

2 Founded in 1923 in Bielefeld, the company was known as Katz & Michel Textiles from 1928. In addition to a linen factory, in 1934 it still owned some 107 department stores in various cities.
3 Siegmund Heymann (b. 1878), retailer; member of the management board, 1924–1937, and managing director from 1926 of Katz Textiles in Bielefeld; emigrated to the United States in 1938.
4 The *Westfälische Neueste Nachrichten* reported, under the headline 'Unerhörte jüdische Frechheit' [Outrageous Jewish audacity], on the conflict between managing director Heymann and the Labour Front functionaries who had voiced complaints in response to his announcement that there were to be reduced working hours and extra work on the following days. The paper maintained that Heymann had behaved in a provoking manner and spat in front of the Labour Front officials. The Gestapo ultimately arrested Heymann after the Labour Front's Kreis leadership intervened along with the Trustees of Labour; *Westfälische Neueste Nachrichten*, 30 Sept. 1936, Bielefelder Stadtanzeiger supplement.
5 On 1 April 1937 the textile company was Aryanized by means of a takeover by a consortium.
6 The newspaper article mentioned here could not be found.
7 On the conditions for grain companies, see Doc. 246, 16 Sept. 1936.

As the special correspondent of the Jewish Telegraphic Agency also learned, for the time being it is not anticipated that there will be a special law prohibiting Jews from owning property (houses and land). However, the project now under consideration by the government concerning property ownership will implement provisions that supply the authorities with the leverage necessary to take away immovable assets belonging to Jews. The Reich Ministry of Economics has expressed its opposition to this legislative project, pointing out that the loss of a large number of Jewish taxpayers would have a significantly adverse effect on the government's coffers. Other ministries, however, are under the influence of the hard-line National Socialists, who insist on the confiscation of Jewish property. It appears that certain concessions must be made to these extremists.

Meanwhile, in Franconia, where Julius Streicher holds power, the first steps have been taken to exert control over the entire system of property ownership. There an office for 'governing the relations between property owners and tenants'[8] has been established: it has the power to regulate the level of rent in any particular case and to decide whether certain persons may rent out their houses and land and to whom. This measure alone gives the authorities in Franconia the opportunity to force Jewish property owners to dispose of their assets.

The Reich Chamber of Culture has just issued instructions to Jewish art dealers in Berlin to relinquish their holdings in the shortest possible time, since Jews are to be prohibited from dealing in works of art before the end of the year.[9]

The Essener National-Zeitung, Göring's personal organ, is calling for Jews to be barred from trading in listed shares because Jewish traders influence share transactions in a way that holds down the demand for shares in German enterprises, even though they pay an average dividend of 4 per cent, while increasing the demand for foreign shares, which only yield 2 per cent.[10]

DOC. 252
On 12 October 1936 the Chief of the Security Police asks the Chief of the Order Police in Berlin to alter the registration system so as to improve the collection of data on baptized Jews[1]

Letter from the Chief of the Security Police (II B 1532/36), signed p.p. by Müller,[2] to the Chief of the Order Police (received on 15 October 1936), Berlin, dated 12 October 1936[3]

Re: surveillance of the Jews.

Since the [National Socialist] entry to power it has been noted that a substantial portion of the Jews living in Germany have had themselves baptized as Protestant or Catholic with the intention of no longer being listed as Jewish after changing their place of resi-

---

8 Further information on this office could not be found.
9 For Göring's criticism regarding the consequences of this action, see Doc. 277, 3 May 1937.
10 See 'Wirtschaftliche Aufgaben der Banken und Börsen', *National-Zeitung*, 3 Oct. 1936, p. 5.

1 GStA PK, I HA, Rep. 77, Tit. 343, Nr. 17, Sonderakte Bd. 2, fol. 269. This document has been translated from German.

dence in the public registries, and in order to make it difficult in individual cases for the authorities, particularly the Political Police forces, to determine Jewish descent.[4]

I would therefore most respectfully suggest that suitable measures be taken to require that a person under obligation to register not only specify his religion, but also whether he is a Jew as defined by the Nuremberg Laws. Such a measure would greatly facilitate State Police investigations as well as the surveillance of the Jews.[5]

I kindly request that you involve me, where appropriate, in the further handling of this matter.[6]

DOC. 253
Invitation from the People's Association for the German Reich Church to a Reformation church service to be held in Grabow on 2 November 1936[1]

Circular from the People's Association for the German Reich Church,[2] Grabow/Mecklenburg congregation, prepared in conjunction with the council of elders and Chairman Günter Niemack,[3] undated [late October 1936], copy (M/X/1862 A)[4]

To all our members and to all loyal, like-minded friends in city and country!

This coming *Monday, 2 November 1936*, we will all be attending the *Reformation church service* at *8:15 p.m.* in Grabow Church.

---

2 Heinrich Müller (1900–1945), aircraft assembler; from 1919 worked at the Munich police headquarters; joined the SS in 1934; transferred to the Gestapo Central Office (Gestapa) in Berlin; deputy chief of the Political Police Office in the Security Police Main Office, 1936; joined the NSDAP in 1938; managing director of the Reich Central Agency for Jewish Emigration and chief of Office IV (Gestapo) in the Reich Security Main Office, 1939.
3 The original contains several handwritten annotations.
4 On the accusation that Jews concealed their origins by being baptized, see also the article in *Der Stürmer* from Jan. 1936, Doc. 222.
5 Starting in Feb. 1937 the police registration system was to meticulously gather information on religion, 'particularly persons of Jewish descent', as part of the implementation of the Reich Citizenship Law: see directive of the Berlin chief of police dated 22 Feb. 1937, supplement C to official bulletins of the *Amtliche Nachrichten des Polizeipräsidiums in Berlin*, no. 14, 26 Feb. 1937.
6 The Chief of the Order Police submitted the letter to Department I of the Reich Ministry of the Interior on 4 Nov. 1936. The Reich Ministry of the Interior replied on 4 Feb. 1937 that there were plans to 'ascertain the blood composition of the German population' in the census scheduled for 1938, adding that these results could then be included on the police registration cards: GStA PK, I HA, Rep. 77, Tit. 343, Nr. 17, Sonderakte Bd. 2, fols. 270–272. In 1937 meetings were held between the Order Police and the Security Police, as well as between the sections for Jewish affairs at the SD and the Gestapo, to discuss what course of action to take, and gathering data on Jews by means of the census was favoured over compulsory registration or a special survey: ibid., fol. 275r–v, and Doc. 288, 12 July 1937.

1 Archiv des Diakonischen Werkes der Evangelischen Kirche Deutschlands, CA, AC-S/73. This document has been translated from German.
2 Volksbund für deutsche Reichskirche.
3 Günter Niemack, author of works including *Die völkische Sendung der Reformation* (1935).
4 Parts of the original have been marked by hand.

Regional Superintendent *Schönrock* of Wittenburg[5] will deliver the sermon and I will give the reading. The congregation's choir will perform.

The Jewish religious movement of the so-called 'Confession Sect'[6] recently used our church improperly on 23 August by having the ousted Superintendent Galley[7] declare there, in his 'Mission Festival sermon', that the mission to the heathen was a Christian purpose unto itself, which is higher than 'the highest national purpose'!

This shameful declaration comes at a time when providing loyal brotherly assistance to German Volksgenossen driven out of Spain by Jewish Bolshevism and supporting the Winter Relief Agency are our highest national and Christian duties!

Our Grabow Church is not an international Jew synagogue, which is what it was to be turned into on 4 October through Provost Burchard's[8] bearing witness to the Jewish Old Testament!

The churches on German soil are and shall remain the property of the German people, whose *Holy Land* – as Alfred Rosenberg proclaimed recently – is *not Palestine* but *Germany*!

We shall all solemnly bear witness to this on Monday evening at the church service to commemorate the German Reformation, which must finally be brought to completion in our lifetime for the benefit of our entire people!

Afterwards we will all gather *at nine in the evening* in the assembly room of '*Fürst Bismarck*' – in the vicinity of the church – *for our annual meeting from nine to ten o'clock*.

All of our like-minded friends in city and country are also cordially invited to attend! And all the more so because of an important announcement.

In the [late] afternoon from six to seven o'clock the council of elders will hold a meeting in the assembly room in Dambeck (Bützow's Beer and Wine Tavern), which *all old fellow fighters (only members)* and founders of the People's Study Group a year ago are also asked to attend.

Let us ensure full attendance of all those German-conscious Volksgenossen who no longer wish to tolerate Jewish clericalism in the church of a unified German people's community.

Heil Hitler!

---

5 Johannes Schönrock (1901–1971), pastor; joined the NSDAP in 1925; from 1934 pastor in Wittenburg and regional superintendent of the Hagenow church district; head of the congregation of the 'German Christians' in the Gau of Mecklenburg, 1937; fought in the war; after 1945 served as a pastor in Schwerin and Hahn, Oldenburg.
6 The author might be referring here to the Confessing Church, though this was not a 'Jewish religious movement'.
7 Alfred Galley (1873–1938), pastor; regional superintendent in Parchim, 1931; compulsorily retired, 1935.
8 Heinrich Burchard (b. 1876), pastor; theological seminary in Schwerin, 1902; headmaster of the private boys' school in Gadebusch, 1903; from 1922 provost in Grabow (Ludwigslust church district).

DOC. 254

On 14 November 1936 the Gestapo Central Office informs local Gestapo offices about the regulations for the Jewish Winter Relief in 1936/1937[1]

Circular decree from the Gestapo Central Office (Gestapa) (II 1 B 2–915/36 J.), signed p.p. by Müller, to all (a) State Police head offices, (b) State Police offices, and (c) Oberpräsidenten and Regierungspräsidenten in Prussia, for information only (received by the Potsdam government on 16 November 1936), dated 14 November 1936[2]

Re: support for Jews from the Winter Relief Agency in 1936/37 and the participation of Jews in the collection of donations.

The Reich Plenipotentiary for the Winter Relief Agency of the German People in 1936/37[3] has issued the following rules for the provision of aid to Jews under the auspices of the Winter Relief Agency and for the participation of Jews in the collection of donations.

I. *Support.*
  (1) Needy Jews shall not receive aid from the Winter Relief Agency of the German People. Sole responsibility for their support lies with the Central Welfare Office of Jews in Germany and its affiliated offices.[4]
  This shall be carried out under my supervision and in accordance with the guidelines approved by me.
  (2) Jewish Mischlinge shall receive support from the Winter Relief Agency of the German People.
  (3) Families resulting from mixed marriages between persons of German blood and Jews shall receive aid:
  (a) from the Winter Relief Agency of the German People if the head of the household is of German blood
  (b) from the Central Welfare Board of Jews in Germany if the head of the household is a Jew.

II. *Participation in the collection of donations.*
  (1) Donations for the Winter Relief Agency of the German People shall not be solicited from Jews, nor shall donations for the Winter Relief Agency of the German People be accepted from them.
  (2) Jewish Mischlinge shall be solicited for donations by the Winter Relief Agency of the German People.

---

1 BLHA, Pr.Br Rep. 2 A I Pol/1919, fols. 249–251. This document has been translated from German.
2 The original contains several annotations. The decree was also sent to the Düsseldorf State Police Office in response to its report dated 19 Sept. 1936 (II 1 B – 71,02/11.9).
3 After 1933 the Reich plenipotentiary was Erich Hilgenfeldt (1897–1945), commercial employee; joined the NSDAP in 1927; from 1933 head of the NSDAP Main Office for People's Welfare.
4 In the winter of 1935/1936, the first winter following the exclusion of Jews from the Winter Relief Agency, the Jewish welfare offices provided aid to 83,761 needy persons, representing 20.5 per cent of the 409,000 Jews still living in Germany: S. Adler-Rudel, *Jüdische Selbsthilfe unter dem Naziregime 1933–1939* (Tübingen: Mohr Siebeck, 1974), p. 163.

(3) Families of mixed marriages between persons of German blood and Jews shall be solicited for donations:
(a) by the Winter Relief Agency of the German People if the head of the household is of German blood
(b) by the Central Welfare Board of Jews in Germany if the head of the household is a Jew.
(4) Jewish fundraising efforts shall be limited to the Jewish community in Germany. It is thus not permitted to conduct fundraising for the Jewish Winter Relief in companies whose owners are not Jewish, for this extends beyond the scope of the Jewish community and is a prohibited form of public collection under the Collections Law of 5 November 1934.[5] Fundraising at incorporated companies (namely, public and private limited companies) shall not be carried out by the Jewish Winter Relief.

III. *Definition of terms.*
The decision as to whether a person is of German blood, a Jew, or a Jewish Mischling is to be based on the Reich Citizenship Law of 15 September 1935 and its implementing regulation of 14 November 1935 (see enclosure).[6] Confessional factors shall not be taken into consideration.[7]

IV. *Needy foreigners.*
Needy foreigners living in the German Reich shall receive aid from the Winter Relief Agency of the German People without consideration of their racial origin, provided that they have proved themselves worthy of this support through their attitude and behaviour towards the German Reich.

Should assertions to the contrary be made at meetings of Jewish organizations or of 'St Paul's Covenant',[8] I request that you arrange for the necessary action to be taken on your own responsibility and that you submit a report to me.
The decree is to be communicated to local and police authorities.

---

[5] According to the Law Regulating Public Collections and Related Events, or Collections Law (5 Nov. 1934), collections made in public places had to be approved: *Reichsgesetzblatt*, 1934, I, p. 1086.
[6] The enclosure mentioned here is not in the file. See Doc. 210, 14 Nov. 1935.
[7] During the previous winter it had not been clear which institutions were responsible for providing aid to which groups of persons. The Winter Relief Agency turned away all Jews, while the Jewish welfare organizations only gave assistance to needy persons of the Jewish faith. See the discussion in the Munich welfare office about providing Jews with heating fuel: memorandum dated 6 Dec. 1935, YVA, M1DN/168, fol. 7.
[8] Originally called the Reich Association of Non-Aryan Christians, the organization was renamed as the St Paul's Covenant in autumn 1936: see Doc. 85, 19 Oct. 1933.

DOC. 255

On 19 November 1936 the retailer Julius Block asks the Berlin police to make an exception and grant him a passport valid for five years[1]

Letter from Julius Block to the Berlin-Charlottenburg Police Station, Neue Grolmannstraße, dated 19 November 1936 (copy)

I, the undersigned Julius Block, am the sole proprietor of the company entered in the commercial register as Block & Simon, Berlin W.8, 58 Kronenstraße (clothing industry).

My passport expires on 24 February 1938. Since the pages of the passport are completely covered with stamps and certificates, I would like to apply for a new passport.

I have been informed that there is a general rule that non-Aryans are issued a passport valid for one year or a maximum two years.[2] I am not familiar with this rule. I would like to apply for a passport valid for five years, for the following reasons:

I invariably make the trips abroad myself in order to maintain the closest possible [business] relationships, especially in view of these difficult times. This is vital because of the sensibility required for the goods I manufacture – namely, highly fashionable women's dresses. As is customary in the industry, it is necessary to travel to each country in each of the four seasons; in addition, a non-Aryan representative is employed both in Switzerland and Holland as well as in Scandinavia.

My success is demonstrated by the following figures. The total exports of my company amounted to:

in 1933	RM 553,000
in 1934	RM 456,000
in 1935	RM 351,000
in the first half of 1936	RM 200,000

These amounts resulted in effective foreign currencies flowing into the German Reich through clearing accounts or in the form of direct currency.

My company holds a 'general permit' for the payment of incidental expenses incurred in the trade in goods, and it is valid for one year at a time.

The main sales territory is England. There I acquire more than a third of my total orders, followed by Sweden, Switzerland, Holland, and Norway. I also recently began operations in France.

My personal visits are necessary to persuade customers to inspect my stock in Berlin. The Reich also benefits from this.

If I am not issued a five-year passport like every German, then I will be faced with great difficulties. The French consuls refuse to issue visas for an extended period to holders of passports valid only for one year. This would force me to apply for a visa for each trip.

In England I would immediately stand out, and probably even arouse the suspicion of the immigration officer, if I carried a passport valid for less than five years. It will be impossible for the officer to understand that a German received a short-term passport

---

1 BArch, R 2/5978, fols. 246–248. This document has been translated from German.
2 It could not be ascertained whether this provision was actually issued.

for any reason other than criminal suspicion. In such a case I would encounter tremendous difficulties from the English border authorities. If I do not have complete freedom to travel freely abroad, it will be impossible to maintain or increase my sales volume. The Reich will suffer losses of foreign currency.

I emphasize that I have never been politically active in any way at any time in my life. My entire wealth lies in my business, which is bound to the soil[3] of the German Reich.

I am a member of the Association of the German Ladies' Outerwear Industry, Berlin W. 62, 1 Kielganstraße (trade association).

My total annual revenue was as follows:

1934	RM 836,754
1935	RM 719,767
1936 (up to and including September)	RM 608,182

Exports make up approximately 55 to 60 per cent of these revenues.

My company employs:
on-site: 25 retail employees
          22 commercial employees
off-site: 10 outworkers
          37 middlemen.

I request the Chamber of Industry and Commerce to verify the accuracy of my statements. It will certainly have to affirm that these are correct and thus agree with the necessity of granting a five-year passport.[4]

I hereby declare under oath that the foregoing information is accurate and complete.

DOC. 256

Deutsches Recht, 15 December 1936: article on a court judgement against a bequeathal to Jews instead of the legal heirs[1]

On German testators appointing Jews as heirs

In a court judgement reached in the *Local Court of Leipzig* on 29 September 1936 (*Deutsche Justiz*, 1936, p. 1579), the bequeathal to a Jew by a German at the exclusion of the legal heir has been declared *null and void* as it contradicts sound public opinion.

3 The German word 'erdgebunden' is underlined by hand, and there is a question mark in the left margin.
4 After depositing a security of 35,000 Reichsmarks, Block received from the tax office a certificate of non-objection for the issuance of a new passport. He had asked the Reich Ministry of Finance, the Reich Ministry of Economics, and the Chamber of Industry and Commerce to intercede on his behalf with the chief of police in Berlin for an arrangement regarding the issuance of passports valid for five years. The head of the Berlin Tax Office saw no reason to comply with Block's request: letter from the head of the Berlin Tax Office to the Reich Ministry of Finance, dated 10 Feb. 1937: ibid., fols. 249–253.

1 'Zur Erbeinsetzung von Juden durch deutsche Erblasser', *Deutsches Recht*, vol. 6 (1936), nos. 23/24, 15 Dec. 1936, pp. 506–507. This article has been translated from German. The newspaper was published from 1931 to 1945 and edited by Hans Frank. Until 1935 it was the voice of the League of National Socialist German Lawyers, and subsequently of the National Socialist Association of Legal Professionals.

The key points in the opinion of the court are:

In no way would it correspond with sound public opinion or the sense of decency of all those with upstanding views, nor would it be in line with the prevailing public consciousness if – contrary to the goals of National Socialism, which demand a pure separation of the races and a distancing from the Jews in social and economic relationships – Aryan national wealth were to be passed into Jewish hands to the exclusion of legal heirs by the bequeathal to a non-Aryan.

This downright revolutionary ruling of a German court will produce – as we've come to expect! – a *storm of indignation* in the Jewish camp on this side of the border. Certain dark forces, which seem hell-bent on undermining National Socialist jurisdiction, sense new evidence of the 'judicial arbitrariness' of German courts. Is it not the case that universally valid 'human rights' are being violated here? Is it not the case that an indisputable claim for purely private property, arising from a formal and valid will, is being declared invalid against the clear wording of the law purely on the grounds of the heir being a *Jew*?

There is no doubt that the ruling of the Local Court of Leipzig corresponds to the law as it is lived by the people – at least not in the case of those whose very essence is that of the German people, those who live by values based on the roots of a völkisch existence and who recognize these values as enshrined in the Nuremberg Laws. For when it comes to the necessity of the racial laws of our völkisch existence the *legal effect of every type of private disposal has its absolute limit*.

Moreover: in a life that is law-abiding, that bases the order of the people upon the order of family and kin, and that specifically orients the creation of property, at least of land and property, again, towards kin, disposal on account of death can under no circumstances remain a private legal transaction. This has indeed, even in times of unadulterated German legal thinking, never been the case. Hereditary succession in traditional German law is primarily an institution of family law – in the broader sense therefore it is also an institution of racial law and popular law. In a discussion of the Leipzig judgement, the Local Court Judge Friedrich[2] of the Reich Ministry of Justice (in *Deutsche Justiz*, loc. cit.) has already proved that, considering the law in terms of the legal history of German inheritance law, the right of succession according to German legal interpretation is rooted in the family and kin, and that, accordingly, particularly strict requirements are to be made upon the issue of free disposal on account of death, an issue previously unknown to German law.

The Leipzig ruling not only is founded upon current legal thinking but also bears the weight of decisive motives that live on throughout German legal history.

---

2 Kurt Friedrich (b. 1902), lawyer; member of the Roßbach Freikorps in Upper Silesia, 1921; joined the NSDAP in 1932; from 1933 local court judge in the Prussian Ministry of Justice; from 1935 section head of the Ministry of Justice group in Gau department X and section head of the Hanns Kerrl Training Camp; from 1936 higher regional court judge; aide to Roland Freisler in the Reich Ministry of Justice, 1938; from 1938/1939 Ministerialrat there.

The Jewish camp will react with a storm of indignation. In this case this has a *rather particular* attraction. For if there is anyone for whom there is no *honest* way to be outraged by this judgement – the factual considerations aside – it is most certainly the Jew! We only need to cast a brief glance at Jewish law and ask ourselves the question of how, according to this law, the same case would have been decided. What would have been the verdict if a Jew had appointed a non-Jew as his heir under the same circumstances and instead of the Civil Code the Jewish book of law, the *Shulchan Aruch*, had been used?[3]

The succession law in the *Shulchan Aruch* is, like the whole of Jewish law, the instrument of an *inexorable racial policy*, and at that of *specifically Jewish bias* – at least as regards the *motives* or *goals*. The *forms* are those of every type of race legislation: in principle Jewish law only recognizes the law of succession bound to family law based on the parentelic system[4] of legal succession. There is no disinheritance and thus no testator freedom.[5] In the relevant section of the *Shulchan Aruch* it states:

> No person shall be appointed as heir who is not a legitimate heir, and who may thus deny the real heir his inheritance. (*Choshen-Mishpat*,[6] section 281, § 1)

Since, according to Jewish law, a non-Jew cannot enter into legal marriage with a Jew,[7] this stipulation alone renders it impossible for a non-Jew to become heir.

Jewish legal thinking, however, is not quite this clear and straightforward. The Talmudic rabbis have devised a legal loophole to circumvent the quoted provision of inheritance law. This does not formally break the law, but leads in practice to cases of disinheritance and *testator freedom*. A gift bestowed during lifetime and in case of death is valid if it is *only categorized as a gift*.[8]

Thus, does this mean that as a consequence of this complete testator freedom, which exists in practice, a non-Jew can after all actually be appointed as heir? Far from it! If the rabbinical legal practice can contrive such a circumvention manoeuvre, then it is purely out of Jewish interest, and, as soon as the interests of the racial laws are jeopardized, an appropriate safeguard provision will be decreed from the very beginning. The danger that a non-Jew could be appointed heir as a consequence of the complete testator freedom that exists in practice will then be averted by means of a *strict legal provision*. We have an example of this here, in rather classic character, which renders all further discussion superfluous:

---

3 Footnote in the original: 'As evidence of the fact that the *Shulchan Aruch* is by all means a living body of laws that is also recognized by Jews themselves – although the Jewish side likes to maintain the contrary – reference can be made at this point to the book by Hermann Schroer *Blut und Geld im Judentum* [Blood and Money in Judaism] (Munich 1936). Schroer has convincingly refuted this contrary claim by the Jews with numerous quotations from jurisprudential works of Jewish rabbis.'
4 System of parentelic succession: a person and that person's descendants constitute one line of relationship or parentela.
5 Testator freedom gives the testator the freedom to bequeath their estate outside the line of hereditary succession (restricted by the law on compulsory portions).
6 Breastplate of Judgement, one of the four main parts of the *Shulchan Aruch*, deals with civil law.
7 Footnote in the original: 'Compare Schroer, op. cit., pages 13 ff.'
8 Footnote in the original: '*Choshen-Mishpat*, section 281, § 1 ff.'

Should he (the testator), however, say that a gift is to be bestowed upon a named *non-Jew* after his death, *this will not be respected* – for this is akin to saying that one should *commit a sin* with his wealth. (*Choshen-Mishpat*, section 256, § 3)

It is scarcely imaginable that from the point of view of such Jewish legal thinking – despite all the differences regarding the motives – the judgement of the Local Court of Leipzig could cause indignation or even alienation in Jewish circles. Or rather: it is only imaginable when one considers how *genuinely and honestly the Jews are accustomed to playing out the comedies of 'human rights' and suchlike on the world stage*.

Probationary Judge Erbslöh,[9] Wuppertal

DOC. 257
On 18 December 1936 State Secretary Wilhelm Stuckart communicates the draft for an anti-Jewish special tax law to the Reich Ministry of Finance[1]

Letter (secret) from the Reich and Prussian Ministry of the Interior/head of department (I B 2 112/ 5012 g), signed Stuckart, to State Secretary Reinhardt[2] (Reich Ministry of Finance), dated 18 December 1936 (copy for State Secretary from Ministerialrat Blümich[3] B 20/1), with enclosure[4]

Dear Party Comrade Reinhardt,

For some time now discussions have been ongoing regarding the foundation of a Jewish Guarantee Association.[5] According to the latest outcome of these discussions, the execution of such a plan only seems possible in the realm of taxation. For your information on the current situation I enclose the copy of the notes recorded by Reich Minister Dr *Gürtner* and a copy of a sketched preliminary draft of the relevant legal regulations.

---

9 Peter Erbslöh (1907–c.1941), lawyer; probationary judge in Wuppertal-Barmen; joined the NSDAP in 1937.

1 BArch, R 2/31097. Document also in Institut für Zeitgeschichte (ed.), *Akten der Partei-Kanzlei der NSDAP* (hereafter *AdP*), part 1, vol. 2 (Munich: Oldenbourg, 1983), no. 10 322 499–10. This document has been translated from German.
2 Fritz Reinhardt (1895–1969), retailer; from 1919 director of the Thuringian Business School; joined the NSDAP in 1923; Gauleiter of Upper Bavaria, 1929–1931; state secretary in the Reich Ministry of Finance, 1933–1945, and at the same time main department head on the staff of the Deputy of the Führer, 1934–1941; imprisoned, 1945–1949; categorized as a 'major offender' at a denazification trial in Munich, 1950; released after consideration of his custody time, then active as a tax advisor; author of works including *Die Herrschaft der Börse* (1927).
3 Dr Walter Blümich (1888–1950), lawyer and political scientist; from 1920 to 1922 worked for the Sagan tax authorities and then in the Reich Ministry of Finance; on the board of the Kolberg tax authorities, 1922–1924; worked for the Berlin regional tax authorities, 1924–1933; employed in the Reich Ministry of Finance, 1933–1938; joined the NSDAP in 1937; senior tax director in Düsseldorf, 1938–1943; senior tax director in Berlin-Brandenburg, 1943–1945; arrested in 1945; until 1948 employed as a construction worker and on the staff of a tax advisor; later head of the tax department of Deutsche Revisions- und Treuhand AG in Düsseldorf; author of works including *Einkommensteuergesetz* (1943).
4 The original contains handwritten annotations.
5 This refers to the demand for a 'collective liability of the Jews under civil law'.

In the meantime the Führer and Reich Chancellor has in principle approved the plan for levying a special Jewish tax after consultation with Minister Dr *Frick* on the continuation of the Jewish legislation, and ordered the acceleration of the preparations for a corresponding draft bill to allow the possibility of announcing the law after the end of the Gustloff trial.[6] The law would be introduced by the Reich Minister of Finance with the involvement of the Reich Minister of the Interior and the Deputy of the Führer.[7]

I kindly request you to inform me of your opinion on the matter as soon as possible.
With best regards
Heil Hitler!
Your very devoted
signed

Copy of no. I B 2 112/5012 g
Draft of a compensation tax law[8]
§ 1
(1) As compensation for the exemption from collective contributions which are compulsory for state subjects of German or related blood, a surcharge on income tax and property tax will be levied on Jews.

(2) A surcharge on corporate tax will be levied on Jewish companies subject to corporate tax.

(3) The rate of the surcharge will be determined annually by the Reich Minister of Finance in consultation with the Deputy of the Führer and the Reich Minister of the Interior.

§ 2
(1) The proceeds from the surcharges (§ 1) are revenue for the Reich. The individual states and municipalities (associations of local authorities) will not partake in the proceeds.

(2) As a special asset of the Reich, the proceeds will be listed and administered separately from other assets.

§ 3
(1) The Reich Minister of the Interior will decide upon the use of the special assets (§ 2) in consultation with the Deputy of the Führer and the Reich ministers involved.

(2) The special assets may be used to fund the emigration of the Jews from the German Reich.

(3) The special assets may also be used to replace damage caused to the German Reich by the actions of individual Jews.

---

6 The trial of David Frankfurter, who killed the head of the Swiss NSDAP Foreign Organization, Wilhelm Gustloff, on 4 Feb. 1936, took place in Dec. 1936. The court of the Swiss canton Graubünden in Chur sentenced Frankfurter to eighteen years of penal servitude on 14 Dec. 1936. For the reaction to the assassination, see Doc. 225, 5 Feb. 1936.

7 On 9 Feb. 1937 State Secretary Fritz Reinhardt issued an invitation to a meeting of departments on 13 Feb. 1937 and sent the document printed here by express letter to the Reich Foreign Office, the Reich Ministry of Economics, the Deputy of the Führer, the Reich Ministry of Public Enlightenment and Propaganda, Göring, and State Secretary Dr Lammers (Reich Chancellery): BArch, R 2/31097 or *AdP*, part 1, vol. 2, no. 10 322 511.

8 This bill was not passed.

§ 4

In consultation with the Deputy of the Führer and the Reich Minister of the Interior, the Reich Minister of Finance enacts the necessary legislative and administrative regulations for the execution and amendment of the law.

Copy of no. I B 2 112/5012 g
Collective liability of the Jews for damage to the German economy if and when caused by Jews.

It seems clear to me that this concept does not entail joint liability of a criminal but of a material nature.

The concept of making a majority of persons liable for damages occurs frequently in the legal system (liability of general partnerships, liability of a husband for his wife, and similar cases). In all of these cases there is a contextual basis of legal relationships or liability among the jointly liable persons.

The concept of making a majority of persons liable whose members have no common context other than that they all belong to a certain race (a certain political or social group, etc.) is not to be found in the legal system. It is a fact that historically, in battles between two peoples or in times of civil war, this kind of liability was often used. This included the practice of taking hostages by the Roman state, as well as the capture and detainment (with goods and life) of those not personally involved in the destructive actions, but only connected to the liable party through a common race, membership of a certain class, etc., which has been done throughout history.

The use of such strategies seems to me to be viable as a means of warfare but hardly imaginable as a legal provision. This concept has also not entered the realm of minority rights.

One concept that in my opinion should be examined very seriously is this: if Germany introduces such a special collective liability for the Jews, would it not pave the way for states in battle with German minorities on their territory to make use of this legal concept themselves, thus rendering all Germans living on their territory liable for all damages that one German might cause to their economy? This thought does not seem so preposterous to me currently when I think of the Czech lands or perhaps even the United States.

Should one, however, manage to lay all of these misgivings to rest, then in my view the problem could only be solved in the realm of taxation, for example in the following way.

1. In cases of unconscionable damage to the German economy, every German state subject is liable to all German people for the damage.

2. If the perpetrator is a Jew, all Jews of German nationality are liable *in addition*.

3. This collective liability will be enforced by a special tax based, for example, on the property tax or the income tax. The costs of the damage will be covered by the proceeds from this special tax.

4. The procedure will be carried out according to the model of the Revolution Damage Law, but not through the courts.[9]

---

9 The Law on Damages Caused by Civil Unrest of 12 May 1920 made provisions in § 1 that the individual states (*Länder*) were responsible for compensating damages and could transfer this task to the municipalities. According to § 6 the authorities of the states (or the municipalities) formed committees, which were to make decision on claims: *Reichsgesetzblatt*, 1920, p. 941.

DOC. 258
On 21 December 1936 the Gestapo Central Office issues a ban on the public gathering of Jews[1]

Circular decree of the Gestapo Central Office (Gestapa) (II 1 B 2–1319/36 J), signed Heydrich, to the State Police head offices, State Police offices, and to the Regierungspräsidenten and Oberpräsidenten in Prussia for information, dated 21 December 1936

Re: the prohibition of Jewish gatherings and meetings
In light of the fact that distorted reports about orders issued by the Gestapo Central Office regarding the Jewish question have repeatedly been appearing in foreign newspapers,[2] there is a strong suspicion that these tendentious Jewish reports have been passed on to the foreign press by representatives of Jewish organizations.

I therefore order that with immediate effect all Jewish political meetings and gatherings (except gatherings of a religious or cultural nature) be banned until 1 February 1937.[3]

DOC. 259
***Zeitschrift des Vereins für Geschichte Schlesiens*: review of the antisemitic book *The Jews in Germany* (1936)**[1]

[Alfred Schellenberg,[2] Breslau]
18. Jews[3]
201. *The Jews in Germany.* Edited by the Institute for the Study of the Jewish Question. Publisher Franz Eher Nachf. Munich 1936, 416 pp., format 8°. Paperback. RM 6.50

The question of the German Jews is discussed in nine chapters, an introduction, and a conclusion.[4] It begins with the emancipation. We see the development of the Jewish population in Germany from the beginning of the nineteenth century until the present day. We learn of the enormous power of the Jews in economic life, in the press, in poli-

---

1 RGVA, 500k-1-290. This document has been translated from German.
2 These reports could not be found.
3 In the original this is followed by: 'Addendum for Berlin State Police: to the reports dated 17 Nov. 1936 (D 1 A.F. 653/36), 25 Nov. 1936 (D 1 a J 2879/36 and 1879/36).'

1 *Zeitschrift des Vereins für Geschichte Schlesiens*, vol. 70 (1936), p. 534. This document has been translated from German. The journal was edited by Wilhelm Dersch until 1934, and from 1935 by Erich Randt. In 1935 the headings 'Racial Studies', 'Folklore Studies', and 'Jews' appeared for the first time in the journal's review section. The *völkisch* historian Hermann Aubin (1885–1969) was also a member of the editorial staff in 1936.
2 Dr Alfred Schellenberg (b. 1888), writer; joined the NSDAP in 1935; lived in Breslau and, from 1941, in Warsaw; author of *Schlesisches Wappenbuch* (1938) and editor of *Der Sippenforscher* (1938).
3 The number 18 denotes a subject section of the review section, and number 201 denotes the running number of the review.
4 The book's chapters include 'Juden als Träger der Korruption' [Jews as the Bearers of Corruption], 'Die Juden und die Unsittlichkeit' [The Jews and Immorality], and 'Die Kriminalität und rassische Degeneration der Juden' [Criminality and the Racial Degeneration of the Jews].

tics, and in the cultural life of the German people, and see exposed those representatives of corruption and immorality that German courts have had to deal with as typical manifestations of racial degeneration. This book is a book of facts. The principal witnesses are Jews themselves, men such as Rathenau, Weininger,[5] Theilhaber,[6] and Krojanker,[7] whose prophecies of doom were ignored by the Jewish people. Furthermore: files in the departments of the authorities or in courts and, finally, the post-war facts that happened right before our eyes, as known to every sentient German.

The aim of this book is to demonstrate the culpability of the Jews towards the German people and to make it clear to all readers why National Socialism was forced, out of self-defence, to create its laws to solve the Jewish question for Germany in order to heal the German people. This collection of facts therefore is not only a terrible indictment of the Jews in Germany but also a shocking testimony for many of our own people who had no sense of the sinister doings of the Jews in our fatherland. No one – not even a philosemite – can deny the facts presented in this book or dismiss them as 'exceptions'. The material is too monstrous in its sheer scale and impact. This is why the portrayal has chiefly been able to restrict itself to the presentation of *facta*. Its language is clear enough for all who can see or wish to see. We were standing on the edge of the abyss. This book is an academic achievement, which avoids hearsay and unprovable theories, providing evidence for all of its statements. Only in this way is it possible also to convince the detractor and make him understand just why our politics had to solve the Jewish question in this way and in no other, in the interests of a healthy future for the German people.

DOC. 260
Reports on antisemitic measures and incidents in Germany (1936)[1]

Memorandum, undated and unsigned

Individual reports.

'New bathing regulations for the municipal river bathing spots'
The *Wuerzburger General-Anzeiger* (no. 96, 24 April 1936) reports:

> The bathing regulations of 2 May 1930 concerning the municipal river bathing spots and their amendments require a revised version, which was presented in yesterday's

---

5 Dr Otto Weininger (1880–1903), philosopher and writer in Vienna.
6 Felix Aaron Theilhaber (1884–1956), physician; as an active Zionist edited the journal *Palästina*, 1907–1910; doctor in Berlin from 1910; founder of the Society for Sexual Research in Berlin, 1913; in 1935 emigrated to Palestine, where he was co-founder and chairman of the Maccabi health insurance company; author of works including *Der Untergang der deutschen Juden: Eine volkswirtschaftliche Studie* (1911).
7 Dr Gustav Krojanker (1891–1945), journalist; Zionist; worked for the newspapers *Jüdische Rundschau* and *Jüdische Revue*; in 1932 he warned German Jews about National Socialism and emigrated to Palestine, where he worked from the early 1940s for the Hebrew daily newspaper *Haaretz*.

1 CZA, S 7/357. The memorandum was located in the 'Central Bureau for the Settlement of German Jews in Palestine' record group. This document has been translated from German.

council meeting by the speaker, City Councillor Rolf Schmitt.[2] Of the seventeen paragraphs that were read out, emphasis was placed on the regulation that spectators, sufferers of skin diseases, and Jews are not allowed entry to the municipal baths. A bathing ticket has to be obtained for every started three-hour period.

'Disciplinary proceedings due to the attendance of a non-Aryan funeral'

The world-famous brain surgeon Professor Heymann,[3] non-Aryan, Protestant, head of a department at the private Kaiserin-Augusta-Hospital, was dismissed from office on 1 January 1936 and since shot himself dead. A ban on attending his funeral was subsequently issued to the doctors and staff. The ban was issued by the [Party] cell organization within the hospital. However, one nurse and the hospital director, the Aryan and National Socialist Professor Schleier,[4] nonetheless attended the funeral. A disciplinary proceeding with the aim of dismissal was subsequently instituted against him.

'Synagogue converted into beer storage'
The *Westpreussische Zeitung* (Elbing, 16 April 1936) reports:

Deutsch Eylau. The synagogue in Deutsch Eylau was sold at auction for RM 9,000. The winning bid was made by the beer wholesaler Willy Kerber, who plans to install a beer warehouse in the building. The auction was a compulsory sale.

German universities, 1936.

Privy Councillor Professor Neckel,[5] literary historian at the University of Berlin, recently asked an Aryan student about Heinrich Heine in an exam. The student subsequently replied that he would give no answer on this Jew. Neckel then dismissed the student. Disciplinary proceedings are now being instituted against the academic. In spite of the University Law, which allows Jews to study under certain circumstances, the Dean of the Faculty of Philosophy at the University of Berlin, Professor Bieberbach,[6] refuses to award degrees to Jewish students who have completed their doctoral thesis, or he bars them on spurious grounds from taking the doctoral exam.[7]

---

2 Rolf (Rudolf) Schmitt (1904–1972), bank clerk; worked at the municipal power station in Würzburg, 1924–1933; joined the NSDAP in 1928 and the SS in 1939; from 1933 Würzburg city councillor; worked in the private sector from 1945.
3 Dr Emil Heymann (1878–1936), physician; chief physician in the department of surgery at the Kaiserin-Augusta-Hospital in Berlin; on leave from 1935; committed suicide in 1936.
4 Correctly: Dr Karl Robert Schlayer (1875–1937), physician; professor in Tübingen, 1912–1913, and in Munich, from 1913; from 1921 director of the Kaiserin-Augusta-Hospital in Berlin; co-editor of the *Zeitschrift für Urologie* and co-author of *Das pathologisch-physiologische Lehrbuch* (1922).
5 Dr Gustav Neckel (1878–1940), philologist; from 1920 professor of Nordic philology at the University of Berlin, in Göttingen from 1935 to 1937, and again in Berlin from 1937.
6 Dr Ludwig Bieberbach (1886–1982), mathematician; joined the SA in 1933 and the NSDAP in 1937; professor of mathematics from 1913 to 1915 in Basel, from 1915 to 1921 in Frankfurt am Main, and from 1921 to 1945 in Berlin, where he was dean of the faculty of philosophy (1935–1936) and dean of the faculty of mathematics and science (from 1936); editor of the journal *Deutsche Mathematik*, 1936–1942.

From German cities and spa towns in the Olympic year

In *Bad Toelz* Jewish spa guests are being refused a spa card, in spite of the Summer Olympics.

In *Bad Brueckenau* Jewish fathers of families were rounded up and imprisoned on 29 March by the SA. They were released the following day.

In *Wuerzburg* spurious excuses are given to arrest particularly wealthy Jews, who are released after paying high fines.

In a *Berlin vocational school* the following topic was set: 'The Jews are our misfortune'. A Jewish pupil who refused to address the topic was given a bad grade.

Only fifteen mourners permitted at Jewish funeral

In the Regierungsbezirk of Arnsberg in Westphalia the Landrat has ordered that Jewish funerals have to be conducted in silence. The city mayor added that Jewish funerals may not take place after 8 a.m. or before 6 p.m. Upon the death of a Jewish war invalid in another city of this district, the relatives requested permission to conduct a funeral procession through the city. This was allowed, but with the instruction that no more than fifteen persons were permitted to follow the coffin.

DOC. 261

Walter Gottheil talks about his life in a small German town in 1936[1]

Submission by Walter Gottheil[2] to a Harvard University competition (1940)

[…][3]

The year 1936 came around. Hitler had already been ruling in Germany for three years. The Nuremberg Laws had been announced. For many Jews, they meant extraordinarily harsh measures. They did not actually apply to me, as our religious community, to which we had to pay tax, was in a neighbouring larger city. The Jews in our town,

---

7 One example was the doctoral candidate Abraham Heller, who was not granted his degree certificate. The degree was not conferred upon him until 1992, when he was living in Israel. See Loose, 'Verfemt und vergessen', pp. 219–241. For more on Heller's doctoral thesis, see Doc. 234, spring 1936.

1 Walter Gottheil, 'Mein Leben in Deutschland vor und nach dem 30. Januar 1933' [My life in Germany before and after 30 January 1933] (Jan. 1940), pp. 49–52; Harvard Competition, no. 81. This document has been translated from German.
2 Walter Gottheil (b. 1888), retailer; emigrated to Palestine in late 1938/early 1939 with his wife and his 16-year-old son.
3 The complete report has sixty-six pages. Gottheil starts with an account of his childhood and of his apprenticeship in a non-Jewish firm and later in a Berlin textile company. At first he was an active Social Democrat, later a Zionist. The final section of the report describes the period after 1933. Gottheil had to give up the shop he had inherited from his father by the end of 1933 as a result of the boycott.

however, wanted to regulate their own cultural affairs and had therefore founded their own religious society. In order to avoid double taxation, they left the official religious community by means of an official declaration of the local court, as a result of religious concerns, as they put it. Now, according to the Nuremberg Laws, they were all fully Jewish, as despite their official dissident status (they still felt Jewish) they all had two Jewish parents.

I, on the other hand, had one Aryan parent and two Aryan grandparents, so I was a first-degree Mischling. I could have had special treatment, which would have meant a separation from my family. Sadly I know of cases where this actually happened. But I also know enough Aryan women who moved abroad with their Jewish husbands, preferring to put up with that hardship than subject themselves to these regulations.

Yes, there were different kinds of people among the Germans, just as there are in other nations too. For thirty years we had been placing joint orders with our neighbour for butter from Schleswig-Holstein, a butter-producing region. Butter started to become scarce. Göring's words 'Guns are more important than butter' came up. So what did our neighbour do? As the portions delivered in the weekly packages started getting smaller, he simply excluded us from further distribution. The increase in *his* butter ration was justified on national political grounds. You could get away with doing anything to the Jews – this idea was gradually becoming widespread in the minds of the German population. Of course they condemned this and that, things that other people did, but when it came to their own self-interest, they thoroughly exploited this motto. At the beginning of the National Socialist regime they always quoted point 24 of the manifesto: 'Public interest above self-interest.' But later it went pretty quiet even when it came to this point.[4]

In the family too I was made to feel the influence of antisemitic slogans. My son was starting his seventh year at school. Almost the whole class was in the Hitler Youth. He was no longer allowed to take part in school trips. When they went swimming he had to be present, as it was school time, but he was not allowed to undress and swim with the others; apparently the little Jewish boy could turn the water in the big river into a health hazard. There was teasing and bullying, which got worse and worse; the children's souls became more antisemitic and more toxic. One day he came home during school time in a flood of tears and said he would rather die than have to put up with it any longer. What could be done? School was still compulsory. There was a Jewish school in a neighbouring village but it was already full and was not taking in any more pupils. So I had to undertake the difficult trip to the school and beseech a remedy to the problem there. But remedy what exactly? Something the state was commanding its citizens to do every day as the most important task in life. In all honesty I have to remark that most of the head teachers from the old days were vehemently opposed to the abuse and bullying of Jewish pupils. Most of them, I emphasize, not all of them! We were lucky. We were promised corrective actions and the punishment of the culprits should it happen again. Yes, one of the teachers, an old conservative, royalist gentleman, again warned the pupils in no uncertain terms not to hurt or scorn anybody on the grounds of their faith. Still, I had had enough of the situation; two months later it was Easter, and at this point I took my boy out of school and sent him to an agricultural training camp near Berlin.

---

4 This is a reference to the NSDAP programme of 1920.

I know of other cases, of parents and children who did not have such a good experience. The attitude of the population, as well as that of the authorities, was always inconsistent. That could be clearly seen in the way the Jews from Poland were treated. The Third Reich needed friends, and it found them in the Polish state.[5] Poland's friendship with Germany was now of benefit to their nationals in the Reich. Almost all of them were Ostjuden; those Ostjuden, Galicians, Planjes, and Polacks,[6] the fight against whom had used up so much rhetorical energy. The Ostjuden thoroughly exploited this privilege – they too turned out to be the sort who had previously always denied their origins. They proudly wore the red and white ribbon with the Polish eagle in their buttonhole. And just as the majority of German Jews did not want to admit that in Germany, too, antisemitism would be a problem for them, the Polish Jews thought that they alone would be safe. But what an ignominious disappointment lay ahead of them all. They had it good in the first years of Hitler's government. Although life was made difficult for them at the fair, one of their main areas of business, as I have already written, still they stayed. Riots followed. Their goods were dragged from the stalls and trampled into the ground or thrown into the gutter; their stands were smashed to bits. But one call to the nearest Polish consulate sufficed and peace was restored. The community paid full compensation.[7] None of this was supposed to reach the higher authorities. Hitler certainly paid for his Polish friendship in his first years of government. I knew a Jewish-Polish market trader who, as an Austrian soldier – his home was in Galicia – had been seriously injured in the World War. He had been wounded as an ally. This man had the canopy of his stall ripped to shreds and was badly set upon. On reporting this to the police, the following suggestion was made to him, with which he agreed. He should give up his market stall, then the other Aryan traders would be happy, and he would be paid decent support from welfare funds, on which he could live. Everyone is happy. That's it! One year later it was a different story. At a company that bought up raw materials, all the suppliers were rounded up and told that they would lose their trading licences if they supplied goods to Jews. That was the end of the line with the Jews too, although this was less painful.

Little by little the appearance of German towns became animated with something that always fills Germans, young and old, with enthusiasm – military presence. Every German is a born soldier, not just men and boys but women too – the female youth in particular goes into raptures over it. When a military band comes, both sexes march along equally to the rigid marching beat. The construction of new barracks and their administrative buildings – all of this contributed to a visible economic upturn, which could also be seen by the increasing number of motor vehicles.

Only the tenant of my shop, who had either missed an opportunity or thought he could teach the Jews a lesson, was dissatisfied and pestered me continually about a reduction in the rent. I assume he believed that once he was in the building, he would take it over, and now progress was too slow for him, as a veteran Party comrade. In any case, he tried everything he could. He reported me to the police for rent extortion, but was

---

5 This is a reference to the German–Polish rapprochement after the non-aggression pact of 26 Jan. 1934: *Reichsgesetzblatt*, 1934, II, pp. 117–119.
6 Galicians, Planjes, and Polacks: pejorative terms for Jews and Poles.
7 On the intervention of Polish diplomats in support of Jewish retailers, see Doc. 45, 22 May 1933.

turned down. Then he tried it with the tenants' association, which was also unsuccessful. The Party came along as the next authority; I was summoned and once told by a man that I should give in, as I would never win in court as a Jew. I rejected this suggestion indignantly and told him that *I* would never have allowed myself this kind of claim. But this constant harassment does wear one down, and that, after all, was its purpose.

Many of my former acquaintances profited from the flourishing economy. Some found employment, or their children did. In brief, every connection to the regime caused one person more to stop greeting us in the street, and there were so many other little details. Lots of Jews moved away. Our stay was made difficult too. We could not go into any village in the neighbourhood any more, as we were greeted everywhere with signs: 'Jews not welcome', 'No Jews allowed', 'No room for Jews here', and whatever other nuances there were.

My old home, where I was born and had lived for over fifty years, where I had been respected and esteemed, in good times and in bad, in which I had lived, felt, and thought, had no place for me and those like me any longer. We had become superfluous. We cleared out our apartment and did the same as many Jews who got rid of their furnishings; the first Four-Year Plan was almost over, it drove us away from our previous domicile, and we moved to Berlin.

[...]8

DOC. 262
Ernst Marcus reports on the fears of the Jewish middle class in Breslau in 1936/1937[1]

Submission by Ernst Marcus[2] to a Harvard University competition (1940)

[...]3

In the years 1936/37 the 'living space' of our existence became ever smaller; fear and danger grew from day to day. We knew that anything careless we might say on the telephone or a thoughtless comment in a letter could lead to interrogations by the State Police, arrests, or a concentration camp. A Breslau retailer was summoned to the State Police and subjected to an interrogation for hours on account of alleged communist connections. He was threatened with imprisonment; he claimed never to have been a communist. What finally transpired was the following: the person concerned had been in a Silesian mountain town a while before. From there he made several telephone calls to his office and occasionally asked about a consignment from *Muskau*, a little town in

---

8 Gottheil subsequently describes his move to Berlin, the year 1938, the November pogroms, and his incarceration in Sachsenhausen concentration camp.

1 Ernst Marcus, 'Mein Leben in Deutschland vor und nach dem 30. Januar 1933' [My life in Germany before and after 30 January 1933] (1940), pp. 48–49; Harvard Competition, no. 124. This document has been translated from German.

2 Dr Ernst Marcus (b. 1890), lawyer; practised law in Breslau, 1922–1938; he emigrated to the USA in 1940.

3 The entire report, sent from New York, comprises 130 pages. At the start of this account, Marcus reports on his youth, the period of his university studies in Breslau and Munich, his work in the judiciary, his time as a lawyer in Breslau, and then the period after 1933.

Lower Silesia. The telephone operator listening in on the call had understood *Moscow* instead of Muskau and informed the police.

At the time a rumour was circulating that the staff at the telephone exchange, who occasionally came to inspect the telephone sets, had built in a bugging device so that everything being said around the telephone set could be heard, even if the telephone set was not in use. It was said that in this way conversations were overheard and those concerned arrested. I have never found out whether these rumours were true. The mere presence of a telephone sufficed to become a source of fear. Many people did not dare to speak loudly in the room where the telephone was.

One can have an idea of life's sense of insecurity if one considers that even abroad we no longer felt safe. People who returned from trips abroad were accused of having read anti-German newspapers such as the *Pariser Tageblatt*, and if they denied it, they were shown photographs taken by spies abroad. In 1936 I wanted to read a pamphlet that had just appeared in Marienbad, in which a former Nazi addressed the Reichstag fire and the events of 30 June 1934,[4] etc. I did not dare to buy the pamphlet in Marienbad, but instead made use of a temporary stay in Carlsbad, read it behind closed doors, and then got rid of it in the woods. As a consequence of these anxieties and the shock upon each return trip, our last trips abroad were hardly relaxing for my wife.

Spending time with friends no longer brought the recuperation and relaxation it once had, either. Only a handful of them managed to distance themselves, at least for a few hours, from the terrors of the day and the fears for the future.

[...][5]

DOC. 263

Pariser Tageszeitung, 28 January 1937: article on the practice of pursuing and punishing cases of race defilement in Germany[1]

One year of judicial practice based on 'The protection of blood'...

Death penalty for 'race defilement' / New 'chambers for the protection of blood' as extraordinary courts against Jews / The exact number of victims of this law in its first year.

As the year came to a close a few weeks ago, the year in which, following the 'Nuremberg Laws' of 1935, the 'protection of German blood' was implemented in practice by the judiciary, exact figures regarding the number of – in almost all cases – Jewish victims of this racial fanaticism were published for the first time. The Reich Ministry of Justice itself informed that part of the world interested in judiciary matters within its reach that, up to the effective date of 25 November 1936, a precise total of 299 legally valid sentenced cases of 'race defilement' are known and a further 125 cases were already pending in the relevant courts. However, what is not included in this one year's 'haul' are the cases that

---

4 The author is referring to the so-called Night of the Long Knives. See Glossary.
5 Passages follow on the persecution in 1938, preparation for emigration, the position of lawyers, and the impact of National Socialism on the German population.
1 'Ein Jahr "Blutschutz"-Justiz', *Pariser Tageszeitung*, 28 Jan. 1937, pp. 1–2. This article has been translated from German.

on the given date were in a preliminary stage of investigation by either the police or the public prosecutor's office.

This official Reich listing of the figures corresponds more or less to the last (December) monthly report of the emigrant chairman of the German Social Democrat Party, who reported around one hundred cases with the exact names of the convicted and locations of the courts, and indeed only such cases that have come to light in Prague in the past four months.[2]

All of the sentences for 'race defilement' ranged between an average of one or two years of prison or penal servitude. Particularly harsh sentences, which are certainly not rare, meant three years of penal servitude and the very 'lenient' sentences, which were even rarer, were four or six months in prison.

Reluctant judges

On the very occasion of the first anniversary of Hitler Germany's 'protection of blood' law, it came to light how little the developments within this most abominable of all neo-barbarisms can be seen as completed, and which truly 'unexpected methods' the National Socialist regime reserves the right to implement against court authorities that out of an instinct of self-preservation are – partly – reluctant and at least passively resistant. In fact this one year in which the 'protection of blood' has been implemented by the judiciary was actually, particularly following the nervous and agitated internal statements of the Reich Ministry of Justice on the subject, filled by a harsh and dogged battle between the highest judicial authorities under the immediate control of the 'Führer' himself and his high-ranking specialist representatives such as Roland Freisler, state secretary in the Reich Ministry of Justice, 'Staatsrat and Reichstag delegate' on the one hand, who have continually and tirelessly pushed for the tightening of the already enacted 'legal' status, and on the other hand the lower-ranking members of the judiciary, chiefly the judges themselves. They, out of self-respect and consideration for public opinion which surrounds them chiefly in the western cities, and certainly for many a good reason otherwise, have rather been striving to achieve the opposite. Barely four months after the legislation on the 'protection of blood' came into force, a circular decree from Gürtner, the Reich Minister of Justice, was issued to all public prosecutors on 2 April 1936 proclaiming that 'the interim period is now over'. This instruction pertained expressly to the practice in court of generally applying leniency in cases where the 'racially defiling' relationship had already begun before the passing of the Nuremberg Laws; this appears now to be 'no longer applicable under any circumstances'. The circular decree ends with the draconian command: 'All average cases are deserving of penal servitude!'[3]

Throughout the year 1936 this 'bridling of men', as practised by Hitler, his man Freisler, and also Gürtner, the Reich Minister of Justice himself, but chiefly by local Nazi

---

2 The list of cases of race defilement for the period Sept. to Dec. 1936 contains the names of the convicted and their sentences, most of which were for more than a year in prison. The report includes twelve cases for Breslau, nine for Hamburg, and six for Berlin that had become known in Prague: Behnken (ed.), *Deutschland-Berichte der Sozialdemokratischen Partei Deutschlands*, vol. 3, pp. 1660–1664. Under the title 'Eine Liste des Grauens' (A List of Horrors), *Der Stürmer*, no. 51, Dec. 1936, lists in a special edition for the whole of Germany 358 verdicts with names and sentences in 1936: DHM, D2A09339.

agencies, who in most cases themselves act as the informers against 'race defilers', continued in the face of clear passive resistance within the German 'self-righteous Reich judiciary'. It furthermore took on an increasingly unequivocal form, which did not stop at widespread threats against the 'reaction of the judiciary'. One internal ministerial circular provides instructions, for example, for what should be done if 'the couple moved abroad to commit their deed', therefore presenting a case of a 'typical attempt to evade laws', which would be a matter above all for the border courts.[4]

One last circular from last autumn[5] even criticizes in the most disparaging tones the 'unjustified, obvious differences in sentences passed in different regions of the Reich'. At the same time it issues an order that puts a new face on the current egregious situation and will characterize the future:

By means of this ministerial ordinance, 'chambers for the protection of blood' – as is the official expression! – are established forthwith in all larger cities of the Reich. Every case of 'defilement of German blood' will now appear before a special court!

That was – up to now – the latest response of a regime faced with what seem to be the last vestiges of judicial morality within its legal profession, the cautious rearing up of a last shred of decency from those who appear to 'conform'. In any case, this has made the situation considerably worse for those, mainly Jews, affected by the law.[6]

The new tightening of the law
This arises chiefly from the following: in one of their last sessions, the so-called 'Criminal Law Commission', now under the chairmanship of the aforementioned State Secretary Freisler, expressly proclaimed: 'In view of the continuation of race defilement in Germany, a tightening of the previous range of sentences is to be undertaken.'[7] Now arising from a semi-official commentary on this decision written by Freisler himself in

---

3 Circular decree issued by the Reich Ministry of Justice (1121 II a 18 501/36) regarding the application of the Law for the Protection of German Blood and German Honour of 15 Sept. 1935: see Walk (ed.), *Das Sonderrecht für die Juden im NS-Staat*, p. 159.
4 This ministerial circular could not be found.
5 Freisler (Reich Ministry of Justice) had demanded stricter sentences for those convicted of race defilement in accordance with the Nuremberg Laws: circular decree issued by the Reich Ministry of Justice (1120 – III a 28 031/36) to the president of the Higher Regional Court, and to the chief public prosecutors for information, 1 Sept. 1936. Published in Ilse Staff (ed.), *Justiz im Dritten Reich: Eine Dokumentation* (Frankfurt am Main: Fischer, 1978), pp. 91–92. Following a decision of the Reich Supreme Court issued on 7 Jan. 1937, race defilement existed even when there was only an attempt at sexual intercourse: ibid., pp. 177–178.
6 In 1936, 102 men (mostly Jews) were accused of race defilement before Berlin courts. Of the accused, 53 were given prison sentences of three to twelve months, 37 were given prison sentences of over one year, and 7 were sentenced to penal servitude. One of the accused received a fine: *Statistisches Jahrbuch der Stadt Berlin*, vol. 14: 1938 (Berlin: Statistisches Amt der Reichshauptstadt Berlin/Kühn, 1939), pp. 206–207. In 1937, 149 men (mostly Jews) were accused of race defilement before Berlin courts, of whom 128 were convicted. Half of them were sentenced to penal servitude: *Statistisches Jahrbuch der Stadt Berlin*, vol. 15: 1939 (Berlin: Statistisches Amt der Reichshauptstadt Berlin/Kühn, 1943), pp. 209–210.
7 For more on the Criminal Law Commission, see Doc. 121, 5 June 1934.

the specialist journal *Deutsches Strafrecht*,[8] which he edits, are the considerations under which the commission came to this conclusion, from which the logical consequences regarding the extent of the planned tightening of sentences arise. From now on, 'race defilement' is to be categorized within a realm of criminal law first introduced by Hitler as the largely confusing complex of 'treason against the people'. The confusion, however, does not prevent this complex from being tied to that of 'treason against the country'. In Hitler's Reich, under aggravating circumstances, both treason against the country and treason against the people are punishable by death. 'Race defilement' would then be regarded as a serious case of 'treason against the people'.

Affection is not affection
Every accused Jewish 'race defiler' now has to stand trial in a special court, one in which the accused has virtually no rights. How else should a situation be described in which the mighty Freisler has issued the following general instructions to the courts to deal with the two different kinds of self-defence of the accused?

1. In the event that the accused Jew claims to have acted not out of passion but out of affection, therefore citing a decent human motive for his misdeed with the aim of receiving a more lenient sentence, Freisler instructs the responsible 'Chambers for the protection of blood' in the following way: 'In the opinion of the legislator, which is alone decisive (!), such "affection" is unnatural. Therefore it is not affection. If it is established that a longer relationship has existed, this is a reason to tighten and not to mitigate the punishment.'

2. The accused Jew claims in his defence not to have acted out of affection but truly out of lust, such as a thoughtless act with a prostitute. According to Freisler, in cases such as this, the special court is to follow this instruction:

> May public prosecutors and courts prevent a race defilement trial from being carried out at the expense of the abused German woman. May the court consider that nothing is more repugnant than allowing a Jew who has violated a German woman to dig around in her past in order to pin something on her which proves her lack of credibility as a witness (mostly as the only witness for the prosecution).[9]

---

8 The criminal law journal *Deutsches Strafrecht* with the subtitle 'Strafrecht, Strafrechtspolitik, Strafprozeß' (Criminal Law, Policy, and Proceedings) appeared from 1934 to 1944 as one of the successors to the *Justiz-Ministerialblatt für die preußische Gesetzgebung und Rechtspflege*, which was founded in 1839. *Deutsches Strafrecht* was published by the Reich Ministry of Justice and State Secretary Freisler.
9 These quotations can be found largely verbatim in Roland Freisler's article on legal practice based on the 'protection of blood': 'Ein Jahr Blutschutzrechtsprechung in Deutschland: Erfahrungen und Lehren', *Deutsches Strafrecht*, nos. 11/12, Nov./Dec. 1936, pp. 385–397.

DOC. 264
On 1 February 1937 Reinhard Heydrich informs the Deputy of the Führer about the granting of public house licences to Jews[1]

Letter from the Reichsführer SS/Chief of the German Police in the Reich and Prussian Ministry of the Interior (S.-PP (II B) 2265/36), p.p. signed by Heydrich, to the Deputy of the Führer in Munich, Brown House, dated 1 February 1937 (copy)[2]

Re: the establishment of Jewish taverns in Munich.
I enclose a copy of[3]

(a) the regulation of 16 March 1936[4] regarding the new establishment of public houses and taverns;

(b) the circular decree issued by the Reich and Prussian Minister of the Interior on 16 March 1936 regarding the new establishment of public houses and taverns;[5]

(c) the circular decree issued by the Reichsführer SS and Chief of the German Police in the Reich Ministry of the Interior on 11 July 1936 on the new establishment of public houses and taverns;[6]

(d) the decree issued by the Reich and Prussian Minister of Economics on 11 December 1936 regarding public house laws.[7]

The question of the establishment of Jewish public houses is now legislated in accordance with the standards applied in the Reich (a–c is the current legal status in Prussia) in such a way that in principle there are no objections to the establishment of Jewish public houses, so long as the requirements stipulated in the decree of the Reichsführer SS and Chief of the German Police dated 11 July 1936 and in the decree of the Reich and Prussian Minister of Economics dated 11 December 1936 are met, and the general preconditions (requirements etc.) are met.

In compliance with the Nuremberg Laws, this accords a further means of driving the Jews back into a ghetto, restraining them from patronizing German public houses and thus separating them more vigorously than before from those of German blood. This regulation should also be approved as regards security and policing aspects. As has already been seen in practice, it grants the police authorities better opportunities for supervision than if Jews and the German-blooded population mix in one place. Given these beneficial conditions, the consideration that Jewish taverns could constitute danger zones for individual actions can be ruled out. Indeed, no such individual actions have been observed of late.

1 BArch, NS 25/836, fols. 3–4. This document has been translated from German.
2 The letter was sent on 18 Feb. 1937 from the NSDAP Deputy of the Führer/Munich Staff to the NSDAP Main Office for Municipal Policy in Munich: ibid., fol. 1.
3 Typewritten note in the margin: 'The regulations referred to here are not enclosed.'
4 According to the decree, Jews in Prussia were only permitted to open public houses if the patrons were exclusively Jewish: Preußisches Staatsministerium (ed.), *Preußische Gesetzsammlung* (Berlin: Decker, 1936), p. 81.
5 This decree could not be found.
6 This decree could not be found.
7 The decree of the Reich Minister of Economics was based on the Prussian regulation of 16 March 1934: BArch, NS 25/836, fol. 2.

DOC. 265

On 8 February 1937 the Israelite Association for Old Age Benefits and Nursing Care applies to the Regierungspräsident in Hanover for a permit to collect donations[1]

Letter from the Israelite Association for Old Age Benefits and Nursing Care in Hanover, 16 Ellernstraße, Wolfes[2] and Spiegelberg,[3] to the Regierungspräsident in Hanover, dated 8 February 1937 (copy)[4]

In line with the Collections Law, we request that a permit be issued to us:
to allow for the distribution of the enclosed business report within the Regierungsbezirk of Hanover and also, in the interests of our association, to collect membership fees and donations.

Please allow us to explain the reason for this application as follows:

Our association was granted legal personhood by royal decree on 22 May 1890. According to the statutes as approved by the Regierungspräsident, the purpose of our association is the operation of a home and hospital for the elderly. It therefore pursues aims that, until recently, were generally recognized as charitable and non-profit-making. As it is necessary to care for the elderly and sick if they are not to become a burden to society, the aims of our association are such that, still today, they are deserving of financial support, since they serve the public interest.

For reasons we do not need to list in detail, revenues have fallen continuously over the previous years. As the running costs can be cut only marginally, the association has been running at a permanently increasing loss. Last year this loss was around RM 9,442. In addition there are costs and write-offs to a sum of around RM 4,500. The loss account for 1936 will therefore close at RM 13,945.64. In order to keep the association running, it is necessary that membership fees and donations now be solicited. We request that the association is thus given this opportunity by granting our permit application.

The Israelite Association for Old Age Benefits and Nursing Care in Hanover[5]
[Hans Wolfes] & Spiegelberg[6]

The Israelite Association for Old Age Benefits and Nursing Care in Hanover.
Annual report 1936.
Unfortunately we have no positive news regarding the reporting year 1936. Even more regrettably, we cannot see the prospect of improvement in the foreseeable future. Rather, we must brace ourselves for a further worsening of the situation. The number of *days when meals are provided* has fallen by around 13 per cent compared with 1935, after a fall of 14 per cent was already recorded in 1935. This negative development is due to the fact

---

1 BArch, R 1501/27713, fols. 418–419. This document has been translated from German.
2 Hans Wolfes (1876–1945), retailer and chairman of the board of trustees of the Jewish hospital in Hanover; emigrated to Luxembourg at the end of June 1939, and later to Argentina.
3 John Spiegelberg (b. 1868), banker and long-serving board member of the Israelite Association for Old Age Benefits and Nursing Care in Hanover; emigrated to the USA in May 1938.
4 The original is underlined by hand in several places.
5 Stamp.
6 Handwritten signatures.

that the health insurance companies make very little use of our establishment, as the proportion of Jewish patients has increased by 36 per cent and their actual number by 16 per cent.

The informative *comparative figures* of the last five business years are as follows:

	1932	1933	1934	1935	1936
Treated cases	773	690	731	702	608
Days when meals provided	17,013	15,760	16,310	14,034	11,933
Percentage of Jewish patients	23.5	26.7	23.5	32.8	44.8
Average occupied beds per day	46.6	43.6	44.7	38.4	33.4
Length of treatment in days	22.1	22.6	22.8	20	19.5

Clinical operations ran as normal.

The *observance of the dietary laws* caused considerable difficulty. The quality of the meat delivered from Paraguay was often poor and supplies from elsewhere were insufficient.[7] As a result, complaints about the food were vociferous. We therefore had to decide, with a heavy heart, to renege on the provision of ritually-prepared food, although we have managed to adhere to the regulations in particular on the separation of dairy and meat dishes. Residents of the home for the elderly and patients for whom it is important continue to be served ritually-prepared food.

Revenue was:	RM 103,582.05
Expenditure was:	RM 113,024.62
Resulting in a deficit of	RM 9,442.57
In addition there is the sum of resulting from the technical transfer of our claims to the health insurance firms.	RM 2,341.19
	RM 11,783.76

---

[7] From April 1933 kosher slaughter was prohibited in Germany. Kosher meat therefore had to be imported for Orthodox Jews.

DOC. 266
On 18 February 1937, 16-year-old Werner Angress describes his reaction to the suicide of his group leader in the Groß-Breesen retraining camp[1]

Handwritten diary of Werner Angress,[2] entry for 18 February 1937

Groß-Breesen,[3] 18 February 1937.

Hannio[4] is dead! Three short, banal-sounding words, but what weight these words have. I didn't write about it straight away, partly because I couldn't and partly because I didn't get around to it. Hannio took his own life in the early hours of 2 February in a hotel in Breslau. It sounds so terribly brutish and cold when I write it like that, but I'm doing it so I don't get too sentimental – that would be worse. Hannio was physically weak, he was ill, he had a kidney disease and didn't feel capable of becoming a settler abroad. After so many failed attempts at other jobs and in other communities, he had finally built his whole life up on Breesen. That was his inner reason. What prompted it was that when the money from the canteen was counted during his shift, several hundred marks were missing. He was summoned and he claimed he didn't know where the money was. Although they believed him, the money was still missing. In this frame of mind, and with the feeling that he might not be able to come along and join the settlers,[5] that he had to leave Groß Breesen due to his illness as well as the unresolved issue of the canteen money, that he didn't want to watch everyone else emigrate one by one while he would have to stay behind, and because he loved Gr[oß] Breesen, he took an overdose of sleeping pills, from which he died on Tuesday, 2 February, at five o'clock in the morning.

When it comes to the canteen matter, Hannio may have been rather slovenly and careless, but he was honest. Hannio was certainly not a dishonest person. Hannio was my leader, ever since he wrested me away from Gert's[6] influence. Most recently he was also my friend. His loss is barely perceptible here any more, at least not on the outside.

---

1 Werner Angress, 'Tagebuch' [early May 1936 until 6 May 1941], (no pagination), Archives of the Leo Baeck Institute, New York, at the Jüdisches Museum Berlin, Sammlung Werner Angress. This document has been translated from German.
2 Dr Werner Thomas Angress (1920–2010), historian; apprenticeship in Groß-Breesen, 1936–1937; emigrated to the Netherlands in Oct. 1937 and from there to the USA in 1939; soldier in the US Army, 1941–1945; later professor of European history, first at Berkeley, then at Stony Brook, New York. Returned to Berlin in 1988. Author of works including …*immer etwas abseits: Jugenderinnerungen eines jüdischen Berliners* (2005). For more on his emigration, see Doc. 310, 20 Nov. 1937.
3 Groß-Breesen (Kreis Trebnitz in Silesia): the facility was set up in a rented manor by the Reich Representation of Jews in Germany in April 1936 as a retraining camp. The purpose was to provide agricultural training to groups of Jewish youths emigrating abroad. From 1939 Groß-Breesen was subject to increasing coercion. Its final residents were deported to Auschwitz in 1943.
4 Hermann Ollendorf (c.1917–1937) came from Breslau. His nickname was Hannio, an amalgamation of two literary figures in Thomas Mann's works, Hanno Buddenbrooks and Tonio Kröger.
5 The purpose of the camp was to organize a group migration abroad, which, however, failed. Nonetheless, most of the youths were able to leave Germany, with or without their families.
6 Gert Lippmann (b. 1914), the last nationwide leader of the youth organization Black Pennant (Schwarzes Fähnlein); emigrated to Paris in 1935 and fought for the Resistance during the German occupation; from 1946 lived in Australia, where he later became the owner of an insurance company.

Life goes on. Just like back then with Stella, there is just a gaping hole inside.[7] Two friends, two boys from the group, from Hannio's group, in just half a year. Hannio is missed everywhere, and now Bondy is the group leader.[8] Jochen[9] is in charge of the technical standards division. But we miss Hannio. Of course we haven't forgotten him. You can't forget a person you liked, one you owe so much to, and one you miss. Hannio's wish was that we go on working, in the group and on ourselves, just the way he showed us. I'm only just writing about it today because I've calmed down a little. I have a heavy responsibility just like all the other lads who are important in the group, in his group. We're still 'Hannio's boys', on the outside at least, and hopefully on the inside too. When I read through what I've just written, I have the feeling I haven't written what I'm really thinking. But I suppose that's a good thing. I want to be tough. 'Toughen up, Töp,[10] you've got to!' was what Hannio said at the end of every talk. Yes, I want to! Without wanting it to sound like a cliché, I keep going, and look ahead. I hope it works out with our group – I'll do my bit to make sure it does. I think the Prinz-Töpper-Stefan friendship is working. I want to do all I can to ensure that too. Hannio showed us all the way, we only have to follow it. 'The path to becoming a personality from being a member of the group is through toughness with oneself!' That's the path Hannio showed me and the one I want to follow.

Hannio was no coward. Hannio never acted on impulse, he was consistent. He did everything for Groß-Breesen! Once he had denounced this idea and saw it crumble, he packed it all in, he thought his life was pointless. People always praise the dead, but I don't. I knew Hannio's faults, but I also knew his strengths. And one of them was 'When I've decided to do something and I think it's right, then I do it.' With this thought in mind, he committed this deed. No, Hannio was not a coward. He will always be my leader.

7 A reference to Herbert Stern (1919–1936) from Nuremberg. He drowned while bathing in Groß-Breesen on 30 August 1936: see the diary entry of Werner Angress for 30 August 1936, Angress, 'Tagebuch'.
8 Dr Curt Bondy (1894–1972), psychologist; worked at the Hahnöfersand prison for young offenders near Hamburg, 1921–1923; later head of the Eisenach juvenile prison; professor of social education in Göttingen, 1930–1933; after his dismissal worked for the Jewish Relief Agency in Frankfurt am Main; leader of the Groß-Breesen retraining camp, 1936–1939; emigrated in 1939 to Britain and in 1941 to the USA, where he was professor at Richmond, VA; professor and head of the Psychology Institute of the University of Hamburg, 1951–1959.
9 Jochen Feingold (1919–c.2002), apprentice in Groß-Breesen from May 1936; emigrated in 1939 to Kenya, where he worked as a farmer and later as an advisor to the Kenyan government; later lived in England.
10 Werner Angress's nickname was Töp or Töpper.

DOC. 267

Advertisement for the antisemitic play *The Dancing Jew*, enclosed in a letter from the Franz Wulf publishing house dated 20 February 1937[1]

Advertising flyer enclosed with a letter from the Franz Wulf publishing house[2] to the National Socialist Association of Teachers,[3] Reich Administration, dated 20 February 1937[4]

The Dancing Jew. A comedy play based on one of Grimm's Fairy Tales
    by *Hermann Homann*[5]

The tale 'The Jew among Thorns'[6] by the Brothers Grimm was the inspiration and basis for this funny and educational play. Just as the old fairy tale expresses the ribald opinion of the people and their justified anger towards the haggling Jew, this play shows even more coherently and clearly, and thus all the more effectively and enduringly, that this anger was and is only too justified. Whereas the Jew's disgraceful behaviour in the fairy tale is simply and correctly assumed, and only his punishment is administered in a very comical and drastic way, the theatre piece requires these acts of disgrace to be portrayed on stage, so that the punishment fits the crime. For this reason a swindling scene takes place that is absolutely typical for the Jewish haggler and extortionist, and has occurred more than once in this or a similar manner in every German village and town. *The Dancing Jew* is a play for theatre troupes wishing to express their opinion through their creative work. This occurs in a highly comical fashion, and is a challenge for all creative skills, as handicraft, music, singing, and also miming are required on stage.

Performance rights granted with seven copies for 7 Reichsmarks.

This order form can be cut off and sent in an open envelope for 3 pfennigs.

---

1 BArch, NS 12/1048. This document has been translated from German.
2 Founded by Franz Wulf (1885?–1940) in 1908 as a publishing house for the Catholic Theatre Groups, the Franz Wulf publishing house in Warendorf published plays, over 200 titles per year from 1919. Following the prohibition of Catholic associations in 1933, the publishing house ran into difficulties and closed in 1939. After the war, Wulf's daughter Maria ran the publishing house until 1968, concentrating on plays written in the Lower German dialect.
3 From 1933 the National Socialist Association of Teachers, founded in 1929, was the sole professional organization for teachers. It was run by Hans Schemm from 1935 and then by Fritz Wächtler. Its official publication was the *Nationalsozialistische Lehrerzeitung*.
4 In the original the title and a drawing are on the left-hand side and the text is on the right.
5 Hermann Homann (1899–1985), teacher; worked in state schools, 1921–1933; member of the Communist Party of Germany (KPD); ran an amateur theatre group in Ostbevern, 1933–1936; soldier from 1939; teacher in Meinberg and a freelancer for the television channels NDR and WDR and for Radio Bremen, 1945–1960; author of various amateur plays, chiefly in Low German; *Wir spielen Soldaten* (1938) was one of the plays that he published with the Franz Wulf publishing house.
6 The fairy tale *Der Jude im Dorn* is about a servant who is cheated out of his wages by his rich master. Aided by a fiddle that makes people dance, the servant randomly takes his revenge on a Jew he meets: *Die Kinder- und Hausmärchen der Brüder Grimm in ihrer Urgestalt*, vol. 2 (Munich: Beck, 1913), pp. 79–84.

However, only the buyer's address should be given in this case. Requested works may only be marked with a sign or a number. Should any further written additions or comments be added, the dispatch has to be sent as a letter for 12 pfennigs.

Franz Wulf Publishing House, Warendorf in Westphalia

DOC. 268
On 2 March 1937 the head of the personnel section of the City of Munich criticizes a staff official in the welfare section for granting too extensive welfare to a Jew[1]

Note from the City of Munich, Personnel Section/Department I (no. 930/36), Tempel,[2] to Welfare Section 6,[3] dated 2 March 1937[4]

With the Rosenbusch welfare file

To Section 6.

For subjective reasons I have distanced myself from instigating disciplinary action against the official V. J. Weiss.[5] I must, however, state that, seen objectively and as a basic rule, the handling of the case was not justified. Even if signs of nervous exhaustion were apparent with Rosenbusch, such complaints, which were barely substantiated, do not justify a convalescent stay in a spa town, even at the risk that Rosenbusch's nervous complaint could worsen and possibly lead to further consequences. This is particularly so because, according to the doctor's report, there were no signs of a serious nervous disorder or severe depression. Such extensive welfare may be arranged in the case of members of the old guard who have served the National Socialist Movement, but not in the case of a Jew. I request that this view is respected when treating similar cases.

---

1 Stadtarchiv München, Wohlfahrt/4599, fol. 84. This document has been translated from German.
2 Dr Karl Tempel (1904–1940), lawyer; took part in the Beer Hall Putsch in 1923; joined the NSDAP in 1929; worked as a lawyer from 1930; from April 1933 head of the food and social affairs section of the City of Munich; from July head of the personnel section; from May 1934 the first deputy mayor; first alderman of the City of Munich, 1935–1940; head of the central office of the NSDAP Main Office for Municipal Policy.
3 Friedrich Hilble (1881–1937), head of the welfare section; member of the Bavarian People's Party (BVP); worked in the Munich city administration from 1917.
4 In the original there are several handwritten annotations.
5 V. J. Weiss, an official in the welfare section in Munich, had treated a Jewish welfare recipient – notwithstanding the discussion in the Welfare Office on the discrimination against Jewish welfare recipients – in accordance with the valid regulations.

DOC. 269

Die Kameradschaft, 10 March 1937: proposal for an antisemitic social evening topic for the Hitler Youth[1]

The Jew as incendiary[2]

Part I: the social evening
   Comrades!

Russia is under the brutal rule of Bolshevism. We have come to know its two apparatuses of power, the Red Army and the Comintern, whose goal it is to conquer the world. We wonder: why does Bolshevik Russia want to conquer the entire world? Is it the *Russian* farmer, worker, soldier, or scholar who has concocted and intends to carry out such plans?

No, it is not the Russian who wants to subjugate all nations. The Russian does not even rule in his own country. He is ruled by an alien power – Bolshevism.

But behind Bolshevism is the Jew!

It is he who has brought the Russian people under his brutal domination and makes it *toil and even go hungry for the sake of his objectives.*

But the objectives of the Jew are to conquer and rule the world.

On this social evening, let us see:

(1) that Russia is ruled not by Russians but rather by Jews;

(2) that the Jew, by means of Bolshevism, intends to conquer the world, and that the Jew's objective of ruling the world did not just emerge in our own times but is already thousands of years old;

(3) that the Jew, who has achieved his objective in Russia, has now established *his* 'paradise' there – and [let us see] what this 'paradise' looks like for the subjugated peoples.

[…][3]

---

1 'Brandstifter Jude', *Die Kameradschaft*, no. 4, 10 March 1937, p. 1. This document has been translated from German. The magazine, subtitled 'Blätter für Heimatabendgestaltung in der Hitler-Jugend' [Organizing Hitler Youth Social Evenings], was published from 1934 to 1939 by the Reich Youth Leadership in Berlin.
2 This was also the title of the entire issue dated 10 March 1937.
3 There follow handouts for the social evening with quotes related to topics 1–3: 'Brandstifter Jude', *Die Kameradschaft*, no. 4, 10 March 1937, pp. 3–16. Part II, 'Leader training', was devoted to the topic 'World Jewry at work': ibid., pp. 17–24.

DOC. 270
Jüdische Rundschau, 16 March 1937: article about two court decisions on making purchases in Jewish shops[1]

From the courts
Buying from a Jewish shop as a marital transgression

The *Hanseatische Rechts- und Gerichts-Zeitschrift*[2] of 27 February/6 March published a decision issued by the *Hanseatic Higher Regional Court* on 19 January 1937 that held the purchase of a coat in a Jewish shop to be a *marital transgression*.

The marriage of the parties concerned, who are still quite young and have lived together for only six months, was regarded as broken as a result of fault on both sides and was dissolved pursuant to § 1568 of the Civil Code. The court notes, among other things, that the fundamentally improper attitude of the female defendant – only 17 years old – towards the plaintiff was revealed by the *purchase of a coat in a Jewish shop*. In this regard, the reasons for the aforementioned decisions included the following:

> A grave marital transgression, however, lies in the fact that she made the purchase in a *Jewish shop*, although she knew that the plaintiff, as a Party comrade and political leader, was not in agreement. The defendant should have shown interest in the political activities of the plaintiff. At least the plaintiff had the right to demand that his wife make allowances for his position in the Party and refrain from causing difficulties for him by making purchases in Jewish shops.[3]

Purchases made from Jews by the wife of a National Socialist
The *Remscheid* Local Court, in a decision reported in *Deutsche Justiz*,[4] has ruled that purchases made *from Jews by the wife of a National Socialist could not place the husband under an obligation*, because they were not within the scope of the powers conferred upon the spouse in the interest of the household (§ 1357 of the Civil Code). The *holding* states:

> Under § 1357(1) of the Civil Code, the wife is entitled to represent her husband in matters concerning the household, and under Amendment 2 of this provision the legal transactions made within these limits are deemed to have been undertaken in the name of the husband. Under the aforementioned provision, however, this principle does not apply if the circumstances give a different picture. The latter condition is present here. In late 1934 and early 1935, when the wife of the male defendant purchased the goods, there was already a generally accepted understanding that it

---

1 'Aus der Rechtssprechung: Kauf im jüdischen Geschäft als Eheverfehlung', *Jüdische Rundschau*, 16 March 1937, p. 5. This document has been translated from German.
2 The *Hanseatische Rechts- und Gerichts-Zeitschrift* was a law and court journal published from 1928 to 1943 as the successor to the *Hanseatische Gerichtszeitung*, founded in 1861. It was divided into section A (treatises) and section B (court decisions). Section A was published monthly; section B weekly.
3 See *Hanseatische Rechts- und Gerichts-Zeitschrift*, section B, no. 9/10, 27 Feb./6 March 1937, pp. 87–88.
4 See the decision of 20 Jan. 1937: *Deutsche Justiz*, edition A, no. 10, 12 March 1937, p. 402.

does not befit a German Volksgenosse to buy from Jews. Such purchases even at that time had already become a definite *exception*. A commitment of the German husband to such a contract must also be routinely viewed as *unacceptable* for him. As a result of these circumstances, the contracts of purchase that the wife concluded with a Jew are to have *no legal effect* with respect to the husband of German blood within the scope of § 1357 of the Civil Code. Rather, the person opposing the contract here as a rule excludes this far-reaching commitment. Circumstances that could justify a different opinion by way of exception have not been demonstrated. The plaintiff is all the less able to show such circumstances, as the defendant had already joined the NSDAP on 28 October 1934. The charge therefore had to be dismissed, without any need for investigating the further pleadings of the parties.

These further pleadings of the parties included the fact that the husband claimed that he and his wife were living separately at the time of the purchases, which she denied.

DOC. 271
On 9 April 1937 Karl Scherk invites the Jewish landowners and householders in Stettin to found an interest group[1]

Circular letter from Karl Scherk,[2] Stettin, 42 Kaiser-Wilhelm-Straße, to the Jewish landowners and householders in Stettin, dated 9 April 1937

In a discussion that took place on the 8th, some Jewish householders decided to found an interest group of Jewish landowners and householders in Stettin.[3]

In connection with this, there will now be an additional and more detailed session in a larger circle on Thursday, the 15th of this month, at 8 p.m. (on the dot) in the hall of the B'nai B'rith Association,[4] 3 Friedrich Karlstr., second staircase, right wing, and I take the liberty of inviting you to attend.

The changed circumstances and particularly the exclusion of Jewish members from the Homeowners' Association make it necessary for us to band together to represent our interests and obligations as householders in compliance with all regulations.

I therefore request that you accept the invitation above.[5]

As prov[isional] head

---

1 RGVA, 503k-1–382. This document has been translated from German.
2 Karl Scherk, retailer and member of the Stettin synagogue congregation.
3 In the left-hand margin of the original is a handwritten comment: '*no* information given by phone', and next to it initials and the date '9 Apr.'. The letter is included in the records of the Stettin Gestapo.
4 The Gestapo forced the Jewish organization B'nai B'rith to close its lodges all over Germany only a few days later, on 19 April 1937, and their property was confiscated: see Doc. 274, 19 April 1937.
5 On 14 April 1937 the Stettin Gestapo had noted on the back of the circular letter that it had prohibited the meeting by means of a decree issued on 5 April 1937 and informed Scherk by telephone. The circular decree of the Gestapo Central Office (Gestapa) (II B 4 – V 12 J) prohibited all events of Jewish organizations, particularly those with an assimilationist leaning, for the period 10 April to 10 June 1937. The only exceptions were events of a religious or cultural nature: BArch, R 58/276.

DOC. 272

On 16 April 1937 Rabbi Wahrmann reports on the grave problems confronting Jewish communities in Silesia[1]

Note, unsigned [Wahrmann], dated 16 April 1937

Report on my activities from 1 April 1936 to 31 March 1937[2]

(1) *General:*

The statements I made in my last activity report with respect to conditions for Jews in the small communities also apply in their entirety to this reporting period. Migration continued in the past year: it was mostly an internal migration. Last year Striegau joined the group of communities that have vacated their places of worship (Festenberg, Freystadt, Neusalz) as a result of the decrease in their number of members. However, while in the places listed only leased prayer rooms were involved, which could no longer be maintained, one community (Winzig) now plans to sell to the city its beautiful house of prayer, even as the seventy-fifth year of its existence is being celebrated, because the Jewish families living there cannot raise the funds required for repairing the roof (400 marks). The continued existence of the communities of Gross-Wartenberg, Bernstadt, and Sagan was also severely threatened during the reporting period. The community in Ohlau has forfeited its prayer room, which for decades had been housed in a municipal building and was renovated and refurbished a few years ago at great expense to the community, because it was forced to vacate the premises at the city's request. It is hoped that the community will manage to obtain a new place for prayer, so that it can continue in future to maintain the active community life that has existed until now.

(2) *In Oels:*

During the reporting period, the community here has also become smaller as a result of emigration, death, and conversion to Catholicism (the dentist Dr Brieger). It was nonetheless possible to maintain Jewish life in its entirety. I delivered sermons here on all the holidays, provided religious instruction in three groups two afternoons each week, and until quite recently also taught a course in modern Hebrew for adults. (Unfortunately, both the children of the manor owner Oliven in Buselwitz near Oels have been having Catholic religious instruction for years; all my previous efforts on this account were therefore completely unsuccessful.) I continued to work as a member of the community board, in that I took part in its meetings, regularly looked after the Jewish inmates of the local prison, and provided help and advice in many instances to the charitable associations and in addition to many community members. Finally, I might also note my participation in the collection for the Reich Representation, which yielded a handsome sum here. Special events in the community included a Hanukkah service for the children with food and drink and gifts for them, a cultural evening of the Prussian Regional Association of Jewish

---

1 CAHJP, P 33/26. This document has been translated from German.
2 See also the report by Wahrmann dated 5 Feb. 1934, Doc. 101.

Communities (Dr Heinrich Stern),³ and two lecture evenings (Director Dr Abt⁴ and Mrs Rose Blum) of the Association of Synagogue Congregations of the Province of Lower Silesia. I discussed the significance of Isaac Abravanel⁵ in the context of my holiday sermon on the second day of Passover.⁶ Both lecture evenings were proposed and overseen by me.

(3) *In the district:*
The constant shrinkage results in the creation of more and more dwarf communities with few families, which must live in relative isolation without any Jewish stimulus and guidance. I regarded it as the most important task of my work in the district to overcome these people's sense of being abandoned, and to help them with words and deeds in their difficult struggle for existence. Therefore, I have often made trips to such dwarf communities, visited the few families in their homes, and discussed their situation with them in detail. Often these visits represented the only contact with the Jewish outside world for quite a long time, and therefore they were always met with heartfelt gratitude. But in order also to raise the morale of these people and give them support from within through words of instruction, I organized, together with a Breslau cantor, religious festivities at centrally located points (such as Löwen, Münsterberg, Strehlen, Sprottau, Städtel, and Steinau), in which several communities participated and which obviously left a lasting impression. In addition, in several communities I held preaching services on Saturdays (where the possibility of compliance with the dietary laws was available) and on Sundays. Towards the end of the reporting period, my district underwent a small change. As a result of the dissolution of the district rabbinate in Gross-Strehlitz, I was assigned the Upper Silesian communities of Konstadt, Kreuzburg, Landsberg, and Pitschen, while the Brieg and Löwen communities are to be looked after in future by the rabbinate in Oppeln. To the work with the district is added my participation in the sessions of the Working Committee of the Association of Synagogue Congregations of the Province of Lower Silesia, and my extensive correspondence with the communities, associations, authorities, and individuals in the various locations. All in all, I made fifty-six trips on official business during the reporting period and visited the following places: Bernstadt, Festenberg, Fraustadt, Gross-Wartenberg, Jauer, Kanth, Konstadt, Kraschnitz, Leubus, Löwen, Militsch, Neumarkt, Namslau, Obernigk, Ohlau, Sagan, Schweidnitz, Sprottau, Städtel, Steinau, Strehlen, Striegau, Trachenberg, Trebnitz, Winzig, and Wohlau. In addition, I dispatched 789 documents during this period.

---

3 Dr Heinrich Stern (1883–1951), lawyer; practised law in Berlin; from 1917 president of the Association of Liberal Judaism; from 1930 chairman of the Assembly of Representatives of the Jewish Community of Berlin and board member of the Central Association of German Citizens of the Jewish Faith (CV); in 1938 emigrated to Britain, where he worked as a retailer and was active in various Jewish organizations.
4 Dr Harry Abt (1900–1977), rabbi and pedagogue; schoolmaster in Berlin, 1927–1936; director of the Jewish grammar school in Breslau, 1936–1939; head of Ezra, an Orthodox Jewish youth association, in 1927; chairman of the League of Observant Jewish Teachers of Germany in 1930; emigrated to South Africa in 1939.
5 Also Abarbanel, Abrabanel, or Abarvanel, Don Isaac ben Judah (1437–1508), religious philosopher and treasurer of King Alfonso V of Portugal.
6 Passover (Pesach): one of the three most important Jewish festivals.

(4) *Pastoral care in institutions:*
While I always provided care and counselling at the prison in Oels, the penal institution in Wohlau, the Leubus Provincial State Hospital and Nursing Home, and the Monastery of the German Order of Samaritans in Kraschnitz, my activity in this area assumed greater dimensions during the reporting period. As the result of an individual case, the necessity of centralizing pastoral care in the penal institutions of my district increased. At the behest of the Association of Synagogue Congregations of the Province of Lower Silesia, pastoral care in all the penal institutions of Lower Silesia that are not under a rabbinate (including Jauer) was assigned to me by order of the chief public prosecutor in Breslau. It is precisely the penal institution in Jauer, in which ten to fifteen inmates from all parts of Prussia are routinely held, that requires, owing to its particular structure (women's correctional institution), more intensive care and extensive correspondence with family members. I teach religion classes there (reading and discussion of religious texts and general Jewish texts), followed by an individual consultation hour. With the help of the Association of Synagogue Congregations of the Province of Lower Silesia and the Jewish Welfare Association for Lower Silesia, I was able to distribute prayer books, *humashim*,[7] and Bibles to the inmates on a number of occasions. In addition, some institutions in which inmates with lengthy sentences are present now receive the *Jüdisches Gemeindeblatt* from Breslau and Berlin on a regular basis, for forwarding to the Jewish inmates. Likewise, the latter were supplied with *matzoth*[8] for the Passover holidays.

(5) *Youth work:*
In every community in the district, without exception, the number of young people has decreased. This was caused partly by migration (see no. 1), but partly also by the transfer of many children to the Jewish schools in Breslau. In many instances the groups for religious education contain only one child apiece. Nonetheless, religious instruction was carried out everywhere in the customary manner and supervised by me in regular inspections. Special emphasis is merited by the large youth festival in Breslau, which was arranged by the Association of Synagogue Congregations of the Province of Lower Silesia with the support of other organizations for the children of the province on the Succoth[9] holiday, and in which I also was instrumental. It was a complete success and left a lasting impression on the children.

(6) *Archives:*
Despite multiple requests by the central associations for superfluous files to be transferred to the Jewish archives, many communities still have archival materials that are threatened with gradual destruction unless they are painstakingly preserved. During the reporting period, I also searched for archival materials on my visits to the communities, and in one instance I also succeeded in transferring a considerable number of papers

---

7 Plural of *humash*, Yiddish. Derived from the Hebrew *hamesh*, meaning 'five', in reference here to the five Books of Moses.
8 Plural of *matzo* or *matzah*: Hebrew for 'unleavened bread'. The eating of matzoth during the Passover holiday is a required aspect of the commemoration of the biblical exodus from Egypt.
9 Feast of Tabernacles: see Doc. 139, fn 3.

and documents to the archives of the Breslau Synagogue Congregation (Fraustadt Community). In two instances, as a result of my mediation, registers of births, deaths, and marriages were loaned to the archives for copying (in Festenberg and Oels).

DOC. 273
On 17 April 1937 the Düsseldorf leather goods salesman Paul Malsch writes to his son from the Netherlands to describe the political situation in Germany[1]

Handwritten letter from Paul Malsch[2] from Venlo (Netherlands), to Willy Malsch,[3] Corona, New York, dated 17 April 1937[4]

My dear Willy,

I travelled here today and collected your dear letter. To get straight to the point, it was not worth the effort & the postage. We were well aware that the 'La Guardia matter'[5] has made you nervous. You have yet to learn to observe everything more coolly. In all the newspaper clippings, there is no news that I did not already know. That Germany is always victorious in German newspapers is obvious. Nobody believes all these announcements any more. Now they are caught up in a new round of agitation against a film that is being shown in churches. None of this disconcerts us. It is encouraging that precisely the better retailers want nothing to do with a boycott of Jewish firms & sales representatives. Leather […][6] is so scarce that everybody takes it whenever they can get it. That all is not well, indeed that many things are quite horrible and vile, is something we know & even the others know. Just think how I would fare if the customers now wanted to carry out the boycott that Streicher desires! They are not doing so, out of a sense of decency & out of *silent* opposition.

It is clear that an even bigger fuss was made of the matter there than here. Window dressing, both here and there. Why does Mr Hull[7] not even once protest against the insults to his millions of subjects of the Jewish faith, who are all affected, all are included in the insults, whenever Streicher, as he did two weeks ago, comes out with accusations

---

1 USHMM, RG 10 086, Malsch family letters. This document has been translated from German.
2 Paul Malsch (1885–1942), sales representative; lived in Düsseldorf with his wife, Amalie, née Samuel (1889–1942). Both were deported on 27 Oct. 1941 on the first Düsseldorf transport to Łódź and murdered in Chełmno in 1942.
3 Wilhelm Malsch, later William Ronald Malsh (1913–1994), emigrated in late 1935/early 1936 to Britain and in Jan. 1937 from there to the USA, where he initially lived with relatives.
4 The letter was written on paper from the Hotel Germania in Venlo.
5 In a speech to the women of the American Jewish Congress on 3 March 1937, the mayor of New York, Fiorello H. La Guardia (1882–1947), had said that at the forthcoming New York World Fair he would like to see Hitler exhibited in a chamber of horrors as the brown-shirted fanatic threatening world peace. The German embassy lodged an official protest, and in response Secretary of State Hull expressed regret for remarks of this nature: *New York Times*, 5 March 1937, pp. 1 and 9.
6 This word is illegible.
7 Cordell Hull (1871–1955) was the US secretary of state from 1933 to 1944.

of ritual murder?[8] That would be a protest that would concern the whole world, one that would gravely wound the Nazi regime. Dr Stefan Wise[9] should see to it that the government over there expresses its indignation!

It's all the same to me if one group of 'victors' or another is telling lies in Spain! For 120 years the Spaniards have depended on nothing but revolutions. Why should they do things any differently? In the Spanish-American War we, that is, our family in Meiningen, were totally on the American side, although all my schoolmates & all the goyim were pro-Spanish! But we had brother Eugen in America & the Spanish Inquisition meant something to us. Let them go ahead and smash each other's heads. Then the business with the pastoral letter of the Pope![10] What does that do for us? A *simha*,[11] even if others stir things up! Don't let yourself be upset or distracted. You are young & quick to join the fray, that is understandable, but keep a cool head. So stop writing to Holland, see that you first create a solid foundation for yourself in American life. Only then can you have a say. I have bought the *Pariser Zeitung* here. There is nothing substantive in it either!

We will write to you tomorrow with the *Europa*![12]

So keep your hands off politics. I read far too many foreign newspapers; I already know what is going on! Except for a few little details, all the newspaper clippings really had nothing new to tell me! I'm sorry to have to possibly disappoint you by saying this. After six weeks I got my passport for – six months. Maybe we'll become millionaires in the meantime & be suspected of tax evasion. Today all that can be said about it is 'nebbich'.[13]

With a warm kiss,
Your loving Papa
Regards to all

---

8 See the article 'Ritualmord: Der Mord an der zehnjährigen Gertrud Lenhoff in Quierschied (Saarpfalz)' [Ritual Murder: the Murder of the 10-Year-Old Gertrud Lenhoff in Quierschied (Saar-Palatinate)], *Der Stürmer*, no. 14, April 1937, pp. 1–2.
9 Correctly: Dr Stephen Samuel Wise. On Wise, see Doc. 14, 27 March 1933.
10 The encyclical of Pope Pius XI entitled 'Mit brennender Sorge' [With Burning Concern] had been reproduced in Germany and read aloud in Catholic parishes on 21 March 1937. Based on a draft by Cardinal Faulhaber, it dealt with the situation of the Church, whose activities were restricted by the National Socialists despite the Reich Concordat of 1933, and criticized National Socialist ideology.
11 Hebrew for 'rejoicing' or 'celebration'.
12 The passenger liner *Europa*, owned by North German Lloyd, regularly worked the sea route between Europe and the USA.
13 Yiddish: 'what a pity'. This letter, posted from the Netherlands, is an exception among the very extensive correspondence of Paul and Amalie Malsch with their son in 1937 by virtue of its open criticism of the National Socialist leadership. Paul Malsch was evidently convinced that letters from Düsseldorf would be opened: on this, see the letter written by Paul Malsch from Venlo to Willy Malsch dated 10 Nov. 1937, USHMM, RG 10 086, Malsch family letters.

DOC. 274

Joseph B. Levy describes the B'nai B'rith Lodge in Frankfurt and how it was closed down by the Gestapo on 19 April 1937[1]

Entry by Joseph B. Levy[2] to a Harvard University competition (April 1940)

[...][3]

F.

For the past thirty years, until 1937, I was a member of the Independent Order of B'nai B'rith,[4] which, as is known, originated in the USA. The ambitions and operating principles of the lodge in Germany are somewhat different from the sphere of activity of the lodge in America. In the selection of its members, too, the order in Germany was certainly more exclusive than it is today in its country of origin. This tendency was especially pronounced in my lodge, one of the oldest branches of the order in Germany, the Frankfurt Lodge. It was founded in 1887 and was just about to celebrate its fiftieth anniversary. The old traditional endeavours of the order were, it was generally acknowledged, rarely pursued as rigorously, as intensely, and as extensively as in this very lodge. Our motto was: 'All for others, nothing for us!' Dissemination of general and Jewish culture, art, and science; self-education; doing good in all areas of charitable work; fraternity and harmony within our narrow circle and dissemination to those outside it; love of fatherland and for our ancestral faith, with exclusion of all political and partisan ambitions; all that is true, beautiful, and good was cultivated in this group. Thus, it also happened that precisely in this city, in this Jewish community with its many splinter groups, elements from all camps came together to support such noble endeavours in this temple of peace and to participate in them to the best of their individual ability and for the good of the whole. As a result of my own personal temperament, I inevitably felt at ease in such a sphere, and thus it came about that I was very soon an active participant in the lodge's work, worked on many committees, and soon assumed a leading role, particularly in the areas of welfare and of education and science. Thus, around 1912 I became and remained for several years the secretary responsible for keeping the log, in this way became part of the leadership, the so-called board of governors, and could now, especially during the war and the following years, take an active part in many works of philanthropy and intellectual betterment. Around 1928 I was elected president for the first time and held this top honorary post five times over the course of the next nine years.

---

1 Joseph B. Levy, 'Mein Leben in Deutschland vor und nach dem 30. Januar 1933' [My life in Germany before and after 30 January 1933], pp. 49–60; Harvard Competition, no. 135. This document has been translated from German.

2 Joseph B. Levy (1870–1950), primary school teacher; teacher and cantor in the Jewish Community in Frankfurt am Main; member of the B'nai B'rith lodge, 1907–1937; arrested on 10 Nov. 1938 but released on grounds of age; emigrated to the USA in 1939.

3 The entire report, posted from Dorchester, Massachusetts, is ninety pages long. In parts A to E, Levy describes his childhood and youth in Bremen, his life in Frankfurt am Main, and the beginning of the National Socialist era.

4 Footnote in the original: 'See enclosure 9.' The enclosure is not reproduced here.

Then, on 30 January 1933, the crisis began to descend upon this noble sphere of activity as well. It can be taken as well known that, under both fascism and National Socialism, Freemasonry is vigorously opposed on account of its worldwide reach and decidedly pacifist ideals, and thus doomed to extinction. Now the UOBB (known in America as the IOBB)[5] admittedly has absolutely nothing to do with Freemasonry and is not close to this much older movement in any way. The name 'lodge', however, led people to suspect and accuse the UOBB of having Freemason ties. As a result, soon after Hitler's seizure of power the Jewish lodges too were temporarily shut down or ceased operations out of caution, until lodge activity could be resumed a few months later (at the time there was talk of intervention by the American mother lodge, which rejected the accusation of international conspiracy). It was resumed to a severely limited extent, however, for all meetings and gatherings, especially all speeches, had to be reported to the 'Geheime Staats-Polizei' (Gestapo). Speeches and lectures had to be submitted verbatim and, once permission was granted (about two weeks later), had to adhere strictly to the manuscript. Naturally, that could only rarely be demanded of our speakers, as they usually were not paid a fee. In addition, it was not to everyone's taste, first, to adhere to the written word and, second, to be monitored and occasionally also interrupted by the Gestapo officials who usually were in attendance. Moreover, it was forbidden to use quotations in Hebrew, again a complication in dealing with the mostly religious and theological and Bible-studies-oriented materials that were popular and favoured in our group, and that constituted the subject matter of our lectures and discussions. Soon these former topics of our lodge evenings were dispensed with, and we contented ourselves with discussions about announced topics, writings, and books, and with recitations or musical offerings. Even these latter were often cancelled by the Gestapo censors, particularly if the authors in question were 'Aryans' (as already stated above). Nonetheless, our gatherings were better attended than before, because for our brothers and sisters they were, after all, a slight substitute for the theatres, concerts, and other evening entertainments that they missed. In addition, people were happy to be able to spend a pleasant hour or so with friends, like-minded persons, and fellow sufferers. – The humanitarian work of the lodge, however, multiplied from day to day. The growing distress and unemployment of all Jewish retailers, tradesmen, artists, doctors, and lawyers took their toll even on our circles. It was no longer possible to uphold our old motto, once our pride, that we selflessly helped only others. Formerly solvent helpers turned into needy and supported persons. The material decline of the formerly financially strong and obliging members – indeed, as a matter of principle, only such persons had been admitted to membership – became ever more visible, and the growth in emigration decreased the number of our brothers, so that by 1937, of our former 600 members, only around half remained. My activities as president and mentor, posts I had held in alternation in the past few years, thus consisted largely in welfare work inside and outside the lodge, and I gained a deep insight into the misery created by hatred and persecution. To intervene here in a helpful way was what I desired, and it made me so happy that, despite all the warnings of my wife and my closest friends, I again took on the serious, responsible, and – perhaps – risky function of lodge leadership, especially as the steady emigration of the intellectuals led to a

---

5 Unabhängiger Orden B'nai B'rith/Independent Order of B'nai B'rith.

perceptible shortage of suitable individuals. The warnings were unfortunately justified, for my willingness, combined with a strong sense of responsibility for the necessary and proper continuation of such an old lodge, respected throughout the order, became a disaster for me personally when misfortune suddenly, 'overnight' – as is customary in the National Socialist state – sought out our association.

In some regions of the Reich, first in Bavaria, but also in some parts of Prussia, the Jewish lodges had been closed even earlier, their activities prohibited and their property confiscated. But, with the reservations described above, we felt safe after a fashion, so that I began preparing to celebrate the anniversary of the lodge. Then – as I recall, it was in early February 1937[6] – one Monday morning, about 7 a.m., two men appeared at my home, ordered the startled maid to lead them to my bedroom and woke me by pounding on the door. I put on a few clothes hastily and enquired as to the reason for this disturbance. The men, still polite despite all their sternness, introduced themselves as officials of the Gestapo, asked to be taken to my study, and questioned me about any lodge files on hand and other papers, books, money, etc. pertaining to the lodge. I was able to give them only a small amount of material, because, as I told them, the lodge files were kept almost exclusively in the office in our lodge building. I thus handed over my portfolio, with few contents, as well as some writings and books. The men undertook a meaningless 'house search', mainly in my bookcase and desk, looking in particular for foreign correspondence and glancing over the few letters on hand. They allowed me to recite my morning prayers and to eat breakfast, and then they led me, or rather I led them, as they admitted they were unfamiliar with the place, to the lodge building, not far away. When I stated my expectation that the building would still be locked, the men revealed to me that the search there had already started at 5 a.m., and I was truly alarmed when I saw upon arrival that the building was already swarming with strangers, who were carrying out a radical inventory, gathering up every movable object, especially desks, tables, chairs, and typewriters, breaking open all the cupboards and thus quickly throwing the once so cosy house into dreadful disarray. I was led, past guards and control points that had been set up, into one of the clubrooms, where a little tribunal (three or four men) was waiting and interrogated me. If I had thought that I would now be questioned about the operations of the lodge, its leanings, activities, members, etc., I was quickly put right. After a very brief recording of my personal data and my position in the lodge, I was asked only short, terse questions about the assets of the lodge, what they consisted of and where, above all, the cash assets were to be found. My information about these financial issues, of course, could not be satisfactory, as these things were not part of my area of responsibility. Along these lines I pointed to the treasurer and the financial secretary, who alone were able to give exact information in this regard. But they were not satisfied with that, because they obviously wanted to know in a hurry and in detail what cash assets were to be expected and obtained. So I gave a superficial summary of the financial circumstances of the lodge, which owned a large, valuable parcel of land in one of the city's most important thoroughfares, worth around 750,000 marks, and a wonderful assembly hall with large rooms and clubrooms, an extensive library, beautiful furnishings, and valuable original paintings, watercolours, and drawings, in

---

6 The events actually occurred on 19 April 1937: see the situation report of the SD Department II 112 for the period 1 April – 30 June 1937 in Wildt (ed.), *Die Judenpolitik des SD*, p. 121.

addition to two large rental apartments in the upper stories. The building was not heavily mortgaged, and one of the small properties adjacent to it had recently been sold to the 'Radio Broadcasting Corporation'. In reply to the repeated brusque questions: 'Where is the money? Where did you hide it?' I was truly unable to give the men an answer that satisfied them. Their suspicions left me cold.

Thus, the entire interrogation, which revolved mainly around the possessions to be confiscated, lasted only around half an hour. Overall, it was conducted in a calm, civilized manner. After it ended, I was sent to the great ceremonial hall, where, with mixed feelings, I had a chance to greet quite a number of fellow sufferers, presidents, ex-presidents, and other officials of my own lodge and the other two lodges in Frankfurt, which had likewise been based in our building. This greeting, however, took the form of only a glance, because all conversation was prohibited by the supervisory officials, more or less friendly, non-uniformed SS men and Gestapo officials. Even smoking was forbidden, with a reference to the risk of fire, while some of those supervising us, especially the younger ones, lit one cigarette after another, lolling on benches and obviously making fun of us older gentlemen. Incidentally, despite the availability of fuel and despite the presence of the stoker we employed, the room was not heated, so that we were painfully cold and tried to get warm by moving around. My modest question to the head officials as to whether we might now go home, because the files of the lodge were at their disposal, after all, and we ourselves could be interrogated again at any time, received a negative response. A certain punishment, too, was apparently connected with our questioning and the entire operation, and I was personally yet to be set straight in this respect and indeed in quite a drastic way.

By 9 a.m. the [SS]-Oberführer of the investigation staff summoned me and solemnly presented me with the decree of dissolution.[7] It was issued by the Ministry of the Interior (Himmler) and signed by the Regierungspräsident.[8] It was addressed to me as the current president of the Frankfurt Lodge, and it contained, with a reference to the relevant 'legislation', the decision that the lodge and the UOBB had pursued and supported 'endeavours hostile to the state' and were therefore dissolved, that all our assets were confiscated pending further disposition, and that, under threat of the most severe punishment, we were not allowed to found or belong to any similar association and were forbidden to arrange any more gatherings. The leader of the operation asked me to put my signature to this decree. I refused to do so, saying I could not possibly acknowledge ever having pursued or supported endeavours hostile to the state. Only after receiving assurance that by signing I was acknowledging solely the receipt of the decree did I sign the death warrant of my lodge, the Frankfurt Lodge. It was one of the most painful moments of my life.

In the meantime, all the other functionaries and officials of our own lodge and the two sister lodges, as well as the three women's associations, had appeared and in some instances been interrogated in a very unfriendly fashion. Even though talking was

---

7 Footnote in the original: 'The original is still in my possession, but unfortunately is in my packing case, which remained behind in Germany.'
8 By circular decree of the Reichsführer SS (S-PP II B 331/36), the 'Independent Order of Bne Briß' was dissolved on 10 April 1937 and its assets were confiscated: *Ministerialblatt des Reichs- und Preußischen Ministerium des Innern*, no. 27, 7 July 1937, p. 1062.

forbidden, I learned from friends who were present that some of the people had already been arrested at 6 a.m. and by very rude and unfriendly individuals, who hurled curses, insults, and suspicions at them in the process. Naturally, the house searches failed to have the desired success. Nonetheless, all kinds of valuable objects were summarily taken away and confiscated. The room filled up. The mood in the building deteriorated visibly as more and more time passed, and the result had obviously not been materially satisfying – it had been assumed that we were richer! Now the investigators resorted to personal suspicions and ordeals of various sorts. For example, one of my friends was accused of having had immoral relations with an allegedly 'Aryan' female employee. At his wish, this lady was fetched – the result of the detailed investigation, which was conducted with all possible harassment and tricky questioning, did not meet the desires of the examiner: there were no personal or indeed indecent relations between the boss and the female employee, who, moreover, was a Jew. – Another friend, a well-known painter and printmaker, was caught committing the 'terrible' crime of creating little sketches to pass the time. The supervising official thought that he himself had been caricatured, and he made the honourable man stand facing the wall like a schoolboy, and also ordered him to pick up pieces of paper that had fallen on the floor and to sweep the hall with a broom.

I myself remained undisturbed until around 2 p.m. Then I was suddenly called for a separate interview. An official, behaving in a very businesslike manner, questioned me about a Frankfurt association, the 'Society of Friends',[9] which allegedly had some connection with the lodge. Naturally it was thought that this rationale, had it stood the test, could be used to confiscate this association's real estate and possessions too. In very strong terms, to the best of my knowledge, I answered in the negative the questions about a link between the two corporations. The association had absolutely nothing to do with the lodge and the order. What I knew of it beyond that was very little. As far as I knew, it had exclusively Jewish members and had solely social objectives. The meetings of its members, I had heard, were devoted solely to card games. I communicated that to the investigator, but at his request could give him the name of only one member, whose affiliation with the aforementioned association I learned of by chance one day, from the gentleman himself, as he was also one of my lodge brothers. – Again, there was obvious dissatisfaction with this meagre information, and around an hour later I was summoned once again, and this time before a larger tribunal. It was made up of several older and younger officials and SS men. While the older and more sensible ones apparently contented themselves with my information, negative this time as well, two younger ones now gained the upper hand. It was easy to note that overall, during the entire operation, the calmer, more gracious, older officials feared the younger go-getters. Now a two- to three-hour ordeal began for me. For the first time, in a drastic fashion, I became acquainted with the investigation methods of the 'Third Reich' and the vicious, harrowing

---

9 The Society of Friends (Gesellschaft der Freunde) – not to be confused with the Religious Society of Friends (or Quakers), founded in England in the mid seventeenth century – was established in Berlin in 1791 by, among others, the writer Isaac Abraham Euchel. In addition to education and enlightenment, it was devoted to charitable pursuits. Similar societies later arose in Breslau, Dessau, Leipzig, and Frankfurt am Main. The originally Jewish Society of Friends promoted understanding with Christians and, during the Weimar Republic, also accepted non-Jewish members.

nature of proceedings against mostly innocent, rarely guilty persons subjected to persecution. No matter what I brought up from my inconsequential and hazy knowledge of the aforementioned association – nothing I said was believed, because they did not *want* to believe anything. I *had to* be familiar with this association, they said. They said that I was one of the elders of the lodge group, an old official of the Jewish Community, had lived in the town for more than four decades, and all my statements were fraudulent, wrong, unsatisfactory. They claimed that I was withholding the truth, which I knew only too well. I *must* know more, both about the purposes of the association and about its members – in short, I was a liar! I pointed out my position in the community and the school, my leading role in the lodge and in many associations and organizations, my lack of a criminal record, my honesty, I offered to swear an oath – nothing helped. 'What does a Jew's oath mean anyway?!' was the insolent retort, which I quite energetically repudiated, however, with these words: 'I claim for myself the complete veracity of my oath.' But all this was of no avail. Apparently they did not believe me: they said they wanted to know the whole truth, even if this came out following my arrest and transfer to prison. I said that everything else I might state about this association could only be invented by me, because I knew the home of the 'Society of Friends' only from the outside and had never entered it. By the way, I added, the building was quite near, one could quickly go there and easily learn there everything one wanted to know. That did not happen – evidence that harassing me was all that was aimed at for now. They became increasingly impassioned, threatened me repeatedly with harsher measures, made me stand facing the wall for hours on end without even being permitted to touch it for support. When I attempted to touch it, my hand was rudely knocked away. I noted that I was 67 years old and had only recently been involved in a serious car accident. 'Doubtless it was your own fault!' was the fatuous, insensitive reply. Every fifteen minutes, one of the tormentors approached me to ask whether I still did not know anything more. Once a fellow came out of the hall and claimed, raising his voice, that among my friends in there were several who had confirmed that they had often seen me in the 'Society of Friends' and that I had often played skat there. I told him that these people were manifest liars. Naturally there was no answer to that, and just as self-evidently no confrontation with these alleged witnesses.

After almost three hours of such torment and medieval methods of interrogation, they seemed to give up hope at last and released me – my strength was giving out and I was about to faint – into the great hall. In this hall, in the meantime, a real reign of terror, under the leadership of a few of the most brazen louts among the 'officials', had gained ground, the outbursts of which I had already heard through the doors of the hall. The men under arrest (mostly between 50 and 60 years old) were arranged in rank and file, and made to march and drill like soldiers (naturally, out of pity, to keep them from freezing in the cold hall!). In the process the coarsest insults and invective were uttered whenever one of the men, who were elderly anyhow, slackened a bit. Allowances were made intermittently only for those with a heart condition, but not until a doctor who was present, one of the men under arrest, confirmed the need for rest, giving his word of honour. After my return to the hall, I tried to participate in the parade-ground drill. One of the older supervising officials, however, noticed how hard it was for me and graciously allowed me to sit down. But then my powers failed me too, and I suffered a severe nervous collapse.

Finally, around 7 p.m., we were released, with another warning against continuation of any and all lodge-like assemblies and activities.

In the next few days, I still had to respond frequently to telephone enquiries regarding the whereabouts of several files and similar documents needed for the pseudo-investigation, and this continued until autumn. My last personal interview took place at the Jewish New Year's holiday, and I could obtain no dispensation from it, despite my protests that the High Holidays were sacred. Like the first interrogation, this one too dealt exclusively with the lodge property that was to be stolen, the buildings and the assets, and besides our financial secretary I was the only person troubled with it. From then on, however, I heard nothing more of our former splendid lodge home. The buildings apparently were in disuse for a long time. Probably there were some difficulties involved in taking possession, as a result of the assumption of the mortgage (the creditor lived in Switzerland). The emblem of the lodge above the entrance was chiselled away by the stonemason a few months later. What became of our valuable library, pictures, and works of art was not known. Naturally, our two sister lodges in Frankfurt and all the other German lodges were treated in the same fashion. Their property too and that of their women's associations was seized, and sometimes the presidents and other officials were even wrongfully imprisoned for several days. The chairwomen also were ruthlessly tormented and harassed, in particular the head of *our* lodge sisters' group. Because she had managed the money through her own postal current account, she even lost a substantial sum of her own money, although she had naturally kept the accounts painstakingly. Also to be pitied were the employees of the lodge, the keeper of the building, a non-Jew, and our secretary, a Jewish woman. With the disbanding and closing of the lodge, both abruptly lost their positions of many years' duration, their incomes, and their pension plans. All this would not have been possible in the former Germany with its excellent provision for old age and disability, particularly in the case of such a reputable association. Concern for our widows and orphans, who until then had drawn a monthly pension from us, up to complete maintenance, weighed heavily, particularly on me as the one formerly in charge. All my efforts and those of my friends in this direction had only very limited success: from other sources, we were able to help the poor for around a year after the dissolution of the lodge, giving them a small fraction of their previous amounts. Then they became subject to the Jewish or general relief scheme for the poor, and thus the relatives and survivors of once well-situated lodge members are now suffering bitter want and hardship.

The fact that our band of friends was no longer allowed to assemble at all and that all the ties, once so close, were dissolved also pained us greatly. But all gatherings, even those for religious purposes, in places other than the synagogues were prohibited and, if not specially approved by way of exception, were threatened at the very least with lengthy deprivation of liberty. Thus the association's activity, which was as valuable and effective as can possibly be imagined, was ended by raw power, lust for the property of others, destructive vandalism, and hatred of other human beings.

[...][10]

---

10 In the following part of his account, Levy describes the years 1938 and 1939, in particular the arrests of Jews in June 1938 and the pogroms of Nov. 1938.

DOC. 275
Hermann Lesser writes to the Reich Association of German Small-Animal Breeders on 27 April 1937 to propose the establishment of a Jewish dog breeders' organization[1]

Letter from Hermann Lesser, Berlin-Wilmersdorf, 53/8 Rudolstädterstraße, to President K. Vetter,[2] Reichstag delegate, Reich Association of German Small-Animal Breeders, Berlin SW 11, 5 Hafenplatz, dated 27 April 1937 (copy)[3]

Dear Mr President,

By order of the previous Reich head official of the Reich Kennel Club, non-Aryan members were urged to resign from the Reich Kennel Club with effect from 1 January 1937.[4]

To prevent harm to the breeding programme as a result of uncontrolled breeding of dogs by non-Aryans, I immediately approached Mr Glockner at that time and enquired whether the founding of an association of non-Aryan dog-lovers might not be a possibility. This association should be completely independent and, without any burdening of the Reich Kennel Club, should monitor the breeding of dogs by non-Aryans and facilitate the recording of these breeding products in the breed registries of the Reich Kennel Club. Thereby, in my view, any harm to dog breeding in Germany would be avoided. – According to my enquiries, many breeding animals are in the hands of non-Aryans.

In addition, the training of service-dog breeds, such as German shepherds, of which I myself own three specimens, is completely prevented by the exit of non-Aryans from the Reich Kennel Club, because work done jointly by those who have resigned would potentially be regarded as prohibited assembly.

Mr Glockner informed me on the 19th of this month that I should contact you on this matter.

For ten years I was a member of the current Section for German Shepherd Dogs, formerly the Society for German Shepherd Dogs.

Should the aforementioned establishment be a possibility, I am ready to provide more detailed explanations to you at any time.

Awaiting your valued communication in this regard,

I remain with the highest esteem

---

1 BArch, R 3601/1859, fol. 317. This letter has been translated from German.
2 Karl Wanfried Vetter (b. 1895), farmer; joined the SA and the NSDAP in 1929, and the SS in 1934; main department head in the Reich Food Estate, 1933–1935; inspector general of the Reich Food Estate, 1935–1937; president of the Reich Association of German Small-Animal Breeders from 1933.
3 Parts of the original have been underlined by hand. The copy was sent by the Reich Association of German Small-Animal Breeders to the Deputy of the Führer on 13 Dec. 1937 with a request for comments: ibid., fol. 316.
4 In comparison to many other organizations, the Reich Kennel Club excluded Jewish members at a very late stage and obviously under pressure from the Supreme SA Command. Max Jüttner (1888–1963) had forbidden the SA in late 1936 to hold joint events with the Reich Kennel Club until the latter 'completely eliminated Jews and persons of Jewish descent from its ranks': circular letter from the Supreme SA Command, dated 12 Nov. 1936, BArch, NS 23/557.

DOC. 276

On 29 April 1937 Adolf Hitler outlines his anti-Jewish strategy to NSDAP Kreisleiter at the Vogelsang National Socialist Castle elite training school[1]

Excerpt from an address given by Adolf Hitler at Vogelsang Castle on 29 April 1937[2]

My fellow Party comrades! [...][3]

We are experiencing this crisis today in the world around us.[4] Just look at France. The French state was not established by means of democratic liberality, but democratic liberality will wreck this state, or it will be replaced by some new form of governance. We too have certainly experienced this problem in Germany, and we ourselves indeed emerged from this crisis. And we have overcome it in Germany. In Germany, this democratic form has been replaced by the National Socialist state based on the leadership principle. In other countries, it is evidently communism that is victorious, but communism also abolishes democracy. In these countries, then, it is ultimately the establishment of the dominance of international Jewry, which forces itself on the peoples by means of the most brutal violence and then also leads these peoples. In other countries, this battle today is partly in a state of development, partly already brightly ablaze, partly in the process of announcing itself.

[...][5]

And the Führer state has no need to fear genius; indeed, that is what distinguishes it from democracy. If, in a democracy, someone were to be, for example, a Gauleiter, he would have to be incredibly afraid that a talented person might appear below him, and he would have to say: 'If the fellow continues like this, he'll have people behind him in short order, and then he'll unseat me. Thump! Then I'll have the reward for all my work.' So in a democracy one must take great care to ensure that no talent comes to light. If a talent does come to light somewhere, then it must be swiftly dispatched. It is the survival instinct in that case [laughter]. In the Führer state, things are not that way at all, because he is well aware that however talented the man is, he still can't get rid of him. Quite the reverse: if he makes a special effort to get rid of him, he sins against discipline and obedience, and by so doing he shows that he himself is not capable of leading. And thus his goose is cooked.

Therefore, in the Führer state, there will be a much greater probability that talent will be fostered. It cannot become a danger to any leader. Quite the contrary; by discovering talent, he provides additional support for himself, he creates exemplary and brilliant associates, and of all these associates, only one who himself, in turn, is absolutely loyal and obedient can expect to get somewhere. Because he demonstrates only that he alone

---

1 DRA, 2 613 005. The speech is published in Hildegard von Kotze and Helmut Krausnick (eds.), 'Es spricht der Führer': Sieben exemplarische Hitler-Reden (Gütersloh: Sigbert Mohn, 1966), pp. 123–177. This document has been translated from German.
2 This is a transcription of the audio recording. Total length of the speech: 137 minutes, 40 seconds.
3 At this point the original contains an introductory passage with background information.
4 Hitler is referring here to the crisis of democracy, about which he had talked in the previous part of the speech.
5 Next there follow passages on the anti-democratic National Socialist approach to governance, the role of the NSDAP, selection of the best among the youth, and discipline and obedience.

is able truly to lead some day. For where would one get if someone who himself is unwilling to practise loyalty and obedience should one day, later on, want to command loyalty and obedience? For he must do so, too, or else it simply doesn't work. These are cast-iron principles, which must be upheld.

In the Party, therefore, as a matter of principle no demands are made; such a thing does not occur. What does it mean anyway, for example, to 'demand' something in the Party? A few days ago, I read these words in a newspaper (I will send for the man and discuss this problem with him very briefly): 'We demand that signs now be placed on Jewish shops, and that Jewish shops be identified.' In the *newspaper*: 'We demand!' Now I must say, you see: 'Of whom does he demand this? Who can mandate this? I alone can do so.' So, the editor demands, in the name of his readers, that I do this. First of all: long before this editor had any inkling of the Jewish question, I was already focused on it in a very exhaustive way [laughter]. Second, this problem of identification has been pondered continuously for two or three years and will one day naturally be brought to completion, too, in one way or another.[6] For the final aim of all our policy is indeed quite clear to us all. For me, it is always solely about not taking a step that I must perhaps take back, and not taking a step that harms us. You know, I always go to the outermost limit of risk, but not beyond it. One just needs a good nose, more or less to smell: 'What can I still do, what can I not do?' [hilarity]. Also in the fight against an opponent [great hilarity and vigorous applause] I don't want to forcibly challenge an opponent to fight right away, I don't say 'Fight!' because I want to fight; instead I say: 'I want to destroy you! And now, may cunning help me to manoeuvre you into a corner so that you have no chance to strike, and then you will be pierced through the heart.' That's the way! [Shouts of 'bravo' and applause.]

But the masses cannot decide that. One must believe that a leadership that has set a goal will ultimately seek also to realize this goal. And then it must be a principle, and then every Party leader, regardless of where he stands, must in turn demand the very same of his subordinates: that it should be left to the person currently in charge. It would be conceivable that, for example, someone who considers such a thing proper would address the relevant office or even communicate it personally and say: 'We now deem it perhaps necessary after all for this to happen.' Then he would be told: 'No, it is not yet the right time.' But it is out of the question that, in this Movement, the masses will ever be used as the decisive means or even just one means of exerting pressure. That does not occur. If we should *ever slip*, then there is no stopping here, my fellow Party comrades. And you, as Kreisleiter, must not tolerate it anywhere either; as a matter of principle, it does not occur. Always there is one person who is in charge, who makes the decision. If a local branch head or a block leader or somebody else has an opinion, he can turn to that person. But he cannot call his block, his cell, or his local group together and say: 'We now demand of the Kreisleiter.' Nor can the Kreisleiter demand it of the Gauleiter, nor can the Gauleiter with their followers demand it of me.

These are principles that must be self-evident. After all, in the Movement there is no appeal to the masses, other than at all times the appeal of the competent authorities.

---

6 On the inter-ministry discussion in 1935, see Doc. 189, 20 August 1935, and Doc. 202, 25 Sept. 1935.

And then our appeal must never be made in order to sway the masses to demand something, but rather in order to make understandable to the masses something that has been accomplished, or to prepare them for something that is in the process of being carried out. For it is surely clear that we now desire, at all times, the closest relationship with the people, and that we know that every decision obtains its ultimate resounding impact only when one gets the greatest possible mass of the people behind it, and that it is therefore expedient to word every decision so succinctly that the people comprehend it, that the people say: 'Naturally, it has to happen now; yes, they are quite right to do it; it is right, they should do it now, we are in favour of it too, quite right.' If anything, it must be the case that, whenever such a decision is made, the people then say: 'I see, well, we've sensed for quite a long time that such a thing would occur [laughter]; it's quite right, too, it had to happen, praise and thanks be to God.'

[...]⁷

DOC. 277
On 3 May 1937 the Office of the Plenipotentiary for the Four-Year Plan summarizes the effects of the Aryanization of the Jewish art trade[1]

Memorandum from the Prussian Minister President, General Göring, Plenipotentiary for the Four-Year Plan (St.M.I.601/37 II, 11 020/36, 12 042/36, 727/37), Section Head von Normann,[2] dated 3 May 1937 (copy)

(1) *Memorandum*
From individual petitions and a collective petition from the lawyer and notary Dr Moral[3] late last year, it became clear that in the area of the German art trade, a development has been in the making that is dangerous in both non-material and economic terms. Because a large number of the art dealers' shops are under Jewish ownership, including the most important ones, the Reich Minister of Propaganda (the Reich Chamber of Culture) summarily eliminated these enterprises over the course of 1936 by prohibiting their continued operation. Because the previous Jewish owners were not even permitted to assist the Aryan buyers of the enterprises, in particular to share their experience with them and transfer their international contacts to them, acquisition by interested Aryan parties was simultaneously made more difficult, if not prevented altogether.

---

7 Here follow passages on the press in the National Socialist state, on personal 'leadership of the people' in place of written communication, against bureaucracy, on the National Socialist way of life, and on the imminent conflict between democracy and the authoritarian state.

1 GStA PK, I HA, Rep. 90 M/44, fols. 5–7. This document has been translated from German.
2 Hans-Henning von Normann (b. 1903), civil servant; joined the civil service in 1926; Regierungsassessor in the Prussian Ministry of State in Berlin, 1933, and later Ministerialrat and head of Section 2 in the office of the Plenipotentiary for the Four-Year Plan; joined the NSDAP in 1937.
3 Dr Reinhard Moral (1894–1958), lawyer; practised law and worked as a notary in Berlin; classed as a *Mischling* as of 1933; advised Jewish emigrants; co-founder of the Association of Berlin Defence Lawyers.

With regard to the various petitions, one heard, via the Minister of Culture, from the director general of the State Museums,[4] who expresses a detailed opinion on the issue in his assessment of 4 January 1937[5] and states, among other things:

> The indigenous art trade ... which a few years ago was still thriving in Germany is pretty much in tatters today ... The destruction of the German art trade, for the most part an accomplished fact, is the work of the Reich Chamber of Fine Arts ... If the shops, because they are Jewish, are closed or taken over by inexperienced non-Jews and thus robbed of their reputation, collectors will no longer have any reason to visit, say, Berlin or Munich ...
>
> In concert with the directors Demmler,[6] Schmidt,[7] Winkler,[8] and Zimmermann,[9] I therefore recommend that the greatest caution be exercised in the dissolution or Aryanization of those Jewish art dealers' shops against whose business conduct the only objection to be made is that their owners are Jews.

To obtain a clearer picture by looking at an individual case, the official in charge here – complying with a wish of Professor Binder[10] – negotiated verbally with the art historian Dr Grosse and in conclusion requested the enclosed note dated 3 February of this year.[11] It makes clear that the actions of the Reich Chamber of Fine Arts apparently have exclusively negative effects. It prohibits Jewish enterprises, does not approve a proposal for Aryanization, but also refrains from making practicable counter-proposals. Also interesting is the assertion by Dr Grosse that since autumn of this year at least 200 art-dealing concerns have been eliminated. Substitutes for these shops, to the extent that they are specialist shops, are scarce or completely non-existent. A transfer of the shops into Aryan hands, he says, is conceivable only if the previous owners are permitted to show the new owner the ropes during a certain transitional period.

With regard to the business and personal calibre of several major Jewish art dealers, a number of positive assessments are on hand: for example, regarding Lederer, reference is made to Oberpräsident Philipp of Hesse, Colonel General von Seeckt, and the also deceased Staatsrat Wiegand; regarding Cramer, to Privy Councillor Zimmermann, the directors Luthmer and Schmidt, etc.

---

4 Dr Otto Kümmel (1874–1952), art historian; director of the Museum of East Asian Art from 1924 and director general of the Berlin State Museums, 1933–1945; NSDAP member.
5 This report could not be found.
6 Dr Theodor Demmler (1879–1944), art historian; director of the Deutsches Museum in Berlin.
7 Dr Robert Schmidt (1878–1952), art historian; director of the Museum of Arts and Crafts (Kunstgewerbemuseum) in Frankfurt am Main, 1918–1927, of the Palace Museum (Schlossmuseum) in Berlin from 1928, and of the Zonal Fine Art Repository in Celle from 1947.
8 Dr Friedrich Horst Winkler (1888–1965), art historian; from 1933 director of the Museum of Prints and Drawings (Kupferstichkabinett) in Berlin.
9 Dr Ernst Heinrich Zimmermann (1886–1971), art historian; director of the Germanic National Museum in Nuremberg, 1920–1936.
10 Presumably Dr Julius Binder (1870–1939), lawyer and political scientist; professor in Rostock and Erlangen, 1900–1913, and in Würzburg from 1913; from 1919 professor of Roman and German civil law and philosophy of law in Göttingen.
11 This note is not in the file.

Because the Minister President[12] takes particular interest in art and the art trade and, moreover, because he, as the Plenipotentiary for the Four-Year Plan – if others do not or cannot do it – must work towards ensuring that preventable damage to our foreign exchange revenue is avoided, it is advisable to ask the Minister of Propaganda for an opinion and thereby call his attention to a matter the effects of which are apparently unknown to him.[13]

DOC. 278
On 7 May 1937 the Office of the Plenipotentiary for the Four-Year Plan discusses the classification of Wertheim as an Aryan company[1]

Memorandum from the Plenipotentiary for the Four-Year Plan (V.A.w.St.M.I. 5153), signed Marotzke,[2] Berlin, dated 7 May 1937 (copy)

(1) *Memorandum:*

On 20 April 1937 the retired Regierungspräsident *Schönner*,[3] chairman of the supervisory board, came by to discuss the Wertheim matter. He explained that the personnel changeover of the Wertheim company has now been carried out, whereby all Jewish associates without exception were removed from leading positions.[4] In these circumstances, the company would welcome seeing the Minister President[5] now assert his influence in order to have Wertheim classified as an Aryan business. I pointed out to Mr Schönner that objections to Aryanization could still exist if, once Mrs Wertheim,[6] née Gilka, is deceased the 51 per cent parcel of shares (which because of the board is in fact currently in the possession of the Aryan Mrs Wertheim, née Gilka) comes into the possession of her children, who are to be regarded as half-Jews. It would remain to be considered, I

---

12 Hermann Göring is meant here.
13 A corresponding draft follows in the file: GStA PK, I HA, Rep. 90 M/44, fols. 6–7.

1 GStA PK, I HA, Rep. 90 B/222, fols. 1–2. This document has been translated from German.
2 Wilhelm Marotzke (b. 1897), civil servant; joined the German National People's Party (DNVP) in 1919 and the NSDAP and the SS in 1937; until 1934 head of the Gestapo office in Elbing; worked in 1934 in the Prussian Ministry of State, from 1936 in the SD, and from 1937 at the office of the Plenipotentiary for the Four-Year Plan, where he was Ministerialdirigent in 1940.
3 Kurt Schönner, lawyer; from the 1920s to 1932 Ministerialrat in the Prussian Ministry of the Interior and from 1932 to 1934 Regierungspräsident in Frankfurt an der Oder.
4 The enterprise had been founded by Abraham Wertheim (1819–1891) with a shop in Stralsund. In 1930 the Wertheim family ran seven department stores. In 1933 Georg Wertheim (1857–1939) transferred his shares to his non-Jewish wife, Ursula. Under official pressure, the remaining shares too had to be Aryanized in 1936. After Georg Wertheim was forced out in 1937, the firm was renamed in 1938 as the Allgemeine Warenhandels-Gesellschaft, or AWAG. The name Wertheim continued to be used, however.
5 This refers to Hermann Göring. He favoured having the Reich Ministry of Economics inform the Gauleitung and the press about the 'consummated Aryanization': memorandum from the Prussian Minister President (Körner), 18 June 1937, GStA PK, I HA, Rep. 90 B/222, fol. 2.
6 Ursula Wertheim, née Gilka (1885–1975), married to Georg Wertheim from 1906. They divorced in 1938 in order to safeguard their shares in the firm. After Georg's death, Ursula married Arthur Lindgens (1899–1976), the chairman of the AWAG consortium, in 1941.

said, whether it might not be possible to reduce this parcel of shares to less than 50 per cent through the sale of shares.

The retired Regierungspräsident Schönner, as chairman of the supervisory board, approved a corresponding clarification of the matter.

A presentation has been made to Staatsrat Neumann.[7]

(2) *Follow-up after one month.*

DOC. 279
On 14 May 1937 Bertha Meyer, who had emigrated to Prague, asks the Foreign Currency Office of the Greater Berlin Tax Office to waive the fees for storage of her household effects[1]

Letter from Bertha Meyer, née Zwindorfer, Prague-Bubenec, to the Foreign Currency Office of the Greater Berlin Tax Office (received on 15 May 1937), dated 14 May 1937[2]

I stored eight crates of used household effects with the Household Goods Repository of the Jewish Community of Berlin, no. 55, 140/141 Greifswalder Strasse, for which I was charged 135 marks as a warehousing fee, and my storage contract was terminated for failure to pay.[3] My request for reduction or waiver of this amount depends on obtaining permission from the tax office, as we are non-resident persons. The Household Goods Repository of the Jewish Community would probably accede to my request if the aforementioned permit were to be issued. The repository is likely to have satisfied itself that a sale of my household effects at auction would not even yield the auction expenses. My husband and I are not able to pay any contributions at all. After seizure of all his goods as a debtor, my husband swore an oath of disclosure on 5 October 1936 at the local enforcement court, file reference E.IV 280/36. As a result of his war-related disability, he cannot do any work at all, and the two of us have no earnings or any other income.

The fact that there is nothing on file against us is probably best demonstrated by the issue of new passports to us by the German embassy in Prague as recently as 1936. We have just received our entry permits for Argentina and, now that we have lost all we have as a result of the seizure, we *urgently* need the contents of the crates mentioned above, which, in the event that our request is granted, we intend to take along with us to Argentina.

---

7 Erich Neumann (1892–1951), lawyer and economist; member of the German National People's Party (DNVP), joined the NSDAP in 1933 and the SS in 1934; from 1920 worked in the Prussian Ministry of the Interior and from 1923 in the Prussian Ministry of Trade; ministerial director in the Prussian Ministry of State, 1932; Prussian Staatsrat, 1933–1942; head of the Foreign Currency Business Group of the Plenipotentiary for the Four-Year Plan, 1936–1942; from 1938 state secretary; attended the Wannsee Conference in 1942; from 1942 director general of the German Potassium Syndicate (Deutsches Kalisyndikat GmbH); interned, 1945–1948.

1 BLHA, Rep. 36 A/2661, fol. 77. This letter has been translated from German.
2 The original contains several notes, including 'To be filed, 25 May 1937'.
3 Many emigrants had to leave household effects behind upon departure, storing them temporarily with forwarding agents or – as in this case – with the Jewish Community.

For all these reasons, I request that you give permission to waive or reduce the storage fees for the eight crates placed by me in the Household Goods Repository of the Jewish Community of Berlin, no. 55, 140/141 Greifswalder Strasse.

Respectfully

DOC. 280
Frankfurter Zeitung, 16 May 1937: article on the increased revenue from the Reich Flight Tax as a result of the mass emigration of Jews[1]

The revenue from the Reich Flight Tax. From deterrent to revenue stream.

Issue no. 2 of 'Wirtschaftskurve' for the year 1937 has just come out.[2] *We take from this issue the following article, which discusses the revenue from the Reich Flight Tax and how the tax has evolved. The Editors.*

The Reich Flight Tax was originally created under the Emergency Decree of 8 December 1931 as a fiscal deterrent to capital flight. Over the course of the years, however, although this was by no means its actual purpose, the tax has come to be a rather abundant source of income for the Reich. In accordance with the aims that were relevant when it was introduced, the Flight Tax was not intended to prevent the legal transfer of assets to another country; rather, it was supposed to make such transfer 'unprofitable' with regard to taxation. Anyone who wanted to transfer his place of residence in order, say, to evade the grasp of the German tax authorities in a foreign tax haven was to be deprived of the hope of really getting a good deal in the process. Originally, therefore, the regulation prohibited neither the transfer of residence to a foreign country nor the taking along of assets. It did, however, provide that every Reich subject who gave up his residence or his habitual abode in Germany in order to relocate to another country had to pay one quarter of his assets as a 'Flight Tax' if he had assets in excess of 200,000 Reichsmarks or an annual income of more than 20,000 Reichsmarks. The tax liability arose independently of whether the assets were taken abroad or not.

If one may draw a conclusion from the relatively small amounts of revenue yielded by the Flight Tax in the early days of its existence, then it appears to have achieved, to some degree, the deterrent effect intended at the time. Since it also covered individuals who had already gone abroad before the issuance of the regulation, since 1 January 1931, there was quite a lot of tax to be recouped at first, but over the course of the entire year of 1932, the monthly tax revenue remained on average below 100,000 Reichsmarks. Only from 1933 onwards did the tax yield begin to increase gradually. Two principal reasons are probably responsible for this: first, the stricter control of the borders and the monitoring of monetary transactions with foreign countries, which over time developed into total foreign exchange control, in combination with tougher practices on the part of the tax authorities; second, Jewish emigration to foreign countries, which began to increase

---

1 'Der Ertrag der Reichsfluchtsteuer: Vom Abschreckungsmittel zur Einnahmequelle', *Frankfurter Zeitung*, 16 May 1937, p. 9. This document has been translated from German.
2 The trade journal *Wirtschaftskurve* was published from 1922 to 1944 in Frankfurt am Main with the assistance of the *Frankfurter Zeitung*.

in 1933. The table shows, for each fiscal year, the development of the tax by calendar quarter.

Until early 1933 the tax revenue remained below 1 million Reichsmarks in almost every quarter; from 1933 on, a level of 4 to 6 million Reichsmarks per calendar quarter was reached. The sharp peak in 1934/35 was caused by an 'extraordinary collection' of 16 million Reichsmarks in August 1934, which was related to the emigration of an especially wealthy Jewish family.[3] Another event in 1934 was a change in the tax legislation, which was calculated to increase its yield: the *threshold* for the assets was lowered from 200,000 to 50,000 Reichsmarks, and in addition the range of taxable assets affected by the Flight Tax was expanded by including items usually exempt from the tax on assets. A second steep rise in the revenue from the Flight Tax began in 1935, doubtlessly in part in connection with the increased emigration of the Jewish population after the introduction of the Nuremberg Laws. From autumn 1935 the average revenue from the tax was at a level of approximately 15 to 16 million Reichsmarks in every calendar quarter. The fiscal year 1935/36 thus ended with a tax yield of 45.3 million Reichsmarks, after the previous year had brought in 38.1 Reichsmarks, or 22.1 million Reichsmarks if one subtracts the one-off special collection. The fiscal year 1936/37, the outcome of which is now available as well, shows a total revenue from taxation of 69.9 million Reichsmarks. Overall, up to the end of March 1937, the Reich Flight Tax has brought in almost 174 million Reichsmarks.

The Reich Flight Tax, 1931 to 1937 (in millions of Reichsmarks)

Fiscal year	April/June	July/Sept.	Oct./Dec.	Jan./March	In total
1931/32	–	–	0,565	1,363	1,938
1932/33	0,689	0,116	0,005	0,129	0,938
1933/34	2,425	5,498	5,710	3,970	17,602
1934/35	6,344	21,471*)	5,533	4,771	38,120
1935/36	2,934	4,651	22,881	14,872	45,337
1936/37	15,221	18,781	15,971	18,938	69,911
				Total	173,846

*) Including RM 16 million from 'extraordinary collection'.

Since the Flight Tax amounts to one quarter of the ascertainable assets, for the entire period of its existence, that is, since the end of 1931, the taxable assets can be calculated to amount to approximately 680 million Reichsmarks. However, this does not mean that assets of this scale or even only three quarters of this amount, hence about half a billion, were taken abroad and burdened the German foreign exchange balance with their full magnitude. For the tax liability arises not from the transfer of assets but rather from the *changing of the place of residence* to a foreign country. Since the transfer possibilities were severely limited right after the increase in tax yield, apart for example from household effects, only a small part of the sum mentioned is likely to have actually been transferred abroad.[4]

3 This report could not be verified.
4 A report on the article from *Wirtschaftskurve* appeared in the *Pariser Tageszeitung*; 'Die Judensteuer: Vom Abschreckungsmittel zur unsauberen Einnahmequelle' [The Jewish Tax: from Deterrent to Tainted Revenue Stream], *Pariser Tageszeitung*, 18 May 1937, p. 2.

DOC. 281

On 19 May 1937 the chief official of the Civil Registry Offices in Frankfurt reports to the mayor about his plan to marry Jewish couples on designated days[1]

Memorandum from the head official of the Civil Registry Offices, Fischer-Defoy,[2] to the mayor of Frankfurt am Main (Main Administrative Office, received on 20 May 1937, C 1745), dated 19 May 1937

Original – with two enclosures – to the mayor[3]
Returned *here*.

I take it for granted that it is not, as the Greater Frankfurt am Main Kreis writes, a matter of comparing Jews and Christians, but rather Jews and *Germans*.[4]

Legal regulations concerning *where* weddings are to take place do not exist. The ministerial directives contain only instructions that certain fees are to be collected if a wish is stated to conduct the wedding 'in a location other than the registry office'. Such cases are considered here only if, for example, it is a question of marrying at a person's sickbed. In addition, *in isolated cases,* weddings in the office building of the Civil Registry Office (53 Mainkai) are also performed – namely, if the couple wishes to be married outside the usual hours for weddings or has not abided by the time set by the registry office.

The statement made in the enclosed proposal that Jews were wed 'until now at random, mixed in with the *Christian* (that is, German) couples'[5] is not accurate. Efforts were subsequently made to schedule such weddings at either the beginning or the end of the likely marriage hours. Nonetheless, this time cannot be precisely determined in advance, because some couples set the date weeks before the intended wedding, while others seek to fix the date only shortly beforehand.

A comparison with the Municipal Welfare Office, where the care of all Jews is now in the hands of *one* Kreis office,[6] is not possible in this form for the Civil Registry Office, because the Civil Registry Office districts are determined by the higher administrative authority. In any event, without legal or ministerial regulation, the establishment of separate Civil Registry Offices for the registration of Germans on the one hand and Jews on the other hand could not be effected. Furthermore, besides marriages, births and deaths are also registered at the Civil Registry Office, and, for example, when there is a request to have the banns published, it is revealed only in the course of the proceedings, on the basis of the documents submitted, whether the future spouses are to be counted as Jews, persons of German blood, or Mischlinge of the first or second degree.

---

1 ISG Frankfurt, Magistratsakten/5850. This document has been translated from German.
2 Dr Werner Fischer-Defoy (1880–1955), physician; doctor in Quedlinburg, 1908–1913; assistant director of the Hygiene Museum in Dresden, 1913–1919; from 1919 physician for the city schools in Frankfurt am Main; joined the NSDAP in 1929; salaried official in Frankfurt, in charge of the Department of the City Health Office, Welfare Office, and Civil Registry Offices, 1934–1945.
3 The mayor was Dr Friedrich Krebs.
4 The NSDAP Kreisleitung in Frankfurt am Main had proposed the plan discussed by Fischer-Defoy. They had demanded a separate space for weddings and had referred the city to their own example of the consolidated service provided to Jewish welfare recipients at one Kreis office. See undated letter from the Kreisleitung, ISG Frankfurt, ibid.
5 See the undated letter of the NSDAP Kreisleitung, ibid.
6 This was done by order of the mayor, starting on 1 Oct. 1936: YVA, M1DN/75, fols. 2–3 and 8.

However, it must be acknowledged that, for the German-minded population, it is undesirable in the extreme to encounter Jews in the waiting room of the marriage hall – that is, on such an important occasion. Therefore, the question of the marriage ceremony would probably be best regulated by having weddings of Jewish couples take place in the marriage hall only on a certain day of the week and even then outside the usual marriage hours – if another day (for example, because of an impending emigration) cannot be declined, in the public office building at 53 Mainkai.

To perform marriage ceremonies for Jews 'at separate premises' as a matter of principle seems questionable, if one keeps in mind that among the Jewish couples there may be a good many foreigners, and it is not known how the Reich government would approach this matter from a foreign policy perspective if applicable.

I will therefore order that marriage ceremonies for Jews in the future be scheduled on a specified day of the week – and separately from the other marriage ceremonies.

DOC. 282

On 21 May 1937 the German Council of Municipalities summarizes the results of a survey on the treatment of Jewish patients in municipal hospitals[1]

Memorandum from the German Council of Municipalities, unsigned, Berlin, dated 21 May 1937 (copy)[2]

Result of a survey conducted on 14 April 1937 (III 2205/37) regarding admission of Jews to municipal hospitals and their treatment.[3]

Several municipal administrations were requested to answer the following questions:

1. Under what conditions and restrictions are Jews admitted to the local municipal hospitals
   (a) in the general unit?
   (b) in the private unit?

2. Are Jews always separated from the non-Jewish patients? How is segregation carried out, particularly in the general unit, that is, in the individual wards?

3. Are hospital chief physicians permitted to counsel and treat Jews during their private consultation hours; if so, under what conditions and restrictions?

4. How is it established that there are no Jews among the persons who turn up to private consultation hours?

5. In which cases are the hospital chief physicians permitted to arrange consultations with Jewish physicians?

---

1 LAB, Rep. 142/7, 3-10-11/Nr. 72. This document has been translated from German.
2 Parts of the original are underlined by hand.
3 The survey was conducted by the German Council of Municipalities (DGT), because in 1936 it had received several enquiries as to how Jewish patients were to be treated in public hospitals. On 10 June 1937 heads of the city welfare offices held a discussion with DGT representatives about the various local practices of discriminating against the Jewish poor in the city welfare system. The written record is published in Lohalm, *Fürsorge und Verfolgung*, appendix, doc. 1, pp. 84–94.

6. Are physicians, laboratories, or institutes of hospitals authorized to examine substances submitted for analysis by Jewish physicians; if so, under what restrictions (primarily bacterial serology assays, chemical and histological analyses)?

7. What restrictions apply to out-patient examination and treatment of Jews in hospital, for example, X-ray examination or treatment, physical treatment, etc.?

For the purpose of this enquiry, all persons of Jewish blood under the Nuremberg Laws, that is, also half- and three-quarter-Jews, are considered to be Jews.

The following responses to this survey were received:

Breslau:
On 1(a): There exist no restrictions on the admission of Jews to the Breslau-Herrnprotsch Sanatorium (TB) and Sanatorium North (neurological disorders). The other hospitals admit only Jews who are looked after by the Welfare Office.

On 1(b): There are no private units in the city hospitals.

On 2: Where possible, the Jews are placed together in designated rooms, so that there generally is no question of placement in wards. In principle, placement in single rooms does not occur, because this would be tantamount to favouritism of Jewish patients over Aryan ones.

On 3: There are no special provisions with respect to counselling Jews during the physicians' private consultation hours. The private consultation hours are held outside the hospitals. As far as is known here, Jewish patients have not yet consulted resident physicians during their private consultation hours. Besides, the guidelines of the Medical Chamber prevail in this respect.

On 4: The physician himself would be able to establish this.

On 5: There exist no provisions for this either, but the chief physicians in the municipal hospitals would of their own accord decline consultations with Jewish physicians, should the occasion arise.

On 6: The hospital laboratories perform analyses only for in-patients.

On 7: Out-patient care of Jews in the out-patient departments, X-ray departments, etc. is possible only for persons looked after by the Welfare Office.

Dortmund:
On 1: Since 1922 the Jews have scarcely made use of the municipal hospitals; instead they go to the two large denominational hospitals. There is no ban on the admission of Jews to either the general unit or the private unit.

On 2: If Jews are admitted to the private unit, they are placed in single rooms. In the general unit, admission still occurs, as a rule, only when the patients in question are assigned to the municipal hospitals by the Welfare Office. There, too, they are then placed in separate rooms.

On 3: There are as yet no regulations for the hospital chief physicians governing the counselling and treatment of Jews during private consultation hours.

On 4: When determining whether Jews are concerned, both the physicians and the admissions nurses must rely on the statements made by the patients.

On 5: There are no restrictions on the examination of substances that Jewish physicians submit for analysis. Likewise, there are no restrictions on the out-patient care of Jews in the hospital.

Frankfurt am Main:
On 1: Admission of Jews to municipal hospitals is subject to the same requirements as admission of sick persons of Aryan origin. There are no restrictions. In general, however, it is a matter of admission to specialist units or infectious disease units, because Jews who are ill generally go to the hospital here that belongs to the Israelite community. There are no restrictions in the private units.

On 2: Segregation of Jews from non-Jewish patients takes place if the latter so desire. If, in such a case, discharge is not justifiable from a medical standpoint, placement in simple, small single rooms results.

On 3: Chief physicians are not forbidden to counsel Jews during private consultation hours. No restrictions have been imposed either. As a matter of principle, treatment does not take place during private consultation hours in the hospital, even for sick persons of Aryan origin.

On 4: On the basis of the statements regarding 3, this automatically ceases to apply.

On 5: A prohibition does not exist. But in a university hospital, consultations with Jewish doctors rarely occur.

On 6: Examination is permitted without restrictions, especially as, in the interest of epidemic control, it frequently cannot be refused.

On 7: No restrictions!

Leipzig:
Admissions of Jewish patients to municipal hospitals are so rare that they are not an issue. But as things stand, admission cannot be refused. In some circumstances, for example, when fighting infectious diseases, it is required for general health-related reasons. Therefore, no particular arrangement has been made in any way for the local municipal hospitals, neither for the general unit nor for the private unit, nor for out-patient care. Besides, Leipzig has a Jewish hospital with ninety-two beds, where Jews go as a rule, unless treatment in a specialist department (dermatology or otology) is necessary. In other respects, too, no general regulations have been put in place here.

Munich:
For the sphere of the municipal hospitals, there exists only the rule that Jews who want to be admitted to a municipal hospital or are hospitalized by a health insurance company or a physician must be placed in special rooms, that is, must be separated from Aryan patients. Naturally, this rule must not result in any disadvantage to Aryan patients with regard to the assignment of hospital rooms; that is to say – apart from emergencies (critical condition, threat of contagion) – if there is a lack of appropriate rooms, Jews can be turned away.

Regulations or guidelines governing cases addressed by questions 3 to 7 have not been issued.

DOC. 283
On 28 May 1937 the SS Security Service discusses preliminary measures against Jews in the event of war[1]

Memorandum from SD II 112[2] (C 422 Hg.), SS-Untersturmführer Wisliceny,[3] Berlin, for Department II 1, dated 28 May 1937

Re: the position of the Jews in Case A.[4]

Just as their performance of military service under § 15 of the Military Service Law remains subject to special regulation,[5] in Case A the Jews of Germany will doubtless be placed under a special law.

However, such a law, the wording of which is not known here, will surely have been drawn up with the enactment of the Military Service Law and documented at the most senior level, so that it could be put into effect at once, if need be.

The preliminary task of the Security Service for Case A at present can be only to compile a registry of Jews[6] and in it to identify, by specially labelling them, Jewish exponents of enterprise, leading figures in Jewish political movements, and Marxist Jews.

---

1 RGVA, 500k-1-485, fol. 6. This document has been translated from German.
2 In 1936 Heydrich had reorganized the SD Main Office: Office II (domestic) took over the surveillance of adversaries. Within its Central Department II 2, Main Department II 11 (ideologies) was divided into Departments II 111 (Freemasons), II 112 (Jews), and II 113 (denominational political movements).
3 Dieter Wisliceny (1911–1948); joined the NSDAP and the SA in 1931, and the SS in 1934; worked as specialist for Freemason affairs in the SD Main Office and from April to Nov. 1937 was head of the section for Jewish affairs (II 112); with the SD in Danzig, 1937–1940; advisor for Jewish affairs in Slovakia, 1940–1943; in 1943 in charge of the Sonderkommando for Jewish Affairs in Thessaloniki; in 1944 co-organizer of the deportation of the Jews from Hungary; arrested in 1945; in 1948 sentenced to death and executed in Bratislava.
4 Code name for war.
5 § 15(5) stated: 'The service of non-Aryans in wartime is subject to special regulation': Military Service Law, 21 May 1935, *Reichsgesetzblatt*, 1935, I, p. 609.
6 The recording of the Jewish population by the Gestapo in a special registry had been under way since 1935 and was also the subject of intense discussion within the SD. See Doc. 188, 17 August 1935, and Doc. 288, 12 July 1937.

DOC. 284
Lecture by Theodor Oberländer on the strengthening of German influence in Eastern Europe, spring 1937[1]

Lecture by Theodor Oberländer,[2] attachment to a letter from the League of the German East (I. 7365/37), Deputy League Head Hoffmeyer,[3] to the German Foundation, Regierungsrat Krahmer-Möllenberg,[4] Berlin, dated 7 June 1937[5]

The fight for the intermediate zone
In the East, we live in a twofold duality. Where two states are working together – as Germany and Poland are – in the German–Polish non-violence pact,[6] peoples are continuing to fight bitterly in a struggle for nationhood. This duality of state and people is clearer to our eastern neighbours than to us, as a result of their long struggle for independent statehood. We must try to draw all the peoples and states situated between the German border and the Soviet Russian border closer to us in ideological terms. In the sphere of ethnic politics the reverse frequently occurs, owing to the defence[7] of ethnic Germans residing in this region, a defence that is naturally supported by the entire populace in the Reich. The fact that Poland defeated the Soviet Union at the Vistula river in 1920, in the 'Miracle at the Vistula', has been of decisive significance for us. It is due to this fact that Czechoslovakia, which believed that the Curzon Line would give it a direct border with Soviet Russia, did not obtain this border.[8] The same is the case for East Prussia. A direct border between Germany and the Soviet Union would have substantially decreased the value of the German–Polish pact. For all the peaceful development work of the past years is scarcely conceivable without the German–Polish pact and without there being several hundred kilometres between the German and Soviet Russian borders. If this assumption is correct, then we have an enormous stake in ensuring that this

---

1 BArch, R 8043/1168, fols. 186–195. This document has been translated from German.
2 Dr Theodor Oberländer (1905–1998), agronomist; took part in the Beer Hall Putsch in 1923; joined the NSDAP in 1933; from 1934 director of the Institute for East European Economics in Königsberg; head of the League of the German East, 1934–1937; professor in Greifswald from 1938 and in Prague from 1940; served in the war; prisoner of war, 1945–1946; in 1951 state secretary for refugee affairs in Bavaria; federal minister for expellees in the Federal Republic of Germany, 1953–1960; sentenced in the German Democratic Republic *in absentia* to life imprisonment in 1960.
3 Horst Hoffmeyer (1903–1944), banker; SA member, 1927–1939; joined the NSDAP in 1937 and the SS in 1939; head of various units for the resettlement of ethnic Germans, 1939–1941; from 1941 head of Sonderkommando R of the Ethnic German Liaison Office in Ukraine; final rank of SS-Brigadeführer and major general of police; took his own life in Soviet captivity.
4 Dr h.c. Erich Krahmer-Möllenberg (1882–1942); worked in the Prussian domestic administration, 1918–1920; chairman of the Deutsche Stiftung, a covert government organization for the promotion of German minorities in foreign countries, 1920–1940.
5 Parts of the original are underlined by hand.
6 This refers to the German–Polish Non-Aggression Pact of Jan. 1934: *Reichsgesetzblatt*, 1934, II, pp. 117–119.
7 This probably means the 'defensive struggle'.
8 After the First World War, Lord Curzon, British foreign secretary, had proposed for the Polish–Russian border a line roughly corresponding to Poland's present eastern border. Under Marshal Piłsudski, Poland conquered large areas on the other side of this line in the Polish–Soviet War of 1919–1921.

intermediate zone remains non-communist and that the Soviet Russians do not succeed in gaining a foothold in this intermediate zone. The ideological domination of this intermediate zone can, in the event of a German/Soviet Russian conflict, conserve military forces. We cannot be unconcerned about whether the 60 to 70 per cent rural population in this region is inclined towards communism or is completely non-communist. At the same time, it is not necessary to promote National Socialism per se; rather, everything that is detrimental to the advance of communism must be strengthened. For the probability that these countries must one day decide in favour of Moscow or Berlin, and that Moscow of its own accord will force such a decision, is extraordinarily great. It is from these perspectives that the region we can succinctly term intermediate Europe or East Central Europe, which shall be demarcated by the German and Soviet Russian borders and by the Baltic and Black Sea or Mediterranean, should be examined, along with the possibilities that Soviet Russia and Germany have in this region.

General features of the intermediate zone
The intermediate zone situated on the other side of the German border (East Central Europe) has few commercial raw materials of its own. Industry is not very developed; it largely dates back to Russian or Austrian times and is highly concentrated. In broad parts of this region, especially in southern Poland, we have a large agrarian overpopulation, which, from the experiences of the Russian Revolution of 1917, must be viewed as a particularly great social threat. Agricultural density with low yields, shortage of livestock, machinery, and equipment, and poor selling conditions are always an element of social unrest. These things find expression in great hardship in the countryside, especially in eastern Poland, where the farmer barely has the money to buy salt or lighting for himself. Marketing difficulties are increasing in this region, with the consequences of the battle for production in Germany and the growth in England's imports of agricultural products from its own dominions. The agricultural surpluses can scarcely be marketed these days without hefty government subsidies (export bounty). Investment of outside capital can bear interest and be paid back only with difficulty. In the entire area, oppression of the nationalities has reached an almost inconceivable level. All entrepreneurship, especially by outside capital, is being suppressed. The state is becoming the great economic leader and entrepreneur. The system of statism could be regarded as the precursor of a communist economic system wherever the state, in contrast to the German economy, dispenses with the formation and maintenance of a separate business community. For a state-managed economy with retention of a separate business community and a state-run economy with suppression of entrepreneurship are completely distinct concepts. The destruction of nationalities has led, and continues to lead, to a forcible unification and destruction of inner cultural values. A great part of the states in this intermediate zone have indeed proceeded to adopt the authoritarian principle, but without having conceptually parted company with liberalism. Today, Poland, with its domestic political difficulties, must be termed an ideological chaos. The Baltic States, despite their presidents and the authorities of these presidents, are still completely stuck in the liberal mindset. Similar things can be said of the south-east.

In the intermediate zone that is so decisive for us, Soviet Russian propaganda is sparing no effort to spread communism. What speaks in Russia's favour? The fact that, in general, in this area Russia can frequently present its own interests as exemplary without being contradicted is due to the massive ignorance that prevails in this entire area with respect to conditions in Russia. Russia makes so-called cultural autonomy part of its propaganda campaign. Throughout Russia the nationalities are being wiped out, despite freedom of speech, by destroying root and branch the family, religion, and the sense of being grounded in one's own native soil. And nonetheless Russia attempts to further its agenda by boasting of its alleged cultural autonomy and its constitution, now transformed into 'democracy'. The collective, too, is repeatedly held up as a means for remedying the land scarcity of the land-poor east Polish or east Romanian farmers. Today we know that the collective is a new form of bondage without real possibilities for progress. Otherwise, how would it be possible that, despite the billions invested in Russian agriculture, the yields of 1914 have not yet been reached? So, there is nothing in Russia's own achievement that speaks in its favour. But we must take a sober view of certain circumstances in the intermediate zone on our outskirts that do speak in favour of the Russian propaganda.

(1) First, in various cities (Łódź, Lwów, Gdynia) we find a commercial proletariat, largely of Jewish origin, which is extraordinarily dissatisfied, given the current labour conditions in Poland. Various riots in Łódź, Lwów, and Gdynia in 1936 have clearly shown that communist propaganda activity, precisely in these centres, is not being abandoned.[9]

(2) The rural proletariat is in part fertile ground for communist propaganda. When 50 per cent of the Polish farmers must work a stretch of land far less than the minimum acreage needed to sustain a family, without the possibility of a secondary income, it is an entirely unhealthy situation. The new Polish agrarian reform, which creates not farming businesses but smallholdings consisting of 3 hectare plots, can be viewed only as a desperate endeavour, with no real solution and redress of land scarcity. Only intensification of agriculture or movement of labour into industry would help to remedy the shortage of land. The former is not possible because of the surpluses in Poznań-Pomerelia, which depress the market; the latter is not possible with an existing overpopulation of around 8 million persons in the agricultural sector. The agricultural question is the future question for Poland. It will decide whether Poland can effectively oppose communist propaganda in future.

(3) The proletarianization of the upper classes is assuming an exceptionally worrying form. For the 8,000–10,000 cities of the union of the three Baltic States, Lithuania, Latvia, and Estonia, can no more be accommodated in the labour market of these three states than the enormous number of cities in Poland and Romania. And once someone has abandoned the plough, he does not return to it again, as is demonstrated precisely by the experiences of these countries. The academic proletariat of East Central Europe is the most active carrier of communist ideas. Through this academic proletariat, a broad propaganda campaign in the countryside is easily possible, especially as it is precisely this proletariat that comes from the countryside.

(4) The East European Jews, unless they are Orthodox rather than assimilationist Jews, are the most active carriers of communist ideas. As Poland alone has 3.5 million Jews, of whom more than 1.5 million can, after all, be regarded as assimilated Jews, and

---

9 In 1936 there were political riots in several Polish cities. During conflicts in Lwów in April 1936 alone, twelve people were shot dead.

as these Jews live in the ghettos of the cities in almost unbelievably poor social conditions, so that they are proletarians in the truest sense of the word, they have little to lose but much to gain. It is they who, as the wholesale buyers in the countryside, most actively and successfully push propaganda on behalf of communism.

(5) The nationality question should not be underestimated in an examination of communist work in East Central Europe. Bolshevism has frequently disguised itself in national dress. After all, the oppressed Belorussians and Ukrainians, if they are not au fait with the situation of nationalities in Soviet Russia, must prefer cultural autonomy with allegedly maximum independence to the attempted assimilation of nation states. Here one should not underestimate the explosive power of 30 million persons who, among the 90 million inhabitants of this East Central European space, are not part of the national population but rather separate ethnic communities. In eastern Poland and eastern Romania, at least, there are groups, especially among the peasantry, that are looking beyond the eastern border, not only for social reasons but also for national ones.

(6) The scant knowledge of Soviet Russia that unfortunately prevails all over East Central Europe is one of the great assets of communist propaganda, as is the lower degree of differentiation that they see in the social development of those peoples before us. The question is: what would the Soviet Union accomplish if it had 5 to 6 million people in this region who were supporters of communism, in contrast to the Belorussians, who most vehemently reject the Soviet Union? The question must be asked so that the counter question can be posed: what potential does Germany have, with its 6 million Germans living abroad in this region, to make the case for its ideas out there?

The six points show that, even though Russia does not have such groups available, the preconditions for communist propaganda are not unfavourable.

What militates against the activity of the Soviet Union is the memory of the presence and behaviour of communist troops in Riga, Lithuania, and eastern Poland shortly before the Miracle at the Vistula, in short, wherever such troops have made an appearance. What could work against the activity of the Soviet Union are certain regional issues that give rise to friction, such as Karelia, Ukraine, and Bessarabia. What is certain is that Russia is using every possible means to force a decision. An extraordinary amount of evidence could be added with respect to the Russian activity, but these questions shall be presented here in brief outline.

What is Germany's status with respect to this region?

(1) Germany is strong, and in Eastern Europe all military power has an impact. An army of 8 million men is a great asset today.

(2) Among the non-Jewish population, antisemitism is an extraordinary asset. The Eastern European peasant, who is dependent on the Jew in buying and selling, and whose monetary transactions are mostly handled by the Jew, is an avowed antisemite. Conversations with various peasants have repeatedly shown that respect for a Germany that has led the fight against Jewry is uncommonly high, and hence the feeling of support for us is great as well, though *only* within the rural population. The strengthening of a sense of rootedness in one's native soil also carries great weight. The Hereditary Farm Law[10] is being discussed by a great many different groups of peasants in Eastern

---

10 This is the Reich Hereditary Farm Law of 29 Sept. 1933: *Reichsgesetzblatt*, 1933, I, p. 685. Under this law, farms of between 7.5 and 125 hectares were classified as 'hereditary farms' and could not be

Europe. The fact that land can be realized and accepted as collateral, which gives great strength precisely to the Jews in East Central Europe, meets with sweeping opposition among the peasantry. The Hereditary Farm Law must be viewed positively and as propaganda for us.

(3) Similar things can be said of our policy on *Volksgruppen* [ethnic communities]. The Führer's speeches in 1933 asserting the rights of German ethnicity [Volkstum] and denouncing all superficial 'Germanization' have been widely welcomed in Eastern Europe. The questions of Ukrainian farmers – how do you treat your ethnic communities; do the Poles in Germany have their own schools with Polish teachers or with German ones??? – indicate what possibilities for a defined ethnic community policy will open up to Germany at some point in the future, under the motto: freedom of nationhood.

(4) Winter Relief and the Labour Service, too, play a decisive role. Winter Relief work has been conducted out there by a large part of the German ethnic community and has also been taken up by the national populations. The Labour Service too has found imitators. So there are a great many things that can have a positive influence on this region, things that are suited for rendering communist propaganda harmless and creating a positive atmosphere for us, especially among the broad masses of peasants.

That means that positive work must be done outwardly and that no effort must be spared to utilize the 6 million Germans in this region fully and completely in this ideological struggle. Against us, for one thing, is a substantial lack of knowledge about Germany. This ignorance is present in the peasant communities in particular, and as a result, nothing of equal value can be offered in response to the acutely anti-German Jewish propaganda. This Jewish propaganda has extraordinary scope and largely has complete control of the cities. Working in opposition to it in the countryside, too, is associated with nothing but difficulties. But this work in opposition is so decisive that no stone ought to be left unturned here. The memories of the occupation period[11] work against us. A period of occupation is always difficult for those who are affected, however just the occupation may be. Jewish propaganda spares no effort today to bring this occupation period to mind over and over, painting it in the most unfavourable colours. Germany's regional losses, which repeatedly awaken the guilty conscience of the beneficiaries, are against us. Lithuania, Poland, and Czechoslovakia perpetually envisage the loss of the territories annexed under the Treaty of Versailles, so that considerable friction must result from these territorial boundaries alone. Certain psychological errors that Germans make whenever they go abroad without appropriate knowledge and appropriate preparation also count against us. All the peoples of the East have a very keen sense of national identity. Wherever the German is present out there as a transmitter of cultural ideas, as a representative of a great people, who wishes to be treated everywhere with respect and deference but looks down on the small peoples with appropriate disdain, the dislike of Germany among those peoples, who are so touchy in matters of national identity, is only increased. The masses of Germans in attendance at the football match

---

divided up on the death of the owner but were instead to pass to the principal heir. They were also unsaleable and not subject to mortgage. The law had the ideological aim of protecting the farming community as the 'blood source of the German people' it stipulated that only men of German or German-related blood could be farmers.

11 This refers to the German occupation of Polish territories in the First World War.

in Warsaw had an effect that was by no means felicitous.[12] Also militating against us is the modest signal strength of the German radio stations in the East, which are drowned out by other broadcasters and are thus unable to provide an adequate link to the German ethnic communities out there or be used for propaganda purposes. Even though our positive features are countered by a host of downsides, the downsides are still offset by the existence of 6 million persons of German blood out there. If the German ethnic communities out there endeavour everywhere, without parading the form of National Socialism in any way and with full loyalty towards the national populations, to present themselves as a little Third Reich through the strengthening of self-help measures, then they can do an immense amount to oppose communism in these countries. Strengthening, differentiation and strengthening of the peasantry are the fundamental principles of our work in Eastern Europe. The utilization of this Germandom abroad, under unified leadership and with the activation of even the last available forces, is a decisive challenge, which cannot be foregone. Granted, scarcely any people has had such enormous losses in terms of national politics over 1½ decades as Germany. Granted, the work of centuries has been largely wiped out in East Central Europe over the past 1½ decades. That does not mean that we must now watch while the sizeable remainder of German influence in Eastern Europe is wiped out because we are unable to offer a new body of our own thought in opposition to all those corrosive liberal and Bolshevik influences. We have no right to ask those Germans to fight and commit themselves for their Germanhood if we do not believe that it can be saved. For if we ever believe that this people will be assimilated, this process need no longer be prolonged and thereby made more painful. But because we believe that every German in Eastern Europe also has a great ideological task, because we believe that Germandom cannot be rescued until the Führer's principles regarding freedom of nationhood have found universal recognition, because we regard every German village and every German person out there as a combat outpost ahead of the great German eastern front, we must spare no effort to strengthen this German ethnic group abroad ideologically and spiritually, without thereby doing anything whatsoever against the government of the national populations but indeed, at times, against the liberal ideas on which this system of government is based today. The example of a few German children from a Galician village, who, returning after spending the holidays in Germany, linked this entire village inwardly with the Reich again and, through their positive reports on Germany, were, for a great many Ukrainian farmers, living witnesses to the fact that the Jewish propaganda about Germany was wrong, should demonstrate to us what a great weapon Germandom abroad presents to us. Thus far we have not put this weapon to full use; until now we have looked on as a struggle of all against all broke out among Germandom abroad. We have not endeavoured, as was natural after the great upheaval in 1933, to spiritually win over Germanhood abroad and thus simultaneously avoid the great rift that must inevitably have a fatal effect, over the long term, in the ethnic communities living under the law of a foreign state. And all that has come about only because the single great task that has existed in East Central Europe since 1933 was not pointed out immediately. Without great tasks, petty fights and conflicts always result. Control of the intermediate zone is one of the great tasks that

---

[12] This evidently refers to the friendly between Poland and Germany on 13 Sept. 1936.

await us in the East, and, as preparation for a power-political contest, it cannot be overestimated. And this task can be performed only when it is recognized by all the key forces of the Movement and when the factors to be deployed in the process are also supported by all the key forces of the Movement.

DOC. 285
On 16 June 1937 the Reich Ministry of Finance asks the Deputy of the Führer for a response on the planned introduction of special taxes for Jews[1]

Letter (secret) from the Reich Ministry of Finance (no. 31/37 III g), signed Hedding,[2] to the Deputy of the Führer, for the attention of Main Department Head Fritz Reinhardt, dated 16 June 1937, with enclosure (copy)

Re: taxation of Jews

I hereby forward the draft of a law on the settlement of damages inflicted on the German Reich by Jews. The wording of the draft corresponds to the outcome of the departmental meeting on 18 February 1937. I request that you advise me of your reaction to the draft.

p.p. signed Hedding

To the Deputy of the Führer
For the attention of Main Department Head Reinhardt in *Berlin*

Secret! On no. 31/37 IIIg

Draft Law on the Settlement of Damages Inflicted on the German Reich by Jews[3]
The Reich government has enacted the following law, which is hereby proclaimed.

§ 1

(1) To ensure compensation for disadvantages caused to the German Reich by Jews, a special fund of the Reich is being created from taxes levied on Jews. This fund will be administered separately from the other assets of the Reich.

(2) To create the special fund (1), surcharges are being added to the income tax (including the wage tax) and the tax on assets for Jews of German nationality who have a residence or their habitual abode in the German Reich. The surcharges amount to, in the case of the income tax ... per cent, in the case of the tax on assets ... per cent.

---

1 BArch, R 2/31097. This document has been translated from German.
2 Dr Otto Hedding (1881–1960), lawyer; practised law, 1909–1914; counsel in the Sal. Oppenheim Company in Cologne, 1918–1920; worked at the Reich Tax Authorities in the Cologne district from 1920 and as departmental director in the Cologne Regional Tax Office, 1926–1930; director of the Upper Silesian Regional Tax Office, 1930–1932; ministerial director from 1932 in the Reich Ministry of Finance, where he was head of Department III (income tax, tax law, etc.) from 1936.
3 Such a special tax law had already been discussed extensively at the end of 1936. See Doc. 257, 18 Dec. 1936.

(3) The surcharges can be changed by the Reich Minister of Finance in consultation with the Reich Minister of the Interior and the Deputy of the Führer, depending on the magnitude of the disadvantages caused by Jews.

§ 2

(1) The decision on the use of the special fund is made by the Reich Minister of the Interior in consultation with the Deputy of the Führer and the Reich ministers involved.

(2) The special fund can also be used to promote the emigration of Jews with low incomes from the German Reich.

§ 3

The surcharges under § 1(2) will be collected for the first time:

for the wage tax, based on the amounts of tax to be withheld for a wage-payment period ending after 31 December 1937;

for the assessed income tax, based on the tax due for the calendar year 1938;

for the tax on assets, based on the amounts of tax to be paid for the fiscal year 1938.

§ 4

The Reich Minister of Finance, in consultation with the Reich Minister of the Interior and the Deputy of the Führer, enacts the legal and administrative provisions required for implementing and supplementing the law.[4]

DOC. 286
On 22 June 1937 the Reich Foreign Office informs the embassies of the German position towards the establishment of a Jewish state in Palestine[1]

Circular decree (strictly confidential!) from the Reich Foreign Office (83–21 A.15/6.), p.p. von Bülow-Schwante,[2] to all missions, the German consulates general in Batavia, Beirut, Danzig, Jerusalem, Calcutta, Memel, Ottawa, Singapore, Sydney, the German consulates in Hong Kong, Tétouan, Geneva, dated 22 June 1937

The riots in Palestine over the course of 1936 led to the institution of a Royal British Commission headed by Lord *Peel*.[3] This commission was tasked with examining the Jewish and Arab claims in Palestine and finding a solution to the Arab-Jewish conflict. The report of the commission, now complete, has not yet been made public. It has become known from press commentaries, however, that this report evidently also gives consideration to the idea of a division of Palestine into an Arab part and a Jewish part.

---

4 The Deputy of the Führer pressed for the passage of this law, but the plan was not realized in 1937 for economic reasons: letter from the Deputy of the Führer to State Secretary Reinhardt, dated 10 Dec. 1937, and letter from Reinhardt to the Deputy of the Führer, 23 Dec. 1937, BArch, R 2/31097.

1 BArch, R 34/3309 (Film), Aufn. 370 133–370138. Published in *Akten zur deutschen auswärtigen Politik 1918–1945*, series D: *1937–1945*, vol. 5: *Polen, Südosteuropa, Lateinamerika, Klein- und Mittelstaaten, Juni 1937 – März 1939* (Baden-Baden: Imprimerie Nationale, 1953), doc. 564, pp. 632–634. This document has been translated from German.

2 Vicco von Bülow-Schwante (1891–1970), diplomat; worked for the Reich Foreign Office from 1914; SA member; from 1934 head of protocol in the Reich Foreign Office and head of the Germany Section; ambassador to Belgium, 1938–1940; worked in the private sector after 1945.

For months, the Jewish press – in Germany too – has been passionately championing the creation of a Jewish state or at least a Jewish-run state structure under a British Mandate, with propaganda being employed to promote the expansion of the Jewish territory to the maximum possible extent. Skilfully, world Jewry is beating the drum in the pro-Jewish press abroad for the establishment of a Jewish state in Palestine. According to reports from the German embassies in Stockholm and Helsinki, known Zionist leaders have called on the Swedish and Finnish governments and attempted to promote the creation of a Jewish state in Palestine.

The Arab world is following this development with burning interest and opposing every measure of the British Mandatory power that could strengthen Jewish influence in Palestine. Arabdom too is beginning to mobilize the world press and direct attention to the danger of a Jewish state in Palestine. In the process, the governments of the Arab states, Iraq in particular but Egypt as well, are entirely on the side of the Arabs in Palestine, according to current reports.

The attitude of the various governments towards the possible founding of a Jewish state in Palestine has not always been clear thus far. What proposals the Peel Commission of the British government will make cannot be discerned for the present. British Foreign Secretary Eden,[4] replying to an enquiry by the German ambassador in London,[5] merely stated that the solution to the Palestine question is one of the most difficult problems of British foreign policy. In fact, the British Mandatory power is probably in the difficult position of faithfully honouring the assent given by Balfour during the war to the establishment of a Jewish 'national home' in Palestine without neglecting the urgent concern of the empire for the Arab world. As affairs now stand, it must probably be assumed that this concern is strong enough to exclude, first of all, a solution that completely satisfies Jewish desires. On the other hand, one must not fail to recognize that international Jewry, particularly in the United States of America, is seeking, not without success, to influence the decision of the British government.

Italian public opinion has adopted a rather clear and in fact adverse stance. Recently, Italian press commentaries devoting critical attention to the Jewish question, even in Italy, have become more frequent. However, in regard to the Italian attitude towards the idea of a Jewish state in Palestine, what carries weight is not so much an antisemitic animosity as the fear that England could parlay the establishment of a Jewish Palestinian state into a platform for its Mediterranean policy. That this fear is not entirely unfounded is demonstrated by the language of the Jewish press, which – although perhaps only as a *captatio benevolentiae*[6] intended for the ear of the Peel Commission – repeatedly points to the identity of Jewish and British interests in Palestine. Mussolini's declaration of

---

3 Lord William Robert Wellesley Peel (1867–1937), lawyer; British transport minister, 1921–1922; secretary of state for India, 1922–1924 and 1928–1929; member of the Indian Round Table Conference, 1931–1932; chairman of the British Royal Commission for Palestine, whose proposal for partition was not implemented, 1936–1937.
4 Sir Anthony Eden (1897–1977), British politician; foreign secretary, 1935–1938; secretary of state for war, 1940, then foreign secretary, 1940–1945 and 1951–1955; prime minister of Britain, 1955–1957.
5 During 1936–1938 the ambassador in London was Joachim von Ribbentrop (1893–1946), businessman; joined the NSDAP in 1932 and the SS in 1933; minister of foreign affairs, 1938–1945; arrested in 1945, sentenced to death at the Nuremberg trials, and executed in 1946.
6 Latin for 'fishing for good will'.

friendship addressed to the Arabs upon his receipt of the 'Sword of Islam'[7] might well also point the way towards an assessment of the Italian attitude towards developments in Palestine.

As far as can be judged to date, French interests in the Mediterranean would not be affected by the establishment of a Jewish state in Palestine to the same extent as the Italian sphere of interest. Nonetheless, one cannot estimate the stance France would adopt towards England's presentation to the Mandate Commission of the League of Nations of a resolution concerning a reorganization of the Palestine Mandate.

The processes described here have led to a revision of the German point of view regarding the problem of creating a Jewish state in Palestine. Until now it was the primary goal of Germany's Jewish policy to promote the emigration of Jews from Germany whenever possible. To achieve this goal, even foreign exchange policy sacrifices are made. Through the conclusion of a transfer agreement with Palestine (the so-called Haavara Agreement), Jews emigrating to Palestine are able to obtain certain funds released by additional German exports to Palestine, as a way of establishing an existence. This German approach, dictated by domestic political reasons, which in effect promotes consolidation of the Jews in Palestine and thus accelerates the building of a Jewish state there, could have contributed to the theory that Germany is sympathetic to the establishment of a Jewish state in Palestine.

In reality, however, Germany has a greater stake in keeping Jewry fragmented. For the Jewish question will not be solved for Germany when there are no more members of the Jewish race residing on German soil. Rather, the developments of recent years have demonstrated that inevitably international Jewry will forever be the ideological and thus the political adversary of National Socialist Germany. The Jewish question is thus simultaneously one of the most significant problems of German foreign policy. Therefore, there is also considerable German interest in the developments in Palestine. For a Palestinian state will not absorb the Jews but rather create for them – corresponding, for example, to the sphere of influence of the Vatican City State – an additional basis in international law, one that could have a disastrous effect on German foreign policy.

Although a direct German intervention in the development of the Palestine question is not envisaged, the German embassy in London, the German legation in Baghdad, and the German consulate general in Jerusalem have received instructions that take this standpoint into account.[8]

(1) The British government has been informed by the German ambassador in London that Germany has indeed promoted the emigration of the Jews to Palestine whenever possible. But, he said, it is wrong to assume that the creation of a state structure more or less under Jewish leadership in Palestine would be welcomed by Germany. Germany, he continued, cannot assume, in view of the agitation against Germany by international

---

7 In March 1937 Mussolini visited the Italian colony of Libya. During an elaborate ceremony in Tripoli on 18 March, two Libyan veterans of the Second Italo-Abyssinian War presented him with the 'Sword of Islam'. In an acceptance speech, Mussolini declared his sympathies for Islam and Muslims throughout the world.
8 On 1 June 1937 Foreign Minister von Neurath had instructed these offices that Germany was now opposed to the establishment of a Jewish state, so that no power base for international Jewry could arise: *Akten zur deutschen auswärtigen Politik 1918–1945*, series D: *1937–1945*, vol. 5, doc. 561, pp. 629–630.

Jewry, that the establishment of a Jewish state in Palestine would be conducive to the peaceful development of the peoples.

(2) The German legation in Baghdad has received instructions to indicate more plainly than before the German interest in Arab national ambitions.

(3) Jerusalem has received identical instructions.

The extent to which the foreign policy instructions will produce a change in domestic policy measures in the area of emigration policy is subject for the moment to the review and decision of the relevant domestic German authorities.

I request a report if perceptible attempts are made by the Jews there to arouse interest among the public or in local government in the establishment of a Jewish state in Palestine.

DOC. 287
Zwischen Weichsel und Nogat, June 1937: article demanding that a Jewish farmer leave the village of Gnojau[1]

How much longer will the Jew Anker continue to own a farm?

Now that Jews and companions of Jews, if they were residents of Kreis Großes Werder,[2] have taken to their heels or are busily packing their bags, it ought to be time also to alert the Jew Anker to the fact that the population of Kreis Großes Werder expects that he too will return to German hands the German land in the village of Gnojau that he at present calls his own.

It is typical Jewish impudence not to have already come to this conclusion himself. It is a disgrace that the land that was cultivated by our ancestors and not by the Jew is being withheld from the indigenous farmers, men of our own people, by foreign and racially alien elements.

---

1 'Wie lange ist noch Jud Anker Besitzer einer Landwirtschaft!', *Zwischen Weichsel und Nogat*, no. 2, June 1937, p. 2. This document has been translated from German. The newspaper *Zwischen Weichsel und Nogat* began publication in 1935. Issue no. 2 from 1937 bore the motto 'Who would oppose the authority of his German blood!'

2 The rural Kreis Großes Werder lay to the east of the Vistula river. It was created in 1920, as a consequence of the Treaty of Versailles, from parts of the Elbing and Marienwerder Kreise and was added to the territory of the city of Danzig. From that time on Danzig, as a free city, was under the protection of the League of Nations.

DOC. 288

On 12 July 1937 the SS Security Service holds talks with the Gestapo to discuss the next census and the racial registration of the Jews[1]

Note by the SD, Department II 112 (Wi./Hrt.), Wisliceny, for II 1, dated 12 July 1937[2]

Submission II 1 verbally for decision, as there is a new state of affairs, Eichm.[3]
Re: *registry of Jews.*

On 12 July 1937, in the Gestapo Central Office, a discussion involving Regierungsrat Dr Haselbacher,[4] Assessor Flesch, and SS-Untersturmführer Wisliceny took place. The subject of the consultation was the planned preparation of a registry of Jews by the SD in cooperation with the Party and state offices concerned.[5]

At the beginning of the conversation, Regierungsrat Dr Haselbacher introduced a letter he had just received from the Chief of the Security Police, which deals with the registration of the Jews in Germany.[6] The letter states that negotiations with the Ministry of the Interior have just taken place and are to be continued in August with the purpose of preparing a registry of the German people on the basis of a population census. In this census, which is scheduled for 1938, detailed enquiries are to be made about racial composition and denominational affiliation.[7] Provision of false information in this survey will be punished with imprisonment. In this way it is possible to also record the quarter- and half-Jews. After the conclusion and evaluation of the census, every local police authority will thus have available a registry of Jews, half-Jews, and persons intermarried with a Jew. All information about race can then be furnished by the police authorities. With this fact in mind, Dr Haselbacher took the view that it is not expedient to have surveys concerning the Jews carried out directly by the Party organizations. There is absolutely no guarantee, he said, that the block and cell leaders of the Party will collect completely precise material. Besides, he said, the SD, by preparing such a registry,

---

1 RGVA, 500k-1-495, fols. 11–12. This document has been translated from German.
2 Parts of the original are underlined by hand.
3 Handwritten note by Eichmann. Adolf Karl Eichmann (1906–1962); originally worked as sales representative; joined the NSDAP and the SS in 1932; worked in the SD Main Office in Berlin, 1934–1938; from summer 1938 headed the Central Office for Jewish Emigration in Vienna and in 1939 the Central Office in Prague; from autumn 1939 worked in the Reich Security Main Office (RSHA) on the organization of the deportations of Jews from Reich territory; from Dec. 1939 special advisor for the evacuation of the Eastern provinces, then head of RSHA Section IV D 4; by March 1941, head of IV B 4 (Jewish affairs, evacuation affairs); incarcerated, 1945–1946; escaped in 1946; in hiding in Argentina, 1950–1960; kidnapped by the Israeli secret service in 1960; sentenced to death and executed in Israel in 1962.
4 Dr Karl Haselbacher (1904–1940), lawyer; joined the NSDAP and the SA in 1933, and the SS in 1934; from 1934 worked in the Gestapo Central Office (Gestapa); in 1936 head of Office II B (churches, Freemasons, Jews, emigrants) there; in 1939 head of the Düsseldorf Gestapo; in 1940 senior commander of the Security Police and the SD in Brussels.
5 See also the memorandum from the Gestapa II B 4, dated 12 July 1937: RGVA, 500k-1-495, fols. 11–12.
6 This letter could not be found.
7 The census planned for 1938 was not carried out until May 1939. Using so-called supplementary cards, respondents had to list the religion of all four grandparents. This information was used to establish 'racial affiliation'.

would become an information office for the Party.[8] He added that the census would take place before the SD's registry of Jews could be ready. Dr Haselbacher therefore took the view that preparation of the registry must be postponed until 1938. He intends to speak with Klopfer[9] along these lines.

Evaluation of the census by the SD is then to be undertaken as follows:

The police stations pass on a duplicate of their file cards for Jews and Mischlinge to the SD sub-districts. The expert within the sub-district then adds to this information in accordance with the SD's guidelines. But to make a start anyway, Dr Haselbacher suggested that the SD take over the organized Jews' membership rosters, which are stored in the Gestapo Central Office. These rosters include around 90 per cent of the full Jews living in Germany.[10] This material will be made available to the SD sub-districts, which will begin preparing a registry of full Jews according to the guidelines of the SD Main Office. After the planned census, this registry will be supplemented only as to the non-organized Jews and the Mischlinge. A great deal of useless duplication of effort will thus be avoided. The rosters of the Jewish organizations will be kept up to date, as the latter are obliged to report their membership every month. In addition, Dr Haselbacher agreed to the immediate forwarding of the aforementioned letter to the Chief of the Security Police.

A decision is requested as to whether a reworking in this regard of the guidelines authorized by C.[11] should take place. Precise instructions can then be given to the sub-district specialists at the conference scheduled for 1 September 1937.[12]

[8] The left-hand margin contains the handwritten word 'correct'.
[9] Presumably Oberregierungsrat Dr Gerhard Klopfer (1905–1987), lawyer; joined the NSDAP and the SA in 1933 and the SS in 1935; on the staff of the Deputy of the Führer from 1935; attended the Wannsee Conference on 20 Jan. 1942; state secretary in the Party Chancellery, 1942; SS-Gruppenführer, 1944; classified as a 'lesser offender' by the Nuremberg denazification tribunal, 1949; worked as a lawyer in Ulm from 1956.
[10] See the Gestapo directive on the preparation of a Jewish registry, dated 17 August 1935, according to which all Jewish organizations, including the Jewish communities, had to furnish the Gestapo with membership lists: Doc. 188.
[11] Chief of the Security Police, Reinhard Heydrich.
[12] The planned conference evidently did not take place until 1 Nov. 1937 in the RSHA.

DOC. 289

Der Fremdenverkehr: reproduction of the decree issued by State Secretary Hans Pfundtner on 24 July 1937 concerning the separation of Jewish from non-Jewish guests in baths and spa resorts[1]

Reich Committee for Tourism[2]

The President:[3] *Directive no. 7*

Jewish visitors to health resorts

The Reich and Prussian Minister of the Interior, with a decree addressed to the regional governments (for Prussia: the Oberpräsidenten and the Regierungspräsidenten, dated 24 July 1937 (I B 3 1043 X/5012 e), has stated:[4]

To the extent that visits by out-of-town Jewish spa guests are regulated for baths and health resorts, the following guidelines are to be observed by state and municipal providers of spa facilities:

(1) Jewish spa guests are to be *accepted* at those *health spas* in which there is a way to accommodate them *separately from the other spa guests* in Jewish spa facilities, hotels, guesthouses, boarding houses, or the like. The *prerequisite* in this case is that no female personnel of German blood under the age of 45 may be employed in these establishments.

Community facilities that serve health-related purposes, such as pump rooms and baths, are *also* to be made available *to Jews*. However, it is permissible, out of consideration for the non-Jewish spa guests, to impose on Jews appropriate *restrictions as to place and time with respect to use*, such as restriction to certain bathing cubicles or bathing hours. Jews can be excluded from the community facilities that do not directly serve health-related purposes, such as spa gardens, sports fields, and spa restaurants.

In all *other baths and health resorts*, Jews can be *excluded in general* or *in part* from the spa facilities or restricted to existing Jewish establishments (number 1, paragraph 1).

Health spas within the meaning of this directive are those spas at which natural or localized curative resources are made available to the public in a fitting way to the public for the purpose of regaining health.

---

1 'Jüdische Kurgäste', *Der Fremdenverkehr*, no. 33, 14 August 1937, p. 5. This document has been translated from German. The Reich organ for German tourism was published from 1936 to 1945 in Berlin by the Reich Committee for Tourism and later by the Reich Tourism Association.
2 The Reich Committee for Tourism emerged in 1931 from the Reich Working Group for the Promotion of German Transport, which had been founded in 1929. The Reich Committee had the status of a Reich authority.
3 Hermann Esser was executive president from 1935 to 1945.
4 Express letter from the Reich and Prussian Minister of the Interior, p.p. signed Pfundtner, to the regional governments, for Prussia: the Oberpräsidenten and the Regierungspräsidenten, dated 24 July 1937, BArch, R 58/276, fols. 83–84. Published in Pätzold (ed.), *Verfolgung, Vertreibung*, p. 138. On the background, see Doc. 244, 30 August 1936.

(2) A Jew is defined on the basis of § 5 of the First Regulation to the Reich Citizenship Law of 14 November 1935 (*Reichsgesetzblatt*, I, p. 1333). No *distinction* is made between native and foreign Jews.

(3) Before issuance of a regulation, the *Reich Committee for Tourism* is to be given an opportunity to state an opinion.

I request that further details be arranged and that, in consultation with the *Reich Committee for Tourism*, action be taken to ensure that these guidelines are also observed by the other providers of spa facilities.

In cases of doubt, my decision should be obtained. This applies in particular even where it is doubtful whether a spa or resort is to be regarded as a health spa.

The guidelines above, which the Reich and Prussian Minister of the Interior has issued with respect to *state* and *municipal* providers of spa facilities, are to be observed also by other providers of spa facilities if and when they wish to regulate the visit of Jewish spa guests.

Berlin, 10 August 1937.

p.p. Dr Hessel.[5]

DOC. 290

Pariser Tageszeitung, 24 July 1937: article about the introduction of a defence tax targeting Jews in the National Socialist state[1]

Germany introduces a national defence tax
Initially 50 per cent surtax on the income tax – a special tax directed primarily against the Jews

Berlin, 23 July.
A new Reich law of 20 July, which is just being promulgated, introduces a 'national defence tax', which is to be paid by those German nationals who are not subject to military service. The defence tax is payable up to the age of 45.[2] During the first two years, the defence tax is to amount to 50 per cent of the income tax. Later it is to be reduced to 6 per cent.

Germans who reside abroad, as well as those who have become unfit for military service as a result of an accident or a disease acquired during labour service, and those with an income below a certain, very low, annual limit, are exempt from the tax. Even so, persons not required to pay income tax must pay a minimum tax.

---

5 Dr August Hessel (1896–1976), lawyer; from 1923 worked in the Bavarian civil service; at the Bavarian State Ministry of Foreign Affairs, 1931–1933; at the Bavarian State Chancellery, 1933–1934; at the Bavarian State Ministry of Economics, 1934–1936; on the Reich Committee for Tourism from 1936; joined the NSDAP in 1937.

1 'Deutschland führt eine Wehrsteuer ein', *Pariser Tageszeitung*, 24 July 1937, p. 1. This document has been translated from German.

2 Law Concerning a Tax on Persons Not Conscripted for Two Years of Active Military Service (Defence Tax), 20 July 1937; *Reichsgesetzblatt*, 1937, I, pp. 821–822.

The defence tax will be applied as of 1 September to young people born in 1914, 1915, and 1916.

In a semi-official statement of grounds, it is said that the young people who are conscripted for military service are at a disadvantage in their working life, while the others can continue their apprenticeship period or pursue their occupation. The defence tax is intended to compensate for this inequality.

Evidently, the defence tax that has existed in Switzerland for fifty years was drawn on here, but in contrast to Switzerland, the new German law targets primarily an entire category of German nationals who are declared unworthy to bear arms.[3] These are the Jewish subjects of Germany, who the Nuremberg Laws have subjected to a state of emergency. Besides, the 50 per cent surtax on the income tax is enormous, and there is not the least certainty that it really will be reduced two years from now.

DOC. 291
In summer 1937 Max Warburg submits to State Secretary Wilhelm Stuckart proposals to encourage Jewish emigration[1]

Position paper for discussion with Stuckart, undated and unsigned (late July/early August 1937)[2]

File copy[3]

I. *Goal: promotion of emigration.*

Notwithstanding the fact that the position of the German government on the Jewish question is fundamentally different from that of the Jews in Germany themselves, both parties meet in the effort to encourage the emigration of the Jews from Germany by all available means.

The promotion of emigration entails creating or improving the conditions for the resettlement of the Jews in other countries.

As the countries that are potential immigration destinations do not accept immigrants randomly, but rather make quite specific demands in terms of the training and economic strength of their future citizens, the Jewish emigrants coming from Germany must be appropriately prepared and equipped with respect to jobs. This applies all the

---

3 The Military Service Law of 21 May 1935 had introduced Aryan origin as a requirement for active military service: *Reichsgesetzblatt*, 1935, I, p. 609.

1 Warburg-Archiv, Hamburg, 'Besprechung mit Staatssekretär Dr. Stuckart' (1937). This document has been translated from German.
2 The position paper was prepared for a meeting between Max Warburg and Stuckart. A letter from Warburg, who saw himself here as the spokesman of the German Jews, on 9 August 1937 makes it clear that the discussion had taken place that day and that he had presented 'in the entirety of its contents' the plan reproduced here: letter from Warburg to Hirsch, 9 August 1937, ibid. After the meeting, Warburg personally informed Reich Minister of Economics Schacht by telephone about his initiative and the conversation with Stuckart: memorandum by Warburg, 10 August 1937, ibid. The memorandum was forwarded to Stuckart on 23 August 1937: see unsigned memorandum dated 10 Nov. 1937, ibid.
3 This is handwritten in the original.

more as they must reckon with strong competition from Japanese and Polish immigrants. *Proper training and adequate equipping of the Jewish emigrants are thus of decisive importance for the promotion of emigration.*

II. *Training of emigrants. Occupational restructuring.*
It is first and foremost *craftsmen, skilled workers, independent farmers, and farm workers* who are needed abroad. In the case of women, whose work is just as important as that of men when it comes to emigrating, *workers trained in housekeeping and nursing* are required.

The general requirement for the *creation of training workshops* for Jewish youths who are willing to emigrate was stated in the decree of the Reich and Prussian Minister of Science, Schooling, and Education, reference number E IV 3842 M, dated 13 July 1936, prepared with the assistance of the Reich and Prussian Minister of the Interior.[4]

However, the training workshops set up on the basis of this decree can only partially meet the need for artisanal training possibilities, as, for many occupations, training cannot be conducted in training workshops but rather must be provided in individual craft and industrial enterprises themselves.

Although the Reich and Prussian Minister of Education stated in the aforementioned decree that 'the learning of a craft can in any event only occur as part of a proper apprenticeship, which Jewish youths are at liberty to undertake', businesses with non-Jewish owners do not accept Jewish apprentices. The Jewish commercial and craft operations are steadily decreasing in number and importance, and in most cases the apprentices in such businesses are not allowed to take the prescribed exams.

In order to meet the need for training positions, therefore, the training of future emigrants should be permitted also in industrial plants that in principle are not entitled to train apprentices within the meaning of the Commercial Code, because the training cannot be performed by a master craftsman.

In order to facilitate acceptance into the firms, this would have to be possible at no charge, and for this purpose, in accordance with legal rulings by several main insurance offices, it must *be guaranteed* that previous recipients of *unemployment, crisis, and welfare benefits* continue to receive this support *even during retraining*, although these persons naturally could be subject to the requirement that they must be available at all times for labour deployment.

For *agricultural training*, on the basis of agreements with the administrative office of the Reich Farmers' Leader, it was possible to set up a number of agricultural training sites for Jewish youth. It must be noted, however, that valuable time has unfortunately been lost here as a result of the frequently protracted approval procedure, which takes more than a year. *This procedure should therefore be accelerated.* In addition, if the very expensive Jewish training sites are not sufficient, *training on large farms or in certain farming businesses* should also be permitted.

Alongside the occupational training, it will be necessary for those Jews who wish to emigrate to acquire language skills and not to leave Germany without a good knowledge

---

4 The circular decree dated 13 July 1936 authorized the setting up of technical schools providing training in skilled crafts and agriculture for Jews in order to prepare them for emigration: Walk (ed.), *Das Sonderrecht für die Juden im NS-Staat*, p. 168.

of the language of the country to which they will go. *No difficulties of any kind should be presented by the government to this language training* at any level (in Jewish schools, houses of learning, courses).

If the emigrants are to meet the serious demands on their physical fitness that await them out there, it will also be necessary to provide them with athletic training. That includes, above all, *instruction in swimming*, which is made impossible for Jewish youth almost everywhere today.

Inducing persons to emigrate who in terms of age, occupation, and physical fitness are *completely unsuited* to the establishment of an existence in a foreign country would absolutely have to be prevented. Not only will such people not be accepted by foreign countries, but in addition their appearance is apt to affect in the gravest way the willingness of the foreign countries to accept immigrants. If such people, for whatever reasons, cannot remain in their present places of residence, then they should be given an opportunity to find a job elsewhere in Germany, whether with relatives or in a different line of work. *It should not be permitted, however, for these alternatives to be closed to them in order to induce them to emigrate 'voluntarily'.*

III. *Equipping of emigrants. Funding.*
Neither the craftsman nor the farmer nor the retailer can establish an existence without himself having modest means or receiving financial assistance. The worker must be able to survive at least the earliest period, until he has found a job.

The increase in the *Reich Flight Tax* for an asset level of RM 50,000 and upwards signifies a very substantial complication of emigration, given the low rate of the blocked mark for emigrants. At an average rate of 20 per cent for the emigrants' blocked mark, this capital is actually worth only RM 10,000 abroad for the emigrant. If he has to surrender an additional 25 per cent of that before emigrating, in the foreign country he is actually left with only RM 7,500 out of domestic assets of RM 50,000.

We ask that you seriously consider whether, given this state of affairs, an increase in the exemption threshold for assets is possible in the case of the Reich Flight Tax, such that at least the low emigrant assets are exempted from the tax and that the emigrants retain an adequate amount for establishing a new existence abroad.[5]

It must be kept in mind that it is precisely the owners of these small assets who are usually middle-aged people, who have accumulated their assets over years of work and now are especially hard hit by emigration and, in addition, can hardly create a new existence abroad without capital. In this regard, we ask that you also consider whether *a part of the revenue from the Reich Flight Tax cannot be diverted* in order to create a fund from which *subsidies can be paid to deserving poor emigrants*. For recipients of welfare benefits who wish to emigrate – in accordance with the practice of several district wel-

---

5 A waiver of the Reich Flight Tax was discussed at a ministerial meeting on 18 Oct. 1937: see Doc. 301, 18 Oct. 1937. However, the validity period of the Reich Flight Tax Law was extended by one year on 19 Dec. 1937. On 23 Dec. 1937 the Reich Ministry of Finance ruled that in the case of 'emigrating Jews or Jewish *Mischlinge*', the prerequisites for an exemption from this tax were generally not present. However, if the levy of the tax was an obstacle to the 'desired emigration of a Jew', applications for reduction or waiver could be submitted to the Reich Ministry of Finance: circular decree of the Reich Ministry of Finance (S 19 115–20 III), 23 Dec. 1937, *Reichssteuerblatt*, no. 96, 29 Dec. 1937, p. 1295.

fare associations – a *contribution to the resettlement costs* should be made in general, as a replacement for the public benefits otherwise to be paid.

If the emigrants' own resources are insufficient, financial assistance must be given to them, as described, in the form of subsidies. The providers of this support are, to the extent it is still possible for them, the Jewish communities in particular, and foreign countries.

The indispensable financial assistance from abroad can be obtained only if a major part of the support is provided by the Jews in Germany. *Every negotiation with the foreign relief organizations begins with the question of the benefits rendered by the Jews in Germany themselves.* It is therefore of the greatest interest that the Jews remaining in Germany should remain in a position to pay; otherwise, they cannot help. If at least most Jews do not remain solvent, they themselves not only can no longer help but also cease to be taxpayers in the Jewish communities. The Jewish communities would then no longer be able to meet the great demands placed on them.

Even now, a great part of the *Jewish communities*, as a consequence of the emigration of productive community members and the impoverishment of the remaining ones, are no longer able to assume a share of the expenses for the training of emigrants and the process of emigration. These communities rely upon the assumption of these costs in their entirety by the central Jewish organizations, particularly the Reich Representation of Jews in Germany. The means for this accrue to the central organizations mainly from donations by foreign Jewish relief organizations and domestic individuals.

Now that, under the Tax Adjustment Law of 16 October 1934 and the law implementing the non-personal tax laws of 1 December 1936, Jewish organizations are no longer recognized as church-related, non-profit, and charitable, such donations have become *subject to the gift tax*.[6] In the case of donations from foreign organizations, very substantial sums are concerned, which would henceforth be subject to the highest rates of the gift tax.

It must be pointed out with the utmost gravity that the foreign relief organizations will not be willing to accept these large deductions from the resources that they make available for the emigration and preparation for emigration of Jews from Germany. Therefore, if the foreign donations, the cessation of which would place in doubt the entire activity of the central Jewish organizations, are not to fall away, remedial action must be taken in this regard. But the donations made by domestic Jews to Jewish organizations should also be *exempted from the gift tax*, at least if they are made for the purpose of emigration and preparation for emigration.

Also to be pointed out in this regard are the recently issued guidelines of the Reich Minister of Finance concerning the *Property Tax Law*, as a result of which Jewish synagogue congregations are subject to a special regulation with respect to property tax.[7] The Jewish communities would lose the remainder of their productive capacity if they were required to pay, for example, property tax on their synagogue and other property as well.

---

6 In § 18(1) of the new version of the Tax Adjustment Law of 16 Oct. 1934, amended on 1 Dec. 1936, the words 'needy persons located in this country or needy Volksgenossen abroad' were replaced with the words 'needy German Volksgenossen': *Reichsgesetzblatt*, 1936, I, p. 977.

7 The Regulation for the Implementation of the Property Tax Law of 1 July 1937 initially stipulated that the real estate of the Jewish communities should remain exempt from the law pending clarification of its status: *Reichsgesetzblatt*, 1937, I, p. 733.

IV. *Systematic emigration! No measures that lead to panic!*

The systematic organization of emigration, as outlined above, and the raising and purposeful use of the requisite means for emigration are possible only *if emigration can take place calmly.* If panic arises in Jewish circles, the German government's objective, to effectuate as complete an emigration from Germany as possible, will never be accomplished. *Nothing threatens that more than a haphazard emigration process* and the dissipation of Jewish assets that is associated with it: in this country, the last economic support of the presumptive emigrants will be lost, and foreign countries will send back persons who are economically weak and ill-prepared for their new work, and will gradually shut themselves off to *all* further immigration.

The German government is aware that the *exclusion of the Jews from gainful activity* is being increasingly expedited, far beyond the provisions of the Nuremberg Laws. With all seriousness, we must point once again to the danger *that, as a result, the economic basis for emigration, a process the German government desires to be as complete as possible, will also be undermined and destroyed.*

Jewish employees are being completely removed from businesses – especially under pressure from the German Labour Front.

All Jewish persons employed by the Reich Food Estate are being systematically excluded from their occupations.

Sales representatives for whose work an identity card is necessary, Jews who work as pedlars, street vendors, etc. can, in many cases, no longer pursue their profession. Often the permits that the traders have obtained from the administrative authorities are taken away from them by the police.

Extremely severe restrictions have recently been issued for Jewish book publishers and distributors. Jewish book distributors are permitted to supply books only to Jews, upon presentation of an identity card, and then only Jewish books. They are not permitted to meet the needs of Jewish schools for general textbooks, nor may they provide to Jewish emigrants the language books and specialist literature required for emigration. A Jewish book distributor is not even permitted to sell to Jewish customers the general literature that is still in stock.[8] The majority of the Jewish bookshops must therefore go under. In this way, the Jewish publishing house also loses its viability, as it lacks the marketing machinery provided by an efficient book trade, quite apart from the difficulty signified for it by the fact that every Jewish book is subject to censorship in advance.

Non-Jewish firms and private persons are forbidden in future to work with their old Jewish business associates. This leads to the dissolution of valuable business connections and, in the long run, must also disrupt firms that can currently still be regarded as sound.

These are merely examples.

V. *Passport system.*

Also of the greatest actual and psychological significance for emigration is the *passport question* and the treatment of so-called 're-migrants'. The validity period of passports

---

8 From 1 July 1937 Jewish booksellers had to restrict their activity to 'Jewish writings' and to a 'Jewish clientele'. Only the publishers and book distributors that were registered on a list for the 'purely Jewish book trade' could continue to operate.

newly issued to Jews is extraordinarily short, usually only six months.⁹ In many cases, this is not even sufficient to enable the Jews to take an *exploratory trip*, in order to determine what prospects present themselves for existence in a foreign country. In many regions of Germany, passports are issued to Jews only on the strength of a certificate from the Chamber of Industry and Commerce or a certificate from a public health officer, or for the purpose of emigration. In other regions, Jews obtain no passports at all, except for the purpose of emigration. Thus, for example, the graduates of a Jewish teacher training school were denied passports for a study trip to Palestine, although the sole purpose of such study trips is to make it easier for Jewish teachers to prepare their school pupils for emigration to Palestine.

Jews who have spent some time abroad, for example, to explore the possibility of establishing an existence in a foreign country, do not know whether they *can return unhindered to Germany*. Problems have been caused at the border even for children and adolescents who attend foreign educational institutions, when they tried to come home to their families on holiday. In many cases, Jews who have emigrated from Germany are turned back at the border or threatened with incarceration in an education camp[10] unless they present a certificate from the German diplomatic mission in their new place of residence stating that there are no objections to their entry. In most cases, the issuance of such certificates is denied, and even in the most favourable cases it takes many weeks.

Most Jewish families are torn apart today under the duress of circumstances. If they are prevented from reuniting, even in cases of emergency, by the fact that the family members remaining in this country are not allowed to travel abroad and the members who have emigrated cannot come to Germany to visit their relatives, in many cases the families will attempt to stay together as long as it is at all possible, even with the greatest hardships. As a result, emigration is not promoted but rather *inhibited*.

VI. *The Reich Representation of Jews in Germany.*

The Jewish relief organizations abroad, without whose further cooperation emigration cannot be sustained at its current rate, let alone expanded in view of the difficult circumstances, require a corresponding Jewish organization in Germany with which they can work. This task until now has been performed by the *Reich Representation of Jews in Germany* as the umbrella association for the Jewish communities, regional associations, and other large organizations. As it is the umbrella organization for the Jewish school system, occupational training and restructuring, and the Jewish welfare system, it has coordinated, in the field of emigration as well, the work of the Palestine Office for emigration to Palestine and the work of the Relief Association of German Jews for emigration to other countries. It has conducted negotiations with the foreign relief organizations, taken responsibility for the resources made available by them, and forwarded them for the stated purposes to the organizations, regional associations, and communities. It and its leading figures, Rabbi Dr Leo Baeck as president and the retired Ministerialrat

---

9 For an example of such a case, see Doc. 255, 19 Nov. 1936.
10 This means a concentration camp. The Bavarian Political Police, for example, had ordered in March 1935 that all returning emigrants be arrested, with men to be sent to Dachau concentration camp and women to Moringen concentration camp.

Dr Otto Hirsch[11] as executive chairman, have succeeded in gaining the full confidence of those Jewish groups abroad that support relief work, and in organizing harmonious teamwork. The effectiveness of this cooperative work, with regard to both raising funds and organizing the emigrants, would be even greater if the *Reich Representation* were to be given the opportunity to air relevant questions with all the official bodies responsible and be *officially recognized as the umbrella organization of the Jews in Germany.*[12]

VII. *English syndicate to advance money.*
On the condition that the organization of Jewish emigration along the lines of the previous statements is possible and guarantees a systematic rather than a hasty transplanting of the emigrants to other countries that allow them to build a new existence, but *only* on this condition, there exists, perhaps, the possibility of releasing additional means abroad on a more commercial basis for the promotion of Jewish emigration from Germany. One year ago both Jewish and non-Jewish banking firms already negotiated along these lines with a first-rate English consortium of both Jewish and non-Jewish banks, and it held out the prospect of a sum of 1.5 million pounds sterling.[13] When these negotiations failed because the preconditions for the financial assistance of the German banks could not be met on the German side at that time, there was a willingness to possibly make smaller sums available through a syndicate that would advance money. *It would now be a matter of resuming these negotiations.*

VIII. *In summary.*
Only if emigration is *systematically organized, economically based,* and *not overhasty* will the goal be reached to which – for different reasons – the German government and the Jews aspire. Proper *training* and adequate economic *endowment* of the emigrants are of decisive importance where it is a matter of carrying out as complete as possible a resettlement of the Jews to other countries.

In order to ensure *training*, the *training workshops, training farms,* and *similar facilities* for vocational preparation of the emigrants must not be hindered in their work, and the *authorization* of new facilities of this kind must be *accelerated.*

Training in independent enterprises, even with non-Jewish owners, must be permitted if Jewish training sites are not sufficient, as well as *training in industrial enterprises.* For participants who are eligible for benefits, attendance should be facilitated by *continued payment of the benefits.*

The language-related preparations of the emigrants must not be hindered, and their physical fitness training must be made possible. *Unsuited persons* must *in no event* be induced to emigrate.

---

11 Dr Otto Hirsch (1885–1941), lawyer; from 1920 Ministerialrat in the Württemberg Ministry of the Interior; from 1919 active in Jewish organizations; from 1933 executive chairman of the Reich Representation of German Jews; arrested in 1941 and murdered in Mauthausen concentration camp.
12 The Reich Representation had already adopted this stance in its reaction to the Nuremberg Laws: see Doc. 201, 24 Sept. 1935.
13 See Doc. 220, early Jan. 1936.

In order to ensure the requisite economic *endowment* of the emigrants, the assets threshold limit of the *Reich Flight Tax* should be lowered, and a part of the revenue from the Reich Flight Tax should be diverted for the endowment of poor Jewish emigrants.

Gift tax should not be collected for donations made by foreign or domestic Jews for the purpose of emigration and preparation for emigration.

In order to avoid bringing to a standstill the ancillary activities of the Jews in Germany on behalf of the emigrants, the Jews who are still in the labour force must *not be discriminated against* and further exclusion of Jews from gainful activity must not be undertaken. In *passport matters*, special treatment of the Jews that impedes emigration cannot be permitted to take place.

In order to achieve the greatest possible concentration of the assistance provided by foreign Jews and to expand organizational measures among the Jews of Germany, the *Reich Representation of Jews in Germany* must *be officially recognized* as their umbrella organization.

DOC. 292
Report by the Jewish Central Information Office dated 11 August 1937 regarding anti-Jewish riots in Upper Silesia following the expiry of the treaty on minorities[1]

Circular (strictly confidential!) from the Jewish Central Information Office,[2] Amsterdam Z., 14 Jan van Eijckstraat, dated 11 August 1937[3]

Dear Sirs,
Dear Sir,

The expiration of the minority-treaty[4] concluded between Germany and Poland regarding the Polish and Jewish minorities in Upper-Silesia has brought the Jewish minority from the 15th of July onward under the special Jewish acts of the German Reich.[5] The transition has led to difficult pogromatic attacks on the Jewish minority, principally on business-circles.

---

1 Wiener Library, 066-WL-1625. The original document is in English.
2 Following his emigration in summer 1933, the literary scholar Alfred Wiener (1885–1964) founded the Information Office in Amsterdam together with Professor David Cohen, a leading member of the Jewish Community of Amsterdam. From 1934 the office published and distributed news reports on the persecution of the Jews in Germany. In 1939 it was transferred to London and provided the basis for the future Wiener Library. On the Wiener Library, see Ben Barkow, *Alfred Wiener and the Making of the Holocaust Library* (London: Vallentine Mitchell, 1997).
3 On the original letterhead, on the left, are the words 'When ordering please quote Ref.: V/37/35'.
4 The author is referring to the Geneva Convention on Upper Silesia (1922), which was valid for fifteen years.
5 By means of the Law on Measures in the Former Upper Silesian Plebiscite Areas (30 June 1937), the anti-Jewish laws in force in Germany were introduced to Upper Silesia, especially the restrictions on Jewish civil servants, lawyers, doctors, dentists, veterinary surgeons, and pharmacists: *Reichsgesetzblatt*, 1937, I, p. 717.

We are in a position to publish an account of this taken on the spot from a most reliable source, which we herewith enclose. We want it to be widely spread, but, as usual our name may not be mentioned as the source.

The account is going to be published besides in the German, also in the English, French and Spanish languages. Further copies are to be had at the price of Dutch fl. 0,50 postage extra.

Yours faithfully
Jewish Central Information Office
Public Service Institute

Introductory remark.
The heavy troubles that broke out in Upper-Silesia[6] were decidedly prepared by a series of essays of the Nürnberg '*Stürmer*' containing the rudest abuse and slander of the Upper-Silesian Jews, especially owners of businesses.

An extra-reporter of the '*Stürmer*' has visited town after town in Upper-Silesia and in long articles has published photographs of Jewish businesses in recent numbers of the '*Stürmer*'. First of all the names of Jews of some importance in those towns were mentioned in full and accused of the greatest crimes.[7] To give an idea of its contents we submit a short quotation from number 30 of the '*Stürmer*' (July-volume, 1937). More or less similar quotations may be found on any page of this number, accompanied by photographs of Jewish businesses. In the number of the '*Stürmer*' the names of all the Jews are mentioned in full; we only give the initials:

> In *Oberglogau* the Jewish doctor Dr. A. B. started a practice. As this Jew also had clients among the members of the Sub-organizations of the Movement, 'Kreisleiter'[8] C. sharply criticized this intolerable situation. And what did the Jew do? He was impudent enough to lodge a complaint with the 'Oberpräsident'[9] of what had been said in the meeting of the Party. –
>
> A similar case has happened in *Klein-Strehlitz*. There the Jewess D. E. has kept before long a public house. By her evil talmudic machinations the German labourers haunting this 'pub' have often spent their entire weekly wages there. The enlightening influence of sincere German men on the people has caused the workmen to avoid the premises. And what did the Jewess do? She brought an action about through the intermediary of lawyer F. at *Beuthen*/U.S. (on whom we'll comment later on. Author

---

6 On the riots, see also the article 'Schwere Pogrome in Oberschlesien', *Pariser Tageszeitung*, 1 August 1937, p. 1.
7 This was a series of articles entitled 'Reise durch Oberschlesien' [Journey through Upper Silesia] by Ernst Hiemer, with contributions such as: 'Unvergeßliche Eindrücke vom Osten des Reiches – Talmudjuden in Neiße, Neustadt, Leobschütz und Ratibor' [Unforgettable Impressions from the East of the Reich – Talmud Jews in Neiße, Neustadt, Leobschütz, and Ratibor] or 'In Hindenburg O.S. – Wie die Juden unter dem Schutze des Genfer Abkommens ihre Sonderrechte mißbrauchten' [In Hindenburg, Upper Silesia – How the Jews Abused their Privileges under the Protection of the Geneva Convention]: *Der Stürmer*, nos. 30–33, July and August 1937 (no pagination).
8 German in the original: 'district leader' of the NSDAP; see Glossary.
9 German in the original. The author means the governor of the provinces of Lower and Upper Silesia, Josef Wagner (1899–1945), who was also NSDAP Gauleiter for Silesia.

of '*Stürmer*') in which she claimed Mk. 10 000.- damages. The fine behaviour of the labourers has finally thwarted her projects.

We leave *Neustadt* and go direction *Ratibor*. The way leads us through the village of *Leobschütz*. Reminiscences awaken. In Leobschütz lived Jew G. H. He was chief-manager of the L.-brewery and a racial violator of the worst kind. Jew H. only took very young and well-proportioned German girls into his service. If they did not do what he required from them, he dismissed them.[10]

Already before the expiration of the Genevese treaty for the protections of the Upper-Silesian minorities between Germany and Poland strong pressure was exercised on Jewish concern[s] and a considerable number was converted into Aryan ones. The day of expiration of the treaty passed without any incident. Also the next week was fairly quiet. In the smaller villages along the Polish frontier Jewish stall-holders were strongly hindered in the markets, thus e.g. at *Klausberg* and *Hindenburg*. At the annual fair at *Kreuzburg* on the 20th of July Jewish merchants could not sell any more, as agitators urged people not to buy from Jews and intending buyers were forcibly pushed away from the stands. At the same time posters [proclaiming] 'Aryan' appeared in the show-windows of all the towns of the industrial district. In a number of towns such as *Kreuzburg, Pitschen, Landsberg, Konstadt* the posters run as follows: 'Business German Aryan – Jews not wanted'.

Owing to this[,] catering to Jews was seriously hampered.

Jews could only obtain foodstuffs through Christian middlemen. Besides these posters screens were stretched across the streets thus e.g. at *Kreuzburg, Langendorf, Gleiwitz*. The text for these screens run[s]: 'He who buys from Jews hates the German people'. At the *Gle[i]witz* townhall we read a placard: 'German compatriots! Only go to German doctors, lawyers and merchants', while at the biggest Gleiwitz's hotel 'Haus Oberschlesien' may be read: 'The Jew lives with falsehood and dies with truth'. In the small village of *Altbandendorf* the placard: 'Do not buy from Jews' has been sticked up by means of a pin to the shop of the only Jewish shopkeeper there.

From day to day the boycott grew more and more perceptible. Especially on market-days Jewish businesses were annoyed by 'Stürmer'-sellers stationed there and the customers prevented from entering Jewish shops. Photographs were taken, besides the threat of taking a film of the customers was used. The sales in all Jewish shops fell by 70 %. Meanwhile came Monday the 26th of July, the day on which the clearance-sales of the drapery shops were to start. This circumstance was used in *Beuthen for great excesses* against some of the bigger Jewish drapery-shops. Supported by hundred[s] of youngsters[,] persons of N.S.-subdivisions clearly used for the purpose were acting as provoking-agents to female customers on entering and leaving these shops. During the evening and nightly hours troubles did not decrease in the least. The youngsters, it is true, were exchanged for boys of from 17 to 20 years old and the crowd artificially stirred smashed all the windows of the synagogue on both sides[,] urged on from three different

---

10 The English translation from *Der Stürmer* is far more mildly formulated than the original: see *Der Stürmer*, no. 30, July 1937 (no pagination).

quarters.[11] *In the afternoon chocolate shops and groceries were ransacked and the panes of show-windows were broken.*

On this and the three or four subsequent days Jewish shops were besieged by a big crowd, who scared away every buyer.

Christian women who nevertheless wanted to buy were spit at.

Also [C]hristian members of the staff were annoyed. In one case the shop was barred on the outside by means of a bicycle-chain so that there was neither entering nor leaving the shop.

In the same week boycott-pickets were stationed in front of Jewish shops and outrages took place.

Thus e.g. at *Guttentag* the interior of the Synagog[u]e which is under the protection of the preservations of monuments has been totally destroyed.

Scremed down benches were over thrown,[12] chandeliers were pulled down, balustrades broken and notwithstanding the great noise caused by all this the police, the office of which is opposite the Synagogue[,] did not intervene. [A]t *Gross-Strehlitz* the big window-panes of four Jewish shops have been smashed. In a considerable number of other shops headings such as 'Jew' or a skull were painted. Below the door-plate of the well-known Jewish doctor, Dr. König[,][13] 'Patient The Jews are fatal to you' has been painted in red. – Jews could not go to any restaurant, as they were not attended to and everywhere posters 'Jews not wanted' or 'Jews not wanted here' have been sticked up. Jewish merchants have been deprived of official privileges such as 'Bedarfsdeckungsscheine'[14] and others partly by official order.

From the '*Beuthner Stadtblatt*' it may be clearly inferred that the boycott is supported and promoted by the officials.[15] At the same time a great num[b]er of Jewish employees of Christian firms have been given notice. Jewish commercial agents have been deprived of their agencies, though the greater part of them has freely carried on their profession for years and years. At *Beuthen* not only swimming baths are forbidden to the Jews but also the medicinal and sanatory baths. As only a few days ago the holidays were over no incidents at schools can be mentioned.

---

11 The *Pariser Tageszeitung* reported on the events in Beuthen under the title 'Die Kinder-Pogrome in Oberschlesien: Einzelheiten von der Judenverfolgung des 27. Juli' [The Child Pogroms in Upper Silesia: Details of the Persecution of the Jews on 27 July], writing that 300 children aged between 8 and 14 years, acting under the direction of members of the National Socialist Women's League and assisted by the Hitler Youth, had defaced and plundered Jewish shops and the synagogue in Beuthen: *Pariser Tageszeitung*, 8 August 1937, p. 1.
12 As in the original. Presumably the author means 'screwed down'.
13 Sussmann König (1888–1943), physician; doctor in Groß Strehlitz; murdered in Auschwitz in Sept. 1943.
14 German in the original: 'subsistence vouchers'. The author probably means the vouchers handed out to the unemployed and recipients of marriage loans, which the licensed sales outlets had to collectively redeem at the tax offices. The Law for the Reduction of Unemployment (1 June 1933) determined in § 25 that the municipal authorities were to decide which sales outlets would be approved for the receipt of subsistence vouchers: *Reichsgesetzblatt*, 1933, I, pp. 323 ff.
15 The local newspaper, issued by the mayor, had called for the boycott of Jewish shops on page 1: 'Deutsche Volksgenossen, kauft nur in deutschen Geschäften' [Fellow Germans, Buy only in German Shops]: *Beuthener Stadtblatt*, 23 July 1937, p. 1.

Especially difficult is the situation of the small number of Jews in the little village of *Langendorf near Tost* and in *Tost* itself. There the inhabitants of the youth-hostels have caused choruses to go through the streets with anti-Jewish slogans etc.

Behind all these anti-Jewish incidents is the '*Stürmer*'.

The '*Stürmer*' is exposed everywhere on special boards. In the small places the putting up of these boards is attended with some festivities such as take place when a monument is unveiled: bands are playing. Besides the well-known headlines on these boards, we also find such as 'The *Stürmer* is the best weapon against the Jewish criminality.'

The authorities have connived at all this and not interfered. Only after repeated complaints, which were unsuccessful with the lesser police authorities, the higher officials (Regierungspräsident)[16] have taken provisional measures for protection.

What they are worth, shows a notice from the *Gleiwitz* police press office (*Ostdeutsche Morgenpost, Gleiwitz, vom 29. 7. 1937*)[.] After this, as is usual, the entirely powerless Jewish minority is blamed for the heavy outrages. At the same time foreign provocations is hinted at, which is frequently used as a hackneyed excuse in such cases.[17]

The official notice is therefore of lasting importance, because it reveals with great clearness the gravity of the anti-Jewish outrages notwithstanding the attempts to make their proportions seem as small as possible.

DOC. 293
On 11 August 1937 the émigré Günter Bodlaender in Prague asks a relief organization to support his emigration to the Philippines[1]

Letter from Günter Bodlaender,[2] Prague III, 7 Sersikovà ul., to HICEM-Emigdirect, Paris, dated [11 August 1937][3] (copy)

I received news today from the local HICEM[4] that you will kindly make efforts to acquire [the] visas for Uruguay for my wife[5] and me. – I was assuming, since I have already been vaccinated and my passport has now been in HICEM's possession for around twelve days, that everything would be in order, which seems by no means to be the case,

---

16 German in the original.
17 A 'Warning against Unlawful Riots' issued by the police press office in Gleiwitz had appeared in the section 'Aus Oberschlesien und Schlesien' ['From Upper Silesia and Silesia']. It referred to demonstrations against Jewish shops on 27 July 1937 in Beuthen and Hindenburg. The crowds had apparently forced their way into several shops. The police declared that the unrest in Upper Silesia was being fomented by subjects in foreign pay: *Ostdeutsche Morgenpost*, 29 July 1937 (no pagination).
1 CJA, 1/75 C Hi 1, Nr. 23-12499, fols. 44–45. This letter has been translated from German.
2 Günt(h)er Bodlaender (b. 1905), retailer and weaver; from 1924 worked for various textile firms in Breslau; in 1929 took over his father's agency business. He was assaulted in 1936 and subsequently emigrated to Prague.
3 The date is missing in the original. A second copy of the letter in the same file contains the date but not the postscript reproduced here at the end of the text: ibid., fols. 37–38.
4 HICEM: see Glossary.
5 Ilse Bodlaender, née Müller (b. 1913), seamstress and milliner; worked in various firms in Breslau until her marriage in 1935.

however, because the letter to me states explicitly: 'the people in Paris will attempt'[6] to get the visas.[7]

At the same time, the letter states that emigration to the Philippines would take too much time; allegedly there would be a delay of six to eight weeks.

Well, believe me, a few weeks really are no longer relevant, since, on the one hand, I know *for sure* that I can get by in Manila and, on the other hand, that in Montevideo today it is *impossible* for *penniless* émigrés to secure any kind of livelihood. Here I am citing only what already appeared in 1936 in the emigration newsletter of the Berlin Relief Association.[8]

Our transportation is not a matter of just getting out of Europe and having two more settled cases appear in the statistics, but of sending emigrants to places where, as far as is humanly possible to tell, a possibility for life is offered to us.

Apart from the fact that we do not know one word of Spanish, *on the other hand we have mastered English.*

I am not a prisoner to be deported, so I do believe I have a right to request politely that you send me to a place where I can live, where I can talk, where I have the chance to be a human being again and am not condemned to ruin in advance as an eternal émigré or at best a vagrant.

The fates of emigrants should not just be treated as 'cases', after all, but rather considered, above all, first from the human aspect alone. I know that changing my travel plans certainly makes a great deal of work for you, and if I have the opportunity, I would gladly show you my gratitude. But it will be of particular interest to you *that I can obtain, from the local American consulate general, for the sum of 15 k.,*[9] *the entry visa for the Philippines, and in fact within five minutes.*

So visa difficulties do not exist at all.

Therefore, I sincerely request once again that you change my emigration so that we can travel to Manila instead of Montevideo. You will surely understand what a significant decision it is to leave Europe, journey into the unknown, land somewhere in the world without a penny in one's pocket, and have only an ounce or so of hope – then it may be understandable if one at least tries to get to a place where one assumes the certainty of being able to work again and rejoin the ranks of normal human beings.

I will go ahead and thank you now for your kindness in pursuing the matter of my emigration in the way I have requested, for I know that you will act humanely and not

---

6 In the copy, the words 'attempt underlined' (*versuchen unterstrichen*) appear here in parentheses.
7 The Paris office of HICEM had refused support in late 1936, saying that the couple should have emigrated directly from Germany. Upon closer scrutiny, HICEM then pledged support, because Bodlaender had married his Christian wife, Ilse, in April 1935 and she now wanted to convert to Judaism and emigrate with him: ibid., fols. 6 and 11.
8 This refers to the *Korrespondenzblatt über Auswanderungs- und Siedlungswesen*, established in 1905. This occasional newsletter was published in Berlin until 1935 by the Relief Association of German Jews. In 1935 it had a circulation of 5,000. From 1936, now published by the Culture League of German Jews, it was known as *Jüdische Auswanderung: Korrespondenzblatt über Auswanderungsfragen und Siedlungswesen*.
9 Koruna: 'crown(s)' Czechoslovak currency.

bureaucratically, and will help us guide our destiny to the best of your judgement and ability, to the extent that it is in human hands.[10]

In this expectation, I commend myself to you

respectfully

(signed Guenther Bodlaender)

NB. Do you know what it means to have had to live here for thirteen months now with no opportunity to pursue any activity, always merely tolerated by the authorities, etc.? *That* ruins one's nerves. I *must* be able *to work* again at last.

DOC. 294
On 13 September 1937 the historian Willy Cohn comments on the failure of his attempts to emigrate to Palestine[1]

Handwritten diary of Willy Cohn, entry for 13 September 1937

13 September 1937. Breslau, Monday. Yesterday I was with Ruth[2] in the Museum of Applied Arts, where I probably have not been for more than four years; it has been newly laid out in a really clear way and set up so that even the layman gets something out of it! There is a bit too much emphasis on prehistory, which is now made very much the focus, especially in Silesia, in order to emphasize the German character of the landscape. – I enjoyed seeing how interested Ruth is in all that; she is now entering an age at which the intellect awakes. Perhaps it is important for her, as someone who will go to Eretz Israel at an early stage,[3] to take all these impressions along with her. – Earlier we were in the Seelig pastry shop, which I had promised Ruth for quite some time. The customers were not very pleasant, an unpleasant selection of our people.

After lunch, a nice nap, then worked on my paper, later put old correspondence in order, and found interesting letters from my youth, written thirty-six and thirty-seven years ago. – In the evening took the usual walk with Trudi[4] in the fine air, still troubled by grievous thoughts in bed; it is very hard to keep one's mind free of bitterness; I woke up early too. – It's really pouring down outside!

---

10 On 3 Oct. 1937 the HICEM office in Paris informed the HICEM office in Prague that Bodlaender's passport for Uruguay as well as the money for the ship passage had been stolen from the travel agency. Later, when it became possible to leave the country after all, Bodlaender declared on 14 Oct. 1937 that it was impossible for him to leave Prague within twenty-four hours because of his family and the settlement of a small business transaction. Departure was postponed until early November. As a result, Bodlaender forfeited the chance to emigrate to Uruguay: CJA, 1/75 C Hi 1, Nr. 23-12499, fols. 52, 54, and 69.

1 Willy Cohn, 'Tagebuch Kudowa, Breslau August-Oktober 1937', fols. 65–69; CAHJP, P 88/80. Abridged English translation in Cohn, *No Justice in Germany*, pp. 467–468. This document has been retranslated from the original German.
2 Ruth Cohn, daughter of Willy Cohn.
3 Ruth Cohn was not able to emigrate to Palestine until the end of 1940.
4 Gertrud Karoline Cohn, wife of Willy Cohn.

13 September 1937. Breslau, Monday. In the morning post today I received a letter that gave me little pleasure. Mrs Borger wrote from Givat Brenner[5] that the *mazkiriuth*[6] has refused to accept us. Certainly, after the long months of waiting I had no longer counted on it, but now that it's here in black and white, it is bad nonetheless. A dream has vanished from my life; perhaps I might have been able to find a piece of home there once again. – At any rate, I was naturally quite upset. I was not given any reasons. Maybe it was partly because Trudi did not really get into the spirit of the community there at the time. People are certainly very sensitive to such things. – Well, I will have to try to get over this blow, too; it remains a heavy blow, and I cannot endure too many more of them; I often have awful troubles. One must be very brave in order to take them in one's stride.

How hard it is to come up with new projects all the time! I think I'll soon give it up. – My mind had firmly latched on to this plan, and it was precisely Givat Brenner that seemed like a haven to me. – Now it is gone, over and done with.

This morning I dictated letters to Miss Cohn for two hours. I wanted to dictate an outline, too, but there were so many letters that I did not get around to it. I also dictated a lengthy letter to Wölfl;[7] he was already quite anxious because he had not received any post from us. – One has many connections all over the world.

Barber, post office, did several errands for Trudi, napped a few minutes before dinner; after dinner I had to toil quite a bit.

DOC. 295

Völkischer Beobachter: Adolf Hitler's closing address on Jewry and Bolshevism at the ninth NSDAP rally in Nuremberg, 13 September 1937[1]

The Führer speaks

Party comrades! / National Socialists!

A few more hours, and the ninth Party rally of the National Socialist Movement will come to a close. For eight days the German nation was again influenced by the impressions of its greatest celebration. What hundreds of thousands experienced themselves or were able to follow with their own eyes commanded the no less rapt attention of millions of Germans inside and outside the Reich. And when could there be a better opportunity to convince oneself of the reality of the new German state than during this week of its greatest and most demonstrative manifestation?

[…][2]

---

5 The kibbutz in Palestine in which the son, Ernst Cohn, lived, and which Willy and Gertrud Cohn had visited in 1937 on an extended trip through Palestine, which they took to prepare themselves for emigration.
6 Correctly: *mazkirut*, Hebrew for 'secretariat' here the administration of a kibbutz.
7 Wolfgang Cohn, Willy's son from his first marriage, was studying in Paris.

1 'Der Führer spricht', *Völkischer Beobachter* (northern German edition), 15 Sept. 1937, pp. 1–5. This document has been translated from German.
2 Passages follow here dealing with the Party rally, just concluded, and with the development of Germany since 1918 and the struggle against a 'world disease of Bolshevism'.

Small racial nuclei – the origin of all the European states
We know today that what stands before us as a fully grown entity, the 'state', was formed as an artificial construct over the course of millennia. And indeed not as, say, the product of a general, voluntarily signed social contract but rather as the result of a developmental process that owed its decisive start and conclusion to the natural law in this world: specifically, to the law of ability and strength, of willpower and the heroic disposition! *All our European states came into being as a result of what were originally small racial nuclei* but are to be regarded as the truly powerful and hence determining factors of these entities.

But we see this fact most clearly confirmed in the states in which, well into our own times, a balance between the masses, shaped and led, and the shaping and leading forces was not achieved, perhaps could not be accomplished, but probably was not even contemplated. One such state was *Russia*. A very thin leadership tier, one that was not racial and national, that is, not Slavic, transformed this state from a jumble of small and very small communities into a literal colossus of a state, which was seemingly indomitable, but whose greatest weakness always lay in the discrepancy between the number and merit of the members of its leading tier, non-Russian by blood, and the number and merit of its national Russian elements.

Russia under the brutal dictatorship of an alien race
Here, therefore, it was also particularly easy for a new racial nucleus to penetrate and to attack with success, deliberately emerging in the guise of a national leader in contrast to the old, official leadership of the state. Here the *Jewish minority*, disproportionately small in comparison to the size of the Russian people itself, succeeded, via the indirect route of appropriating the leadership of the national Russian proletariat, in ousting the previous social and governmental leaders from their positions. Precisely for this reason, however, present-day Russia is fundamentally no different from the Russia of two or three hundred years ago. A brutal dictatorship led by an alien race has seized total control over true Russiandom and is exercising this authority accordingly.

To the extent that this process of creating a new state has now been concluded in Russia, one might be able to simply take note of the event, as with any similar one, as a historical reality and otherwise make the best of it. But to the extent that this Jewish racial nucleus now seeks to achieve the same outcome among other peoples as well, and, at the same time, views present-day Russia as its already conquered base and a bridgehead for further expansion, *this problem has gone from being a Russian problem to being a global problem*, which will be decided one way or the other, because it must be decided.

My Party comrades, you are familiar with the course taken so far by this phenomenon, the most notable phenomenon of our times.

The Jewish race, without having been summoned, forces its way into the peoples and attempts first of all to secure a certain economic influence for itself as a class of foreign merchants who engage for the most part in trade and the exchange of goods. After centuries, as a result of this process, the economic power of the interlopers gradually gives rise to strong reactions on the part of the host people. This natural resistance accelerates the efforts of the Jews to feign gradual assimilation, seeking not only to eliminate their chief vulnerability, which is their status as an alien people, but also to gain a direct, specifically a *political*, influence on the country in question. Partly because of economic interests, but partly also out of innate middle-class inertia, the dangers of this development go unrecognized by many. At the same time, the warning voice of influential or quick-witted men is deliberately ignored, as is indeed always customary in history whenever the predicted consequences are of an unpleasant nature.

From trade to politics – that is the path of the Jew
In this way, this Jewish community of race, which operates, however, in the language of the host peoples, starting with influence on trade, succeeds in gaining more and more influence on political developments. In the process, it circulates just as much in the camp of the rulers as, conversely, in the camp of their opponents. To the very same extent to which its activity also succeeds in shaking the position of a dynastically established kingdom that is gradually weakening for other reasons as well, it shifts its interests more in the direction of promoting democratic popular movements. Democracy, however, then first provides the basis for the organization of those terrorist entities that we know as social democracy, the Communist Party, or the Bolshevik International. However, while the lively will to resist is gradually stifled as a result of democracy, by a thousand formalities, and above all by the deliberate *breeding* of state representatives who are as weak as possible, the vanguard of the Jewish world revolution develops in the radical revolutionary movements. Social and economic weaknesses also help to facilitate the subversive attack of this Bolshevik International, *organized solely by Jewish elements*.

The ultimate goal – the final Bolshevik revolution
Thus, the same process as in the preceding stage repeats itself during this stage. While one part of the 'Jewish fellow citizens' demobilizes democracy, especially through the influence of the press, or even infects democracy with its poison by linking up with revolutionary phenomena in the form of *popular fronts*, the other part of Jewry is already carrying the torch of the Bolshevik revolution into the midst of the bourgeois-democratic world, without needing to fear any effective resistance by this world.

The ultimate goal is then the final Bolshevik revolution, meaning, however, not something like the establishment of the leadership of the proletariat by the proletariat but rather the *subjugation* of the proletariat under the leadership of its new alien master.

Just as the hatred-filled, crazed, and demented masses, supported by the antisocial elements released from prisons and penal institutions, once wiped out the natural, native intelligentsia of the peoples and caused it to bleed to death on the scaffold, the Jew remains as the last carrier of intellectual knowledge, albeit abysmal knowledge. For one thing must be recorded here: *this race is neither intellectually nor morally a superior one but rather in both respects thoroughly inferior!* For unscrupulousness and lack of conscience can never be equated with authentic, brilliant natural ability.

My Volksgenossen, just take a look at the significance of Jewry in a commercial respect and then another look at the truly valuable inventions or great achievements of mankind that derive from creative fantasy, genius, and honest work. If the observation applies anywhere that *what counts is not* dealing with the facts but rather *creating the facts*, then this is true above all in assessing the true merits of Jewry. In some countries, the Jews may hold 90 per cent of all the intellectual positions, but they have not found, created, or produced the elements of knowledge, culture, art, etc. They can, through certain manipulations, take possession of trade, but the basis of trade, that is, its values, has not been discovered, invented, and developed by Jews. They are, *in terms of creativity, a thoroughly untalented race.*

Therefore, if this race ever wants to rule anywhere for a prolonged period, it must engage in the rapid extermination of the former intellectual upper classes of the other peoples. Otherwise it would be defeated again in a short time by their superior intelligence. For, in everything that has to do with *true accomplishment*, the Jews have *always been bunglers* and nothing but bunglers.

How has National Socialism, contrary to the prophecies of our wise critic, been able to cope with these arrogant incompetents? As democrats, they have not even mastered the possibilities that lay in democracy, nor have they, as social democrats, been able to lead the masses. As stakeholders in our economy, they have neither prevented its decline nor, as communists, succeeded in drawing the anticipated conclusions from this collapse. And only *because a perceptive National Socialism consciously confronted them.*

And that is why we National Socialists are also so self-confident and so convinced of the indestructibility of our state. However, we view the rest of the world in part as very much under threat, because it deliberately closes its eyes to this issue, and above all refuses to see that the dictatorship of the proletariat is nothing other than the dictatorship of Jewish intellectualism.

In the past year, through a series of distressing pieces of statistical evidence, we have proved that *in the present-day Soviet Russia of the proletariat, more than 98 per cent of the leading positions are held by Jews.* This means, therefore: it is not the proletariat that is the dictator but rather the race whose Star of David has finally also become the symbol of the so-called proletarian state. We have made comparisons with the situation in Germany, where, without doubt, the most capable minds are selected and trained for leadership as a result of the work of National Socialism, without distinction of person, origin, or even of fortune. At that time, the Jewish world press and also the press of Soviet Russia, that is, Soviet Judea, had written about a great many things, but not a word was published about this statistical proof of the all-Jewish leadership of the so-called 'state of workers and peasants'. They *had to* be silent on this subject as well. Here there was nothing to either lie away or distort, but there was indeed a danger of enlightenment for other peoples!

By the way, we ourselves have experienced the same thing in Germany. Who were the leaders of our *Bavarian Council Republic*?[3] Who were the leaders of *Spartacus*? Who were the real leaders and financiers of our Communist Party? Now even the most sympathetic world democrats cannot smooth this away or change it: they were exclusively *Jews!*

And thus it was in *Hungary*, and in the part of *Spain* that has not yet been reconquered by the true Spanish people!

There is therefore no doubt, either, that in every country it is not the fascists but rather the *Jewish* elements that try to undermine democracy. And in addition, there is no doubt that the destruction of national production also serves as a means to achieve that end. For if someone, using certain methods, deliberately destroys the national

---

3 Bayerische Räterepublik; the short-lived attempt to establish an independent socialist state in Bavaria in April 1919.

economy of a country and thereby creates a general shortage of goods, this can take place only in the hope of being able to politically exploit the resulting dissatisfaction.

In Germany too, the proletariat was Jewry's battering ram for decades
For decades, in our country too, these Jews utilized the Marxist parties of the proletariat as a battering ram, not, for example, against the parasites feeding on our national and economic life, no, just the reverse: *in the service of the parasites*, always *against* national production. The Jews pressed this national production hard, until at last 7 million unemployed lay in the streets. And all this only in the hope of at last being able, after all, to erect the Bolshevik revolutionary army from these 7 million unemployed. With this army they then hoped to be able to wipe out the national intelligentsia in our people exactly as they are now attempting to do in Spain and have done in Russia.

But in this struggle, which the Jew, of all people, is organizing and guiding as the leading element of social justice, not a single Jew is himself being attacked as a socially harmful element. The ultimate instincts of the Jew begin to run free only in places where a leadership that is tied to the people is no longer present. The most inferior leaders imaginable for human beings then begin, as in Soviet Russia, to slaughter each other and wipe each other out. But if someone wages this seemingly social global struggle only, in the end, to forcibly bring the members of foreign peoples under the leadership of this race in the form of a most brutal dictatorship, and in the process tries hard to *expand* this event into a *world revolution*, then not only everyone directly concerned but also *everyone indirectly threatened thereby* has a stake in such a development.

And this applies to Germany! For during the past year we had ample opportunity to reflect on how necessary it is to deal with this problem.

To open revolution via the indirect route of democracy
As you know, in *Spain* this Jewish Bolshevism has proceeded to the point of open revolution by a similar method, via the indirect route of democracy. It is a major distortion of the facts whenever it is asserted that the Bolshevik oppressors of the people there were the supporters of a legal power, while the fighters of nationalist Spain were illegal revolutionaries. *No! In General Franco's men we see the genuine and, above all, enduring Spain, and in the usurpers of Valencia*[4] *the international revolutionary forces in the pay of Moscow, which are afflicting Spain today and will perhaps afflict another country tomorrow.*

Can we now be indifferent to these events? Allow me to first make a short statement:

In the press of our Western democracies and from the speeches of some politicians, we repeatedly hear how large the natural spheres of interest of these powers are. It seems quite self-evident to the representatives of these states that their interests include both every sea and every country in Europe and are, even beyond Europe, straightforward interests that are universally bestowed by nature. Conversely, we immediately experience outbursts of indignation as soon as a people that does not belong to this exclusive circle of international power holders also dares to speak of certain interests that lie beyond its own borders. I would now like to state the following here, in opposition to this arrogance:

---

4 This refers to the Popular Front government, which relocated from Madrid to Valencia.

From England and France we repeatedly hear the assertion that they have sacred interests in Spain. Now, what is the nature of these interests? Are they political or economic? If they are political, we have as little understanding of this as we would if someone were to claim to have political interests in Germany. Whoever governs Germany, for example, concerns nobody but us, as long as this regime is not contemplating or actually engaging in hostilities against other countries. But if, in England and France, one has an eye on certain economic interests in Spain, let us allow for that without further ado but also note that we claim exactly the same economic interests for ourselves too, that is, in other words:

National Socialist Germany follows, for example, the attempted Jewish revolutionization of the world in Spain with keen interest, and specifically in two directions:

1. Just as England and France do not wish a shift to occur in the balance of power in Europe, perhaps in favour of Germany or Italy, no more do we wish a shift in power to occur in the sense of an increase in Bolshevik power, because: if fascism rules in Italy, it is a purely Italian national affair. It would be foolishness to imply that instructions or even orders could be given to this fascist Italy by an authority outside the country.

It would be even more foolish to claim that this fascist Italy is, for example, a component of a larger, superordinate fascist international organization. On the contrary. The fact that political doctrines are concerned here, whose ideology and effectiveness *lie only within the bounds of the respective peoples*, is deeply inherent in fascism and National Socialism.

Similarly, it is certain that a national Spain will be *national*, that is, Spanish, just as, conversely, it cannot be denied that Bolshevism is consciously *international* and has only one centre but apart from that knows only branches of this centre. Just as one professes in England and France to be alarmed at the thought that Spain could perhaps even be occupied by Italy or Germany, we are equally aghast at the possibility that it might be conquered by Soviet Russia! What is more, this conquest by no means has to take the form of an occupation by Soviet Russian troops. Rather, it is a fait accompli at the moment when a Bolshevized Spain has become a branch, that is, an integral component, of the Bolshevik central headquarters in Moscow, a subsidiary that receives both its political directives and its material subsidies from Moscow.

In general:

We view any attempt at a further expansion of Bolshevism in Europe categorically as a shifting of the European balance of power.

(Tumultuous applause!) And just as England is interested in preventing such a shift in accordance with its views, we are interested in the same prevention in accordance with our view!

In the process, we must categorically *refuse to accept instructions* regarding the nature of such a Bolshevik shift in the balance of power from statesmen who, in this area, do not have the knowledge we possess and were also not in a position to acquire the practical experience that we unfortunately were forced to acquire.

2. In addition, no less important is the fact that such a Bolshevik shift in the political equilibrium, first and foremost, is identical to an economic development, the consequences of which can only be catastrophic in the closely linked European constellation of states.

For the first visible success of every Bolshevik revolution is, first of all, not an increase in production but a *total destruction* of the existing economic values and all economic functions in the countries affected. But the world does not subsist on the global economic conferences that are held somewhere from time to time – as experience has proved – rather, it subsists on the exchange of its goods and thus primarily on the production of goods. If, therefore, the production of goods in the individual states is gradually destroyed by means of a criminal madness, the consequences cannot be remedied by global economic conferences. Instead, they will inevitably spread even to those peoples who themselves are secured against Bolshevism within their own borders but will lose important economic ties, owing to the nature of their economic integration with the afflicted peoples. We now witness in practice all sorts of experiences in this area. When Bolshevism erupted in Spain, overall national production was so damaged that a momentary slowdown in an economically valuable exchange of goods occurred. Whenever, on the other hand, it is pointed out to me that other countries were able to do good business with Red Spain, this concerns payment for their deliveries in gold, which did not gain its value through Spanish Bolshevism but rather, being an expression of the value of previous national Spanish work and achievement, was *stolen* and looted by Spanish Bolshevism and taken to foreign countries. Upon that footing, however, one cannot build enduring and solid economic transactions, for they can be based only on the exchange of fair values and not on dealing in stolen goods!

Production of real values, however, is first wiped out utterly by Bolshevism and cannot – as proved by Soviet Russia – be set to rights again by it, even after twenty years, while it is based on a real dog's life for its workers! Now, this may be of no interest at all, for example, to wealthy Great Britain. Perhaps it also does not matter at all to England whether *Spain becomes a wasteland*, is economically ruined and brought to the point of the familiar Bolshevik turmoil or not. Perhaps, in this Spanish question, England is really thinking only in political terms. However, *for us Germans, who have no way to shift our flow of trade to a global empire of our own, Europe, and indeed Europe as it is today, is one of the prerequisites for our own existence.*

A Bolshevized Europe would make all trade policy of our country impossible, and not because we do not want to trade, but rather because we would no longer get any trading partners.

Therefore, for us this is not a matter of theoretical observations or moral concern, though also not a problem for international complaints either – for we do not have so much respect for the international institutions that we would think, even for a second, that we could obtain any practical help from them, apart from slogans – rather, it is one of the *essential questions*.

We know this with certainty: if Spain, in the end, had become Bolshevik and this wave had then continued to spread perhaps throughout the rest of Europe, or if it should spread once again – and Bolshevism itself asserts that it surely will, and wants it to do so, at any rate – this would signify a grave economic crisis for Germany.

For we simply must participate in the mutual exchange of goods with these countries, namely in the sheer interests of preserving the existence of the German people itself. But this exchange is possible only when these countries themselves also manufacture goods under regulated, normal conditions. If this were to cease, however, as a result of a Bolshevik catastrophe, Germany too would be in for economically grave times.

Now, we all are aware that in the event of such a development, the Geneva *League of Nations* would presumably gain the same power that our domestic German Frankfurt

Parliament once had. But today we already see how little is to be expected from such international assistance in general.

The Bolshevik plague must never spread further across Europe!
Scarcely had the Bolshevik uproar in Spain begun when not only did trade with Germany decline but also, above all, more than 15,000 Reich subjects had to leave this country, which was torn by civil unrest. Their shops were looted, German schools destroyed, the assembly halls set on fire in some cases, the assets of all these industrious people wiped out at one blow. They lost the results of years of honest labour. Now, I hardly think that the League of Nations will indemnify them for these losses. We take cognizance of this while making no request of this body at all. We know that it has its own problems and tasks. For example, for years it has had to attempt to support the various Marxist and Jewish emigration processes in order to keep them alive in this way! (Jubilant applause.)

Indeed, I am just stating the facts! We thus have a serious stake in ensuring that this Bolshevik plague does not spread any further across Europe. Apart from that, we have naturally had many conflicts with nationalist France, for example, over the course of its history. However, *somehow and somewhere, we belong together in the great European family of peoples after all,* and especially when we all look deep into our innermost core.

Hence, I believe, we would not want to feel the absence of, or even just wish away, any of the real European cultural nations. We have each other to thank not only for quite a bit of trouble and grief but also for enormous cross-fertilization. We have given each other many models, examples, and cautionary lessons, just as we have also given each other many a pleasure and much that was beautiful. If we are truthful, we have every reason to hate each other less than to admire each other!

In this community of European cultural nations, Jewish world Bolshevism is an absolutely alien element, which makes not the slightest contribution to our economy or our culture but only creates confusion. It cannot put forward a single positive achievement at an international exhibition of life in Europe and the world, but has only propagandistic charts, falsified numbers, and rabble-rousing posters to show.

In the process, I also do not want to neglect to reply to those who tenaciously put the case for the necessity of international global economic ties, their continual improvement, and, in connection with that, international solidarity, and who now believe they must complain that National Socialist Germany, in their view, is attempting to retreat into a planned isolation.

I have already emphasized the magnitude of the error made by the statesmen or editorial writers who seriously believe such a thing. It is compellingly refuted by practical reality. We have neither the desire nor the intention to be hermits, politically or economically!

Germany has not isolated itself at all, either politically or economically!

It is not politically isolated, because, on the contrary, it is trying hard to work together with all those who have a truly European shared goal in their sights. We now categorically refuse to let ourselves be coupled together with those whose plan is the destruction of Europe and who also make absolutely no secret of this plan!

Even though we feel that we ourselves are secure against this destruction, it nonetheless seems to us to be a contradiction in terms to make agreements for European solidarity with people who plan to destroy this very solidarity.

To refuse to go along with these elements does not mean, therefore, to isolate oneself. Instead, it means only to *safeguard* oneself. All the greater, therefore, is our determination to seek and find an understanding with all those who do not merely talk about solidarity but, above all, also *seriously desire* it, and not a solidarity in the negative sense of a mutual destruction but rather in the positive sense of a mutual development. Even more insane, however, is the charge that we are pursuing economic isolation. I believe that our trade figures are the best rebuttal of this foolish opinion, which is completely unfounded. But even if our trade were to fail to increase, we would not desire economic isolation. Rather, we would at most incur it, and in fact against our wishes. This economic isolation, however, must inevitably come about at the point that Europe becomes Bolshevik. We are witnessing, however, an amusing spectacle: the members of the press in the countries where it is deemed necessary to keep encouraging our greater participation in the global economy are precisely the ones who immediately start shouting when, for example, it becomes known that we are doing business with nationalist Spain! That we are supplying to this nationalist Spain machinery and so forth, and this nationalist Spain is giving us natural resources and foodstuffs in return. Yes, here we are doing what these apostles of the world economy constantly want! Why now, suddenly, the outrage at this? No! We are too well aware of the internal reasons for this attitude.

Germany has the weapons to bring down, with lightning speed, every Bolshevik attempt at interference.

There is anger that we are simply not willing under any circumstances to reintroduce in Germany, as commodities, those contagious Marxist materials that brought us once before to the edge of the abyss. We certainly reject this trade transaction. There is anger about the fact that we not only are not isolating ourselves but just the opposite, that we have found *firm support* from states with similar ideals and leaders who think and act in a similar way. But I can only repeat here that for Germany, *another orientation* is *not possible at all*. For we are more interested in Europe than some other countries perhaps need to be. Our country, our people, our culture, our economy have developed from the general European circumstances. We must therefore be the foe of every attempt to carry into this European family of peoples an element of disintegration and destruction specifically and on the whole.

In addition, to us Germans the thought that this Europe could be directed or ruled from Moscow, of all places, is simply intolerable.

When such a presumption is tolerated as a political demand in other countries, we can note this only with astonishment and regret. For us, at any rate, even the mere notion of receiving directives from a world so very far beneath us is both ludicrous and outrageous. Further, the aspiration of an uncivilized Jewish Bolshevik guild of criminals to rule from Moscow over Germany, an established civilized country in Europe, is effrontery as well. Moscow is Moscow and Soviet Russia, for all we care, is Soviet Russia. But be that as it may, the name of our German capital is Berlin, and besides, thank God, Germany is still Germany!

One should therefore not succumb to a delusion concerning another point, either.

National Socialism has exorcized the global Bolshevik menace inside Germany. It has made sure that in this country it is not the Jewish intellectual scum, alien to our people, that commands the proletariat, meaning the German worker. Instead, it is the German people that, at last, understands its destiny and finds its self-governance. National Socialism has made our people and hence the Reich in other respects immune to Bolshevik contamination. Apart from that, nor will it shy away from confronting, with the most forceful means, any repetition of the earlier internal encroachments upon the sovereignty of our people.

We National Socialists have grown up fighting against this enemy. Over the course of more than fifteen years we have destroyed this foe in Germany, intellectually, ideologically, and in reality. Neither its countless murders and other acts of violence nor the support it obtained through the Marxist rulers of the Reich at the time was able to prevent our triumphal march. We will keep a careful watch today, to ensure that such a menace never again descends upon Germany.

But should anyone dare to bring this menace towards or into Germany from without, let him know that the National Socialist state has also created for itself the weapons to crush such an endeavour with lightning speed.

The fact that we were good soldiers is something the world has surely not forgotten. The fact that we are even better soldiers today is something they can take our word for. But the fact that the National Socialist state will join in and fight for its existence with a fanaticism different from that of the bourgeois empire of yesteryear is something no one should doubt! (Tumultuous agreement, repeated surges of applause.)

[…]5

DOC. 296
On 15 September 1937 the chief public prosecutor in Frankfurt requests permission from the Reich Minister of Justice to initiate criminal proceedings on account of defamation of the SS newspaper *Das Schwarze Korps*[1]

Letter (detention order) from the chief public prosecutor at the Frankfurt am Main Regional Court as the head of the prosecuting authority at the Special Court (6 S Js 549/37), unsigned, to the Reich Ministry of Justice, dated 15 September 1937 (carbon copy)[2]

I am enclosing the proceedings against the subscription agent Dr Eduard *Schreiber*,[3] born on 11 April 1892 in Frankfurt am Main, resident of said town at 55 Burgfeld, married, Israelite, no criminal record (fol. 15 of the file[4]), currently in custody in the remand prison in Frankfurt am Main on this matter since 25 August 1937, with the request for a criminal prosecution order to be issued.

---

5 Statements follow here about Britain, the strength of the German Wehrmacht, and the unity of the German people.
1 Hessisches Hauptstaatsarchiv Wiesbaden, Abt. 461/16835, Handakte, fols. 3–4. Printed in abridged form (with altered names) in Noam and Kropat (eds.), *Juden vor Gericht*, pp. 201–202. This document has been translated from German.
2 The original contains several annotations.
3 Dr Eduard Schreiber, later Edward Schreiber (1892–1968); emigrated to the USA.
4 This page is not reproduced here.

The accused is a Jew. Until 1934 he was a judge at the district and regional courts in the district of the Frankfurt am Main Higher Regional Court, and was most recently active at the courts in Limburg an der Lahn. He was sent into early retirement in accordance with § 6 of the Law for the Restoration of the Professional Civil Service. He draws a monthly pension of 276 Reichsmarks. Since January 1937 he has been working as a subscription agent for the magazine *Der Morgen*.[5] He fought in the war. After being seriously wounded he was imprisoned in England in 1918 and was released in October 1919. He has no criminal record. So far there is no information regarding his political leanings.

On the morning of 13 August 1937 at around 10:30 a.m., the accused was walking along the Bockenheimer Landstraße in Frankfurt am Main. Outside Post Office no. 4 he stopped in front of a display case of the local North-West branch of the NSDAP.

National Socialist journals are displayed in this case. On the day in question, the issue of *Das Schwarze Korps* from 12 August 1937 was on display. The accused read the article published on the front page, the 'Letter to Mr Feilchenfeld'.[6] While the accused was standing in front of the display case, the witness Völp passed by. When he saw that the accused, whom he recognized as a Jew, was standing in front of the display case, he stopped, and stood behind the accused. The accused noticed this and wanted to leave. Before he turned around to continue on his way, he spat hard against the glass of the display case. The witness Völp took hold of him. The accused tried to apologize and agreed to wipe off the saliva, which he proceeded to do. He then tried to get away, but the witness Völp and the witness Zinnel, who in the meantime had also come along, detained him and brought him to the SS guardhouse.

The accused has verified the facts of the case. He claims to have acted in a state of agitation. He claims to have been ill two days before the act and not to have earned anything, which exacerbated his agitation. He cannot say which information in the mentioned article in *Das Schwarze Korps* agitated him so much.

The act of the accused constitutes a criminal offence as described in § 134b of the Criminal Code.[7] The newspaper *Das Schwarze Korps* is the organ of the SS Reich leadership. The issue in question was on display in an official Party display case. It follows from these circumstances, which are known to and recognized by the accused, that by spitting on the display case, his intention was to strike at the Party and the SS in particular, and to slur them, maliciously and deliberately. The fact that the act was committed in public requires no further explanation.

Considering the base disposition exhibited by the accused, I recommend that an order be issued for criminal prosecution. With his level of education, one would have expected the greatest restraint from the accused who, as a Jew, still claims a not insub-

---

5 The magazine *Der Morgen*, founded by Julius Goldstein (1873–1929), appeared every two months from 1925 until it was banned in 1938. It focused on Jewish cultural, social, and religious history.
6 This pertains to a blatantly antisemitic editorial: *Das Schwarze Korps*, 12 August 1937, pp. 1–2.
7 § 134 of the Criminal Code penalized those who wilfully removed or damaged announcements of the authorities on public display. In 1935 this was extended to include the NSDAP and its symbols by adding § 134b.

stantial pension from the German Reich. The fact that the accused did his duty on the battlefield cannot be considered to weigh decisively in his favour. In the case of an order for criminal prosecution, conviction is expected.[8] [...][9]

DOC. 297
On 30 September 1937 a Berlin local branch of the NSDAP demands the termination of leases to Jewish tenants of the municipal housing associations[1]

Special report by the NSDAP Gau of Berlin/Kreis I Charlottenburg, dated 30 September 1937[2]

Re: housing issues.
The Heerstrasse local branch reports the following:
In our district there are hardly any apartments available at affordable prices. In new buildings, as already reported on several occasions, the asking price for 3½ rooms is RM 150 to 170. The construction of such apartments is to be rejected on the grounds that it is antisocial as long as families with many children are still seeking affordable housing in vain.

In the houses belonging to the Non-Profit Building Society of Berlin-Heerstrasse (an association of the Berlin city administration), at 72–76 Westendallee, several Jewish families live in apartments that are not subject to tenant protection. As these apartments could be made available to Volksgenossen with larger families, with subsidies from the authorities, it appears to be of urgent necessity to advise the Berlin city administration to make the apartments available to German Volksgenossen at a suitable opportunity.[3] This desire is also understandable on the grounds that Volksgenossen and Party comrades already resident in the building do not wish to share their housing community with Jews.

---

8 The Reich Ministry of Justice rejected the application for criminal prosecution. The accused was subsequently convicted of disorderly conduct and defamation and sentenced to four months in prison: Noam and Kropat (eds.), *Juden vor Gericht*, pp. 202–205.
9 Technical notes 1 to 6 follow here.

1 LAB, A Rep. 009/31419, fol. 15. This document has been translated from German.
2 The original is marked and underlined in several places.
3 Several municipal residential and housing associations in Berlin had already terminated Jewish tenant leases for smaller apartments in 1935/1936.

DOC. 298

On 3 October 1937 Gary Samuelis writes to Kurt Polley in Berlin
about his difficult start in the USA[1]

Letter from Gary Samuelis,[2] Portland, Oregon, c/o Mrs Becher, 735 SW Hall Street, to Kurt Polley,[3] Berlin, dated 3 October 1937

My dear Mr Polley,

I haven't died yet and I haven't forgotten you yet either. I can explain why it's taken me so long to write. I've been working like a madman to gain a foothold in the six months since I've been here, but I haven't managed it yet. However, I'm hoping to have taken the first step. From tomorrow I'll be working in the stationery department of one of the largest department stores in the United States (around 5,000 employees). What has happened in the meantime is simply impossible to describe. Have you ever been to war, or spoken to a soldier who has been to the front? I think it is the same thing. One has gone through so much, experienced and seen so many terrible things that one is simply incapable of finding words for it without it sounding flat. But I think the biggest hurdle is behind me – that is to say now I'm a lowly employee with the lowest salary and it will take a few more years before I even see the ladder of success. Whenever you hear from other folks that it's easier and faster to make a go of it, they are the exceptions or the lucky ones, the loudmouths with rich relatives. I want to try and paint you a picture of *my* America, in just a few words, so here we go. A fabulous crossing, my aunt gives me a great welcome, takes me out, I see all the great sights of the huge city, after eight days a job offer – which my aunt rejects, because she wants me to herself for a bit longer. After four weeks a start: looking for work. June, summer heat, everyone is firing staff, I try to get a foot in the door of any old department store, it doesn't work out. Attempts at becoming a carpenter, a chauffeur, a waiter, a busboy, I give everything a try. My aunt has no connections at all and absolutely no idea of business. I run around like a lunatic for two months, all in vain. Feel pretty down. Then I get an offer from the council to go west – I accept. My aunt is in tears, calls me ungrateful, I clear off after three days, travel 3,000 miles without a break in 3½ days, arrive in the afternoon, go into the store (a gentlemen's outfitter for work wear) and have to work immediately until nine o'clock in the evening. I work like a dog from eight in the morning until nine in the evening, Saturdays until eleven o'clock, Sundays from 9 a.m. to 6 p.m. I gradually get used to it, in the rest of the time I write applications, letters to committees, etc. After two months I ask for two days' holiday (which is docked from my pay) and set off at night, travelling eight hours. I meet various people from the committee, get some references, go for interviews, all in vain. I make one attempt on my own – it worked out.

---

1 Jüdisches Museum Berlin, DOK-97-5-32, fols. 1–2. This document has been translated from German.
2 Probably Gerhard Samuelis (1912–1984), commercial employee; employed in the N. Israel department store, Berlin, in the fabrics department and under the supervision of Kurt Polley; emigrated to the USA.
3 Kurt Polley (b. 1898), commercial employee; head of the fabrics department of the N. Israel company, 1921–1938. His attempts at emigration failed. He later had to work as a forced labourer for the Siemens company and on 19 April 1943 was deported from Berlin to Auschwitz, where he was last registered in 1943 in the infirmary of the Buna-Monowitz camp.

Can hardly believe it, like a gift from heaven. Within three days I'm back again, I pack everything, pay, back off to Portland, look for a room, in the meantime have operations (two) on my toe, insufficient hygiene due to a lack of time. Have to run around in slippers for four days, twice. Had to go into the store, as otherwise pay would be docked again and it's not much anyhow. Now I'm here in Portland. Got a nice room, plenty of hot water, was able to take my first bath in two months.

Yes, that's how it is. In just a few words. The work, time, efforts, and thoughts one has in the process, well, they can't be described. But with a little success, one is quick and happy to forget all that and see just how much has been gained. The freedom is indescribably wonderful. Can you understand that?

Once I've been working for a little while and feel safer, then the preparations for my girl will begin. A difficult but wonderful goal. May God give me the strength to manage it after all. Now my dear Mr Polley, how are you? How are the NI[4] staff and store doing? How is the atmosphere? Is there anything new, anything nice to report? I would be so pleased to hear from you, just a few lines. I'm just thinking about my farewell evening. Wasn't it nice? When will it be like that again, at least a little bit?

Very warmest regards from your

DOC. 299
Position paper dated 16 October 1937 on the establishment in Munich of Europe's largest library for the study of the Jewish question[1]

Document, unsigned, dated 16 October 1937 (copy)[2]

Position paper
on the establishment of Europe's largest library in the capital city of the Movement for the study of the Jewish question.

The Jewish question has been settled within the frontiers of the German Reich by the passage of the Nuremberg Laws. In the territories bordering the German Reich, however, the issue still needs to be urgently addressed. National Socialist Germany is surrounded by a ring of international Jewry that seeks to impose not only an economic boycott, but also an intellectual and moral one. The Four-Year Plan has been put in place to counter the Jewish economic boycott. A similar four-year plan for an intellectual and moral fightback against the intellectual and moral boycott imposed by Jewry is also needed. This poses a major new challenge, not least for German scientists and academics. On the whole, their track record on the study of racial issues, and in particular of the Jewish question, has been deeply disappointing. It is only as a result of the National Socialist Revolution that things have changed.

---

4 N. Israel department store in Berlin, Spandauer Straße. The department store was Aryanized in 1939 and transferred to the Emil Köster company.

1 BayHStA, StK 6411, fols. 17–21. This document has been translated from German.
2 The original contains several stamps and abbreviations, including the receipt stamp of 'The Bavarian Minister President'. The document presumably comes from the Reich Institute for History of the New Germany.

When the Reich Institute for History of the New Germany³ was established in Munich it turned its attention immediately to the Jewish question and set up a special Research Department for the Jewish Question. This was opened in the autumn of 1936 at a ceremony attended by the Deputy of the Führer, Reich Minister Hess, Bavarian Minister President Siebert, and numerous dignitaries representing the Party, the state, and the Wehrmacht. (Appendix: speeches delivered at the opening ceremony for the Research Department for the Jewish Question.⁴)

The department is headed by the president of the Bavarian Academy of Sciences, Professor Karl Alexander von Müller,⁵ with Dr Wilhelm Grau as managing director. It has a large staff of experts specializing in different aspects of the Jewish question, leading figures drawn not only from academia, but also from the practical, political, and military spheres, who meet once a year for a conference extending over several days to hear presentations and discuss the issues. The proceedings of this conference are published in the journal *Forschungen zur Judenfrage*, volume 1 of which has already appeared,⁶ while volume 2 is due to be published shortly.⁷ The department also has a number of permanent research associates, mostly junior academics, who are working on specific topics of importance relating to the Jewish question. Examples of their work include historical statistics for Jewish baptisms and mixed marriages in the nineteenth century; a history of the expulsion of the Jews from Spain and the Marrano problem;⁸ the role of Jewry in the Enlightenment; the role of the Talmud; and finally a study by the director himself, Dr Grau, which is a comprehensive history of the Jewish question from the French Revolution to the National Socialist Revolution.

*To enable this work to continue, preparations are now finally in hand to establish, in Munich, the largest international library for the study of the Jewish question.*⁹

---

3 Established in the summer of 1935 for the purpose of studying modern German history since the French Revolution, the Reich Institute was under the supervision of the Reich Ministry of Education.

4 See the speeches delivered by Karl Alexander von Müller, Theodor Vahlen, and Walter Frank, in Walter Frank, *Deutsche Wissenschaft und Judenfrage*, Schriften des Reichsinstituts für Geschichte des neuen Deutschlands (Hamburg: Hanseatische Verlagsanstalt, 1937).

5 Dr Karl Alexander von Müller (1882–1964), lawyer and historian; professor at the University of Munich, 1917–1945; joined the NSDAP in 1933; sat on the advisory committee of the Reich Institute for the History of the New Germany from 1935; editor of the *Historische Zeitschrift*, 1935–1944; author of works including *Deutsche Geschichte und deutscher Charakter* (1926).

6 *Sitzungsberichte der 1. Arbeitstagung der Forschungsabteilung Judenfrage des Reichsinstituts für Geschichte des neuen Deutschlands vom 19. bis 21. November 1936* (Hamburg: Hanseatische Verlagsanstalt, 1937).

7 *Sitzungsberichte der 2. Arbeitstagung der Forschungsabteilung Judenfrage des Reichsinstituts für Geschichte des neuen Deutschlands vom 12. bis 14. Mai 1937* (Hamburg: Hanseatische Verlagsanstalt, 1937).

8 In 1492 the Spanish Jews were expelled from Spain on the orders of the monarch, Ferdinand of Aragon, and his wife, Isabella of Castile. Those Jews who converted to Christianity, and were therefore allowed to remain, were known as Marranos.

9 In August 1937 the German Research Foundation (DFG) approved a grant of 10,000 Reichsmarks for the purchase of books for the new library dedicated to 'the study of the Jewish question': see the letter of thanks from Walter Frank to the president of the DFG, Rudolf Mentzel, dated 1 Sept. 1937, BArch, R 1/51.

As yet, no such library exists anywhere in the world. Initiatives to create one have hitherto come only from the *Jewish* side, and with a *Jewish* bias. Earlier, for example, the Jews established a large library of Judaica in Frankfurt am Main, the largest facility of its kind in Germany. It belongs to the city of Frankfurt, *and use of the library is still largely confined to Jews.*[10]

The Reich Institute for History of the New Germany initially sought to have the library of Judaica transferred from Frankfurt to the Research Department for the Jewish Question in Munich – either by purchase or on loan – since this was the only place where *the academic utilization of this resource for the benefit of National Socialist Germany* was guaranteed.[11] It need hardly be said that the transfer of the Jewish library from the former citadel of Jewry to the capital city of the National Socialist Movement would also have been a highly visible, *politically symbolic* act.

The request made to Mayor Krebs in Frankfurt am Main by the Reich Institute was endorsed by Reich Minister of Science *Rust*, Reich Minister of the Interior *Frick*, and the Deputy of the Führer, Reich Minister *Hess*, all of whom wrote to the mayor supporting the proposal.

However, the mayor rejected this request most brusquely, refusing either to sell or to loan the collection. His refusal was not only confirmed by a resolution of the city council, but also *published in the 'Frankfurter Zeitung'* in November 1936. From here it was picked up by *the Jewish press abroad*, which welcomed the fact that the library was thereby 'saved' from 'antisemitic exploitation' by the Reich Institute.

It should be noted that the 'counter-proposal' made by Mayor Krebs, to the effect that he is prepared to support the establishment of a separate branch of the Reich Institute in Frankfurt, is just a diversionary tactic, an empty gesture, since the mayor must be aware that the Reich Institute's Research Department for the Jewish Question has been quite deliberately located *in the capital city of the Movement*, and self-evidently cannot be uprooted from Munich.

The city of Frankfurt cannot be *compelled* to surrender its property by any Party or state agency – not unless the Führer and Reich Chancellor himself chooses to intervene in the matter.

The *second* possibility – which the Reich Institute for History of the New Germany sought to bring about following the breakdown of negotiations in Frankfurt – is to open a library of Judaica in Munich with the aid of special funding, even if it means buying new copies of some of the same books that the Jews in Frankfurt am Main have already collected.

---

10 The holdings of Judaica in the Frankfurt city library, which numbered over 20,000 volumes in 1932, had been acquired through Jewish endowments and gifts.

11 Wilhelm Grau had attempted to purchase the collection as early as 1935. The library in Frankfurt am Main considered the price offered by Grau – up to 40,000 Reichsmarks – to be too low, and was only prepared to sell the holdings in conjunction with a second collection of Hebrew works, which also numbered 20,000 volumes. In 1936 Grau asked the Reich Ministry of Education to intervene to secure the acceptance of his proposals and to provide the necessary funding. A report commissioned by the ministry put the value of the collection at several hundred thousand Reichsmarks. The ministry ruled out the purchase option on grounds of cost; the collection would have to be obtained on long-term loan. Following the intervention of Mayor Krebs, who wanted to retain the collection in his city, the library in Frankfurt refused either to sell or to lend the collection to Munich.

To that end the Reich Institute had applied to the Reich Minister of Science for a *one-off grant* of some 150,000 marks (one hundred and fifty thousand Reichsmarks) to be made available by the Reich Minister of Finance for the coming 1938 fiscal year. This sum would enable the purchase of all the major works on the Jewish question published prior to 1936. The year-on-year cost of buying new books on the Jewish question published after 1936 could be met out of a normal annual budget of 15,000 (fifteen thousand) Reichsmarks.

The Reich Ministry of Science has now informed me in a letter of 4 October that in the light of the pressing programme that the Führer has set out for the Reich, the application for the aforementioned special grant for the library has been refused, as requests of this kind for additional funding have no chance of succeeding.

While I entirely understand the position adopted by the Reich Ministry of Science, I believe that in this particular instance it is appropriate for me to ask the Führer and Reich Chancellor for a review of the matter, to examine whether – given what is at stake here – special funding could be allocated for this purpose within the Reich budget.

What could be achieved with the relatively modest outlay of RM 150,000 is quite extraordinary.

The capital city of the Movement would acquire the first major library of its kind devoted to the study of the Jewish question in the whole of Europe. The capital city of the Movement, and the capital of German art, would thus necessarily become a magnet for all politicians and scholars who have a special interest in the Jewish question. At the same time those critics who accuse the new Germany of 'anti-intellectualism' would find that the boot was on the other foot, in that the real 'anti-intellectuals' would then be those who have nothing in their own countries to compare with this great project for the scientific study of the Jewish question.

It is also worth mentioning that if the Jewish library in Munich were to carry on expanding, the question would surely arise in a few years' time as to whether a large and imposing new building might be constructed – the 'Library for the Study of the Jewish Question' – as part of the Führer's building programme for Munich.

In conclusion, it is right to point out that the establishment of a scientific centre for the study of the Jewish question would be an important part of an *intellectual rearming* of the German nation against the global Jewish enemy. International Jewry has fully recognized the advantages of a struggle conducted in the cultural and academic arena, or at least under the cloak of culture and scholarship. *It has been calculated that the Jews spend twelve million each year to fund this struggle. It must surely be possible for National Socialist Germany to find the sum of 150,000 marks as a one-off allocation for the same purpose.*[12]

---

12 After Müller and Grau had both appealed in person to Rudolf Heß and secured his approval, Walter Frank sent a request directly to Hitler, supported by recommendations from the Bavarian Minister President and Mayor Fiehler of Munich. Hitler gave his consent, and at the beginning of 1938 the head of the Reich Chancellery instructed the Reich Ministry of Finance to approve a grant of 130,000 Reichsmarks for the purchase of books for the Munich library for the study of the Jewish question: Helmut Heiber, *Walter Frank und sein Reichsinstitut für Geschichte des neuen Deutschlands* (Stuttgart: Deutsche Verlags-Anstalt, 1966), pp. 430–435.

DOC. 300

Haynt, 17 October 1937: article on the situation in Germany and resistance on the part of Jews in Poland[1]

Dr M[oshe] Kleinbaum[2]
We're throwing it back – the yellow patch!

After Hitler's *coup d'état* in Germany, as blow upon blow, persecution upon persecution, calamity and the limiting of rights started to pour down upon German Jewry, when 500,000 citizens were suddenly thrown out of political life – they replied: 'Let's wear the yellow patch with pride!'[3]

A process of inner-Jewish immersion began, a process of embellishment and improvement of the enforced ghetto-life, of the development of Jewish national-cultural institutions, of the return to one's own Jewish origins. In the 'Third Reich' it was the only way for Jews, the only option because there was not even the smallest chance of standing up against the brutal superior power. Because the human, the humane Germany has in general disappeared from the surface and has been thrown down into the underground world; because the brown Nazism has achieved an autocracy over the entire country. The fight is (in any case for many years) over, lost; the defeat is – one hundred per cent, and nothing more remains but to 'wear the yellow patch with pride'.

In Poland, however, the fight for the face of the republic, for the political order, for the internal and external policies, is far, far from over. The struggle between two worlds within the Polish nation continues, and though the reactionary world wins battle upon battle, they have not yet won the war. On the surface of Polish life there are still forces that have an effect, strong and pure, that do not want to and will not make peace with the thought that in Poland forces should rule that fight under the banner of darkness and racial hatred. In Poland there are still possibilities for legal resistance – limited, reduced to a minimum, but they are still there. Not to take advantage of this last possibility for fighting and resisting would mean: *capitulation* at the outset, capitulation of one's own will, from fatigue, from despondency, from despair and brokenness. And precisely *that* is not allowed, that will not happen!

National Judaism, in the broadest sense of the word, the Judaism that does not want to perish, that wants to hold on to and further develop its own character and distinctiveness, the historic continuity of its culture, defends itself, naturally, against the stream of assimilation and also wants to build up its own Jewish world within the conditions of

---

1 *Haynt*, 17 Oct. 1937, p. 4. This document has been translated from Yiddish.
2 Moshe Kleinbaum, later Moshe Sneh (1909–1972), physician, journalist, and politician; politically active for the General Zionists; in 1940 emigrated via Vilna to Palestine, where he became head of the national staff of the Haganah in 1941; member of the Jewish Agency Executive, 1945; joined Mapam (United Workers' Party) in 1948 and headed its left-wing camp, which split from the party in 1954 and merged with the Israeli Communist Party; from 1949 delegate for Mapam and, later, for the Israeli Communist Party in the Knesset.
3 After the anti-Jewish boycott of 1 April 1933, Robert Weltsch had published a keynote article in the *Jüdische Rundschau* with the title: 'Tragt ihn mit Stolz, den gelben Fleck!' [Wear the Yellow Patch with Pride!]: see Doc. 25, 4 April 1933.

the diaspora. In political terms, this means: the pursuit of national-cultural autonomy. Let us keep ourselves from mixing up this term with the term ghetto.

Both have a common character trait – their distinctiveness. But ghetto means a forced isolation from lepers, a separateness from the despised creatures contrived from the outside, a closed storehouse of pariahs, of the unclean, contact with whom disgusts the 'wellborn'. We, however, strive for the acknowledgement of our distinctiveness as a people, for equality of rights without paying the price of national decline, for full equality not merely as individuals and citizens, but as a national-cultural community that will, however, not be closed off with a ghetto wall from the surrounding world, but will have a continuing relationship with the outside world through the exchange of values, a peaceful and brotherly symbiosis.

The idea to renew the ghetto is, therefore, nothing but a weakening and an injury to our pursuit of a national character, of our demand for cultural autonomy. And when the vice chancellors of the Polish universities assign Jewish students special benches[4] due to the demand by the Endecja,[5] the ONR,[6] and 'Young Poland',[7] we instinctively see in this an announcement of the renewal of the ghetto, the yellow patch, the symbols from the Middle Ages. And because we can still, for the present, state that which our German brothers can no longer bring themselves to pronounce, we say:

'Tear it off with disgust – the yellow patch!'

'Shun them with fury and contempt – the yellow ghetto benches!'

Fate wanted the students to form the avant-garde in the Jewish national minority's struggle against extermination in Poland. They did not come forward for this role, they are not a volunteer avant-garde, but they are placed – not for the first time – in the position of the avant-garde, and they must stand on the front lines. Not for the first time. The economic repudiation and displacement of the Jewish masses began with the practice of the *numerus clausus* in the more important university faculties. The physical antisemitic terror started within the walls of the universities, and from there the waves first spilled out on to the streets. And now, when our enemies propagandize day in and day out that one should deprive Jews even of their official, formal rights, the first blow has again hit this sphere – the Jewish students.

Yes, the '*numerus clausus*' started with students, but the sequel was the boycott of the Jewish shopkeepers, craftsmen, and workers. The excesses began with the beating of Jewish students, but continued in Jewish cities and shtetls, until they came to a most tragic head at Przytyk, Minsk, Brest, and Częstochowa.[8] Thus, *all Jews* must consider the ghetto decrees for our students as *their business* and the Jewish students' fight as the fight of the entire Jewish community.

---

4 From 1937, in response to the demands of radical right-wing students, separate benches for Jewish students were set up in the lecture theatres of numerous Polish universities. These measures are referred to in the text printed here as 'ghetto benches' or 'ghetto regulations'.
5 From the abbreviation ND for Narodowa Demokracja (National Democracy). Founded in 1886 as the secret Liga Polska and known from 1897 as National Democracy, this was a popular party with an antisemitic and anti-German orientation.
6 Obóz Narodowo-Radykalny (ONR): National Radical Camp; founded in 1934 as Endecja's youth organization, especially for students.
7 Probably the radical right-wing youth organization Zwiazek Młodej Polski (Union of Young Poland) of the pro-government Camp of National Unity Party; founded in 1937 and led by ONR functionaries.

The strike, called by the vast majority of Jewish parties for Tuesday,[9] will be a clear demonstration that not only the young students are opposing the ghettoization in the universities, but also the entire Jewish community – men, women, and schoolchildren. Some 4.5 million Jews[10] will strike on Tuesday and demonstrate that we will not return to the ghetto, but that we will rip off the yellow patch and fling it back into the black grimace of our enemy.

DOC. 301
Conference at the Reich Ministry of the Interior on 18 October 1937 on the mass emigration of Jews[1]

Memorandum (secret) from the Reich and Prussian Ministry of the Interior (I B 191 VI/5012 d g), unsigned, dated 28 October 1937 (copy)[2]

Memorandum regarding the conference on 18 October 1937.
It was chaired by Ministerialdirigent and Privy Councillor Hering.

The director of the Reich Office for Emigration Affairs[3] first gave an overview of the overall level of Jewish emigration since 1933, of the emigration to Palestine, and of the present level of Jewish emigration. According to this data, the total number of Jewish emigrants can be put at around 105,000, of whom one third have chosen Palestine as their destination. In the last half-year a marked decline in Jewish emigration has become evident. The reasons for this lie in the opposition to Jewish immigration by a large number of countries, the unrest in Palestine, the extension of the so-called negative list of the Haavara scheme,[4] and ultimately the economic upswing in Germany. It will be important to pursue internal policies that help Jews in Germany maintain the desire to emigrate. One must, however, be clearly aware that such measures will lead chiefly to the emigration of rich Jews, while Jews who are not wealthy will be an even greater burden on the welfare services than has hitherto been the case.

---

8 Anti-Jewish pogroms had taken place in Przytyk and Minsk Mazowiecki in 1936 and in Brest and Częstochowa in 1937. After the pogrom in Brest, Jewish parties organized a strike by all Jewish companies and stores in Poland, which lasted for several hours on 24 May 1937.
9 At a meeting, multiple Jewish parties decided to protest against the introduction of the 'ghetto benches' on 19 Oct. 1937.
10 At the time, there were fewer than 3.5 million Jews living in Poland.

1 BArch, R 2/56269, fols. 65–68. This document has been translated from German.
2 The original has been underlined in several places. On 28 Oct. 1937 the memorandum was passed on via a circular from State Secretary Stuckart (Reich and Prussian Ministry of the Interior) to the Deputy of the Führer, the Reich Foreign Office, the Reich and Prussian Ministry of Economics, the Chief of the Security Police, the director of the Reich Office for Foreign Exchange Control, the director of the Reich Office for Emigration Affairs, and the Foreign Organization of the NSDAP, with the following note added: 'I would be grateful if you could inform me of what findings have been made with respect to the investigation into the issue of increasing the number of Jewish business owners who are permitted to train Jewish apprentices': ibid., fol. 64.
3 The director was Dr Schmidt. On the Reich Office for Emigration Affairs, see Doc. 133, 29 August 1934.
4 The German authorities registered all goods that were excluded from export within the scope of the Haavara Agreement in so-called negative lists because, among other reasons, they contained valuable raw materials.

Following a brief presentation of the Haavara scheme by a representative of the Reich Office for Foreign Exchange Control,[5] the discussion addressed the present value of the Haavara Agreement. The extensive debate led to the conclusion that given the substantial decline in Jewish emigration to Palestine, the drawbacks of the agreement so greatly outweigh its advantages that an interest in the agreement no longer exists from the standpoint of Germany's domestic Jewish policy and it no longer seems justified to continue to uphold the agreement. This position taken by the chairman for the Reich Ministry of the Interior was also adopted by the representatives of the Reich Foreign Office and the Deputy of the Führer as well as the Foreign Organization of the NSDAP. However, the representatives of the Ministry of Economics and the Prussian Minister President[6] stressed that the Haavara Agreement was – from a foreign exchange perspective – still the least expensive way of facilitating Jewish emigration.

In accordance with the earlier decision made by the Führer and Reich Chancellor, there was agreement that we should continue to work towards achieving the most extensive possible emigration of Jews. The policy pursued so far regarding leaving the implementation of the emigration to the Jews themselves should also remain in place. Although the state should not participate directly in the organization of Jewish emigration, it must become involved in *finding new countries of destination* for Jewish emigration. The Reich Foreign Office will continue to pursue this issue. Furthermore, Palestine will not completely cease to be a country of destination if the Haavara scheme is scaled back or discontinued, for so far only 37.8 per cent of all Jews emigrating to Palestine have made use of the Haavara scheme (capitalists),[7] while a larger number have emigrated using worker certificates. This option will continue to be available.

There was also agreement that given the current situation of foreign exchange control, it is necessary to limit to the minimum possible amount the *foreign currency made available* to promote Jewish emigration, because the vital interests of the German people must take precedence over interest in encouraging Jewish emigration. We thus have to aim first and foremost at supporting the emigration of Jews without means. In this regard the *training and re-education* of younger Jews in *agriculture and the skilled crafts* will primarily be considered. The task of establishing the required schools and camps should continue to be entrusted to the Jews. The state and the Party should not, however, place any difficulties in their way.[8] The representative of the Deputy of the Führer

---

5 The Reich Office for Foreign Exchange Control was established by the regulation of 19 Dec. 1933 (*Reichsgesetzblatt*, 1933, I, p. 1088), which thus removed foreign exchange control from the remit of the Reich Ministry of Economics. As part of the reorganization of the Office of the Four-Year Plan and the Reich Ministry of Economics, the Reich Office was closed down in 1938. Its responsibilities were taken on by the foreign exchange section in the Reich Ministry of Economics.
6 A representative of the Foreign Exchange Group took part in the conference on behalf of Göring in his capacity as Plenipotentiary for the Four-Year Plan. An activity report of the Foreign Exchange Group for the period from 16 to 31 Oct. 1937 stated that various parties were opposed to the policy on Palestine emigration because they believed the Haavara scheme's problems significantly outweighed its benefits. While investigating the willingness of other countries to accept emigrants, it was discovered that large-scale emigration would not be possible without sacrificing foreign currency: GStA PK, I HA, Rep. 90 M/42, fol. 36.
7 Persons in possession of at least 1,000 British pounds could emigrate to Palestine on so-called capitalist certificates.
8 On the discussion that took place in 1934, see Doc. 107, 27 Feb 1934, and Doc. 122, 13 June 1934.

declared himself willing to influence the Party's local administrative offices and the crafts organizations along these lines. In view of the low number of apprenticeships for Jews and with regard to the fact that German business owners cannot be reasonably expected to train Jewish apprentices, the representatives of the Ministry of Economics agreed to assess how far it would be possible to broaden the ability of Jewish businesspeople to provide *training to Jewish apprentices*. In each and every case, precautions should be taken to preclude the possibility of the trained and re-educated Jews from subsequently pursuing their trade in Germany.

There was, furthermore, agreement that the establishment of *language schools* to prepare Jews for emigration should not be hampered in any way. The Reich Ministry of the Interior will approach the Ministry of Education regarding this matter. The representatives of the Security Police Main Office declared themselves willing to discuss a change in the provisions regarding the treatment of returning Jewish migrants in a way that would allow in appropriate cases those Jews to enter Germany who are to be employed as teachers, and in particular those who are to work as language teachers at Jewish emigrant schools.

The representatives of the Reich Office for Foreign Exchange Control proposed that those Jews who emigrate as capitalists should be induced to take with them a certain number of poor Jews. This [proposal] was approved.[9]

It was recognized that the *Reich Flight Tax* acts as a deterrent to emigration. On this point, the representatives of the Reich Office for Foreign Exchange informed us that the Ministry of Finance is currently reviewing the possibility of relaxing the rules on the Reich Flight Tax, and that the effective date for [assessing] the value of assets should be changed from 1933 to 1935.[10] Moreover, the Reich Ministry of the Interior suggested that consideration should be given to lowering the *tax on gifts* for donations made by foreign Jews to promote Jewish emigration, since this tax acts as a deterrent to gift-giving. In fact, there is an interest in [enabling] the maximum possible amount of contributions from abroad. The Reich Ministry of the Interior will approach the Ministry of Finance regarding this issue. The representative of the Deputy of the Führer promised his support for these tax law revisions.

There was also agreement that the policy for *the issuance of passports* to Jews should not act as a deterrent to emigration.[11] With this in mind, the representatives of the Security Police Main Office agreed to conduct a further review of the regulations, which have been in preparation for quite some time already. The publication of these regulations will be expedited.[12]

---

9 On the plans of the Reich Office for Foreign Exchange Control, see Doc. 304, 26 Oct. 1937.
10 The validity period of the Reich Flight Tax provisions was later extended to 31 Dec. 1938, despite the reservations of the Reich Ministry of Economics and the Reich Ministry of Finance; Law on the Reich Flight Tax, 19 Dec. 1937, *Reichsgesetzblatt*, 1937, I, pp. 1385–1386. On these reservations, see the memorandum by Kurt Zülow's section (Reich Ministry of Finance), dated 26 Nov. 1937: BArch, R 2/56269, fol. 63.
11 In the summer of 1937 Max Warburg had submitted several of these proposals to the Reich Ministry of the Interior: see Doc. 291.
12 On 16 Nov. 1937 the Reich Ministry of the Interior enacted a decree restricting the issuance of passports to Jews. It stipulated that passports were only to be issued to emigrants and persons whose trips abroad corresponded to Germany's economic interests, or in case of sickness or death of a family member abroad: Bruno Blau, *Das Ausnahmerecht für die Juden in Deutschland 1933–1945* (Düsseldorf: Verlag Allgemeine Wochenzeitung der Juden in Deutschland, 1965), no. 135, p. 40.

DOC. 302

On 18 October 1937 Julius Salinger writes to Kaspar Arendt in Berlin to tell him about conditions for immigrants in South Africa[1]

Letter from Julius Salinger,[2] Cape Town, to Kaspar Arendt,[3] Berlin, dated 18 October 1937

Dear Kaspar,

Thank you for your letter of 5 Oct., which arrived today. I was already beginning to think that your letter might have been lost, because the airmail [plane] crashed somewhere. However, the mail was not damaged. Nothing from me was lost. Your letter no longer caused much of my hair to stand on end. Besides, I get a little mad with joy every now and then at the thought that I will be able to clasp you, my dear ones, in my arms again soon. If only this peculiar Immigration Society does not ruin everything. But now to your various questions and points:

(1) 'I ask you, by all means, to find somebody' etc. Why, that's splendid! My only hope at present is to win someone over by offering him the prospect of quick repayment. You would not believe how fast the people in this hot country get cold feet as soon as cash is involved. By now you will have received my letter of 11 October detailing what the immigration official said to our envoy, namely, that each person [should] deposit £35 here so that they won't have to carry anything with them. I'll therefore send money if I can. Otherwise [get] a receipt for the funds you deposit here; preferably on the ship in Southampton. (2) The invitation can in any event be sent. Notarial certification is not necessary. Absolutely nothing is predictable here; [it depends on] what side of bed the people get out of that morning. As a matter of fact, I caution you against saying anything to the immigration official here about the submitted application. Because even if you are right, the people here are utterly self-opinionated, and by the time you have convinced the official of this (if he lets himself be convinced at all), the ship will already have left port again. Particularly if you have to deal with the one who eats three immigrants for breakfast every day. I tell you there are such people here, you wouldn't believe it. Mr O has still not heard if the protest of his parents-in-law was successful. The lawyer's agent in the Pretoria office was told when the documents were recovered that a decision should be made on Peter's[4] applications during the week concerned. But this in no way means that this has indeed happened (the decision), because everything here proceeds at an unbelievably slow pace, and you cannot depend on anything unless you have it in writing. And even then you cannot be absolutely certain. So this could possibly take forever. I don't think that Peter will be able to study here with the state examinations but without a doctorate. This was possible earlier, I believe. But

---

1 Jüdisches Museum Berlin, DOK-89-2-242–4. This document has been translated from German.
2 Julius Salinger (b. 1884), physician; practised in Berlin; from 1910 married to Marta Salinger, née Saft. Both emigrated to South Africa around 1936.
3 Kaspar Arendt, architect; in 1929 married Liesbeth, the sister of Julius Salinger. Because of his marriage to a 'non-Aryan', Arendt was hindered from practising his profession from 1936 onwards. The couple emigrated to South Africa, probably in August 1938. Kaspar Arendt died in Cape Town in 1994.
4 Peter Salinger was the son of Julius and Marta Salinger; he became a physician in South Africa.

I do hope that he receives his doctorate. Are there any problems here? It is doubtful that it can be pushed through by having someone intercede on his behalf. He must by all means try to get his doctorate.

!! I would have the South African Embassy give me the information in writing regarding [issuance of] a visitor's permit upon submitting an application, for instance, in the form of a reply to a written enquiry. This might perhaps, if necessary, make more of an impression on the officials here, and would in any case show that Peter is acting in good faith! You must also have a certificate (if at all possible) stating that you have purchased a return journey. Have you got this from the shipping line? You must have this since you wrote that you received notification that the money for the return journey was deposited. So make sure you bring this letter with you.

Well, for now, I'll keep trying to raise money. Peter should also try to establish connections with Albert Schweitzer. He must certainly have relations with the missions, [which could be useful] in the event that East Africa still remains a possibility. Incidentally, according to the German pastor here, the missions in East Africa are run by Bethel-Bielefeld (that is, Bodelschwingh).[5] Peter wrote something about recommendations. I can also make some enquiries concerning this matter. Peter should by all means bring a *large* package of Laryngsan[6] with him, and you should, too, later on. I'm still waiting on the promised intermediate shipment of Laryngsan to arrive. I need it badly! A Mr Guericke and his wife will probably be travelling on the ship with you, Kaspar. He is [the] brother of the lady who works in the archives here (I wrote about it) and who spoke to the immigration official for us. His wife is said to be greatly interested in art. But they will surely travel first class. They are only coming to visit, that is, he is travelling for business purposes to the south-west (Ottawi mines or something like that). Peter and Hilda should in any event push the matter concerning the A T 10, that is, speak to Prof. H. and try to get as many recommendations as possible. It is a great pity that it could not be done earlier, so that the people would have had more of an interest in granting an entry permit; well, perhaps it will come in handy in this respect later on. For the matter is by no means closed after a single rejection.

I'm enclosing a letter to Lieschen.[7] I've already written one to Uncle Engel. I'll wait and put it in the next post because of the weight. I'll send it directly by airmail; he'll surely grumble about it being a waste.

Rike has gone to choir practice. In the afternoon she is going to cast [models of] Father Christmases again; she's already able to do it very well. Miss Guericke gave us a large, very nice lampshade for our floor lamp; in exchange I made her a floor lamp for her lampshade. That's how one helps each other here. People who don't have anything help each other here as well, which is always very nice.

Well, give everyone my best regards. Everything will work out somehow.

---

5 This is a reference to a Protestant social welfare organization in Bethel named after Pastor Friedrich von Bodelschwingh (1831–1910). From 1872 he headed the institution, which was later renamed Bethel. It is still in operation today, providing care and support to people with physical, mental, and psychological disabilities. From 1890 Friedrich von Bodelschwingh was a member of the executive board of the Protestant Missionary Society for German East Africa.
6 A drug used to treat colds, coughs, and hoarseness.
7 This is a reference to Liesbeth Salinger.

Don't you think so? But how on earth can one do that to Eva and Trine!?⁸ I'll keep sending you the architectural supplements from the *Argus*.⁹ It will give you a rough idea of what's being built here, and how it's being built. A tremendous amount of building work is also taking place in C[ape] T[own], and this is particularly so in the case of the new building plans for around the pier, where a whole new district is being built as it were into the sea, and which will provide all sorts of work opportunities over the next ten years. (That's how long it's supposed to take to complete everything.)

Greetings to everyone.

*Be sure to send the p. back soon!*¹⁰

DOC. 303
On 18 October 1937 Police Detective Ernst Patzer appeals to Adolf Hitler for a new post after being dismissed due to his 'mixed marriage'¹

Letter from Ernst Patzer,² Elbing police headquarters, to the Führer and Reich Chancellor, Adolf Hitler, dated 18 October 1937³

My Führer,

As a combat veteran and severely war-disabled, I take the liberty today of addressing a request to our Führer, because all the authorities involved thus far have reached their decision without giving me a hearing and because I firmly believe that our Führer, a combat veteran himself, will help me in my difficult situation.⁴

I was born on 29 September 1895 and voluntarily joined the army on 15 October 1912. On 30 September 1914, at the age of only 19, I was severely wounded outside Verdun. I have a stiff left leg, and my physical development has been stunted ever since then. There are probably few combat veterans of my age who have made this sacrifice for the fatherland, setting aside all personal interests and future prospects. My contemporaries who did not voluntarily venture into the field secured jobs for themselves, were deferred from military service in some instances, and today occupy elevated posts, whereas I have had

---

8 Eva was the daughter of Julius and Marta Salinger. She died in Britain in 1978. Trine was probably their niece Katherine.
9 *Cape Argus*: a newspaper published in Cape Town from 1863 to 1969; the name was changed to *The Argus* in 1969.
10 This was added by hand in the original. It probably refers to post or papers.

1 DHM, D2Z16728. This letter has been translated from German.
2 Ernst Patzer (b. 1895), soldier and police officer; military career from 1912; worked for the main border police commissariat of the Marienwerder government, 1922–1927, and for the Criminal Police in Elbing, 1927–1937.
3 On the same day, Patzer forwarded copies of the petition to Hitler to the Reich Ministry of the Interior and the Reich Ministry of Labour: DHM, D2Z16727 and D2Z16731.
4 The Elbing chief of police had dismissed Patzer on 29 Sept. 1937, with an effective date of 1 April 1938, on the grounds that he was 'intermarried with a Jew' on account of his marriage to a Jew in 1925. On 11 Oct. 1937 Patzer lodged an appeal with the Regierungspräsident/Main Welfare Office for the War-Disabled in Königsberg. However, the office rejected the appeal on 16 Oct. 1937: ibid., D2Z16723–26.

to suffer many a disadvantage only because I put myself at the fatherland's disposal at a difficult time. I hold the Iron Cross 2nd Class, the Honour Cross for Combat Veterans, and the Wound Badge in black.

Before my military service I did not learn a profession, because I worked in my father's house and had planned to join the army. Although after being wounded I was initially granted leave until my discharge and returned home, I had to rejoin my regiment since a regulation was issued forbidding re-enlisted men from being discharged during the war. This made my plans at that time to undertake professional training unviable.

I continued my service until 1919 as a non-commissioned officer in the Posen district command, as a deputy civil servant directly at the commissariat, as a maintenance sergeant at the Royal Ammunition Factory in Spandau, and at the ordnance depot in Breslau, and was then discharged due to a reduction in the size of the armed forces.

On 1 March 1922 I found employment with the border police in Marienwerder, and was transferred to the newly established Elbing police headquarters on 1 April 1927. I have already completed twenty-five years of service, including fifteen consecutive years in my current position in the police force.

I am a member of the DAF,[5] the RLB,[6] the Sacrifice League,[7] and the NSV.[8] As a trainer for the German Shorthand Writers' Association and head of an allotment garden association, I have contributed with all my strength, since 1933, to the reconstruction of the fatherland in accordance with the wishes of our Führer.

As far as my powers have enabled me, I have acted in the interests of the NSDAP at all times. With regard to this, I request that you consult the present head of the [NSDAP] district office, Thebud,[9] who was previously an employee of the *Elbinger Tageblatt* (now the *Westpreussische Zeitung*) and whom I was frequently able to assist in dealing with the difficulties encountered under the former system. Furthermore, I supported the development [of the grounds] of the veterans' housing estate by contributing garden plants etc. for setting up its gardens (and I was, to the best of my knowledge, the only allotment gardener in Elbing to do so). I submit as a witness to this SA-Sturmhauptführer Kiesser[10] from the Elbing police headquarters.

As further witnesses who can attest that I have lived and acted at all times according to National Socialist principles, I submit the veteran Party comrades District Detective Sergeant Hänke[11] from the State Criminal Police in Elbing and Detective Sergeant Kurt Schulz[12] from the State Criminal Police in Königsberg, Prussia. Both are long-time Party members, and I have frequently had the opportunity to join them in championing the goals of the NSDAP. Should it be necessary, I can submit the names of further witnesses at any time. The heads of the NSV and RLB offices have lived for years in the same building as me. I am acquainted with long-time members of the SS and the State Police.

---

5 Deutsche Arbeitsfront: German Labour Front.
6 Reichsluftschutzbund: Reich Federation for Air Raid Protection.
7 Opferring: an organization established to provide support to the NSDAP.
8 Nationalsozialistische Volkswohlfahrt: National Socialist Welfare Organization.
9 Franz Thebud (b. 1909), editorial assistant; joined the NSDAP in 1930.
10 Probably Walter Kießer (b. 1910), police officer; joined the NSDAP in 1930 and the SA in 1932.
11 Heinrich Hänke (b. 1883), police detective; joined the NSDAP in 1932.
12 Kurt Schulz (b. 1898), police detective; joined the NSDAP in 1933; member of the SS.

If I now refrain from providing further witnesses, it is only because the highest priority might be given to the testimonials of veteran comrades.

On 30 September 1937, the same day that I was wounded outside Verdun in 1914, I received notice of dismissal, effective as of 31 March 1938, of which a copy is enclosed. The Main Welfare Office in Königsberg, Prussia, gave its consent to this decision on 11 October 1937. I also enclose a copy of the notification from this office. The decisions were reached without taking into account my difficult situation, without providing a means for legal redress, and without citing the statutory provisions governing such a dismissal. I have thus far not been given a hearing from any authority despite the efforts I have taken to receive one.

My marriage took place in 1925. This mixed marriage was at that time neither prohibited nor punishable by law. It was unfortunately not yet possible to foresee today's developments. I met my wife at the military hospital during the handing out of Christmas presents. My nurse was also a Jew, who did much good for the wounded. Furthermore, my experience of the time was unfortunately that other young ladies acted in a hostile manner towards me and could not be induced to enter into a union for life. I was young and inexperienced myself, and the war and its impact had taken such a toll on me that, without taking time for due consideration and without seeking advice from anyone else, I made the mistake whose present consequences for me are not only the loss of my post but also the complete destruction of my means of livelihood.

There was no doubt about the German convictions of my wife's family. Her father was a craftsman (a master tailor). Two of her brothers served in the military as infantryman and foot artilleryman, respectively, with one earning the Iron Cross and the other the Honour Cross for Combat Veterans. Another brother, who was not yet of military age, was interned by the Poles for a considerable time after the rebellion in Posen because of his German convictions. Her father suffered a heart attack due to all this agitation and died before they left Poland. I can also produce impeccable witnesses who will attest to the German convictions of my wife.

I am at present 42 years old, have no professional training, am severely war-disabled, and in very fragile health as a result of my wound. Judging from the experiences I have had thus far, in spite of all my efforts, it will be impossible for me to find new employment if, without regard to the protective regulations for older employees and severely war-disabled persons issued on 31 March 1938,[13] I lose not only my post but also the rights and the protection from dismissal I have earned throughout my long career. Even as an Aryan, I would be worse off than a Jew, who, though only a combat veteran, receives his full salary upon dismissal until pensionable age if he held a post in the civil service.

As I have had the privilege of serving the state for what is now twenty-five years, and also since 1933, I hope that it will be possible to find further employment for me in some other post, particularly considering the circular decree of the Reich and Prussian Minister of the Interior dated 8 April 1937, II S B 6 100/1 091, according to which even civil servants intermarried with a Jew are permitted to remain in their post if they are combat veterans or severely disabled.[14]

---

13 Year incorrect in the original. A corresponding regulation from an earlier date could not be verified.

Should it not be possible to continue my employment in my present capacity, a post will become vacant as a result of my dismissal. I therefore ask that further employment in another post be facilitated through an exchange [of personnel], so that I will not, stripped of all my rights on 1 April 1938, be turned out onto the street and left to perish.[15]

I again most imploringly beseech our Führer hereby to give me the opportunity to continue to faithfully serve the state, and I vow that I will conscientiously fulfil my duties at all times and continue to demonstrate my National Socialist convictions.

Should this petition in any way fail to conform to regulations, I beg your indulgence as I have found no other alternative, being left to my own devices and owing to my difficult situation.

Heil Hitler!

DOC. 304

On 26 October 1937 the Reich Office for Foreign Exchange Control disseminates information about changes in the financing of mass Jewish emigration[1]

Circular of the Reich Office for Foreign Exchange Control (A4/53704/37), signed Wohlthat, Berlin, to the Reich and Prussian Ministry of the Interior, the Reich Ministry of Finance (received on 28 October 1937), the Deputy of the Führer, Minister President General Göring, the Plenipotentiary for the Four-Year Plan (for the attention of Ministerialdirigent Gramsch),[2] the Reich Foreign Office, the Managing Board of the Reichsbank, the Deutsche Golddiskontbank, the Foreign Organization of the NSDAP, and the Reich Office for Emigration Affairs, dated 26 October 1937[3]

In order to facilitate the emigration of low-income and impoverished Jews in greater numbers within the scope of the funds already committed to emigration purposes, I have extended the scope of immigrant and emigrant clearing accounts with regard to the permitted assets of Jewish emigrants, which had thus far been regulated by circular

---

14 See circular decree of the Reich Ministry of the Interior from 8 April 1937 regarding the implementation of the Reich Citizenship Law: Walk (ed.), *Das Sonderrecht für die Juden im NS-Staat*, p. 187.
15 The petitions to Hitler and the Ministry of the Interior were forwarded to the Regierungspräsident in Marienwerder, who issued a negative decision on 10 Nov. 1937. However, he referred Patzer to the mayor of Elbing, who was to assist him in obtaining a post in the office of the Oberpräsident sponsored by the Welfare Office for the War-Disabled: DHM, D2Z16732. Since this evidently did not have any effect, Patzer submitted further petitions, in mid Dec. 1937, to the employment office in Elbing and to Field Marshal von Mackensen, under whom he had served as a soldier in the First World War: ibid., D2Z16736-37.

1 BArch, R 2/14518, fols. 34–36. This document has been translated from German.
2 Dr Friedrich Gramsch (1894–1955), lawyer; Regierungsrat in Kreis Heiligenbeil, 1927; Ministerialrat in the Prussian Ministry of the Interior, 1933; Ministerialdirigent, 1937; ministerial director in the Office of the Four-Year Plan from 1938; executive director of the Council of German Rural Districts, 1953–1955, and member of the executive board of the German Association for Public and Private Welfare.
3 The original contains several handwritten notes, including '(1) the procedures [are] considerably outdated and therefore to be viewed as completed, to be filed […] 18/2'.

decrees nos. 153/36 D.St.-Ue.St[4] and 73/37 D.St.-Ue.St.[5] In the future, the assets of applicants participating in the scheme should not exceed:

if three or more persons are emigrating	RM 50,000
if two persons are emigrating	RM 40,000
if one person is emigrating	RM 30,000

The transfer rate is determined by the amount of the capital sum and the number of persons emigrating. The enclosed transfer table,[6] which was prepared in accordance with these guidelines, envisages a minimum transfer rate of 27 per cent and a maximum transfer rate of 50 per cent. The 'Altreu'[7] will transfer the surplus amounts – which it generates by purchasing foreign currency from the Deutsche Golddiskontbank at a markup of 100 per cent, and disbursing it to Jewish emigrants at higher markups in accordance with the transfer table – to the Reich Representation of Jews in Germany for the establishment of a special fund. This fund will be used solely to support the emigration of indigent Jews from Germany. Indigent persons will be allocated a maximum average amount of RM 1,800 per head in the form of a loan, 50 per cent of which the 'Altreu' will convert to foreign currency. The amount of foreign currency that may be paid through this 'subsidy category' to immigrant and emigrant clearing accounts is therefore foreign currency valued at a maximum average of RM 900 per head. By linking together impoverished emigrants with emigrants possessing assets of up to RM 50,000, it will be possible to ensure that the overall average of foreign currency (both categories together) allotted to an emigrant amounts to an estimated RM 1,700, but under no circumstances more than RM 1,800. The new scheme will accomplish the following:

(1) the emigration of Jews with low and moderate levels of assets (up to RM 50,000) will increase significantly;

(2) through the establishment of the subsidy fund, emigration will now be possible for indigent Jews who previously were unable to emigrate;

(3) the amount of foreign currency allotted to an emigrant will be reduced to a maximum average of RM 1,800 per head;

(4) many of the small deposits made by emigrants will no longer be made.

The details of the new scheme can be found in the enclosed general confidential decree no. 131/37 D.St.-Ue.St. as well as in the other enclosures.[8]

This arrangement will make no more foreign currency from immigration available than under the scheme hitherto in force, pursuant to circular decrees 153/36 D.St.-Ue.St. and 73/37 D.St.-Ue.St. It will only distribute it differently so as to achieve the emigration

---

4 Circular decree 153/36 of the Reich Office for Foreign Exchange Control dated 26 Oct. 1936 supplemented the circular decree 1/36 with regard to duty-free amounts, household goods, and the export of merchandise, as well as the purchase of emigrant deposits by the Deutsche Golddiskontbank at only 50 per cent of their face value: *Reichssteuerblatt*, no. 58, 3 Nov. 1936, pp. 1067–1068.

5 Circular decree 73/37 of the Reich Office dated 24 May 1937 stipulated that allocations of foreign currency to people emigrating to Palestine were not to exceed the amounts required for the purchase of the various categories of immigrant certificates in Palestine: *Reichssteuerblatt*, no. 37, 27 May 1937, pp. 631–632.

6 The enclosure is not printed here.

7 General Trust Agency for Jewish Emigration. See Glossary.

8 In a decree issued to the regional tax directors on 26 Oct. 1937 concerning the purchase of foreign currency at the Altreu, which included the provisions listed here, the Reich Office for Foreign Exchange Control rescinded its confidential decree of 24 May 1937: BArch, R 2/14518, fols. 37–38rs.

of a larger number of Jews. Independently of the now revised emigration scheme, I intend in the near term to bring about a fundamental decision among the parties involved regarding to which extent the foreign currency can still be made available in the future for the purpose of emigration, and in particular whether foreign currency from immigrants should be used for the emigration of Jews at the level expended hitherto.

DOC. 305

Jüdisches Gemeindeblatt für Rheinland und Westfalen, 29 October 1937: article on conditions for the Jews in the communities of Cologne and Breslau[1]

[Dr Fritz Becker][2]
From East to West / Glimpses of two large Jewish communities

For more than four years now there has been a steady stream of Jewish people emigrating from all parts of Germany to nearly every country and continent on earth. At the same time there is an equally significant, and indeed steadily increasing, *internal migration* of Jews, which principally involves Jews from country villages and hamlets moving into larger town and city communities in the vicinity, but which also involves a good deal of migration from one community to another, whether these be medium-sized or large, urban communities. Nearly all medium-sized and large Jewish communities are affected by this internal migration, and in many cases the loss of population due to emigration has to a greater or lesser extent been made good by this internal migration.

The reasons why there is so much internal migration of German Jews – including the present writer, who came from the large Silesian community of *Breslau* in eastern Germany, to the west, to the large Rhineland community of *Cologne* – are well known. Our migration is still under way, and nobody knows where it will lead us, or when and where it will end. It has already changed the make-up of some communities quite substantially, and continues to affect it on a daily basis. Nor is there any immediate prospect of consolidation, given the present state of things. The concentration [in urban centres] will continue, and many small communities will cease to be sustainable.

For all the other differences between them, the situation of the Jews in different parts of Germany, when viewed from this perspective, has become very similar in many ways. It is said that when a Jew enters the temple he feels at home, regardless of where he comes from. These days, it seems to us, he feels at home in other ways besides. The conversations between Jews are much the same everywhere: the same questions, the same concerns, the same joys, and the same afflictions, from the eastern extremities of this Reich to the far west. The names may be different, but otherwise there are no great

---

1 'Von Osten nach Westen: Streiflichter aus zwei jüdischen Großgemeinden', *Jüdisches Gemeindeblatt für Rheinland und Westfalen*, no. 38, 29 Oct. 1937, pp. 337–338. This article has been translated from German. The *Jüdisches Gemeindeblatt* was published in Cologne in the period 1937–1938. Its predecessor was the *Gemeindeblatt für die jüdischen Gemeinden in Rheinland und Westfalen*, established in 1931.
2 Dr Fritz Becker (b. 1895), editor; lived in Cologne until around 1941, then emigrated to Britain.

differences, not even in people's faces – with one exception, which relates to the face of the community, so to speak, and about which there is more to be said later.

The uncertainty that characterizes our existence, which springs from the severe blow dealt to our economic livelihoods, and which was accompanied or followed by deep emotional trauma, has left its mark on us in the west in much the same way as it has in the east. To all outward appearances, life in two such large urban communities – the one in Breslau, with just under 17,000 Jews, being slightly larger than the one in Cologne – is much the same, despite the considerable distance that separates them. Our segregation from the general life of society and our isolation [are] just as complete here as they are there, and every reasonable and responsible person has adapted to the situation we find ourselves in. The home has once again become the focus and locus of our private and social lives, while Jewish firms are providing opportunities for socializing for those who want them.

If the general conditions of life for the Jews in these two large urban communities are very similar, there are also quite a few parallels in terms of the way people actually live their day-to-day lives. The employment profile of the Jews in Cologne and the Rhineland does not exhibit quite the same degree of concentration in a relatively small number of trades and occupations. Anything we say about this necessarily applies more to the past than to the present, when circumstances have in part changed dramatically, and continue to change on a daily basis. As far as the employment situation of the Jews is concerned, the occupational profile in the west presents a healthier picture. Here the distribution of occupations in retailing, wholesaling, and industrial manufacturing is better than it is where certain lines of work, such as the ready-made garment industry, the wholesale trade in linen and cotton goods, and the grain trade, have always been dominated by the Jews. One important difference is that the Silesian province, even if we include Upper Silesia, has never had such a large Jewish population as the Rhineland. Today there are some 3,000–4,000 Jews living in Silesia/Upper Silesia outside Breslau, whereas in the Rhineland there are still some 25,000 Jewish souls living in a large number of villages and hamlets. It is obvious that this is an important factor both in economic terms and in every other respect, even if conditions for the Jews in the Rhenish province, which we will soon be covering in a separate report, are steadily deteriorating. The general economic situation of the Jews in Silesia can only be described as bad, although we have to remember that the province of Silesia has always been one of Germany's most depressed economic regions. Even the years of crisis prior to 1933 dealt many severe blows to the Jewish economic sector in Silesia. According to figures published by the Jewish Winter Relief (Berlin) for last winter (1936/37), Silesia accounted for 5.83 per cent of all Germany's Jewish aid recipients, yet Silesia's Jewish population makes up only 5.04 per cent of the national Jewish population. In the Rhineland, however, which accounts for 9.78 per cent of Germany's Jewish population, those receiving aid comprised only 9.66 per cent of the national total. Donations for winter relief in Silesia amounted to 3.90 per cent of the national total, and in the Rhineland 8.39 per cent, which means that Silesia did rather worse when these figures are measured against the two regions' respective shares of the national Jewish population. The [Jewish] Community in Breslau itself had to give aid to some 4,500 persons, compared with approximately 2,500 in Cologne. While these statistics speak for themselves, the figures for the Breslau Jewish Community budget give an even clearer picture of the worse situation of this large urban community. The situation of individual institutions that rely directly or indirectly on the Jewish Community tells the same story, just one example being the serious financial crisis with which the Jewish Hospital in Breslau has been struggling for a number of years, despite significant injections of cash by the Jewish Community. In the budget estimate for 1937/38, expenditure by the welfare office of the Breslau Jewish Community accounted for some 33 per cent of the total budget.

It is gratifying to note that the poor economic situation has not adversely affected the Jewish life of the Breslau Community. In many respects things here are much the same as in Cologne. Jewish life centres on the Jewish schools, the Jewish Theological Seminary, the Jewish house of learning, the Culture League, and the Jewish political and ideological groupings, which are all very active. Community politics probably count as part of 'Jewish life', and in Breslau they have played a very big part in recent years, and continue to do so. Relations in this area cannot exactly be described as harmonious, and it would seem that these things run much more smoothly in Cologne. A series of controversial issues have repeatedly caused great unrest within the Breslau Community. To conclude from this that people take the problems of the Jews much more seriously there than they do in Cologne would probably not be entirely correct. But the fact remains that despite the compromise that has held for some years now, Party policy has repeatedly served to aggravate many a difficult situation, and the chairman of the Breslau Jewish Community, Councillor (retired) *Less*,[3] who has always made a point of standing aloof from party politics, has, it seems to us, a much less easy job than his colleague Consul *Bendix*.[4] It is also quite true that these things are affected by the differing temperaments of people in the east and in the west. The influence that geographical, economic, and sociological factors have on people is plainly apparent in the Rhineland Jews, just as people in general differ in the west of Germany from their compatriots in the east.

In terms of Jewish religious practices, Breslau has only the unified congregation with conservative and liberal ordinances. It has no separate secessionist congregation. There are no significant differences in religious observance; minor variations in practices, prayers, and chants have always been a well-known feature of Jewish congregations both in the west and in the east. Religious life and Jewish life in general receive much help and encouragement from the rabbinic seminary mentioned above, whose teachers and students make themselves fully available to the community. Unfortunately this institution – the only one in Germany apart from Berlin – is now threatened with closure, unless the necessary funding can continue to be found. The seminary contains one of the largest and most important Jewish libraries.

In general terms there has been a revival of Jewish life in recent years, and a renewed interest in Jews and the Jewish tradition. But as in Cologne and elsewhere in the German Reich, this has been followed by a backlash. The delicate plant, placed in soil that has

---

3 Georg Less (1871–1953), entrepreneur and local politician; chairman of the advisory committee of the Chamber of Industry and Commerce and of the advisory committee of the Breslau Municipal Bank; from 1932 he was a member of the executive of the Breslau synagogue congregation, and served as its chairman from 1934 to 1941; emigrated to Uruguay in 1941.
4 Albert Bendix (1879–1940), banker; manager of various branches and later owner of the Barmer Bank-Verein Hinsberg, Fischer & Co. until its merger in 1932 with the Commerzbank; chairman of the executive of the Cologne synagogue congregation, 1933–1939; consul for Lithuania; took his own life in 1940.

been much dug over and loosened, has been given too much artificial fertilizer and worked over by far too many gardeners. This seems to us to be the main reason for all the misdirections and wasted time and effort that everyone now complains about all the time.

It is well known that the Breslau Community cannot compare with the Cologne Community when it comes to longevity. Cologne's proud claim to be the oldest Jewish community in Germany cannot be disputed. Even so, the community in Breslau dates back to the early thirteenth century, and Jews from the western part of Germany, who constantly migrated to the east from the time of the Crusades onwards, can be seen as the forefathers of the Breslau Jews. We have documentary evidence of Jews living in Breslau as early as 1203. Some of the Silesian Jews appear to have come from the Orient, as the oldest known name of a Breslau Jew (David b. Sar Scholaum) suggests. This is not the place, however, to go into more detail about the significant role that the congregation there subsequently played in the period following the emancipation of the Jews in Germany, or its part in the religious struggles of the last century (Geiger–Tiktin).[5]

Jewish communities in Germany all have their history, their traditions; they had a time when economic, intellectual, and social life flourished; and today they all exhibit much the same signs of decay, because they are no longer able to cope with the hardships of the present day. This brief comparative survey makes no claim to being an exhaustive portrayal, but we would like to think that the peace and harmony that the Cologne Community has managed to achieve is an example and model deserving of universal emulation in these present times.

---

5 This is a reference to the quarrel between Abraham Geiger and the Breslau rabbi Salomon Abraham Tiktin, seen here as exemplifying the conflict between the reformist and traditionalist tendencies in Jewry. In 1838 the reformist Geiger was elected as rabbi in Breslau against the will of the Orthodox chief rabbi Tiktin. The latter prevented Geiger from taking up his post until 1840.

DOC. 306

On 9 November 1937 the chairman of the Berlin City Council writes to the Reich Minister of Education to justify his decision to limit the number of pupils at a Jewish private school[1]

Letter from the chairman of the City Council of the Reich Capital of Berlin/General Affairs Department (I 9a. 201/37.), signed Lippert, to the Reich Ministry of Education (received on 11 November 1937), dated 9 November 1937[2]

Re: Kaliski Jewish Private School[3] in Berlin-Dahlem, limiting the number of pupils.
Decree dated 11 October 1937 – C. III.b.Nr. 2598. –[4]
Rapporteurs: Oberregierungsrat and Chief Building Official Klemme.[5]
                Oberregierungsrat von Lettow-Vorbeck.[6]

After re-examining the matter[7] I find that I must adhere to my earlier decision. The right to run the Jewish school in a residential area does not exist as this requires an exemption from the relevant provisions of § 8(25) of the Berlin Building Code, and such a decision falls within the discretion of the appropriate officials. I availed myself of this discretion in that I, in response to the negative opinion of the Building Inspection Authorities, judged a total of 100 pupils to be reasonable and decided accordingly in the complaints procedure. This should generally promote the establishment of Jewish schools. I believe, however, that it is not possible to permit Jewish schools to have a larger number of pupils in a residential area of such importance as Dahlem, as the residents must rightfully consider this to be a severe disturbance. In addition to this, only about a quarter of the pupils presently attending the school come from Dahlem; the rest reside in city districts further away, such as Charlottenburg.

---

1 BArch, R 4901/5368, fol. 13r–v. This document has been translated from German.
2 The original contains several handwritten notes.
3 In 1932 the teacher Lotte Kaliski (1908–1995) founded the non-denominational Kaliski Private Forest School in the Berlin district of Charlottenburg. All pupils and teachers classed as Aryan, however, had to leave the school by Easter 1934. From 1936 the school was located in the Berlin district of Dahlem, at the address 2–6 Im Dol, and was forced to change its name to Kaliski Jewish Private School. As of summer 1938, 405 pupils attended the school. In 1938 Lotte Kaliski emigrated to the United States, where she started a nursery school for refugee children and in 1947 she founded the New Kaliski Country Day School for Children with Learning Disabilities. Dr Paul Jacob continued to run the Berlin school until its closure in March 1939.
4 Letter from the Reich Ministry of Education, dated 11 Oct. 1937: BArch, R 4901/5368, fol. 12.
5 Emil Klemme (b. 1876), civil servant; entered the civil service in 1900; served as Oberregierungsrat and chief building official in the General Affairs Department of the Chairman of the City Council of the Reich Capital of Berlin, 1937–1942.
6 Kurt von Lettow-Vorbeck (1879–1960), lawyer; entered the Prussian civil service, 1917; member of the German National People's Party (DNVP), 1925–1927, and member of the German Nationalist Party (DVP), 1928–1931; joined the SA in 1933; from 1934 section head for the state commissioner for Berlin and the chairman of the Berlin City Council.
7 In March 1937 Julius Lippert had granted a permit to run the school on the condition that the number of pupils be limited to 100. On 17 August 1937 the school submitted a petition to the Reich Minister of Education, seeking to have the limit overturned: ibid., fols. 1–5. On 11 Oct. 1937 the Reich Ministry of Education declared that it would agree to reduce the number of pupils to 100 only if all dismissed pupils could be enrolled in other private Jewish institutions: ibid., fol. 12.

At the moment, it is not possible for me to ascertain whether and to what extent the limit decided upon will place a burden on the public schools through their admission of the 351–100 = 251 dismissed Jewish pupils.⁸

The Prussian Minister of Finance, as the minister responsible for building inspection matters, has received a copy of this report.

DOC. 307
Paul Malsch from Düsseldorf writes about the opening of the propaganda exhibition 'The Eternal Jew' (around 10 November 1937)[1]

Handwritten note by Paul Malsch, undated and unsigned, probably enclosed in his letter from Venlo, the Netherlands, to Willy Malsch, USA, dated 10 November 1937[2]

Well, in Munich they have opened an exhibition entitled 'The Eternal Jew'.[3] The exhibition is sponsored by the German Reich!! Hence, a highly official show. Its contents consist of affronts, insults, jibes, and slights against German Jews and Jews worldwide.

All the outlandish old wives' tales, all the mean and base practices spawned in the Dark Ages, are all the Nazis' new lies; the vile and slanderous association of Jewry with Bolshevism is 'pictorially' presented here. The protest planned by German rabbis was promptly quashed through the threat of concentration camps in the event of domestic protest, and of penal servitude in the event of protest from outside [Germany]!! The vile scoundrel and slanderer Streicher, the Führer's friend (that's why the slanderer runs with the Führer; the Nazis think they have risen to the heights of humanity!!), was allowed to open this exhibition and Dr Göbbels had to put in his official two cents![4] Fools, thieves, Nazi minions, prostituted judges, and 'men of letters' applauded [the remarks]. Decent Germans who are still capable of thinking for themselves feel only the deepest shame about such villainy. Indeed, no one is copying Germany in this respect: cruelly kicking the muzzled and silently suffering German Jewry, a dwindling minority; disgracing and torturing the defenceless; only Hitler is capable of such acts![5]

And what has been the response of the King of England – the ruler of Palestine?[6] He has closed the territory's doors and in the splendour of the throne has no compassion for the mental agony of those who look to him full of hope! He has sent congratulatory

---

8 In consultation with the Reich Ministry of Education, on 18 Dec. 1937 the Prussian Ministry of Finance decided to limit the number of pupils only to 300: ibid., fol. 17.

1 USHMM, RG 10 086, Malsch family letters. This document has been translated from German.
2 The original contains an illegible comment in the bottom margin.
3 The exhibition's title, 'The Eternal Jew', alludes to the thirteenth-century myth of the Jew Ahasverus who taunted Jesus on his way to the cross only to then be condemned to wander the earth until Judgement Day. The propaganda exhibition opened on 8 Nov. 1937 at the Deutsches Museum in Munich, and by December had already attracted some 210,000 visitors, including many school classes and Strength through Joy groups. The exhibition was later shown in other cities, including Berlin and Vienna.
4 Correctly: Goebbels. See the newspaper article reporting on Goebbels's opening address 'Eröffnung der Ausstellung "Der ewige Jude": Gauleiter Streicher über die jüdische Weltpest – Eröffnungsansprache Dr Goebbels', *Völkischer Beobachter* (northern German edition), 9 Nov. 1937, p. 2.

telegrams to the Reich Chancellor and Führer, who assaults the defenceless with sadistic brutality.

Is it possible to imagine that a civilized or even a half-civilized people is capable of falling so far?

They are no longer humans; they are ghouls for whom an honest soldier has only one thing left! The bullet of salvation.

DOC. 308
On 12 November 1937 the Relief Association of Jews in Germany issues a report on the progress and organization of emigration[1]

Report by the Relief Association of Jews in Germany, 12 November 1937 (reprint)[2]

I. Emigration of Jews from Germany to overseas countries: current status and future possibilities

Overseas migration: current status and future possibilities
The total number of Jews emigrating from Germany in 1936 is estimated at 24,000. The breakdown by destination is as follows:

Emigration to Palestine:	9,000
Migration overseas:	10,000
Migration within Europe:	1,500
Return migration (foreigners returning home):	3,500
	24,000

In the first six months of 1937 the total Jewish emigration (aided and non-aided emigration combined) is estimated at approximately 12,000 people.

This report is concerned solely with those instances of emigration to countries other than Palestine that have been processed by the Relief Association. It is divided into the following sections:

I. Extent of overseas emigration in 1936 and 1937
II. Current status of overseas emigration to individual countries
III. Principles and possibilities for promoting and assisting overseas emigration.

---

5 US Consul Bower in Munich, on the other hand, wrote in an extensive report for the US Secretary of State that the NSDAP had failed in its attempt to vilify the Jews. He stated that the exhibition provided often unexpected proof of Jewish creativity: Voluntary Report, 'The Eternal Jew: The Great Political Show', by Roy E. B. Bower, US Consul in Munich, to the Secretary of State, 11 Dec. 1937, NACP, RG 59, General Records, decimal file 862 4016/1696.
6 George VI (1895–1952) was the king of 'Great Britain, Ireland and the British Dominions beyond the Seas' from 1936 until his death. Palestine was administered by Britain under a League of Nations mandate.

1 Archives of the Leo Baeck Institute, New York, at the Jüdisches Museum Berlin, MF 57, reel 2. This report has been translated from German.
2 In the original, which is entitled 'Zwei Berichte' (Two reports), part I, as published here (pp. 1–14), is followed by part II (pp. 1–18).

I

Over the last four years the emigration of Jews from Germany to countries other than Palestine has taught us a great deal about how to manage the emigration of German Jews in the future. Most of what has been learned relates to those who have emigrated with the advice and financial assistance of the Relief Association. The figures show a steady increase in emigration overseas, while emigration to other European countries has declined. In line with this trend, the Relief Association is endeavouring to direct the flow of emigrants under its charge towards overseas countries.

In 1936 a total of 5,555 persons were able to emigrate with financial assistance from the Relief Association. Of these, 4,738 went to countries overseas.

In the first ten months of 1937, a total of 3,532 persons emigrated overseas with assistance from the Relief Association. In the same period of the previous year the number of persons whom the Relief Association helped to emigrate (excluding those persons taken to South Africa on board the steamer *Stuttgart*[3]) totalled 3,586.

This shows that emigration overseas remained more or less at the level of the previous year, even though key destination countries such as South Africa[4] and Brazil[5] were virtually closed to Jewish emigrants altogether in 1937, when new immigration restrictions were imposed. It was only possible to keep the numbers up by exploiting all other emigration options to the full, and by opening up new countries (such as Australia) to Jewish emigration.

The total cost of funding Jewish emigration to countries other than Palestine was RM 2,319,639.07. It is safe to assume that a similar sum will need to be raised in 1937. However, it was only possible to meet these costs because the Jewish communities in Germany were able to raise a large proportion of the money to fund emigration themselves, and because the Jewish aid organizations in other countries provided substantial grants towards these costs.

II

To give a clear picture of the present situation, the emigration opportunities offered by the most important overseas countries will be summarized briefly.

In 1937 a number of key countries accepting Jewish immigrants, such as Brazil and South Africa, have tightened their immigration regulations or enforced them more rigorously, while at the same time no country has relaxed its immigration requirements. Apart from Brazil and South Africa, countries that have imposed new restrictions include Chile,[6] Peru, Paraguay,[7] and Bolivia.[8] Meanwhile, countries such as Colombia and Ecuador[9] – and apparently Uruguay as well, according to recent reports – have effectively made emigration more difficult by increasing the proof of means and the landing deposit required by law. The immigration restrictions imposed by South Africa and Bra-

---

3 In 1936 the steamer *Stuttgart* sailed from Hamburg with 537 refugees on board, but was initially refused permission to dock in South Africa.
4 The Union of South Africa had introduced a proof of means of 100 pounds in 1936, then passed a law at the beginning of 1937 imposing strict restrictions on immigration. Immigrants were now selected on the basis of their financial independence, their occupational qualifications, and their 'assimilability'.
5 Brazil stopped issuing visas to stateless persons at the beginning of 1937, and in July of that year imposed a general visa ban.

zil are particularly damaging for Jewish emigration from Germany, given that these large countries would otherwise be well placed to absorb large numbers of Jewish immigrants in terms of their economic resources.

This tightening up of immigration requirements is due in large part to the fact that the sometimes uncontrolled and disorganized emigration of recent years has led to the arrival in these countries of a number of unsuitable persons, who lack occupational qualifications and adequate language skills, are for the most part almost entirely without means, and are therefore a burden on the labour market, making these countries less willing to accept further emigrants. The willingness of overseas countries to accept Jewish emigrants is largely dependent on the economic and moral perception of Jewish emigration as such. When considering the overseas immigration options it is important to distinguish between individual migration and group migration. Individual migration will undoubtedly remain the more important of the two in future, since in the case of individual emigrants and their families it is much easier to take into account the immigration requirements of the destination countries, the prospects for economic integration there, and any special personal or family connections. Group migration, on the other hand, is essentially conditional upon the availability of a suitable settlement site, suitable settlers, and the necessary resources for agricultural colonization. Under the present circumstances, these conditions can be met only to a limited extent. Where families suitable for resettlement are available in sufficient numbers, group migration is particularly significant because for people who would otherwise be unable to emigrate it offers opportunities to move to another country and settle there. For that reason it is important that the existing opportunities for group migration be exploited to the full. However, this is only feasible on a reasonably large scale if the settlement is managed by an experienced colonization organization, which can make land available to the settlers and assist with their resettlement. Outside Palestine itself, only one colonization organization meeting these criteria has really emerged so far, and that is the Jewish Colonization Association. Following negotiations with the JCA, this body has been persuaded to draw up a colonization plan that provides for the resettlement of several hundred families in the near future.[10] Alongside this collaboration with the JCA, another priority must be the establishment in the first instance of small agricultural settlements in various suitable countries.[11] A number of suitable farmers have already been resettled in Paraguay, Ecuador, Colombia, and Kenya. Meanwhile all other opportunities for group resettlement must be explored and exploited to the full. The number of Jewish families in Germany suitable for resettlement abroad is limited, however, and can only be gradually

6 Since 1933 Chile had been progressively tightening its entry requirements. Quotas were established for Jewish immigration, and immigration was restricted to farmers and agriculturalists.
7 Paraguay banned the immigration of Jews at the beginning of 1937.
8 Bolivia did not relax its entry restrictions on Jewish refugees until the end of 1938.
9 In Ecuador heads of families were required to produce a proof of means of 400–1,000 dollars.
10 The plan envisaged the establishment of group settlements in Argentina through the Jewish Colonization Association (JCA or ICA).
11 The Relief Association of Jews in Germany planned resettlement projects in Brazil, Colombia, Argentina, and Kenya.

increased by appropriate agricultural training.[12] For this reason Jewish emigration from Germany in the future will necessarily continue to focus primarily on individuals and families.

In the case of individual emigrants, it is fair to say that emigration is significantly dependent on the emigrant's occupational qualifications and language skills. As far as the opportunities for immigration are concerned, experience has shown that qualified tradesmen, skilled workers, and persons with detailed knowledge of a particular branch of trade or commerce are likely to be accepted in all countries that are open in principle to Jewish immigrants from Germany. The same applies to women qualified in specific women's occupations, such as housekeeping, nursing, and childcare. On the other hand, it is extremely difficult to place and integrate workers in trade and commerce who lack specialist knowledge of a particular sector, and university graduates who have not undergone occupational retraining or otherwise been prepared for the destination country, especially would-be immigrants with no knowledge of the language and no start-up capital.

In order to give an overview of emigration to the most important overseas countries, the following table shows the numbers of Jews who were assisted to emigrate over a ten-month period in 1936 and 1937, respectively, listed by country to which they emigrated.

Assisted overseas emigration, country by country for the first 10 months of 1936 and 1937 (provisional figures)

	1936	1937
The Americas		
United States and Canada	978	1,768
Argentina	450	663
Brazil	788	254
Chile	53	31
Colombia	52	178
Ecuador	26	47
Mexico	18	4
Peru	23	25
Paraguay	269	39
Uruguay	183	195
Other American countries	25	39
Africa		
Union of South Africa[13]	668	142
British East Africa	4	17
Other African countries	11	5

---

12 On the obstacles to agricultural instruction in retraining camps, see Doc. 107, 27 Feb. 1934, and Doc. 122, 13 June 1934.
13 Footnote in the original: 'excluding the special transport on the steamer *Stuttgart*'.

Asia		
All countries	23	29
Australia and New Zealand		
Australia	15	92
New Zealand	- -	4
	3,586	3,555[14]

The above figures show what a serious impact the withdrawal of such major emigration destinations as Brazil, South Africa, and Paraguay has had. But this has been largely offset by an increase in emigration to North America, Argentina, Colombia, Ecuador, and, in particular, Australia. The increased emigration to North America and Argentina is largely due to the fact that the emigration of Jews from Germany in earlier years has led to the establishment of family ties, which, given the particular nature of the immigration requirements for these two countries (written application from a relative or sponsorship by existing residents), are a key condition of follow-on immigration.

The increase in emigration to countries such as Colombia, Ecuador, and Uruguay, however, is largely the result of concerted efforts to open up new immigration opportunities in countries that have hitherto hardly been affected by Jewish immigration. Australia is a special case: as a result of collaboration with British and Australian Jewish organizations, a not insignificant number of immigrants have already been accepted this year, and the prospects for future immigration appear promising.

The opening up of these new immigration opportunities is of crucial importance for the overall planning of Jewish emigration as such, since any sudden increase in emigration to one particular country can lead to difficulties in absorbing and accommodating the immigrants, or indeed to the imposition of statutory restrictions on immigration, as in the case of South Africa.

III

It is safe to assume that German Jews in general are very ready and willing to emigrate. In practice, however, the willingness to emigrate is constrained by individual circumstances and by the existing immigration requirements.

The Jewish population of Germany is currently estimated at around 365,000 souls, allowing for emigration to date of 120,000 and an annual surplus of deaths over births of around 4,000.

The previous emigrants came largely from the younger age groups. Because the decline in the Jewish birth rate in Germany has been greatly accelerated by the emigration of those age groups capable of conceiving and bearing children, the Jewish population in Germany is not only shrinking in numbers, but is also an increasingly ageing population. Only a limited number of older persons will be able or willing to emigrate for family reasons, by means of children who have already emigrated applying for their parents or other relatives to join them. So in planning our future emigration strategy, we need to prioritize the emigration, and subsequent integration in the destination country, of those young persons who may reasonably be expected to generate follow-on

---

[14] The correct figure is 3,532. Incorrectly calculated in the original.

emigration of relatives. Apart from this, it will in general be necessary to cater primarily for the younger age groups when planning the emigration strategy, because only these groups are likely to be in a position to emigrate in large numbers. For persons of the middle generation, who have previously worked in occupations that they cannot pursue in the countries of immigration, integration is likely to prove much more difficult. Such individuals can only emigrate after an in-depth personal consultation, and in many cases only after extensive retraining.

Apart from the constraints of personal circumstance, the willingness to emigrate is also constrained by the rules and regulations and conditions of life in the countries to which people emigrate. In some countries, such as Argentina and in North America, immigration is basically only possible if an application is made by relatives. In other countries immigration is conditional upon the ability to put up a more or less substantial sum of money as proof of means or as a landing deposit. Apart from such statutory disincentives, a lack of capital to start a new life in the immigration country is often a further obstacle to immigration. For some occupations there are many countries where economic integration is not possible. This is partly due to the economic make-up of these countries, and partly due to specific legal restrictions on the pursuit of those occupations.

Subject to limitations of this kind on emigration, which are effectively beyond our control, we shall do everything in our power to promote the emigration of Jews from Germany on the largest possible scale.

In order to ensure that overseas migration continues to grow, it is important that the emigration of Jews from Germany be conducted in an *orderly* and *carefully planned* manner. Pressure to emigrate, which could result in over-hasty and ill-planned emigration, carries with it the risk that the immigration countries might effectively close their borders, on the grounds that a sudden influx of poorly prepared immigrants could place an intolerable burden on the labour market, even in countries that in principle welcome immigrants. For this reason any emigration scheme must allow sufficient lead time for the emigrants to be adequately prepared and trained, in terms of both occupational and linguistic capabilities, for the intended immigration country, so that they can be integrated as smoothly as possible without prejudicing future immigration. This means, particularly for the younger age groups, thorough training in a skilled trade or agricultural work, both of which require an extended training period.

In order to carry out this training, it is necessary for German Jews to have access to appropriate training facilities in schools, farm academies, and training workshops. These training facilities, and the maintenance of trainees during their period of training, cost a great deal of money, which even now can only be raised at great personal sacrifice by the Jewish community in Germany. Raising sufficient money in future to fund vocational training and emigration programmes will only be possible if the economic circumstances of the Jews in Germany permit it. Since financial support from foreign Jewish relief organizations will only be forthcoming on condition that a substantial portion of the money needed to prepare emigrants and fund emigration programmes is raised by the Jews in Germany themselves, it will not be possible to maintain the previous level of emigration, let alone increase it, unless the economic livelihoods of the remaining Jews in Germany are protected. Any significant impoverishment of the Jewish population would jeopardize present levels of emigration and seriously damage the prospects for any future increase. The number of persons receiving aid from the Jewish Winter

Relief agency in the winter of 1936/37 – approximately 82,000 – shows the extent to which the population is already impoverished.¹⁵

Subject to these preconditions for the planning of Jewish emigration from Germany, our aim must be to increase emigration to the maximum extent possible. There are three areas in particular where action is needed.

(a) Emigration opportunities must be expanded and developed through negotiations with the Jewish relief organizations in the immigration countries.

(b) The numbers of emigrants among those who are less well off or in need of care must be increased.

(c) The obstacles to Jewish emigration that exist here in Germany must be removed.

(a)
Negotiations must be conducted with the Jewish relief organizations in other countries in an effort to ensure that immigrants with suitable occupational training can be integrated into the local economy in greater numbers. It is important to identify jobs that allow Jewish emigrants without means to make full use of their knowledge and skills in the country to which they emigrate. We must also seek to increase the volume of group migration, especially under the auspices of the JCA. Furthermore, we need to make greater use of the services of foreign Jewish relief organizations in procuring the necessary immigration papers.

(b)
A further increase in emigration is achievable if it is made easier for emigrants in possession of capital to establish a new life in the country to which they emigrate by transferring funds there. In the meantime the responsible authorities have agreed in principle to an extension of the existing transfer process used by the General Trust Agency for Jewish Emigration GmbH, which should make it possible for emigrants to transfer capital of up to RM 50,000 in future. In order to ensure that persons who are less well off can also emigrate in larger numbers, the so-called Altreu Fund is being set up within this transfer process by the Reich Representation of Jews in Germany, from which Jewish emigrants of limited means can draw loans up to an average value of 900 gold marks per head in the currency of the country to which they emigrate, on condition that emigration is only possible if such a loan is forthcoming, and that they would not be able to emigrate in the absence of such a loan.¹⁶ In this way it will be possible to get more persons and families who are less well off and/or in need of care into those immigration countries where integration is only possible for those who can produce proof of means, a landing deposit, or a start-up loan.

We are proposing to publish a separate report looking at ways and means of promoting the emigration of persons who are less well off.

(c)
Regarding the domestic obstacles to Jewish emigration, attention is drawn to the following points in particular:

The emigration process and the preparations for emigration are dependent on the emigrant possessing a valid regular *passport* that is still well within its expiry date.

---

15 See the progress report for 1937 compiled by the Reich Representation of Jews in Germany, Doc. 320.
16 On the Altreu process, see Doc. 304, 26 Oct. 1937.

Special restrictions on the passport in terms of time or place make emigration to certain countries impossible, because the immigration authorities will not issue an immigration visa to the holder of a restricted passport. In many cases the aspiring emigrant is required to go on a fact-finding visit to the destination country as a prerequisite for emigration; such a visit is often required anyway in order to procure the necessary immigration papers. Hitherto such fact-finding visits have been dogged by two difficulties: first, the issue of a passport for the purpose of undertaking a fact-finding visit has quite often been refused, or else approved only after a considerable delay. In certain countries, such as the USA, the issue of a tourist visa is conditional upon the passport being valid for a minimum of sixty days after the date of return. Secondly, such visits, necessary as they are, are often avoided for fear that the traveller might be treated on his return as a returning migrant. Since the emigration of children is generally a first step in the emigration of the entire family, the issue of passports to the parents for the purpose of visiting their children from time to time after they have gone abroad to learn a trade would make the parents much more willing to part from their children, and this in turn would serve indirectly to encourage more child emigration. It would therefore help to promote Jewish emigration in general if the issue of passports to Jews were mandated, if the time between applying for a passport and receiving it were shortened, and if the validity of the passport could be extended beyond six months.[17]

Nearly all immigration countries make the issue of a visa dependent on evidence of good character – and, more specifically, a full and complete *police clearance certificate* for the past five years. Even minor and insignificant previous convictions recorded in the police certificate often result in the refusal of a visa. In many cases, therefore, a successful emigration will be dependent on the ability to produce a complete and unblemished police certificate. It would therefore help to facilitate further emigration if it were possible – in appropriate cases, and provided there are no serious or long-standing previous convictions – to devise a speedy and simplified process for obtaining a limited injunction for the disclosure of information from an applicant's police record.

A large number of countries accepting immigrants require persons practising certain types of occupation, particularly a skilled trade of some sort, to produce *documentary evidence, in the form of certificates, that they have undergone appropriate training*. In many cases, therefore, a completed apprenticeship is a necessary prerequisite for emigration. Since Jewish training workshops do not have enough places for all those seeking training, and money is not available to provide additional training workshops, allowing Jewish apprentices and journeymen to undergo training in skilled trade enterprises and industrial firms in order to prepare them for emigration would put a significant number of persons in a position to emigrate. If, furthermore, it were made possible for journeymen and master craftsmen to take their examination, perhaps before a Jewish examination board constituted under the supervision of, and with the involvement of, the local chamber of commerce, and to issue them with the appropriate certificates, this would also do much to facilitate and encourage emigration.

---

17 On such cases where passports were issued for a period of six months only, see Doc. 255, 19 Nov. 1936, and Doc. 273, 17 April 1937.

In conclusion, we believe it is fair to say, allowing for the various considerations mentioned in this report and subject to the present immigration requirements remaining essentially unchanged, that it should be possible to increase the overall volume of Jewish emigration from Germany by approximately 15 per cent compared with the previous year.

[...]¹⁸

DOC. 309
On 18 November 1937 the physician Hertha Nathorff bemoans the surveillance by the Gestapo of her lecture at the League of Jewish Women¹

Diary of Hertha Nathorff, entry for 18 November 1937 (typescript from 1940)

18 November 1937. I gave a lecture on women's hygiene. Just for the sake of my fellow women in the League of Jewish Women – I didn't enjoy it one bit – first submitting the manuscript to the Gestapo – then reading the lecture aloud in the presence of a state official!! – How preposterous, how depressing – I was so accustomed to speaking freely at all times – but I could very well have said something against the government! It is as stupid as it is ridiculous what they put you through, just to harass and insult you. And we had to finish at 10 o'clock sharp.

But the Women's League is the only opportunity left for us to meet. Everything else is forbidden.

DOC. 310
On 20 November 1937 the 17-year-old Werner Angress describes his flight from Germany¹

Handwritten diary of Werner Angress, entry for 20 November 1937

London, 20 November 1937.
I haven't written any entries for a very, very long time. Much has taken place; lots of nice things have happened and quite a number of sad things as well. I have been away from

---

18 In the original, part II now follows, under the heading 'Assisting the emigration of less well-off emigrants'. This part of the report is divided into sections – 'Individual emigration', 'Family emigration', and 'Group emigration' – and deals with assistance for emigrants in the form of loans, job placement, follow-on emigration of family members, and the organization of resettlement projects.

1 Hertha Nathorff, 'Tagebuch 30.1.1933 bis 9.5.1965', p. 33: ZfA, Lebensgeschichtliche Sammlung, Hertha Nathorff. Published in Nathorff, *Das Tagebuch der Hertha Nathorff*, pp. 99–100. This diary entry has been translated from German.

1 Werner Angress, 'Tagebuch' [early May 1936 until 6 May 1941], (no pagination): Archives of the Leo Baeck Institute, New York, at the Jüdisches Museum Berlin, Sammlung Werner Angress. This diary entry has been translated from German.

Breesen[2] since 30 October. My father[3] had to give up his business and rescued his money abroad, contrary to all foreign currency laws.[4] I had to leave too; otherwise I might have been held hostage in a concentration camp. On the night of the 30th I travelled alone to Amsterdam, while my father went to Prague. The money and my mother and my brothers[5] were already abroad, in London. I stayed alone in Amsterdam for a week and met Meui[6] there. We became friends, the two of us, who had never set eyes on one another before but quickly got acquainted because of one goal, Germany.

Breesen means a lot to me, indeed everything, even though I'm physically separated from the people there. There is, first of all, Leus,[7] the girl I love and who loves me, my sweetheart. Then Stef,[8] Prinz,[9] Jochen, Bondy, Traut,[10] Büh,[11] and all the others who in some way matter and mean very much to me. I left Germany, and Groß-Breesen, against my will. I love Breesen and the people there, as well as the three people who sealed their [stay] with their lives; they should also help me to stay faithful to Breesen, and to do everything to remain together with those people who are important to me.[12] One and a half years at Breesen is a long time.[13] It creates ties that bind.

Saying farewell to Breesen was difficult, and tough. I also stayed tough, for the first time in my life. But this time it was of vital importance. When my parents informed me of their desperate plan, I fled Berlin and ran away to Breesen. I had left behind a letter for my parents in which I threatened to commit suicide. I was serious about it. Life had

2 Groß-Breesen was set up by the Reich Representation of Jews in Germany in 1936 as an agricultural training camp. Its purpose was to prepare potential migrants for group emigration: see Doc. 266, 18 Feb. 1937.
3 Ernst Angress (1883–1943), banker; from 1918 head procurator and from 1932 partner of the Königsberger and Lichtenhein private bank; emigrated to London in 1937, and then to Amsterdam in 1938; imprisoned in Amsterdam in 1941 and convicted of currency violations in Berlin; from 1941 to 1942 imprisoned in the Brandenburg penal institution, from which he was deported at the end of 1942; died in Auschwitz in Jan. 1943.
4 On the revision in 1937 of the foreign currency legislation to the disadvantage of Jewish emigrants, see Doc. 304, 26 Oct. 1937.
5 Werner Angress's mother was Henny Angress, née Kiefer (1892–1985). She survived in hiding in Amsterdam, and remarried and moved to Britain in 1947. His two younger brothers, Fritz Peter (b. 1923) and Hans Herbert (b. 1928), emigrated to the United States in 1947 and later lived in California.
6 Dr Werner Warmbrunn (1920–2009). Angress received his address when he left Groß-Breesen. Warmbrunn emigrated in 1941 to the United States, where he later became professor of history at Pitzer College in Claremont, CA; author of works including *The Dutch under German Occupation, 1940–1945* (1963).
7 Anneliese Fränkel (b. 1921), daughter of a Nuremberg sawmill owner; later lived in the United States.
8 Stefan Katz (1920–c.2004), friend and roommate of Angress at Groß-Breesen.
9 Hermann Neustadt, later Harvey P. Newton (1920–1998); came from Breslau; emigrated to the United States; served in the US Army for four years; worked as an agronomist; at his death, resided in Costa Rica.
10 Traut Fleischer (c.1922–1947); emigrated to London, where she worked as a household help and nurse.
11 Gerd Bühler (1922–1944) came from Cologne and emigrated in 1939 first to the Netherlands, and then to the United States with his parents; he died in Normandy while serving in the US Army.
12 During Werner Angress's stay, two youths died in accidents and a good friend committed suicide: see Doc. 266, 18 Feb. 1937.
13 Angress was a resident of the Groß-Breesen camp from May 1936 until Oct. 1937.

no meaning to me without Breesen. That was weak of me, for Breesen is so strong inside me that it gives me meaning even from far away, and ensures that I am still a Hanniot[14] and remain subject to the laws of Breesen.

In mid December I want to visit Meui, go hitch-hiking, and take to the road with him. We two boys who are emigrants and yet harbour no hatred for Germany, but rather boundless love for it, for the country, and for its vigour, beauty, and strength, which have already been implanted in our blood. We are under its spell and will continue to hold on to it fondly. I now want to write more often, record all of my doings and assert control over myself. I want to write down here my longings, my poems, my thoughts, and see some day if I have actually been able to govern myself independently as I now intend to do. Upright, honest, faithful, firm, and German; in spite of everything and everyone: German.

DOC. 311

On 23 November 1937 the Reich Foreign Office urges the head of the Reich Chancellery to ensure that Jewish shops are marked as such[1]

Letter from the state secretary at the Reich Foreign Office (83–21 D.5./11.), signed von Mackensen,[2] addressed to the state secretary and head of the Reich Chancellery, Lammers,[3] dated 23 November 1937 (copy)[4]

Dear Mr Lammers,

As you know, civil servants and employees of the Reich are not permitted to buy goods in Jewish shops. The actual implementation of this prohibition has constantly led to major issues within the Reich Foreign Office because civil servants employed in the foreign service have not always been able to determine with certainty whether or not a company is to be classified as Jewish. This kind of assessment is particularly difficult for those civil servants currently posted outside Germany, who order goods from abroad or

---

14 Member of the group at Groß-Breesen led by Hannio until his suicide. The groups at the camp were named after the oldest person in the dormitory.

1 BArch, R 3601/1859, fol. 289r–v. This document has been translated from German.
2 Dr Hans Georg von Mackensen (1883–1947), military officer and lawyer; served in the Prussian judiciary from 1911 and was employed in the Reich Foreign Office from 1919; joined the NSDAP in 1934 and the SS in 1937; envoy in Budapest, 1933–1937; became a state secretary in the Reich Foreign Office in March 1937; ambassador in Rome, 1938–1943; compulsorily retired in 1944.
3 Dr Hans Heinrich Lammers (1879–1962), lawyer; initially a judge, then employed in the Reich Ministry of the Interior from 1921; joined the NSDAP in 1932 and the SS in 1933; became a state secretary and head of the Reich Chancellery in 1933, tasked with the preparation of government business; held the rank of Reich minister from 1937; administered the business of the Ministerial Council for the Defence of the Reich; sentenced to twenty years' imprisonment in 1949 at the Ministries (Wilhelmstrasse) Trial in Nuremberg and released in 1951.
4 A copy of the letter was also forwarded for the attention of the Supreme Reich Authorities. Reich Minister for Ecclesiastical Affairs Kerrl wrote to the Reich ministers on 2 Dec. 1937 noting that this issue had also been brought to his attention a number of times. He asked for a speedy resolution of the matter in light of the upcoming holiday shopping season and in the interests of the public at large: ibid., fol. 290.

go shopping while on home leave. For example, we have already corresponded at length with the pertinent authorities in order to determine whether the Wertheim department store is to be classified as Jewish or not.[5] The Reich Minister of Foreign Affairs,[6] in the interest of those civil servants in the Reich Foreign Office entrusted to his care who would face major difficulties if they were to violate this prohibition, believes that it is necessary to clarify which businesses *in Berlin*, at least, are to be considered Jewish.

To the best of my knowledge, the Reich and Prussian Ministry of the Interior has already presented a draft law that provides for the identification of Jewish businesses as well as the compilation of a register of Jewish businesses.[7] But, it seems to me that at least this aspect of the matter needs to be clarified immediately. I would therefore be grateful if you would ensure that the proposed measures are carried out as quickly as possible.

Moreover, the Reich Minister of Foreign Affairs would also welcome a decision about how to deal with those businesses that may have non-Aryan elements, but whose wages provide for the livelihoods of hundreds or, in the case of large department stores, even thousands of pure Aryan Volksgenossen.

With best regards and Heil Hitler!

Your very devoted

DOC. 312
On 26 November 1937 Minister of Propaganda Joseph Goebbels advocates the exclusion of Jews from German cultural life[1]

Address delivered by Joseph Goebbels at the annual conference of the Reich Chamber of Culture and the National Socialist organization Strength through Joy, Berlin, 26 November 1937

[...]²

Only in this way have we been able to solve in the realm of German cultural life, without appreciable commotion, a problem that was regarded as simply intractable, precisely in this realm, in pre-National Socialist times: we have removed the Jews and placed

---

5 See Doc. 278, 7 May 1937.
6 The Reich Minister of Foreign Affairs at the time was Baron Konstantin von Neurath.
7 The registration and identification of Jewish businesses was later enacted through the Third Regulation to the Reich Citizenship Law (14 June 1938): *Reichsgesetzblatt*, 1938, I, p. 627.

1 DRA, FHB NM 59/5/3, transcription: 5.45–12.25 min; published in Walter Roller and Susanne Höschel (eds.), *Judenverfolgung und jüdisches Leben unter den Bedingungen der nationalsozialistischen Gewaltherrschaft* (Potsdam: Verlag für Berlin-Brandenburg, 1997), vol. 1, pp. 98–100. This document has been translated from German.
2 The total length of the speech was 35 minutes. Goebbels introduced his address with comments on the essence of the 'organization', which, he said, played a decisive role in the life of the nations. He said that for the benefit of 'a greater and broader law of life', the 'surrender of certain individual civil laws' must be called for. Then Goebbels raised the subject of the 'cleansing' of the art scene. The speech was printed in condensed form in the *Völkischer Beobachter* (northern German edition), 27 Nov. 1937, p. 2.

again into German hands the leadership and representation of German intellectual life with respect to the nation and the world. What that means can be gauged only by someone who has a notion of how deeply the Jewish influence had penetrated right into Germany's cultural life. Nowhere did the Jew rule and dominate so unrestrictedly and unimpededly as here. If one realizes that since 1933 – quite apart from the Jews who in a timely fashion took to their heels as emigrants at the onset of the National Socialist revolution – we have removed close to 3,000 Jews[3] from German cultural life, but have simultaneously also filled the vacated positions with Germans, without this enormous replacement causing even a hint of stagnation in Germany's cultural life; if one considers in addition that on the whole these were, of course, pivotal positions – indeed, in general they performed leading functions in public life – then one can get some idea of how much work was accomplished here and how lightly one personnel mistake or another weighs in comparison with the objective that was achieved. Today, no Jew writes for a German newspaper, and the newspapers nonetheless keep being published, more numerous and better presented than ever before. Today, no Jew appears on a stage, and the theatres nonetheless keep putting on plays, and they are more crowded than ever before. Today, no Jew performs in a film, and we nonetheless keep producing films, more numerous and successful than ever before.[4]

The clamour of our opponents still rings in our ears, saying that it was impossible to remove the Jews from German cultural life, since they could not be replaced. We have done so, and things are better than before! In this area, the demand of National Socialism has been carried out well and truly, and the world has before its eyes the proof that the cultural life of a people can also be governed, conducted, and represented exclusively by its own sons, and in a corresponding and suitable manner at that.

How deeply the Jewish demon had penetrated into Germany's cultural life was demonstrated in alarming and downright blood-curdling ways in the 'Degenerate Art' exhibition held in Munich as a warning example.[5] We have frequently been attacked in the so-called world press on account of this exhibition, but to this day no foreign enthusiast has turned up who would be willing, say, to make reparations for this cultural barbarism by buying the 'art treasures' exhibited in Munich and thereby saving them for eternity. *(Applause)* They do not like them, but they defend them. And they defend them not for cultural reasons but merely for political ones. It takes scarcely a dismissive wave of the hand to deal with their arguments. But in Germany, too, this course of action has caused misunderstandings here and there.

One was in agreement with the general trend towards redressing a cultural crisis, to be sure, but reserved the right to raise low-keyed objections in specific instances. These objections sounded very much like those formerly raised on account of our hostility towards Jews: one must not throw the baby out with the bathwater, one is naturally

---

3 In its reproduction of the speech, the *Völkischer Beobachter* used the words 'Jews and Jews' cronies' (Juden und Judengenossen): ibid.
4 With the exception of the last sentence of the document, the following text was omitted from the account of the speech in the *Völkischer Beobachter*: ibid.
5 The 'Degenerate Art' exhibition opened in Munich on 19 July 1937 and was later shown in twelve cities. The exhibition, which was viewed by 3 million persons in all, presented in a defamatory way expressionist, Dadaist, and other works of art that had been confiscated from German museums.

antisemitic as well, but enough is simply enough. – We know this refrain: let me have my cake and eat it, too.

For the paintings and sculptures of the 'Degenerate Art' exhibition denounced in Munich, not a single resounding argument was presented in earnest. A case was made not in favour of the documents of decadence exhibited there, but rather against the so-called method.

These fabricators of filth, it was said, possessed a strong volition, were representative, in their activism, of a new artistic world and however else these lame excuses were worded. It was opined that one should allow this development to run its course, and in this way it would peter out sooner rather than later. The same could have been said in domestic politics about Marxism or parliamentarianism, in the economic sector about the class struggle or class snobbery, in foreign affairs about the Treaty of Versailles or the taking away of Germany's rights of sovereignty. Something of this sort does not peter out; it must be removed. The more thoroughly, quickly, and sweepingly this is done, the better! [Applause]

It has nothing at all to do with the suppression of artistic freedom and youthful progress. On the contrary, the substandard works that were exhibited here and their creators are outmoded, ancient history now. They are senile, no longer to be taken seriously, representatives of an era that we have long since overcome intellectually and politically, and whose dreadful mutations continued to haunt our times only in the area of the fine arts.

The salubrity of such a cleansing regimen is demonstrated by the public's reaction and, in particular, among the groups of buyers at the Great German Art Exhibition in the House of German Art in Munich.[6]

[...][7]

---

[6] The first Great German Art Exhibition took place from 18 July to 31 Oct. 1937 and attracted 400,000 visitors. The sales exhibition was staged eight times in all before 1944, in the House of German Art in Munich, which was specially built for this purpose.

[7] In the following part of the speech, Goebbels asserted that the general public had never before taken such an intense interest in the visual arts as in the National Socialist state. The government, he said, had taken action in the cultural sector by awarding grants and commissions. In addition to the promotion of young artists, provision was also being made, he added, for ageing artists by funding retirement and convalescent homes: *Völkischer Beobachter* (northern German edition), 27 Nov. 1937, p. 2. On the use of Aryanized assets to provide assistance for artists, see Doc. 180, 24 July 1935, fn. 4.

DOC. 313

The Jewish Community of Merzig writes to the Reich commissioner for the Saarland on 29 November 1937 regarding the repair of the damaged synagogue[1]

Handwritten letter from Leo Weil,[2] state commissioner of the synagogue congregation of Merzig (Saar), to the Reich commissioner for the Saarland, Dept. III, Cultural Affairs and Schools (received on 30 November 1937), Saarbrücken, dated 29 November 1937[3]

Recently, in our affiliate congregation of Brotdorf, [subordinated to the] Merzig-Land regional mayor's office, the windowpanes in the synagogue have quite often been smashed. On the evening of 12 November, once again, approximately twenty panes were smashed. Since our community now consists of only a few very poor persons, they are no longer able to bear the expenses. The offenders were identified in the schools.

I approached the Merzig-Land mayor's office responsible with the request that the Brotdorf local authority be induced to replace the windows. Thus far I have had no reply. Religious services were always held there, which is no longer possible in this cold weather. What am I supposed to do now? Please prevail upon the Brotdorf local authority to repair the damage. Awaiting your favourable decision, respectfully[4]

---

1 Landesarchiv des Saarlands, MK, Nr. 3314, fol. 187. Published in Landesarchivverwaltung Rheinland-Pfalz (ed.), *Dokumentation zur Geschichte der jüdischen Bevölkerung in Rheinland-Pfalz und im Saarland*, vol. 6, pp. 440–441. This document has been translated from German.
2 Leo Weil (1870–1944); from 1925 a member and from 1932 the chairman of the Representation of the Synagogue Congregation of Merzig; deported to Gurs in Oct. 1940 and then from Drancy to Auschwitz in May 1944.
3 Parts of the original are underlined by hand.
4 According to the response of the mayor of Merzig-Land, his office refused to recognize the town council's obligation to replace the windows; Landesarchivwerwaltung Rheinland-Pfalz (ed.), *Dokumentation zur Geschichte der jüdischen Bevölkerung*, pp. 440–441.

DOC. 314

On 7 December 1937 the German Labour Front plans to push through the legal exclusion of Jews as factory leaders[1]

Letter (confidential!) from the DAF Central Office/Department of the Councils of Trust (Wy/St, V 01.24, diary no. A 2231/2357), Head of Department Weygold,[2] addressed to the Office for Work Committees, Council of Trust Section, DAF Gau Administration in Silesia, dated 7 December 1937 (carbon copy)

I require as soon as possible – though without reference to our proposition – a letter containing roughly the following:

A future revision of the AOG[3] must include a provision prohibiting Jews from holding posts as factory leaders as defined by the AOG, i.e. that they cannot be in charge of others. – We cannot expect that a German worker gives his pledge to work for the Führer and the people to a Jew. – Cases are known to us in which the refusal of members of the Council of Trust to make their pledges before a Jew meant that they could not be duly appointed (and granted the corresponding protection against dismissal!).

Such letters – with examples provided, if available – should be submitted *immediately*.[4] (Backdated by up to two months!)[5]

Heil Hitler!

DOC. 315

On 15 December 1937 Hermann Göring, as acting Reich Minister of Economics, limits the foreign currency and raw material allocations for Jewish companies[1]

Circular decree issued by the Reich and Prussian Minister of Economics tasked with conducting the affairs of the ministry: signed Göring,[2] Prussian Minister President (II R 45 578/37), addressed to the Reich Plenipotentiaries for the Supervisory Offices[3] VII to XXVII (private), dated 15 December 1937 (copy)

Re: foreign currency and raw material allocations for Jewish companies.

The allocation of foreign currency and raw materials according to reference points dated prior to the rationing of foreign currency and raw materials or during its early phase has resulted in the continued participation of Jewish companies in trade and the production

---

[1] BArch, NS 5 IV/199, fol. 155. This document has been translated from German.
[2] Karl Josef Weygold (1897–1982), retailer; joined the NSDAP in 1929; became the chairman of the General Health Insurance Company for the city of Munich in 1933; later became head of department in the Central Office of the German Labour Front until 1943; from 1943 head of labour and social organization affairs within the Nazi Party organization responsible for the Eastern territories.
[3] *Arbeitsordnungsgesetz*: Law for the Regulation of National Labour, 20 Jan. 1934: *Reichsgesetzblatt*, 1934, I, pp. 45–56.
[4] The file does not contain any response to this letter.
[5] A corresponding regulation was later enacted in the Regulation on the Exclusion of Jews from German Economic Life, 12 Nov. 1938: *Reichsgesetzblatt*, 1938, I, p. 1580.

[1] BArch, R 3601 II/1859, fols. 359–360. This document has been translated from German.

of goods at a level today that is incongruent with the general intention to eliminate Jewish influence within the economy and fails to reflect recent developments. In terms of the import of goods, the General Confidential Decree of the Reich Office for Foreign Exchange Control dated 8 June 1936 (88/36 Ü.St.)[4] already stipulates that the foreign currency allowances are not to be determined strictly according to the respective extent of a company's involvement in the import of goods within a given period of comparison. On 27 November 1937 the supervisory offices received new instructions regarding the allocation of foreign currency and raw materials to Jewish companies.[5] In addition to these provisions, I stipulate the following:

I. In addition to reviews mandated by the decree dated 27 November 1937 (II R 40 181/37), the supervisory offices must determine whether the use of earlier points of reference for Jewish companies is still justified. This review is to be extended on a case-by-case basis to the foreign currency and raw materials quotas.

As a rule, the volume of imports when the rationing of foreign currency commenced or in its early phase shall no longer serve as a standard for determining the import quotas for Jewish companies. Instead, these foreign currency quotas are to be based on the share of imports in more recent years (for instance 1936/37).

From now on, the allocation of quotas falling under the rubric of domestic German business (processing, purchasing, storage, and trade quotas) is to be re-evaluated in a similar way in order to determine whether the implementation of the aforementioned principles is compatible with the retention of points of comparison for Jewish companies that were mostly established in 1933 and 1934. Generally speaking, a later point of comparison should also be chosen for Jewish companies in this respect. Moreover, the 10 per cent quota reduction envisaged in the decree of 27 November 1937, which is the absolute minimum, may be increased in appropriate cases.

II. According to the decree dated 27 November 1937, the amounts of foreign currency and raw materials saved as a result are to be used primarily for the following:
(1) special allocations for worthy German companies,
(2) the alleviation of hardship in the border regions,
(3) the creation of new German companies in predominantly Jewish economic sectors.

Furthermore, I would also like to draw your attention in particular to the decree dated 28 May 1937 (II R 18 659/37) regarding the special provisions for long-time combatants of

---

2 Following Hjalmar Schacht's dismissal, Göring headed the Reich Ministry of Economics from autumn 1937 to spring 1938.
3 In March 1934 the Reich Ministry of Economics began to set up so-called supervisory offices tasked with overseeing the acquisition, storage, and allocation of goods: *Reichsgesetzblatt*, 1934, I, p. 212. Such supervisory offices also later existed for agricultural and industrial products.
4 *Allgemeiner vertraulicher Erlaß der Reichsstelle für Devisenbewirtschaftung*; *Überwachungsstelle*: supervisory office.
5 With the decree dated 27 Nov. 1937, the Reich Ministry of Economics had stipulated, among other things, that the 'import quotas for Jewish companies' were to be continually re-evaluated and reduced if customer demand waned. An increase in these import quotas or additional foreign currency allocations was ruled out: decree of the Reich and Prussian Minister of Economics (Posse) addressed to the Reich Plenipotentiaries for the Supervisory Offices VII to XXVII, 27 Nov. 1937: BArch, R 3601 II/1859, fols. 357–358v.

the Movement.⁶ I request the retention of a certain portion of what has been saved in order to serve such purposes. The decree dated 28 May 1937 shall also apply to the allocation of import quotas from now on.

III. If there are any doubts as to whether a company is to be classified as Jewish, the supervisory offices can request an expert assessment from the respective chamber of industry and commerce. The chambers of industry and commerce will receive further instructions from me. Any uncertain cases are to be reported to me for the time being, until a final legal regulation has been issued.

Any necessary clarification regarding such uncertain cases shall not delay the implementation of appropriate measures against those companies known to be Jewish.

DOC. 316

On 18 December 1937 State Secretary Hans Pfundtner sends the head of the Reich Chancellery the draft of a regulation directed against Jewish physicians¹

Letter (secret) from the state secretary in the Reich and Prussian Ministry of the Interior (I B 215/ 5016 g), Pfundtner, to the head of the Reich Chancellery, Lammers, dated 18 December 1937²

Re: elimination of Jewish physicians.
In response to the courteous letter dated 25 August 1937 (Rk. 13 354 A).³
Dear Mr *Lammers*,
For your information, I am sending you a preliminary draft at section-head level of a fourth regulation to the Reich Citizenship Law, which I ask you to treat confidentially for the time being.⁴

My general comments regarding this draft follow:

The draft of this regulation goes beyond the scope of the matter of excluding Jewish physicians, as raised in the speech of the Reich Physicians' Leader⁵ before the Führer and Reich Chancellor on 14 June of this year,⁶ to cover the exclusion of Jews from a number of other professions as well. Decisive in this regard was the consideration that it seemed expedient to address the issue of a general regulation regarding the elimination of Jews in certain professions from which they will have to be expelled at some point

---

6 This decree could not be found.

1 BArch, R 43 II/733, fols. 60–66. Published in Friedrich Hartmannsgruber (ed.), *AdR*, part IV, pp. 678–682. This document has been translated from German.
2 The original contains handwritten notes.
3 Lammers had informed State Secretary Pfundtner on 25 August 1937 that the 'question of the elimination of the physicians still practising' would be dealt with at a meeting planned for 1 Sept. 1937 in Berchtesgaden: BArch, R 43 II/733, fols. 44–45.
4 Not printed here: ibid., fols. 67–69.
5 Gerhard Wagner had been Reich physicians' leader since 1935.
6 Hitler told Wagner that he wanted to see Jewish physicians 'excluded' in the event of a war. Hitler decided that Lammers was to prepare the legal foundation for removing the remaining practising physicians by retracting their medical licences: memorandum dated 14 June 1937, ibid., fol. 43. Published in Hartmannsgruber (ed.), *AdR*, part IV, pp. 351–352.

sooner or later. I must emphasize, however, that the inclusion of lawyers and patent lawyers in the draft was done without consulting the Reich Ministry of Justice in advance. This was done with the policy on Jews in mind, for which we are responsible, and with the intention of conclusively outlining the circle of professions to be included.

Moreover, the creation of a special law was purposely avoided. The Reich Citizenship Law is the law that provides the foundation for the exclusion of Jews from the body and life of the German people.[7] Consequently, additional measures intended to further the achievement of this goal should logically take the form of an implementing regulation under the Reich Citizenship Law. Insofar as such a regulation substantively alters statutory laws – only the Reich Physicians' Code[8] and the Law on Measures in the Former Upper Silesian Plebiscite Territory can be considered here[9] – then there should be no objections, especially if the envisioned regulation bears the signature of the Führer and Reich Chancellor, which I believe it must.

My comments regarding individual points of the draft are as follows:

On § 1[10]
In my opinion, before the problem of the exclusion of Jewish physicians can be addressed legislatively, the following preliminary issues must be clarified – by means of a binding statement issued by the Reich Chamber of Physicians.

1. (a) If all of the 4,000 Jewish physicians are expelled, can sufficient medical care be guaranteed for the entire country during times of peace and war?

In particular, it must be taken into account that practising physicians of German blood are currently and will in the future be very busy due to the many new tasks constantly being assigned to them.

(b) What preparatory measures might be necessary?

2. If the answer to question 1(a) is 'yes', when would it be safe to exclude the Jewish physicians?

Once these preliminary questions have been settled favourably, nothing else stands in the way of the proposed regulation.

In terms of *how* to go about this, it does not make sense to bring about the exclusion of the Jewish physicians by repealing their licences, as outlined in the Reich Physicians' Code, because the sheer number of cases would prove to be such a burden for the administration that it does not seem justifiable. Therefore, the plan is to terminate the licences of Jewish physicians by legal decree, as has also been stipulated in § 12 of the Law on Measures in the Former Upper Silesian Plebiscite Territory dated 30 June 1937 (*Reichsgesetzblatt*, I, p. 717). The planned date is tentatively 31 March 1938. The final determination of the date will also depend largely on when the necessary number of prospective physicians for health insurance companies can be duly accredited.

---

7 See Doc. 198, 15 Sept. 1935.
8 According to the Reich Physicians' Code (*Reichsärzteordnung*), dated 13 Dec. 1935, the granting of a new licence could be refused if the percentage of Jewish physicians exceeded the percentage of Jews within the overall population: *Reichsgesetzblatt*, 1935, I, p. 1433.
9 This law, dated 30 June 1937, introduced the 'race laws' in Upper Silesia, including the limitations imposed for Jewish physicians: *Reichsgesetzblatt*, 1937, I, pp. 717–720.
10 According to § 1 of the draft regulation, the licences of Jewish physicians were to be terminated: BArch, R 43 II/733, fol. 67.

In particular, it must be determined whether Jewish physicians are to be excluded without exception. In making this decision, it must be kept in mind that charitable Jewish hospitals still exist in some cities in Germany (around nine or ten establishments with about 1,500 beds). There is no reason to allow institutions such as these, which are paid for by the Jews, to fold, as it would lead to an increased reliance on public funds. These establishments are also essential for training Jewish nurses, who are still needed for the care of Jewish patients because we can hardly expect nurses of German blood to go into Jewish households to care for the sick. The inability to care for the sick at home, however, would mean that the Jews would have to rely on public hospitals and, in the case of the compulsorily insured, it would lead to an increased burden on the insurance companies to the benefit of the Jews. After all, given the heavy load already carried by physicians of German blood, it does not seem reasonable to assign them the additional task of treating Jewish patients, especially in the districts in which larger numbers of Jews live – such as Berlin, Breslau, Frankfurt am Main – as this would cut back even further on the time they have to treat patients of German blood.

In light of these considerations, the draft law leaves room for certain exceptions to the termination of the licences of Jewish physicians. In order to ensure that these Jewish physicians serve only the Jewish portion of the population, it is envisaged not only that the certificates of exemption may be retracted and that they may contain specific requirements, but also that a prohibition will apply, punishable by law, against treating German nationals of German or related blood, provided that the general penal provisions do not stipulate that they are obligated to give medical assistance.

Section 4 of § 1 is provided for in the current version of the Reich Physicians' Code. Section 5 is designed to ensure that the necessary amendments to the Reich Physicians' Code can be easily implemented.

On § 2[11]

There is no problem of potential shortage resulting from the exclusion of Jewish dentists and veterinarians. According to the Chamber of Dentists, there are [only] 606 Jews among the 16,217 practising dentists. Among the 8,500 to 9,000 veterinarians, there are only 78 Jews.

In contrast to the Reich Physicians' Code, an amendment of the Reich Veterinarians' Code is not necessary. A Reich Dentists' Code has not yet been issued. The examination regulations for dentists can be amended at any time, at our own discretion, without any special permission being required.

On § 3[12]

With regard to the non-accredited Jewish dental practitioners, non-medical practitioners, and midwives, it seems undesirable to exclude Jews from these professional groups, not only to avoid having to deal with the issue of the legality of non-accredited practitioners offering treatment in a ruling with a completely different intended scope, but also because the percentage of Jews in these professions is insignificant. The prohibition against treating people of German blood is sufficient in this case.

---

11 § 2 of the draft regulation stipulated that the licences of Jewish dentists and veterinarians were to be terminated on 31 March 1938: ibid., fol. 67.

On § 4[13]

As emphasized above, the inclusion of lawyers and patent lawyers initially took place without consulting the Reich Ministry of Justice. Undoubtedly, however, the legal profession will demand the exclusion of Jews among their ranks as soon as the Jewish physicians, dentists, and veterinarians are expelled from their professions.

On § 5 and § 6

The intended stipulations correspond to the existing laws, as outlined in § 2 and § 4 of the Second Regulation to the Reich Citizenship Law dated 21 December 1935 (*Reichsgesetzblatt*, I, p. 1524).[14]

On § 7

The stipulation that Jews dismissed from the civil service on the basis of § 4 of the First Regulation to the Reich Citizenship Law receive a pension in the full amount of their current salary until they reach full retirement age provoked much opposition among the civil servants of German blood because they, in contrast to these Jews, were only entitled to a percentage of their salaries if they retired early. At the time, this regulation was enacted mainly for foreign policy reasons that no longer apply today. Moreover, it also seems appropriate for financial reasons to retract this preferential treatment afforded to Jewish civil servants. The same also applies to the Jewish civil servants who, according to § 2, no. 1, of the Law on Measures in the Former Upper Silesian Plebiscite Territory, were retired as of 31 August 1937 and retained their full salaries. An explicit amendment of the Law on Measures in the Former Upper Silesian Plebiscite Territory is not necessary because the stipulations referred to in sentence 2 in no. 1 of § 2 loc. cit. have been repealed under § 7(1) of the draft regulation in such a way that the reference in this provision lapses automatically.

The Reich Foreign Office, the Reich Minister of Finance, the Reich Minister of Education, the Reich Minister of Labour, and the Reich Minister of War have all shown considerable interest in the draft. Before I allow for the further preparation of this draft,

---

12 § 3 of the draft regulation prohibited 'Jewish dentists and non-medical practitioners' from treating non-Jews: ibid., fols. 67–68.

13 § 4 of the draft regulation stipulated that the licences of Jewish lawyers and patent lawyers were to be terminated on 31 March 1938: ibid., fol. 68.

14 §§ 2 and 4 of the Second Regulation to the Reich Citizenship Law (21 Dec. 1935) regulated the possibility of subsistence allowances for needy civil servants and the application of the provisions of the Law on the Termination of Rental Contracts by Persons Affected by the Law for the Restoration of the Professional Civil Service: *Reichsgesetzblatt*, 1935, I, pp. 1524–1525.

I feel that it is very important for me to discuss its fundamental principles with you first. Please contact me so that we can arrange a suitable time.[15]

Heil Hitler!

DOC. 317
On 28 December 1937 the SS Security Service demands information from the SD Main Districts on the practice of approving itinerant trade licences for Jews[1]

Circular order from the SD (II 112 o/C 4222 Hg/Pi), Hagen,[2] addressed to the SD officers of the SS Main Districts, dated 28 December 1937[3]

Re: new rules for the issuance of itinerant trade licences to Jews
Case file: none
At a meeting held with Main Department II 22[4] regarding new rules for the issuance of itinerant trade licences to Jews, we learned that the main department has already been working on a draft law to this effect for over six months. The preparations have been undertaken in consultation with State Secretary Stuckart.[5] The planned law would make it impossible for administrative courts to modify a decision made by the Gestapo regarding the issuance of itinerant trade licences, peddling licences, and identity cards to Jews. To all intents and purposes, this would mean that the issuance of these papers would be entirely dependent on the decision of the Gestapo Central Office.

Given that the renewal of the itinerant trade licences etc. has to be done at the end of the year, we ask that you get in contact with Department II 22 in the [SD] Main Districts and hand over to the administrators all the materials on file at II 112 pertaining to this question and inform the department heads regarding your experiences gained on this matter.

2. Resubmission: II 112
3. II 22 to countersign before copying[6]

---

15 Hitler later decided that the scope of the Fourth Regulation would be limited exclusively to physicians; letter from State Secretary Pfundtner to Lammers dated 24 Jan. 1938, BArch, R 43 II/733, fols. 76–77. The Fourth Regulation to the Reich Citizenship Law was enacted on 25 July 1938. The licences of all Jewish physicians expired accordingly on 30 Sept. 1938. Only a limited number of these physicians were certified as 'practitioners for the sick' (*Krankenbehandler*) for Jews: *Reichsgesetzblatt*, 1938, I, p. 969.

1 RGVA, 500k-1-290, fol. 203. This document has been translated from German.
2 Herbert Hagen (1913–1999), clerk; joined the SS in 1933; worked for the SD from 1934; head of Department II 112 (Jewish affairs) of the SD, 1937–1939; from 1940 worked for the SD in France, where he served as the personal assistant to the Higher SS and Police Leader from 1942 to 1944; interned, 1945–1948; later managing director of a mechanical engineering company; sentenced in absentia in Paris in 1954 to lifelong penal servitude for war crimes; sentenced in Cologne in 1980 to twelve years' imprisonment, and released after serving four years.
3 The original contains several handwritten annotations.
4 Department II 22 (communal life) was part of Central Department II 2 (assessment of living environments) of SD Office II (domestic affairs).
5 This was planned with the Law on the Amendment of the Commercial Code: letter from Pfundtner x (Reich and Prussian Ministry of the Interior) to the Regierungspräsident in Magdeburg, 15 July 1937, LASA, C 20 Ib/2523 IV, fol. 169.
6 Several departmental abbreviations and handwritten markings follow here in the original.

DOC. 318

In the 1937 *Reich Medicinal Almanac*, Jewish physicians are indicated with a colon[1]

§ 1194–1196   (Seite 562)   Thüringen

Bad Köstritz (Thür.) 2489 E
Engelhardt ○, Max 99
Gerdes, Louis 19
Helwig, Ernst 18, BadeA

○**Großenstein** 934 E
über Schmölln (Thür.)
Jelke, Walter 24

○**Hundhaupten** 196 E
über Gera
Engelstädter ○, Alfred 21, Hom,
   VertrauensA d. AOK Gera

○**Kleinaga** 359 E
über Gera
Franke, Manfred 20

Kraftdorf (Thür.) 793 E
Hardt, Karl 21

Langenberg (Thür.) 3998 E
Börner ○, Johannes 89, SR
Heubel, Heinrich 24,
Mulert ♀, Friederike 22
Mulert, Martin 20,

○**Liebschwitz (Elster)** 1295 E
[Gera]
Focke, Werner 20

○**Mannichswalde** 781 E
über Crimmitschau
: Hirsch, Ernst 22

Münchenbernsdorf 3117 E
(Thüringen)
Händel, Paul 85, SR
Höller, Ernst 19
Vierhuth, Walter 26
Willgeroth, Wilhelm 96

Neustadt (Orla) 7890 E
Grimm, John 11,   d.
   Städt. Kh
Heck, Richard 04
Lautenschläger, Karl 27
Rupprecht, Paul 16
Schilling, Hermann 99
Schlipp, Friedrich 00
Wendel ♀, Käthe, geb. Stapff 36,
   AssÄ a. Städt. Kh

○**Nöbdenitz (Kr. Gera)** 462 E
[Schmölln (Thür.)]
Nordbeck, Johann 14

H Anst Tannenfels
f. und -kranke
Cauer ♀, Johanna geb. Gläser
   20, Ä
Lemmer, Ludwig 13,
Tecklenburg, Arthur 94,

○**Pölzig über Zeitz 2** 1057 E
[Zeitz 1]
Gerth, Emil 04

Ronneburg (Thür.) 7852 E
Engelberg, Georg 14,
    d. Städt. Kh
Findeisen, Georg 09
Müller, Fritz 22
Paulus, Gustav 20
Waurick, Ernst-Otto 26

○**Töppeln (Kr. Gera)** 437 E
[Gera]
Luft, Johannes 25

Triptis (Thür.) 3068 E
Gäbler, Rudolf 09
Laraß, Paul 04

Weida 11 040 E
Bahl, Johannes 21
Hegewald, Hans 21
Hollesen, Thomas 19
Leuthäusser ♀, Hilde 36, AssÄ a.
   Städt. Kh
Sauer, August 35, AssÄ a. Städt.
   Kh
Schiffler, Heinrich 26,
Welcker, Hans 20
Zum Winkel, Karl-Gustav 14
Zum Winkel ♀ ○, Martha, geb.
   Geber 14

Wünschendorf (Elster) 1606 E
Hoßmann, Arthur 16

1195
Stadtkreis Gotha

47 848 E   48 qkm
ÄKam . . . . Thüringen
BzVgg . . . . Gotha

Gotha
[Postzeitungsverkehr:]
○~ Siebleben [~]
Baerwolf, Fritz 20, (a. ZA),
Becker, Gerhard 35, Vertreter
   (ständ. Anschrift)
Brehm, Willy 11,
Crusius, Fritz 30,
Crusius ♀ ○, Margarete, geb.
   Baumann 22
Dracklé ○, Walter 22, AmtsA,
   Leiter d. Staatl. Gesundh-
   Amts Gotha-Stadt
Drewes ○, Herbert 35, A a.
   Staatl. GesundhAmt Gotha-
   Land
Ehrsam ○, Alexander 00,
   ORegMR, Leiter d. VAmt
Engler, Horst 32, AssA a. Thür.
   LKh
: Falkenstein ♀, Auguste 21, ~
   Siebleben
: Falkenstein, Leo 14, ~Sieb-
   leben
Fischer, Fritz 10,   , I. BankA
   d. Goth. LebensversichBank
Florschütz ○, Georg 84, Prof
Fürbringer ○, Julius 03,
   Prof, OMR, ,   a. Thür.
   LKh
Glanz, Franz 18,
Greffrath, Karl 83, SR
Gries, Karl 26,
Günther ♀, Willy 09, Ver-
   trauensÄ d. AOK
Haertel, Wolf 36, Vertreter,
   Kunstmühlenweg 1 (ständ.
   Anschrift)
Hager, Konrad 94, SR,
Hascrodt, Hans 10, StadtA

: Heilbrunn, Max 24
Heym ○, Hans 36, A a. Staatl.
   GesundhAmt Gotha-Stadt
Hochheim, Kurd 00
Janssen ○, Vincent 86, SR
Juhl ♀, Elisabeth, geb. Stein
   22
Jusatz ○, Helmut J. 31, Doz f.
   Hyg. u. Bakteriol. a. d.
   Unv Marburg, Liebetrau-
   str. 17 (zZ Berlin)
Käckell, Rudolf 14, , OA a.
   Thür. LKh
Kleinsorgen ○, Wilhelm 14, ,
   MR, Leiter d. Staatl. Bak-
   teriol. UAmst
Knauf ○, Max 83, SR, OStA a. d.
König, Hugo 99
Krüger, Gerhard 27
Krusch, Hans 27, -FürsA f.
   Stadt- u. Landkreis
Krusch ♀ ○, Martha, geb. Klein
   31
Krumhaar, Friedrich 14,
Liebolt, Herbert 35, AssA a.
   Thür. LKh
Lose, Peter 23,
Meyburg, Hans Joachim 33,
    d. ~Abt a. Thür.
   LKh
: Meyer, Adolf 83, SR
: Meyer, Kurt 17
Müller, Erich 31
Mueller, ♀ Ilse 26
Müller, Willy 96, HofR
Nagel, Viktor 19, PolMR aD,
Noltmann, Ernst 22,
Plaesterer, Ludwig 21
Prillipp, Wilhelm 24, , StA d.
   Luftw.
Reichenbächer, Wilhelm 21,
Schauer, Wilhelm 27, OA a.
   Thür. LKh
Schlichting, Walter 14,
Schmidt, Friedrich 20, O-
   FeldA d. Luftw.
Schmidt, Paul 96, SR,
: Schulenklopper, Richard 21
Schulz, Ernst 25, , OStA d.
   Luftw.
Schulz, Josef 29
Schuster ♀, Erika 37
Schuster ○, Paul 04, VertragsA
   b. VAmt
Schulze, Horst 36, AssA a. Thür.
   LKh
Stockmann ○, Herbert 34, A d.
   VersichBank Gotha
Sporberg ○, Otto 03, , OStA
   aD, RegMR a. VAmt
Trautmann, Max 96, SR
Versmold, Heinrich 34
Vierheilig, Max 35, AssÄ a.
   Thür. LKh
Waldeck, Anton 34, , StA d.
   Luftw.
: Wassermann, Wilhelm 20
Winkler ○, Herbert 27, ,
   MR, AmtsA, Leiter d.
   Staatl. GesundhAmts Go-
   tha-Land
Zengeler, Hermann 28
Zimmermann, Werner 14,

1196
Landkreis Gotha

106 262 E   998 qkm
ÄKam . . . . Thüringen
BzVgg . . . . Gotha

○**Bischleben (Kr. Gotha)** 1752 E
[Erfurt]
Gehrhardt, Hans 23

○**Crawinkel (Kr. Gotha)** 1966 E
[Ohrdruf]
Schellmann ○, Friedrich 97,
   GenOA aD
Schellmann, Rolf 27

○**Finsterbergen** 1445 E
○**(Thüringerwald)**
[Friedrichroda]
Kleinschmidt, Georg 03

Friedrichroda 5521 E
Bieling, Kurt 98, SR,
    d. Sanat Tannen-
   hof,
Bieling, Kurt 36, AssA a. Sanat
   Tannenhof
Bracknann, Erich 34, AssA a.
   Sanat Tannenhof
Braun, Willy 01
Bucerius, Gerhard 25,
Jaeger, Martin 34
: Kawalek-Cohn ♀, Leonie, geb.
   Kawalek 21
Ortlepp, Max 03
Rauch, Walter 13
Ries, Adam 24, ,   d.
   Sanat Thüringerwald

○**Friemar** 1262 E
über Gotha
Lehmann, Herbert 18

○**Georgenthal** 1610 E
(Thüringerwald)
Köhler, Christian 93, GenOA aD
Mayer-Faulborn ♀, Helene 22
Pagel, Max 90, SR

○**Gräfentonna** 1907 E
[Gotha]
Pfeifer, Ernst

○**Großenbehringen** 862 E
über Eisenach
Salzmann, Otto 31

○**Herbsleben (Kr. Gotha)** 3050 E
[Gotha]
Jordan, Gerhard 30
Jordan, Michael 92, SR

○**Mechterstädt** 1059 E
über Wutha (Thür.)
Kindt, Alfred 01

○**Molschleben** 1083 E
über Gotha
Keller, Max 36, Dr med et jur,
   Vertreter (ständ. Anschrift)

Neudietendorf 701 E
Diener, Helmut 24
Lottmann, Curt 20,

Ortsnamen für Briefverkehr: fette Schrift. Zeichen ○ und Zusätze in [ ] gelten nur für Postzeitungsverkehr[2]

---

1 Hermann Lautsch and Hans Dornedden, eds., *Verzeichnis der deutschen Ärzte und Heilanstalten: Reichs-Medizinal-Kalender für Deutschland Teil II. Zugleich Fortsetzung des Ärzteverzeichnisses des Verbandes der Ärzte Deutschlands* (Hartmannbund), vol. 58 (Leipzig: Georg Thieme, 1937), p. 562. The foreword (p. vi) elaborates on the labelling of Jewish physicians: 'The current handbook contains a supplement that has been repeatedly requested since 1933 and was recently called for in official circles. This supplement comes in the form of a labelling of those regarded as Jewish physicians in accordance with the Nuremberg Laws by means of the addition of a colon (:) in front of their names in the main directory of physicians. This constitutes an evaluation of the questionnaires completed by the physicians themselves for the Reich Chamber of Physicians.' The enclosure with the Reich Medicinal Almanac contains the following explanation: ': = Jew in accordance with the "First Regulation to the Reich Citizenship Law, 14 November 1935" (Reichsgesetzblatt, I, page 1333)'.

2 The italicized text at the bottom of the page reads: 'Place names for correspondence: bold typeface. Symbol ○ and additions in [ ] apply only for newspaper subscriptions by post'.

DOC. 319

The executive of the Jewish Community of Berlin reports on vocational training and retraining measures in 1937[1]

Administrative report of the executive of the Berlin Jewish Community for 1937.

(Delivered by the chairman of the community's executive at a meeting of the assembly of representatives on 20 Dec. 1937.)

[...][2]

A. *Occupational restructuring*

The occupational restructuring agency provides in-depth counselling and advice and runs retraining courses for adults as well as training courses for young persons; the agency is responsible for setting up these courses, as well as for the planning and development of new projects.

The purpose of occupational reassignment is almost exclusively to facilitate emigration to Palestine and other overseas countries. In order to further this aim, ongoing negotiations were conducted for the first time in 1937 with the Relief Association of German Jews and the Palestine Office, with the result that so far approximately 50 per cent of participants were able to emigrate after completing the retraining course. The requirement that all course participants must learn at least one foreign language, if necessary with the financial support of the local congregation, is likewise aimed at facilitating emigration. To ensure that the skills needed for working abroad are successfully acquired, the growing number of requests from applicants for short training courses in 1937 had to be routinely refused. This policy has paid off: the present indications are that those who took a retraining course and emigrated upon completion of their course have consistently been able to make a living for themselves overseas with their newly acquired occupation.

If necessary, the occupational restructuring agency can also arrange *funding* for training courses. This can be made available, strictly on a loan basis, in the form of training grants, food allowances, subsidized travel, and work clothing, provided a review of the economic circumstances of the applicant and his family indicates a genuine need that warrants such support.

The entire training operation of the Jewish Community is overseen by the 'Directorate of Technical Training Courses' in association with an advisory panel of experts drawn from the skilled trades.

(*a*) *Occupational restructuring for men*

At the beginning of 1937 the Jewish Community was offering the following courses:

(1) retraining course for metalworking, Berlin-Siemensstadt, 4 Nonnendamm (machine fitters), with 30 places,

(2) retraining course for woodworking at the same location (joiners), with 25 places,

---

[1] *Verwaltungsbericht des Vorstandes der Jüdischen Gemeinde zu Berlin für das Jahr 1937* [Berlin 1937/1938], pp. 24–28. This document has been translated from German.
[2] In the original this section is preceded by chapters I ('General points') to VI ('Youth Welfare Department'). The section reprinted here is taken from chapter VII ('Economic assistance').

(3) retraining course for construction and site development, 74 Fruchtstr. (bricklayers), with 30 places,

(4) retraining course in cemetery gardening, Weißensee.

During 1937 a further *course in fusion welding* was started at 30 Melchiorstr., with 40 places.

The course in cemetery gardening, which only accepts participants recommended by the appropriate organizations, is generally intended as a transition to intensive agricultural training courses at other training centres, designed to prepare people for emigration to Palestine.

Unlike the other courses, the newly established training course for fusion welders also offers an opportunity *for older people* (in the general age range 35–45 years) to learn a new trade. The training period here is only nine months, as opposed to 1½ years for the other courses.

At the end of the year under review, the staff available to train course participants in matters of theory numbered a total of six master craftsmen, seven journeymen, and five qualified teachers.

As well as training in the aforementioned courses run by the Jewish Community, persons wishing to retrain were also given the opportunity to train with foremen in industrial enterprises and so on (e.g. cutting out men's underwear and work clothing, making pockets and linings, steam ironing, belt making and the like, knitters, soap makers, makers of board games, etc.). Likewise trainees were sent to private schools, where they had the opportunity to train in trades such as decorating, making posters and advertising placards, fashion illustration, and photography. Finally we should also mention that after consultation with a private Jewish music school, a Beth Hachasanim[3] has been established for the training of cantors, and is now taking in students on a regular basis.

The total number of persons applying to the occupational reassignment agency for men in 1937 was 3,927. Places were found for 316 persons to retrain in a new occupation.

The average age of those seeking advice was higher than in previous years: in 1936 only 22 per cent of men were older than 35, but in 1937 that figure increased to 38 per cent.

(b) Occupational restructuring for women

The retraining programme for *women* provided by the Jewish Community in 1937 consisted of the following courses: five retraining courses for tailoring, two for cleaning work, and one for hairdressing. The existing private Jewish schools offering training in tailoring and cleaning also received a steady stream of new applicants. The occupational restructuring agency sought to meet the need for training opportunities in other types of occupation by obtaining traineeships and encouraging existing private schools to extend their range of offers – with some degree of success. These included garment making, sewing underwear, making lampshades, photography, stain removal, and invisible mending. Persons wishing to emigrate were also placed in greater numbers on private courses for cosmetics, manicure, pedicure, massage, medical gymnastics, and baby and toddler gymnastics, as well as in retraining courses in trade and commerce to meet requirements both here in Germany and abroad.

---

3 House of cantors: a training centre or school for cantors. From Hebrew *chasan*, cantor, who leads the congregation in singing and prayer in the synagogue.

The total number of persons applying to the occupational reassignment agency for women in the year under review was 1,654. Places were found for 332 persons to retrain in a new occupation. Here too the percentage of older applicants has risen. In 1937, 45 per cent of the women who applied to the agency were over 35, compared with only 38 per cent in 1936.

B. *Labour welfare*

Careers advice and an apprenticeship placement service for *young persons* has not been provided by the Jewish Community since 1 January 1937, when the entire responsibility for careers advice and apprenticeship placement was transferred to government employment offices.[4]

Since that time the work of the labour welfare office has largely been confined to referring applicants to Jewish training centres, providing information about apprenticeship matters, and receiving applications for loans to fund training.

Because the availability of apprenticeship placements for individuals, and in particular boys, has been severely curtailed, there was a need to create more *collective training centres*. This need was addressed in 1937, and the following opportunities are now available:

(a) To accommodate *boys*: the community-run training workshops, which are partly maintained in conjunction with the retraining courses for adults set up by the occupational reassignment agency, namely training workshops for building fitters, machine fitters, joiners, bricklayers; the training workshops run by the 'Ort' Society[5] for mechanics, electrical engineers, gas fitters, and plumbers; training workshops run by Jewish organizations in the Reich; a chemistry school; a commercial school; draughtsmen's schools; and teacher-training establishments.

(b) To accommodate *girls*: housekeeping schools and homes offering training in housekeeping; hospitals and nurseries for training nurses, infant nurses, baby carers; the course offered by the Jewish Children's Aid agency for training childcare assistants; the community-run course training girls for educational work; the Jewish Seminary for Nursery School Teachers; teacher-training establishments; a chemistry school; a commercial school; draughtsmen's schools.

(c) In addition, for *boys and girls*: placements in farming academies, under the Youth Aliyah programme, and in medium-sized hachsharah centres in association with the labour unions.

The number of cases where the Jewish Community had to make grants to needy applicants for placements in these collective training facilities was substantial during the year under review. It is not just a matter of bearing the actual costs of training (tuition fees, maintenance during institutional training), but also of paying out for apprenticeship allowances, subsidized travel, and work clothing.

---

4 Under a law passed on 5 Nov. 1935, exclusive responsibility for labour placement, careers advice, and apprenticeship placement had been transferred to the Reich Institute for Labour Placement and Unemployment Insurance: *Reichsgesetzblatt*, 1935, I, p. 1281.

5 Correctly: ORT, an acronym derived from the original Russian term *Obshchestvo Remeslennogo i Zemledel'cheskogo Truda* and known in English as the 'Society for Trades and Agricultural Labour' or the 'Organization for Rehabilitation through Training': see Glossary.

During the year under review a total of 3,252 boys and 1,635 girls applied to the labour welfare office for assistance. Grants were approved for 354 boys and 247 girls.

C. *Employment agency*
The Jewish Community's own employment agency had to cease all placement work when responsibility for these matters was transferred to government employment offices. Its work is now confined to *placing persons in jobs abroad* that are advertised in the Jewish press after prior approval by the regional employment office. It is to be hoped that this work, which began in 1937 and serves to encourage emigration, will continue to grow and develop.
[...]⁶

DOC. 320
The Reich Representation of Jews in Germany reports on the development and the problems of Jewish welfare support in 1937[1]

Progress report for 1937 compiled by the Reich Representation of Jews in Germany [Berlin, 1938], (typescript)

[...]²
B. *Welfare support*

1. *General welfare provision.* In the period under review, the mismatch between the means to assist and the requirements of the work became very apparent. While in recent years it was still possible to meet all legitimate claims for welfare support, we now find ourselves increasingly in a situation where we are ruled by the budget, and even the most urgent claims for welfare provision can no longer be met owing to a lack of means. This is particularly evident in the work of the *Central Welfare Board for Jews in Germany*, the department of the Reich Representation of Jews in Germany responsible for dealing with matters of welfare. Under the direct control of the Central Welfare Board are the regional and provincial welfare offices, which are responsible for looking after those communities that are no longer able to finance their own welfare work. It is here that the discrepancy between needs and the means of satisfying those needs is greatest.

The Central Welfare Board received applications from every district for increased funding on the grounds that the need was now greater. It was with a heavy heart that all these applications had to be refused. That refusal was particularly painful where it affected persons who had previously been able to earn a living thanks to their possession of an itinerant trader's licence, but who were now denied the opportunity to provide for

---

6 In the original this section is followed by chapters VIII ('Collections') to XV ('Conclusion').

1 'Arbeitsbericht der Reichsvertretung der Juden in Deutschland für das Jahr 1937', pp. 43–49; ZfA, Arbeitsberichte, Mikrofilm 2. This report has been translated from German.

2 In the original this section is preceded by chapters I ('Introduction') and II ('Capacity and Aid Provision'). Chapter III ('Specific Activities') is subdivided into 'Migration' and 'Welfare support'.

themselves by the refusal to renew their licence.³ While the Jewish Winter Relief agency was able to provide some support in the first three months and the last three months of the year, this resource was not available in the period from 1 April to 1 October 1937.

Increasingly, the money allocated to the provincial welfare offices for specific purposes is being fixed for longer periods of time, so that it is becoming harder to give favourable consideration to new applications for assistance. Meanwhile all current cases are kept under constant review to see if it might be possible to suspend assistance temporarily, or at least to reduce the payments. This is not possible, however, in any of those cases where persons have been rehoused in old people's homes with the aid of public assistance and assistance provided by us. The demand for places in old people's homes is growing all the time, and as it is we are not able to satisfy that demand. The number of places has been increased again during the period under review, thanks to measures taken by the Central Welfare Board and the communities involved, but there is still a lack of affordable places for old people. This lack is felt particularly acutely when, as is very often the case, old people receive only about 30 Reichsmarks per head in public welfare. When the minimum cost of rehousing someone in an old people's home is 50 Reichsmarks, the welfare offices cannot continue to make up the difference over time, even with the help of the Central Welfare Board. During the period under review, therefore, a substantial number of requests for assistance from elderly people had to be refused for financial reasons.

Bearing in mind that half of the persons in need of assistance are over the age of 45, the outlook for the future is bleak indeed. The economic situation in small rural communities is getting steadily worse. The migration of tax-paying members of these communities to larger urban communities or to other countries is now on such a scale that the burden of maintaining the remaining population now falls increasingly on welfare support.⁴ Deciding whether these persons in need of assistance should be advised to move to the larger cities, or whether they should remain in their present place of residence for as long as this is possible and affordable, is extremely difficult. Generally speaking, remaining in their present place of residence – assuming that emigration is not an option – is the cheapest solution, because here, in their familiar surroundings, people are able to get by with very little.

With this in mind, welfare offices and economic aid offices worked hard to help people retain their modest properties in small communities, as this is still a less costly option than relocating to a larger community, where the full cost of maintenance is borne by social welfare. In many cases, however, people are unable to pay the interest on the mortgage for their house, or to raise sufficient capital to pay off a mortgage that has been called in. They then have no choice but to give up the house, and generally speaking there is hardly anything left over from the sales proceeds after they have paid off their accumulated liabilities.

Migrating to the big towns and cities makes people completely rootless, and also gets them into financial difficulties: housing costs are significantly higher there, and newly arrived residents do not get the public assistance they need.

3 See Doc. 317, 28 Dec. 1937.
4 See Doc. 305, 29 Oct. 1937.

In other areas of general welfare provision, too, the shortage of funding is being increasingly felt. One example is:

2. *Welfare provision for persons at risk.* For the year under review the service's budget allocation of 12,000 Reichsmarks was overspent by 4,300 Reichsmarks, despite the fact that officials were strict to the point of hard-heartedness in refusing applications for aid. We cite here just two cases by way of illustration: *Kurt H. in East Prussia*, a mentally retarded boy, who lives in a small East Prussian village in complete isolation, as the only young Jewish person in the community. His widowed mother runs a very small shop which barely supports them. The plan was to send the boy to a farm, where they were prepared to take him in for a monthly care allowance of 45 Reichsmarks. A brother living in Berlin was willing to pay 10 Reichsmarks towards the cost, while the provincial association was ready to contribute another 10 Reichsmarks. An application was therefore made for welfare assistance of 25 Reichsmarks a month. The application was denied, due to lack of funds, even though the farm, for which the boy would have been eminently well suited, had agreed to take him.

Hildegard B., Kassel district, 13 years old. After the family had become totally impoverished, the household was broken up so that the parents could take jobs. The children, who would otherwise have had nobody to care for them, were admitted to the orphanage in Kassel. Family relatives were able to pay 20 Reichsmarks towards the monthly fees of 45 Reichsmarks, and the Kassel welfare office contributed another 10 Reichsmarks. An application for the remaining 15 Reichsmarks per month was submitted to the Central Welfare Board's care service for persons at risk, but it was rejected owing to shortage of funds.

The same problems arose with the work of the

3. Schoolchildren's Fund, which despite rigorous frugality was unable to manage on its allocated budget of 50,000 Reichsmarks. Requests for assistance for children who are the only young Jewish persons in their village, and who can hardly be expected to attend a state school any more, are constantly being refused because of lack of funds. To demonstrate how difficult it has become to undertake even the most essential expenditure any more, we cite the figures for a small provincial association, namely the association for the Border Province of Posen-West Prussia[5] in Schneidemühl. Lack of funding means that more than 140 children are unable to attend a Jewish school, which, given the present circumstances, would be highly desirable. A Jewish district school urgently needs to be established in Schneidemühl. It would then be possible for 29 children from Schneidemühl itself to attend the school, a further 47 children would be able to travel to the school by train, and a place in Schneidemühl would offer the only chance of an education for 71 children from outlying rural communities. For day pupils a monthly subsidy of 250 Reichsmarks would be required, and for boarders a monthly subsidy of 2,306.25 Reichsmarks, making a monthly total of 2,556.25 Reichsmarks. In other words, for *one* single province an annual sum of 30,675 Reichsmarks would be needed to alleviate the worst of the hardships suffered by these young people. We are talking here about a very small

---

5 Part of the former Prussian province of Posen and the western part of West Prussia that had remained German after the Treaty of Versailles. It had one Regierungsbezirk, Schneidemühl.

district, where currently only 1,600–1,700 Jews are still living: yet the Schoolchildren's Fund only had a budget allocation of around 50,000 Reichsmarks *for the whole of Germany*.

Another example to illustrate the problem: until Easter 1937 there was a Jewish school in Birstein (Hesse), which was also attended by children from Hellstein. This school had to close because of insufficient pupil numbers. The parents of the children from Hellstein then requested that their children be placed elsewhere. These children are now attending the state school again, where they are completely isolated, both in the classroom and the playground. They urgently need to be relocated to a Jewish school. But the request to accommodate them elsewhere had to be refused – again, due to lack of funds.

We cite these examples, which could be endlessly multiplied, simply to show the yawning gap that already exists between essential needs and the funding that is available to meet them.

4. Jewish Winter Relief 1936/37.
As already stated in the last annual report,[6] responsibility for Jewish Winter Relief has been transferred by order of the Reich plenipotentiary for the Winter Relief Agency of the German People to the Central Welfare Board for Jews in Germany and its affiliated Jewish welfare support organizations. Guidelines approved by the Reich plenipotentiary were drawn up, covering eligibility, circumstances and benefits, providers, fundraising, publicity, burden sharing, and invoicing.[7] With regard to eligibility, it was determined that Jewish Winter Relief should apply to all persons living in the German Reich – with the exception of the Upper Silesian plebiscite area – who are Jews as defined under the Reich Citizenship Law. Families from mixed marriages between persons of German blood and Jews would also be eligible for Jewish Winter Relief, provided that the head of the household is a Jew as defined under the Reich Citizenship Law. Publicity for fundraising and the delivery of care to those in need was coordinated by the local Jewish Community welfare offices. The Central Welfare Board made direct provision for those in need in smaller communities through the provincial welfare offices. Alongside the propaganda work for Jewish Winter Relief carried out by the larger Jewish communities in direct publicity campaigns, the Central Welfare Board also conducted a coordinated publicity campaign in collaboration with the major Jewish newspapers, organizations, and aid agencies. The office kept a central record of receipts and payments, and was responsible for *burden sharing*, which ensures that smaller rural communities that are unable to raise much money are not deprived of winter relief. After deduction of costs, 15 per cent of all donations were to be channelled to the Central Welfare Board as the central provider of Jewish Winter Relief, which would then be able to make money available to the smaller Jewish communities from this central fund. In the guidelines for Jewish Winter Relief, *fundraising* was to be regulated according to the same principles laid down for the Winter Relief Agency of the German People. Thus, funds were raised through monthly donations, stew donations,[8] and the pound [food] collections.[9] Given

---

6 'Arbeitsbericht des Zentralausschusses für Hilfe und Aufbau bei der Reichsvertretung der Juden in Deutschland für das Jahr 1936', pp. 61–69: ZfA, Arbeitsberichte, Mikrofilm 2.
7 On the guidelines for 1936/1937, see Doc. 254, 14 Nov. 1936.

the increasing hardships suffered by a substantial portion of the Jewish population, the collections for Jewish Winter Relief could only be carried out by stretching all available resources to the limit. Compared with the previous year, the existing organizational structure of Jewish Winter Relief proved to be an asset. The work of Jewish Winter Relief also benefited from the cooperation of all Jewish organizations and the support of all Jewish congregations. The engagement of all sections of the Jewish population in the work of Winter Relief is also evidenced by the fact that in addition to the full-time staff working in the central offices, a total of *10,366 voluntary helpers* (4,486 of them in Berlin) had offered their services. It was only thanks to this enormous joint effort, combined with repeated urgent appeals to the Jewish Community's own sense of responsibility, that the results were at least sufficient to provide assistance to all those who needed it. But, like all Jewish fundraising activities this winter, the collections for Jewish Winter Relief showed a clear decline for the first time since 1933, with an average 12–15 per cent decrease in the funds raised. In the face of constantly growing need, this decline gives very great cause for concern for the immediate future.

In the winter of 1936/37 Jewish Winter Relief had a total of *82,067 persons* on its books. Although the actual number of persons in need of relief therefore fell slightly short of the previous year's figure (83,761 for the winter of 1935/36), the proportion of the overall Jewish population in receipt of Jewish Winter Relief rose, since the population itself is now significantly smaller as a result of emigration and a surplus of deaths over births.

The increase in the number of persons in need as a proportion of the overall population is most dramatically illustrated by the following statistics. Compared with the previous year, the number of persons in need has fallen by around 1,000, while the overall Jewish population has declined by something like 20,000. Another factor that has to be taken into account is that, with each passing year, new sections of the population find themselves in need, so that even if the number of persons in need of relief were to fall even more sharply as a result of emigration, this would always be outweighed by the increased hardships suffered by sections of the Jewish population that have not hitherto been affected.[10]

The fact that over half the people supported by Jewish Winter Relief are over 45 years old also acts as a major obstacle to emigration by this demographic, since people in this age group cannot normally emigrate unless they have relatives in the destination country who can support them for an extended period of time.

The number of people receiving Jewish Winter Relief exceeds a fifth of Germany's total Jewish population. The difficult conditions affecting the most depressed areas also made themselves felt in the fact that there was an increase in the number of those districts that were exempted from contributing to the general compensation fund, or that had to be given substantial grants of money by way of burden sharing. Thus, parts of the provinces of Pomerania and Schleswig-Holstein were added to the existing list of depressed areas. The total cost of providing assistance to the 82,067 persons in need

---

8 Germans were encouraged to eat a cheap stew or 'one-pot' (*Eintopf*) meal one Sunday a month, and to donate the money thereby saved for welfare purposes.
9 Food items were collected by weight.
10 The number of Jewish unemployed at this time was estimated at around 40,000. This figure too had hardly changed from the previous year, while the total number of Jews had declined sharply: 'Arbeitsbericht der Reichsvertretung der Juden in Deutschland für das Jahr 1937', p. 70.

came to 3,630,353.63 *Reichsmarks*. The geographical distribution of aid recipients and the amount of aid provided for each area are listed in the following table:

Number of aid recipients and payments made under the Jewish Winter Relief programme for the winter of 1936/37

District	No. of aid recipients	Amount of aid provided (in Reichsmarks)
Baden	2,836	140,605.29
Bavaria	3,847	169,772.64
Hanseatic cities	3,795	195,082.60
Hesse	2,825	96,975.55
Mecklenburg	131	5,018.95
Saxony	3,228	130,315.40
Württemberg	1,258	51,280.84
Berlin	29,610	1,501,068.77
Brandenburg	1,152	45,585.94
Border Province of Posen-West Prussia	530	15,723.85
Hanover-Braunschweig	2,086	86,846.67
Hesse-Nassau	7,865	350,429.59
Hohenzollern	46	1,405.23
Eastern West Prussia	1,409	52,813.78
Palatinate (Rhine Palatinate)	949	36,965.68
Pomerania	1,113	38,238.49
Rhine Province	8,109	321,339.25
Saarland	308	7,986.24
Saxony-Anhalt	1,120	42,410.79
Southern Saxony-Thuringia	603	40,654.87
Silesia	4,921	144,376.52
Schleswig-Holstein	1,027	44,072.46
Westphalia (incl. Lippe)	3,299	111,384.23
	82,067	3,630,353.63

The *aid provided by Jewish Winter Relief* consisted of grants of food, drink, and tobacco, linen and clothing, and coal coupons. Only exceptionally, in communities where there were fewer than ten people in need of relief, and where there were significant obstacles to providing directly for their physical needs, was aid made available in the form of a cash payment. The need for clothing, underwear, and household linen among aid recipients has continued to increase, because a large proportion of those in need often lacked the most basic items of attire. The distribution of warm clothing was particularly necessary for those living on the land and for those young persons in need who were undergoing some form of agricultural or technical training. As a rule, linen and clothing were distributed under the special winter relief initiative timed to coincide with the Hanukkah festival in December.

[...][11]

---

11 This section is followed in chapter III by sections C–F ('Schooling', 'Economic assistance', 'Occupational restructuring', and 'Payment arrangements for education in other countries'), then by chapters IV–V ('Financial Report' and 'Conclusion').

Glossary

Aliyah (Hebrew for 'ascent')
Jewish emigration to Palestine with the aim of establishing a Jewish homeland.

Altreu (Allgemeine Treuhandstelle für die jüdische Auswanderung GmbH; General Trust Agency for Jewish Emigration)
Agency established in May 1937 to support emigration to countries other than Palestine (in addition to the Paltreu-Haavara, which had been responsible for Palestine since 1933). Emigrants could transfer a certain amount of Reichsmarks into an Altreu account, in return for which they received foreign currency at a markdown of 50 per cent.

American Jewish Congress (AJC)
Association founded in 1918 of Jewish-American organizations which served as a platform for Jewish interests following the First World War and throughout the Second World War. It was involved in organizing the boycott of German goods and protest rallies in the United States and across Europe between 1933 and 1945, and worked to influence the policies of American and European governments, especially with regard to immigration restrictions.

American Jewish Joint Distribution Committee (JDC, Joint)
Committee founded in the United States in 1914 to coordinate the relief efforts of American Jewish aid organizations. It provided funding and aid to Jews and Jewish organizations, especially in Eastern Europe. Following the outbreak of the Second World War, its efforts extended to Nazi-occupied and -controlled territories, including the ghettos, where it supported schools, orphanages, cultural institutions, and other important areas of Jewish life.

Aryan (*Arier*)
Term used to describe the peoples supposedly descended from the Indo-Europeans. It was used in Nazi Germany to support the thesis of the inequality of human races and the superiority of those with 'German and related blood' over 'non-Aryan races', above all Jews and Sinti and Roma.

Aryan Paragraph (*Arierparagraph*)
Clause in the statutes of an organization, corporation, or the civil service that reserved membership solely for Aryans. It blocked all non-Aryans, particularly Jews, from membership in economic establishments, political parties, social clubs, volunteer organizations, sports groups, and other institutions, and was used as a legal stepping stone to increased persecution prior to the formulation of the Nuremberg Laws.

Aryanization (*Arisierung*)
The process of expropriating Jews and excluding them from a 'racially purified' economy. It involved the closure or confiscation of Jewish property, assets, and businesses and the forced transfer of these to Aryans or to the Reich.

Beer Hall Putsch
The failed attempt by Adolf Hitler and other right-wing opponents of the Weimar Republic to seize power in Germany on 8–9 November 1923 in Munich.

B'nai B'rith (Hebrew for 'Sons of the Covenant')
: Jewish fraternal organization founded in New York for 'benevolence, brotherly love, and harmony' by German migrants in 1843. The first branch in Germany was established in 1882 in Berlin, and by 1933 there were more than 100 lodges in the country with approximately 12,000 members. Their tasks included the elimination of general poverty, aid for widows and orphans, and the promotion of science and the arts, as well as the moral support of their members. The Nazi regime ordered the closure of the German lodges in 1937.

British Mandate for Palestine
: League of Nations mandate granted to Britain in 1922. The Mandate ended on 15 May 1948, one day before the proclamation of the State of Israel.

Central Association of German Citizens of the Jewish Faith (Centralverein deutscher Staatsbürger jüdischen Glaubens, CV)
: Association founded by Jewish intellectuals in 1893 in Berlin with the aim of opposing increasing antisemitism in Imperial Germany and defending the rights of German Jews. In the 1930s it had over 60,000 members and was the largest organization of Jews in Germany.

Central Committee of the German Jews for Relief and Reconstruction (Zentralausschuss der deutschen Juden für Hilfe und Aufbau)
: Committee created in April 1933 which coordinated socio-economic aid for German Jews between 1933 and 1938, in particular by providing assistance to Jews who had lost their jobs and businesses as a result of anti-Jewish legislation. It comprised various German-Jewish communal, political, and welfare organizations, and in April 1934 was incorporated into the Reich Representation of German Jews (later the Reich Representation of Jews in Germany).

Confessing Church (Bekennende Kirche)
: Protestant movement led by Martin Niemöller and others, founded in 1934 to oppose attempts to bring the Church under the control of the Nazi regime and in line with Nazi ideology. The conflict between the Confessing Church and the Nazi-oriented 'German Christian' movement, both of which remained part of German Protestantism, was termed the 'Church struggle' (*Kirchenkampf*).

Criminal Police (Kriminalpolizei, Kripo)
: Criminal investigation force that, together with the Gestapo, constituted the Security Police (Sipo). The Kripo mainly dealt with non-political crimes including offences against the war economy (black market, slaughtering animals without permit, contravention of the rationing regulations), rape, murder, and arson.

Denazification (*Entnazifizierung*)
: Allied efforts to remove Nazis and National Socialist ideology from public life and to re-educate Germans politically after 1945. One of the first initiatives was the distribution of questionnaires by the Western Allies in order to identify Nazi Party members and sympathizers by placing them into five categories: major offenders, offenders, lesser offenders, 'followers' (*Mitläufer*), or exonerated. In 1946 the Western Allies transferred the responsibility for denazification to the German administration, which concluded the process in 1951. In the Soviet zone, denazification efforts ended in March 1948.

Deutsche Golddiskontbank (German Gold Discount Bank, Dego)
: Bank established in 1924 as a subsidiary of the Reichsbank. Starting in 1925 it functioned mainly as an export credit bank that granted short-term foreign-currency loans to German banks and industrial enterprises. In addition to the Reich Flight Tax, the so-called Dego tax – or fee ('Dego-Abgabe') – was levied on every Jewish emigrant. By mid 1938 both taxes applied to more than 90 per cent of declared assets and property. Dego was closed down after the war and liquidated in 1969.

Emigdirect (abbreviation for Emigrationsdirektorium, EM)
: Migration organization founded in Berlin in 1921 as the United Committee for Jewish Emigration. In 1927 the organization merged with the Hebrew Sheltering and Immigrant Aid Society (HIAS) and the Jewish Colonization Association (JCA, ICA) to form HICEM, but it was forced to withdraw from the merger in 1934. It was dissolved in 1945.

Enabling Act (*Ermächtigungsgesetz*)
: Law passed by the Reichstag on 24 March 1933 transferring legislative authority from the Reichstag to the Hitler cabinet, which was thereby granted dictatorial powers. The National Socialists used lobbying, intimidation, and persecution to secure the two-thirds majority required to enact the law.

Eretz Israel (Hebrew for the 'Land of Israel' or the 'Holy Land')
: Biblical term used in Jewish writings to refer to Palestine. The Zionist movement sought to establish a state in Eretz Israel within the British Mandate for Palestine in order to revive the Jewish people as a modern nation and provide a refuge for diaspora Jews. Zionists in the diaspora often used the shortened version, 'Eretz'.

Ethnic Germans (*Volksdeutsche*)
: People of German descent with a shared language and culture living beyond German borders. Under National Socialism, the term distinguished ethnic Germans from Reich Germans (*Reichsdeutsche*), who were German citizens.

Four-Year Plan
: A series of economic measures initiated by Hitler in 1936 and managed by the Office of the Four-Year Plan under the leadership of plenipotentiary Herman Göring. The plan aimed to prepare Germany for war within four years. It focused on rearmament of Germany and the mobilization of the economy, and aimed to make the country self-sufficient in terms of raw materials.

Freikorps (Free Corps)
: Anti-democratic, nationalist, and anti-revolutionary paramilitary groups formed in the wake of Germany's defeat in the First World War. Members included former soldiers and university students. In the Weimar Republic, the Freikorps were often used to suppress domestic left-wing revolts and protect the eastern borders of the German Reich. In 1919 the Freikorps had approximately 200,000 members.

Führer principle (*Führerprinzip*)
: Autocratic method of governmental organization whereby all power – legislative, executive, and judicial – was concentrated in the hands of Hitler and extended downward through each level of the hierarchy. The principle professed authority over all subordinates and responsibility towards all superiors.

Gau (NSDAP term for 'region')
: The largest NSDAP administrative category below Reich level. After the National Socialists assumed power in 1933, the Gaue increasingly replaced the individual states (Länder) as the effective regional subdivision of the Third Reich. As the regional units of the NSDAP, the Gaue were divided into Kreise (districts), consisting of 'local branches' (Ortsgruppen, covering several villages or towns), 'cells' (Zellen), and 'blocks' (Blöcke, neighbourhoods within the cells). The number of Gaue varied over time, with new ones created following territorial annexations.

Gauleiter (Gau leader)
: Head of an NSDAP Gau.

Gendarmerie
: Branch of the German police force deployed in rural areas and small communities.

Geneva Convention on Upper Silesia (Deutsch-polnisches Abkommen über Oberschlesien)
: Bilateral minority agreement signed on 15 May 1922 between the Republic of Poland and the German Reich. In force until July 1937, the accord regulated the protection of minorities and economic conditions in the territories of Upper Silesia ceded by the German Reich to Poland in the aftermath of the First World War.

German Christians (Deutsche Christen)
: Protestant movement that aimed to combine Lutheran Christianity with racist and nationalist ideals. Its support for Nazi principles led to a split in the German Lutheran Church and the creation of the Confessing Church, which opposed Nazi control over religious life.

German Council of Municipalities (Deutscher Gemeindetag, DGT)
: Council founded in 1934 as a result of the *Gleichschaltung* of the central municipal associations. All local governments had to belong to the DGT. It established a number of committees to discuss topical issues. These committees contributed to the expansion of anti-Jewish measures at local government level, for example with regard to the use of municipal facilities by Jews.

German Labour Front (Deutsche Arbeitsfront, DAF)
: Compulsory National Socialist organization of workers and employers, set up to replace trade unions following their dissolution in 1933. It had approximately 25 million members.

German Reich (Deutsches Reich; German Empire)
: From 1871 to 1945 official term for Germany, comprising Imperial Germany (Kaiserreich, 1871–1918), the Weimar Republic (1918–1933), and the Third Reich (1933–1945).

Gestapa (abbreviation for Geheimes Staatspolizeiamt; Secret State Police Central Office)
: Central office of the Gestapo, based in Berlin. It was initially headed by Hermann Göring and from 1934 by Heinrich Himmler.

Gestapo (abbreviation for Geheime Staatspolizei; Secret State Police)
: Secret State Police in Nazi Germany and German-occupied Europe, established by Hermann Göring in 1933 with the aim of combating internal 'enemies of the state'. From 1934 it was led by Heinrich Himmler and in 1936 it became part of Reinhard Heydrich's Security Police. In 1939 the Security Police merged with the SD to form the Reich Security Main Office. Thereafter it became known as RSHA Amt IV and was headed by Heinrich Müller. It was divided into five departments: (a) Political

Opponents, (b) Sects and Churches, (c) Administration and Party Affairs, (d) Occupied Territories, (e) Security and Counter-intelligence. The Gestapo had a smaller staff than is often imagined; by the end of 1944 it employed 32,000 officials.

Gleichschaltung ('synchronization' or 'enforced coordination')
Synchronization of all areas of life (political parties, professional associations, cultural organizations, etc.) and their subordination to National Socialist ideology.

Goy/Goyim (Hebrew for 'nation')
Term commonly used in Jewish discourse to refer to a Gentile.

Haavara Agreement (Hebrew for 'transfer' agreement)
In effect between 1933 and 1939, an agreement between the Jewish Agency for Palestine and Nazi Germany that enabled Jewish emigrants to receive German goods in Palestine in exchange for money they deposited in Germany and was also intended to promote German exports. The arrangement made it possible for emigrants to indirectly transfer a part of their assets without the National Socialist state incurring foreign exchange costs. The Berlin-based Paltreu was responsible for overseeing the financial transactions. Nearly 140 million Reichsmarks were transferred to Palestine while the agreement was in force.

Hachsharah (also hakhsharah; Hebrew for 'preparation')
Occupational and agricultural training of young Jews on Zionist collective farms in preparation for emigration to Palestine.

Hanukkah (Hebrew for 'consecration' or 'inauguration'; also known as the Festival of Lights)
Eight-day Jewish festival commemorating the victory of the Maccabees over the Seleucids (167–160 BC). The festival begins on the twenty-fifth day of the Jewish month Kislev (November/December).

Harvard University competition
Essay competition held in 1940 on the theme 'My life in Germany before and after Jan. 30, 1933'. The contest was sponsored by Harvard University, which invited submissions 'for the purely scientific purpose' of studying the 'social and psychological effects of National Socialism on German society and the German people'. The project was open to Jews and non-Jews.

Hehalutz (Hebrew for 'the pioneer')
Organization founded in the United States in 1905 to prepare halutzim (pioneers) for life in Palestine. A German branch was established in 1922.

HIAS (Hebrew Immigrant Aid Society)
Aid organization founded in the United States in 1881, initially to support Jews fleeing pogroms in Russia and Eastern Europe. HIAS worked with HICEM to support and organize the emigration of German Jews and played a key role in helping to resettle displaced persons after the war.

HICEM
Acronym for three Jewish advocacy organizations that merged in 1927: the Hebrew Immigrant Aid Society (HIAS), the Jewish Colonization Association (JCA, ICA), and Emigdirect (EM). HICEM was based in Paris until Germany's invasion of France in mid 1940, and subsequently in Lisbon. Its purpose was to organize Jewish emigration and to financially support the emigrants in the destination countries; it enabled approximately 90,000 Jews to escape persecution.

Histadrut (Union of Hebrew Labourers in Eretz Israel)
: The largest association of trade unions for Jewish workers in Palestine (and later Israel), founded in 1920. It was involved in supporting and expanding social and medical services and in cultural activities.

Immigration certificates
: Compulsory requirement introduced by the British Mandate for Palestine in an attempt to limit Jewish immigration into Palestine. A certificate was issued only if the candidate could prove that he or she had relatives, significant assets, or skills that were needed in Palestine. From the beginning of the 1930s there were annual quotas for several categories, for example young people. The certificates were distributed via Palestine Offices of the Jewish Agency for Palestine in Germany and other countries.

Imperial Germany (also Wilhelmine Germany; Kaiserreich)
: German monarchy established following the unification of Germany in 1871. It lasted until the end of the First World War in 1918, when the November Revolution led to the abdication of Kaiser Wilhelm II and the establishment of the Weimar Republic.

Jewish Agency for Palestine ('Jewish Agency')
: Agency founded in 1929 to represent Jewish interests in the British Mandate for Palestine. It cooperated with the British Mandate government and advised it on socio-economic issues. The Jewish Agency served as the political leadership of the Jewish community in Palestine until the establishment of the State of Israel in 1948. It also worked to help Jews emigrate to Palestine under the Haavara Agreement.

Jewish Colonization Association (JCA, ICA)
: Paris-based organization founded in 1891 by Baron Maurice de Hirsch. The JCA supported agricultural colonies for Jewish refugees in Argentina, the United States, Canada, Brazil, Russia, Bessarabia, and Poland. In 1896 it expanded its activities to include Palestine (PICA). The JCA also worked with HICEM to support the emigration of Jewish refugees during the years 1933–1941.

Jewish Culture League (Jüdischer Kulturbund)
: Organization founded in 1933, and known until 1935 as the Culture League of German Jews (Kulturbund deutscher Juden), which supported and promoted Jewish music, art, theatre, and publishing for Jewish-only audiences after the Nazis had excluded Jews from German cultural life. By 1935 the league had thirty-six branches and over 70,000 members.

Jewish Telegraphic Agency (JTA)
: Jewish news agency originally founded by the journalist Jacob Landau in 1917 as the Jewish Correspondence Bureau; from 1919 it was called the Jewish Telegraphic Agency (JTA). It maintained offices in Berlin, Warsaw, Jerusalem, and New York, among other cities. The antisemitic incidents reported by the JTA attracted wide international attention. The JTA exists to this day.

Jewish Women's League (Jüdischer Frauenbund, JFB)
: Organization founded in Germany in 1904 by Bertha Pappenheim, which offered a feminist approach to social welfare and was the first national organization to promote the interests of German-Jewish women. It had a total of 50,000 members in 1935. The JFB exists to this day.

Kreis
: An administrative subdivision of a Gau.

Kreisau Circle (Kreisauer Kreis)
: Resistance movement (1940–1944), led by Count Helmuth James von Moltke, that sought to bring about the demise of the Third Reich and to plan a new form of government for after the war. Many of its approximately forty members were from an aristocratic background and tended to hold conservative, albeit diverse, political views. A number of members of the group supported or were directly involved in the failed plot to assassinate Hitler on 20 July 1944, after which many of them were sentenced to death and executed.

Kreisleiter (district leader)
: Head of an NSDAP Kreis.

Kurfürstendamm
: One of the most famous avenues in Berlin, lined with boutiques, residences, hotels, cafes, and restaurants. The boulevard was a centre of leisure and nightlife during the 1920s. In 1931 and 1935 it became the site of antisemitic riots (Kurfürstendamm Krawalle) and other acts of violence that culminated in the destruction of Jewish-owned shops and businesses.

Landrat
: Civil service official in charge of a rural district and subordinate to the Regierungspräsident.

Law for the Protection of German Blood and German Honour (Blood Protection Law) (Gesetz zum Schutz des deutschen Blutes und der deutschen Ehre [Blutschutzgesetz])
: One of the Nuremberg Laws promulgated in September 1935. The Blood Protection Law prohibited marriages and extramarital sexual relations between Jews and citizens with German or related blood. It further excluded Jews from the *Volksgemeinschaft* by prohibiting them from displaying the Reich flag and the national colours, and from employing Aryan females under the age of 45 as domestic staff.

Law for the Protection of the Hereditary Health of the German People (Marital Health Law) (Gesetz zum Schutz der Erbgesundheit des deutschen Volkes [Erbgesundheitsgesetz])
: One of the Nuremberg Laws promulgated in September 1935. The law stipulated that all prospective spouses had to have a 'certificate of fitness for marriage', which was issued by the local health authorities. Certificates were denied to those with serious infectious and 'hereditary' diseases.

Law for the Restoration of the Professional Civil Service (Civil Service Law) (Gesetz zur Wiederherstellung des Berufsbeamtentums [Berufsbeamtengesetz])
: Law issued on 7 April 1933 which excluded Jews and political opponents of the National Socialists from all civil service positions. Initially it exempted persons who had been civil servants since August 1914, veterans of the First World War, and those whose father or son had been killed in action in the war, but this exemption was revoked following President Hindenburg's death in 1934.

Law on the Revocation of Naturalization and the Deprivation of German Nationality (Gesetz über den Widerruf von Einbürgerungen und die Aberkennung der deutschen Staatsangehörigkeit)

One of the first legislative steps towards stripping Jews and 'enemies of the Reich' of German citizenship. Issued on 14 July 1933, the law made it possible to revoke naturalization granted between 9 November 1918 and 30 January 1933. Approximately 39,000 individuals and their family members lost their citizenship as a result.

Lebensraum ('living space')

Central tenet of Nazi ideology, referring to the planned eastward expansion of German territory in order to acquire more space for the German people. The 'racial superiority' of the German Aryan race was considered to justify the resulting subjugation, enslavement, and decimation of the 'inferior' populations living in the territories conquered.

Minister President

Head of a German Land (state within the Reich).

Ministerial director (*Ministerialdirektor*)

Head of a department within a ministry.

Ministerialdirigent

Civil service rank subordinate to ministerial director.

Ministerialrat

Civil service rank subordinate to Ministerialdirigent.

Mischling ('half-caste' or person of 'mixed blood')

Classification under Nazi racial law to describe an individual of combined Aryan and non-Aryan, particularly Jewish, descent. The Nuremberg Laws of 1935 categorized *Mischlinge* according to the number of Jewish grandparents: *Mischlinge* of the first degree (half Jewish – one Jewish parent or two Jewish grandparents) and *Mischlinge* of the second degree (quarter Jewish – one Jewish grandparent). In order to prevent the birth of children of 'mixed blood', marriage was effectively prohibited between Aryans and '*Mischlinge* of the first degree' (those with two Jewish grandparents).

Mixed marriages (*Mischehen*)

Marriages between Jews and non-Jews, prohibited by the Nuremberg legislation of 1935 in order to preserve the 'racial purity' of the *Volksgemeinschaft*. In 1938 mixed marriages were subdivided into 'privileged' (Jewish wife married to a non-Jewish husband, or if there were children who were raised as Christians and under the age of eighteen) and 'non-privileged' (when the children were considered Jews, the couple was childless, or a Jewish husband was married to a non-Jewish wife). Jews in both types of mixed marriages suffered under most of the anti-Jewish measures that applied to 'full Jews', although they were not deported from Germany systematically.

National Socialist Factory Cell Organization (Nationalsozialistische Betriebszellenorganisation, NSBO)

A workers' organization, the first cells of which were founded in 1927–1929 in Berlin, the Ruhr, and Saxony. Its members were mainly foremen, skilled workers and clerks opposed to workers' parties and trade unions. The NSBO was the only official workers' organization in Germany until its absorption by the German Labour Front in 1935.

National Socialist Welfare Organization (Nationalsozialistische Volkswohlfahrt, NSV)

A social welfare organization founded in Berlin in 1933. Its welfare work was restricted to 'valuable members of the *Volksgemeinschaft*' and included annual charity drives for the poor, funding holiday homes for mothers, food distribution to large families, the evacuation of children from urban areas, and assistance to bombing victims during the war.

Night of the Long Knives
Purge of the SA leadership, including Ernst Röhm, carried out by the SS on Hitler's orders between 30 June and 2 July 1934. The purge was also used to kill other political enemies, primarily on the German nationalist right, and former supporters believed to have betrayed the Nazi movement. In all, sources estimate that up to 200 persons were killed, with over 100 persons taken into 'protective custody'. The Reich government claimed that the purge had been carried out to prevent a planned coup by Röhm. On 2 July 1934 it issued a law that retroactively legitimated the murders by declaring them a necessary response to a 'state of emergency'.

NS-Hago (abbreviation for NS-Handwerks-, Handels- und Gewerbe- Organisation; National Socialist Organization of Crafts, Trade, and Commerce)
Organization founded in 1933 responsible for all matters related to commerce, including the production and advertising of items in wholesale and retail trade. The NS-Hago published the monthly periodical *Der Aufbau*. It merged with the German Labour Front (DAF) in 1935.

NSDAP (Nationalsozialistische Deutsche Arbeiterpartei; National Socialist German Workers' Party or Nazi Party)
Anti-Marxist, antisemitic, and racist political party founded in Munich in 1919 as the Deutsche Arbeiterpartei (German Workers' Party) and renamed in 1920. Adolf Hitler became its leader in July 1921. In July 1933 the NSDAP became the only legal political party in the German Reich. In 1945 there were between 8 and 8.5 million NSDAP members.

Numerus clausus (Latin for 'closed number')
Restriction on the number of applicants who may be admitted to an academic institution or licensed in a given profession, either as a yearly quota or as a maximum number that may not be exceeded at any given time. Under the Nazi regime it generally referred to restrictions on access to schools, universities, and certain professions on the basis of Jewish ancestry.

Nuremberg Laws
Laws proclaimed at the annual Nazi Party congress in Nuremberg in September 1935. They excluded German Jews from Reich citizenship and prohibited them from marrying or having sexual relations with persons of 'German or related blood'.

Oberpräsident
Official in charge of a Prussian province, in the Third Reich usually also a Gauleiter.

Oberregierungsrat
Senior civil service rank subordinate to Regierungsdirektor.

Occupational restructuring (*Berufsumschichtung*)
Movement emerging in the second half of the nineteenth century within liberal Jewish discourse in Germany that aimed to improve Jews' employment opportunities and emigration chances by training them for work in agriculture and skilled crafts. Its proponents sought to counter the high proportion of Jews in certain professions (i.e. academia and trade) and direct them into fields in which they were permitted to work.

Old Reich (Altreich)
: Germany within its 1937 borders, prior to the Anschluss (annexation) of Austria in March 1938 and the annexation of the Sudetenland in October of the same year.

Order Police (Ordnungspolizei, Orpo)
: German uniformed police between 1936 and 1945 composed of the urban police (Schutzpolizei), municipal police (Gemeindepolizei), and the rural police (Gendarmerie). The Order Police was administered by the Interior Ministry but led by the SS from 1936, with Kurt Daluege as its head. During the war, several of its military battalions were tasked with policing the civilian population in the occupied territories, while others were directly involved in killing operations as part of the 'final solution'.

ORT (Russian acronym for the 'Society for Trades and Agricultural Labour', also known as the 'Organization for Rehabilitation through Training)
: Society established in Russia in 1880 by a small group of Jewish philanthropists to help impoverished Jews acquire skills that would enable them to become self-sufficient through education and training. It organized vocational training and supplied workshops with materials and tools, in addition to overseeing agricultural settlements. In 1921 the World ORT was established in Berlin, and in the following years it expanded its activities to Western and Eastern Europe, the Americas, and South Africa. ORT exists to this day.

Ostjuden ('Eastern Jews')
: Yiddish-speaking, mainly non-assimilated Jews who had migrated from Eastern Europe, particularly Poland, to Western Europe, North and South America and Palestine from the nineteenth century onwards. The term initially emerged as a result of the division between these Jews and the emancipated Jews in the countries to which they migrated. *Ostjuden* were early targets of the Nazi regime and the negative stereotype associated with them played a central role in Nazi propaganda.

Palestine Office (Palästina-Amt)
: Branch of the Jewish Agency for Palestine (in Germany and other countries) that helped Jews prepare for and organize their emigration to Palestine. The Palestine Office distributed the immigration certificates required by the British Mandate for Palestine.

Paltreu (acronym for Palästina Treuhandstelle zur Beratung deutscher Juden GmbH; Palestine Trust Agency to Advise German Jews)
: Agency founded in late 1933 together with the Trust and Transfer Office Haavara in Tel Aviv to assist with the implementation of the Haavara Agreement.

Political Police
: Common term for the Secret Police of the German state of Prussia in the nineteenth and twentieth centuries. The Prussian Secret Police was renamed the Gestapo in 1933.

Protective custody (*Schutzhaft*)
: Arrest and detention of persons suspected of acting against the state's interests, carried out without warrant or judicial review. The Gestapo in particular used protective custody as an instrument to crush dissent and to enforce Nazi racial and social policy. Those arrested were either imprisoned or sent to concentration camps.

Race defilement (*Rassenschande*)
: Extramarital sexual relations between Aryans and non-Aryans. Race defilement was criminalized in 1935 under the Law for the Protection of German Blood and German Honour.

Regierungsassessor
: Junior civil service rank attained after passing the qualifying examinations for the civil service.

Regierungsbezirk
: Administrative subdivision of a Land, Prussian province, or Gau, the level above Kreis; approximately equivalent to a British county.

Regierungsdirektor
: Senior civil service rank subordinate to Ministerialrat.

Regierungspräsident
: Civil service official in charge of a Regierungsbezirk.

Regierungsrat
: Senior civil service rank subordinate to Oberregierungsrat.

Reich Citizenship Law (*Reichsbürgergesetz*)
: One of the Nuremberg Laws proclaimed in September 1935. The Reich Citizenship Law did not strip Jews of their German citizenship but introduced a new distinction between 'subject of the state' (*Staatsangehörige*) and 'Reich citizen' (*Reichsbürger*); only those with 'German or related blood' could be the latter.

Reich Flight Tax (*Reichsfluchtsteuer*)
: Emigration tax, introduced during the Weimar Republic to prevent capital flight during the Great Depression, which increasingly targeted Jews forced to flee Nazi Germany. At first the tax only applied to emigrants with assets worth over 200,000 Reichsmarks, but from 1934 it was extended to those with assets of 50,000 Reichsmarks or more. Initially levied at a rate of 25 per cent, in 1938 the rate increased to 90 per cent.

Reich League of Jewish Combat Veterans (Reichsbund jüdischer Frontsoldaten, RjF)
: Organization founded in 1919 with the aim of preserving soldierly traditions, maintaining camaraderie, promoting the physical fitness of members in sports associations, and providing support to war victims. The RjF published the weekly newspaper *Der Schild*.

Reich Representation of Jews in Germany (Reichsvertretung der Juden in Deutschland)
: Central representative organization of German Jewry, founded in 1933 by Rabbi Leo Baeck and Otto Hirsch as the Reich Representation of German Jews (Reichsvertretung der deutschen Juden). Its goal was to confront the problems faced by German Jews in Nazi Germany by dealing with German authorities and Jewish organizations outside Germany. It administered all aspects of Jewish life: education, employment training, general support for the poor, economic assistance, and emigration. In 1935 the authorities forced the change of name to the 'Reich Representation of Jews in Germany'. In 1939 its name was changed once again, to 'Reich Association of Jews in Germany' (Reichsvereinigung der Juden in Deutschland). The organization was dissolved in July 1943.

Reich Security Main Office (Reichssicherheitshauptamt, RSHA)
: Office created by Heinrich Himmler on 27 September 1939 by merging the SD and the Security Police into one, and headed by Reinhard Heydrich. The RSHA played an important role in the regime's policies of persecution and extermination. It was responsible for intelligence gathering and criminal investigation. Through the work of Section IV D 4, run by Adolf Eichmann, it played a leading role in implementing the 'final solution'.

Reichsbank
: The central bank of Germany between 1876 and 1945. In 1939 it was placed under Hitler's direct control, with Walther Funk as the Reichsbank's last president, from 1939 to 1945. The Reichsbank benefited from property confiscation, especially the personal assets of Jews and the gold reserves of the countries invaded by the Germans.

Reichsgesetzblatt (*Reich Law Gazette*, *RGBl*)
: Official gazette of the German Reich between 1871 and 1945, which published laws and regulations.

Reichsleiter (Reich leader)
: The most senior political rank in the NSDAP, second only to the Führer. Hitler appointed Reichsleiter to oversee a range of portfolios (propaganda, law, finance, foreign policy). They were collectively designated as the Reich leadership (Reichsleitung).

Reichsstatthalter (Reich governor)
: Political officials appointed to head the Länder (German states) and implement political orders from Hitler after 1933. The Gauleiter frequently also served as Reichsstatthalter.

Relief Association of German Jews (Hilfsverein der deutschen Juden)
: Association founded in 1901 in Berlin to improve the cultural and sociopolitical conditions of Jews in the Levant and Eastern Europe. It was dissolved in 1939.

SA (abbreviation for Sturmabteilung; 'Storm Troopers', colloquially 'Brownshirts')
: Paramilitary wing of the NSDAP established in 1920 to provide protection during Party gatherings and rallies and to disrupt those of its opponents through systematic intimidation. The SA was instrumental to Hitler's rise to power in the early 1930s and was heavily involved in the escalating violence against Jews. Headed by Ernst Röhm until 1934, the SA aimed to uphold the National Socialist 'revolution'. However, its leadership was purged in 1934 during the 'Night of the Long Knives' and its influence gradually waned due to the increased importance of the SS.

Schools
- Academic secondary school (*höhere Schule*)
  School preparing pupils for university-level education.
- Grammar school (*Gymnasium*)
  Secondary school preparing pupils for university-level education.
- Middle school (*Mittelschule*)
  Prepared pupils for the higher level of secondary education (*Gymnasium* / *höhere Schule*).
- Primary school (*Volksschule*)
  Provided education up to the compulsory school-leaving age of 14.

- School providing compulsory education [up to the school-leaving age of 14] (*Pflichtschule*)
- Secondary school (*Realschule*); upper secondary school (*Oberrealschule*)
- Technical school (*Fachschule*)
- Vocational school (*Berufsschule*)

Provided general and technical education for pupils aged 14 and above.

SD (abbreviation for Sicherheitsdienst; SS Security Service)

Intelligence service of the SS and NSDAP, founded in 1931 by Heinrich Himmler and headed by Reinhard Heydrich. Its tasks included the detection and surveillance of those classed as political and ideological enemies, especially Jews, communists, Social Democrats, and Freemasons. In 1939 it was incorporated into the Reich Security Main Office (RSHA) along with the Security Police (Gestapo and Criminal Police). It played an instrumental role in the planning and implementation of the 'final solution'.

Security Police (Sicherheitspolizei, Sipo)

One of the two police branches after Himmler's reorganization of the entire police apparatus in 1936 (the other being the Order Police). The Security Police was headed by Reinhard Heydrich between 1936 and 1939 and consisted of the Gestapo and the Criminal Police. It was incorporated into the Reich Security Main Office in 1939.

Sopade

The exiled executive of the Social Democratic Party of Germany (SPD) that operated in Prague (1933–1938), Paris (1938–1940), and London (until 1945). It collected and analysed reports and newspaper articles about the political, cultural, economic, and social situation in Germany, which it published on a monthly basis from May 1934. The Sopade reports are among the most valuable historical sources about public opinion in Nazi Germany.

Special court (Sondergericht)

Courts created by decree of 21 March 1933, mainly concerned with eliminating political threats. Many of the 'crimes' tried by the courts concerned verbal exchanges and were based on denunciation. Special courts were also set up in countries under German occupation.

SS (abbreviation for Schutzstaffel; 'protection squadron')

Force established in 1925 under the leadership of Heinrich Himmler. From 1934 it was responsible for running the concentration camps and from 1941 for the extermination camps. It was instrumental in planning and implementing the genocide of Jews and other groups.

SS Race and Settlement Main Office (Rasse- und Siedlungshauptamt der SS, RuSHA)

Office responsible for conducting racial checks as a prerequisite for individuals to be accepted into SS organizations, founded in 1931 by Heinrich Himmler and Richard Walther Darré. In some cases it also carried out racial assessment of individuals and communities prior to resettlement, deportation, and extermination.

Staatsrat

Member of the Prussian State Council.

State minister (Staatsminister)

Head of a ministry in a Land government.

State secretary (*Staatssekretär*)
: The most senior grade of permanent civil service official in a ministry. There were sometimes several state secretaries in one ministry.

Strength through Joy (Kraft durch Freude)
: Founded in November 1933, a subsidiary of the German Labour Front that organized a wide range of leisure and tourism activities and offered subsidized holidays to workers.

Der Stürmer
: Vehemently antisemitic weekly tabloid published by the Gauleiter of Franconia, Julius Streicher, from 1923 to 1945. Although not an official Party publication, it became an integral part of Nazi propaganda. Its readership was even larger than circulation figures suggest, as it featured each week's issue in public display cases throughout Germany.

Treaty of Versailles
: Peace treaty signed at the end of the First World War by the Allied and associated powers and by Germany in the Palace of Versailles in France on 28 June 1919. The treaty stipulated that Germany disarm, make territorial concessions, pay reparations to the Entente powers, and accept responsibility for the war (war guilt clause).

Undersecretary (*Unterstaatssekretär*)
: Civil service official within a ministry; rank below state secretary.

Urban police (Schutzpolizei, Schupo)
: Uniformed state protection police in towns and cities; branch of the Order Police. The Schupo comprised the patrol police, barracked police, traffic police, waterways police, mounted police, and aviation and communications branches.

Völkisch (literally 'folkish', roughly meaning 'ethno-nationalist')
: Term dating back to the nineteenth century and denoting the organic unity of people bound by blood, soil, history, and culture. In the second half of the nineteenth century the central tenet of *völkisch* thinking was a racial ideology that later became a key element of National Socialism.

Volksgemeinschaft (usually translated as 'people's community' or 'national community')
: Under National Socialism, the notion of a racially homogeneous, 'Aryan' national community, restricted to those of 'German blood'. The concept evoked a utopian order that promised material well-being and self-fulfilment, and provided Nazi functionaries with a framework for social engineering.

Volksgenosse/-in ('ethnic comrade')
: Member of the German *Volksgemeinschaft*.

Volljude ('full Jew')
: Classification under Nazi racial laws to describe an individual with at least three Jewish grandparents.

Wehrmacht
: Collective term for the German armed forces – army, air force (Luftwaffe), and navy – from 1935 to 1945. The Wehrmacht was the successor to the Reichswehr (1919–1935). The Armed Forces High Command (Oberkommando der Wehrmacht, OKW) under Wilhelm Keitel coordinated military activities, although each of the three military branches had their respective high command: OKH (army), OKM (navy), and OKL (air force).

Weimar Republic
: The designation for the German state between 1918 and 1933. It takes its name from the town of Weimar, where the constituent assembly first met. National Socialist propaganda depicted the Weimar Republic as corrupt, degenerate, and ruled by Jews, socialists, and Bolsheviks. It also denounced the Weimar government leaders as the 'November Criminals' for having signed the armistice on 11 November 1918.

Winter Relief Agency (Winterhilfswerk, WHW)
: A joint initiative of private welfare organizations that originated in the late years of the Weimar Republic. In 1933 it came under the jurisdiction of the National Socialist People's Welfare. Funding was obtained from street campaigning, wage/salary deductions, and house-to-house collections. The purpose of the WHW was not only to raise money to help those in need of food, clothing, or medical assistance, but also to inculcate readiness to make sacrifices for the national good.

Youth Aliyah
: A department of the Jewish Agency for Palestine formed in 1932 with the aim of aiding Jewish children and young people in Europe to emigrate to Palestine.

Zionism
: Movement that originated in Central and Eastern Europe in the late nineteenth century and continues to support the reestablishment of a Jewish nation in what is now Israel.

Zionist Federation for Germany (Zionistische Vereinigung für Deutschland)
: Organization which supported Jewish settlement in Palestine and the reinvigoration of Jewish national identity, founded in 1897 in Cologne by Max Bodenheimer. With its headquarters in Berlin, it had a membership of more than 7,000 in 1932 and more than 22,000 in 1935. It was dissolved following the November pogroms in 1938.

Approximate Rank and Hierarchy Equivalents

NSDAP and Civil Service

NSDAP	Civil Service
Reichsleiter	Staatssekretär
–	Oberpräsident (only in Prussia)
Gauleiter	Unterstaatssekretär
Hauptbefehlsleiter	Ministerialdirektor
Oberbefehlsleiter	Regierungspräsident
Befehlsleiter	–
Hauptdienstleiter	Ministerialdirigent
Oberdienstleiter	–
Hauptbereichsleiter	Ministerialrat
Kreisleiter	
Oberbereichsleiter	Regierungsdirektor
Bereichsleiter	–
Hauptgemeinschaftsleiter	Amtsrat
Ortsgruppenleiter	
Obergemeinschaftsleiter	Oberinspektor
Gemeinschaftsleiter	Inspektor
Haupteinsatzleiter	–
Einsatzleiter	–
Hauptbereitschaftsleiter	Obersekretär
Oberbereitschaftsleiter	Sekretär
–	Verwaltungsassistent
Bereitschaftsleiter	–
–	Assistent
Hauptarbeitsleiter	Assistent
Oberarbeitsleiter	Amtsgehilfe
Arbeitsleiter	–
Oberhelfer	–
Helfer	–
Polit. Leiter-Anwärter	–

Source: Michael Buddrus, *Totale Erziehung für den totalen Krieg: Hitlerjugend und nationalsozialistische Jugendpolitik* (Munich: De Gruyter, 2003).

Approximate Rank and Hierarchy Equivalents

SS, Wehrmacht, British Army, US Army

SS	Wehrmacht	British Army	US Army
Reichsführer-SS	Reichsmarschall	—	—
—	Generalfeldmarschall	Field Marshal	General of the Army
SS-Oberstgruppenführer	Generaloberst	—	General
SS-Obergruppenführer	General der Waffengattung (Infanterie, Artillerie, etc.)	General	Lieutenant General
SS-Gruppenführer	Generalleutnant	Lieutenant General	Major General
SS-Brigadeführer	Generalmajor	Major General	Brigadier General
SS-Oberführer	—	Brigadier	—
SS-Standartenführer	Oberst	Colonel	Colonel
SS-Obersturmbannführer	Oberstleutnant	Lieutenant Colonel	Lieutenant Colonel
SS-Sturmbannführer	Major	Major	Major
SS-Hauptsturmführer	Hauptmann	Captain	Captain
SS-Obersturmführer	Oberleutnant	First Lieutenant	First Lieutenant
SS-Untersturmführer	Leutnant	Second Lieutenant	Second Lieutenant
SS-Sturmscharführer	Stabsoberfeldwebel	Regimental Sergeant Major (Warrant Officer Class 1)	Sergeant Major
—	Oberfähnrich	—	Senior Officer Candidate
SS-Hauptscharführer	Oberfeldwebel	Staff Sergeant Major (Warrant Officer Class 1)	Master Sergeant
SS-Oberscharführer	Feldwebel	Warrant Officer Class 2	Technical Sergeant
—	Fähnrich	Ensign	Officer Candidate
SS-Scharführer	Unterfeldwebel	Staff Sergeant	Staff Sergeant
SS-Unterscharführer	Unteroffizier	Sergeant	Sergeant
—	Stabsgefreiter	Corporal (senior)	—
—	Obergefreiter	Corporal	Corporal

SS-Rottenführer	Gefreiter	Lance Corporal
SS-Sturmmann	Obersoldat	Private (senior)
SS-Mann	Soldat	Private
SS-Anwärter	—	—

Acting Corporal	
Private First Class	
Private	
—	

Sources:

SS/Wehrmacht ranks: Heinz Antzt, *Mörder in Uniform: Organisationen, die zu Vollstreckern nationalsozialistischer Verbrechen wurden* (Munich: Kindler, 1979).

Wehrmacht/US army ranks: Tim Ripley, *The German Army in World War II, 1939–1945* (Hoboken: Taylor and Francis, 2014).

Wehrmacht/British army ranks: Ben H. Shepherd, *Hitler's Soldiers: The German Army in the Third Reich* (New Haven: Yale University Press, 2017).

Security Police (SIPO)

Sicherheitspolizei (SIPO)

Chef der deutschen Polizei / Chief of the German Police
Chef der SIPO / Chief of the SIPO
Kriminaldirigent
Reichskriminaldirektor
Regierungs-und Kriminaldirektor
Oberregierungs- und Kriminalrat
Regierungs- und Kriminalrat
Kriminaldirektor
Kriminalrat / detective chief superintendent
Kriminalkommissar / detective superintendent
Kriminalinspektor / detective inspector
Kriminalobersekretär / detective chief sergeant
Kriminalsekretär / detective sergeant
Kriminaloberassistent / detective chief constable
Kriminalassistent / detective constable
Kriminalassistentenanwärter / detective constable candidate

Source: Hans-Christian Harten, *Die weltanschauliche Schulung der Polizei im Nationalsozialismus* (Paderborn: Ferdinand Schöningh, 2018).

List of Abbreviations

§	section (of a German law, code, or regulation)
§§	sections (of a German law, code, or regulation)
AAD	Arbeitsgemeinschaft der Automobilbesitzer Deutschlands (Association of German Motor Car Owners)
AdP	*Akten der Partei-Kanzlei* (Files of the Party Chancellery); published source collection
AdR	*Akten der Reichskanzlei* (Files of the Reich Chancellery); published source collection
AdsD	Archiv der sozialen Demokratie der Friedrich-Ebert-Stiftung (Archive of Social Democracy of the Friedrich Ebert Foundation)
AEG	Allgemeine Elektrizitäts-Gesellschaft (General Electric Company)
AG	Aktiengesellschaft (public limited company)
AJA	American Jewish Archives
AJC	American Jewish Congress
Altreu	Allgemeine Treuhandstelle für die jüdische Auswanderung GmbH (General Trust Agency for Jewish Emigration GmbH)
AOG	Arbeitsordnungsgesetz = *Gesetz zur Ordnung der Nationalen Arbeit* (Law for the Regulation of National Labour)
Art.	article (of a German law, code, or regulation)
AWAG	Allgemeine Warenhandels-Gesellschaft; a chain of department stores
b.	born
BArch	Bundesarchiv (German Federal Archives)
BayHStA	Bayerisches Hauptstaatsarchiv (Bavarian Main State Archives)
Bd.	Band (volume)
BDM	Bund Deutscher Mädel (League of German Girls)
BEWAG	Berliner Städtische Elektrizitätswerke AG (Berlin Municipal Electric Works)
BLHA	Brandenburgisches Landeshauptarchiv (Brandenburg Main State Archives)
BNSDJ	Bund Nationalsozialistischer Deutscher Juristen (League of National Socialist German Lawyers)
BSSR	Belorussian Soviet Socialist Republic
BT	Berliner Turnerschaft (Berlin Gymnastics Association)
BVP	Bayerische Volkspartei (Bavarian People's Party)
BVP	Beauftragter für den Vierjahresplan (Plenipotentiary for the Four-Year Plan)
CAHJP	Central Archives for the History of the Jewish People
CDU	Christlich Demokratische Union Deutschlands (Christian Democratic Union of Germany)
cf.	*conferre* (compare with)
CJA	Archiv der Stiftung Neue Synagoge Berlin – Centrum Judaicum (Archive of the New Synagogue Berlin – Centrum Judaicum Foundation)
Comintern	Communist International
Comp. / Co.	company
CSU	Christlich-Soziale Union in Bayern (Christian Social Union in Bavaria)
CT	Connecticut

CV	Centralverein deutscher Staatsbürger jüdischen Glaubens (Central Association of German Citizens of the Jewish Faith)
CZA	Central Zionist Archives
D. Phil-Blatt	*Deutsches Philologenblatt*
DAAD	Deutscher Akademischer Austauschdienst (German Academic Exchange Service)
DAF	Deutsche Arbeitsfront (German Labour Front)
DAP	Deutsche Arbeiterpartei (German Workers' Party)
DAZ	*Deutsche Allgemeine Zeitung*
DC	Deutsche Christen (German Christians)
DC	District of Columbia
DDP	Deutsche Demokratische Partei (German Democratic Party)
Dept.	department
DFG	Deutsche Forschungsgemeinschaft (German Research Foundation)
DGO	Deutsche Gemeindeordnung (German Municipal Code)
DGT	Deutscher Gemeindetag (German Council of Municipalities)
DHM	Deutsches Historisches Museum (German Historical Museum)
dnb	Deutsches Nachrichtenbüro (German News Agency)
DNVP	Deutschnationale Volkspartei (German National People's Party)
Doc.	document (citation for a document in the present PMJ volume)
doc.	document (citation for a document in a non-PMJ source collection)
Dr	doctor
Dr h.c.	*doctor honoris causa* (honorary doctor)
DRA	Deutsches Rundfunkarchiv (German Broadcasting Archives)
DSP	Deutschsoziale Partei (German Social Party)
DT	Deutsche Turnerschaft (German Gymnastics Association)
DVP	Deutsche Volkspartei (German People's Party)
EAF	Erzbischöfliches Archiv Freiburg (Archiepiscopal Archives Freiburg)
ed.	edited by / editor
edn	edition
eds.	editors
EI	Eretz Israel (Hebrew for 'the land of Israel')
Emigdirect	Emigrations-Direktorium (Emigration Directorate)
Encl.	enclosure
Epa	Einheitspreis AG; a chain of department stores
et al.	*et alii* (and others)
e. V.	eingetragener Verein (registered charitable/non-profit society)
fn.	footnote
fol.	folio (of an archival source)
fols.	folios (of an archival source)
Gestapa	Geheimes Staatspolizeiamt (Secret State Police Central Office)
Gestapo	Geheime Staatspolizei (Secret State Police)
GmbH	Gesellschaft mit beschränkter Haftung (private limited company)
GS / GS.	*Preußische Gesetzsammlung* (Prussian statute book)
GStA PK	Geheimes Staatsarchiv Preußischer Kulturbesitz (Secret State Archives Prussian Cultural Heritage Foundation)
h.c.	see Dr h.c.
HE	His Excellency

List of Abbreviations

HG	Handel und Gewerbe (trade and commerce); department in the Reich Ministry of Economics
HHStA	Hessisches Hauptstaatsarchiv (Hessian Main State Archives)
HIAS	Hebrew Immigrant Aid Society
HICEM	amalgamation of *HIAS*, *ICA* and *Em*igdirect
HStAD	Hessisches Staatsarchiv Darmstadt (Hessian State Archives Darmstadt)
HWA	Heereswaffenamt (Army Ordnance Department)
HZ	*Historische Zeitschrift*
IB	*Illustrierter Beobachter*
ibid.	*ibidem* (in the same place)
ICA	Jewish Colonization Association
IfZ-Archives	Archiv des Instituts für Zeitgeschichte München – Berlin (Archives of the Institute of Contemporary History Munich – Berlin)
IGdJ	Institut für die Geschichte der deutschen Juden (Institute for the History of the German Jews)
IOBB	Independent Order of B'nai B'rith
ISG Frankfurt	Institut für Stadtgeschichte Frankfurt am Main (Frankfurt Institute of Local History)
JCA	Jewish Colonization Association
JDC	American Jewish Joint Distribution Committee
JMBl.	*Justizministerialblatt*
JTA	Jewish Telegraphic Agency
KdF	Kraft durch Freude (Strength through Joy)
KfdK / KFDK	Kampfbund für deutsche Kultur (Combat League for German Culture)
KG	Kommanditgesellschaft (limited partnership)
KH	Keren Hayesod
KKL	Keren Kayemeth Leisrael
KPD	Kommunistische Partei Deutschlands (Communist Party of Germany)
KPÖ	Kommunistische Partei Österreichs (Communist Party of Austria)
KY	Kentucky
LAB	Landesarchiv Berlin (Berlin State Archive)
LASA	Landesarchiv Sachsen-Anhalt (State Archives of Saxony-Anhalt)
Lawohl	Landeswohlfahrtsamt (regional welfare office)
LHAS	Landeshauptarchiv Schwerin (Main State Archives of Schwerin)
loc. cit.	*loco citato* (in the cited place)
Ltd	limited company
MA	Massachusetts
MBliV	*Ministerialblatt der inneren Verwaltung*
NACP	National Archives at College Park
NB.	*nota bene* (take note)
ND	Narodowa Demokracja (National Democracy)
n.d.	no date
NDR	Norddeutscher Rundfunk (Northern German Broadcasting Company)
NH	New Hampshire
NJ / N.J.	New Jersey
no.	number
n.pub.	no publisher
nos.	numbers

n.p.	no place (of publication)
NS	nationalsozialistisch (National Socialist)
NSBO	Nationalsozialistische Betriebszellenorganisation (National Socialist Factory Cell Organization)
NSDAP/ N.S.D.A.P.	Nationalsozialistische Deutsche Arbeiterpartei (National Socialist German Workers' Party)
NS-Hago	Nationalsozialistische Handwerks-, Handels- und Gewerbe-Organisation (National Socialist Organization of Crafts, Trade, and Commerce)
NSK	Nationalsozialistische Partei-Korrespondenz (National Socialist Party Correspondence)
NSKOV	Nationalsozialistische Kriegsopferversorgung (National Socialist Welfare for War Victims)
NSLB	Nationalsozialistischer Lehrerbund (National Socialist Association of Teachers)
NSV	Nationalsozialistische Volkswohlfahrt (National Socialist Welfare Organization)
NY	New York (state)
ONR	Obóz Narodowo-Radykalny (National Radical Camp)
ORT	Obshchestvo Remeslennogo i Zemledel'cheskogo Truda (Society for Trades and Agricultural Labour)
p.	page
PA AA	Politisches Archiv des Auswärtigen Amts (Political Archives of the Federal Foreign Office)
Paltreu	Palästina Treuhandstelle zur Beratung deutscher Juden GmbH (Palestine Trust Agency to Advise German Jews Ltd)
PhD	Doctor of Philosophy
PI	Pädagogisches Institut der Technischen Hochschule Dresden (Pedagogical Institute of the Technical University in Dresden)
PMJ	*The Persecution and Murder of the European Jews by Nazi Germany, 1933–1945*
P.O.	Parteiorganisation (Party Organization)
pp.	pages
p.p.	*per procurationem* (by proxy)
preuß. FM	Preußisches Finanzministerium (Prussian Ministry of Finance)
Prof.	professor
r–v	recto and verso (of an archival source)
RAG	Reichsarbeitsgesetz/-gebung (Reich labour law / legislation)
RDM	Reichsverband Deutschler Makler (Reich Association of German Estate Agents)
Ref.	reference
ref. no.	reference number
RGO	Revolutionäre Gewerkschafts-Opposition der KPD (Revolutionary Trade Union Opposition of the Communist Party of Germany)
RGVA	Rossiiskii Gosudarstvennyi Voennyi Arkhiv (Russian State Military Archives)
RjF	Reichsbund jüdischer Frontsoldaten (Reich League of Jewish Combat Veterans)
RLB	Reichsluftschutzbund (Reich Federation for Air Raid Protection)
RM	Reichsmark(s)
RMdI	Reichsministerium des Innern (Reich Ministry of the Interior)
RMEuL	Reichsministerium für Ernährung und Landwirtschaft (Reich Ministry of Food and Agriculture)
RMfVuP	Reichsministerium für Volksaufklärung und Propaganda (Reich Ministry of Public Enlightenment and Propaganda)

RSHA	Reichssicherheitshauptamt (Reich Security Main Office)
RWM	Reichswirtschaftsministerium (Reich Ministry of Economics)
RWZ	*Rheinisch-Westfälische Zeitung*
SA	Sturmabteilung (Storm Troopers)
SD / S.D.	Sicherheitsdienst (SS Security Service)
SLUB	Sächsische Landesbibliothek, Staats- und Universitätsbibliothek Dresden (Saxon State and University Library Dresden)
SNG	Senckenbergische Naturforschende Gesellschaft (Senckenberg Natural History Society)
Sopade	Sozialdemokratische Partei Deutschlands im Exil (Social Democratic Party of Germany in Exile)
SOS	save our souls (international code signal of extreme distress)
SPD	Sozialdemokratische Partei Deutschlands (Social Democratic Party of Germany)
SS	Schutzstaffel ('Protection Squadron')
str.	Straße (street / road)
TB	tuberculosis
trans.	translated by
UA–HUB	Universitätsarchiv der Humboldt-Universität zu Berlin (Humboldt University Archives)
UFA	Universum Film AG
UOBB	Unabhängiger Orden B'nai B'rith (Independent Order of B'nai B'rith)
US / U.S.	United States
USA	United States of America
USHMM	United States Holocaust Memorial Museum
USPD	Unabhängige Sozialdemokratische Partei Deutschlands (Independent Social Democratic Party of Germany)
USSR	Ukrainian Soviet Socialist Republic
UuF	Herbert Michaelis and Ernst Schraepler (eds.), *Ursachen und Folgen: Vom deutschen Zusammenbruch 1918 und 1945 bis zur staatlichen Neuordnung Deutschlands in der Gegenwart Eine Urkunden- und Dokumentensammlung zur Zeitgeschichte*, 29 vols. (Berlin, 1958–1979)
v	verso (of an archival source)
VA	Virginia
VB	*Völkischer Beobachter*
Vg. / Vgn.	Volkgenosse/-in
Viag	Vereinigte Industrieunternehmungen AG (United Industrial Enterprises)
vol.	volume
vols.	volumes
VSH	Verband der Sittichliebhaber (Association of Budgerigar Enthusiasts)
WDR	Westdeutscher Rundfunk (Western German Broadcasting Company)
WI	Wisconsin
WJC	World Jewish Congress
WTB	Wolffsches Telegraphenbüro (Wolff Telegraph Office)
YVA	Yad Vashem Archives
ZfA	Zentrum für Antisemitismusforschung (Centre for Research on Antisemitism)
ZVfD	Zionistische Vereinigung für Deutschland (Zionist Association for Germany)

List of Archives, Sources, and Literature Cited

Primary Sources

Archives

American Jewish Archives (AJA), Cincinnati, OH
Archiv der Max-Planck-Gesellschaft (Archives of the Max Planck Society), Berlin
Archiv der Senckenberg Gesellschaft für Naturforschung (Archives of the Senckenberg Nature Research Society), Frankfurt
Archiv der sozialen Demokratie der Friedrich-Ebert-Stiftung (AdsD, Archive of Social Democracy of the Friedrich Ebert Foundation), Bonn
Archiv der Stiftung Neue Synagoge Berlin – Centrum Judaicum (CJA, Archives of the New Synagogue Berlin – Centrum Judaicum Foundation)
Archiv des Diakonischen Werkes der Evangelischen Kirche Deutschlands (Archives of the Social Welfare Organization of Germany's Protestant Churches), Berlin
Archiv des Instituts für Zeitgeschichte München – Berlin (IfZ Archives, Archives of the Institute of Contemporary History Munich – Berlin), Munich
Archives of the Leo Baeck Institute, New York, at the Jüdisches Museum Berlin
Archiwum Państwowe we Wrocławiu (State Archives in Wrocław)
Bayerisches Hauptstaatsarchiv (BayHStA, Bavarian Main State Archives), Munich
Brandenburgisches Landeshauptarchiv (BLHA, Brandenburg Main State Archives), Potsdam
Bundesarchiv (BArch, German Federal Archives), Berlin
Central Archives for the History of the Jewish People (CAHJP), Jerusalem
Central Zionist Archives (CZA), Jerusalem
Deutsche Nationalbibliothek/Deutsches Exilarchiv 1933–1945 (German National Library: German Exile Archives, 1933–1945), Frankfurt
Deutsches Historisches Museum (DHM, German Historical Museum), Berlin
Deutsches Rundfunkarchiv (DRA, German Broadcasting Archives), Frankfurt
Erzbischöfliches Archiv Freiburg (EAF, Archiepiscopal Archives Freiburg)
Erzbischöfliches Archiv München (Archiepiscopal Archives Munich)
Geheimes Staatsarchiv Preußischer Kulturbesitz (GStA PK, Secret State Archives Prussian Cultural Heritage Foundation), Berlin
Hessisches Hauptstaatsarchiv (HHStAW, Hessian Main State Archives), Wiesbaden
Hessisches Staatsarchiv Darmstadt (HStAD, Hessian State Archives Darmstadt)
Houghton Library, Harvard University, Cambridge, MA
Institut für die Geschichte der deutschen Juden (IGdJ, Institute for the History of the German Jews), Hamburg
Institut für Stadtgeschichte Frankfurt am Main (ISG Frankfurt, Frankfurt Institute of Local History)
Jüdisches Museum Berlin (Jewish Museum Berlin)
Landesarchiv Berlin (LAB, Berlin State Archives)
Landesarchiv des Saarlands (Saarland State Archives), Saarbrücken
Landesarchiv Sachsen-Anhalt (LASA, Saxony-Anhalt State Archives), Magdeburg
Landeshauptarchiv Schwerin (LHAS, Schwerin Main State Archives)
National Archives at College Park, MD (NACP)
Politisches Archiv des Auswärtigen Amts (PA AA, Political Archives of the Federal Foreign Office), Berlin
Privatarchiv Gerhard Lüdecke (Gerhard Lüdecke Private Archives)
Privatarchiv Trapp (Trapp Private Archives)

Rossiiskii Gosudarstvennyi Voennyi Arkhiv (RGVA, Russian State Military Archives), Moscow
Sächsische Landesbibliothek, Staats- und Universitätsbibliothek Dresden (SLUB, Saxon State and University Library, Dresden)
Sächsisches Staatsarchiv, Hauptstaatsarchiv Dresden (Saxon Main State Archives, Dresden)
Sächsisches Staatsarchiv Leipzig (Saxon State Archives, Leipzig)
Staatsarchiv Hamburg (Hamburg State Archives)
Staatsarchiv Nürnberg (Nuremberg State Archives)
Stadtarchiv Braunschweig (Braunschweig Municipal Archives)
Stadtarchiv Duisburg (Duisburg City Archives)
Stadtarchiv Düsseldorf (Düsseldorf City Archives)
Stadtarchiv Hannover (Hanover City Archives)
Stadtarchiv Leipzig (Leipzig City Archives)
Stadtarchiv München (Munich City Archives)
United States Holocaust Memorial Museum (USHMM), Washington, DC
Universitätsarchiv der Humboldt-Universität zu Berlin (UA-HUB, Humboldt University Archives)
Warburg-Archiv (Warburg Archives), Hamburg
Wiener Library, London
Yad Vashem Archives (YVA), Jerusalem
Zentrum für Antisemitismusforschung (ZfA, Centre for Research on Antisemitism), Berlin

Newspapers and Magazines

12 Uhr Blatt
Akademischer Beobachter
Amtliche Nachrichten des Polizeipräsidiums in Berlin
Amtsblatt der Preußischen Regierung zu Königsberg
Berliner Beobachter (daily supplement to the Völkischer Beobachter)
Berliner Börsen-Zeitung
Berliner Tageblatt
Beuthener Stadtblatt
Braunschweiger Neueste Nachrichten
C.V.-Zeitung
Daily Telegraph
Danziger Echo
Das Schwarze Korps
Der Angriff
Der Kicker: Mitteldeutschland
Der National-Sozialistische Erzieher
Der Schild: Zeitschrift des Reichsbundes jüdischer Frontsoldaten e. V.
Der Stürmer
Deutsche Allgemeine Zeitung
Deutsche Immobilien-Zeitung: Zeitung des Reichsverbandes Deutscher Makler (RDM) für Immobilien, Hypotheken und Finanzierungen E.V.
Deutsche Juristen-Zeitung
Deutsche Justiz: Rechtspflege und Rechtspolitik: Amtliches Blatt der deutschen Rechtspflege
Deutsche Reichsanzeiger und Preußischer Staatsanzeiger
Deutsche Volksgesundheit aus Blut und Boden: Gesundheitserziehung auf rassischer Grundlage
Deutsches Ärzteblatt
Deutsches Philologen-Blatt
Deutsches Recht
Die Deutsche Studentenschaft: Nachrichtendienst
Die Kameradschaft
Die Neue Welt: Revue
Die neue Weltbühne
Dienstblatt des Magistrats von Berlin
Frankfurter Zeitung
Gesetz- u. Verordnungsblatt für den Freistaat Bayern
Hanseatische Rechts- und Gerichts-Zeitschrift
Haynt
Hessisches Regierungsblatt
Historische Zeitschrift
Internationales Ärztliches Bulletin
Jewish Telegraphic Agency: Latest Cable Dispatches
Jüdische Rundschau
Jüdisches Gemeindeblatt für Rheinland und Westfalen
Junge Kirche
Juristische Rundschau
Juristische Wochenschrift
Kirchliches Gesetz- und Verordnungsblatt

Le Temps
Manchester Guardian
Meeraner Zeitung
Meldung des Deutschen Nachrichtenbüros
Ministerialblatt der inneren Verwaltung
Ministerialblatt der Preußischen Verwaltung
Ministerialblatt des Reichs- und Preußischen Ministerium des Innern
Münchner Neueste Nachrichten, Stadtnachrichten und General-Anzeiger
Nachrichtenblatt der Berliner Turnerschaft
National-Zeitung
Nationalsozialistische Monatshefte
Nationalsozialistische Partei-Korrespondenz
Neue Augsburger Zeitung
Neue Zürcher Zeitung
Neuer Vorwärts
New York Herald Tribune Magazine
New York Times
Ostdeutsche Morgenpost
Pariser Tageblatt
Pariser Tageszeitung
Preußische Gesetzsammlung
Reichsgesetzblatt
Reichssteuerblatt
Rote Erde
Sächsisches Justizministerialblatt
Sächsisches Verwaltungsblatt
The Times
Verordnungsblatt der Obersten SA-Führung
Völkischer Beobachter
Vossische Zeitung
Werdauer Zeitung
Westfälische Neueste Nachrichten
Zeitschrift des Vereins für Geschichte Schlesiens
Zwischen Weichsel und Nogat

Diaries and Memoirs

Blumenthal, W. Michael, *The Invisible Wall: Germans and Jews. A Personal Exploration* (Washington, DC: Counterpoint, 1998).
Cohn, Willy, *No Justice in Germany: The Breslau Diaries, 1933–1944*, ed. Norbert Conrads, trans. Kenneth Kronenberg (Stanford, CA: Stanford University Press, 2012 [German edn, 2006]).
Goebbels, Joseph, *Die Tagebücher von Joseph Goebbels*, part 1: *Aufzeichnungen 1923–1941*, vol. 2, no. 3: *Oktober 1932 – März 1934*, ed. Elke Fröhlich (Munich: Saur, 2006).
Goebbels, Joseph, *Die Tagebücher von Joseph Goebbels*, part 1: *Aufzeichnungen 1923–1941*, vol. 3, no. 1: *April 1934 – Februar 1936*, ed. Elke Fröhlich (Munich: Saur, 2005).
Gyssling, Walter, *Mein Leben in Deutschland vor und nach 1933, und Der Anti-Nazi: Handbuch im Kampf gegen die NSDAP*, ed. Leonidas Hill (Bremen: Donat, 2003).
Herzfeld, Albert, *Ein nichtarischer Deutscher: Die Tagebücher des Albert Herzfeld 1935–1939*, ed. Hugo Weidenhaupt (Düsseldorf: Triltsch, 1982).
Klemperer, Victor, *I Shall Bear Witness: The Diaries of Victor Klemperer, 1933–1941*, trans. Martin Chalmers (London: Weidenfeld & Nicolson, 1998 [German edn, 1995]).
König, Joel [Ezra Ben-Gershom], *David: Aufzeichnungen eines Überlebenden* (Frankfurt am Main: Fischer, 1979).
Lansing, Robert, *The Peace Negotiations: A Personal Narrative* (New York/Boston, MA: Houghton Mifflin, 1921).
Nathorff, Hertha, *Das Tagebuch der Hertha Nathorff: Berlin–New York. Aufzeichnungen 1933 bis 1945*, ed. Wolfgang Benz (Frankfurt am Main: Fischer, 1988).
Schacht, Hjalmar, *76 Jahre meines Lebens* (Bad Wörishofen: Kindler und Schiermeister, 1953).
Schottlaender, Rudolf, *Trotz allem ein Deutscher: Mein Lebensweg seit Jahrhundertbeginn* (Freiburg im Breisgau: Herder, 1986).
Schwab, Hermann, *1933: Ein Tagebuch* (Zurich: Jüdischer Volksschriftenverlag, 1953).

Works Published before 1945

'Antisemitismus, Geschichte (Deutschland)', in *Jüdisches Lexikon: Ein enzyklopädisches Handbuch des jüdischen Wissens in vier Bänden*, vol. 1 (Berlin: Jüdischer Verlag, 1927), pp. 342–348.

Ausstellungs-, Messe- u. Fremdenverkehrs-Amt der Stadt Berlin (ed.), *Amtlicher Führer durch Berlin: Mit Plan der Innenstadt* (Berlin: abc, 1933).

Baumgart, Gertrud, *Frauenbewegung: Gestern und heute* (Heidelberg: C. Winter, 1933).

Baur, Erwin, Eugen Fischer, and Fritz Lenz, *Menschliche Erblichkeitslehre und Rassenhygiene*, vol. 1, 3rd edn (Munich: Lehmann, 1927).

Das Judentum in der Rechtswissenschaft: Ansprachen, Vorträge und Ergebnisse der Tagung der Reichsgruppe Hochschullehrer des NSRB am 3. und 4. Oktober 1936, vol. 1 (Berlin: Deutscher Rechtsverlag, 1936).

Die Kinder- und Hausmärchen der Brüder Grimm in ihrer Urgestalt, vol. 2 (Munich: Beck, 1913).

Dohm, Christian Wilhelm, *Concerning the Amelioration of the Civil Status of the Jews*, trans. Helen Lederer (Cincinnati, OH: Hebrew Union College, 1957 [German edn, 1781]).

Entscheidungen des Reichsgerichts in Zivilsachen, vol. 145 (Berlin/Leipzig: De Gruyter, 1935).

Europäischer Nationalitäten-Kongress: Sitzungsbericht des Kongresses der organisierten Nationalen Gruppen in den Staaten Europas, Bern, 16. bis 19. September 1933 (Vienna/Leipzig: Braumüller, 1934).

Feder, Gottfried, *The Programme of the N.S.D.A.P. and Its General Conceptions*, trans. E. T. S. Dugdale (Munich: Eher, 1932 [German edn, 1927]).

Feuchtwanger, Lion (ed.), *Der Gelbe Fleck: Die Ausrottung von 500 000 deutschen Juden* (Paris: Carrefour, 1936).

Fischer, Eugen, *Die Rehobother Bastards und das Bastardisierungsproblem beim Menschen* (Jena: Gustav Fischer, 1913).

Fraenkel, Ernst, *Der Doppelstaat: Recht und Justiz im 'Dritten Reich'* (Frankfurt am Main: Fischer, 1984 [English edn, 1941]).

Fraenkel, Ernst, *The Dual State: A Contribution to the Theory of Dictatorship* (New York: Oxford University Press, 1941).

Frank, Walter, *Deutsche Wissenschaft und Judenfrage: Schriften des Reichsinstituts für Geschichte des neuen Deutschlands* (Hamburg: Hanseatische Verlagsanstalt, 1937).

Frankenthal, Käthe, 'Ärzteschaft und Faschismus', *Der sozialistische Arzt*, vol. 8, no. 6 (1932), pp. 101–107.

Freisler, Roland, 'Ein Jahr Blutschutzrechtsprechung in Deutschland: Erfahrungen und Lehren', *Deutsches Strafrecht*, nos. 11–12 (Nov./Dec. 1936), pp. 385–397.

Frymann, Daniel [Heinrich Claß], *Wenn ich der Kaiser wär': Politische Wahrheiten und Notwendigkeiten* (Leipzig: Dieterich, 1912).

Gürtner, Franz (ed.), *Das kommende deutsche Strafrecht. Allgemeiner Teil: Bericht über die Arbeit der amtlichen Strafrechtskommission* (Berlin: Vahlen, 1934).

Gürtner, Franz (ed.), *Das kommende deutsche Strafrecht. Besonderer Teil: Bericht der amtlichen Strafrechtskommission* (Berlin: Vahlen, 1935).

Hauptmann, Gerhart, 'The Conflagration' [Der rote Hahn], in Ludwig Lewisohn (ed.), *The Dramatic Works of Gerhart Hauptmann*, 7 vols. (New York: B. W. Huebsch, 1912–1917), vol. 1: *Social Dramas*, pp. 511–649.

Heller, Abraham, *Die Lage der Juden in Rußland von der Märzrevolution 1917 bis zur Gegenwart* (Breslau: Marcus, 1935).

Henry, Matthew, *An Exposition of the Old and New Testaments: Wherein Each Chapter Is Preceded by an Analysis of Its Contents, the Sense Given and Largely Illustrated, with Practical Remarks and Observations*, vol. 2 (New York: H. C. Sleight, 1833).

Hilfsausschuss der Vereinigten Jüdischen Organisationen in Hamburg (ed.), *Hilfe und Aufbau in Hamburg: April 1933 bis Dezember 1934* (Hamburg: Hilfsausschuss der Vereinigten Jüdischen Organisationen in Hamburg, 1935).

Hitler, Adolf, *Mein Kampf*, trans. from German (New York: Reynal & Hitchcock, 1941 [German edn, 1925–1926]).

Jüdisches Lexikon: Ein enzyklopädisches Handbuch des jüdischen Wissens in vier Bänden, vol. 1 (Berlin: Jüdischer Verlag, 1927).

Keiser, Günther, 'Der jüngste Konzentrationsprozeß', *Die Wirtschaftskurve*, vol. 18 (1939), pp. 136–156.

Kerrl, Hanns (ed.), *Nationalsozialistisches Strafrecht: Denkschrift des Preußischen Justizministers* (Berlin: R. v. Decker, 1933).

Künneth, Walter, *Antwort auf den Mythus: Die Entscheidung zwischen dem nordischen Mythus und dem biblischen Christus* (Berlin: Wichern, 1935).

Lautsch, Hermann, and Hans Dornedden (eds.), *Verzeichnis der deutschen Ärzte und Heilanstalten: Reichs-Medizinal-Kalender für Deutschland*, part 2: *Zugleich Fortsetzung des Ärzteverzeichnisses des Verbandes der Ärzte Deutschlands (Hartmannbund)*, vol. 58 (Leipzig: Georg Thieme, 1937).

McDonald, James G., *Lettre de démission adressée au Secrétaire général de la Société des Nations: Avec une annexe contenant l'analyse des mesures prises en Allemagne contre les 'non-Aryens' et de leurs effets sur la question des réfugiés* (Geneva: n.pub., 1936).

Mały rocznik statystyczny Polski, wrzesień 1939 – czerwiec 1941 (Warsaw: Główny Urząd Statystyczny, 1990 [1941]).

Mann, Heinrich, *Es kommt der Tag: Deutsches Lesebuch*, ed. Peter-Paul Schneider (Frankfurt am Main: Fischer, 1992 [1936]).

Marr, Wilhelm, *Der Sieg des Judenthums über das Germanenenthum* (Bern: Costenoble, 1879).

Masaryk, Thomas G., *Zur russischen Geschichte und Religionsphilosophie: Soziologische Skizzen* (Jena: Diederichs, 1913).

Maunz, Theodor, *Gestalt und Recht der Polizei* (Hamburg: Hanseatische Verlagsanstalt, 1943).

Metternich, Klemens Wenzel Lothar von, 'Die Deutsche Frage: Genesis, Verlauf und gegenwärtiger Stand derselben. Denkschrift an Erzherzog Johann, Reichsverweser, London, August 1848', in Richard von Metternich-Winneburg (ed.), *Aus Metternichs nachgelassenen Papieren*, vol. 8 (Vienna: Braumüller, 1884), pp. 443–453.

Müller, Karl Alexander von, address in Walter Frank (ed.), *Deutsche Wissenschaft und Judenfrage: Schriften des Reichsinstituts für Geschichte des neuen Deutschlands* (Hamburg: Hanseatische Verlagsanstalt, 1937), pp. 5–14.

Neumann, Franz, *Behemoth: The Structure and Practice of National Socialism, 1933–1944* (Chicago: Ivan R. Dee, 2009 [German edn, 1942/1944]).

Oettinger, Eduard M., *Offenes Billet-doux an den berühmten Hepp-Hepp-Schreier und Juden-Fresser Herrn Wilhelm Richard Wagner* (Dresden: Wolf, 1869).

Preußisches Staatsministerium (ed.), *Preußische Gesetzessammlung* (Berlin: Decker, 1936).

Reichsbund jüdischer Frontsoldaten (ed.), *Die jüdischen Gefallenen des deutschen Heeres, der deutschen Marine und der deutschen Schutztruppen 1914–1918: Ein Gedenkbuch* (Berlin: Der Schild, 1932).

Rosenberg, Arthur, 'Treitschke und die Juden: Zur Soziologie der deutschen akademischen Reaktion', *Die Gesellschaft: Internationale Revue für Sozialismus und Politik*, vol. 7, no. 2 (July 1930), pp. 78–83.

Rumpelstilzchen [Adolf Stein], *Nee aber sowas! Rumpelstilzchen*, vol. 15: *1934/1935* (Berlin: Brunnen, 1935).

Schmidt, Kurt Dietrich (ed.), *Die Bekenntnisse und grundsätzlichen Äußerungen zur Kirchenfrage des Jahres 1933* (Göttingen: Vandenhoeck & Ruprecht, 1934).

Schnabel, Franz, *Deutsche Geschichte im neunzehnten Jahrhundert*, vol. 2: *Monarchie und Volkssouveränität* (Freiburg im Breisgau: Herder, 1933).

Schnabel, Franz, *Deutsche Geschichte im neunzehnten Jahrhundert*, vol. 3: *Erfahrungswissenschaft und Technik* (Freiburg im Breisgau: Herder, 1934).

Schuster, Hans, *Die Judenfrage in Rumänien* (Leipzig: Meiner, 1939).

Schwarz, Karl, *Die Juden in der Kunst* (Berlin: Der Heine-Bund, 1928).

Segel, Benjamin, *Rumänien und seine Juden: Zeitgemäße Studien* (Berlin: Nibelungen, 1918).

Silbergleit, Heinrich (ed.), *Die Bevölkerungs- und Berufsverhältnisse der Juden im*

Deutschen Reich, part 1: *Freistaat Preußen, Tabellen* (Berlin: Akademie, 1930).

Simmel, Georg, *Sociology: Inquiries into the Construction of Social Forms*, vol. 1, trans. and ed. Anthony J. Blasi, Anton K. Jacobs, and Mathew Kanjirathinkal (Leiden/Boston, MA: Brill, 2009 [German edn, 1908]).

Sitzungsberichte der 1. Arbeitstagung der Forschungsabteilung Judenfrage des Reichsinstituts für Geschichte des neuen Deutschlands vom 19. bis 21. November 1936 (Hamburg: Hanseatische Verlagsanstalt, 1937).

Sitzungsberichte der 2. Arbeitstagung der Forschungsabteilung Judenfrage des Reichsinstituts für Geschichte des neuen Deutschlands vom 12. bis 14. Mai 1937 (Hamburg: Hanseatische Verlagsanstalt, 1937).

Statistik des Deutschen Reichs, vol. 451: *Volks-, Berufs- und Betriebszählung vom 16. Juni 1933: Volkszählung. Die Bevölkerung des Deutschen Reichs nach den Ergebnissen der Volkszählung 1933*, no. 3: *Die Bevölkerung des Deutschen Reichs nach der Religionszugehörigkeit*, compiled by the Statistisches Reichsamt (Berlin: Verlag für Sozialpolitik, Wirtschaft und Statistik, 1936).

Statistik des Deutschen Reichs, vol. 451: *Volks-, Berufs- und Betriebszählung vom 16. Juni 1933: Volkszählung. Die Bevölkerung des Deutschen Reichs nach den Ergebnissen der Volkszählung 1933*, no. 5: *Die Glaubensjuden im Deutschen Reich*, compiled by the Statistisches Reichsamt (Berlin: Verlag für Sozialpolitik, Wirtschaft und Statistik, 1936).

Statistisches Jahrbuch der Stadt Berlin, vol. 14: *1938* (Berlin: Statistisches Amt der Reichshauptstadt Berlin/Kühn, 1939).

Statistisches Jahrbuch der Stadt Berlin, vol. 15: *1939* (Berlin: Statistisches Amt der Reichshauptstadt Berlin/Kühn, 1943).

Strack, Hermann L., *Das Blut im Glauben und Aberglauben der Menschheit: Mit besonderer Berücksichtigung der Volksmedizin und des jüdischen 'Blutritus'* (Munich: Beck, 1900 [1891]).

The Jewish Peril: Protocols of the Learned Elders of Zion, trans. George Shanks (London: Eyre & Spottiswoode, 1920 [Russian edn, 1905]).

Traub, Michael, *Die jüdische Auswanderung aus Deutschland: Westeuropa, Übersee, Palästina* (Berlin: Jüdische Rundschau, 1936).

Treitschke, Heinrich von, 'Our Prospects', in Marcel Stoetzler, *The State, the Nation, and the Jews: Liberalism and the Antisemitism Dispute in Bismarck's Germany* (Lincoln, NE: University of Nebraska Press, 2009), pp. 309–316.

Verwaltungsbericht des Vorstandes der Jüdischen Gemeinde zu Berlin für das Jahr 1937 ([Berlin]: M. Lessmann, [1937/1938]).

Zionisten-Congress in Basel (29–31 August 1897), Officielles Protocol (Vienna: Verlag des Vereines 'Erez Israel', 1898).

Primary Source Collections

Akten zur deutschen auswärtigen Politik 1918–1945, series C: *1933–1937*, vol. 4, no. 1: *1. April bis 13. September 1935* (Göttingen: Vandenhoeck & Ruprecht, 1975).

Akten zur deutschen auswärtigen Politik 1918–1945, series D: *1937–1945*, vol. 5: *Polen, Südosteuropa, Lateinamerika, Klein- und Mittelstaaten, Juni 1937 – März 1939* (Baden-Baden: Imprimerie Nationale, 1953).

Arendt, Hannah, and Heinrich Blücher, *Briefe 1936–1968*, ed. Lotte Köhler (Munich: Piper, 1996).

Behnken, Klaus (ed.), *Deutschland-Berichte der Sozialdemokratischen Partei Deutschlands (Sopade) 1934–1940*, 7 vols. (Frankfurt am Main: Zweitausendeins, 1980).

Behörde für Schule, Jugend und Berufsbildung, Amt für Schule, Hamburg (ed.), *'Aus Kindern werden Briefe': Dokumente zum Schicksal jüdischer Kinder und Jugendlicher in der NS-Zeit* (Hamburg: Hamburg Freie und Hansestadt Hamburg, Amt für Schule, 1999).

Bonhoeffer, Dietrich, *Dietrich Bonhoeffer Werke*, ed. Eberhard Bethge et al., vol. 12: *Berlin 1932–1933*, ed. Carsten Nicolaisen and Ernst-

Albert Scharffenorth (Munich: Chr. Kaiser, 1997).

Commission nationale pour la publication de documents diplomatiques suisses (ed.), *Documents Diplomatiques Suisses. Diplomatische Dokumente der Schweiz. Documenti Diplomatici Svizzeri 1848–1945*, vol. 11: *1934–1936*, ed. Mauro Cerutti, Jean-Claude Favez, and Michèle Fleury-Seemüller (Bern: Benteli, 1989).

Erhart, Hannelore, Ilse Meseberg-Haubold, and Dietgard Meyer, *Katharina Staritz, 1903–1953: Dokumentation*, vol. 1: *1903–1942* (Neukirchen-Vluyn: Neukirchener, 1999).

Eschwege, Helmut (ed.), *Kennzeichen J: Bilder, Dokumente, Berichte zur Geschichte der Verbrechen des Hitlerfaschismus an den deutschen Juden 1933–1945* ([East] Berlin: VEB Verlag der Wissenschaften, 1981).

Friedenberger, Martin, Klaus-Dieter Gössel, and Ebergard Schönknecht (eds.), *Die Reichsfinanzverwaltung im Nationalsozialismus: Darstellung und Dokumente* (Bremen: Temmen, 2002).

Friedlander, Henry, and Sybil Milton (eds.), *Archives of the Holocaust: An International Collection of Selected Documents*, vol. 7 (New York: Garland, 1990).

Friesel, Evyatar, *Atlas of Modern Jewish History* (New York/Oxford: Oxford University Press, 1990).

Geisel, Eike, and Henryk M. Broder, *Premiere und Pogrom: Der Jüdische Kulturbund 1933–1941. Texte und Bilder* (Berlin: Siedler, 1992).

Hartmannsgruber, Friedrich (ed.), *Akten der Reichskanzlei: Regierung Hitler, 1933–1945*, part 2: *1934/35*, vol. 2: *Juni bis Dezember 1935* (Munich: Oldenbourg, 1999).

Hartmannsgruber, Friedrich (ed.), *Akten der Reichskanzlei: Regierung Hitler, 1933–1945*, part 3: *1936* (Munich: Oldenbourg, 2002).

Hartmannsgruber, Friedrich (ed.), *Akten der Reichskanzlei: Regierung Hitler, 1933–1945*, part 4: *1937* (Munich: Oldenbourg, 2005).

Hepp, Michael (ed.), *Die Ausbürgerung deutscher Staatsangehöriger 1933–1945 nach den im Reichsanzeiger veröffentlichten Listen*, 3 vols. (Munich: Saur, 1985–1988).

Hofer, Walther (ed.), *Der Nationalsozialismus: Dokumente 1933–1945*, new edn (Frankfurt am Main: Fischer, 1988 [1957]).

Institut für Zeitgeschichte (eds.), *Akten der Partei-Kanzlei der NSDAP*, part 1, vol. 2 (Munich: Oldenbourg, 1983).

Institut für Zeitgeschichte, Munich, and Research Foundation for Jewish Immigration, New York, *International Biographical Dictionary of Central European Emigrés, 1933–1945*, 3 vols. (Munich: Saur, 1999 [1980–1983]).

Jäckel, Eberhard, and Axel Kuhn (eds.), *Hitler: Sämtliche Aufzeichnungen* (Stuttgart: Deutsche Verlags-Anstalt, 1980).

Kommission für Zeitgeschichte (ed.), *Akten deutscher Bischöfe über die Lage der Kirche 1933–1945*, vol. 2: *1934–1935*, ed. Bernhard Stasiewski (Mainz: Matthias Grünewald, 1976).

Kommission zur Erforschung der Geschichte der Frankfurter Juden (ed.), *Dokumente zur Geschichte der Frankfurter Juden 1933–1945* (Frankfurt am Main: Kramer, 1963).

Kotze, Hildegard von, and Helmut Krausnick (eds.), *'Es spricht der Führer': Sieben exemplarische Hitler-Reden* (Gütersloh: Sigbert Mohn, 1966).

Krieger, Karsten (ed.), *Der 'Berliner Antisemitismusstreit' 1879–1881: Eine Kontroverse um die Zugehörigkeit der deutschen Juden zur Nation. Eine kommentierte Quellenedition*, 2 vols. (Munich: Saur, 2003).

Kulka, Otto Dov (ed.), *Deutsches Judentum unter dem Nationalsozialismus*, vol. 1: *Dokumente zur Geschichte der Reichsvertretung der deutschen Juden 1933–1939* (Tübingen: Mohr Siebeck, 1997).

Kulka, Otto Dov, and Eberhard Jäckel (eds.), *The Jews in the Secret Nazi Reports on Popular Opinion in Germany, 1933–1945*, trans. William Templer (New Haven, CT/London: Yale University Press, 2010 [German edn, 2004]).

Landesarchivverwaltung Rheinland-Pfalz in association with the Landesarchiv Saarbrücken (ed.), *Dokumentation zur Geschichte der jüdischen Bevölkerung in Rheinland-Pfalz und im Saarland von 1800 bis 1945*, vol. 6 (Koblenz: Landesarchivverwaltung Rheinland-Pfalz, 1974).

List, Friedrich, *Schriften, Reden, Briefe*, vol. 1: *Der Kampf um die politische und ökonomische Reform 1815-25* (Aalen: Scientia, 1971).

Michaelis, Herbert, and Ernst Schraepler (eds.), *Ursachen und Folgen: Vom deutschen Zusammenbruch 1918 und 1945 bis zur staatlichen Neuordnung Deutschlands in der Gegenwart. Eine Urkunden- und Dokumentensammlung zur Zeitgeschichte*, vol. 9: *Das Dritte Reich: Die Zertrümmerung des Parteienstaates und die Grundlegung der Diktatur* (Berlin: Wendler, 1964); vol. 11: *Das Dritte Reich: Innere Gleichschaltung. Der Staat und die Kirchen. Antikominternpakt – Achse Rom-Berlin. Der Weg ins großdeutsche Reich* (Berlin: Wendler, 1966).

Minuth, Karl Heinz (ed.), *Akten der Reichskanzlei: Regierung Hitler, 1933-1938*, part 1: *1933/34*, vol. 1: *30. Januar bis 31. August 1933* (Munich: Oldenbourg, 1983).

Mommsen, Hans, and Susanne Willems (eds.), *Herrschaftsalltag im Dritten Reich: Studien und Texte* (Düsseldorf: Schwann, 1988).

Noam, Ernst, and Wolf-Arno Kropat (eds.), *Juden vor Gericht, 1933-1945: Dokumente aus hessischen Justizakten* (Wiesbaden: Kommission für die Geschichte der Juden in Hessen, 1975).

Pätzold, Kurt (ed.), *Verfolgung, Vertreibung, Vernichtung: Dokumente des faschistischen Antisemitismus 1933-1942* (Leipzig: Reclam, 1983).

Pross, Harry (ed.), *Die Zerstörung der deutschen Politik: Dokumente 1871-1933* (Frankfurt am Main: Fischer, 1959).

Regge, Jürgen, and Werner Schubert (eds.), *Quellen zur Reform des Straf- und Strafprozeßrechts*, part 2: *NS-Zeit (1933-1939) Strafgesetzbuch*, vol. 2: *Protokolle der Strafrechtskommission des Reichsjustizministeriums* (Berlin: De Gruyter, 1988).

Richarz, Monika (ed.), *Bürger auf Widerruf: Lebenszeugnisse deutscher Juden 1780-1945* (Munich: Beck, 1989).

Rürup, Reinhard (ed.), *1936: Die Olympischen Spiele und der Nationalsozialismus. Eine Dokumentation* (Berlin: Argon, 1996).

Sammons Jeffrey L. (ed.), *Die Protokolle der Weisen von Zion: Die Grundlage des modernen Antisemitismus – eine Fälschung. Text und Kommentar* (Göttingen: Wallstein, 1998).

Sauer, Paul (ed.), *Dokumente über die Verfolgung der jüdischen Bürger in Baden-Württemberg durch das nationalsozialistische Regime 1933-1945*, vols. 1 and 2 (Stuttgart: W. Kohlhammer, 1966).

Staff, Ilse (ed.), *Justiz im Dritten Reich: Eine Dokumentation* (Frankfurt am Main: Fischer, 1978).

Volk, Ludwig (ed.), *Akten Kardinal Michael von Faulhabers*, vol. 1 (Mainz: Matthias Grünewald, 1975).

Walk, Joseph (ed.), *Das Sonderrecht für die Juden im NS-Staat: Eine Sammlung der gesetzlichen Maßnahmen und Richtlinien. Inhalt und Bedeutung* (Heidelberg: Müller Juristischer, 1981).

Weiss, Georg (ed.), *Einige Dokumente zur Rechtsstellung der Juden und zur Entziehung ihres Vermögens 1933-1945* (Berlin: n.pub., 1954).

Weltsch, Robert, *Tragt ihn mit Stolz, den gelben Fleck: Eine Aufsatzreihe der 'Jüdischen Rundschau' zur Lage der deutschen Juden* (Nördlingen: Greno, 1988).

Wildt, Michael (ed.), *Die Judenpolitik des SD 1935 bis 1938: Eine Dokumentation* (Munich: Oldenbourg, 1995).

Secondary Literature

Adam, Uwe Dietrich, *Judenpolitik im Dritten Reich* (Düsseldorf: Droste, 1972).

Adam, Uwe Dietrich, 'An Overall Plan for Anti-Jewish Legislation in the Third Reich?', *Yad Vashem Studies*, vol. 11 (1976), pp. 33-55.

Adler, H. G., *Der verwaltete Mensch: Studien zur Deportation der Juden aus Deutschland* (Tübingen: Mohr, 1974).

Adler-Rudel, Salomon, *Jüdische Selbsthilfe unter dem Naziregime 1933–1939: Im Spiegel der Berichte der Reichsvertretung der Juden in Deutschland* (Tübingen: Mohr, 1974).

Ahlheim, Hannah, *'Deutsche, kauft nicht bei Juden!' Antisemitismus und politischer Boykott in Deutschland 1924 bis 1935* (Göttingen: Wallstein, 2011).

Aly, Götz, *Why the Germans? Why the Jews? Envy, Race Hatred, and the Prehistory of the Holocaust*, trans. Jefferson Chase (New York: Metropolitan, 2014 [German edn, 2011]).

Aly, Götz, and Karl Heinz Roth, *Die restlose Erfassung: Volkszählen, Identifizieren, Aussondern im Nationalsozialismus*, new edn (Frankfurt am Main: Fischer, 2000 [1984]).

Angress, Werner T., 'Das deutsche Militär und die Juden 1914–1918', *Militärgeschichtliche Mitteilungen*, vol. 19 (1976), pp. 77–146.

Angress, Werner T., *Between Fear and Hope: Jewish Youth and the Third Reich*, trans. Christine Granger (New York: Columbia University Press, 1988 [German edn, 1985]).

Appelbaum, Peter G., *Loyal Sons: Jews in the German Army in the Great War* (Edgware/Portland, OR: Vallentine Mitchell, 2014).

Arendt, Hannah, *The Origins of Totalitarianism*, new edn (New York: Harcourt, 1973 [1951]).

Arendt, Hannah, *Rahel Varnhagen: The Life of a Jewess*, ed. Liliane Weissberg, new edn (Baltimore, MD: Johns Hopkins University Press, 1997 [1957]).

Aschheim, Steven E., *Brothers and Strangers: The East European Jew in German and German Jewish Consciousness, 1800–1923* (Madison, WI: University of Wisconsin Press, 1982).

Babel, Isaak, *Exemplarische Erzählungen: Erwachen – Geschichten aus Odessa – Die Reiterarmee – Petersburg – Paris und ich* (Vienna: Europaverlag, 1985).

Bajohr, Frank, *Aryanisation in Hamburg: The Economic Exclusion of Jews and the Confiscation of their Property in Nazi Germany* (New York/Oxford: Berghahn, 2002).

Bajohr, Frank, *'Unser Hotel ist judenfrei': Bäder-Antisemitismus im 19. und 20. Jahrhundert* (Frankfurt am Main: Fischer, 2003).

Bajohr, Frank, and Dieter Pohl, *Der Holocaust als offenes Geheimnis: Die Deutschen, die NS-Führung und die Alliierten* (Munich: Beck, 2006).

Bankier, David (ed.), *Probing the Depths of German Anti-Semitism: German Society and the Persecution of the Jews, 1933–1941* (New York: Berghahn, 1999).

Barkai, Avraham, *From Boycott to Annihilation: The Economic Struggle of German Jews, 1933–1943*, trans. William Templer (Hanover, NH: University Press of New England, 1989 [German edn, 1987]).

Barkai, Avraham, *'Wehr Dich!' Der Centralverein deutscher Staatsbürger Jüdischen Glaubens (C.V.) 1893–1938* (Munich: Beck, 2002).

Barkai, Avraham, *Oscar Wassermann und die Deutsche Bank: Bankier in schwieriger Zeit* (Munich: Beck, 2005).

Barkai, Avraham, 'Jewish Self-Help in Nazi Germany, 1933–1939: The Dilemmas of Cooperation', in Francis R. Nicosia and David Scrase (eds.), *Jewish Life in Nazi Germany: Dilemmas and Responses* (New York: Berghahn, 2012), pp. 71–88

Barkai, Avraham, and Paul Mendes-Flohr, *Deutsch-Jüdische Geschichte in der Neuzeit*, vol. 4: *Aufbruch und Zerstörung 1918–1945* (Munich: Beck, 1997).

Barkow, Ben, *Alfred Wiener and the Making of the Holocaust Library* (London: Vallentine Mitchell, 1997).

Bartal, Israel, *The Jews of Eastern Europe, 1772–1881*, trans. Chaya Naor (Philadelphia, PA: University of Pennsylvania Press, 2002 [Hebrew edn, 2002]).

Barth, Hans Paul, 'Gesellschaftliche Voraussetzungen des Antisemitismus', in Werner E. Mosse (ed.), *Entscheidungsjahr 1932: Zur Judenfrage in der Endphase der Weimarer Republik* (Tübingen: Mohr, 1966), pp. 135–155.

Bauer, Yehuda, *My Brother's Keeper: A History of the American Jewish Joint Distribution Committee, 1929–1939* (Philadelphia, PA: Jewish Publication Society of America, 1974).

Beddies, Thomas (ed.), *Jüdische Ärztinnen und Ärzte im Nationalsozialismus: Entrechtung, Vertreibung, Ermordung* (Berlin: De Gruyter, 2014).

Bennathan, Esra, 'Demographische und wirtschaftliche Struktur der Juden', in Werner E. Mosse (ed.), *Entscheidungsjahr 1932: Zur Judenfrage in der Endphase der Weimarer Republik* (Tübingen: Mohr, 1966), pp. 87–131.

Benz, Wolfgang, Arnold Paucker, and Peter Pulzer (eds.), *Jüdisches Leben in der Weimarer Republik / Jews in the Weimar Republic* (Tübingen: Mohr Siebeck, 1998).

Berg, Matthias, *Karl Alexander von Müller: Historiker für den Nationalsozialismus* (Göttingen: Vandenhoeck & Ruprecht, 2014).

Beutner, Gunnar, 'Das Pogrom von Gunzenhausen 1934: Anfänge des NS-Terrors in Westmittelfranken', in Heike Tagsold (ed.), *'Was brauchen wir einen Befehl, wenn es gegen die Juden geht?' Das Pogrom von Gunzenhausen 1934* (Nuremberg: ANTOGO, 2006), pp. 7–30.

Birnbaum, Pierre, and Ira Katznelson (eds.), *Paths of Emancipation: Jews, States, and Citizenships* (Princeton, NJ: Princeton University Press, 1995).

Blau, Bruno, *Das Ausnahmerecht für die Juden in Deutschland 1933–1945* (Düsseldorf: Verlag Allgemeine Wochenzeitung der Juden in Deutschland, 1965).

Block, Ernst, *'Wir waren eine glückliche Familie': Zur Geschichte und den Schicksalen der Juden in Salzwedel/Altmark* (Salzwedel: Renner & Meineke, 1998).

Boas, Jacob, 'The Shrinking World of German Jewry, 1933–1938', *Leo Baeck Institute Year Book*, vol. 31 (1986), pp. 241–266.

Boehlich, Walter (ed.), *Der Berliner Antisemitismusstreit* (Frankfurt am Main: Insel, 1965).

Bornemann, Elke, *Der Frieden von Bukarest 1918* (Frankfurt am Main: Peter Lang, 1978).

Borut, Jacob, 'Antisemitism in Tourist Facilities in Weimar Germany', *Yad Vashem Studies*, vol. 28 (2000), pp. 7–50.

Bracher, Karl Dietrich, *The German Dictatorship: Origins, Structure, and Consequences of National Socialism*, trans. Jean Steinberg (New York: Praeger, 1970 [German edn, 1969]).

Brechtken, Magnus et al. (eds.), *Die Nürnberger Gesetze – 80 Jahre danach: Vorgeschichte, Entstehung, Auswirkungen* (Göttingen: Wallstein, 2017).

Breitman, Richard D., and Alan M. Kraut, *American Refugee Policy and European Jewry, 1933–1945* (Bloomington: Indiana University Press, 1987).

Brenner, Michael, *The Renaissance of Jewish Culture in Weimar Germany* (New Haven, CT/London: Yale University Press, 1996).

Broszat, Martin, *The Hitler State: The Foundation and Development of the Internal Structure of the Third Reich*, trans. John W. Hiden (London: Longman, 1981 [German edn, 1969]).

Broszat, Martin, 'Zur Erklärung des nationalsozialistischen Judenmords', in Hermann Graml and Klaus-Dietmar Henke (eds.), *Nach Hitler: Der schwierige Umgang mit unserer Geschichte. Beiträge von Martin Broszat* (Munich: Oldenbourg, 1988 [1986]).

Browder, George C., *Foundations of the Nazi State: The Formation of Sipo and SD* (Lexington, KY: University Press of Kentucky, 1990).

Brustein, William I., *Roots of Hate: Anti-Semitism in Europe before the Holocaust* (Cambridge: Cambridge University Press, 2003).

Buchheim, Hans, 'The SS: Instrument of Domination', in Hans Buchheim, Martin Broszat, Hans-Adolf Jacobsen, and Helmut Krausnick, *Anatomy of the SS State*, trans. Richard Barry, Marian Jackson, and Dorothy Long (London: Collins, 1968 [German edn, 1965]), pp. 127–301.

Bullock, Alan, *Hitler: A Study in Tyranny* (London: Hamlyn, 1973).

Bund der Antifaschisten, Region Dresden, and Helfried Wehner (eds.), *Radeberger Land unterm Hakenkreuz: Fakten und Ereignisse aus unserer Stadt und umliegenden Orten während des 'Dritten Reiches'* (n.p.: privately published, n.d. [c.1999]).

Burleigh, Michael, *The Third Reich: A New History* (London: Macmillan, 2000).

Dahm, Volker, *Das jüdische Buch im Dritten Reich*, 2nd edn (Munich: Beck, 1993).

Dalaman, Cem, 'Die Türkei in ihrer Modernisierungsphase als Fluchtland für deutsche Exilanten', doctoral thesis, Freie Universität, Berlin, 1998: http://www.diss.fu-berlin.de/diss/receive/FUDISS_thesis_000000000526 (2001).

Dams, Carsten, and Michael Stolle, *The Gestapo: Power and Terror in the Third Reich* (Oxford: Oxford University Press, 2014)

Deichmann, Ute, *Biologen unter Hitler: Vertreibung, Karrieren, Forschung* (Frankfurt am Main: Campus, 1992).

Ericksen, Robert P., *Theologians under Hitler: Gerhard Kittel, Paul Althaus and Emanuel Hirsch* (New Haven, CT/London: Yale University Press, 1985).

Essner, Cornelia, *Die 'Nürnberger Gesetze' oder die Verwaltung des Rassenwahns 1933-1945* (Paderborn: Schöningh, 2002).

Evans, Richard J., *The Third Reich in Power, 1933-1939* (London: Allen Lane, 2005).

Falter, Jürgen W., *Hitlers Wähler* (Munich: Beck, 1991).

Feilchenfeld, Werner, Dolf Michaelis, and Ludwig Pinner, *Haavara-Transfer nach Palästina und Einwanderung deutscher Juden 1933-1939* (Tübingen: Mohr, 1972).

Fetheringill Zwicker, Lisa, *Dueling Students: Conflict, Masculinity, and Politics in German Universities* (Ann Arbor, MI: University of Michigan Press, 2011), pp. 103-117.

Fine, David J., *Jewish Integration in the German Army in the First World War* (Berlin: De Gruyter, 2012).

Fink, Carole, *Defending the Rights of Others: The Great Powers, the Jews, and International Minority Protection, 1878-1938* (Cambridge: Cambridge University Press, 2004).

Fischer, Albert, 'Jüdische Privatbanken im "Dritten Reich"', *Scripta Mercaturae*, vol. 28, nos. 1-2 (1994), pp. 1-54.

Frei, Norbert, *National Socialist Rule in Germany: The Führer State, 1933-1945*, trans. Simon B. Steyne (Oxford: Blackwell, 1993 [German edn, 1987]).

Friedländer, Saul, *Nazi Germany and the Jews*, vol. 1: *The Years of Persecution, 1933-1939* (New York: HarperCollins, 1997).

Friedländer, Saul, *Nazi Germany and the Jews*, vol. 2: *The Years of Extermination, 1939-1945* (New York: HarperCollins, 2007).

Friedrich, Eckhardt, and Dagmar Schmieder-Friedrich (eds.), *Die Gailinger Juden: Materialien zur Geschichte der jüdischen Gemeinde Gailingen aus ihrer Blütezeit und den Jahren der gewaltsamen Auflösung* (Konstanz: Arbeitskreis für Regionalgeschichte e.V., 1981).

Fritsch-Vivié, Gabriele, *Gegen alle Widerstände: Der Jüdische Kulturbund 1933-1941* (Berlin: Hentrich & Hentrich, 2013).

Gerlach, Christian, *The Extermination of the European Jews* (Cambridge: Cambridge University Press, 2016).

Gerwarth, Robert, *Hitler's Hangman: The Life of Heydrich* (New Haven, CT: Yale University Press, 2011).

Gellately, Robert, *The Gestapo and German Society: Enforcing Racial Policy, 1933-1945* (Oxford: Clarendon, 1990).

Gellately, Robert, *Backing Hitler: Consent and Coercion in Nazi Germany* (Oxford/New York: Oxford University Press, 2001).

Gerwarth, Robert, and John Horne (eds.), *War in Peace: Paramilitary Violence in Europe after the Great War* (Oxford/New York: Oxford University Press, 2012).

Giles, Geoffrey J., *Students and National Socialism in Germany* (Princeton, NJ: Princeton University Press, 1985).

Graf, Philipp, 'Die "Bernheim-Petition" 1933: Ein Fall jüdischer Diplomatiegeschichte', *Leipziger Beiträge zur jüdischen Geschichte und Kultur*, vol. 2 (2004), pp. 283-299.

Grady, Tim, *The German-Jewish Soldiers of the First World War in History and Memory* (Liverpool: Liverpool University Press, 2011).

Grady, Tim, *A Deadly Legacy: German Jews and the Great War* (New Haven, CT: Yale University Press, 2017).

Gruner, Wolf, 'Die Reichshauptstadt und die Verfolgung der Berliner Juden 1933–1945', in Reinhard Rürup (ed.), *Jüdische Geschichte in Berlin: Essays und Studien* (Berlin: Hentrich, 1995), pp. 229–266.

Gruner, Wolf, 'Die NS-Judenverfolgung und die Kommunen: Zur wechselseitigen Dynamisierung von zentraler und lokaler Politik 1933–1941', *Vierteljahrshefte für Zeitgeschichte*, vol. 48, no. 1 (Jan. 2000), pp. 75–126.

Gruner, Wolf, *Öffentliche Wohlfahrt und Judenverfolgung: Wechselwirkung lokaler und zentraler Politik im NS-Staat (1933–1942)* (Munich: Oldenbourg, 2002).

Grüttner, Michael, *Studenten im Dritten Reich* (Paderborn: Schöningh, 1995).

Grüttner, Michael, and Sven Kinas, 'Die Vertreibung von Wissenschaftlern aus den deutschen Universitäten', *Vierteljahrshefte für Zeitgeschichte*, vol. 55, no. 1 (Jan. 2007), pp. 123–188.

Haumann, Heiko, *A History of East European Jews*, trans. James Patterson (New York: Central European University Press, 2002 [German edn, 1998]).

Heiber, Helmut, *Walter Frank und sein Reichsinstitut für Geschichte des neuen Deutschlands* (Stuttgart: Deutsche Verlags-Anstalt, 1966).

Heim, Susanne, '"Deutschland muß ihnen ein Land ohne Zukunft sein": Die Zwangsmigration der Juden 1933 bis 1938', in Eberhard Jungfer et al. (eds.), *Arbeitsmigration und Flucht: Vertreibung und Arbeitskräfteregulierung in Zwischeneuropa* (Berlin: Schwarze Risse; Göttingen: Rote Strasse, 1993), pp. 48–81.

Herbert, Ulrich, '"Generation der Sachlichkeit": Die völkische Studentenbewegung der frühen zwanziger Jahre', in *Arbeit, Volkstum, Weltanschauung: Über Fremde und Deutsche im 20. Jahrhundert* (Frankfurt am Main: Fischer, 1995), pp. 31–58.

Herbert, Ulrich, *Best: Biographische Studien über Radikalismus, Weltanschauung und Vernunft 1903–1989* (Bonn: Dietz, 1996).

Herbert, Ulrich, *Geschichte der Ausländerpolitik in Deutschland: Saisonarbeiter, Zwangsarbeiter, Gastarbeiter, Flüchtlinge* (Munich: Beck, 2001).

Herbst, Ludolf, *Das nationalsozialistische Deutschland 1933–1945* (Frankfurt am Main: Suhrkamp, 1996).

Herrmann, Klaus J., *Das Dritte Reich und die deutsch-jüdischen Organisationen 1933–1934* (Cologne: Heymanns, 1969).

Heuberger, Georg, and Fritz Backhaus (eds.), *Leo Baeck 1873–1956: Aus dem Stamme von Rabbinern* (Frankfurt am Main: Jüdischer Verlag, 2001).

Hilberg, Raul, *The Destruction of the European Jews*, vol. 1, 3rd edn (New Haven, CT/London: Yale University Press, 2003 [1961]).

Hildebrand, Klaus, *Das vergangene Reich: Deutsche Außenpolitik von Bismarck bis Hitler, 1871–1945* (Stuttgart: Deutsche Verlags-Anstalt, 1995).

Hildebrand, Klaus, *The Third Reich*, trans. P. S. Falla (London: G. Allen & Unwin, 1984 [German edn, 1979]).

James, Harold, *Die Deutsche Bank und die 'Arisierung'* (Munich: Beck, 2001).

Jarausch, Konrad H., 'Jewish Lawyers in Germany, 1848–1938: The Disintegration of a Profession', *Leo Baeck Institute Year Book*, vol. 36 (1991), pp. 171–190.

Jochmann, Werner, *Gesellschaftskrise und Judenfeindschaft in Deutschland* (Hamburg: Christians, 1988).

Johnson, Eric A., *Nazi Terror: The Gestapo, Jews, and Ordinary Germans* (New York: Basic, 2000).

Kampe, Norbert, *Studenten und 'Judenfrage' im deutschen Kaiserreich: Die Entstehung einer akademischen Trägerschicht des Antisemitismus* (Göttingen: Vandenhoeck & Ruprecht, 1988).

Kaplan, Marion A., *Between Dignity and Despair: Jewish Life in Nazi Germany* (Oxford: Oxford University Press, 1998).

Kempter, Klaus, *Joseph Wulf: Ein Historikerschicksal in Deutschland* (Göttingen: Vandenhoeck & Ruprecht, 2013).

Kershaw, Ian, *Hitler, 1889-1936: Hubris* (London: Allen Lane, 1998).

Klemperer, Victor, *The Language of the Third Reich: LTI, Lingua Tertii Imperii: A Philologist's Notebook*, trans. Martin Brady (London: Athlone, 2000 [German edn, 1947]).

Knütter, Hans-Helmuth, 'Die Linksparteien', in Werner E. Mosse (ed.), *Entscheidungsjahr 1932: Zur Judenfrage in der Endphase der Weimarer Republik* (Tübingen: Mohr, 1966), pp. 323-345.

Koselleck, Reinhart, 'Deutschland – Eine verspätete Nation?', in *Zeitschichten: Studien zur Historik* (Frankfurt am Main: Suhrkamp, 2003), pp. 359-380.

Krach, Tillmann, *Jüdische Rechtsanwälte in Preußen: Über die Bedeutung der freien Advokatur und ihre Zerstörung durch den Nationalsozialismus* (Munich: Beck, 1991).

Kraus, Hans-Joachim, 'Die evangelische Kirche', in Werner E. Mosse (ed.), *Entscheidungsjahr 1932: Zur Judenfrage in der Endphase der Weimarer Republik* (Tübingen: Mohr, 1966), pp. 249-270.

Kreutzmüller, Christoph, *Ausverkauf: Die Vernichtung der jüdischen Gewerbetätigkeit in Berlin 1930-1945* (Berlin: Metropol, 2012).

Kümmel, Werner F., 'Die Ausschaltung rassisch und politisch missliebiger Ärzte', in Fridolf Kudlien (ed.), *Ärzte im Nationalsozialismus* (Cologne: Kiepenheuer und Witsch, 1985), pp. 56-81.

Kwiet, Konrad, 'Gehen oder bleiben? Die deutschen Juden am Wendepunkt', in Walter Pehle (ed.), *Der Judenpogrom 1938: Von der 'Reichskristallnacht' zum Völkermord* (Frankfurt am Main: Fischer, 1988), pp. 132-145.

Lambart, Friedrich (ed.), *Tod eines Pianisten: Karlrobert Kreiten und der Fall Werner Höfer* (Berlin: Hentrich, 1988).

Leibfried, Stephan, and Florian Tennstedt, *Berufsverbote und Sozialpolitik 1933: Die Auswirkungen der nationalsozialistischen Machtergreifung auf die Krankenkassenverwaltung und die Kassenärzte* (Bremen: Universität Bremen, 1979).

Leiser, Erwin, *'Deutschland Erwache!' Propaganda und Film des Dritten Reiches*, new edn (Reinbek bei Hamburg: Rowohlt, 1978 [1968]).

Liepach, Martin, *Das Wahlverhalten der jüdischen Bevölkerung: Zur politischen Orientierung der Juden in der Weimarer Republik* (Tübingen: Mohr, 1996).

Lohalm, Uwe, *Völkischer Radikalismus: Die Geschichte des Deutschvölkischen Schutz- und Trutzbundes 1919-1923* (Hamburg: Leibniz, 1970).

Lohalm, Uwe, *Fürsorge und Verfolgung: Öffentliche Wohlfahrtsverwaltung und nationalsozialistische Judenpolitik in Hamburg 1933 bis 1942* (Hamburg: Ergebnisse, 1998).

Longerich, Peter, *Politik der Vernichtung: Eine Gesamtdarstellung der nationalsozialistischen Judenverfolgung* (Munich: Piper, 1998).

Longerich, Peter, *Holocaust: The Nazi Persecution and Murder of the Jews*, trans. Shaun Whiteside, new edn (Oxford: Oxford University Press, 2010 [German edn, 1998]).

Longerich, Peter, *Heinrich Himmler: A Life*, trans. Jeremy Noakes and Lesley Sharpe (Oxford: Oxford University Press, 2012 [German edn, 2008]).

Loose, Ingo, 'Verfemt und vergessen: Abraham Hellers Dissertation "Die Lage der Juden in Rußland von der Märzrevolution 1917 bis zur Gegenwart" an der Berliner Universität 1934-1992', *Jahrbuch für Antisemitismusforschung*, vol. 14 (2005), pp. 219-241.

Maurer, Trude, *Ostjuden in Deutschland: 1918-1933* (Hamburg: Christians, 1986).

Mendelsohn, Ezra, *The Jews of East-Central Europe between the World Wars* (Bloomington: Indiana University Press, 1983).

Mendes Flohr, Paul R., and Jehuda Reinhard, *The Jew in the Modern World: A Documentary History* (Oxford: Oxford University Press, 1995).

Meyer, Beate, 'Jüdische Mischlinge': Rassenpolitik und Verfolgungserfahrung 1933–1945 (Hamburg: Dölling und Galitz, 1999).

Meyer, Michael A., Response to Modernity: A History of the Reform Movement in Judaism (Detroit, MI: Wayne State University Press, 1988).

Michalczyk, John J. (ed.), Nazi Law: From Nuremberg to Nuremberg (London: Bloomsbury Academic, 2017).

Miron, Guy, The Waning of Emancipation: Jewish History, Memory, and the Rise of Fascism in Germany, France, and Hungary (Detroit, MI: Wayne State University Press, 2011).

Möller, Horst, Exodus der Kultur: Schriftsteller, Wissenschaftler und Künstler in der Emigration nach 1933 (Munich: Beck, 1984).

Möller, Horst, Die Weimarer Republik: Eine unvollendete Demokratie, 8th edn (Munich: dtv, 2006 [1985]).

Mommsen, Hans, 'Cumulative Radicalisation and Progressive Self-Destruction as Structural Determinants of the Nazi Dictatorship', in Ian Kershaw and Moshe Lewin (eds.), Stalinism and Nazism: Dictatorships in Comparison (Cambridge: Cambridge University Press, 1997), pp. 75–87.

Mommsen, Hans, 'The Realization of the Unthinkable: The "Final Solution of the Jewish Question" in the Third Reich', in Gerhard Hirschfeld (ed.), The Policies of Genocide: Jews and Soviet Prisoners of War in Nazi Germany (London: Allen & Unwin, 1986), pp. 97–144.

Mommsen, Hans, Das NS-Regime und die Auslöschung des Judentums in Europa (Göttingen: Wallstein, 2014).

Morris, Douglas G., 'Discrimination, Degradation, Defiance: Jewish Lawyers under Nazism', in Alan E. Steinweis and Robert D. Rachlin (eds.), The Law in Nazi Germany: Ideology, Opportunism, and the Perversion of Justice (New York: Berghahn, 2015).

Mosse, Werner E. (ed.), Entscheidungsjahr 1932: Zur Judenfrage in der Endphase der Weimarer Republik (Tübingen: Mohr, 1966).

Müller, Klaus-Jürgen, Das Heer und Hitler: Armee und nationalsozialistisches Regime 1933–1940 (Stuttgart: Deutsche, 1969).

Neliba, Gunter, Wilhelm Frick: Der Legalist des Unrechtsstaates. Eine politische Biographie (Paderborn: Schöningh, 1992).

Nicosia, Francis R., The Third Reich and the Palestine Question, new edn (New Brunswick, NJ/London: Transaction, 2000 [1985]).

Niewyk, Donald L., The Jews in Weimar Germany, new edn (New Brunswick, NJ/London: Transaction, 2001 [1980]).

Noach, Franck, Veit Harlan: The Life and Work of a Nazi Filmmaker (Lexington, KY: University Press of Kentucky, 2016).

Nolte, Ernst, Three Faces of Fascism: Action Française, Italian Fascism, National Socialism, trans. Leila Vennewitz (New York: Holt, Rinehart & Winston, 1966 [German edn, 1963]).

Nolzen, Armin, 'The Nazi Party and Its Violence against the Jews, 1933–1938/39: Violence as a Historiographical Concept', Yad Vashem Studies, vol. 31 (2003), pp. 245–285.

Olsen, Niklas, History in the Plural: An Introduction to the Work of Reinhart Kolloseck (New York: Berghahn, 2012).

Pätzold, Kurt, Faschismus, Rassenwahn, Judenverfolgung: Eine Studie zur politischen Strategie und Taktik des faschistischen Imperialismus 1933–1935 (Berlin: Deutscher Verlag der Wissenschaften, 1975).

Prieberg, Fred K., Musik im NS-Staat (Frankfurt am Main: Fischer, 1982).

Przyrembel, Alexandra, 'Rassenschande': Reinheitsmythos und Vernichtungslegitimation im Nationalsozialismus (Göttingen: Vandenhoeck & Ruprecht, 2003).

Pulzer, Peter G. J., The Rise of Political Anti-Semitism in Germany and Austria (New York: J. Wiley, 1964).

Richter, Gabriel, 'Blindheit und Eugenik: Zwischen Widerstand und Integration', in Blinde unterm Hakenkreuz: Erkennen, Trauern, Begegnen (Marburg an der Lahn: Deutscher Verein der Blinden und Sehbehinderten in Studium und Beruf, 1991), pp. 16–34.

Roller, Walter, and Susanne Höschel (eds.), *Judenverfolgung und jüdisches Leben unter den Bedingungen der nationalsozialistischen Gewaltherrschaft*, vol. 1 (Potsdam: Verlag für Berlin-Brandenburg, 1997).

Rosenstock, Werner, 'Exodus, 1933–1939: A Survey of Jewish Emigration from Germany', *Leo Baeck Institute Year Book*, vol. 1 (1956), pp. 373–390.

Rosenthal, Jacob, *'Die Ehre des jüdischen Soldaten': Die Judenzählung im Ersten Weltkrieg und ihre Folgen* (Frankfurt am Main: Campus, 2007).

Rovit, Rebecca, *The Jewish Kulturbund Theatre Company in Nazi Berlin* (Iowa City, IA: University of Iowa Press, 2012).

Rürup, Reinhard, *Emanzipation und Antisemitismus: Studien zur 'Judenfrage' der bürgerlichen Gesellschaft* (Göttingen: Vandenhoeck & Ruprecht, 1975).

Rürup, Reinhard, 'Emanzipation und Krise: Zur Geschichte der "Judenfrage" in Deutschland vor 1890', in Werner E. Mosse and Arnold Paucker (eds.), *Juden im Wilhelminischen Deutschland* (Tübingen: Mohr, 1976).

Sabrow, Martin, *Der Rathenaumord: Rekonstruktion einer Verschwörung gegen die Republik von Weimar* (Munich: Oldenbourg, 1994).

Schleunes, Karl, *The Twisted Road to Auschwitz: Nazi Policy towards German Jews, 1933–39* (London: Andre Deutsch, 1972).

Schrafstetter, Susanna and Alan Steinweis (eds.), *The Germans and the Holocaust: Popular Responses to the Persecution and Murder of the Jews* (New York: Berghahn, 2015).

Schuster, Frank M., *Zwischen allen Fronten: Osteuropäische Juden während des Ersten Weltkrieges (1914–1919)* (Cologne: Böhlau, 2004).

Steinweis, Alan E., *Studying the Jew: Scholarly Antisemitism in Nazi Germany* (Cambridge, MA/London: Harvard University Press, 2006).

Stern, Fritz, *The Politics of Cultural Despair: A Study in the Rise of the Germanic Ideology* (Berkeley: University of California Press, 1961).

Stoetzler, Marcel, *The State, the Nation, and the Jews: Liberalism and the Antisemitism Dispute in Bismarck's Germany* (Lincoln, NE: University of Nebraska Press, 2009).

Strauss, Herbert A., 'Jewish Emigration from Germany: Nazi Policies and Jewish Responses, I', *Leo Baeck Institute Year Book*, vol. 25 (1980), pp. 313–361.

Strauss, Herbert A., 'Jewish Emigration from Germany: Nazi Policies and Jewish Responses, II', *Leo Baeck Institute Year Book*, vol. 26 (1981), pp. 343–409.

Szobar, Patricia, 'Telling Sexual Stories in the Nazi Courts of Law: Race Defilement in Germany, 1933 to 1945', in Dagmar Herzog (ed.), *Sexuality and German Fascism* (New York: Berghahn, 2005), pp. 131–163.

Thamer, Hans-Ulrich, *Verführung und Gewalt: Deutschland 1933–1945* (Berlin: Siedler, 1986).

Thieme, Karl, 'Deutsche Katholiken', in Werner E. Mosse (ed.), *Entscheidungsjahr 1932: Zur Judenfrage in der Endphase der Weimarer Republik* (Tübingen: Mohr, 1966), pp. 271–288.

Tooze, Adam, *The Wages of Destruction: The Making and Breaking of the Nazi Economy* (London: Allen Lane, 2006).

Trapp, Joachim, *Kölner Schulen in der NS-Zeit* (Cologne: Böhlau, 1994).

Treue, Wilhelm, 'Hitlers Denkschrift zum Vierjahresplan 1936', *Vierteljahrshefte für Zeitgeschichte*, vol. 3, no. 2 (April 1955), pp. 184–210.

Volkov, Shulamit, *Die Juden in Deutschland 1780–1918*, 2nd edn (Munich: Oldenbourg, 2000).

Vollnhals, Clemens, 'Jüdische Selbsthilfe bis 1938', in Wolfgang Benz (ed.), *Die Juden in Deutschland 1933–1945: Leben unter nationalsozialistischer Herrschaft* (Munich: Beck, 1988), pp. 314–411.

Volsansky, Gabriele, *Pakt auf Zeit: Das Deutsch-Österreichische Juli-Abkommen 1936* (Vienna: Böhlau, 2001).

Vuletić, Aleksandar-Saša, *Christen jüdischer Herkunft im Dritten Reich: Verfolgung und organisierte Selbsthilfe 1933–1939* (Mainz: P. von Zabern, 1999).

Walter, Dirk, *Antisemitische Kriminalität und Gewalt: Judenfeindschaft in der Weimarer Republik* (Bonn: Dietz, 1999).

Weingart, Peter, Jürgen Kroll, and Kurt Bayertz, *Rasse, Blut und Gene: Geschichte der Eugenik und Rassenhygiene in Deutschland* (Frankfurt am Main: Suhrkamp, 1988).

Wertheimer, Jack, *Unwelcome Strangers: East European Jews in Imperial Germany* (New York: Oxford University Press, 1987).

Wetzel, Juliane, 'Auswanderung in Deutschland', in Wolfgang Benz (ed.), *Die Juden in Deutschland 1933–1945* (Munich: Beck, 1989), pp. 412–498.

Wiener, P. B., 'Die Parteien der Mitte', in Werner E. Mosse (ed.), *Entscheidungsjahr 1932: Zur Judenfrage in der Endphase der Weimarer Republik* (Tübingen: Mohr, 1966), pp. 288–321.

Wildt, Michael, 'Gewalt gegen Juden in Deutschland 1933–1939', *WerkstattGeschichte*, vol. 6, no. 18 (1997), pp. 5–80.

Wildt, Michael, *An Uncompromising Generation: The Nazi Leadership of the Reich Security Main Office*, trans. Tom Lampert (Madison, WI: University of Wisconsin Press, 2010 [German edn, 2002]).

Wildt, Michael, *Hitler's Volksgemeinschaft and the Dynamics of Racial Exclusion: Violence against Jews in Provincial Germany, 1919–1939*, trans. Bernard Heise (New York: Berghahn, 2012 [German edn, 2007]).

Wulf, Joseph, *Die bildenden Künste im Dritten Reich* (Gütersloh: S. Mohn, 1963).

Wulf, Joseph, *Literatur und Dichtung im Dritten Reich* (Gütersloh: S. Mohn, 1963).

Wulf, Joseph, *Musik im Dritten Reich* (Gütersloh: S. Mohn, 1963).

Wulf, Joseph, *Theater und Film im Dritten Reich* (Gütersloh: S. Mohn, 1963).

Wulf, Joseph, *Presse und Funk im Dritten Reich* (Gütersloh: S. Mohn, 1964).

Yahil, Leni, *The Holocaust: The Fate of European Jewry, 1932–1945*, trans. Ina Friedman and Haya Galai (New York: Oxford University Press, 1990 [Hebrew edn, 1987]).

Zechlin, Egmont, *Die deutsche Politik und die Juden im Ersten Weltkrieg* (Göttingen: Vandenhoeck & Ruprecht, 1969).

Zinke, Peter, 'Der Strick mit dem Knoten: Suizid oder Mord bei Max Rosenau und Jakob Rosenfelder?', in Heike Tagsold (ed.), *'Was brauchen wir einen Befehl, wenn es gegen die Juden geht?' Das Pogrom von Gunzenhausen 1934* (Nuremberg: ANTOGO, 2006), pp. 31–44.

Index

Newspapers and periodicals are included in the index only if the text contains information about them (e.g. publication period, editors), and not if they are merely mentioned or cited as a source.

A

Aachen 300
Aaron, Helo 162
Aaron, Otti 162
Abarbanel, Isaak 680
Abt, Harry 680
Abyssinia 357
Academic Assistance Council 298, 456
Ackermann, Johann 121
Ackermann, Otto 553
Action Committee for the Defence against Jewish Atrocity and Boycott Propaganda 121–122
Adam (employee, Johannes Jeserich AG, Berlin) 129
Adenauer, Konrad 330
Adler (Protestant bishop, Münster) 438
Advertising Council for the German Economy 541
Agudas Israel 351
Ahr, Helmut 169–170
Aid Committee for Catholic Non-Aryans 437, 440–442
Aid Committee of Hamburg's United Jewish Organizations 421–427
Alexander-Katz, Günther 285
Alfonso V of Portugal 680
Alldeutscher Verband, *see* Pan-German League
Allenstein (Olszytn) 354, 420
Albany, New York 109
Allgemeine Treuhandstelle für die jüdische Auswanderung GmbH Berlin (Altreu), *see* General Trust Agency for Jewish Emigration
Alliance Israélite Universelle 124
Alsace 18
Altbandendorf 729

Altdamm 436
Altona 221
Aman, Dudley Leigh 357
American Jewish Committee 189
American Jewish Congress (AJC) 108–111, 113, 189
American Jewish Joint Distribution Committee (JDC) 51, 187, 189–190, 234, 297–298
Ammende, Ewald 265
Ammon, Wahrhold 410
Amsterdam 778
Andermann, Martin 427–430
Anders, Max 567
Angermünde 406
Angress, Ernst 778
Angress, Fritz Peter 778
Angress, Hans Herbert 778
Angress, Henny, née Kiefer 778
Angress, Werner T. 672–673, 777
Anker (farmer, Gnojau) 715
Ansbach 343
Apfel, Alfred 250
Apfel, Isadore 189
Arbeitsgemeinschaft deutsch-arischer Fabrikanten der Bekleidungsindustrie e.V. (Adefa), *see* Association of German-Aryan Clothing Manufacturers
Arendt, Hannah 46
Arendt, Kaspar 756–757
Arendt, Martha 46
Argentina 393, 423, 563, 622, 633, 771–774
Army Ordnance Department (Heereswaffenamt) 396, 460
Arndt, Ernst Moritz 19
Arnsberg 661
Arnswalde 54

arrests, *see also* concentration camps; protective custody 128, 163, 301–302, 493–494, 645, 688–690
Aryan Paragraph 47–48, 141, 151, 186, 244, 258, 260–262, 272–274, 277, 290–291, 293, 333, 340–342, 352, 391, 414–415, 488, 509
Aryanization/expropriation, *see also* fines, levies, and taxation issues 32, 39, 60, 162, 251, 374, 400, 443–444, 460–462, 483, 512, 559–561, 572, 644–645, 686–688, 690, 694–696, 785
Asch, Shalom 172
Association for Jewish Museums 174
Association for Liberal Judaism 527, 529
Association for Settlement Abroad GmbH, Berlin 392
Association of Bavarian Israelite Communities 529
Association of Budgerigar Enthusiasts 257–258
Association of German-Aryan Clothing Manufacturers (Adefa) 590–591
Association of German Engineering Institutions 122
Association of German Motor Car Owners 419
Association of German Patent Lawyers 131
Association of German Zionists-Revisionists 350
Association of National German Jews (Verband nationaldeutscher Juden) 45, 56, 352
Association of Persecutees of the Nazi Regime (VVN) 190
Association of Physicians in Germany (Hartmann League) 248, 286
Association of Statutory Health Insurance Physicians 286
Association of Synagogue Congregations of the Province of Lower Silesia 324, 680–681
Association of Synagogue Congregations of the Province of Upper Silesia 243–244
Association of the German Ladies' Outerwear Industry 652
Association of Württemberg Footwear Retailers 179
Asthalter, Wilhelm 127
Astrophysical Observatory, Potsdam 230–231

Atlantic City 189
Atzmon, Ruth, *see* Cohn, Ruth
Aubin, Hermann 658
Auerbach, Walter 256
Augsburg 407
Aurich 354
Ausgleichsstelle der Länder, *see* Compensation Office of the States
Australia 394, 423, 443, 770, 773
Austria 58, 295, 394, 424, 441, 621, 640
Austria-Hungary 27
Auswärtiges Amt, *see* Reich Minister of Foreign Affairs/Reich Foreign Office
Auto-Club 1927 419

B

Bab, Julius 255–256
Bacharach, Bella 446
Bacharach, Harry 189
Bacharach, Hermann 400
Bacharach, Ida 85
Bacharach, Manfred 446
Bacharach, Moses 446
Bacharach, Sally 85
Bachrach, Raphael Z. 222
Backe, Herbert 331, 497, 503
Bad Arendsee 483
Bad Brückenau 661
Bad Karlshafen 474
Bad Kissingen 626–627
Bad Kudowa (Kudowa-Zdrój) 619
Bad Muskau 664
Bad Tölz 661
Baden 18, 391, 507, 800
Badler, Elias 324
Badt, Hermann 94–95
Baeck, Leo 44, 50, 187–188, 256, 465, 725
Baer, Maximilian Adelbert 303
Baerwald, Leo 93, 173
Baghdad 714–715
Balfour, Arthur James Lord 713
Ballin, Albert 26
Balzer, Albrecht 548
Bamberger, Hans 190
Bang (state secretary, Reich Ministry of Economics) 96
banks
– Bett, Simon & Co. 362, 364

banks (contd.)
- Deutsche Bank 234, 238, 240–241, 243
- Deutsche Bank and Disconto-Gesellschaft, Berlin 129, 162, 234–236, 241, 243
- Deutsche Genossenschaftskasse 143
- Deutsche Golddiskontbank 59, 143, 235, 761–762
- Deutsche Rentenbank-Kreditanstalt 143
- Disconto-Gesellschaft 234–236, 240–241
- Dresdner Bank 241
- Reichsbank 48, 54, 143, 148, 235, 237, 241–242, 497, 504–505, 512, 594, 625, 761
- Reichs-Kredit-Gesellschaft 143, 241
- Rheinische Kreditbank 239

Bar Kokhba Association 328–329, 351
Bär, Kurt 345
Barmat, Julius 473
Barnowsky, Victor 255
Bartels, Friedrich 414–415
Bartenstein (Bartoszyce) 420
Barthou, Louis 412
Basel 20, 30
Bätz (director, Simson Works) 395
Bauer, Manfred 222
Bauermeister (painter, Braunschweig) 411
Baumann, Kurt 255
Baumgart, David 256
Baumgart, Gertrud 332–335
Baur, Erwin 30
Bavaria 283–284, 391, 584, 800
Bavarian Academy of Sciences 748
Bavarian People's Party (BVP) 93, 164
Bavarian State Ministry of Education and Culture 283–284
Bearsted, 2nd Viscount, *see* Samuel, Sir Walter Horace
Beck, József 643
Becker, Anni, née Bohlert 346–347
Becker, Fritz 763
Becker, Heinrich 346–347
Becker, Rudolf 138, 140
Beddelhausen 483
Beer Hall Putsch 33
Behrendt, David 243
Behrendt, Ernst Josef 321–322
Belarus 708
Belbe (district farmers' leader) 629
Belgium 112, 295, 393–394, 424, 441, 621

Belloc, Hilaire 605
Benario, Rudolf 166
Bendix, Albert 765
Benz, Ottomar 129
Berchtesgaden 786
Bérenger, Henry 297
Berger, Julius 472
Bergmann, Alexander 599
Bergner, Elisabeth 356, 472
Berkutz (businessman, Suhl) 462
Berlin 18, 22–23, 35–37, 50, 52, 137, 156, 159, 170, 172, 178, 182–184, 197, 213–216, 255, 259, 283, 290–293, 304, 315, 391–392, 397, 427, 432–434, 437, 440, 471–473, 477–479, 481–482, 484, 489–490, 499, 539, 558, 571, 580, 584, 589, 625–626, 633, 638, 645–646, 651, 698, 706, 745–746, 767, 778, 780, 788, 795, 799–800
Berlin Antisemitism Dispute 18, 23
Berlin Gymnastics Association 227–228, 277, 279
Berne 463
Bernard, Anna 620
Bernhard, Georg 251, 302, 363
Bernheim, Franz 181
Berning, Wilhelm 437–439, 441, 443
Bernstadt (Bierutów) 323–324, 679–680
Bernstein, Arnold 458
Bernstein, Otto 235–236
Bertram, Ludwig Theodor 589, 591
Bessarabia 708
Best, Werner 57, 468–469, 494, 513, 560, 571
Bethke, Hermann 495–496
Beumelburg, Werner 398–399
Beuthen (Bytom) 243, 245, 300, 494, 728, 730
Bieberbach, Ludwig 610, 660
Bielefeld 645
Bigart, Jacques 124
Binder, Julius 695
Birobidžan 357
Birstein 798
Bischoff, Karl 554
Bismarck, Otto von 27
Bistritzky, Marcus 222
Black Pennant 433
Blankenstein, Hans 325
Blaschko, Hermann Karl Felix 162
Blaschko, Johanna, née Littauer 162

Blau (judicial counsellor, Jewish Community, Frankfurt am Main) 529
Blinzig, Alfred 241–242
Bloch, Paul 191–194
Block, Julius 651–652
Blomberg, Werner von, *see also* Reich Minister/Ministry of the Army/of War 395, 465, 532
Blome, Kurt 634, 637
Blum, Rose 680
Blumenfeld, Walter Georg 456
Blumenstein (banker) 240
Blumenthal, Emanuel (Max) 447
Blumenthal, Moses 446
Blumenthal, W. Michael 50
Blümich, Walter 505, 655
Blutschutzgesetz, *see* Law for the Protection of German Blood and German Honour (Blood Protection Law)
B'nai B'rith, Independent Order of (IOBB) 145, 189, 350, 678, 684–687, 689–690
Bochum 179
Bode (official, Gestapa) 374
Bodelschwingh, Friedrich von 757
Bodelschwingh Institution 757
Bodenheimer, Wilhelm 220
Bodlaender, Günt(h)er 731–733
Bodlaender, Ilse, née Müller 731
Boehm, Simon 629, 631
Boerner, Karl 601
Bohlert, Anni, *see* Becker, Anni
Bohlmann, Johannes 324
Böhm, Franz 42
Bojano, Fillipo 171
Bökenkamp, Hans 548
Bolivia 393, 770–771
Bondy, Curt 673
Boner, Franz 234
Bonhoeffer, Dietrich 277
Bonn 167, 239–240
Bonn, Ferdinand 471
book burnings 172
Borberg, William 297
Borchard, Lucy 457–458
Borchardt (school caretaker, Altdamm) 436
Borchardt, Walter 436
Borchheim (relative of Alex Löwenstein, Berlin) 633
Borger (resident, Givat Brenner Kibbutz) 734
Bormann, Martin 48, 263
Bose, Herbert von 285
Bourquin (Belgian representative, High Commission for Refugees) 297
Bower, Rob 769
boycotts 41, 48–50, 106–108, 130, 153–154, 183, 244–245, 268, 318, 320, 343–345, 434, 444–445, 470, 498–500, 502, 515, 527, 559, 561, 568, 583, 601, 640, 752, 786
– of lawyers 246, 318, 344, 432
– national boycott on 1 April 1933 41–42, 47–48, 116–117, 119–121, 124–128, 132–137, 156, 246–247, 301, 310–312, 344, 486, 751
– passive or silent 559
– of physicians 246, 318, 344, 432, 444, 450–451, 623–624
– refusal to sell to Jewish firms 559, 573
– of shops 42, 52, 225, 245–246, 340, 343, 353, 410–412, 418, 432, 443–444, 466, 478, 482–483, 532, 566–567, 583, 589–590, 598, 629–632, 641, 645, 682, 729–730, 779
Brandenburg 489, 800
Brandt (Oberregierungsrat, Karlsruhe Regional Tax Office) 591
Brandt (SS-Sturmbannführer, RuSHA) 415
Branner, Per-Axel 477
Braun (director, Johannes Jeserich AG) 129
Braun, Carl Maria 327
Braun, Otto 363
Braun, Sally 346–347
Braunsberg (Braniewo) 420
Braunschweig 410–411
Bravmann, Salomon Stefan 226
Brazil 392–394, 423, 622, 770–773
Brecht, Arnold 94–95
Brehm, Bruno 398
Breithaupt, Franz 432
Breitscheid, Rudolf 251, 363
Breitung, G. 131
Bremen 394
Brenner, Joseph Chaim 457
Breslau (Wrocław) 97, 99–100, 171, 197, 212, 218, 323–324, 383, 392, 508–509, 658, 664, 672, 680–681, 702, 733, 763–766, 788
Breslauer, Walter 259

Index

Breslauer, Wilhelm 529
Brest 752–753
Brieg (Brzeg) 680
Brieger (dentist, Oels) 679
Brilling, Bernhard 323
Brinkmann (NS-Hago leader, Braunschweig) 411
Briske, Leonie, later Saulmann 223
Britain, *see* United Kingdom of Great Britain and Northern Ireland
B'rith Abraham, Independent Order 189
Brith Trumpeldor, *see* Herzlia
British East Africa 772
British Empire, *see* United Kingdom of Great Britain and Northern Ireland
British Union of Fascists 379
Brixlegg 108
Brodnitz, Friedrich 529
Brodnitz, Julius 110–111, 404, 529
Brotdorf 783
Brück, Paul-Richard 474
Brückner, Helmuth 243–244
Brüggemann (SA member, Lübeck) 88
Bruhn (negotiator, Flick Corporation) 462
Brüning, Heinrich 305
Brunswig, Peter 240–242
Buber, Martin 256
Buch, Gustav Friedrich von 225
Buch, Konrad 190
Buch, Walter 415
Buchental 644
Büchs (colonel, Army Ordnance Department) 462
Buenos Aires 633–634
Bühler, Gerd 778
Bulgaria 424
Bülow, Bernhard Wilhelm von 497, 502–503, 522
Bülow-Schwante, Vicco von 138, 178, 712
Bund Deutscher Mädel, *see* League of German Girls
Burchard, Heinrich 648
Bürckel, Josef, *see also* Reich commissioner for the reintegration of the Saarland/for the Saarland 588
Burgdörfer, Friedrich 448, 532
Burwig (official, Reich Ministry of the Interior) 440
Busch, Fritz 225
Busch, Walther 470–471
Buselwitz (Bogusławice) 679
businesses and companies, *see also* department stores and shops; publishing houses
– Adler & Oppenheimer leather factory, Neustadt-Glewe 483
– Allgemeine Warenhandels-Gesellschaft (AWAG) 696
– Arno Schlesier, Dresden 631
– Arno Vieth, Berlin 630
– [Arnold] Bernstein Shipping Company 458–459
– Bata, Czechoslovakia 281
– Beiersdorf AG Hamburg 432
– Berlin Municipal Electrical Works (BEWAG) 177
– Block & Simon, Berlin 651
– Central Union of Agricultural Cooperatives of Lower Silesia GmbH (Raiffeisen) 631
– Central Union of Agricultural Cooperatives of Pomerania 631
– Ernst Nehring & Co., Deutsch-Krone 630
– Ernst Rosenberg & Co. GmbH, Berlin 381
– Fairplay Schleppdampfschiffs-Reederei Richard Borchard GmbH (Fairplay Towage), Hamburg 425, 458
– Flick Corporation 396, 460–461
– Fromms Act, Julius Fromm rubber works (Julius Fromm Gummiwerke), Berlin Köpenick 303–306
– Gebrüder Guttstein Steam Mill, Osterode 482
– General Trust Agency for Jewish Emigration GmbH (Altreu) 762, 775
– Georg Fromberg & Co., Berlin 381
– German Moving Pictures Syndicate (Syndikat-Film GmbH) 138
– Gustav Noeske & Kirstein, Schneidemühl 630
– Haase & Schrodt, Frankfurt an der Oder 630
– Herz-Licht, Berlin 484
– Hirsch Kupfer- und Messingwerke AG, Eberswalde 472
– Illerwerke AG, Regensburg 108

businesses and companies (contd.)
- Joachim Hagenow AG, *see* Nebel & Sander
- Johannes Jeserich AG, Berlin 129
- Johannes Wenzel, Pomerania 631
- Julius Berger Tiefbau AG 472
- Kathreiner GmbH 630
- Katz & Michel Textiles AG 645
- Kaufmann, Cologne 179
- Landhandel GmbH, Ratzebuhr 631
- Laussing haulage firm, Cologne 179
- Ludwig Bertram 589
- Max Gagelmann, Meyenburg 629
- Maxhütte, *see also* Flick Corporation 461
- Meyer-Brüggemann, Meyenburg 400
- Mitteldeutsche Stahlwerke (Central German Steel Works), *see also* Flick Corporation 460
- Mosse, Frankfurt am Main 192
- Nebel & Sander, Hamburg 403
- Paul Vangerow GmbH, Breslau 175
- Rappolt & Söhne (Eres), Hamburg 590
- Reichselektrowerke 143
- Salzwedel sugar factory 401
- Schiff, Frankfurt am Main 192
- Schmidt, Braunschweig 411
- Schüller und Rubruck, Cologne 179
- Schultheiss-Patzenhofer 630
- Siemssen & Co. China Furs, Shanghai 156
- Silesian Farmers' Trading Company 631
- Simson, Suhl 395–396, 460–462
- Städte-Reklame billboard advertising company 280–281
- Stargard & Reuter, Berlin 492
- Swedish Linen Industry, Regina (Canada) 305
- Theodor Althoff, Leipzig 226
- Trust and Transfer Office Haavara Ltd, Tel Aviv, *see* Haavara Agreement
- Viag (Vereinigte Industrieunternehmungen AG) 143
- von Schirach & Co., Munich 107
- Wilhelm Gustloff Foundation, *see also* Simson, Suhl 396, 462

Bütow (Bytów) 180
Buttmann, Rudolf 448
Buxbaum, Samuel 446

C

Cairo 463
Callies (parishioner, Altdamm) 436
Callmann (Jewish Community representative, Cologne) 529
Calonder, Felix Ludwig 146–147
Cameroon 394
Canada 393, 423, 772, 774
Cannstadt 179
Cape Town 756, 758
Cardinal, von (Regierungsrat, Königsberg) 602
Caritas Association (Caritasverband), *see* German Caritas Association
Caritasnotwerk 439
Carl Schurz Association 474
Carlebach, Emil 190–194
Carlebach, Ezriel, *see* Karlebach, Ezriel
Carlsbad 665
Castiglioni (industrialist, Austria) 473
Castro, Brazil 392
Catholic Centre Party (Zentrumspartei) 26, 33, 82, 156, 309, 580
Catholic Church 152–153, 273, 437–439, 441–442, 488, 580–582
Catholic German Women's League 442
Cecil, Robert 294, 297
Central Association of German Banks and Bankers (Centralverband des deutschen Bank- und Bankiersgewerbes) 234–236, 241
Central Association of German Citizens of the Jewish Faith/of Jews in Germany (CV) 24, 34–35, 44–45, 56, 110–112, 188, 223–226, 317, 321, 325–326, 352, 404, 421, 426, 433, 435, 443, 450, 470–471, 482, 527, 529
Central British Fund for German Jewry 51
Central Committee for Inland Mission (Centralausschuß für Innere Mission) 488
Central Committee for the Defence against Jewish Atrocity and Boycott Propaganda (Zentralkomitee zur Abwehr der jüdischen Greuel- und Boykotthetze) 119, 134
Central Committee of German Jews for Relief and Reconstruction (Zentralausschuß der deutschen Juden für Hilfe und Aufbau) 44, 51, 426

Central League of German Trade
  Representatives' Associations 342
Central Procurement Agency for the Army
  and the Navy, Berlin 154
Central Welfare Board of German Jews 649–
  650, 795–798
Centralverein deutscher Staatsbürger
  jüdischen Glaubens/Centralverein der
  Juden in Deutschland (CV), *see* Central
  Association of German Citizens of the
  Jewish Faith
Chamber of the Interior, Swabia and
  Neuburg 406
Chamber of the Interior, Upper Bavaria 408
Chamberlain, Arthur Neville 176
Chamberlain, Joseph P. 297
Chemnitz 42, 156, 223–225, 300
Chicago 302
chief of police
- Berlin, *see also* Helldorf, Count Wolf
  Heinrich von; Levetzow, Magnus 303,
  306–307, 397, 489
- Braunschweig 410
- Breslau 212
- Düsseldorf 476
- Elbing 758
- Leipzig 223
chief of the Order Police, *see also* Daluege,
  Kurt 646
chief of the Reich Chancellery, *see also*
  Lammers, Hans Heinrich 96, 157, 511, 750,
  779, 786
Chief of the Security Police and the SD, *see
  also* Heydrich, Reinhard 57, 646, 716–717,
  753
Chief Public Prosecutor's Office, Frankfurt
  am Main 190, 192
children/adolescents 384–385, 398, 467–468,
  558
Chile 393, 423, 622, 770–772
Chimowicz, Moses Hersch 179
China 189, 423
Chodzko (Polish representative, High
  Commission for Refugees) 297
Christian Social Party (CSP) 35
Chur, Switzerland 656
Church Congress of Electoral Hesse 272

citizenship
- denaturalization 47, 145, 250–251, 303–304,
  306–307, 370–371, 562
- deprivation of rights, *see also* Nuremberg
  Laws 16, 47, 54, 468, 514–515, 519, 551, 573,
  593–594, 651, 776, 787
Claß, Heinrich 25
Clemente, Otto 327
Code of Criminal Procedure 493
Codreanu, Corneliu Zelea 379
Cohen, Abraham H. 113
Cohen, David 124, 727
Cohen, Frederic 103
Cohen, Hermann 18
Cohn, Ernst Abraham 508, 734
Cohn, Gertrud Karoline (Trudi), née
  Rothmann 396, 508–509, 733–734
Cohn, Ruth, later Atzmon 396, 733
Cohn, Wilhelm 221
Cohn, Wilhelm (Willy) 396, 508–509, 619–
  620, 733
Cohn, Wolfgang 508, 734
Cohnstaedt, Ruth 191–194
Cologne 179, 197, 329, 392, 558, 763–766
Colombia 393, 423, 770–773
Combat League for German Culture 101–102,
  327
Combat League for Small and Medium-Sized
  Businesses 107–108, 213, 225, 245–246
Comité de placement des Intellectuels
  Réfugiés 298
Comité des Délégations Juives 181, 297
Comité National de Secours aux
  Réfugiés 295–296, 298
Communist Party in Germany (KPD) 155,
  176, 190–191, 193, 195
Community Representation of the Hanseatic
  Towns 529
Compensation Office of the States
  (Ausgleichsstelle der Länder) 153–154
concentration camps, *see also* arrests;
  protective custody 128, 386, 495, 664, 768,
  778
- Brandenburg 386
- Dachau 164–167, 725
- Moringen 725
- Oranienburg 386
- Osthofen 347

concentration camps (contd.)
- Sachsenburg 568
- Sonnenburg 386

Condell, Heinz 256
Confessing Church (Bekennende Kirche) 272, 429–430, 485, 487–488, 648
Congress of European Nationalities 265–271
Congress of Organized National Groups in the European States 37
Constantinople, *see* Istanbul
Costa Rica 423
Cottbus 368
Coty, François 379
courts 190–191, 454
- higher regional courts (Oberlandesgerichte)
  - Berlin (Kammergericht) 336–337
  - Cologne 599
  - Darmstadt 475
  - Frankfurt am Main 744
  - Hanseatic 677
  - Kassel 191
- labour courts (Arbeitsgerichte)
  - Frankfurt am Main 414
  - Hanau 413–414
  - Leipzig 226
- local courts (Amtsgerichte)
  - Berlin 41
  - Breslau 99
  - Leipzig 652, 655
  - Remscheid 677
- People's Court (Volksgerichtshof) 365
- regional courts (Landgerichte)
  - Ansbach 345
  - Breslau 97–99, 101
  - Frankfurt am Main 743
  - Schwerin 445
- Reich Fiscal Court (Reichsfinanzhof) 51, 382–383
- Reich Labour Court (Reichsarbeitsgericht) 226, 309, 311, 313
- Reich Supreme Court (Reichsgericht) 55, 468
- special courts (Sondergerichte) 416, 667–668, 743

Cracow 175–176
Cremers, Paul Joseph 104
Criminal Code 369–372, 493, 744
Criminal Police (Kripo) 57
- Berlin 305
- Munich 173

Crivitz 443
Cuba 393, 423
cultural and religious practices, restrictions on 244–245, 259, 636, 690
Culture League of German Jews (Jüdischer Kulturbund) 50, 255–257, 283–284, 355, 471–473, 612, 732, 765
Curzon, George Nathaniel 705
Customs Investigation Service 592
Cyrus, Margarete, *see* Löwenstein, Margarete
Czechoslovakia 51, 295, 394, 424, 499, 621, 705, 709
Częstochowa 752–753
Czollek (Jewish religious instructor, Lower Silesia) 323

D

Daber (Dobra) 436
Dachau, *see* concentration camps
Dahm, Georg 369
d'Alquen, Gunter 481
Dalton, Baron Hugh 188
Daluege, Kurt, *see also* chief of the Order Police 130
Dammann, Paul M. 547
Dannecker, Theodor 58–59
Dannenbaum, Sophie, *see* Rathenau, Sophie
Danzig 176–177, 304
Dargel, Paul 495
Dargun 445
Darmstadt 475
Darré, Richard Walther, *see also* Reich Farmers' Leader; Reich Minister/Ministry of Food and Agriculture 331, 400, 414, 513, 534
Dauster, Rudolf 567
David, Bernhard 220, 222, 529
Davos 57, 588–589
Delmer, Sefton 171
Dember, Harry 456
Demmler, Theodor 695
denaturalization, *see* citizenship
Denmark 295, 394, 424
denunciation 121, 212–213, 230–231, 326–327, 403–404, 436, 481, 547

department stores and shops 21
- Adolf Frank, Braunschweig 411
- Bach, Munich 418
- Bamberger & Hertz, Munich 418
- Deininger, Munich 418
- Deutsch-Amerikanisches Schuhgeschäft, Munich 418
- Deutsches Schuhwarenhaus (owner Fritz K.) 309–310
- Diegel, Munich 418
- Ehrlich, Parchim 444
- Eichengrün, Munich 418
- Eid, Munich 418
- Einheitspreis AG (Epa), Munich 417–418
- Felber, Munich 418
- Fuchsberger, Munich 418
- Geigl, Munich 418
- Gerstle & Löffler, Munich 418
- Goldene 19, Munich 418
- Gottlieb, Munich 418
- Hartlmaier, Munich 418
- Heene, Munich 418
- Hermann Tietz & Co., later Hertie Waren- und Kaufhaus GmbH 417–418
- Hertie Waren- und Kaufhaus GmbH 417
- Hollenkamp 590
- Horn, Munich 418
- Indanthrenhaus, Munich 418
- Jakob, Munich 466
- Josephson, Munich 418
- Kaufhaus des Westens (KaDeWe) 128, 417
- Kaufhaus Heinrich Uhlfelder GmbH, Munich 417–418
- Kellner, Munich 418
- Kleinmann Schuhe, Munich 418
- Knagge & Peitz, Munich 418
- Koch music shop, Munich 466
- Kröninger, Munich 418
- Kübler, Munich 418
- Lewkowitz, Munich 418
- Lodenfrey, Munich 418
- Loewenthal, Munich 418
- Lun, Munich 418
- Maier, Munich 418
- Mössbauer, Munich 418
- Mühlhäuser, Munich 418
- Neubert & Ebert, Munich 418
- N. Israel, Berlin 747
- Oberpollinger, Munich 418
- Obletter, Munich 418
- Orliansky, Munich 466
- Pauson, Munich 418
- Posega, Munich 418
- Ried, Munich 418
- Rieger, Munich 418
- Roman Mayr, Munich 418
- Rosa Klauber, Munich 418
- Rotschild, Munich 418
- Rudolf Karstadt AG Leipzig 226, 402
- Salamander shoe retailer 418, 499
- Salberg, Munich 466
- Schleich, Munich 418
- Schlicht, Munich 418
- Schmidt, Munich 418
- Schokoladenbuck, Munich 418
- Schubert, Munich 418
- Schuhkönig, Braunschweig 411
- Schuhwaren-Haus Brück, Munich 418
- Schulhoff, Munich 418
- Schwarz, Munich 418
- Sigurd, Munich 418
- Silberbauer, Munich 418
- Speier, Munich 418
- Spielmann, Munich 418
- Spier, Munich 418
- Stalf, Munich 418
- Strumpfsachs, Munich 418
- Tiarks, Munich 418
- Traphöner, Munich 418
- Weinberger & Bissinger, Munich 418
- Wertheim AG 696, 780
- Wiedling, Munich 418
- Winter, Munich 418
- Wohlworth (Woolworth), Munich 418
- Zuckerbär, Munich 418
- Zum Strauß, Görlitz 402
deportation and expulsion 41, 56, 58, 86, 96, 110, 112, 145–146, 179, 186, 222, 270, 531, 562–563
Deputy of the Führer, see also Heß, Rudolf 47–48, 138, 263, 348, 395, 414–415, 434, 480, 484, 497, 500, 513, 520–521, 525, 550, 565, 568–569, 571, 595, 599, 634, 656–657, 669, 711–712, 748–749, 753–755, 761
Dersch, Wilhelm 658
Deschauer, Robert 190, 192, 194

Desgranges, Pierre 398
Dessau 403, 558
destruction of
- homes 85, 93, 164, 397, 447, 466, 482–483
- Jewish cemeteries 33, 35, 224
- shops and businesses 41, 444, 466, 468, 483–484, 566, 572
- synagogues 35, 783
Deuter (NS-Hago leader, Braunschweig) 411
Deutsch, Bernard S. 109–111
Deutsch Eylau 660
Deutsche Arbeitsfront (DAF), see German Labour Front
Deutsche Reichsbahn-Gesellschaft, see German Reich Railways
Deutsche Stiftung 705
Deutsche Studentenschaft (German Students' Union) 34, 172, 530
Deutsche Turnerschaft (DT), see German Gymnastics Association
Deutscher Gemeindetag, see German Council of Municipalities
Deutscher Industrie- und Handelstag, see German Association of Chambers of Industry and Commerce
Deutsches Beamtengesetz, see German Civil Service Law
Deutsches Museum, Munich 768
Deutschnationaler Handlungsgehilfenverband, see German National Association of Commercial Employees
Deutschvölkischer Schutz- und Trutzbund, see German-*Völkisch* Protection and Defiance League
Dieckhoff, Hans Heinrich 214
Diels, Rudolf, see also Regierungspräsident, Cologne/Hanover 138
Dienemann, Gaby, later Jacobi 628
Dienemann, Mally 628
Dienemann, Max 628
Dietrich, Otto 214
Dimitrov, Georgi 358
Dingelstedt, Franz von 472
Dinter, Artur 30
Dobrodzień, see Guttentag
Dohm, Christian Wilhelm 17
Dohnanyi, Johann von 369

Dominican Republic 393, 423
Domrös (civil servant, Altdamm) 436
Dopheide, Wilhelm 444, 623–624
Dorpmüller, Julius, see also Reich Minister/Ministry of Transport 511
Dortmund 103, 179, 197–198, 702
Doude von Trootswijk (Dutch representative, High Commission for Refugees) 297
Dresden 42, 197, 223–225, 392, 631
Dresden State Opera House 224
Dreyse, Friedrich Wilhelm 241
Driesen, Adolf 602–603
Driesen Foundation 602
Driest, Emil 250
Dubnow, Simon 245
Duisburg 103
Dunn, John J. 109
Dürr, Alfred 369
Düsseldorf 179, 300, 475–476, 682

E

East Prussia 420, 482, 495, 644, 705, 797
East European Jews, see also Ostjuden 20–21, 23, 36, 47, 420, 476, 619–621
Ebbutt, Norman 127
Eberlein, Hellmut 616
Eckart, Dietrich 399
Eckstein, Manfred 475–476
Ecuador 357, 393, 423, 770–773
Eden, Sir Anthony 713
Edenkoben 406
Eggeling, Joachim Albrecht 400
Egypt 713
Ehrlich (Jewish religious instructor, Neumarkt) 323
Eichmann, Adolf 44, 58, 716
Eidmann, Bernhard 589, 591
Einödshofer, Julius 376
Einstein, Albert 105, 129, 230, 250–251
Einstein, Alfred 256
Eisner, Kurt 33
Elbing (Elbląg) 420, 759, 761
Elbogen, Ismar 256
Elfriede Salomon Foundation 126
Eloesser, Arthur 256
Elsner, Rosalie, see Gehrike, Rosalie
Elsoff 483
Eltz-Rübenach, Baron Paul von 241, 511

embassies and consulates
- Chinese consulate, Leipzig 226
- German embassy, Warsaw 642
- German embassy, Washington DC 105
- Japanese consulate, Leipzig 226
- Persian consulate, Leipzig 226
- Polish consulate, Essen 476
- Swiss embassy, Berlin 539

Emergency Association of German Scientists Abroad 456

Emergency Committee in Aid of Displaced German Scholars 298, 456

emigration 46, 49, 51–52, 59, 231, 328, 350, 356, 372–374, 382, 390–391, 416, 420, 449, 512–513, 516, 518, 563, 568–570, 592–594, 612, 620, 624, 635, 642, 656, 672, 685, 698–699, 714–715, 753–754, 761–763, 792, 796, 799
- destinations 45–46, 50–52, 112, 162, 189, 216, 226, 350–351, 354, 356–357, 391–394, 422–424, 442, 561, 563, 620–622, 633, 637, 731–732, 756–757, 769–770, 772–774
- obstacles 392, 672, 755, 773, 775, 792, 799
  - international restrictions and quotas 52, 118, 356, 393, 563, 598, 770–771, 774, 776
- preparation and planning 162, 187–188, 216–217, 226, 318–319, 351, 422, 594, 597, 720, 723–724, 726, 755–757, 773, 775–776
  - retraining 331–332, 351, 354–355, 391, 396, 421, 424–425, 437, 439–440, 528, 598, 636–637, 662, 672, 721–722, 726, 754, 772, 774, 776, 778, 792–794, 800
- relief efforts and aid 44, 51–52, 189, 357, 391, 393–394, 422–423, 426, 563, 575–576, 636, 722–723, 727, 731, 733, 755, 769–770, 772, 774–775, 794

Emmendingen 300
Enabling Act (*Ermächtigungsgesetz*)
Engel, Johannes 213
England, *see* United Kingdom of Great Britain and Northern Ireland
Ephraim, Sally 278
Epp, Emil 346
Epp, Franz Xaver Ritter von 92–93
Epstein, David 223
Epstein, Hella 223
Epstein, Max 223
Erbslöh, Peter 655

Erck, Erich (Eisner, Erich) 283
Erfurt 300
Erhardt, Hermann 386
Ermächtigungsgesetz, *see* Enabling Act
Erzberger, Matthias 26, 33, 399
Essen 101–103, 179, 197–198
Esser, Hermann 92, 326–327, 718–719
Esslingen 179
Estonia 394, 707
Euringer, Richard 102
European Office for Inter-Church Aid 297–298
Euskirchen 179
Evangelische Kirche, *see* Protestant Church
exclusion of Jews from
- clubs and societies 33–34, 43, 47, 49–50, 55, 115, 227–228, 258, 277–279, 290–291, 300, 338–339, 350, 400–401, 408–409, 415, 419, 481, 554, 614, 616, 636, 639, 691
- education 38, 225, 244–245, 268, 318, 370, 516–518, 525, 558, 565, 636, 660, 752
- professional life and economy, *see* Aryanization/expropriation; unemployment
- public amenities 48, 50, 172, 224, 232, 244–245, 320, 348, 490, 498, 500, 502, 510, 595–596, 627, 659, 661, 669, 700–701, 718–719, 752

F

Fajtlowicz, David 180
Falk, Alfred 252
Falkenheim 529
Farchi (Jewish delegate, Congress of Nationalities) 266
Faulhaber, Michael von 43, 152–153
Faustmann (retailer, Braunschweig) 411
Fechheimer, Hedwig 256
Feder, Gottfried 399
Federation of Bavarian Regimental Officers' Associations 408–409
Feer, Eduard Albert 539
Fehr (businessman, Georg Fromberg & Co.) 239–240, 381
Fehst, Hermann 605
Feingold, Jochen 673
Feingreber, Miss 495
Felsberg 300

Fendt, Julius 405
Fengler (chairman, Factory Cell Organization of the NSDAP, Charlottenburg) 130
Festenberg 323–324, 679–680, 682
Feuchtmann, Eugen 129
Feuchtwanger, Lion 106, 252
Fiehler, Karl 106–107, 750
Fiessler, Karl August 440
fines, levies, and taxation issues 225, 247, 382, 454, 505–508, 518, 543, 592, 655–657, 711–712, 719–720, 723
Fink, Ernst 221
Finland 394
First World War 16, 26–28, 30, 32
Fischer (Major, head of association) 138
Fischer (residents, Wuppertal-Barmen) 249
Fischer, Christian Otto 241
Fischer, Eugen 30, 537
Fischer, Hugo 493
Fischer, Ruth 250
Fischer-Defoy, Werner 700–701
Flach, Heinrich Daniel 346–347
Flatow, Alfred 278
Fleischer, Traut 778
Flemke, Hugo 390
Flesch (assessor) 716
Flick, Friedrich 460–462
Floret (politician, Pyritz) 406
Foerster, Friedrich Wilhelm 252
forced labour, *see also* concentration camps 167
Foreign Exchange Investigation Office (Devisenfahndungsamt) 59
Foreign Organization of the NSDAP 640, 753–754, 761
Four-Year Plan, *see* Plenipotentiary for the Four-Year Plan
Fränkel, Anneliese 778
France 51, 112, 295–296, 393, 412, 423–424, 435, 441, 621, 714, 739, 741
Franck, James 172
Franco, Francisco 738
Franconia 560, 646
Frank, Erich 382
Frank, Hans 224, 263, 560–561, 652
Frank, Theodor 234–235, 240–242
Frank, Walter 605, 748, 750
Frankenstein 323

Frankenstein, Ernst 554
Frankfurt am Main 22, 36, 114, 190, 192, 197, 229, 389–393, 558, 596, 684, 687, 690, 700, 703, 743, 749, 788
Frankfurt an der Oder 362
Frankfurter, David 57, 589, 656
Franz Ferdinand, Austrian archduke 463
Franz Josef, emperor of Austria-Hungary 81
Fraustadt (Wschowa) 324, 680, 682
Free Trade Unions 173
Freemasonry 685
Freiburg 592
Freikorps 33–34
Freimann (rabbi) 259
Freisler, Roland 369, 522, 653, 666–668
Fremdenpolizei, *see* Police for Foreign Nationals
Frercks, Rudolf 138
Freundlich, Erwin Finlay 172, 230–231
Freundlich, Herbert Max Finlay 172, 230
Freystadt 679
Freytag, Alfred 630
Frick, Wilhelm, *see also* Reich (and Prussian) Minister/Ministry of the Interior 41, 48, 54, 96–97, 146, 152, 156, 180, 250, 257, 286, 341, 477, 479–480, 484, 497, 500, 502, 505, 519–521, 523, 541, 546, 552, 557, 565, 586, 589, 656, 749
Friedemann, Heinrich Walter 437–439, 441–442
Friedmann, Alfred 130
Friedrich (NSDAP Kreisleiter) 363
Friedrich, Carl Georg 235–236
Friedrich, Gustav 285
Friedrich, Kurt 653
Friedrich, Werner 602, 604
Friedrich Wilhelm III, King of Prussia 17, 140, 617
Frijda, Herman 188
Fritsch, Karl 223
Fritsch, Theodor 314, 479
Fröhlich, Eugen 466
Fromm, Edgar 304
Fromm, Ernst 585, 587
Fromm, Herbert 304
Fromm, Julius (Israel) 303–307
Fromm, Max 304
Frymann, Daniel, *see* Claß, Heinrich

Fuchs, Erwin 130
Fuhrmann, Otto 408
Fuld, Lothar 129–131
Fuld, Ludwig 130
Fulda 484
Funk-Stunde 170
Fürth 300
Furtwängler, Wilhelm 48

G

Garda de Fier 379
Gärtner (Hamburg resident) 329
Gärtner (official, Regional Contract Office for the State of Saxony) 153
Gärtnerplatz Theatre, Munich 327
Gagelmann, Max 630
Gagelmann, Wilhelm 400–402
Gailingen 22, 35
Galley, Alfred 648
Gareis, Heinrich 408
Garmisch-Partenkirchen 57, 326–327
Gaus, Friedrich 180, 522–523
Gayer, Feiga, née Zonstein 626
Gayer, Leo 626
Gayer, Salomon (Sally) 626
Gdynia (Gdingen) 707
Geheimes Staatspolizeiamt (Gestapa), see Gestapo Central Office
Gehrte 179
Gehrike, Rosalie, née Elsner 633
Geiger, Abraham 766
Geilenkirchen 300
General Trust Agency for Jewish Emigration GmbH (Altreu), see business and companies
Geneva 37, 46, 180, 642–643
Geneva Convention on Upper Silesia 146, 181, 243, 246, 495, 578, 612, 727, 729
George VI, King of England 768–769
Gercke, Achim 155, 185, 187, 415
Gerdauen 483
Gerlach, Helmuth von 252, 363
German Agrarian League (Bund der Landwirte) 24
German Association of Chambers of Industry and Commerce 280, 349
German-Atlantic Telegraph Company 241
German Automobile Club 419

German Bar Association 560
German Caritas Association 297–298, 437–439, 441–443, 466
German Christians 290, 486
German Civil Code 150, 264, 309, 336–337, 654, 677–678
German Civil Service Law (*Deutsches Beamtengesetz*) 273
German Committee – with Hindenburg for Volk and Reich 306–307
German Council of Municipalities (Deutscher Gemeindetag) 232, 280–281, 454, 595–596, 701
German Democratic Party (DDP) 35
German East Africa 394, 757
German Football League 158
German Gymnastics Association 160, 228, 277–279, 300
German Labour Front (DAF) 320, 348–349, 411, 418, 458, 463, 491, 498, 512, 530, 546, 559, 623, 645, 724, 759, 784
German Language Association
German League (Deutschland) 24
German League for Human Rights 156, 252, 435
German League of Gymnasts 33
German Medical Association 286
German Municipal Code (Deutsche Gemeindeordnung) 543, 595, 644
German National Association of Commercial Employees (Deutschnationaler Handlungsgehilfenverband) 24, 33
German National People's Party (DNVP) 33
German News Agency (dnb) 386, 509, 516
German Order of Samaritans 681
German Pharmacists' Association 311–312
German Reich-Auto Club 419
German Reich Committee for Physical Exercise 157–158
German Reich Railways 148, 154, 246, 472, 499, 511, 559
German Rowing Association 300
German South-West Africa 394
German Student Fraternities 33
German Swimming Association 300
German University Circle (Deutscher Hochschulring) 34

German *Völkisch*-Protection and Defiance League 30, 277
Gesetz für den Aufbau der Wehrmacht, see Law for the Establishment of the Wehrmacht
Gesetz gegen die Überfüllung deutscher Schulen und Hochschulen, see Law against Overcrowding in German Schools and Institutions of Higher Education
Gesetz gegen Mißbräuche bei der Eheschließung und bei der Annahme an Kindesstatt, see Law against the Abuse of Marriage and Adoption
Gesetz gegen Verrat der Deutschen Volkswirtschaft, see Law against Betrayal of the German National Economy
Gesetz gegen Wirtschaftssabotage, see Law against Economic Sabotage
Gesetz über Änderungen von Stiftungen, see Law on Changes to Foundations
Gesetz über das Kündigungsrecht der durch das Gesetz zur Wiederherstellung des Berufsbeamtentums betroffenen Personen, see Law on the Termination of Rental Contracts by Persons Affected by the Law for the Restoration of the Professional Civil Service
Gesetz über das Schlachten von Tieren, see Law and Regulation on the Slaughter of Animals
Gesetz über den Ausgleich von Schäden, die dem Deutschen Reich durch Juden zugefügt werden, see Law on the Settlement of Damages Inflicted on the German Reich by Jews
Gesetz über den Widerruf von Einbürgerungen und die Aberkennung der deutschen Staatsangehörigkeit, see Law on the Revocation of Naturalization and the Deprivation of German Nationality
Gesetz über die Änderung von Familien- und Vornamen, see Law on Changes to Surnames and Forenames
Gesetz über die Ausübung der Reisevermittlung, see Law on Operating a Travel Agency

Gesetz über die durch innere Unruhen verursachten Schäden, see Law on Damages Caused by Civil Unrest
Gesetz über die Einziehung kommunistischen Vermögens, see Law Concerning the Confiscation of Communist Property
Gesetz über die Einziehung staats- und volksfeindlichen Vermögens, see Law Concerning the Confiscation of Subversive Property
Gesetz über die Stellung der Juden, see Law on the Status of Jews
Gesetz über die Zulassung zur Rechtsanwaltschaft, see Law on Admission to the Legal Profession
Gesetz über eine Steuer der Personen, die nicht zur Erfüllung der zweijährigen aktiven Dienstzeit einberufen werden, see Law Concerning a Tax on Persons Not Conscripted for Two Years of Active Military Service
Gesetz über Maßnahmen im ehemaligen oberschlesischen Abstimmungsgebiet, see Law on Measures in the Former Upper Silesian Plebiscite Areas
Gesetz zum Schutz der Erbgesundheit des deutschen Volkes (Erbgesundheitsgesetz), see Law for the Protection of the Hereditary Health of the German People
Gesetz zum Schutz des deutschen Blutes und der deutschen Ehre (Blutschutzgesetz), see Law for the Protection of German Blood and German Honour
Gesetz zum Schutz des Einzelhandels, see Law for the Protection of Retail Trade
Gesetz zur Änderung des Gesetzes über die Devisenbewirtschaftung, see Law for the Amendment of the Law on Foreign Exchange Control
Gesetz zur Änderung der Gewerbeordnung, see Law on the Amendment of the Commercial Code
Gesetz zur Änderung des Strafrechts und des Strafverfahrens, see Law Amending Criminal Law and Criminal Procedure
Gesetz zur Behebung der Not von Volk und Reich, see Enabling Act

Gesetz zur Ordnung der Arbeit in öffentlichen Verwaltungen und Betrieben, see Law for the Regulation of Labour in Public Administrations and Enterprises
Gesetz zur Ordnung der nationalen Arbeit, see Law for the Regulation of National Labour
Gesetz zur Regelung der öffentlichen Sammlungen und sammlungsähnlichen Veranstaltungen, see Law Regulating Public Collections and Related Events
Gesetz zur Verhütung erbkranken Nachwuchses, see Law for the Prevention of Offspring with Hereditary Diseases
Gesetz zur Vorbereitung des organischen Aufbaues der deutschen Wirtschaft, see Law for the Preparation of the Organic Development of the German Economy
Gesetz zur Wiederherstellung des Berufsbeamtentums, see Law for the Restoration of the Professional Civil Service
Gestapa, see Gestapo Central Office (Gestapa)
Gestapo 51, 55, 57, 141–142, 353, 387–388, 408, 419, 433, 435, 469, 494, 496, 500, 504, 518, 591, 593, 611, 645, 647, 664, 685, 704, 716, 777, 790
- Berlin 471, 489
- Bielefeld 645
- Dresden 568
- Frankfurt am Main 684, 686–687
- Freiburg 592
- Karlsruhe 515, 592
- Königsberg 482
- Krefeld 57
- Stettin 436
Gestapo Central Office (Gestapa) 56–57, 138, 250–251, 321, 331, 349–350, 354–356, 372, 374, 403, 410, 414, 419, 433–435, 448, 468, 472, 479, 489, 496–497, 504, 513, 571, 592, 649, 658, 716–717, 790
Gilka, Ursula, see Wertheim, Ursula
Giwat Brenner (Kibbutz) 457
Glatz (Kłodzko) 620
Glauchau 223
Gleispach, Count Wenzel von 369
Gleiwitz (Gliwice) 181, 243, 246, 494, 729, 731
Globke, Hans 480, 596–597

Glockner (member, Reich Kennel Club) 691
Głubczyce, see Leobschütz
Gnojau (Gnojewo) 715
Gobineau Society 24
Goebbels Foundation for Stage Artists 483
Goebbels, Joseph, see also Reich Minister/Ministry of Public Enlightenment and Propaganda 40, 42, 48, 54, 104–105, 117, 136, 173, 314–316, 345, 359, 391, 477–478, 519, 768, 780, 782
Goerdeler, Carl Friedrich 450
Gohlke, Elfriede, see Fischer, Ruth
Gold, Peter 179
Goldap 420
Goldmann, Ernst 166
Goldmann, Felix 226
Goldschmidt, Jacob 221
Goldschmidt, James Paul 219–220
Goldschmit, Kurt Walter 256
Goldstein, Julius 744
Goldstein, Kurt 163
Gommlich, Hellmuth 395
Göpfert, Arthur 456
Góra, see Guhrau
Gordon, George Anderson 214
Göring, Hermann, see also Minister President, Prussia; Prussian Minister/Ministry of the Interior 41, 48, 58–60, 98, 104–105, 112, 139, 156, 161, 167–168, 180, 184, 195, 249, 448, 513, 519, 646, 656, 662, 694, 696, 754, 761, 784–786
Görlitz 402
Gorzów Śląski, see Landsberg
Gottheil, Walter 661–664
Gotthold, John 220
Göttingen 52
Gottinger, Balthasar 165
Gottschalk (lawyer, Palestine Shipping Company) 458
Gottschalk, Max 123
Grabow 445, 647
Graetz (board of directors, Jewish Community, Berlin) 259
Graetz, Heinrich 245
Gramsch, Friedrich 761
Gransow (parishioner, Altdamm) 436
Grau, Fritz 369–372
Grau, Wilhelm 321–322, 605, 610, 748–750

Grauert, Ludwig 180
Great Britain, see United Kingdom of Great Britain and Northern Ireland
Greece 424
Green, William 109
Grimmsmann, Erna 375–376
Gronau, Westphalia 179
Gronemann, Sammy 125
Gross, Alfred 347
Groß, Walter 414–415, 448, 497, 530–533
Groß-Breesen 672–673, 778
Groß-Gaglow 368
Groß Gerau 405
Groß-Karben 346–347
Gross-Strehlitz 246, 680, 730
Gross-Wartenberg (Syców) 324, 679–680
Grosse (art historian) 695
Größer, Max 438–439, 442
Großes Werder 715
Grossmann, Kurt R. 252
Grün, Ridi 326–327
Grünberg 405
Grund, Peter 615
Grundsteuergesetz, see Property Tax Law
Gruner, Carl 407–408
Grünewald 529
Grynszpan (Grynspan, Grynßpan, Grünspan), Hershel (Herszel, Herschel) 358
Grzesinski, Albert 250, 363
Guani (Uruguayan representative, High Commission for Refugees) 297
Guatemala 423
Gubitz, Paul 566
Guericke (archivist, South Africa) 757
Guericke (businessman, South Africa) 757
Guggenheim, Leopold
Guhrau 324
Gumpert, Charlotte, née Blaschko 161–163
Gumpert, Martin 161–162, 624–625
Gumpert, Nina 162–163, 624–625
Gumprich (procurator) 458
Gundolf, Friedrich 453
Gürtner, Franz, see also Reich Minister/Ministry of Justice 180, 369, 497, 502, 521–523, 564, 599–600, 655, 666
Gütt, Arthur 535

Gunzenhausen 344–345
Gustloff, Wilhelm 57, 588–589, 656
Guttentag 730
Gutzeit (co-owner, Johannes Wenzel) 631
Gwinner, Arthur von 238
Gyssling, Walter 92–94

H

Haake, Rudolf 450–451, 498, 509–510
Haavara Agreement 351, 442, 576, 637, 714, 753–754
Haber, Fritz 172
Haber, Mendel Zelig 179
hachsharah, see emigration
Hachsharah Association, Hamburg 423
Hackelsberger, Albert 442
Haegert, Wilhelm 497, 503
Hafemann, Wilhelm Wolfgang 213
Haffmann, Arthur 495–496
Hagen, Herbert 58, 790
Hagenow 445, 623–624
Hagenow, Joachim 403–404
Haifa 457
Haiti 393
Halberstadt 224
Halle 224
Hallgarten, Gustav 257
Hamburg 34, 43, 52, 197, 221–223, 260, 328, 375, 391–392, 394, 403, 421–423, 425–426, 431, 458, 547, 558
Hamburg Culture League, see Jewish Society of Arts and Sciences, Hamburg
Hamburg Medical Association 233
Hamburg State Lottery 547–548
Hamburger (resident, Berlin) 440
Hammenhög, Waldemar 477
Hanau 413–414
Hänke, Heinrich 759
Hanover 300, 454, 670
Hanover-Braunschweig 800
Hansmann, Wilhelm 252
Hapt, P. 131
Hardt, Ludwig 256
Harlan, Veit 40
Harling, Otto von 42
Hartman, Gustave 189
Hartmann League, see Association of Physicians in Germany

Hartmann, Hermann 248
Harvard University competition (1940) 92, 97, 122, 125, 159, 164, 226, 255, 332, 383, 427, 465, 661, 664, 684
Haselbacher, Karl 716–717
Hassel, Erich 287
Hassenstein, Fritz 293
Hauptmann, Gerhard 24, 398
Hausding, Alfred 305
Hausmann, Margarete 483
Hausmann, Wilhelm 483
Hausmann Foundation, Arendsee 483
Hayes (cardinal, New York) 109
Health and Welfare Office, Hamburg 431–432
Hebrew Immigrant Aid Society (HIAS) 189
Hecker 375–376
Heckert, Friedrich 253
Heckscher, Cäsar 221
Heckscher, Jacob 220–222
Heckscher, Julius 547
Heckscher, Maria, née Frank 547
Hedding, Otto 711
Hehalutz 50, 331, 350–351, 354, 425, 459
Heidelberg 52, 592
Heidtmann (state commissioner, Upper Silesia) 246
Heilberg, Adolf 99
Heilmann, E. 131
Heine, Heinrich 660
Heinen (engineer, Suhl) 462
Heines, Edmund 100, 212–213
Heinz (head of Combat League for German Culture) 327
Helfferich, Emil 260
Helldorf, Count Wolf Heinrich von, *see also* chief of police, Berlin 35, 477, 489
Heller, Abraham 605–610
Hellstein 798
Hengeler, Hans 615
Henry and Emma Budge Foundation 426
Heppmer (Hamburg resident) 223
Hergert, Nikolaus 447
Hering, Hermann 250–251, 476, 753
Herman, Abraham 189
Hermann, Georg 256
Hermannswalde 644
Herriot, Édouard 358

Herrnstadt-Oettingen, Edith 256
Hertzog, James Barry Munnick 443
Herxheimer, Karl 472
Herzfeld, Albert 552–553, 614–616
Herzfeld, Annemarie 552
Herzfeld, Elsa, née Volkmar 552–553
Herzfeld, Franz 566
Herzl, Theodor 133–134, 509, 606
Herzlia 350
Heß, Rudolf, *see also* Deputy of the Führer 47, 54, 138–140, 263, 348–349, 388–389, 395, 434, 484, 519, 521, 552, 588, 748–750
Hesse 280, 404–405, 482, 487, 508, 560, 584, 800
Hesse-Kassel 272
Hesse-Nassau 800
Hessel, August 719
Heun, Wilhelm 85
Heuser, Adolf 303
Heusser, Oskar 431
Heydrich, Reinhard, *see also* Chief of the Security Police and the SD 56–57, 59, 414, 419, 489, 496–497, 504, 658, 669, 704, 717
Heymann, Emil 660
Heymann, Siegmund 645
HICEM 123, 731
high commissioner of Palestine 576
Hilble, Friedrich 675
Hildebrandt, Susi 455
Hilfsverein der deutschen Juden, *see* Relief Association of German Jews
Hilgenfeldt, Erich 649
Himmler, Heinrich, *see also* Reichsführer SS and Chief of the German Police 56–57, 408, 414, 460, 518, 687
Hindenburg (Zabrze) 245, 247, 729
Hindenburg, Paul von, *see also* Reich President 37, 81–82, 338, 389–390, 398, 465
Hinkel, Hans 355, 561, 615
Hirsch, Emanuel 40
Hirsch, Otto 726
Hirsch, Siegmund 472
Hirschberg, Alfred 226
Hirschfeld, Magnus 172
Hirschland, Albert 474, 529
Hirtsiefer, Heinrich 94–95
Histadrut 457

Hitler, Adolf 83, 106, 399, 448, 511
- anti-Jewish boycott 41, 117, 500, 532
- anti-Jewish legislation and policy 16, 41, 47, 54–55, 58, 112, 142, 152, 263, 479–480, 500, 504, 510, 513, 520–521, 527, 530–532, 544, 552, 556, 564, 568–569, 583, 641, 656, 666, 668, 754, 786–787, 790
- approval of 40, 58, 91–92, 167, 305, 313–316, 410–412, 580
- criticism of 94–95, 106, 108, 124, 161, 163–164, 195, 231, 302, 378, 682, 768–769
- early years and rise to power 16, 33, 37, 81–82
- executive power 54, 57, 96, 98, 286, 386, 395, 408, 416, 462, 477, 500, 524, 530, 546, 619, 749–750, 758–759, 761
- and fellow Party members 344, 401, 519
- first months of government 29, 47, 189, 386, 661, 663, 751
- on Jewry and Marxism 31–32, 57, 409, 530–533, 692–693, 735–743
- *Mein Kampf* 32, 314–316, 399
- as public speaker 112, 173, 181, 290, 464, 519, 692–694, 709–710, 734–743
Hitler Youth 43, 54–55, 225, 398–399, 418, 429, 433, 467, 566, 624, 662, 676
Hoetzsch, Otto 610
Höfer, Werner 40
Hoffmann (official, Reich Chamber of Visual Arts) 615
Hoffmann (rabbi, Organized Orthodox Community) 529
Hoffmann (trustee, Suhl) 461–462
Hoffmann, Jacob 259
Hoffmann, Walter 156
Hoffmeyer, Horst 705
Höfler, Heinrich 438, 442
Hofmann, Chaskel 179
Hofmann, Ernst 301–302
Hofstein, Franz 566
Hohenzollern 800
Holland, *see* Netherlands, the
Holländer, Ludwig 86
Holy See, *see also* Pius XI 35
Holz, Karl 474
Hölz, Max 253
Holzmann, Willy 233
Holzschuh (magistrate, Garmisch) 326

Homann, Hermann 674
Hopf, Volkmar 232
Hoppe (parishioner, Altdamm) 436
Hoppe, Alfred 634, 639
Hoppe, Werner 177
Hoßbach, Friedrich 448
Hossenfelder, Joachim 290
house searches 93, 164, 686, 688
housing
- ownership and lease, terminations and restrictions 745
- restrictions on place of residence 504, 510, 514, 543, 558, 587
Hünfeld 446–447
Hull, Cordell 682
Humbert (government assessor) 634
Hummel, Fritz 191
Hungary 28, 424, 737
Hungen 405

I

Ichenhäuser, Emil 547
Ihering, Herbert 40
Ikenberg, Rosa, *see* Schaefer, Rosa
Iława, *see* Deutsch Eylau
Ilse, Rudolf 464
Independent Mizrachi Organization of Germany 350
Insterburg 420
Institute for Sexual Research 172
Institute of Solar Physics (Einstein Institute) 230
International Association of Socialist Physicians 386
International Federation of Trade Unions 298
International Jewish Women's League 334
International Student Service 298
Invalidendank 306
Iraq 713
Isak, David 479
Isakowitz, Lore, later Petzal 455
Israelite Association for Old Age Benefits and Nursing Care 670
Israelite Community, *see* Jewish Community
Israelite Medical Care Association for Women and Girls 549

Israelite Men's Health Insurance
    Companies 549
Israelite Men's Medical Care
    Associations 549
Israelite Nursing Care Association for the
    Elderly 549
Israelite Women's Benevolent Association
    for Sick Women and Women in
    Childbed 549
Israelite Women's Health Insurance
    Companies 549
Israelite Women's Medical Care
    Associations 549
Istanbul 383, 456
Italy 195, 295, 394, 424, 441, 621, 713, 739

J

Jacob, Paul 767
Jacobovits (rabbi) 259
Jakob, Plawner 179
Janentzky, Christian 455
Jansen (schoolboy, Cologne) 330
Jarres, Karl Rudolf 157–158
Jauer 680–681
Jawor, see Jauer
Jedwab, Abraham 179
Jedwab, Ester, see Stern, Ester
Jedwab, Isidor-Julius 179
Jedwab, Jakob 179
Jena 20
Jerusalem 714–715
Jewish Agency for Palestine 234, 297–298,
    351, 423, 621
Jewish Auto Club, see Auto-Club 1927
Jewish Boxing Club Maccabi 351
Jewish Central Information Office 727–728
Jewish Colonization Association (ICA,
    JCA) 51, 123, 297–298, 563, 771, 775
Jewish Community 29, 426–427
- Berlin 44, 117, 182–184, 216, 259, 529, 626,
    697–698, 765, 792–795
- Breslau 529, 764–766
- Cologne 529, 766
- Deutsch-Krone 321
- Essen 529
- Frankfurt am Main 229, 529, 684, 703
- Hamburg 421, 424–426
- Königsberg 529
- Leipzig 597–598
- Mannheim 529
- Merzig 783
- Munich 173–174, 283–284
- Nuremberg 529
- Stavenhagen 443
Jewish Culture League, see Culture League of
    German Jews
Jewish everyday life 162, 170–171, 322–323,
    328, 383, 397, 427–428, 508, 620, 628, 664–
    665, 679–680, 684, 729, 733, 763–764
Jewish Gymnastics and Sports Association
    Bar Kokhba Hanover 300
Jewish League of Combat Veterans, see Reich
    League of Jewish Combat Veterans
Jewish Museum
- Berlin 184, 216
- Breslau 509
Jewish organizations, dissolution of and
    restrictions on 229, 318, 356, 374, 679, 684–
    687, 690
'Jewish question' 16, 23, 54, 59, 82–83, 89,
    132–134, 136, 143, 168–169, 177, 185–186, 215,
    288, 300, 314, 332, 334, 349, 354, 372–373,
    384, 398, 409, 415–416, 444, 463, 497, 499–
    501, 504, 513, 530, 533, 535, 537, 545–548,
    565, 571, 582–583, 585–588, 600, 605, 607,
    611, 635, 642, 658–659, 693, 713–714, 747–
    748, 750
- academic research on 30, 39, 287–289,
    307–308, 535, 537, 545, 605, 610, 658–659,
    747–748, 750
Jewish Society of Arts and Sciences,
    Hamburg 422
Jewish Telegraphic Agency 344, 412, 575–576,
    611, 644, 646
Jewish Welfare Association for Lower
    Silesia 681
Jewish Winter Relief 51, 649–650, 764, 774,
    796, 798–800
Jochimsen (ship's captain) 458
Joerger, Kuno 438, 442
Jordan, E. 131
Josephy (representative, Supreme Council,
    Jewish Regional Community,
    Mecklenburg-Schwerin) 529
Judendorf 644

Jüdischer Kulturbund, *see* Culture League of German Jews
Jungdeutscher Orden, *see* Young German Order
Jüttner, Max 691

K
Kahn, Arthur 166
Kahn, Bernhard 123–125
Kahn, Erwin 166
Kahn, Richard 240
Kaiser Wilhelm Institute for Breeding Research 30
Kaiser Wilhelm Institute of Anthropology, Human Heredity, and Eugenics 30
Kaiser Wilhelm Society for the Advancement of Science 469–470
Kaliski, Lotte 767
Kalthof 644
Kamnitzer, Bernhard 224
Kampfbund für den gewerblichen Mittelstand, *see* Combat League for Small and Medium-Sized Businesses
Kampfbund für deutsche Kultur, *see* Combat League for German Culture
Kanth 680
Kantorowicz (Kantorowitz), Hans 227–228, 278–279
Kantorowicz, Hermann 219
Karelia 708
Karlebach, Ezriel 378, 380
Karlovy Vary, *see* Carlsbad
Karlsruhe 515, 592
Kassel 797
Kassel, Martha 487–488
Kąty Wrocławskie, *see* Kanth
Katz, Stefan 778
Katz, Theodor D. 167
Katzenstein, Isaak 446
Katzenstein, Jakob 220, 446
Kaufmann, Karl 375, 377
Kautzsch, Emil 87
Kehl (banker) 239–240
Keller, Friedrich von 181
Kelter, Will (Willi) 102
Kempner, Robert M. W. 52
Kenya 771
Keppler, Wilhelm 460–462, 513

Kerber, Willy 660
Keren Hayesod 351, 426, 528
Keren Kayemeth Leisrael Jewish National Fund 351
Kerr, Alfred 40, 111, 253, 473
Kerrl, Hanns, *see also* Prussian Minister/Ministry of Justice 100, 180, 249, 369, 779
Kestenberg, Leo 81, 91
Kiefer, Henny, *see* Angress, Henny
Kiel 42, 126
Kießer, Walter 759
Kilian, Hanns 326
Killy, Leo 349
Kimmich, Karl 234, 243
Kitzinger, Elisabeth Rachel 174
Klagges, Dietrich 410
Klausberg 729
Klebe, Jakob 446
Klebe, Sally 446–447
Klee, Alfred 529
Klee, Karl 369
Kleemann (student) 508
Kleinbaum, Moshe, later Sneh 751
Klein Silsterwitz (Sulistrowiczki) 396
Klein-Strehlitz 728
Klein, Wilhelm 213
Klemme, Emil 767
Klemperer, Eva, née Schlemmer 56, 457
Klemperer, Victor 42, 56, 455–456
Klöckner, Peter 461
Klopfer, Gerhard 717
Klopstock, Friedrich Gottlieb 17
Kluczbork, *see* Kreuzburg
Knickerbocker, Hubert Renfro 171
Knips (schoolboy, Cologne) 330
Knofe, Oskar 224
Koch (lawyer, Suhl) 461–462
Koch, Erich 644
Koch, Robert 498
Kochmann, Arthur 243
Köhler (Reich economic advisor) 108, 498
Kohlau (Kolzowo) 324
Kohlrausch, Eduard 369
Kohn (resident, Schweidnitz) 620
Kohn, Hedwig 218–219
Kollenscher, Max 259
Kolonial-Kriegerdank 306
Komarnicki, Tytus 643

Index

König (assessor, Friedberg) 347
König, Joel, later Ben Gershôm, Ezra
König, Sussmann 730
Königsberg (Kaliningrad) 46, 354, 420, 427–428, 430, 482, 495, 602–603, 644
Konstadt 680, 729
Konstanz 407
Köpke, Gerhard 522–523
Körner, Paul 696
Korschelt (speaker at church meeting, resident of Daber) 436
Kortner, Fritz 472
Kotze, Hans Ulrich von 250
Kożuchów, see Freystadt
Kraft durch Freude (KdF), see Strength through Joy
Krahmer-Möllenberg, Erich 705
Krakow, Harris, see Levinsky, King
Krämer, Emil 130
Kraschnitz 680–681
Krauel, Wolfgang 643
Krause, Reinhold 290
Krebs, Friedrich 114–115, 389, 700, 749
Krekels (court clerk, Frankfurt am Main) 190, 192
Kreutz, Benedikt 438
Kreutzer, Leonid 256
Kreuzburg 246, 680, 729
Krogmann, Carl Vincent 260, 547
Krohn, Johannes 497, 503
Krojanker, Gustav 659
Krone, Heinrich 438–439, 441–442
Krośnice, see Kraschnitz
Krug, Georg 403–404
Krug, Karl 249
Krüger (police inspector, Berlin) 481
Kube, Wilhelm, see also Oberpräsident, Brandenburg 585
Kuchel (block leader, Hamburg) 375
Kühlmann, Richard von 27
Kühlungsborn 483
Kühne, Walter 505
Kulturbund deutscher Juden/Kulturbund der Juden Deutschland, see Culture League of German Jews
Kümmel, Otto 695
Kümmell, Richard 233
Kunig, Rudolf Bonifaz 327

Kunisch, Siegmund 565
Künneth, Walter 485–488
Kurchinskii, Michail 271
Kyffhäuser League, see Reich Veterans' League

L

La Guardia, Fiorello H. 682
Lachmann, Hans 382–383
Lachmann-Mosse, Hans 473
Lachs (representative, Jewish Community, Breslau) 529
Ladewig, Hans Carl 278
Lagemann, Paul 101–105
Lammers, Hans Heinrich, see also chief of the Reich Chancellery 96, 157, 317, 368, 395, 409, 656, 779, 786, 790
land ownership, restrictions and prohibition 415, 490, 504, 515, 560
Landau, Anneliese 256
Landau, Karl 177
Landsberg 680, 729
Landshut 328
Lange, Helene 335
Langendorf 729, 731
Lansing, Robert 20
Lanz, Heinrich 347
Laski, Neville Jonas 123
Latvia 424, 707
Lau, Elly 481
Lau, Fritz 481
Laue, Max von 231
Lauret, René 171
Lausanne 298
Lauterbach 405
Law against Betrayal of the German National Economy (*Gesetz gegen Verrat der Deutschen Volkswirtschaft*) 625
Law against Economic Sabotage (*Gesetz gegen Wirtschaftssabotage*) 59
Law against Overcrowding in German Schools and Institutions of Higher Education (*Gesetz gegen die Überfüllung deutscher Schulen und Hochschulen*) 172, 221, 268, 517–518, 558
Law against the Abuse of Marriage and Adoption (*Gesetz gegen Mißbräuche bei der Eheschließung und bei der Annahme an Kindesstatt*) 370

Law Amending Criminal Law and Criminal Procedure (*Gesetz zur Änderung des Strafrechts und des Strafverfahrens*) 365

Law and Regulation on the Slaughter of Animals (*Gesetz über das Schlachten von Tieren*) 142, 259

Law Concerning a Tax on Persons Not Conscripted for Two Years of Active Military Service (*Gesetz über eine Steuer der Personen, die nicht zur Erfüllung der zweijährigen aktiven Dienstzeit einberufen werden*) 719

Law Concerning the Confiscation of Communist Property (*Gesetz über die Einziehung kommunistischen Vermögens*) 362, 374

Law Concerning the Confiscation of Subversive Property (*Gesetz über die Einziehung staats- und volksfeindlichen Vermögens*) 362, 374

Law for the Amendment of the Law on Foreign Exchange Control (*Gesetz zur Änderung des Gesetzes über die Devisenbewirtschaftung*) 59

Law for the Establishment of the Wehrmacht (*Gesetz für den Aufbau der Wehrmacht*) 465

Law for the Preparation of the Organic Reconstruction of the German Economy (*Gesetz zur Vorbereitung des organischen Aufbaues der deutschen Wirtschaft*) 342

Law for the Prevention of Offspring with Hereditary Diseases (*Gesetz zur Verhütung erbkranken Nachwuchses*) 153, 288, 370

Law for the Protection of German Blood and German Honour (Blood Protection Law) (*Gesetz zum Schutz des deutschen Blutes und der deutschen Ehre* [*Blutschutzgesetz*]) 54, 144, 403, 415, 469, 492, 502, 504, 514, 519–520, 522–524, 539, 551, 555, 596, 616, 640

Law for the Protection of Retail Trade (*Gesetz zum Schutz des Einzelhandels*) 489

Law for the Protection of the Hereditary Health of the German People (Marital Health Law) (*Gesetz zum Schutz der Erbgesundheit des deutschen Volkes* [*Erbgesundheitsgesetz*]) 524, 596

Law for the Regulation of Labour in Public Administrations and Enterprises (*Gesetz zur Ordnung der Arbeit in öffentlichen Verwaltungen und Betrieben*) 543

Law for the Restoration of the Professional Civil Service (Civil Service Law) (*Gesetz zur Wiederherstellung des Berufsbeamtentums* [*Berufsbeamtengesetz*]) 32, 47, 60, 141, 143–144, 147–151, 155–156, 177, 182–183, 186, 218–220, 226, 231, 248, 261, 264, 268, 283, 287, 312, 320, 338, 341, 370, 415, 437, 455, 502, 516, 530–531, 744

Law on Admission to the Legal Profession (*Gesetz über die Zulassung zur Rechtsanwaltschaft*) 144, 215, 312

Law on Changes to Foundations (*Gesetz über die Änderungen von Stiftungen*) 604

Law on Changes to Surnames and Forenames (*Gesetz über die Änderung von Familien- und Vornamen*) 145

Law on Damages Caused by Civil Unrest (*Gesetz über die durch innere Unruhen verursachten Schäden*) 657, 711

Law on Measures in the Former Upper Silesian Plebiscite Areas (*Gesetz über Maßnahmen im ehemaligen oberschlesischen Abstimmungsgebiet*) 727

Law on Operating a Travel Agency (*Gesetz über die Ausübung der Reisevermittlung*) 638

Law on Reich Ministers (*Reichsministergesetz*) 150–151

Law on the Amendment of the Commercial Code (*Gesetz zur Änderung der Gewerbeordnung*) 638, 790

Law on the Expropriation of Goods used for Anti-National Purposes (Bavaria) (*Gesetz über die Enteignung von zu antinationalen Zwecken verwendetem Gut*)

Law on the Regulation of National Labour (*Gesetz zur Ordnung der nationalen Arbeit*) 348, 413–415, 503, 543, 784

Law on the Reich Chamber of Culture (*Reichskulturkammergesetz*) 615

Law on the Revocation of Naturalization and the Deprivation of German Nationality (*Gesetz über den Widerruf von Einbürgerungen und die Aberkennung der*

deutschen Staatsangehörigkeit) 47, 145, 251, 303, 306, 370
Law on the Settlement of Damages Inflicted on the German Reich by Jews (Gesetz über den Ausgleich von Schäden, die dem Deutschen Reich durch Juden zugefügt werden) 32
Law on the Status of the Jews (Gesetz über die Stellung der Juden) 47, 138–140, 144–146
Law on the Termination of Rental Contracts by Persons Affected by the Law for the Restoration of the Professional Civil Service (Gesetz über das Kündigungsrecht der durch das Gesetz zur Wiederherstellung des Berufsbeamtentums betroffenen Personen) 148, 789
Law Regulating Public Collections and Related Events (Collections Law) (Gesetz zur Regelung der öffentlichen Sammlungen und sammlungsähnlichen Veranstaltungen [Sammlungsgesetz]) 650, 670
Law to Remedy the Distress of the People and the Reich (Gesetz zur Behebung der Not von Volk und Reich), see Enabling Act
Lazarus Gumpel Foundation 426
League of Blinded War Veterans 47
League of German Female Physicians 159
League of German Girls 384, 418
League of Jewish Employees 374
League of Jewish Women 44, 527, 529, 777
League of National Socialist German Lawyers (Bund Nationalsozialistischer Deutscher Juristen) 100, 243–244, 263
League of Nations 146, 180–181, 188, 294, 296, 412, 577, 579, 613, 642–643, 714, 740–741
League of Nations High Commissioner for Refugees Coming from Germany 294, 296–299, 577
Lebeck (teacher, Breslau) 509
Leber, Julius 88
Lederberger, Simon 222
Lederer (art dealer) 695
Leeb, Baronet Wilhelm von 460
Leers, Johann von 86–88, 138
Lehman, Herbert Henry 109–110
Lehmann, Ernst 40
Leipold, Artur 130

Leipzig 55, 197, 225–226, 450, 498, 500, 509–510, 546, 597, 652, 703
Lemberg, see Lwów
Lenk, Georg 566
Lenz, Fritz 30–31
Lenz, Max 285–286
Leobschütz 729
Leopold, Joseph Arnold 601
Leroy-Beaulieu, Anatole 134
Less, Georg 765
Lesser (journalist, Argentina) 171
Lesser, Hermann 691
Lessing, Gotthold Ephraim 17, 50, 491
Lessing, Theodor 491
Lester, Seán 181
Lettow-Vorbeck, Kurt von 767
Leubus (Lubiąż) 324, 680
Leubus Provincial State Hospital and Nursing Home 323, 681
Levetzow, Magnus, see also chief of police, Berlin 303–304, 477
Lévi, Israel 123
Levi, Leopold 529
Levinger, Wilhelm 31
Levinsky, King (born Harris Krakow) 302–303
Levy, Aaron J. 189
Levy, Bertold 103
Levy, Ernst 222
Levy, Joseph B. 684–690
Lewald, Theodor Otto 157–158
Lewaldt, G. 615–616
Lewin, Reinhold 420
Ley, Robert 546
Libya 714
Lichtwitz, Leopold 162
Lichtwitz, Max 317
Liebenthal, Kurt 278
Liebermann, Max 50, 172–173, 256
Liegner, Martin 566
Liegnitz 402
Lieres und Wilkau, Joachim Friedrich von 146
Liese, Kurt 460, 462
Lima 456
Lindemann (Protestant pastor) 438
Linder, Karl 114
Lindgens, Arthur 696

Linnemann, Felix 157–158
Lippe 800
Lippert, Julius 116, 138, 182, 184, 213, 397, 767
Lippmann, Gert 672
Lissauer, Ernst 26
List, Friedrich
Lithuania 394, 707–709
Littauer (physician, Breslau) 385
Littauer, Margot 383–385
Litterscheid, Richard 102–103
Litvinov, Maxim 609
Lobkowicz, Maximilian 297
Łódź (Litzmannstadt) 175, 313–316, 707
Loeffler, Lothar 545
Loeper, Wilhelm Friedrich 401
Loewe, Heinrich 81
Loewen, Hanns van (born Löwenstein, Hans) 103
Loewenberg, Ernst 43
Loewenberg, Karl 255
London 188, 473, 714, 777–778
Löns, Hermann 398
looting and theft, see also Aryanization/expropriation 42, 93, 662
López Oliván, Julio 412
Lorenz, Erwin 331
Lorenz, Gerhard 369
Lösener, Bernhard 369, 497, 634
Lossen (official, Reich Ministry of the Interior) 440
Louis, Joe 303
Löwen (Lewin Brzeski) 680
Löwenstein, Alex 633–634
Löwenstein, Hans, see Loewen, Hanns van
Löwenstein, Karl 121
Löwenstein, Leo 338, 367–368, 529
Löwenstein, Margarete, née Cyrus 633
Lubiąż, see Leubus
Lübz 443
Lucerne 509
Ludendorff, Hans 230
Ludwig, Heinz 625
Ludwig, Renate 485
Ludwigslust 444
Lueger, Karl 81
Lüer, Carl 280
Lummer (physicist, Breslau) 218
Luther, Martin 276, 291

Luxembourg 295, 394, 435
Luxemburg, Rosa 33
Lwów 707

M

Maccabi 351, 434
Machol, Josef 180
Mackensen, Hans Georg von 779
Magdeburg 224, 300, 474
Main Welfare Office for the War-Disabled, Königsberg 758, 760
Majoni, Giovanni Cesare 297
Malsch, Amalie, née Samuel 682
Malsch, Paul 682–683, 768
Malsch, Wilhelm, later William Ronald Malsh 682–683, 768
Manasse (Community Representation of the Hanseatic Towns, Altona) 529
Manila 732
Mankiewitz, Paul 238
Mann, Heinrich 253, 571
Mann, Thomas 171
Mannes, Bruno 326
Mannheim 592
Mannheim, Karl 455
Mannheimer, Emil 475
Manning, William T. 109
Marahrens, August 488
Marba, Theodor 130
Marburg 52, 272
Marcus, Ernst 664–665
Marcus, Paul 444
Maretzky, Oskar 213
Margulies, Emil 266–267
Marienbad (Mariánské Lázně) 665
Marienwerder 420, 495, 761
Maritime Office Hamburg 458
marking of Jews and their possessions
- compulsory Jewish names 479–480, 491–492
- identification of individuals 47, 145, 515, 791
- shops and businesses 411, 489, 532, 541–543, 546, 640–641, 693, 779–780, 791
Marks, Simon 575–576
Marotzke, Wilhelm 696
Marr, Erich 233
Marshall, James

Martini, Oskar 431
Marx, Ernst 229
Marx, Heinrich, later Henry Marx 137, 170–171
Marx, Otto 164–167
Masaryk, Tomáš Garrigue 26
Massfeller, Franz 335
Mayer (Regional Association of Israelite Religious Communities of Hesse, Mainz) 529
Mayer (SS-Untersturmführer, RuSHA) 415
Mayer, Kurt 448
McConnell, Francis J. 109
McDonald, James Grover 294, 296–299, 577–579
Mecklenburg 443, 445, 482–483, 507, 800
Medicus, Franz 286
Meier, Alexander 138
Mein Kampf, see Hitler, Adolf
Meiningen 395
Meinshausen, Hans 293
Meißen 470–471
Melchior, Carl 26, 189
Meldau, R. 131
Memel (Klaipėda) 394
Mendel, Gregor 288
Mendelsohn, Bruno 626
Mendelssohn-Bartholdy, Felix 40
Menge, Arthur 300
Mentzel, Rudolf 748
Merkur association, Nuremberg 225
Merzbach, Ernst 224
Merzig 783
Messersmith, George S. 214
Metternich, Prince Klemens von 20
Mexico 423, 772
Meyer (archivist, Hamburg) 375
Meyer, Alfred 249
Meyer, Bertha, née Zwindorfer 697–698
Meyer, Franz 529
Meyer, Isaac 229–230
Meyer, Richard 147
Meyer-Brüggemann, Johannes 400–401
Meyerhof, Otto 162
Mezger, Edmund 369
Miaskowski, Karl Woldemar Kurt von 224
Michaelis, Rudolf 618
Michel, Elmar 417

military and political symbols, ban on using 387–388, 402–403, 542, 553, 640
Military Service Law (*Wehrgesetz*) 60, 143, 448, 465, 704, 720
Militsch (Milicz) 324, 680
Minister President
– Bavaria, see also Siebert, Ludwig 626, 748, 750
– Braunschweig 410–411
– Prussia, see also Göring, Hermann 182, 184, 249, 754, 761
Minsk 752–753
Mischlinge, see also Nuremberg Laws 55–56, 58, 141, 145–146, 186, 415–416, 448–450, 468, 509, 523, 530–532, 537–538, 551, 555–556, 565–566, 600, 637, 639, 641, 649–650, 662, 700, 716–717
mixed marriages (*Mischehen*) 37, 54, 56, 60, 141, 144, 198, 263–265, 293, 333, 335–337, 371, 415, 449, 468–469, 484, 490, 504, 508–509, 514, 520, 535, 537–538, 637, 649–650, 748, 758, 760, 798
Möbius, Erich 369
Möbus, Johannes 362
Moffit, James P. 343
Möller (civil servant, Cologne) 374, 419
Mommsen, Theodor 18
Monka, Friedrich 398
Montevideo 732
Moral, Reinhard 694
Moringen, see concentration camps
Moro-Giafferi, Vincent de 358
Moscow 706, 742
Moses, Iwan 328–329
Moses, Rifka (Becky) 328–329
Moses, Ruth 328
Moses, Siegfried 259, 529
Mosler, Eduard 234, 236, 241
Mosley, Oswald 379
Moszkowski, Alexander 308
Motzkin, Leo 266
Mowrer, Edgar Ansel 171
Mühsam, Erich 386–387
Mühsam, Kreszentia (Zenzl) 386–387
Müller, A. (resident, Bonn) 167
Müller, Adolf 390
Müller, E. (resident, Leipzig) 509
Müller, Heinrich 646–647, 649–650

Müller, Ilse, *see* Bodlaender, Ilse
Müller, Karl Alexander von 39, 605, 748, 750
Münch, Wilhelm 231
Münder am Deister 263
Münster 388, 438
Münsterberg (Ziębice) 680
Münzenberg, Wilhelm (Willi) 253
Mulrooney, Edward 109
Munich 32–33, 39, 92–94, 97, 107, 121, 173–174, 197, 283–284, 391–392, 408, 414, 417–419, 466–467, 669, 675, 703, 747–750, 768, 781–782
municipal authorities
- Angermünde 406
- Berlin 116, 182–184, 213, 292–293, 397, 478, 489–490, 767
- Beuthen 245
- Edenkoben 406
- Elbing 761
- Frankfurt am Main 389–390, 749
- Gailingen
- Groß Gerau 405
- Grünberg 405
- Hamburg 547
- Hanover 300
- Hindenburg 247
- Hungen 405
- Königsberg 602–603
- Konstanz 407
- Lauterbach 405
- Leipzig 498, 509–510
- Merzig 783
- Nördlingen 407
- Ortenberg 405
- Pyritz 406
- Stuttgart 595
murder, *see also* violence 33, 42, 48, 249, 345, 386, 487
Mussolini, Benito 713
Mutschmann, Martin 223, 455

N

Nachmansohn, David 162
Nagler, Johannes 369
Namslau (Namysłów) 324, 680
Napoleon I 492
Nathorff, Hertha 159, 777

National Democracy (Narodowa Demokracja) 752
National Radical Camp (Obóz Narodowo-Radykalny) 752
National Socialist Association of Lawyers 115, 224, 365, 560
National Socialist Association of Teachers 115, 366, 596, 674
National Socialist Civil Service Department 115, 230
Nationalist Socialist commissioner for Jewish cultural affairs 561
National Socialist Factory Cell Organization (Nationalsozialistische Betriebszellenorganisation, NSBO) 115, 119, 129–130, 193–195, 305
National Socialist German Association of Students 34, 565
National Socialist German Reich Estate Agents' League 169–170
National Socialist German Workers' Party (NSDAP) 16, 25, 31–35, 37–38, 41–42, 45, 48, 54, 56–57, 117–118, 162, 164–165, 169–170, 195, 263–264, 281, 387–389, 410, 412, 418, 429–430, 434, 436, 443–444, 447, 495–496, 500–501, 504, 511–513, 518–521, 552, 734, 748, 755
- Foreign Policy Office of the NSDAP 175, 313
- Gau/Gauleitung
  - Berlin 130, 290, 489–490, 745
  - East Prussia 495–496
  - Essen 102–104
  - Franconia 342, 344
  - Kurmark 230–231, 585–586
  - Magdeburg-Anhalt 401
  - Munich-Upper Bavaria 121, 467, 497, 501, 504
  - Rhineland 180
  - Saxony 154, 223
  - Thuringia 462
  - Westphalia North 102, 104
  - Westphalia South 102, 104
- Kreis/Kreisleitung
  - Ansbach 343
  - Berlin 305
  - Bruchsal 346
  - Dresden 567

National Socialist German Workers' Party (NSDAP), Kreis/Kreisleitung (contd.)
- Frankfurt am Main 700
- Oberglogau 728
- Parchim 444
- Salzwedel 400–402
- Seelow 363
- Zwickau 224
- local branch
  - Berlin 35, 305, 745
  - Beuthen 495
  - Chemnitz 225
  - Frankfurt am Main 744
  - Görlitz 402
  - Munich 419
  - Stavenhagen 443
  - Zwickau 463
- Racial Policy Office (Rassenpolitisches Amt) 440, 448–449, 497, 516, 530, 533, 545
- Reichsleitung 117, 153–154, 263, 432, 493, 571, 595

National Socialist Motor Corps 403
National Socialist Observatories Department 230–231
National Socialist Organization of Crafts, Trade and Commerce (NS-Hago) 48, 410–411, 489, 498, 755
National Socialist Physician' League 115, 286, 309
National Socialist Welfare Organization (NSV) 496, 759
National Socialist Welfare for War Victims 418–419
National Socialist Women's League (NS-Frauenschaft) 418, 430, 496
Naumann, Max 352
Naumann, Rupert 227–228, 277, 279
Nazi Party, *see* National Socialist German Workers' Party
Neander, August 276
Necheles-Magnus, Henriette 125
Neckel, Gustav 660
Neideck (schoolboy, Cologne) 330
Netherlands, the 51, 112, 188, 295, 297, 358, 393, 423–424, 441, 621, 682
Netter, Arnold 124
Neubrandenburg 445
Neubukow 443

Neuendorff, Edmund 158, 228, 277, 279
Neukirchen 446
Neumann (head, National Socialist Women's League, Marienwerder) 496
Neumann, Erich 697
Neumann, Heinz Werner 254
Neumark, Ernst 566
Neumarkt (Środa Śląska) 323–324, 680
Neumeyer, Alfred 173, 529
Neurath, Baron Konstantin Hermann Karl von 131, 180, 412, 522, 714, 780
Neusalz (Nowa Sól) 324, 679
Neustadt (Prudnik) 729
Neustadt, Hermann 778
Neustadt an der Aich 345
Neustadt-Glewe 483
Neustrelitz 444
New Synagogue, Berlin 23, 184
New York 393, 436
New Zealand 394, 773
newspapers and periodicals
- *8-Uhr-Abendblatt* 116
- *Abend, Der* 35
- *Angriff, Der* 88–89, 136, 645
- *Berliner Tageblatt* 35, 116, 308
- *Berliner Volkszeitung* 35
- *Bulletin of the Reich Association of Non-Aryan Christians* 440
- *Cape Argus* 758
- *C.V.-Zeitung* 352, 561
- *Daily News*, New York 156
- *Danziger Echo* 577
- *Danziger Volksstimme* 176–177
- *Deutsche Allgemeine Zeitung* 48, 173, 213
- *Deutsche Immobilien-Zeitung* 169
- *Deutsche Juristen-Zeitung* 219
- *Deutsche Justiz* 335
- *Deutsche Volksgesundheit aus Blut und Boden* 498
- *Deutsches Ärzteblatt* 248
- *Deutsches Philologen-Blatt* 287
- *Deutsches Recht* 652
- *Frankfurter Rundschau* 190
- *Frankfurter Zeitung* 308, 340, 545
- *Fremdenverkehr, Der* 718
- *Hakenkreuz-Banner* 406
- *Haynt* 378, 380
- *Historische Zeitschrift* 605

newspapers and periodicals (contd.)
- *Illustrierter Beobachter* 315
- *Illustrowany Kuryer Codzienny* 175
- *Internationales Ärztliches Bulletin* 386
- *Israelitisches Familienblatt*, Hamburg 561
- *Jüdische Rundschau* 37, 132, 160, 508–509, 527, 620, 622, 677, 751
- *Jüdisches Gemeindeblatt für Rheinlandland und Westfalen* 763
- *Junge Kirche* 272
- *Juristische Wochenschrift* 263, 309, 413
- *Kameradschaft, Die* 676
- *Kicker, Der* 158
- *Komet, Der* 408
- *Manchester Guardian* 472
- *Meeraner Zeitung* 474
- *Mitteilungsblatt des Reichsverbandes der nichtarischen Christen*, see Bulletin of the Reich Association of Non-Aryan Christians
- *Morgenpost, Die* 116
- *National-Sozialistische Erzieher, Der* 307, 398
- *Nationalsozialistische Monatshefte* 185–186
- *Nationalsozialistische Partei-Korrespondenz* 133, 342
- *Neue Welt, Die* 344
- *Neue Weltbühne, Die* 571
- *Neue Zürcher Zeitung* 477–478
- *New York Times* 105, 108, 189
- *New Yorker Staats-Zeitung* 113
- *NS-Funk* 315
- *Pariser Tageblatt* 302, 348, 420, 478–479, 554
- *Pariser Tageszeitung* 611, 644, 665, 719
- *Pretoria News* 187
- *Preußische Zeitung* 483
- *Rote Erde* 179
- *Rote Fahne* 176, 254
- *Schwarze Korps, Das* 479, 481, 487, 493, 743–744
- *Seele: Monatsschrift im Dienste christlicher Lebensgestaltung* 152
- *Stürmer, Der* 48, 160, 378, 380, 399, 430, 470, 478–479, 487, 502, 558, 580, 582, 584–585, 590, 728–729, 731
- *Tempo* 116
- *Temps, Le* 495
- *Times, The* 126
- *Verordnungsblatt der Obersten SA-Führung* 388–389
- *Völkischer Beobachter* 41, 89, 102, 107, 117, 126, 133–135, 172, 176, 315, 359, 479, 734, 768, 780–781
- *Vorwärts* 35
- *Vossische Zeitung* 116, 251
- *Welt am Montag* 35
- *Westpreussische Zeitung* 759
- *Wirtschaftskurve, Die* 698
- *Zeitschrift des Vereins für Geschichte Schlesiens* 658
- *Zwischen Weichsel und Nogat* 715

Nicaragua 423
Niederwipper (schoolboy, Cologne) 330
Niemack, Günter 647
Niemöller, Martin 277, 485
Non-Sectarian Anti-Nazi League to Champion Human Rights 358
Nördlingen 407
Norkus, Herbert 399
Normann, Hans-Henning von 694
Norway 394
Nothmann, Samuel 101
NS-Hago, see National Socialist Organization of Crafts, Trade and Commerce
NSDAP, see National Socialist German Workers' Party
Nuremberg 54, 378, 381, 487, 512, 519–521, 734
Nuremberg Laws, see also Law for the Protection of German Blood and German Honour (Blood Protection Law); Reich Citizenship Law 46, 48, 54–56, 58, 60, 527, 530, 549, 554, 556–558, 560, 582, 585–586, 596, 611–613, 624, 647, 653, 662, 665–666, 699, 702, 720, 724, 747, 791
Nußbaum, Bella 447
Nußbaum, Max 447
Nußbaum, Nathan 446
Nussbaum, Sally 447

O

Oberdörffer, Wilhelm 222
Oberglogau (Głogówek) 728
Oberländer, Theodor 705
Obernigk (Oborniki Śląskie) 680
Oberpräsident
- Brandenburg, see also Kube, Wilhelm 293

- East Prussia 644
- Prussian 588, 649, 658, 718
O'Brien, John P. 109
Obst 230
Oceania 394
Oels (Oleśnica) 323–324, 679, 681–682
Oettinger, Eduard Maria 581
Offenbach 628
Ofterdinger, Friedrich 431
Ohel Jakob, Munich 174
Ohlau (Oława) 679–680
Old Prussian Union, *see* Protestant Church of the Old Prussian Union
Oliven (manor owner, Buselwitz) 679
Ollendorf, Hermann 672–673, 778–779
Olympic Games, Berlin 57–58, 611, 618–619, 627
Oppeln (Opole) 247, 300, 680
Oppenheim, Isaak 446
Oppenheim, Siegfried 446
Oppenheimer, Franz 217, 256
Oppermann, Hermann Walther 309
Oranienburg, *see* concentration camps
Organized Orthodox Community 527, 529
ORT (Society for Trades and Agricultural Labour) 331, 351, 354, 794
Ortenberg 405
Osborn, Franz Joachim 216–217
Osborn, Max 216–217, 256
Osterode 420, 482
Osthofen, *see* concentration camps
Ostjuden, see also East European Jews 27–28, 32, 39, 41, 86, 96–97, 110, 113, 187, 308, 399, 476, 538, 598, 663
Oungre, Edouard 123
Oungre, Louis 123

P

Pagenstecher, Wolfgang 615
Paintbox (Malkasten) Artists' Association 553
Pakula (Jewish religious instructor, Gross-Wartenberg) 323–324
Palestine 50–52, 161–163, 188–189, 216, 260, 295, 319, 322, 328, 350–351, 355–356, 391–394, 397, 422–423, 425, 427, 433–434, 442–443, 457–458, 527–528, 561, 575–576, 598, 607, 621, 624, 637, 642–643, 648, 712–715, 725, 733–734, 753–754, 762, 768–771, 792–793
Palestine Office 243, 350, 423, 426, 459, 529, 563, 620, 725, 792
Palestine Shipping Company 457
Palestine Trust Agency to Advise German Jews (Paltreu) 392
Palme, Erich 402
Pan-German League 25, 307
Papen, Franz von 98, 285, 306
Paraguay 393, 423, 770–773
Parchim 444, 483
Paris 46, 123, 473
Patschowski, Günther, later Palten 387
Patzer, Ernst 758, 761
Pauli, Heinrich 157–158
Paulus-Bund, *see* Reich Association of Non-Aryan Christians
Peel, William Robert Wellesley 712–713
Pels, James 221
Penzlin 445
People's Association for the German Reich Church 647
Perfall, Baron Erich von 614
Peritz, Edith 163
Peritz, Georg 163
Peru 393, 423, 770, 772
Peters (instructor, Offenbach am Main) 628
Peters, H. (NSDAP member, Hamburg) 547
Petzal, Lore, *see* Isakowitz, Lore
Pfitzner, Hans 103
Pforzheim 592
Pfundtner, Johannes (Hans) 147, 157, 250, 285, 372, 374, 448, 541, 626–627, 634, 718, 786–787, 790
Philipp, Hermann 220, 222
Philippines 731–732
Phillips, William 106
Physicians' Association of Chemnitz and the Surrounding Area 247
Pieck, Wilhelm 250
Piłsudski, Józef Klemens 314, 705
Pitschen (Byczyna) 680, 729
Pius XI 437, 442
Planck, Max 231
Platen, Count von 473
Plath, Otto 214
Plauen 42, 224

Plaut, Julius 375–377
Pleißner, Paul 463
Plenipotentiary for the Four-Year Plan, *see also* Göring, Hermann 58–59, 694, 696, 754, 761
plenipotentiary of the Führer for economic matters 461, 513
Plesch, Johann 469–470
Plischke, Kurt 345
pogroms and riots 85, 92, 94, 344–345, 466, 477, 498–499, 503, 727, 753
Pohl, Wolfgang 541
Poland 18, 28, 37, 112, 175–177, 195, 295, 313, 315–316, 394, 424, 499, 509–510, 621, 642–643, 705–707, 751–752, 760
Polanyi, Michael 172
Police Administration Law (*Polizei-Verwaltungsggesetz*) 419
Police for Foreign Nationals (*Fremdenpolizei*) 96, 476–477
police headquarters
– Berlin 176, 489
– Düsseldorf 476
– Elbing 758–759
– Freiburg 593
– Kiel 127
– Mönchengladbach-Rheydt 402
– Munich 94, 284
Polish Legation in Berlin 178–180
political police, *see also* Gestapo 138, 165, 173, 408, 504, 518, 571, 647
– Bavarian 56, 284, 408
Polke, Max Moses 97–98, 101
Polley, Kurt 746–747
Pomerania 631, 799–800
Popitz, Johannes, *see also* Prussian Minister/Ministry of Finance 497, 502
Portland, Oregon 393
Portugal 424, 621
Posen (Poznań) 177, 760
Posen-West Prussia 797, 800
Posner (Klein Silsterwitz) 396
Posse, Hans Ernst 541, 634–638, 640
Potsdam 112, 585, 599
Prague 112, 181, 386, 473, 499, 582, 731, 778
Pravdinsk, *see* Prussian Friedland
Pretoria 756
Prill (SA member, Hamburg) 376

Pringsheim 218
Prinz, Joachim 44, 256, 451–453
Prittwitz und Gaffron, Friedrich Wilhelm von 105
propaganda
– alleged Jewish atrocity propaganda 105–106, 114, 117–120, 122–123, 128, 175–176, 212, 214, 311–312, 354–357, 359–361, 373, 471, 515–516, 586–587, 708–710, 714
– antisemitic 25, 32, 35, 47–48, 54, 86, 88–90, 109, 112, 117–118, 120, 139, 187, 225, 243, 245, 343–346, 385, 398–399, 417–418, 432, 443–444, 463–464, 477–478, 499, 502, 504, 512–513, 530, 532–533, 535, 547, 558, 567, 571, 582–584, 605, 607, 609–610, 654–655, 676, 715, 768, 781–782
Property Tax Law (*Grundsteuergesetz*) 507–508, 723
protective custody (*Schutzhaft*), *see also* arrests; concentration camps 344, 347
Protestant Church 260–262, 272–273, 275–277, 290, 438, 440, 488
Protestant Church of the Old Prussian Union 47, 272, 277
Protocols of the Elders of Zion 30, 86, 88
Provincial Federation of East Prussian Communities 420
Prussia 17–18, 28, 36, 57, 388, 391, 449, 454, 517
Prussian Academy of the Arts 173
Prussian Friedland (Pravdinsk) 232
Prussian Minister/Ministry
– Prussian Minister/Ministry of Finance 362, 448, 497, 502, 768
– Prussian Minister/Ministry of Science, Art and Education, *see also* Rust, Bernhard 34, 219–220, 283–284, 383
– Prussian Minister/Ministry of the Interior, *see also* Göring, Hermann 146, 184, 250–251, 307, 321, 402, 460
– Prussian Minister/Ministry of Justice, *see also* Kerrl, Hanns 219, 234, 249
Prussian Regional Association of Jewish Communities 44, 259, 323, 529, 679
Prussian Regional Statistical Office 138
Prussian-South German Class Lottery 502
Przytyk 752–753

publishing houses
- C. H. Beck 596
- Deutscher Verlag KG 162
- Franz Eher Nachfolger GmbH 162, 658
- Franz Wulf 674
- NS-Druck und Verlag 345
- NS-Schlesien GmbH 243
- Ullstein, Berlin 162, 308
Puerto Rico 393
Puls, Margarete 305
Pyritz (Pyrzyce) 406

Q
Queck, Johannes 324
Quedlinburg 225

R
Raabe, Hans 103
Rabinowitsch, Michael 222
race defilement (*Rassenschande*) 47, 54, 57, 332, 344, 346–347, 372, 415, 474–476, 494, 504, 514, 520, 545, 573, 611, 665–668
Racial Policy Office of the NSDAP, *see* National Socialist German Workers' Party
Radeberg 566
Radek, Karl 609
Radmann, Helmuth 585
Raeke, Walter 564
Ramin, Günther 41
Randt, Erich 616, 658
Rastenburg (Kętrzyn) 420
Rathenau (Breslau) 463
Rathenau, Fritz 381–382
Rathenau, Kurt 381–382
Rathenau, Sophie, née Dannebaum 382
Rathenau, Walther 26, 35, 659
Ratibor (Racibórz) 729
Rechenbach, Horst 415, 534
Red Cross 159, 306, 496
Regensburg 108
Regierungspräsident
- Breslau 616
- Cologne, *see also* Diels, Rudolf 374
- Düsseldorf, *see also* Schmid, Carl Christian 476
- Frankfurt an der Oder 362
- Hanover, *see also* Diels, Rudolf 670

- Königsberg, *see also* Friedrich, Werner 602, 758
- Liegnitz 402
- Marienwerder 761
- Potsdam, *see also* Fromm, Ernst 585
- Prussia 658, 718
Regional Association of Israelite Religious Communities of Hesse 529
Regional Contract Office 153–154
registration of Jews and their assets 36, 58, 60, 141, 196–211, 496, 616, 646–647, 704, 716–717
Regulation for the Protection of People and State (*Verordnung zum Schutze von Volk und Staat*) 419
Regulation of the Reich President against Betrayal of the German People and Highly Treasonous Activities (*Verordnung des Reichspräsidenten gegen Verrat am Deutschen Volke und hochverräterische Umtriebe*) 191, 193, 311
Regulation of the Reich President for the Defense against Treacherous Attacks on the Government of the National Uprising (*Verordnung des Reichspräsidenten gegen heimtückische Angriffe auf die Regierung der nationalen Erhebung* [*Heimtückegesetz*]) 311
Regulation on the Admission of Doctors for Employment with the Medical Insurance Companies (*Verordnung über die Zulassung von Ärzten zur Tätigkeit bei den Krankenkassen*) 144, 264, 268, 312, 320, 451
Regulation on the Exclusion of Jews from German Economic Life (*Verordnung zur Ausschaltung der Juden aus dem deutschen Wirtschaftsleben*) 784
Regulation on the Granting of Marriage Loans (*Verordnung über die Gewährung von Ehestandsdarlehen*) 370
Reich Agricultural League (Reichslandbund) 33
Reich Association of Christian German Citizens of Non-Aryan or Not Pure Aryan Descent, *see* Reich Association of Non-Aryan Christians
Reich Association of German Artists 614

Reich Association of German Estate Agents 169–170, 342
Reich Association of German Small-Animal Breeders 691
Reich Association of Itinerant Traders 213
Reich Association of Non-Aryan Christians (later St Paul's Covenant and the 1937 Association) 55, 285–286, 352, 438, 440, 615, 650
Reich Association of the German Press 214
Reich Banner Black-Red-Gold 35, 156
Reich Chamber of Culture 532, 614–615, 646, 694, 780
Reich Chamber of Economics 241, 549
Reich Chamber of Physicians 787, 791
Reich Chamber of Visual Arts 615–616
Reich Chancellery 286, 348, 367, 410, 479
Reich Circle for Propaganda and Public Enlightenment 618
Reich Citizenship Law (*Reichsbürgergesetz*) 47, 54–55, 141, 144, 155, 415, 504, 519–520, 522–523, 525–526, 538, 550, 555–556, 565, 596, 616, 637, 641, 650, 719, 761, 780, 786–790, 798
Reich Commercial Code 279, 291
Reich commissioner
- for banking 497
- at the Berlin stock exchange 628
- for the Central Medical Associations, *see also* Wagner, Gerhard 248
- for the economy 182
- for Prussia 95
- for the Prussian Ministry of Justice, *see also* Kerrl, Hanns 100
- for the reintegration of the Saarland, *see also* Bürckel, Josef 588, 599
- for the Saarland, *see also* Bürckel, Josef 783
- for sport, *see also* Tschammer und Osten, Hans von 257

Reich Committee for Jewish Youth Organizations 527, 529
Reich Committee for Tourism 718–719
Reich Farmers' Leader, *see also* Darré, Richard Walther 400, 414, 721
Reich Federation for Air Raid Protection 368, 759
Reich Flight Tax (*Reichsfluchtsteuer*) 59, 382, 569–570, 592–593, 698–699, 722, 727, 755

Reich Food Estate 400–401, 533, 724
Reich German Association of the Middle Class (Reichsdeutscher Mittelstandsverein) 24
Reich government 45, 57, 81, 147, 157, 285–287, 317–320, 340–342, 355, 369, 373, 386, 410–411, 471, 484, 489, 499, 542, 548, 550, 711
Reich Group of University Teachers 40
Reich Hammer League 24
Reich Hereditary Farm Law (*Reichserbhofgesetz*) 288, 370, 516, 708–709
Reich Institute for Labour Placement and Unemployment Insurance (Reichsanstalt für Arbeitsvermittlung und Arbeitslosenversicherung) 332
Reich Institute for History of the New Germany 39, 605, 748–749
Reich Kennel Club 691
Reich Labour Community for German Labour Service Obligation 305
Reich League of German Tenants' Associations 389
Reich League of Jewish Combat Veterans 45, 50, 174, 188, 226, 300, 317, 338, 352, 356, 367–368, 421, 433, 435, 486, 527, 529, 636
Reich League of Jewish Settlement 425
Reich Minister/Ministry
- Reich (and Prussian) Minister/Ministry of Economics, *see also* Schacht, Hjalmar 434, 497, 499, 502, 505, 513, 541, 566, 568–571, 595, 611, 628, 634–635, 638, 646, 753–755, 784–785
- Reich (and Prussian) Minister/Ministry of Science, Schooling and Education, *see also* Rust, Bernhard 398, 438, 441–442, 448, 455, 509, 516–518, 565, 721, 749–750, 755, 767–768, 789
- Reich (and Prussian) Minister/Ministry of the Interior, *see also* Frick, Wilhelm 48, 141, 149–151, 155, 178, 185, 231, 247–248, 250–251, 285–286, 293, 341, 390, 402, 410, 438, 440, 448–449, 466, 469, 476, 479–480, 482, 484, 497, 500, 502, 505, 513, 520–522, 525, 535, 541–542, 544, 546, 550, 557, 568, 571, 586, 588–589, 595–596, 599, 602, 626, 634, 640–641, 655–657, 669, 712, 716, 718–

719, 721, 749, 753–755, 758, 760–761, 780, 786
- Reich Minister of Church Affairs, *see also* Kerrl, Hanns 779
- Reich Minister of Foreign Affairs/Reich Foreign Office, *see also* Neurath, Baron Konstantin Hermann Karl von 48, 105, 138, 146, 173, 178, 181, 187, 214, 231, 243, 250, 325, 383, 438, 463, 476, 494, 497, 522–523, 541, 642, 712–715, 753–754, 761, 779–780, 789
- Reich Minister/Ministry of Finance, *see also* Schwerin von Krosigk, Count Johann Ludwig (Lutz) 149–151, 153, 383, 504–505, 568, 591, 655–657, 711–712, 723, 750, 755, 761, 789
- Reich Minister/Ministry of Food and Agriculture, *see also* Darré, Richard Walther 372, 400, 497, 503, 513, 560, 570, 628, 635–636
- Reich Minister/Ministry of Justice, *see also* Gürtner, Franz 220, 325, 468, 479–480, 497, 502, 504, 513, 521–522, 524, 541, 564, 653, 665–666, 743, 787
- Reich Minister/Ministry of Labour, *see also* Seldte, Franz 247–248, 332, 348, 354, 497, 503, 544, 758, 789
- Reich Minister/Ministry of Public Enlightenment and Propaganda, *see also* Goebbels, Joseph 54, 138, 497, 503, 513, 541, 613, 635, 639, 694, 696
- Reich Minister/Ministry of the Army/of War, *see also* Blomberg, Werner von 143, 395, 410, 461, 465, 789
- Reich Minister/Ministry of Transport, *see also* Dorpmüller, Julius 241, 503, 511

Reich Navy 143
Reich Office for Emigration Affairs (Reichsstelle für das Auswanderungswesen) 390, 448, 753, 761
Reich Office for Foreign Exchange Control (Reichsstelle für Devisenbewirtschaftung) 753–755, 761–762
Reich Office for Grains, Feeding Stuffs and Other Agricultural Products 629, 631
Reich Office for Kinship Research (Reichsstelle für Sippenforschung) 448–449

Reich Organization of German Students 565
Reich Physicians' Leader, *see also* Wagner, Gerhard 248, 286, 415, 565, 786
Reich Postal Service 154, 282, 559
Reich President, *see also* Hindenburg, Paul von 81, 117, 389–390
Reich Press Law (*Reichspressegesetz*) 192–193
Reich Propaganda Leadership 493, 619
Reich Railways, *see* German Reich Railways
Reich Representation of German Jews (Reichsvertretung der Juden in Deutschland) (1933–1935)/of Jews in Germany (1935–1939)/Reich Association of Jews in Germany (from 1939) 45, 117, 188, 221, 243, 317–320, 352, 426, 527–529, 620–622, 679, 723, 725–727, 762, 775, 778, 795–800
Reich Representation of Jewish Regional Associations in Germany 44, 188, 247–248
Reich Sports Leader, *see also* Tschammer und Osten, Hans von 434
Reich Statistical Office 196, 199, 448, 532
Reich Veterans' League 409
Reich Youth Leader 356, 388, 434
Reichenau, Walter von 460
Reichmann, Hans 404
Reichsärztekammer, *see* Reich Chamber of Physicians
Reichsbahn, *see* German Reich Railways
Reichsbank, *see* banks
Reichsbund jüdischer Frontsoldaten, *see* Reich League of Jewish Combat Veterans
Reichsbürgergesetz, *see* Reich Citizenship Law
Reichserbhofgesetz, *see* Reich Hereditary Farm Law
Reichsfluchtsteuer, *see* Reich Flight Tax
Reichsführer SS and Chief of the German Police, *see also* Himmler, Heinrich 414, 432, 461, 491, 515, 669
Reichskulturkammergesetz, *see* Law on Reich Chamber of Culture
Reichsministergesetz, *see* Law on Reich Ministers
Reichsstatthalter
- Hamburg 375, 377
- Saxony, *see also* Mutschmann, Martin 223
- Thuringia, *see also* Sauckel, Ernst Friedrich (Fritz) 395

Reichstag 26, 41, 54, 92, 112, 144, 181, 214, 251, 253–254, 257, 264, 286, 306, 386, 464, 519–520, 525, 527, 550, 553, 581, 665–666
Reichsverband christlich-deutscher Staatsbürger nichtarischer oder nicht reinarischer Abstammung, see Reich Association of Non-Aryan Christians
Reichsverband der nichtarischen Christen (later Paulus-Bund and Vereinigung 1937), see Reich Association of Non-Aryan Christians
Reichsvertretung der deutschen Juden (1933–1935)/Reichsvertretung der Juden in Deutschland (1935–1939)/Reichsvereinigung der Juden in Deutschland (from 1939), see Reich Representation of German Jews
Reichswehr, see also Wehrmacht 143, 395–396
Reimer, Werner 369
Rein, Richard 287
Reinhardt, Fritz 655–656, 711
Reinhardt, Max 40, 356
Reis, Theodor 130
Reismann-Grone, Theodor 102, 104
Relief Association of German Jews 44
Republican Association of Judges 156
responses to persecution and antisemitic measures
– German 34–35, 42–43, 46, 48, 52, 56, 126, 129, 131–132, 152–153, 218, 285, 341, 343, 364–366, 409–410, 412, 430–431, 467–468, 485, 487, 495, 511, 582–585
– international 35, 41, 44, 48, 51–52, 108–111, 113, 156, 189, 260, 294–296, 298–299, 357, 412, 423, 426, 476, 499, 577–579, 768
– Jewish, see also emigration; suicide; Zionism 24, 37, 44–46, 48–51, 123–125, 132–133, 135–137, 160, 171, 190–191, 193, 243–244, 255, 260, 349, 404, 420–422, 424–427, 451–454, 563, 664, 679, 685, 751–753, 764–765, 768, 796, 799
Reuter, Fritz 492
Reuter, Baron Paul Julius von 492
Reuter's Telegram Company 492
Revolutionary Trade Union Opposition 193, 195
Reye, Edgar 233
Rheinland 763–765

Rhina 446–447
Rhine province 800
Rhineland 391
Rhineland Palatinate 406, 800
Ribbentrop, Joachim von 713
Richter, Rudolf 229
Ridder, Bernard H. 113
Rieger, Josef 329–330
Riesa 499
Riga 708
Ritter, Karl Ludwig 389
Röchling, Hermann 461
Röhm, Ernst 92–93, 386
Röhrecke (official, Reich Foreign Office) 497
Romania 27–28, 37, 424, 707–708
Rose, Adam Karol 642
Rosenau, Max 345
Rosenberg, Alfred 83, 101, 104, 264, 313, 486–487, 648
Rosenberg, Arthur 23
Rosenbloom, Maxie 303
Rosenbusch (Munich resident) 675
Rosenfelder, Fritz 160
Rosenfelder, Jakob 345
Rosenstock, Josef 255–256
Rosenthal (Jewish Community, Berlin) 259
Rosenthal (resident in Palestine) 217
Rosenthal, Hans 457–459
Rosenthal, Johanna 282
Rosenzweig (commercial counsellor) 529
Rosmarin, H. 266
Ross, Albion 127
Ross, Julius 347
Rostock 445
Roth, Hans Otto 267
Rothenkirchen 446–447
Rothmann, Eva 163
Rothmann, Gertrud Karoline, see Cohn, Gertrud Karoline (Trudi)
Rothmund, Heinrich 297
Ruben, Otto 220, 222
Rügen, Richard 191
Rummel (Deutsche Bank official) 234
Rupprecht, Luise 212–213
Russell, Ernst Enno 234–236, 238, 240
Russia, see also Soviet Union 18, 27, 30, 394, 606–607, 609, 735, 738, 740

Rust, Bernhard, *see also* Reich (and Prussian) Minister/Ministry of Science; Prussian Minister/Ministry of Science 101, 103, 172, 180, 257, 398, 509, 516–518, 558, 636, 749–750

Rydzówka, *see* Kalthof

S

SA, *see also* Supreme SA Command 41, 48, 54, 93–94, 97–99, 120, 125–126, 163, 165, 193, 225, 245, 301–302, 310, 315, 345, 347, 386, 389, 397, 403–404, 418, 427, 431, 444, 477, 489, 495, 618

Saala, A. W. 245

Saar/Saarland 295, 412, 433, 435, 448, 783, 800

Sabatzky, Kurt 224–226, 325, 450

Sabel (wife of Rudolf Sabel, Munich) 121

Sabel, Rudolf 121

Sachsenburg, *see* concentration camps

Sack (retailer, Braunschweig) 411

Sacrifice League (Opferring) 759

Saft, Marta, *see* Salinger, Marta

Sagan (Żagań) 324, 679–680

Sahm, Heinrich 178, 213–214

Salinger, Eva 758

Salinger, Julius 756

Salinger, Liesbeth 756–757

Salinger, Marta, née Saft 756

Salinger, Peter 756–757

Salm-Horstmar, Otto zu 306

Salomon, Alice 335

Salzwedel 400–401

Samson, Hermann Jacob 220–222

Samuel, Amalie, *see* Malsch, Amalie

Samuel, Sir Herbert Luis 576

Samuel, Sir Walter Horace 575–576

Samuelis, Gary (Gerhard) 746

Sandermayer (solicitor, Frankfurt am Main) 191–192

Sanders, Leon 189

Sandler (Jewish Community, Berlin) 259

Santo Domingo, *see* Dominican Republic

Sar Scholaum, David ben 766

Sauckel, Ernst Friedrich (Fritz) 395, 462

Saulmann, Leonie, *see* Briske, Leonie

Save the Children International Union 298

Saxon Association of Israelite Communities 529

Saxon State Ministry for Education 225

Saxon Ministry of Economics 225, 324

Saxony 223, 388, 546, 582, 800

Saxony-Anhalt 223, 400, 800

Schaale (bailiff, Dresden Police) 154

Schacht, Hjalmar, *see also* Reich (and Prussian) Minister/Ministry of Economics 48, 54, 234–236, 240, 242, 479, 497–501, 504–505, 512, 531–532, 541, 560, 576, 635, 639, 720, 785

Schaefer, Clemens 218–219

Schaefer, Franz 566

Schaefer, Rosa, née Ikenberg 566

Schäfer, Ernst 369

Schäfer, Leopold 369

Schapiro, Mr 240

Scheidemann, Philipp 254

Schellenberg, Alfred 658

Schemm, Hans 283–284, 596, 674

Schenker, R. 440

Scherk, Karl 678

Schickedanz, Arno 83

Schiedermair (government assessor) 634

Schild (Jewish sports organization) 434

Schildberger, Hermann 256

Schilling (radio host, Berlin) 171

Schindler, Julius 458

Schindler, Karl 620

Schindler, Robert 458

Schinkel, von (Deutsche Bank official) 234

Schirach, Baldur von, *see also* Reich Youth Leader 356

Schirach, Friedrich von 107

Schlageter, Albert Leo 399

Schlayer, Karl Robert 660

Schlegelberger, Franz 564–565

Schleicher, Kurt von 386

Schlemmer, Eva, *see* Klemperer, Eva

Schlemmermeyer (managing director, Kurmark Wheat Trade Association) 630

Schlempp, Hans 595

Schlenger, Fred-Egon 285

Schleswig-Holstein 799–800

Schletzenrod 446

Schlieper, Gustav 234, 241

Schlitter, Oscar 234–238, 240–242

Schloss, Heinemann 220

Schlösser, Ludwig 530

Schmeling, Max 302–303
Schmid, Carl A. 170
Schmid, Carl Christian 476
Schmidmann, Gottfried 272
Schmidt (director, Reich Office for Emigration Affairs) 390, 753
Schmidt, Robert 695
Schmitt, Carl 38, 40
Schmitt, Fritz 307
Schmitt, Kurt 348
Schmitt, Rolf (Rudolf) 660
Schmitz, Elisabeth 485, 487–488
Schnabel, Franz 19
Schneidemühl (Piła) 797
Schneider, Ludwig Eduard 591
Schneider Franke, Josef Rudolf 327
Schnitzer, Joseph 179
Scholz (interim executive board member, Hamburg Medical Association) 233
Schönewald, Ottilie 529
Schönfeld, Leo 321
Schönner, Kurt 696
Schönrock, Johannes 648
schools and universities 22, 34, 50, 383–385, 398, 454, 516–518, 558, 661
- Dresden Institute of Technology 455
- Higher Institute for Jewish Studies in Berlin (Hochschule für die Wissenschaft des Judentums Berlin) 483
- Humboldt School in Beuthen 245
- Israelite Girls' School, Hamburg (Israelitische Töchterschule Hamburg) 328
- Kaliski Jewish Private School, Berlin 516, 767
- Neukloster Teacher Training College 624
- Reed College, Portland 393
- Rudolf Sabel Business School 121
- Talmud Torah School, Hamburg 220–222, 425
- University of Berlin 172, 610, 660
- University of Breslau 218–219
- University of Erlangen 272
- University of Göttingen 40
- University of Greifswald 178
- University of Halle 366
- University of Istanbul 382–383
- University of Königsberg 545
- University of Leipzig 366
- University of Marburg 272, 277
- University of New York 393
Schottlaender, Rudolf 22
Schoyer, Adolf 259
Schräpel, Johannes 257–258
Schreiber, Eduard 743–744
Schroeder, Gustav Wilhelm 601
Schüller, Moses 179
Schultze (ministerial director) 415
Schultze, Walter 375–376
Schulz, Edgar Hans 138, 140
Schulz, Kurt 759
Schulz, Robert 446
Schumann, Hubert 170
Schumm, Friedrich 126–127
Schünemann, Fritz 107
Schurz, Carl 474
Schwaab, Otto 407
Schwaan 444
Schwarz, Karl-Israel 216–217, 245
Schweidnitz (Świdnica) 680
Schweitzer, Albert 757
Schwerin 444–445
Schwerin von Krosigk, Count Johann Ludwig (Lutz), see also Reich Minister/Ministry of Finance 152, 156
SD, see SS Security Service
Security Police, see also Gestapo 57, 755
Seeckt, Hans von 695
Seel (official, Reich Foreign Office) 243–244
Seelow 362–363
segregation of Jews and non-Jews, see also exclusion of Jews from; housing 44, 343, 388–389, 432, 492, 552–553, 557, 660, 664, 745
Seibert, Theodor 609
Seikel (Cologne family) 162
Seldte, Franz, see also Reich Minister/Ministry of Labour 247, 348–349
Senckenberg, Johann Christian 229
Senckenberg Natural History Society 229–230
Severing, Carl 363
Sicher, Dudley David 190
Siebert, Ludwig, see also Minister President 627, 748
Siegel, Michael 94
Siegl, Engelbert 177–178

Siekmeyer, Emil 614
Siemens, Carl von 234
Siemroth, Werner 403
Sigle, Jacob 499
Silbergleit, Heinrich 138
Silesia 583, 616, 679, 763–764, 766, 800
Simon, Ernst
Simon, Hugo 362–363, 473
Simon, Kurt 278
Simson, Arthur 395–396, 461–462
Simson, Julius 395–396
Simson, Löb 395
Simson, Moses 395
Singer, Kurt 50, 255–256
Skalawski, Louis 291
Sklarek scandal 473
Smith, Alfred E. 109
Sneh, Moshe, see Kleinbaum, Moshe
Social Democratic Party of Germany (SPD), see also Sopade 26, 164, 251–252, 254, 666
Society for Literature and the Performing Arts 327
Society of Friends 297, 688–689
Soden, Baron Hans von 277
Sohn, Friedrich Wilhelm 169–170
Solidarité française 379
Solmssen, Georg Adolf 234–236, 241
Soltau, Fritz 628–629
Sommer, Karl 292
Sommer, Walther 634–638
Sommerfeld, Hans 623–624
Sonnenburg, see concentration camps
Sopade, see also Social Democratic Party of Germany 254, 364
South Africa 52, 187, 391, 394, 423, 443, 499, 622, 756–757, 770, 772–773
Soviet Union, see also Moscow; Russia 28, 424, 607–608, 705–706, 708–709, 737
Spain 295, 424, 441, 621, 737–742
Spiegelberg, John 670
Spier, Arthur 220–222
Spiess (representative, Reich Association of Non-Aryan Christians) 615
Spiewok, Karl Eduard 214, 321, 478
Spiro, E. 256
Spitta, Philipp 276
Spitzer, Leo 456
Spitzer, Samuel 220

Spranger, Eduard 172
Sprottau (Szprotawa) 324, 680
SS Race and Settlement Main Office (RuSHA) 414–415, 534–535
SS Security Service (SD) 44, 57–60, 141, 349, 481, 491, 497, 704, 716–717, 790
SS, see also Reichsführer SS and Chief of the German Police 41, 54, 57, 120, 164–166, 301–302, 386, 418, 432–433, 467, 479, 481, 491, 533–535, 687–688
St Paul's Covenant, see Reich Association of Non-Aryan Christians
St Raphael Society for the Protection of Catholic Emigrants 437–439, 441–442
Städtel (Miejsce) 680
Staemmler, Martin 307, 309
Stahl, Heinrich 182, 259, 529
Stahlhelm 33, 41
Stampfer, Friedrich 254
state commissioner for Berlin, see also Lippert, Julius 116, 138, 182, 184, 397
State Police, see Gestapo
State Zionist Organization 350
Stauss, von (banker) 239–240
Stavenhagen 443
Steckelsdorf
Steeg, Ludwig 489
Stein (Supreme Council of Jews, Baden, Karlsruhe) 529
Stein, Adolf (Rumpelstilzchen) 471, 473
Stein-Hardenberg Reforms 17
Steinau (Ścinawa) 324, 680
Steinbrenner, Hans 166–167
Steinbrinck, Otto 460
Steinhardt, Jacob 161, 163, 624
Steinhardt, Josefa 161–162, 624–625
Steinhardt, Minni 161, 216–217, 624
Steinhausen, Wilhelm 276
Steinthal 234
sterilization 153, 288, 531, 538
Stern, E. 256
Stern, Ernst 130–131
Stern, Ester, née Jedwab 179
Stern, Heinrich 529, 680
Stern, Herbert 673
Stern, Max 179
Stettin (Szczecin) 436, 596, 678
Steubing, Walter 218

Stoppelmann, Willy 222
Storm Troopers, see SA
Stoutz, Maxime de 539
Strack, Hermann L. 87
Straßer, Gregor 89
Straßmann, Paul Ferdinand 278–279
Straus, Simon 345
Strauss, Erwin 256
Strauß, Richard 472
Strehlen (Strzelin) 323, 680
Streicher, Julius 119, 127, 129, 133, 138, 344, 378, 411, 487, 498, 530, 582–583, 646, 682, 768
Streim, Siegfried 222
Strength through Joy 427, 780
Striegau (Strzegom) 679–680
Strölin, Karl 595
Strzelce Opolskie, see Gross-Strehlitz
Strzeleczki, see Klein-Strehlitz
Stuckart, Wilhelm 522, 541–542, 565, 596–597, 634–635, 637, 639, 655, 720, 753, 790
Stuermer, Paul 307
Stutterheim, Hermann von 367–368
Stuttgart 160, 595
Stützel, Karl 93
Suesmann, Herbert 402
Suhl 395, 460, 462
suicide committed by Jews, see also responses to persecution and antisemitic measures 160, 171, 189, 344–345, 487, 613, 660, 672–673, 778
Supreme Council of Jews in Baden 529
Supreme Council of the Jewish Regional Community of Mecklenburg-Schwerin 529
Supreme Council of the Jewish Religious Community of Württemberg 529
Supreme SA Command 388–389, 618
surveillance, see also Gestapo 349–350, 355, 647, 669, 685, 777
Sweden 394, 424
Swiss National Council 509
Switzerland 51, 57, 112, 162, 295, 394–395, 424, 441, 509, 539–540, 588–589, 621
synagogue congregations 45, 723
– Breslau 682, 765–766
– Brotdorf 783
– Gleiwitz 243
– Hanover 454
– Königsberg 603–604
Syria 357, 424, 443
Syrup, Friedrich 331–332
Szczawnica 510
Szikowitz, Nathalius 212–213
Szüllö, Géza von 271

T

Tanke, Walter 436
Taube, Michael 256
Taubert, Eberhard 331
Tax Adjustment Law (Steueranpassungsgesetz) 723
taxation issues, see fines, levies and taxation issues
tax authorities 51, 59, 129, 221, 351, 382–383, 518–519, 567, 591–594, 626, 652, 697
Tax Investigation Service (Steuerfahndungsdienst) 592–593
Teichgräber, Lotte 494–495
Tel Aviv 161–162, 216–217, 473
Tempel, Karl 675
Tenants' Protection Association Frankfurt am Main 389
Terra Nova, Brazil 392
Theatre Law (Theatergesetz) 473
Thebud, Franz 759
Theilhaber, Felix Aaron 659
Thuringia 395, 800
Tiefenau (Dębin) 496
Tießler, Walter 618
Tietz (doctor) 189
Tietz, Hermann 417
Tiktin, Salomon Abraham 766
Tilsit (Sovetsk) 420
Tobias, Paula 332, 335, 465
Toller, Ernst 254
Törne, Gerhard 400
Tost (Toszek) 247, 731
Trachenberg (Żmigród) 324, 680
Transjordan 188
Trapp (schoolboy, Cologne) 330
Traub, Michael 622
Traumann, Lilli 328
Traumann, Susi S. 328
Treaty of Bucharest (1918) 27

Treaty of Versailles 16, 20, 31–32, 37, 58, 110, 195, 214, 395, 399, 412, 709, 782
Trebnitz (Trzebnica) 324, 680
Treitschke, Heinrich von 18, 23
Treplin, Lorenz 233
Treuchtlingen 46
Trust and Transfer Office Haavara Ltd, Tel Aviv, *see* business and companies 52
Tschammer und Osten, Hans von 157, 228, 257, 434
Tucholsky, Kurt 250, 473
Turkey 424
Tuttle, Charles H. 109
Twardogóra, *see* Festenberg

U

Ufa Theatre Berlin 477
Ukrainian Soviet Socialist Republic (USSR) 609, 708–709
Ulbersdorf (Wojcieszyn) 324
unemployment, *see also* Law for the Restoration of the Professional Civil Service (Civil Service Law) (*Gesetz zur Wiederherstellung des Berufsbeamtentums* [*Berufsbeamtengesetz*]) 16, 43, 47–49, 51, 97–98, 100–101, 107–108, 120–121, 136, 143, 168, 246–248, 279, 291–292, 318, 320, 324–325, 331–332, 340–341, 349, 353–354, 370, 391, 404–408, 414, 457, 489, 501, 542–544, 557, 560–562, 564, 568, 598, 614–615, 638, 645–646, 685, 724, 781, 784–789, 791
– dismissals 39, 50, 101, 103, 114–115, 129–130, 147–149, 219, 224, 226, 231, 233–234, 237, 240, 242, 246, 255, 309–312, 341, 413–414, 455, 547–548, 559–560, 789
– revocation of permits and licences 49, 219–220, 246–247, 515, 541, 564, 787, 790, 796
Unger, Naftali 457–459
Union of Christian Farmers' Associations (Vereinigung christlicher Bauernvereine) 24
Union of South Africa, *see* South Africa
Union of Young Poland (Związek Młodej Polski) 752
United Kingdom of Great Britain and Northern Ireland (UK) 51, 295, 394, 423–424, 441, 621, 713–714, 739–740

United States of America (USA) 28, 52, 189, 295, 358, 392–393, 423, 499, 622, 624, 713, 746, 769, 772, 774, 776
Universal Christian Council for Life and Work 297–298
universities, *see* schools and universities
Unna (rabbi, Mannheim) 259
Untermeyer, Samuel 358–359
Unterwellenborn 462
Upper Silesia 146–147, 180–181, 243–245, 247, 494, 612–613, 727–728, 764, 787
Upper Silesian Chamber of Skilled Crafts, Oppeln 247
Upper Silesian Regional Theatre 247
Urbanus (Regierungsrat, Königsberg) 602
Urbig, Franz 234–238, 240–242
Uruguay 393, 423, 731, 770, 772–773

V

Vahlen, K. Theodor 748
Valencia 738
Vangerow, Oskar 175
Varnhagen, Rahel 18
Vasmer, Max Julius Friedrich 610
Vellguth, Hermann 533
Venezuela 393, 423
Verordnung des Reichspräsidenten gegen Verrat am Deutschen Volke und hochverräterische Umtriebe, *see* Regulation of the Reich President against Betrayal of the German People and Highly Treasonous Activities
Verordnung über die Gewährung von Ehestandsdarlehen, *see* Regulation on the Granting of Marriage Loans
Verordnung über die Zulassung von Ärzten zur Tätigkeit bei den Krankenkassen, *see* Regulation on the Admission of Doctors for Employment with the Medical Insurance Companies
Verordnung zum Schutze von Volk und Staat, *see* Regulation for the Protection of People and State
Verordnung zur Ausschaltung der Juden aus dem deutschen Wirtschaftsleben, *see* Regulation for the Exclusion of Jews from German Economic Life
Vetter, Karl 691

Vienna 108, 177–178
Vieth, Arno 630–631
Viktor I, Moritz 447
Viktor II, Samuel 447
violence, *see also* murder
- physical abuse 35, 46, 48, 54, 85, 92–94, 166–167, 224, 301–302, 344, 386, 446–447, 466–467, 477, 482–484, 493–494, 558, 573, 661, 688–690, 729–731, 752
- public humiliation 94, 302, 346–347, 482–483, 494
- verbal abuse 35, 385, 662, 689, 768
Vogel, Wilhelm 436
Vogt (solicitor, Frankfurt am Main) 191–192
Volkmann, Erich Otto 399
Volkmar, Elsa, *see* Herzfeld, Elsa
Vollkommer, Max 326–327
Völp (Frankfurt am Main resident) 744
Volz (agronomist, Seelow) 363
Voss (member, Dutch Parliament) 123
Voß, Fritz 474
Vossler, Karl 456

W

Wachspress, Frieda 179
Wachtel, Alexander Siegfried 597
Wächtersbach 483
Wächtler, Fritz 596, 674
Wäckerle, Hilmar 167
Wagner, Adolf 467, 497, 501, 504
Wagner, Gerhard, *see also* Reich Physicians' Leader 248, 286, 414–415, 522, 565, 786
Wagner, Josef 728
Wagner, Richard 492
Wagner, Robert F. 109
Wagner Society 24
Wagschal, Wilhelm 323
Wahrmann, Nachum 322, 679–681
Wallach, Ernst 110
Walter, Bruno 111
Walther, Heinrich 509
Walzel, Oskar 456
Wandervogel movement 429
Wandsbek 125, 404
Warburg, Felix M. 190, 234, 357
Warburg, Max Moritz 26–27, 221–222, 260, 529, 720, 755
Waren (Müritz) 445, 601

Warmbrunn, Werner 778–779
Warsaw 175–176, 358, 710
Warszewo, *see* Hermannswalde
Wassermann, Jakob 50, 234, 238, 256
Wassermann, Oscar 234–243
Weerth, Wilhelm de 234
Wehner, Josef Magnus 399
Wehrmacht, *see also* Reichswehr 15, 58, 448, 465, 561, 748
Weiden 164–165
Weil, Leo 783
Weinberg 259
Weinberger, Fritz 223
Weininger, Otto 659
Weinmann, Leopold 466
Weinold 305
Weiß, Bernhard 250, 363
Weiss, V. J. 675
Weissenberg (industrialist, Wieblingen) 442
Weißenberg, Kurt 244
Weissmann, Georg 243
Weitzel, Friedrich (Fritz) 476
welfare benefits, subsidies, and loans, withdrawal of 50–51, 149–151, 244, 246, 320, 558, 560, 562–563, 649, 675
Wels, Otto 254
Weltmann, Lutz 256
Weltner, Armin 103
Weltsch, Robert 132, 136, 189, 751
Werner, Friedrich 262
Werner, Kurt 540
Wertheim, Abraham 696
Wertheim, Georg 696
Wertheim, Ursula, née Gilka 696
Wesche (shoemaker, Braunschweig) 411
Wessel, Horst 399
West Prussia 800
Westman (Swedish representative, High Commission for Refugees) 297
Westphalia 482–483, 800
Wetterhahn, Hermann 446
Weweler, August Benedikt 102
Weygold, Karl Josef 784
Weyrich (court assessor, Frankfurt am Main) 190
Wheat Trade Association (Getreidewirtschaftsverband), Kurmark 629–630

Wiegand (Staatsrat) 695
Wielowieś, see Langendorf
Wienbeck, Erich 279
Wiener, Alfred 727
Wienken, Heinrich 438–439, 442–443
Wilfan, Josip 265–271
Wilhelminenhöhe 425
Will, Hellmuth 602
Will, Phillipp 447
Wilson, Woodrow 20
Winkler, Friedrich Horst 695
Winter Relief Agency of the German People (Winterhilfswerk) 51, 315, 321, 648–650, 709, 798
Wintermantel, Fritz 234, 243
Winzig (Wińsko) 679–680
Wirth, Richard 131
Wise, Jonah Bondi 190
Wise, Stephen Samuel 109–111, 683
Wisliceny, Dieter 58, 704, 716
Wismar 444
Witte (NSDAP branch leader, Görlitz) 402
Witte, Max 99–100
Wittmund, Harry 222
Wohlau (Wołów) 324, 680–681
Wohlthat, Helmuth 568, 761
Wöhrmann (probationary judge, Münder am Deister) 263
Wołczyn, see Konstadt
Wolf (sergeant, Kassel) 446
Wolfes, Felix 103
Wolfes, Fritz 300–301
Wolfes, Hans 670
Wolff, Leo 188, 529
Wolff, Richard 285, 440
Wolff, Theodor 111
Wolff, Walter 220
Wolfram, Karl 191
World Economic Conference, London (1933) 187
World Jewish Congress 109
Wrobel, Ignaz, see Tucholsky, Kurt
Wrocław, see Breslau
Wulf, Franz 674
Wulf, Joseph 41
Wurm, Alois 152–153
Württemberg 17, 19, 178, 391, 560, 800
Würzburg 661
Wuttke, Bernhard 495–496

Y

Young Plan 195
Young German Order (Jungdeutscher Orden) 33
Youth Aliyah 396, 794
Youth Welfare Association, Munich 174
Yugoslavia 175, 424, 621

Z

Ząbkowice Śląskie, see Frankenstein
Zagreb 175
Zarek, Hermann 323
Zarnack, Wolfgang 493
Zeidelhack, Johann Martin (Max) 460–462
Zelle 590
Ziegler, Wilhelm 138
Zimmermann (schoolboy, Cologne) 330
Zimmermann, Ernst 695
Zinnel (Frankfurt am Main resident) 744
Zint, Hans 99
Zinten (Kornevo) 420
Zintgraff, Alfred 443
Zionism 20, 37, 45, 50, 133–134, 136, 186, 234, 322, 350–353, 367, 396, 422, 433, 486, 508, 516, 528, 532, 575, 606–607, 713
Zionist Congress (1897) 20
Zionist Federation for Germany 44, 50, 188, 317, 322, 350–351, 426, 527, 529, 622
Zionist World Organization 133
Zittau 224
Zonstein, Feiga, see Gayer, Feiga
Zörner (agronomist, Seelow) 363
Zschimmer (official, Reich Ministry of Labour) 247
Zuckermann, Dora 163
Zülow, Kurt 755
Zuntz, Hugo 220
Zweig, Arnold 111
Zweig, Stefan 172, 472
Zwickau 224, 463
Zwindorfer, Bertha, see Meyer, Bertha

www.ingramcontent.com/pod-product-compliance
Lightning Source LLC
Chambersburg PA
CBHW080052170426
42814CB00048BA/296